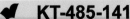
ON THE ROAD

YOUR COMPLETE DESTINATION GUIDE
In-depth reviews, detailed listings
and insider tips

TOP EXPERIENCES MAP **NEXT PAGE**

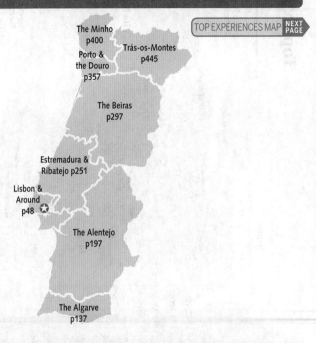
PAGE 517 **SURVIVAL GUIDE**

YOUR AT-A-GLANCE REFERENCE
How to get around, get a room,
stay safe, say hello

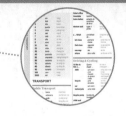

THIS EDITION WRITTEN AND RESEARCHED BY

Regis St Louis

Kate Armstrong, Gregor Clark, Adam Skolnick

Portugal

Top Experiences ›

Braga
Climb a splendid, baroque staircase (p402)

Parque Nacional da Peneda-Gerês
Scale boulder-strewn peaks (p435)

Vila Nova de Foz Côa
Uncover ancient rock art (p396)

Parque Natural da Serra da Estrela
Hike the high-country trails (p331)

The Beiras
Tour picturesque villages (p297)

Viana do Castelo
Devour fresh, top-quality seafood (p417)

Barcelos
Shop at a famed outdoor market (p409)

Alto Douro
Imbibe in the world's oldest wine region (p395)

Porto
Sip port in a romantic city (p359)

Velha Universidade
Wander through Portugal's oldest university (p303)

Batalha, Alcobaça & Tomar
Marvel at medieval Christian monuments (p251)

SPAIN

Valença do Minho, Monção, Ponte de Lima, Viana do Castelo, Barcelos, Vila do Conde, Espinho, Ovar, Aveiro, Mira, Figueira da Foz, Leiria, Pombal, Porto, Braga, Guimarães, Amarante, Peso da Régua, Vila Real, Chaves, Mirandela, Bragança, Miranda do Douro, Mogadouro, Pocinho, Vila Nova de Foz Côa, Barca de Alva, Pinhel, Guarda, Vilar Formoso, Sortelha, Covilhã, Fundão, Castelo Branco, Gouveia, Mangualde, Viseu, Lamego, São Pedro do Sul, Tondela, Luso, Lousã, Coimbra, Zamora, Salamanca, Plasencia

80 km
40 miles

MINHO, DOURO, ALTO DOURO, BEIRA ALTA, BEIRA BAIXA, BEIRA LITORAL

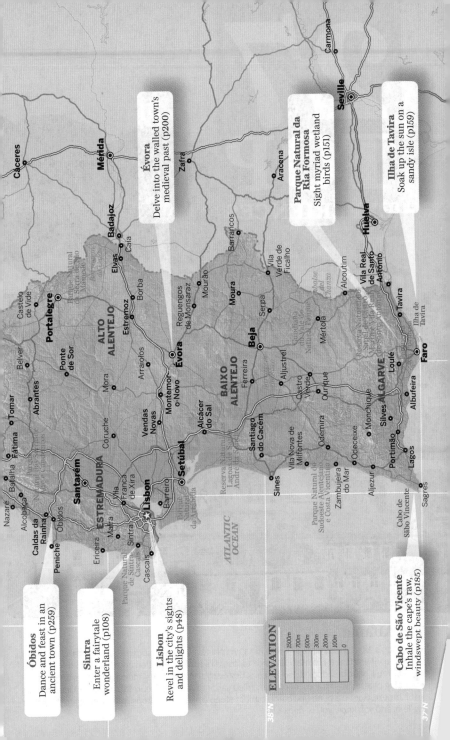

Óbidos
Dance and feast in an ancient town (p259)

Sintra
Enter a fairytale wonderland (p108)

Lisbon
Revel in the city's sights and delights (p48)

Évora
Delve into the walled town's medieval past (p200)

Parque Natural da Ria Formosa
Sight myriad wetland birds (p151)

Ilha de Tavira
Soak up the sun on a sandy isle (p159)

Cabo de São Vicente
Inhale the cape's raw, windswept beauty (p185)

ELEVATION

1500m
700m
500m
300m
200m
100m
0

ATLANTIC OCEAN

ESTREMADURA

ALTO ALENTEJO

BAIXO ALENTEJO

ALGARVE

38°N

37°N

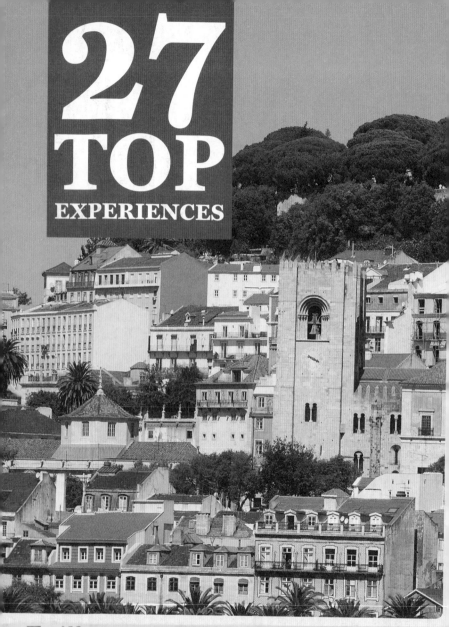

27 TOP EXPERIENCES

The Alfama

1 Lisbon's Alfama district (p57), with its labyrinthine alleyways, hidden courtyards and curving shadow-filled lanes, is a magical place to lose all sense of direction and delve into the soul of the city. You'll pass breadbox-sized grocers, brilliantly tiled buildings and cosy taverns filled with easygoing chatter, with the scent of chargrilled sardines and the mournful rhythms of fado drifting in the breeze. Round a bend and catch sight of steeply pitched rooftops leading down to the glittering Tejo, and you know you're hooked...

Nightlife in the Bairro Alto

2 It's midnight in the Bairro Alto (p92) and electricity crackles over the narrow cobblestone streets. As the moon rises over Lisbon's hillsides, eye-catching urban art and graffiti-stained buildings guide revellers to the heart of this night-loving neighbourhood. The chatter of drink-toting celebrators blends with the urban rhythms of brassy local bands and House-spinning DJs. Traditional taverns and glossy dining rooms lure late-night diners, while others opt for mojitos and sangria sipped on sidewalks – front-row seating to one of Europe's finest evening shows.

Wooded Wonderland

3 Less than an hour by train from the capital, Sintra (p108) feels like another world. Like a page torn from a fairytale, Sintra is a quaint village sprinkled with stone-walled taverns and with a whitewashed palace looming over town. Forested hillsides form the backdrop to the storybook, with imposing castles, mystical gardens, strange mansions and centuries-old monasteries hidden among the woodlands. The fog that sweeps in by night adds another layer of mystery, and cool evenings are best spent fireside in one of Sintra's many charming B&Bs. Palácio Nacional de Sintra, below

Porto

4 It would be hard to dream up a more romantic city than Portugal's second largest (p359). Laced with narrow pedestrian laneways, it is blessed with countless baroque churches, epic theatres and sprawling plazas. Its Ribeira district – a Unesco World Heritage Site – is just a short walk across a landmark bridge from centuries-old port wineries in Vila Nova de Gaia, where you can sip the world's best port. And though some walls are crumbling, renewal – in the form of spectacular modern architecture, cosmopolitan restaurants, burgeoning nightlife and a vibrant arts scene – is palpable. Ribeira district, Porto, left

BRENT WINEBRENNER

DAVID BORLAND

The Cliffs of Cabo de São Vicente

6 There's something thrilling about standing at Europe's most southwestern edge, a headland of barren cliffs to which Portuguese sailors bid a nervous farewell as they sailed past, venturing into the unknown during Portugal's golden years of exploration. The windswept cape is redolent of history – if you squint hard (really hard), you'll see the ghost of Vasco da Gama sailing past. These days, a fortress and lighthouse perch on the cape. A new museum (p185) beautifully highlights Portugal's maritime navigation history.

PAUL BERNHARDT

Historic Évora

5 The Queen of the Alentejo and one of Portugal's most beautifully preserved medieval towns, Évora (p200) is an enchanting place to spend several days delving into the past. Inside the 14th-century walls, Évora's narrow, winding lanes lead to striking architectural works: an elaborate medieval cathedral and cloisters, Roman ruins and a picturesque town square. Historic and aesthetic virtues aside, Évora is also a lively university town, and its many attractive restaurants serve up excellent, hearty Alentejan cuisine.

Sipping the Douro

7 The exquisite Alto Douro wine country (p395) is the oldest demarcated wine region on earth. Its steeply terraced hills, stitched together with craggy vines that have produced luscious wines for centuries, loom on both sides of the sinuous Rio Douro. Whether you get here by driving the impossibly scenic back roads, or catch a train or boat from Porto, take the time to hike, cruise and taste. Countless vintners receive guests for tours, tastings and overnight stays, and if you find one that's still family-owned, don't be surprised if you sample something very old and very special.

WSIT/IMAGEBROKER

GREG ELMS

Fado

8 Born in a working-class neighbourhood of Lisbon, the melancholic music of fado (p97) has been around for centuries. Despite its years, fado remains a living art, heard in tiny mom-and-pop restaurants and elegant music halls alike. A lone, powerful voice coupled with the 12-string Portuguese *guitarra* are all the tools needed to bring some listeners to tears, as songs recall broken hearts, unfulfilled dreams and lost days of youth. In fado, raw emotion often conveys more than mere lyrics can; even non-Portuguese speakers find themselves moved by great *fadistas*.

Ilha de Tavira

9 This place has the lot for sun-seekers, beach bums, nature lovers (and naturists): mile after mile of golden beach (think sand, sand, sand, as far as the eye can see), designated nudist area, transport via miniature train, busy restaurants and a campground. To top it off, it's part of the protected Parque Natural da Ria Formosa. Outside the high season, the island (p159) feels wonderfully remote and empty, but be warned: during high season (July and August) the hordes descend.

ROBERT HARDING PICTURE LIBRARY LTD/ALAMY

Parque Natural da Ria Formosa

10 This special spot feels like it's in the middle of wilderness, yet it's right off the Algarvian coast (p151). Enclosing a vast area of *sapais* (marshes), *salinas* (salt pans), creeks and dune islands, the protected lagoon system stretches for an incredible 60km and encompasses 18,000 hectares. And it's all accessible to a traveller from various towns – have a boat drop you at a deserted beach, or amble along the nature trail among the precious wetland birdlife. View from Cacela Velha over the Ria Formosa lagoons, above

Magnificent Megaliths

11 Spiritual, magical, historical, incredible – a visit to the many ancient megaliths around Évora (p210) will make your hairs stand on end. As a traveller, you will more often than not have these sites to yourselves. And what better way to ponder the mysteries of places so ancient they cannot fully be explained? How did such massive rocks get hauled into place? Were they fertility symbols or proprietal land boundaries? They beg questions, yet – refreshingly in a world of reasoning – provide few answers. Somehow, their appeal is in not knowing. Cromeleque dos Almendres, above

Castelo de Vide

12 High above the rolling countryside and a brief crow's flight west of the beautiful ancient village of Marvão, Castelo de Vide (p228) is one of the country's most underrated villages. Head here for a hilly vantage point, quaint houses and flower-lined lanes. History has left some fascinating legacies – a tiny synagogue (now a museum) in a former Jewish district, beautiful fountains which spout the town's crystal-clear mineral water, and a hilltop castle. The real beauty, however, is watching the local world go by.

Living Like Royals

13 Portugal has its share of boutique hotels and lavish beach resorts, but some of its most memorable lodging is found inside its government-run *pousadas* (p519). The settings are historic and jaw-dropping: 300-year-old castles, atmospheric monasteries and cliff-top mansions are among the 40 different pousadas sprinkled across the country. Where else can you lodge in antique-filled rooms where dukes once slept, contemplating the age-old beauty of the landscape? Pulling aside curtains, you'll gaze upon rolling vineyards, boulder-strewn mountains or the glimmering coastline.

Batalha, Alcobaça & Tomar

14 These medieval Christian monuments – all Unesco World Heritage Sites – constitute one of Portugal's greatest national treasures. Each has its own magic: the whimsy of Manueline adornments and haunting roofless shell of the unfinished Capelas Imperfeitas at Batalha's monastery (left; p269); the great kitchen at Alcobaça's monastery (p267), where a multistorey chimney and fish-stocked river once stoked the appetites of countless monks; or the labyrinthine courtyards and mysterious 16-sided chapel of the Knights Templar at Tomar's Convento de Cristo (p283).

Parque Natural da Serra da Estrela

15 Portugal's highest mountains (p331) blend rugged scenery, outdoor adventure and vanishing traditional ways. At Torre (p339), the country's highest point (artificially pushed up to 2000m by the addition of a not-so-subtle stone monument!), you can slalom down the country's only ski slope. Hikers can choose from a network of high country trails with stupendous vistas. Oh, and did we mention the furry sheepdog puppies that frolic by the roadside? You'll long to take one home.

Villages of the Beiras

16 From schist-walled communities spilling down terraced hillsides to spiky-edged sentinels that once guarded the eastern border against Spanish incursions, the inland Beiras are filled with picturesque and historical villages: Piódão, Trancoso, Sortelha, Monsanto, Idanha-a-Velha... Today mostly devoid of residents but not yet overwhelmed by mass tourism, they make some of the country's most peaceful and appealing destinations. String a few together into the perfect road trip (p353) – or better yet, don your walking shoes and experience these ancient places at a medieval pace.

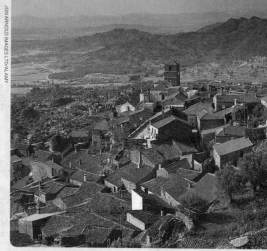

JON ARNOLD IMAGES LTD/ALAMY

Festivals

17 There's always something to celebrate in Portugal (p23). For Easter processions, head to Braga. Romantics will love Lisbon's mid-June Festa de Santo António, with ubiquitous parties and locals plying sweethearts with poems and pots of aromatic basil. In August, catch Viana do Castelo's Romaria de Nossa Senhora d'Agonia (left), where *gigantones* (giants) parade down sawdust-painted streets alongside gold-and-scarlet-clad women. And in winter, young lads wear masks and colourful garb in Trás-os-Montes' villages during the pagan-derived Festa dos Rapazes.

PAUL BERNHARDT

Seafood

18 Always a seafaring culture, the Portuguese know a thing or two about cooking fish. Taste the culinary riches of Portugal's coast in dishes like *caldeirada de peixe* (fish stew layered with tomatoes, potatoes and rice), *açorda de camarãoes* (a tasty stew of shrimp, garlic and cilantro thickened with bread crumbs), *cataplana* (shellfish stewed with wine, garlic and tomatoes in a traditional domed copper pan) or *ensopada de enguias* (eel stew). Or content yourself with the simplest of all Portuguese treats – fresh-grilled sardines, straight out of the ocean and onto the fire! *Caldeirada*, right

SIMON REDDY/ALAMY

ANDERS BLOMQVIST

IZZET KERIBAR

Óbidos

20 Wandering through tangle of ancient streets and whitewashed houses of Óbidos is enchanting any time of year, but come during one of its festivals (p261) and you're in for a special treat. Whether attending a jousting match or climbing the castle walls at the medieval fair, searching for the next Pavarotti at the Festival de Ópera, or sampling chocolate at the Festival Internacional do Chocolate, you couldn't ask for a better backdrop.

Coimbra

19 Portugal's atmospheric college town, Coimbra (p298) rises steeply from the Rio Mondego to a medieval quarter housing one of Europe's oldest universities. Students roam the narrow streets clad in black capes, while strolling fado musicians give free concerts beneath the Moorish town gate or under the stained-glass windows of Café Santa Cruz. Kids can keep busy at Portugal dos Pequenitos (p305), a theme park with miniature versions of Portuguese monuments; grown-ups will appreciate the upper town's student-driven nightlife and the new cluster of bars and restaurants in the riverside park below.

Azulejos

21 Some of Portugal's most captivating works of art are out on the streets – free viewing for anyone who happens to stroll past. A great legacy of the Moors, the *azulejo* (hand-painted tile) was adopted by the Portuguese, and put to stunning use over the centuries. Exquisite displays cover Porto's train station and iconic churches, with larger-than-life stories painted on the ceramic tiles. Lisbon has even more eye candy, with *azulejo*-adorned buildings all over town. The best place to start the hunt: Museu Nacional do Azulejo (p62), home to *azulejos* dating back 400 years.

GREG ELMS

ANDERS BLOMQVIST

Rock Hopping in Vila Nova de Foz Côa

22 Whether you travel by mountain bike, 4WD or on foot under a full moon, this enormous Palaeolithic rock art gallery (p396) is a must-see. Discovered by archaeologists in the 1990s and nearly flooded by a misguided dam, hundreds of drawings can be glimpsed at three public sites. Knowledgeable, passionate national park guides will lead you to the most interesting and visible sites, but new finds are common. If you arrive in springtime, wildflowers will only add to the ancient beauty.

Sweet Hearts

23 One of the great culinary wonders of Portugal, the cinnamon-dusted *pastel de nata* (custard tart), with its flaky crust and creamy centre, lurks irresistibly behind pastry counters across the country; the best are served piping hot in Belém (p91). Of course, when it comes to dessert, Portugal is more than a one-hit wonder, with a dazzling array of regional sweets – from jewel-like Algarve marzipan to Sintra's heavenly almond-and-egg *travesseiros* to Serpa's cheesecake-like *queijadas*. Freshly baked *pastéis de nata*, Belém, right

PAUL BERNHARDT

Braga's Monuments

24 Portugal's third-largest city (p402) is blessed with terrific restaurants, a vibrant university and raucous festivals, but when it comes to historic sites it is unparalleled in Portugal. Here's the remarkable 12th-century cathedral (left), there's a 14th-century church. Braga has not one, but two sets of Roman ruins, countless 17th-century plazas and an 18th-century palace turned museum. Then there's that splendid baroque staircase: Escadaria do Bom Jesus, the target of penitent pilgrims who come to make offerings at altars on the way to the mountaintop throughout the year.

Barcelos Market

25 The Minho is famous for its sprawling outdoor markets, but the largest, oldest and most celebrated is the Feira de Barcelos (p409), held every Thursday in this ancient town on the banks of the Rio Cávado. Most outsiders come for the yellow-dotted louça de Barcelos ceramics and the gaudy figurines à la local potter Rosa Ramalho, while rural villagers are more interested in the scrawny chickens, hand-embroidered linen, hand-woven baskets and hand-carved ox yokes.

Viana do Castelo

26 Whether glimpsing the waves from the tower of Monte de Santa Luzia or riding them on your kiteboard at Praia de Cabedelo, it's hard not to love the jewel of the Costa Verde (p417). The old quarters seem downright sophisticated, with leafy, 19th-century boulevards and narrow lanes crowded with Manueline manors and rococo palaces. The cobbled fishing quarter is rough around the edges, but sprinkled with the some of the finest seafood kitchens in the country. And fun-loving university students rule the night. Monte de Santa Luzia, Viana do Castelo, below

WST/IMAGEBROKER

JENNY JONES

Parque Nacional da Peneda-Gerês

27 The vast rugged wilderness of Portugal's northernmost park (p435) is home to dramatic peaks, meandering streams and rolling hillsides covered with wildflowers. Its age-old stone villages seem lost in time and, in remote areas, wolves still roam. As always, the best way to feel nature's power is on foot along one of more than a dozen hiking trails. Some scale peaks, a few link to old Roman roads, others lead to castle ruins or waterfalls. Sunbaking by a waterfall, Parque Nacional da Peneda-Gerês, left

Medieval castles, cobblestone villages, captivating cities and golden-sand beaches: the Portugal experience can mean many things. History, great food and wine, idyllic scenery and blazing nightlife are just the beginning...

...e to
...gal

Daily
...get

...et less than
...0

...rm bed: €14–€22
...elf-catering
...lan sightseeing
...ound free-admission
...ays (often Sunday
...mornings)
...» Youth cards save on
sights and transport

Midrange
€50–€120

» Double room in
a midrange hotel:
€50–€100
» Lunch and dinner
in a midrange
restaurant: €20–€30
» Book online to
save money on
accommodation

Top end more
than €120

» Boutique hotel
room: from €120
» 3-course meal in a
top restaurant: from
€40

...nier
...ezing
...s in the

...ices,
...ds.
...tions keep
...hours.
...d ocean
...ratures.

Christians all left their mark on the Iberian nation. ...e to face with the great mysteries of the past. You ...arvings in the Vila Nova de Foz Côa, watch the ...Évora or lose yourself in the elaborate corridors ...Belém, Alcobaça or Batalha. You can pack an ...ered woodlands, craggy cliff-top castles and

...isp *vinho verde,* chargrilled fish, *cata-* ...se have perfected the art of cooking ...table means experiencing the rich- ...tryside. Of course, you don't have ...ard tart) standing up at an 1837 ...sipping the velvety ports of the ...h. You can shop the produce- ...le picnic for the beach, and ...ning rooms, where talented

...ty. You can overnight ...nd olive groves, go ...ake in the pristine ...coast offer more ...he-world cliffs, ...ands fronting ...g and kayak- ...s all across

...ugh all- ...oão. There ...orld-music fests ...ournful music of fado ...ars in Porto, Coimbra and

need to know

Currency
» The euro (€)

Language
» Portuguese

When to Go?

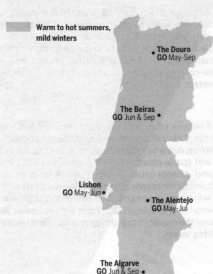

Warm to hot summers, mild winters

The Douro
GO May-Sep

The Beiras
GO Jun & Sep

Lisbon
GO May-Jun

The Alentejo
GO May-Jul

The Algarve
GO Jun & Sep

High Season
(Jul–Aug)

» Accommodation prices increase 30%.

» Expect big crowds in the Algarve and coastal resort areas.

» Sweltering temperatures are commonplace.

» Warmer ocean temperatures.

Shoulder
(May, Jun & Sep)

» Wildflowers and mild days make it ideal for hikes and outdoor activities.

» Lively festivals take place in June.

» Crowds and prices are average.

» Colder ocean temperatures.

Low Season
(Dec–Mar)

» Shorter, rainy days with freezing temperatures in the interior.

» Lower prices, fewer crowds.

» Attractions keep shorter hours.

» Frigid ocean temperatures.

Your Budget

Budget
€5...

» ...
» S...
» ...

Money

» ATMs widely available. Credit cards accepted at most midrange and top-end hotels and restaurants.

Visas

» Generally not required for stays of up to 90 days; some nationalities will need a Schengen visa.

Mobile Phones

» Local SIM cards can be used in unlocked European, Australian and quad-band US mobiles.

Transport

» Trains provide good service between major towns; buses (sometimes infrequent) serve smaller towns.

Websites

» **Lonely Planet** (www.lonelyplanet.com/portugal) Destination information, hotel bookings, traveller forum and more.

» **Portugal Tourism** (www.visitportugal.com) Portugal's official tourism site.

» **Inside Portugal Travel** (www.insideportugaltravel.com) The Portuguese National Tourist Office site in North America.

» **ViniPortugal** (www.viniportugal.pt) Fine overview of Portugal's favourite beverage, covering wine regions, grape varieties and wine routes.

Exchange Rates

Australia	A$1	€0.70
Canada	C$1	€0.74
Japan	¥100	€0.88
New Zealand	NZ$1	€0.55
UK	£1	€1.20
USA	US$1	€0.76

For current exchange rates see www.xe.com.

Important Numbers

Country Code	☏351
International Access Code	☏00
Ambulance	☏112
Fire	☏112
Police	☏112

Arriving in Portugal

» **Aeroporto de Lisboa (Lisbon)**
AeroBus – €3.50; every 20 minutes from 7.45am to 8.15pm
Taxi – €12–€16; around 20 minutes to the centre

» **Aeroporto Francisco Sá Carneiro (Porto)**
Metro – €1.50; 45 minutes to the centre; frequent departures
Taxi – €22–€28; around 30 to 60 minutes to the centre

» **Aeroporto de Faro (Faro)**
Bus – €1.60; every 30 minutes weekdays, every two hours weekends
Taxi – €10–€14; around 20 minutes to the centre

Dangers & Annoyances

Compared with other European countries, Portugal's crime rate remains low, but some types of crime – including car theft – are on the rise. Crime against foreigners is of the usual rush-hour-pickpocketing, bag-snatching and theft-from-rental-cars variety. Take the usual precautions: don't flash your cash; keep valuables in a safe place; and, if you are challenged, hand it over – it's not worth taking the risk.

Take care in the water; the surf can be strong, with dangerous ocean currents.

if you like...

Food

Renowned for its seafood, hearty country cooking and the many regional specialities, Portugal offers many temptations to the food-minded traveller. Celebrated new chefs have brought much attention to many dining rooms; while those who enjoy the simple things – freshly baked bread, olives, cheeses, roast meats, fish sizzling on the grill – will enjoy memorable meals in traditional restaurants all across the country.

Chiado district This Lisbon neighbourhood is home to some of Portugal's most elegant dining rooms (p86)

Food festivals The Algarve elevates its seafood and regional delicacies to high art in these food-minded celebrations (p180)

Vila Joya Overlooking the beach, this two-Michelin-starred restaurant is one of Portugal's finest (p167)

Cataplana This decadent seafood stew is a south-coast speciality; Olhão serves an excellent version (p153)

Taberna do Valentim One of several great traditional restaurants in a fishing neighbourhood in Viana do Castelo (p422)

Wine & Port

Home to some of the oldest vineyards on earth, Portugal has some fantastic (and deliciously affordable) wines. Each region has its enticements, from full-bodied Alentejan reds to Minho's refreshing *vinho verde,* along with the famous ports from the Douro. Stylish wine bars and bucolic vineyards provide memorable settings to taste Portugal's great fruits of the vine.

Wine Bar do Castelo Sample the country's finest – over 150 Portuguese wines – at Lisbon's best wine bar (p95)

Herdade do Esporão An acclaimed winery outside Reguengos de Monsaraz, with vineyards dating back hundreds of years (p213)

Palácio de Mateus Inside a palace, drink in the grandeur while sipping distinctive and rare Alvarelhão (p446)

Solar do Vinho do Porto With views over the Douro, the elegant garden bar serves an astounding variety of ports (p377)

Douro Vineyards Breathtaking views from 18th-century manors and velvety rich wines make the Douro a requisite stop for wine lovers (p394)

Architecture

Portugal's wildly varied architecture encompasses royal palaces, baroque churches and modernist masterpieces. Taking in the country's icons means delving into the past as you gaze upon 400-year-old monasteries, imposing hilltop castles and ancient ruins.

Fortaleza de Sagres Contemplate Portugal's seafaring past from this cliff-top perch over the Atlantic (p184)

Casa da Música Rem Koolhaas' stunning music hall, completed in 2005, is an architectural gem (p378)

Mosteiro dos Jerónimos Dom Manuel I's fantastical tribute to the great explorers of the 15th century (p74)

Convento de Cristo Former headquarters of the Knights Templar, this Unesco World Heritage Site is stunning to behold (p283)

Conimbriga The best-preserved Roman ruins on the Iberian Peninsula provide a window into the rise and fall of the once great empire (p311)

Palácio Nacional de Mafra The construction of this exuberant palace with its 1200 rooms nearly bankrupted the nation (p125)

» Sample a port or 10 in a Portuguese wine bar

ANDERS BLOMQVIST

Outdoor Activities

Basking in the sun on a lovely beach fronting the Atlantic is activity enough for some. Those seeking something a bit more adventurous can go surfing, kitesurfing or even diving. You can also head to the hills for birdwatching, hiking or cycling.

Kitesurfing One of the top places for riding a kiteboard over the kicking waves is Praia do Cabedelo (p419)

Parque Nacional da Peneda-Gerês Portugal has many great places to hike, and this mountainous national park in the north has some fantastic trails (p435)

Surfing There's no lack of great surf spots off Portugal's pretty beaches, but the captivating island of Baleal has consistently good breaks (p257)

Via Algarviana The ambitious can walk the entire breadth of Portugal on this 300km trail (p145)

Diving Some of Portugal's best diving happens around the rocky island of Berlenga Grande; you'll find dive operators in nearby Peniche (p257)

Music

The national music of Portugal is undoubtedly fado, that stirring, melancholic sound that's so prevalent in Lisbon (its birthplace) and Coimbra. Other genres also have their followers, and you can catch live rock, jazz and a wide range of world sounds.

Museu do Fado Learn the history of this musical art form at this intriguing Lisbon museum (p61)

The Alfama The birthplace of fado has many authentic places in which to hear live fado – as well as tourist traps to avoid; see our picks on p97

A Capella Coimbra also has a fado-loving heart; this converted 14th-century chapel is the best place to hear it live (p310)

Onda Jazz Bar Vaulted ceilings and stone walls set the scene at this medievalesque jazz space in Lisbon (p99)

Casa da Música Sure it's an architectural masterpiece, but the acoustics at this Porto concert hall are no less stunning (p378)

Art

In the Portuguese art world, quality trumps quantity. You may not find massive art institutions here, but you will find wondrous galleries showcasing unique works from past and present – including Portugal's own home-grown legends.

Museu de Calouste Gulbenkian One of Lisbon's finest museums houses an epic collection of magnificent artwork from East and West (p66)

Museu Colecção Berardo In Belém, this free museum hosts some of Portugal's most daring exhibits (p69)

Casa das Histórias Paula Rego Cascais' newest exhibition space celebrates the artwork of Paula Rego, one of Portugal's finest living painters (p118)

Casa de Serralves Porto's art lovers don't miss the cutting-edge exhibits inside this art-deco mansion in the park (p366)

Museu da Tapeçaria de Portalegre Guy Fino Be dazzled by colour at this fine tapestry museum in the Alentejo (p226)

If you like... craggy castle towns
Monsanto has majestic beauty, plus hiking trails to other historic villages (p327)
If you like... scenic train rides
the Douro line heading east to Pocinho (p395) has stunning views of the river and vineyard-covered hillsides

Beaches

With 830km of coastline, Portugal has you covered when it comes to beaches. You'll find sun-kissed shores of every type here, from festive, people-packed coves to remote windswept shores that invite endless wandering. There are photogenic cliff-backed beaches, surf-loving beaches (for novices and experts alike) and even idyllic island beaches.

Ilha de Tavira This sandy island off the southern coast is a remarkable getaway (p159)

São Jacinto To escape the crowds, head to this wild beach backed by dunes west of Aveiro (p320)

Vila Nova de Milfontes Star of the Alentejo coastline is the lovely and vibrant village overlooking several beautiful beaches (p248)

Costa da Caparica Just across the Tejo from Lisbon, you'll find 8km of pretty coastline, with stylish beach bars sprinkled along it (p127)

Lagos This popular Algarve resort town offers a mix of lively surfing beaches and secluded sandstone-backed shorelines further out of town (p175)

Festivals

Praying and playing go hand in hand in this traditional Catholic country, where the calendar is packed with colourful processions followed by music, dancing and feasting. Portugal also throws down film and music festivals, food and wine fests and good old-fashioned country fairs.

Festa de Santo António
Lisbon's favourite saint is feted with fervour at all-night street parties erupting across town (p77)

Medieval Fun Óbidos' Mercado Medieval is the go-to place for jousting and sword-fighting, wandering minstrels, pig roasts and grog (p261)

Festa de São João Porto and Braga go wild for St John, with bonfires, concerts, fireworks and plenty of good-natured mayhem (p369 and p405)

Queima das Fitas Coimbra's students go wild at the academic year's end with parties, concerts and exhibitions (p303)

Festival do Sudoeste One of Portugal's biggest music fests erupts each August in the seaside town of Zambujeira do Mar (p249)

Nightlife

When the sun goes down, things start to get interesting – or so it goes for those on the trail of Portugal's best bars, lounges and nightclubs. Whether you want to party like a rock star or sip cocktails with a more laid-back, bohemian crowd, you'll find these and dozens of other scenes in Portugal.

Lagos Packed with music-filled bars and lounges, Lagos is the nightlife centre of the Algarve (p181)

Forte São João Baptista In a striking 17th-century fort, this hotel, restaurant and nightclub throws some of the best summer parties in the north (p385)

Bairro Alto Portugal's nightlife capital, this blazing hilltop 'hood is packed with eclectic bars and revellers at all hours nearly every night of the week (p92)

Lux Still one of Lisbon's best nightclubs after all these years, riverside Lux always reels in a stylish, dance-loving crowd (p95)

month by month

Top Events

1 **Semana Santa**, April

2 **Queima das Fitas**, May

3 **Festa de Santo António**, June

4 **Festa de São João**, June

5 **Festival do Marisco**, August

February

Few travellers visit Portugal during winter and you'll net substantial savings on accommodation. Coastal temperatures are cool but mild, while inland sees frigid days, particularly in the Serra da Estrela, when skiing is at its peak. Winter also brings abundant rainfall, particularly in the north. In the south, many resorts remain shuttered until spring.

Carnaval

Although small by Brazilian standards, Portugal's Carnaval features much merry-making in the pre-Lenten celebrations. Loulé boasts the best parades, while Lisbon, Nazaré and Viana do Castelo all throw a respectable bash.

Fantasporto

World-renowned two-week international festival (www.fantasporto. com) of fantasy, horror and just plain weird films that takes place in Porto.

March

March days are rainy and chilly in much of Portugal, though the south sees more sunshine than the north. Prices remain low, and foreign travellers few and far between.

Festival Internacional do Chocolate

For several days in early March Óbidos, in Estremadura, celebrates the sweet temptation of the cacao bean (see p261).

April

Spring arrives, bringing warmer temperatures and fewer rainy days, with abundant sunshine in both the north and the south. Following the winter rains, late April sees a profusion of wildflowers in the south.

Semana Santa

The build-up to Easter is magnificent in the Minho's saintly Braga (see p405). During Holy Week, barefoot penitents process through the streets, past rows of makeshift altars, with an explosion of jubilation at the cathedral on the eve of Easter.

Ovibeja

This huge nine-day agricultural fair in Beja, the Alentejo, features concerts every night, with handicrafts booths and abundant food stalls.

May

Lovely, sunny weather and the lack of peak-season crowds makes May an ideal time to visit. The beaches of the Algarve awake from their slumber and see a smattering of travellers passing through.

Feira das Cantarinhas

In the far north, this is a huge three-day street fair of traditional handicrafts in Bragança, Trás-os-Montes.

Queima das Fitas

Join the mayhem of Burning of the Ribbons at the University of Coimbra

(Portugal's Oxford) in the Beiras, as students celebrate the end of the academic year with concerts, a parade and copious amounts of drinking.

Festa das Cruzes

Barcelos, in the Minho, turns into a fairground of flags, flowers, coloured lights and open-air concerts at the Festival of the Crosses. The biggest days are 1 to 3 May. Monsanto, in the Beiras, also celebrates, with singing and dancing beside a medieval castle.

Festa do Mar

Celebrating the age-old love of the sea (and the patron saints of fishermen), this lively fest brings a flotilla of fishing boats to Nazaré's harbour, Estremadura, as well as a colourful parade of elaborately decorated floats. There's plenty of eating and drinking.

Fátima Romaris

Hundreds of thousands make the pilgrimage to Fátima each year to commemorate the apparitions of the Virgin that occurred on 13 May 1917. The pilgrimage also happens in October (12–13).

Feira do Alvarinho

The great wine of the Minho, as well as plenty of food, music and folkloric dancing, is the raison d'être of this five-day festival (www.feiraalvarinho. pt.vu) in Monção, the self-described birthplace of the refreshing Alvarinho wine.

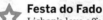
June

Early summer is one of the liveliest times to visit, with a packed festival calendar. Warm sunny days are the norm, and although tourism picks up, the hordes have yet to arrive.

Festa do Fado

Lisbon's love affair with fado reaches a high point at this annual songfest held at the cinematic Castelo de São Jorge. You can also hear free fado on trams every Thursday and Sunday in June.

Festival Ollin Kan Portugal

Erupting in Vila do Conde, just north of Porto, is this world-music fest (www. ollinkanportugal.com). Hear top acts for free during the three-night event on the banks of the Rio Ave.

Festa do Corpo de Deus

This religious fest happens all across Northern Portugal on Corpus Christi, but is liveliest in Monção, with an old-fashioned medieval fair, theatrical shows and over-the-top processions.

FestivalMed

In the Algarve, Loulé's world-music festival (www.festivalmed.com. pt), held over three days, brings more than 50 bands playing an incredible variety of music including jazz, blues and soul as well as Arabic, Latin, African, Caribbean and Brazilian sounds. There's also world cuisine to go with the global beats.

Vaca das Cordas & Corpus Christi

Ponte de Lima gets rowdy during this unusual event, which features a bull on a rope let loose on the streets. A more solemn event follows suit with religious processions along flower-strewn streets.

Festas de Junho

One of the Douro's liveliest summertime fests happens in Amarante, when the town goes wild for its favourite saint and patron of lovers, São Gonçalo: all-night music, fireworks, markets and processions mark the occasion.

Feiras do Cavalo

In June, the pretty riverside town of Ponte de Lima hosts a fair in honour of its favourite quadruped, with horse-and-carriage races, live music and abundant food and drink.

Festa de Santo António

The lively Festival of St Anthony is celebrated with particular fervour in Lisbon's Alfama and Madragoa districts, with feasting, drinking and dancing in some 50 *arraiais* (street parties); see p77.

Festa de São João

St John is the favourite up north, where Porto, Braga and Vila do Conde celebrate with elaborate processions, music and feasting, while folks go around whacking each other with plastic hammers.

Feira Nacional da Agricultura

One of Portugal's biggest country fairs, this family-fun event turns Santarém, Ribatejo, into an oversized playground for horse-racing, bullfights, live music, feasting, dancing and bull-running through the streets; there's loads of entertainment for kids.

Festas Populares

Celebrating the feast days of São João and São Pedro, Évora hosts a lively 12-day event that kicks off in late June. There's a traditional fairground, art exposi-tions, gourmet food and drink, cultural events and sporting competitions.

July

The summer heat arrives, bringing with it a profusion of sun-seekers who pack the resorts of the Algarve. Lisbon and other popular destinations swell with crowds and prices peak in July and August. Open-air concerts and other events make good use of the warm nights.

Festival Internacional de Folclore

The week-long Internation-al Folk Festival in late July brings in costumed dancers and traditional groups to Porto from across Portugal and beyond.

Curtas

Held in the seaside hamlet of Vila do Conde, this edgy, popular short-film fest (www.curtas.pt)

has been running annually since 1993. It runs for eight days in early July.

Mercado Medieval

Don your armour and head to the castle grounds for this lively two-week medieval fair in Óbidos, Estremadura. Attractions include wandering min-strels, jousting matches and plenty of grog. Other medi-eval fairs are held in Silves and other castle towns.

August

The mercury rises even higher in August, with sweltering days best spent along the coast. This is one of Portugal's busiest tourist months, and advance booking of accommodation is essential. Big fests – the last of the summer – happen countrywide.

Festas de Cidade e Gualterianas

The old city of Guimarães brings revellers from across the region to its colourful processions with allegorical floats, plus folk dancing, fireworks and live bands (www.aoficina.pt).

Festival do Sudoeste

The Alentejan Glastonbury, in Zambujeira do Mar, at-tracts a young, surfy crowd with huge parties and big-name bands headlining.

Festival do Marisco

Seafood lovers should not miss this grand culinary fest in Olhão, the Algarve. High-lights including an endless array of regional specialities including chargrilled fish, *caldeirada* (fish stew) and *cataplana* (a kind of Portu-guese paella); there's also live music and refreshing wines and other drinks. For other eating festivals in the Algarve, see p180.

Romaria de Nossa Senhora d'Agonia

The Minho's most spec-tacular festival, in Viana do Castelo, has elaborate street paintings, folk cos-tume parades, drumming, giant puppets and much merry-making (see p421).

Feira de São Mateus

Folk music, traditional food and fireworks rule the day at St Matthew's Fair in Viseu, the Beiras.

Folkfaro

A musician's treat, the Folkfaro brings local and international folk per-formers to the city of Faro for staged and impromptu performances all across town. Street fairs accom-pany the event.

Noites Ritual Rock

Towards the end of sum-mer, Porto hosts a free weekend-long rock bash (www.noitesritual.com) that sees up-and-coming bands from around Por-tugal work big crowds at the Jardins do Palácio de Cristal.

Festa de Nossa Senhora dos Remédios

Head to Lamego, in the Douro, for a mix of reli-gious devotion and secular revelry. In early September, rock concerts and all-night celebrations happen in one part of town, while pious and beautifully elaborate processions wind through the streets.

September

Peak tourist season officially runs until mid-September, when ongoing warm weather ensures beaches remain packed. Things cool down a bit, and prices dip, as the crowds dissipate by late September.

Nossa Senhora da Nazaré

The festival of Our Lady of Nazaré brings much life to this eponymous town in Estremadura, with rich processions, folk music and dancing, bullfights and other competitions.

Feiras Novas

One of Portugal's most ancient ongoing events, the New Fairs festival has a massive market and fair, with folk dances, fireworks and brass bands at Ponte de Lima, the Minho.

October

Early autumn can be a magical time to visit, with crisp mornings and warm, pleasant sunny days. A lull descends on beach resorts (though many remain open) as the crowds disperse. October also brings lower lodging prices.

Feira de Santa Iria

Santa Iria (St Irene) may be obscure in some parts, but Faro puts her front and centre at processions, fairground fun, food and drink stalls, and art shows; there are plenty of amusements for kids.

November

November generally sees more rainy days and cooler temperatures, with fewer sunny days the further north you go. The Algarve remains pleasant and relatively dry, while northern regions can be quite wet and cold.

Feira de São Martinho

In the heart of horse country, this fair has a running of the bulls, bullfights, parades and nightly parties on the town square of Golegã, the Ribatejo.

December

December means more rain and colder temperatures. Few travellers venture south, where many resorts close for the winter. The buzz of Christmas and New Year's Eve brings merriment to the somewhat dreary season.

Festa dos Rapazes

Just after Christmas, the so-called Festival of the Lads is a rollicking time of merry-making by young unmarried men who light bonfires and rampage around in rags and wooden masks. Catch it in Miranda do Douro, Trás-os-Montes (see p469).

New Year's Eve

Ring in the Ano Novo in Lisbon with fireworks, free concerts and DJs down by the Tejo.

itineraries

Two Weeks
Lisbon to Porto: Highlights of Portugal

The great Portugal journey begins in **Lisbon**. Spend three days exploring the city's enchanting neighbourhoods, fado-filled taverns, atmospheric cafes and restaurants and late-night street parties. Take in vertiginous tram rides, the hilltop castle and viewing points, museums and historic sites. On day four, head to nearby **Sintra**, for quaint village life amid woodlands and palaces. Next enjoy two days exploring fascinating **Évora** and its nearby megaliths. From there, go south and spend a day in peaceful **Tavira**, one of the Algarve's prettiest towns, followed by a day in beach- and nightlife-loving **Lagos**. Head back to Lisbon, stopping en route in the laid-back coastal town of **Vila Nova de Milfontes**. Spend one day in **Tomar**, home of the staggering **Convento do Cristo**. Then book two nights in the prestigious university town of **Coimbra**, wandering the old quarters and enjoying some nightlife. Spend your last two days in **Porto**, Lisbon's rival in beauty. Enjoy a day exploring the Ribeira, then head across the river to **Vila Nova de Gaia**, for an intro to the country's great ports. If time allows, take a boat trip along the Rio Douro, taking in some dramatic gorge scenery.

Two to Three Weeks
Porto to Lisbon: Exploring the Atlantic Coast

> Scenic shorelines, captivating towns and Unesco World Heritage Sites set the stage for this memorable journey down the Atlantic coast. Begin in **Porto**, the port-wine capital at the mouth of the Douro. Spend two days exploring its historic centre, museums, parks and gardens, plus the beach neighbourhood of Foz do Douro. On the third day go north to the seaside town of **Vila do Conde**, a quick and popular beach getaway with a historic centre. Next, head south to **Aveiro**, for rides along its scenic canals from high-prowed *moliceiros* (traditional boats). For a fine day trip from here take a bus and ferry out to the **Reserva Natural das Dunas de São Jacinto**, a scenic nature reserve and birdwatching site. The popular resort town of **Figueira da Foz** is the next stop; you'll find prime surfing, a touch of nightlife and wide people-packed beaches, with more isolated sands out of town. After a day of sunbaking, make an inland day trip to the striking mountain-top castle of **Montemor-o-Velho**. The picturesque and fun-loving beach town of **Nazaré** is next and here you can frolic in the waves, enjoy traditional seafood restaurants and take the funicular to a cliff-top promontory for superb views. Nazaré is also a good base for exploring the architecturally stunning monasteries (and Unesco World Heritage Sites) in **Alcobaça** and **Batalha**. From there, head south to the historic centre of **Óbidos**, with its cobblestone lanes and upmarket inns. Go west back to the coast to reach **Peniche**, where you'll find excellent beaches, particularly in the picturesque island village of nearby **Baleal**. From Peniche, be sure to take a boat out to the rocky and remote island of **Berlenga Grande**. You can even stay overnight (reserve well ahead). Continue south to **Ericeira**, a whitewashed village perched atop sandstone cliffs. Explore the beaches, feast on seafood, then continue on to the fairy-tale setting of **Sintra**, whose picturesque guest houses make a fine overnight stay. The next stop is the pretty village of **Cascais**, home to narrow pedestrian lanes, lively outdoor restaurants and bars, gardens, and a coastal path that leads 9km out to the gorgeous, windswept beach of **Praia do Guincho**. End your journey in **Lisbon**, spending a few days discovering the many charms of Portugal's vibrant capital.

Two Weeks
Southern Beauty

This trip will give you a chance to see spectacular contrasts in scenery by following Portugal's southern rivers, beaches and ridges. From **Lisbon** head to the **Costa da Caparica**, taking in the festive beaches near the town, and then escaping the crowds on wilder beaches to the south. Next head down to **Praia do Meco** for more sandy action and some great seafood. Keep going south to reach the desolate cliffs of **Cabo Espichel**. A good place to stay for the night is at rural guest houses outside of **Sesimbra**, a former fishing-village-turned-resort with open-air restaurants and family-friendly beaches. On the next day, continue east, stopping for a picnic on the incredibly photogenic shores of the wooded **Parque Natural da Arrábida**. At night, stay in **Setúbal** for more seafood feasting and a wander through the sleepy old-town quarters. The next day, book a dolphin-watching boat trip along the **Sado Estuary**. From Setúbal, take the ferry across to handsomely sited Tróia. Continue south to overnight in **Vila Nova de Milfontes**, a lovely seaside town with fine beaches and charming guest houses. Next is **Zambujeira do Mar**, a tiny village perched above a pretty beach. Follow the coast to **Aljezur**, with its unspoilt, cliff-backed sands, and into the rustic town of **Carrapateira**, with more wild, untouched beaches, plus cafes and guest houses catering to the surf-loving crowd.

Head south, and you'll reach the southern coast at pretty, laid-back **Sagres**, another surf-loving town, with both high-end and budget restaurants and guest houses. Visit Sagres' famous sea-cliff fortress as well as the surreal cliffs of **Cabo de São Vicente**.

Go east to **Lagos**, one of the Algarve's liveliest towns with loads of good sleeping, eating and drinking options. Afterwards, go inland to **Monchique**, with its densely wooded hillsides that offer picturesque walking, cycling and pony-trekking opportunities, followed by a spa visit in **Caldas de Monchique**. Back on the coast, stay overnight in the old town centre of lively **Faro**, before journeying out to the **Parque Natural da Ria Formosa**, a lagoon system full of marsh, creeks and dune islands. From there, head to **Tavira**, set with genteel 18th-century buildings straddling the Rio Gilão. This picturesque river town is a fine base for a boat trip across to the long idyllic beach of **Ilha de Tavira**.

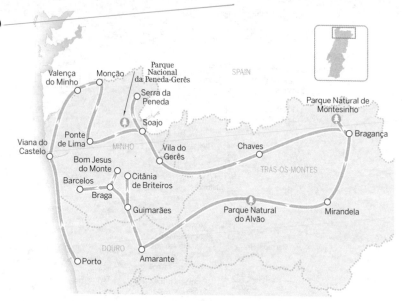

Two Weeks
Around the Minho & Trás-os-Montes

> Portugal's oft-ignored northern region makes a great destination for exploring preserved villages and pristine national parks ripe for outdoor adventure. It's also home to colourful markets and the nation's most traditional festivals. From **Porto**, head up the coast to the beautifully set town of **Viana do Castelo**, which is also just a short ferry ride from the north's best beaches. Continue up to the border fortress of **Valença do Minho** and tiny **Monção**, both perched scenically over the Minho River.

From here, travel south to the charming town of **Ponte de Lima**, with its garden-lined riverbanks and picture-book Roman bridge; stock up here before heading to the remote stone village of **Soajo**, a great base for walks amid untouched mountain scenery. For more outdoor adventures inside the **Parque Nacional da Peneda-Gerês**, go hiking in the little-visited **Serra da Peneda**, the northern part of the park, where low-lying forests meld into glacially formed peaks. Afterwards, loop east to the spa town **Vila do Gerês** and nearby spots for canoeing, mountain biking and more great hiking.

Continue east to **Chaves**, where its Roman bridge and fascinating old centre attest to its many layers of history. Overnight in **Bragança**, home to a 12th-century citadel and cradle of the Portuguese royal family. Strike out into the **Parque Natural de Montesinho** with its ancient stone villages and lush forests.

Loop back south and then west through pretty **Mirandela** and **Parque Natural do Alvão**, windswept high country of waterfalls, schist villages and traditional lifestyles.

Heading west, visit **Amarante**, famous for its monastery, pastries and pretty riverside. Then go north to **Guimarães**, birthplace of Portugal and home to an immaculately preserved medieval centre. While here, visit the Celtic ruins of **Citânia de Briteiros** for a dose of early history.

Nearing the journey's end go to beautiful **Braga**, a town of magnificent churches and manicured plazas set with fine restaurants and outdoor cafes. For great city views, take in the hilltop sanctuary of **Bom Jesus do Monte**. If you're passing on a Thursday, take a day trip to **Barcelos** for its famous weekly market.

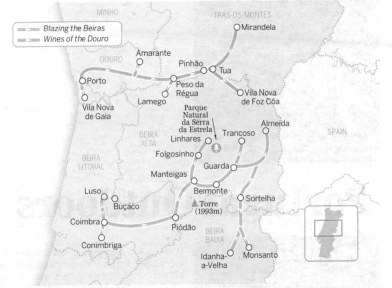

One to Two Weeks
Blazing the Beiras

❭ Natural scenery, frozen-in-time villages and cliff-top castles make for a charming journey through the Beiras. Start in lively, historic **Coimbra**, soaking up the sights and taking a day trip to the Roman ruins at **Conimbriga**. Nearby is the royal retreat and spa of **Luso** and **Buçaco**. Go back through Coimbra and continue east for an overnight in the old stone village of **Piódão**.

Next, explore the **Parque Natural da Serra da Estrela**, with mountainous scenery, great hiking and Portugal's highest point (and only ski resort), **Torre**. Base yourself at cobblestone **Manteigas**, near hot springs and forested slopes, and spend a day poking around **Linhares** and **Folgosinho**, captivating hilltop villages with small castles to the north. To the east is beautiful **Belmonte**, a peaceful hill town overlooking the Serra da Estrela.

Descend via the highland town of **Guarda**, then head north to **Trancoso**, a medieval walled town. From here, loop back through Guarda and northeast to the castle-village of **Almeida**. Head south to **Sortelha**, another fortified cliff-top stunner. Continue south to the fairy-tale village of **Monsanto**, and neighbouring **Idanha-a-Velha**, with Roman and Visigoth roots.

One Week
Wines of the Douro

❭ Wine lovers have their work cut out for them on a leisurely journey through the Douro Valley, Portugal's premier wine-growing region. Any self-respecting wine tour will begin in **Porto**, gateway to the world's most famous port-wine region. Across the river is the historic **Vila Nova de Gaia**, where you can sample countless varieties at its many port-wine lodges.

Continue the journey east following the Douro. Detour north to **Amarante**, famous for its monastery, pastries and pretty riverside. Back on the river continue to **Peso da Régua**, set at the heart of vineyard country. Wine-taste your way to the quaint riverside village of **Pinhão**, a great place to base for a few nights, with scenic guest houses, good restaurants and vineyards sprinkling the area. A fine day or overnight trip from here is the scenic narrow-gauge railway from **Tua** through almond-blossom country to **Mirandela**.

East of Pinhão, take the picturesque drive over the mountains to **Vila Nova de Foz Côa**, famed for the Palaeolithic stone carvings in the surrounding countryside. On the way back to Porto, visit the attractive food- and wine-loving town of **Lamego**, producer of a fine sparkling wine.

Portugal Outdoors

10 Great Beaches

Cabedelo (Minho)
Figueira da Foz (Beiras)
São Martinho do Porto (Estremadura)
Foz do Arelho (Estremadura)
Guincho (Lisbon Coast)
Portinho da Arrábida (Lisbon Coast)
Costa da Caparica (Lisbon Coast)
Zambujeira (Alentejo)
Ilha de Tavira (Algarve)
Dona Ana (Algarve)

Best Places to Walk

Parque Nacional da Peneda-Gerês (Minho)
Parque Natural da Serra da Estrela (Beiras)
Via Algarviana (Algarve)
Parque Natural de Montesinho (Trás-os-Montes)

Best Places to Cycle

Costa Azul near Setúbal (Lisbon Coast)
Douro valley (Douro)
Ecovia do Rio Lima (Minho)
Ecovia do Litoral (Algarve)

Best Places to Watch Wildlife

Parque Natural da Ria Formosa (Algarve)
Sado estuary (Lisbon Coast)
Parque Natural do Douro Internacional (Trás-os-Montes)

With 830km of coastline and beaches for every taste, Portugal attracts its fair share of sun worshippers. Perfect waves and winds make the country a paradise for surfers and windsurfers, and there's a seemingly endless range of other pursuits to enjoy along the country's Atlantic shores: diving, dolphin watching, golfing, kayaking...

Outdoors enthusiasts will find plenty to appreciate in Portugal beyond sun, surf and sand. Inland, landscapes of cork and olive trees, granite peaks, limestone heights and precipitous river gorges form the backdrop for a host of other activities – from walking to birdwatching, horse riding to paragliding. And as you leave the coast behind, the crowds grow thinner and the prices – already among Europe's lowest – go down.

Thanks to Portugal's geographic compactness, there's no reason you can't combine multiple outdoor adventures in a single trip. It's not unreasonable to plan a rock-climbing/surfing vacation or even – in late winter – to trade in your waterskis for a day slaloming down the snowy slopes of Torre, Portugal's highest mountain.

But if all you're really after is the perfect beach, you've come to the right place. Roughly half of Portugal's border is formed by its long Atlantic shoreline, and there's a beach for just about every taste – from tranquil moon-shaped coves to rocky shores pounded by raging surf; from kilometres of nearly untouched sand to party beaches where holidaymakers pack like sardines under the sandstone cliffs. So pack your bathing suit and towel, get out and explore!

Surfing

Portugal has some of Europe's most curvaceous surf, with 30 to 40 major reefs and beaches. It picks up swells from the north, south and west, giving it remarkable consistency. It also has a wide variety of waves and swell size, making it ideal for surfers of all levels. Numerous surf schools in the Algarve and along Portugal's western Atlantic coast offer classes and all-inclusive packages for all skill levels, from beginners to advanced.

When to Surf

The best waves in southern Portugal are generally in the winter from November to March. Further north, spring and autumn tend to be the best seasons for surfing action. Waves at these times range from 2m to 4.5m high. This is also the low season, meaning you'll pay less for accommodation, and the beaches will be far less crowded. Even during the summer, however, the coast gets good waves (1m to 1.5m on average) and, despite the crowds, it's fairly easy to head off and find your own spots (with your own wheels, you can often be on your own stretch of beach just by driving a few minutes up the road).

What to Take

The water temperature here is colder than it is in most other southern European countries, and even in the summer you'll probably want a wetsuit. Board and wetsuit rental are widely available at surf shops and surf camps; you can usually score a discount if you rent long-term – otherwise, you'll be paying around €20 to €30 per day for board and wetsuit rental, or €15 to €25 per day for the board only.

WORLD CHAMPIONSHIP WAVES

In 2009, Portugal's surf scene got a real shot in the arm when **Supertubos** beach near Peniche was chosen as one of 10 stops on the ASP World Tour, the most prestigious international competitive surfing event. For 12 days in October, the beach was packed with surfers from around the world showing off their best moves. The event's organisers apparently liked what they saw – Supertubos hosted the international contest again in 2010.

Prime Spots

One of Portugal's best breaks is around Peniche (p256), where you can count on good waves with just about any wind. An excellent hostel and several residential surf camps make this an affordable base. Supertubos and Baleal are the most popular local beaches.

Other fabled surf spots include Ribeira d'Ilhas (p253) in Ericeira and Praia do Guincho (p119) near Cascais, which often host international championships. Another break that's famous among the global surfing community is Carrapateira (p189) in the western Algarve. Schools and clubs head over this way from Lagos and further afield to take advantage of the crashing waves. Nearby, the area around Praia do Penedo is a good choice for beginners.

There are countless other good surf spots up and down the coast, including but by no means limited to the following, from north to south: Viana do Castelo, Praia da Barra,

SURFER SITES

For information on wave conditions, competitions and more, surf on over to one of these helpful sites.

» **www.ligaprosurf.com** Official site of the Portuguese National Surfer's Association, which organises the national Liga ProSurf competition

» **www.magicseaweed.com** International site with English-language surf reports for many Portuguese beaches

» **www.surfingportugal.com** Official site of the Portuguese Surfing Federation

» **www.surftotal.com/pt** Another Portuguese-language site with news about the national surf scene and webcams showing conditions at a dozen popular beaches around Portugal

Portugal Outdoors

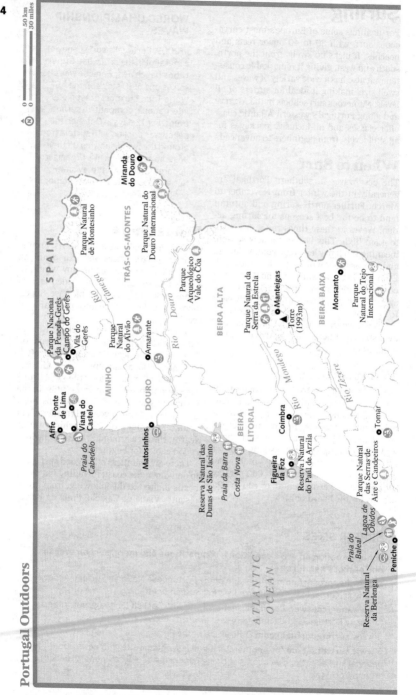

50 km
30 miles

ATLANTIC OCEAN

SPAIN

MINHO

DOURO

TRÁS-OS-MONTES

BEIRA ALTA

BEIRA LITORAL

BEIRA BAIXA

Parque Nacional da Peneda-Gerês
Campo do Gerês
Vila do Gerês

Parque Natural de Montesinho

Miranda do Douro

Parque Natural do Douro Internacional

Parque Natural do Alvão

Amarante

Parque Arqueológico Vale do Côa

Parque Natural da Serra da Estrela

Manteigas

Torre (1993m)

Monsanto

Parque Natural do Tejo Internacional

Afife
Ponte de Lima
Viana do Castelo

Praia do Cabedelo

Matosinhos

Reserva Natural das Dunas de São Jacinto

Praia da Barra
Costa Nova

Coimbra

Figueira da Foz

Reserva Natural do Paúl de Arzila

Parque Natural das Serras de Aire e Candeeiros

Tomar

Praia do Baleal
Lagoa de Óbidos

Reserva Natural da Berlenga

Peniche

Rio Tâmega
Rio Douro
Rio Douro
Rio Mondego
Rio Zêzere

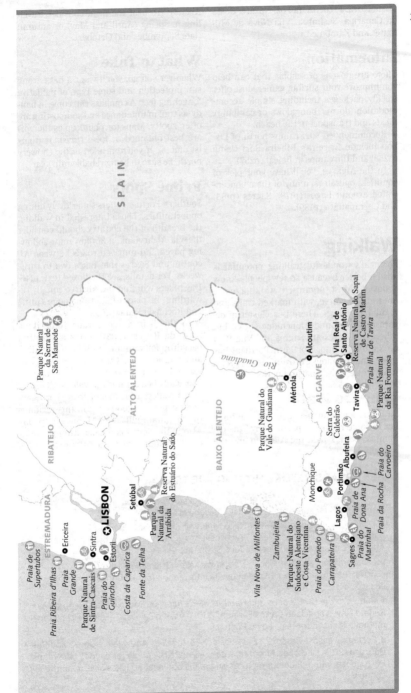

Costa Nova, Figueira da Foz, Nazaré, Costa da Caparica, Sesimbra, Vila Nova de Milfontes and Zambujeira.

Information

There are dozens of schools that can help you improve your surfing game. Most offer weekly packages including simple accommodation (dorms, bungalows or camping), meals and transport to the beach.

Recommended surf camps north of Lisbon include Ericeira's Ribeira Surf Camp (p253) and the camps at Baleal (p257).

In the Algarve, you'll have your pick of countless operators, many of them concentrated around Lagos (p178), Sagres (p185) and Carrapateira (p189).

Walking

Portugal's wonderful walking potential is all the better because so few people know about it. Most organised walking clubs are in the Algarve, with marked trails and regular meetings. There is a cluster of organisations around Monchique (p193) but other good bases are Sagres and Vila Real de Santo António. Northern Portugal has more mountainous terrain and several lovely, little-visited natural parks.

When to Walk

Summer temperatures can get stiflingly hot in some regions – particularly Trás-os-Montes, Beira Baixa, the Alentejo and the Algarve. To beat the heat, consider travelling in spring (April and May) or autumn (late September and October).

What to Take

Wherever you go, you'll want a hat, strong sun protection and some type of palliative for aching feet. A compass can come in handy, as trail maintenance and signposting are often spotty. Maps (or photocopies thereof) are best obtained at local *turismos* (tourist offices). If you're headed to the showery north, be sure to bring reliable rain gear.

Prime Spots

Southern Portugal offers some lovely hiking opportunities. Those interested in walking the breadth of the country should consider the Via Algarviana, a 300km route following paved and unpaved roads between Alcoutim and Sagres that takes two to three weeks. For details, see the boxed text, p145. Day hikers will find the Algarve equally rewarding, in places like Monchique (p192) and Rocha da Pena (p165).

In the Beiras, the Parque Natural da Serra da Estrela (p331) forms a beautiful backdrop for walking, with both day hikes and multiday itineraries. In many places you're likely to have the trail to yourself. Especially beautiful is the Vale do Zêzere, a glacial valley at the foot of Torre, Portugal's highest peak. A good base in this region is the mountain village of Manteigas (p336). Also in the Beiras is the beautiful multiday GR-22 walking route, a 540km circuit of

---

BEST READS BEFORE HITTING THE TRAIL

The following books, available online or at bookstores in Lisbon and Porto, are great planning aids for some of the country's best hikes.

» *Walking in the Algarve: 40 Coastal & Mountain Walks*, by Julie Statham and June Parker (2006), Cicerone Press – An excellent guide co-authored by British-born Algarve resident and tour leader Julie Statham

» *Landscapes of Algarve: Car Tours and Walks*, by Brian and Eileen Anderson (2007), Sunflower Books – Lots of useful information for exploring the southern coast

» *Routes to the Landscapes and Habitats of Portugal*, by Pedro Castro Henriques, Renato Neves and João Carlos Farinha (2001), Assirio & Alvim – Features environmentally focused routes all over Portugal

» *Portugal Passo-a-Passo: 20 Passeios por Portugal*, by Abel Melo e Sousa and Rui Cardoso (2004), Edições Afrontamento – A great little guide for anyone who reads Portuguese, with full-colour pictures and maps outlining 20 hikes all around the country

GREAT OUTDOOR ADVENTURES FOR FAMILIES

» Mountain bike through the outback to see the Palaeolithic petroglyphs at Parque Arqueológico do Vale do Côa (p397)

» Kayak with your kids down the Rio Mondego from Penacova to Coimbra (p305)

» Learn to surf with the whole family at Hooked Surf School in Costa da Caparica (p127)

» Take the invigoratingly bouncy boat ride from Peniche to Berlenga Grande, then stay overnight in a 17th-century fort converted into a hostel (p259)

» Look for dolphins – and learn about them from an onboard marine biologist – as you ply the Atlantic waters off the Algarve coast (p178)

» Walk through a landscape of dramatic mountains and stone shepherds' huts as you climb the glacial Zêzere Valley, then cool off with icy water from a natural spring in Parque Natural Serra da Estrela (p337)

» Scan the horizon for pirates from the 17th-century fort, play king of the castle at the Moorish *castelo*, or build sandcastles of your own on the beach at Sesimbra (p133)

» Take the narrow-gauge train to the lovely, wild beaches along Costa Caparica (p127)

» See dinosaur footprints – yes, *real* dinosaur footprints! – at Cabo Espichel (p136) or Monumento Natural das Pegadas dos Dinossáurios (p276)

aldeias históricas (historic villages) including medieval hill towns such as Sortelha, Linhares and Monsanto.

Perhaps the country's best walking is in the far north, where Parque Nacional da Peneda-Gerês (p436) offers gorgeous hikes over mountainous terrain, encompassing forests, villages, high-altitude boulder fields, archaeological sites and ancient Roman milestones. A quiet base for adventure is Campo do Gerês, while a busier touristy base (but with lots of services) is Vila do Gerês. In neighbouring Trás-os-Montes, the natural parks of Montesinho (p461), Alvão (p449) and Douro Internacional (p468) also have some splendid trails connecting the region's remarkably picturesque stone villages.

Closer to civilisation, there are some great day hikes in prime tourist areas, including the walk along the top of Évora's 16th-century aqueduct (p201) and the climb from Sintra to its 9th-century Moorish castle (p112).

Walking Tours

If you love to walk but hate to plan, why not consider an organised walking tour? The companies listed here offer both group walking tours – complete with tour leader – and self-guided tours where you walk independently, following an itinerary provided by the tour company, with pre-arranged meals and lodging included in the price.

About 10km north of Sagres, walking-guide author Julie Statham runs **Portugal Walks** (www.portugalwalks.com), which offers weeklong packages (self-guided/group walks from €450/590) in mainland Portugal as well as Madeira and the Azores.

SANTIAGO DE COMPOSTELA

Every year thousands of walkers from around the world hike the **Camino de Santiago**, the classic pilgrimage route from France to Santiago de Compostela, Spain. But what if you're already in Portugal? Portuguese pilgrims have their own route to Santiago, less crowded but just as interesting for lovers of long-distance walking. Like its sister trail to the north, the **Caminho Português** has multiple starting points, but the best-known section originates in Porto. Information is available through the Associação dos Amigos do Caminho Português de Santiago (www.caminho portuguesdesantiago.com).

Another dependable Portuguese outfitter offering guided walks throughout the country is **A2Z Adventures** (www.a2z-adventures.com).

Also try these UK-based companies:

ATG Oxford (www.atg-oxford.co.uk) Offers weeklong guided walking holidays between Sintra and Cascais, and also in the Azores.

Headwater (www.headwater.com) Weeklong jaunts in the Serra da Estrela and Alentejo regions.

Ramblers Holidays (www.ramblersholidays.co.uk) Guided one- to two-week walking holidays in the Minho, the Douro, Trás-os-Montes and the Algarve.

Sherpa Expeditions (www.sherpa-walking-holidays.co.uk) Self-guided walks in the Alentejo and Madeira.

Sistemas de Ar Livre (www.sal.pt) More suitable for long-term, Portuguese-speaking visitors than for casual tourists, this local organisation of outdoor enthusiasts schedules regular low-cost outings.

VBT Bicycling & Walking Vacations (www.vbt.com) Guided weeklong walking tours in the Douro, Minho and Beiras regions.

Information

Many *turismos* and natural-park offices offer free brochures about local walks, although materials frequently go out of print due to insufficient funding. Other organisations that produce free maps of their own trails include Odiana in the Algarve (p162) and the Centro de Interpretação da Serra da Estrela (CISE) in the Serra da Estrela (p333).

Portugal uses a system of coloured blazes to mark its trails. White and red are the colours of choice for the major multiday trails known as Grandes Rotas, while red and yellow blazes indicate Pequenas Rotas (shorter day hikes). Common blaze patterns and their meanings are outlined here.

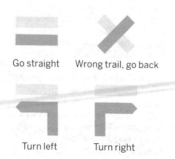

Go straight	Wrong trail, go back

Turn left	Turn right

Other Outdoor Activities

While walking and cycling can be done at the drop of a hat, many other outdoor activities need a bit more organisation – and often specialist kit, as well as guides or instructors. Below are a few ideas to inform and inspire. If you need more details while you're travelling in Portugal, *turismos* can advise about specialist local operators and adventure centres.

Climbing, Paragliding & Adrenalin Sports

In the far north, the granite peaks of Parque Nacional da Peneda-Gerês (p435) are a climber's paradise. Other popular places are the schist cliffs at Nossa Senhora do Salto east of Porto; the rugged 500m-tall granite outcropping of Cántaro Magro (p339) in the Serra da Estrela; the limestone crags of Reguengo do Fetal near Fátima; the sheer rock walls of Penedo da Amizade, just below Sintra's Moorish castle; the dramatic quartzite ridge of Penha Garcia, near Monsanto in Beira Baixa; and Rocha da Pena (p152) in the Algarve.

Useful organisations for climbers include Clube Nacional de Montanhismo (www.cnm.org.pt) and Grupo de Montanha e Escalada de Sintra (www.gmesintra.com). The latter publishes free downloadable topo guides to popular climbing spots as well as the online climbing magazine Vertigem (www.vertigem-mag.com).

Paragliding is also popular in the north. Two prime launch sites are Linhares in the Serra da Estrela and Alvados in the Parque das Serras de Aire e Candeeiros.

Several local adrenalin-sports outfitters have English-language websites.

Capitão Dureza (www.capitaodureza.com) This Coimbra-based group organises high-adrenalin activities including rafting, canyoning, mountain biking and trekking.

Freetour (www.freetour.pt) This Leiria-based agency sponsors a similar mix of activities, plus paragliding, skydiving and other adrenalin sports throughout Portugal.

Trilhos (www.trilhos.pt) A Porto-based company promoting environmental tourism, offering climbing, caving, canyoning, trekking and other adventure sports.

SKI PORTUGAL?

Switzerland it isn't – or not even Spain! – but believe it or not, Portugal has a downhill ski run. The country's highest peak, 1993m-high Torre in Parque Natural da Serra da Estrela, offers basic facilities including three lifts and equipment rental (p339). Truth be told, Torre offers more curiosity value than actual skiing excitement, and the mountain landscape is so fragile that it's hard to recommend this as sustainable tourism. If you're really hard-up, and want a (slightly) less environmentally damaging alternative, you can always hit the rather surreal 'dry ski' run at SkiParque east of Manteigas (p338).

Vertente Natural (www.vertentenatural.com) An all-round outfitter in Sesimbra that can organise everything from parasailing to coasteering, climbing to spelunking.

Boating

Along the coast, especially in the Algarve, pleasure boats predominate, offering everything from barbecue cruises to grotto tours to dolphin-spotting excursions. Inland, Portugal's rivers, lagoons and reservoirs offer a wide variety of boating opportunities, including kayaking, sailing, rafting and canoeing. Rivers popular for boating include the Guadiana (see p195), Mondego, Zêzere, Paiva, Minho and Tâmega.

Companies that rent boats and/or operate boat trips can be found in Lagos (p178), Mértola (p236), Barragem do Alqueva (p214), Tomar (p286), Coimbra (p305), Ponte de Lima (p429), Rio Caldo (p441) and Amarante (p386), just to name a few.

Cycling

Portugal has many exhilarating opportunities for **mountain biking** (*bicicleta todo terreno;* BTT). Monchique and Tavira in the Algarve, Sintra and Setúbal in central Portugal and Parque Nacional da Peneda-Gerês in the north are all popular starting points.

Bicycle trails are also growing in popularity. Along the Rio Lima in the north, cyclists can ride the Ecovia do Rio Lima (p429), a 32km rails-to-trails greenway that will eventually extend to Viana do Castelo on the Atlantic coast. Another brand new rail-to-trails initiative, the 52km Ecopista between Viseu and Santa Comba Dão in the Beiras, is just opening as this book goes to press. Down south, the ambitious Ecovia do Litoral (p145) is a 214km cycling route across the Algarve that will eventually connect Cabo de Sao Vicente at Portugal's southwestern tip to Vila Real de Santo António on the Spanish border. Meanwhile, bike paths have become fixtures of the urban landscape around Lisbon (p79) and in northern cities like Porto, Coimbra and Guarda; popular bike trails have also cropped up in coastal venues such as the Estremadura's Pinhal de Leiria and the Lisbon coast between Cascais and Praia do Guincho.

Cycling Tours

If you're looking for a good day trip or a longer cycling holiday, the following excellent local companies can point you in the right direction.

Blue Coast Bikes (www.bluecoastbikes. com), an American-Portuguese partnership based in Setúbal, offers both guided and self-guided tours countrywide, with good maps and a special emphasis on their home territory, Alentejo and the Costa Azul. Their mechanic is a former Portuguese downhill and cross-country champion.

Pedal in Portugal (www.pedalinportugal. com) is another well-established, Portugal-based company offering both guided and self-guided road- and mountain-bike tours throughout the country, from the Algarve to the Douro wine country.

You can also try the following UK- and US-based companies.

Backroads (www.backroads.com) Offers guided cycling tours in the Douro and Minho regions.

PENNILESS PEDALLING

Fancy a ride without spending a euro-cent? An increasing number of Portuguese towns have adopted **free bike programs**. In places like Aveiro (p323) and Cascais (p119) you can show up at the local free bike agency, provide a photo ID, fill out a short form and presto! – off you go on your very own bicycle.

Easy Rider Tours (www.easyridertours.com) Features several guided cycling itineraries in the Minho, Alentejo and Algarve and along the Lisbon coast near Sintra.

Saddle Skedaddle (www.skedaddle.co.uk) Offers a weeklong self-guided tour through the eastern Beiras and Alentejo, along the border with Spain.

Saranjan Tours (www.saranjan.com) High-end cycling tours in the Algarve, Alentejo, Minho and Douro regions.

Sherpa Expeditions (www.sherpa-walking-holidays.co.uk) Self-guided cycling tours on Portugal's southwest coast.

For additional practical information on cycling in Portugal, see p530.

Diving

Portugal's best dive sites are concentrated in the Algarve. The water temperature is a bit crisp (around 14°C to 16°C, though it doesn't vary much between summer and winter); most divers prefer a 5mm suit. Visibility is usually between 4m and 6m; on the best days, it can range from 15m to 20m.

One of the best places for beginners to learn to dive is off Praia do Carvoeiro, with several operators offering PADI-accredited courses in English (p168). PADI-accredited courses are also offered in Lagos (p178) and Sagres (p186), among other Algarve locations.

Closer to Lisbon, there are diving outfits at Costa da Caparica (p127), Sesimbra (p134) and Reserva Natural da Berlenga (p257).

Golf

Portugal is a golf mecca, and its championship courses are famous for their rolling greens and ocean vistas. Although many courses are frequented mainly by club members and local property owners, anyone with a handicap certificate can play here. Greens fees usually run from €70 to €100 per round.

Estoril has nearly a dozen spectacular courses. Golf do Estoril, one of Portugal's best-known, has hosted the Portuguese Open Championship 20 times. It's 5262m long and set among eucalyptus, pine and mimosa. Two other Portuguese Open venues lie nearby: Oitavos Dunes, which rolls over windblown dunes and rocky outcrops; and Penha Longa, ranked one of Europe's best courses, with superb views of the Serra de Sintra. See www.estorilsintragolf.net or the Estoril and Cascais *turismos* for full details of all courses.

Two other well-regarded courses around Lisbon are Troia Golf near Setubal and Praia d'El Rey Golf & Beach Resort near Óbidos.

The Algarve has three-dozen courses at last count – including the renowned Vilamoura Oceânico Victoria, San Lorenzo, Monte Rei and Vale do Lobo courses. For a general overview, see the complete course guide at www.algarve-golf.com.

For golfing packages around Lisbon and in the Algarve, try UK-based **3D Golf** (www.3dgolf.com).

Bear in mind that golf courses' toll on the environment can be significant, especially in dry and fragile coastal settings like the Algarve (see p150).

Horse Riding

Riding is a fantastic way to experience Portugal's countryside. Lusitano thoroughbreds hail from Portugal, and experienced riders can take dressage lessons in Estremadura. Otherwise, there are dozens of horse-riding centres – especially in the Alentejo, and in the Algarve at places like Silves (p171), Lagos (p179), Portimão (p173) and Albufeira (p166). Northern Portugal also offers some pleasant settings for rides, including Campo do Gerês (p442) at the edge of Parque Nacional da Peneda-Gerês. Rates are usually around €20 to €30 per hour.

Switzerland-based **Equitour** (www.equitour .com) offers eight-day riding holidays costing €1292 to €2325 per person, including accommodation and some meals. Its signature tour follows the Alentejo Royal Horse Stud Trail, with stays at grand country estates. Other destinations include the Alentejo coast and the Algarve.

The Wyoming-based outfit **Equitours** (www.ridingtours.com), America's largest and oldest, offers a year-round classical dressage program on Lusitano horses at the Escola de Equitação de Alcainça, near Mafra, including accommodation plus 90 minutes/three hours of riding per day for €235/285.

Wildlife Watching

Portugal provides excellent opportunities for **birdwatching**, especially in Atlantic coastal lagoons and the deep river canyons along the Spanish border. In the south, prime birdwatching spots include the Serra do Caldeirão (p152), Parque Natural da Ria Formosa (p151), Parque Natural do Vale do Guadiana (p235) and the Reserva Natural do Sapal de Castro Marim e Vila Real de Santo Antonio (p161).

North of Lisbon, the Berlenga Islands make a perfect place to observe seabirds (p259). Other good places for birdwatching

NATURAL PARKS & RESERVES

Portugal's mixed bag of natural parks and reserves is worth the effort. The Parque Nacional da Peneda-Gerês is the country's only bona fide *parque nacional* (national park), but there are 24 other *parques naturais* (natural parks), *reservas naturais* (nature reserves) and *paisagens protegidas* (protected landscape areas). These areas total some 6500 sq km – just over 7% of Portugal's land area.

The **Instituto da Conservação da Natureza e da Biodiversidade** (ICNB; www.icnb.pt; Rua de Santa Marta 55, Lisbon) is the government agency responsible for the parks. It has general information, but detailed maps and English-language materials are sometimes hard to come by. Standards of maintenance and facilities vary wildly, but there are signs of improvements of trails and resources within the parks. For a picture of all the rich wildlife and diverse landscapes on offer, browse the table below.

PARK OR RESERVE NAME	FEATURES
Parque Nacional da Peneda-Gerês (p435)	lushly forested mountains, rock-strewn plateaus; deer, birds of prey, hot springs, wolves, long-horned cattle
Parque Natural da Arrábida (p134)	coastal mountain range, damaged by wildfire; birds of prey, diverse flora
Parque Natural da Ria Formosa (p151)	salty coastal lagoons, lakes, marshes & dunes; rich bird life, beaches, Mediterranean chameleons
Parque Natural da Serra da Estrela (p331)	pristine mountains – Portugal's highest; rich bird life, rare herbs
Parque Natural das Serras de Aire e Candeeiros (p277)	limestone mountains, cave systems; covered in gorse & olive trees
Parque Natural de Montesinho (p461)	remote oasis of peaceful grassland & forest; last wild refuge for Iberian wolf
Parque Natural de Sintra-Cascais (p116)	rugged coastline & mountains; diverse flora
Parque Natural do Alvão (p449)	granite basin, pine forest, waterfalls; rich bird life, deer, boar
Parque Natural do Douro Internacional (p468)	canyon country with high cliffs & lakes; home to many endangered birds of prey
Parque Natural do Vale do Guadiana (p235)	gentle hills & plains, rivers; rare birds of prey, snakes, toads, prehistoric sites
Parque Natural do Sudoeste Alentejano e Costa Vicentina (p189)	coastal cliffs & remote beaches; unique plants, otters, foxes, 200 bird types
Reserva Natural da Berlenga (p259)	remote islands in clear seas, rock formations, caves; seabirds
Reserva Natural das Dunas de São Jacinto (p320)	thickly wooded coastal park; rich in bird life
Reserva Natural do Estuário do Sado (Sado estuary; p129)	estuary of mud, marshes, lagoons & dunes; bird life including flamingos; molluscs, bottlenose dolphins
Reserva Natural do Sapal de Castro Marim e Vila Real de Santo António (p161)	marshland & salt pans; flamingos, spoonbills, avocet, caspian terns, white storks

include Reserva Natural do Paúl de Arzila near Coimbra (p314), Dunas de São Jacinto near Aveiro (p320) and the Tejo and Douro gorges, where vultures and eagles nest in the Parque Natural do Tejo Internacional (p327) and Parque Natural do Douro Internacional (p468).

Portugal's leading ornithological society is the Sociedade Portuguêsa para o Estudo de Aves (www.spea.pt; 2nd fl, Av da Liberdade 105, Lisbon), which runs government-funded projects to map the distribution of Portugal's breeding birds.

For birdwatching and other nature-oriented **guided excursions** in the Algarve, there are several excellent options:

Formosamar (www.formosamar.pt) The local environmental organisation offers two-hour tours in Parque Natural da Ria Formosa, employing marine biologists and raptor specialists as guides.

Wildaway (www.wildaway.com), based in Portugal, offers day tours of the Algarve's lagoons, wetlands, salt marshes and tidal flats. Prices for a guided seven-hour day trip start at €91 for one to three people, or €136 for four to six people.

Naturetrek (www.naturetrek.co.uk), UK-based, runs an eight-day birdwatching excursion around southern Portugal starting at £1295.

Various companies in the Algarve and around the Sado estuary near Setubal offer **dolphin-spotting** trips, including Mar Ilimitado (p186), Dolphins Driven (p166), and Dizzy Dolphins, Algarve Dolphins and Dolphin Seafaris (p179).

Windsurfing & Kitesurfing

Praia do Guincho (p119), west of Sintra, and Portimão (p173) in the Algarve are both world-championship windsurfing sites. Other prime spots include (from north to south) Viana do Castelo's Praia do Cabedelo; Lagoa de Óbidos, a pretty lagoon that draws both sailors and windsurfers; and (closer to Lisbon) the Costa da Caparica's Fonte da Telha. In the Algarve, Sagres attracts pros (its strong winds and fairly flat seas are ideal for free-riding), while Lagos, Albufeira and Praia da Rocha cater to all.

Popular venues for windsurfing and kitesurfing lessons include the beaches around Viana do Castelo (p420), Foz do Arelho (p263), Peniche (p257), Praia do Guincho (p119), Lagos (p178) and Tavira (p156).

regions at a glance

Lisbon & Around

History ✓✓✓
Food & Wine ✓✓✓
Nightlife ✓✓✓

History
Phoenicians, Romans, Visigoths and Moors all left their mark on Lisbon. History lurks around every corner, from roofless cathedrals that bore witness to Europe's most devastating earthquake, to the 1000-year-old castle on the hill – scene of bloody Crusades battles. There are Roman ruins, medieval churches, 18th-century plazas, and World Heritage–listed 16th-century monuments, Torre de Belém and Mosteiro dos Jerónimos.

Food & Wine
Lisbon's dining scene has grown in recent years, with first-rate chefs competing for top honours as local gourmands celebrate (while bemoaning their expanding waistlines). The bounty from field and ocean features in ever-inventive menus alongside traditional restaurants serving Spanish, Italian, Indian, French and other cuisines. Cinematic views, al-fresco meals and historic dining rooms complete the Lisbon culinary experience.

Nightlife
Nights out range from strolling the graffiti lanes of party-loving Bairro Alto to pulling up a chair and sinking into the sorrowful rhythms of fado inside a tiny Alfama bar. Put your hands in the air at Lux, or enjoy live jazz, a big-ticket rock show or a stylish lounge bar. For a peaceful place to catch the sunset look to the hills, where esplanades and outdoor bars provide the perfect setting for a sundowner.

p48

The Algarve

Beaches ✓✓✓
Food & Wine ✓✓
Activities ✓✓

Beaches
Sun-kissed beaches come in many forms in the Algarve: scenic coves, family-friendly bays, long open stretches of pounding surf. Beaches along the rugged west coast are more remote, rough and natural. Those further east have bigger tourist infrastructures, and swell with holidaymakers in summer.

Food & Wine
Seafood plays a starring role in the Algarve – with superb *cataplanas* (paella-like seafood platters) and grilled fish of all varieties. You'll find all levels of restaurants, from Michelin-starred to beachside shacks. Algarve vineyards are also gaining acclaim, with more wineries opening each year.

Activities
The Algarve offers a plethora of organised activities, especially for children, with water parks, horse riding and pirate-ship cruises. There's also birdwatching, walking, thermal baths, surfing classes and boat trips.

p137

The Alentejo

Medieval Delights ✓✓
Food & Wine ✓✓
Natural Scenery ✓✓

Medieval Delights
Medieval hilltop villages proliferate in the Alentejo. Marvão, Monsaraz, Mértola, Estremoz, Estremadura and Elvas all have striking castles that played roles in shaping Portugal's history. These living fortress museums also offer bird's-eye views over their surrounds.

Food & Wine
The Alentejo is known for its produce, especially *porco preto* (black pork), and its *doces conventuais* (sweets). Vineyards cover the region, with a well-established network of *adegas* (wineries) offering tastings.

Natural Scenery
This multifaceted region boasts many great settings for walks and scenic drives. Highlights include craggy mountains, rivers and gorges, and rolling golden hillsides dotted with cork trees, olive groves, wildflowers and eucalypts. The lush environs of Parque Natural do Vale do Guadiana are particularly striking.

p197

Estremadura & Ribatejo

Monasteries ✓✓✓
Seafood ✓✓✓
Surfing ✓✓✓

Monasteries
A cluster of Unesco World Heritage Sites, Tomar, Batalha and Alcobaça are three splendid religious monuments all easily reachable from Lisbon. With soaring arches, Manueline ornamentation and pretty courtyards, these medieval-Renaissance masterpieces are *the* reason to visit central Portugal.

Seafood
Ask a Lisboeta where to go for seafood, and chances are they'll point you to Ericeira. This whitewashed coastal village is full of restaurants where you choose the catch of the day straight out of the case and watch them grill it on the spot.

Surfing
Estremadura's appeal as a surfing capital is no secret. The waves of Baleal, Supertubos and Ribeira d'Ilhas draw throngs from around the globe, and national championships are often held here.

p251

The Beiras

Frontier Towns ✓✓✓
Natural Scenery ✓✓✓
University Life ✓✓

Frontier Towns
The inland Beiras are filled with castles and fortresses that once guarded the country's eastern frontier with Spain. From Folgosinho's fairy-tale minicastle to the elaborate star-shaped ramparts of Almeida, they tell tales of a rambunctious time in Portugal's history.

Natural Scenery
The rocky heights of Serra da Estrela are a revelation of cool air, magnificent vistas and great walks. Portugal's highest mountain range, once the exclusive domain of shepherds, now sees an increasing stream of outdoor enthusiasts.

University Life
Portugal's oldest university town, Coimbra, wears its tradition proudly, as evidenced in its medieval architecture and the black capes still worn by students. The city also knows how to party, especially during the 10-day Queima das Fitas festival in May.

p297

Porto & the Douro

History ✓✓✓
Wine & Port ✓✓✓
Nightlife ✓✓

History

Baroque churches, 18th-century squares and Roman foundations: Porto is awash in history. Other Douro stars include Visigothic ruins and 12th-century monasteries near Lamego, and 30,000-year-old rock carvings at Vila Nova de Foz Côa.

Wine & Port

Oenophiles and port lovers will have a packed itinerary sampling the great produce of the Douro. You can taste the world's best ports in Vila Nova de Gaia followed by a wine-tasting ramble through vineyard country, overnighting at historic guest houses.

Nightlife

Porto's wine bars, bohemian art-music spaces and ocean-fronting bars are found in the seaside district of Foz do Douro. There's a lively drinking scene in Vila Nova de Gaia and great nightlife (including summer parties in an old fortress) in Vila do Conde.

p357

The Minho

History ✓✓✓
Food & Wine ✓✓✓
Outdoor Activities ✓✓✓

History

Head to medieval Guimarães to discover Portugal's birthplace. Even more stunning is Braga, with its 1000-year-old cathedral and colourful festivals. Then there's the Celtic settlement of Citânia de Briteiros, atmospheric Viana do Castelo and cinematic citadel Valença do Minho.

Food & Wine

Minho chefs make fine use of simple ingredients. Braga has a first-rate selection of restaurants, while Viana do Castelo and Guimarães also have gems. Home to *vinho verde* (green wine), the Minho produces some great wines, including the refreshing Alvarinho.

Outdoor Activities

There's top surfing in Minho, particularly off Praia do Cabedelo. Parque Nacional da Peneda-Gerês has great hiking amid forest and mountain scenery. Walkers and cyclists can also explore the new greenway along the Minho River.

p400

Trás-os-Montes

Natural Scenery ✓✓✓
Stone Villages ✓✓✓
Wine ✓✓

Natural Scenery

Trás-os-Montes offers walking trails for all abilities in three natural parks: Montesinho, Alvão and Douro Internacional. Watch eagles soar over the Rio Douro canyon, cross the medieval bridge at Moimenta, and swim in pristine pools above the Fisgas de Ermelo waterfall.

Stone Villages

For a tramontane experience, visit the region's ancient stone villages. Crazy slate roofs and piled slabs of schist form the backdrop for a vanishing rural lifestyle, where shepherds bring their flocks to the high country and villagers pile hay onto horse-drawn carts.

Wine

The vineyard country of southern Trás-os-Montes offers steep terraced hillsides and fine wines reminiscent of the neighbouring Douro region. Taste a few local vintages at the picturesque Palácio de Mateus just outside Vila Real.

p445

Look out for these icons:

 Our author's recommendation

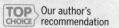 A green or sustainable option

 No payment required

On the Road

Lisbon & Around

POP 580,000

Best Places to Stay

» Hotel Britania (p82)
» Olissippo Castelo (p81)
» Altis Belém (p83)
» Internacional Design Hotel (p77)
» Fortaleza do Guincho (p119)

Best Places to Eat

» 100 Maneiras (p88)
» Olivier (p86)
» Alma (p90)
» Santo António de Alfama (p89)
» Azenhas do Mar (p117)

Why Go?

Spread across steep hillsides that overlook the Rio Tejo, Lisbon has captivated visitors for centuries. Windswept vistas reveal the city in all its beauty: Roman and Moorish ruins, white-domed cathedrals, grand plazas lined with sun-drenched cafes. The real delight of discovery though, is delving into the narrow cobblestone lanes.

As yellow trams clatter through tree-lined streets, *lisboêtas* stroll through lamplit old quarters, much as they've done for centuries. Gossip is exchanged over fresh bread and wine at tiny patio restaurants as fado singers perform in the background. In other parts of town, Lisbon reveals her youthful alter ego at stylish dining rooms and lounges, late-night street parties, riverside nightspots and boutiques selling all things classic and cutting-edge.

Just outside Lisbon, there's more – enchanting woodlands, gorgeous beaches and seaside villages – all ripe for discovery.

When to Go?

Lisbon

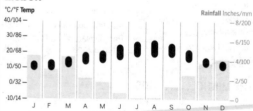

May
After the winter rains, late spring is lovely with sunny days and flowers in bloom.

June
Early summer brings festivals and warm weather, with perfect beach days in late June.

September
Lisbon is pure magic, with cooler days and nights and a lack of summer crowds.

History

Imperial riches, fires, plague, Europe's worst recorded earthquake, revolutions, coups and a dictatorship – Lisbon has certainly had its ups and downs.

It's said that Ulysses was here first, but the Phoenicians definitely settled here 3000 years ago, calling the city Alis Ubbo (Delightful Shore). Others soon recognised its qualities: the Greeks, the Carthaginians and then, in 205 BC, the Romans, who stayed until the 5th century AD. After some tribal chaos, the city was taken over by North African Moors in 714. They fortified the city they called Lissabona and fended off the Christians for 400 years.

But in 1147, after a four-month siege, Christian fighters (mainly British crusader hooligan-pillagers) under Dom Afonso Henriques captured the city. In 1255, Afonso III moved his capital here from Coimbra, which proved far more strategic given the city's excellent port and central position.

In the 15th and 16th centuries Lisbon boomed as the opulent centre of a vast empire after Vasco da Gama found a sea route to India. The party raged on into the 1800s, when gold was discovered in Brazil. Merchants flocked to the city, trading in gold, spices, silks and jewels. Frenzied, extravagant architecture held up a mirror to the era, with Manueline works such as Belém's Mosteiro dos Jerónimos.

But at 9.40am on All Saints' Day, 1 November 1755, everything changed. Three major earthquakes hit, as residents celebrated Mass. The tremors brought an even more devastating fire and tsunami. Some estimate that as many as 90,000 of Lisbon's 270,000 inhabitants died. Much of the city was ruined, never to regain its former status. Dom João I's chief minister, the formidable Marquês de Pombal, immediately began rebuilding in a simple, cheap, earthquake-proof style that created today's formal grid.

Two bloodless coups (in 1926 and 1974) rocked the city. In 1974 and 1975 there was a massive influx of refugees from the former African colonies, changing the demographic of the city and culturally, if not financially, adding to its richness.

After Portugal joined the European Community (EC) in 1986, massive funding fuelled redevelopment, which was a welcome boost after a 1988 fire in Chiado. Streets became cleaner and investment improved facilities. Lisbon has spent recent years dashing in and out of the limelight as 1994 European City of Culture, and host of Expo '98 and the 2004 European Football Championships. Major development projects throughout the city have continued recently, from the reopening of the restored Campo Pequeno bullring to ongoing work on the metro and, most importantly, much needed building rehab in the Alfama.

Sights

At the riverfront is the grand Praça do Comércio. Behind it march the pedestrian-filled streets of Baixa (lower) district, up to Praça da Figueira and Praça Dom Pedro IV (aka Rossio). From Baixa it's a steep climb west, through swanky shopping district Chiado, into the narrow streets of nightlife-haven Bairro Alto. Eastwards from the Baixa it's another climb to Castelo de São Jorge and the Moorish, labyrinthine Alfama district around it. The World Heritage Sites of Belém lie further west along the river – an easy tram ride from Praça do Comércio.

BAIXA & ROSSIO

After the devastating earthquake of 1755, the Baixa was reborn as a grid – the world's first ever – as envisioned by the Marquês de Pombal. Wide commercial streets were laid, with grand plazas, fountains and a triumphal arch evoking the glory of Portuguese royalty. Today the main drag, pedestrianised Rua Augusta, buzzes with bag-toting shoppers, camera-wielding tourists and shrill-voiced buskers. For a taste of the trades that once flourished here, stroll down streets named after *sapateiros* (shoemakers), *correeiros* (saddlers), *douradores* (gilders), *fanqueiros* (cutlers) and even *bacalhoeiros* (cod-fishing vessels).

Praça do Comércio   PLAZA

With its grand 18th-century arcades, lemon-meringue facades and mosaic cobbles, the riverfront Praça do Comércio (Map p54) is a square to out-pomp them all. Everyone arriving by boat used to disembark here, and it still feels like the gateway to Lisbon, thronging with activity and rattling trams. At its centre rises the dashing equestrian statue of Dom José I, hinting at the square's royal roots as the pre-earthquake site of Palácio da Ribeira. In 1908 the square witnessed the fall of the monarchy, when anarchists assassinated Dom Carlos I and his son. The biggest

Lisbon Highlights

1 Get lost in the narrow village-like lanes of the **Alfama** (p57), searching for the soul of fado

2 Bar-hop your way through the cobblestone streets of nightlife-loving **Bairro Alto** (p92)

3 Take in the pleasant outdoor cafes and restaurants of elegant **Chiado** (p86)

4 Hop aboard **tram 28** (see boxed text, p63) for a rattling, roller-coaster ride through the city.

5 Bid *bom dia* (good morning) to sharks and sea otters at the mind-blowing **Oceanário** (p71)

6 Gaze upon the Manueline fantasy of **Mosteiro dos Jerónimos** (see boxed text, p74)

7 Stride through enchanted forests to above-the-clouds palaces and castles in **Sintra** (p108)

8 Spend the day taking in the beaches, village lanes and outdoor eateries of laid-back **Cascais** (p118)

9 Frolic in the waves off the beautiful forest-backed beaches of **Parque Natural da Arrábida** (p134)

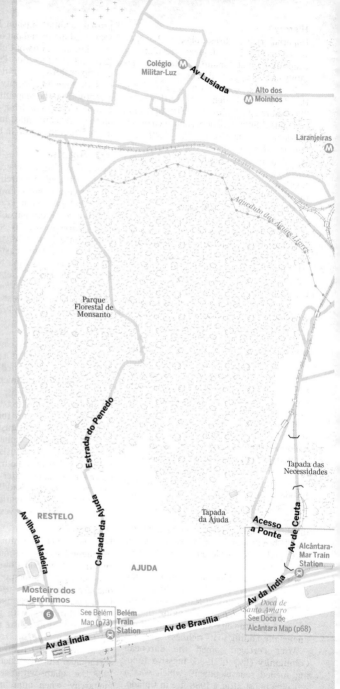

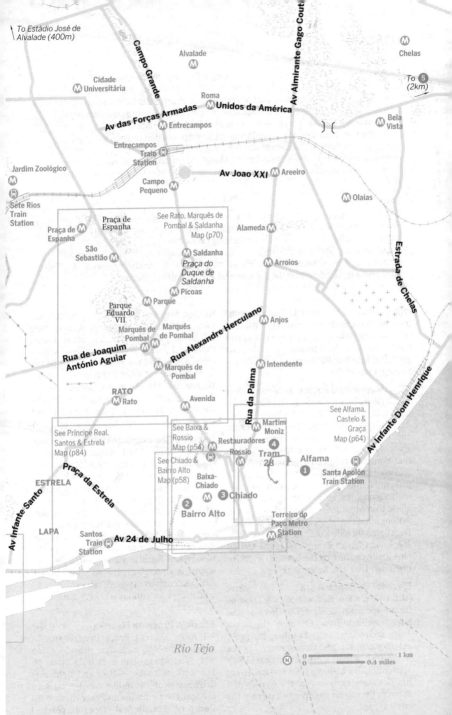

LISBON IN...

Two Days

Take a roller-coaster ride on tram 28, hopping off to scale the ramparts of Castelo de São Jorge. Sample Portugal's finest at Wine Bar do Castelo, then stroll the picturesque lanes of Alfama, pausing for a pick-me-up in arty Pois Café. Glimpse the fortress-like sé (cathedral) en route to shopping in pedestrianised Baixa. By night, return to lantern-lit Alfama for first-rate fado at Mesa dos Frades.

On day two, breakfast on cinnamon-dusted pastries in Belém, then explore the fantastical Manueline cloisters of Mosteiro dos Jerónimos. River gaze from the Torre de Belém and see cutting-edge art at the Museu Colecção Berardo. Head back for sundowners and magical views at Noobai, dinner at 100 Maneiras and bar-crawling in Bairro Alto.

Four Days

Go window-shopping and cafe-hopping in well-heeled Chiado, then head to futuristic Parque das Nações for riverfront gardens and the head-spinning Oceanário. That night, dine at Bocca or Alma, then go dancing in clubbing temple Lux.

On day four, catch the train to Sintra, for walks through boulder-speckled woodlands to fairy-tale palaces. Back in Rossio, toast your trip with cherry liqueur at A Ginjinha and alfresco dining on the cobbled steps of Calçada do Duque.

---

crowd-puller is Verissimo da Costa's triumphal **Arco da Victória**, crowned with bigwigs such as 15th-century explorer Vasco da Gama; come at dusk to see the arch glow gold. Pop into **ViniPortugal** to taste Portuguese wines for free.

FREE **Museu de Design e da Moda** MUSEUM (Map p54; www.mude.pt; Rua Augusta 24; ☺10am-8pm Tue-Thu & Sun, 10am-10pm Fri & Sat) Baixa's newest star is the Museum of Design and Fashion, a cavernous concrete-walled space – set in an abandoned bank building – that contains furniture, industrial design and couture dating from the 1930s to the present. Exhibits are arranged by decade, with signage in both English and Portuguese to contextualise the trends and innovations amid the larger historical backdrop. Highlights include iconic furniture by Arne Jacobsen, Charles Eames and Frank Gehry, plus haute couture by the likes of Givenchy, Christian Dior and Balenciaga.

Elevador de Santa Justa ELEVATOR (Map p54; cnr Rua de Santa Justa & Largo do Carmo; admission €2.80; ☺7am-11pm) If the lanky, wrought-iron Elevador de Santa Justa seems uncannily familiar, it's probably because the neo-Gothic marvel is the handiwork of Raul Mésnier, Gustave Eiffel's apprentice. It's Lisbon's only vertical street lift. Get there early to beat the crowds and zoom to the top for sweeping views over the city's skyline.

Núcleo Arqueológico HISTORIC SITE (Map p54; Rua dos Correeiros 9; tours free; ☺10am-5pm Mon-Sat) Hidden under Banco Comercial Portuguesa is the Núcleo Arqueológico, a web of tunnels believed to be the remnants of a Roman spa dating from the 1st century AD. You can descend into the depths on a fascinating guided tour run by the Museu da Cidade. Stop by to find out the schedule for English-language tours.

Igreja de São Domingos CHURCH (Map p54; Largo de São Domingos; admission free; ☺7.30am-7pm Mon-Fri, noon-6pm Sat) It's a miracle that the enigmatic Igreja de São Domingos still stands, having barely survived the 1755 earthquake and fire in 1959. A sea of tea lights illuminates gashed pillars, battered walls and ethereal sculptures in its musty, yet enchanting, interior. Note the Star of David outside marking the spot of a bloody anti-Semitic massacre in 1506. The square is a popular hang-out with Lisbon's African community and, at dusk, locals who gather for sundown cherry liqueurs at A Ginjinha (p92).

Rossio & Praça da Figueira PLAZAS All roads lead to Praça Dom Pedro IV, which *lisboêtas* nickname **Rossio** (Map p54). The square has a 24-hour buzz: office workers, hash-peddlers and sightseers drift across its wave-like cobbles, bask in the spray of fountains and gaze up to **Dom Pedro IV** (Brazil's first emperor), perched high on a marble pedestal. Standouts feature the filigree horseshoe-shaped arches of neo-Manueline **Rossio train station**, where trains depart for Sintra, and neo-classical **Teatro Nacional de Dona Maria II** (p99) hiding a dark past as the seat of the Portuguese Inquisition.

Rossio's sidekick is bustling **Praça da Figueira**, flanked by Pombaline town houses and alfresco cafes ideal for sipping a *bica* (espresso), admiring the castle on the hillside and watching gravity-defying skateboarders tear past the statue of Dom João I.

CHIADO & BAIRRO ALTO

Framed by the ethereal arches of Convento do Carmo, well-heeled Chiado harbours old-world cafes with literary credentials, swish boutiques, grand theatres and elegant 18th-century town houses. Designer divas seeking Portuguese couture, art buffs hunting Rodin originals and those content to people-watch from a cafe terrace flock here.

Sidling up to Chiado is the party-loving Bairro Alto, whose web of graffiti-slashed streets is sleepy by day. The district comes alive at twilight when hippy chicks hunt for vintage glitz in its retro boutiques and revellers hit its wall-to-wall bars and bistros. For daytime chilling, head to the leafy squares around Príncipe Real.

Convento do Carmo & Museu Arqueológico   MUSEUM
(Map p58; Largo do Carmo; adult/child €3.50/free; ☺10am-7pm Mon-Sat) Soaring high above Lisbon, the skeletal Convento do Carmo was all but devoured by the 1755 earthquake

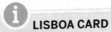

and it's precisely that which makes it so captivating. Its shattered pillars and wishbone-like arches are completely exposed to the elements. The **Museu Arqueológico** shelters archaeological treasures from Lisbon and beyond, such as 4th-century sarcophagi, griffin-covered column fragments from the 10th-century, 18th-century *azulejo* (hand-painted tile) panels, a curious belt buckle from Visigothic times and two gruesome 16th-century Peruvian mummies.

Museu do Chiado   MUSEUM
(Map p58; www.museudochiado-ipmuseus.pt; Rua Serpa Pinto 4; adult/under 14yr/concession €4/free/2.50, admission free 10am-2pm Sun; ☺10am-6pm Tue-Sun) Contemporary art fans flock to Museu do Chiado, housed in the strikingly converted Convento de São Francisco. Temporary exhibitions lean toward interactive multimedia installations, while the gallery's permanent collection of 19th-

Baixa & Rossio

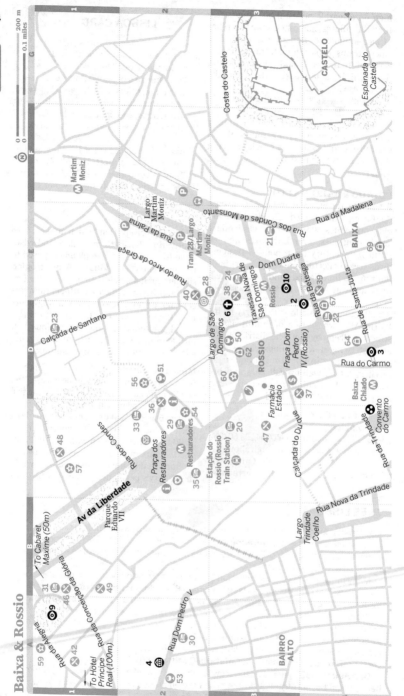

0 200 m
0 0.1 miles

CASTELO

Costa do Castelo

Esplanada do Castelo

Martim Moniz

Largo Martim Moniz

Rua da Palma

Rua do Arco da Graça

Tram 28/Largo Martim Moniz

Rua dos Condes de Monsanto

Rua da Madalena

BAIXA

69

Dom Duarte

Travessa Nova de São Domingos

Rossio

Largo de São Domingos

Calçada de Santano

ROSSIO

Praça Dom Pedro IV (Rossio)

Rua da Betesga

Rua de Santa Justa

Rua do Carmo

Rua dos Condes

Praça dos Restauradores

Restauradores

Estação do Rossio (Rossio Train Station)

Farmácia Estácio

Calçada do Duque

Baixa-Chiado

Convento do Carmo

Rua da Trindade

Av da Liberdade

Parque de Eduardo VII

To Cabaret Maxime (50m)

Rua do Alecrim

Rua da Conceição da Glória

To Hotel Príncipe Real (100m)

Rua Dom Pedro V

Rua Nova da Trindade

Largo Trindade Coelho

BAIRRO ALTO

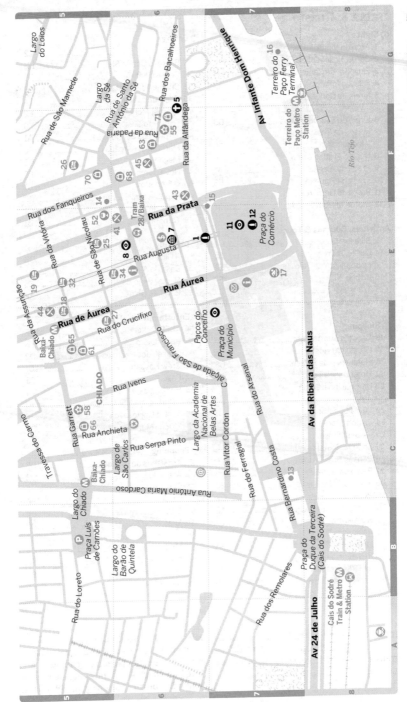

Largo do Loios

Largo da Sé

Rua de São Mamede

Rua de Santo António da Sé

Rua dos Bacalhoeiros

Av Infante Dom Henrique

⊕ 5

71
55

Rua da Padaria

63

Rua da Alfândega

26

70

45 ✕

68

Rua dos Fanqueiros

43 ✕

Rua da Prata

15

Tram 28/Baixa

14

52

Rua da Vitória

Rua de São Nicolau

25

41 ✕

Terreiro do Paço Ferry Terminal

16

Terreiro do Paço Metro Station

Rio Tejo

11 ⊙

12

Praça do Comércio

7

Rua Augusta

⊖ 1

8 ⊙

Rua da Assunção

19

34

32

27

Rua Áurea

17

Rua de Áurea

44 ✕

18

Baixa-Chiado Ⓜ

65

61

Rua do Crucifixo

Paços do Concelho ⊙

Praça do Município

CHIADO

Rua Ivens

Calçada de São Francisco

Rua do Arsenal

Largo do Chiado

Travessa do Carmo

Rua Garrett

58

66

Rua Anchieta

Largo de São Carlos

Rua Serpa Pinto

Largo da Academia Nacional de Belas Artes

Rua Vítor Cordon

Av da Ribeira das Naus

Rua do Loreto

Praça Luís de Camões Ⓟ

Largo do Barão de Quintela

Baixa-Chiado Ⓜ

Rua António Maria Cardoso

Rua Ferragial

Rua Bernardino Costa

⊙ 13

Praça do Duque da Terceira (Cais do Sodré)

Rua dos Remolares

Av 24 de Julho

Cais do Sodré Train & Metro Ⓜ Station

LISBON & AROUND

and 20th-century works features pieces by Rodin, Jorge Vieira and José de Almada Negreiros. Revive over coffee in the sculpture garden.

Miradouro de Santa Catarina VIEWPOINT
Students bashing out rhythms, pot-smoking hippies, stroller-pushing parents, and loved-up couples – all meet at this precipitous **viewpoint** (Map p58) in boho Santa

Catarina. The views are fantastic, stretching from the river to the Ponte 25 de Abril and Cristo Rei. If you're coming from Cais do Sodré, it's fun to take the arthritic, 19th-century Elevador da Bica funicular up chasm-like Rua da Bica de Duarte Belo to reach the lookout. When Lisbon twinkles, enjoy the same vista over drinks at laid-back **Noobai Café** (p92).

Igreja & Museu São Roque   CHURCH, MUSEUM
(Map p58) Largo Trindade Coelho; admission €2.50; ⊙10am-6pm Tue, Wed & Fri-Sun, 2-9pm Thu) The plain facade of 16th-century Jesuit Igreja de São Roque belies its dazzling interior of gold, marble and Florentine *azulejos* – bankrolled by Brazilian riches. Its star attraction is **Capela de São João Baptista**, to the left of the altar, a lavish confection of amethyst, alabaster, lapis lazuli and Carrara marble. The newly restored museum adjoining the church is packed with elaborate sacred art and holy relics; the bamboo-lined courtyard restaurant is a treat.

Miradouro de São Pedro de Alcântara
VIEWPOINT
Hitch a ride on vintage Elevador da Glória (Map p58) from Praça dos Restauradores, or practise step-aerobics climbing the steep Calçada da Glória to this terrific viewpoint atop one of Lisbon's seven hills. Plant yourself next to the fountains and Greek busts for a picnic with castle views. Across the street is **Solar do Vinho do Porto** (p93), where you can taste some of Portugal's finest ports.

ALFAMA, CASTELO & GRAÇA
Unfurling like a magic carpet at the foot of Castelo de São Jorge, Alfama is Lisbon's Moorish time capsule: a medina-like district of tangled alleys, palm-shaded squares and skinny, terracotta-roofed houses that tumble down to the glittering Tejo. These cobbles have been worn smooth by theatre-going Romans, bath-loving Moors who called it *al-hamma* (Arabic for 'springs'), and stampeding Crusaders.

Here life is literally inside out: women dish the latest *mexericos* (gossip) over strings of freshly washed laundry, men gut sardines on the street then fry them on open grills, plump matrons spontaneously erupt into wailful fado, kids use chapel entrances as football goals, babies cry, budgies twitter, trams rattle and in the midday heat the web of steep lanes falls into its siesta slumber.

Add some altitude to your sightseeing by edging north to Graça, where giddy *miradouros* afford sweeping vistas and the pearly-white Panteão Nacional and Igreja de São Vicente de Fora punctuate the skyline.

Castelo de São Jorge   CASTLE
(Map p64; St George's Castle; www.castelodesao jorge.pt; adult/child €7/free; ⊙9am-9pm) Towering dramatically above Lisbon, the hilltop fortifications of Castelo de São Jorge sneak into almost every snapshot. These smooth cobbles have seen it all – Visigoths in the 5th century, Moors in the 9th century, Christians in the 12th century, royals from the 14th to 16th centuries, and convicts in every century. Roam its snaking ramparts and pine-shaded courtyards for superlative views over the city's red rooftops to the river.

Inside the **Ulysses Tower**, a camera obscura offers a unique 360-degree angle on Lisbon, with demos every half-hour. There are also a few galleries displaying relics from past centuries, but the standout attraction is the view – as well as the anachronous feeling of stepping back in time amid fortified courtyards and towering walls.

Bus 737 from Praça Figueira goes right to the gate. Tram 28 also passes near.

GET LOST IN ALFAMA

There's no place like the labyrinthine Alfama for ditching the map to get lost in sun-dappled alleys and squares full of beauty and banter. Its narrow *becos* (cul de sacs) and *travessas* (alleys) lead you on a spectacular wild goose chase past chalk-white chapels and tiny grocery stores, patios shaded by orange trees, and João's freshly washed underpants. The earthy, working-class residents, *alfacinhas*, fill the lanes with neighbourly chatter, wafts of fried fish and the mournful ballads of fado. Experiencing Alfama is more about luxuriating in the everyday than ticking off the big sights. Take a serendipitous wander through lanes fanning out from Rua de São Miguel, Rua de São João da Praça and Rua dos Remédios.

Chiado & Bairro Alto

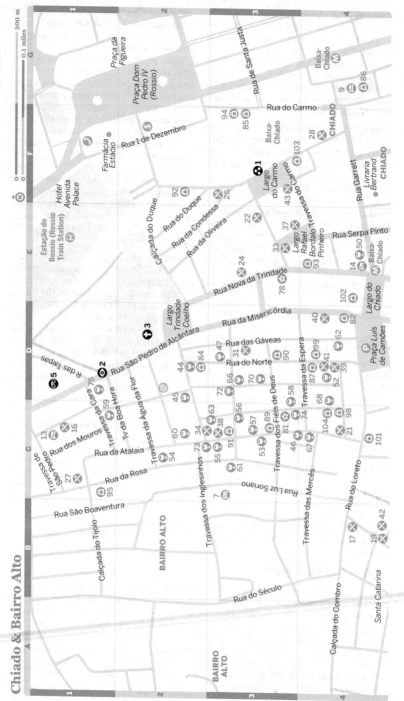

200 m
0.1 miles

Praça da Figueira

Praça Dom Pedro IV (Rossio)

Estação do Rossio (Rossio Train Station)

Hotel Avenida Palace

Farmácia Estácio

Rua 1 de Dezembro

Rua de Santa Justa

Baixa-Chiado

9 86

Rua do Carmo

94 85

Baixa-Chiado

103 28

CHIADO

CHIADO

Rua Garrett

Livraria Bertrand

Largo do Carmo

1

43

Rua do Carmo

Travessa do Carmo

Rua Serpa Pinto

92

Rua do Duque

26

22

37

Largo Rafael Bordalo Pinheiro

50

Rua do Condessa

Rua da Oliveira

33

14

Baixa-Chiado

93

Calçada do Duque

24

Rua Nova da Trindade

78

102

Largo do Chiado

Largo Trindade Coelho

Rua da Misericórdia

40

82

Rua São Pedro de Alcântara

3

Rua das Gáveas

47

31

90

99

62

Praça Luís de Camões

R. das Taipas

2

44

84

Rua do Norte

66

70

87

41

52

39

5

75

59

Travessa da Boa Hora

Tv da Boa Hora

Tv da Água da Flor

45

72

56

58

Travessa da Espera

68

104

21

98

13

16

Rua dos Mouros

Rua da Cara

60

34

63

38

91

89

81

74

67

101

27

Rua da Atalaia

54

55

53

57

46

Travessa de São Pedro

95

Rua da Rosa

73

61

Travessa dos Fiéis de Deus

Rua Luz Soriano

Rua São Boaventura

7

Travessa dos Inglesinhos

Travessa das Mercês

17

19

42

BAIRRO ALTO

Calçada do Tijolo

Rua do Loreto

Calçada do Combro

Rua do Século

Santa Catarina

BAIRRO ALTO

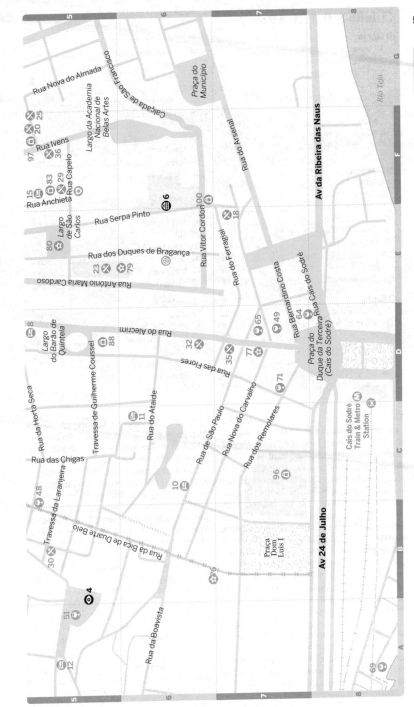

Praça do Município

Rua Nova do Almada

Calçada de São Francisco

Largo da Academia Nacional de Belas Artes

Rua do Arsenal

Av da Ribeira das Naus

Rio Tejo

97
20 25
36
Rua Ivens

Rua Capelo

15 83 29
Rua Anchieta

Rua Serpa Pinto

6

Rua Vitor Cordon
100
18

Largo de São Carlos

80

Rua dos Duques de Bragança

Rua do Ferragial

23 79

Rua António Maria Cardoso

8

Largo do Barão de Quintela

88

Rua do Alecrim

65
49

Rua Bernardino Costa

Rua Cais do Sodré

Rua da Terceira

Praça do Duque da Terceira (Cais do Sodré)

64

Rua das Flores

32

35
77

Travessa de Guilherme Coussel

Rua da Horta Seca

Rua do Ataíde

11

Rua de São Paulo

Rua Nova do Carvalho

Rua dos Remolares

71

Rua das Chigas

10

96

Cais do Sodré Train & Metro Station

48

Travessa da Laranjeira

Rua da Bica de Duarte Belo

30

Praça Dom Luís I

Av 24 de Julho

4

51

Rua da Boavista

12

69

Sé   CATHEDRAL

(Map p64; admission free; ⊗9am-7pm Tue-Sat, 9am-5pm Mon & Sun) One of Lisbon's biggest icons is the fortresslike *sé*, built in 1150 on the site of a mosque soon after Christians recaptured the city from the Moors. It was sensitively restored in the 1930s. Despite the masses outside, the rib-vaulted interior, lit by a rose window, is calm. History buffs shouldn't miss the less-visited **Gothic cloister** (admission €2.50; ⊗10am-6pm Mon-Sat, 2-6pm Sun), which opens onto a deep pit full of archaeological excavations going back more than 2000 years. You have to squint hard to imagine it, but you'll see remnants of a Roman street and shopfronts, an Islamic-era house and dump, as well as a medieval cistern. The **treasury** (admission €2.50) showcases religious gems. Stroll around the cathedral to spy leering gargoyles peeking above the orange trees; the *sé* looks its best when the late-afternoon sun makes its bricks glow honey-gold.

Igreja de São Vicente de Fora   CHURCH

(Map p64; Largo de São Vicente; admission €5; ⊗10am-6pm Tue-Sun) Graça's serene, gorgeous Igreja de São Vicente de Fora was founded as a monastery in 1147, revamped by Italian architect Felipe Terzi in the late 16th century, and devastated in the 1755 earthquake when its dome collapsed on worshippers. Elaborate blue-and-white *azulejos* dance across almost every wall, echoing the curves of the architecture, across the white cloisters and up to the 1st floor. Here you'll find a one-off collection of panels depicting La Fontaine's moral tales of sly foxes and greedy wolves. Under the marble sacristy lie the crusaders' tombs. Seek out the weeping, cloaked woman holding stony vigil in the eerie mausoleum. Have your camera handy for the superb views from the tower.

Panteão Nacional   MUSEUM

(Map p64; Campo de Santa Clara; adult/child €3/ free, admission free 10am-2pm Sun; ⊗10am-5pm Tue-Sun) Perched high and mighty above

Graça's Campo de Santa Clara, the porcelain-white Panteão Nacional is a baroque beauty. Originally intended as a church, it now pays homage to Portugal's heroes and heroines, including 15th-century explorer Vasco da Gama and *fadista* Amália Rodrigues. Lavishly adorned with pink marble and gold swirls, its echoing dome resembles an enormous Fabergé egg. Trudge up to the 4th-floor viewpoint for a sunbake and vertigo-inducing views over Alfama and the river.

Museu do Fado   MUSEUM
(Map p64; www.museudofado.egeac.pt; Largo do Chafariz de Dentro; admission €3; ⊙10am-6pm Tue-Sun) Fado was born in the Alfama. Immerse yourself in its bittersweet symphonies at Museu do Fado. This engaging museum traces fado's history from its working-class roots to international stardom, taking in discs, recordings, posters, a hall of fame and a re-created guitar

workshop. Afterwards, pick up some fado of your own at the shop.

Museu de Artes Decorativas   MUSEUM
(Map p64; Museum of Decorative Arts; www.fress.pt; Largo das Portas do Sol 2; admission €4; ⊙10am-5pm Tue-Sun) Set in a petite 17th-century palace, the Museu de Artes Decorativas creaks under the weight of treasures including blingy French silverware, priceless Qing vases and Indo-Chinese furniture. It's worth a visit alone to admire the lavish apartments, embellished with baroque *azulejos,* frescos and chandeliers.

FREE **Museu do Teatro Romano** MUSEUM
(Map p64; Pátio do Aljube 5; ⊙10am-1pm & 2-6pm Tue-Sun) The ultramodern Museu do Teatro Romano catapults you back to Emperor Augustus' rule in Olisipo (Lisbon). Head upstairs and across the street for the star attraction – a ruined **Roman theatre** extended in AD 57, buried in the 1755 earthquake and finally unearthed in 1964.

MUSEU NACIONAL DO AZULEJO

You haven't been to Lisbon until you've been on the tiles at the **Museu Nacional do Azulejo** (National Tile Museum; Map p50; Rua Madre de Deus 4; adult/child €5/2.50, admission free 10am-2pm Sun; ☺2-6pm Tue, 10am-6pm Wed-Sun). Housed in a sublime 16th-century convent, the museum covers the entire *azulejo* spectrum, from early Ottoman geometry to zinging altars, scenes of lords a-hunting to Goan intricacies. Star exhibits are a 36m-long panel depicting pre-earthquake Lisbon, a Manueline cloister with weblike vaulting and exquisite blue-and-white *azulejos*, and a gold-smothered baroque chapel. Food-inspired *azulejos* – ducks, pigs and the like – adorn the restaurant opening onto a vine-clad courtyard. For more on *azulejos*, see p509.

Casa dos Bicos
HISTORIC SITE

(Map p64; Rua dos Bacalhoeiros 10) The pincushion facade of Casa dos Bicos, the eccentric 16th-century abode of Afonso de Albuquerque, former viceroy to India, grabs your attention with 1125 pyramid-shaped stones. Long closed to the public, the Casa was at the time of writing on its way to housing the José Saramago Foundation, which will host literary readings

and contain the library of the Nobel Prize–winning author.

PRÍNCIPE REAL, SANTOS & ESTRELA

West of Bairro Alto, these serene and affluent tree-fringed neighbourhoods slope down to the Rio Tejo, and are dotted with boutique hotels, art galleries, vine-clad courtyards and antique shops. This offbeat corner of Lisbon harbours a handful of must-sees including a neoclassical basilica, exotic gardens, a cavernous ancient art museum, plus the neoclassical Palácio da Assembleia da República, home to Portugal's parliament.

Casa Museu de Amália Rodrigues
MUSEUM

(Map p84; Rua de São Bento 193; admission €5; ☺10am-1pm & 2-6pm Tue-Sun) A pilgrimage site for fado fans, Casa Museu de Amália Rodrigues is where the Rainha do Fado (Queen of Fado) Amália Rodrigues lived; note graffiti along the street announcing it as Rua Amália. Born in Lisbon in 1920, the diva popularised the genre with her heartbreaking trills and poetic soul. Short tours take in portraits, glittering costumes and crackly recordings of her performances.

Museu da Marioneta
MUSEUM

(Puppet Museum; Map p84; www.museuda marioneta.egeac.pt; Rua da Esperança 146; adult/child €3/2; ☺10am-1pm & 2-6pm Tue-Sun) Discover your inner child at the enchanting Museu da Marioneta, a veritable Geppetto's workshop housed in the 17th-century Convento das Bernardas. Alongside superstars such as impish Punch and his Russian equivalent Petruschka are rarities:

STAIRWAYS TO HEAVEN

You might curse the cobbles as you're puffing up the steep stairways lacing Alfama and Graça at times, but take heart in the fact that they lead to heavenly *miradouros*. Have your digicam handy:

» **Largo das Portas do Sol** (Map p64) This original Moorish gateway affords stunning angles over Alfama's jumble of red rooftops and pastel-coloured houses, underscored by the true blue Tejo.

» **Miradouro de Santa Luzia** (Map p64) A fountain trickles at this lookout shaded by bougainvillea and vines, offering superlative vistas over Alfama's blushing rooftops to the river. At the back, notice the blue-and-white *azulejos* depicting scenes from the Siege of Lisbon in 1147.

» **Miradouro da Graça** (Map p64) Young *lisboêtas* flock to this pine-fringed square at dusk for sundowners and sweeping vistas over central Lisbon.

» **Miradouro da Senhora do Monte** (Map p50) Lisbon spreads out before you at Graça's highest of the high, Miradouro da Senhora do Monte. Come for the relaxed vibe and the best views of the castle on the hill opposite. It's a short walk west (along Rua da Senhora do Monte) of the tram 28 stop on Rua da Graça.

A WONDROUS ART COLLECTION

Set in a lemon-fronted, 17th-century palace, the Museu Nacional de Arte Antiga (National Museum of Ancient Art; Map p84; www.mnarteantiga-ipmuseus.pt; Rua das Janelas Verdes 9; admission €5, admission free 10am-2pm Sun; ☺2-5.30pm Tue, 10am-5.30pm Wed-Sun) is Lapa's biggest draw. It presents a star-studded collection of European and Asian paintings and decorative arts. Keep an eye out for highlights such as Nuno Gonçalves' naturalistic *Panels of São Vicente*, Albrecht Dürer's *St Jerome*, Lucas Cranach's haunting *Salomé* and Gustave Courbet's bleak *Snow*. Other gems include golden wonder the *Monstrance of Belém*, a souvenir from Vasco da Gama's second voyage, and 16th-century Japanese screens depicting the arrival of the *namban* (southern barbarians), namely big-nosed Portuguese explorers.

Vietnamese water puppets, Sicilian opera marionettes and intricate Burmese shadow puppets. Tots can try their hand at puppetry. The museum also hosts periodic performances and puppet-making workshops.

Basílica da Estrela   CHURCH
(Map p84; Praça da Estrela; admission free; ☺8am-1pm & 3-8pm) The curvaceous, sugar-white dome and twin belfries of Basílica da Estrela are visible from afar. The neoclassical beauty was completed in 1790 by order of Dona Maria I (whose tomb is here) in gratitude for a male heir. The echoing interior is awash with pink-and-black marble, which creates a kaleidoscopic effect when you gaze up into the cupola. Climb the dome for far-reaching views over Lisbon.

Jardim da Estrela   GARDENS
(Map p84; Largo da Estrela; admission free; ☺7am-midnight) Seeking green respite? Opposite the basilica, this garden is perfect for a stroll, with paths weaving past pine, monkey puzzle and palm trees, rose and cacti beds and the centrepiece – a giant banyan tree. Kids love the duck ponds and animal-themed playground.

Jardim Botânico   GARDENS
(Botanical Garden; Map p84; Rua da Escola Politécnica 58; admission €2; ☺9am-8pm Mon-Fri, 10am-8pm Sat & Sun) Nurtured by green-fingered students, the Jardim Botânico is a quiet pocket of lushness just north of Bairro Alto. Look out for Madeiran geraniums, sequoias, purple jacarandas and, by the entrance, a gigantic Moreton Bay fig tree.

Palácio da Assembleia da República
NOTABLE BUILDING
(Assembly of the Republic; Map p84; Rua de São Bento; closed to the public) The columned, temple-like Palácio da Assembleia da República is where Portugal's parliament, the Assembleia da República, makes its home. It was once the enormous Benedictine Mosteiro de São Bento. Its lofty Doric columns and graceful statues of temperance, prudence, fortitude and justice give visitors the shutterbug.

Cemitério dos Ingleses   CEMETERY
(English Cemetery; Map p84; Rua de São Jorge; ☺daylight hours) Overgrown with cypress trees, the Cemitério dos Ingleses was founded in 1717. Expats at rest here include Henry Fielding (author of *Tom Jones*), who died during a fruitless visit to Lisbon in 1754 to improve his health. At the far corner are the remains of Lisbon's old Jewish cemetery.

DOCA DE ALCÂNTARA
Near the scenic but gratingly noisy suspension bridge Ponte 25 de Abril, the reborn

HITCH A RIDE ON TRAM 28

Vintage tram 28 offers the ultimate spin of Lisbon's blockbuster sights – from Basílica da Estrela to the back-streets of Baixa – for the price of a €1.40 ticket. The route from Campo Ourique to Martim Moniz is 45 minutes of astonishing views and absurdly steep climbs. The most exciting bit is when the tram commences its rattling climb to Alfama, where passengers lean perilously out of the window for an in-motion shot of the *sé* or hop out for postcard-perfect views from Miradouro de Santa Luzia. The final stretch negotiates impossibly narrow streets and hairpin bends up to Graça, where most folk get out to explore Igreja de São Vicente de Fora.

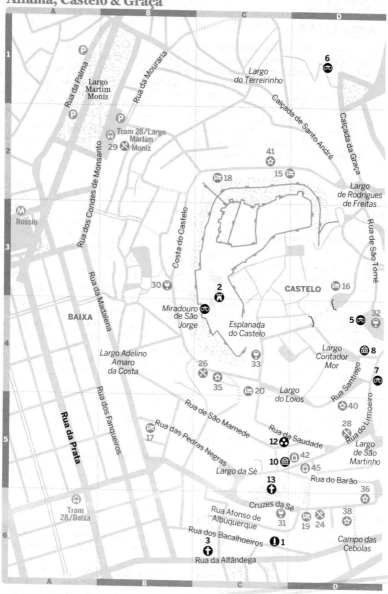

Alcantara dock is sprinkled with outdoor restaurants and drinking spots. For sightseers, the star attraction is the impressive Museu do Oriente; this spectacularly converted warehouse turns the spotlight on Portugal's links with Asia.

Getting here on westbound tram 28 or 25 is fun. You can also get here by taking the new riverside bike path from Cais do Sodré.

Museu do Oriente MUSEUM
(Map p68; www.museudooriente.pt; Doca de Alcântara; adult/child €5/2, admission free

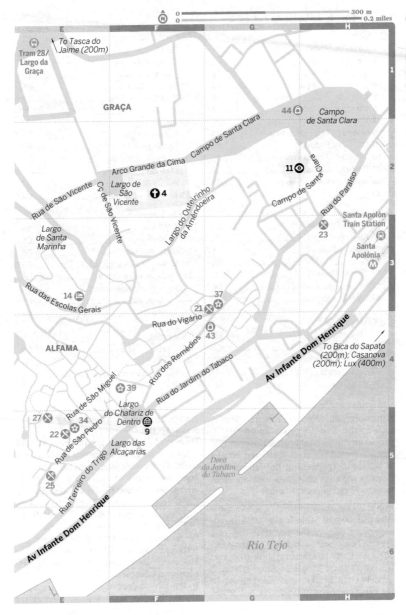

6-10pm Fri; ⊙10am-6pm Tue-Sun, 10am-10pm Fri) Opened to much fanfare in 2008, the stunning Museu do Oriente highlights Portugal's ties with Asia from colonial baby steps in Macau to ancestor worship. The cavernous museum occupies a revamped 1940s *bacalhau* (dried salt-cod) warehouse – a €30 million conversion. Strikingly displayed in pitch-black rooms, the permanent collection focuses on Portuguese presence in Asia, and Asian gods. Standouts on the 1st floor feature rare Chinese screens and

Ming porcelain, plus East Timor curiosities such as the divining conch and delicately carved umbilical-cord knives. Upstairs, cult classics include peacock-feathered effigies of Yellamma (goddess of the fallen), Vietnamese medium costumes and an eerie, faceless Nepalese exorcism doll

Ponte 25 de Abril
LANDMARK

(Map p68; Doca de Santo Amaro) Most people experience déjà vu the first time they clap eyes on bombastic suspension bridge Ponte 25 de Abril. It's hardly surprising given that it's the spitting image of San Francisco's Golden Gate Bridge, was constructed by the same company in 1966, and, at 2.27km, is almost as long. The thundering bridge dwarfs Lisbon's docks and is dazzling when illuminated by night. It was called Ponte Salazar until the 1974 Revolution of the Carnations (see p485), when a demonstrator removed the 'Salazar' and daubed '25 de Abril' in its place; the name stuck, the dictatorship crumbled.

RATO, MARQUÊS DE POMBAL & SALDANHA

Up north Lisbon races headlong into the 21st century with gleaming high-rises, dizzying roundabouts, shopping malls and Parisian-style boulevard Avenida da Liberdade, which poet Fernando Pessoa dubbed 'the finest artery in Lisbon'. The contrast to the olde-worlde riverfront districts is startling.

Though often overlooked, these parts reveal some gems: from René Lalique glitterbugs at Museu Calouste Gulbenkian to Hockney masterpieces at Centro de Arte Moderna, hothouses in Parque Eduardo VII to the lofty arches of Aqueduto das Águas Livres. Foodies flock here to dine at top tables like Bocca and Restaurante 33.

Museu Calouste Gulbenkian
MUSEUM

(Map p70; www.museu.gulbenkian.pt; Av de Berna 45A; adult/child €4/free, admission free Sun; ⏰10am-6pm Tue-Sun) Famous for its outstanding quality and breadth, Museu Calouste Gulbenkian showcases an epic collection of Western and Eastern art. The chronological romp kicks off with highlights such as gilded Egyptian mummy masks, Mesopotamian urns, elaborate Persian carpets and Qing porcelain (note the grinning Dogs of Fo). Going west, art buffs bewonder masterpieces by Rembrandt *(Portrait of an Old Man),* Van Dyck and Rubens (including the frantic *Loves of the Centaurs).* Be sure to glimpse Rodin's passionate *Spring Kiss.* The grand finale is the collection of exquisite René Lalique jewellery, including the otherworldly *Dragonfly.* Periodically hosts free classical concerts at noon on Sunday.

Centro de Arte Moderna MUSEUM
(Modern Art Centre; Map p70; adult/child €4/free, admission free Sun; ◷10am-6pm Tue-Sun) Situated in a sculpture-dotted garden alongside Museu Calouste Gulbenkian, the Centro de Arte Moderna reveals a stellar collection of 20th-century Portuguese and international art, including works by David Hockney, Anthony Gormley and José de Almada Negreiros. Feast your eyes on gems like Paula Rego's warped fairy-tale series *Contos Populares* and Sonia Delaunay's geometrically bold *Chanteur Flamenco.* There's also a well-stocked bookshop and garden cafe.

Parque Eduardo VII PARK
(Map p70; Alameda Edgar Cardoso; admission free; ◷daylight hours) An urban oasis with British roots, Parque Eduardo VII is named after his highness Edward VII, who visited Lisbon in 1903. The sloping parterre affords sweeping views over the whizzing traffic of Praça Marquês de Pombal to the river. The estufas (greenhouses; admisison €2; ◷9am-4.30pm Oct-Apr, 9am-5.30pm May-Sep) are a highlight, with lush foliage and tinkling fountains. Look out for tree ferns and camellias in the *estufa fría* (cool greenhouse), coffee and mango trees in the *estufa quente* (hot greenhouse) and cacti in the *estufa doce* (sweet greenhouse).

Mãe d'Água GALLERY
(Mother of Water; Map p70; Praça das Amoreiras; admission €3; ◷10am-6pm Mon-Sat) The king laid the aqueduct's final stone at Mãe d'Água, the city's massive 5500-cu-metre main reservoir. Completed in 1834, the reservoir's cool, echoing chamber (check out the start of the narrow aqueduct passage) now hosts art exhibitions.

BELÉM
Belém translates as Bethlehem but despite its villagey trappings, this is no little town. Picture stepping into a watercolour painting on the Age of Discovery: mighty caravels setting sail for Asia, coffers overflowing with spices, salt-bedraggled sailors washing up on distant shores and Manuel I using his newfound wealth to parade on an elephant and send the Pope a rhino. Belém catapults you back to the nautical adventures and architectural exuberance of the 15th and 16th centuries, when the world was Portugal's oyster and Vasco da Gama's timely discovery of a sea route to India in 1498 kick-started the age of empires.

GREAT ESCAPES

Some of Lisbon's greenest and most peaceful *praças* (town squares) are perfect for a crowd-free stroll or picnic. A few of our favourites:

» **Praça da Alegria** (Map p54) Swooping palms and banyan trees shade tranquil Praça da Alegria, which is actually more round than square. Look out for the bronze bust of 19th-century Portuguese painter and composer Alfredo Keil.

» **Praça do Príncipe Real** (Map p84) A century-old cedar tree forms a giant natural parasol at the centre of this palm-dotted square, popular among grizzled card players by day and gay cruisers by night. There's a kids playground and a relaxed cafe with alfresco seating.

» **Praça das Flores** (Map p84) Centred on a fountain, this romantic, leafy square has cobbles, pastel-washed houses and enough doggie-do to make a Parisian proud.

» **Campo dos Mártires da Pátria** (Map p70) Framed by elegant buildings, this grassy square is dotted with pine, weeping willow and jacaranda trees, with a pond for ducks and a pleasant indoor-outdoor cafe. *Lisboêtas* in search of cures light candles before the statue of Dr Sousa Martins, who was renowned for his healing work among the poor.

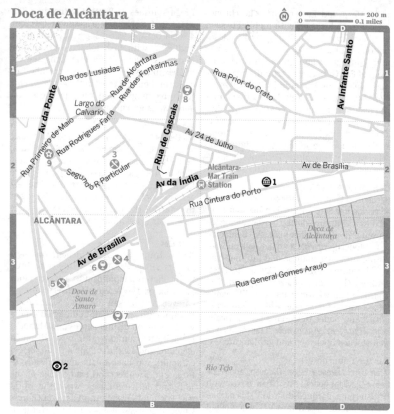

0   200 m
0   0.1 miles

Rua dos Lusiadas
Rua de Alcântara
Rua das Fontainhas
Rua Prior do Crato
Av Infante Santo
Largo do Calvario
Av da Ponte
Rua Primeiro de Maio
Rua Rodrigues Faria
Segundo R Particular
Rua de Cascais
Av 24 de Julho
Av da Índia
Alcântara-Mar Train Station
Av de Brasília
Rua Cintura do Porto
ALCÂNTARA
Av de Brasília
Doca de Alcântara
Rua General Gomes Araujo
Doca de Santo Amaro
Rio Tejo

As well as Unesco World Heritage–listed Manueline stunners such as Mosteiro dos Jerónimos and the whimsical Torre de Belém, this district 6km west of the centre offers a tranquil botanical garden, fairy-tale golden coaches, Warhol originals, Lisbon's tastiest *pastéis de nata* (custard tarts) and a whole booty of other treasures.

The best way to reach Belém is on the zippy tram 15 from Praça da Figueira or Praça do Comércio. Note that most sights here close on Monday.

Museu de Marinha   MUSEUM
(Naval Museum; Map p73; Praça do Império; adult/child €4/2, admission free 10am-2pm Sun; ☺10am-6pm Tue-Sun) The Museu de Marinha is a nautical flashback to the Age of Discovery with its armadas of model ships, cannonballs and shipwreck booty. Dig for buried treasure such as Vasco da Gama's portable wooden altar, 17th-century globes (note Australia's absence) and the polished private quarters of UK-built royal yacht *Amélia*. A separate building houses ornate royal barges, 19th-century fire-fighting machines and several seaplanes.

Padrão dos Descobrimentos   MUSEUM
(Discoveries Monument; Map p73; Av de Brasília; viewpoint €2.50, viewpoint & film €4; ☺10am-7pm, closed Mon in low season) Like a caravel frozen in mid-swell, the monolithic Padrão dos Descobrimentos was inaugurated in 1960 on the 500th anniversary of Henry the Navigator's death. The 52m-high limestone giant is chock-full of Portuguese bigwigs. At the prow is Henry, while behind him are explorers Vasco da Gama, Diogo Cão, Fernão de Magalhães and 29 other greats. The main event is a film that distills the history of the city down to 25 (sometimes overly sentimental) minutes. Film or not, do take the lift (or puff up 267 steps) to the windswept *miradouro* for 360-degree views over the river. The mosaic in front of

Doca de Alcântara

the monument charts the routes of Portuguese mariners.

Torre de Belém   FORT
(Map p73; Av da Índia; adult/child €4/free, admission free 10am-2pm Sun; ◷10am-6.30pm Tue-Sun) Jutting out onto the Rio Tejo, the World Heritage–listed fortress of Torre de Belém epitomises the Age of Discoveries. Francisco de Arruda designed the pearly-grey chess piece in 1515 to defend Lisbon's harbour and nowhere else is the lure of the Atlantic more powerful. The Manueline show-off flaunts filigree stonework, meringue-like cupolas and – just below the western tower – a stone rhinoceros. The ungulate depicts the one Manuel I sent Pope Leo X in 1515, which inspired Dürer's famous woodcut. Breathe in to climb a narrow spiral staircase to the tower, affording sublime views over Belém and the river. Crowds can be intense on weekends (especially Sunday) – a warning to claustrophobes.

Museu Colecção Berardo   MUSEUM
(Berardo Collection Museum; Map p73; www.museuberardo.pt; Praça do Império; admission free; ◷10am-7pm, 10am-10pm Sat) Culture fiends get their contemporary art fix for free at Museu Colecção Berardo, the latest addition to the Centro Cultural de Belém (p99). The ultrawhite, minimalist gallery displays billionaire José Berardo's eye-popping collection of abstract, surrealist and pop art. Don't miss Warhol's blue-eyed girl *Judy Garland*, Lichtenstein's utterly dotty *Interior with Restful Painting*, Paula Rego's magical realism in *The Barn* and Magritte's fantastical *The Silvery Chasm*.

Outside in the sculpture park, Niki de Saint Phalle's buxom *Swimmers* hog the limelight.

Museu Nacional de Arqueologia   MUSEUM
(National Archaeology Museum; Map p73; Praça do Império; adult/child €5/free, admission free 10am-2pm Sun; ◷10am-6pm, closed Mon in low season) It mightn't sound it, but the Museu Nacional de Arqueologia is a fascinating way to spend an hour. Housed in Mosteiro dos Jerónimos' western wing, the intriguing stash contains Mesolithic flintstones, Egyptian mummies inside elaborately painted sarcophagi and beautifully wrought Bronze Age jewellery. Even more curious is the collection of statues dedicated to Roman deities.

Museu Nacional dos Coches   MUSEUM
(National Coach Museum; Map p73; Praça Afonso de Albuquerque; adult/child €5/2.50, admission free 10am-2pm Sun; ◷10am-6pm Tue-Sun) Cinderella wannabes feel right at home at the palatial Museu Nacional dos Coches, which dazzles with its world-class collection of 17th- to 19th-century coaches. The stuccoed, frescoed halls of the former royal riding stables display gold coaches so heavy and ornate, it's a wonder they could move at all. Stunners include Pope Clement XI's scarlet-and-gold *Coach of the Oceans*.

Jardim Botânico Tropical   GARDENS
(Overseas Garden; Map p73; Calçada do Galvão; adult/child €2/free; ◷9am-6pm Mon-Fri, 11am-7pm Sat & Sun) Far from the madding crowd, these botanical gardens bristle with hundreds of tropical species from date palms

---

WATER FEATURE

The 109 arches of the **Aqueduto das Águas Livres** (Aqueduct of the Free Waters; Map p70) lope across the hills into Lisbon from Caneças, more than 18km away; they are most spectacular at Campolide, where the tallest arch is an incredible 65m high. Built between 1728 and 1835, by order of Dom João V, the aqueduct is a spectacular feat of engineering and brought Lisbon its first clean drinking water. Its more sinister claim to fame is as the site where 19th-century mass murderer Diogo Alves pushed his victims over the edge. No prizes for guessing why the aqueduct was closed to the public soon after.

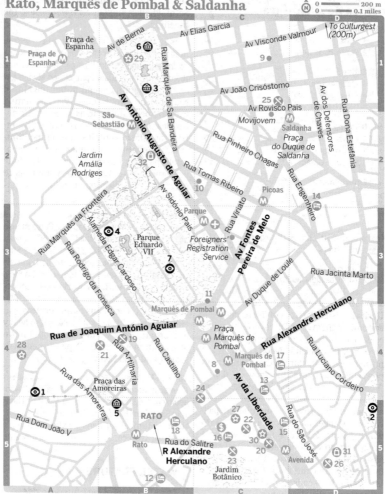

to monkey puzzle trees. Spread across 7 hectares, it's a peaceful, shady retreat on a sweltering summer's day. A highlight is the Macau garden complete with mini pagoda, where bamboo rustles and a cool stream trickles. Tots love to clamber over the gnarled roots of a banyan tree and spot the waddling ducks and geese.

PARQUE DAS NAÇÕES

Parque das Nações blossomed out of an industrial estate for Expo '98. Polluting factories were demolished and progressive architects from Nick Jacobs to Santiago Calatrava pooled their creative vision to shape a futuristic glass-and-steel playground with an ocean theme and impeccable eco credentials. Today, the waterfront is a cocktail of contemporary style with sci-fi edifices, public art installations, riverfront cafes, lush gardens and kiddie wonderlands such as the Oceanário. It's proof that Lisbon is not beyond the reaches of modernisation.

To reach the Parque das Nações, take the train or metro to Gare do Oriente and follow the signs to the waterfront. The riverside promenade is great for two-wheel adventures. To rent your own set of wheels, check out **Tejo Bike** (p79). For a bird's-eye view of the park, take a ride on the **Teleférico** (aerial tram; Passeio do Tejo; adult/child one-way €4/2), which glides above the river's edge.

Oceanário AQUARIUM
(Oceanarium; www.oceanario.pt; Doca dos Olivais; adult/child €12/6; ☺10am-8pm) The closest you'll get to scuba-diving without a wet-suit, Lisbon's Oceanário is mind-blowing. No amount of hyperbole about it being Europe's second-largest aquarium, where 8000 species splash in 7 million litres of seawater, does it justice.

Huge wraparound tanks make you feel as if you are underwater, as you eyeball zebra sharks, honeycombed rays, gliding mantas and schools of neon fish. Keep your peepers open for oddities such as filigree seadragons, big 'n' dopey ocean sunfish and flying saucer–like moon jellyfish. The superstars, though, are frolicsome sea otters Eusébio and Amália. You'll also want to see the recreated rainforest, Indo-Pacific coral reef and Magellan penguins on ice. The conservation-oriented oceanarium arranges family activities from behind-the-scenes marine tours to sleeping – yeah right! – with the sharks.

Pavilhão do Conhecimento MUSEUM
(Knowledge Pavilion; www.pavconhecimento.pt; Alameda dos Oceanos; adult/child €7/4; ☺10am-6pm Tue-Fri, 11am-7pm Sat & Sun) Kids won't grumble about science at the interactive Pavilhão do Conhecimento, where they can launch hydrogen rockets, lie unhurt on a bed of nails, experience the gravity on the moon and get dizzy on a high-wire bicycle. Budding physicists have fun whipping up tornadoes and blowing massive soap bubbles, while tots run riot in the adult-free unfinished house.

PARK PASS

Save euros by buying the **Cartão do Parque** (adult/concession €19/10) offering admission to Parque das Nações' top attractions including the Oceanário and Pavilhão do Conhecimento, plus a 20% discount on bike rental. The pass is valid for one month and allows you to jump the queues at ticket offices. Buy yours at the **Posto de Informação** (Information Post; Alameda dos Oceanos; ☺10am-7pm).

Gare do Oriente
TRAIN STATION

(Oriente Station) Designed by acclaimed Spanish architect Santiago Calatrava, the space-age Gare do Oriente is an extraordinary vaulted structure, with slender columns fanning out into a concertina roof to create a kind of geometric, crystalline forest. The *Starship Enterprise*-like entrance adds a sci-fi dimension to the organic edifice. Calatrava, it seems, is a trainspotter at heart, having put his signature on other stations in Zurich, Lyon and Valencia. Keep an eye out for bold murals by celebrated artists such as Friedensreich Hundertwasser, Antonio Seguí and Arthur Boyd at the metro station.

Jardim Garcia de Orta
GARDENS

(Garcia de Orta Garden; Rossio dos Olivais) Bristling with exotic foliage from Portugal's former colonies, the Jardim Garcia de Orta is named after a 16th-century Portuguese naturalist and pioneer in tropical medicine. Botanical rarities feature Madeira's bird of paradise and serpentine dragon tree. Stroll the Brazilian garden, shaded by bougainvillea, silk-cotton, frangipani and Tabasco pepper trees. There's also a music garden where kids can bash out melodies on giant triangles and gongs.

Torre Vasco da Gama
MONUMENT, VIEWPOINT

(Vasco da Gama Tower; Rua Cais das Naus) Nope, you're not in Dubai, even if it feels like it, gazing up at the 145m-high, concrete-and-steel Torre Vasco da Gama, shaped like the sail of explorer Vasco da Gama's mighty caravel. The brainchild of architects Leonor

Janeiro and Nick Jacobs, the tower was on its way to becoming a swish five-star hotel run by **Sana** (www.sanahotels.com).

Ponte Vasco da Gama
BRIDGE

(Vasco da Gama Bridge) Vanishing into a watery distance, Ponte Vasco da Gama is Europe's longest bridge, stretching a head-spinning 17.2km across the Rio Tejo. Its incredible scale makes everything around it seem toy-town tiny. The architects took every last detail into account when building the six-lane, cable-style bridge for Expo '98, from the curvature of the earth to its rock-solid 85m foundations, which can withstand a major earthquake and winds of up to 250km/h.

🏃 Activities

Reserva Natural do Estuário do Tejo
BIRDWATCHING

(☑212 348 021; Av dos Combatentes da Grande Guerra 1, Alcochete) Birdwatchers will want their binoculars handy for Reserva Natural do Estuário do Tejo, upriver from Lisbon. The vast wetland nature reserve hosts more than 120,000 migrant wading birds, including black cowbirds and flocks of pink flamingos. It's accessible from Montijo, a ferry ride from Lisbon's Terreiro do Paço (p105), then the TST bus to Alcochete.

🎓 Courses

There is a handful of places where you can take a crash course in Portuguese. **Cambridge School** (Map p70; ☑213 124 600; www.cambridge.pt; Av da Liberdade 173) and **Cen-**

OUTDOOR ART

You can feast your eyes on some weird and wonderful public art in Parque das Nações. Commissioned pieces for Expo '98 comprise works by prolific sculptors such as Antony Gormley (of *Angel of the North* fame) and the late Jorge Vieira. As you wander, look for the famous five:

» Amy Yoes' loopy *Cursiva*, two lime-green iron squiggles that apparently symbolise the capitulary of a medieval manuscript

» Antony Gormley's loose-limbed frenzy *Rhizome* on Rossio dos Olivais – the abstract iron sculpture represents nine life-sized human figures that harmoniously slot together

» Jorge Vieira's iron-oxide *Homem-Sol* (Sun Man), a 20m anthropomorphic giant whose sharp, angular bulk rises above Alameda dos Oceanos

» Fernando Conduto's ocean-inspired *Mar Largo* on Rossio dos Olivais, a wavy mosaic pathway reflecting the tides of the Tejo

» João Cutileiro's saucy *Lago das Tágides*, partially submerged marble sculptures of voluptuous female nudes evoking poet Luís de Camões' mythical *Tágides* (nymphs of the Tejo)

Belém

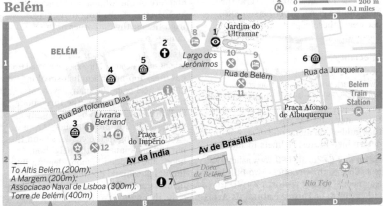

tro de Linguas (CIAL; Map p70; ☑217 940 448; www.cial.pt; Av da República 41) both give group language courses (from about €320 for a 30- to 40-hour intensive course; individual lessons cost €25 and up). **Centro de Informação e Documentação** (CIDAC; Map p70; ☑021 317 28 60; www.cidac.pt; Rua Pinheiro Chagas 77) runs accredited courses in Portuguese, which start at €26.50 for individual and €13 for group lessons per hour.

☞ Tours
Jeep, Bus & Tram Tours

We Hate Tourism Tours (☑911 501 720; www.wehatetourismtours.com; tours per person €15-30) One memorable way to explore the city is with Bruno, a friendly native *lisboêta* who takes travellers around in his iconic open-topped UMM (a Portuguese 4WD once made for the army). In addition to his King of the Hills tour, he leads nightlife tours, beach trips and excursions to Sintra.

Carristur (☑213 582 334; www.carristur.pt; tour adult €15-18, child €8-9) Tram 28 covers the major sights, but if you'd prefer to join a group, Carristur runs 1½-hour tram tours of city highlights in Alfama and Baixa departing from Praça do Comércio. A Belém-bound Carristur departs from Praça Figueira.

Cityrama (☑213 191 090; www.cityrama. pt) This outfit runs open-topped double-decker bus tours of Lisbon (adult/child €15/8), plus Sintra and the western beaches (€39). All depart from Marquês de Pombal (Map p70).

Belém

◉ Sights

◎ Sleeping

⊗ Eating

✿ Entertainment

⊜ Shopping

River Cruises & Dinner Cruises

Transtejo (Map p54; ☑218 824 674; www. transtejo.pt; Terreiro do Paço terminal; adult/ child €20/10; ◎3pm Apr-Oct) These 2½-hour river cruises are a laid-back way to enjoy Lisbon's sights with multilingual commentary.

Lisboa Vista do Tejo (Map p54; ☑213 913 030; www.lvt.pt; Terreiro do Paço terminal; ferry ticket one-way/return €12/15; ☏) This outfit sails twice daily between Caís do Sodré and Belém, where it docks near the Torre de Belém. LVT also offers several three-hour dinner cruises (per person €80) per week; these depart from Docas de Alcântara.

Speciality Tours

GoCar Touring (Map p54; ☑210 965 030; www.gocartours.pt; Rua dos Douradores 16; per hr/day €25/89) These self-guided tours put you behind the wheel of an open-topped two-seater mini-car with a talking GPS that guides you along one of several pre-determined routes. Helmets included.

Naturway (☑213 918 090; www.naturway.pt; tours €50) Naturway offers two full-day excursions, taking visitors by 4WD to either Sintra or Parque Natural da Arrábida (see boxed text, p134). Tours take in coastal scenery and include hotel pick-up and drop-off.

Walking Tours

Lisbon Walker (Map p54; ☑218 861 840; www.lisbonwalker.com; Rua dos Remédios 84; 3hr walk adult/child €15/free; ☺10am & 2.30pm) This excellent company, with well-informed, English-speaking guides, offers themed walking tours through Lisbon such as 'Old Town' (the history

and lore of the Alfama) and 'Legends and Mysteries'. Walking tours depart from the northwest corner of Praça do Comércio.

Lisbon Explorer (☑961 198 781; www.lisbonexplorer.com; 2-3hr walk adult/child from €34/free) Top-notch English-speaking guides peel back the many layers of Lisbon's history during the three-hour walking tours offered by this highly rated outfit. Top picks include 'Around Alfama', taking in the castle, *sé* and the narrow back lanes of the neighbourhood; and 'Hidden Lisbon', delving into the Baixa, Chiado and Bairro Alto. Fee includes admission and public transport costs during tour.

✦ Festivals & Events

Lisboêtas celebrate their seasons with fervour. Rio-style carnivals and indie flicks heat up the cooler months, while summer spells high-octane concerts, sparkly pride parading and saintly celebrations of feasting and indecent proposals. *Fazer a festa* (partying) is considered a birthright in Portugal's live-wire capital. For up-to-date listings, pick up the tourist board's free magazine *Follow Me Lisboa*.

DON'T MISS

MOSTEIRO DOS JERÓNIMOS

Belém's undisputed heart-stealer is the Unesco-listed **monastery** (Hieronymites Monastery; Map p73; www.mosteirojeronimos.pt; Praça do Império; adult/child €6/free, admission free 10am-2pm Sun; ☺10am-6pm Tue-Sun). The *mosteiro* is the stuff of pure fantasy; a fusion of Diogo de Boitaca's creative vision and the spice and pepper dosh of Manuel I, who commissioned it to trumpet Vasco da Gama's discovery of a sea route to India in 1498.

Wrought for the glory of God, Jerónimos was once populated by monks of the Order of St Jerome, whose spiritual job for four centuries was to comfort sailors and pray for the king's soul. When the order was dissolved in 1833, the monastery was used as a school and orphanage until about 1940.

Entering the church through the western portal, you'll notice tree-trunk-like columns seem to grow into the ceiling, which is itself a spiderweb of stone. Windows cast a soft golden light over the church. Superstar Vasco da Gama is interred in the lower chancel, just left of the entrance, opposite venerated 16th-century poet Luís Vaz de Camões. From the upper choir, there's a superb view of the church; the rows of seats are Portugal's first Renaissance woodcarvings.

There's nothing like the moment you walk into the honey-stone Manueline **cloisters**, dripping with organic detail in their delicately scalloped arches, twisting augershell turrets and columns intertwined with leaves, vines and knots. It's just wow. Keep an eye out for symbols of the age like the armillary sphere and the cross of the Military Order, plus gargoyles and fantastical beasties on the upper balustrade.

If you plan to visit both the monastery and Torre de Belém, you can save a little by purchasing an €8 admission pass valid for both.

INDIA AHOY!

Fed up with the Venetian monopoly on overland trade with Asia, Portuguese explorer Vasco da Gama set sail from Lisbon in 1497 for distant shores, with a motley crew aboard his handsome caravel. He skirted the coast of Mozambique and Mombasa before finally washing up on the shore of Calicut, India, in May 1498. The bedraggled crew received a frosty welcome from the Zamorin (Hindu ruler) and when tensions flared, they returned from whence they came. The voyage was hardly plain sailing – monsoon tides were fraught with danger, scurvy was rife and more than half of Vasco da Gama's party perished. For his pains and success at discovering a sea route to India, Manuel I made him a lord when he returned in 1499 and he was hailed 'Admiral of the Indian Ocean'.

But in 1502, mounting hostilities in Calicut meant Vasco da Gama was forced to return to establish control. No more Mr Nice Guy, he seized an Arab ship and set it alight with hundreds of merchants onboard, then banished Muslims from the port. He returned to Europe with coffers full of silk and spices. Luís Vaz de Camões recounts the fascinating adventures of Portugal's *facundo Capitão* (eloquent captain) in his epic poem, *The Lusiads*.

February

Lisbon Carnival (www.visitlisboa.com) From Friday to Tuesday before Ash Wednesday, Lisbon celebrates with abandon at music-filled street parties and big events (including costume balls) at nightclubs.

April

Dias da Música (www.ccb.pt) Classical-music buffs see world-renowned orchestras perform at this three-day festival held at Centro Cultural de Belém.

Indie Lisboa (www.indielisboa.com) This spring filmathon brings 10 days of indie features, documentaries and shorts to Lisbon's big screens.

Peixe em Lisboa (www.peixemlisboa.com) Seafood lovers won't want to miss this week-long culinary extravaganza, put on by a dozen restaurants (including chefs with Michelin stars).

May

Alkantara Festival (www.alkantarafestival.pt) The cutting-edge Alkantara Festival lures theatregoers with a fortnight of innovative, boundary-crossing performances.

Lisboa Downtown (http://lisboadowntown. sapo.pt) Lisbon's wackiest race is this downhill boneshaker through Alfama. Competitors rattle across the cobbles, negotiating hairpin bends and gravity-defying jumps. First down gets the crown...

Rock in Rio (http://rockinrio-lisboa.sapo.pt) Lisbon's biggest music bash, the biannual Rock in Rio (held on even-numbered years) takes over Parque da Bela Vista with a star-studded line-up. The Cidade do Rock spins nonstop electronica.

June

Festa do Fado (Fado Festival) Classic and new-generation *fadistas* perform in the atmospheric setting of an illuminated Castelo de São Jorge. Catch free fado performances on trams every Thursday and Sunday in June.

Lisbon Pride (www.portugalpride.org) Feel the pride as whistling, rainbow flag-waving gays and lesbians parade from Marquês de Pombal to Praça do Município. Expect sizzling after-parties.

July

BaixAnima Baixa's summertime shindig entertains the crowds for free on weekends from July to September with circus acts and live music, improvised theatre and mime.

Delta Tejo (www.deltatejo.com) Alto Ajuda's environmentally sustainable festival stages three days of live music under a starry sky – from reggae and fado to mellow Brazilian grooves.

August

Festival dos Oceanos (www.festivaldos oceanos.com) Dive into Lisbon's seafaring heritage at this two-week festival of swashbuckling parades, world beats, regattas and riverside fireworks.

START **MIRADOURO DA SENHORA DO MONTE**
FINISH **NEAR PRAÇA DO COMÉRCIO**
DISTANCE **2KM**
DURATION **TWO TO THREE HOURS**

Walking Tour
Exploring the Alfama

This viewpoint-to-viewpoint route starts on tram 28 from Largo Martim Moniz or the Baixa, taking in the city's best tram route *and* avoiding uphill slogs. Take the tram up to Largo da Graça. From here, stroll north and turn left behind the barracks for breathtaking views from Lisbon's highest lookout, **1** **Miradouro da Senhora do Monte** (see boxed text, p62). Or, walk south and turn right to pine-shaded **2** **Miradouro da Graça** (see boxed text, p62), where central Lisbon spreads out before you. Retrace your steps and head east to admire the exquisitely tiled cloisters of **3** **Igreja de São Vicente de Fora,** and the cool, echoing **4** **Panteão Nacional.** If it's Tuesday or Saturday, make a detour to the buzzy **5** **Feira da Ladra** (Thieves Market; p102) to hunt for buried treasure. Otherwise, go west along Arco Grande da Cima until you reach Largo de Rodrigues de Freitas. Take the Costa do Castelo

fork, continuing west to skirt the castle battlements along narrow cobbled streets affording stunning views. Pass in front of **6** **Solar dos Mouros** (p81), then turn left up to the **7** **Castelo de São Jorge** (p57) and its **8** **viewpoint**. Next, head down the steep lanes to Largo das Portas do Sol, and another fine vista from bougainvillea-clad **9** **Miradouro de Santa Luzia**. From here wander northward, past whitewashed **10** **Igreja de Santa Luzia** and turn right into the atmospheric lane of Beco de Santa Helena, threading through labyrinthine Alfama to Largo das Alcaçarias. Take Rua de São João da Praça westwards, pausing for coffee and flaky apple strudel at arty, Austrian-run **11** **Pois Café** (p89), to the fortresslike **12** **sé** (p60) and **13** **Igreja de Santo António**. Downhill from here, your final stop is gazing at the intricate Manueline facade of **14** **Igreja da Conceição Velha**, just east of Praça do Comércio.

SAINTLY CELEBRATIONS

Come all ye faithful lovers of *vinho*-swigging, sardine-feasting, dancing and merry-making to June's **Festas dos Santos Populares** (Festivals of the Popular Saints), three weeks of midsummer madness. In Lisbon, the key saintly festivities are these:

» **Festa de Santo António** (Festival of St Anthony) This lively fest is celebrated with particular fervour in Alfama and Madragoa from 12 to 13 June, with feasting, drinking, *bailes* (balls) and some 50 *arraiais* (street parties). St Anthony has a bit of a reputation as a matchmaker. *Lisboêtas* declare their undying love by giving *manjericos* (basil plants) with soppy poems. Around 300 hard-up couples get hitched for free!

» **Festa de São Pedro** (Festival of St Peter) Lisbon pulls out all the stops for St Peter, the patron saint of fishermen, from 28 to 29 June. There are slap-up seafood dinners and river processions in his barnacled honour.

Jazz em Agosto (www.musica.gulbenkian.pt) Fundação Calouste Gulbenkian (p99) welcomes established and fresh talent to the stage at this soulful jazz fest.

September

Festival de Cinema Gay e Lésbico (www.queerlisboa.pt) Lisbon's pinkest 10-day flick fest screens 100 homegrown and international gay and lesbian films in late September.

November

Arte Lisboa In the spotlight: the contemporary art of 60 Portuguese and international galleries at this massive fair in Parque das Nações.

December

Lisbon Marathon (www.lisbon-marathon.com) 'Tis the season to work up a festive appetite at Lisbon's pre-Yuletide dash from Praça do Comércio to Belém.

New Year's Eve Ring in the *ano novo* (new year) with fireworks, free concerts and DJs down by the river.

🛏 Sleeping

Finally waking up to smell those tourist euros, Lisbon has seriously raised the slumber stakes with an excellent array of design-conscious boutique hotels and upmarket backpacker digs. Be sure to book ahead during the high season (mid-July to mid-September). If you arrive without a reservation, head to a tourist office (p105), where staff can call around for you.

A word to those with weak knees and/or heavy bags: many guest houses lack lifts, meaning you'll have to haul your luggage up three flights or more. If this disconcerts, be sure to book a place with an elevator.

BAIXA & ROSSIO

Sandwiched between the Alfama and Bairro Alto, this central area has seen a huge influx of both style-conscious boutique hotels as well as fanciful, award-winning hostels. Those looking for modestly priced private rooms can survey the simple, old-fashioned *pensões* (guest houses) that sprinkle the area. Baixa and Rossio are both within staggering distance of the main sights, shops and nightlife, yet they are quieter than rowdy Bairro Alto.

Lavra Guesthouse   GUEST HOUSE €€
(Map p54; ☎218 820 000; www.lavra.pt; Calçada de Santana 182; s/d from €40/50) Set in a former convent that dates back two centuries), the Lavra Guesthouse has a range of rooms, from basic quarters facing onto an inner courtyard, to brighter, more stylishly set rooms with wood floors and tiny balconies. Some bathrooms are cramped. It's a short stroll from the Elevador da Lavra, or a steep climb from Largo de São Domingos.

Internacional Design Hotel
BOUTIQUE HOTEL €€€
(Map p54; ☎213 240 990; www.internacional designhotel.com; Rua da Betesga 3; d from €250; ❉) Raising the ante in the city's design stakes, this high-concept hotel has four types of rooms, each conjuring a radically different aesthetic: Urban, with grey walls and brightly coloured artwork and duvets; Tribu, which has more earthy appeal, with light and dark woods and tree silhouettes on the walls; Zen, which aims for simple elegance; and Pop, which takes things up a notch with eye-catching art on the walls and bubblegum-coloured floors and walls.

Brown's Apartments APARTMENTS €€
(Map p54; ☎218 874 128; www.brownsapart
ments.com; Rua da Vitória 88; d from €80; ✿⬚)
This new apart-hotel offers small, smartly
decorated rooms in an excellent location in
Baixa. Comfortable beds, black-and-white
photos on the walls, artful lighting, elevator access and oversized showerheads are
nice touches – though minuses include the
minimal service (rooms aren't cleaned daily) and minor design flaws (lack of closets/
storage space, thin walls).

Lisbon Story Guesthouse GUEST HOUSE €€
(Map p54; ☎211 529 313; www.lisbonstoryguest
house.com; Largo de São Domingos 18; d with
shared bathroom incl breakfast €45-80; @⬚)
Overlooking Praça São Domingos, Lisbon
Story is a small, welcoming guest house
with nicely maintained rooms, some of
which sport Portuguese themes (the river-
blue Tejo room, a handicraft-lined 'Culturas'
room). Rooms range from cramped to spacious, and the best room has fine views and
pays homage to Portugal's greatest writers.
All eight rooms share three bathrooms. The
shoe-free lounge, with throw pillows and
low tables, is a nice touch.

Hotel Avenida Palace HOTEL €€€
(Map p54; ☎213 218 100; www.hotelavenida
palace.pt; Rua 1 de Dezembro 123; d from €200;
✿@) Palatial certainly sums up this belle-
époque hotel with its blingy chandeliers,
polished marble and skylight. Rooms are
lavish with plump beds, high-thread-count
sheets and gilt mirrors. There's a tiny gym,
a wood-panelled bar and a sublime lounge
where high tea is served.

Residencial Alegria GUEST HOUSE €€
(Map p54; ☎213 220 670; www.alegrianet.com;
Praça da Alegria 12; d €58-78;✿) Overlooking
a palm-dotted plaza, this lemon-fronted
belle-époque gem is ablaze with pink geraniums in summer. Rooms are peaceful and
airy with plaids and chunky wood, while
corridors reveal stucco and antiques.

Travellers House HOSTEL €
(Map p54; ☎210 115 922; http://travellershouse.
com; Rua Augusta 89; dm from €22;@) Our readers enthuse about this super-friendly hostel
set in a converted 250-year-old house on
Rua Augusta. As well as cosy dorms, there's
a retro lounge with beanbags, an internet
corner and a communal kitchen. Tiago and
Gonçalo know what makes travellers tick,
from scrambled eggs for breakfast to activi-

ties such as wine-tasting, and – like it! – an
honour system for the minibar.

Goodnight Hostel HOSTEL €
(Map p54; ☎213 430 139; http://goodnighthostel.
com; Rua dos Correeiros 113; dm/d €20/50;@⬚)
Set in a converted 18th-century town
house, this glam hostel rocks with its fab
location, retro design and friendly owner
João. Goodnight has everything backpackers crave: from free wi-fi and breakfast to
a communal kitchen and lounge. The high-
ceilinged dorms offer vertigo-inducing
views over Baixa.

Hotel Lisboa Tejo HOTEL €€€
(Map p54; ☎218 866 182; www.evidenciahoteis.
com; Rua dos Condes de Monsanto 2; s/d incl
breakfast €113/130; ✿@⬚) Once a broom-
maker's, this town house has scrubbed up
nicely into a contemporary hotel, combin-
ing original features such as brick vaulting
with quirky wavy ceilings. Wood-floored
rooms are cushy with cornflower-blue hues,
theatrical chairs and satellite TV. Don't miss
the Roman *poço* (well) near the entrance.

Lounge Hostel HOSTEL €€
(Map p54; ☎213 462 061; www.lisbonlounge
hostel.com; Rua de São Nicolau 41; dm/d incl
breakfast €20/60;@) These ultrahip Baixa
digs have a party vibe. Bed down in immaculate dorms and meet like-minded travellers in the hip lounge watched over by a
wacky moose head. The fun team regularly
organises events such as the Portuguese
dinner with wine for €7. Free internet and
breakfast sweeten the deal.

VIP Eden APARTMENTS €€
(Map p54; ☎213 216 600; www.viphotels.com;
Praça dos Restauradores 24; apt from €95;
✿@⬚⬚) The art deco Eden theatre has
morphed into this apart-hotel on buzzy
Praça dos Restauradores. Studios with
kitchenettes are functional and clean. The
biggest draw, though, is the rooftop pool,
where you can splash, sunbathe and enjoy
fine Lisbon views.

Residencial Duas Nações GUEST HOUSE €€
(Map p54; ☎213 460 710; Rua da Vitória 41; d
with/without bathroom €75/50) Bang in the
heart of pedestrianised Baixa, this bright
guest house makes a good sightseeing and
shopping base. Painted in blues and yel-
lows, rooms are decent, though the microscopic bathrooms are a blast from the '70s.
Rooms on upper floors are quieter and open
onto verandas.

Residencial Florescente   GUEST HOUSE €€
(Map p54; ☎213 426 609; www.residencial florescente.com; Rua das Portas de Santo Antão 99; s/d from €45/65; ✴@🛜) On a vibrant street lined with alfresco restaurants, lemon-fronted Florescente has comfy rooms in muted tones with shiny new bathrooms and free wi-fi. It's a two-minute walk from Rossio.

Pensão Brasil-África   GUEST HOUSE €
(Map p64; ☎218 869 266; www.pensaobrasil africa.com; Travessa das Pedras Negras 8; s/d €25/35) Tucked down a quiet street, this old-school guest house near the *sé* offers sunny, wood-floored rooms with floral prints. Shared bathrooms are spotless. There's everything you need to rustle up a light breakfast in the lounge.

Pensão Imperial   GUEST HOUSE €
(Map p54; ☎213 420 166; 4th fl, Praça dos Restauradores 78; s/d with shower €25/40) Cheery Imperial has a terrific location, but you'll need to grin and lug it, as there's no lift. The high-ceilinged rooms with wooden furniture are nothing flash, but some have flower-draped balconies overlooking the *praça*.

Pensão Galicia   GUEST HOUSE €
(Map p54; ☎213 428 430; Rua do Crucifixo 50; s/d with shared bathroom €25/40) Central for Baixa, this homey, no-frills guest house exudes crusty charm. Its 11 small rooms are decked out in chintzy pastels, rag rugs and old-style furnishings; the best have little balconies.

Pensão Gerês   GUEST HOUSE €€
(Map p54; ☎218 810 497; www.pensaogeres. com; Calçada do Garcia 6; s/d €45/55;@) Near bustling Largo de São Domingos, this petite and family-run Gerês has basic but bright and airy rooms decorated with dark wood furniture and thin blue carpeting. Mattresses are a bit on the firm side.

CHIADO, BAIRRO ALTO & AROUND
Well-heeled Chiado has high-quality accommodation options, with both boutique hotels and high-end hostels – though little in between. If you want to be central for nightlife, crash in loud and lively Bairro Alto, which is better for all-night partying than quality shut-eye. Light sleepers should pack earplugs. The hip Santa Catarina district is giving rise to a new breed of stylish hostels.

Hotel do Chiado   HOTEL €€€
(Map p58; ☎213 256 100; www.hoteldochiado. com; Rua Nova do Almada 114; d from €150;✴🛜) Fusing 19th-century charm with 21st-century cool, the well-located Hotel do Chiado offers plush rooms with perks such as cable TV and fluffy bathrobes. Go for a top-floor room with a bougainvillea-clad terrace affording views to the river and castle; room 712 is most coveted. Open from noon to midnight, the 7th-floor bar offers superb vistas for all.

Pensão Londres   GUEST HOUSE €€
(Map p54; ☎213 462 203; www.pensaolondres. com.pt; Rua Dom Pedro V 53; s/d €50/75) Opposite Miradouro de São Pedro de Alcântara lookout, Londres oozes art-nouveau charm with its cage elevator and stuccowork. Its high-ceilinged rooms feature decorative balconies and polished wood furniture; those on the 4th floor afford sweeping city views.

BIKING THE TEJO

With its steep, winding hills and narrow, traffic-filled lanes, Lisbon may not seem like the ideal place to hop on a bicycle. The city however is redefining itself with the addition of a new biking/jogging path that opened in 2010. Coursing along the Tejo for nearly 7km, the path connects Cais do Sodré with Belém, and has artful touches – including the poetry of Pessoa printed along parts of it. It passes beside a rapidly changing landscape – taking in ageing warehouses that are being converted into open-air cafes, restaurants and nightspots.

A handy place to rent bikes is a short stroll from Cais do Sodré: **Bike Iberia** (Map p54; www.bikeiberia.com; Largo Corpo Santo 5). Those looking for a longer ride, can bike out to Belém, catch the ferry to Trafaria, and then continue on another **new bike path** (also separate from traffic) that runs for about 6km down to the pretty beach of Costa da Caparica.

You can also hire bikes for short spins along the Tejo out at Parque das Nações, where **Tejo Bike** (www.tejobike.pt) rents quality mountain bikes, kids' bikes, go-carts and inline skates.

SELF-CATERING IN STYLE

If you're travelling with family or a group of friends in high season (July to mid-September), it may work out cheaper to rent a self-catering apartment, particularly if you're staying for more than a few nights. Rates for modern, fully equipped apartments in central districts such as Alfama, Baixa and Chiado range from €50 to €150 per night, with many places offering substantial discounts for stays of more than a week. There are some excellent deals out there, but you'll need to do your homework online. Good websites to try include www.travelingtolisbon.com, www.lisbon-apartments.com and www.lisbon-holiday-apartments.com.

Lisbon Old Town Hostel
HOSTEL €€

(Map p58; ☑213 465 248; www.lisbonoldtown hostel.com; Rua do Ataíde 26; dm/d incl breakfast from €18/50; ❋@☎) In a quiet area a short stroll from Bairro Alto, the Lisbon Old Town Hostel earns high marks for its friendly staff and clean, spacious dorm rooms with high ceilings and original details. There's a good traveller vibe here, and staff occasionally organises group dinners.

Poets Hostel
HOSTEL €

(Map p58; ☑213 461 058; www.lisbonpoets hostel.com; 5th fl, Rua Nova da Trindade 2; dm €21;@☎) Backpackers wax lyrical about this poetry-themed hostel in well-heeled Chiado. The 17th-century town house has been lovingly reincarnated as a charming hostel with high-ceilinged, light-flooded dorms. There's a relaxed lounge with free wi-fi and beanbags.

Shiado Hostel
HOSTEL €

(Map p58; ☑213 429 227; 3rd fl, Rua Anchieta 5; dm/d with shared bathroom incl breakfast from €21/60; @☎) Beautifully located on an elegant street in the Chiado, this handsomely maintained hostel has bright, Zen-like rooms with polished floors and a simple, but inviting, colour scheme, with touches of artwork around the common areas. It's a welcoming, but quiet, place – not ideal for those seeking a more social experience.

Lisbon Calling
HOSTEL €

(Map p58; ☑213 432 381; www.lisboncalling.net; 3rd fl, Rua de São Paulo 126; dm incl breakfast €20;@☎) This stylish, unsigned backpacker favourite near Santa Catarina features original frescos, azulejos and hardwood floors – all lovingly restored by the friendly English-Portuguese owners. It's a charming pad with bright, spacious dorms, a groovy lounge with internet, and a brick-vaulted kitchen where breakfast is served.

Oasis Lisboa
HOSTEL €

(Map p58; ☑213 478 044; www.oasislisboa.com; Rua de Santa Catarina 24; dm incl breakfast €20;@☎) Behind yellow wonder walls, this self-defined backpacker mansion offers wood-floored dorms, a sleek lounge and kitchen, and a rooftop terrace with stunning views to the river. There's free breakfast, internet and coffee. The young team arranges activities from cocktail hours to barbecues. Play ping-pong or snuggle by an open fire.

Pensão Globo
GUEST HOUSE €€

(Map p58; ☑213 462 279; www.pensaoglobo -lisbon.com; Rua do Teixeira 37; r from €50) Tucked down a quietish street, this guest house offers 16 tidy, individually decorated rooms – from scarlet ones with postage-stamp-sized courtyards to lime-green and leafy jobs; all have ultramodern bathrooms. Payment is cash only.

Anjo Azul
HOTEL €€

(Map p58; ☑213 478 069; www.anjoazul.com; Rua Luz Soriano 75; d €50-80;@) You can't miss the dazzling blue-tiled facade of this gay-friendly hotel, named after smouldering Blue Angel Marlene Dietrich. Adorned with homoerotic artwork, rooms stretch from scarlet-and-black love nests with heart pillows to chocolate-caramel numbers. Clean bathrooms and teeny balconies.

Bairro Alto Hotel
HOTEL €€€

(Map p58; ☑213 408 288; www.bairroaltohotel.com; Praça Luís de Camões 2; s/d incl breakfast from €330/365; ❋@☎) Bairro Alto's funkiest boutique hotel bears the hallmark of interior designer José Pedro Vieira. Note the esoteric Rui Chafes' sculptures in the lobby. Decked out in bold colours, the plush rooms offer five-star trappings such as plasma TVs, wi-fi and shiny marble bathrooms. A Ferrero Rocher–style gold lift zooms to the 6th-floor lounge, a great place to sip cocktails at sundown.

Hotel Príncipe Real HOTEL €€€
(213 407 350; www.hotelprincipereal.com; Rua da Alegria 53; s/d incl breakfast €120/150;) Hidden in a quiet pocket of Bairro Alto, this boutique hotel has stylish rooms with flat-screen TVs and marble bathrooms; most have balconies with superb views. Wake up to a full English breakfast.

ALFAMA, CASTELO & GRAÇA
Alfama's cobbled lanes generally offer peaceful slumber, though choose wisely or else you might find yourself being serenaded to sleep by a warbling *fadista*. On its hilltop perch above Lisbon, leafy Graça has dramatic views.

Palácio Belmonte LUXURY HOTEL €€€
(Map p64; 218 816 600; www.palaciobelmonte .com; Páteo Dom Fradique 14; ste from €400;) Nestled beside Castelo de São Jorge, this 15th-century palace turns on the VIP treatment with its 11 suites, named after Portuguese luminaries and lavishly adorned with 18th-century *azulejos*, silks, marble and antiques. There's a pool framed by herb gardens, a wood-panelled library where classical music plays and numerous other luxuries that justify the price tag.

Olissippo Castelo GUEST HOUSE €€€
(Map p64; 218 820 190; www.olissippohotels. com; Costa do Castelo 112-126; d incl breakfast from €190;) Up the cobbled hill lies this bubblegum-pink hotel offering sweeping views and silent nights. The spacious rooms are classically elegant with huge windows, deep-pile carpets and sparkly marble bathrooms; pick one on the 3rd floor for a private veranda. Wi-fi and a hearty breakfast are other pluses.

Solar dos Mouros BOUTIQUE HOTEL €€€
(Map p64; 218 854 940; www.solardosmouros. com; Rua do Milagre de Santo António 6; d with castle/river view from €120/180;) Blink and you'll miss this boutique pad near the castle. Its art-slung interior reveals a passion for Africa and primary colours. Affording castle views or more panoramic vistas over the river, the 12 rooms bear the imprint of artist Luís Lemos and offer trappings such as flat-screen TVs and minibars. There's a water garden for catnapping between sights.

Albergaria Senhora do Monte HOTEL €€
(Map p50; 218 866 002; senhoradomonte@ hotmail.com; Calçada do Monte 39; s/d from €50/65;) Well off the beaten path, this friendly hotel has clean but slightly dated rooms with stunning views, and the price-to-value ratio here is excellent. It's worth shelling out extra for a veranda. There's also a restaurant and sunny terrace – both with panoramic views. Tram 28 passes close by. It's a short stroll to the magnificent lookout of Miradouro da Senhora do Monte.

LISBON FOR CHILDREN

Amusing kids is child's play in Lisbon, where even little things spark the imagination – from bumpy rides on bee-yellow trams to gooey *pastéis de nata*, acting out fairy tales at Castelo de São Jorge to munching colourful *pipocas* (popcorn).

Lisboêtas are well prepared for families, with free or half-price tickets for little 'uns at major sights, half portions (ask for *uma meia dose*) at many restaurants, and free transport for under-fives. Hotels will often squeeze in cots or beds for tots at no extra charge.

Prime kiddie territory is Parque das Nações, where little nippers love to spot toothy sharks and sea otters at the eye-popping Oceanário, launch rockets and ride the high-wire bicycle at the hands-on Pavilhão do Conhecimento, then get utterly soaked at the splashy Jardins d'Água.

Most of Lisbon's squares and parks have playgrounds for tykes to let off excess energy, including Parque Eduardo VII and an animal-themed one at Jardim da Estrela.

Go west to relive the nautical adventures of the Age of Discovery in Belém's barge-stuffed Museu do Marinha, or marvel at the puppets in Lapa's enchanting Museu da Marioneta. Hard-to-please teens in tow? Take them shopping in Bairro Alto's groovy boutiques such as Sneakers Delight.

When weather warms, take the train to Cascais for some ice-cream-licking, bucket-and-spade fun. Kids can make finny friends on a dolphin-watching tour in Setúbal, or play king of the castle in the fantastical turrets and woodlands of Sintra.

Alfama Patio Hostel HOSTEL €€
(Map p64; ☑218 883 127; www.flashhostel.com;
Rua dos Escola Gerais 3; dm/d from €17/60; @🛜)
In the heart of the Alfama, this beautifully
run hostel is a great place to meet other
travellers, with loads of activities (from
pub crawls through the Bairro Alto to day
trips to the beach), plus regular barbecues
on the hostel's laid-back garden-like patio.
There's free wi-fi, a stylish lounge and fantastic staff.

Pensão Ninho das Águias GUEST HOUSE €
(Map p64; ☑218 854 070; Costa do Castelo 74;
s/d/tr with shared bathroom €30/40/60) It isn't
called 'eagle's nest' for nothing: this guest
house has a Rapunzel-esque turret affording magical 360-degree views over Lisbon.
Let your hair down in the light and breezy
rooms, or on the flowery terrace. Service is
grumpy.

Pensão São João da Praça GUEST HOUSE €
(Map p64; ☑218 862 591; 2nd fl, Rua de São João
da Praça 97; d with/without bathroom €50/35)
So close to the *sé* you can almost touch the
gargoyles, this 19th-century guest house
has a pick-and-mix of sunny rooms with
fridges and TVs; the best have river-facing
verandas.

PRÍNCIPE REAL, SANTOS & ESTRELA

Leafy neighbourhoods and plenty of style
set the scene for an overnight stay in the
top-notch boutique hotels here. It's an ideal
for escapists that prefer pin-drop peace to
central bustle.

Lapa Palace LUXURY HOTEL €€€
(Map p84; ☑213 949 494; www.lapapalace.
com; Rua do Pau de Bandeira 4; d from €350;
❋@🛜▨) Set in landscaped gardens, this
belle-époque mansion offers the red-carpet
treatment in swanky quarters with five-
star trimmings: from precious porcelain
to Oscar-winning flicks and marble bathrooms with toasty towels. Flash the cash
to upgrade to the Count of Valenças suite
complete with a turret affording 360-
degree views. The outdoor pool, Zen-style
treatment rooms, cocktail lounge and Italian restaurant are, as befits a palace, first
class. To get here, take tram 25E west from
Praça do Comércio to the Rua de São Domingos à Lapa stop. It's a five-minute walk
further along Rua do Sacramento.

As Janelas Verdes BOUTIQUE HOTEL €€€
(Map p84; ☑213 968 143; www.heritage.pt; Rua
das Janelas Verdes 47; d €250; ❋@) This romantic 18th-century mansion inspired
Eça de Queirós' novel *Os Maias*. Spacious
and classically elegant, the rooms feature
perks such as flat-screen TVs, DVD players,
shiny marble bathrooms and complimentary port. Retreat to the wood-panelled library for sweeping views to the river and
a stargazing telescope. When the sun's out,
take breakfast in the bougainvillea-draped
courtyard.

Maná Guesthouse GUEST HOUSE €€
(Map p84; ☑213 931 060; pensaomana@sapo.
pt; Calçada do Marquês de Abrantes 97; d with/
without bathroom incl breakfast €35/55; 🛜)
Small and welcoming, Maná has ultra-
clean rooms with polished wood floors,
high ceilings and decorative balconies.
Breakfast is served under the fruit trees in
the garden.

RATO, MARQUÊS DE POMBAL & SALDANHA

Hotel Britania HOTEL €€€
(Map p70; ☑213 155 016; www.heritage.pt; Rua
Rodrigues Sampaio 17; d from €160; ❋@🛜) Art
deco rules the waves at Britania, a boutique
gem near Avenida da Liberdade. Cassiano
Branco put his modernist stamp on the
rooms with chrome lamps, plaid fabrics
and shiny marble bathrooms. Hobnob over
a G&T at the bar, chat with the affable staff
and let this 1940s time capsule work its
charm.

Inspira Santa Marta HOTEL €€€
(Map p70; ☑210 440 900; www.inspirasanta
martahotel.com; Rua de Santa Marta 48; s/d from
€125/140; ❋@🛜) New in 2010, the 89-room
Inspira Santa Marta is an ecofriendly designer hotel set in a converted 19th-century
building. Rooms are stylish but functional
and incorporate five different feng shui
themes, including earth-toned Terra rooms
and cork-floored Arvore (tree) rooms with
sky-blue details. There's an inviting bras-
serie that showcases locally grown ingredients, a bar with fireplace, a games room
with billiards table and a spa.

Lisbon Dreams GUEST HOUSE €€
(Map p70; ☑213 872 393; www.lisbondreams
guesthouse.com; Rua Rodrigo da Fonseca 29; s/d/
tr incl breakfast €40/60/75; @🛜) On a quiet
street lined with jacaranda trees, Lisbon
Dreams offers excellent value for its bright
modern rooms (some on the spacious side)
with high ceilings and excellent mattresses
with crisp white linens. The green apples

are a nice touch, and there are attractive common areas to unwind in. All bathrooms are shared, but are spotlessly clean.

Fontana Park Hotel
HOTEL €€€
(Map p70; ☑210 410 600; www.fontanaparkhotel. com; Rua Engenheiro Vieira da Silva 2; d from €100; ❉@) The new design kid on Saldanha's block is this 1908 iron factory turned cutting-edge hotel, flaunting smooth contours, space-age lighting and sylvan flourishes. The monochrome rooms are temples to minimalism, with wall-mounted flat-screen TVs, wi-fi and granite bathrooms with transparent walls. Zen is the word in the Japanese restaurant and the bamboo-fringed garden with gurgling fountain.

Hotel Eurostars das Letras
HOTEL €€€
(Map p70; ☑213 573 094; www.eurostarsdas letras.com; Rua Castilho 6; d from €100; ❉@☎) The handsomely designed Hotel Eurostars, which opened in 2008, has high-tech rooms (Grundig stereos, flat-screen TVs, free wi-fi) that are done up in earthy tones – with wood floors, walnut headboards, black armchairs and satiny brown comforters. Rooms have a literary bent, with quotes by famous writers (Shakespeare, Borges, Pessoa) over the beds. Top-floor rooms have balconies.

Casa de São Mamede
GUEST HOUSE €€€
(Map p70; ☑213 963 166; www.casadesaoma mede.com; Rua da Escola Politécnica 159; s/d incl breakfast €100/120; ❉) This 18th-century, family-run villa has class: from the red carpet gracing the stone staircase to the tinkling chandeliers in the exquisitely tiled breakfast room. Large and serene, rooms sport period furnishings. It's a short stroll from Bairro Alto and the botanical gardens.

Dom Sancho I
GUEST HOUSE €€
(Map p70; ☑213 513 160; www.domsancho.com; 2nd fl, Av da Liberdade 202; s/d from €50/60; ❉@☎) In a grand 18th-century edifice overlooking the leafy, but busy, Avenida da Liberdade, Dom Sancho I offers small but comfortably furnished rooms – the best with polished wood floors, marble bathrooms and decorative balconies. Breakfast and wi-fi are available, but may cost extra (depending on where you booked).

BELÉM

Altis Belém
HOTEL €€€
(Map73; ☑210 400 200; www.altisbelem hotel.com; Doca do Bom Sucesso; d from €200; P❉@☎) New in 2009, this hypermodern

boutique hotel and spa near the waterfront offers stylish rooms that range from small to large with all the high-end fittings (Egyptian-cotton bed linen, glass-walled marble bathrooms, outdoor jacuzzis in some suites). All have balconies, and the best have enviable views over the Tejo. There's also a full-service spa and several enticing restaurants (one with an outdoor deck facing the marina).

Jerónimos 8
BOUTIQUE HOTEL €€€
(Map73; ☑213 600 900; www.jeronimos8hotel. com; Rua dos Jerónimos 8; s/d €120/130; ❉@☎) Belém's first boutique hotel, Jerónimos 8 ups the style ante with clean lines, floor-to-ceiling windows and designer flourishes aplenty. The slick rooms, dressed in cream and caramel hues with natural fabrics, feature cable TV, minibar and wi-fi. Chill in the pepper-red bar or on the deck. The monastery views are superb.

Pensão Residencial Setúbalense
GUEST HOUSE €
(Map73; ☑213 636 639; www.pensaosetub alense.pt; Rua de Belém 28; s/d from €35/45; ❉) A short toddle east of the monastery, this 17th-century guest house has twee but comfy rooms with tiled floors, floral fabrics and modern bathrooms. Corridors are a tad dark, but *azulejos* and potted plants add a homely touch.

✖ Eating

Sparky new-generation chefs at the stove, first-rate raw ingredients and a generous pinch of world spice means Lisbon no longer makes diners meow with *bacalhau*. Today's exciting, varied offerings span everything from ubercool dockside sushi lounges to designer Michelin-starred restaurants. Gourmet trailblazers such as Olivier, Joachim Koerper and Henrique Sá Pessoa have put the Portuguese capital back on the gastro map with boldly creative, seasonally inspired cuisine.

With the Atlantic on the doorstep, fish is big on most menus and tastes terrific served with a glass of Alentejo white on the cobbles. Even vegetarians find more to like about Lisbon nowadays. Euro-economisers should check out daily specials costing as little as €6. Many one-pan, family places close on Sunday or Monday.

BAIXA & ROSSIO
Many of Baixa's old-school bistros and outdoor cafes heave with tourists, but tiptoe

Jardim Botânico

Rua da Escola Politécnica

To Pavilhão Chinês (100m)

Rua da Palmeira

PRÍNCIPE REAL

Rua do Jasmim

ESTRELA

Rua de São Bento

Rua de Santo Amaro

Rua da Imprensa Nacional

Jardim da Estrela

Rua da Estrela

Praça da Estrela

BAIRRO ALTO

Largo de Jesus

Calçada da Estrela

Rua dos Na vagantes

Calçada do Combro

Rua do Poço dos Negros

Av Dom Carlos 1

To Lapa Palace Hotel (200m)

Rua das Praças

Rua do Sacramento a Lapa

MADRAGOA

LAPA

Rua Garcia da Horta

Calçada Ribeiro Santos

Rua do Instituto Industrial

Av 24 de Julho

Av de Brasília

Rua das Janelas Verdes

Santos Train Station

SANTOS

Cais da Viscondessa

Rio Tejo

---

away from the main drag Rua Augusta and you'll find some gems in streets such as Rua dos Correeiros and Rua dos Sapateiros. For alfresco dining with dazzling castle views, make for the cobbled steps of Calçada do Duque.

Solar dos Presuntos   PORTUGUESE €€€
(Map p54; ☑ 213 424 253; Rua das Portas de Santo Antão 150; mains €15-24; ☺lunch & dinner Mon-Sat) Don't be fooled by the smoked *presunto* (ham) hanging in the window, this iconic restaurant is renowned for its excellent seafood – as well as its smoked and grilled meats. There's a pleasant buzz to the folksy

and welcoming space, with photos of admirers lining the restaurant's walls. Prawn and lobster curry, salt-baked sea bass and delectable seafood paella are among the top choices.

República da Cerveja   INTERNATIONAL €€
(Map p54; Largo Duque de Cadaval 17; mains €7-14; ☺noon-midnight) Overlooking a hidden plaza behind Rossio train station, this bistro-pub sports high ceilings and an airy wood-filled interior, plus terrace seating. Smoked pork chops, steaks, burgers and other meaty fare fill out the menu, best ordered with a refreshing microbrew on draught.

Everest Montanha　　　　NEPALESE €€
(Map p54; Calçada do Garcia 15; mains €7-10; ☺lunch & dinner Mon-Sat;☑) Tucked just north of Praça da Figueira, this unassuming restaurant reaches Himalayan heights with flavourful lamb kormas, gobis and so-smooth mango lassis.

Jardim dos Sentidos　　　VEGETARIAN €€
(Map p54; Rua Mãe d'Água 3; lunch buffet €8-10; ☺lunch Mon-Fri, dinner Mon-Sat) Vegetarian-minded diners flock to this attractive restaurant with back garden and extensive lunch buffet. Among the offerings: four-cheese lasagna, vegetarian chilli, warm goat's-cheese salad and stuffed eggplant, plus a substantial tea menu.

Martinho da Arcada　　　PORTUGUESE €€€
(Map p54; Praça do Comércio 3; dishes €14-25; ☺breakfast, lunch & dinner Mon-Sat) Sizzling since 1782, this old-world restaurant was once a haunt of poet Fernando Pessoa. Dapper waiters bring pepper steak and grilled cod to the outdoor tables beneath a colonnade; prime people-watching territory.

Nova Pombalina　　　　　PORTUGUESE €
(Map p54; Rua do Comércio 2; sandwiches €3.50; ☺7am-8pm) The reason this bustling traditional restaurant is always packed around midday is its delicious *leitão* (suckling pig) sandwich, served on freshly baked bread in

60 seconds or less by the lightning-fast crew behind the counter. Other sandwich favourites include prosciutto and roast chicken.

Chaminés do Palácio　　GOURMET BURGERS €€
(Map p54; Largo de São Domingos 11; mains €8-10; ☺lunch Mon-Fri) Hidden on the 2nd floor of the Palácio da Independencia, you'll find a charming open-air courtyard where locals and a few well-informed visitors enjoy gourmet burgers – codfish, beef, garlicky sausage – served with tasty fixings.

Fragoleto　　　　　　　ICE CREAM €
(Map p54; Rua da Prata 74; 1/2 scoops €1.90/3; ☺9am-8pm Mon-Sat; ☑) Fragoleto serves creamy, rich Italian-style gelato, made from fresh, seasonal fruit – and there are even vegan options. Our favourites: pistachio and green tea. Get it to go, as there's no place to sit.

Confeitaria Nacional　　　PATISSERIE €
(Map p54; Praça da Figueira 18; lunches from €6; ☺8am-8pm Mon-Sat) Expanding waistlines since 1829, this stuccoed patisserie entices with strong *bica,* macaroons and *pastéis de nata.* Upstairs, the restaurant dishes up hearty quiches and soups.

Brown's Coffee Shop　　　　CAFE €
(Map p54; Rua da Vitória 86; mains €5-7; ☺8am-11pm; ☎) Although it looks and feels like

LET THEM EAT PASTÉIS!

Londoners have pubs, Parisians boulangeries and lisboêtas have pastelerias (pastry and cake shops) – temples to cream-filled treats that are never more than a few paces away. Everywhere, you'll see locals devouring flaky pastéis de nata or whiling away afternoons sipping bicas. Take this as your cue to follow those whiffs of butter, sugar and freshly roasted coffee. You can kiss the diet goodbye in this sugar-coated city, which sees pastelerias as life-enriching rather than waistline-expanding. But calorie counters take heart: for every blob of cream, there's another step to climb in Lisbon's steeply twisting streets, so you can counteract the indulgence with a vigorous urban workout.

Starbucks, with its dark wood interior and soft leather armchairs, Brown's is Portuguese owned and run. Lots of hot and iced coffee drinks, plus sandwiches, juices and pastries, plus free wi-fi.

Tamarind
INDIAN €€
(Map p54; ☎213 466 080; Rua da Glória 43; dishes €12-16; ⓦlunch Sun-Fri, dinner daily;✔) Dave Walia cooks up an Indian storm at this calm restaurant in Ayurveda-inspired pink and blue tones. His rich prawn kormas and lamb curries are inflected with chilli, ginger and fresh herbs.

Bonjardim
PORTUGUESE €€
(Map p54; Travessa de Santo Antão 11; mains €6-13; ⓦlunch & dinner) Juicy, spit-roast frango (chicken) is served with a mountain of fries at this local favourite. Add piri-piri for extra spice. The pavement terrace is elbow-to-elbow in summer.

O Fumeiro
PORTUGUESE €€
(Map p54; ☎213 474 203; Rua da Conceição da Glória 25; mains €12-20; ⓦlunch & dinner) This cosy blue-and-white-tiled restaurant specialises in the earthy, aromatic cuisine of the mountainous Beira Alta. Suckling pig and cataplana (seafood stew) pair well with Portuguese wines.

Celeiro Dieta
ORGANIC GROCERY, RESTAURANT €
(Map p54; Rua 1 de Dezembro 65; lunches around €6; ⓦ9am-6pm Mon-Fri, 9am-5pm Sat; ✔) Stop in Celeiro to assemble a tasty, organic picnic. You can also head downstairs where a no-fuss cafe serves daily specials like gazpacho, grilled vegie burgers and codfish soufflé. There's another restaurant-only branch a few doors down at Rua 1 de Dezembro 51.

Mega Vega
VEGETARIAN €
(Map p54; Rua dos Sapateiros 113; lunches €6.50-10; ⓦ8.30am-11pm Mon-Fri, 10am-11pm Sat;✔) This cheery vegetarian cafe rustles up fresh salads, tasty tarts and juices, and spreads a lunch buffet.

CHIADO
The elegant back streets of Chiado have some memorable dining options, some of which have vistas overlooking peaceful tree-fringed plazas.

Olivier
FRENCH €€€
(Map p58; ☎213 422 916; Rua do Alecrim 23; mains €19-27, tasting menu €38; ⓦdinner Mon-Sat) Lisbon master chef Olivier da Costa continues to wow diners at this intimate Chiado restaurant, with its beautifully prepared French-inspired dishes served amid gilded banquettes, low-hanging chandeliers and vintage wallpaper. The tasting menu features nine starters, a main and sorbet with vodka for dessert. Recent favourites included duck magret with port-wine sauce and fish, prawns and spinach in puff pastry. Reservations recommended.

Tavares Rico
PORTUGUESE €€€
(Map p58; ☎213 421 112; Rua da Misericórdia 37; mains €32-38, tasting menu €90; ⓦlunch & dinner Tue-Sat) Tavares is the fairest of them all, with its all-gold 18th-century interior lit by chandeliers. Signature dishes such as scallops with Alentejo bacon are beautifully cooked, artfully presented and marry well with Portuguese wines.

Kaffee Haus
CAFE €€
(Map p58; Rua Anchieta 3; mains €6-10; ⓦ11am-midnight Tue-Thu, 11am-2am Fri & Sat, 11am-8pm Sun) Kaffee Haus has a bright interior with classic lines and big windows overlooking a peaceful corner of the Chiado, and it's a favourite eating and drinking spot among a cool but unpretentious crowd. Check the chalkboard for daily specials – including big salads, tasty schnitzels, strudels, cakes and more. Expect big crowds (and great food) at weekend brunches.

Fábulas
CAFE €€

(Map p58; Calçada Nova de São Francisco 14; mains €6-10; ⊙10am-midnight Mon-Sat, 10am-8pm Sun;🗑) Exposed stone walls, low lighting and twisting corridors that open onto cosy nooks and crannies do indeed conjure a *fábula* (storybook fable). Couches and wooden tables are fine spots to while away a few hours over coffee or a bottle of wine, though Fábulas also prepares imaginative salads, penne and sundried-tomato pasta, burritos, crepes and daily specials.

Faca & Garfo
PORTUGUESE €

(Map p58; Rua da Condessa 2; mains €6-8; ⊙lunch & dinner Mon-Sat) The sweet *azulejo*-filled Faca & Garfo (which means 'knife and fork') has earned a loyal local following for its tasty, carefully prepared Portuguese recipes, reasonable prices and friendly service. Try the authentic *alheira de Mirandela* (chicken sausage) or the *bife à casa* (steak with cream and port-wine sauce).

Café no Chiado
PORTUGUESE €€

(Map p58; Largo do Picadeiro 10; mains €12-16; ⊙10am-2am) Near the Teatro São Luís, this laid-back cafe attracts an eclectic crowd who come for Portuguese classics such as *bacalhau espiritual* (shredded cod with carrot and bechamel sauce), *arroz de pato* (oven-cooked duck with rice) and creamy desserts. Tram 28 rattles right by the shaded sidewalk terrace, which is great for people-watching.

Aqui Há Peixe
SEAFOOD €€€

(Map p58; 🖉213 432 154; Rua da Trindade 18; mains €15-20; ⊙lunch Tue-Fri, dinner Tue-Sun) One of Lisbon's top seafood restaurants, this Chiado newcomer has stone walls, sea-green banquettes and walls adorned with nautical accoutrements (fish images, wooden sailboats), reminding one that indeed '*aqui ha peixe*' ('here there is fish'). Prices are high, but so is the quality in favourites such as oysters, octopus salad, grilled sea bass and lobster.

Royale Café
CAFE €

(Map p58; Largo Rafael Bordalo Pinheiro 29; snacks €4-7; ⊙10am-midnight Mon-Sat, 10am-8pm Sun;🖉) Media types and yummy mummiesflock to this chichi cafe – all monochrome walls and funky chandeliers. When the sun comes out, retreat to the vine-clad courtyard for zingy gooseberry juices, wild-rosebud teas and create-your-own sandwiches.

Oriente Chiado
VEGETARIAN €€

(Map p58; Rua Ivens 28; dishes €8-16; ⊙lunch & dinner;🖉) A rarity in Lisbon, this feng shui-inspired restaurant serves 100% vegan and macrobiotic food. Tasty dishes include polenta, hummus and tofu curries. There's a salad and juice bar.

Amo.te Chiado
CONTEMPORARY €€

(Map p58; Calçada Nova de São Francisco 2; mains €8-16; ⊙10am-midnight Mon-Thu, 10am-2am Fri & Sat;🖉) Giggly *lisboêtas* adore this *Sex and the City*-style haunt, kissed with silver and jazzed up with bubble-shaped lights. Lounge music plays as hipsters sip strawberry-vodka cocktails and devour couscous or octopus with roast peppers.

Nood
JAPANESE €

(Map p58; Largo Rafael Bordalo Pinheiro 20; mains €6-10; ⊙noon-midnight Sun-Thu, noon-2am Fri & Sat;🖉) Young and buzzy, this sleek Japanese eatery whips up tempting sushi and sashimi plates, steaming noodle dishes and satisfying appetisers such as shrimp gyoza and chicken or vegetable yakitori. The scene: chilli-red walls, communal tables and flaming woks.

Cervejaria da Trindade
PORTUGUESE €€

(Map p58; Rua Nova da Trindade 20C; dishes €8-20; ⊙lunch & dinner) This 13th-century monastery turned clattering beer hall oozes atmosphere with its vaults and *azulejos* of quaffing clerics and seasonal goddesses. Feast away on humungous steaks or lobster stew, washed down with foaming beer.

Jardim das Cerejas
VEGETARIAN €€

(Map p58; Calçada do Sacramento 36; buffet lunch/dinner €7/9; ⊙lunch & dinner) On a restaurant-lined stretch of Chiado, Jardim das Cerejas spreads a small but tasty lunch buffet, with many vegan items.

Vertigo Café
CAFE €

(Map p58; Travessa do Carmo 4; snacks €4-7; ⊙10am-midnight;🖉) Artists lap up the boho vibe at this glam Chiado cafe, where they can relax, read the papers and play draughts. Speciality teas, such as violet and jasmine, pair nicely with bagels or smoked-salmon salads.

ACISJF
PORTUGUESE €

(Map p58; top fl, Travessa do Ferragial 1; mains €7; ⊙lunch Mon-Fri) Sweet nuns dressed as lunch ladies run this small, sunny cafeteria, dishing up a daily soup (the gazpacho is great!), several mains – of the beef, sardines or codfish variety – and fresh fruit for dessert. The river views from the sun-drenched terrace are astounding. Free lunch on your birthday.

Mar Adentro
CAFE €

(Map p58; Rua do Alecrim 35; snacks €3-6; ☺10am-11pm Mon-Thu, 1pm-midnight Fri & Sat;✐) Gay-friendly Mar Adentro reveals a razor-sharp industrial design with a stainless steel arch, concrete walls and moulded plastic chairs. Lisbon creatives flock here for healthy breakfasts, yummy sandwiches (such as feta, pepper and olive) and free wi-fi.

BAIRRO ALTO & AROUND

For a preclubbing vibe, *caipirinhas* and a side order of cool, it has to be loud and lively Bairro Alto. The rhythmic sizzle of grills, wafts of garlic and pumping music fill the narrow lanes come twilight.

100 Maneiras
FUSION €€€

(Map p58; ✐210 990 475; Rua do Teixeira 35; tasting menu €35; ☺dinner Mon-Sat) One of Lisbon's best-rated restaurants, 100 Maneiras has no menu, just a 10-course tasting menu that changes daily and features creative, delicately prepared dishes. The courses are all a surprise – part of the charm – though the chef will take special diets and food allergies into consideration. There's a lively buzz to the elegant and small space. Reservations essential.

Flor da Laranja
MOROCCAN €€

(Map p58; ✐213 422 996; Rua da Rosa 206; mains €10-15; ☺lunch Mon, lunch & dinner Tue-Sat) A great place to linger over a meal, Flor da Laranja earns rave reviews for its warm welcome, cosy ambience and delicious Moroccan cuisine. Top picks include dolmas, mouth-watering couscous dishes, lamb tagine, and for dessert fresh berry crepes. Catch belly-dancing on weekend nights.

Le Petit Bistro
FUSION €€

(Map p58; Rua do Almada 31; mains €7-12; ☺lunch & dinner Tue-Sun) On a lively stretch of Bica, the bohemian Petit Bistro serves both tapas-size plates and heartier mains from France and beyond (gazpacho, endive salad, quiche, Israeli couscous, fava bean guacamole). Good brunches on weekends.

Antigo Primeiro de Maio
PORTUGUESE €€

(Map p58; Rua da Atalaia 8; mains €10-12; ☺dinner Mon-Sat, lunch Mon-Fri) Always packed with regulars, this small but festive *tasca* (tavern) serves excellent traditional Portuguese

dishes, amid tiled walls, a garrulous crowd and harried but friendly waiters.

Toma Lá-Dá-Cá
PORTUGUESE €€

(Map p58; Travessa do Sequeiro 38; dishes €6-10; ☺lunch & dinner) There's always a buzzing crowd filling this Santa Catarina gem, which is famed for its simple classics such as grilled fish and roasted meat dishes.

A Camponesa
PORTUGUESE €€

(Map p58; ✐213 464 791; Rua Marechal Saldanha 23; dishes €7.50-15; ☺lunch & dinner Mon-Fri, dinner only Sat;✐) This Santa Catarina hot spot attracts arty types with its poster-plastered walls, jazzy grooves and tables full of holiday snapshots. Savour home-grown flavours like Algarve oysters and cuttlefish with fried egg.

Barrigas
PORTUGUESE €€

(Map p58; ✐213 471 220; Travessa da Queimada 31; mains €10-17; ☺dinner Thu-Tue) With a name meaning 'the bellies', there are no prizes for guessing what you'll be nursing at this low-lit bistro. Red-and-white tiles and candles create the backdrop for flavours like braised rabbit and fluffy *bacalhau espiritual* (salt-cod soufflé).

Lisboa à Noite
PORTUGUESE €€€

(Map p58; ✐213 468 557; Rua das Gáveas 69; mains €14-26; ☺dinner Mon-Sat) Deliciously prepared traditional recipes are served with panache at this atmospheric restaurant with stone archways, tangerine walls and night shots of Lisbon. Recent favourites include tiger prawns with lobster risotto, oven-baked *bacalhau*, and pork loin with garlic and clams.

Sul
FUSION €€

(Map p58; ✐213 462 449; Rua do Norte 13; dishes €12-18; ☺dinner Tue-Sun) Quirkily lit by ostrich-egg lamps, Sul is a fixture on Lisbon's late-night dining circuit. The mint-walled, gallery-style restaurant churns out tasty grilled meats, as well as salmon, duck magret and beef bourguignon.

Simplesmente
PIZZERIA €€

(Map p58; Rua da Atalaia 108; pizzas €9-12; ☺dinner) Open late on weekends (till 3am), Simplesmente serves tasty thin-crust pizzas in a small warmly lit space in the heart of Bairro Alto.

Tease
CAFE €

(Map p58; Rua do Norte 31; cupcakes €2.50; ☺noon-11pm) This rock 'n' roll bakery specialises in decadent cupcakes, piled high with frosting, as well as scones and freshly brewed teas. The gold disco ball, delicate armchairs and black skull wallpaper add to the fun.

Adamastor
PORTUGUESE €
(Map p58; Rua Marechal Saldanha 24; mains €5-8; ⊙lunch & dinner Mon-Sat) Wedge-shaped Adamastor serves inexpensive specials like roast chicken and sardines with refreshing homemade lemonade. Try to snag an outdoor table.

Pastelaria São Roque
PATISSERIE €
(Map p58; Rua Dom Pedro V; pastries €1-3; ⊙7am-7pm) This wedding cake of a patisserie drips with exquisite *azulejos*, gold-topped columns and mirrors. Bag a seat in one of the alcoves to indulge in buttery cakes, freshly made bread and window-watching.

ALFAMA, CASTELO & GRAÇA
Peppered with hobbit-sized family bistros whose owners might spontaneously break out in song, Alfama's twisting, lantern-lit lanes are made for romantic tête-à-têtes. Come for alfresco dining on the cobbles, views of the castle illuminated and impromptu *fado vadio* (street fado).

Santo António de Alfama
PORTUGUESE €€
(Map p64; ☎218 881 328; Beco de Saõ Miguel 7; mains €13-16; ⊙lunch & dinner) This bistro wins the award for Lisbon's loveliest courtyard: all vines, twittering budgies and fluttering laundry. The interior is a silver-screen shrine, while the menu stars tasty *petiscos* (appetisers): gorgonzola-stuffed mushrooms, roasted aubergines with yoghurt, as well as more filling traditional Portuguese dishes.

Pois Café
CAFE €
(Map p64; Rua de São João da Praça 93; mains €5-12; ⊙11am-8pm Tue-Sun) All hail Austrian-run Pois for its laid-back boho vibe. Its sofas invite lazy afternoons spent reading novels and guzzling coffee. Creative salads and sandwiches with names like 'Sepp' (olive, pesto and Emmental) go nicely with tangy juices. There's a kids' play area.

Chapitô
CONTEMPORARY €€
(Map p64; ☎218 867 334; Costa do Castelo 7; tapas €4-5, mains €10-17; ⊙7.30pm-2am Mon-Fri, noon-2am Sat & Sun) Part of the Chapitô arts cooperative (p98), this tree-filled courtyard hums with arty types tucking into tapas or barbecued steaks. Zebra and giraffe prints glam up the top-floor restaurant, affording mesmerising views over Lisbon.

Senhora Mãe
CONTEMPORARY €€
(Map p64; Largo de São Martinho 6-7; mains €10-18; ⊙lunch & dinner) Senhora flaunts minimalist chic with blonde wood, clean lines and zinc flourishes. Seasonally inspired dishes might include ravioli in cuttlefish ink or game in chestnut and *ginjinha* sauce.

O Faz Figura
PORTUGUESE €€€
(Map p64; ☎218 868 901; Rua do Paraíso 15B; dishes €18-22; ⊙lunch & dinner Tue-Sun, dinner Mon) This stylish restaurant feels like a well-kept secret. Polished wood, white linen and art-slung walls set the scene for seasonal Portuguese fare like stewed boar with wild mushrooms. The views from the conservatory are stunning.

Bica do Sapato
FUSION €€€
(☎218 810 320; Cais da Pedra á Bica do Sapato; mains €24-36; ⊙lunch Tue-Sat, dinner Mon-Sat) Part-owned by John Malkovich, this uber-hip dockside venue is all glass walls, UFO-style lighting and chocolate-black hues. Upstairs, hipsters nibble sushi in the spacey bar, while downstairs the design-conscious restaurant serves highlights such as tender roast lamb with citrus jelly.

Malmequer Bemmequer
PORTUGUESE €€
(Map p64; Rua de São Miguel 23; dishes €6-13; ⊙lunch & dinner Wed-Sun) Look for the daisy at this bright check-tablecloth-and-tile number, overlooking a pretty square. It rolls out charcoal-grilled dishes such as lamb with rosemary.

Casanova
PIZZA €€
(☎218 877 532; Cais da Pedra á Bica do Sapato; mains €6-13; ⊙lunch & dinner Tue-Sun) Casanova seduces with wood-fired pizza that's thin, crisp and authentically Italian. Bag a table on the riverside terrace (heated in winter).

Porta d'Alfama
PORTUGUESE €
(Map p64; Rua de São João da Praça 17; dishes €6-10; ⊙lunch & dinner) Tiny Porta d'Alfama serves simple fare like grilled sardines. But food is secondary at Saturday afternoon's free *fado vadio*, where the family gathers for a gutsy warble. Take a pew on the sunny terrace with a pitcher of white wine and enjoy.

Grelhador de Alfama
PORTUGUESE €€
(Map p64; Rua dos Remédios 135; mains €9-12; ⊙lunch & dinner Mon-Sat) Exposed stone and fado paraphernalia create a cosy-meets-kitsch setting for barbecued fish or steak

at this no-fuss grill house. The pocket-sized terrace fills up fast in summer.

Tentações de Goa
INDIAN €€

(Map p64; ☑218 875 824; Rua São Pedro Mártir 23; mains €6-12; ☺lunch Tue-Sat, dinner Mon-Sat) Friendly and usually full, this family affair is tucked down a backstreet near Martim Moniz. Reserve a table to munch on spicy Goan nosh such as crab curry with perfectly fluffy basmati.

PRÍNCIPE REAL, SANTOS & ESTRELA

Elegant Príncipe Real with its peaceful streets and leafy plazas has a mix of charming outdoor cafes and local-loving restaurants. Santos, closer to the waterfront, has some innovative, beautifully designed dining rooms currently in vogue with Lisbon's style set.

Alma
CONTEMPORARY €€€

(Map p84; ☑213 963 527; Calçada Marquês de Abrantes 92; 3-/5-course menu €28/39; ☺dinner Tue-Sat) Henrique Sá Pessoa, one of Portugal's most talented chefs, consistently receives stellar reviews for the nouveau Portuguese cuisine (suckling pig confit with fondant sweet potatoes, tempura with sardines and sundried tomatoes) he so masterfully prepares at this stylish, all-white restaurant in Santos. The multicourse tasting menus provide excellent value for the money and the service is first-rate.

Estado Líquido
SUSHI €€€

(Map p84; ☑213 972 022; Largo de Santos 5A; dinner for 2 people €60-80; ☺8pm-2am Sun-Wed, to 3am Thu, to 4am Fri & Sat) A feng shui–inspired lounge, club and sushi bar rolled into one, Estado Líquido is an uberpopular destination. Get your back rubbed, nibble sushi, sip kiwi *caipirinhas*, then shake your sumo belly to house and electro on the dance floor.

Nova Mesa
FUSION €€

(Map p84; ☑213 966 287; Rua Marcos Portugal 1; 3-course lunch/dinner €14/24; ☺lunch & dinner Tue-Sat) Overlooking the peaceful Praça das Flores, Nova Mesa serves innovative world cuisine, including Tahia curry with scallops and prawns, lamb with couscous and organic vegetables and fruit crumble for dessert. Nearby are several other cafe terraces facing the plaza.

Terra
VEGETARIAN €€

(Map p84; Rua da Palmeira 15; buffet €15; ☺lunch Sat & Sun, dinner Tue-Sun; ☑) Vegetarians sing the praises of Terra for its superb buffet (including vegan options) of salads, kebabs and curries, plus organic wines and juices. A fountain gurgles in the tree-shaded courtyard, lit by twinkling lights after dark.

Esplanada
CAFE €

(Map p84; Praça do Príncipe Real; mains €6-10; ☺9am-8pm Mon, 9am-11pm Wed-Sun) This indoor-outdoor cafe is ideal for a coffee break among the palms and twittering birds. Sweet-toothed folk love the sharp lemon tart and homemade ice cream.

DOCA DE ALCÂNTARA

There's a string of waterfront restaurants around the Docas area, near the grating noise of traffic on Ponte 25 de Abril. Take a stroll to see what takes your fancy. After dark, the riverfront switches into party mode.

Doca Peixe
SEAFOOD €€

(Map p68; Doca de Santo Amaro; mains €15-30; ☺lunch & dinner Tue-Sun) Famous for market-fresh seafood, Doca Peixe is practically under Ponte 25 de Abril. Savour lemony oysters or cod with clams on the terrace.

Artisani
ICE CREAM €

(Map p68; Doca de Santo Amaro; 1/2 scoops €2.50/4; ☺10am-10pm) Artisani serves some of Lisbon's best ice cream, with creamy rich flavours, and there's ample, open-air sitting on their stylish terrace.

Alcântara Café
FUSION €€€

(Map p68; ☑213 621 226; Rua Maria Luisa Holstein 15; mains €16-34; ☺8pm-1am) This one-time printing factory now rolls out innovative cuisine in industrial-baroque surrounds. Lisbon's fashionistas love the celebrity treatment and decor: a fusion of red velvet, dark wood and steel pipework.

RATO, MARQUÊS DE POMBAL & SALDANHA

Head north of the centre to splurge at some of Lisbon's top restaurants.

Bocca
FUSION €€€

(Map p70; ☑213 808 383; Rua Rodrigo da Fonseca 87; mains €15-30; ☺lunch & dinner Tue-Sat) Since opening in 2008, this elegant, award-winning restaurant has been dazzling Lisbon diners and critics alike with inventive, beautifully turned-out meat and seafood dishes (lamb loin stuffed with dried figs, braised scallops on spicy wakame seaweed). The gastrobar serves inventive plates meant for sharing as well as tasty cocktails. Excellent wine list, including 90 wines by the glass.

Olivier Avenida
CONTEMPORARY €€€

(Map p70; ☑213 174 105; Rua Júlio César Machado 7; mains €18-30; ⊗breakfast, lunch & dinner) Star chef Olivier heads this gorgeous pearl-kissed restaurant, lit by teardrop chandeliers and centred on a horseshoe-shaped bar where DJs spin lounge music in the evening. Signatures such as tender Kobe beef are polished off nicely with tangy apple sorbet.

Restaurante 33
PORTUGUESE €€€

(Map p70; ☑213 546 079; Rua Alexandre Herculano 33; mains €16-30; ⊗lunch Mon-Fri, dinner Mon-Sat) Well worth a trip to the Rato neighbourhood, Restaurante 33 serves beautifully prepared seafood and grilled meat dishes. You can eat in the elegant but rustic dining room or the peaceful bougainvillea-clad garden in back.

Cervejaria Ribadouro
SEAFOOD €€

(Map p70; ☑213 549 411; Av da Liberdade 155; mains €8-20; ⊗lunch & dinner) Bright, noisy and full to the gills, this bustling beer hall is popular with the local seafood fans. The shellfish are plucked fresh from the tank, weighed and cooked to lip-smacking perfection.

Zé Varunca
PORTUGUESE €€

(Map p70; Rua de São José 54; mains €10-13; ⊗lunch & dinner Mon-Sat) Beamed ceilings, crafty wall hangings and colourful ceramic place settings lend a rustic charm to this warmly lit restaurant. Zé specialises in Alentejo cooking, with a changing menu of regional favourites such as roast pork with clam sauce, gazpacho with fried fish and *migas de bacalhau* (a bread-based dish cooked with cod).

La Trattoria
ITALIAN €€

(Map p70; ☑213 853 043; Rua Artilharia 79; mains €12-18; ⊗lunch Mon-Fri, dinner daily) The all-you-can-eat lunch buffet (€12) is the best reason to make the trip out to the sleek and polished dining rooms of La Trattoria. You'll find average pastas and pizzas, but fantastic antipasti – tomato and *mozzarella di bufala* salad, prosciutto and other cured meats, beet and orange salads and more. At night, it's à la carte.

Cinemateca Portuguesa
CAFE €

(Map p70; Rua Barata Salgueiro 39; mains €6-8; ⊗3-11.30pm Mon-Sat) Hidden on the 2nd floor of the indie-loving cinema, this bright, wood-filled cafe with its sunny terrace makes a fine retreat for an afternoon or evening pick-me-up. Menu features light snacks, drinks and daily specials.

Versailles
PATISSERIE €

(Map p70; Av da República 15A; pastries €2-4; ⊗7.30am-10pm) With a marble chandelier and icing-sugar stucco confection, this sublime patisserie is where well-coiffed ladies come to devour cream cakes and gossip.

Os Tibetanos
TIBETAN €€

(Map p70; ☑213 142 038; Rua do Salitre 117; mains €8-12; ⊗lunch & dinner Mon-Fri; ☑) Part of a Tibetan Buddhism school, the mantra here is fresh vegetarian food, with daily specials such as quiche and curry. Sit in the serene courtyard if the sun's out and save room for rose-petal ice cream.

BELÉM

Antiga Confeitaria de Belém
PATISSERIE €

(Map p73; Rua de Belém 84-92; pastéis de belém €0.90; ⊗8am-midnight) Since 1837, this patisserie has been transporting locals to sugar-coated nirvana with heavenly *pastéis de belém*: crisp pastry nests filled with custard cream, baked at 200°C for that perfect golden crust, then lightly dusted with cinnamon. Admire *azulejos* in the vaulted rooms or devour a still-warm tart at the counter to try to guess the secret ingredient. And another, and another...

A Margem
FUSION €€

(☑918 225 584; Doca do Bom Sucesso; salads €10-12; ⊗10am-1am) Well-sited near the river's edge, this small sundrenched cube of glass and white stone boasts an open patio and large windows facing the Tejo. Locals come to A Margem for fresh salads, cheese plates, bruschetta and other light bites that go nicely with wine and other drinks. Sunglasses are essential. To get here, follow the river's edge 200m west from the Padrão dos Descobrimentos.

Assoçiação Naval de Lisboa
SEAFOOD, PORTUGUESE €€€

(☑213 635 329; Doca do Belém; mains €16-30; ⊗12.30-3pm & 8-10.30pm Mon-Sat) A long-standing classic, this wood-panelled restaurant near the Torre de Belém serves some of Lisbon's best seafood. Standouts include the *cataplana*, grilled fresh fish of the day and a decadent lobster soup. Reserve ahead (and try for a table upstairs, near a window, for memorable river views).

Cafetaria Quadrante
CAFE €

(Map p73; Centro Cultural de Belém; buffet per kg €17; ◷10am-8pm; 🐾) Revive museum-weary eyes over salads and soups at this light-filled cafe, there's also a good self-serve buffet at lunchtime. Don't miss the Henry Moore sculpture on the terrace. Free summer jazz concerts on Thursday bring in the music-loving crowds.

Bem Belém
PORTUGUESE €

(Map p73; Rua Vieira Portuense 72; mains €8-12; ◷lunch Wed-Mon, dinner Wed-Sun) Bem Belém's sunny patio facing the park is a magnet for lunchtime crowds, who refuel over generous portions of chargrilled sardines and other Portuguese classics.

PARQUE DAS NAÇÕES

Many of the waterfront cafes and restaurants have outdoor seating and do double duty as pulsating bars after dark.

Art Cafe
CAFE €

(Alameda dos Oceanos; snacks €1.50-5; ◷8am-8pm Tue-Fri, noon-8pm Sat & Sun; 🐾) Scarlet walls and vibrant paintings give this high-ceilinged cafe an arty feel. It's a relaxed spot for a *bica* or light bites such as quiches and salads. Free wi-fi.

Origami
JAPANESE €€

(Alameda dos Oceanos; sushi €5-20; ◷lunch & dinner Mon-Sat) Blonde wood and clean lines define this gallery-style restaurant. Between mouthfuls of great sushi and sashimi, try your hand at folding paper animals to add to the origami zoo.

🍷 Drinking

All-night street parties in Bairro Alto, sunset *ginjinhas* on Rossio's sticky cobbles, drinks and gigs with indie kids in precipitous Santa Catarina – Lisbon is swiftly establishing a reputation as having one of Europe's liveliest and most eclectic nightlife scenes.

Most bars offer free admission, open from 10pm until 3am, and have a relaxed dress code.

BAIXA & ROSSIO

Cabaret Maxime
NIGHTCLUB

(www.cabaret-maxime.com; Praça da Alegria 58) Formerly a strip joint and Parisian-style cabaret, Maxime has bid farewell to the leggy showgirls. Nowadays, young *lisboêtas* flock here for club nights where DJs play old-school tunes, or loud, sweaty gigs

of both established and upcoming local bands.

Casa do Alentejo
BAR, RESTAURANT

(Map p54; Rua Portas de Santo Antão 58; ◷9am-8pm Mon-Sat) Hidden behind a plain facade, the Casa do Alentejo has a magnificent Moorish-style interior; head upstairs to the spacious bar and gilded dining room. The food and service receive mixed reviews, but the bar makes a great pre-dinner meeting spot over wine and appetisers.

A Ginjinha
BAR

(Map p54; Largo de São Domingos 8; ◷9am-10pm) Hipsters, old men in flat caps, office workers and tourists, all meet at this microscopic *ginjinha* bar for that moment of cherry-licking, pip-spitting pleasure their euro buys. Watch the owner line 'em up at the bar under the beady watch of the drink's 19th-century inventor, Espinheira. It's less about the grog, more about the event.

Néctar Wine Bar
WINE BAR

(Map p54; Rua dos Douradores 33; ◷12.30-3pm Mon-Thu, to midnight Fri & Sat) This attitude-free restaurant and bar attracts a young crowd with modern art, Portuguese wines by the glass and relaxed lounge music. Good-value lunch specials (mains €6 to €7).

CHIADO & BAIRRO ALTO

Bairro Alto is like a student at a house party: wasted on cheap booze, flirty and everybody's friend. At dusk, the nocturnal hedonist rears its head with bars trying to out-decibel each other, hash-peddlers lurking in the shadows and kamikaze taxi drivers forcing kerbside sippers to leap aside. For a more sophisticated and more artistically minded crowd, head a few blocks south to Bica.

Noobai Café
CAFE

(Map p58; Miradouro de Santa Catarina; ◷noon-9pm Sun-Thu, to midnight Fri & Sat) Great views, winning cocktails and a festive crowd make Noobai a popular draw for a sundowner. Though it's next to Miradouro de Santa Catarina, most people don't realise this bar is here until descending the steps and a terrace unfurls before them. The vibe is laid-back, the music funky jazz and the views over the Tejo are magical.

Bairro Alto Hotel
BAR

(Map p58; Praça Luís de Camões 2; ◷12.30pm-midnight) Rise in the gold-mesh lift to the 6th floor of Bairro Alto Hotel (p80) for sundowners and dazzling views over the rooftops to the river. It's a smart, grown-up lounge for cocktails and conversation as Lisbon starts to sparkle.

Bicaense
BAR

(Map p58; Rua da Bica de Duarte Belo 42A) Indie kids have a soft spot for this chilled Santa Catarina haunt, kitted out with retro radios, projectors and squishy beanbags. DJs spin house to the preclubbing crowd and the back room stages occasional gigs. There are lots of other great drinking spots nearby – and it's less of a frat-house scene than Bairro Alto.

Maria Caxuxa
BAR

(Map p58; Rua Barroca 6; ⊙8am-2am) Set in a former bakery, Maria Caxuxa has effortless style – its several rooms decked with giant mixers, 1950s armchairs and sofas, marble- and *azulejo*-lined walls and incongruous photos. Funk-laden jazz plays overhead with DJs adding to the eclectic setting. Go early to enjoy a hip, laid-back scene before the crowds arrive.

A Brasileira
CAFE

(Map p58; Rua Garrett 120-122; ⊙8am-2am) All gold swirls and cherubs, this art-deco cafe has been a Lisbon institution since 1905. Sure it's touristy, but the terrace is brilliant for watching street entertainers beside the bronze statue of poet Fernando Pessoa. Order a *bica*, which takes its name from A Brasileira's 1905 catchphrase: *beba isto com açúcar* (drink this with sugar).

Catacumbas
BAR

(Map p58; Travessa da Água da Flor 43) Moodily lit and festooned with portraits of legends such as Miles Davis, this den is jam packed when it hosts live jazz on Thursday night. Musicians bash out bluesy rhythms on the piano, as the relaxed crowd sip *vinho tinto* (red wine).

Frágil
NIGHTCLUB

(Map p58; Rua da Atalaia 126) In the beginning there was Frágil, Manuel Reis' first love before Lux. This small, loud and sweaty club has been rocking Bairro Alto for 25 years and shows no signs of waning. DJs spin progressive house and electronica to a mixed gay-straight crowd.

Clandestino
BAR

(Map p58; Rua da Barroca 99) Keep your eyes peeled for this well-hidden, old-skool Bairro Alto den. Battered and lovable, its walls are smothered in scribblings of the 'X luvs Y 4ever' and 'hasta la victoria siempre' variety. The playlist: Pearl Jam, Manu Chao, The Ramones...

Capela
NIGHTCLUB

(Map p58; Rua da Atalaia 45) Once a Gothic chapel, today Capela's gospel is an experimental line-up of electronica and funky house. Get there early (before midnight) to appreciate the DJs before the crowds descend. Frescos, Renaissance-style nude murals and dusty chandeliers add a boho-chic touch.

Majong
BAR

(Map p58; Rua da Atalaia 3) Bairro Alto's gay-friendly cabbage-patch kid, Majong oozes shabby chic with pak-choi lights, deep-red walls and school chairs. Mojitos flow as DJs spin minimalist techno, rock and reggae.

Portas Largas
BAR

(Map p58; Rua da Atalaia 105) Once a *tasca*, this well-loved Bairro Alto linchpin retains original fittings including black-and-white tiles, columns and porticos. It throws open *portas largas* (wide doors) to a mishmash of gays, straights and not-sures, who prop up the marble bar or spill onto the cobbles with zingy *caipirinhas*.

Solar do Vinho do Porto
WINE BAR

(Map p58; Rua São Pedro de Alcântara 45; ⊙11am-midnight Mon-Sat) The glug, glug of a 40-year-old tawny being poured is music

NIGHTCLUBS

Superstar DJs heating up dance floors at clubbing temples such as Lux have put Lisbon firmly on Europe's must-party map. Sleep is overrated in a city where locals don't even think about showing up at a club before 2am. Clubbing here is not late-night, it's all-night, with waterfront haunts pumping out grooves from electro to deep house really warming up at 4am.

Though getting in is not as much of a beauty contest as in other capitals, you'll stand a better chance of slipping past the fashion police if you dress smartish and don't rock up on your lonesome. Most clubs charge entry (around €5 to €20, which usually includes a drink or two), and some operate a card-stamping system to ensure you spend a minimum amount. Many close Sunday and Monday.

MONASTIC LIBATIONS

Come dusk, the area around Largo de São Domingos and the adjacent Rua das Portas de Santo Antão buzzes with locals getting their cherry fix in a cluster of *ginjinha* bars. A Ginjinha (p92) is famous as the birthplace of the sugary sweet tipple thanks to a quaffing friar from Igreja Santo Antonio who revealed the secret to an entrepreneurial Galician by the name of Espinheira. Nearby are other postage-stamp-sized bars to try. Order your €0.90 *ginjinha sem* (without) or – our favourite – *com* (with) the alcohol-soaked cherries. It's a fine way to start or end your evening.

to port-lovers' ears. Part of an 18th-century mansion, the low-lit, beamed cavern is ideal for nursing a glass of Portugal's finest.

Club Carib
BAR

(Map p58; Rua da Atalaia 78) A dance-loving crowd flocks to Carib, drawn by DJs spinning a dizzying variety of world beats – Afro-Cuban jazz, Brazilian MPB and samba, African funk, salsa, tango and more.

Heidi Bar
BAR

(Map p58; Rua da Barroca 129) Deliciously out of sync with the neighbourhood, Heidi is an alpine hideaway complete with edelweiss-like chandeliers, mountain landscape paintings and cosy wood furnishings.

Bedroom
BAR

(Map p58; Rua do Norte 86) It's a bedroom, but these beauties aren't sleeping. Join them on the dance floor for electro and hip hop, or recline on the beds in the lounge shimmering with gold wallpaper and chandeliers.

Alfaia Garrafeira
WINE BAR

(Map p58; Rua Diário de Notícias 125) On a quiet stretch of Bairro Alto, this tiny wine shop and charcuterie serves wines by the glass and cheeses and smoked meats. Arrive early to score one of the few wine-cask tables in front.

Friends of Bairro Alto
CAFE, BAR

(Map p58; Rua da Rosa 99; ☺3pm-2am; @🛜) Painted in red, desertlike hues, this gay-friendly spot has a circular bar that seems to hover above the floor, a mishmash of low, '70s-style armchairs and disco balls sparkling over the entrance. The staff and crowd are friendly and laid-back, and there's free internet (two computers), a book exchange and wi-fi.

Ginjinha das Gáveas
BAR

(Map p58; Rua das Gáveas 17A) This hole-in-the-wall *ginjinha* bar is a popular hang-out for young *lisboêtas* and travellers, with plenty of buzz and incredibly cheap drinks.

Lounge
LIVE MUSIC

(Map p58; Rua da Moeda 1) Little miss popular on the Cais do Sodré circuit, this laid-back indie club is jam-packed and pumping most nights. DJs, live acts and rock gigs are first-rate.

PRÍNCIPE REAL, SANTOS & ESTRELA

Just north of Bairro Alto, Príncipe Real is the epicentre of Lisbon's gay scene and home to some quirky drinking dens.

Pavilhão Chinês
BAR

(Rua Dom Pedro V 89-91) Pavilhão Chinês is an old curiosity shop of a bar with oil paintings and model spitfires dangling from the ceiling, and cabinets brimming with glittering Venetian masks and Action Men. Play pool or bag a comfy armchair to nurse a port or beer. Prices are higher than elsewhere, but such classy kitsch doesn't come cheap.

Cinco Lounge
LOUNGE

(Map p84; Rua Ruben António Leitão 17; ☺9pm-2am Tue-Sat) Take an award-winning London-born mixologist, add a candlelit, gold-kissed setting and give it a funky twist – *et voilà* – you have Cinco Lounge. Come here to converse and sip legendary cocktails – from Milli Vanillis (hazelnut-vanilla mojitos) to Bloody Shames (vodka-free Bloody Marys).

Incógnito
NIGHTCLUB

(Map p84; Rua Poiais de São Bento 37) No-sign, pint-sized Incógnito offers an alternative vibe and DJs thrashing out indie rock and electropop. Sweat it out with a fun crowd on the tiny basement dance floor, or breathe more easily in the loft bar upstairs.

K Urban Beach
NIGHTCLUB

(Map p84; www.grupo-k.pt; Cais da Viscondessa; ☺6pm-4am) Jutting out over the Tejo, this stylish and airy club has a lively dance floor, a restaurant (open 6pm to 10pm) and outdoor seating that makes fine use of its scenic riverside setting.

Kapital
NIGHTCLUB

(Map p84; Av 24 de Julho 68) Being young, gorgeous and loaded helps you to get the nod from the picky doormen at Kapital. It's the super-slick haunt of 20- to 30-something *lisboêtas* out spending daddy's pension on cocktails in the VIP lounge. The too-cool crowd defrosts in the *madrugada* (wee hours) grooving to '80s and garage tunes.

Kremlin
NIGHTCLUB

(Map p84; Escadinhas da Praia 5) Until Lux pinched its crown, Kremlin was Lisbon's undisputed megaclub. It's still the home of house, though slipping past the Stalin-esque bouncers can be a challenge. A pick 'n' mix of gays, straights, models and wannabes come to bop to deep house in wacky Oriental surrounds. The place heats up around 3am.

The Loft
NIGHTCLUB

(Map p84; www.theloft.pt; Rua do Instituto Industrial 6) Hipsters love the ultraglam design of this dockside lounge – think violet lighting, polka-dot walls, beanbags, primary-colour cube stools and mirrors for slyly checking your look. Grab a *caipirinha* and join the house party.

A Lontra
NIGHTCLUB

(Map p84; Rua de São Bento 155) Near Bairro Alto, A Lontra attracts mostly African-Portuguese clubbers bumping and grinding to African sounds, R 'n' B and hip hop. It fills up about 2am and stays open late.

ALFAMA, CASTELO & GRAÇA

Alfama and Graça are perfect for a relaxed drink with a view.

Lux
NIGHTCLUB

(Map p50; www.luxfragil.com; Av Infante Dom Henrique) Lisbon's ice-cool, must-see club, Lux is run by ex-Frágil maestro Marcel Reis and part-owned by John Malkovich. The wacky design features an oversized shoe, mirrored tunnels and violet light. Special but not snooty, Lux hosts big-name DJs, like Leonaldo de Almeida and Pinkboy, spinning electro and house. Grab a spot on the roof terrace to see the sun rise over the Tejo. Style policing is heartwarmingly lax but get here after 4am on a Friday or Saturday and you might have trouble getting in because of the crowds.

Bar das Imagens
CAFE, BAR

(Map p64; Calçada Marquês de Tancos 1; ⊙11am-2am Tue-Sat, 3-11pm Sun) With a terrace affording vertigo-inducing views over the city, this cheery bar serves potent Cuba libres and other well-prepared cocktails. Jazz plays in the background.

Wine Bar do Castelo
WINE BAR

(Map p64; Rua Bartolomeu de Gusmão 13; ⊙noon-11pm) Located near the entrance to the Castelo São Jorge, this laid-back wine bar serves more than 150 Portuguese wines by the glass, along with gourmet smoked meats, cheeses, olives and other tasty accompaniments. Nuno, the multilingual owner, is a welcoming host and a fount of knowledge about all things wine-related.

Chapitô
BAR

(Map p64; Costa do Castelo 7; ⊙noon-midnight) This alternative theatre offers fantastic views from its bar and is a top choice for a

BAIRRO ALTO BAR-CRAWL

Still fizzing with energy? Test your stamina bar-hopping among the rest of the best:

» **A Tasca** (Map p58; Travessa de Queimada 13) Sloshed stags, Latino grooves and tequila till the sun rises.

» **Bar 21** (Map p58; Rua da Atalaia 9) Friendly '80s kid with chart-toppers from The Clash to Culture Club.

» **Café Suave** (Map p58; Rua do Diário de Notícias 6) Futuristic forest decor, cubby holes and a preclubbing vibe.

» **Cuba a la Vista** (Map p58; Rua do Diário de Notícias 6) *Caipirinhas*, booty-shaking to merengue, and Che beaming down from the wall.

» **Jürgen's Bar** (Map p58; Rua do Diário de Notícias 68) Big-screen sports, killer cocktails and people-watching.

» **Nova Tertúlia** (Map p58; Rua do Diário de Notícias 60) Low-lit den with house beats and a laid-back feel.

» **Páginas Tantas** (Map p58; Rua do Diário de Notícias 85) Relaxed soul man with live jazz and NYC style.

sundowner or a late-night drink overlooking the city.

Miradouro da Graça — OUTDOOR BAR

(Map p64; ☺10.30am-3am) There are far-reaching vistas from this terrace, with soothing music during the day, getting heavier as the night wears on.

Portas do Sol — BAR

(Map p64; Largo das Portas do Sol; ☺10am-midnight Sun-Thu, to 2am Fri & Sat) Near one of Lisbon's iconic viewpoints, this spacious new sun-drenched terrace has a mix of sofas and white patio furniture on which to sip cocktails while taking in magnificent river views. DJs bring animation to the darkly lit wood-and-concrete interior on weekends.

Cruzes Credo Café — CAFE

(Map p64; Rua Cruzes da Sé 29; snacks €3-6; ☺8am-2am) In the shadow of the grand cathedral, this friendly, jazz-loving cafe has already earned a local following despite its youth (new in 2010). Stop in for coffees, stiff drinks, salads and toasted sandwiches.

CAIS DO SODRÉ

Locals hit this upbeat nightlife area when they feel like a change from Bairro Alto. During the Salazar years, it was the only place for a bit of night-time sleaze, and some areas retain this seedy feel, particularly Rua Nova do Carvalho.

Music Box — NIGHTCLUB

(Map p58; Rua Nova do Carvalho 24; www.music boxlisboa.com) Under the brick arches on Rua Nova do Carvalho lies one of Lisbon's hottest clubs. The pulsating Music Box hosts loud and sweaty club nights with music shifting from electro to rock, plus ear-splitting gigs by up-and-coming bands.

Meninos do Rio — OUTDOOR BAR

(Map p58; Rua da Cintura do Porto de Lisboa, Armação 255; ☺12.30pm-1am Sun-Thu, to 4am Fri & Sat) Perched on the river's edge, Meninos do Rio has palm trees, wooden decks, reggae-playing DJs and tropical cocktails, giving it a vibe that's more Caribbean than Iberian. Needless to say, it's a great spot at sunset.

Jamaica — NIGHTCLUB

(Map p58; Rua Nova do Carvalho 8) Yep, most dancing on this street involves laps but not at Jamaica, man. Gay and straight, black and white, young and old – everyone has a soft spot for this offbeat club. It gets going around 2am at weekends with DJs pumping out reggae, hip hop and retro.

O'Gilíns — PUB

(Map p58; Rua dos Remolares 10) To be sure the best craic in Lisbon, O'Gilíns serves Guinness, big-screen sports and live music from Wednesday to Saturday. 'Tis a lively affair with fiddles, singing and the odd punter jigging on the table.

British Bar — BAR

(Map p58; Rua Bernardino Costa 52; ☺Mon-Sat) Resembling an early-20th-century railway bar, this bottle-lined watering hole has an old-fashioned clientele and a backwards clock.

Hennessy's — PUB

(Map p58; Rua Cais do Sodré 32-38) This is another relaxed Irish pub with banter, occasional live music and Kilkenny on tap.

DOCA DE ALCÂNTARA & DOCA DE SANTO AMARO

The dockside duo of Doca de Alcântara and Doca de Santo Amaro harbour wall-to-wall bars with a preclubbing vibe. Many occupy revamped warehouses, with terraces facing the river and the lit-up Ponte 25 de Abril. Most people taxi here, but you can take the train from Cais do Sodré to Alcântara Mar or catch tram 15 from Praça da Figueira.

Art — BAR

(Map p84; Av 24 de Julho 66) Kate Moss wannabes and Moët-guzzling all-comers sway to house at this ubercool lounge before sashaying over to Kremlin (p95). The monochrome decor is fabulously over the top – think feather-filled columns, black velvet and teardrop chandeliers.

Belém Bar Café — LOUNGE

(Map p68; Av Brasília, Pavilhão Poente; ☺10pm-2am Tue & Wed, midnight-5am Fri & Sat) The self-consciously cool BBC attracts fashionistas to its glass-walled lounge bar and terrace with cracking views of Ponte 25 de Abril. DJs fill the dance floor with hip hop and R 'n' B at the weekend.

Op Art Café — CAFE, BAR

(Map p84; Doca de Santo Amaro) Located on the water's edge, this slightly hidden glass-and-wood cafe attracts a more laid-back bunch than other Docas bars. On Saturday nights, the DJs spin house and lounge till dawn.

Paradise Garage NIGHTCLUB
(Map p68; Rua João Oliveira Miguens 38-48) For garage freaks this *is* paradise. Resident DJs Enrage and VJ Water keep the dance floor rammed, particularly at Saturday night's Baby Loves Disco party. It also hosts some of Lisbon's hottest live gigs.

☆ Entertainment

Lisbon entertains with high culture, experimental art and everything in between. One minute it's sumptuous strings and street theatre in Chiado, the next it's the melancholic soul of fado in Alfama's atmospheric lanes.

For event listings during your stay, grab a copy of the free monthly *Follow Me Lisboa* from tourist offices. If you speak Portuguese, click onto **Time Out Lisboa** (http://timeout.sapo.pt), **Guia da Noite** (www.guiadanoite.com) and **Agenda Cultural Lisboa** (www.lisboacultural.pt) for info on performances and screenings; cinema listings can also be found in the daily *Diário de Notícias*. Tickets are available in a number of outlets:

ABEP (Map p54; ☎213 475 824; Praça dos Restauradores)

Fnac (Map p54; ☎213 221 800; www.fnac.pt; Armazéns do Chiado, Rua do Carmo 3)

Ticket Line (☎210 036 300; www.ticketline.pt)

Fado

Infused by Moorish song and the ditties of homesick sailors, bluesy, bittersweet fado encapsulates the Lisbon psyche like nothing else. Ask 10 *lisboêtas* to explain it and each will give a different version. This is because fado is deeply personal and explanations hinge on the mood of the moment. Recurring themes are love, destiny, death and the omnipresent *saudade* or 'nostalgic longing' (see p510); a kind of musical soap opera.

Though a *fadista* is traditionally accompanied by a classical and 12-string Portuguese guitar, many new-generation stars such as Mariza, Ana Moura and Joana Amendoeira are putting their own spin on the genre, giving it a twist of Cuban *son* or a dash of Argentine tango. For more, see p512.

At Bairro Alto's touristy, folksy performances, you'll only be skating the surface. For authentic fado, go to where it was born – Alfama. You'll be serenaded by mournful ballads wandering the narrow lanes here by night. There's usually a minimum cover of €15 to €25 and, as food is often mediocre, it's worth asking if you can just order a bottle of wine. Book ahead at weekends. If you prefer a spontaneous approach, seek out *fado vadio* where anyone can – and does – have a warble.

A Baîuca FADO RESTAURANT
(Map p64; ☎218 867 284; Rua de São Miguel 20; ⊙dinner Thu-Mon) On a good night, walking into A Baîuca is like gatecrashing a family party. It's a special place with *fado vadio,* where locals take a turn and spectators hiss if anyone dares to chat during the singing. The food stops around 10pm but the fado goes on until midnight. Reserve ahead.

Clube de Fado FADO RESTAURANT
(Map p64; ☎218 852 704; www.clube-de-fado.com; Rua de São João da Praça; ⊙9pm-2.30am Mon-Sat) Clube de Fado hosts the cream of the fado crop in vaulted, dimly lit surrounds. Big-name *fadistas* performing here include Joana Amendoeira and Miguel Capucho, alongside celebrated guitarists such as José Fontes Rocha.

Mesa de Frades FADO RESTAURANT
(Map p64; ☎91 702; Rua dos Remédios 139A; minimum €15; ⊙dinner Wed-Mon) A magical place to hear fado, tiny Mesa de Frades used to be a chapel. It's tiled with exquisite *azulejos* and has just a handful of tables. The show begins around 11pm.

Parreirinha de Alfama FADO RESTAURANT
(Map p64; ☎218 868 209; Beco do Espírito Santo 1; minimum €15; ⊙8pm-2am) Owned by fado legend Argentina Santos, this place offers good food and ambience; it attracts an audience that often falls hard for the top-quality *fadistas*. Book by 4pm.

Senhor Vinho FADO RESTAURANT
(Map p84; ☎213 972 681; Rua do Meio á Lapa; minimum €15; ⊙8pm-2am) Fado star Maria da Fé owns this small place, welcoming first-rate *fadistas*. Even the legendary Mariza has performed here.

Tasca do Jaime FADO RESTAURANT
(Map p50; Rua da Graça 91) This low-key restaurant in Graça hosts authentic, sing-for-your-dinner fado on weekends from about 4pm to 8pm. Decorated with *azulejos* and photos of prominent *fadistas,* it's a tiny space, so arrive early to score a table.

Fado in Chiado CONCERTS
(Map p58; ☎213 430 184; Espaço Chiado, Rua da Miséricordia 14; admission €15; ⊙7pm Mon-Sat)

GAY & LESBIAN LISBON

The Gay and Lesbian community had much to celebrate in 2010, with the passing of a bill that legalised gay marriage. The big events worth looking out for are **Lisbon Pride** (www.portugalpride.org) in June, and the **Festival de Cinema Gay e Lésbico** (www.queerlisboa.pt) in late September.

The Scene

From camp to cruisy, Praça do Príncipe Real, just north of Bairro Alto, is king of Lisbon's gay and lesbian scene. Other gay-friendly spots are the cafes Mar Adentro and Friends of Bairro Alto. For more listings, visit www.gaylisbon4u.com and the more comprehensive but less up-to-date www.portugalgay.pt.

» **Bar 106** (Map p84; www.bar106.com; Rua de São Marçal 106) Young and fun with an upbeat, preclubbing vibe and crazy events such as Sunday's message party.

» **Bar Água No Bico** (Map p84; Rua de São Marçal 170) Cheery bar with art exhibitions, shows and music from jazz to chill-out.

» **Chueca** (Map p58; Rua da Atalaia 97) Tiny bar popular with lesbians and gay men.

» **Clube da Esquina** (Map p58; Rua da Barroca 30) DJs playing hip hop and house to an eye-candy crowd.

» **Finalmente** (Map p84; Rua da Palmeira 38) This popular club has a tiny dance floor, nightly drag shows and wall-to-wall crowds.

» **S&S** (Map p84; Calçada da Patriarchal 38; ⊘Fri & Sat) Atmospheric setting with oil paintings, comfy sofas, a lively dance floor and drag shows.

» **Sétimo Céu** (Map p58; Travessa da Espera 54) A mainstay of the Bairro Alto scene, this old-school bar attracts a young festive crowd. Excellent *caipirinhas*.

» **Trumps** (Map p84; www.trumps.pt; Rua da Imprensa Nacional 104B) Lisbon's hottest gay club with cruisy corners, a sizeable dance floor and events from live music to drag.

Inside a small theatre, the nightly shows feature high-quality fado – a male and a female singer and two guitarists – and it is held early so you can grab dinner afterwards.

Alternative Culture

Lisbon may flirt with high culture and embrace fado, but she also has an ongoing relationship with the underdog. Individuality trumps conformity and alternative culture rules in these offbeat cultural centres.

Bacalhoeiro ECLECTIC
(Map p54; Rua dos Bacalhoeiros 125;@) Nonconformist, laid-back Bacalhoeiro shelters a cosy bar and hosts everything from alternative gigs to film screenings, salsa nights and themed parties. Free wi-fi.

Chapitô ECLECTIC
(Map p64; www.chapito.org; Costa do Castelo 1-7;@) Chapitô offers physical theatre performances, with a theatre school attached. There's a jazz cafe downstairs with dentist-chair decor and live music Thursday to Saturday. Come for the spectacular views and excellent restaurant.

Santiago Alquimista CONCERTS, THEATRE
(Map p64; www.santiagoalquimista.com; Rua de Santiago 19; ⊘ closed Sun) This multicultural space in the Alfama hosts local and foreign bands, dance groups and more. Even when nothing is on, the stone-walled cafe-bar is an atmospheric spot for a drink.

Crew Hassan ECLECTIC
(Map p54; Rua das Portas de Santo Antão 159; @🖉) Grungy Crew Hassan smells like teen spirit. Alternative types dig its graffiti, threadbare sofas, cheap vegie fare and free internet. Its line-up spans films, gigs, exhibitions and DJs playing music from reggae to minimalist techno.

Culturgest ECLECTIC
(www.culturgest.pt; Rua do Arco do Cego) Culturgest's experimental and occasionally provocative line-up encompasses exhibitions, dance, poetry, music and theatre.

Zé dos Bois ECLECTIC
(Map p58; www.zedosbois.org; Rua da Barroca 59) Focusing on tomorrow's performing arts and music trends, Zé dos Bois is an experi-

mental venue with a graffitied courtyard for chilling. The boho haunt has welcomed bands such as Black Dice and Animal Collective to its stage.

Cinemas

For blockbusters try the multiplexes in **Complexo das Amoreiras** (Map p70; ☏ 213 810 200), **Centro Comercial Colombo** (www. colombo.pt) and **Centro Vasco da Gama** (www.centrovascodagama.pt) malls. More-traditional cinemas are the **São Jorge** (Map p70; ☏ 213 579 144; Av da Liberdade 175) and, just around the corner, **Cinemateca Portuguesa** (National Film Theatre; Map p70; ☏ 213 596 200; www.cinemateca.pt; Rua Barata Salgueiro 39), screening offbeat, art-house, world and old films.

For details of screen times and venues, visit www.7arte.net.

Music, Theatre & Dance

Teatro Nacional de Dona Maria II   THEATRE
(Map p54; ☏ 213 250 835; www.teatro-dmaria.pt; Rossio) Rossio's graceful neoclassical theatre has a somewhat hit-and-miss schedule because of underfunding. There's a charming cafe on-site.

Teatro Nacional de São Carlos
OPERA, BALLET
(Map p58; ☏ 213 253 045; www.saocarlos.pt; Rua Serpa Pinto 9) Worth visiting just to see the sublime gold-and-red interior, this theatre has opera, ballet and theatre seasons.

Teatro Municipal de São Luís   OPERA, BALLET
(Map p58; ☏ 213 257 640; Rua António Maria Cardosa 38) This venue stages opera, ballet and theatre.

Teatro Taborda   CONTEMPORARY DANCE
(Map p64; ☏ 218 854 190; Costa do Castelo 75; @) This cultural centre shows contemporary dance, theatre and world music. It also

has spectacular views and an excellent restaurant.

Teatro da Trindade   THEATRE
(Map p58; ☏ 213 420 000; http://teatrotrindade. inatel.pt; Largo da Trindade 7) Bairro Alto's early-20th-century gem stages an assortment of national and foreign productions as well as the popular Fado in Chiado.

Centro Cultural de Belém   THEATRE
(CCB; Map p73; ☏ 213 612 444; www.ccb.pt; Praça do Império, Belém) CCB presents a diverse program, spanning experimental jazz, contemporary ballet, boundary-crossing plays and performances by the Portuguese Chamber Orchestra.

Coliseu dos Recreios   CONCERT HALL
(Map p54; ☏ 213 240 580; www.coliseulisboa. com; Rua das Portas de Santo Antão 96) This concert hall stages big-name concerts, theatre, dance and opera. The recent roll-call has included *fadista* Ana Moura and flamenco star Rafael Amargo.

Fundação Calouste Gulbenkian
CLASSICAL MUSIC
(Map p70; ☏ 217 935 131; www.musica.gulben kian.pt; Av de Berna) Home to the Gulbenkian Orchestra under the baton of Lawrence Foster, this classical music heavyweight stages first-rate concerts and ballets.

Hot Clube de Portugal   JAZZ
(Map p54; ☏ 213 467 369; www.hcp.pt; Praça da Alegria 39) As hot as its name suggests, this small, poster-plastered cellar has staged top-drawer jazz acts since the 1940s. At the time of research it was on the verge of re-opening following a disastrous fire.

Onda Jazz Bar   JAZZ
(Map p64; www.ondajazz.com; Arco de Jesus 7) This vaulted cellar features a menu of mainstream jazz, plus more-eclectic beats

---

DON'T MISS

FACTORY OF THE ARTS

Set in a converted 19th-century industrial complex, **LX Factory** (Map p68; ☏ 213 143 399; ww.lxfactory.com; Rua Rodrigues de Faria 103) is Lisbon's new hub of creativity. In 2007 some 23,000 sq metres of abandoned warehouses were transformed into art studios, galleries and printing and design companies. Today LX Factory hosts a dynamic menu of events from live concerts and film screenings to fashion shows and art exhibitions. There's a rustically cool cafe as well as a restaurant, Cantina (open 9am to 11pm Tuesday to Friday and 8pm to 11pm Saturday), plus a bookshop and other design-minded shops. Weekend nights see parties with a dance-loving and art-loving crowd. Check website for upcoming events.

of bands hailing from Brazil and Africa. Don't miss Wednesday's free jam session.

Pavilhão Atlântico ROCK CONCERTS
(☎218 918 409; www.pavilhaoatlantico.pt; Parque das Nações) Sporting an energy-efficient zinc roof, this UFO-shaped arena is Portugal's largest, hosting big international acts from Moby to Madonna.

Teatro Camões BALLET
(☎218 923 477; www.cnb.pt; Parque das Nações) Teatro Camões is home to the Portuguese National Ballet Company under the direction of innovative choreographer Vasco Wellenkamp.

Sport
Football
Lisboêtas are mad about football. It's hardly surprising given that the capital is home to two of Portugal's 'big three' clubs – SL Benfica and Sporting Club de Portugal. Lisbon's main stadiums were given a multimillion-euro facelift for Euro 2008.

The season runs September to mid-June, with most league matches on Sunday; check details in the papers (especially *Bola*, the daily football paper) or ask at the tourist office. Tickets cost €20 to €55 at the stadium on match day or, for higher prices, at the ABEP ticket agency (Map p54; ☎213 475 824; Praça dos Restauradores).

Estádio da Luz STADIUM
(☎217 219 555; www.slbenfica.pt) SL Benfica plays at this 65,000-seat stadium in the northwestern Benfica district. The nearest metro station is Colégio Militar-Luz.

Estádio Nacional STADIUM
(☎214 197 212; Cruz Quebrada) The national stadium hosts the Portuguese Cup Final each May. Take the train from Cais do Sodré.

Estádio José de Alvalade STADIUM
(☎217 514 069) This state-of-the-art 54,000-seater stadium hosted Euro 2004 matches. Just north of the university; take the metro to Campo Grande.

Bullfighting
Whether it makes your pulse race or blood boil, you can't ignore *tauromaquia* (bullfighting). The red-brick, neo-Moorish Campo Pequeno (Bullring; ☎217 932 442; Av da República; tickets €10-75) reopened in 2006 following six years of restoration. Fights are held on Thursday from May to October.

Tickets are sold outside the bullring, or at higher prices from the ABEP ticket agency (Map p54; ☎213 475 824; Praça dos Restauradores). For the lowdown on bullfighting, see p515.

Shopping
Le freak, c'est retro chic in grid-like Bairro Alto, attracting vinyl lovers and vintage devotees to its cluster of late-opening boutiques. Remember those days spent shopping with dear old gran? You can relive them in the backstreets of Alfama, Baixa and Rossio, where stuck-in-time stores deal exclusively in buttons and kid gloves, tawny port and tinned fish. Literary Chiado is the go-to place for high-street and couture shopping to the backbeat of buskers, while Santos is upping the design ante with avant-garde galleries.

Books
Fnac BOOKS, MUSIC
(Map p54; Armazéns do Chiado) One of the city's biggest book and music stores.

Livraria Bertrand BOOKS
(Map p54; Rua Garrett 73) Amid 18th-century charm Bertrand has excellent selections, including titles in English, French and Spanish.

CE Livrarias BOOKS
(Map p70; Rua Duque de Palmela 4) Sizeable collection of literature in Portuguese, English, French and German, plus in-store readings and concerts.

Crafts & Souvenirs
A Arte da Terra HANDICRAFTS
(Map p64; Rua Augusto Rosa 40) In the stables of a centuries-old bishop's palace, this cobbled store brims with authentic Portuguese crafts including Castelo Branco embroideries, love hankies and hand-painted *azulejos*.

A Vida Portuguesa PORTUGUESE PRODUCTS
(Map p58; Rua Anchieta 11) A flashback to the late 19th century with its high ceilings and polished cabinets, this store lures nostalgics with all-Portuguese products from retro-wrapped Tricona sardines to lime-oil soap and Bordallo Pinheiro porcelain swallows.

Fábrica Sant'Anna AZULEJOS
(Map p58; ☎213 422 537; Rua do Alecrim 95) Hand-making and painting *azulejos* since 1741, this is the place to get some porcelain

pizzazz for your home with classics ranging from blue-and-white geometric tiles to cherubs and candlesticks.

Omlet
ACCESSORIES

(Map p58; Calçada Nova de São Francisco 10; ⊙Tue-Sat) Tucked down a restaurant-lined lane in the Chiado, Omlet is a fanciful little store selling delicate handmade trams, graphically rich over-the-shoulder bags, whimsical hats and wall hangings and the popular Paez slipper-shoes.

Ponte Lisboa
HANDICRAFTS

(Map p64; Rua Augusto Rosa 21) Kids love Joana Areal's bright, touchy-feely felt animals at this hole-in-the-wall workshop, presenting crafts by 15 Brazilian and Portuguese artists. Also look out for Sebastião Lobo's glittering silver dragonflies.

Santos Ofícios
HANDICRAFTS

(Map p54; ☏218 872 031; Rua da Madalena 87) If you have always fancied a hand-embroidered fado shawl, check out this brick-vaulted store. Santos is a must-shop for Portuguese folk art including Madeira lace, blingy Christmas decorations and glazed earthenware.

Wrong Shop
KITSCH

(☏213 433 197; Calçada do Sacramento 25) Sick of Barcelos cockerels and 'I love Lisbon' tees? This Chiado shop gets it right with tongue-in-cheek souvenirs. Our favourites: gay roosters emblazoned with the rainbow flag, ever-so-friendly fly-catchers (with an escape route), and the blank-paged books Pessoa never wrote.

Vista Alegre
CERAMICS

(Map p58; Largo do Chiado 20) Vista Alegre produces exquisitely crafted ceramics that have graced the tables of royalty and heads of state since 1824.

Design & Concept Stores

Matéria Prima & GDE
MUSIC, FASHION

(Map p58; Rua da Rosa 197) This store has two sides: the first devoted to music – cutting-edge electronica, indie rock and esoteric sounds, plus art and culture mags; the adjoining space is a boutique, devoted to recycled fashion and local designers.

Fabrico Infinito
DESIGN

(Map p54; Rua Dom Pedro V 74A) Set in a former coach house, this virginal white gallery showcases avant-garde designs that give recycled items a luxury twist. There's a garden cafe out back, where decadent desserts are served on golden crockery.

Fashion & Accessories

Agência 117
CLOTHING

(Map p58; Rua do Norte 117) No place for wallflowers, Agência revamps wardrobes with tartan wellies, candy-bright dresses and Miss Sixty garb. Marilyn Monroe, velvet crucifixes, a hair salon – it's all at this eccentric Bairro boutique.

Espaço B
CLOTHING

(Map p73; Centro Cultural de Belém) Belém's progressive concept store tempts design lovers with gadgets and knick-knacks for home and garden, with surreal 'foot' vases, elegant fado espresso cups, Warhol-print T-shirts and bags made from recycled materials (like computer keyboards).

Lisboa Carmo
CLOTHING, ACCESSORIES

(Map p58; Calçada do Carmo 26) Lisboa Carmo beckons passers-by with its eye-catching graphic T-shirts (for men, women and children), Pessoa mugs, scarves and other

SHOP 'N' STROLL

If you prefer to mooch rather than target specific shops, Lisbon has some terrific streets for walking. Baixa's pedestrianised main drag, **Rua Augusta**, is a mix of high-street stores and souvenir kitsch; pause for chestnuts (winter) or popcorn (summer) and street entertainment between purchases. Nearby, olde-worlde **Rua da Conceição** is a classic stitch-up, where thimble-sized, wood-panelled haberdasheries recall an era when folk still used to darn their stockings. Chiado's well-heeled **Rua do Carmo** harbours designer names and smart cafes, while leafy boulevard **Avenida da Liberdade** cranks up the swank-o-meter with labels from Gucci to Louis Vuitton. Divas live out vintage dreams in the alleys of boho **Bairro Alto**, peppered with idiosyncratic boutiques playing scratchy vinyl and selling everything from glittering platforms to glam hairdos and tattoos. It's out with the old at the all-new **Santos Design District** (www.santosdesigndistrict.com), luring design fiends to its forward-thinking galleries.

mementos highlighting the city's iconic designs.

Articula
CLOTHING

(Map p64; www.teresamilheiro.com; Rua dos Remédios 102) This anticonformist gallery-workshop displays Teresa Milheiro's rebellious, recycled creations made from bones, medical tubes and aluminium. Look out for the doll's-eye necklace 'Big Brother is watching you' and syringe chain 'be botox, be beautiful'.

El Dorado
VINTAGE CLOTHING

(Map p58; Rua do Norte 23) A gramophone plays vinyl classics as divas bag vintage styles from psychedelic prints to 6in platforms and pencil skirts at this Bairro Alto hipster. There's also a great range of clubwear.

Happy Days
CLOTHING

(Map p58; Rua do Norte 60) Sadly no Fonz, but this boutique still rocks with its collection of glittering bauble necklaces, sequin clutch bags, FLY London footwear and shimmery gold pumps. Kids' toys, from toy cars to plastic fish, give grown-up styles a wacky twist.

Outra Face da Lua
CLOTHING, CAFE

(Map p54; Rua da Assunção 22) Vintage divas make for this retro boutique in Baixa, crammed with puffball dresses, lurex skirts and wildly patterned '70s shirts. Jazz and electronica play overhead. Revive over salads, sandwiches and cosmic iced tea at the in-store cafe.

Sneakers Delight
SHOES

(Map p58; Rua do Norte 30) Funk up your feet with limited edition Adidas trainers at this groovy store, where ogres and monsters beam down from the walls. DJs spin on weekends.

Story Tailors
CLOTHING

(Map p58; Calçada do Ferragial 8) Luís and João bewitch with floaty, feminine polka-dot, gingham and ruffle designs at their enchanted forest of fashion, bedecked with a hanging swing, chandeliers and gnarled wood.

Zed's Dad
CLOTHING

(Map p58; Rua da Barroca 7) German-born designer Nicole puts her own stamp on vintage at this boutique-cum-workshop in Bairro Alto, with bold prints, lurex, denim and faux snakeskin.

Markets

Feira da Ladra
SECONDHAND GOODS

(Thieves Market; Map p58; Campo de Santa Clara; ⊙7am-5pm Sat, 8am-noon Tue) Browse for back-of-the-lorry treasures at this lively flea market. You'll find old records, coins, baggy pants, dog-eared poetry books and other attic junk. Haggle hard and watch your wallet – it isn't called 'thieves market' for nothing.

Mercado da Ribeira
FOOD

(Map p54; Av 24 de Julho; ⊙6am-2pm Mon-Sat) Lisbon's premier food market buzzes with locals shopping for fruit and vegetables, crusty bread and silvery sardines fresh from the Atlantic.

Music

Carbono
CDS, RECORDS

(Map p70; Rua Telhal 6B) The staff may be grumpy, but it's hard not to like Carbono, with its impressive selection of new and secondhand vinyl and CDs. World music – West African boogaloo, Brazilian tropicalia – is especially well represented.

Louie Louie
RECORDS

(Map p58; Rua Nova da Trinidade 8) Clued-up DJs head for this funky music store stocking secondhand vinyl and the latest house, dance and electronica grooves.

Discoteca Amália
MUSIC

(Map p54; Rua de Áurea 272) This shrine to *fadista* Amália Rodrigues stocks an excellent range of fado and classical CDs.

Shopping Malls

Most malls and department stores open daily until 10pm or midnight.

Armazéns do Chiado
SHOPPING MALL

(Map p58; Rua do Carmo 2) Fashion, books, music and cosmetics in the heart of Chiado.

Centro Comercial Colombo
SHOPPING MALL

(www.colombo.pt; Av Lusíada) Colossal with 420 shops, cinemas, restaurants and a health club. To get there, take the blue metro line northwest to the Colégio Militar/Luz stop.

Centro Vasco da Gama
SHOPPING MALL

(www.centrovascodagama.pt; Parque das Nações) Glass-roofed mall sheltering high-street stores, a food court and a cinema.

Complexo das Amoreiras
SHOPPING MALL

(Map p70; Av Duarte Pacheco) Modernist mall with 275 stores.

El Corte Inglês SHOPPING MALL
(Map p70; Av António Augusto de Aguiar 31)
Spanish giant with nine floors of fashion, design and food.

Dolce Vita SHOPPING MALL
(www.dolcevita.pt; Ave Cruzeiro Seixas & Radial da Pontinha, Amadora) New in 2009, this massive shopping mall – over 300 stores, 30 restaurants and an 11-screen cinema – is a siren song for weak-willed shop-goers. It's located in Amadora, about 10km northwest of Baixa and best reached by car.

Speciality Stores

A Carioca COFFEE, TEA
(Map p58; Rua da Misericórdia 9) Little has changed since this old-world store opened in 1924: brass fittings still gleam, the coffee roaster is still in action and home blends, sugared almonds and toffees are still lovingly wrapped in green paper.

Azevedo Rua HATS
(Map p54; Praça Dom Pedro IV 73) Lisbon's maddest hatters have been covering bald spots since 1886. Expect old-school service and wood-panelled cabinets full of flat caps and Ascot-worthy headwear.

Conserveira de Lisboa TINNED FISH
(Map p54; Rua dos Bacalhoeiros 34) In Rua dos Bacalhoeiros (cod-vessel street) lies a store dedicated wholly to tinned fish, and whose walls are a mosaic of retro wrappings. An elderly lady and her son tot up on a monstrous old till and wrap purchases in brown paper.

Luvaria Ulisses GLOVES
(Map p58; ☎213 420 295; Rua do Carmo 87A) So tiny it's almost an optical illusion, this magical art-deco store is chock-full of soft handmade leather gloves in kaleidoscope shades. Breathe in and squeeze in to find a glove that fits.

Manuel Tavares FOOD, WINE
(Map p54; Rua da Betesga 1A) For a lingering taste of Lisbon, nip into this wood-fronted store, which has been tempting locals since 1860 with *pata negra* (cured ham), pungent cheeses, *ginjinha,* port and other Portuguese treats.

Napoleão WINE, PORT
(Map p54; Rua dos Fanqueiros 70) This friendly, English-speaking cellar is the go-to place for Portuguese wines and ports, with hundreds of bottles to choose from. Ships worldwide.

Saboeiro SOAPS
(Map p58; Rua das Salgadeiras 32) Saboeiro has all you need for a scrub-a-dub-dub in the tub, from clove-and-cinnamon bath tea to rosehip oil and citrusy exfoliating soap bars.

Silva & Feijó FOODS
(Map p54; Rua dos Bacalhoeiros 117) Planning a picnic? Stop by this beamed store for sheep's cheese from the Seia mountains, sardine pâté, rye bread, *salsichas* (sausages) and other Portuguese goodies.

Vellas Loreto CANDLES
(Map p58; Rua do Loreto 53) *Lisboêtas* have been waxing lyrical about this specialist candle-maker since 1789. The wood-panelled, talc-scented store sells myriad candles, from cherubs and peppers to Christmas trees and water lilies.

ⓘ Information

Dangers & Annoyances

Lisbon is generally a safe city with a low crime rate, though you'll definitely want to mind your wallet on tram 28 – a major hot-spot for

---

CATWALK QUEENS

Make way for Lisbon's trio of catwalk queens, revamping wardrobes with their majestic collections:

» **Ana Salazar** (Map p58; Rua do Carmo 87) Ana's sassy, feminine styles reveal a passion for stretchy fabrics, bold prints and earthy hues. Her flagship boutique, with a striking arched glass ceiling, is in the heart of Chiado.

» **Fátima Lopes** (Map p58; Rua da Atalaia 36) Divas love Fátima's immaculate collection of figure-hugging, Latin-inspired threads – from slinky suits to itsy-glitzy prom dresses and hot-pink ball gowns.

» **Lena Aires** (Map p58; Rua da Atalaia 96) Lena's funky Bairro Alto boutique brims with citrus-bright knits and fresh-faced fashion.

pickpockets – and at other tourist hubs such as Rua Augusta. You're also certain to be offered hash and sunglasses from swarthy characters in Baixa and in Bairro Alto; a firm but polite 'no' keeps hawkers at bay. Main streets are relatively safe to walk along at night, but be wary around metro stations such as Anjos, Martim Moniz and Intendente, where there have been muggings. Take care in the dark alleys of Alfama and Graça.

Emergency

Police, Fire & Ambulance ☎119

Police headquarters (Map p54; ☎217 654 242; Rua Capelo 13)

Tourist police post (Map p54; ☎213 421 634; Palácio Foz, Praça dos Restauradores; ☺24hr)

Internet Access

Some cafes in Lisbon offer free wireless surfing, including Mar Adentro (p88), Brown's Coffee Shop (p85) and Fábulas (p87), which also has computers for internet. Cheap internet cafes that double as international call centres huddle around Largo de São Domingos. The places listed here charge around €2 to €4 per hour:

Cyber Bica (Map p58; Rua dos Duques de Bragança; ☺11am-midnight Mon-Fri) Groovy cafe-bar.

Portugal Telecom (Map p54; Praça Rossio 68; ☺8am-11pm)

Web Café (Map p58; Rua do Diário de Notícias 126; ☺7pm-2am)

Internet Resources

www.timeout.pt Details on upcoming gigs, cultural events and interesting commentary, in Portuguese.

www.askmelisboa.com Multilingual site with info on discount cards.

www.golisbon.com Up-to-date info on sightseeing, eating, nightlife and events.

www.visitlisboa.com Lisbon's comprehensive tourism website, with the lowdown on sightseeing, transport and accommodation.

Media

In addition to Portuguese dailies such as *Diario de Noticias* and the tabloid bestseller *Correiro da Manhã*, the *Portugal News* (http://theportugal news.com) is an English-language daily.

Medical Services

British Hospital (☎217 213 400; Rua Tomás da Fonseca) English-speaking staff and English-speaking doctors.

Clínica Médica Internacional (Map p70; ☎213 513 310; Av António Augusto de Aguiar 40) A quick (though not cheap), private clinic with English-speaking doctors.

Farmácia Estácio (Map p54; ☎213 211 390; Rossio 62) A central pharmacy.

Money

Multibanco ATMs are widespread throughout the city.

Barclays Bank (Map p70; ☎217 911 100; Av da República 50)

Cotacâmbios (Map p54; ☎213 220 480; Rossio 41; ☺8am-10pm) The best bet for changing cash or travellers cheques is a private-exchange bureau like this one.

Post

Airport (☺9am-8pm Mon-Fri, 9am-1pm & 2-5pm Sat & Sun)

Main post office (Map p54; Praça do Comércio) Has poste restante.

Post office (Map p54; Praça dos Restauradores) Another central post office.

THE KITSCH COLLECTION

Seeking quality kitsch? Look no further than cock-a-doolally Rua Augusta, where souvenir shops and stalls will help you part with your euros. Top of the tacky pops:

» **Galo de Barcelos** Portugal's beloved feathered friend is this punk cockerel with a heart, who miraculously escaped a piri-piri fate. Keyrings, coasters, watches, you name it – the rooster's there.

» **'I love Pessoa' T-shirt** Show poetic soul wearing a T-shirt graced with Fernando Pessoa's mug.

» **Lisbon landmark boxer shorts** Hmmm, what could be more entertaining than planning your next sightseeing trip on the loo? There's tram 28, the castle, Elevador de Santa Justa...

» **Fado shawl** Ignore the fashion slaves and set the trend with your very own embroidered lace creation; perfect for those warble-in-front-of-the-mirror moments.

» **Virgin Mary** Day-Glo or sprayed gold, a porcelain Virgin Mary is a must for the mantelpiece.

Telephone

Equipped with a phone card, including the Portugal Telecom card, you can make international direct-dial (IDD) phone calls from most pay phones. At Portugal Telecom booths in post offices you can pay after you've made the call.

Portugal Telecom (Map p54; Rossio 68; ⊙8am-11pm) Has rows of booths.

Tourist Information

ASK ME LISBOA The largest and most helpful tourist office in the city faces Praça Restauradaures inside the **Palácio Foz** (Map p54; www. askmelisboa.com; Praça dos Restauradores; ⊙9am-8pm). Staff here doles out maps and information, books accommodation or reserves rental cars. Nearby, the smaller **Y Lisboa** (Map p54; Praça dos Restauradores; ⊙9am-8pm) branch does much the same; there's also left luggage here (full day €1.50) and internet access (€2.50 per hour). **Lisboa Welcome Centre** (Map p54; www.visitlisboa.com; Praça do Comércio; ⊙9am-6pm) Is another helpful branch.

INFORMATION KIOSKS Lisboa runs several information kiosks, which are handy places for maps and quick information:

Airport (⊙7am-midnight)

Belém (Map p73; Largo dos Jernónimos; ⊙10am-1pm & 2-6pm Tue-Sat)

Rua Augusta (Map p54; near Rua Conceição; ⊙10am-1pm & 2-6pm)

Santa Apolónia (door 47, inside train station; ⊙8am-1pm Tue-Sat)

ⓘ Getting There & Away

Air

Situated around 6km north of the centre, the ultramodern **Aeroporto de Lisboa** (Lisbon Airport; ☑218 413 500; www.ana.pt) operates direct flights to major international hubs including London, New York and Berlin. For details on airlines, see p527).

Boat

The **Transtejo ferry line** (www.transtejo. pt) has several riverfront terminals. From the eastern end of the Terreiro do Paço terminal (Map p54), catamarans zip across the Tejo to Montijo (€2.10, 30 minutes) and Seixal (€1.75, 30 minutes, half-hourly weekdays, every hour or so weekends). From the main part of the terminal, called Estação do Sul e Sueste, Soflusa ferries run very frequently to Barreiro (€1.75, 30 minutes), for rail connections to the Alentejo, Algarve and Setúbal. From Cais do Sodré ferry terminal (Map p54), passenger ferries go to Cacilhas (€0.81, 10 minutes, every 10 minutes all day). Car (and bicycle) ferries also go from Cais do Sodré to Cacilhas.

From Belém, ferries depart for Trafaria and Porto Brandão (€0.85, every 30 to 60 minutes), about 3.5km and 5km respectively from Costa da Caparica town.

Bus

Lisbon's long-distance bus terminal is **Sete Rios** (Rua das Laranjeiras), linked to both Jardim Zoológico metro station and Sete Rios train station. The big carriers, **Rede Expressos** (☑213 581 460; www.rede-expressos.pt) and **Eva** (☑213 581 466; www.eva-bus.com), run frequent services to almost every major town. You can buy your ticket up to seven days in advance.

The other major terminal is **Gare do Oriente** (near Parque das Nações), concentrating on services to the north and to Spain. On the 1st floor are bus company booths (mostly open 9am to 5.30pm Monday to Saturday, to 7pm Friday, closed for lunch; smaller operators only open just before arrival or departure). The biggest companies operating from here are **Renex** (☑218 956 836; www.renex.pt) and the Spanish operator **Avanza** (☑218 940 250; www.avanzabus.com).

Many Renex buses take passengers 20 minutes early at Campo das Cebolas in Alfama, before Gare do Oriente.

Several regional companies with destinations in the north include **Mafrense** (www.mafrense. pt) for Ericeira and Mafra and **Barraqueiro Oeste** (www.barraqueiro-oeste.pt) for Malveira and Torres Vedras. These companies operate from **Terminal Campo Grande** (☑217 582 212) outside Campo Grande metro station.

Buses to Sesimbra and Costa da Caparica go from a bus terminal at Sete Rios bus station (Map p50).

Eurolines (☑218 957 398; www.eurolines portugal.com; Loja 203, Gare do Oriente) runs coaches to destinations all over Europe.

Information and tickets for international departures are scarce at weekends, so try to avoid that last-minute Sunday dash out of Portugal.

Car & Motorcycle

Scooters, ranging from 50cc to Vespa LXVs, are available for hire from **Scooter Mania** (☑213 467 144; www.scooter-mania.pt); prices start at €30 for the day. You can rent more substantial motorbikes (750cc Suzukis) in Cascais (see p123).

The big-name car-hire companies are all on hand, though you can often save by using local agencies; most offer pick-up and delivery service to your hotel. The tourist offices have loads of car rental fliers where you can compare prices. Staff will even call and book a vehicle for you.

Autojardim (☑213 549 182; www.auto-jardim. com)

Avis (☑800 201 002; www.avis.com.pt)

Europcar (☑219 407 790; www.europcar.pt)

Hertz (📞219 426 300; www.hertz.com)

Holidays Car (📞217 150 610; www.holidays car.com)

Sixt (📞218 407 927; www.e-sixt.com)

Train

Lisbon is linked by train to other major cities. See p533 for domestic services and p529 for international services. Check www.cp.pt for schedules. The table (p107) shows sample 2nd-class direct journeys from Lisbon. The abbreviations relate to international train services (IN) and express services (*intercidade;* IC).

Lisbon has several major train stations. Santa Apolónia (Map p64) is the terminal for trains from northern and central Portugal. It has a helpful **information desk** (📞808 208 208; ⏰7.30am-9pm Mon-Fri, 8pm-4.30pm Sat & Sun) at door 8.

All of Santa Apolónia's services also stop at the Gare do Oriente, where there are departures to the Algarve and international destinations. Ticket booths are on the 1st floor (platforms are on the 2nd) and car-rental offices, banks and shops are at street level. Left-luggage lockers are on the basement metro level.

Another major terminal is Sete Rios (Map p50), which is connected to the Jardim Zoológico metro station and serves the northern suburbs. Most services continue on to Entrecampos station (Map p50). Either of these stations provides services across the Ponte 25 de Abril to Setúbal, among other destinations.

Cais do Sodré (Map p58) is the terminal for train services to Cascais and Estoril.

Reopened in all its neo-Manueline glory in 2008, **Rossio** (Map p54) is the most central station operating frequent services to Sintra via Queluz.

ℹ Getting Around

To/From the Airport

The AeroBus (91) departs from outside Arrivals (€3.50, 25 to 35 minutes, roughly every 20 minutes from 7.45am to 8.15pm). It goes via Marquês de Pombal, Avenida Liberdade, Restauradores, Rossio and Praça do Comércio to Cais do Sodré. The ticket gives free passage on the entire city bus network for the rest of the day.

Local buses 43, 44 and 45 (single €1.40) also run from central stops including Cais do Sodré and Praça dos Restauradores and are a better deal if you arrive in the afternoon. They take slightly longer than the AeroBus and are best avoided during rush hour if you have a lot of luggage.

Expect to pay about €10 for a taxi into central Lisbon, plus €1.60 if your luggage needs to be placed in the boot. Avoid long queues by flagging down a taxi at Departures.

Bicycle

Traffic, trams, hills, cobbles and disgruntled drivers make cycling a challenging prospect. There are pleasant rides along a new bike lane along the Tejo, however (see boxed text, p79).

Car & Motorcycle

Lisbon can be quite stressful to drive around, thanks to heavy traffic, maverick drivers, narrow one-way streets and tram lines, but at least the city is small. There are two ring roads useful for staying out of the centre: the inner Cintura Regional Interna de Lisboa (CRIL) and the outer Cintura Regional Externa de Lisboa (CREL).

Once in the centre, parking is the main issue. Spaces are scarce, parking regulations are complex, pay-and-display machines are often broken and car-park rates are expensive (about €10 to €12 per day). On Saturday afternoon and Sunday parking is usually free.

Upmarket hotels usually have their own garages. If you need to park for more than a few days, there are cheaper car parks near Parque das Nações (metro Gare do Oriente – the multistorey here costs around €5 per day) or Belém (free car parks), then catch a bus or tram to the centre. Always lock up and don't leave any valuables inside, as theft is a risk.

Public Transport

BUS, TRAM & FUNICULAR **Companhia Carris de Ferro de Lisboa** (Carris; 📞213 613 054; www.carris.pt) operates all transport except the metro. Its buses and trams run from about 5am or 6am to 1am; there are some night bus and tram services.

Pick up a transport map, *Planta dos Transportes Públicos da Carris* (including a map of

BUSES FROM LISBON

DESTINATION	PRICE (€)	DURATION (HR)	FREQUENCY (PER DAY)
Évora	12	1½	10-20
Coimbra	13	2½	15-25
Porto	18	3½	10-20
Faro	19	3½	4-8

DESTINATION	SERVICE	PRICE (€)	DURATION (HR)	FREQUENCY (PER DAY)
Coimbra	IC/IN	16	2	10-20
Faro	IC	18	4	3-6
Porto C	IC	20	3	7-18

night-time services) from tourist offices or Carris kiosks, which are dotted around the city. The Carris website has timetables and route details.

Individual tickets cost €1.35 on board or €0.81 if you buy a *bilhete único de coroa* (BUC; a one-zone city-centre ticket) beforehand. These prepaid tickets are sold at Carris kiosks – most conveniently at Praça da Figueira, at the foot of the Elevador de Santa Justa, and at Santa Apolónia and Cais do Sodré train stations.

The Carris kiosks also sell a one-day (€3.70) Bilhete Carris/Metro valid for buses, trams, funiculars *and* the metro.

The Lisboa Card (see boxed text, p53) is good for most tourist sights as well as bus, tram, funicular and metro travel.

Don't leave the city without riding tram 28 from Largo Martim Moniz or tram 12 from Praça da Figueira through the narrow streets of the Alfama.

Two other useful lines are tram 15 which runs from Praça da Figueira and Praça do Comércio via Alcântara to Belém, and tram 18 from Praça do Comércio via Alcântara to Ajuda. Tram 15 features space-age articulated trams with onboard machines for buying tickets and passes. Tram

stops are marked by a small yellow *paragem* (stop) sign hanging from a lamp post or from the overhead wires.

METRO The **metropolitano** (underground; www.metrolisboa.pt; 1-/2-zone tickets €0.85/1.15, 24hr day pass €3.75; ☺6.30am-1am) is useful for short hops and to reach the Gare do Oriente and nearby Parque das Nações.

Buy tickets from metro ticket machines, which have English-language menus; see Transport Cards for more details. The Lisboa Card (see boxed text, p53) is also valid.

Entrances are marked by a big red 'M'. Useful signs include *correspondência* (transfer between lines) and *saída* (exit to the street). There is some impressive contemporary art on the metro, including Angelo de Sousa at Baixa-Chiado and Hundertwasser at Oriente.

Watch out for pickpockets in rush-hour crowds.

Taxi

Táxis in Lisbon are reasonable and plentiful. If you can't hail one, try the ranks at Rossio and Praça dos Restauradores, near stations and ferry terminals, and at top-end hotels, or call **Rádio Táxis** (☎218 119 000) or **Autocoope** (☎217 932 756).

The fare on the meter should read €2.50 (daytime flag-fall). You will be charged extra for luggage and an additional 20% for journeys between 9pm and 6am. Rip-offs occasionally occur (the airport route is the main culprit). If you think you may have been cheated, get a receipt from the driver, note the registration number and talk to the tourist police.

For more information about taxis, see p533.

AROUND LISBON

Most frazzled urbanites hop on a plane when the sun-and-sea urge hits them. Not *lisboêtas*. When the city sizzles in summer, they don't have to go far to keep their cool – it's all in their backyard. Enchanting beaches lie north and south of the capital, offering a mix of great surfing, charming seaside restaurants and guest houses. There are also

TRANSPORT CARDS

There are two useful cards for catching public transport around the city; both can be purchased from kiosks in the metro station. The Viva Viagem card costs €0.50, to which you can then add credit in various denominations. When adding credit to the card, make sure you select the option 'add credit' option, rather than a single trip, otherwise you can only ride the metro. This credit allows the card to be used on the metro, buses, trams and funiculars. Each ride will deduct €0.80 from the card. The other card is the day pass, which costs €3.75 and allows unlimited travel over a 24-hour period on the aforementioned transport network.

rippling woods brushed with pine and eucalyptus, marshy reserves where bottlenose dolphins splash, hills studded with fanciful palaces and limestone cliffs where dinosaurs left their footprints 150 million years ago. And you'll find it all within an hour of the capital.

Drenched in shades of green, Sintra is often touted as the must-do day trip and you can believe the hype – it's stunning. Moors, blue-blooded eccentrics and even Lord Byron let their vivid imaginations loose in above-the-clouds palaces, woods scattered with enormous boulders and subtropical gardens. To the southwest, Cascais is a cocktail of beach, culture and lively bars, and neighbouring Estoril (p123) might just tempt you to roll the dice at its once ritzy casino of James Bond 007 fame. Go northwest for royal decadence in Mafra's (p125) baroque palace of Versailles proportions.

Sintra

POP 26,000 / ELEV 280M

With its rippling mountains, dewy forests thick with ferns and lichen, exotic gardens and glittering palaces, Sintra is like a page torn from a fairy tale. Its Unesco World Heritage—listed centre, Sintra-Vila, is dotted with pastel-hued manors folded into luxuriant hills that roll down to the blue Atlantic.

Celts worshipped their moon god here, the Moors built a precipitous castle and 18th-century Portuguese royals swanned around its dreamy gardens. Even Lord Byron waxed lyrical about Sintra's charms: 'Lo! Cintra's glorious Eden intervenes, in variegated maze of mount and glen', which inspired his epic poem *Childe Harold's Pilgrimage*. Extravagant and exquisite, Sintra has ivy-clad Rapunzel-esque turrets, nature-gone-wild botanical gardens and forests strewn with granite boulders.

It's the must-do day trip and, if time's not an issue, has enough allure to keep you there for several days. Try to come midweek to avoid the masses.

If arriving by train, go to the last stop – Portela de Sintra – from which it's a pleasant 1km walk (or short bus ride) into the village.

◉ Sights

Palácio Nacional de Sintra   PALACE
(Sintra National Palace; Map p112; Largo Rainha Dona Amélia; adult/child €7/free; ◉10am-

5.30pm Thu-Tue) The icing on Sintra-Vila's Unesco World Heritage cake is this palace, whose iconic twin conical chimneys set imaginations into overdrive and cameras snapping. Of Moorish origins, the palace was first expanded by Dom Dinis (1261–1325), enlarged by João I in the 15th century (when the kitchens were built), then given a Manueline twist by Manuel I in the following century.

The whimsical interior is a mix of Moorish and Manueline styles, with arabesque courtyards, barley-twist columns and 15th- and 16th-century geometric *azulejos* that figure among Portugal's oldest. Highlights include the octagonal **Sala dos Cisnes** (Swan Room), adorned with frescos of 27 gold-collared swans. Suspicious? You will be in the **Sala das Pegas** (Magpie Room), its ceiling emblazoned with magpies. Lore has it that the queen caught João I kissing one of her ladies-in-waiting. The cheeky king claimed the kisses were innocent and all *'por bem'* ('for the good'), then commissioned one magpie for every lady-in-waiting.

Other standouts are the wooden Sala dos Brasões, bearing the shields of 72 leading 16th-century families, the shipshape Galleon Room and the Palatine chapel featuring an Islamic mosaic floor. Finally, you reach the kitchen of twin-chimney fame, where the flutes work their magic. You can almost hear the crackle of a hog roasting on a spit for the king – he didn't only have an appetite for infidelity!

Castelo dos Mouros   CASTLE
(Map p110; www.parquesdesintra.pt; adult/child €6/5; ◉9.30am-8pm) Soaring 412m above sea level, this mist-enshrouded ruined castle looms high above the surrounding forest. This 9th-century Moorish castle's dizzying ramparts stretch across the mountain ridges and past moss-clad boulders the size of small buses. When the clouds peel away, the vistas over Sintra's palace-dotted hill and dale to the glittering Atlantic are – like the climb – breathtaking.

The best walking route here from Sintra-Vila is not along the main road but the quicker, partly off-road route via Rua Marechal Saldanha. The steep trail is around 2km, but quiet and rewarding.

Parque da Pena   GARDENS
(Map p110; www.parquesdesintra.pt; adult/child €6/5, combined ticket with Palácio Nacional da Pena €12/9; ◉9.30am-8pm) A further 200m

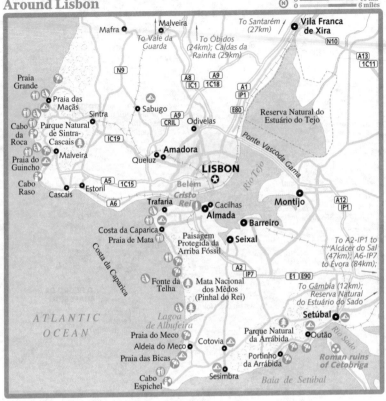

up the road from Castelo dos Mouros is Parque da Pena, filled with tropical plants, huge redwoods and fern trees, camellias, rhododendrons and lakes (note the castle-shaped duck houses for web-footed royalty!). It's cheaper to buy a combined ticket if you want to visit Palácio Nacional da Pena too.

Palácio Nacional da Pena PALACE
(Pena National Palace; Map p110; www.parques desintra.pt; adult/child €8/6; ⊙9.45am-7pm) Rising up from a thickly wooded peak and often enshrouded in swirling mist, Palácio Nacional da Pena is pure fantasy stuff. The wacky confection is a riot of onion domes, Moorish keyhole gates, writhing stone snakes and crenellated towers in pinks and lemons. Ferdinand of Saxe Coburg-Gotha, the artist-husband of Queen Maria II, commissioned Prussian architect Ludwig von Eschwege in 1840 to build the Bavarian-Manueline epic (and as a final flourish added an armoured statue of him-

self, overlooking the palace from a nearby peak).

The kitschy, extravagant interior is equally extraordinary, brimming with precious Meissen porcelain, Eiffel-designed furniture, *trompe l'oeil* murals and Dom Carlos' unfinished nudes of buxom nymphs. The ballroom has a chandelier holding 72 candles, and just in case those didn't do it, there are four statues of Turks bearing electric candles. A bas-relief showing a terrible cholera outbreak dominates Queen Amélia's teak-furnished tearoom.

Buses to the park entrance leave from Sintra train station and near the *turismo* (tourist office). A taxi costs around €8 one way. The steep, zigzagging walk through pine and eucalyptus woods from Sintra-Vila is around 3km.

Convento dos Capuchos MONASTERY
(Capuchin Monastery; www.parquesdesintra.pt; adult/child €5/4; ⊙9.30am-8pm) Hidden in

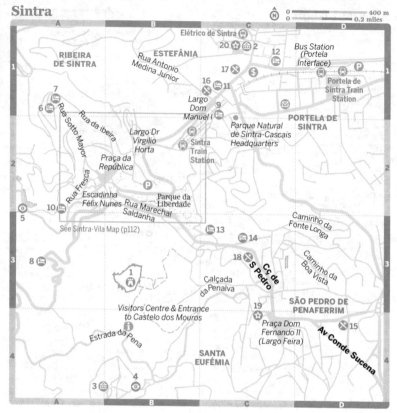

the woods is the bewitchingly hobbit-hole-like Convento dos Capuchos, which was originally built in 1560 to house 12 monks who lived in incredibly cramped conditions, their tiny cells having low, narrow doors. Byron mocked the monastery in his poem *Childe Harold's Pilgrimage,* referring to recluse Honorius who spent a staggering 36 years here (before dying at age 95 in 1596).

It's often nicknamed the Cork Convent, because its miniscule cells are lined with cork. Visiting here is an *Alice in Wonderland* experience as you squeeze through to explore the warren of cells, chapels, kitchen and cavern. The monks lived a simple, touchingly well-ordered life in this idyllic yet spartan place, hiding up until 1834 when it was abandoned.

You can walk here – the monastery is 7.3km from Sintra-Vila (5.1km from the turn-off to Parque da Pena) along a remote, wooded road. There is no bus connection to the convent (taxis charge around €16 return; arrange for a pick-up ahead). Admission is by guided visit (lasting 45 minutes) and it is preferable to book your visit in advance.

Monserrate Park   GARDENS, PALACE
(www.parquesdesintra.pt; adult/child €6/5; ☺9.30am-8pm) Wild and rambling Monserrate Park is a 30-hectare garden created in the 18th century by wealthy English merchant Gerard de Visme, then enlarged by landscape painter William Stockdale (with help from London's Kew Gardens). Its wooded hillsides bristle with exotic foliage, from Chinese weeping cypress to dragon trees and Himalayan rhododendrons. Seek out the Mexican garden nurturing palms, yuccas and agaves, and the bamboo-fringed Japanese garden abloom with camellias. The park is 3.5km west of Sintra-Vila.

A manicured lawn sweeps up to the whimsical, Moorish-inspired **palácio** (⊙10am-1pm & 2-6.30pm), the 19th-century romantic folly of English millionaire Sir Francis Cook. A Gothic-style villa previously stood on the site, rented by the rich, eccentric British writer William Beckford in 1794 after he fled Britain in the wake of a homosexual scandal.

Museu do Brinquedo   MUSEUM
(Toy Museum; Map p112; www.museu-do-brinquedo.pt; Rua Visconde de Monserrate; adult/child €4/2; ⊙10am-6pm Tue-Sun) Sintra's toy story is Museu do Brinquedo. João Arbués Moreira's fascinating 20,000-piece collection presents a chronological romp, from 3000-year-old Egyptian stone counters to a 1999 Barbie Burberry. Standouts include vintage Barbies from a more demure, housewifely era and arch-rival Sindy dolls.

Also note the tin soldiers used to drum up Nazi support, WWII Action Men, penny toys and Japanese kokeshi wooden dolls. On the 3rd floor is a toy-repair workshop, where you can sometimes find a man studiously working in a glass case, beside a bizarre tray of disembodied heads.

Museu de Arte Moderna   MUSEUM
(Map p110; www.berardocollection.com; Av Heliodoro Salgado; admission free; ⊙10am-6pm Tue-Sun) The Museu de Arte Moderna hosts world-class rotating exhibitions covering the entire modern art spectrum from kinetic and pop art to surrealism and expressionism. Sheltering Hockney, Lichtenstein and Warhol originals, the permanent collection is part of billionaire José Berardo's stash, which also graces the walls of Museu Colecção Berardo. Exhibits change frequently because of space limitations.

DON'T MISS

A SURREAL MANSION & GARDENS

Exploring the **Quinta da Regaleira** (www.regaleira.pt; Rua Barbosa du Bocage; adult/child €6/3; ⊙10am-8pm) is like delving into another world. This neo-Manueline extravaganza was dreamed up by Italian opera-set designer Luigi Manini under the orders of Brazilian coffee tycoon, António Carvalho Monteiro, aka Monteiro dos Milhões (Moneybags Monteiro). Enter the villa to begin the surreal journey, with ferociously carved fireplaces, frescos and Venetian glass mosaics. Keep an eye out for mythological and Knights Templar symbols.

The playful gardens are fun to explore – footpaths wriggle through the dense foliage to follies, fountains, grottoes, lakes and underground caverns. All routes seem to eventually end at the revolving stone door leading to the initiation well, **Poço Iniciáto**, plunging down some 30m. You walk down the nine-tiered spiral (three by three – three being the magic number) to mysterious hollowed-out underground galleries, lit by fairy lights.

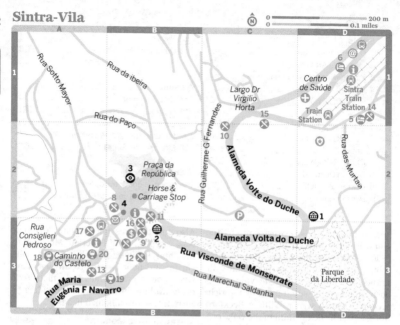

Museu Anjos Teixeira   MUSEUM
(Map p112; Alameda Volta do Duche; admission free; ☺10am-6pm Tue-Fri, 2-6pm Sat & Sun) Set in a former watermill, this small museum displays works by the father and son duo of Anjos Teixeira – two of Portugal's greatest sculptors. Most of the pieces here are the work of Pedro Augusto (1908–97), the son, who enjoyed greater success than his father, and was connected to the neorealism of the 1940s. Some of his best works are on display here, from sensual Rodin-like works of feminine beauty to grand pastoral sculp-

tures that capture the hardships of life in the countryside. Access is via steps, leading down from the main road opposite Parque da Liberdade.

🏃 Activities

Sintra is a terrific place to get out and stride, with waymarked **hiking trails** (look for red-and-yellow stripes) that corkscrew up into densely wooded hills strewn with giant boulders. Justifiably popular is the gentle 50-minute trek from Sintra-Vila to Castelo dos Mouros. You can continue to Palácio Nacional da Pena (another five minutes). From here you can ascend Serra de Sintra's highest point, the 529m Cruz Alta (High Cross), named after its 16th-century cross, with amazing views all over Sintra. It's possible to continue on foot to São Pedro de Penaferrim and loop back to Sintra-Vila. Click onto www.cm-sintra.pt for basic trail maps.

If you're up for a challenge, Sintra is great terrain for **mountain biking**, with uphill climbs and exhilarating downhill rushes. On the bitumen, take care: many drivers speed along the narrow, windy roads around Sintra.

Ozono Mais   ADVENTURE TOURS
(☎219 619 927; www.ozonomais.com) Offers a variety of outdoor excursions, includ-

---

SINTRA BY BIKE

One new way to see the sights is via electric bicycle, offered by **MVP** (www.mvp.pt). You pedal, but the 250W motor assists (the lighter you are, the more boost you get on those hills). These are available from the **Torre do Relógio** (Map p112; ☺10am-6pm) near the tourist office in Sintra-Vila. Half-day rental costs €19, which is great value considering it includes free admission to four sites – Castelo dos Mouros, Palácio Nacional da Pena, Monserrate Park and Convento dos Capuchos.

Sintra-Vila

ing canoeing, rafting, mountain biking and jeep tours. Call ahead for times and prices.

Cabra Montêz   ADVENTURE TOURS
(☏917 446 668; www.cabramontez.com) 'Mountain goat' arranges all kinds of adventurous pursuits including trekking/rafting/canyoning trips for €25/45/40 per person.

🎊 Festivals & Events

From late May to early July, the long-running **Festival de Sintra** (www.festivalde sintra.pt) features classical recitals, ballet and modern dance, world music and multimedia events, plus concerts for kids.

🛏 Sleeping

It's worth staying overnight, as Sintra has some magical places to snooze, from quaint villas to lavish manors. The *turismo* can advise on apartments (€50 to €70). Book ahead in summer.

Lawrence's Hotel   GUEST HOUSE €€
(Map p110; ☏219 105 500; www.lawrences hotel.com; Rua Consiglieri Pedroso 38; d/ste €90/180; ❄@🖥) Lord Byron once stayed at this 18th-century mansion turned boutique hotel. It oozes charm in its lantern-lit, vaulted corridors and snug bar. Wood floors creak in the individually designed rooms, decorated with *azulejos* and antique trunks; some rooms have views over the wooded valley. There's also an excellent restaurant (p114).

Quinta da Capela   GUEST HOUSE €€€
(☏219 290 170; www.quintadacapela.com; s/d incl breakfast €130/150; ⊙mid-Mar–mid-Oct;🏊) Slip into your role as lord or lady of the manor at this sublime 16th-century estate just beyond Monserrate Park. Its nine antique-filled rooms offer complimentary port and superb views. Stroll the manicured gardens, populated by peacocks and gliding swans, or take a dip in the pool with vistas over the valley to the Atlantic.

Pensão Residencial Sintra   GUEST HOUSE €€
(Map p110; ☏219 230 738; www.residencial sintra.blogspot.com; Travessa dos Avelares 12; d incl breakfast from €80; @🖥🏊) This stately 1850s manor overlooks rambling gardens and an inviting pool, and offers captivating views to the castle. The bright, high-ceilinged rooms are decorated in crisp hues with shiny wood floors. Wake up to birdsong and a hearty breakfast.

Quinta das Murtas   GUEST HOUSE €€
(Map p110; ☏219 240 246; www.quinta-das-mur tas.com; Rua Eduardo Van Zeller 4; d/apt from €75/100; 🅿) A grand manor surrounded by lush greenery, this retreat charms with sweeping views, a trickling fountain and a grand lounge room with carved columns and an elaborate ceiling. The traditional, tiled-floor rooms are light and spacious; the roomier apartments also have kitchenettes.

Chalet Relogio   GUEST HOUSE €€
(Map p110; ☏219 241 550; www.chaletrelogio.com; Estrada da Pena 22; d from €60; 🅿) This quirky, castle-style villa was designed by Luigi Manini of Quinta da Regaleira fame. The owners are welcoming, the country-style rooms huge, and the views of the Moorish castle amazing. A stream runs through the verdant gardens. It's 700m from Sintra-Vila en route to Palácio Nacional da Pena.

Casa do Valle
B&B €€

(Map p110; ☑219 244 699; www.casadovalle.com; Rua da Paderna; d €80; @🛜🗙🏊) Just downhill from the historical centre, Casa do Valle has seven spacious, handome rooms set around a garden with an inviting pool. There are fine views onto the lush hillsides rising above the valley and friendly multi-lingual service.

Quinta das Sequóias
GUEST HOUSE €€€

(☑219 243 821; www.quintadasequoias.com; d incl breakfast €160; @🗙) Nestled among red-wood forest near Monserrate Park, this an-tique-filled five-bedroom manor has elegant rooms. All have enchanting views of the sur-rounding rolling hills. No children under 12.

Casa Miradouro
GUEST HOUSE €€€

(Map p110; ☑219 107 100; www.casa-miradouro.com; Rua Sotto Mayor 55; s/d incl breakfast €125/135) An imposing Battenberg cake of a house, built in 1890, with eight elegant, stuccoed rooms and panoramic views. The best have small balconies.

Pensão Nova Sintra
GUEST HOUSE €€

(Map p110; ☑219 230 220; www.novasintra.com; Largo Afonso de Albuquerque 25; s/d incl breakfast €55/75; ✲@🛜) This renovated late-19th-century mansion is set above the main road. The big drawcard is the sunny terrace overlooking Sintra, where you can take breakfast. Front-facing doubles offer picturesque views, back rooms more peace-ful slumber. Best of all are the attic rooms.

Piela's
GUEST HOUSE €€

(Map p110; ☑219 241 691; www.cafepielas.com; Av Dr Cambournac 1-3; s/d €40/60; @🛜) Reno-vated in 2006, Pielas has clean, comfortable, fairly spacious rooms and friendly service. It's located near the Museum of Modern Art on a busy street – light sleepers should ask for a back room. There's a cafe downstairs.

OFF DAYS

Unlike most other tourist sights, the Palácio Nacional de Sintra closes on Wednesday. Following suit, some restaurants close on Wednesday as well. Some other places, including the Palácio Nacional da Pena and the Museu de Arte Moderna, close on Monday, the traditional day off. If you plan to see Sintra's star attractions, make sure you plan accordingly.

Casa de Hóspedes Dona Maria da Parreirinha
GUEST HOUSE €

(Map p112; ☑219 232 490; Rua João de Deus 12-14; d €45-55) A short walk from the train station, this small, homely guest house has spotless, old-fashioned rooms, with big windows, dark-wood furnishings and floral fabrics.

Monte da Lua
GUEST HOUSE €

(Map p112; ☑219 241 029; Av Dr Miguel Bombarda 51; d €35-40) Opposite the station, this quiet marshmallow-pink villa offers clean but dowdy rooms with blue carpeting and flo-ral or plaid details; the best overlook the wooded valley at the back.

Dois ao Quadrado
HOSTEL €

(☑219 246 160; Rua João de Deus 68; dm/d with shared bathroom from €15/35;@🛜) Above a smokey, rock-loving bar, this no-frills hos-tel has bright and airy dorms, though mat-tresses are thin and communal bathrooms could do with a scrub.

🍴 Eating

Lawrence's Restaurant
PORTUGUESE €€€

(Map p110; ☑219 105 500; Rua Consiglieri Pedroso 38; mains €12-26; ⊙lunch & dinner) Perfect for romantic tête-à-têtes with its classical mu-sic, candlelight and rose-clad terrace, the restaurant at Lawrence's Hotel (p113) serves modern Portuguese cuisine. Signatures such as veal with turnip tops and tarragon sauce are beautifully cooked and presented.

Tulhas Bar & Restaurante
PORTUGUESE €

(Map p112; Rua Gil Vicente 4; mains €9-14; ⊙closed Wed) This converted grain ware-house is dark, tiled and quaint, with wrought-iron chandeliers and a relaxed, cosy atmosphere. It's renowned for its *bacalhau com natas* (shredded cod with cream and potato).

Saudade
CAFE €

(Map p112; Av Dr Miguel Bombardo 8; snacks €2-4; ⊙8am-10pm Tue-Sun) This former bakery where Sintra's famous *queijadas* were made has cherub-covered ceilings and a rambling interior, making a fine spot for pastries or lighter fare (with a different soup, salad, fish- and meat-dish of the day). A gallery in back features changing art exhibitions.

Tasca do Xico
TAPAS €€

(Map p112; Rua Arco do Teixeira 6; tapas €4-6; ⊙noon-10pm Tue-Sun) On a quiet lane in the old quarter, the petite Tasca do Xico pre-pares tasty tapas plates (prawns with gar-lic, mussels in vinaigrette) as well as a few heartier changing specials such as grilled fresh fish of the day. There's just one table inside and a few tables outside.

G-Spot
FUSION €€

(Map p110; ☑927 508 027; Alameda dos Combatentes da Grande Guerra 12; mains €16-18; ⊘7.30-10.30pm Tue-Sat) The name may not whet your appetite, but the cooking is top-notch at this small, elegant restaurant well off the beaten path. The menu, which changes weekly, features imaginative combinations such as hake loin with goat's cheese and coriander toast, and there's an excellent wine list. Reservations recommended.

Tacho Real
PORTUGUESE €€

(Map p112; ☑219 235 277; Rua da Ferraria 4; mains €7-18; ⊘closed Wed) Take a pew on the cobbled patio or retreat to the 17th-century vaulted interior, bedecked with century-old *azulejos*, at this charming haunt. Dapper waiters bring specialities, from juicy steaks to stuffed king crab, to the table.

Páteo do Garrett
PORTUGUESE €€

(Map p112; Rua Maria Eugénia Reis F Navarro 7; mains €10-22; ⊘lunch & dinner Thu-Tue) Don't be put off by the rustic-meets-kitsch decor; the major draw here is the patio, shaded by a huge plane tree and affording far-reaching views over Sintra's rooftops. Home-cooked classics include spicy black sausage and garlicky clams with coriander.

Bica São Pedro
PORTUGUESE €€

(Map p110; Rua 1 de Dezembro 16; mains €4-8; ⊘7am-10pm) On a peaceful lane in São Pedro, a friendly welcome and good-value daily specials await – steak, salads, *bacalhau* dishes and crepes and quiches are among the selections. There's garden dining in back.

Mourisca de Sintra
PORTUGUESE €€

(Map p110; Calçada de San Pedro 54; mains €9-12; ⊘lunch & dinner Tue-Sat) Above a low-key cafe, this charming tavern, with blond woods and black-and-white photos on the walls, prepares tasty Portuguese fare including grilled sea bass, *bacalhau* dishes and rib-eye steak.

Sabores da Vila
PORTUGUESE €

(Map p112; ☑219 241 040; Av Augusto Freire 2; lunch buffet €7; ⊘lunch Mon-Sat;☑) Painted in zesty lemon-and-lime tones, this modern cafe attracts lunchtime locals with its wallet-pleasing lunch buffet (with vegetarian options).

Maggie's Tea Spot
CAFE €

(Map p112; Rua Costa do Castelo 1; ⊘10am-8pm Thu-Tue) Tucked away in the upper reaches of Old Sintra, Maggie's makes a pleasant spot for tea and scones, as well as toasted sandwiches, salads and oh-so-tempting desserts.

Restaurante Tirol Pastelaria
PATISSERIE €

(Map p110; Largo Afonso de Albuquerque 9; snacks €1-4.50; ⊘7.30am-8.30pm) This buzzy cafe tempts with cream-filled desserts and almond biscuits. Sit on the terrace when the sun's out.

Café de Paris
INTERNATIONAL €€

(Map p112; ☑219 232 375; Praça da República 32; mains €6-14; ⊘10am-8pm) This opulent cafe is a pink marble, stucco and chandelier confection facing the palace. *Oui,* the crunchy baguettes, bistro specials, light crepes and even the snooty service are indeed very Parisian.

🍷 Drinking

Sintra is no party town, but there are several bars in the side streets where you can converse over a cold one. Rua das Padarias and Rua Fonte da Pipa are quite lively on summer weekends.

Binhoteca
WINE BAR

(Map p112; Rua das Padarias 16; tapas €3-8; ⊘noon-10pm) Jazzy music and exposed stone set the scene at Binhoteca, serving Portugal's finest, from full-bodied Douros to woody Madeira whites. Nibblers graze *pata negra,* cumin-and-apple blood sausage and pungent cheeses with pumpkin chutney.

Fonte da Pipa
BAR

(Map p112; Rua Fonte da Pipa 11-13) A hip tiled bar, this has craggy, cavelike rooms and comfy seats.

Estrada Velha
BAR

(Map p112; Rua Consiglieri Pedroso 16) Jazzy music place at this popular den with a laid-back, pubby vibe. Its sign – a fallen angel, guzzling beer and smoking – causes a few giggles.

Xentra
BAR

(Map p112; Rua Consiglieri Pedroso 2A) This cellar bar has a vaguely medieval feel with stone walls and an arched ceiling.

☆ Entertainment

Taverna dos Trovadores
LIVE MUSIC

(Map p110; ☑219 233 548; Praça Dom Fernando II 18; mains €11-15) This atmospheric restaurant and bar features live music (folk and

SWEET DREAMS

Sintra is famous for its luscious sweeties. **Fábrica das Verdadeiras Queijadas da Sapa** (Map p112; Alameda Volta do Duche 12; ⊘closed Mon) has been fattening up royalty since 1756 with bite-sized *queijadas* – crisp pastry shells filled with a marzipan-like mix of fresh cheese, sugar, flour and cinnamon. Since 1952, **Casa Piriquita** (Map p112; Rua das Padarias 1-5; ⊘closed Wed) has been tempting locals with another sweet dream: the *travesseiro* (pillow), light puff pastry turned, rolled and folded seven times, then filled with delicious almond-and-egg-yolk cream and lightly dusted with sugar.

acoustic) on Friday and Saturday nights – an institution that's been around for over two decades. Concerts run from 11.30pm to 2am. It's located in São Pedro de Penaferrim.

Centro Cultural Olga Cadaval

CULTURAL CENTRE
(Map p110; ☎219 107 110; www.ccolgacadaval.pt; Praça Francisco Sá Carneiro) Sintra's major cultural venue, staging concerts, theatre and dance, is the Centro Cultural Olga Cadaval, beautifully converted from an old cinema.

ⓘ Information

Emergency

Police station (Map p112; ☎219 230 761; Rua João de Deus 6)

Internet Access

Sabot (Map p112; Rua Dr Alfredo Costa 74; per hr €2.50; ⊘1pm-midnight Mon-Fri, 9.30pm-midnight Sat) Internet access near the station.

Medical Services

Centro de saúde (medical centre; Map p112; ☎219 247 770; Rua Dr Alfredo Costa 34)

Money

There's an ATM at the train station and in the tourism office, or try one of the banks (with ATMs):

Montepio Geral (Map p110; ☎214 248 000; Av Heliodoro Salgado 42)

Totta (Map p112; Rua das Padarias 4)

Post

Post office Sintra-Vila (Map p112; Rua Gil Vicente); Portela de Sintra (Map p110; Av Movimento das Forças Armadas) Has NetPost.

Tourist Information

Parques de Sintra – Monte da Lua (www.parquesdesintra.pt) Runs the gardens and parks, most of which have visitors centres.

Parque Natural de Sintra-Cascais Headquarters (Map p110; ☎219 247 200; Rua Gago Coutinho 1) Opens usual business hours.

Turismo (⊘9am-7pm Oct-May, 9am-8pm Jun-Sep); Main office (Map p112; ☎219 231 157; www.cm-sintra.pt; Museu Regional, Praça da República 23); Train station (Map p112; ☎219 241 623) These *turismos* provide a free, informative map and help with accommodation.

ⓘ Getting There & Away

Buses run by **Scotturb** (Map p112; ☎214 699 100; www.scotturb.com; Av Dr Miguel Bombarda) or **Mafrense** (☎261 816 150; www.mafrense.pt) leave regularly for Cascais (€3.50, 60 minutes), sometimes via Cabo da Roca (€3.35). Buses also head to Estoril (€3.50, 40 minutes), Mafra (45 minutes) and Ericeira (45 minutes). Most services leave from Sintra train station (which is *estação* on timetables) via Portela de Sintra. Scotturb's useful information office, open from 9am to 1pm and 2pm to 8pm, is opposite the station.

Trains (€2, 40 minutes) run every 15 minutes between Sintra and Lisbon's Rossio station.

ⓘ Getting Around

Bus

From the station, it's a 1km scenic walk into Sintra-Vila – a good way to get your bearings – or you can hop on bus 433, which runs regularly from Portela Interface to São Pedro (€1) via Estefânia and Sintra-Vila. A handy bus for accessing the castle is the Scotturb bus 434 (€4.60), which runs from the train station via Sintra-Vila to Castelo dos Mouros (10 minutes), Palácio da Pena (15 minutes) and back. It operates every 15 minutes from 9.15am to 7.50pm. One ticket gives you hop-on, hop-off access.

Horse & Carriage

Horse-driven carriages clip-clop all over Sintra, even as far as Monserrate. The *turismo* has a full list of prices (starting at €30 for a 25-minute ride). The best place to pick up a carriage is by the *pelourinho* (stone pillory) below Palácio Nacional de Sintra.

Taxi & Car

Taxis are available at the train station or opposite Sintra-Vila post office. They are metered, so fares depend on traffic. Count on about €8 one way to Palácio Nacional da Pena, or €16 return to Convento dos Capuchos.

There's a free car park below Sintra-Vila; follow the signs by the *câmara municipal* (town hall) in Estefânia. Alternatively, park at Portela Interface and take the bus.

Tram

On weekends, Sintra's restored electric tram, the **Elétrico de Sintra** (Map p110; one-way €2) offers convenient access to the coast, running from Rua Alves Roçadas near Portela de Sintra train station, arriving at Praia das Maçãs 45 minutes later. Trams depart approximately every 50 to 60 minutes from 9.20am to 6.05pm from Friday to Sunday. The last tram back leaves the beach at 7pm.

West of Sintra

Precipitous cliffs and crescent-shaped bays pummelled by the Atlantic lie just 12km west of Sintra. Previous host of European Surfing Championships, **Praia Grande** lures surfers and bodyboarders to its big sandy beach with ripping breakers. Clamber over the cliffs to spot dinosaur fossils. Family-friendly **Praia das Maçãs** has a sweep of gold sand, backed by a lively little resort. **Azenhas do Mar**, 2km further, is a cliff-hanger of a village, where a jumble of whitewashed, red-roofed houses tumble down the crags to a free saltwater pool (only accessible when the sea is calm).

En route to the beaches, ridgetop **Colares** makes a great pit stop with its panoramas, stuck-in-time village charm and wines dating back to the 13th century. The vines grown today are the only ones in Europe to have survived the 19th-century phylloxera plague, saved by their deep roots and sandy soil. To purchase some of the venerable wines, visit **Adega Regional de Colares** (Alameda Coronel, Linhares de Lima 32).

Wild and wonderful **Cabo da Roca** (Rock Cape) is a sheer 150m cliff, facing the roaring sea, 18km west of Sintra. It's Europe's westernmost point and a terrific sunset spot. Though a steady trickle of visitors come to see the lighthouse and buy an I've-been-there certificate at the *turismo*, it still has an air of rugged, windswept remoteness.

🛏 Sleeping

Residencial Real　　GUEST HOUSE €
(☎219 292 002; Rua Fernão Magalhães, Praia das Maçãs; d with/without view incl breakfast €45/35) For spacious, immaculate rooms with expansive ocean views, you can't beat this homely guest house right on the beach at Praia Grande.

Estalagem de Colares　　GUEST HOUSE €€€
(☎219 282 942; estalagemdecolares@yahoo.com; Estrada Nacional 247, Colares; s/d €80/110; 🅿❋) Peeking above lush greenery, this whitewashed villa is a calm retreat with large, clean rooms and a peaceful garden.

Hotel Arribas　　HOTEL €€
(☎219 289 050; www.hotelarribas.com; Av Alfredo Coelho 28, Praia Grande; s/d €70/82; ❋@) While this 39-room, scallop-shaped hotel isn't a pretty face, its sea views over Praia Grande and 100m-long ocean-water pool are magnificent. Light, breezy rooms feature fridges, TVs and balconies that are ideal for watching surfers ride the waves.

Casal St Virginia　　GUEST HOUSE €€€
(☎219 283 198; www.casalstvirginia.com; Av Luis Augusto Colares 17; d €125;❋) On a cliff facing the Atlantic, this manor house near the small village of Azenhas do Mar exudes charm with its antique-filled corridors and sunny terrace. The individually designed rooms include one with a skylight through which you can stargaze by night. Sunbathe on the lawns or swim laps in the pool.

🍴 Eating

Many cafes and seafood restaurants are scattered along Praia Grande; Praia das Maçãs also has a few options.

Moinho Dom Quixote　　INTERNATIONAL €€
(☎219 292 523; Rua do Campo da Bola, Azoia; mains €6-10; ⊙noon-2am) This colourfully decorated, kitsch-filled restaurant serves salads, quiches, baguette sandwiches, burritos and burgers (both vegie and beef), but the real draw is the breezy terrace with magnificent views over the coast. Look for the large, white, blue-trimmed *moinho* (windmill) in Azoia, 2.5km south of the Cabo da Roca.

Azenhas do Mar　　SEAFOOD €€€
(☎219 280 739; www.azenhasdomar.com; Azenhas do Mar; mains €10-18; ⊙lunch & dinner; ❋) Perched above the saltwater pool in Azenhas do Mar, you'll find delicious seafood dishes and grilled fish (some of which is caught by the fisherman-owner). The sea views are stunning, especially from the deck. And there's a private pool (also with views) for restaurant-goers. Step up to the bar to glimpse the old water mill.

Bus 441 from Portela Interface goes frequently via Colares to Praia das Maçãs (€3, 25 minutes) and on to Azenhas do Mar (€3, 30 minutes), stopping at Praia Grande (€3, 25 minutes) three times daily (more in summer). Bus 440 also runs from Sintra to Azenhas do Mar (€3, 35 minutes). On weekends, the tram (Elétrico de Sintra, €2) goes from Sintra to Praia das Maçãs via Colares.

Bus 403 to Cascais runs regularly via Cabo da Roca (€3.60, 45 minutes) from Sintra station.

Cascais

POP 35,000

Cascais (kush-*kaish*) has rocketed from sleepy fishing village to much-loved summertime playground of wave-frolicking *lisboêtas* ever since King Luís I went for a dip in 1870. Its trio of golden bays attracts sun-worshipping holidaymakers, who come to splash in the ice-cold Atlantic. Don't expect to get much sand to yourself at the weekend, though.

There's plenty of post-beach life, with winding lanes leading to small museums, cool gardens, a shiny new marina and a pedestrianised old town dotted with designer boutiques and alfresco fish restaurants. After dark, lively bars and clubs fuel the party. Active bods can ride the waves at Praia do Guincho, 9km northwest, or pedal along the palm-fringed coastline to Estoril.

The train station and nearby bus station are about 250m north of the main pedestrianised drag, Rua Frederico Arouca.

◉ Sights

OLD CASCAIS

The hubbub of the fish market near Praia da Ribeira races you back to when Cascais was but a little fishing village. An auctioneer sells the day's catch in rapid-fire lingo at about 5pm Monday to Saturday.

Weave through the back alleys west of the *câmara municipal* to the palm-fringed square that is home to the whitewashed Igreja de Nossa Senhora da Assunção (Largo da Assunção; admission free; ⊙9am-1pm & 5-8pm), adorned with *azulejos* predating the 1755 earthquake.

The citadel is where the royal family used to spend the summer. It's currently occupied by the military, but plans are under way to transform it into a new cultural space. Beyond lies the modern Marina de Cascais with its postcard-perfect lighthouse, sleek yachts and too-cool lounge bars.

PARKS & MUSEUMS

Sintra's stellar new attraction, the Casa das Histórias Paula Rego (www.casadas historiaspaularego.com; Av da República 300; admission free; ⊙10am-8pm) showcases the evocative paintings of one of Portugal's finest living artists. Exhibits span Rego's career, from early work with collage in the 1950s to twisted fairy tale–like tableaux of the 1980s, and up to the disturbing realism of more recent years.

Nearby, the wild and shady Parque Marechal Carmona, (Av da República; ⊙8.30am-7.45pm) provides a shady retreat from the seaside crowds, with birch and pine trees, palms and eucalyptus, rose gardens and flowering shrubs. Kids love the duck pond and playground with a sandpit, but the cramped and grimy minizoo is a letdown.

The grounds harbour the Museu Condes de Castro Guimarães (admission €2; ⊙10am-5pm Tue-Sun), the whimsical early-19th-century mansion of Irish aristocrat Jorge O'Neill, complete with castle turrets and Arabic cloister. But the clover leaves inside didn't bring him luck – he went bankrupt and had to sell up. His successor, Count of Castro Guimarães, lavishly decorated the abode with 17th-century Indo-Portuguese cabinets, Oriental silk tapestries and 17th-century *azulejos*. Don't miss the rare 16th-century manuscript depicting pre-earthquake Lisbon.

Nearby, the colourful Centro Cultural de Cascais (Av Rei Humberto II de Itália; admission free; ⊙10am-6pm Tue-Sun), in what was a barefooted Carmelite convent, hosts contemporary exhibitions and cultural events. It has a great cafe.

Set in Jardim da Parada, the small Museu do Mar (Rua Júlio Pereira de Mello; admission €2, Sun free; ⊙10am-5pm Tue-Sun) spells out Cascais' maritime history with costumes, tools, nets and boats, accompanied by quotes (in English) from the fisherfolk.

Boca do Inferno

Atlantic waves pummel craggy Boca do Inferno (Mouth of Hell), 2km west of Cascais. Taxis charge €6 return, or you can walk along the coast (about 20 minutes). Expect a mouthful of small splashes unless a storm is raging.

Activities

Cascais' three sandy bays – Praia da Conceição, Praia da Rainha and Praia da Ribeira – are great for a sunbake or a tingly Atlantic dip, but don't expect much towel space in summer.

The best beach is wild, windswept Praia do Guincho, 9km northwest, a mecca to surfers and windsurfers (the site of previous World Surfing Championships) with massive crashing rollers. The strong undertow can be dangerous for swimmers, but Guincho still lures nonsurfers with powder-soft sands, fresh seafood and magical sunsets.

If you're keen to ride the waves, grab your boardies and check out the surfing courses available at Moana Surf School (964449436; www.moanasurfschool.com; introductory 75min lesson €25, 4 lessons €85). It also rents boards and wetsuits. Guincho Surf School (917 535 719; www.guinchosurfschool.com), also offers classes.

John David's Watersports Centre
AQUATIC SPORTS

(10am-7.30pm) At Praia da Duquesa, midway between Cascais and Estoril, you can rent pedaloes, canoes and arrange waterskiing jaunts and windsurfing (€25 per hour).

Exclusive Divers
DIVING

(965 455 991; www.exclusive-divers.net) Next door, Exclusive Divers can take you scuba-diving around the Cascais coastline and beyond with equipment rental and courses.

Festivals & Events

Festas do Mar This festival in late August celebrates Cascais' maritime heritage with nautical parades, fireworks and fado. Wackier events include placing bets on which hole a mouse will run down and a bull race on the beach.

Estoril Jazz This 10-day jazz fest takes place in Cascais and Estoril in July.

Festival de Música da Costa do Estoril This festival brings classical and jazz concerts to both towns in July.

Free outdoor entertainment Cascais and Estoril entertain the summertime crowds from July to mid-September with live bands nightly, usually at Estoril's Praia de Tamariz and/or Cascais' Praia de Moitas, and fireworks on Saturdays around midnight.

Sleeping

It's worth booking in advance if you're visiting in summer, as the best places fill up in a flash.

Fortaleza do Guincho
LUXURY HOTEL €€€

(214 870 491; www.guinchotel.pt; Estrada do Guincho; s €205, d incl breakfast from €280;) Set in a 17th-century fortress perched over the sea, this dramatic five-star guest house is a great place for a splurge. Rooms are small but beautifully set with solid antique furnishings, and the best boast magnificent sea views. The restaurant has a Michelin star (one of two in the Lisbon area).

Farol Design Hotel
BOUTIQUE HOTEL €€€

(214 823 490; www.farol.com.pt; Av Rei Humberto II de Itália 7; d from €170;) Self-consciously cool, this hotel reveals a razor-sharp design – picture chilli-red walls, floor-to-ceiling windows facing the Atlantic, a poolside chill-out lounge and a creative restaurant with Med-sushi fusion cuisine. The more expensive rooms have sea views and were designed by Portuguese fashion royalty such as Ana Salazar and Fátima Lopes.

FREE WHEELS

Cascais has recently boosted its eco-credentials by offering **free bike hire**. The bikes are available from 8am to 7pm daily at various points around town, including Largo da Estação near the train station. Demand is naturally high, so arrive early and bring some form of ID. There's a bicycle path that runs the entire 9km stretch from Cascais to Guincho. A shorter route is along the attractive seafront promenade to Estoril, 2km east.

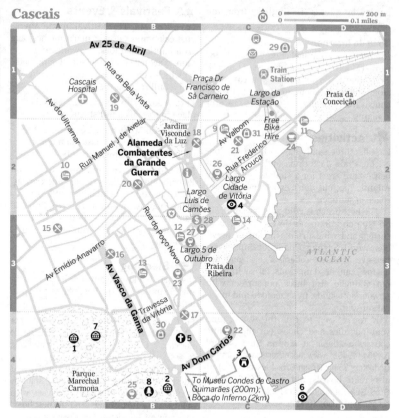

Hotel Albatroz BOUTIQUE HOTEL €€€
(☑214 847 300; www.albatrozhotels.com; Rua Frederico Arouca 100; d from €205; [P][✳][@][≋]) Take a 19th-century cliff-top villa, give it an avant-garde twist with glass walls and streamlined aesthetic and you get this boutique gem. The snazzy rooms feature wi-fi, complimentary port, and bathrooms with copper basins and Molton Brown cosmetics. Upgrade for a free-standing tub or private tower. There's a saltwater pool overlooking the bay and a panoramic restaurant serving Mediterranean-style cuisine.

Casa da Pergola B&B €€€
(☑214 840 040; Av Valbom 13; d incl breakfast with/without balcony €147/127) An oasis of calm with a lush garden and bougainvillea-draped facade, this century-old manor is a family heirloom. A marble staircase sweeps up to six classically elegant rooms with stucco, dark-wood trappings and sparkling bathrooms; several have garden-facing balconies. Relax in the antique-filled sitting room or with a glass of complimentary port in the evening.

Villa Albatroz BOUTIQUE HOTEL €€€
(☑214 863 410; www.albatrozhotels.com; Rua Fernandes Tomás 1; s/d incl breakfast from €182/224; [✳][@][☎][≋]) Facing the bay, this smaller sibling of Hotel Albatroz has has just 11 individually decorated rooms – some flowery, some with ornamental fireplace. The best rooms sport terraces, jacuzzi tubs and ocean views.

Residencial Solar Dom Carlos
GUEST HOUSE €€
(☑214 828 115; www.solardomcarlos.pt; Rua Latino Coelho 104; s/d incl breakfast €55/70; [P][@]) Hidden down a sleepy alley, this 16th-century former royal residence turned guest house retains lots of original features, from chandeliers to wood beams, *azulejos* and a frescoed breakfast room. The high-

ceilinged rooms are spacious and traditional. Don't miss the 400-year-old chapel where Dom Carlos used to pray.

Residencial Parsi GUEST HOUSE €€
(☎214 861 309; www.residencial-parsi.com; Rua Afonso Sanches 8; d with/without bathroom €100/50) In a crumbling, characterful building near the waterfront, Parsi's rooms have been spruced up with zingy colours, parquet floors and flat-screen TVs. The stuccoed front room has sea views. It's intimate and friendly.

Cascais Beach Hostel HOSTEL €€
(☎309 906 421; www.cascaisbeachostel.com; Rua da Vista Alegre 10; dm/d €20/50; @🛜🏊) This funky newcomer is central for Cascais' beaches and nightlife. Dorms and doubles sport shiny wood floors and citrus hues. There's a lounge, a communal kitchen, a small pool in the garden and free bike rental.

Agarre o Momento HOSTEL €
(☎214 064 532; www.agarreomomento.com; Rua Joaquim Ereira 458; dm/d from €20/40;@🛜) These groovy new backpacker digs, in a bubblegum-pink house and 10 minutes' walk north of the station, offer clean, airy dorms, plus a few other perks such as a garden, free wi-fi, a shared kitchen and bike rental.

Camping Orbitur do Guincho
CAMPGROUND €
(☎214 870 450; www.orbitur.pt; bungalows from €40, sites per adult/tent/car €4.50/5.10/4.40;🛜) Set back behind the dunes of Praia do Guincho, 9km from Cascais, this pine-shaded site has a restaurant and tennis court. It gets busy in July and August. Buses run frequently to Guincho from Cascais.

🍴 Eating

You'll find a glut of restaurants with alfresco seating along pedestrianised Rua Frederico Arouca and cobbled Largo Cidade de Vitória. For seafood and sunsets, make for the beach-shack restaurants by the waterfront in Guincho.

Fortaleza do Guincho CONTEMPORARY €€€
(☎214 870 491; www.guinchotel.pt; Estrada do Guincho; mains around €32; ✸@🛜) Inside the striking 17th-century fortress turned luxury guest house (doubles including breakfast from €205), the Michelin-starred Fortaleza do Guincho wows diners with its complex,

delicately prepared dishes – from sea bass with oyster tartare to roasted Alentejo pork with gnocchi and glazed vegetables. The ocean views are magical.

Furnas do Guincho
SEAFOOD €€€
(☑214 869 243; Estrada da Guincho; mains €16-30; ☺lunch & dinner) Straddling a rocky outcrop looking out to the Atlantic, this smart seafood restaurant is about 1km along the road to Guincho. Savour house specials such as goose barnacles and lobster over dramatic sea views.

Confraria Sushi
JAPANESE €€
(Rua Luís Xavier Palmeirim 16; mains €8-13; ☺noon-midnight Tue-Sun) It's hard to know where to look first at this Smartie-bright, art-slung cafe, jazzed up with flower prints, zebra stripes and technicolour glass chandeliers. It's a fun spot for sushi and yummy salads such as goat's cheese with forest fruits. There's a handful of tables on the sunny patio.

A Carvoaria
SOUTH AFRICAN €€
(☑214 830 406; Rua João Luís de Moura 24; mains €10-20; ☺dinner Mon-Sat) A well-kept local secret, this rustic South African haunt is always packed thanks to its friendly service and terrific food. On the menu: spicy *boerewors* (sausage), garlicky ostrich fillet, oxtail stew and the roll-me-out-the-door 'steak big boss'.

Santini
ICE CREAM €
(Av Valbom 28F; ice creams €2.50; ☺11am-11pm Tue-Sat, 11am-8pm Sun) All hail Santini for its creamy rich 100% natural gelati, made to an age-old family recipe. Join the line, grab a cone and skedaddle to the beach before it melts.

Restaurante Galerias
PORTUGUESE €€
(Rua Afonso Sanches 38; mains €6-11; ☺lunch & dinner Mon-Sat) Tucked down a quiet lane, Restaurante Galerias attracts a mix of locals and well-informed visitors who enjoy delicious, no-nonsense fare – grilled fish of the day, lamb chops, sizzling shish kebab – in a small dining room decorated with fishing nets and old photos. Service can sometimes be a bit slow.

Le Meli-Melo
CREPERIE €
(Rua Visconde da Luz 43; crepes €7; ☺noon-midnight) Colourful paintings adorn the walls of quaint, candlelit Meli-Melo, which proffers savoury and sweet crepes, plump salads and daily specials.

Jardim dos Frangos
CHICKEN €€
(Av Marginal; mains €7-11; ☺lunch & dinner Mon-Sat) Whiffs of grilled chicken and piri-piri lure hungry locals to the pavement terrace of this no-frills joint. Waiters can be moody, but the *frango no churrasco* is first-class.

Apeadeiro
SEAFOOD €€
(Av Vasco da Gama 252; mains €7-12; ☺lunch & dinner) With chequered tablecloths, big windows and walls hung with fishing nets, this sunny restaurant is known for its superb chargrilled fish – shrimp piri-piri is delicious.

Esplanada Santa Marta
PORTUGUESE €€
(Praia de Santa Marta; mains €8-10; ☺10am-10pm Tue-Sun) Perched above a bay, this cute place is a family favourite because of its after-dinner paddling potential. Tuck into dishes such as shrimp kebabs and halibut on the palm-shaded terrace with lighthouse views.

 Drinking

Bars huddling around Largo Luís de Camões are publike, lively and packed with a good-time crowd that gets crazy after too many rays.

Baluarte
LOUNGE
(Av Dom Carlos I 6) Ubercool Baluarte draws a see-and-be-seen crowd with its glam-meets-retro decor of swirly gold wallpaper, tub chairs and bold purple splashes. It offers sea views, well-mixed cocktails and regular events from DJ nights to karaoke.

Buvigis
LOUNGE
(Rua do Poço Novo) A hip lounge bar close to the waterfront, Buvigis is packed with 20- and 30-somethings who gather over fruity cocktails, games of pool and laid-back old-school tunes.

Rock 'n' Shots
BAR
(Largo Luís do Camões 36) This funky bar does what the label says – expect thumping Portuguese rock, a dash of reggae and potent shots and cocktails. Sip a cool Rui Veloso (vodka, peach and pineapple juice).

O Luain's
PUB
(☑214 861 627; Rua da Palmeira 4A) For the craic in Cascais, it has to be this cheery Irish watering hole, run by Ivor and Karen. Pull up a stool for Guinness and – at 10.30pm, Thursday to Sunday – live music, including the popular banjo jam sessions.

O'Neill's
PUB

(☏214 868 230; Rua Afonso Sanches 8) Another Irish number with banter and a passion for the pint, O'Neill's has live music at around 11pm from Thursday to Saturday.

Esplanada Rainha
OUTDOOR BAR

(Largo da Rainha; ⊘10am-10pm) For sundowners with a sea view, head to this outdoor place with a pleasant vista overlooking Praia da Rainha beach.

Jardim Cerveja
OUTDOOR BAR

(Parque Marechal Carmona; ⊘1pm-1am) Inside the leafy Parque Marechal Carmona, this stylish bar has a large open-air terrace that hosts DJs and live music from Tuesday to Sunday nights (Thursdays are fado nights, weekends salsa).

🛍 Shopping

Label lovers head down Rua Frederico Arouca for boutiques from Max Mara to Hugo Boss.

Cascais Villa Shopping Centre
SHOPPING MALL

(Av Marginal) Near the bus station, this mall shelters a cinema, supermarket and a string of other shops.

Mercado Municipal
MARKET

(Av Dom Pedro I; ⊘morning Wed & Sat) Cascais' bustling municipal market tempts with fresh local produce such as juicy Algarve nectarines, glossy olives, wagon wheel-sized cheeses and bread. An entire hall is given over to fish.

Ceramicarte
FINE ART, HANDICRAFTS

(☏214 840 170; Largo da Assunção 3) This eye-catching gallery showcases Luís Soares' bright, abstract fused-glass creations, from jewellery to tableware.

Livraria Galileu
BOOKS

(☏214 866 014; Av Valbom 24A) Good source of secondhand English, Spanish, Italian, French and German books.

ℹ Information

Banco Espírito Santo (☏214 864 302; Largo Luís de Camões 40) Has an ATM.

Cascais Hospital (☏214 827 700; Rua Padre JM Loureiro)

International Medical Centre (☏214 845 317; Instituto Médico de Cascais, Av Pedro Álvares Cabral 242)

Main police station (☏214 861 127; Rua Afonso Sanches)

Post office (Av Marginal; ⊘8.30am-6pm Mon-Fri) Also has NetPost.

Tourist police post (☏214 863 929; Rua Visconde da Luz) Next to the *turismo*.

Turismo (☏214 868 204; www.visiteestoril. com; Rua Visconde da Luz 14; ⊘9am-7pm Mon-Sat) Can assist with accommodation. Hands out free maps and brochures.

ℹ Getting There & Away

Buses go frequently to Sintra from both Estoril and Cascais (€3.50, 40 minutes) and to Cabo da Roca (€2.60, 30 minutes). You pay more on board than at the kiosk. If you're planning on travelling a lot by bus, it's worthy buying a day pass for €4.

Trains run from Lisbon's Cais do Sodré to Cascais via Estoril (€1.70, 40 minutes, every 20 minutes).

It's only 2km to Estoril, so it doesn't take long to walk the seafront route.

ℹ Getting Around

Transrent (☏214 864 566; www.transrent. pt; basement level, Centro Comercial Cisne, Av Marginal) rents bikes, scooters, cars and motorbikes. Buses 405 and 415 go to Guincho (€2.60, 20 minutes, seven daily).

Often waiting at Jardim Visconde da Luz are horse-drawn carriages, which do half-hour trips to Boca do Inferno.

Near the bus station are numerous car-rental agencies including **Ausocar** (☏214 822 472; www. ausocar-rentacar.pt; loja D, Edificio Sol de Cascais, Av 25 de Abril 16). For a taxi, call ☏214 660 101.

Free bike hire (see p119) offers a more eco-friendly way to explore Cascais.

Estoril

POP 24,000

With its swish hotels, turreted villas and glitzy casino, Estoril (shtoe-*reel*) once fancied itself as the Portuguese Riviera. The rich and famous came here to frolic in the sea, stroll palm-fringed landscaped gardens and fritter away their fortunes. Though it still has a whiff of faded aristocracy, those heady days of grandeur have passed. Today, there isn't much to Estoril aside from its beach and casino, and overnight guests may end up wishing they'd stayed in livelier Cascais. During the day, Estoril's big draw is the sandy bay of Praia de Tamariz, which tends to be slightly quieter than the beaches in neighbouring Cascais in summer.

Estoril was where Ian Fleming hit on the idea for *Casino Royale,* as he stalked Yugoslav double agent Dusko Popov at its casino. During WWII, the town heaved with exiles and spies (including Graham Greene, another British intelligence man and author).

The bus and train stations are a stone's throw from the beach on Avenida Marginal, opposite shady Parque do Estoril. The casino is at the north end of the park.

👁 Sights & Activities

The glitzy, temple-like **casino** (☏214 667 700; www.casino-estoril.pt; Praça José Teodoro dos Santos; gaming/slot machine rooms €4/free; ⏰3pm-3am) has everything from roulette to poker, blackjack and the ubiquitous slot machines. Its cavernous main restaurant, **Preto e Prata** (☏214 684 521; show €21, dinner €35-44), stages a sparkly floor show nightly.

Estoril's sandy **Praia de Tamariz** tends to be quieter than the bays in Cascais and has showers, cafes, beachside bars and a free ocean **swimming pool**, east of the train station.

For details on Estoril's world-famous golf scene, see p40.

🛏 Sleeping

Pica-Pau   GUEST HOUSE €€
(☏214 667 140; www.picapauestoril.com; Rua do Afonso Henriques 48; s/d €55/80; ☒) Occupying a white-fronted, red-roofed villa 400m west of the casino, Pica-Pau's big draw is its pool framed by sunloungers. The marble-floored rooms with cable TV and safes are spacious and well kept, though beds can be on the springy side.

Hotel Smart   GUEST HOUSE €€
(☏214 682 164; www.hotel-smart.net; Rua Maestro Laçerda 6; s/d €70/80; ℗☒) This little guest house is smart alright. The affable owner runs the place with pride – think manicured lawns, a clean swimming pool and gleaming marble floors. The light-filled rooms have lots of polished wood and tiny balconies.

Palacio Estoril Hotel   HOTEL €€€
(☏214 648 000; www.palacioestorilhotel.com; Rua Particular; d from €180; ✳@☒) Built in 1930 this elegant, five-star hotel earns high marks for its grand atmosphere and doting service; the rooms are modern and comfortably furnished, but are less impressive than the ornate common areas. There's

also a lovely spa, fine restaurant, bar and pool.

✕ Eating

Garrett do Estoril   PORTUGUESE €
(☏214 680 365; Av de Nice 54; snacks €1-4; ⏰8am-7pm) Overlooking the park, this handsomely set *pastelaria* and restaurant impresses the small dog-toting clientele with its teas, sandwiches, daily specials and sticky pastries.

Praia de Tamariz   PORTUGUESE €€
(☏214 681 010; Praia de Tamariz; mains €10-18; ⏰lunch & dinner) Overlooking the beach of the same name, this traditional restaurant serves decent, if unsurprising, traditional fare. More memorable are the ocean views from the breezy terrace.

Mandarim   CHINESE €€€
(☏214 667 270; Av Dr Stanley Ho; mains €12-24; ⏰lunch & dinner Wed-Sun) Inside the Casino Estoril, Mandarim is considered Portugal's best Chinese restaurant – and is priced accordingly. Fresh-tasting and exquisitely spiced dishes come beautifully presented. There's pleasant outdoor seating overlooking the park, with the sea visible in the distance.

ℹ Information

Turismo (⏰9am-7pm Mon-Sat Sep-Jun, to 8pm Mon-Sat Jul & Aug, 10am-6pm Sun year-round) Faces the train station.

ℹ Getting There & Away

Bus 412 goes frequently to Cascais (€1.80, five minutes), or it's a pleasant 2km walk or cycle along the seafront. For other train and bus services, see p123.

Queluz

Versailles' fanciful cousin-once-removed, the powder-puff **Palácio de Queluz** (☏214 343 860; adult/child €5/free; ⏰9.30am-5pm Wed-Mon) was once a hunting lodge, converted in the late 1700s to a royal summer residence. It's surrounded by queen-of-hearts formal gardens, with oak-lined avenues, fountains (including the Fonte de Neptuno, ascribed to Italian master Bernini) and an *azulejo*-lined canal where the royals went boating.

The palace was designed by Portuguese architect Mateus Vicente de Oliveira and French artist Jean-Baptiste Robillon for Prince Dom Pedro in the 1750s. Pedro's niece and wife, Queen Maria I, lived here for most of her reign, going increasingly mad. Her scheming Spanish daughter-in-law, Carlota Joaquina, was quite a match for eccentric British visitor William Beckford. On one occasion she insisted that Beckford run a race with her maid in the garden and then dance a bolero, which he did 'in a delirium of romantic delight'.

Inside is like a chocolate box, with a gilded, mirror-lined Throne Room and Pedro IV's bedroom where he slept under a circular ceiling, surrounded by *Don Quixote* murals. The palace's vast kitchens now house a palatial restaurant, Cozinha Velha (⏺214 356 158; ◷lunch & dinner Wed-Mon).

You've seen the palace, now live the life. The Royal Guard of the Court quarters in this ice cream–pink rococo palace have been converted into the dazzling **Pousada de Dona Maria I** (⏺214 356 158; www.pousadas.pt; d incl breakfast from €120;✳), with high-ceilinged rooms that will make you feel as if you're at home with the royals.

ⓘ Getting There & Away

Queluz (keh-*loozh*) is 5km northwest of Lisbon and makes an easy day trip. Frequent trains from Rossio station stop at Queluz-Belas (€1.30, 15 minutes).

Mafra

POP 11,000 / ELEV 250M

Mafra, 39km northwest of Lisbon, makes a superb day trip from Lisbon, Sintra or Ericeira. It is home to Palácio de Mafra, Portugal's extravagant monastery-palace hybrid with 1200 rooms. Nearby is the beautiful former royal park, Tapada de Mafra, once a hunting ground and still teeming with wild animals and plants.

The monumental palace facade dominates the town. Opposite is a pleasant square, Praça da República, which is lined with cafes and restaurants. Mafra's bus terminal is 1.5km northwest but buses also stop in front of the palace. A Mafrense bus **ticket office** (Terreiro Dom João V 21) is located near the square. You can get basic info on the town in the tourist office attached to the palace.

⊙ Sights

Palácio Nacional de Mafra   PALACE
(⏺261 817 550; adult/child €6/3; ◷10am-5pm Wed-Mon) Wild-spending Dom João

V poured pots of Brazilian gold into this baroque palace, covering a mind-boggling 4 sq km and comprising a monastery and basilica. Begun in 1717, the exuberant mock-marble confection is the handiwork of German master Friedrich Ludwig, who trained in Italy and clearly had a kind of Portuguese Vatican in mind. No expense was spared: around 45,000 artisans worked on building its 1200 rooms and two bell towers, which shelter the world's largest collection of bells (92 in total).

When the French invaded Portugal in 1807, Dom João VI and the royals skedaddled to Brazil, taking most of Mafra's furniture with them. Imagine the anticlimax when the French found nothing but 20 elderly Franciscan friars. General Junot billeted his troops in the monastery, followed by Wellington and his men. From then on the palace became a military haven. Even today, most of it is used as a military academy.

On a self-guided visit, you'll take in treasures such as the antler-strewn hunting room and a walled bed for mad monks (maybe sent over the edge by all those corridors!). The biggest stunner is the 83.6m-long barrel-vaulted library, housing some 40,000 15th- to 18th-century books, many hand-bound by the monks. It's an appropriate fairy-tale coda to all this extravagance that they're gradually being gnawed away by rats. The basilica of twin bell-tower fame is strikingly restrained by comparison, featuring multihued marble floors and Carrara marble statues.

Tapada Nacional de Mafra   FOREST
(⏺261 817 050; www.tapadademafra.pt; walker €4.50-6, cyclist €10; ◷9am-6pm) The palace's 819-hectare park, Tapada Nacional de Mafra is where Dom João V used to go a-hunting. Enclosed by an original 21km wall, the grounds are now an environmentally aware game park, home to free-roaming wild boar and red deer, plus smaller numbers of foxes, badgers and eagles.

To appreciate the different ecosystems, hike through its woodlands of Portuguese oak, cork oak and pine; don't miss the 350-year-old cork oak saved from fire in 2003. The 4km trail (€4.50) is a good introduction to the park, but you have a greater chance of spotting animals on the more remote 7.5km route (€6). Also on the grounds is a simple but pleasantly furnished guest house (singles/doubles €65/75).

A WOLF IN THE WOODS

There's no need to be afraid of the wolves at the **Centro de Recuperação do Lobo Ibérico** (Iberian Wolf Sanctuary; ☑261 785 037; http://lobo.fc.ul.pt; Vale da Guarda, Picão; adult/concession €5/3; ☉4-8pm Sat & Sun May-Sep, 2.30-6pm Sat & Sun Oct-Apr) located near Malveira, 10km east of Mafra. The centre is home to a pack of around 20 wolves that can no longer live in the wild. Set in a forested valley, the centre aims to boost the rapidly dwindling numbers of Portugal's Iberian wolf population (now just 300 in the wild) by affording them safe shelter in a near-to-natural habitat. As the wolves are free to roam in their large enclosures, there's no guarantee that you'll spot them, but encounters are frequent. Advance bookings are essential. The sanctuary is best reached by private transport.

The Tapada is about 7km north of Mafra, along the road to Gradil. It's best reached by private transport, as buses are erratic; from Mafra, taxis charge around €8 one way.

Sobreiro   MINIATURE VILLAGE
(admission free; ☉10am-6pm) At the village of Sobreiro, 4km northwest of Mafra (take any Ericeira-bound bus), sculptor José Franco has created an enchanting miniature, vaguely surreal craft village of windmills, watermills and traditional shops. José himself can often be seen crafting clay figures at the entrance. Kids love it here; so do adults, especially when they discover the rustic *adega* (winery) serving good red wine and snacks. Ramped walkways make it accessible for wheelchair users.

🛏 Sleeping & Eating

Hotel Castelão   HOTEL **€€**
(☑261 816 050; Av 25 de Abril; s/d incl breakfast €55/75) If you want to stay overnight, Castelão offers comfy, though corporate, rooms with minibar and satellite TV. It has a pizzeria and bar.

Café Paris   PORTUGUESE **€**
(☑261 815 797; Praça da República 14; mains €6-9; ☉lunch & dinner Mon-Sat) This smartish, genteel pink place is among several cafe-restaurants around Praça da República and rustles up decent Portuguese dishes.

If you want something lighter, there are lots of nice *pastelarias* around the square selling local crusty Mafra bread and traditional cakes, such as *pastéis de feijão*, a concoction of eggs, sugar and almonds.

❶ Getting There & Around
There are regular **Mafrense** (☑261 816 159; Av Dr Francisco Sá Carneiro) buses to/from Ericeira (€2, 20 minutes, at least hourly), Sintra (€4, 45 minutes) and Lisbon's Campo Grande ter-

minal (€4, 75 minutes, at least hourly). Mafra's train station is 6km away from the town centre with infrequent buses (taxis charge around €9 between the train station and the town centre); go to Malveira station instead for easier connections (20 minutes) to Mafra.

Taxis are available in Praça da República.

SETÚBAL PENINSULA

As the mercury rises, the promise of sun, sea and mouth-watering grilled fish lures *lisboêtas* south to the Setúbal Peninsula for weekends of ozone-enriched fun. Beach bums make for the Costa da Caparica's 8km sweep of golden sand to laze on a lounger, dip in the chilly Atlantic and unwind over sundowners in beachside cafes. The coast gets wilder the further south you venture and Cabo Espichel is wildest of all – a vertiginous cape thrashed by the Atlantic, where you can trace the footprints of dinosaurs.

Edging further south, the vibrant port of Setúbal provides a tonic for a UV overdose. It's a fine place to munch *choco frito* (fried cuttlefish) and spot bottlenose dolphins on a breezy cruise of the marshy Sado estuary. To the west lies Parque Natural da Arrábida, lined with scalloped bays flanked by sheer cliffs that are home to birds of prey. It leads to the fishing town and bay of Sesimbra (p133), laced with cobbled backstreets and overshadowed by a Moorish castle. The coast is great for outdoorsy types, offering activities from scuba-diving and surfing to hiking and canyoning.

Cacilhas

This sleepy seaside suburb lies just across the Rio Tejo from the capital. Its star attraction, visible from almost everywhere in Lisbon, is 110m-high **Cristo Rei**. Perched on a pedestal, the statue of Christ with outstretched arms is a slightly more baroque version of Rio de Janeiro's Christ the Redeemer. It was erected in 1959 to thank God for sparing Portugal from the horrors of WWII. A **lift** (adult/concession €4/2; ⊙9.30am-6pm Apr-Sep, 9.30am-5pm Oct-Mar) zooms you up to a platform, from where Lisbon spreads magnificently before you. It's a fantastic place for photos. To reach the statue from Cacilhas, take bus 101.

Lisboêtas also flock to Cacilhas for the *cervejarias* (beer halls) serving fresh seafood, refreshing brews and fine views of the sun setting over the river.

Near the ferry terminal, **Cervejaria O Farol** (☎212 765 248; Largo Alfredo Diniz Alex 1; mains €8-12; ⊙9am-midnight Thu-Tue) is a buzzy haunt that cooks crustaceans, including garlicky clams and shrimps, to finger-licking perfection. Note the tiled panel depicting the *farol* (lighthouse) that once stood here.

A 15-minute stroll along the waterfront brings you to Brazilian restaurant **Atira-te ao Rio** (Cais do Ginjal 69; mains €12-18; ⊙1pm-midnight). Its terrace is a wonderful spot to feast on coconut-rich shrimp moqueca and sip *caipirinhas*, as Ponte 25 de Abril starts to twinkle. Come on Saturdays for a *feijoada* feast (pork-and-black-bean stew).

ⓘ Getting There & Away

Ferries to Cacilhas (€0.81, 10 minutes) run frequently from Lisbon's Cais do Sodré.

Costa da Caparica

Costa da Caparica's seemingly never-ending beach attracts sun-worshipping *lisboêtas* craving all-over tans, surfer dudes keen to ride Atlantic waves, and day-tripping families seeking clean sea and soft sand. It hasn't escaped development, but head south and the high-rises soon give way to pine forests and mellow beach-shack cafes. The town has the same name as the coastline, and is a cheery place with shops and lots of inflatable seaside tack.

During the summer a narrow-gauge railway runs most of the length of the beach and you can jump off at any one of 20 stops. The nearer beaches, including **Praia do Norte** and **Praia do São Sebastião**, are great for families, while the further ones are younger and trendier. **Praia do Castelo**

(stop 11) and **Praia da Bela Vista** (stop 17) are more-secluded gay and nudist havens.

Costa da Caparica town focuses on Praça da Liberdade. West of the *praça*, pedestrianised Rua dos Pescadores, with hotels and restaurants, leads to the seaside and a helpful **tourist office** (⊙9.30am-1pm & 2-5.30pm Mon-Fri, 9.30am-1pm Sat). The main beach (called Praia do CDS, or Centro Desportivo de Surf), with cafes, bars and surfing clubs along its promenade, is a short walk north. The **bus terminal** (Av General Humberto Delgado) is 400m northwest of the Praça da Liberdade; additional stops are by the *praça*.

🏃 Activities

Atlantic rollers pounding the shore are all the encouragement surfers need to grab their boards and hit the waves, particularly along the northern stretch of coast.

Among the hottest **surfing** spots are São João da Caparica, Praia da Mata and Praia da Sereia. **Fonte da Telha** (where the train terminates) is the best beach for **windsurfing** and has plenty of water-sports facilities. Check the handy *Tabela de Marés* booklet (available at the *turismo*), listing tide times, surf shops and clubs.

Caparica Surfing School (☎212 919 078; www.caparicasurf.com; Praia do CDS; ⊙10am-6pm Sat & Sun) is the main surfing school. Brian Trigg runs the excellent **Hooked Surf School** (☎913 615 978; www.hookedsurf. com; intro lesson €25, 4 lessons €80), offering lessons and a kids' surf club at Costa da Caparica, Praia do Guincho (p119) and Praia Grande (p117). Call ahead for a pick-up from your accommodation. It also rents boards and wetsuits.

Cabana Divers (☎212 977 711; www.cabana divers.com; Fonte da Telha), with a nicely set-up bar and wicker basket chairs by the beach, provides scuba diving lessons and all the necessary equipment.

Da Wave (p128) rents out surf- and bodyboards, wetsuits and beach gear (footballs, frisbees and in-line skates). You can also arrange surf lessons.

You can rent bikes for cruising along the beach path from **Bicla** (per hr/half-day €3/6; ⊙10am-7pm), which operates out of Dragão Vermelha, the trendy beachside restaurant near Hotel Costa da Caparica.

🛏 Sleeping

Residencial Mar e Sol GUEST HOUSE €€ (☎212 900 017; www.residencialmaresol.com; Rua dos Pescadores 42; s/d €45/65; ❄ @ 🛜)

Mar e Sol offers simple yet comfy rooms in warm hues with parquet floors. There is free internet, bike hire and an Italian restaurant next door, which serves decent pizzas.

Hotel Costa da Caparica · HOTEL €€

(📞212 918 900; www.costacaparicahotel. com; Avenida General Humberto Delgado 47; r with/without view incl breakfast from €80/60;❄@🖥🐕) This boxy, nine-story hotel facing the beach has comfortable carpeted rooms with balconies, and it's worth paying extra for the unobstructed ocean views. There's an inviting pool, a spa and an 8th-floor restaurant with panoramic views.

Residencial Real · GUEST HOUSE €

(📞212 918 870; www.hotel-real.pt; Rua Mestre Manuel 18; s/d €45/60;❄) A young crew runs this guest house, 30m from the beach. Rooms have simple wood furnishings and paisley patterned bedspreads; the upstairs rooms are brighter.

Costa da Caparica · CAMPGROUND €

(📞212 901 366; bungalows from €56, camp sites per adult/tent/car €4.50/5.10/4.40; 🐕) Orbitur's campground, 1km north of town, is the closest and the best. Situated 200m from the beach, the pine-shaded campground has tent sites, bungalows and excellent facilities such as a cafe, tennis court and playground.

🍴 Eating & Drinking

In Costa da Caparica town, seafood restaurants line Rua dos Pescadores. You'll find a wide mix of restaurants and open-sided bars on the beach, which crank up during the summer months.

A Merendeira · SANDWICHES €

(Rua dos Pescadores 20; sandwiches €1.80) This cafe on the main drag serves *merendeiras,* which are oven-baked sandwiches (chorizo, beef or cod), and filling daily soups and desserts.

Da Wave · CAFE €€

(Praia Nova; mains €7-9; ⏰10am-2am; 🐕) One of many open-sided cafe-restaurants along the beach, Da Wave has a laid-back vibe with its beanbag chairs, hammocks and reggae playing overhead. American-style breakfasts, sandwiches, pizzas and juices make up the menu. Find it by heading 500m from town in the direction of the narrow-gauge train.

Napoli · ITALIAN €€

(📞212 903 197; Rua dos Flores 1; mains €7-13; ⏰dinner) Pizzas, pasta dishes and other Italian fare draw hungry locals to this unassuming Italian joint at Residencial Mar e Sol.

Bar Waikiki · BAR, RESTAURANT

(📞212 962 129; Praia da Sereia; snacks €3-7; ⏰10am-2am Apr-Sep) Nicely on its own, this beachfront bar is popular with surfers and has a cool lounge vibe. Great for sundowners, you'll find it at stop 15 on the train.

ℹ️ Information

Turismo (⏰9.30am-1pm & 2-5.30pm Mon-Fri, 9.30am-1pm Sat) Helpful staff in the modern brown building on the beach.

ℹ️ Getting There & Away

Transportes Sul do Tejo (TST; 📞217 262 740; www.tsuldotejo.pt) runs regular buses to Costa da Caparica from Lisbon's Praça de Espanha (€2.70, 20 to 60 minutes).

The best way to get here is by ferry to Cacilhas (every 15 minutes) from Lisbon's Cais do Sodré, where bus 135 runs to Costa da Caparica town (€3, 30 to 45 minutes, every 30 to 60 minutes); buses 124 and 194 also run here but are slower, and also stop at the train station. Bus 127 runs from Cacilhas to Fonte da Telha (50 minutes, at least hourly). Bus 130 runs from Trafaria to Fonte da Telha (45 minutes, at least hourly) via Costa da Caparica and Pinhal do Rei (near Praia do Rei).

ℹ️ Getting Around

The train along the beach runs every half-hour from 9am to 7.30pm between Praia Nova and Fonte da Telha (€6.50 return), about 1km before the end of the county beach. Although this is the end of the line, the beaches continue along the coast.

Setúbal

POP 114,000

Though hardly a classic beauty, the thriving port town of Setúbal (*shtoo*-bahl) makes a terrific base for exploring the region's sublime natural assets. Top of the must-do list is a cruise to the marshy wetlands of the Sado estuary, the splashy playground of around 30 bottlenose dolphins, flocks of white storks (spring and summer), and 1000 wintering flamingos that make the water fizz like pink champagne. Outdoorsy types can hike or bike along the dramatic, pine-brushed coastline of Parque Natural da Arrábida, while sun-seekers can bliss out on nearby sandy beaches.

Back in town, it's worth taking a stroll through the squares in the pedestrianised old town, seeking out Igreja de Jesús, Portugal's first-ever Manueline church, and clambering up to the hilltop fortress for giddy views over the estuary. The fish reeled the Romans to Setúbal in 412, so it's no surprise that seafood here is delicious. On Avenida Luísa Todi, locals happily while away hours polishing off enormous platters of *choco frito* and carafes of white wine.

Most sights are within easy walking distance of the mostly pedestrianised centre. The bus station is about 150m northwest of the centre; the main train station is 700m north of the centre. Frequent ferries shuttle across the Rio Sado to the Tróia peninsula from terminals around Doca do Comércio.

⊙ Sights

Praça do Bocage   PLAZA

All streets in the pedestrianised old town seem to lead to this mosaic-cobbled square, presided over by the arcaded pink-and-white town hall. It's a sunny spot for a wander amid the palms and fountains, or for coffee and people-watching on one of the pavement terraces.

Castelo São Filipe   CASTLE

(⊙7am-10pm) Worth the 500m schlep uphill to the west, the castle was built by Filipe I in 1590 to fend off an English attack on the invincible Armada. Converted into a *pousada* (upmarket inn) in the 1960s, its hulking ramparts afford precipitous views and its chapel is festooned in blue-and-white 18th-century *azulejos* depicting the life of São Filipe – you can view them through a glass wall if the door is locked. Arrive early morning and you'll be able to watch fishermen unload their catch in the harbour below.

Igreja de Jesus   CHURCH

(Praça Miguel Bombarda; admission free; ⊙9am-1pm & 2-5.30pm Tue-Sun) Setúbal's architectural stunner is the sand-coloured Igreja de Jesus, one of the earliest examples of Manueline architecture, adorned with gargoyles and twirling turrets. The facade, however, is eclipsed by its interior of twisted pillars, like writhing snakes, that spiral upwards to the ceiling. Nebulous-seeming and organic, they are made from pink-tinged Arrábida marble. Around the altar, 18th-century blue-and-white geometric *azulejos* contrast strikingly with the curling arches of the roof.

Constructed in 1491, the church was designed by Diogo de Boitaca, better known for his later work on Belém's fantastical Mosteiro dos Jerónimos.

Museu do Trabalho Michel Giacometti

MUSEUM

(Largo Defensores da República; admission €1.20; ⊙9.30am-6pm Tue-Sat) How does the sardine get in the tin and 1001 other fishy mysteries are solved at this quirky yet often empty museum, set in a cavernous former sardine-canning factory. There's also an entire 1920s grocery, transported from Lisbon wholesale.

Museu de Arqueologia e Etnografia

MUSEUM

(Museum of Archaeology & Ethnography; Av Luísa Todi 162; admission free; ⊙9am-12.30pm & 2-5.30pm Tue-Sat) This small, rambling museum showcases several intriguing pieces such as Roman mosaics and 19th-century devotional paintings on wood, showing invalids having holy visions.

🏃 Activities

While most visitors are rather underwhelmed with Setúbal itself, the coastal scenery outside of town is truly spectacular. Don't miss the chiselled cliffs, pine-brushed hills and picturesque beaches of Parque Natural da Arrábida (p134).

Alternatively, It's an easy 20-minute ferry ride – look out for dolphins on the way – to Tróia, where the soft sandy beaches are flanked by dunes. A new resort there somewhat diminishes the natural beauty, but provides a great setting for exploring beaches going south.

👉 Tours

Cycling Tours

For two-wheel adventures, check out the new and highly recommended **Blue Coast Bikes** (📱265 092 172; www.bluecoastbikes.com; Rua das Fontaínhas 82; bike hire per day from €15, guided tours from €70). Hire a bike to pedal along the coast, or join one of the guided tours (advance bookings essential) to local vineyards, beaches or native cork forests.

Cruises & Dolphin-Watching

A highlight of any trip to Setúbal is the chance to spot resident bottlenose dolphins on a cruise of the Sado estuary. The frolicsome fellas show off their dorsal fins to a happy-snappy crowd; listen for their high-pitched clicking. Plenty of companies run half-day trips around the estuary (leaving from Doca do Comércio). Book ahead.

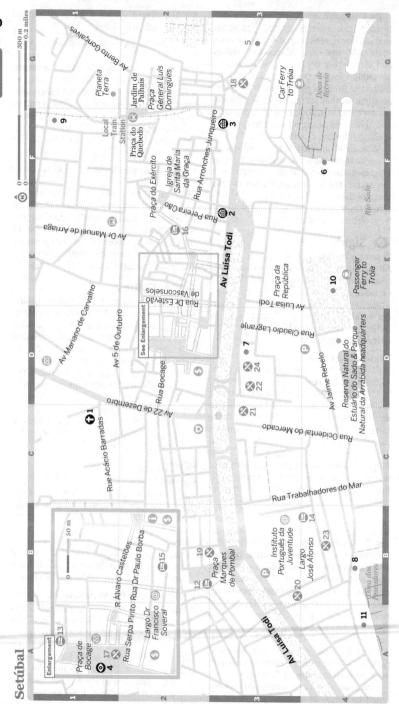

Setúbal

Enlargement

Praça de Bocage

Av Luísa Todi

Setubal

Nautur (☎265 532 914; www.nautur.com; Rua Praia da Saúde 15E) Offers a variety of cruises, starting on the Sado estuary, then visiting Arrábida beach, before returning to the river for some dolphin-spotting (from €44).

Mil Andanças (☎265 490 750; www.mil-andancas.pt; Av Luísa Todi 121) Runs dolphin-spotting river tours (€30 per person).

Troiacruze (☎265 228 482; www.troiacruze.com; Rua das Barroças 34) Offers dolphin-spotting (five-hour trip per person €30 to €40) and other cruises, such as a sailing galleon along the Sado estuary (€65 including meals).

Vertigem Azul (☎265 238 000; www.vertigemazul.com; Rua Praia da Saúde 11D) Offers sustainable three-hour dolphin-watching tours in the Sado estuary (€35). It's located 500m west of the centre.

Jeep Tours

Blue Coast Bikes (☎265 092 172; www.bluecoastbikes.com; Rua das Fontaínhas 82; tours from €45) In addition to bike tours, Blue Coast runs jeep tours in and around Arrábida, plus wine-tasting and cellar tours.

Mil Andanças (☎265 490 750; www.mil-andancas.pt; Av Luísa Todi 121; half-day €30) Offers jeep tours in Arrábida.

Walking

The ecotourism company **Sistemas de Ar Livre** (SAL; ☎265 227 685; www.sal.pt; Av Manuel Maria Portela 40; per person €7; ⊙10am Sat & Sun Sep-Jun) arranges activities including three-hour guided walks in or around Setúbal.

Wine Tours

Wine-lovers shouldn't miss the cellar tours of **José Maria da Fonseca** (☎212 198 940; www.jmf.pt; Rua José Augusto Coelho 11; visits €3-4; ⊙10am-12.15pm & 2-5.30pm), the oldest Portuguese producer of table wine and Moscatel de Setúbal, in nearby Vila Nogueira de Azeitão. The winery is now run by the sixth generation of the family. Ring ahead to arrange a visit to the house and museum. From Setúbal, buses leave frequently to Vila Nogueira de Azeitão (20 minutes).

The tourist office has a free useful leaflet, *Rota de Vinhos da Costa Azul,* detailing all the wine producers you can visit in the area.

🛏 Sleeping

Pousada de São Filipe LUXURY HOTEL **€€€** (☎265 550 070; www.pousadas.pt; d from €150; ✳) Perched high and mighty above Setúbal is this green-shuttered retreat, hidden inside the town's hilltop fortress. Expect vaulted corridors filled with antiques, spacious quarters and dramatic ocean panoramas.

Há Mar ao Luar GUEST HOUSE **€€€** (☎265 220 901; www.hamaraoluar.com; Alto S Filipe; d €100-130) Romantic types love this peach-hued villa near the castle for its large, strikingly decorated apartments with plump beds, tranquil shaded terraces and sea views. Book ahead to stay in the windmill.

Blue & Green Tróia Design Hotel
 RESORT **€€€** (☎265 498 000; www.troiadesignhotel.com; Tróia Marina, Tróia; d from €200; ✳🛜🏊) Looming large over Tróia beach, this new luxury

resort opened in 2010 and offers stylish modern rooms with balconies overlooking either the Rio Sado or the Arrábida mountains. The facilities are extensive, with a spa, restaurants, bars and several pools; a casino was in the works. It's best reached by ferry from Setúbal.

Albergaria Solaris
GUEST HOUSE €€

(☑265 541 770; www.albergariasolaris.com; Praça Marquês de Pombal 12; s/d incl breakfast €50/60; ❋ @) Overlooking a lively square, Solaris is a small and friendly option. Rooms have a neat, trim design with dark wood floors and red, quilted bedspreads; some have small balconies. Breakfast is above-par, with eggs and fresh fruit.

Casa de Hóspedes Bom Amigo
GUEST HOUSE €

(☑265 526 290; 2nd fl, Rua do Concelho 7; d with/without shower €30/25) Anyone who believes silence is golden is bemvindo in this homely pad, where 'silêncio' signs rule out late-night shenanigans. Still, it's a bargain and the chintzy rooms – think lace doilies, plastic roses and baby pinks and blues – are immaculate.

Residencial Bocage
GUEST HOUSE €€

(☑265 543 080; www.residencialbocage.pt; Rua de São Cristóvão 14; s/d incl breakfast €35/45; ❋) Decorated inside with earthy hues and striped curtains, the renovated rooms at Bocager sport parquet floors, comfy beds and squeaky-clean bathrooms. Rooms in the older separate building need a serious makeover.

Residencial Setúbalense
GUEST HOUSE €€

(☑265 525 790; Rua Major Afonso Pala 17; s/d incl breakfast €40/50; ❋ @) Tucked down a quiet backstreet, Setúbalense's old-style rooms are nothing flash but they're clean and comfy with wood furnishings and cable TV. Other bonuses include a hearty breakfast, free parking and internet access.

Pousada de Juventude
HOSTEL €

(☑265 534 431; setubal@movijovem.pt; Largo José Afonso; dm/d €12/27; 🛜) Attached to the IPJ, this curved building is near the busy fishing harbour. The four-bed dorm rooms are spick and span, though fluorescent lights may depress. There's a curfew from 11pm till 7am.

Parque de Campismo
CAMPGROUND €

(☑265 238 318; Outão; www.roteiro-campista. pt; camp sites per adult/tent/car €4.20/5.50/3) Situated 4km west of Setúbal, this green and shady site is right on the coast, perfect for those who want to snorkel or windsurf. It's accessible by regular bus (25 minutes).

🍴 Eating & Drinking

Head to the western end of Avenida Luísa Todi for lip-smacking, fresh-from-the-Atlantic seafood. Here you'll find a cluster of simple, buzzy restaurants with alfresco seating. Be sure to sample local specialities such as caldeirada, a hearty fish stew prepared in a covered brass pot, or choco frito washed down with sweet Moscatel de Setúbal wine.

Pousada de São Filipe
SEAFOOD €€€

(☑218 442 001; mains €17-23; ☺lunch & dinner) Great for special occasions, this smart restaurant has a top-of-the-world sea-view terrace. Service is attentive and food beautifully presented – try the monkfish stew or tender lamb. It's also a great setting for a drink at sunset.

Champanheria
SEAFOOD €€

(Av Luísa Todi 414; mains €14-15; ☺lunch & dinner Mon-Sat) This dapper restaurant and tapas bar serves up rich Rio Sado oysters, best enjoyed with a glass of bubbly. Five-course tasting menus are a fine way to sample the variety of seafood from the region.

Xica Bia
SEAFOOD €€

(☑265 522 559; Av Luísa Todi 131; mains €9-14; ☺lunch & dinner Mon-Sat) Fado shawls, wrought-iron chandeliers and copper pots jazz up this brick-vaulted restaurant. Xica Bia serves market-fresh seafood alongside other flavoursome fare such as herby salsichas.

Solar do Lago
PORTUGUESE €€

(☑265 238 847; Parque das Escolas 40; mains €8-16; ☺lunch & dinner) This high-ceilinged restaurant exudes rustic charm with its chunky wooden tables and terracotta tiles. Tasty seafood dishes include garlicky caldeirada and grilled squid. A handful of outdoor tables overlook a quiet plaza.

Casa Santiago
SEAFOOD €€

(☑265 221 688; Av Luísa Todi 92; mains €6-12; ☺lunch & dinner Mon-Sat) Wafts of fish sizzling on the grill will reel you into this local favourite, where the hungry lunchtime crowds feast on huge portions of choco frito, served with a squirt of lemon and mounds of fries, rice and salad. It's the best along the strip with a covered terrace and plenty of buzz.

Duarte dos Frangos
CHICKEN €

(☑265 522 603; Av Luísa Todi 285; mains €5-10; ⊙lunch Fri-Wed, dinner Fri-Tue) This cosy spot just south of the old town whips up succulent roast chicken. The yellow-and-blue decor is cheery, but service can border on matronly.

Botequim de Bocage
CAFE €

(☑265 534 077; Praça de Bocage 128; pastries €2-3) Pull up a chair at this cafe terrace on Setúbal's sunny main square. Light bites include quiche, pizza and sweets such as almond tart. It makes a good coffee pit stop.

For self-caterers there's the supermarket **Pingo Doce** (Av Luísa Todi 149; ⊙8am-9pm) and the large *mercado municipal* (municipal market) next door selling excellent fish and fresh produce.

ℹ Information

Caixa Geral de Depósitos (Av Luísa Todi 190) Has an ATM.

Hospital (☑265 549 000) Near the Praça de Touros (bullring), off Avenida Dom João II.

Municipal turismo (Av Luísa Todi 486)

Police station (☑265 522 022; Av 22 de Dezembro)

Regional turismo (☑265 539 130; www.costa-azul.rts.pt; Travessa Frei Gaspar 10;) Has a glass floor revealing the remains of a Roman *garum* (fish condiment) factory. The office hands out a free booklet, *Parques e Reservas Naturais* (Parks & Natural Reserves), with an English translation, plus other leaflets on the area.

ℹ Getting There & Away

Boat

Car ferries and passenger-only catamarans to Tróia depart half-hourly to hourly every day (car and driver €9.50; passenger €2). Note that car ferries, catamarans and cruises all have different departure points. See www.atlanticferries.pt for departure times.

Bus

Buses run between Setúbal and Lisbon's Praça de Espanha (€4 to €6, 45 to 60 minutes, at least hourly) – or from Cacilhas (€4, 50 minutes, every 15 minutes Monday to Friday, every two hours Saturday and Sunday).

Train

From Lisbon's Oriente station five IC trains run daily (weekdays only) to Setúbal (€7.50, one hour). You can also catch a frequent ferry from Lisbon's Terreiro do Paço terminal to Barreiro

HAVE YOUR SAY

Found a fantastic restaurant that you're longing to share with the world? Disagree with our recommendations? Or just want to talk about your most recent trip?

Whatever your reason, head to lonelyplanet.com, where you can post a review, ask or answer a question on the Thorntree forum, comment on a blog, or share your photos and tips on Groups. Or you can simply spend time chatting with like-minded travellers. So go on, have your say.

station (€1.80, 30 minutes), from where there are frequent *suburbano* (suburban) trains to Setúbal (€1.75, 45 minutes).

ℹ Getting Around

Cycling is a great way to discover the coast at your own pace. Hire a bike from Blue Coast Bikes (p129).

Car-rental agencies include **Avis** (☑265 538 710; Av Luísa Todi 96).

Sesimbra

POP 38,000

Sesimbra has been reeling in nets for centuries and today the picture-perfect town also hooks day-tripping *lisboêtas* and holidaymakers. But the fishermen haven't hung up their salt-encrusted boots yet. As well as fine sands, turquoise waters and a Moorish castle slung high above the centre, Sesimbra offers tasty seafood in its waterfront restaurants.

Though it can be cheek by jowl on the beach in summer, the town has kept its low-key charm with narrow lanes lined with terracotta-roofed houses, outdoor cafes and a palm-fringed promenade for lazy ambles. Cruises, guided hikes and scuba-diving activities here include trips to Cabo Espichel, where dinosaurs once roamed. It's 30km southwest of Setúbal, sheltering under the Serra da Arrábida at the western edge of the beautiful Parque Natural da Arrábida.

⊙ Sights

Castelo
CASTLE

(admission free; ⊙7am-8pm Mon-Wed, Fri & Sat, 7am-7pm Sun & Thu) For sweeping views over

PARQUE NATURAL DA ARRÁBIDA

Thickly green, hilly and edged by gleaming, clean, golden beaches and chiselled cliffs, the Arrábida Natural Park stretches along the southeastern coast of the Setúbal Peninsula from Setúbal to Sesimbra. Covering the 35km-long Serra da Arrábida mountain ridge, this is a protected area rich in Mediterranean plants, from olive, pistachio and strawberry to lavender, thyme and chamomile, with attendant butterflies, beetles and birds (especially birds of prey such as eagles and kestrels) and even 70 types of seaweed. Its pine-brushed hills are also home to deer and wild boar.

Highlights here are the long, golden beaches of windsurfer hot-spot **Figueirinha** and the sheltered bay of **Galapo**. Most stunning of all is **Portinho da Arrábida** with fine sand, azure waters and a small 17th-century fort built to protect the monks from Barbary pirates. There are some *quartos* (private rooms) right on the beach here.

Local honey is delicious, especially that produced in the gardens of the whitewashed, red-roofed **Convento da Arrábida** (☑212 180 520), a 16th-century former monastery overlooking the sea just north of Portinho (best days to visit are Tuesday or Thursday, but call ahead). Another famous product is Azeitão ewe's cheese, with a characteristic flavour that owes much to lush Arrábida pastures and a variety of thistle used in the curdling process.

Public transport through the middle of the park is nonexistent; some buses serve the beach from July to September (around four daily to Figueirinha). Your best option is to rent a car or motorcycle, or take an organised trip by jeep and/or boat. Be warned: parking is tricky near the beaches, even in the low season.

---

dale and coast, roam the snaking ramparts of the Moorish castle, rising 200m above Sesimbra. It was taken by Dom Afonso Henriques in the 12th century, retaken by the Moors, then snatched back by Christians under Dom Sancho I. The hilltop battlements glow gold when illuminated by night.

The ruins harbour the 18th-century, chalk-white **Igreja Santa Maria do Castelo**; step inside to admire its heavy gold altar and exquisite blue-and-white *azulejos*. The shady castle grounds are ideal for picnics.

The grandest castle on the sand is 17th-century **Fortaleza de Santiago** (admission free; ⊗8am-8pm). Once part of Portugal's coastal defences and the summertime retreat of Portuguese kings, the fort is now open to the public and boasts fine views out to sea.

Porto de Abrigo   PORT
Brightly painted boats bob on the water at Porto de Abrigo, 1km west of town, where grizzled fishermen unload, gut and auction their catch at the bustling fish market in the early morning and late afternoon.

🏃 Activities
Sesimbra is a great place to get into the outdoors with a backyard full of cliffs for climbing, clear water for scuba diving, Atlantic waves for windsurfing and miles and miles of unspoilt coastal trails for hiking and cycling. Adrenaline junkies get their thrills with vigorous pursuits from canyoning to rappelling.

Vertente Natural   ADVENTURE SPORTS
(☑210 848 919; www.vertentenatural.com; Santana; tours from €20) An eco-aware, one-stop shop for adventure sports, offers excursions from trekking and canyoning to canoeing, diving and rappelling. It's headquartered a few kilometres northwest of town.

Aquarama   CRUISE
(☑965 263 157; www.aquarama.com.pt; Av dos Náufragos; adult/child €17/10) Runs two to four trips per day to Cabo Espichel on a glass-bottomed partially submerged boat. Buy tickets at the office or on the boat.

Nautilus   DIVING
(☑212 551 969; www.nautilus-sub.com; Porto de Abrigo) PADI dive centre offering courses (including some for kids) and dives in the Sesimbra area.

Surf Clube de Sesimbra   SURF LESSONS
(☑210 875 139; www.scs.pt; Edificio Mar de Sesimbra, Rua Navegador Rodrigues Soromenho, Lote 1A, Loja 5) Offers lessons and board hire.

✨ Festivals & Events

Cabo Espichel festival Spectacularly set, this festival celebrates an alleged apparition of the Virgin Mary during the 15th century; an image of the Virgin is carried through the parishes, ending at the Cape. It takes place on the last Sunday in September.

Senhor Jesus das Chagas In early May, a procession stops twice to bless the land and four times to bless the sea, carrying an image of Christ that is said to have appeared on the beach in the 16th century (usually kept in Misericórdia church).

🛏 Sleeping

Sesimbra Hotel & Spa LUXURY HOTEL €€€
(☑212 289 800; www.sesimbrahotelspa.com; Praça da Califórnia; d from €190; ❄@🏊) Looming over the beach, this massive spa hotel has comfortable modern rooms that sport a clean geometric design. Balconies with ocean views are the real draw. There's a spa, an infinity pool, a kids' club, a gym, several bars and a good restaurant.

Quinta do Rio RURAL INN €€
(☑212 189 343; www.estalagemquintadorio.com; Alto das Vinhas; s/d €45/70;🏊) Nestled among orange groves and vineyards, this converted *quinta* (estate), 7km from Setúbal, is a calm hideaway with light, spacious rooms and mountain views. Ideal for families, the country retreat offers horse riding, tennis and minigolf, plus helicopter tours.

Residencial Náutico GUEST HOUSE €€
(☑212 233 233; www.residencialnautico.com; Av dos Combatentes 19; d incl breakfast from €85;❄) Set 500m uphill from the waterfront, this cheery guest house has airy tiled-floor double rooms in citrus shades. The best have terraces that overlook Sesimbra's sun-bleached red rooftops.

Forte do Cavalo CAMPGROUND €
(☑212 288 508; www.mun-sesimbra.pt; camp sites per adult/tent/car €3/5/2) Camp under the pines at this hilltop municipal site, 1km west of town. It's a shady, quiet spot with sea views, an on-site restaurant and a kids' playground.

Parque de Campismo de Valbom CAMPGROUND €
(☑212 687 545; camp sites per adult/tent/car €4/4/7; 🏊) Situated 5km north of Sesimbra in Cotovia, this leafy, well-equipped site has excellent facilities for families including a swimming pool, a playground and minigolf. To get here from Sesimbra, take any Lisbon-bound bus.

🍴 Eating & Drinking

Sea-foodies are in heaven in Sesimbra, where what swims in the Atlantic in the morning lands on plates by midday. Check out the fish restaurants by the waterfront just east of the fort.

Isaías SEAFOOD €
(Rua Coronel Barreto 2; mains €6-8; ⊘lunch & dinner Mon-Sat) No menu, no frills, just *the* tastiest grilled fish and cheapest plonk in town at this *tasca* run with love and prowess by Senhor Isaías, his son Carlos and chip maven Maria. You might well share your table with a band of merry fishermen. Sole, sardines, swordfish – it's all uniformly delicious.

Tony Bar SEAFOOD €€
(Largo de Bombaldes 19; mains €8-16; ⊘lunch & dinner) This smart restaurant on the square serves up deliciously grilled fish. Menu standouts include the swordfish with tomatoes and the succulent lobster. Portions are generous and the service is attentive.

Ribamar SEAFOOD €€
(☑212 234 853; Av dos Náufragos 29; mains €10-20; ⊘lunch & dinner) One of Sesimbra's best, this sleek restaurant faces the beach. Feast away on large seafood platters for two. Choosing a bottle from the arm-long wine list is quite a challenge.

ℹ Information

Turn right when you reach the bottom of the *avenida* and pass the small 17th-century Forte de Santiago to the helpful **turismo** (Largo da Marinha 26; ⊘9am-8pm Jun-Sep, 9am-12.30pm & 2-5.30pm Oct-May), set back slightly from the seafront.

ℹ Getting There & Away

Buses leave from Lisbon's Praça de Espanha (€4, 60 to 90 minutes, at least 10 daily); from Setúbal (€3.30, 45 minutes, at least nine daily Monday to Saturday, six Sunday); and from Cacilhas (€3.50, around one hour, at least hourly). There are runs to Cabo Espichel (€2.50, 25 minutes, two daily) and more frequent runs to the village of Azóia (€2.50, 10 daily Monday to Saturday, six Sunday), about 3km before the cape.

DINO PAWS

Step back in time 150 million years hunting for the footprints of dinosaurs on the craggy limestone cliffs just north of Cabo Espichel. The clearly visible imprints are near the small cove of Praia dos Lagosteiros. Rare and remarkably well preserved, the tracks date back to the Late Jurassic Age when this area was the stomping ground of four-legged, long-necked, herbivorous sauropods. Apparently, they were first discovered in the 13th century by fishermen who believed they were made by a giant mule that carried Our Lady of the Cape. Kids and dino fans should take a short ramble to see how many footprints they can find.

Around Sesimbra

ALDEIA DO MECO

Like nearby Alfarim, this tiny village 12km northwest of Sesimbra is famous for its seafood restaurants. Praia do Meco is an unspoilt sweep of golden sand, flanked by low-rise cliffs; try to catch one of its mesmerising sunsets.

The big summertime event is the **Super Bock Super Rock fest** in mid-July, with three stages of top-name performers lighting up the crowds (Prince played in 2010).

🛏 Sleeping & Eating

Country House   RURAL INN €€
(📞212 685 001; www.countryhouse-meco.com; Rua Alto da Carona, Alfarim; d €50, 2-/4-person apt €65/80) In a quiet wooded setting 1.4km north of the village, this big, fairly modern whitewashed house offers four spacious rooms (with coffeemakers and fridge) and three apartments, most with balconies. It's located 2km from the beach and is well signposted.

Campimeco   CAMPGROUND €
(📞212 683 393; camp sites per adult/tent/car €3.85/3.35/3.30; 🐾) Right up on the cliff top and offering lots of shade, this large camp site is 3km from the village, above Praia das Bicas and close to several beaches. Its facilities include barbecue areas and a kids' playground.

Bar do Peixe   SEAFOOD €€
(📞212 684 732; Praia do Meco; mains €7-11; ⏰11am-11pm Wed-Mon) This beachfront restaurant, north of Praia das Bicas, has a chilled vibe and a sea-facing terrace. It

serves light bites and fresh seafood. Other top seafood spots are scattered throughout the village, particularly on the main street Rua Central do Meco.

Amo-te Meco   CONTEMPORARY €€
(📞212 684 522; Rua Praia Moinho Baixo; mains €10-15; ⏰10am-2am) The food at this airy place near the beach is hit or miss, but the view from the terrace is stunning, making it a great spot for a sunset sangria. On weekends, a trendy crowd packs the back garden.

ℹ Getting There & Away

Buses run from Sesimbra (€2.50, 25 minutes, four to eight daily).

CABO ESPICHEL

At strange, bleak Cabo Espichel, frighteningly tall cliffs plunge down into piercing blue sea, some met by swaths of beach. The only building on the cape is a huge church, the 18th-century Nossa Senhõra do Cabo, flanked by two arms of desolately empty pilgrims' lodges.

It's easy to see why Wim Wenders used this windswept spot as a location when he was filming *A Lisbon Story,* with its lonely, brooding, outback atmosphere. It's worth your while trying to catch the Cabo Espichel festival if you are visiting in September (p135).

Buses to Cabo Espichel run direct from Sesimbra (€2.50, 25 minutes, two daily), while more frequent buses terminate at the village of Azóia (€2.50, 10 daily Monday to Saturday, six Sunday), about 3km before the cape.

The Algarve

Best Places to Stay

» Vila Joya (see the boxed text, p167)

» Monte da Vilarinha (p189)

» Aldeia Da Pedralva (p190)

Best Places to Eat

» Vila Joya (see the boxed text, p167)

» A Eira do Mel (p188)

» Jardim das Oliveiras (p193)

» A Forja (p180)

» Mesa dos Mouros (p147)

» Pastelaria Chicca (p183)

Why Go?

The Algarve is alluring. Coastal Algarve receives much exposure for its breathtaking cliffs, golden beaches, scalloped bays and sandy islands. But the letter 'S' (for sun, surf and sand) is only one letter in the Algarvian alphabet: activities, beach bars (and discos), castles (both sandy and real), diving (and a plethora of beach activities), entertainment, fun...

Let's be frank: Portugal's premier holiday destination sold its soul to tourism in the 1960s and never looked back. Behind sections of the south coast's beachscape loom massive conglomerations of bland holiday villas and brash resorts. The west coast is another story. Relatively low key and relaxed, this enchanting area is more about nature and less about development.

But Coastal Algarve is a 'drop in the ocean' for any visitor. The enchanting inner Algarve boasts pretty castle towns and historic villages, cork-tree- and flower-covered hillsides, and birdlife. The Via Algarviana walking track passes through here.

When to Go

Lagos

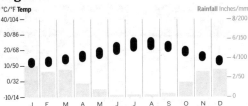

Anytime
The region is blessed with good weather; a mild winter and sun almost year-round

February & March See and smell the abundance of almond and orange blossoms

April & May Hike inland amid the wildflowers and leafy hillsides

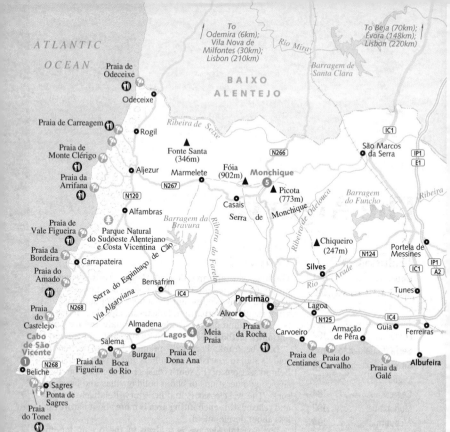

The Algarve Highlights

1 Wind your way up the stunning – and secluded – west coast, after peering over the cliffs of **Cabo de São Vicente** (p185)

2 Lounge in waters off untouched sand islands in the **Parque Natural da Ria Formosa** (p151)

3 Explore the inner Algarve on foot, by bicycle or in a car, especially the villages of **Alte** and **Salir** in and around **Serra do Caldeirão**

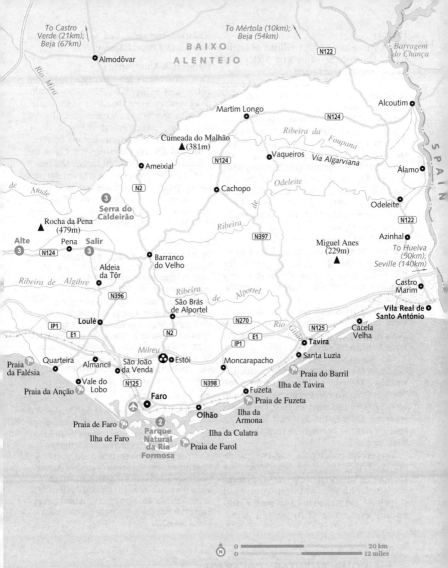

To Castro
Verde (21km);
Beja (67km)

To Mértola (10km);
Beja (54km)

BAIXO
ALENTEJO

N122

Barragem
do Chança

Almodôvar

Rio Mira

Alcoutim

Martim Longo

N124

Cumeada do Malhão
▲(381m)

Ribeira da Foupana

Vaqueiros

Via Algarviana

Álamo

S
P
A
I
N

Ameixial

N124

de Ave

de

Cachopo

Odeleite

N2

Odeleite

3
Serra do
Caldeirão

de

Ribeira

N122

▲ Rocha da Pena
(479m)

Alte
3
N124

Pena

Salir
3

N397

Miguel Anes
(229m)
▲

Azinhal

To Huelva
(50km);
Seville (140km)

Ribeira de Algibre

Aldeia
da Tôr

N396

Barranco
do Velho

Ribeira

de Alportel

Castro
Marim

IP1
E1

Loulé

São Brás
de Alportel

N270

Rio Guadiana

N125

Vila Real de
Santo António

N2

E1
IP1

Tavira

Cacela
Velha

Milreu

Quarteira

Almancil

Estói

Santa Luzia

Praia
da Falésia

São João
da Venda

Moncarapacho

Praia do Barril

Vale do
Lobo

N125

Faro

N398

Fuzeta

Ilha de Tavira

Praia da Anção

Praia de Fuzeta

Olhão

Ilha da
Armona

Praia de Faro

Ilha de Faro

2
Parque
Natural
da Ria
Formosa

Ilha da Culatra

Praia de Farol

N

0   20 km
0   12 miles

4 Find your inner hedonist at
the beaches and nightclubs of
Lagos (p175)

5 Unwind in the spas of
Monchique (p192) after hiking
in the surrounding hills

History

The Algarve has a long tradition of settlement. Phoenicians came first and established trading posts some 3000 years ago, followed by the Carthaginians. Next came the industrious Romans, who, during their 400-year stay, grew wheat, barley and grapes and built roads and palaces. Check out the remains of Milreu (p149), near Faro.

Then came the Visigoths and, in 711, the North African Moors. They stayed 500 years, but later Christians obliterated what they could, leaving little trace of the era. Many place names come from this time, easily recognised by the article 'al' (eg Albufeira, Aljezur, Alcoutim). The Syrian Moors called the region in which they settled (east of Faro to Seville, Spain) 'al-Gharb al-Andalus' (western Andalucía), later known as 'Algarve'. Another Arabic legacy is the flat-roofed house, originally used to dry almonds, figs and corn, and to escape the night heat.

Trade, particularly in nuts and dried fruit, boomed, and Silves was the mighty Moorish capital, quite independent of the large Muslim emirate to the east.

The Reconquista (Christian reconquest) began in the early 12th century, with the wealthy Algarve as the ultimate goal. Though Dom Sancho I captured Silves and territories to the west in 1189, the Moors returned. Only in the first half of the 13th century did the Portuguese claw their way back for good.

Two centuries later the Algarve had its heyday. Prince Henry the Navigator chose the appropriately end-of-the-earth Sagres as the base for his school navigation, and had ships built and staffed in Lagos for the 15th-century exploration of Africa and Asia – seafaring triumphs that turned Portugal into a major imperial power.

Dangers & Annoyances

This is Portugal's most touristed area, and petty theft is prevalent. Never leave valuables unattended in the car or on the beach.

Swimmers beware temperamental coast conditions, especially on the west coast. This means dangerous ocean currents, strong winds and sometimes fog. Check the coloured flags: chequered means the beach is unattended, red means don't even dip your toe in, yellow means wade but don't swim, and green means wade or swim. Blue is an international symbol that means the beach is smashing – safe, clean, good facilities.

ℹ Information

INTERNET RESOURCES Far and away the best of many websites is www.visitalgarve.pt, with information on hidden beaches, upcoming events and festivals, activities and more.

MEDIA The monthly *Algarve Guide* covers what's on, as does the quarterly *Welcome to the Algarve*. Major towns often have a monthly *Agenda Cultural* magazine. *Algarve Tourist Yellow Pages* is another freebie, with town maps and local information. Useful for up-to-date tips on local spots are privately produced free maps, often available at resorts, bars and shops.

ℹ Getting Around

A good bus network runs along the Algarve and to Loulé. From here, you can access inland Algarve, although services become more limited. Eva Transportes and Renex are the two main companies (see the boxed text, p141). Most main towns have reliable car-hire outlets (some are listed in this chapter). Trains run along the coast between Faro and Vila Real de Santo António, and Faro and Lagos (and Loulé). Express trains run to/from the region's main towns to Lisbon.

ℹ COMPLEMENTARY COVERAGE

The Associação Turismo do Algarve (Algarve Tourism Association; www.visitalgarve.pt) has strongly branded tourist offices in main destinations in the Algarve. These, along with some municipal tourist offices, dole out information, maps and free leaflets, much of it on the Algarve. The Association has produced some excellent, full-colour **information guides** covering the Algarve – everything from wine trips, driving routes, best beaches and the Via Algarviana walking track, among others. These are available from the association's tourist offices for €7 (with the exception of the full-colour waterproof diving booklet; €20) and are a handy complement to the **Lonely Planet** guide if you want to explore a bit further.

For local town information, don't overlook the municipal tourist offices (listed in this chapter where relevant), which often have better local information.

BUSSING IT

Two big bus companies, **Eva Transportes** (☏289 899 700; www.eva-bus.com) and **Rede Expressos** (☏707 22 33 44; www.rede-expressos.pt) zip frequently between the Algarve and elsewhere in Portugal. Smaller lines include Renex and Frota Azul. If you're travelling by bus, consider buying Eva's **Passe Turístico** (€25.50), available from major bus stations and good for three days of unlimited travel on most main routes in one direction with Eva Transportes, and on Frota Azul between Lagos and Loulé. Bus service slows down considerably on weekends – particularly on Sunday.

Faro

POP 58,000

Algarve's capital has a more distinctly Portuguese feel than most resort towns. Many visitors only pass through this underrated town – it makes an enjoyable stopover. It has an attractive marina, well-maintained parks and plazas and a historic old town full of pedestrian lanes and outdoor cafes. Its student population of 8000 ensures a happening nightlife, and its theatre scene is strong. Marvellously preserved medieval quarters harbour curious museums, churches and a bone chapel. The lagoons of the Parque Natural da Ria Formosa and nearby beaches, including the island sands of Ilha de Faro to the southwest and Ilha da Barreta (aka Ilha Deserta) to the south, add to Faro's allure.

History

After the Phoenicians and Carthaginians, Faro boomed as the Roman port Ossonoba. During the Moorish occupation, it became the cultured capital of an 11th-century principality.

Afonso III took the town in 1249 – making it the last major Portuguese town to be recaptured from the Moors – and walled it.

Portugal's first printed works – books in Hebrew made by a Jewish printer – came from Faro in 1487.

A city from 1540, Faro had a brief golden age that slunk to a halt in 1596, during Spanish rule. Troops under the Earl of Essex, en route to England from Spain in 1597, plundered the city and carried off hundreds of priceless theological works from the bishop's palace, now part of the Bodleian Library in Oxford.

Battered Faro was rebuilt, only to be shattered by an earthquake in 1722 and then almost flattened in 1755. Most of what you see today was built postquake, though the historic centre largely survived. In 1834 Faro became the Algarve's capital.

◉ Sights & Activities

Cidade Velha   HISTORIC SITE, CATHEDRAL

Within medieval walls, the picturesque Cidade Velha (Old Town) consists of winding, peaceful cobbled streets and squares, reconstructed in a melange of styles following successive batterings – first by marauding British and then two big earthquakes.

Enter through the neoclassical **Arco da Vila**, built by order of Bishop Francisco Gomes, Faro's answer to the Marquês de Pombal (see p480), who oversaw Faro's reconstruction after the 1755 earthquake. The top of the street opens onto the orange-tree-lined Largo da Sé, with the *câmara municipal* (town hall) on the left, the Paço Episcopal (Bishop's Palace) on the right and the ancient *sé* (cathedral) in front of you.

The *sé* (admission €3; ◷10am-5pm Mon-Fri Dec-Feb, to 6pm Jun-Aug, 10am-1pm Sat) was completed in 1251, on what was probably the site of a Roman temple, then a Visigoth cathedral and then a Moorish mosque. Only the tower gate and several chapels remain of the original Romanesque-Gothic exterior – the rest was devoured in 1755. It was rebuilt in a polygamy of Gothic, Renaissance and baroque styles, with intense gilded carving alongside elaborate tilework inside. The baroque organ is worth noting. Climb up to the rooftop *miradouro* (lookout) for views across the pretty walled town to the sea. If you're lucky, you might see storks nesting in the bell towers. The cathedral buildings also house the **Museu Capitular**, with an assortment of sacred artwork (vestments, chalices, saint statues in glass boxes), and a small 18th-century shrine built of bones to remind you of your mortality.

Facing the cathedral is the 18th-century **Paço Episcopal** (no longer open to visitors), with a pointy roof and finished in multicoloured *azulejos* (hand-painted tiles); it's the successor to the previous Episcopal dwelling trashed by British troops in

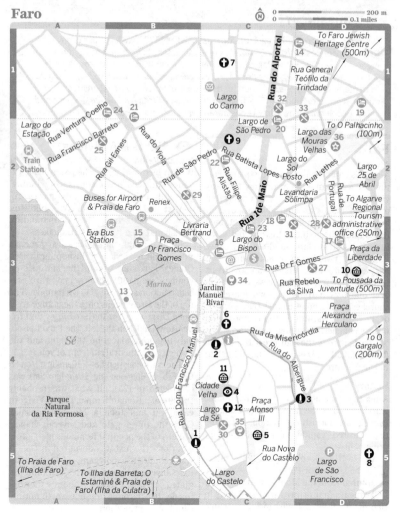

1596. At the southern end of the square is a small 15th-century town gate, the **Arco da Porta Nova**, leading to the ferry pier.

Next to the cathedral is the stately 16th-century **Convento de Nossa Senhora da Assunção**, now housing the Museu Municipal, also known by its former name, Museu Arqueológico (p143).

Also nearby is **Trem Municipal Gallery of Art** (Rua do Trem; admission free; ⊘10am-6pm Tue-Fri, 10.30am-5pm Sat & Sun). This attractively converted building houses temporary exhibitions by known locals and international artists – painters, photogra-phers, installation artists and sculptors. It's worth popping in here to see what's on.

From here you can leave the old town through the medieval **Arco de Repouso** (Gate of Rest) – apparently Afonso III, after taking Faro from the Moors, put his feet up and heard Mass nearby. Around the gateway are some of the town walls' oldest sections – Afonso III's improvements on the Moorish defences.

Igreja de Nossa Senhora do Carmo & Capela dos Ossos CHURCH
(Our Lady of Carmel; Largo do Carmo; ⊘10am-1pm & 3-5.30pm Mon-Fri Dec-Feb, to 6pm Jun-

Aug, 10am-1pm Sat) The twin-towered, baroque Igreja de Nossa Senhora do Carmo was completed in 1719 under João V and paid for (and gilded to death inside) with Brazilian gold. The facade was completed after the 1755 earthquake.

A more ghoulish attraction lies behind the church. The 19th-century **Capela dos Ossos** (admission €1) was built from the bones and skulls of over a thousand monks as a blackly reverent reminder of earthly impermanence, and the ultimate in recycling. There's a similar chapel at Évora (p201).

For more dazzling woodwork, head to the frenzied 18th-century baroque interior of the **Igreja de São Francisco** (Largo de São Francisco; ⊙Mass 6.30pm), with tiles depicting the life of St Francis.

The 16th-century **Igreja de Misericórdia** (not open to the public), opposite Arco da Vila, has a remarkable Manueline portico, the only remnant of an earlier chapel to withstand the 1755 earthquake.

At the southern end of Largo do Carmo is the 16th-century **Igreja de São Pedro** (⊙10am-1pm & 3-5pm Mon-Sat). The plain exterior hides an interesting interior of 18th-century *azulejos* and fine-carved woodwork.

Museu Municipal   MUSEUM
(⊋289 897 400; Largo Dom Afonso III; adult/ student €3/1.50; ⊙10am-6pm Tue-Fri, 10.30am-5pm Sat & Sun) Faro's domed and splendid 16th-century Renaissance Convento de Nossa Senhora da Assunção, in what was once the Jewish quarter, houses the Museu Municipal, formerly called the Museu Arqueológico. Highlights are the 3rd-century *Mosaic of the Ocean,* found in 1976 on a building site; 9th- to 13th-century domestic Islamic artefacts; and works by a notable Faro painter, Carlos Filipe Porfírio, depicting local legends. Ask for the informative pamphlets in English about some of the exhibits, including the interesting *Paths of the Roman Algarve,* an atmospheric display of large rocks and plinths,

and *Walks Around the Historic Centre (The Inward Village)*.

Faro Jewish Heritage Centre

JEWISH CEMETERY

(☑289 829 525; www.farojewishheritagecentre.org; ◷9.30am-12.30pm & 2-5pm) The last vestiges of the first post-Inquisition Jewish presence in Portugal are found at the extraordinary Jewish cemetery, which has 76 beautiful marble gravestones. The small site also has a tiny museum and recreated synagogue (complete with a reconstructed wedding). Interested parties can ring in advance to arrange a guide. The centre is located north of town, near the Faro hospital; local buses (*circuito* bus 3) leave from in front of the Eva terminal. Alight at the Rotunda de Bombeiros bus stop and cross the road, the Estrada da Penha.

Museu Regional do Algarve

MUSEUM

(☑289 827 610; Praça da Liberdade; adult/concession €1.50/1; ◷9am-1.30pm & 2.30-6pm Mon-Fri) Elements of old peasant life – such as a small fishing boat and a wooden water cart (used until the owner's death in 1974) – are on display at the Museu Regional do Algarve, plus ceramics, fabrics and dioramas of typical interiors. Labelling is scarce – basic written information is available in English and other languages.

Beaches

The town's beach, Praia de Faro, with miles of sweeping sand, windsurfing operators and some cafes, is on the Ilha de Faro, 10km away. It's crammed in July and August. Take bus 14 or 16 from opposite the bus station (€1.65, half-hourly June to August, via the airport). Ferries go out to Praia de Farol (Ilha da Culatra) and Ilha da Barreta (aka Ilha Deserta; see p149), a stunning, remote and long narrow strip of sand just off the mainland. Here, you will find ☑O Estaminé (☑917 811 856), a new environmentally friendly restaurant built on boardwalks and run by solar power.

Tours

Formosamar

BOAT TRIPS, BIRDWATCHING

(☑289 817 466, 967 073 846; www.formosamar.pt, www.lands.pt; Clube Naval, Faro Marina) Ria Formosa and Lands are highly recommended outfits working under the name Formosamar to genuinely embrace and promote environmentally responsible tourism. Among the excellent tours it provides are two-hour birdwatching trips around the Parque Natural da Ria Formosa (see p151; €25, minimum four people), 2½-hour guided cycling tours (€17) and numerous guided walking tours inland from Faro. Accompanying guides may include a marine biologist and raptor specialist. Its two-hour boat trips take small boats (up to eight people) in some of the narrower channels in the lagoon (€20), providing participants with a close-to-nature experience.

Natura

BOAT TRIPS

(☑918 056 674; www.natura-algarve.com) Another recommended eco-responsible operator, offering a range of activities from all-day boat tours with a focus on birdwatching, or the region's fishing history (with visits to fish markets) or the islands (each tour including lunch €60; minimum four people). Other trips include two-hour dolphin-watching experiences (€30) and exploring inland Algarve, including Serra Caldeirão and sections of the Via Algarviana (see the boxed text, p145).

Animaris

BOAT TRIPS

(Ilha Deserta; ☑917 811 856; www.ilha-deserta.com) Offers more basic, short trips in the area; see p149.

GETTING YOUR HEAD (& BODY) AROUND THE ALGARVE

The Algarve coastline is 155km long, with five regions: the leeward coast (Sotavento), from Vila Real de Santo António to Faro, largely fronted by a chain of sandy offshore *ilhas* (islands); the central coast, from Faro to Portimão, featuring the heaviest resort development; the increasingly rocky windward coast (or Barlavento), from Lagos to Sagres, culminating in the wind-scoured grandeur of the Cabo de São Vicente, Europe's southwesternmost corner; and the hilly, thickly green interior, which rises to two high mountain ranges, the Serra de Monchique and less-visited Serra do Caldeirão. The Costa do Ouro (Golden Coast) borders the Costa de Sagres (Bay of Sagres), while the Costa Vicentina stretches north of here on the windy, wild rim of a national park.

Covering some of the most beautiful scenery in the Algarve, the 300km Via Algarviana walking trail crosses the breadth of Portugal from Alcoutim to Cabo de São Vicente, taking in the wooded hillsides of the Serras de Caldeirão and Monchique. It takes about 14 days to walk the trail. You may hear the contrary, but a local resident who completed the trail in May 2010 assures us that the Via Algarviana is definitely *not* yet fully marked and some signs have been vandalised. New military maps are accurate. The best times to walk the trail are between March and May (note: hunting season takes place on Thursday and Sunday from October to June – *do not walk* on these days). For more information, visit www.viaalgarviana.org (run by environmental group Almargem) or www.algarveway.com (a private website run by enthusiasts). The official Via Algarviana route booklet (€7) is available from the Algarve Tourist Association's tourist offices.

Cyclists might like to check out Algarve Tourism's Ecovia do Litoral, a cycling route that links Cabo de São Vicente and Sagres in the west to Vila Real de São António on the Spanish border. Spanning 214km, it encompasses both secondary roads and rural paths across 12 Algarve municipalities. The initiative was launched in 2008, but at the time of writing, several municipalities were still officially approving their patches and signage was poor in some parts – so to save a bumpy (or traffic-clogged) ride, check with tourism authorities before heading out.

⚑ Festivals & Events

Festival Internacional de Música do Algarve MUSIC

(FIMA) Brings together an impressive range of international artists who perform in Faro's Teatro Lethes and the modern Teatro Figuras. Usually between April and June.

FolkFaro FOLK

The city's big folk festival features lots of dance (with local and international folk groups), live music and street fests. It's held in late August over a week at various venues around town.

Feira de Santa Iria RELIGIOUS

In late October Faro's biggest traditional event honours St Irene with fairground rides, stalls and entertainment. It takes place in a temporary fairground to the northeast, by the municipal fire station.

🛏 Sleeping

Unless stated otherwise, rates for the budget options listed here do not include breakfast. Outside high season, prices can halve.

Hotel Faro HOTEL €€€

(☎289 830 830; www.hotelfaro.pt; Praça Dr Francisco Gomes 2; s €136-156, d €171; ❉) We're not sure how this modern cubist block made it past the town planners. But it has comfortable, sleek rooms with large beds and marble-filled bathrooms and flat-screen TVs. The small top-floor bar-restaurant with terrace is great for a sunset cocktail.

Hotel Eva HOTEL €€€

(☎289 001 000; www.tdhotels.pt; Av da República 1; s/d/ste €140/170/250; ❉❂❄) This 134-room hotel has spacious, pleasant rooms. Those facing east have balconies and views. There's a rooftop swimming pool for more marina-gazing. An extra €15 gets you a more upmarket 'superior' room – worth it for the extra space, but there's no balcony.

Hotel Residencial Sun Algarve HOTEL €€

(☎289 895 700; www.residencialalgarve.com; Rua Infante Dom Henrique 52; s/d/tr €60/75/90; ⓟ@) This efficiently run hotel has 38 bright, spick-and-span motel-style rooms, some with balconies. Parking costs €5 per night.

Hotel Santa Maria HOTEL €€€

(☎289 898 080; www.jcr-group.com; Rua de Portugal, 17; s €91-98, d €107-120) Don't be fooled by the exterior of this plain hotel. Renovated in 2006, this modern motel-style option offers clean rooms with contemporary, stylish decor, though rooms are cramped. Low-season prices are significantly cheaper.

Residencial Oceano GUEST HOUSE €€

(☎289 805 591; Travessa Ivens 21; s/d/tr €37/47/61) This simple and friendly option has tidy rooms with tiled floors. Some rooms are stuffy. There's a very steep, tile-lined stairway.

FINDING A BED

During July and August, thousands of Portuguese and foreign visitors flock to the Algarve. Faro airport – the region's main transport hub – experiences tens of daily inbound and outbound flights a day. During this time, most visitors have prebooked package accommodation. For the independent traveller, it can be tricky to front up and expect to find a bed with no reservations; try and reserve a night or two in advance. Prices, too, are at their highest (as listed in this chapter). In most places you can expect to pay considerably less in *mais tranquilo* (quieter) times. Check hotel websites for special deals.

Residencial Adelaide   GUEST HOUSE €€
(☎289 802 383; www.adelaideresidencial.
net; Rua Cruz dos Mestres 9; s/d incl breakfast
€40/50; 🅿️📶) This modern and pleasant guest house is good value. It has slightly worn but clean and light rooms, some with terraces and all with cable TV. A cheap laundry service is available.

Pensão Residencial Central GUEST HOUSE €€
(☎289 807 291; Largo do Bispo 12; s €40, d €50-55) The eight rooms at this small guest house are cool and tiled, and vary in size. Those rooms with balconies overlook the pretty square; rooms at the back are quieter.

São Filipe Hospedária   GUEST HOUSE €€
(☎/fax 289 824 182; www.guesthouse-saofilipe
.com; Rua Infante Dom Henrique 55; s/d/tr
€45/55/65; 🅿️📶) The 11 rooms in this friendly guest house are small but shipshape. Great out-of-season deals available.

Residencial Dandy   GUEST HOUSE €€
(☎289 824 791; Rua Filipe Alistão 62; s with shared bathroom €35, d with/without bathroom from €55/40) Find pot plants, plastic flowers, African masks and museum-style paraphernalia at rambling Residencial Dandy. The owner has personality, too. The best of the 18 rooms have antique furniture, high ceilings and wrought-iron balconies. Smaller, tile-floored rooms are in the back.

Hotel Dom Bernardo   HOTEL €€€
(☎289 889 800; www.hoteldombernardo.com;
Rua General Teófilo da Trindade 20; s/d incl break-
fast from €91/150; 🅿️📶) Part of the Best Western chain, Dom Bernardo's rooms are spotless and modern, if a little 'a là the '80s' (although some rooms have been renovated). Prices are significantly less in low season; beware – it's a popular group option.

Pousada da Juventude   HOSTEL €
(☎289 826 521; www.pousadasjuventude.pt; Rua da Polícia de Segurança Pública; dm incl breakfast €14, d with/without bathroom €40/32) Part of the Instituto Português da Juventude, this hostel adjoins a small park. It offers basic clean rooms with no frills and is a good ultrabudget option. Reception is open 24 hours.

Pensão Residencial Oliveira GUEST HOUSE €
(☎289 812 154; Rua Horta Machado 28; d/tr without bathroom from €30/45) In real-estate terms, this place (and its owner) has character. The eight well-worn rooms are cluttered and have flowery bedspreads and floral odours.

Eating

Several midrange eateries are clustered around Praça Ferreira de Almeida. They serve similar fare in similar settings, mainly to tourists. Faro's big, daily *mercado municipal* (municipal market) is in Largo Mercado.

Adega Nova   PORTUGUESE €€
(Rua Francisco Barreto 24; mains €6-16; ⏱lunch & dinner) This popular place buzzes with tourists and country charm. It has a lofty beamed ceiling, rustic cooking implements on display and long, communal tables and bench seats. The meat and fish dishes are reliable and service is efficient.

O Palhacinho   PORTUGUESE €€
(Largo Dr Francisco Sá Carneiro; mains €8-13; ⏱7am-midnight Mon-Fri, lunch Sat) Located within the market complex, this unfancy yet treat of a place is frequented by everyone and anyone, including – we are told – the town's lawyers. It serves traditional Portuguese cuisine – fish and meat dishes – in a pleasant, airy environment. Generous and tasty plates of the day are around €8.

Gengibre e Canela   VEGETARIAN €
(Travessa da Mota 10; buffet €7.50; ⏱lunch Mon-Sat; 🅿️) Give the taste buds a break from meat and fish dishes, and veg out (literally) at this Zen-like vegetarian restaurant. The buffet changes daily; there may be vegetable lasagne, *feijoada* (bean casserole) and tofu dishes.

Gardy
PATISSERIE €

(Rua de Santo António 16 & 33; mains €3-10; ☺all day Mon-Sat) The place to head for your patisserie fix and *the* place to be seen. Has a wide variety of homemade specialities.

Restaurante A Taska
PORTUGUESE €€

(Rua do Alportel 38; mains €10-15; ☺lunch & dinner Mon-Sat) This cosy, busy trattoria-style restaurant serves delicious regional food such as *xarém* (corn meal), and has daily specials on a blackboard.

O Gargalo
ITALIAN €€

(Largo do Pé da Cruz; mains €7-15; ☺lunch & dinner Wed-Mon) Hefty portions of pasta and pizza – with an occasional Portuguese influence – come out of Mama's kitchen at this large but enjoyable place. Served by smart, multilingual waiters.

Faro e Benfica Restaurante
SEAFOOD €€

(Marina; mains €10-20; ☺lunch & dinner) Candle-lit at night, with a marina setting, big open windows and a plant-filled terrace, this is a slightly upmarket, romantic seafood choice.

Mesa dos Mouros
PORTUGUESE, INTERNATIONAL €€€

(☎966 784 536; Largo da Sé 10; mains €11-18; ☺lunch & dinner Mon-Sat) With cosy indoor seating and a small outdoor terrace right by the cathedral, this place is blessed with high-quality cuisine (as confirmed by us and the comments book!). Excellent choices include the seafood dishes or hearty gourmet-style mains such as rabbit with chestnuts.

La Pizza
ITALIAN €€

(Travessa José Coelho 13; mains €6.50-13; ☺lunch & dinner) On a narrow pedestrian lane near the bars (follow your nose), this small pizzeria whips up delicious tasty thin-crust pizzas plus other dishes.

Algartalhos (Largo do Carmo) and small **Minipreço** (Praça Ferreira de Almeida 8) are centrally located supermarkets.

🍷 Drinking

Faro's student-driven nightlife clusters around Rua do Prior and surrounding alleys, with bars and clubs open most days till late, though things pick up considerably on weekends.

Taverna da Sé
BAR

(Praça Afonso III 26; ☺11am-2am Mon-Sat) This small in-crowd taverna in the old town comes alive at night. There are some outdoor tables in its very quaint square.

Columbus Bar
BAR

(Rua Dr Francisco Gomes) A popular place for drinks, parties, music and events.

☆ Entertainment

Estádio Intermunicipal do Algarve
SPORTS

(www.parquecidades-eim.pt) This 30,000-seat, state-of-the-art football stadium, built for Euro 2004, is located at São João da Venda, 8km northwest of Faro. Here you can watch Faro's own team, SC Farense, and Loulé's Louletano.

Teatro Lethes
THEATRE

(☎289 820 300; www.teatrolethes.pt; Rua Lethes) This tiny and exquisite Italianate theatre hosts drama, music and dance performances. Adapted into a theatre in 1874 (from a building dating to 1603), it was once the Jesuit Colégio de Santiago Maior and is now owned by the Portuguese Cruz Vermelha (Red Cross). Ask the tourist office for a list of what's on. Other performances are often held in the modern Teatro Figuras.

ℹ Information

Emergency & Medical Services
Hospital de Gambelas (☎289 892 000; www.hpalg.com; Largo de Camões) Faro's newest private hospital

Police station (☎289 822 022; Rua da Polícia de Segurança Pública 32) Around 100m southeast of Praça da Liberdade, before the Youth Hostel

Tourist support line (☎808 781 212)

Internet Access
Free wi-fi connection is available in Jardim Manuel Bivar and Alameda João de Deus.

Café Aliança (Rua Dr Francisco Gomes; per hr €2.50; ☺8am-10pm Mon-Sat)

Money
Cotacâmbios/Western Union (☎289 822 044; Av da República 16; ☺9am-8pm) A private exchange bureau. Also located at the airport.

Post
Main post office (Largo do Carmo)

Tourist Information
Algarve Regional Tourism administrative office (☎289 800 400; www.visitalgarve.pt; Av 5 de Outubro 18; ☺9am-12.30pm & 2-5.30pm Mon-Fri) Provides a map and leaflets of the region.

Faro Tourist Office (☎289 800 400; www.visitalgarve.pt, www.cm-faro.pt; Rua da Misericórdia 8; ☺9.30am-1pm & 2-5.30pm

THE ALGARVE

MARKET MANIA

Look out for local specialities – warm woollens, brassware and Moorish-influenced ceramics – at the region's many local, buzzy markets:

Every Saturday Loulé, São Brás de Alportel
Every Wednesday Quarteira
First Saturday Lagos
First Sunday Almancil, Azinhal, Olhão-Fuseta, Portimão
First Monday Portimão
First and third Tuesday Albufeira
Second Friday Monchique
Third Monday Aljezur, Silves
Third Thursday Alte

Mon-Fri Dec-Feb, 9.30am-7pm Jun-Aug) Run by the regional tourism administrative office, this efficient, busy and helpful place offers information on Faro.

Turismo de Aeroporto Internacional (289 818 582; ⊗8am-11.30pm) Based at the airport; good for basic information on arrival.

🛈 Getting There & Away
Air

For international services, see p527.

Portugália and TAP (Air Portugal) have multiple daily Lisbon–Faro flights (40 minutes) and Lisbon–Porto flights (45 minutes).

For flight inquiries call the **airport** (general inquiries 289 800 800, flight information 289 800 801). An office of **TAP** (707 205 700; www.tap.pt) is located at the airport.

Bus

Buses arrive at and depart from **Eva bus station** (289 899 760; www.eva-bus.com; Av da República 5). Eva services run to Seville in Spain (€16, 4½ hours, four daily) via Huelva (€12, 3½ hours).

Renex (289 812 980; ⊗9-11.15am & 1.30-8pm Mon-Sat, 12.30-8pm Sun), located opposite the bus terminal, has express coaches to Lisbon (€19, five hours, at least hourly). Tickets for the Renex Lisbon express bus cost €18, eight daily. For Sagres, change at Lagos.

Services include:

Vila Real de Santo António (€5, 1¾ hours, six to nine daily) Via Tavira (€3.15, one hour)

Albufeira (€4.20, 1¼ hours, at least hourly) Some go on to Portimão (€5, 1½ hours, seven daily weekdays, four daily weekends) and Lagos (€5.35, 1¾ hours)

Olhão (€1.75, 20 minutes, every 20 minutes weekdays)

São Bras de Alportel (€3.55, 35 minutes, nine daily) Via Estói (€2.75, 15 minutes)

Car

The most direct route from Lisbon to Faro takes about five hours. A alternative to the motorway is the often-traffic-clogged N125. Tollways on this route cost around €18.

Major car-rental agencies are at the airport:

Auto Rent (free call 800 212 011, 289 818 580; www.autorent.pt) In a small office located in the car park, bay 4.

Gerin (289 800 883; www.guerin.pt)

Auto Jardim (289 800 881; www.auto-jardim.com)

Faro's easiest parking is in Largo de São Francisco (free).

Train

There are trains from Lisbon (€18.50 to €21, three to 3¾ hours, five daily); 1st-class fares are slightly higher. You can also get to Porto (€50, six to eight hours, three daily), sometimes changing at Lisbon.

Regional services include the following:

Albufeira (€2.50, 30 minutes, 11 daily)

Vila Real de Santo António (€4.15, 1¼ hours, 10 daily) Via Olhão (€1.05, 10 minutes).

Lagos (€5.85, 1¾ hours, nine daily, fewer on weekends)

Loulé (€1.40, 20 minutes, 10 daily)

🛈 Getting Around
To/From the Airport

Eva (289 899 740; www.eva-bus.com) buses 14 and 16 run to the bus station (€1.65, 20 minutes, half-hourly June to August, every two hours on weekends December to February). From here it's an easy stroll to the centre.

A taxi into town costs between €10 and €12 (20% more after 10pm and on weekends; €1.60 for each luggage item).

Bicycle

You can rent bikes (including kids' bikes) from **Formosamar** (/fax 289 817 466, 967 073 846;

www.formosamar.pt; Clube Naval, Faro Marina; per hr/day €2.50/12).

Boat

From May to September, **Ilha Deserta** (Animaris; ☑917 811 856; www.ilha-deserta.com) operates four ferries a day to/from Ilha da Barreta (€5 one way). The same company also runs 2½-hour year-round boat trips (€20) through Parque Natural da Ria Formosa (p151). Boats leave from the pier next to Arco da Porta Nova. Taxi boats also operate from here, or from the nautical centre.

Taxi

Ring for a **taxi** (☑289 895 790) or find one at the taxi rank outside the train station.

Milreu & Estói

Ten kilometres north of Faro, the Roman ruins at Milreu make a pleasant brief excursion. Several hundred metres up the road is the sleepy but attractive village of Estói, which boasts a charming derelict 18th-century rococo palace and gardens, some of which has been recently renovated into a posh *pousada* (inn).

⊙ Sights

Milreu Ruins   ROMAN RUINS
(adult/under 25yr €2/1; ⊙10.30am-1pm & 2-6.30pm May-Sep, 9.30am-1pm & 2-5pm Oct-Apr) Set in beautiful countryside, the ruins of this grand Roman villa provide a rare opportunity to gain insight into Roman life. The 1st-century-AD ruins reveal the characteristic form of a peristyle villa, with a gallery of columns around a courtyard. In the surrounding rooms geometric motifs and friezes of fish were found.

Tantalising glimpses of the villa's former glory include the **fish mosaics** in the bathing chambers, which are located to the west of the villa's courtyard.

The remains of the bathing rooms include the **apodyterium** (changing room; note the arched niches and benches for clothes and postbath massage) and the **frigidarium**, which had a marble basin to hold cold water for cooling off postbath, and a basin with stunning fish mosaics.

Other luxuries included underground heating and marble sculptures (now in Faro and Lagos museums).

To the right of the entrance is the site's water sanctuary, a temple devoted to the cult of water. The interior was once decorated with polychrome marble slabs and its exterior with fish mosaics. In the 6th century the late Romans converted it into a church, adding a baptismal font and a small mausoleum, and in the 8th century it was converted into a mosque. In the 10th century it collapsed, possibly due to an earthquake, and the site was abandoned. In the 15th century, a rural house was constructed within the abandoned site (the house you see today).

🛏 Sleeping & Eating

The recently-reopened, rococo-style **Pousada do Palácio de Estoi** (☑289 990 150; www.pousadas.pt; d €290) provides a luxurious stay. The incredible Versailles-style gardens are currently being restored.

Simple local cafes front Estói's small main square. Alternatively, **V Terra** (☑912 447 051; Sítio do Guelhim; mains €8-20; ⊙lunch & dinner Mon-Fri, dinner Sat), a cheery spot next to the old Roman bridge at Milreu, serves a range of changing international dishes. There's a sunny terrace on the top floor.

❶ Getting There & Away

Buses run from Faro to Estói, passing through Milreu (€2.10, 20 minutes, four to 10 buses daily Monday to Friday), continuing to São Brás de Alportel. Estói is nearly 1km from Milreu.

São Brás de Alportel

POP 10,030

Seventeen kilometres north of Faro, this quiet country town provides a welcome break from the coast. São Brás de Alportel has few attractions in the town proper, but it's a pleasant place to stroll. There are some excellent activities in the surrounding area, including walks and a guided cork route. The town was a hot spot in the 19th-century heyday of cork and has stayed true to its agricultural roots. It lies in a valley in the olive-, carob-, fig- and almond-wooded Barrocal region, a lush limestone area sandwiched between the mountains and the sea.

⊙ Sights & Activities

Museu Etnográfico do Trajo Algarvio   MUSEUM
(☑289 846 100; Rua Dr José Dias Sancho 61; admission €2; ⊙10am-1pm & 2-5pm Mon-Fri, 2-5pm Sat, Sun & holidays) This constantly expanding and beautifully maintained museum, 200m east of the Largo (along the Tavira

(OVER)EXPOSING THE ALGARVE

Tourism accounts for 80% of Portugal's GDP, and much of this comes from the Algarve. Tourists are not international travellers alone; local visitors comprise a large part of the industry, numerous Portuguese have homes in this sun-kissed region, and many foreigners have moved here permanently. The massive influx of visitors has led to ongoing heavy development in the region – large (mainly concrete) hotels, apartments, shops and restaurants – along much of the Algarve's southern coastline. Some say the Algarve's tourist industry provides work – albeit seasonal – to thousands of people, especially the young, thereby enhancing their skills and improving service mentality. But, others argue, the departure of Portuguese from their villages has devastating consequences – it is causing an irreversible disintegration of traditions and village life. Then there are the obvious environmental problems caused by heavy construction: destruction of coastal areas including cliffs and beaches, pressure on water resources, and the building of major roads. Construction is said to be controlled (although it is not always sensitive to its surrounds).

More recently, tourism authorities have focused their efforts on promoting special-interest activities beyond sun, surf and sand. While this is a positive initiative – with the region's spectacular nature, walks and inland villages being increasingly highlighted – it also means that thousands flock to visit some of the Algarve's 30-plus golf courses. These have a major environmental impact on an already stretched region, although some courses are adopting environmentally friendly maintenance practices.

Visitors to the Algarve should think carefully about their impact on this sensitive region: don't stick only to the coast – head inland (responsibly), be selective about which enterprises you select, and consider the impact of the type of activities you undertake.

The Algarve Tourism Board has some excellent publications to help you get off the beaten track. These include *Rotas: tours around the Algarve* (ideal for those with their own wheels) and *Trails in the Algarve*, which outlines some nature trails and cross-country day (or shorter) hikes. Both cost €7.

road, known as Rua Dr José Dias Sanco), is a labour of love for the curator and Friends of the Museum. It's housed in a former cork magnate's mansion (which is stunning in itself – note the original kitchen). The building displays a rambling collection of local costumes, while the garden has agricultural implements. In the stables, there is a fascinating exhibit, including a video, of the town's once-buoyant cork industry, which is part of the local cork route (see p150 for details of tours organised by the municipality). Very kid-friendly.

Old Town HISTORIC SITES

For a fine stroll, follow Rua Gago Coutinho south from the Largo to the 16th-century **igreja matriz** (parish church), which has breezy views of orange groves and surrounding valleys. Nearby, below what was once a bishop's palace, is **Jardim da Verbena,** a pretty garden with an interesting fountain. Also here is the **municipal swimming pool** (☎289 841 243; ⏱Jun-Sep) and a children's playground.

The **Calćadinha de Sào Brás de Alportel** is an ancient road constructed in Roman times, possibly linking Faro (Ossonoba) with Beja (Pax Julia). It was used by mules and shepherds until the 19th century. You can wander along two branches – one is around 100m, the other 500m. It starts near the **Information Centre** (Centro Explicativo e de Acolhimento da Calçadinha; Rua do Matadouro 2; admission free). The centre provides a text-heavy explanation of the route (in English and Portuguese).

An English-speaking guide from the municipality office takes a fascinating guided tour along a **cork route** (☎960 070 806; www.rotadacortica.pt; per person €15), which includes anything and everything from visiting a traditional cork factory to cork stacks in the surrounding countryside, known as the *barrocal* (limestone) coastal region. Participants learn about the cork industry – from the extraction of cork from the trees to its production, processes and use. Minimum numbers may apply.

Sleeping

Hospedaria São Brás   GUEST HOUSE €

(☑/fax 289 842 213; Rua Luís Bívar 27; s/d €30/50) Around the corner from the bus station (along the Loulé road), this guest house is jam-packed with attractive antiques (note the gramophone), pretty *azulejos* and plants. The delightful owner is happy to show you the full range of eclectic rooms.

Estalagem Sequeira   HOTEL €

(☑289 843 444; fax 289 841 457; Rua Dr Evaristo Gago 9; s/d €35/55) Although its facade is uninspiring and decor a bit dated, this hotel's rooms are decent, with a trim if flowery design.

Eating

Vila Velha   PORTUGUESE €€

(Rua Gago Coutinho 45; mains €13-17; ⊙lunch & dinner Mon-Sat) Just south of the Largo, this warm and intimate restaurant has tasteful decor and a tasty menu of regional specialities such as *lombinho de porco aromatizado come ameixas* (pork with prunes; €14).

Café Regional   PATISSERIE €

(Largo de São Sebastião 7; pastries from €1; ⊙breakfast, lunch & dinner) In the centre of town and overlooking the square, this São Brás institution (it's been around since 1952) sells tasty pastries, made on the premises.

Luís dos Frangos   GRILL HOUSE €

(Estrada de Tavira 8150; mains €5-9; ⊙lunch & dinner Tue-Sun) Five hundred metres east of the Largo (beyond the museum), this is another local institution, famous for its grilled mains – particularly its chicken. It's a large, busy and friendly place.

ⓘ Information

Ponte de Informacão Turística (www.cm
-sbras.pt; ⊙9.30am-12.30pm & 1-6.30pm) The municipality's tourist point, next to the municipal swimming pool and Jardim da Verbena has some excellent resources, including copies of *Percursos Pedestres* (Pedestrian Routes), self-guided walking tours in the surrounding valleys and countryside.

Turismo (☑289 843 165; www.visitalgarve. pt; Largo de São Sebastião; ⊙9.30am-1pm & 2-5.30pm Mon-Fri) Distributes maps and information on the region and town.

ⓘ Getting There & Away

Buses run to/from Faro (via Estói €3.55, 30 minutes, three to 11 daily) and to Loulé (€2.75, 25 minutes, five weekdays).

POP 15,000

A short hop east of Faro, Olhão (pronounced *ol-yowng*) is the Algarve's biggest fishing port, with an active waterfront and pretty, bustling lanes in its old quarters. There aren't many sights, but the flat-roofed Moorish-influenced neighbourhoods and North African feel make it a pleasant place to wander. The town's fish restaurants draw the crowds, as does the morning fish and vegetable market on Av 5 de Outubro, best visited on Saturday.

Olhão is also a springboard for Parque Natural da Ria Formosa's sandy islands, Culatra and Armona, plus the park's environmental centre in Quinta Marim.

⊙ Sights & Activities

Bairro dos Pescadores   NEIGHBOURHOOD

Just back from the market and park is the Bairro dos Pescadores (Fishermen's Quarter), a knot of whitewashed, cubical houses, often with tiled fronts and flat roofs. Narrow lanes thread through the *bairro* (neighbourhood), and there's a definite Moorish influence, probably a legacy of long-standing trade links with North Africa. Similar houses are found in Fuzeta (10km east).

Parque Natural da Ria Formosa   NATURE RESERVE

Ria Formosa Natural Park is mostly a lagoon system stretching for 60km along the Algarve coastline and encompassing 18,000 hectares, from west of Faro to Cacela Velha. It encloses a vast area of *sapal* (marsh), *salinas* (salt pans), creeks and dune islands. To the west there are several freshwater lakes, including those at Ludo and Quinta do Lago; the marshes are an important area for migrating and nesting birds. You can see a huge variety of wetland birds here, along with ducks, shorebirds, gulls and terns. This is the favoured nesting place of the little tern and rare purple gallinule (see the boxed text, p152).

The **park headquarters and visitor interpretation centre** (☑289 700 210; www. icn.pt; Quinta de Marim; ⊙11am-1pm & 2-4pm) is 3km east of Olhão, within the 60-hectare Centro Educação Ambiental de Marim (Environmental Education Centre of Marim; commonly known as Quinta Marim). A 3km nature trail takes you through various ecosystems – dunes, saltmarshes, pine woodlands. If open (this section was closed at the time of research), don't miss visiting

Although not the most fauna-rich region of the country, the Algarve is home to some fascinating wildlife. The purple gallinule (aka the purple swamp-hen or sultan chicken) is one of Europe's rarest and most nattily turned-out birds – a large violet-blue water creature with red bill and legs. In Portugal it only nests in a patch of wetland spilling into the exclusive Quinta do Lago estate, at the western end of the Parque Natural da Ria Formosa, 12km west of Faro. Look for it near the lake at the estate's São Lourenço Nature Trail.

Another bizarre Algarve resident is the Mediterranean chameleon (*Chamaeleo chamaeleon*), a 25cm-long reptile with independently moving eyes, a tongue longer than its body and skin that mimics its environment. It only started creeping around southern Portugal about 75 years ago, and is the only chameleon found in Europe, its habitat limited to Crete and the Iberian Peninsula. Your best chance of seeing this shy creature is on spring mornings in the Quinta Marim area of the Parque Natural da Ria Formosa or in Monte Gordo's conifer woods, now a protected habitat for the species.

Bird-lovers should consider a trip to the Serra do Caldeirão foothills. Approximately 21km northwest of Loulé, the dramatic Rocha da Pena, a 479m-high limestone outcrop, is a classified site because of its rich flora and fauna. Orchids, narcissi and native cistus cover the slopes, where red foxes and Egyptian mongooses are common. Among many bird species seen here are the huge eagle owl, Bonelli's eagle and the buzzard.

There's a *centro ambiental* (environmental centre) in Pena village, and you can walk up to the top of Rocha itself (see the boxed text, p165).

the refuge kennels of the remarkable Portuguese water-dog. These were formerly fishermen's helpers – known for their distinctively matted waterproof coats, they helped herd the fish into nets.

To get to Quinta Marim, take a municipal bus to the camping ground (200m before the visitor centre).

Boat Trips

For around €10 per hour, you can grab a ride on a traditional boat offered by several private boat operators.

Natura-Algarve (☑918 056 674; www.natura-algarve.com; per person 2½hr €25, per day €47-60) offers guided trips with a multilingual guide in a very swish, comfortable boat through the park. A gourmet lunch is provided on longer trips. Different tours focus on the islands, birdwatching, dolphin-spotting and the history of fishing in the area. Children under 10 years are half price. The company also explores the inner Algarve with trips to the Serra do Caldeirão (see p165).

Beaches

Fine beaches, sparsely sprinkled with holiday chalets, include those on the sandbank *ilhas* (islands) of Parque Natural da Ria Formosa: **Ilha de Farol**, **Ilha da Culatra** and

Ilha da Armona. There are ferries to both islands from the pier just east of Jardim Patrão Joaquim Lopes. Unfortunately, at the time of research, much of Ilha Fuzeta had been destroyed due to the heavy December–February rains in 2010.

✹ Festivals & Events

Festival do Marisco, a seafood festival with food and folk music, fills the Jardim Patrão Joaquim Lopes some time in the middle of August.

🛏 Sleeping

There are few places to stay and they fill up quickly in summer.

Pensão Bicuar GUEST HOUSE € (☑289 714 816; www.pension-bicuar.com; Rua Vasco da Gama 5; dm €15, s €30-40, d €40-50, f €50-60) Run by a welcoming Dutch couple, this guest house offers a range of pleasant rooms, featuring old-fashioned details. Some have bathrooms, others don't. It's well serviced with a guests kitchen, a roof terrace and a book exchange. Head to the left (east) of the parish church.

Pensão Bela Vista GUEST HOUSE €€ (☑289 702 538; Rua Teófilo Braga 65; s/d/tr €35/50/60; ✹) A short walk west of the *turismo*, this friendly and efficient place has clean, tiled rooms and a plant-filled courtyard. Some singles don't have a bathroom or external-facing window.

Parque de Campismo de Fuzeta
CAMPGROUND €

(☎289 793 459; camping@jf-fuseta.pt; camp sites per adult/tent/car €3.50/2.80/3.75; ☺year-round) This small, shady municipal site is on the waterfront in peaceful Fuzeta, about 10km east of Olhão.

Camping Olhão
CAMPGROUND €

(☎289 700 300; www.sbsi.pt; camp sites per adult/tent/car €4.10/3/3.30, family bungalows €45; ☒) This large, well-equipped, shady camping ground is 2km east of Olhão. The upside? It's near Quinta Marim. The downside? It's by a train line and trains run between 6.45am and midnight. To get here, you can catch a municipal bus from the bus station.

✖ Eating

Av 5 de Outubro has a market (☺7am-2pm Mon-Sat) and is lined with seafood restaurants open for lunch and dinner (closed in between). Follow your whim – nearly all serve good *cataplanas* (seafood stews) and *xerém* and charge between €7 and €15.

For a departure from the *avenida* seafood scene:

Ta Pronto (Market Bldg, Av 5 de Outubro) Handy because it's open all day, unlike most restaurants, and serves up some good local dishes, including shellfish.

Sabores do Churrasco (Av 5 de Outubro 162) An authentic-as-they-come Brazilian *churrasqueira* and an incredible all-you-can-eat extravaganza – five different kinds of grilled meats for €7 or, for an even greater protein injection, 12 kinds for €11.

❶ Information

Espaço Internet (Rua Teófilo Braga; ☺10am-1.30pm & 3-6.30pm Mon-Fri) Free internet access.

Centro de saúde (health centre; ☎289 700 260; Rua Associação Chasfa)

Police (☎289 710 770; Av 5 de Outubro 176)

Post office (☎289 700 600; Av da República) A block north of the parish church, opposite a bank with an ATM.

Turismo (☎289 713 936; Largo Sebastião Martins Mestre; ☺9.30am-7pm May-Sep, 9.30am-1pm & 2-5.30pm Mon-Fri) In the centre of the pedestrian zone; from the bus station bear right at the fork beside the parish church.

❶ Getting There & Away

Bus
Eva (www.eva-bus.com) express buses run to Lisbon (€19, four hours, four to five daily), as do **Renex** (Av da República 101).

Buses run frequently to/from Faro (€1.75, 20 minutes), some continuing to the waterfront at Bairro dos Pescadores, and from Tavira (€2.40, 40 minutes).

Train
Regular trains connect to Faro (€1.05, 10 minutes, every one to two hours) or east to Fuzeta (€1.05, 10 minutes) and Tavira (€1.75, 30 minutes).

❶ Getting Around

Handy municipal buses run 'green and yellow routes' around town, including to the camp site and supermarkets.

Ferries run out to the *ilhas* from the pier at the eastern end of Jardim Patrão Joaquim Lopes. Boats run to Ilha da Armona (€3.10 return, 15 minutes, at least nine daily June to mid-September, hourly July and August, four daily mid-September to May); the last trip back from Armona in July and August leaves at 8.30pm.

Boats also go to Ilha da Culatra (€3.60, 30 minutes) and Praia de Farol (€3.70, one hour), with six daily from June to September and four daily from mid-September to May.

Tavira

POP 12,600

Set on either side of the meandering Rio Gilão, Tavira is a charming town. The ruins of a hilltop castle, an old Roman bridge and a smattering of Gothic and Renaissance churches are among Tavira's historic attractions. Its enticing assortment of restaurants and guest houses makes it an excellent base for exploring the Algarve's eastern section.

Tavira is ideal for wandering; the warren of cobblestone streets hides pretty, historic gardens and shady plazas. There's a small, active fishing port and a modern market. Only 3km from the coast, Tavira is the launching point for the stunning, unspoilt beaches of Ilha de Tavira.

If you're arriving by public transport, the bus station is a 200m walk west of central Praça da República while the train station is on the southern edge of town, 1km from the centre.

History
The Roman settlement of Balsa was just down the road from Tavira, near Santa Luzia (3km west). The seven-arched bridge

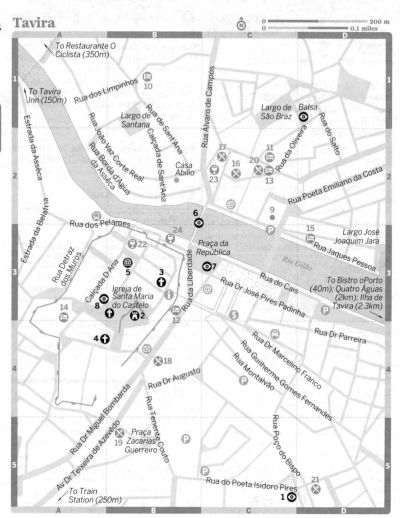

the Romans built at Tavira (which was then called Tabira) was an important link in the route between Baesuris (Castro Marim) and Ossonoba (Faro).

In the 8th century, the Moors occupied Tavira. They built the castle, probably on the site of a Roman fortress, and two mosques. In 1242 Dom Paio Peres Correia reconquered the town. Those Moors who remained were segregated into the *mouraria* (segregated Moorish quarter) outside the town walls.

As the port closest to the Moroccan coast, Tavira became important during the

Age of Discoveries (p479), serving as a base for Portuguese expeditions to North Africa, supplying provisions (especially salt, wine and dried fish) and a hospital. Its maritime trade also expanded, with exports of salted fish, almonds, figs and wine to northern Europe. By 1520 it had become the Algarve's most populated settlement and was raised to the rank of city.

Decline began in the early 17th century when the North African campaign was abandoned and the Rio Gilão became so silted up that large boats couldn't enter the port. Things got worse when the plague struck in 1645, followed by the 1755 earthquake.

After briefly producing carpets in the late 18th century, Tavira found a more stable income in its tuna fishing and canning industry, although this too declined in the 1950s. Today, tourists have taken the place of fish as the biggest money-earners.

◉ Sights

Old Town   HISTORICAL SITE

Enter the old town through the Porta de Dom Manuel (by the *turismo*), built in 1520 when Dom Manuel I made Tavira a city. Around the back, along Calçada da Galeria, the elegant **Palácio da Galeria** (adult/concession €2/1; ⊙10am-12.30pm & 2-5.30pm Tue-Sat Dec-Feb, 10am-12.30pm & 3-6.30pm Jun-Aug) holds exhibitions.

Nearby, the **Torre da Tavira** (admission €4; ⊙10am-5pm Mon-Sat), which was formerly the town's water tower (100m), now houses a *câmara obscura*. A simple but ingenious object, the camera obscura reveals a 360-degree panoramic view of Tavira, its monuments and local events, in real time – all while you are stationary.

Just south of the castle is the whitewashed 17th-century **Igreja de Santiago** (⊙Mass 8.30am Mon-Fri, 6pm Sun), built where a small mosque probably once stood. The area beside it was formerly the Praça da Vila, the old town square.

Downhill from here is the **Largo da Porta do Postigo**, at the site of another old town gate and the town's Moorish quarter.

Igreja da Misericórdia   CHURCH

(Rua da Galeria; admission free; ⊙9.30am-12.30pm, 2-5.30pm Tue-Sat) Built in the 1540s, this church is the Algarve's most important Renaissance monument, with a magnificent carved, arched doorway topped by statues of Nossa Senhora da Misericórdia, São Pedro and São Paulo. The church's stone mason, André Pilarte, also worked on Mosteiro dos Jerónimos (see the boxed text, p74).

Castelo   CASTLE

(admission free; ⊙8.30am-5pm Mon-Fri, 10am-7pm Sat & Sun Mar-Nov, 9am-5pm Sat & Sun Dec-Feb) What's left of the castle is surrounded by a small and very appealing garden. The defence might date back to Neolithic times; it was rebuilt by Phoenicians in the 8th century and later taken over by the Moors. What stands today dates mostly from 17th-century reconstruction. The restored octagonal tower offers fine views over Tavira. Note: don't set the kids free here – ramparts and steps are without railing.

Ponte Romana   LANDMARK

This seven-arched bridge that loops away from Praça da República may predate the Romans but is so named because it linked the Roman road from Castro Marim to

CACELA VELHA

Enchanting, small and cobbled, Cacela Velha is a huddle of whitewashed cottages edged with bright borders, and has a pocket-sized fort, orange and olive groves, and gardens blazing with colour. It's 12km east of Tavira, above a gorgeous stretch of sea, with a couple of excellent cafe-restaurants, splendid views and a meandering path down to the long white beach.

Unfortunately, there's no direct bus from Tavira, but Cacela Velha is located only 1km south of the N125 (2km before Vila Nova de Cacela; €1.75), which is on the Faro–Vila Real de Santo António bus route.

Tavira. The structure you see dates from a 17th-century reconstruction. The latest touch-up job was in 1989, after floods knocked down one of its pillars.

Praça da República   PLAZA

For centuries, this sociable town square on the riverfront served as promenade and marketplace, where slaves were traded along with less ignominious commodities such as fish and fruit. The market moved to Jardim do Coreto in 1887 to improve hygiene, only moving again in 2000 to a new riverside location. The *mercado municipal* is held mornings from Monday to Saturday.

Biblioteca Municipal
Álvaro de Campos   LIBRARY

(☉10am-7pm Tue-Fri, 2-7.30pm Mon & Sat) Aspiring architects or anyone who appreciates modern design should pay a visit to Tavira's municipal library, which was originally the town prison. Architect João Luís Carrilho da Graça sympathetically and cleverly converted the former prison's facade and cells into a fabulous modern and harmonious cultural space. Opened in 2006, the building now houses books, exhibitions and computers.

Arraial Ferreira Neto   MUSEUM

(admission free; ☉9am-6pm) The original name of a former fishing community, which operated between 1943 and around 1970. Now incorporated within a hotel resort, this is nevertheless worth visiting to see the site's original school and chapel and for the small but very quaint tuna fishing museum, said to be the only museum in Portugal dedicated to tuna fishing. A highlight is the miniature model showing how the fishing boats operated with a complex series of nets to catch the fish. There is little in the way of description but 45-minute guided tours are available (€5; ask at reception).

Salt Pans to Quatro Águas
WALKING, BIRDWATCHING

You can walk 2km east along the river, past the fascinating, snowlike salt pans to Quatro Águas. The salt pans produce tiptop table salt and in summer attract feeding birds, including flamingos. As well as being the jumping-off point for Ilha de Tavira, the seaside hub of Quatro Águas has a couple of seafood restaurants and a former tuna-canning village – now a luxury hotel, across the river. For information on buses to Quatro Águas, see p159.

🏃 Activities

Sport Nautica   KAYAKING

(☎281 324 943; Rua Jacques Pessoa 26; kayak per half-/full day €15/25; ☉9.30am-1pm & 3.30-7.30pm Mon-Fri, to 6pm Sat) Rent kayaks for a paddle along the river.

Tourist Train   TRAIN TOURS

(40min tours €5; ☉hourly 10am-7pm Sep-May, to 8pm Jun, to midnight Jul & Aug) Starts from the northern side of Ponte Romana and visits the main sights.

Guided walks   WALKING TOURS

(☎919 441 871; Rua da Galeria; tours from €12; ☉10am-6pm) Cultural tours of the city centre and surrounds in English and Spanish; minimum numbers apply.

South Adventures   WATER SPORTS

(☎916 126 305; www.southadventures.com.pt; Cabanas) Highly professional outfit based at Cabanas, around 6km east of Tavira, offering reader-recommended kitesurfing classes and a range of other water sports.

🎉 Festivals & Events

You can't go wrong with free sardines, and that's what you'll get at **Festa de Cidade**, Tavira's biggest festival, held from 23 to 24 June. Myrtle and paper flowers decorate the streets, and the dancing and festivities carry on till late.

🛏 Sleeping

Rates for the budget places listed here do not include breakfast. Rates for most places can halve in low season.

Quinta da Lua
B&B €€€

(📞281 961 070; www.quintadalua.com.pt; Bernardinheiro, Santo Estevão; d/ste €190/205; ✷🛜) Peace and serenity. Set among orange groves 4km northwest of Tavira, this delightful place has eight bright and very stylish rooms set around a large, saltwater swimming pool. The extensive gardens feature an outdoor lounge area. Superb breakfasts (anything from homemade muesli to eggs) included.

Quinta do Caracol
GUEST HOUSE €€€

(📞281 322 475; www.quintadocaracol.com; Rua do São Pedro; s/d €100/140; P🛜✷) Overlooking a large garden, this 17th-century farmhouse has maintained its patch of paradise despite surrounding suburban development. Each of its nine individual apartments is tastefully designed with traditional Algarve furnishings and rustic artwork; all have kitchenettes. It's child- and pet-friendly. From Tavira's train station, cross the railway and turn left at Rua de Sao Pedro. The entry is 200m further on to the left – look for the blue and white arch.

Tavira Inn
GUEST HOUSE €€

(Casa do Rio; 📞917 356 623; www.tavira-inn.com; Rua Chefe António Afonso 39; d €105; ✷🛜✷) In a quirky spot nestled by the train bridge and in front of the river, the five rooms in this comfortable place have style...and effective double-glazed windows. There's a lot of terracotta, the owner's own artwork, a small saltwater swimming pool and a bar. Children not permitted and, unfortunately, breakfast is not included.

Ilha de Tavira
CAMPGROUND €

(📞281 321 709; www.campingtavira.com; camp sites per 1/2 people incl tent €11/16; ⊙May-Oct) Tavira's nearest camping site has a great location on the island (see p159). It gets crowded and noisy in the high season (mid-June to mid-September). There's no car access.

Hotel Vila Galé Albacora
HOTEL €€

(📞281 380 800; www.vilagale.pt; Quatro Águas; r from €99; ✷🛜✷) Two kilometres east, overlooking Ilha de Tavira, this four-star 162-room hotel has been converted from, and cleverly incorporates, a former tuna village, complete with the original school and chapel. It has cheerful modern rooms (the former tuna workers' living premises), plus spa, pool and restaurant.

Pousada Convento da Graça
LUXURY HOTEL €€€

(📞281 329 040; www.pousadas.pt; Rua Dom Paio Peres Correia; s/d €278/290; ✷✷) If you can get past the front door (there's a bit of attitude here), you'll find an elegant converted convent, with attractive and plush rooms – some with modern four-poster beds – a pool and a pricey restaurant.

Hotel Porta Nova
HOTEL €€€

(📞281 329 700; Rua António Pinheiro; s/d €98/123; ✷@✷) On a hill in a newer area above town, this modern whitewashed hotel offers a predictably safe, international hotel-style experience, complete with pleasant top-floor bar. Rooms with fine views over the pool and town cost more.

Residencial Princesa do Gilão
GUEST HOUSE €€

(📞/fax 281 325 171; Rua Borda d'Água de Aguiar 10; s €50, d €60-65, tr €80; ✷) This '80s-style place on the river has tight but neat rooms with identical decor. Get a room with a river view.

Pensão Residencial Lagoas
GUEST HOUSE €

(📞281 322 252; Rua Almirante Cândido dos Reis 24; s/d/tr without bathroom €20/30/50, s €40, d €40-50) A long-standing favourite, Lagoas has endearing owners and small (some cramped), spotless rooms. There's a plant-filled courtyard and a sunny terrace with views.

Pensão Residencial Castelo
GUEST HOUSE €€

(📞281 320 790; fax 281 325 877; Rua da Liberdade 22; s/d/apt €40/60/70; ✷✷) A blast from the past, the Castelo offers dated but pleasant rooms. Some have balconies and/or castle views. It has wheelchair access.

Pensão Residencial Almirante
GUEST HOUSE €

(📞281 322 163; Rua Almirante Cândido dos Reis 51; d €30) One block from the river, this cosy family house is full of clutter, but its six rooms are spacious and charmingly old-fashioned.

✖ Eating

You can take your pick of eateries along the waterfront's Rua Dr José Pires Padinha. To get off this well-trodden taste-bud path, we recommend the following places and/or locations.

Vela Dois   SEAFOOD €€
(mains €10; ⊙lunch & dinner Mon-Sat) Soccer fanatics will love this atmospheric, buzzing Benfica-crazy restaurant (which looks like it has raided the Benfica fan club premises). Its winning secret would have to be the €10 for all-you-can-eat (very good) seafood feast. This restaurant is opposite the library.

Bistro 'oPorto'   INTERNATIONAL €€
(Rua Dr José Pires Padinha 180; mains €9.50-14; ⊙lunch & dinner Tue-Sat) An intimate bar and a relaxed riverside setting make for a pleasant time at this French-owned spot. Dishes combine Portuguese and French flavours and vegetarians are usually catered for.

Restaurante O Ciclista
PORTUGUESE, SEAFOOD €€
(Rua João Vaz Corte Real; mains €8-12, fish per kg €25-50; ⊙lunch & dinner Tue-Sun, lunch Mon) Just beyond the EN125 bridge, this isolated barnlike spot rightly stands out on its own. Seafood here is fresh (and don't the locals know it), grilled and served by the kilo. It gets packed to the gills with locals.

Restaurante Avenida
PORTUGUESE, SEAFOOD €€
(Av Dr Mateus Teixeira de Azevedo 6; mains €7.50-15; ⊙lunch & dinner Wed-Mon) This charming, well-maintained Portuguese place with gold and blue tablecloths has an air of the 1960s, and a loyal clientele. Good home-style Portuguese plates include the seafood risotto and grilled tuna.

Micromania   CAFE €
(Rua da Liberdade; mains €3.50-4.50; ⊙8am-7pm Mon-Fri, 8am-1pm Sat) This small, casual spot serves bargain meals of the day plus snacks. Frequented by local workers.

Restaurante Bica   SEAFOOD €€
(Rua Almirante Cândido dos Reis 24; mains €7-16; ⊙lunch & dinner) Deservedly popular. Here you can eat reliable food, such as fresh grilled fish, and down cheap bottles of decent Borba wine.

Portas do Mar   PORTUGUESE, SEAFOOD €€
(Quatro Águas; mains €10-20; ⊙lunch & dinner Wed-Sun) This place has attentive service and good seafood. Serves everything from lobster *cataplana* to pig's ear. It's 2km southeast of Tavira.

Aquasul   SEAFOOD €€
(☎281 325 166; Rua Dr Augusto Silva Carvalho 13; mains €9.50-14, set menus €14-25; ⊙dinner Tue-Sun) You won't hear too much Portuguese spoken here, given this place's popularity among foreigners and expats, but this Dutch-run place serves up some tasty international dishes in a fun, mosaic-filled environment.

Quatro Águas   PORTUGUESE €€
(Quatro Águas; mains €12.50-22.50; ⊙lunch & dinner Tue-Sun) Despite its touristic hum, this is a lovely place, and serves good seafood, fish and meat dishes in a smart environment. The outside area overlooks the river and is ideal for lunches.

Churrasqueira O Manel   GRILL HOUSE €
(Rua Dr António Cabreira 39; mains €5-8) There's plenty of great takeaway *frango no churrasco* (grilled chicken) on offer at this place. There are plenty of cafes in town and around the plaza. There's a modern **mercado municipal** (⊙most stalls morning only) on the eastern edge of town, and a Pingo Doce Supermarket.

🍸 Drinking & Entertainment
Bars are interspersed throughout town; most are on the northern bank, with a couple along Rua Dr José Padinha.

Tavira Lounge   BAR, CAFE
(☎281 381 034; Rua Goncal Velho 16-18; ⊙11.30am-2am Mon-Sat) By day it's a cafe-restaurant; by night a cafe-bar. Whatever it is, it's cosy and a lovely place to chill over delicious tapas snacks, or kick back with a cocktail or smoothie. Free internet and several cosy spaces ensure a long and comfortable visit. There are even distractions for the kids.

Refcafé   BAR
(Rua Gonçalo Velho 23; ⊙Tue-Sun) A casual place where nothing is quite what it seems: it's more of a bar (despite its name, although it serves good smoked-salmon sandwiches), its space has a 1970s feel (but it plays contemporary music) and the ladies' bathroom is behind the blue (not yellow) curtain. Can be fun.

Távila   SNACK BAR
(Praça Dr António Padinha 50) Overlooking a small tree-filled plaza, this low-key spot is popular with locals. It has outdoor tables, ideal for an afternoon or evening drink.

For a higher-velocity night, head to the *mercado municipal*, which hosts a row of dancier, preclub bars that play music from hands-in-the-air house to African. The area buzzes in July and August. After that, head to **UBI** (Rua Almirante Cândido dos Reis; ☻midnight-6am Tue-Sun May-Sep, Sat & Sun Nov-Apr), an extraordinary nightclub, in a former tuna factory, that churns out music (and an experience) across umpteen sleek spaces and bar areas. Join the party with up to 3999 others.

ⓘ Information

Banks with ATMs lie around Praça da República and Rua da Liberdade.

Biblioteca Municipal Álvaro de Campos (Rua Comunidade Lusiada 21; ☻2-7.30pm Mon & Sat, 10am-7pm Tue-Fri) Free access plus wi-fi.

Centro de Saude (Health Centre; ☑281 329 000; Strada de Santa Luzia; ☻3-8pm) Public clinic; these hours are for tourists.

Cotacâmbios/Western Union (Rua Marcelino Franco 7; ☻9am-8pm) Private exchange bureau.

Cyber-Café Anazu (Rua Jacques Pessoa 4; per hr €3; ☻9am-midnight)

Espaço Internet (Câmara municipal, Praça da República; ☻9am-noon, 12.30-5pm & 5.30-8pm Mon-Fri, 10am-1pm Sat) Free access.

Police station (☑281 322 022; Campo dos Mártires da Pátria)

Post office (Rua da Liberdade)

SOS Clinic (☑281 380 660; Rua Almirante Cândido dos Reis; ☻24hr) Private clinic.

Turismo (☑281 322 511; www.visitalgarve.pt; Rua da Galeria 9; ☻9.30am-1pm & 2-5.30pm Mon-Fri Sep-Jun, 9am-7pm Mon-Fri Jul & Aug) Provides local and some regional information and helps with accommodation.

ⓘ Getting There & Around

BICYCLE Bike rental is available through **Casa Abilio** (☑281 323 467; Rua Joáo Vaz Corte Real 21-23; per day around €7). Other options are **Sport Nautica** (☑281 324 943; Rua Jacques Pessoa 26; per day from €6) and **Balsa** (☑697278374; Rua Álvares Botelho 51; per day normal/tandem/scooter €7/12/18), although this place is more interesting for the ceramics shop and the friendly owner than the bike quality.

BUS The **bus station** (☑281 322 546) has the following services:

Faro (€3.15, one hour, 11/eight daily weekdays/weekends) Via Olhão (€2.40).

Vila Real (€3, 40 minutes, seven/10 weekdays/weekends)

Express buses also go to Lisbon (€19, up to five hours, four to five daily) and Huelva (Spain; €11, two hours, twice daily), with connections to Seville (€15, three hours).

TRAIN Trains run daily to Faro (€2.30, 40 minutes, 15 daily) and Vila Real (€1.70, 35 minutes).

TAXIS A reliable rank for **taxis** (☑281 321 544, 281 325 746) is located near the cinema on Rua Dr Marcelino Franco.

Around Tavira

ILHA DE TAVIRA

Sandy islands (all part of the Parque Natural da Ria Formosa) stretch along the coast from Cacela Velha to just west of Faro, and this is one of the finest. The huge beach at the island's eastern end, opposite Tavira, has water sports, a camping ground and cafe-restaurants. Outside high season, the island feels wonderfully remote and empty, but during July and August it's busy.

A kilometre west of the jetty is an unofficial nudist area. A few kilometres further west along the island is **Praia do Barril**, accessible by a miniature train that trundles over the mud flats from **Pedras d'el Rei**, a resort 4km southwest of Tavira. About half a kilometre further west is the official nudist beach. There are some eateries where the shuttle train stops, then sand, sand, sand as far as the eye can see.

ⓘ Getting There & Away

Ferries make the five-minute hop to the *ilha* (€1.40 return, from 8am to 8pm) from Quatro Águas, 2km southeast of Tavira. Times are subject to change – ask the crew when the last one runs! In July and August they usually run till midnight and can be very busy. From July to mid-September a boat normally runs direct from Tavira from around 8am (return €1.80, 15 minutes) – ask at the *turismo* for details.

In addition to the local ferry, **Áqua-Taxis** (☑964 515 073, 917 035 207) operates 24 hours a day from July to mid-September, and until midnight from May to June. The fare from Quatro Águas-Tavira to the island is around €15 for six people.

A bus goes to Quatro Águas from the Tavira bus station from July to mid-September (eight daily). A taxi to Quatro Águas costs around €5.

For Praia do Barril, take a bus from Tavira to Pedras d'el Rei (10 minutes, around eight daily weekdays), from where the little train runs regularly to the beach from March to September. Out of high season the timetable depends on the mood of the operating company.

Vila Real de Santo António

POP 11,000

Perched on the edge of wide Rio Guadiana, low-key but pleasant Vila Real de Santo António stares across at Spanish eyes. Its small pedestrian centre is architecturally impressive: in 1774, the Marquês de Pombal stamped the town, in five months, with his hallmark gleaming grid-pattern of streets (like Lisbon's Baixa district) after the town was destroyed by floods. From here you can head off to Castro Marim or on boat or biking trips along the Rio Guadiana (see the boxed text, p195).

🛏 Sleeping

Villa Marquês HOTEL €€
(☏281 530 420; Rua Dr José Barão 61; s/d €55/60)
Two streets back from the waterfront, near the bus station, this modern, yellow place has bright and airy – if a little cramped – rooms and a rooftop terrace with views over town. The best value in town.

Residência Matos Pereira GUEST HOUSE €€
(☏281 543 325; Rua Dr Sousa Martins 57; s/d €35/60) This family-home guest house near the *turismo* has small lace-filled rooms, some with a terrace and very steep steps.

Hospedaria Arenilha GUEST HOUSE €€
(☏281 512 565; Rua Dom Pedro V, 53-55; s/d/tr/ste €50/70/80/90; 🅿) Owned by those of Churrasqueira Arenilha fame, and in the centre of town, this place is modern and very new. The jury is still out – let's hope the quality holds up. At the time of research, it offers small, clean rooms with all the mod cons.

🍴 Eating

Associação Naval do Guadiana SEAFOOD €€
(Av da República; mains €8-14; ⊙lunch & dinner) Quaintly dated, this big blue waterfront building has a terrace with views over the river and good seafood, as attested by the locals.

Os Arcos PORTUGUESE €€
(Av da República 45; mains €8-15; ⊙lunch & dinner) Unpretentious and slightly barnlike, Os Arcos offers efficient service in a typically gruff Portuguese don't-mess-with-me-it's-service-time manner. Large selection of meat and fish.

Two pocket-sized places have good-value Portuguese nosh:

Snack-Bar Mira PORTUGUESE €
(Rua da Princesa 59; mains €6-10; ⊙lunch & dinner Mon-Sat)

Snack-Bar Cuca PORTUGUESE €
(Rua Dr Sousa Martins 64; mains €8-14; ⊙lunch & dinner)

❶ Information

Espaço Internet (Rua Candid do Reís; ⊙9am-9pm) Free internet access (note: free wi-fi connections are available on Praça Marquês de Pombal and along the marina).

Turismo (☏281 510 045; Rua Teófilo Braga; ⊙10am-1pm & 3-7pm) A tiny support office in high season to the principal **turismo** (☏281 544 495; Av Marginal) at Monte Gordo, 4km west.

❶ Getting There & Away

Boat

Ferries cross the river border every hour to whitewashed Ayamonte; buy tickets (€1.50/5/0.90 per person/car/bike) from the waterfront office, open 9am to 6.30pm Monday to Saturday, 9.15am to 5.40pm Sunday. Note: there is a one-hour time difference between Portugal and Spain.

Bus

Buses (☏281 511 807) service the following:
Faro (€5, 1¾ hours, six to nine daily) Some go on to Lisbon (express €18 to €19, 4¾ hours, eight daily).
Mértola (€9.40, one hour, one daily)
Monte Gordo (€2.75, 10 minutes, seven to eight daily)
Tavira (€2.95, 30 to 45 minutes, six to nine daily)
To get to Spain, you must head to Huelva (€10, one hour, two daily), and connect there to Seville (total fare from Vila Real de Santo António €15, 3½ hours).

Train

Trains to Lagos (€7.40, 3¾ hours, seven daily) require changes at Faro and/or Tunes. There are regular train services to Faro (€2.35, 45 minutes, 10 daily).

❶ Getting Around

The nearest place to rent bikes is in Monte Gordo, from **Riosul** (☏281 510 200; www.riosul travel.com; Rua Tristão Vaz Teixeira 15C).

Castro Marim

POP 3100

Slumbering in the shadows of a 14th-century castle, Castro Marim is a picturesque village that sees few foreign visitors, but deserves to see more. It has a quaint, tree-shaded centre, several restaurants and impressive fortifications. These afford views across salt pans, the bridge to Spain, and the marshes of the Reserva Natural do Sapal de Castro Marim, which is famous for its flamingos. For walkers, there are some good trails around the area. It's 3km north of Vila Real de Santo António.

⊙ Sights

Castelo & Around   HISTORIC SITE

(admission free; ⊙9am-7pm Apr-Oct, 9am-5pm Nov-Mar) In the 13th century, Dom Afonso III built Castro Marim's castle on the site of Roman and Moorish fortifications in a dramatic and strategic position for spying on the Spanish frontier. In 1319 it became the first headquarters of the religious military order known as the Order of Christ, the new version of the Knights Templar (see the boxed text, p283). Until they moved to Tomar in 1334, the soldiers of the Order of Christ used this castle to keep watch over the estuary of the Rio Guadiana and the border with Spain, where the Moors were still in power.

The grand stretch of ruins today, however, dates from the 17th century, when Dom João IV ordered the addition of vast ramparts. At the same time Forte de São Sebastião, a smaller fort, was built on a nearby hilltop (currently closed to the public). Much of the area was destroyed in the 1755 earthquake, but the ruins of the main fort are still amazing.

Inside the wonderfully derelict castle walls is a 14th-century church, the **Igreja de Santiago**, where Henry the Navigator, also Grand Master of the Order of Christ, is said to have prayed. A small museum (admission free; ⊙10am-1pm & 2-5pm Nov-Mar, 10am-1pm & 3-6pm Apr-Oct) displays some pots and vases dating back to the Iron Age, discovered during excavations. A fun spectacle, the **Feira Mediéval**, takes place at the castle for four days encompassing the last weekend of August. There's a parade on the first (from the village to the castle) and last days (from the castle to the village, emulating medieval times). Food stalls with local products, music, fencing competitions and a medieval banquet create an authentic atmosphere.

Reserva Natural do Sapal de Castro Marim e Vila Real de Santo António
NATURE RESERVE

(⏚administrative office 281 510 680; Sapal de Venta Moínhos; ⊙9am-12.30pm & 2-5.30pm Mon-Fri) Established in 1975, this nature reserve is Portugal's oldest, covering 20 sq km of marshland and salt pans bordering the Rio Guadiana north of Vila Real. Important winter visitors are greater flamingos, spoonbills and Caspian terns. In spring it's busy with white storks.

The park's administrative office is 2km from Monte Francisco, a five-minute bus ride north of Castro Marim; get directions from the *turismo* at Castro Marim, as there are few signs.

TOP 10 BEACHES OF THE ALGARVE

From small, secluded coves to wide stretches of rugged, dune-backed shores, the Algarve has enticing choices when it comes to sunbaking and wave frolicking. Our highly subjective picks:

» **Odeceixe** (p191) Small and pretty, with decent swimming and good surfing.

» **Meia Praia** (p178) Vast, popular and scenic, with options for water sports.

» **Ilha de Tavira** (p159) Crown jewel of the east-coast beaches, with a nudist area.

» **Ilha da Barreta** (Ilha Deserta; p161) In the Parque Natural da Ria Formosa, this sandy island is accessed by boat through nature-filled lagoons.

» **Vale Figueira** (p190) Long stretch of wild coast that's little frequented.

» **Praia da Galé** (p167) Attractive cove beach with striking rock formations.

» **Praia da Bordeira** (p189) Wild untamed beauty (and surfing).

» **Praia da Arrifana** (p190) Lovely setting along a bay framed by black cliffs.

» **Alcoutim** (p195) Novel because it's a tiny riverside beach; it comes with lifeguard!

» **Praia de Dona Ana** (p178) Enchanting, golden rock formations make this cove beach a photographer's favourite.

There are two accommodation centres in the park but you need to book ahead, as they are used by groups (mainly scientists and schools). Birdwatchers should also head to Cerro do Bufo, 2km southwest of Castro Marim, another rewarding area for spotting the park's birdlife. There are three short walks in the area (only one is signed). Ask staff at the park office or at Castro Marim's *turismo* for details.

ℹ️ Information

Odiana (📠/fax 281 531 171; www.odiana.pt; Rua 25 de Abril; ⏱9am-1pm & 2-5.30pm) This excellent organisation promotes the more rural Baixo (lower) Guadiana region. It distributes an excellent guide (published in 1999, but still useful in the most part) covering regional culture, with suggestions for day trips. A must for keen walkers are the trail brochures of 19 signposted trails within the region (these are in short supply; if you can, download them from the Odiana website). The trails encompass diverse areas, from salt pans and river areas to ruins and villages.

Turismo (📞281 531 232; Rua Dr José Alves Moreira; ⏱9.30am-1pm & 2-5.30pm Mon-Fri) Below the castle in the village centre.

ℹ️ Getting There & Away

Buses from Vila Real run to Castro Marim (€1.90, eight minutes) and go on to Monte Francisco, a short distance north. Weekend buses are extremely limited.

Loulé

POP 21,700

One of the Algarve's largest inland towns, and only 16km northwest of Faro, Loulé (lo-*lay*) is a reasonable base from which to explore the inland Algarve. A busy commercial centre, it is one of the fastest-growing towns in Portugal, as people use this as a base to work (or seek work) in the Algarve. Loulé has an attractive old quarter and Moorish castle ruins and its history spans back to the Romans. A few of Loulé's artisan traditions still survive; crafty folk toil away on wicker baskets, copperworks and embroidery at hole-in-the-wall workshops about town. Loulé's small university lends it some verve, as does its wild Carnaval (just before Lent) and FestivalMed, an annual music festival.

If arriving by train, note that the train station is 5km southwest of town (take any Quarteira-bound bus).

◎ Sights & Activities

The restored castle ruins house the **Museu Municipal** (📞289 400 600; Largo Dom Pedro I; admission €1.50; ⏱9am-5.30pm Mon-Fri, 10am-2pm Sat), which currently contains beautifully presented fine fragments of Bronze Age and Roman ceramics. A glass floor exposes excavated Moorish ruins. The admission fee includes entry to a stretch of the castle walls and the **Cozinha Tradicional Algarvia** (⏱same as museum), a re-creation of a traditional Algarve kitchen, featuring a cosy hearth, archaic implements and burnished copper.

Situated opposite the castle, **Nossa Senhora da Conceição** dates from the mid-17th century. It's a small chapel with a plain facade nonchalantly hiding a heavily decorated mid-18th-century interior with a magnificent gold altarpiece. During recent excavations, an Islamic door, dating from the 3rd century, was uncovered under the floor where it stays, protected by glass.

An environmental group, **Almargem** (📞289 412 959; www.almargem.org; admission free), is responsible for the Via Algarviana (see the boxed text, p145) and welcomes visitors on its Sunday walks.

★彡 Festivals & Events

Carnaval   VILLAGE, RELIGIOUS
Just before Lent, Loulé shimmies into something sexy and sequinned, with parades, tractor-drawn floats and lots of musical high jinks. Friday is the children's parade, and Sunday the big one. Held in late February or early March.

FestivalMed   WORLD MUSIC
(www.festivalmed.com.pt) Having been an attraction since 2006, this is fast gaining a reputation as a quality world-music festival, attracting the likes of Jamaican performer Jimmy Cliff and international performers. Held in late June.

Loulé International Jazz Festival
                    INTERNATIONAL JAZZ
(www.ccloule.com) In July the town dons jazz boots on selected evenings; international and Portuguese musicians jam in the convent and castle.

Nossa Senhora da Piedade   RELIGIOUS
Linked to ancient maternity rites, this *romaria* (religious festival) is the Algarve's most important. On Easter Sunday a 16th-century image of Our Lady of Pity (or Piety)

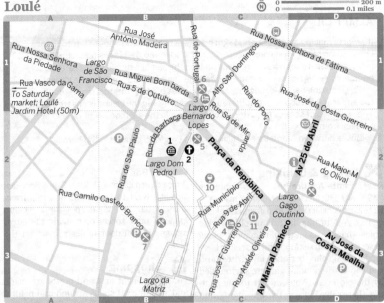

is carried down from its hilltop chapel, 2km north of town, to the parish church. Two weeks later, a procession of devotees lines the steep route to the chapel to witness its return.

🛏 Sleeping

Loulé Jardim Hotel   HOTEL **€€**
(☎289 413 094-5; www.loulejardimhotel.com; Praça Manuel D'Arriaga; s/d/tr €56/73/94, d with terrace €78; 🏢🛜🏊) A late-19th-century building with tasteful, airy and spacious rooms, this well-run place overlooks a pretty square. Book ahead for a terrace.

Casa Beny   GUEST HOUSE **€€**
(☎289 417 702; casabeny@portugalmail.com; Rua São Domingos 13; d €50-65; 🏢) In a pleasantly restored mansion dating from 1897, Casa Beny offers nine peachy rooms, each with Brazilian hardwood floors, a touch of '80s-style pine, tall ceilings and French doors. The rooftop terrace has castle views.

Hospedaria Dom Fernando GUEST HOUSE **€€**
(☎289 415 553; Travessa do Mercado; s/d €65/80; 🏢🛜) This option offers two different choices: a newer section, above the owner's restaurant, with simple, modern rooms, or those in the neighbouring build-

ing, which are showing signs of age in the decor department, but are adequate (you are probably able to negotiate lower rates for these). In an excellent location, behind the market, although you'll be in the thick of it (think noise and action) during festival times.

THE ALGARVE

ALMANCIL

It's worth making a detour here, 13km northwest of Faro and about 6km south of Loulé, to visit the marvellous **Igreja de São Lourenço de Matos** (Church of St Lourenço; admission free). The church was built on the site of a ruined chapel after local people, while digging a well, had implored the saint for help and then struck water.

The resulting baroque masterpiece, which was built by fraternal master-team Antão and Manuel Borges, is smothered in *azulejos* – even the ceiling is covered in them. The walls depict scenes from the life of the saint. In the earthquake of 1755, only five tiles fell from the roof.

Buses between Albufeira (40 minutes) and Loulé (15 minutes) stop here.

✖ Eating & Drinking

Restaurante A Muralha   PORTUGUESE €€
(☑967 347 530; Rua Martim Moniz 41; mains €8-17; ⊙lunch & dinner) Set in a former bakery, quaint A Muralha is full of olde-worlde knick-knacks. Its new management plans to serve up fresh seafood and *mariscos* (seafood stews), plus regional favourites, and you can eat in a small garden, surrounded by the old ovens. You can eat to the beat, too: there's live fado on Tuesday nights, and other live music on Saturday nights.

Espaços Gastronómicos Perdição
INTERNATIONAL   €€
(☑919 669 953; Rua Camilo Castelo Branco; mains €6-15; ⊙lunch Mon-Sat, dinner Thu-Sat) This place lives up to its name: gastronomic delights in the form of daily vegetarian, fish, meat and pasta dishes. Has a good selection of juices, teas and desserts, too.

Cantina dos Sabores   VEGETARIAN €
(Rua de Portugal 22; ⊙lunch & dinner Mon-Sat; ☑) You might have to queue to get a place at this buzzing vegetarian eatery, as does everyone from professionals to butch-looking meat-eating guys (okay, so it has chicken on the menu). It's deservedly popular for its daily specials (€5 to €6), juices and desserts. Generous portions are filling and enjoyable.

Café Calcinha   CAFE €
(Praça da República 67; snacks €1-7; ⊙8am-11pm Mon-Fri, to 4pm Sat) This traditional 1920s-style cafe (Loulé's oldest) has marble-topped tables and sidewalk tables. The statue outside depicts António Aleixo, an early-20th-century poet and former regular of the cafe.

Restaurante A Moagem   PORTUGUESE €€
(Rua Maria Campina 37A; mains €8-19; ⊙lunch & dinner Mon-Sat) Recommended for its good-quality Algarvian and Alentejan specialities, from cod dishes to rabbit.

Campus Bar   BAR
(Praça da República; ⊙11.30am-2pm & 8pm-2am Mon-Sat) Next to the university, this lively student bar is a good spot for a pick-up game of table soccer or hearing the latest uni gossip. Outdoor tables are set on the plaza.

🛍 Shopping

Loulé's excellent arts and crafts are made and sold in craft shops around and behind the castle (Rua Barbaca). The *mercado municipal* also has traditional craft stalls.

On Saturday morning there's a large open-air **market** (⊙9am-1pm) northwest of the centre, selling clothes, shoes, toys and souvenirs.

ℹ Information

Espaço Internet (Largo de São Francisco ⊙9.30am-7.30pm Mon-Fri, to 2.30pm Sat) Free internet access.

Souvenir shop (Praça da República) Has a good range of guidebooks and maps.

Turismo (☑289 463 900; www.atalgarve.pt; Av 25 de Abril 9; ⊙9.30am-1pm & 2-5.30pm Mon-Sat Oct-Jun, 9.30am-5.30pm Mon-Sat Jul-Sep) Maps and 'what's on' brochures available here.

ℹ Getting There & Around

BUS Daily **bus** (☑289 416 655) connections head to the following:

Faro (€2.75, 40 minutes, one to three daily),

Albufeira (€4.20, 55 minutes, four to six daily). If heading to Portimão on a weekday, change at Albufeira. On weekends there are direct buses (€5.40, 1½ hours). Express buses head to Lisbon (€19, 3¾ hours, four to five daily).

CAR If driving, parking can be tricky in Loulé – park on the edge of town. Note, however, never leave valuables in your car – travellers have reported theft.

TRAIN Services from Loulé station, 5km south of town:

Faro (€1.40, 15 minutes, 11 daily)

Lagos (€5, 1½ hours, nine daily)

Serra do Caldeirão

Lying around 30km north of Loulé is the stunning, undulating region of Serra do Caldeirão, a beautiful protected area of undulating hills, cork trees and harsh scrubland. The area is renowned for its bird varieties. It's an excellent place to hike – the Via Algarviana goes through here – and a wonderful spot to base oneself to meander through some ancient villages and enjoy the region's cuisine. A feature of the region is its *fontes* (traditional water sources, many of which comprise exquisite taps and fountains), highlighted by signs that have been erected in recent years.

ALTE & SALIR

Perched on a hillside on the edge of Serra do Caldeirão, Alte, located 45km northwest of Loulé, is a quaint and very pretty little village. In high season visitors are disgorged from buses for a quick-see experience. Boasting flower-filled streets, whitewashed buildings and several *fontes* (traditional water taps and streams), it's a pleasant place to wander for an hour or so. These were traditionally used for the mills and former wells; Fonte Grande passes through dykes, weirs and watermills. Several *artesanatos* (handicrafts shops) are dotted around town, as are several restaurants and cafes.

The helpful **tourist office** (☑289 478 666) is on the main road and provides a suggested walking 'tour'. Opened in 2009 in a cleverly converted house, the museum-cultural space of **Pólo Museológico Cândido Guerreiro e Condes de Alte** (☑289 478 058; Rua Condes de Alte; admission free; ◷9.30am-12.30pm & 2-6pm) pays homage to Alte's famous poet, Guerreiro, and the Counts of Alte who lived there. It displays the books and paraphernalia of all.

If travelling by car, pass through the small, sleepy and attractive town of Salir. It's a pleasant, very genuine village set on two hills with castle walls dating from the 12th century and an attractive church. There's a small **tourist office** (☑289 489 733) on the main street.

Buses depart Loulé for Alte (€3, 45 minutes, five weekdays) and Salir (€3.15, 30 minutes, three weekdays).

⨉ Sleeping & Eating

Quinta do Freixo   RURAL INN   €€
(☑289 472 185; www.quintadofreixo.org; Benafim; s/d incl breakfast €48/65; ⊛) This delightful place – a converted barn – is located on Quinta do Freixo, a functioning farm well-known for producing traditional foodstuffs (marketed under the same name). It's a more upmarket rural experience, where accommodation errs on the 'moo', not the 'poo'; you can see animals from the windows in the comfortable communal areas, but don't have to leave the complex's green lawns and swimming pool. The 10 comfortable rooms feature Alentejan (painted wooden) furniture. Popular with small European groups.

Quinta do Coração   GUEST HOUSE   €€
(☑/fax 289 489 959; www.algarveparadise.com; Carrasqueiro; r incl breakfast €55, self-catering studios €60, 2-person cottages €65; ⊛) On a wooded hill, encircled by a eucalypt, olive-grove and cork-tree paradise, the rooms, studios and cottage (with kitchenette) in the remote, converted farmhouse have a rustic-with-a-wee-touch-of-hippy ambience. Carrasqueiro is located around 7km east of Salir.

Casa da Mãe   GUEST HOUSE   €€
(☑289 489 179; www.casadamae.com; Almeijoafra; s incl breakfast €40-75; d incl breakfast

WALKS IN SERRA DO CALDEIRÃO

The tourism offices at **Salir** (☑289 489 733; Rua José Viegas Guerreiro) and **Alte** (☑289 478 666) sometimes stock basic maps. Otherwise, they sell copies of *Routes of the Algarve* (€7), which outlines a couple of walks in the region.

A walk well worth doing is **Rocha da Pena**, a limestone rock just east of Alte and off the N124. Keen walkers can do a signed 4.7km circuit walk up the mountain; follow the road signs to the mountain. A return walk takes about two to three hours. Carry water and snacks; there's a small shop-cafe at the base and another in Penina village but no other refreshment stops for miles. Note fire-danger times – bushfires occur in this area, too.

€70-100; @❦) This friendly unpretentious complex offers a series of good-value, if slightly dated, rooms and apartments. It has a lovely garden – with pool – and superb views of greenery and Salir in the distance. Good breakfasts with homemade produce.

Monte da Eira PORTUGUESE €€€
(☏289 438 129; Clareanes; mains €12-17; ⊙lunch & dinner Tue-Sat, lunch Sun) On Rte 396, 5km north of Loulé in the village of Clareanes, is this smart restaurant, the stables of a converted threshing mill, now several rooms and two outdoor terraces. People come from afar to feast on dishes of *javali* (wild boar), lamb and bean casserole and stewed rabbit. Little living beasts (err, children) also welcome. To top it off, choose from one of 96 wines – *hic* – and that's the red alone. Vegetarians are catered for, too.

Albufeira

POP 20,200

Once a scenic fishing village, Albufeira has tragically lost its vestiges to its past – fishermen's boats are now moored at the ultramodern new marina southwest of town. These days, the town is a den of mass-market tourism; the old town – and its pretty cobblestone streets and Moorish influences – is concealed by neon signs, English menu boards and rowdy bars. It is the destination for cheap package deals, mainly catering to Brits and Germans and focused on cheap food, grog and fine nearby beaches.

It has good transport links to lovely beaches, such as Praia da Galé to the west. To explore the pretty inland villages and the area's high-quality restaurants, you will need your own transport.

Arrival here can be slightly overwhelming. A snapshot orientation: the old town lies below the N526 (Av dos Descobrimentos), and 3km east of here is 'the Strip', a road with more shops and bars, leading up from crowded Praia da Oura. The new marina 'tourist complex' is at the southwestern edge of town, and the train station is 6km north at Ferreiras.

◉ Sights

Museu Municipal de Arqueologia MUSEUM
(admission €1; ⊙10.30am-4.30pm Dec-Feb, 2-8pm Jun-Aug) This museum showcases items excavated from the municipality and surrounds (such as the castle in the village of Paderne). Pieces date from the prehistoric era to the 16th century. A highlight is a beautifully complete Neolithic vase from 5000 BC.

Museum of Sacred Art MUSEUM
(admission €1; ⊙10am-4.30pm Dec-Feb, 10am-noon Jun-Aug) The town's other cultural site, the tiny museum is housed in the beautifully restored 18th-century Chapel of San Sebastian. It has a stunning gold wooden

FOR THE KIDS

A plethora of agencies in and around Albufereira sell a variety of trips, from horse riding to cruising on pirate ships. Most boat trips leave from the marina. Other kid-friendly activities include the following:

Albufeira Riding Centre HORSE RIDING
(☏289 542 870; Vale Navio Complex; 1hr ride €30) On the road to Vilamoura. Offers one- to three-hour horse rides for all ages and abilities.

Aqualand WATER PARK
(☏282 320 230; www.aqualand.pt; Alcantarilha; adult/child €20/15.50; ⊙10am-6pm Jun-Sep) Huge loop-the-loop slide and rapids.

Aqua Show WATER PARK
(☏289 389 396; www.aquashowpark.com; adult/child €25/15; ⊙10am-6pm Jun-Sep, to 7pm Aug) In Quarteira, 10km east of Albufeira, with parrots, reptiles and a wave pool.

Dolphins Driven BOAT TRIPS
(☏913 113 095; www.dolphins.pt; Marina de Albufeira) Offers three boat trips from Albufeira (from 2½ hours to full day) to caves, beaches, up the Rio Arade and to Ria Formosa.

Zoomarine WATER PARK
(☏289 560 306; www.zoomarine.com; adult/child €24/15; ⊙10am-7.30pm Jul–mid-Sep, to 5pm rest of year, closed Dec) Will satisfy all desires for aqua-entertainment, with huge swimming pools and slides, as well as lakes, an aquarium and dolphin shows. Located at Guia, 8km northwest of Albufeira.

WORTH A TRIP

VILA JOYA – JOY INDEED

Vila Joya (☎289 591 795; www.vilajoya.com; Apt 120 Praia da Galé; incl breakfast from €160) is a luxury resort and spa located several kilometres from Albufeira – yet a planet away in every respect – right on the beachfront near Praia da Galé. The decor and surrounds have a touch of Africa about them. Pool areas, lush green lawn, views of the sea and a health spa add to an ultraplush and relaxing experience. If your purse strings don't stretch to staying here, consider saving your pennies for a meal at the restaurant, the only eatery in the Algarve with Michelin stars (not one, but two!). You'll enjoy impeccable service, exquisite locally sourced produce and the best of the *best* cuisine from chef Dieter Koschina at **Vila Joya Restaurant** (mains €42-112; ☺lunch & dinner).

altar and exhibits sacred art from surrounding churches that survived the 1775 earthquake.

🏃 Activities

Besides strolling cheek-to-jowl with others along the pedestrianised seafront, most come here for the beaches. **Praia do Peneco**, through the tunnel near the *turismo*, is usually head-to-toe with sunloungers. East and west of town are beautifully rugged coves and bays, though the nearest are heavily developed and often crowded. These include **Praia da Oura**, at the bottom of 'the Strip' 3km to the east; **Praia da Falésia**, a long beach 10km to the east; **Balaia** and **Olhos de Água**. Buses run to Olhos de Água (€1.60, 10 minutes, half-hourly), mostly continuing to Praia da Falésia (20 minutes).

One of the best beaches to the west, **Praia da Galé**, about 6km away, is long and sandy, not so crowded and a centre for jet-skiing and water-skiing. It's easily accessible by car, but there's no direct bus service to this beach or the others en route, though local buses to Portimão do run along the main road about 2km above the beaches (get off at Vale de Parra).

🛏 Sleeping

Most places are associated with travel companies; bagging a room in July and August is impossible without reservations. Many places close in low season (November to March).

Dianamar GUEST HOUSE €€
(☎289 587 801; www.dianamar.com; Rua Latino Coelho 36; s/d/tr incl breakfast €50/60-65/75) If you must stay in Albufeira, this is one good reason to do so. Friendly, Scandinavian-run Dianamar has lovely details, with fresh

flowers and attractive rooms, many with balconies and two with sea views. Excellent and oh-so-generous breakfasts and afternoon teas. Best to reserve ahead.

Vila São Vicente BOUTIQUE HOTEL €€€
(☎289 583 700; www.hotelsaovicentealbufeira. com; Largo Jacinto D'Ayet; s/d/ste €120/140/175; ❄❄) This peaceful, classically decorated boutique-style hotel has handsome rooms with polished-wood floors. It's a welcome relief from the town's theme-park atmosphere.

🍴 Eating & Drinking

British breakfasts? Thai curries? Tasty? Bland? Albufeira has every conceivable range of dining options. The small market has fruits, vegetables and fish. Browse the menus near Largo Cais Herculano, the main plaza or any streets leading off here, for foodstuffs and flavours that will best appease your hunger pangs.

You can bar-hop your brain cells away in Albufeira. Bars throng the area around Largo Engenheiro Duarte Pacheco and nearby Rua Cândido dos Reis. Nearly all offer happy hours (at various times of the day) and similar cocktails, and are open until at least 4am in summer.

ℹ Information

Centro de saúde (medical centre; ☎289 598 400; ☺24hr) Two kilometres north of the old town.

Clioura Clinic (☎289 587 000; ☺24hr) A private clinic in Montechoro.

GNR police station (☎289 590 790; Av 25 de Abril)

Turismo (☎289 585 279; www.visitalgarve.pt; Rua 5 de Outubro 8; ☺9.30am-5.30pm Mon-Fri, 9.30am-7pm daily Jul-Sep) By a tunnel that leads to the beach.

ℹ Getting There & Away

BUS The **main bus station** (☏289 580 611; Rua dos Caliços) is 2km north of town. Passengers travelling to Lisbon can purchase tickets at a more conveniently located **bus shop** (☏289 588 122; Av da Liberdade), outside of which buses leave for the main bus station (€1.10) every 30 minutes from 7am to 10pm.

Lagos (€4.95, 65 to 75 minutes, 12 daily)

Faro (€4.20, 40 minutes, hourly)

Silves (€3.75, 40 minutes to one hour, three to seven daily)

Loulé (€3.55, 40 minutes, seven to 10 daily).

Two buses head to Huelva in Spain (€13, 4¼ hours, via Faro), and on to Seville (€17, 5½ hours). Services shrink from October to May.

TRAIN Services from Albufeira:

Lagos (€3.60, 1¼ hours, 10 daily)

Faro (€2.40 to €7.50, 35 minutes, 16 daily)

ℹ Getting Around

To reach the train station, take the *estação* (station) Eva bus (€2, 20 minutes, at least hourly 6.45am to 8pm) from the main bus station.

For car hire:

Auto Jardim (☏289 580 500; www.auto -jardim.com; Edifício Brisa, Av da Liberdade)

Auto Prudente (☏289 542 160; www.auto -prudente.com; Estrada de Santa Eulália, Edifíccio Ondas do Mar, Loja 1) Another option with competitive rates.

Carvoeiro

Carvoeiro is a cluster of whitewashed buildings rising up from tawny, gold and green cliffs and backed by hills. Shops, bars and restaurants rise steeply from the small arc of beach that is the focus of the town, and beyond lie hillsides full of sprawling holiday villas. This diminutive seaside resort 5km south of Lagoa is prettier and more laid-back than many of the bigger resorts, but its size means that it gets full to bursting in summer. Note: parking is difficult in summer – you are best to head to Estrada do Farol and walk.

◉ Sights & Activities

The town's handkerchief-sized little sandy beach, **Praia do Carvoeiro**, is surrounded by the steeply mounting town. About 1km east on the coastal road is the bay of **Algar Seco**, a favourite stop on the tour-bus itinerary thanks to its dramatic rock formations.

If you're looking for a stunning swimming spot, continue east along the main road, Estrada do Farol, to **Praia de Centianes**, where the secluded cliff-wrapped beach is almost as dramatic as Algar Seco. Buses heading for **Praia do Carvalho** (nine daily from Lagoa, via Carvoeiro) pass nearby – get off at Colina Sol Aparthotel, the Moorish-style cliff-top hotel. The nearest water park is **Slide & Splash** (☏282 341 685; www.slidesplash.com; Estrada Nacional 125; adult/child €18/14.50), situated 2km west of Lagoa.

Golfers can be choosy: there's the **Pestana Gramacho** (☏282 340 900; www.pestanagolf.com) and **Pestana Vale da Pinta** (☏282 340 900; www.pestanagolf.com), both at Pestana Golf Resort; and **Vale de Milho** (☏282 358 502; www.valedemilhogolf.com) near Praia de Centianes.

The (German) family-run **Divers Cove** (☏282 356 594; www.diverscove.de; Quinta do Paraíso; ⊘9am-7pm) diving centre provides equipment, dives and PADI certification (three-hour introduction €80, one-day discovery €135, two-day scuba diver €260, four-day open water €440).

🛏 Sleeping

In July and August it may be impossible to find a room, so reserve well ahead. Some guest houses may require a minimum three-night stay.

Casa von Baselli　GUEST HOUSE €€
(☏282 357 159; Rua da Escola; s without bathroom €30, d €50-55) This homely, antique-filled five-room place is run by a delightful German owner. A shared terrace, high above the bay, is a highlight for breakfast and sunset.

O Castelo　GUEST HOUSE €€
(☏282 357 416; www.ocastelo.net; Rua do Casino 59; d without view €48-50, d with view €55-78) To the west of the bay, behind the *turismo*, this welcoming guest house gets the sunrise view and offers spotless well-kept rooms with parquetry floors. Some rooms share a large terrace and sea views. Guests even have use of a kitchen.

Casa Luiz　GUEST HOUSE €€
(☏282 354 058; www.casaluiz.com; Rampa da Nossa Senhora da Encarnação; d/studios/apt €60/70/80) The owner prefers reservations at this well-situated place. Once ensconced, you'll enjoy clean and modern rooms or studios (with kitchen) overlooking the beach.

🍴 Eating & Drinking

There is a handful of restaurants clustered near the beach and scattered along Estrada do Farol.

Marisqueira   SEAFOOD, GRILL HOUSE €€
(Estrada do Farol; mains €7-16; ⊘lunch & dinner Tue-Sun) This local, well-established place has an outdoor terrace and is known for its seafood and grilled dishes.

Julio's Bar Restaurante   PORTUGUESE €€€
(☑282 358 368; www.julios-restaurant.com; Vale do Milho; mains €11-20; ⊘dinner Mon-Sat) This smart but unstuffy place is set in a pretty garden around 2km east of town. Its clientele are mainly tourists who come here for the excellent international cuisine. Best to reserve.

Restaurante Boneca Bar   BAR €€
(⊘10am-midnight) Hidden in the rock formations out at Algar Seco, this long-standing place is a novel spot for a cocktail.

ℹ️ Information

The post office and several banks are located on Rua dos Pescadores (the one-way road in from Lagoa).
Turismo (☑282 357 728; ⊘9.30am-1pm & 2-5.30pm Fri-Mon, 9.30am-6pm Tue-Thu)

ℹ️ Getting There & Around

Buses run on weekdays from Portimão to Lagoa (€2, 20 minutes, hourly) and to Carvoeiro (€2.75, 10 minutes, one to seven daily).

You can rent scooters from **Motorent** (☑282 356 551; Rua do Barranco) on the road back to Lagoa. Several car-rental agencies are also along this road.

Silves

POP 10,800

Silves is a gorgeous town of jumbling orange rooftops scattered above the banks of the Rio Arade. It boasts one of the best-preserved castles in the Algarve, attractive red-stone walls and winding sleepy backstreets on a hillside. After dark, not much happens around town, but it's the perfect place to base yourself, if you're after a less hectic, noncoastal Algarvian pace. Around Silves, there are some lovely rural accommodation options. It's 15km northeast of Portimão.

The train station is located 2km south of town, but you'll need to catch a cab as it's along a major highway.

History

The Rio Arade was long an important route into the interior for the Phoenicians, Greeks and Carthaginians, who wanted the copper and iron action in the southwest of the country. With the Moorish invasion from the 8th century, the town gained prominence due to its strategic hilltop, riverside site. From the mid-11th to the mid-13th centuries, Shelb (or Xelb), as it was then known, rivalled Lisbon in prosperity and influence: according to the 12th-century Arab geographer Idrisi, it had a population of 30,000, a port and shipyards, and 'attractive buildings and well-furnished bazaars'.

The town's downfall began in June 1189, when Dom Sancho I laid siege to it, supported by a horde of (mostly English) hooligan crusaders, who had been persuaded (with the promise of loot) to pause in their journey to Jerusalem and give Sancho a hand. The Moors holed up inside their impregnable castle with their huge cisterns, but after three hot months of harassment they ran out of water and were forced to surrender. Sancho was all for mercy and honour, but the crusaders wanted the plunder they were promised, and stripped the Moors of their possessions (including the clothes on their backs) as they left, tortured those remaining and wrecked the town.

Two years later the Moors recaptured the town. It wasn't until 1249 that Christians gained control once and for all. But by then Silves was a shadow of its former self. The silting up of the river – which caused disease and stymied maritime trade – coupled with the growing importance of the Algarvian ports hastened the town's decline. Devastation in the 1755 earthquake seemed to seal its fate. But in the 19th century, local cork and dried-fruit industries revitalised Silves, hence the grand bourgeois architecture around town. Today tourism and agriculture are the town's lifeblood.

◉ Sights

Castelo   CASTLE
(☑282 445 624; adult/concession/under 10yr €2.50/1.25/free, joint ticket with Museu Municipal €3.60; ⊘9am-5pm Dec-Feb, to 6.30pm Jun-Aug) The russet-coloured, Lego-like castle has great views over the town and surrounding countryside. It was restored in the 1940s and you can walk around its chunky sandstone walls. The whole site is Islamic and Christian (8th to 13th centuries).

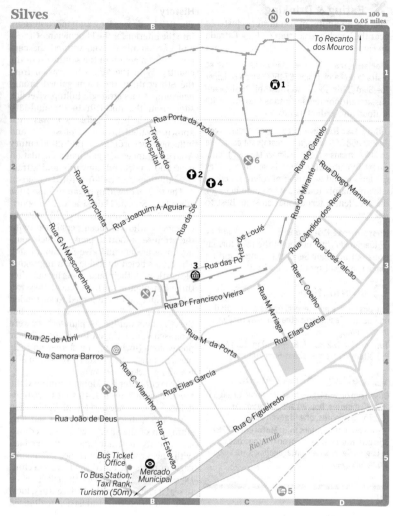

In the north wall you can see a treason gate, an escape route through which turncoats would sometimes let the enemy in, typical of castles at the time. The Moorish occupation is recalled by a deep well and a rosy-coloured water cistern, 5m deep and constructed at the end of the 12th century. Inside, the cistern's four vaults are supported by 10 columns. Most probably built in the 11th century, the castle was abandoned by the 16th century. Recent restorations include the red-brick interior walkway and the tearoom (not operating at time of research).

Sé & Igreja da Misericórdia CHURCH
(Cathedral; admission €1; ⊙10am-noon & 3-7pm)
Just below the castle is the *sé*, built in 1189 on the site of an earlier mosque, then rebuilt after the 1249 Reconquista and subsequently restored several times following earthquake damage. The stark, fortresslike building has a multiarched Portuguese-Gothic doorway, and some original Gothic touches left, including the nave and aisles and a dramatically tall, strikingly simple interior. There are several fine tombs, one of which is purported to be of João do Rego, who helped to settle Madeira. Nearby is

Silves

the 16th-century **Igreja da Misericórdia**
(◷9am-1pm & 2-5pm), plain apart from its
distinctive, fanciful Manueline doorway
(not the main entrance) decorated with curious heads, pine cones, foliage and aquatic
emblems.

Museu Municipal de Arqueologia MUSEUM
(☏282 444 832; Rua das Portas de Loulé; adult/
under 10yr €2/free, joint ticket with Castelo €3;
◷9am-5.30pm Mon-Sat) Just below the cathedral is the impressive, well-laid-out Museu
Municipal de Arqueologia. In the centre is
a well-preserved 4m-wide, 18m-deep Moorish well surrounded by a spiral staircase,
which was discovered during excavations.
The find, together with other archaeological discoveries in the area, led to the establishment of the museum on this site;
it shows prehistoric, Roman and Moorish
antiquities. One wall is of glass, showing
a section of the fort wall (also of Almohad
origin) that is used to support the building.

⊀ Activities
See p173 for information about **boat trips**
from Portimão to Silves.

Country Riding Centre HORSE RIDING
(www.countryridingcentre.com; lessons from
€22.50) Located about 4km east of Silves,
left off the road to Messines (it is signposted); offers hour-long to half-day hacks at
all levels, with swimming opportunities as
well (open daily).

Krazy World WATER PARK
(☏282 574 134; www.krazyworld.com; adult/child
€15/8; ◷10am-6pm) Near São Bartolomeu de
Messines, about 17km northwest, there's
Krazy World, an animal and crocodile park

with minigolf, pony rides and two swimming pools.

✹ Festivals & Events
Over one week each August (dates vary annually), Silves relives its past at the **Medieval
Fair**. The town's important events and people are reconstructed, from Al Muthamid,
the governor of Silves, to the town being
awarded its charter. Think bawdy costumes,
dances, jesters, feasts, traditional food and
handicrafts...all evoking life in the 11th to
13th centuries.

⛏ Sleeping
Duas Quintas RURAL INN €€
(☏919 729 799; www.algarveguesthouse.com; d/
studios incl breakfast €95/115; São Estevão; ☒)
This charming but unpretentious place, a
converted farmhouse, screams 'relax!' Set
within greenery and rolling hills, it has six
pleasant rooms, a living space, terraces and
a pool. The friendly Irish owners serve up
scrumptious gourmet breakfasts – great
energy for the excellent walks in the surrounds. Prices are significantly less outside
high season. To get here, head 5.5km northeast (en route to São Bartolomeu de Messines) to Sítio São Estevão.

Quinta da Figueirinha RURAL INN €€
(☏282 440 700; www.qdf.pt; 2-/4-/6-person
apt €64/92/125; ☎☒) This 36-hectare organic farm and botanic (drought-resistant)
garden, run by the kindly agronomist Dr
Gerhard Zabel, offers simple apartments in
peaceful farmlike surroundings. The surrounding exotic orchards are yours (more
than 50 species of plants) for picking and
wandering. Leaving Silves and crossing the
bridge, take the first left to Fragura and continue for 4km. The *quinta* (estate) is signposted. You can self-cater, or there is a basic
restaurant serving delicious, wholesome
buffet-style food.

Casa das Oliveiras RURAL INN €€
(☏282 342 115; www.casa-das.oliveiras.com; s
€47-53, d €57-65; ☎☒) This peaceful place
offers an old-style B&B with a British flavour, with five slightly dated rooms in a
relaxed setting. There's a lovely garden and
pool area. It's 4km from Silves train station.
Ring for directions.

Vila Sodre GUEST HOUSE €€
(☏282 443 441; www.vilasodresilves.sapo.pt/
index; Estrada de Messines; s incl breakfast €40,
d €55-70; ❄☒) This modern blue-and-white

villa is 1.4km east of the newer bridge. It's good value, with smart, if faded, rooms that overlook orange orchards. The highlight is the owner – ask to see his extraordinary wine collection.

Residencial Restaurante Ponte Romana
GUEST HOUSE €

(282 443 275; Horta da Cruz; s/d €20/35) At the end of the old bridge on the other side of the river from town, this long-standing place has clean rooms with frilly bedspreads. Some of the rooms have idyllic views across the river to the castle. There's a cheery restaurant, too. To get here by car, drive over the larger bridge towards Portimão and take the first right (west) after the big bridge.

Eating

There are plenty of cafe-restaurants in the pedestrianised streets leading up to the castle or down by the river, where you'll also find a reasonable *mercado municipal* (just west of the old pedestrian bridge).

TOP CHOICE Restaurante O Barradas
PORTUGUESE €€€

(282 443 308; www.obarradas.com; Palmeirinha; mains €8.50-25; dinner Thu-Tue) The star choice for fine dining is this delightful spot (follow the road to Lagoa and then to Palmeirinha; it's 3km from Silves). The German chef creates her own Portuguese wonders, always using Mediterranean ingredients, sourced where possible from local suppliers. The country's finest organic meats and fresh, not farmed, fish are used. Desserts use seasonal fruits (don't miss the figs with muscatel). An elegant atmosphere, gourmet dishes, and too many fine wines (did we mention her husband is a winemaker?) make for a taxi booking (seriously, think about it).

Recanto dos Mouros
PORTUGUESE €€

(282 443 240; Monte Branco; mains €9-13; lunch & dinner Thu-Tue) Situated a kilometre or so behind the castle (follow the signs), this is one of Silves' most popular places. As the Portuguese attest, it's *bom preço-qualidade* (damn good value) for lots of hearty Algarvian delights.

Café Inglês
BAR, RESTAURANT €€

(mains €6-14; 9.30am-5.30pm Mon, 9.30am-late Tue-Sat) Located below the castle entrance, the Café Inglês has a wonderful, shady terrace and is everyone's favourite spot. The food is excellent (don't miss the

chocolate St Emilion dessert). One of the Algarve's liveliest restaurants north of the coast, it has an elegant interior and on weekends has occasional live jazz, fado and African music.

Restaurante Marisqueria Rui
SEAFOOD €€

(282 442 682; Rua Commendador Vilarinho 27; mains €7-16; lunch & dinner Wed-Mon) Situated in the old town, this place is Silves' finest seafood restaurant. Join the locals – it gets busy – and savour plates from cockles, clams and crabs to bass and seafood rice.

Pastelaria Rosa
PATISSERIE €

(Largo do Município; 7.30am-late Mon-Sat) On the ground floor of the town hall building, this long-standing, tile-lined place is lovely for coffee and pastries. You can sit outside next to a small tree-shaded plaza or inside for rustic charm.

Restaurante Ponte Romana
PORTUGUESE €

(Horta da Cruz; mains €5-11) Adjoining the Ponte Romana *residencial,* this basement restaurant has decorations – keys, cowbells and harnesses – as antiquated as its prices (which haven't moved in years) and clients (ditto). Great value, hearty country fare.

Information

Internet Cafe (Rua Pintor Bernardo Marques; per hr €2; 10am-1.30pm & 3-7.30pm)

Post office (Rua Samora Barros)

Turismo do Algarve (www.visitalgarve.pt; 9.30am-1pm & 2-5.30pm Mon-Fri) Next to the main car park. The unrelated but informative municipality website is www.cm-silves.pt.

Getting There & Around

Much of the hilly, compact centre of Silves is easily done on foot; many streets are pedestrianised areas only. Drivers are advised to park their car in the large car park on the city side (north) of the river and southwest of the city centre (no charge).

BUS There are no direct buses between Lagos and Silves; change at Portimão (40 minutes).

Albufeira (€3.75, 40 minutes, four to seven daily)

Portimão (€2.75, 20 minutes, five to nine daily)

All buses leave from the riverfront, with fewer running at weekends. The **bus ticket office** (282 442 338; 8am-6pm Mon-Fri, to 1pm Sat, 9am-noon Sun) is on the western side of the market.

TRAINS Local buses travel daily between Silves and its train station (€1.90, five to 10 daily). Services from Silves:

Lagos (€2.15 35 minutes, eight daily)

Faro (€4.10, 1¼ hours, eight daily)

Portimão

POP 37,000

Bustling Portimão is the western Algarve's main commercial centre and the second-most populous city in the Algarve. It used to be the region's fishing and canning centre but, although it still has a sprawling port, only a small fishing fleet remains. The messy outskirts of the city hide a small, friendly hub, whose focal point is the Praça Manuel Teixeira Gomes, a pleasant waterfront, an assortment of outdoor cafes, and sizzling fish restaurants in the old quarter and quayside. You can also arrange a boat trip up the Rio Arade. Most tourists only pass through en route to Praia da Rocha.

Portimão was an important trading link for Phoenicians, Greeks and Carthaginians (Hannibal is said to have visited). It was called Portos Magnus by the Romans and was fought over by Moors and Christians. In 1189 Dom Sancho I and a band of crusaders sailed up the Rio Arade from here to besiege Silves. Almost destroyed in the 1755 earthquake, it regained its maritime importance in the 19th century. Since the 1970s, the fishing and related industries have been in decline, but in recent years there has been much investment in marina and waterfront redevelopment for tourism and leisure boats.

Sights

The town's parish church, the igreja matriz (admission free), stands on high ground to the north of the town centre and features a 14th-century Gothic portal – all that remains of the original structure after the 1755 earthquake. Other echoes of the past can be found in the narrow streets of the old fishing quarter, around Largo da Barca, just before the old highway bridge.

Museu de Portimão   MUSEUM
(☎282 405 230; admission €3; ☻2.30-6pm Tue & 10am-6pm Wed-Sun 1 Sep-14 Jul, 7.30-11pm Tue & 3-11pm Wed-Sun 15 Jul-31 Aug) The modern Museu de Portimão, housed in a converted fish cannery, is one excellent reason to visit Portimão. Opened in 2008, the museum focuses on three areas: archaeology, underwater finds and, the most fascinating, the re-creation of the fish cannery (mackerel and sardines). The museum re-creates former production lines, complete with sound effects – clanking and grinding and the like. An excellent video (in Portuguese) of the fishing industry reveals each step

in the process, from netting the shoals to packaging.

Activities

Operators galore line the riverside promenade offering **boat trips**. These include cruises up coast and/or the Rio Arade, visiting caves along the way. Prices start at around €25. There are also **dolphin-spotting** opportunities. Some trips are in fishing boats for 10 people, others are in sailing boats for 35. Santa Bernarda (☎282 422 791, 967 023 840; www.santa-bernarda.com; trips adult/child from €30/15) runs trips visiting the caves and coast on a 23m wooden sailing ship with wheelchair access. The full-day trip includes a beach barbecue and time to swim.

Ask at the tourist office for a copy of *Get in touch with Nature,* which outlines several **self-guided nature walks**, **bikes** and boat trips in the region.

Centro Hípico Vale de Ferro   HORSE RIDING
(☎282 968 444; www.algarvehorseholidays.com; per hr €25) The nearest place to go for a gallop is Centro Hípico Vale de Ferro, near Mexilhoeira Grande (4.2km west of Portimão); it also offers riding-holiday packages.

Sleeping

Globo Hotel   HOTEL €€€
(☎282 405 030; www.hoteisalgarvesol.pt; Rua 5 de Outubro 26; s/d €98/130; ❄) Rooms here have a snazzy design, with contemporary fittings and abundant natural light. Each floor has a colour scheme, from lilac to green.

Pousada de Juventude   HOSTEL €
(☎282 491 804; Rua da Nossa Senhora da Conceição; dm/d €16/45) This place is just out of the centre, but it's a good budget option.

Eating & Drinking

The fountain-lined pedestrian street Rua Direita, about 300m west of the river, is a good destination for restaurant browsing. For open-air seafood grub, head to Largo da Barco – a strip of restaurants under the arches of the bridge – where for decades, charcoal-grilled sardines and barbecued fish were enjoyed by hungry fishermen and, in later years, by hoards of locals and visitors.

Casa Inglesa   CAFE €
(Praça Manuel T Gomes; mains €3-7; ☻8am-11pm; ☻) Central to Portimão life, this large cafe

THE ALGARVE

on the main square has a charming 1920s feel (make sure you look upstairs), with lots of snacks on offer, as well as tasty marzipan.

Taska Porta Velha　　BAR, RESTAURANT　€€
(☑918 053 169; Travessa Manuel Dias Barão; tapas €4-8; ☉10pm-4am Mon-Sat) This atmospheric bar is the kind of place you can kick back and relax in. It's been lovingly restored and decorated; spread across several rooms are antique knick-knacks and modern artworks. The tables are made of wood and stone slabs and in one room the ceiling is made entirely of corks. *Petiscos* (snacks) and drinks only. It's near the modern square (an extension of Rua Direita).

ⓘ Information
There are several banks with ATMs around the riverside Praça Manuel Teixeira Gomes.

Municipal turismo (☑282 470 732; www. cm-portimao.pt; Av Zeca Afonso; ☉9am-6pm Mon-Fri, 9am-1pm Sat Jun-Aug, 9am-12.30pm & 2-5.30pm Mon-Fri Sep-May) Opposite the football stadium, about 600m west of the river.

Sodeal (☑282 424 061; Rua Mouzinho de Albuquerque 39; ☉9am-1pm & 3-7pm Mon-Fri, 9am-1pm Sat) A handy same-day laundry service (€1.65 per kg).

ⓘ Getting There & Around
Bus

Local buses shuttle between Praia da Rocha and Portimão (€1.30 on the bus, €10.50 for 10 prepurchased tickets on a card, at least half-hourly).

To head further afield, Portimão has excellent bus connections; local buses cover some inner-city routes.

You can get information and tickets for Eva and Intersul (Eurolines) services at the **Eva office** (☑282 418 120; Largo do Duque 3), located by the riverside. Buses leave from near the Repsol petrol station along the riverside on Av Guanaré.

Services include the following:

DESTINATION	FARE (€)	DURATION (HR)	FREQUENCY (NORMAL/EXPRESS PER DAY)
Albufeira	4.05	1	14/6
Cabo São Vicente	5.45	1½	1/0
Faro	5	1¾	7/2
Lagos	3.75	¾	12/5
Lisbon	19	3¼	6/4
Loulé	5.40	1¾	6 (weekends only; change in Albufeira on weekdays)
Sagres	5.40	1¼	2/0
Salema	3.75	1	1/0

Car
If you have your own wheels, the easiest parking is a free riverside area by the Repsol station.

Train
Eight daily trains connect Portimão with Tunes (via Silves €2.15) and Lagos (€1.40, 20 minutes). Change at Tunes for Lisbon.

Praia da Rocha

One of the Algarve's finest beaches, Praia da Rocha is a wide stretch of sand backed by ochre-red cliffs and the petite 16th-century Fortaleza da Santa Catarina, built in the 16th century to stop pirates and invaders from sailing up the Rio Arade to Portimão.

Behind the beach looms the town; this has long known the hand of development, with high-rise condos and luxury hotels sprouting along the cliffside, and a row of restaurants, bars and dance clubs packed along the main thoroughfare. If you look hard beyond the ugly concrete facade, Praia da Rocha has several vestiges from an elegant past, including some 19th-century mansions, which are now atmospheric guest houses.

There's also a sleek marina, Marina de Portimão, painted autumnal colours (to match the cliffs) and a casino where you can double (or deplete) your savings.

⏢ Sleeping
Accommodation is almost impossible to find in the high season if you don't have a prior reservation.

Albergaria Vila Lido　　GUEST HOUSE　€€€
(☑282 241 127; www.hotelvilalido.com; Av Tomás Cabreira; d from €130; ℗※) Near the fort, this hotel was converted from a 19th-century mansion and has a slightly Brighton (UK) guest-house feel, with great sea views and 10 bright rooms, most of which have terraces.

Hotel da Rocha　　LUXURY HOTEL　€€€
(☑282 424 081; www.hoteldarocha.com; d from €150; ℗※@※) Praia da Rocha's newest hotel is bang in the middle of a busy strip opposite the beach. The rooms are simple,

yet sleek and modern, with good light. All feature kitchenettes.

Eating

Restaurante Marisqueira   PORTUGUESE €€
(mains €7-17, 3-course menus €15; ☺lunch & dinner Mon-Sat) An unusually traditional restaurant for Praia da Rocha, this popular and low-key place opposite Algarve Mor hotel offers decent Portuguese fare, with a hearty array of daily specials.

Snack Bar Scorpíus   RESTAURANT €
(Rua Bartolomeu Dias; mains €6-8; ☺10am-1am Tue-Sun) A bit off the beaten path, this popular local cafe is a good spot to enjoy simple but nicely prepared plates of seafood, omelettes and desserts.

The marina has a row of romantic, upmarket dining and drinking spots, some of which stare across at the beautiful Praia Meia Grande:

Restaurante Almeida   RESTAURANT €€
(☎282 424 304; mains €12-18; fish per kg €45-95) Almeida has a pleasant setting on the marina and is a safe, conservative bet for your standard fish and meat cuisine. *Cataplanas* also on offer.

Dockside   RESTAURANT €€€
(www.restaurantedockside.com; mains €10-20; ☺10am-midnight) One of the newer, best situated and most highly recommended places on the marina. Serves up live shellfish and flambéed meat dishes.

☆ Entertainment

Praia da Rocha bristles with bars that are packed with sun-kissed faces, satellite TV, live music and karaoke. Many are owned or run by foreign residents. You might as well be in Dublin, for the plethora of Irish bars, including Ireland's Eye and Celt Bar (barhopping directions not needed, just follow the craic). They're open all day (and nearly all night).

Voxx (Av Tomás Cabreira) is a sleek discotheque that makes good use of its waterside setting and plays anything from pop to African to hip-hop. Monster **Discoteca Katedral** (Rua António Feu) gets busy with pop house, until 6am nightly during summer. The marina has some sleek, fun alternatives with karaoke and regular live music.

Casino   GAMING
(☎282 402 000; Av Tomás Cabreira; admission free; ☺4pm-3am) The glitzy casino, midway along the esplanade in Hotel Algarve, has the gaming lot.

ⓘ Information

The post office is near the *turismo*.

Police (☎281 419 183; Av Tomas Cabrera; ☺9am-12.30pm & 2-5pm Mon-Fri)

Turismo (☎282 419 132; Av Tomas Cabrera; ☺9.30am-7pm Jul & Aug, 9.30am-5.30pm Mon-Fri Sep-Jun) In the centre of the esplanade.

Unicâmbio/Western Union (☺9.30am-9pm) Next door to the *turismo*, this has telephone booths and internet.

ⓘ Getting There & Around

BUS A regular shuttle heads to Portimão (around €2 on the bus, €10.50 for 10 pre-purchased trips, every 15 to 30 minutes). Eva bus services run to Albufeira (€3.80, four to six daily, 45 minutes) and Lagos (€3.60, four to six daily, 45 minutes). Frota Azul has regular trips to Lagos as well (€2.60, regular, 45 minutes). Eva runs to/from Lisbon (€19, five daily). The bus terminus in Praia da Rocha is by Club Praia de Rocha.

CAR Auto Rent (☎282 417 171; www.auto rent.pt; Av Tomás Cabreira) offers good car-rental deals.

Lagos

POP 17,500

As far as touristy towns go, Lagos (*lah-goosh*) has, fortunately – or unfortunately – got the lot. It lies along the bank of the Rio Bensafrim, with 16th-century walls enclosing the old town's pretty, cobbled streets and picturesque plazas and churches. Beyond these lies a modern, but not overly unattractive, modern sprawl. The town's good restaurants and range of fabulous beaches nearby add to the allure. With every activity under the sun (literally) on offer, plus a pumping nightlife, it's not surprising that people of all ages are drawn here. In season, with all the crowds and action, the town can feel hectic and claustrophobic.

Aside from its hedonistic appeal, Lagos has historical clout, having launched many naval excursions during Portugal's extraordinary Age of Discoveries (see p479).

History

Phoenicians and Greeks set up shop at this port (which later became Roman Lacobriga) at the mouth of the muddy Rio Bensafrim. Afonso III recaptured it from the Moors in 1241, and the Portuguese continued harassing the Muslims of North Africa

THE ALGARVE

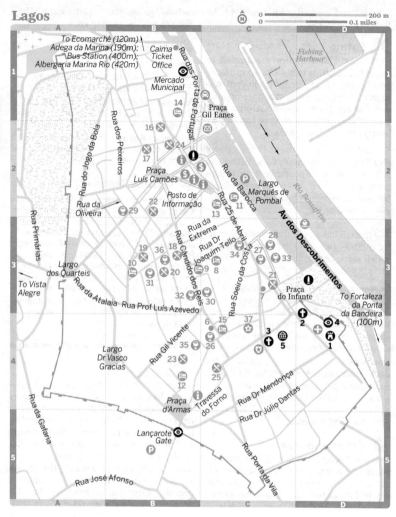

from here. In 1415 a giant fleet set sail from Lagos under the command of the 21-year-old Prince Henry the Navigator to seize Ceuta in Morocco, thereby setting the stage for the Age of Discoveries.

The shipyards of Lagos built and launched Prince Henry's caravels, and Henry split his time between his trading company here and his navigation school at Sagres. Local boy Gil Eanes left Lagos in 1434 as commander of the first ship to round West Africa's Cape Bojador. Others continued to bring back information about the African coast, along with ivory, gold

and slaves. Lagos has the dubious distinction of having hosted (in 1444) the first sale of black Africans as slaves to Europeans, and the town grew into a slave-trading centre.

It was also from Lagos in 1578 that Dom Sebastião, along with the cream of Portuguese nobility and an army of Portuguese, Spanish, Dutch and German buccaneers, left on a disastrous crusade to Christianise North Africa, which ended in a debacle at Alcácer-Quibir in Morocco. Sir Francis Drake inflicted heavy damage on Lagos a few years later, in 1587.

Lagos was the Algarve's high-profile capital from 1576 until 1755, when the earthquake flattened it.

◎ Sights

Igreja de Santo António & Museu Municipal
CHURCH, MUSEUM

(Rua General Alberto da Silveira; ◎9.30am-12.30pm & 2-5pm Tue-Sun) The little Igreja de Santo António, bursting with 18th- and 19th-century gilded, carved wood, is a stupendous baroque extravaganza. Beaming cherubs and ripening grapes are much in evidence. The dome and *azulejo* panels were installed during repairs after the 1755 earthquake.

Enter from the adjacent **Museu Municipal** (☑282 762 301; Rua General Alberto da Silveira; adult/concession €2.60/1.30; ◎9.30am-12.30pm & 2-5pm Tue-Sun), a glorious and fascinating historic mishmash. There's an entrancing haphazardness about it all, from Roman nails found locally and opium pipes from Macau to bits of the Berlin wall sharing a case with scary-looking surgical instruments.

Fortaleza da Ponta da Bandeira
FORTRESS

(Av dos Descobrimentos; adult/concession €2/1; ◎9.30am-12.30pm & 2-5pm Tue-Sun) This little fortress, at the southern end of the avenue, was built in the 17th century to protect the port. Now restored, it houses an exhibition on the Portuguese discoveries and a quaint chapel, Santa Bárbara, Protector of Storms.

Ponta da Piedade
VIEWING POINT

Protruding south from Lagos, Ponta da Piedade (Point of Piety) is a stunning, dramatic wedge of headland. Three windswept kilometres out of town, the point is well worth a visit for its contorted, polychrome sandstone cliffs and towers, complete with lighthouse and, in spring, hundreds of nesting egrets. The surrounding area is brilliant with wild orchids in spring. On a clear day you can see east to Carvoeiro and west to Sagres.

Parque Zoológico de Lagos
ZOO

(☑282 680 100; www.zoolagos.com; Quinta Figueiras; adult/child €12/6; ◎10am-7pm Apr-Sep, 10am-5pm Oct-Mar, restaurant closed Mon) This zoo is a shady 3-hectare kid-pleaser, with many small primates, and a children's farm housing domestic animals. It's near the village of Barão de São João, 8km west of Lagos.

Around the Town

Igreja de Santa Maria (Praça do Infante) dates from the 15th and 16th centuries

KIDDIE FUN – THE ALGARVE FOR CHILDREN

The Algarve is a fun kid-focused area, with loads of attractions, family-friendly beaches and cultural activities. Try thrilling water parks (see the boxed text, p166 and p168); a great zoo in Lagos (p177); and, at Silves, an imagination-firing castle (p195). There are some excellent museums, too. In São Bras de Alportel there's a simple cork display in the Museu Etnográfico do Trajo Algarvio (p149), and in Portimão, the wonderful Museu de Portimão re-creates a former fish cannery (p173).

Many towns along the coast run boat trips (see individual destinations), and several have little trains. Horse riding is another option (see the boxed text, p166 and p171). See the Directory chapter (p520) for more details on keeping little ones happy.

and retains a 16th-century entrance; the rest dates largely from the mid-19th century when it was restored after a fire. Don't overlook the strange orange and purple battling-angels mural behind the altar.

Just south of Praça do Infante is a restored section of the stout **town walls**, built (atop earlier versions) during the reigns of both Manuel I and João III in the 16th century, when the walls were enlarged to the existing outline. They extend intermittently, with at least six bastions, for about 1.5km around the central town.

Rua da Barroca once formed the boundary between the town and the sea, and retains some Arabic features.

Castelo dos Governadores (Governors Castle), in the southeast part of town at the back of the present-day hospital, was built by the Arabs. After the Reconquista in the 13th century, the Algarve's military government was established here in the 14th century. It's said that the ill-fated, evangelical Dom Sebastião attended an open-air Mass here and spoke to the assembled nobility from a small Manueline window in the castle, before leading them to a crushing defeat at Alcácer-Quibir (Morocco).

Near Praça do Infante is a less-than-glorious site – where slaves were auctioned off in Portugal in the 15th century. It now houses an art gallery.

🏃 Activities

Beaches & Water Sports

Meia Praia, the vast expanse of sand to the east of town, has outlets offering sailboard rental and water-skiing lessons, plus several laid-back restaurants and beach bars. South of town the beaches – **Batata**, **Pinhão**, **Dona Ana**, **Camilo** among others – are smaller and more secluded, lapped by calm waters and punctuated with amazing grottoes, coves and towers of coloured sandstone). A **ferry** runs from the waterfront in Lagos to Meia Praia.

Lagos is a popular **surfing** centre and has good facilities; surfing companies head to the west coast for the waves.

Lagos Surf Center SURFING
(☑282 764 734; www.lagossurfcenter.com; Rua da Silva Lopes 31; 1-/3-/5-day courses €45/120/180) Will help you catch a wave and head to where there are suitable swells. Children must be accompanied by a family member over 14 years of age. It also rents out wetsuits (€5 per day) and boards (€20) and offers beach kayaking trips (€25 per person).

Jah-Shaka SURFING
(☑915 896 536; www.jah-shaka.eu; Rua Cândido dos Reis 112; equipment hire & B&B per day €55, 1-/3-/5-day course or safari €45/120/180) Another swell option plus board hire available.

Blue Ocean Divers DIVING
(☑964 665 667; www.blue-ocean-divers.de; Motel Ancora, Porto de Mos) For those who want to go diving or snorkelling. Offers a half-day discovery experience (€30), a full-day dive (€90) and a five-day divemaster PADI scuba course (€510). It also offers kayak safaris (€30/45 half/full day, child under 12 years half price).

Windsurf Point WINDSURFING
(☑282 792 315; www.windsurfpoint.com; Marina) Windsurfing courses (beginners full-day €180) at Meia Praia, kitesurfing, board rental (per hour/half-day €30/45) and a shop.

Boat Trips & Dolphin Safaris

Numerous operators have ticket stands at the marina or along the promenade opposite. They operate a bit like sausage factories but offer some fun outings. The following are a mere selection. Local fishermen offering jaunts to the grottoes by motorboat trawl for customers along the promenade and by the Fortaleza da Ponta da Bandeira.

Bom Dia BOAT TRIPS
(☎282 764 670; www.bomdia-boattrips.com)
The oldest operator and based at the marina, Bom Dia runs trips on traditional schooners, including a five-hour barbecue cruise (adult/child €49/25), with a chance to swim; a two-hour grotto trip (€27.50/12.50; four daily) or family fishing (€45/35).

Frota do Infante BOAT TRIPS
(☎912 545 431; www.frotadoinfante.pt) Offers one-hour trips to the grottoes beneath Ponta da Piedade (€10).

Kayak Adventures KAYAKING
(☎913 262 200; www.kayakadventures-lagos.com) Has kayaking trips from Batata Beach, including snorkelling, between April and October. Trips last around 2½ hours (€25).

Some outfits offer dolphin-spotting trips:

Dizzy Dolphins DOLPHIN WATCHING
(☎938 305 000; www.dizzydolphin.com) In summer, trips are led by novelist Kit Thackeray.

Algarve Dolphins DOLPHIN WATCHING
(☎282 087 587; www.algarve-dolphins.com; trips from €35) Also supports the research and protection of dolphins.

Dolphin Seafaris DOLPHIN WATCHING
(☎282 799 209; www.dolphinseafaris.com; trips €35; ⊘Apr-Oct)

Other Activities

Tiffany's KAYAKING
(☎282 697 395; www.valegrifo.com/tiffanysriding/; Vale Grifo, Almádena; ⊘9am-dusk) About 10km west of Lagos, this outfit charges €33 an hour for horse riding and has other options, including a three-/five-hour trip (€85/140); the latter includes a champagne picnic. Another centre with similar activities is **Quinta Paraíso Alto** (☎282 687 596; www.qpahorseriding.com; Fronteira), 7km north of Lagos.

Mountain Bike Adventure CYCLING
(☎916 726 739; www.themountainbikeadventure.com; Porta da Vila) Bike geeks will have some fun with this company, which offers a range of trips for all standards, from shorter scenic trips, to full-on technical rides with shoots, drops and jumps.

🛏 Sleeping

Accommodation options are extensive in Lagos, with more places out on Meia Praia and on Praia da Dona Ana. Rooms are pricier and scarcer from July to mid-

September. Locals often meet the buses to tout their private homes; head to the tourist office for a list of officially approved individuals.

Pensâo Marazul GUEST HOUSE €€
(☎282 770 230; www.pensaomarazul.com; Rua 25 de Abril 13; s/d €40/50, without bathroom €30/40;@🖥🛜) Also central, this well-run and delightfully welcoming place has comfortable, neat rooms, some with sea views. Those facing the (busy) front have double-glazed windows. A simple breakfast is an added bonus. Excellent value.

Pousada da Juventude HOSTEL €
(☎282 761 970; www.pousadasjuventude.pt; Rua Lançarote de Freitas 50; dm/d €17/43, d without bathroom €37;@) One of Portugal's best, this well-run hostel is a great place to meet other travellers. There's a kitchen and pleasant courtyard, and the reception is very helpful. It's open 24 hours.

Vila Galé Lagos LUXURY HOTEL €€€
(☎282 771 400; www.vilagalelagos.pt; Meia Praia; d from €300; P❄🛀) This is Lagos' newest and finest hotel, offering all the creature comforts for resort-loving visitors and business clients. Everything seems to come in multiples – pools, restaurants, activities and zeros (as in the price – but promotions are available).

Pensão Caravela GUEST HOUSE €
(☎282 763 361; Rua 25 de Abril 16; s €25, d €30-35) In the central pedestrian zone, Caravela hasn't been renovated in years...but 'keeps on keeping on'. Some of the ageing rooms have their own rickety showers, but none have toilets.

Hotel Riomar HOTEL €€
(☎282 763 091; hotelriomar@sapo.pt; Rua Cândido dos Reis 83; s/d €50/80; ❄) Rooms here are small but comfortable, with parquetry wood floors and balconies (no view). Rooms boast a recent facelift, and now boast new bathrooms.

Cidade Velha GUEST HOUSE €€
(☎282 762 041; Rua Dr Joaquim Tello 7; s/d/tr from €45/65/75; ❄@) Closed at the time of research for a bit of a pep up, but past visits indicate light, airy and tidy rooms. Breakfast not included.

Sol a Sol HOTEL €€
(☎282 761 290; www.residencialsolasol.com; Rua Lançarote de Freitas 22; s/d/tr from €60/65/80) This central, small hotel has rooms with

tiny balconies and views over the town; it's a bit dated on the outside but, inside, the rooms are neat and clean.

Hotel Lagosmar HOTEL €€
(☎282 763 722; www.lagosmar.com; Rua Dr Faria da Silva 13; s/d €85/95; ❄️🛜) Lagosmar had a makeover in 2009. It boasts a new orange, brown and yellow retro look and offers simple and plain but comfortable motel-style rooms, some with tiny verandas.

Albergaria Marina Rio HOTEL €€€
(☎282 780 830; www.marinario.com; Av dos Descobrimentos; s €92-102, d €95-105; 🅿️❄️ @🛜) Overlooking the harbour, this hotel has comfortable rooms with contemporary decor and balconies. On the downside, it faces the road and backs onto the bus station. Most rooms are twins. There's a tiny pool and roof terrace.

✖️ Eating

Lagos has some great dining spots, serving both Portuguese and international cuisine. Budget travellers should focus their attentions on lunchtime *pratos do dia* (daily specials), which often cost around €6. Many excellent cafes are dotted around town. A daily fish market sells its catch.

TOP CHOICE A Forja PORTUGUESE €€
(Rua dos Ferreiros 17; mains €6.50-15; ⊙lunch & dinner, closed Sat) The secret is out. This buzzing place pulls in the crowds – locals, tourists, expats – for its overhearty, top-

quality traditional food served in a bustling environment at great prices. Plates of the day are always reliable, as are the fish dishes.

Casinha do Petisco PORTUGUESE, SEAFOOD €€
(Rua da Oliveira 51; mains €6.90-12; ⊙lunch & dinner Mon-Sat) Blink – or be late – and you'll miss this tiny traditional gem. It's cosy and simply decorated and comes highly recommended by locals for its seafood grills and shellfish dishes.

Vista Alegre PORTUGUESE €€
(Rua Ilha Terceira 19B; mains €13-17; ⊙lunch & dinner Tue-Sun) Beyond the town walls is this warm, intimate eatery. The chef is French, his wife Portuguese, and the menu an enticing mix of both. Think lamb *provençal* and quail (with a *jus* to die for). True panache.

No Patio PORTUGUESE, INTERNATIONAL €€€
(☎282 763 777; Rua Lançerote de Freitas 46; 2-/3-course dinner €18.50/22.50; ⊙dinner Tue-Sat, lunch Sun) When you hear the song 'Food, Glorious Food' (from the musical of *Oliver Twist*) playing in the background of this cosy place, you know that either you're immersed in a British theme, or the owner-chef loves his food. Correct on both accounts. The menu and clientele err towards lamb rumps, pork fillets and summer pudding, you don't hear much Portuguese spoken, and it might stretch the budget. But it doesn't matter. The quality cuisine hits a high note.

ALGARVE FOOD FESTIVALS

Epicureans shouldn't miss a chance to eat and drink their way into a tizzy – Algarve-style.

» **Feira Concurso Arte Doce** (Lagos) Dessert is elevated to high art at this three-day sweets fair, with marzipan, an Algarvian favourite, taking centre stage. The fair takes place in July.

» **Feira da Serra** (São Brás de Alportel) This down-home country fair held in late July sells locally produced cheese and meats, cakes, wine and other belly fillers; there are also games for the kiddies and plenty of folkloric song and dance performances.

» **Feiras dos Enchidos Tradicionais** (Monchique) Head for the hills in early March, if you want to get a taste of Monchique's country cooking at this traditional sausage festival. You'll also catch performances by folklore troops and find handicrafts for sale.

» **Festival da Cerveja** (Silves) Usually held around July/August, this spirited fest is dedicated to beer, though you'll also find traditional cuisine and singing and dancing to accompany all that beer-guzzling.

» **Festival do Marisco** (Olhão) Held in mid-August, this lively seafood festival features all the great Algarvian oceanic dishes, including *caldeirada* (fish stew) and *cataplana*. Bands add to the fun – the Village People played in 2006.

Cervejaria Dois Irmãos
TAPAS €€

(Travessa do Mar 2; tapas per plate €5; ⊘lunch & dinner) Hordes of local businessfolk head to this relaxing and stylish place – which is housed in a quaint historical building on Praça do Infante. The sublime selection of *petiscos* (Portuguese tapas) includes everything from pipis to pork ear.

Casa Rosa
CAFE €

(Rua do Ferrador 22; dishes €3-7; ⊘5pm-midnight, 9am-midnight Jun-Aug) Backpacker-favourite Casa Rosa serves up simple, great-value mains such as veggie stir-fry, chilli con carne and fajitas. The friendly owner serves up drinks at the bar.

Adega da Marina
PORTUGUESE €€

(Av dos Descobrimentos 35; mains €6-10; ⊘lunch & dinner) This barnlike place is a bit like a Portuguese grandmother – she hasn't changed her hairstyle in a while. But she dishes out generous portions of reliable (and economical) tasty grilled chicken and seafood favourites to grateful guests (who queue to eat here in summer). Her accessories include iron chandeliers and farming implements.

Pastelaria Alemã
PATISSERIE €

(Rua São Gonçalo 10; snacks €1.50-4; ⊘8am-6pm Mon-Fri, 8am-1pm Sat) This German-run patisserie sells a variety of tempting fresh-baked goods, including cheesecakes, *sachertorte* and flaky croissants.

Mimar Café
CAFE €

(Rua António Barbosa Viana 27; snacks €3-8; ⊘7.30am-9pm Mon-Sat, to midnight Jun-Aug) One of the few places to open early, this is excellent for coffees, breakfasts and snacks. The quiche and salad is a scrumptious luncheon special (€3.50).

O Pescador
SEAFOOD €€

(Rua Gil Eanes 6; mains €7.50-15; ⊘lunch & dinner Mon-Sat) Don't let the pictures of dishes in the menu display put you off. This plain and unpretentious place is far from a fast-food joint, but can be recommended for its blackboard specials.

Bora Café
CAFE €

(Rua Conselheiro Joaquim Machado 17; mains €3-7; ⊘8.30am-7pm; @) Tiny Bora is the ideal place for your healthy fruit and vegie fix, delicious *batidos* (fruit milkshakes) and a cool outdoor setting.

Café Gombá
CAFE €

(Rua Cândido dos Reis 56) This place has been around since 1964 and the friendly owner has a loyal local clientele for the coffee and cakes.

Écomarché
SUPERMARKET

(Av dos Descobrimentos 2; ⊘8am-9pm) For self-caterers, this is a small but accessible supermarket.

🍷 Drinking

Taberna de Lagos
BAR

(Rua Dr Joaquim Tello 1) Boasting a stylish space and brooding electronic music, this airy and atmospheric bar attracts a somewhat savvier bar-goer (higher cocktail prices also keep some punters away).

Taverna Velha
BAR

(Rua Lançarote de Freitas 34) The snug Old Tavern is an old favourite and continues to haul in a lively more mature crowd with its feel-good cocktail of pop classics.

Mullen's
BAR

(Rua Cândido dos Reis 86) This long-established *adega típica* (wine bar) starts as a cosy restaurant and morphs into a bar later in the evening.

Grand Café
BAR

(Rua N Senhora da Graça) This classy place has three bars, lots of gold leaf, kitsch, red velvet and cherubs, over which are draped dressed-up local and foreign hipsters.

Amuras Bar
BAR

(Marina) One of half a dozen restaurant-bars overlooking the marina, this one attracts a slightly more staid crowd, which comes for fruity cocktails and live music most nights.

Duna Beach Club
BAR

(☎282 762 091; Meia Praia; ⊘9pm-2am) Chill out with the smart set at this bar-restaurant, open day and night. It's located bang on the beach, with a pool and attitude. At night it's the bar for A-listers.

Stevie Ray's Blues Jazz Bar
BAR

(Rua da Senhora da Graça 9) This intimate two-level candlelit joint is the best live music bar in town. On weekends it has live blues, jazz and oldies. It attracts a smart-casual older crowd.

Dozens of bars – party palaces and local beer stops – litter the streets of Lagos, with some of the Algarve's most diverse and most clichéd drinking holes on hand. These gather plenty of surfers, backpackers and younger party animals. They are generally open until the wee hours of the morning, and a few are open during the day. Most offer a drinking gimmick – anything from 'happy hours' to sculling from funnels or guzzling progressive shots of hard liquor. Such bars include, but are by no means limited to:

Eddie's Bar (Rua 25 de Abril 99)

Whytes (Rua do Ferrador 7A)

Three Monkeys (Rua Lançarote de Freitas 26)

Green Room (Rua de Oliveira 44)

Irish Rover (Rua do Ferrador 9)

Inside Out (Rua Cândido dos Reis 19)

Meia Praia has some beachfront gems just seconds from sun, swimming and sand, including Linda's Bar, with fab food, good salads, cocktails and tunes; and Bahia Beach Bar, an essential hang-out with live music on Friday and Sunday. Further around the beach and side by side are Bar Quim, renowned for its prawn dishes, and Pôr do Sol, a great place to enjoy the Angolan dish, *muamba de galinha,* chicken in palm oil.

Entertainment

Centro Cultural   CULTURAL CENTRE
(282 770 450; Rua Lançarote de Freitas 7; 10am-8pm) This is Lagos' main venue for classical performances, including popular fado concerts, as well as contemporary art exhibitions.

Shopping

Owl Story   BOOKS
(Rua Marreiros Neto 67; 10am-7pm Mon-Fri, 10am-1pm Sat) Owl Story has an excellent supply of new and secondhand English books as well as sailing almanacs and boating books.

Information

For entertainment information, check the listings in the *Best of Lagos, Luz & Burgau* (www.freemaps.net), a privately produced free map available at *residencials,* shops and bars.

Praça Gil Eanes has banks with ATMs.

Cotacâmbios/Western Union (Praça Gil Eanes 11; 9am-8pm Mon-Sun) A private exchange bureau.

Cyber Café Gélibar (Rua Lançarote de Freitas 43A; per hr €2.50; 9am-10pm) Cafe with internet.

Hospital (282 770 100; Rua Castelo dos Governadores) Just off Praça do Infante. Free treatment if you're prepared to queue.

Police station (282 762 930; Rua General Alberto da Silveira)

Post & telephone office Centrally located just off Praça Gil Eanes.

Saó Gonçalo (282 790 700; www.hppsaude.pt; Av D Sebastião) Private hospital.

Turismo (282 763 031; www.visitalgarve.pt; Praça Gil Eanes; 9.30am-8.30pm Mon-Fri, 9.30am-1pm & 3-6pm Sat & Sun) The helpful staff offers excellent maps (including a suggested walking route) and historical leaflets.

Unicâmbio (Largo Marquês de Pombal) Also has telephones and internet (€2 per hour).

Getting There & Away

Bus

From the **bus station** (282 762 944; www.eva-bus.com; Rua Vasco da Gama) buses travel to the following:

Albufeira (€5, one hour, 13 daily, four on weekends)

Cabo de São Vicente (€3.55, one hour, one on weekdays only)

Lisbon (€19, 4¼ hours, six express daily)

Portimão (€2.60, 20 minutes, 14 daily)

Sagres (€3.40, one hour, nearly hourly on weekdays, seven daily Saturday and Sunday) Via the crossroads to Salema (€2.30, 20 minutes; several run into Salema) from where you must walk for around 1km along a narrow road.

Vila do Bispo (€3, 1½ hours, 13 daily)
To get to/from Carrapateira or Monchique, change at Aljezur (€3.40, 50 minutes, one to two daily) or Portimão. Buses to Aljezur serve Odeceixe (€3.80, 1½ hours).

Renex also operates an express service from Lagos to Lisbon (€18); tickets are available from the **Caima ticket office** (282 768 931/2; Rua das Portas de Portugal 101), which can also arrange minibus transfers to Faro airport (€20 to €28).

Buses also go to Seville (via Huelva) in Spain (€20, 5½ hours, two to four times daily Monday to Friday, more frequently in summer).

Train

Lagos is at the western end of the Algarve line, with direct regional services to the following:

Loulé (€4.90; 1½ hours)

Faro (€5.85, 1¾ to two hours, nine daily), via Albufeira (€3.60), and with onward connections from Faro to

Vila Real de Santo António (€4.15, 1¼ hours) via Tavira (¾ hour).

Trains go daily to Lisbon (all requiring a change at Tunes; €20 to €25, 3½ hours, five daily).

ⓘ Getting Around

Boat

In summer, ferries run to and fro across the estuary to the Meia Praia side from a landing just north of Praça do Infante.

Bus

Two local bus services provide useful connections around town, as well as to Meia Praia, Luz, Odiáxere and the zoo in Barão de João. Tickets cost between €1 and €2 (or buy a book of 10 tickets – this costs less; a one-day ticket with Onda costs €3). Buses run from Monday to Saturday between 7am and 8pm (7pm on Saturday). A few run on Sunday.

Car, Motorcycle & Bicycle

Local agencies offering competitive car-rental rates:

Auto Jardim (☑282 769 486; www.auto-jardim.com; Rua Victor Costa e Silva 18A; ⊗8.30am-1pm & 2.30-7pm)

Luzcar (☑282 761 016; www.luzcar.com; Largo das Portas de Portugal 10; ⊗9am-1pm & 3-6pm)

Motorent (☑282 769 716; www.motorent.pt; Rua Victor Costa e Silva; ⊗9am-1pm & 3-7pm) You can hire both bicycles (€10 per day, €21 three days) and scooters (50/125cc per three days from €55/65).

Passeios do Sudoest (☑282 761 720; Rua Vasco da Gama) Good selection of suspension and mountain bikes (from €10/18 per one/three days) and scooters (per three days from €50).

Drivers are advised to leave their cars in one of the free car parks on the outskirts (look for the large parking signs). At the time of research, a new underground car park was being constructed on Av dos Descobrimentos; but this road is usually congested. Street parking spaces close to the centre are metered – watch out or you'll be wheel-clamped.

Taxi

You can call for **taxis** (☑282 763 587) or find them on Rua das Portas de Portugal.

Lagos to Sagres

To the west of Lagos, the coastline is sharp and ragged, and much less developed, though the area is certainly not undiscovered. Once-sleepy fishing villages set above long beaches have now woken up to the benefits of tourism and, in some cases, developers have moved in. Out of the high season, these places remain bewitchingly calm.

LUZ

Six kilometres west of Lagos, the small resort of Luz is packed with Brits. It's fronted by a sandy beach that's ideal for families. Most accommodation is prebooked by those on a package deal. Luz is a convenient side trip from Lagos. Buses run frequently from Lagos (around €2, 15 minutes) and arrive by the village church on the waterfront.

If you do end up here for the night, you can try **Camping de Espiche** (☑282 789 265; www.turiscampo.com; sites per adult/tent/car €6.20/7/5.25; ⊛) a Turiscampo-run, shady site 2km from Luz.

If there's only one reason to visit Luz (dare we stretch it to the Algarve), it's to dine at **Pastelaria Chicca** (☑282 761 334; www.pastelariachiccaluz.com; Rua da Várzea 3; meals €5-14; ⊗lunch & dinner). Owner Chicca is Portugal's answer to Nigella Lawson (or so *we* think). Her presentations of the dishes – all her creations – are as elaborate as the treats themselves. All ingredients are organic, all are imaginatively combined, and all are superb. Think savoury bread-and-butter pudding, vegetable stacks (and other vegie options), amazing salads, fish and meats, and *the* best desserts (don't miss the white-chocolate-and-raspberry tart) and cakes, all made on the premises. Come with time and an empty stomach. You can always work off the calories by walking back along the cliff track between Luz and Lagos.

SALEMA

This charmingly small coastal resort has an easygoing atmosphere; it's set on a wide bay 17km west of Lagos, surrounded by developments that manage not to overwhelm it. It's ideal for families, and there are several small, secluded beaches within a few kilometres – **Praia da Salema** by the village, **Praia da Figueira** to the west and **Boca do Rio** to the east. Dinosaur prints exist in the area.

🛏 Sleeping

Quinta dos Carriços   CAMPGROUND **€** (☑282 695 201; www.quintadoscarricos.com; camp sites per adult/tent/car €5.45/5.45/5.45, studios/apt from €72/82; ⊛) Just 1.5km north of Salema, this camping ground is in a peaceful, tree-filled setting with abundant birdlife (no radios allowed!). It has studios and apartments and a designated nudist camping area.

Hospedaria A Maré GUEST HOUSE €€

(☑282 695 165; www.the-mare.com; s/d incl breakfast €60/75, self-catering apt €70-85) Just off the main road into town, this welcoming blue-and-white guest house has light and bright rooms, some with sea views, a pretty garden and a guests kitchen. It's a short stroll downhill to the beach. There's a two-night minimum stay.

Hotel Residencial Salema HOTEL €€

(☑282 695 328; www.hotelsalema.com; s/d incl breakfast €81/94; ✳) Fifty metres from the beach, Salema offers bright rooms with terraces (most with sea views) in a modern whitewashed building.

✗ Eating

For a place of its size, Salema boasts excellent eateries.

Água na Boca SEAFOOD, INTERNATIONAL €€

(☑282 695 651; Rua dos Pescadores; mains €13-18; ⏰lunch & dinner Mon-Fri, lunch Sat) This is the upmarket choice in Salema and said to be one of the best in town.

Boia SEAFOOD €€

(ww.boiabar.com; Rua dos Pescadores 101; mains €8-17; ⏰lunch & dinner) This attractive fish eatery has a sea-facing terrace.

Restaurante Lourenço SEAFOOD €€

(Rua 28 de Janeiro; mains €8.50-15; ⏰lunch & dinner Mon-Sat) Behind the car park, this unpretentious place is recommended for its fish (the owner happens to be a keen hobby fisherman).

ℹ Getting There & Away

At least six buses daily connect Lagos and Salema (€2.30, 30 minutes).

Sagres

POP 1940

Overlooking some of the Algarve's most dramatic scenery, the small, elongated village of Sagres has an end-of-the-world feel with its sea-carved cliffs and empty, wind-whipped fortress high above the ocean. Despite its connection to Portugal's rich nautical past, there isn't much of historical interest in town. Its appeal lies mainly in its sense of isolation (refreshing after the hectic Algarve), plus access to fine beaches. It has a laid-back vibe, and simple, cheery cafes and bars. It's especially popular, particularly in the last decade, with a surfing crowd. Outside town, the striking cliffs of Cabo de São Vicente make for an enchanting visit.

One kilometre east of the square, past holiday villas and restaurants, is the port, still a centre for boatbuilding and lobster fishing, and the marina.

Sagres is where dashing Prince Henry the Navigator built a new, fortified town and a semimonastic school of navigation that specialised in cartography, astronomy and ship design, steering Portugal on towards the Age of Discoveries.

At least, that's according to history and myth. Henry was, among other things, governor of the Algarve and had a residence in its primary port town, Lagos, from where most expeditions set sail. He certainly did put together a kind of nautical think-tank, though how much thinking went on out at Sagres is uncertain. He definitely had a house somewhere near Sagres, where he died in November 1460.

In May 1587 the English privateer Sir Francis Drake, in the course of attacking supply lines to the Spanish Armada, captured and wrecked the fortifications around Sagres. The Ponta de Sagres was refortified following the earthquake of 1755, after which there was little of verifiable antiquity left standing.

Sagres has milder temperatures than other parts of the Algarve, with Atlantic winds keeping the summers cool. Note that there is no car rental in Sagres; it's advisable to hire cars in Lagos instead.

Sights

Fortaleza de Sagres FORTRESS

(☑282 620 140; adult/child €3/1.50; ⏰9.30am-8pm May-Sep, 9.30am-5.30pm Oct-Apr) Blank, hulking and prisonlike, Sagres' fortress has a forbidding front wall balanced by two mighty bastions. Inside, a few buildings dot the vast, open expanse, but otherwise a visit here is mostly about the striking views over the sheer cliffs, and all along the coast to Cabo de São Vicente.

Splash out on the printed guide (€1) that's sold at the entrance.

Inside the gate is a curious, huge stone pattern that measures 43m in diameter. Named the rosa dos ventos (literally, 'wind rose'), this strange paving pattern is believed to be a mariner's compass. Excavated in 1921, the paving may date from Prince Henry's time – probably the only thing that does apart from the foundations.

Although not much is known about the life of the Spanish-born St Vincent, his death is of such legendary stuff that both Spain and Portugal claim him as their own. In Portugal he is considered the patron saint of wine and sea voyages.

Born in the 4th century AD, St Vincent was a Spanish preacher who was killed by the Romans in 304. During his torturous death (he was burnt at the stake), he is said to have maintained such composure, praising God all the while, that he converted several of his torturers on the spot. Following his martyrdom, his remains were gathered, at which point two differing accounts emerge. Spain claims his final resting place is in Ávila. Portugal claims that his remains washed up on the shores of the Algarve, near Sagres, in a boat watched over by two protective ravens. A shrine in his honour, which Muslim chronicles refer to as the Crow Church, became an object of Christian pilgrimage, though it was destroyed by Muslim fanatics in the 12th century.

Afonso Henriques, Portugal's first king, had the remains moved by ship to Lisbon in 1173, again accompanied by ravens. St Vincent became Lisbon's patron saint (his remains now rest in the Igreja de São Vicente de Fora). A raven features in the city's coat of arms – some *lisboêtas* claim that ravens inhabited the church's bell tower for years afterwards.

The village's oldest buildings, which include a cistern tower to the east; a house and the small, whitewashed, 16th-century **Igreja da Nossa Senhora da Graça**, with its golden altar (of wood), to the west; and the remnants of a wall, are possibly replacements for what was there before.

Many of the gaps you will see between buildings are the result of a 1960s spring-clean of 17th- and 18th-century ruins that was organised to make way for a reconstruction (later aborted) that was to coincide with the 500th anniversary of Henry's death.

Smack in the centre is a modern, rather unsightly exhibition hall (closed at time of research). A small auditorium shows a short film on Sagres' role in maritime navigation history (English subtitles; every 40 minutes). Near the southern end of the promontory is a **lighthouse**. Death-defying anglers balance on the cliffs below the walls, hoping to land bream or sea bass.

Cabo de São Vicente   LANDMARK, MUSEUM

A trip to Cabo de São Vicente (Cape St Vincent), Europe's southwesternmost point, is a must. At sunset you can almost hear the hissing as the sun hits the sea. This barren, thrusting headland is the bleak last piece of home that nervous Portuguese sailors would have seen as they launched into the unknown.

The cape – a revered place even in the time of the Phoenicians and known to the Romans as Promontorium Sacrum – takes its present name from a Spanish priest martyred by the Romans. The old fortifications, trashed by Sir Francis Drake in 1587, were later pulverised by the 1755 earthquake.

At the end of the cape there's a wind-whipped red **lighthouse** (hundreds of ocean-going ships round this point every day) and a former convent. On-site, and opened in 2010, is the small, but excellent, **Museu dos Faróis** (admission €3; ◷10am-6pm Tue-Sun). It showcases the importance of Sagres in Portugal's maritime navigation history, along with replicas of 16th-century cartography and the history of the Cape's lighthouse.

At the 4.5km mark you'll pass the remains of **Fortaleza do Beliche**, built in 1632 on the site of an older fortress. Inside is a small chapel on the site of the ruined Igreja de Santa Catarina (and possibly an old convent). It was once a hotel, but sadly it's crumbling, along with the cliff, and is now strictly off-limits.

🏃 Activities

There are four good beaches a short drive or long walk from Sagres: **Praia da Mareta**, just below the town; lovely **Praia do Martinhal** to the east; **Praia do Tonel** on the other side of the Ponta de Sagres, and especially good for surfing; and the isolated **Praia de Beliche**, on the way to Cabo de São Vicente.

Sagres

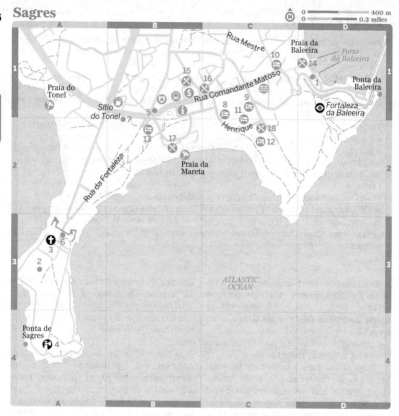

Mar Ilimitado BOAT TRIPS
(✆916 832 625; www.marilimitado.com) A team
of marine biologists offers a variety of 'educational' boat trips, from dolphin-spotting
trips (€30) to excursions up to Cabo de São
Vicente (€20).

Sagres Natura WATER SPORTS
(✆282 624 072; www.sagres-surfcamp.com; Rua
São Vicente; per day €15) Rents out bodyboards
(€10 per day), surfboards (€15) and wetsuits
(€5). The company also offers canoeing trips
(€30). Bikes can also be hired (€15).

Free Ride Sagres Surfcamp SURFING
(✆916 089 005; www.freeridesurfcamp.com;
1-/3-/5-day lessons €45/120/180) Gives lessons and offers free transport from Sagres
and Lagos.

DiversCape DIVING
(✆965 559 073; www.diverscape.com; Porto da
Baleeira) Diving centres are based at the
port. Recommended is the PADI-certified.

It organises dives of between 12m and 30m
around shipwrecks. A dive and equipment
costs €45/210/320 for one/six/10 dives,
while the four-day PADI open-water course
is €380. Beginners' courses (from €80) are
available.

Walkin' Sagres GUIDED WALKS
(✆925 545 515; www.walkinsagres.com) Started in 2010, this company offers a much-
needed service – guided walks around and
near Sagres and Cabo São Vicente. Led
by a multilingual guide (English, French,
Spanish and Portuguese) who focuses on
history and explanation of the surrounds,
the walks head through pine forests to the
Cape's cliffs. These vary from shorter 6km
options (2½ hours; €25) to a longer 14.5km
walk (three hours; €40). There's even a one-
hour walk for parents with young children
(€15, children free).

Surfing is possible at all beaches except
Praia do Martinhal and Praia da Baleeira.

Several places offer surfing and bodyboarding lessons:

Sagres Natura (☎282 624 072; www.
sagresnatura.com; Rua São Vicente; 1-/3-/5-day courses €45/120/180)

International Surf School (☎914 482 407; www.internationalsurfschool.com; 1-/3-/5-day courses €45/120/180)

Maretta Shop (☎931940711; www.sagreson line.com; Av Comandante Matoso; 1-/3-/5-day courses €55/150/220)

✯ Festivals

Sleepy Sagres goes into overdrive during its annual **Surf Festival**, which is held during one weekend in mid-August and features music (with reggae bands taking centre stage) and surf crowds.

🛏 Sleeping

Sagres fills up in summer, though it's marginally easier to find accommodation here than in the rest of the Algarve during the high season, thanks partly to the number of private houses in Sagres that advertise private rooms or apartments (at the time of research, these were being formalised into a category known as '*alojamento local*') and informal 'hostels'. Doubles generally cost around €40 and flats cost from €45 to €80.

Elsewhere prices can halve outside high season, including the top-end options.

Mareta View Boutique B&B
BOUTIQUE HOTEL €€€
(☎282 620 000; www.maretaview.com; Praça da República; s/d from €98/108; ❄@🛜) The

Mareta View (and its neighbour Mareta Beach) brings sleek – and some classy attitude – to Sagres. White- and aquamarine-hued decor gives it a futuristic feel (the rooms' funky mood lighting rivals the Cape Vincent lighthouse beacon). It has wonderful sea views (these rooms cost €10 more), excellent breakfasts and a top location on the old plaza.

Memmo Baleeira Hotel BOUTIQUE HOTEL €€€
(☎282 624 212; www.memmobaleeira.com; s/d €170/190; P❄@🛜🏊) Reopened in 2008 with a facelift, and not a wrinkle on-site. Think clean, smooth, white and minimalist design, from the contemporary glass reception area, to the retro footrests in brown, white and powder-blue coverings. The corridors may resemble a morgue, but you'd be pretty pleased to be entombed in one of the contemporary-style rooms, decked out in stylish white interiors. Heaven comes at a price; ask about promotional deals.

Pousada do Infante LUXURY HOTEL €€€
(☎282 620 240; www.pousadas.pt; Rua Patrão Antonio Faustino; d from €270; ❄@🛜🏊) This modern *pousada* has large rooms in a great setting near the cliff-top. Count on green or orange interiors, handsome public areas and picture-perfect views from the terraces.

Pontalaia APARTMENTS €€
(☎282 620 280; www.pontalaia.pt; Rua Infante Dom Henrique; apt from €125; ❄🏊) Next door to Navigator, this small, condolike complex offers attractive airy apartments set with blond woods and stylish furnishings, each with a balcony.

Orbitur Sagres
CAMPGROUND €

(☎282 624 371; www.orbitur.pt; camp sites per adult/tent/car €5/5.80/5) Situated some 2.5km from town, off the road to Cabo de São Vicente, this is a shady, well-maintained camping ground with lots of trees. You can hire bikes here.

Casa do Cabo de Santa Maria
GUEST HOUSE €€

(☎/fax 282 624 722; casacabosantamaria@sapo. pt; Rua Patrão António Faustino; r from €50-60, apt from €80) You could eat off the floors of these squeaky-clean, welcoming rooms and apartments. They might not have sweeping views, but they are handsome and nicely furnished rooms – excellent value (breakfast not included).

Aparthotel Navigator
HOTEL €€

(☎282 624 354; www.hotel-navigator.com; Rua Infante Dom Henrique; 1-/2-person apt €88/93; ✳@🛜🛏) It certainly ain't five-star (and breakfast isn't included), yet it's large (think groups), and has spacious, cheaply furnished apartments with million-dollar views over the cliffs. Each has a balcony and satellite TV. Prices halve outside high season.

🍴 Eating & Drinking

Many places close or operate shorter hours during the low season (November to April). The *mercado municipal* provides great supplies for long beach days. There are cafes on Praça de República and restaurants along the way to Cabo São Vicente.

Cafe-Bars

It's Groundhog Day (albeit a pleasant one), such is the row of atmospheric and good-value cafe-bars located cheek-to-cheek along Rua Comandante Matoso. Common features include opening hours between 10am to 2am (or later); great snacks (with vegie options, between €3.50 to €8); free internet and/or wi-fi; and good music, depending on your taste.

Dromedário
CAFE, BAR €€

The legitimate founder of such cafe-bars and still going strong (it celebrated 25 years in 2010), good food (a weekly surfers' meal is €7 for all you can eat), karaoke on Thursdays and the practice of 'mixology', aka creative cocktails.

Agua Salgada
CAFE, BAR €€

Said to have the best crêpes and has a DJ in the evenings.

Pau de Pita
CAFE, BAR €€

The funkiest of its neighbours (at least in its design – think disco ball for tasteful mood lighting), this place has great salads and juices and plays pleasant house music.

Mitic
CAFE, BAR €€

Hefty toasted sandwiches, good cocktails, friendly environment.

Restaurants

TOP CHOICE A Eira do Mel
PORTUGUESE €€€

(☎282 639 016; www.eiradomel.com; Estrada do Castelejo, Vila do Bispo; mains €12-30; ☉lunch & dinner Mon-Sat)
It's worth driving 10km further north to Vila do Bispo to enjoy the fine foods of chef José Pinheiro at this charming, Michelin-listed restaurant. The meat leans towards the Algarvian; the seafood has a more contemporary touch. Think rabbit in red-wine sauce, octopus *cataplana* with sweet potatoes (€35 for two people), curried Atlantic wild shrimps (€18) and *javali* (€17). Mouthwatering stuff.

Vila Velha
INTERNATIONAL €€€

(☎282 624 788; Rua António Faustino; mains €12-25; ☉dinner Tue-Sun;🅿) In a house with a lovely rose garden in front, the more upmarket Vila Velha offers consistently good seafood mains, rabbit, grilled salmon and good vegetarian dishes.

A Tasca
SEAFOOD €€€

(☎282 624 177; Porto da Baleeira; dishes €12-25; ☉lunch & dinner Thu-Tue) Overlooking the marina and out to sea, this converted fish warehouse specialises in, you guessed it, seafood. The cosy interior is filled with hanging strands of dried garlic and chillies, bottles and clay jugs are embedded in the walls. The kitchen is open and there's a sunny terrace. Note – solo travellers – one of the few places in Portugal where you can have a *cataplana* for one person (rather than two).

A Sagres
PORTUGUESE €€

(mains €8-13; ☉lunch & dinner Thu-Tue) This popular local restaurant offers great fish and meat fare (from *arroz de polvo* to grilled meats) that won't break the bank. It's opposite the Galp petrol station at the first roundabout, direction Lagos.

Raposo
PORTUGUESE €€

(mains €8-12; ☉10am-9pm) On the beach, laid-back Raposo enjoys an ideal setting, with lapping waves a few steps from the terrace.

Bossa Nova Restaurante PIZZA €€
(off Rua Comandante Matoso; mains €8-18; ⊗lunch & dinner) The owner of Dromedário runs this pizza place, where decor is nonexistent 'cos it's all about the food (read good pizza).

Elsewhere, there are several inviting restaurants on the sands of Praia do Martinhal, including **Nortada** (mains €5-25; ⊗10am-10pm) and **Restaurante-Bar Martinhal** (Praia do Martinhal; dishes €10-15; ⊗10am-9pm Tue-Sun).

❶ Information
There's a bank and ATM just beyond the **Turismo** (☑282 624 873; Av Comandante Matoso; ⊗9.30am-12.30pm & 1.30-5.30pm Tue-Sat), which is 100m east of Praça da República; the post office is just east of there.

Internet is available at many of the town's cafe-bars.

❶ Getting There & Around
The bus stop is by the *turismo*. You can buy tickets on the bus. For more information call ☑282 762 944.

Buses come from Lagos via Salema (€3.40, one hour, around 12 daily), and Portimão (€5.40, 1¾ hours, one on weekdays). On weekends there are fewer services. It's only 10 minutes to Cabo de São Vicente (twice daily on weekdays only; €1.10).

Bike rental is available at Sagres Natura (see p186).

For a taxi, call ☑282 624 501.

North of Sagres
Heading north along the Algarve's western coast you'll find some amazing beaches, backed by beautiful wild vegetation. Thanks to building restrictions imposed to protect the Parque Natural do Sudoeste Alentejano e Costa Vicentina, it's relatively well preserved (but there's the odd shock – construction is occurring, although it's said to be 'controlled'). Protected since 1995, it's rarely more than 6km wide, and runs for about 120km from Burgau to Cabo de São Vicente and up nearly the entire western Algarve and Alentejo shore. Here there are at least 48 plant species found only in Portugal, and around a dozen or so found only within the park.

It's home to otters, foxes and wild cats, and some 200 species of birds enjoy the coastal wetlands, salt marshes and cliffs, including Portugal's last remaining ospreys. Although the seas can be dangerous,

the area has a growing reputation for some of Europe's finest surf and attracts people from all over the world.

CARRAPATEIRA
Surf-central Carrapateira is a tranquil, pretty, spread-out village, with two exhilarating beaches nearby whose lack of development, fizzing surf and strong swells attract a hippy, surf-dude crowd. The coast along here is wild, with copper-coloured and ash-grey cliffs covered in speckled yellow and green scrub, backing creamy, wide sands.

Praia da Bordeira (aka Praia Carrapateira) is a mammoth swath merging into dunes, 2km off the road on the north side of the village, while the similarly stunning **Praia do Amado** (more famous for its surf) is at the southern end of the village. Note: despite the number of campervans you see around the place, camping here is definitely illegal – please think twice before joining the camping fray.

For surfing courses contact **Algarve Surf School** (☑962 846 771; www.algarvesurfschool. com; 1-week accommodation incl breakfast & lunch, equipment hire, lessons €485-600), or try **Amado Surfcamp** (☑925 748 228, 927 831 568; www.amadosurfcamp.com; 1-week accommodation incl breakfast, equipment hire & lessons €395, if camping €295), run by local brothers. They built the camp (made up of basic but well-made three-bed wooden huts, with a communal kitchen) on family farmland, in a beautiful remote setting.

Opened in May 2008, the compact **Carrapateira Land & Sea Museum** (☑282 970 000; Rua de Pescador; ⊗11am-5pm; adult/child €2.50/1) is a must for visitors – surfers or otherwise. Its contemporary design space has small exhibits covering everything from the fishing industry to daily life of the locals, and stunning photograph collages depicting Carrapateira of yesteryear (there's minimal English labelling). The vista from the museum's ingenious viewing window is sublime.

🛏 Sleeping & Eating
Cafes and snack bars line the town's tiny plaza and keep long hours.

Monte da Vilarinha RURAL INN €€€
(☑282 973 218; www.montedavilarinha.com; Vilarinha; r from €160) Several kilometres south of Carrapateira and set within a gorgeous valley is this new, stylish rural refuge-cum-mini-resort. The resort's sleek

studios and apartments are equipped with the lot...all except mobile-telephone coverage – the hills block reception here (yay, say some). Prices are considerably lower outside high season.

Pensão das Dunas GUEST HOUSE €€
(☎282 973 118; www.pensao-das-dunas.pt; Rua da Padaria 9; d without bathroom €40, 1-/2-room apt €60/75) This pretty guest house has basic but pleasant and colourful rooms overlooking a flower-filled courtyard. It's 100m from the road at the southern end of the village.

Bamboo GUEST HOUSE €€
(☎282 973 323; Sitio do Rio; d/tr €50/75, apt €80) About 500m from Praia da Bordeira, on the main road, this friendly, ecologically minded guest house has four lovely, colourful rooms and friendly owners. It has a wonderful open-plan apartment.

Aldeia da Pedralva LUXURY HOTEL €€€
(☎282 639 342; www.aldeiadapedralva.com; Pedralva; d €135, 4-person house €175) The place is reads like a quirky fairy tale: 'Once upon a time there was a beautiful village called Pedralva, located 7km southeast of Carrapateira. The community gradually dwindled as old people died and young people left; the crumbling village almost became a ghost town. Investors waved their magic wand: they rebuilt the village, gradually buying up and restoring the homes, along with the quaint streets (in an authentic, not Disneyland, manner). These days, each converted house provides comfortable accommodation with kitchenette. Around nine permanent residents – some of them former inhabitants – still live in the village, including a talented German artist. Staying here provides a 'different' experience, although it currently lacks the more genuine Portuguese life that you may get in a community elsewhere. There are lovely walks and birdwatching and you're a 10-minute car ride from the beach.' 'The end?' Definitely not. The owners hope that tourism will revitalise this little dot on the map.

TOP CHOICE **Sítio do Rio** GRILL HOUSE, SEAFOOD €€
(mains €9-15; ☉lunch & dinner Wed-Mon; ✐) Right on the dunes near Praia da Bordeira, this restaurant cooks up excellent grilled-fish and meat mains; there are also vegetarian choices. It has an appealing indoor area, with fishing nets on the walls, and outdoor seating under large brollies.

It's hugely popular at weekends and is good value.

TOP CHOICE **Sítio do Forno** SEAFOOD €€
(mains €9-20; ☉noon-9pm Tue-Sun) On the cliff overlooking Praia do Amado, this large place grew from a tiny fisherman's cabana. It's considered *the* eatery to visit; we think the value is in the setting – the magnificent ocean views – not so much in the cuisine. That said, it's worth mooching here.

ALJEZUR

Some 20km further north, Aljezur is an attractive village that straddles a river. The western part is Moorish, with a collection of cottages below a ruined 10th-century hilltop castle; the eastern side, called Igreja Nova (meaning 'new church'), is 600m up a steep hill. Aljezur is close to some fantastic beaches, edged by black rocks that reach into the white-tipped, bracing sea – surfing hot spots. The countryside around, which is part of the natural park, is a tangle of yellow, mauve and green wiry gorse and heather.

◉ Sights & Activities
Nearby wonderful, unspoilt beaches include **Praia da Arrifana** (10km southwest, near a tourist development called Vale da Telha), a dramatic curved black-cliff-backed bay with one restaurant, balmy pale sands and some big northwest swells (a surfer's delight); and **Praia de Monte Clérigo**, about 8km northwest. **Praia de Amoreira**, 6km away, is a wonderful beach where the river meets the sea. More difficult to reach but worth the effort getting there is the more remote **Praia de Vale Figueira**, about 15km southwest of Aljezur on rugged dirt roads.

Surfing lessons are available through **Arrifana Surf School** (☎917 862 138; www.surfinginaljezur.com; 1-/3-/5-day course €45/120/180).

🛏 Sleeping
In Praia da Arrifana locals sometimes rent out private rooms (look for *'quartos'* signs). There are a few other options outside town.

Amazigh Hostel HOSTEL €
(☎282 997 502; www.amazighostel.com; Rua da Ladeira 5; dm/d €22/35, f per person €25; ☎) Meet the setting for *Gidget* (1960s) with a Gen Y twist: this hip, hop and happening place has to be one of the world's most in-

telligently designed and funky hostels. It boasts the lot: inbuilt lockers under the bunks, steel staircases, surfboard and gear storage, the coolest of living areas (including a sun terrace with superlative views), plus a communal kitchen. It suits travellers of all kinds; those who don't want to squeeze into a dorm might prefer the private rooms with en suite.

Pousada da Juventude HOSTEL €
(282 997 455; www.pousadasjuventude.pt; Praia Arrifana; dm €16, d with/without bathroom €45/37) This grey and yellow hostel is decked out in plastic furniture that is of cutting-edge design. The hostel offers light and airy rooms, great communal areas including a sunny terrace, a storeroom for surf gear and a washing and drying room. It's a few minutes' walk away from Arrifana Beach.

Restaurante-Bar A Lareira GUEST HOUSE €€
(282 998 440; Rua 3 de Janeiro; d incl breakfast €60) Located in Igreja Nova, this place has 12 clean and tidy rooms with wood details, and each opens onto a shared terrace with lovely views.

Residencial Dom Sancho II GUEST HOUSE €€
(282 997 070; Largo Igreja Nova; s/d €40/50) In Igreja Nova, just off the main square, this friendly guest house has handsome rooms and a great restaurant below. It's excellent value.

Parque de Campismo Serrão CAMPGROUND €
(282 990 220; www.parque-campismo-serrao. com; camp sites per adult/tent/car €5.50/5/4; @🛜🐾) This calm, shady site is 4km north of Aljezur, then 1km off the main road (turn at Chill Out restaurant). It has wheelchair access, tennis courts, a playground and apartments, plus bike rental.

🍴 Eating & Drinking

Cafe-bars overlook the main square around Igreja Nova. In Praia da Arrifana there's a string of seafood restaurants (packed with Portuguese at weekends) on the road above the beach, where you can expect to pay around €10 for grilled fish.

Pontá Pé SEAFOOD, GRILL HOUSE €€
(282 998 104; Largo da Liberdade; mains €7.50-12; ☺lunch & dinner Mon-Sat) Friendly, with wooden floors and a beamed ceiling, Pontá Pé does tasty fish dishes and good barbecue chicken. Adjoining it is a cheery bar.

Restaurante Ruth o Ivo PORTUGUESE €€
(282 998 534; Rua 25 de Abril 14; mains €8-11; ☺lunch & dinner) This is a casual nautical-themed eatery, often recommended by locals for its seafood dishes and honest fare.

Restaurante Portal da Várzea PORTUGUESE €€
(282 995 443; mains €10-14; ☺lunch & dinner Thu-Tue) This popular restaurant has a friendly feel and lovely garden area. Serves up everything from fish dishes to *feijoada* (pork and bean casserole) delights.

Restaurante Paraíso do Mar SEAFOOD €€
(282 991 088; mains from €7-15, fish per kg from €38; ☺lunch & dinner) At Praia da Amoreira, try Paraíso do Mar, which offers fantastic panoramas overlooking the beach.

Mercado municipal MARKET €
(☺8am-2pm Mon-Sat) Next to the *turismo*, the municipal market is a good place to buy fresh fruits and vegies. There's also a Minipreço supermarket near Igreja Nova.

ℹ Information
Post office (Rua 25 de Abril)

Turismo do Algarve (282 998 229; ☺9.30am-1pm & 2-5.30pm Mon-Fri) Next to the town market, just before the bridge leading to the Lagos N120 road (Rua 25 de Abril). Buses stop near here.

ℹ Getting Around
If you're driving, there's a free car park next to the *turismo*. Eva buses run between Lagos and Aljezur (€4, four on weekdays only, one on Saturday) via Odexeice. There's a twice-weekly service to Praia de Arrifana from Aljezur (€2, 35 minutes).

ODECEIXE
Around here the countryside rucks up into rolling, large hills. As the Alentejo turns into the Algarve, the first coastal settlement is Odeceixe, an endearing small town clinging to the southern side of the Ribeira de Seixe valley, and so snoozy it's in danger of falling off, apart from during high season, when Portuguese and European visitors pack the place.

The sheltered **Praia de Odeceixe**, 3.5km down the valley, is a wonderful bite of sand surrounded by gorse- and tree-covered cliffs. **Odeceixe Surf School** (963 170 493; 1-/3-/5-day courses €45/120/180) offers surfing classes (and board and wetsuit rental) – look for its signs on the beach.

THE ALGARVE

🛏 Sleeping & Eating

There is a handful of unofficial, but well-advertised *quartos* (private rooms) in the village, especially along Rua Nova (en route to the beach). Expect to pay at least €35 to €40 for a double.

Several pleasant eateries are around Largo 1 Mai, a great spot to sit and watch the world amble by and on Rua Estrada Nacional, the road into town. On the way to the beach there are a couple of restaurants, and at the beach there are snack-bars competing for hungry beachgoers.

Casa Hospedes Celeste GUEST HOUSE €€
(✆282 947 150; www.casaceleste.web.pt; Rua Nova 9; d incl breakfast €60) This renovated, clean and bright spot is excellent value, in a great central location and run by delightful owners. Rooms are smallish, but have colourful bedspreads and TV.

Parque de Campismo São Miguel CAMPGROUND €
(✆282 947 145; www.campingsaomiguel.com; camp sites per adult/tent/car €6.40/5.90/5.40, bungalows from €80; ☀) Facility-loaded and pine-shaded, this camping ground-cum-miniresort is 1.5km north of Odeceixe; wooden bungalows are also available.

Casa Vicentina RURAL INN €€€
(✆282 947 447; www.casavicentina.pt; Monte Novo; d €125, ste €165; ☀) For a touch of indulgence, head to this stylish complex, set in tranquil, rural surrounds. The interior-decorator owner has gone to town in the rooms and suites; these are arranged around a lush green lawn, with pool and lily ponds. Some rooms have kitchenettes. It's 2km from Odeceixe, near Maria Vinagre and signposted.

Pensão Luar GUEST HOUSE €€
(✆282 947 194; www.pensaoluar.blogspot.com; Rua da Várzea 28; d/tr €65/75, 4-person apt €100) At the western edge of the village, this friendly place is an excellent bargain (prices are almost half outside high season), with modern and white spick-and-span rooms.

Pensão Restaurante Dorita GUEST HOUSE €€
(✆282 947 581; www.naturalmenteportugal.com; d with/without bathroom €50/60) You pay for the gorgeous beach view – but not much more – at this place. Rooms are worn and basic; the best have terraces with a vista.

Taberna do Gabão PORTUGUESE €€
(Rua do Gabão 9; mains €6.50-13.50; ⊙lunch & dinner Wed-Mon) Odeceixe's best option, this

welcoming restaurant features good-value traditional dishes served in a charming old-fashioned wooden dining room. There's outdoor seating.

❶ Getting There & Away

Express buses run between Lagos and Odeceixe (€8.50, 80 minutes, at least twice daily) via Aljezur (€5.70, 35 minutes). Buy tickets at the *papelaria* (newsagent) next to the market.

One daily bus connects Vila do Bispo with Carrapateira (€4, one hour). There's a twice-weekly service to Praia de Arrifana from Aljezur (€2, 35 minutes).

Monchique

POP 2800

High up above the coast, in cooler mountainous woodlands, the picturesque hamlet of Monchique makes a lovely base for exploring the surrounding area, with some excellent options for walking, biking or canoeing.

An enticing spa town nearby is another alluring factor. It's set in the forested Serra de Monchique, the Algarve's mountain range, lying some 24km north of Portimão. Monchique is also known for having the best brews of the fiery *medronho,* a locally made liqueur.

Fires regularly affect this area during the summertime – the last major ones were in 2003 and 2004. These cause widespread damage and ongoing frustration at the lack of measures to prevent the devastation.

❷ Sights

A series of brown pedestrian signs starting near the bus station directs visitors up into the town's narrow old streets and major places of interest.

The **igreja matriz** (parish church; admission free; ⊙9am-5pm) has an extraordinary, star-shaped Manueline porch decorated with twisted columns that look like lengths of knotted rope, and a simple interior, with columns topped with more stony rope, and some fine chapels, including one whose vault contains beautiful 17th-century glazed tiles showing St Francis and St Michael killing the devil.

Keep climbing and you'll eventually reach the ruins of the 17th-century Franciscan monastery of **Nossa Senhora do Desterro**, which overlooks the town from its wooded hilltop.

Activities

All of the activities listed here require advance reservations.

Dutch-run **Outdoor Tours** (✆282 969 520, 916 736 226; www.outdoor-tours.com; Mexilhoeira Grande) offers biking (€24 to €35), kayaking (€23) and walking trips (€19) both in and around the Serra Monchique.

Alternativtour (✆282 913 204, 965 004 337; www.alternativtour.com) offers many activities, including guided walks (€20), mountain-biking tours (€35), canoeing trips (€25) or combined mountain-biking and canoeing trips (€55). A minimum number of people is required, however.

Sleeping

Villa Vina   RURAL INN €€

(✆965 753 393; www.vv.web.pt; r €78) Hidden up a tiny pathway (note: the only access is by steps) and signed as you cross the Ribeira do Banho, around 500m after the turn-off to Caldas de Monchique, this lovely rural villa with pretty garden is perfect for those who crave seclusion, rather than village infrastructure. Reservations required.

Albergaria Bica-Boa   GUEST HOUSE €€

(✆282 912 271; bica-bao@sapo.pt; d incl breakfast €75; P ⊛) One kilometre out of town on the Lisbon road, this pretty four-room place overlooks a wooded valley. There's a decent restaurant here, too (mains €8.50 to €12).

Residencial Miradouro   GUEST HOUSE €

(✆282 912 163; Rua dos Combatentes do Ultramar; s/d/tr €35/40/50) Up steep Rua Engenheiro Duarte Pacheco (signposted to Portimão), near the *turismo*, this 1970s hilltop place, run with great seriousness, offers sweeping, breezy views and neat rooms, some with balcony.

Eating & Drinking

TOP
CHOICE **Jardim das Oliveiras** PORTUGUESE €€€

(✆282 912 874; mains €10-25; ⊙lunch & dinner) About 2km from Monchique just off the road to Fóia (signposted), this atmospheric place, with beamed ceilings, serves up regional dishes. Outdoors, the garden, shady trees, hammocks and seating scream 'long lunch'. It is known for its *javali* (wild boar), wild rabbit and game dishes.

TOP
CHOICE **A Charrette**   PORTUGUESE €€

(✆282 912 142; Rua Dr Samora Gil 30-34; mains €9-16; ⊙lunch & dinner Thu-Tue) Touted

as the town's best eatery for its regional specialities, this place serves reliably good cuisine amid country rustic charm. A few favourites include cabbage with spicy sausages and an award-winning honey flan for dessert.

Barlefante   BAR €

(Travessa das Guerreiras; mains €3-5; ⊙noon-2am Mon-Thu, 1pm-4am Fri-Sun) Signposted off the town's main drag, this fun place has a touch of the burlesque, with hot-pink walls, red-velvet alcoves, ornate mirrors and chandeliers. The TV-lined dance floor is hip; it's young Monchique's coolest haunt.

Restaurante O Parque   PORTUGUESE €€

(mains €6-12.50; ⊙lunch & dinner) Directly opposite the tourist office, this cosy local haunt serves good, honest down-to-earth dishes. Many workers head here for lunch.

Also on the road to Fóia, many restaurants offer piri-piri chicken.

Shopping

Distinctive, locally made 'scissor chairs' (wooden folding stools) are a good buy here (smaller children's versions start at €25). Try shops along Rua Estrada Velha and Rua Calouste Gulbenkian.

Information

Espaço Internet (✆282 910 235; Quinta da Vila; ⊙3-9pm Mon-Fri, 9am-9pm Sat)

Turismo (✆282 911 189; www.cm-monchique. pt; Largo da São Sebastião; ⊙9.30am-1pm, 2-5.30pm Mon-Fri) A useful spot for picking up maps, but frustratingly, limited (or no) information on walks. It's uphill from the bus stop, up Rua Engenheiro Duarte Pacheco.

Getting There & Away

Buses run to/from Portimão (€2.80, 45 minutes, five to eight daily).

Around Monchique

FÓIA

The 902m Fóia peak, 8km west of Monchique, is the Algarve's highest point. The road to the summit climbs through eucalyptus and pine trees and opens up vast views over the rolling hills. On the way are numerous piri-piri pit stops offering spicy chicken. Telecommunication towers spike the peak, but ignore them and look at the panoramic views. On clear days you can see out to the corners of the western Algarve – Cabo de São Vicente to the southwest and Odeceixe to the northwest.

CALDAS DE MONCHIQUE

Caldas de Monchique is a bit like the set of *The Truman Show*. It's a slightly sanitised, faintly fantastical hamlet, with a therapeutic calm, and pastel-painted buildings nestling above a delightful valley full of birdsong, eucalyptus, acacia and pine trees, 6km south of Monchique (and 500m below the main road).

It has been a popular spa for over two millennia – the Romans loved its 32°C, slightly sulphurous waters, which are said to be good for rheumatism and respiratory and digestive ailments. Dom João II came here for years in an unsuccessful attempt to cure his dropsy.

Floods in 1997 led to the closure of the spa hospital, after which it was redeveloped into a spa resort, and its picturesque buildings repainted pale pink, green and yellow.

⊙ Sights & Activities

The most peaceful patch is a pretty, streamside garden above the hamlet's central square. Down the valley is the spa itself and below this is the huge unattractive bottling plant where the famous Caldas waters are bottled.

Termas de Monchique Spa
SPA, THERMAL SPRINGS
(☑282 910 910; www.monchiquetermas.com; admission €25, hotel guests €15; ☉10.30am-7pm Tue, 9am-7pm Wed-Mon) In the wooded valley below town, admission allows access to the sauna, steam bath, gym and swimming pool with hydromassage jets. You can then indulge in special treatments, from a Cleopatra bath to a chocolate-mask wrapping.

🛏 Sleeping

Albergaria Lageado HOTEL €€
(☑282 912 616; www.albergariadabagado.com; s/d €45/55; ☉ May-Oct; ☒) In the village, Albergaria Lageado is an attractive hotel with a red-sloped roof and cosy ambience. It provides spotless rooms, a small plant-surrounded pool and a restaurant. Packages with board are also available.

The four other hotels all belong to Termas de Monchique. Rates include breakfast, and you can book weekend or week-long packages that include treatments. Prices are cheaper in low season.

Hotel Termal HOTEL €€€
(s/d €100/130) Situated next to the spa is the oldest, biggest (and least modern) of them.

Hotel Central HOTEL €€€
(s/d €105/140) Next to Termas' main reception, has 13 beautifully furnished rooms.

Estalagem Dom Lourenço HOTEL €€€
(s/d €105/140) Opposite reception, is the most luxurious option.

Hotel Dom Carlos HOTEL €€€
(s/d €105/140) The newest and most contemporary in style.

Apartamentos Turísticos Dom Francisco HOTEL €€€
(apt €170) A self-catering option also run by Termas de Monchique.

🍴 Eating

Restaurante 1692 RESTAURANT €€
(mains €9-18; ☉lunch & dinner) This upmarket place has tables in the tree-shaded central square, and a classy interior.

Café Império GRILL HOUSE €
(☑282 912 290; ☉lunch & dinner Wed-Mon) From the outside there's nothing particularly hot, although the view it offers of the valley is lovely. Locals flock to this place for what is reputedly the best piri-piri chicken in the region. Heading north, it's 700m on the left-hand side past the turn-off to Caldas – look for the tiled 'Schweppes' sign on the wall.

ℹ Information

At reception (the first building on your left), you can book accommodation. Spa treatments and other luxuries are available at the spa.

ℹ Getting There & Away

The Monchique–Portimão bus service goes via Caldas de Monchique (€1.25); the bus stop is on the road above the hamlet near Restaurant Rouxinol. It's easy to miss – ask the driver to alert you.

Alcoutim

POP 1100

Strategically positioned along the idyllic Rio Guadiana, Alcoutim (ahl-ko-*teeng*) is a small village just across the river from the Spanish town of Sanlúcar de Guadiana. What-are-you-looking-at fortresses above both villages remind one of testier times. Phoenicians, Greeks, Romans and Arabs have barricaded themselves in the hills here, and centuries of tension have bubbled across the river, which forms the Algarve's entire eastern boundary. In the 14th century, Dom Fernando I of Portugal and Don Henrique II of Castile signed a tentative peace treaty in Alcoutim. Tragically, today Alcoutim is said to be one of the fastest-diminishing towns in Portugal, as younger people leave the village to find jobs elsewhere. Tourism authorities are desperately trying to maintain this pleasant spot, as they well should. It boasts a lovely riverside beach, a fascinating castle and museum, and some interesting sites.

Sights & Activities

The main attraction for most day-trippers is the small riverside beach, equipped with sand, palm-leaf umbrellas, and even a lifeguard! The setting is breathtaking, but in summer it's hot, hot, hot. At the bridge, follow the signs to Praia Fluvial. The flower-ringed 14th-century castelo (admission €2.50; 9.30am-7pm Jun-Aug, to 5.30pm Dec-Feb) has sweeping views. Inside the grounds are the small, excellent Núcleo Museológico de Arqueologia (archaeological museum), displaying ruined medieval castle walls and other artefacts and an exhibition on Islamic 'board' games.

You can cross the river on the Fun River ferry (www.fun-river.com; tickets €1.25, half-hourly 10.15am-5.45pm). Rent bikes or canoes from the Pousada da Juventude (see p195).

Entrance fee to the castle also includes entry to small museums (núcleos museológicos) in Alcoutim and around. In Alcoutim, this includes Museu de Arte Sacra

in Capela de Santo António (9.30am-5.30pm Sep-May, to 7pm Jun-Aug).

Inland Adventures (922173183; www.inland-adventures.com; Apartado 24) offers riverboat trips and bicycle tours along the Guadiana and surrounds.

Sleeping

Guerreiros do Rio
HOTEL €€

(281 540 170; www.guerreirosdorio.com; s/d €95/105; @) Ten kilometres south of Alcoutim, this incongruous hotel on the banks of the lovely Rio Guadiana is smart, if slightly institutional. Prices are significantly less outside high season. Meals also available.

Pousada da Juventude
HOSTEL €

(281 546 004; www.pousadasjuventude.pt; dm €14, d €37-43, apt €80; reception 8am-noon & 6pm-midnight;) On the river, 1km north of the square, past the new town and fire station, is this well-appointed hostel, with an excellent pool and kitchen facilities, plus bikes and canoes for rent.

The town's only two private houses with beds:

Ilda Afonso
GUEST HOUSE €

(967 933 300; Rua Dr João Dias; r €35) Rooms are plain, but the owners are friendly and it's central.

Brisas do Guadiana
GUEST HOUSE €

(968 162 508; www.visitaralcoutim.blogspot.com; Rua do Bairro das Casas Pré-Fabricadas; s/d €40/50) Contrary to the street name ('Prefabricated Houses St'), this smart new yellow place on top of the hill behind the castle offers smart rooms.

GLIDING ALONG THE GUADIANA

One of the major rivers of Portugal, the slow-flowing Rio Guadiana makes an idyllic setting for a bit of adventure. Several outfits offer excursions along the river, which forms the border with Spain for some 50km.

In Alcoutim, Fun River (926 682 605; www.fun-river.com) offers river jaunts from anywhere between 20 minutes (€5) to a half day (€35).

Riosul (281 510 200; www.riosultravel.com; Monte Gordo) runs small-scale trips from Vila Real de Santo António to Foz de Odeleite at least four times weekly in summer and twice-weekly the rest of the year. The trips cost €41, including lunch and a stop for a swim. Periodically, Riosul also offers night-time cruises, which cost €40 and include dinner.

The quiet back road along the river from Foz de Odeleite to Alcoutim (14km) is also popular with bikers. Along this scenic route are several villages worth visiting, including Álamo, with its Roman dam, and Guerreiros do Rio, with its small Museu do Rio (River Museum; 281 547 380; admission €1; 9am-12.30pm & 2-5.30pm Tue-Sat) about traditional river life.

✗ Eating

You can take a safe pick from one of the town's three main restaurants, all of which serve up traditional cuisine with Algarvian flavours:

Ti Afonso   PORTUGUESE €€
(Rua 1o de Maio; mains €8-15; ⊙lunch & dinner Thu-Tue)

Restaurante os Cadavais   PORTUGUESE €€
(Rua João Dias 28; mains €7.50-10; ⊙lunch & dinner Tue-Sun)

**Snack Bar Restaurante
O Soeiro**   PORTUGUESE €
(Rua do Município; daily specials €6-7; ⊙lunch Mon-Fri) Cheap and cheerful but renowned for its chicken piri-piri and setting near the river.

ℹ Information

Casa dos Condes (☑281 540 500; ⊙9am-12.30pm & 2-5.30pm) Opposite the *turismo;* has free internet access (including wi-fi), a small display of local crafts. The municipality has a desk here offering guided visits of Alcoutim.

Turismo (☑281 546 179; Rua 1 de Maio; ⊙9.30am-1pm & 2-5.30pm Oct-Jun, 9.30am-5.30pm Jul-Sep) Behind the central square, just a few steps from the river, this office distributes maps and other information.

ℹ Getting There & Around

Bus services run to/from Vila Real de Santo António (€4, 1¼ hours, one to three daily Monday to Friday); on Monday and Friday these go to/from Beja (two hours, around €5) via Mértola (50 minutes).

The Alentejo

Best Places to Stay

» Quinta do Barrieiro (p233)

» Herdade do Touril (p250)

» Convento de São Francisco (p236)

» Casa do Terreiro do Poço (p219)

» Pousada de Rainha Santa Isabel (p217)

Best Places to Eat

» Tasca do Celso (p249)

» Tomba Lobos (p227)

» Botequim da Mouraria (p208)

» Dom Joaquim (p207)

» Adega do Isaías (p218)

Why Go?

To be bewitched. Covering a third of the country, Portugal's largest region truly captivates. Think dry, golden plains, rolling hillsides and lime-green vines. A rugged coastline, traditional whitewashed villages, marble towns and majestic medieval cities. Plus a proud, if melancholic, people (so their countrymen say), who valiantly cling to their local crafts.

Centuries-old farming traditions continue here, ongoing economic stalwarts in Portugal's poorest (but arguably most beautiful) region.

Alentejo's rich past offers Palaeolithic carvings, fragments from Roman conquerors and stolid Visigothic churches. There are Moorish-designed neighbourhoods and the awe-inspiring fortresses built at stork-nest heights.

As for the cuisine? Alentejo is 'it' for traditional food. Gastronomic delights are plentiful – pork, game dishes, breads, cheeses, wines, and seafood along the Alentejan coastline.

Bird life and rare plants are prolific, and excellent walking opportunities abound.

When to Go

Évora

°C/°F Temp   Rainfall Inches/mm

April & May
Red and yellow flowers mingle with golden plains, and it's baby stork time!

September & October Festival frenzy hits; enjoy while missing the crowds and the heat.

June & July Pre-August beaches await, plus Festas Populares, Évora's bounciest annual country fair.

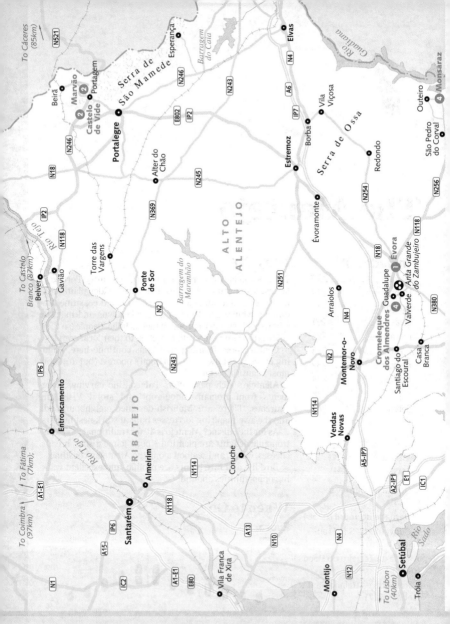

The Alentejo Highlights

1 Sample the history, culture and cuisine of historically rich **Évora** (p200), a Unesco World Heritage–listed city

2 Gaze out over the countryside from the castle perches of enchanting **Marvão** (p232) and **Castelo de Vide** (p228)

3 Stroll with spirits of past civilisations and religions in **Mértola** (p234) and at the nearby **Convento de São Francisco** (p235)

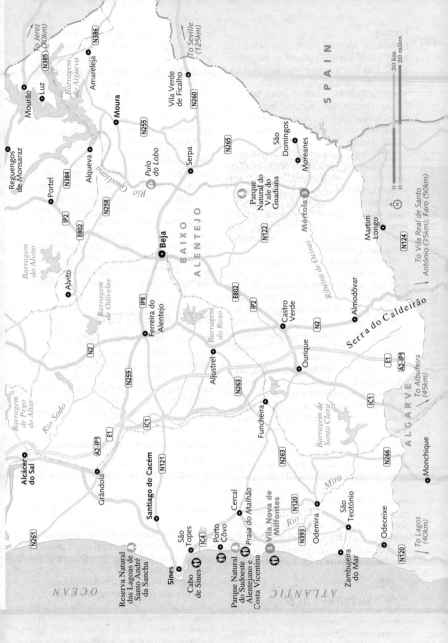

4 Watch the shadows play on the megaliths at **Cromeleque dos Almendres** (p211) and **Monsaraz** (p213)

5 Soak up the sun and sunset cocktails of **Vila Nova de Milfontes** (p248)

History

Prehistoric Alentejo was a busy place, and today's landscape is covered in megaliths. But it was the Romans who stamped and shaped the landscape, introducing vines, wheat and olives, building dams and irrigation schemes and founding huge estates called *latifúndios* to make the most of the region's limited rivers and poor soil.

The Moors, arriving in the early 8th century, took Roman irrigation further and introduced new crops such as citrus and rice. By 1279 they were on the run to southern Spain or forced to live in *mouraria* (segregated Moorish quarters) outside town walls. Many of their hilltop citadels were later reinforced by Dom Dinis (p477), who threw a chain of spectacular fortresses along the Spanish border.

Despite Roman and Moorish development, the Alentejo remained agriculturally poor and backward, and increasingly so as the Age of Discoveries (p479) led to an explosive growth in maritime trade and seaports became sexy. Only Évora flourished, under the royal patronage of the House of Avis, but it too declined once the Spanish seized the throne in 1580.

During the 1974 revolution (p485) Alentejo suddenly stepped into the limelight; landless rural workers who had laboured on the *latifúndios* for generations rose up in support of the communist rebellion and seized the land from its owners. Nearly 1000 estates were collectivised, although few succeeded and all were gradually reprivatised in the 1980s. Most are now back in the hands of their original owners.

Today Alentejo remains among Europe's poorest and emptiest regions. Portugal's entry into the EU (and its demanding regulations), increasing mechanisation, successive droughts and greater opportunities elsewhere have hit the region hard: young people have headed for the cities, leaving villages –

and their traditions – to die out. Although its cork, olives, marble and granite are still in great demand, and the deep-water port and industrial zone of Sines is of national importance, this vast region contributes only a small fraction to the gross national product. Locals are still waiting for the benefits promised by the construction of the huge Barragem do Alqueva (Alqueva Dam) and its reservoir (see boxed text, p246).

ℹ Getting Around

Trains run between some of the region's towns, but buses are a good way to access the region's smaller towns and villages. Two bus companies service the Alentejo: **Rede Expressos** (www.rede-expressos.pt) and the national company, **Rodalentejo** (www.rodalentejo.pt). Their websites publish up-to-date bus schedules. To get to remote places, including some mountaintop villages and the Alqueva Dam, a hire car is your best option.

ALTO ALENTEJO

The northern half of the Alentejo is a medieval gem, with a scattering of walled fortress towns (like Elvas and Estremoz) and remote cliff-top castles (like Marvão and Castelo de Vide). Only a handful of visitors to Alto Alentejo travel beyond Évora, so once outside the city you'll see traditional life at its most authentic.

Évora

POP 41,000

One of Portugal's most beautifully preserved medieval towns, Évora is an enchanting place to delve into the past. Inside the 14th-century walls, Évora's narrow, winding lanes lead to striking architectural works: an elaborate medieval cathedral and cloisters; the cinematic columns of the Templo Romano (near the intriguing Roman baths); and a picturesque town square, once the site of some rather gruesome episodes courtesy of the Inquisition. Aside from its historic and aesthetic virtues, Évora is also a lively university town, and its many attractive restaurants serve up hearty Alentejan cuisine. Outside of town, Neolithic monuments and rustic wineries make for fine day trips.

Évora climbs a gentle hill above the Alentejo plain. Around the walled centre runs a ring road from which you can enter the

INTERNET RESOURCE

A handy website on Alentejo is www.visitalentejo.pt presented in several languages. Detailed maps show highlights, bike trails, restaurants, everything for the tourist. Choose your interest, from gastronomy, wine, nature, heritage or just the rhythm of the seasons.

town on one of several 'spoke' roads. The town's focal point is Praça do Giraldo, 700m from the bus station to the southwest. The train station is outside the walls, 1km south of the square. If you're driving, it's advisable to park outside the walls at one of the many signposted car parks (eg at the southern end of Rua da República in Parking Rossio de São Brás). Except on Sunday, spaces inside the walls are limited and usually metered; pricier hotels have some parking.

History

The Celtic settlement of Ebora had been established here before the Romans arrived in 59 BC and made it a military outpost, and eventually an important centre of Roman Iberia, when it was known as 'Ebora Liberalitas Julia'.

After a depressing spell under the Visigoths, the town got its groove back as a centre of trade under the Moors. In AD 1165 Évora's Muslim rulers were hoodwinked by a rogue Portuguese Christian knight known as Giraldo Sem Pavor (Gerald the Fearless). The well-embellished story goes like this: Giraldo single-handedly stormed one of the town's watchtowers by climbing up a ladder of spears driven into the walls. From there he distracted (some say killed) municipal sentries while his companions took the town with hardly a fight.

Évora's golden age was from the 14th to 16th centuries, when it was favoured by the Alentejo's own House of Avis, as well as by scholars and artists. Declared an archbishopric in 1540, it got its own Jesuit university in 1559.

When Cardinal-King Dom Henrique, last of the Avis line, died in 1580 and Spain seized the throne, the royal court left Évora and the town began wasting away. The Marquês de Pombal's closure of the university in 1759 was the last straw. French forces plundered the town and massacred its defenders in July 1808.

Ironically, it was decline itself that protected Évora's very fine old centre – economic success would have led to greater redevelopment. Today the population is smaller than it was in the Middle Ages.

◎ Sights

Igreja de São Francisco &
Capela dos Ossos   CHURCH
(Praça 1 de Maio; Capela dos Ossos adult/concession €2/1.50, photography €1; ⊙9am-12.50pm & 2.30-5.40pm Mon-Sat, from 10am Sun) Évo-

ra's best-known church is a tall and huge Manueline-Gothic structure, completed around 1510 and dedicated to St Francis. Exuberant nautical motifs celebrating the Age of Discoveries deck the walls and reflect the confident, booming mood of the time. It's all topped by a cross of Christ's order and dome. Legend has it that the Portuguese navigator Gil Vicente is buried here.

What draws the crowds, though, is the mesmerising Capela dos Ossos (Chapel of Bones). A small room behind the altar has walls and columns lined with carefully arranged bones and skulls of some 5000 people. Visitors here describe the sight as macabre, artistic, ghoulish or beautiful (and, tasteful or not, we even heard several people humming 'Dem bones, dem bones, dem dry bones'). According to records, 17th-century Franciscan monks constructed this as a *memento mori* (reminder of death) to meditate on the human condition. An inscription over the entrance translates as: 'We bones await yours'.

Adding a final ghoulish flourish are two hanging mummified corpses; explanations in English highlight a legend. The entrance is to the right of the main church entrance.

TOP
CHOICE   Aqueduto da Água de Prata
                                          AQUEDUCT
Jutting into the town from the northwest is the beguilingly named Aqueduto da Água de Prata (Aqueduct of Silver Water), designed by Francisco de Arruda (better known for Lisbon's Tower of Belém) to bring clean water to Évora and completed in the 1530s. At the end of the aqueduct, on Rua do Cano, the neighbourhood feels like a self-contained village, with houses, shops and cafes built right into its perfect arches, as if nestling against the base of a hill.

It's possible to **walk** for around 8.5km along the aqueduct, starting outside of town, on the road to Arraiolos. There are three access points – the tourist office provides maps. Unfortunately, it's not a circuit walk and heads in one direction only, so transport back can be a problem if you don't have your own wheels. Take plenty of liquids – ironically, there's no potable water along the way.

Museu do Évora   MUSEUM
(Largo Conde de Vila Flor; adult/senior/youth €4/2/1.80; ⊙2.30-6pm Tue, 10am-6pm Wed-Sun) Adjacent to the cathedral, in what used to be the archbishop's palace (built in the 16th century), is this elegant

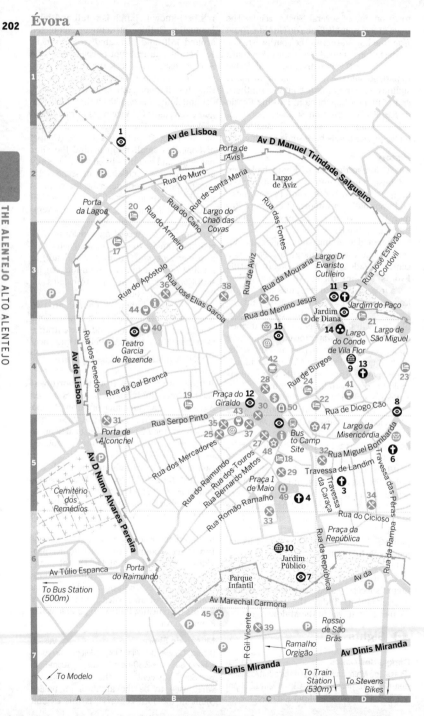

museum (reopened in 2010 after five years' renovation). The cloistered courtyard reveals Islamic, Roman and medieval remains. In polished rooms upstairs are former Episcopal furnishings and a gallery of Flemish paintings. Most memorable is *Life of the Virgin*, a 13-panel series originally part of the cathedral's altarpiece, created by anonymous Flemish artists working in Portugal around 1500.

Praça do Giraldo   PLAZA
The city's main square has seen some potent moments in Portuguese history, including the 1483 execution of Fernando, Duke of Bragança; the public burning of victims of the Inquisition in the 16th century; and fiery debates on agrarian reform in the 1970s. Nowadays it's still the city focus, hosting less dramatic activities such as sitting in the sun and coffee drinking.

The narrow lanes to the southwest were once Évora's *judiaria* (Jewish quarter). To the northeast, Rua 5 de Outubro, climbing to the *sé* (cathedral), is lined with handsome town houses wearing wrought-iron balconies, while side alleys pass beneath Moorish-style arches.

Palácio dos Duques de Cadaval   PALACE
Just northwest of the Igreja de São João is the 17th-century facade of a much older palace and castle, as revealed by the two powerful square towers that bracket it. The Palácio dos Duques de Cadaval (Palace of the Dukes of Cadaval) was given to Martim Afonso de Melo, the governor of Évora, by Dom João I, and it also served from time to time as a royal residence. A section of the palace still serves as the private quarters of the de Melo family; the other main occupant is the city's highway department.

Town Walls   HISTORIC SITE
About one-fifth of Évora's residents live within the town's old walls, some of which are built on top of 1st-century Roman fortifications. Over 3km of 14th-century walls enclose the northern part of the old town, while the bulwarks along the southern side, such as those running through the *jardim público* (public gardens), date from the 17th century.

Largo da Porta de Moura   PLAZA
The Largo da Porta de Moura (Moura Gate Square) stands just southeast of the cathedral. Near here was the original entrance to town. In the middle of the square is a strange-looking, globular 16th-century

Évora

Renaissance **fountain**. Among the elegant mansions around the square is **Casa Cordovil**, built in Manueline-Moorish style. Across the road to the west have a look at the extraordinary knotted Manueline stone doorway of the **Igreja do Carmo**.

Jardim Público   GARDEN
For a lovely tranquil stroll, head to the light-dappled public gardens (with a small outdoor cafe) south of the Igreja de São Francisco. Inside the walls of the 15th-century **Palácio de Dom Manuel** is the **Galeria das Damas** (Ladies' Gallery), an indecisive hybrid of Gothic, Manueline, neo-Moorish and Renaissance styles. It's open when there are (frequent) temporary art exhibitions.

From the town walls you can see, a few blocks to the southeast, the crenellated, pointy-topped Arabian Gothic profile of the **Ermida de São Brás** (Chapel of St Blaise), dating from about 1490. It's possibly an early project of Diogo de Boitaca, considered the originator of the Manueline style.

Sé   CATHEDRAL
(Largo do Marquês de Marialva; cathedral €1.50, plus cloister €2.50, plus tower €3.50, plus muse-

um €4.50; ☺9am-12.20pm & 2-4.50pm) Évora's cathedral looks like a fortress, with two stout granite towers. It was begun around 1186, during the reign of Sancho I, Afonso Henriques' son – there was probably a mosque here before. It was completed about 60 years later. The flags of Vasco da Gama's ships were blessed here in 1497.

You enter the cathedral through a portal flanked by 14th-century stone apostles, flanked in turn by asymmetrical towers and crowned by 16th-century roofs. Inside, the Gothic influence takes over. The chancel, remodelled when Évora became the seat of an archdiocese, represents the only significant stylistic change since the cathedral was completed. Golden light filters through the window across the space.

The cool **cloister** is an early-14th-century addition. Downstairs are the stone tombs of Évora's last four archbishops. At each corner of the cloister a dark, circular staircase (at least one will be open) climbs to the top of the walls, from where there are good views.

Climb the steps in the south tower to reach the choir stalls and up to the **museum**, which demonstrates again the enormous wealth poured into the church, with ecclesiastical riches, including a revolving jewelled reliquary (containing a fragment of the true cross). Encrusted with emeralds, diamonds, sapphires and rubies, it rests on gold cherubs and is flanked by two Ming vases and topped by Indo-Persian textiles.

Templo Romano   ROMAN RUINS
(Largo do Conde de Vila Flor) Opposite the museum are the remains of a Roman temple dating from the 2nd or early 3rd century. It's among the best-preserved Roman monuments in Portugal, and probably on the Iberian Peninsula. Though it's commonly referred to as the Temple of Diana, there's no consensus about the deity to which it was dedicated, and some archaeologists believe it may have been dedicated to Julius Caesar. How did these 14 Corinthian columns, capped with Estremoz marble, manage to survive in such good shape for some 18 centuries? The temple was apparently walled up in the Middle Ages to form a small fortress, and then used as the town slaughterhouse. It was uncovered late in the 19th century.

Termas Romanas   ROMAN RUINS
(admission free; ☺9am-5.30pm Mon-Fri) Inside the entrance hall of the *câmara municipal* on Praça de Sertório are more Roman vestiges, discovered only in 1987. These impressive Roman baths, which include a *laconicum* (heated room for steam baths) with a superbly preserved 9m-diameter circular pool, would have been the largest public building in Roman Évora. The complex also includes an open-air swimming pool, discovered in 1994.

Universidade de Évora   UNIVERSITY
Just outside the walls to the northeast is the **university's main building** (Colégio do Espírito Santo; admission free; ☺9am-7pm Mon-Fri, 9am-1pm Sat), a descendent (reopened

---

WORTH A TRIP

ARRAIOLOS: THE GREAT CARPETS OF PORTUGAL

About 20km north of Évora, the small town of Arraiolos is famed for its exquisite *tapetes* (carpets). These handwoven works show a marked influence from Persian rugs, and they have been in production here since the 12th century. It seems half the town is involved in this artistry, and on a casual stroll through town, you might encounter several women stitching in front of their homes. Rug patterns are based on abstract motifs, *azulejo* designs or flower, bird or animal depictions. Shops are abundant, and you can pay anything from €50 for a tiny runner to €2000 for the most beautiful pieces, which feature more elaborate designs.

The village itself dates from the 2nd or 3rd century BC, and is laid out along traditional lines, with whitewashed blue-trimmed houses topped with terracotta roofs and the ruins of a castle overlooking the town. The plain facade of the **Igreja da Misericórdia** hides a beautiful interior with a golden altar and 18th-century *azulejo*-lined walls.

Take a peak at the centuries-old dye chambers in the main square, which is also where you'll find the **turismo** (✆266 490 254; www.cm-arraiolos.pt). There are cafes in town for lingering, and a flashy **pousada** (✆266 419 340; www.pousadas.pt; d €270) just outside Arraiolos.

in 1973) of the original Jesuit institution founded in 1559 (which closed when the Jesuits got shooed out by Marquês de Pombal in 1759). Inside are arched, Italian Renaissance-style **cloisters**, the Mannerist-style **Templo do Espírito Santo** and beautiful *azulejos* (hand-painted tiles).

Igreja de São João & Convento dos Lóios CHURCH

(admission €3, plus Salas de Exposição do Palácio €5; ⊘9am-12.30pm & 2-6pm Tue-Sun) The small, fabulous Church of St John the Evangelist, which faces the Templo Romano, was founded in 1485 by one Rodrigo Afonso de Melo, count of Olivença and the first governor of Portuguese Tangier, to serve as his family's pantheon. It's still privately owned, by the Duques de Cadaval, and notably well kept.

Behind its elaborate Gothic portal is a nave lined with glorious floor-to-ceiling *azulejos* created in 1711 by one of Portugal's best-known tile-makers, António de Oliveira Bernardes. The grates in the floor reveal a surprising underworld: you'll see a deep Moorish cistern that predates the church and an ossuary full of monks' bones. In the sacristy beyond are fragments of even earlier *azulejos*.

The former **Convento dos Lóios**, to the right of the church, has elegant Gothic cloisters topped by a Renaissance gallery. A national monument, the convent was converted into a top-end *pousada* (upmarket inn) in 1965 (the Pousada dos Lóios). If you want to wander around, wear your wealthy-guest expression – or have dinner at its upmarket restaurant.

Igreja da Nossa Senhora da Graça CHURCH

Down an alley off Rua da República is the curious baroque facade of the Igreja da Nossa Senhora da Graça (Church of Our Lady of Grace), topped by four ungainly stone giants – as if they've strayed from a mythological tale and landed up on a religious building. An early example of the Renaissance style in Portugal is found in the cloister of the 17th-century **monastery** next door.

☞ Tours

Agia GUIDED TOURS

(☎963 702 392; www.alentejoguides.com; adult/under 12yr €12/free, minimum 2 people; ⊘tours at 10am) Agia offers daily 90-minute guided tours of Évora from outside the *turismo* (tourist office) on Praça do Giraldo.

TOP CHOICE Rota dos Frescos CULTURAL TOURS

(☎284 475 413; www.rotadofresco. com; per person €20) Offers fascinating cultural tours led by an art historian to Baroque sites filled with frescos and *azulejos* (tiles). Every Friday in English at 10am.

✵ Festivals & Events

Rota de Sabores Tradicionais FOOD

A gastronomic festival that lasts from January to May, celebrating game in January, pork in February, soups in March, lamb in April and desserts in May – traditional restaurants throughout the city serve specialities accordingly.

Festas Populares RURAL

Évora's biggest, bounciest annual bash, and one of Alentejo's best country fairs is held in late June.

Évora Classical Music Festival MUSIC

This five-day event (usually held in early July) formerly featured a strictly classical program, but today encompasses a wide range of contemporary and world musical styles. Concerts are held at various indoor and outdoor venues in Évora.

⌂ Sleeping

In high season it's essential to book ahead. Budget choices are limited.

TOP CHOICE Albergaria do Calvário BOUTIQUE HOTEL €€€

(☎266 745 930; www.albergariadocalvario.com; Travessa dos Lagares 3; s/d/studios €82/108/125) Elegant (yet unpretentious), friendly (yet not in your face), comfortable (but not awkwardly can't-put-your-feet-up-uberluxurious), this place has an ambience and *je ne sais quoi* that travellers adore. The delightful American owners love their cuisine and play a hands-on role in your experience. Breakfasts are among the best around: locally sourced organic produce and fresh juices. Pleasant lounge areas, books, and classical music plus comfortable beds and flat-screen TVs, ensure a homely stay. It's located in a delightful part of town, near Porta Lagoa, and has a pleasant garden patio area.

Residencial Riviera HOTEL €€

(☎266 737 210; www.riviera-evora.com; Rua 5 de Outubro 49; s/d/ste €64/80/97; ❄☎) Only one block from the *praça* (town square), this charming and well-renovated place has bright, stylish rooms with *boveda* (brick-arched) ceilings and carved bed-heads. Bathrooms are gleamingly tiled. Prices are significantly less outside high season.

Convento do Espinheiro
LUXURY HOTEL €€€

(☑266 788 200; www.conventodoespinheiro. com; r from €200) Housed in a restored 15th-century convent, several kilometres north-east of Évora, is this elegant hotel and spa complex with facilities galore (heliport, anyone?). The rooms feature heavy fabrics and rugs, and there are several restaurants on the premises.

M'ar De Ar Aqueduto
LUXURY HOTEL €€€

(www.mardearhotels.com; Rua Cândido dos Reis 72; r €255) Despite its location in a 16th-century former palace, with chapel, domed ceilings and three Manueline windows, this is Évora's newest hotel and up there as the city's most luxurious. It's a sleek number, and where the beautiful people stay, although you could be anywhere in the world (that said, you have a great view of Évora's aqueduct.) Prices fluctuate and you must consult the website for quotes.

Pousada dos Lóios
LUXURY HOTEL €€€

(☑266 730 070; www.pousadas.pt; Largo do Conde de Vila Flor; d €290; ✸✸) Occupying the former Convento dos Lóios, opposite the Templo Romano, this beautiful *pousada* has gorgeously furnished rooms in a contemporary style (mint green and white) set around the pretty cloister. Note the original walkie-talkie 'devices' in the room doors. There's a flash restaurant on the ground floor of the cloister (mains €22 to €25).

Best Western Hotel Santa Clara
HOTEL €€

(☑266 704 141; www.hotelsantaclara.pt; Travessa da Milheira 19; r €74; ℙ✸✸) A whitewashed building tucked away in a quiet back street, this efficiently run and reliable hotel has plain but comfortable rooms.

Casa dos Teles
GUEST HOUSE €

(☑266 702 453; Rua Romão Ramalho 27; s €25, d with shared bathroom €30-35, r with bathroom €40; ✸) These nine mostly light and airy rooms are the best of the *quartos* (rooms in private houses); quieter rooms at the back overlook a pretty courtyard and have their own bathrooms.

Residencial Diana
GUEST HOUSE €€

(☑266 702 008; www.softline.pt/residencial -diana/; Rua de Diogo Cão 2; s/d with bathroom

€50/55, without bathroom €42/47; ✸☎) Diana is a bit long in the tooth with slightly saggy mattresses. Nevertheless, it's charming in a caught-in-a-time-warp, high-ceilinged, wood-floored kind of way. Corner rooms are appealing, if potentially noisy. Breakfast is served in the *salão de chá* (tearoom).

Residencial Policarpo
GUEST HOUSE €€

(☑266 702 424; www.pensaopolicarpo.com; Rua da Freiria de Baixo 16; s/d with bathroom €52/57, without bathroom €30/35; ℙ@) This hotel is the former holiday home of a 16th-century count – the family was purged by the Pombals in the 18th century. While atmospheric (with the odd musty wall), it's somewhat faded. All rooms are different in layout and decor and have a mix of carved wooden and traditionally hand-painted Alentejan furniture.

Parque de Campismo
CAMPGROUND €

(☑266 705 190; www.orbitur.pt; sites per adult/tent/car €5.40/6.10/5.30) Flat, grassy and tree-shaded, with disabled access, Orbitur's well-equipped camp site is 2km southwest of town. Yellow line bus 41 (€1.20) from Praça do Giraldo, via Avenida de São Sebastião and the bus station, goes close by.

✗ Eating

Scattered around Praça do Giraldo are a handful of attractive cafes with outdoor seating – a good spot for coffee or an early evening drink. Most of the town's many snack bars serve basic, cheap eats – try those along Rua de Vasco da Gama and Praça de Sertorio.

Snack-Bar Restaurante
A Choupana
PORTUGUESE €€

(☑266 704 427; Rua dos Mercadores 18; mains €5-13; ◷lunch & dinner Mon-Sat) This is a tiled, busy place where many locals opt to sit on stools at a long bar. There's a TV, lots of knick-knacks and tasty, good-value daily mains (including generous half serves). At-tached is an appealing restaurant served by efficient bow-tied waiters.

Dom Joaquim
PORTUGUESE €€

(☑266 731 105; Rua dos Penedos 6; mains €11-13; ◷lunch & dinner Thu-Tue) Housed in a reno-vated building, Dom Joaquim offers fine dining in a contemporary setting. Modern artworks line the stone walls, and cane chairs grace clothed tables. While it's smart and trendy, it offers excellent traditional cuisine. Chef Joaquim adores his clients as much as they love his skills; he serves up big tastes with great enthusiasm: meats (including game and succulent, fall-off-the-bone oven lamb) and seafood dishes, such as *perdiz* (partridge) and *caçao* (dogfish). For dessert, we dare you to try the *toucinho ransoso dos santos*, which literally translates as 'rancid lard of the saint'. Oh so sweet.

Pastelaria Conventual Pão de Rala

PASTISSERIE €

(Rua do Cicioso 47; ⊙7.30am-8pm) Out of the centre, but still within the walls, this delightful spot specialises in convent cakes, all made on the premises and the recipes for which originated in the local convents. Don't miss the *pão de rala* (we'll let you find out what it is) – it's sweet stuff (and wonderfully sinful).

Botequim da Mouraria

PORTUGUESE €€

(☑266 746 775; Rua da Mouraria 16A; mains €12.50-14; ⊙lunch & dinner Mon-Fri, lunch Sat) Local gastronomes believe this is Évora's culinary shrine. Poke around the old Moorish quarter to find this cosy spot serving some of Évora's finest food and wine (the owner currently stocks more than 150 wines from the Alentejo alone). There are no reservations, just 12 stools at a counter. Rumour is that it's moving to larger premises – a pity, in our opinion – but will be worth seeking out.

Vinho e Noz

PORTUGUESE €€

(Ramalho Orgigão 12; mains €8.50-11; ⊙lunch & dinner Mon-Sat) The delightful owner and family run this efficient and unpretentious establishment, which has professional service, a large wine list and good-quality cuisine. One of the best-value places to eat in town.

Um Quarto para as Nove

SEAFOOD €€

(☑266 706 774; Rua Pedro Simões 9A; mains €10-15; ⊙dinner Thu-Tue) We'll let you establish the reason for this eatery's name (the owner bought the object secondhand – it never worked). This cheerful place has clocked up 30 years experience, and with that, some of Évora's best seafood dishes. It's hard to go past the generous and tasty *arroz* (risotto) dishes.

Café Alentejo

PORTUGUESE €€

(Rua do Raimundo 5; mains €10-15; ⊙lunch & dinner Mon-Sat) Housed in a 16th-century building, Café Alentejo is full of arches and smart decor (with beautiful floors). Not to mention the amazing aromas: a heady mix of red wine and herbs that hit you on

entry. The *rabo de boi estufado em vinho tinto* (oxtail stew in red wine; €12.50) and *arroz de pato* (duck risotto) are both highly recommended.

Adega do Neto

PORTUGUESE €

(Rua dos Mercadores 46; mains €6-8; ⊙lunch & dinner Mon-Sat) This cheap and cheerful eatery has daily specials, such as fried chicken and *feijoada* (pork-and-bean casserole). There is a handful of tables and counter service.

Café Arcada

CAFE, RESTAURANT €

(Praça do Giraldo 10; meals €6.50-10; ⊙breakfast, lunch & dinner) This busy, barn-sized cafe is an Évora institution, serving up coffee, crepes and cakes. You can sit at an outdoor table on the lovely plaza.

Restaurante Cozinha de Santo Humberto

PORTUGUESE €€€

(Rua da Moeda 39; mains €9-16; ⊙lunch & dinner Fri-Tue) This is a traditional, long-established place, in a grand arched, whitewashed cellar hung with brass and ceramics. It offers hearty servings of rich regional fare. An excellent plaza-side cafe serves similar (but lighter) bites.

Restaurante O Fialho

PORTUGUESE €€€

(☑266 703 079; Travessa dos Mascarenhas 16; mains €14.50-18; ⊙lunch & dinner Tue-Sun) Évora's long-standing culinary institution. Spread over several small rooms and with wood panelling and white tablecloths, this restaurant serves up professional service and good Alentejan cuisine. Photos of visiting dignitaries line the walls.

Gelataria Zoka

ICE CREAM €

(Largo de São Vicente 14, Rua Miguel Bombarda; ice creams from €1.75; ⊙8am-midnight) Ice-cream lovers can head here for heaven-in-a-cone – experienced at tables on the pedestrianised street.

Cafe Restaurante Repas

PORTUGUESE €€

(Praça 1 de Maio 19; mains €6-12; ⊙breakfast, lunch & dinner Thu-Tue) Repas may be nothing special cuisine-wise, but its location near the Igreja São Francisco is pleasant. In summer, this is the spot for *caracois* (snails) and beer.

Mercado Municipal

MARKET €

(municipal market; Praça 1 de Maio; ⊙8am-5pm Tue-Sun) You can pick up fruit and vegetables at the municipal market. Or try Modelo Hypermarket, a supermarket beyond the town limits on the road to Alcáçovas.

Drinking

Most bars open late and don't close until at least 2am (4am at weekends). There are no cover charges at these places.

Cup of Joe
CAFE-BAR

(Praça de Sertório 3; mains from €5-8; ⊙noon-2am; ♪) Part of a coffee chain, this attractive cafe has a peaceful outdoor seating overlooking a plaza, and a good selection of lighter fare – crepes, salads, wraps and plenty of caffeine. Electronic music and a friendly cocktail-sipping crowd arrive by night.

Bar do Teatro
BAR

(Praça Joaquim António de Aguiar; ⊙8pm-2am) Next to the theatre, this small and inviting bar has high ceilings and old-world decor that welcomes a friendly mixed crowd. The bar's soundtrack tends towards lounge and electronica.

Tuareg
BAR

(Praca Joaqium António de Aguiar; ⊙9pm-2am Mon-Fri, 10pm-3am Sat) Position, position, position. Right on the plaza, near the main theatre, this plays to a Moroccan theme. It's surprisingly laid-back and attracts a younger crowd, who enjoy the reasonably priced cocktails and chilled ambience.

Oficin@Bar
BAR

(Rua da Moeda 27; ⊙8pm-2am Mon-Fri, 9pm-3am Sat) Attracting all ages, this is an appealing, relaxed bar with little wooden tables in a white-arched cave-like space. It's convivial, with jazz and blues playing gently in the background.

Bar UÉ
BAR

(Rua de Diogo Cão 21; ⊙Mon-Sat) At the Associação de Estudantes da Universidade de Évora, this is the main central student hang-out with a laid-back atmosphere.

☆ Entertainment

For theatre, film, concerts and art expositions, stop in at the imaginative cultural centre **Sociedade Harmonia Eborense** (☑266 746 874; Praça do Giraldo 72) to see what's on.

Praxis
NIGHTCLUB

(Rua de Valdevinos; ⊙midnight-6am) Praxis has one big dance floor, one small dance floor and DJs spinning house, R&B and hip hop. It's a lively, good-time crowd, but the place doesn't get busy until around 2am after the other places have closed.

Casa dos Bonecos
PUPPET THEATRE

(☑266 703 112) Actors from the grand municipal Teatro Garcia de Resende studied for several years with the only surviving master of a traditional rural puppetry style called *bonecos de Santo Aleixo* (Santo Aleixo puppets). They occasionally perform this, other styles, and hand-puppet shows for children at this little theatre off Largo de Machede Velho. Ask at the tourist office for their schedule.

Aréna de Évora
BULLFIGHTING

Évora has a *praça de touros* (bullring) outside the southern walls, near the *jardim público*. Several bullfights usually take place between March and October.

🛍 Shopping

Rua 5 de Outubro has rows of *artesanatos* (handicrafts shops) selling pottery, knick-knacks and cork products of every kind. A couple of shops in the modern *mercado municipal* sell pottery. There are more up-market shops along Rua Cândido dos Reis, northwest of the centre.

On the second Tuesday of each month a vast open-air market sprawls across the big Rossio de São Brás, just outside the walls south of Rua da República.

Feiras no Largo
MARKETS

(Praça 1 de Maio; ⊙8am-2pm Sat & Sun) Each weekend sees the Feiras no Largo, one of four different markets – antiquities, used books and collectables, art and *artesanato* – near the aqueduct.

Livraria Nazareth
BOOKS

(☑266 741 702; Praça do Giraldo 46) Head up the stairs of Évora's oldest shop, for maps, including *Alentejo & Évora* (€4.95), and some books in English.

ℹ Information

Emergency & Medical Services

Évora district hospital (☑266 740 100; Largo Senhor da Pobraza) East of the centre.

PSP police station (☑266 702 022; Rua Francisco Soares Lusitano) Near the Templo Romano.

Internet access

Câmara municipal (town hall; Praça de Sertório; ⊙9am-12.30pm & 2-5pm Mon-Fri) Free internet access in the same building as the old Roman baths.

Cybercenter (Rua Serpa Pinto 36; per hr €2; ⊙10.30am-11pm Mon-Fri, 2-10pm Sat & Sun)

Oficin@Bar (Rua da Moeda 27; per hr €3; ◷9pm-2am Tue-Thu, 9pm-3am Fri & Sat)

Money
There are several banks with ATMs on and around Praça do Giraldo, including **Caixa de Crédito Agrícola** (Praça do Giraldo 13).

MundiTransfers (266 761 025; Rua Serpa Pinto 40A; ◷10am-1.30pm & 3-7pm) Changes money.

Post
Branch post office (Largo da Porta de Moura)

Main post office (Rua de Olivença)

Tourist Information
Rota dos Vinhos do Alentejo headquarters (Wine Route Office; ☑266 746 498; www .vinhosdoalentejo.pt; Praça Joaquim António de Aguiar 20-21; ◷2-7pm Mon, 11am-7pm Tue-Fri, 10am-1pm Sat) Head here for details of a *rota dos vinhos* (wine route) to *adegas* (wineries) in the Alentejo, plus wine tastings and cellar visits (free).

Turismo (tourist office; ☑266 777 071; www. cm-evora.pt; Praça do Giraldo 73; ◷9am-7pm Apr-Oct, 9am-6pm Nov-Mar) This helpful place offers a *Historical Itineraries* leaflet (€1.05) and free publications including a town map and the listings guide *Viva por Cá*. Excellent tourist guides can be downloaded from www.cm-evora. pt/guiaturistico (in English, Spanish, French and Portuguese).

Travel Agencies
Abreu (☑266 769 180; www.abreu.pt; Rua da Misericórdia 16)

TopAtlántico (☑266 746 970; www.topatlan tico.pt; Rua 5 de Outubro 63)

ⓘ Getting There & Away
Bus
The **bus station** (☑266 769 410) is off Avenida de São Sebastião.

Beja (normal/express €6/8, 1½ hours, three to five daily)

Coimbra (€17, 4½ hours, two daily) Alternatively, change in Lisbon.

Elvas(normal/express €6.25/11, 2¼/1¼ hours, one to six weekdays)

Estremoz (normal/express €4.50/9, 1½ hours/30 minutes, two daily)

Faro (€16, 5¼ hours, three daily) Via Albufeira.

Lisbon (€12, 1½ to two hours, hourly)

Portalegre (normal/express €6.60/12, 2½/1½ hours, three to five daily)

Reguengos de Monsaraz (normal/express €3.50/7.50, 1¼/¾ hours, three to four every weekday)

Vila Viçosa (normal/express €5.50/9, 90/60 minutes, one to six weekdays)

Train
The **Évora station** (☑266 742 336), 600m south of Jardim Público, is on a branch of the Lisbon–Funcheira (via Beja) train line. At the time of research this was closed for renovation. When operating, trains head to Lisbon, Beja, Lagos and Faro.

ⓘ Getting Around
Car & Bicycle
If you want to rent a car, get in touch with Abreu or TopAtlántico.

You can rent a bike from **Stevens Bikes** (☑939 046 864; www.solarbike.com.pt; Combatentes da Grande Guerra 27; per half-/full day €10/15; ◷10am-1pm & 3-7pm Mon-Fri, 10am-1pm Sat).

If you're driving, it's best to park outside the walls at a signposted car park (eg at the southern end of Rua da República in Parking Rossio de São Brás). Spaces inside the walls are limited and usually metered.

Taxi
Taxis (☑266 734 734) congregate in Praça do Giraldo and Largo da Porta de Moura. On a weekday you can expect to pay about €6 from the train station to Praça do Giraldo.

Around Évora

Megaliths – the word is derived from the ancient Greek for 'big stones' – are found all over the ancient landscape that surrounds Évora. Such prehistoric structures, built around 5000 to 6000 years ago, dot the European Atlantic coast, but here in Alentejo there is an astounding amount of Neolithic remains. Dolmens (Neolithic stone tombs – *antas* in Portuguese) were probably temples and/or tombs, covered with a large flat stone and usually built on hilltops or near water. Menhirs (individual standing stones) point to fertility rites – as phallic as skyscrapers, if on a smaller scale – while *cromeleques* (cromlechs, stone circles) were also places of worship.

Évora's *turismo* sells *Historical Itineraries* (€1.05), a leaflet that details many sites. Dolmen devotees can buy the book *Paisagens Arqueologicas A Oeste de Évora*, which has English summaries.

You can see more megaliths around Reguengos de Monsaraz, Elvas and Castelo de Vide.

Wines here, particularly the reds, are fat, rich and fruity. But tasting them is much more fun than reading about them, so drop in on some wineries. The **Rota dos Vinhos do Alentejo** (Alentejan Wine Route) splits the region into three separate areas – the Serra de São Mamede (dark reds, full bodied, red fruit hints), Historic (around Évora, Estremoz, Borba and Monsaraz; smooth reds, fruity whites), and the Rio Guadiana (scented whites, spicy reds). Some wineries also have accommodation options.

You'll see the brown signs all over the place, announcing that you are on the wine trail, and can pick up the booklet that lists wineries and their details at any local tourist office. Otherwise visit the helpful **Rota dos Vinhos do Alentejo headquarters** (☎266 746 498; Praça Joaquim António de Aguiar 20-21, Évora; ☺2-7pm Mon, 11am-7pm Tue-Fri, 10am-1pm Sat).

ⓘ Getting There & Away

To get to this area, your only option is to rent a car or bike (note that about 5km of the route is rough and remote), or hire a taxi for the day (around €60).

With your own wheels, head west from Évora on the old Lisbon road (N114) for 10km, then turn south for 2.8km to Guadalupe. Follow the signs from here to the Cromeleque dos Almendres (4.3km).

Return to Guadalupe and head south for 5km to Valverde, home of the Universidade de Évora's school of agriculture and the 16th-century Convento de Bom Jesus. Following the signs to Anta Grande do Zambujeiro, turn into the school's farmyard and onto a badly potholed track. After 1km you'll see the Great Dolmen.

Continue west from Valverde for 12km. Before joining the N2, turn right for the cave at Santiago do Escoural.

CROMELEQUE DOS ALMENDRES

Set within a beautiful landscape of olive and cork trees – unfortunately the dirt road almost impinges onto the site – stands the Cromeleque dos Almendres (Almendres Cromlech). This huge, spectacular oval of standing stones, 15km west of Évora, is the Iberian Peninsula's most important megalithic group and an extraordinary place to visit.

The site consists of a huge oval of some 95 rounded granite monoliths – some of which are engraved with symbolic markings – spread down a rough slope. They were erected over different periods, it seems with geometric and astral consideration, probably for social gatherings or sacred rituals.

Two and a half kilometres before Cromeleque dos Almendres stands **Menir** dos Almendres, a single stone about 4m high, with some very faint carvings near the top. Look for the sign; to reach the menhir you must walk for a few hundred metres from the road.

ANTA GRANDE DO ZAMBUJEIRO

The Anta Grande do Zambujeiro (Great Dolmen of Zambujeiro), 13km southwest of Évora, is Europe's largest dolmen and a rather neglected one at that. Under a huge sheet-metal shelter in a field of wildflowers and yellow broom, seven stones, each 6m high, form a huge chamber more than 50m in diameter. Unfortunately, you cannot enter; the entrance is blocked, but the setting is pretty.

Archaeologists removed the capstone in the 1960s. Most of the site's relics are in the Museu de Évora (currently closed).

Feeling peckish? **Restaurante O Ricardo** (☎266 711 115; Valverde; mains €7-13; ☺lunch & dinner Tue-Sat, lunch Sun) is the perfect place to sate your menhir-like appetite. The owner cooks seasonal dishes, carrying on the tradition of her grandparents. Summer dishes include asparagus and gazpacho; winter feasts include *feijoadas* (rich kidney- or butter-bean-and-meat stews) and *açorda* (bread soup). Organic produce is used where possible. The restaurant is on your return leg (after you visit Zambujeiro) in the village of Valverde.

Évoramonte

POP 700

Northeast of Évora, this tiny village, with its quaint 16th-century castle, makes an interesting detour on your way through the region. There are fine views all around across the low hills.

The **castelo** (adult/senior €1.50/.75; ⏰10am-1pm & 2-5pm Wed-Sun, 2-5pm Tue, closed last weekend of every month) dates from 1306, but was rebuilt after the 1531 earthquake. Exterior stone carving shows unwarlike small bows, the symbol of the Bragança family – the knot symbolises fidelity. The interior is neatly restored, with impressively meaty columns topped by a sinuous arched ceiling on each cavernous floor. The roof provides sweeping panoramas.

You can stay at **A Convenção** (☎268 959 217; Rua de Santa Maria 26; d with/without terrace €35/30), where the three rooms – particularly the one with a terrace – have fantastic views from this peaceful spot.

This place has an unexpectedly smart **restaurant** (mains €9-12; ⏰Mon) with indoor-outdoor seating and views. There are also several restaurants in the village below.

One to two buses a day stop in Évoramonte from Évora (€1.40, 30 minutes), though it's a long uphill walk (1km) from the bus stop to the castle.

São Pedro do Corval

Known for its fine pottery traditions, this tiny village, 5km east of Reguengos de Monsaraz, has dozens of **pottery workshops** where you can see both the potters and artists in action and purchase a few pieces of cheap and cheerful plates, pots, jugs, candlesticks and floor tiles.

With more than 20 *olarias* (pottery workshops), the village is one of Portugal's largest pottery centres. It's difficult to recommend one *olaria* over the other; wander along Rua da Primavera and the nearby streets (follow the *'olarias'* signs). Ask at the Reguengos and Monsaraz tourist offic-

---

WORTH A TRIP

ALVITO

Situated only 38km northwest of Beja and 37km southwest of Évora, beautiful Alvito is well worth visiting, for a day at least. Be aware though, such is its appeal, it's the kind of place you get to and wished you'd packed your toothbrush, and excellent accommodation options abound. The town was the home of the Portuguese Barons; the first baron, Dom João Fernandes da Silveira, decided to make Alvito an artistic landmark. (The Festa do Barão – Baron's Feast – is held each year at the end of June.)

You can visit parts of a 15th-century former **castle**, now a **luxury pousada** (☎284 480 700; www.pousadas.pt; r €270) and several important **churches**. The 16th-century **Ermida de Sao Sebastião** has some extraordinary revived **frescos**.

Throughout the village, you can see beautiful **Manueline features** – pick up a brochure from the tourist office and play 'spot the Manueline doorway' (these are stunning).

Turismo (☎284 480 808; www.cm-alvito.pt; Rua dos Lobos 13; ⏰9am-12.30pm & 2-5.30pm Mon-Fri, 10am-12.30pm & 2-5.30pm Sat, plus Sun Jun-Aug) has a great selection of brochures showing the town's Manueline doors.

The community-focused **Rota do Fresco** (Fresco Route; ☎284 475 413; www.rotadofresco.com; Rua 5 de Outubre 20, Vila Nova da Baronia; see also p206) arranges fun and informative cultural and heritage tours, including – as the name suggests – trips to the region's extraordinary historic frescos. It also runs themed gastronomy tours and workshops (including wine, honey, herbs and bread-making). Minimum numbers apply and prices vary (see website for further information).

If you decided to stay the night in Alvito, our pick is the delightful **Horta do Padre** (☎961 865 502, 284 485 400; Quinta da Esperança, Apartado 16; s/d €25/35), a renovated blue-and-white traditional Alentejan farm house 1km from Alvito's centre, with comfortable rooms and excellent breakfasts. The multilingual owners are passionate about preserving Portuguese traditional practices. Best to ring in advance, and consider renting the whole place, per night €150. Wow. Eight beds, two-night minimum.

Traditional bread-making workshops are offered by the Horta do Padre team in conjunction with Rota dos Frescos, as part of Rota dos Frescos' gastronomy tours. Here you prepare and then bake bread in the *horta*'s own wood-fired oven. Minimum numbers apply.

es for a map locating the *olarias*. Buses between Reguengos and Monsaraz stop here.

Reguengos de Monsaraz
POP 11,300

This small working-class town, once famous for its sheep and wool production, is a stopping point and transport hub for Monsaraz. It's also close to the pottery centre of São Pedro do Corval as well as to an impressive half-dozen dolmens and menhirs (out of around 150 scattered across the surrounding plains). Near here, too, are some excellent wineries.

The rocket-like local church (built in 1887) was designed by José António Dias da Silva, who was also responsible for Praça de Touros, the Lisbon bullring.

◉ Sights

There are several **wineries** around Reguengos (part of the wine route), including the acclaimed **Herdade do Esporão** (☑266 509 280; www.esporao.com), 7km out of town. The property's border was defined in 1267 and it has vestiges of Roman times. It produces a wide variety of wines for the domestic and overseas markets. The winery offers various tours, and not only of the vineyards and extraordinary cellars (among the largest in Portugal, parts of the cellars were sourced from the same factory that supplied the underground/metro in Lisbon). **Birdwatching** trips head to one of the two water courses, while **history tours** cover the archaeological excavations of the Herdad's neighbouring estate, Perdigões. The small on-site museum features the original artwork done for the wine labels of Esporão's annual reserve collection; each year a famous Portuguese artist is given the honours. It's worth splurging at the wine cellar or the restaurant. Phone ahead to arrange a tour.

🛏 Sleeping & Eating

Residencial O Gato   GUEST HOUSE €

(☑266 502 353; www.residencialogato.com; Praça da Liberdade 11; s/d €25/35; ❊) This friendly guest house has pleasant rooms that are nicely maintained. The best have small balconies (with flower boxes) overlooking the sleepy *praça*. A restaurant is downstairs.

Restaurante Central   TRADITIONAL €€

(☑266 502 219; Praça da Liberdade; mains €8.50-15) Since 1918, Central has been in the same family, has offered tasty Portuguese mains

and still keeps up a busy trade. The original wooden tables and chairs are still in use, although covered in crisp cloths.

🛍 Shopping

The local handicraft is *mantas alentejanas* (handwoven woollen blankets). The making of these beautiful pieces is, sadly, a declining craft.

Fabrica Alentejana de Lanifícios   HANDICRAFTS

(☑266 502 179; Rua Mendes; ⊙9am-5pm Mon-Fri) This extraordinary factory is the last remaining hand-loom producer of *mantas alentejanas*. Only two women are at the looms these days but demand for the *mantas* was again increasing at the time of research. It's worth visiting, if only to support the craft (purchases can be made). The weavers are happy to show you around. The factory is southeast of the *praça* (take the road to Monsaraz and turn right at Rua Mendes). The factory's shop is in Monsaraz (see p215).

ℹ Information

Espaço Internet (Rua do Conde de Monsaraz 32) About 100m northeast of the *praça*. Free internet access.

Saberes & Encantos (☑962 501 387; www.sabereseencantos.org) Offers personalised tours around the region including bike, vineyard and lake tours.

Turismo (☑266 503 052; Rua 1 de Maio; ⊙9am-12.30pm & 2-5.30pm Mon-Fri, 10am-1pm & 2.30-4.30pm Sat & Sun) Just off the *praça*.

ℹ Getting There & Away

BUS Buses run daily to Évora (€7.40 express, normal/express 1¼ hours/45 minutes, two to nine daily) and direct to Lisbon (€13, 2½ hours, two daily).

Monsaraz
POP 20

Perched high over the surrounding countryside, tiny Monsaraz is a charming village with a looming castle at its edge, great views over the Alqueva Dam and olive groves sprinkling the landscape. The narrow streets here are lined with unevenwalled, whitewashed cottages. Sadly, as with other villages in the region, Monsaraz struggles to maintain its inhabitants; permanent residents are mainly elderly people.

But it has not lost its magic. In the streets, you'll see flat-capped men watch the day unfold and women chatting on stoops.

Today, the village prospers on tourism, with a handful of restaurants, guest houses and artisan shops. It's worth coming here to taste a slice of traditional Portugal, wander the slumbering streets and sample Alentejan cuisine. It's at its best as it wakes up in the morning, in the quiet of the evening, or during a wintry dusk.

Settled long before the Moors arrived in the 8th century, Monsaraz was subsequently recaptured by the Christians under Giraldo Sem Pavor (Gerald the Fearless) in 1167, and then given to the Knights Templar as thanks for their help. The castle was added in 1310.

As for your arrival? Like historic times – on foot through one of the four arched entrances. Coaches or cars have to be parked outside the walled village.

☉ Sights & Activities

Igreja Matriz
CHURCH

(☉2-7pm) The parish church, near the *turismo,* was rebuilt after the 1755 earthquake and again a century later. Inside (if you can get in, hours can be vague) is an impressive nave and a 14th-century marble tomb carved with 14 saints. An 18th-century *pelourinho* (stone pillory) topped by a Manueline globe stands outside. The 16th-century Igreja da Misericórdia is opposite, but is rarely open.

Museu de Arte Sacra
MUSEUM

(Museum of Sacred Art; admission €1.80; ☉10am-7pm) Housed inside a fine Gothic building beside the parish church, the Museu de Arte Sacra houses a small collection of 14th-century wooden religious figures and 18th-century vestments and silverware. Its most famous exhibit is a rare example of a 14th-century secular fresco, a charming piece depicting a good and a bad judge, the latter appropriately two-faced.

Castelo
CASTLE

(☉24hr) The castle at the southwestern end of the village was one in the chain of Dom Dinis' defensive fortresses along the Spanish border. It's now converted into a small bullring, and its ramparts offer a fine panoramic view over the Alentejan plains.

Barragem do Alqueva
BOAT TRIPS

A great way to explore the lake is by boat. Capitão Tiago (☎962 653 711; www.sem-fim.

com; Telheiro) runs excellent voyages in his 17m Dutch sail boat. Several trips are available – the standard is a two-hour trip with the chance to swim and visit some of the islands (€50 per person if alone, less if in a group). Other packages include a meal at Tiago's restaurant, Sem Fim (☎962 653 711; Telheiro), and a boat trip (€20). You can also rent bikes and canoes. Telheiro is about 2km from Monsaraz; call in advance for advice on mooring on the lake.

✦ Festivals & Events

Accommodation must be booked far in advance at these times.

Bullfights
BULLFIGHTING

If you want to see a bullfight, Easter Sunday is a good time to visit.

Museu Aberto
MUSIC

Monsaraz heaves with jollity during its week long Museu Aberto (Open Museum) music festival, held in July in even-numbered years.

Festa de Nosso Senhor
VILLAGE

Bullfights and processions feature in this festival on the second weekend of September.

⌂ Sleeping

Some villagers have converted their ancient cottages to guest houses, most of which are along Rua Direita. Unless otherwise mentioned, all the following rates include breakfast. Book ahead in high season.

Casa Saramago de Monsaraz
RURAL INN €€

(☎266 557 494; www.casasaramago-monsaraz.com.pt; Telheiro; s/d €50/60; ✸✸) Based in Telheiro, at the foot of Monsaraz, this delightfully converted blue and white *quinta* is great value for money. Rooms are tastefully decorated in old-style – but not too twee – furniture. The Portuguese owners are friendly and accommodating. Rooms in the former *celeiros* (silos) have verandahs and face Monsaraz. Four-legged friends are welcome too – a horse hotel and *cão* (dog) kennels are on the premises.

Casa Paroquial
B&B €

(☎266 557 181; Rua Direita 4; s/d/tr €35/40/70) Owned by a *padre* and managed by a friendly local, this charming place has five cool rooms (great when the mercury hits 40°C) with wooden trimmings, whitewashed walls and heavy wooden furniture.

Casa Pinto
B&B €€€

(☎266 557 076; www.casapinto.es; Praça Dom Nuno Alvares Pereira 10; d incl breakfast €90-120) A touch of class and the downright quirky hits Monsaraz. Under construction at the time of research, this place stretches the imagination. Each of the five rooms – decorated by the Spanish owner–interior designer – has a theme based around Portuguese former colonies. Think Macau to Mombasa. We're talking themed touches, from a waterfall shower (Dili) to elephant tusks (Asilah, Morocco – no, the tusks are not real) and much more besides. Fabulous terrace views and pleasant living spaces.

Casa Dona Antónia
B&B €€

(☎266 557 142; www.casadantonia-monsaraz.com; Rua Direita 15; d €60-75, ste €90; ❋) The four pleasant rooms in this traditional house vary in size, but all are pleasant and comfortable; the suite is huge and includes a terrace.

Estalagem de Monsaraz
HOTEL €€€

(☎266 557 112; www.estalagemdemonsaraz.com; Largo São Bartolomeu 5; s/d/ste €74/99/105; ❋❀) Just outside the village walls, this atmospheric place with a guest-house feel has reasonable rooms across three areas. The older sections have dark-wood furniture and shuttered windows; the more recent ones have unusual touches, such as recycled-door bedheads. All rooms have glorious views. There's a restaurant, pool and playground, as well as a lounge area with an open fire.

✖ Eating

Monsaraz has a handful of restaurants, all offering traditional Alentejan mains such as *borrego assado* (roast lamb).

Café-Restaurante Lumumba
CAFE, RESTAURANT €€

(Rua Direita 12; mains €6.50-8.50; ⏱lunch & dinner) This small place has a more local, less touristy clientele as well as more atmosphere than other cafes. It also boasts a terrace with great views.

A Casa do Forno
PORTUGUESE €€

(Travessa da Sanabrosa; mains €10-14; ⏱lunch & dinner Wed-Mon) The menu is fairly standard here (although the walls display lots of prizes for cuisine from previous decades), but the ambience is pleasant – there are checked tablecloths, attractive wooden chairs and an outdoor terrace with 'those' views.

Xarez
INTERNATIONAL €€

(www.xarez-monsaraz.com; Rua de Santiago 33; mains €7-12; ⏱11am-8pm) A tourist-magnet for its views and reasonable *petiscos* and mains. Seems to be open when nothing else is.

🔒 Shopping

Loja da Mizette
HANDICRAFT

(Rua do Celeiro; ⏱9.30am-1pm & 2-7pm Mon-Fri, 10am-1pm & 2-8pm Sat & Sun) Sells beautiful Alentejano *mantas* made by one of two workers in its factory in nearby Reguengos, the last of its kind (see p213). Well worth a visit.

ℹ Information

Multibanco ATM (Travessa da Misericórdia 2) Off the main square.

Turismo (☎266 557 136; Praça Dom Nuno Álvares Pereira; ⏱10am-12.30pm & 2-5.30pm) Stocked with some regional information, including bus timetables and basic maps of the area's megalithic monuments.

ℹ Getting There & Away

BUS Buses run to/from Reguengos de Monsaraz (€3, 35 minutes, four daily on weekdays). The last bus back to Reguengos, where you can pick up connections to Évora, is around 5.15pm.

Around Monsaraz

Neolithic megaliths are scattered throughout the landscape around Monsaraz – it is great to explore and discover these (they're signposted, but finding each one is an adventure) amid the tangles of olive groves and open fields of wildflowers. Most spectacular is **Cromeleque do Xerez**, an ensemble with the triumphant 7-tonne menhir at its centre. The rocks once stood 5km south of Monsaraz but were moved before flooding by the massive Barragem do Alqueva. A remaining highlight is the **Menhir de Bulhoa**, another phallic stone with intriguing carved circles and lines, 4km north of Monsaraz off the Telheiro–Outeiro road. A map outlining the region's megalithic circuit is available at the tourist office.

Estremoz

POP 9000

Along with neighbouring Borba and Vila Viçosa, Estremoz is one of the region's well-known marble towns. Because there is so much fine marble in this region – rivalling

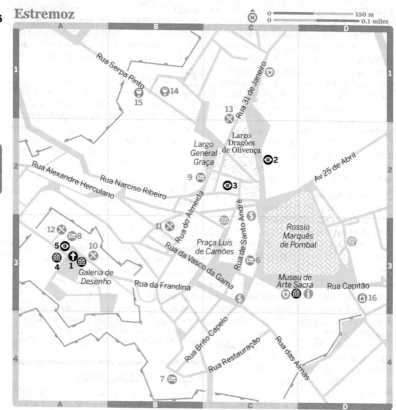

that in Carrara, Italy – it's used all over the place: even the cobbles are rough chunks of marble.

Ringed by an old protective wall, Estremoz has a centre set with orange tree–lined lanes, a 13th-century hilltop castle enclosed in an old quarter, and peaceful plazas (the main one being **Rossio Marquês de Pombal**, or 'the Rossio'). This simple provincial town is a busy trading centre, with lots of shops selling farm tools, though visitors can also load up on crafts, earthenware pottery and gourmet delights – all of which are available at the great market that fills the huge central square on Saturday.

⊙ Sights

Lower Town

On the fringes of the Rossio are imposing old churches, former convents and, just north of the Rossio, monastic buildings converted into **cavalry barracks**. Oppo-

site these, by Largo General Graça, is a marble-edged water tank, called the **Lago do Gadanha** (Lake of the Scythe) after its scythe-wielding statue of Neptune. Some of the prettiest marble streets in town are south of the Rossio, off Largo da República.

Upper Town

The upper town is surrounded by dramatic zig-zagging ramparts and contains a gleaming white palace. The easiest way to reach it on foot is to follow narrow Rua da Frandina from Praça Luís de Camões and pass the inner castle walls through the Arco da Frandina.

Museu Municipal MUSEUM
(☑268 333 608; adult/senior €1.50/.75; ⊙9am-12.30pm & 2-5.30pm Tue-Sun) This museum is housed in a beautiful 17th-century almshouse near the former palace. Pretty hand-painted furniture sits alongside endearing, locally carved wooden figures (charming

rural scenes by Joaquim Velhinho) and a collection of typical 19th-century domestic Alentejan items. On the ground floor is an amazing display of the unique Estremoz pottery figurines – some 500 pieces covering 200 years, including lots of ladies with carnivalesque outfits, explosively floral headdresses and wind-rippled dresses. There's even an entire 19th-century Easter Parade.

Royal Palace & Torre das Três Coroas
PALACE

At the top of the upper town is the stark, glowing-white, fortress-like former royal palace, now the Pousada de Santa Rainha Isabel.

Dom Dinis built the palace in the 13th century for his new wife, Isabel of Aragon. After her death in 1336 (Dinis had died 11 years earlier) it was used as an ammunition dump. An inevitable explosion, in 1698, destroyed most of the palace and the surrounding castle, though in the 18th century João V restored the palace for use as an armoury. The 27m-high keep, the Torre das Três Coroas (Tower of the Three Crowns), survived and is still the dominant feature. It's so-called because it was apparently built by three kings: Sancho II, Afonso III and Dinis.

Visitors are welcome to view the public areas of the *pousada* and climb the keep, which offers a superb panorama of the old town and surrounding plains. The holes at the keep's edges were channels for boiling oil – a good way of getting rid of uninvited guests.

Capela de Santa Isabel
CHAPEL

(admission free) This richly adorned chapel behind the keep was built in 1659. The narrow stairway up to the chapel, and the chapel itself, are lined with 18th-century *azulejos,* most of them featuring scenes from the saintly queen's life.

Isabel was famously generous to the poor, despite her husband's disapproval. In one legend, the king demanded to see what she was carrying in her skirt; she let go of her apron, and the bread she had hidden to donate to the poor was miraculously transformed into roses.

To visit the chapel, ask for the custodian in the Santa Maria church.

🎉 Festivals & Events

The town's biggest event is the **Feira Internacional de Artesanato e Agro-Pecuária de Estremoz** (FIAPE), a baskets, ceramics, vegetables and livestock bonanza, held for several days at the end of April. **Cozinha dos Ganhões** (Festival de Gastronomia Alentejana), the town's fun culinary festival, is held from the end of November to the beginning of December.

🛏 Sleeping

TOP CHOICE **Pousada de Rainha Santa Isabel**
LUXURY HOTEL €€€

(☑268 332 075; www.pousadas.pt; d €240; ❄ ☒) In the restored former palace, this lavish *pousada* offers spacious rooms with antique furnishings and views over the Alentejo plains. There are lovely palace gardens, a pool with views and common areas set with museum-quality tapestries.

Residencial O Gadanha GUEST HOUSE €
(☑268 339 110; www.residencialogadanha.com; Largo General Graça 56; s/d/tr €20/32.50/42.50; ❄) This whitewashed house is one of Portugal's best-value sleeping options. It has

bright, fresh, white and clean rooms that overlook the square. Rooms come with satellite TV (and even hairdryers).

Monte dos Pensamentos   RURAL INN €€
(☎268 333 166; montedospensamentos@yahoo.com; Estrada da Estação do Ameixal; d/ste incl breakfast €60/80, apt 90; ☀) This lovely manor house offers attractive, traditionally furnished rooms and apartments in a pretty setting 2km west of Estremoz. There's a pool surrounded by citrus trees. Mountain bikes are available to guests.

Páteo dos Solares   HOTEL €€€
(☎268 338 400; www.pateosolares.com; Rua Brito Capelo; s/d from €170/200; ❀☀) This sumptuous place, partly situated on the old city walls, is housed in a converted bread factory. Spacious, well-furnished rooms, a charming sitting room, a large terrace, a restaurant and a pool add to the appeal.

✕ Eating

TOP CHOICE / **Adega do Isaías**   PORTUGUESE €€
(☎268 322 318; Rua do Almeida 21; mains €8-12; ☉lunch & dinner Mon-Sat) To enter this award-winning, rustic *tasca* (tavern), you pass by a sizzling grill cooking up tender fish, meat and Alentejan specialities. Inside, a wine cellar awaits, crammed with tables and huge wine jars.

São Rosas   INTERNATIONAL, PORTUGUESE €€€
(☎268 333 345; Largo de Dom Dinis; mains €13-18; ☉lunch & dinner Tue-Sun) White tablecloths under whitewashed arches equal rustic-meets-smart, and the food is great, featuring some unusual starters (such as smoked salmon and buttery, garlic-covered clams), pork and gazpacho in summer. It's near the former palace.

A Cadeia   INTERNATIONAL, PORTUGUESE €€€
(☎268 323 400; www.cadeiaquinhentista.com; Rua Rainha Santa Isabel; mains €9.50-22; ☉lunch & dinner) Unlock your purses at this place, housed in the former judicial jail, which dates from the 16th century; the two storeys of the quadrangle separated male and female prisoners. The restaurant serves *petiscos* and main dishes. There's also an area for coffee and drinks under the building's arch and a classy, romantically lit bar upstairs.

Café Alentejano   CAFE, RESTAURANT €€
(Rossio Marquês de Pombal 14; mains €7-11; ☉lunch & dinner) Generations of country folk meet at this pleasant spot, which has art-deco wood-and-mirror panels and tiled tabletops. Outdoor tables face the square. Upstairs, a wood-floored, white-tablecloth restaurant offers heartier traditional and great-value fare.

Zona Verde Restaurante   PORTUGUESE €€
(Largo Dragões de Olivença 86; mains €8.80-16; ☉lunch & dinner Fri-Wed) This smart restaurant may have had a modern renovation (original *azulejos* were replaced), but thankfully, it hasn't changed its traditional cuisine. It serves massive portions of excellent regional specialities, including *ensopado de borrego* (lamb stew). Warning: even the half servings are massive.

♟ Drinking

Reguengo Bar   BAR
(Rua Serpa Pinta 126; ☉8am-2am Tue-Sun) This big barnlike space with a vaulted ceiling is where Estremoz youth kick up their heels. Live bands play most Friday nights. In summer the party continues in the garden outside.

Até Jazz Café   BAR
(Rua Serpa Pinta 65) This cosy bar delivers a varied schedule of jazz or fado most weekends to an arty crowd that's older than Reguengo's.

🔒 Shopping

The *turismo* can provide a list of artisans who work with cork, clay, wood and iron, making figurines, bells, sculptures and unique pieces (most work from their homes, but many are happy to receive customers – it makes a great visit).

The weekly Saturday market held on the Rossio provides a great display of Alentejan goodies and Estremoz specialities, from goat's- and ewe's-milk cheeses, to a unique style of unglazed, ochre-red pots.

Casa Galileu   RURAL, HANDICRAFT
(Rua Victor Cordon 16) If you miss the Saturday market, visit this shop southeast of the Rossio. It is crammed with locally made ceramic figurines, as well as other essentials such as flat caps and cowbells.

ℹ Information

Caixa Geral de Depósitos Bank & ATM (Rossio Marquês de Pombal 43)

Centro de saúde (medical centre; ☎268 332 042; Av 9 de Abril) At the northeastern end of town.

Espaço Internet (Rossio Marquês de Pombal; ⊘2-8pm) Free internet access inside the Centro Ciência Viva.

Police station (☑268 338 470; Rua 31 de Janeiro)

Post office (Rua 5 de Outubro; ⊘9am-6pm Mon-Fri)

Turismo (☑268 333 541; www.estremozmarca .com, www.cm-estremoz.pt; Casa de Estremoz/ câmara municipal, Rossio Marquês de Pombal; ⊘10am-1pm & 2-6pm)

ⓘ Getting There & Around

All buses stop at and depart from Av 25 de Abril by the old train station.

Estremoz has services to Évora (three daily Monday to Friday), Évoramonte (two daily, Monday to Saturday), Portalegre (three daily Monday to Friday, one Saturday) and Vila Viçosa (one daily Monday to Friday). Services are considerably reduced or non-existent on weekends. Regular buses also head further afield to Faro in the Algarve, and Lisbon.

Around Estremoz

BORBA
POP 5000

The least visited of the marble towns, Borba glows with a peculiar rosy light. Its marble wealth hasn't brought it many obvious riches, so its marble-lined houses and public buildings have a remarkable simplicity.

This quiet small town is encircled by marble quarries and is famous for its great red wines. It comes to life once a year in early November, when it hosts the All Saints Fair.

◉ Sights

The Alentejo Wine Route lists several *adegas* in this region (see p211). The **Adega Cooperativa de Borba** (☑268 891 660; www .adegaborba.pt; Rua Gago Coutinho Sacadura Cabral; ⊘2-7pm Mon, 11am-7pm Tue-Fri, 10am-1pm Sat) is one of the region's largest *adegas*, producing the famous Borba full-bodied red and white *maduro* (mature) and rosé wines. You can buy wine at the Adega's large **shop** (☑268 891 660; ⊘9am-7pm Mon-Sat), 100m further up the road from the co-op.

⨄ Sleeping & Eating

TOP
CHOICE **Casa do Terreiro do Poço**
                           BOUTIQUE HOTEL €€€
(☑917 256 077; www.casadoterreirodopoco.com; Largo dos Combatentes da Grande Guerra 12; r incl breakfast €75-150) Another 'sigh-ain't-

it-great-to-be-in-Portugal' moment. This dreamy place offers a range of rooms, all located in a sensitively restored mansion. The owners have maintained the building's quirky aspects (mind your head – some doors are low) and have filled the rooms with stunning antiques and items from around the world. Beautiful outdoor spaces, a pool and massive breakfasts of local produce make it hard not to feel, dare we say, smug.

Residencial Inaramos   GUEST HOUSE €
(☑268 894 563; Av do Povo 22; s/d without breakfast €25/30) Up a marble staircase, this pleasant option offers bright, good-value rooms. It's nicely located on a street sprinkled with cafes, 1½ blocks east of the *praça*.

Tasca Real   PORTUGUESE €
(Dr Ramos de Abreu 20; mains €5.50-7.50; ⊘lunch & dinner) Trade in the fancy settings for a cellar-like space, nouveau-cuisine for plates of local *petiscos* and hearty mains, and snooty waiters for down-to-earth owners. One of the most authentic and delightful experiences you'll get in Alentejo. Pigs' trotters are a speciality. As for the price-to-quality ratio? The best value around.

ⓘ Information
Turismo (⊘10am-12.30pm & 2-5.30pm Mon-Fri) Half a block from Praça da República.

ⓘ Getting There & Away
BUS Buses stop just east of the *praça*.

Estremoz (€5.70, 15 minutes, around five buses daily) Obtain times and tickets from **Café Brinquete** (Av do Povo 31).

Vila Viçosa (around €1.30) Buy tickets from driver on Rodoviária do Alentejo bus.

VILA VIÇOSA
POP 8000

If you visit just one marble town in the region, Vila Viçosa is the one to hit. It features Praça da República, a long attractive plaza set with orange trees, a marvellous marble palace, one of the country's largest, and a castle.

This was once home to the Bragança dynasty, whose kings ruled Portugal until it became a republic (Dom Carlos spent his last night here before his assassination). There is also a fine castle – one of the few nonmarble structures in town – an excellent archaeological museum, appealing churches and a friendly laid-back citizenry who are proud of their sparkling town.

◉ Sights

Terreiro do Paço & Paço Ducal PALACE

The **palace square** covers 16,000 sq metres, and it's ringed by the palace, the heavy-fronted Agostinhos Convent and graceful Chagas Nunnery. In the centre is a statue of Dom João IV.

The dukes of Bragança built their **palace** (🕿268 980 659; www.fcbraganca.pt; adult/under 10yr €6/free; ◷2.30-5.30pm Tue, 10am-1pm & 2.30-5.30pm Wed-Sun Apr-Sep, 2-5pm Tue, 10am-1pm & 2-5pm Wed-Sun Oct-Mar) in the early 16th century when the fourth duke, Dom Jaime, decided he had had enough of his uncomfortable hilltop castle. The wealthy Bragança family, originally from Bragança in Trás-os-Montes, had settled in Vila Viçosa in the 15th century. After the eighth duke became king in 1640, it changed from a permanent residence to just another royal palace, but the family maintained a special fondness for it and Dom João IV and his successors continued to visit the palace.

The palace's best furniture went to Lisbon after Dom João IV ascended the throne, and some went on to Brazil after the royal family fled there in 1807, but there are still some stunning pieces on display, such as a huge 16th-century Persian rug in the Dukes Hall. Lots of royal portraits put into context the interesting background on the royal family.

The **private apartments** hold a ghostly fascination – toiletries, knick-knacks and clothes of Dom Carlos and his wife, Marie-Amélia, are laid out as if the royal couple were about to return (Dom Carlos left one morning in 1908 and was assassinated in Lisbon that afternoon).

A compulsory Portuguese-speaking guide leads the hour-long tours. English guidebooks cost €5.

Other parts of the Ducal Palace, including the **16th-century cloister**, house more museums containing specific collections and with separate admission fees (armoury/coach collection/Chinese Porcelain/treasury €3/2/2.50/2.50).

Castelo CASTLE

The fascinating Dom Dinis' walled hilltop castle was where the Bragança family lived before the palace was built. It has been transformed into the **Museu de Arqueologia and Museu de Caça** (Archaeological Museum and Game Museum & Hunting Museum; admission €3; ◷2.30-5.30pm Tue, 10am-1pm & 2.30-5.30pm Wed-Sun Apr-Sep, 2-5pm Tue, 10am-1pm & 2-5pm Wed-Sun Oct-Mar). A visit to these museums is a must – if only as an excuse to wander through the castle itself (think 'secret' tunnels, giant fireplaces and wonderful vaulted ceilings). The extraordinary (and under-promoted) archaeological collection is housed in the castle's many rooms and spans various eras from the Palaeolithic to the Roman. It even has Ancient Egyptian treasures. The less interesting hunting museum is stuffed with guns and the dukes' animal trophies.

Surrounding the castle is a cluster of village houses and peaceful overgrown gardens. There's a 16th-century Manueline *pelourinho* (the prison used to be nearby), with sculpted frogs. Also near the castle is

---

USING YOUR MARBLES

The marble towns gleam with rosy-gold or white stone, but the effect is enhanced by the houses, which have a Hollywood-smile brightness. As if locals hadn't found enough uses for the stone stuff, with their marble doorsteps, pavements and shoes (OK, we made that last one up), a process has been cooked up to create marble paint: marble is recrystallised limestone, so if you heat marble chips in a clay oven for three days they turn into calcium oxide, which is mixed with water to become whitewash. Cheaper than paint. People take pride in the whiteness of their house and retouch them annually.

While we're on the subject of colour, apparently the yellow borders keep away fever, while blue is the bane of flies (you can add these colours to the oxide). The blue theory may have some truth, or at least international adherents – in Rajasthan (India) local people also apply pale blue to their houses to ward off mosquitoes.

Vila Viçosa has an interesting little marble museum housed in the quaint former train station, the walls of which are covered with stunning blue-and-white *azulejos*.

the brilliantly tiled 15th-century **Igreja de Nossa Senhora da Conceição** (☺8.30am-12.30pm & 2.30-6.30pm). An image of Nossa Senhora da Conceição, the Patron Saint of Portugal, is in the chancel.

Marble Museum   MUSEUM
(☑268 889 314; admission €1; ☺9am-12.30pm & 2-5.30pm Tue-Sat) The modest marble museum is worth going to for its location alone – it's housed in the town's former train station, which is covered in stunning tiles. Spanning seven small rooms, the museum's basic exhibits illustrate the marble industry and its processes.

✯✯ Festivals & Events
On the second weekend of September the **Festa dos Capuchos** takes place, with a bullfight and a *vacada* (a bull is released and locals try to jump over it to show how brave they are) in the main square.

⊨ Sleeping
Hospedaria Dom Carlos   GUEST HOUSE €
(☑/fax 268 980 318; Praça da República 25; s/d/tr without breakfast €30/40/50; ❆) In an excellent location on the main square, the Dom Carlos offers tidy and comfortable rooms with wood finishing and a small, fancy lobby.

Herdade da Ribeira de Borba   RURAL INN €€
(☑268 980 709; www.hrb.com.pt; Cilados; r €75-90; ❆ ▨) Five kilometres out of Vila Viçosa and on a working farm (think rural tranquillity, walks, birdwatching), this lovely option offers everything from contemporary apartments with kitchens in former workers' cottages to plainer, but pleasant, rooms in the main building. Perfect for longer term stays.

São Paulo   LUXURY HOTEL €€€
(☑266 989 160; www.hotelconventospaulo.com; Aldeia da Serra; d from €90; ❆ ▨) A marvellously romantic huge monastery on a 240-hectare estate, this hotel has big, grand, striking rooms and a restaurant with a lofty painted ceiling.

Pousada de Dom João IV   LUXURY HOTEL €€€
(☑268 980 742; www.pousadas.pt; d €270; ❆ ☏ ▨) Next to the Ducal Palace, this former royal convent was once the 'House of the Ladies of the Court'. Today, this regal spot offers spacious rooms – one with original frescos – terraces and classic furnishings. Rooms open onto a striking inner courtyard.

✗ Eating
Os Cucos   PORTUGUESE €€
(mains €8-12; ☺lunch & dinner Mon-Sat) Hidden in the pretty gardens near the *mercado municipal*, this is the pick for quality food and shady location. It has an airy, semicircular interior, and you can eat snacks at garden tables. The changing daily specials (Monday, *bacalhau*, Tuesday, *arroz de pato* etc) feature regional cuisine.

Other good choices for regional cuisine:

Ouro Branco   PORTUGUESE €€
(Alameda das Varandinhas 43; mains €8.50-13; ☺lunch & dinner) The smart and elegant of the trio.

Tasca O Necas   PORTUGUESE €€
(Cristóvão de Brito Pereira 12; mains €6-10; ☺lunch & dinner) Robust in every sense – cuisine and clientele (many labourers).

O Forno   PORTUGUESE €€
(Cristóvão de Brito Pereirano; mains €8-13; ☺lunch & dinner Mon-Sat) You can choose your own combinations here.

☆ Entertainment
Classical **concerts** (☑268 980 659; www.fcbraganca.pt; admission free) are held year-round in the chapel of the Ducal Palace on the last Friday of the month at 9pm.

❶ Information
Espaço Internet (Rua Padre Joaquim Espanca 19; ☺10am-1pm & 3.30-6.30pm Mon-Fri, 10am-12.30pm Sat) Free web access; around the corner from the *turismo* .

Turismo (☑268 881 101; www.cm-vilavicosa.pt; Praça da República 34; ☺9.30am-12.30pm, 2-5.30pm) Pick up a town map and *Agenda Cultural* (with listings) here.

❶ Getting There & Away
BUS There are limited buses to/from Évora (normal/express €5/8.40, 1¾/one hour, one on weekdays), and Estremoz (€3, 35 minutes, two on weekdays).

Elvas
POP 15,100

The impressive fortifications zig-zagging around this pleasant little town reflect some of the most sophisticated military technology of 17th-century Europe. Its moats, fort and heavy walls would indicate a certain paranoia if it weren't for Elvas' position, only 15km west of Spain's Badajoz. Inside the stout town walls, you'll

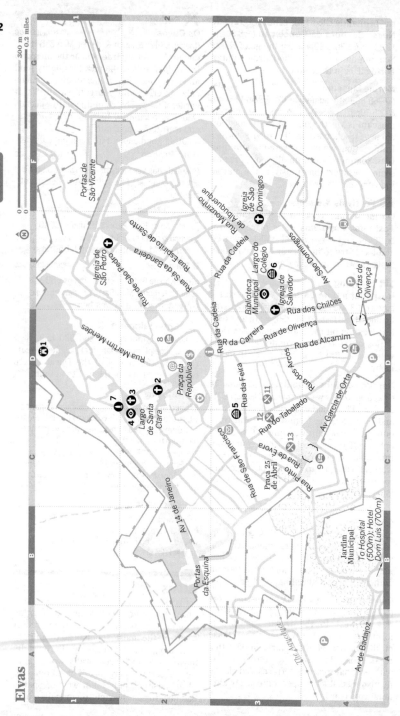

Elvas

300 m
0.2 miles

Elvas

find a lovely town plaza, some quaint museums and very few foreign visitors – aside from the occasional flood of Spanish daytrippers. Although there's not much to hold your attention beyond a day, Elvas is a fascinating place to visit, with its evocative frontier-post atmosphere, its narrow medina-like streets and its extraordinary, forbidding walls and buttresses.

Drivers be aware – it's possible to find central parking, but not always easy; if you don't like narrow one-way streets, park on the outskirts of town (or just inside Portas de Olivença). Train travellers will find themselves disembarking at Fontaínhas, 4km northeast of town off the Campo Maior road.

History
In 1229 Elvas was recaptured from the Moors after 500 years of fairly peaceful occupation. The following centuries saw relentless attacks from Spain, interrupted by occasional peace treaties. Spain only succeeded in 1580, allowing Felipe II of Spain (the future Felipe I of Portugal) to set up court here for a few months. But the mighty fortifications were seldom breached: in 1644, during the Wars of Succession (1640–68), the garrison held out against a nine-day Spanish siege and, in

1659, just 1000 – an epidemic had wiped out the rest – withstood an attack by a 15,000-strong Spanish army.

The fortifications saw their last action in 1811, when the Duke of Wellington used the town as the base for an attack on Badajoz during the Peninsular War.

Sights

Museu de Arte Contemporânea
de Elvas   CONTEMPORARY ART MUSEUM
(268 637 150; www.cm-elvas/mace; adult/concession €2/1; ☉3-6.30pm Tue, 10am-1pm & 3-6.30pm Wed-Sun) The Museu de Arte Contemporânea de Elvas is a must-see. Opened in 2007, the museum is housed in a cleverly renovated baroque-style building from the 1700s, formerly the Misericórdia Hospital, and houses exhibitions of modern Portuguese artists from the collection of António Cachola. Each six months or so a different selection of the 300 contemporary pieces (installations, paintings and photographs) is on display. Artists include the likes of Francisco Vidal, Rui Patacho and Ana Pinto. One of the rooms contains the original chapel with exquisite tiles. Upstairs is a small funky all-white cafe with a stunning city vista from the terrace.

Aqueduto da Amoreira   AQUEDUCT
It took an unsurprising 100 years or so to complete this breathtakingly ambitious aqueduct. Finished in 1622, these huge cylindrical buttresses and several tiers of arches stalk from 7km west of town to bring water to the marble fountain in Largo da Misericórdia. It's best seen from the Lisbon road, west of the centre.

Castelo   CASTLE
(adult/concession €1.50/0.75; ☉9.30am-1pm & 2.30-5.30pm Mon-Fri) You can walk around the battlements at the castle for dramatic views across the baking plains. The original castle was built by the Moors on a Roman site, and rebuilt by Dom Dinis in the 13th century, then again by Dom João II in the late 15th century.

FREE Igreja de Nossa Senhora da
Assunção   CHURCH
(Praça da República; ☉closed Mon & Tue morning) Francisco de Arruda designed this sturdy fortified church in the early 16th century, and it served as the town's cathedral until Elvas lost its episcopal status in 1882. Renovated in the 17th and 18th centuries, it retains a few Manueline touches, such

as the south portal. Inside is a sumptuous 18th-century organ and some pretty, but somewhat lost, 17th- and 18th-century tiling.

FREE Igreja de Nossa Senhora da Consolação CHURCH
(Largo de Santa Clara; ☺closed Mon & Tue morning) This plain church hides a thrilling interior. There are painted marble columns under a cupola, gilded chapels and fantastic 17th-century *azulejos* covering the surface. The unusual octagonal design was inspired by the Knights Templar chapel, which stood on a nearby site before this church was built in the mid-16th century. It was once the church of the Dominicans, and is all that is left of the original monastery.

Largo de Santa Clara PLAZA
This delightful cobbled square facing the Igreja de Nossa Senhora da Consolação has a whimsical centrepiece – a polka-dotted **pelourinho**. This pillory was a symbol of municipal power: criminals would once have been chained to the metal hooks at the top. The fancy **archway** with its own loggia at the top of the square is pure Moorish artistry – a flourish in the town walls that once trailed past here.

Museu Fotográfico João Carpinteiro
MUSEUM
(☎268 636 470; Largo Luis de Camões; adult/child €2/1; ☺10am-1pm & 2-5pm Tue-Sun Dec-Feb, 10am-1pm & 3-7pm Tue-Sun Jun-Aug) Housed in the old town cinema is the Photography Museum João Carpinteiro, with an impressive collection of cameras, the oldest a pocket-vest number dating from 1912. Changing photography exhibits, however, are often the highlight of a visit here.

Fortifications & Military Museum MUSEUM
Walls encircled Elvas as early as the 13th century, but it was in the 17th century that Flemish Jesuit engineer Cosmander designed the formidable defences that you now see, adding moats, ramparts, seven bastions, four semibastions and fortified gates in the style of the famous French military architect the Marquis de Vauban. To give you an idea of the level of security, you cross a drawbridge to get to the main gate; inside is a 150-sq-metre square, surrounded by bastions, turrets and battlements, a covered road and three lines of trenches, some of which are carved out of rock.

Also added was the miniature, zig-zagwalled **Forte de Santa Luzia**, just 1.4km south of the *praça*. This now houses the **military museum** (☎268 628 357; admission €2; ☺10am-1pm & 3-7pm Tue-Sun). The **Forte de Nossa Senhora da Graça**, 3km north of town, with a similar shape, was added in the following century; it's still in use as an army base and is closed to the public.

⚑ Tours

Agia WALKING TOURS
(☎933 259 036; www.alentejoguides.com) This licensed guide association organises two-hour walking tours (€12) that explore Elvas' historic sites. Tours take place on Saturdays and depart from Praça 25 Abril.

🎊 Festivals & Events

Elvas starts to tap its blue suede shoes in late September, celebrating the **Festas do Senhor da Piedade e de São Mateus**, with everything from agricultural markets and bullfights to folk dancing and religious processions (especially on the last day).

🛌 Sleeping

Hotel Convento São João de Deus
LUXURY HOTEL €€
(☎268 639 220; www.hotelsaojoaodeus.com; Largo João de Deus 1; s/d Sun-Thu €64/70, Fri & Sat €74/80; ✳@≋) Spanish-owned and operated since 2004, this is Elvas' grandest hotel. It's a pleasant, although not always sympathetic, conversion of a 17th-century convent. Each room is different in size and decor – the larger ones are lovely, a couple of smaller ones less so. Most, however, have handsome wood floors and heavy fabrics. One has a bed head made of tiles.

Hotel Dom Luís LUXURY HOTEL €€€
(☎268 622 710; www.elpohoteis.com; Av de Badajoz; s/d incl breakfast €52/62; ✳🛜) This modern establishment is slightly tattered around the edges. There are two sections: older rooms with worn carpets and traditional Alentejano decor, and newer rooms with contemporary decor in browns and beiges. It's 700m west of the centre, just outside the town walls and near the aqueduct.

Residencial Luso Espanhola GUEST HOUSE €
(☎/fax 268 623 092; Rua Rui de Melo; s/d €25/35; ✳) A short way from town (2km north on the Portalegre road), this friendly 14-room hostelry has smallish, modern rooms with

balconies giving a fine view of the countryside. There are two restaurants next door. You'll need your own transport to get here.

António Mocisso e Garcia Coelho Quartos
GUEST HOUSE €

(268 622 126; Rua Aires Varela 15; s/d/tr €25/30/45; 🌐) The best of the budget places in the town centre has 14 small but clean rooms. Single rooms are less appealing and some rooms have small windows.

Senhor Jesus da Piedade Parque de Campismo
CAMPGROUND €

(268 628 997; sites per adult/tent/car €3.50/5/3.50; ⊙Apr–mid-Sep) Elvas' nearest camping ground is on the southwestern outskirts of Elvas, off the N4 Estremoz road. It's a small tree-shaded camp, with a municipal pool 1km away.

Residência Garcia de Orta
GUEST HOUSE €

(268 623 152; Av Garcia de Orta 3a; s/d/tr €25/35/45) A pillow-for-the-night type place; the pine-clad rooms in this old building are worn and stuffy and the floors slope, but it's nonetheless clean. Note: rooms are at the top of a short, but steep marble staircase.

✖ Eating

A Coluna
PORTUGUESE €€

(Rua do Cabrito 11; mains €7-10, tourist menu €10; ⊙lunch & dinner Wed-Mon) This tavern-cavern offers an elegant space with *azulejos* on the walls. Pork and *bacalhau* (cod fish) dishes are its forte.

O Lagar
PORTUGUESE €€

(Rua Nova da Vedoria 7; mains €8-15; ⊙lunch & dinner Fri-Wed) Smart and buzzing, O Lagar dishes up excellent regional cooking, with good-value, high-quality *açordas* (a kind of bread soup) and *bacalhau*. Service can be a bit slow, but it's a pleasant enough place to linger over a meal.

Adega Regional
PORTUGUESE €€

(Rua João Casqueiro 22B; mains €7.50-12; ⊙Wed-Mon) Locals love this small place where it's all about the food – lashings of *plumas de porco preto* (pork) and *choquinhos á alentejana* (squid), or a great-value three-course daily meal for €7.

🛍 Shopping

On alternate Mondays there's a big lively market around the aqueduct, just off the Lisbon road west of town. The weeks it's not on, there's a flea market in Praça da República.

ℹ Information

Banco Espirito Santo & ATM (268 939 240; Praça da República) There are many banks with ATMs around town, including this one.

District hospital (268 637 700; Av de Badajoz) Opposite the Pousada de Santa Luzia.

Espaço Internet (Praça da República; ⊙10am-7pm Mon-Fri, 10am-5pm Sat) Free internet access. Enter from Rua dos Sapateiros.

Police station (268 639 470; Rua Isabel Maria Picão)

Post office (Rua da Cadeia; ⊙8.30am-6pm Mon-Fri, 9am-12.30pm Sat)

Turismo (268 622 236; www.cm-elvas.pt; Praça da República; ⊙9am-7pm Mon-Fri, 10am-12.30pm & 2-5.30pm Sat & Sun) Distributes pamphlets and a rudimentary town map.

ℹ Getting There & Around

BUS The bus station is outside the city walls, on the road to Spain. It's an 800m walk mostly uphill (or a €6 taxi ride) to the main *praça*. Cheaper but considerably slower 'carreira normal' (bus) services are also available to these destinations:

Estremoz (€8, 45 minutes, six daily)

Évora (€11, 1¼ to 1¾ hours, three daily)

Portalegre (€12.50, 1¼ hours, one daily)

Faro (€19, 6½ hours, one daily)

Lisbon (€15, 3¼ to 3½ hours, seven daily)

TAXI Taxis (268 623 526) charge around €5 from the train station at Fontaínhas into town.
TRAIN Two train services run daily to Lisbon (€13, 4¼ to 5¼ hours), with a transfer necessary at Entroncamento.

Portalegre

POP 15,200 / ELEV 520M

Alto Alentejo's capital, Portalegre, is bunched up on a hilltop at the foot of Serra de São Mamede. This pretty, whitewashed, ochre-edged city makes for a charming, low-key, off-the-beaten-track experience. A lively student population and handy transport links to nearby mountaintop villages add to its appeal.

Inside the city walls, faded baroque mansions – relics of the town's textile-manufacturing heyday – are all dressed up with no place to go. In the 16th century, the town boomed through tapestry, and in the 17th century, silk. Bust followed boom after the 1703 Treaty of Methuen brought English competition. But, even today,

Portalegre stays true to its legacy of natty threads – there is a factory here producing extraordinary tapestries of artworks by famous modern artists, and an impressive museum showcasing the work.

◉ Sights

Sé CHURCH
(⊙2.30-6pm Tue, 9am-noon & 2.30-6pm Wed-Sun) In 1550 Portalegre became the seat of a new diocese and soon got its own cathedral. The pyramid-pointed, twin-towered 18th-century facade, with a broken clock, sombrely presides over the white-washed Praça do Município. The sacristy contains an array of fine *azulejos*.

FREE Castelo CASTLE
(⊙9.30am-1pm & 2.30-6pm Tue-Sun) Portalegre's castle, off Rua do Carmo, dates from the time of Dom Dinis, with three restored towers that offer good views across the town. In the 1930s, part of the castle walls were destroyed to open the streets to traffic. In 2006, a controversial renovation was completed – a modern wooden structure now links the walls of the castle to the tower. Designed by Portuguese architect Cândido Chuva Gomes, the you-either-love-it-or-hate-it construction is intended to resemble rocks, marking the difference between the 13th and 21st centuries. There is a temporary exhibition gallery on the 1st floor.

Mansions MANSIONS
The town's former glory is recorded in stone: faded 17th-century baroque town houses and mansions dot Rua 19 de Junho to the southeast

Museu da Tapeçaria de Portalegre Guy Fino CONTEMPORARY ART GALLERY
(☎245 307 530; Rua da Figueira 9; admission €2; ⊙9.30am-1pm & 2.30-6pm Tue-Sun) If there's one thing you must visit in Portalegre, it's this splendid museum. Opened in 2001, it contains brilliant contemporary creations from Portalegre's unique tapestry factory. It's named after the factory founder, who created an innovatory 'stitch' by hand weaving. The museum shows a selection of the 7000 colours of thread used. French tapestry artist Jean Lurçat at first dismissed the technique, then the factory made a copy of one of his works – a cockerel – and asked him to identify the one made at Aubusson, in France. He chose the more perfect Portalegre copy – you can see them juxtaposed here. The huge tapestries are vastly expensive, and the museum includes copies of works by some of the most famous names in Portuguese 20th-century art, including Almada Negreiros and Vieira de Silva.

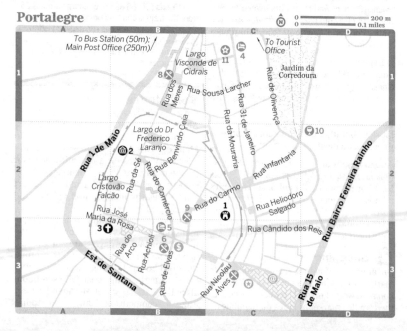

Portalegre

Museu José Regio
MUSEUM

(Rua Poeta José Régio; ⊙9.30am-12.30pm & 2-6pm Tue-Sun) This small museum is in poet José Regio's former house, and shows his magpie-like collection of popular religious art, with around 400 Christ figures. There are lots of rustic ceramics from Coimbra, which 18th-century migrant workers used to swap for clothes.

🛏 Sleeping

TOP CHOICE Convento da Provença
LUXURY HOTEL €€

(☎245 337 104; www.provenca.pt; Monte Paleiros; s/d/ste €85/95/105; ❄🛜❄) Mother Superior may not have approved of this luxury sleeping option, but *we* do. This renovated former convent has an austere white exterior, but its interior is another story. Shiny sabres and suits of armour fill the grand lounge room and entrance hall. The spacious rooms and suites are decked out in masculine hues and stylish wooden trimmings, and all have lovely green views. There's a massive games room (and kids' nursery). Unfortunately, one bad habit – smoking – is permitted in the rooms. The Convento is located north of Portalegre at Monte Paleiros on the road to Marvão.

Quinta da Dourada
RURAL INN €€

(☎937 218 654; www.quintadadourada.com; d €65-85; ❄🛜❄) Seven kilometres northeast of Portalegre, in the Parque Natural da Serra de São Mamede, this picture-perfect, modern-looking place is surrounded by glorious vegetation – lime trees and flowers. The individual rooms are smartly furnished and have granite floors.

Residencial Mansão Alto Alentejo
GUEST HOUSE €

(☎245 202 290; www.mansaoaltoalentejo.com.pt; Rua 19 de Junho 59; s/d incl breakfast €35/45; ❄) The stone staircase is steep, but it's the pick of the bunch for its small, bright rooms with traditional hand-painted Alentejan furniture and charming lounge area. Good, central location.

Solar das Avenças
GUEST HOUSE €€

(☎245 201 028; www.rtsm.pt/solardasavencas; Jardim da Corredoura 11; s/d/ste incl breakfast €55/65/80; ❄🛜) Near the park, this extraordinary old-fashioned 18th-century manor house has five ornate rooms, stuffed with antique furnishings. Some rooms have fireplaces. The spacious suites will take you back a few centuries.

Pousada da Juventude
HOSTEL €

(☎245 330 971; www.pousadasjuventude.pt; Estrada do Bonfim; dm/d with shared bathroom €10/22; ⊙8-10am & 6pm-midnight) A big white tower block labelled 'Centro de Juventude', 700m north of the Rossio, this youth hostel provides the usual not-fancy-but-fine bunks and bathrooms; the adjacent Instituto Português da Juventude (IPJ) is the town's main youth centre.

Pensão Nova
GUEST HOUSE €

(☎245 331 212; fax 245 330 493; Rua 31 de Janeiro 26; s/d €25/40; ❄) Pensão Nova is one of the few budget options around and is looking a bit long in the tooth these days: its small, slightly fuggy rooms are crammed with large pieces of wooden furniture. If it's full, guests are housed in the proprietors' other, and similar, hotel, Pensão Residencial São Pedro.

🍴 Eating

Portalegre has some excellent restaurants. Cheap eats include sandwich and pizza places. Praça da República is the place for cheap eats and bars. A garrulous young crowd arrives in the evenings.

TOP CHOICE Tomba Lobos
INTERNATIONAL, PORTUGUESE €€

(☎245 331 214; www.tombalobos.com; mains €12-15; ⊙lunch & dinner Tue-Sat, lunch Sun) Simply put, this restaurant, headed by Chef José Júlio Vintém, is regarded as one of the best –

for its cuisine – in Alentejo. It's located 5km from Portalegre at Bairro Pedra Basta (direction Reguengos).

Restaurante O Escondidinho

PORTUGUESE €€

(☑245 202 728; Travessa das Cruzes 1; mains €7-14; ☺lunch & dinner) A Portalegre charmer, this cosy spot has quaint country-style dining areas, a bar lined with tiles and a massive selection of traditional mains. Try the *espetados de toreiro bravo* (wild bull kebabs; €14). Half servings are available.

O Poeiras Restaurante

PORTUGUESE €€

(Praça da República 9-15; mains €6-11) This great value, popular restaurant has a meaty smell and whips up fabulous Alentejano cuisine, including *bacalhau* dishes.

O Abrigo

PORTUGUESE €€

(Rua de Elvas; mains €8-10; ☺lunch & dinner Wed-Mon) This cheerful, cosy place is renowned for its delicious local dishes, including *migas* (pork and fried bread; €8).

Restaurante-Cervejaria Santos

PORTUGUESE €€

(Largo Serpa Pinto 4; mains €5-10; ☺lunch & dinner Thu-Tue) This little place has a small outdoor wooden terrace under umbrellas, and great *migas* and so on.

Drinking

Portalegre's student population adds some life to the old streets. For **outdoor drinking**, take your pick of the spots around Praça da República and to a lesser extent Largo do Dr Frederico Laranjo.

☆ Entertainment

Crisfal

DISCO

(Av George Robinson) This renovated former cinema is the place to join the late-night disco crowd.

Centro de Artes do Espectáculo de Portalegre

OUTDOOR THEATRE

(☑245 307 498; www.caeportalegre.blogspot.com; Praça da República 39) Overlooking Praça da República is Portalegre's major performance space, hosting fado singers, rock, jazz and acoustic groups, as well as dance and theatre. Check the latest *Agenda Cultural* or the tourist office for current shows.

ⓘ Information

In the Rossio, the Millennium, BPI and Montepio banks all have ATMs.

Caixa Geral de Depósitos & ATM (☑245 339 100; Rua de Elvas) Bank with ATM in the old town.

Espaço Internet (Praça da República; ☺10.30am-8pm Mon-Fri, 2-6pm Sat) Free access, but often packed.

Hospital (☑245 301 000) About 400m north of town.

Instituto Português de Juventude (Estrada do Bonfim; ☺9am-12.30pm & 2-5.30pm Mon-Fri) Free internet access; 700m north of the Rossio.

Main post office (cnr Av da Liberdade & Rua Alexandre Herculano; ☺8.30am-6pm Mon-Fri, 9am-12.30pm Sat) About 250m north of the Rossio.

Police station (☑245 300 620; Praça República) Just outside Porta de Alegrete.

Turismo (☑245 307 445; Rua Guilherme Gomes Fernandes 22; ☺9.30am-1pm & 2.30-6pm Mon-Sun) Helpful staff dole out information and a town map. The monthly *Agenda Cultural* promotes concerts which are sometimes held in the Jardim do Tarro.

ⓘ Getting There & Around

BUS The **bus station** (☑245 330 723) has regular services to the following destinations:

Lisbon (€14, 4½ hours)

Estremoz (€5.10/8.50 normal/express, 80/50 minutes, two daily weekdays)

Évora (€6.30 to €11, 1½ hours, two daily weekdays)

Castelo Branco (€10, one hour 50 minutes, one daily)

Elvas (€5.10, 1½ hours, two daily weekdays)

Marvão (€2.60, 45 minutes, two daily)

Castelo de Vide (€2.30, two daily)

TAXI There are sometimes **taxis** (☑245 203 842) outside the bus station and in the nearby Rossio.

TRAIN Services from Lisbon run daily (€11.50, 3½ to four hours, two daily); change at Entroncamento. The station is 12km south of town.

Castelo de Vide

POP 4100 / ELEV 570M

High up above lush, rolling countryside, Castelo de Vide is one of Portugal's most attractive and underrated villages. Its fine hilltop vantage point, dazzlingly white houses, flower-lined lanes and proud locals are reason alone to visit. There aren't many attractions in town, but there don't need to be. Absorb this pleasant place for a day and a night; at dusk and early morning you can experience the town at its most disarming. You'll see elderly ladies crocheting on doorsteps, children playing in the narrow streets, and neighbours chatting out of upper-storey windows.

By the castle is a small *judiaria* – the former Jewish district, strongest here in the early 15th century after the expulsion of the Jews from Spain. A small synagogue (now a museum) is the main memento of this era. Castelo de Vide is famous for its crystal-clear mineral water, which spouts out of numerous pretty public fountains; several of these are surrounded by hedged gardens.

⊙ Sights

Old Town & Judiaria   HISTORIC SITE
A sizeable community of Jews settled here in the 12th century, then larger waves came in the 15th. At first they didn't have an exclusive district, but Dom Pedro I restricted them to specific quarters. The highlight of this area is the **synagogue and museum** (☺9.30am-12.30 & 2-5.30pm Tue-Sun, to 6pm Jun-Aug). Reopened in 2009 after being converted into a museum, the site comprises the original synagogue – two rooms (one for women and one for men), a wooden tabernacle and Holy Ark for Torah scrolls. The remaining rooms (part of the original village home from which the synagogue was originally converted) house a superb collection of items illustrating the history of the Jewish communities of Castelo de Vide. Following Manuel I's convert-or-leave edict in 1496, many Jews returned to Spain, though some headed to Évora.

FREE Castelo   CASTLE
(admission free; ☺9.30am-12.30pm & 2-6pm) Originally Castelo de Vide's inhabitants lived within the castle's sturdy outer walls; even now there remains a small inner village with a church, the 17th-century **Igreja da Nossa Senhora da Alegria**.

You can take in some brilliant views from here over the town's red roofs, surrounded by green and olive hills. The **castle**, built by Dom Dinis and his brother Dom Afonso between 1280 and 1365, is topped by a 12m-high brick tower, thought to be the oldest part. Feel like the king of the castle and catch the great views from the roof of the tower's fine vaulted hall (the hall itself is unfortunately covered in graffiti).

The castle houses the **Centro de Interpretação do Megalitismo**. Its wordy information boards explain the background, history and characteristics of the area's megaliths (unfortunately, all in Portuguese), and there are some ancient stone tools. In the room above, the **Museu da História e Arquitectura Militares** outlines the chronology of the castle's kings between the 12th and 14th centuries, and displays a few muskets, cannonballs and stone tools. All information is in Portuguese only.

Fonte da Vila   FOUNTAIN
In a pretty square just below and east of the *judiaria* is the worn-smooth 16th-century marble Fonte da Vila, with a washing area. This, along with several other fountains in the village, spouts out the delicious mineral water for which Castelo de Vide is known.

FREE Centro Municipal de Cultura   EXHIBITIONS
(Rua 5 de Outubro 21; ☺9am-4pm Mon-Fri) This cultural centre hosts a range of temporary exhibitions – photographs of traditional and rural life in the Alentejo and the like.

Anta dos Coureleiros & Menhir da Meada   MEGALITHS
In the wild, boulder-strewn landscape around Castelo de Vide are dozens of ancient megaliths. The two most impressive are the Anta dos Coureleiros, 8km north of town (with three other megaliths nearby making up what's called a Parque Megalítico) and the 7m-high Menhir da Meada, 8.5km further on – supposedly the tallest menhir in the Iberian Peninsula – a large phallus for keeping the fields fertile and acting as a territory-marker (one of the few believed to have done both things).

Both megaliths are best accessible by car. At the time of research, no maps showed walking routes, although it is possible to reach them on foot.

⚝ Festivals & Events

Carnaval   VILLAGE
Held in February/March, this festival is great fun, with everyone out to watch processions of fantastically costumed folk, many in traditional dress (males as females and vice versa).

Easter festival   EASTER
Castelo de Vide's big bash – and one of the most traditional of its festivals – is the four-day fair in March/April when hundreds of lambs go through the highs and lows of blessings and slaughter; processions, folk dances, band music and much revelry all take place.

Castelo De Vide

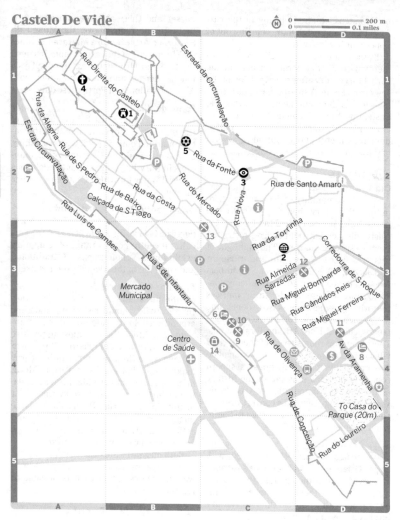

Rua Direita do Castelo
Estrada da Circunvalação
Est da Circunvalação
Rua da Alegria
Rua de S Pedro
Rua de Baixo
Rua da Costa
Calçada de S Tiago
Rua Luís de Camões
Rua da Fonte
Rua do Mercado
Rua Nova
Rua de Santo Amaro
Rua 8 de Infantaria
Rua da Torrinha
Rua Almeida Sarzedas
Rua Miguel Bombarda
Rua Cândidos Reis
Corredoura de S Roque
Rua Miguel Ferreira
AV da Aramenha
Rua de Olivença
Rua de Conceição
Rua do Loureiro
Mercado Municipal
Centro de Saúde
To Casa do Parque (20m)

Sleeping

Casa Amarela   GUEST HOUSE €€€
(☑ 245 905 878; www.casaamarelath.com; Praça Dom Pedro V 11; s/d/ste €80/120/140) This beautifully restored 18th-century building on the main square, with views over the *praça*, is a luxurious choice. It has stone staircases and antiques-filled common areas. The 10 rooms drip with rich fabrics and feature massive, marble-filled bathrooms.

Casa de Hóspedes Melanie   GUEST HOUSE €
(☑ 245 901 632; Largo do Paça Novo 3; s/d/tr €25/35/45; ✸) Situated near a leafy square,

this clean spot is up there with Portugal's best-value accommodation. Its has five neat and light rooms with cork-tile floors. Longer stayers are invited to enjoy the roof terrace.

Quinta da Bela Vista   RURAL INN €€
(☑ 245 968 125; www.quintabelavista.net; Póvoa e Meadas; s €65, d from €80; ☒) This is an olde-worlde country house 13km north of Castelo de Vide. It's been in the same family since the 1920s and is a lovely choice.

Casa de Hóspedes Machado   GUEST HOUSE €
(☑ 245 901 515; Rua Luís de Camões 33; s €25, d €28-30) On the western edge of town,

THE ALENTEJO CASTELO DE VIDE

this friendly and efficiently run place has airy, modern and spotless rooms. There's a small, shared kitchen and outdoor patio.

Casa do Parque GUEST HOUSE €
(☑245 901 250; www.casadoparque.net; Av da Aramenha 37; s/d €35/48) Overlooking the park, and in a historic building (a former girls' school – even the receptionist has a school matron's manner), this spot has inviting, slightly worn, rooms with tile floors and big windows. A decent restaurant adjoins the lobby.

Eating & Drinking

Dom Pedro V PORTUGUESE €€
(☑245 901 236; www.dpedrov.com.pt; Praça Dom Pedro; mains €8-13; ⊗lunch & dinner Tue-Sun) The town's best for regional cuisine and up there for quality produce and service. Hearty helpings (think about sharing) of *ensopado do borrego* (lamb stew) and *sopa de tomate* (tomato soup – the English translation just doesn't do it justice). Those with big appetites will revel in the fresh-from-the-beast (read 'meaty meat') filet mignon with mussels and tiger prawns (platter for two is €40). Desserts? 'Sweets sinners' will love the amazing selection of locally baked convent treats.

O Paladar INTERNATIONAL, VEGETARIAN €€
(Rua de Santa Maria de Baixo, 10; mains €8-16; ⊗lunch & dinner Tue-Sun; ☑) Your taste buds might go into pork-withdrawal mode...and they will love you forever. The owners, a passionate young Dutch and Portuguese couple, whip up excellent Asian and vegie (with a

touch of Portuguese) delights. Exotic dish names – such as Cupid at Sea (grilled fish) or Devine Duo (squid and shrimp kebab) – bring a colour and sensuality back into your palate.

Doces & Companhia PATISSERIE €
(Praça Dom Pedro V 6; mains €3-5; ⊗breakfast, lunch & dinner Mon-Sat) Serving great cakes and ice creams, this is the place to ease your sugar cravings. Also on offer are set-menu lunches and a lovely terrace (head through the restaurant to find it).

Two good eateries serving traditional cuisine:

O Miguel PORTUGUESE €€
(Rua Almeida Sarzedas 32-34; mains €6.50-9; ⊗lunch & dinner Mon-Sat)

O Alentejano PORTUGUESE €€
(Largos dos Mártires de República 14; mains €7-11)

Shopping

Every week there's a **Friday market** (but the biggest is the last Friday of the month) in a car park just outside the old walls.

❶ Information

Caixa Geral de Depósitos (☑245 339 100; Praça Valência de Alcántara)

Centro de Interpretação (☑245 905 299; Rua de Santo Amaro 27; ⊗9am-12.30pm & 2-5.30pm Mon-Fri) Information centre for the Parque Natural da Serra de São Mamede.

Centro de saúde (medical centre; ☑245 900 160; EN246-1) On the southern exit out of town.

Police station (☑245 901 314; Av da Aramenha)

Post office (Rua de Olivença)

Turismo (☑245 901 361; www.cm-castelo-vide .pt, turismo.cmcv@gmail.com; Praça Dom Pedro V; ☺9am-5.30pm daily Oct-Apr, to 7pm Tue-Sat May-Sep) Stocks some reasonable printed matter, including maps and leaflets.

ⓘ Getting There & Away

Buses (☑245 901 510) run to/from Portalegre (normal/express €2.50/5, 20 minutes, one to three daily) and Lisbon (€15, 4¼ hours, two daily). All buses stop beside the garden (Praça Valência de Alcântara). Ask at the *turismo* for bus times.

Taxis (☑245 901 271) are available from outside the *turismo*.

Marvão

POP 150 / ELEV 862M

On a jutting crag high above the surrounding countryside, the narrow lanes of Marvão feel like a retreat far removed from the settlements below. The whitewashed village of picturesque tiled roofs and bright flowers has marvellous views, a splendid castle and a handful of low-key guest houses and restaurants. Since the 16th century, the town has struggled to keep inhabitants, and today, the friendly locals survive mainly on tourism. It's worth spending a night here.

Arriving by car or bus you'll approach Portas de Ródão, one of the four village gates, opening onto Rua de Cima, which has several shops and restaurants. Drivers can park outside or enter this gate and park in Largo de Olivença, just below Rua de Cima.

History

Not surprisingly, this garrison town just 10km from the Spanish frontier has long been a prized possession. Romans settled here, and Christian Visigoths were on the scene when the Moors arrived in 715. It was probably the Moorish lord of Coimbra, Emir Maraun, who gave the place its present name.

In 1160 Christians took control. In 1226 the town received a municipal charter, the walls were extended to encompass the whole summit, and the castle was rebuilt by Dom Dinis.

Marvão's importance in the defence against the Castilians was highlighted during the 17th-century War of Restoration, when further defences were added. But by the 1800s it had lost its way, a garrison town without a garrison, and this lack of interest is why so many 15th- and 16th-century buildings have been preserved. Its last action was at the centre of the tug-of-war between the Liberals and Royalists; in 1833 the Liberals used a secret entrance to seize the town – the only time Marvão has ever been captured.

◉ Sights & Activities

Castelo　　　　　　　　　　　　CASTLE
(admission free; ☺24hr) The formidable castle, built into the rock at the western end of the village, dates from the end of the 13th century, but most of what you see today was built in the 17th century. The views from the battlements are staggering. There's a huge vaulted cistern (still full of water) near the entrance and it's landscaped with hedges and flowerbeds. You can walk around the town on the castle walls.

Museu Municipal　　　　　　　　MUSEUM
(adult/concession €1.25/free; ☺9am-12.30pm & 2-5.30pm Tue-Sun) Just southeast of the castle, the Igreja de Santa Maria provides graceful surroundings for the small museum. The approach to history is a bit scattershot, with displays of muskets and bayonets, medieval grave markers, carved stonework dating from the 3rd millennium BC, costumes and Roman pottery shards.

FREE Casa da Cultura　　　　EXHIBITIONS
(Largo do Pelourinho; ☺9.30am-1pm & 2-5.30pm) In a restored building, this cultural centre hosts changing exhibitions, and you can check out the rustic upstairs court room, dating from 1809. There's also a small handicrafts **shop** on site.

Walking Trail　　　　　　　WALKING TRAIL
Ask at the tourist office for instructions on the interesting 7.5km circuit walk from Marvão to Portagem via Abegoa and Fonte Souto (or 2.5km direct to Portagem), following a medieval stone-paved route (note: the return journey is steep).

Megaliths　　　　　　　　　MEGALITHS
You can make a brilliant 30km round-trip via Santo António das Areias and Beirã, visiting nearby *antas* (dolmens). Tour maps are available from the *turismo* for €1 but these can, and do, go out of print. Follow the '*antas*' signs through a fabulously quiet landscape of cork trees and rummaging pigs. Some megaliths are right by the roadside, while others require a 300m-to-500m

walk. Be sure to bring refreshments: there's no village en route. You can continue north of Beirã to visit the megaliths in the Castelo de Vide area (p229). Ask at the *turismo* about bikes to rent.

Cidade de Ammaia MUSEUM
(adult/concession €2; ⊘9am-1pm & 2-5pm Mon-Fri, 10am-1pm & 2-5pm Sat & Sun) This excellent little Roman museum lies between Castelo de Vide and Marvão in São Salvador de Aramenha. From São Salvador head 700m south along the Portalegre road, then turn left, following the signs to Ammaia.

In the 1st century AD this area was a huge Roman city called Ammaia, flourishing from the area's rich agricultural produce (especially oil, wine and cereals). Although evidence was found (and some destroyed) in the 19th century, it wasn't until 1994 that thorough digs began.

Here you can see some of the finds, including engraved lintels and tablets, jewellery, coins and some incredibly well-preserved glassware. You can also follow paths across the fields to where the forum and spa once stood and see several impressive columns and ongoing excavations.

🛏 Sleeping

TOP CHOICE **Quinta do Barrieiro** GUEST HOUSE €€
(☑245 964 308; www.quintadobarrieiro.com; r incl breakfast from €85, 6-person apt €225; ❄🤶🛏) Special occasion anyone? Bah! You shouldn't need an excuse to come to this rural tourism abode. Home to two creative Portuguese – a sculptor and an architect – this superb place, made up of several *casinhas* (little houses) and rooms, provides luxury, creativity, outdoors (there are some great walks around the property and to a dam). The garden is full of the owner's sculptures, as are the light and airy communal living areas. Superb breakfasts are included (brought to your accommodation – all have kitchenettes). Ring for directions as it's several kilometres from Marvão.

Hotel El Rei Dom Manuel HOTEL €€
(☑245 909 150; www.turismarvao.pt; Largo da Olivença; s/d incl breakfast €65/75; 🤶) Rooms in this charming, friendly and professional hotel have tiled floors and sizeable windows. The best rooms are the suites-with-a-view and there's a restaurant (mains €9 to €12).

Casa da Árvore GUEST HOUSE €€
(☑245 993 854; Rua Dr Matos Magalhães 3; s/d incl breakfast €50/75) This elegant guest house has five country home–style rooms and an attractive lounge area with a stunning view. It boasts a Roman funerary stone and a João Tavares tapestry.

Casa da João GUEST HOUSE €
(☑245 993 437; Travessa de Santiago 1; s/d €25/30) This welcoming little house offers two spotless rooms. Look for the bright red door.

Pousada de Santa Maria LUXURY HOTEL €€€
(☑245 993 201; www.pousadas.pt; Rua 24 de Janeiro; d €220; ❄) Converted from several village houses, this is the most elegant and intimate option in town, with marvellous views from some rooms.

Camping Asseiceira CAMPGROUND €
(☑245 992 940; www.campingasseiceira.com; Santo António Das Areias; sites per adult/tent/car €3/4/2) Simple rooms, too. Readers praise this neat camp site for its organisation and location, in the quaint village of Santo António Das Areias, located 4km northeast of Marvão.

Casa Dom Dinis GUEST HOUSE €€
(☑245 993 957; www.casaddinis.pa-net.pt; Rua Dr Matos Magalhães 7; s/d incl breakfast €45/55, d with terrace €63; 🤶) Near the *turismo*, the friendly Dom Dinis has eight quirkily painted but slightly tired rooms of varying sizes, one of which has a terrace.

Casa das Portas de Ródão GUEST HOUSE €
(☑933 828 093; Largo da Silveirinha 2; r with shared bathroom €30-35) At the entrance to town, this two-storey, three-bedroom house has a rustic, old-fashioned feel with curly iron bedsteads and original knick-knacks. There's a kitchen and a terrace. You can rent by room or the whole house. For info, ask at the handicraft shop Muralhas da Vila nearby.

🍴 Eating

Marvão is light on for great quality restaurant options. If cuisine rates over views, then you're better off heading to Portagem on the Rio Sever, several kilometres down the road.

Restaurante Sever PORTUGUESE €€
(☑245 993 318; Portagem; mains €9-14; ⊘lunch & dinner) The pick of the restaurants around the traps, this smart place is in a beautiful location, just over the bridge in Portagem, on the Rio Sever. It comes highly recommended by locals and serves first-class Alentejan cuisine. For both price and quality, it's at the higher end of the scale.

Restaurante Casa do Povo
PORTUGUESE €

(Rua de Cima; mains €7-12; ⊙lunch & dinner Fri-Wed) Boasting the town's loveliest terrace, Casa do Povo has wonderful views across the countryside. The menu is OK, but won't knock your culinary socks off. A speciality is shark with garlic and coriander.

Bar-Restaurante Varanda do Alentejo
PORTUGUESE €€

(Praça do Pelourinho 1; mains €8-12; ⊙lunch & dinner, lunch Sun) This popular place serves up lots of pork-based regional specialities, which you can enjoy with a sangria on the terrace.

Bar O Castelo
CAFE-BAR €

(Rua Dr Matos Magalhães; snacks €2-4; ⊙9am-10pm) This cosy, local snack bar serves daily simple specials (pasta and sandwiches) and has a shady, casual terrace at front.

ⓘ Information

There's a Caixa Geral do Depósitos bank (with ATM) on Rua do Espírito Santo. Access the internet for free at the **Casa da Cultura** (Largo do Pelourinho; ⊙9.30am-1pm & 2-5.30pm Mon-Fri). Near the castle is the helpful **turismo** (☑245 909 131; www.cm-marvao.pt; Largo de Santa Maria; ⊙9am-noon & 2-5.30pm Sep-Jun, 9am-7pm Jul & Aug), which also has free internet.

ⓘ Getting There & Away

BUS Two buses run daily between Portalegre and Marvão (€2.50, 45 minutes). There are two services from Castelo de Vide, but one may require a change of buses at Portagem, a major road junction 7.5km northeast.

TRAIN The nearest train station, Marvão-Beirã, is 9km north of Marvão, and has beautiful *azulejo* panels. Three trains run daily to/from Lisbon (€12 to €27, 4½ hours); change at Abrantes and Torre das Vargens. The daily Lisbon–Madrid *Talgo Lusitânia* train also stops here. Taxis charge around €13 to the station.

TAXI A **taxi** (☑245 993 272; Praça do Pelourinho) to Castelo de Vide costs around €15.

BAIXO ALENTEJO

Mértola
POP 2000

Spectacularly set on a rocky spur, high above the peaceful Rio Guadiana, the cobbled streets of medieval Mértola are a delightful place to roam. A small but imposing castle stands high over town, overlooking the jumble of dazzlingly white houses and a picturesque church that was once a mosque. A long bout of economic stagnation at this remote town has left many traces of Islamic occupation intact, so much so that Mértola is considered a *vila museu* (open-air museum). To let Mértola's magic do its thing, you need more than a quick visit here.

In the heat of the day – up to 47°C – the only sound is insects buzzing. Nearby is an enchanting botanic garden in the grounds of a restored convent, and further afield, the beautiful, bleak, disused copper mines of São Domingos. The pretty gorge and cascades of Pulo do Lobo are around 30km away.

History

Mértola follows the usual pattern of settlement in this area: Phoenician traders, who sailed up the Guadiana, then Carthaginians, then Romans. Its strategic position, as the northernmost port on the Guadiana, and the final destination for many Mediterranean routes, led the Romans to develop Mértola (naming it Myrtilis) as a major agricultural and mineral-exporting centre. Cereals and olive oil arrived from Beja, copper and other metals from Aljustrel and São Domingos. It was a rich merchant town.

Later the Moors, who called it Martulah and made it a regional capital, further fortified Mértola and built a mosque. Dom Sancho II and the Knights of the Order of Santiago captured the site in 1238. But then, as commercial routes shifted to the Tejo, Mértola declined. When the last steamboat service to Vila Real de Santo António ended and the copper mines of São Domingos (the area's main employer) closed in 1965, its port days were over.

◉ Sights & Activities

Stepping through the thick outer walls into the old town makes you feel as if you have stepped back in time. It's enchanting just to wander around the snoozy, sun-baked streets (but take plenty of water).

Castelo & Torre de Menagem (Nucleo do Castelo)
CASTLE

(⊙9am-12.30pm & 2-5.30pm Tue-Sun) Above the parish church looms Mértola's fortified castle, most of which dates from the 13th century. It was built upon Moorish foundations next to an Islamic residential, the *alcáçova* (citadel), which itself overlaid the

Roman forum. For centuries the castle was considered western Iberia's most impregnable fortress.

From its prominent tower, the Torre de Menagem, and the walls, there are ultrafabulous views – the *alcáçova* is on one side, and the old town and the river on the other.

Largo Luís de Camões   PLAZA

This is the administrative heart of the old town, a picturesque square lined with orange trees, with the *câmara municipal* at its western end. To reach the *largo* (small square), enter the old town and keep to the left at the fork in the road.

The **Torre do Relógio**, a little clock tower topped with a stork's nest and overlooking the Rio Guadiana, is northeast of the square. Alongside it is a municipal building with a rooftop worthy of Van Gogh.

Igreja Matriz   CHURCH

(Rua da Igreja; admission free; ☺Tue-Sun) Mértola's striking parish church – square, flat-faced and topped with whimsical little conical decorations – is most well known because in a former incarnation it was a mosque, one of the few in the country to have survived the Reconquista. It was reconsecrated as a church in the 13th century. Look out for an unwhitewashed cavity in the wall, behind the altar; in former times this served as the mosque's mihrab (prayer niche). Note also the goats, lions and other figures carved around the peculiar Gothic portal and the typically Moorish horseshoe arch in the north door.

Torre do Rio   TOWER

At the river's edge, near its confluence with the Ribeira de Oeiras, is the ruined, Roman-era Torre do Rio (River Tower), which once guarded the vital port.

TOP CHOICE Convento de São Francisco

BOTANIC GARDEN & ART GALLERY

(☎286 612 119; www.conventomertola.com/en; adult €5; ☺by appointment only) This 400-year-old former convent, across the Ribeira de Oeiras, 500m southwest of Largo Vasco da Gama, has been owned since 1980 by Dutch artist Geraldine Zwanikken and her family. In a true labour of love, they have gradually transformed the ruins into an extraordinary place, most simply described as a nature reserve and art gallery. The organic garden – overseen by Geraldine's youngest son, Louis, is full of herbs, rare plants and flowers, watered by a restored Islamic irrigation system. Highlights include Geraldine's modern artworks, and, gracing the former chapel (if they are not in temporary exhibitions elsewhere), the kinetic installations of renowned artist Christiaan Zwanikken, Geraldine's eldest son. The nearby riverside is devoted to specially constructed nests for storks and lesser kestrels.

Museums

Mértola's wonderful group of **museums** (1 museum adult/concession €2/1, combined ticket €5/2.50; ☺9am-12.30pm & 2-5.30pm Tue-Sun) have the same opening hours and form an excellent tour of the town.

Casa Romana   ROMAN RUINS

(Roman House; Largo Luís de Camões) In the cellar of the *câmara municipal* is the enchanting Casa Romana. This clever display allows the visitor to walk 'through' the foundations of the Roman house upon which the building rests, and brings it to life with its small collection of pots, sculpture and other artefacts.

Museu Islâmico   MUSEUM

At the southern end of the old town, the Museu Islâmico (Islamic Museum) is a small but dramatic display of inscribed funerary stones, jewellery, pots and jugs from the 11th to 13th centuries.

Museu de Arte Sacra   MUSEUM

(Museum of Ecclesiastical Art; Largo da Misericórdia) Housed in the former Misericórdia church nearby, the Museu de Arte Sacra exhibits religious statuettes from the 16th to 18th centuries and several impressive 16th-century retables from the village and castle churches; some portray the battle against the Moors.

Museu Paleocristão   ROMAN RUINS, MUSEUM

(Palaeo-Christian Museum; Rossio do Carmo) North of the old town is the Museu Paleocristão, this features a partly reconstructed line of 6th-century Roman columns and poignant funerary stones, some of which are beautifully carved with birds, hearts and wreaths. It was the site of a huge Palaeo-Christian basilica, and the adjacent cemetery was used over the centuries by both Roman-era Christians and medieval Moors.

Parque Natural do Vale do Guadiana

NATURE RESERVE

Created in 1995, this zone of hills, plains and deep valleys around Serpa and Mértola shelters the Rio Guadiana, one of Portugal's largest and most important rivers. Among its rich variety of flora and fauna are several rare or endangered species, including the black stork (sightings of the shy creatures are rare), lesser kestrel (most likely around Castro Verde and at Convento do São Francisco), Bonelli's eagle, royal owl, grey kite, horned viper and Iberian toad. The park also has many prehistoric remains. Ask at the park headquarters for details of walking trails and where to spot wildlife – they can advise you and provide you with a basic map. Note: hunting takes place in the park throughout the year; this not only creates controversy about the park's status (and frightens birds away) but can be dangerous for walkers. Check with headquarters before venturing out.

Kayaking

You can rent kayaks for trips down the lazy river at the Nautical Club (☎286 612 044; www.nauticodemertola.com; Rua Serrão Martins; per day €18) below the Restaurante O Naútico. Beira Rio rents out kayaks, which is handy on weekends when the Nautical Club is closed.

🛏 Sleeping

The *turismo* has a brochure listing more accommodation options in rural areas.

TOP CHOICE 🌿 **Convento de São Francisco**
GUEST HOUSE €€

(☎286 612 119; www.conventomertola.com; apt €65) This hauntingly beautiful and rustic former convent overlooking Mértola and the Rio Guadiana should be a mandatory sleepover for all tranquil souls. Rustic, fully-equipped apartments are converted from former stables, arteliers and the like. There's a cottage (solar powered) on the grounds for those looking for complete seclusion. Note, however, that minimum nights apply. An artist-in-residence program is also available.

Residencial Beira Rio GUEST HOUSE €
(☎286 611 190; www.beirario.pt; Rua Dr Afonso Costa 108; s from €35, d €45-50, tr €60, incl breakfast; ❄) Great at self-promotion and forever expanding, Beira Rio offers more polished rooms than Oasis, but lacks the same character. Most have superb river views and some have breezy terraces.

Monte do Alhinho RURAL INN €
(☎286 655 115; www.montedoalhinho.com; Estrada Nacional 265; s/d €50/60; ❄ ❄) Try the

appealing Monte do Alhinho, 8km from Mértola on the road to São Domingos. This tastefully converted farmhouse-cum-hacienda has massive rooms, fluffy white towels, and a superb kitchen, where breakfast – an onslaught of Alentejan delights – is served. Discounts apply for long-term stays.

Hospedaria Rita GUEST HOUSE €
(☎969 210 537; hospedariarita@gmail.com; r €40) Also overlooking the river, this is a new, modern option. It's the first lane after the roundabout, off Dr Afonso Costa.

Residencial Oasis GUEST HOUSE €
(☎286 612 404; Rua Dr Afonso Costa 104; d €25-40; ❄) Overlooking the river, rooms in this excellent-value place are basic but tidy (some have superb views). Price doesn't include breakfast.

🍴 Eating

Mértola's speciality is game, including *javali* (wild boar) and the regional pork dish *migas* – great labouring fuel, but perhaps heavier than necessary for sightseeing.

Café-Restaurante Alentejo PORTUGUESE €€
(☎286 655 133; Moreanes; mains €6-10; ⏰lunch & dinner Tue-Sun) This attractive place in Moreanes, 10km from Mértola on the way to São Domingos, is almost a museum thanks to its antique exhibits (including the local clients themselves!). It serves great-value, hearty helpings of true Alentejan cuisine.

A Esquina PORTUGUESE €€
(Rua Dr Afonso Costa 2; mains €9-12; ⏰lunch & dinner Wed-Mon) Several boars' heads mounted on the wall (not to mention the array of *presuntos* – hams hanging at the bar) attest to this eatery's hearty Alentejan cuisine, which is of high quality and served with gusto. It's situated on the roundabout into town.

Terra Utópica MEDITERRANEAN €€
(Rua D Sancho II 41; mains €8-10; ⏰lunch & dinner) A radical departure from Mértola's other traditional eateries, this place has a touch of Asia, Africa and the Mediterranean. The setting is pleasant, spread over several rooms and overlooking the Guadiana; the fare (mainly Meditteranean)? Only okay.

Other eateries dishing up traditional cuisine:

Restaurante Alengarve PORTUGUESE €€
(Av Aureliano Mira Fernandes; mains €6-11; ⏰lunch & dinner Tue-Thu) Run by the same family for over 40 years and consistent.

O Brasileiro PORTUGUESE €€
(mains €8-10; ☺lunch Mon, lunch & dinner Tue-Sun) Great quality traditional cuisine. Known for its *javali* and *migas* dishes.

Migas PORTUGUESE €
(mains €8) Another place with the oink factor.

Self-caterers should head to the mercado municipal (municipal market; Praça Vasco da Gama; ☺8am-4pm Mon-Sat), which sells fresh fruit and vegetables and other produce. There's also a wonderful unsigned bakery (Rua Dr Afonso Costa 96), where you can buy fresh-baked bread (go early or in the evening for hot rolls).

🍷 Drinking

Lancelote Bar BAR
(Rua Nossa Senhora da Conceição; ☺9pm-4am) This vaguely medieval-feeling bar has friendly barkeeps and eclectic decor (colourful paintings and a wall of skeleton keys), with a shady wooden terrace attached.

Alsafir BAR
(Rua dos Combatentes da Grande Guerra 9; ☺9pm-4am) A more tavern-like bar, Alsafir hosts the occasional dance-party nights.

🛍 Shopping

Oficina de Tecelagem HANDICRAFTS
(Rua da Igreja; ☺9am-5.30pm) A small wool-weaving workshop next to the *turismo*, this place hangs on by a thread through tourist sales of beautiful handmade products, including rugs and ponchos. Weaving is done onsite.

ℹ️ Information

Biblioteca Municipal (municipal library; Rua 25 de Abril 16; ☺10.30am-12.30pm Tue & Wed, 2-7pm Mon & Fri) Provides free internet access.

Centro de saúde (☏286 610 900; Cerca Carmo) Medical centre.

Millennium BCP Bank (Rua Dr Afonso Costa) Has an ATM. Three other banks are about town.

Parque Natural do Vale do Guadiana headquarters (☏286 610 090; ☺9am-12.30pm & 2-5.30pm Mon-Fri, 10am-1pm & 3-6pm Sat) In smart new premises by the *câmara municipal*, displays information on the fauna and flora of the 600-sq-km park, plus brochures on walks (note: these are fairly basic; serious walkers should buy the Serviço Cartográfico do Exército (ie army maps) labelled 'Mertola' from *papelarias*.

Police station (☏286 612 127; Rua Dr Afonso Costa)

Post office (Rua Alves Redol; ☺9am-12.30pm & 2-5.30pm)

Turismo (☏286 610 109; Rua da Igreja 31; ☺9am-12.30pm & 2-5.30pm mid-Sep–Jun, 9.30am-12.30pm & 2-6pm 1 Jul-15 Sep) Just inside the walled town, this place has a town map, list of *quartos* and free internet access.

ℹ️ Getting There & Away

BUS There are services by **Rede Expressos** (☏286 611 127; www.rede-expressos.pt) to Lisbon (€14.80, 4¼ hours, one or two daily) and **Rodoviária do Alentejo** (www.rodalentejo.pt) to Vila Real de Santo António (€9.40, 1½ hours); and a slower local Vila Real service (€6, two hours, one daily) via Alcoutim (50 minutes), which runs on Monday and Friday. Three weekday services run to/from Beja (normal/express €5/9, 75 minutes/one hour).

Around Mértola

The ghost town of São Domingos consists of desolate rows of small mining cottages. Once the mine closed in the 1960s, many miners emigrated or moved to Setúbal. But the nearby contemporary village is set amid beautiful countryside and next to a huge lake, where you can swim or rent a paddleboat or canoe.

The São Domingos mine itself is over 150 years old – though mining has been taking place here since Roman times – and is a deserted, eerie place to explore, with crumbling old offices and machinery. The rocks surrounding it are clouded with different colours, and the chief mine shaft is filled with deep, unnatural dark-blue water, shot through with it-doesn't-bear-thinking-about-substances (read: contaminated). Locals have no fondness for the firm that established the mines, which kept its workers in line with a private police force.

A small museum, Casa do Mineiro (Rua Santa Isabel 31-33; ☺9am-12.30pm & 2-5.30pm Mon-Fri, plus weekends Jun-Aug) recreates a typical miner's cottage.

Set in some of the mine's former administrative buildings, the grand Hotel São Domingos (☏286 640 000; www.hotelsaodomingos.com; s/d from €92/110; ❄) features extensive facilities. The hotel's rooms are bright and spacious, with attractive furnishings. There's a saltwater pool, games room and elegant common areas, including a library. Packages are available.

Best visited with your own transport, São Domingos is 15km east of Mértola.

Beja

POP 21,600

Baixo Alentejo's principal town is easy-going, welcoming and untouristed, with a walled centre and some beguiling sights, all of which are within an easy walk of each other; these often follow old Roman routes. Often dismissed as Évora's 'plainer cousin', Beja has an inferiority complex, but it shouldn't. Its inexpensive guest houses, quaint plazas and excellent eateries make for a relaxing stop and a very genuine Portuguese experience.

Beja is at the heart of the regional tourist area called Planície Dourada (Golden Plain) – meaning it's surrounded by an endless sea of wheat fields. On Saturday there's the bonus of a traditional market, spread around the castle.

Drivers are advised to park their cars in the clearly marked car parks outside the walled centre.

History

Settlements have existed on the site of Beja since the Iron Age. Vestiges of this period have been discovered as recently as the 1990s, and some of these finds are proudly displayed in the town's archaeological museum. During Roman and Muslim times, Beja was considered an important administrative centre (wrongly, as locals will stress, attributed to Évora alone). The Romans called the city Pax Julia (shortened to Pax, which then became Paca, Baca, Baju and finally Beja), after Julius Caesar restored peace between the Romans and rebellious Lusitanians. It became an important agricultural centre, booming on wheat and oil.

Little evidence remains of the 400 years of subsequent Moorish rule, except for some distinctive 16th-century *azulejos* in the Convento de Nossa Senhora da Conceição (now the Museu Regional). The town was recaptured from the Moors in 1162.

Beja

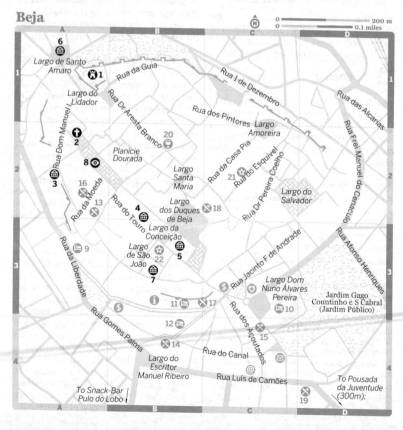

⊙ Sights

Museu Jorge Vieira CONTEMPORARY ART MUSEUM
(Rua do Touro 33; admission free; ⊙10am-12.30pm & 2.30-6.30pm Tue-Sat, 2-6.30pm Sun)
A charming, small museum, devoted to the work of renowned Portuguese sculptor Jorge Vieira, who donated his works to Beja. His monumental bulbous figures and strange creatures capture the imagination, calling to mind Maurice Sendak's *Where the Wild Things Are*. Look out for Viera's linked ellipses on Praça Diogo Fernandes de Beja.

Praça da República PLAZA
This renovated attractive town square with a *pelourinho* (stone pillory) is the historic heart of the old city. Dominating the square is the 16th-century Igreja de Misericórdia, a hefty church with an immense porch – its crude stonework betrays its origins as a meat market. The Planície Dourada building features an elegant Manueline colonnade.

Convento de Nossa Senhora da Conceição & Museu Regional MUSEUM
(Largo da Conceição; adult/child €2/free; ⊙9.30am-12.30pm & 2-5.15pm Tue-Sun) Founded in 1459, this Franciscan convent was the location for the romance between a nun and soldier that inspired *Letters of a Portuguese Nun* (see p240).

Indeed a romantic setting, it's a delicate balance between no-nonsense Gothic and Manueline flights of fancy. The interior is lavish – amazing highlights are the rococo chapel with 17th- and 18th-century gilded woodwork, and a chapel inlaid with intricate marble. The chapterhouse is incongruously Arabian, with a beautiful ceiling painted with unfurling ferns, 16th-century tiles and a carved doorway. The cloister has some splendid 16th- and 17th-century *azulejos*.

Tucked inside this convent is the **Museu Regional**, displaying Roman lamps, glass bottles and stelae, and 16th- and 17th-century paintings. The admission fee includes entry to the Museu Visigótico.

FREE **Núcleo Museológico da Rua do Sembrano** ROMAN RUINS
(Rua do Sembrano; ⊙9.30am-12.30pm & 2-5.45pm) Opened in 2008, there is more to this modern museum than meets the eye – the exhibition is underfoot and displayed through a glass floor. Iron Age finds were discovered here during building works in the 1980s, and the site was deemed important enough to excavate and protect. Peer through the glass floor at 2200-year-old remains, over which were laid subsequent Roman walls, indicating that this

THE ALENTEJO BEJA

Beja

BEJA'S LOVE LETTERS

A series of scandalous, passionate 17th-century love letters came from Beja, allegedly written by one of the convent's nuns, Mariana Alcoforado, to a French cavalry officer, Count Chamilly. The letters immortalised their love affair while the count was stationed here during the time of the Portuguese war with Spain.

The *Letters of a Portuguese Nun* first emerged in a French translation in 1669 and subsequently appeared in English and many other languages. Funnily enough, the originals were never found.

In 1972 three Portuguese writers, Maria Isabel Barreno, Maria Teresa Horta and Maria Velho da Costa published *The Three Marias: New Portuguese Letters*, a collection of stories, poems and letters that formed a feminist update of the letters – for which they were prosecuted under the Salazar regime.

location was important for millennia. A curator will explain the site.

Museu Visigótico MUSEUM
(Largo de Santo Amaro; adult/concession €2/1; ☉9.30am-12.30pm & 2-5pm Tue-Sun) Found just beyond the castle, the unusual Visigothic museum is housed in the former Igreja de Santo Amaro, parts of which date from the early 6th century when it was a Visigothic church – so it's one of Portugal's oldest standing buildings. Inside, the original columns display intriguing, beautiful carvings. The admission fee includes entry to the Museu Regional.

Castelo CASTLE
Dom Dinis built the castle on Roman foundations in the late 13th century. There are grand views from the top of the impressive 42m-high **Torre de Menagem**. The *turismo* (see p242) is located here.

Sacred Art Museums
Several museums of religious artworks opened in 2008. So great was the wealth of the Catholic Church that no single space can display all of the paintings and other items. The most attractive, for its church, is housed in the restored Igreja de Nossa Senhora dos Prazeres e Museu Episcopal (adult/child €1.50/free; ☉10am-12.30pm & 2.30-6pm Wed-Sun Jun-Aug, 10am-12.30pm & 2-5pm Dec-Feb) While the church is stunning, perhaps only those interested in religious art might appreciate the museum (enter from near the altar).

★✰ Festivals & Events
The nine-day Ovibeja agricultural fair, one of the largest in the country's south, has music by day and a show every night. Held in the Parque de Feiras e Exposições, which is on the town's southeastern outskirts, the fair has grown from a livestock market to a music, handicrafts and cuisine bonanza. It starts in the last weekend of April.

🛏 Sleeping

Pousada de São Francisco LUXURY HOTEL €€€
(✆284 313 580; www.pousadas.pt; Largo Dom Nuno Álvares Pereira; d €270; ✲✎) Located in the 13th-century São Francisco Convent, this *pousada* provides gorgeous rooms, formerly cells, and a restaurant (open all day) with a magnificent vaulted ceiling. A Gothic chapel and Chapter House (with billiards table) add to the unique and luxurious atmosphere.

Residencial Bejense GUEST HOUSE €€
(✆284 311 570; www.residencialbejense.com; Rua Capitão João Francisco de Sousa 57; s/d/tr incl breakfast €40/55/65; ✲) This pleasant family-run option, with bright and airy rooms (slightly tizzy decor) is hard to beat for value. Front rooms have small balconies. The hallways are trimmed with tiles. Breakfast is a small, but excellent, buffet.

Hospedaria Rosa do Campo GUEST HOUSE €
(✆284 323 578; Rua da Liberdade 12; s €28, d €35-40; ✲☏) This sparkling guest house has polished floors and mostly spacious rooms, each with a small refrigerator. There are even fly-wire window coverings. Breakfast is included. Incredible value.

Pousada da Juventude HOSTEL €
(✆284 325 458; www.pousadasjuventude.pt; Rua Professor Janeiro Acabado; dm €12, d without/with bathroom €28/30) Next to the Instituto Português da Juventude (IPJ), 300m southeast of the bus station, this yellow-and-blue, spick-and-span hostel is one of the

cleanest and best around. There's a kitchen for guest use and a continental breakfast is included.

Residencial Santa Bárbara   GUEST HOUSE €€
(☑284 312 280; www.residencialsantabarbara.pt; Rua de Mértola 56; s €30, d €42-45, tw €65, incl breakfast; ✳⑳) This reliable and good-value choice has neat, motel-style rooms set in masculine tones – all dark woods and plaid curtains – and it's well located in the pedestrianised town centre.

✖ Eating
Casa de Chá Maltesinhas   TEAROOM €
(Rua dos Açoutados 12 & Terreiro dos Valentes 7; snacks €1-5; ⊘9am-7pm Mon-Fri, 9am-2pm Sat) These not-to-be-missed tearooms serves delicious regional *doces conventuais* (desserts traditionally made by nuns). Try the *pasteis de toucinho,* a delicious thin pastry and almond creation with, believe it or not, a smidgeon of pork lard. Worth the pig out.

Sabores do Campo   VEGETARIAN €
(Rua Bento de Jesus Caraçça 4; ⊘lunch & dinner Mon-Thu, lunch Fri; ⑳) This simple place serves 100% vegetarian food – perfect for those in need of a tasty fill of pork-free tarts, vegetables and salads. Prices are by weight (€14 per kilogram).

Luiz da Rocha   CAFE €
(Rua Capitão João Francisco de Sousa 63; mains €7-12; ⊘lunch & dinner) Founded in 1893, this is one of Beja's oldest cafes and best-known institutions. It gathers a chatty neighbourhood crowd day and night and is justly famous for its cakes: *trouxas de ovos* (literally 'sweet egg yolks') and *porquinhos de doce* ('sweet little pigs'). It also serves up Alentejan staples.

Restaurante Alentejano   PORTUGUESE €€
(Largo dos Duques de Beja 6; mains €7.50-10; ⊘lunch & dinner Sat-Thu) This lively local eatery is a good bet for filling Alentejan plates of roasted pork or cod dishes. Its plain exterior hides a dapper but relaxed interior. Popular among the lunching businessfolk.

Adega Típica 25 Abril   PORTUGUESE €€
(Rua da Moeda 23; mains €6-11; ⊘lunch & dinner Tue-Sun) Packed to the basket-lined rafters with locals, this cavernous, rustic *adega* serves typical food, with good daily specials.

Casa de Pasto a Pipa   PORTUGUESE €€
(Rua da Moeda 8; mains €7.50-10; ⊘lunch & dinner Mon-Sat) This rustic eatery has a wood-beamed ceiling, bright blue wooden chairs

and checked tablecloths. It dishes up the usual standards such as *migas alentejana* (a tasty bread and pork dish).

🍷 Drinking
Enoteca Magna Casa   BAR
(Rua Dr Aresta Branco 45; snacks €1-7; ⊘6pm-midnight Mon-Sat) An atmospheric, contemporary wine bar (note the fabulous green-tiled exterior). The passionate owner serves delicious *petiscos* (appetisers) to match his long list of Portuguese wines.

Snack-Bar Pulo do Lobo   CAFE, RESTAURANT
(Av Vasco da Gama; ⊘8am-midnight Mon-Sun) A cafe and restaurant with outdoor seating, this is a favourite for an evening get-together over snails and *petiscos* and cold beer. Great quality plates of the day cost between €9 and €15.

☆ Entertainment
Galeria do Desassossego   BAR
(Rua da Casa Pia 26-28; www.myspace.com/galeriadodesassossego; ⊘7pm-4am Tue-Sat) Try saying *'desassossego'* after a few drinks. Literally meaning 'unquiet', this gallery is anything but. Its unique concept brings a bar and snacks, shows and exhibitions together in the one place. *Petiscos* are sometimes shared with neighbours, live music ranges from jazz to rock (no covers allowed!) and creativity is in the air. There is no signage – follow the vibe.

Pax Julia Teatro Municipal   CINEMA, THEATRE
(☑284 315 090; www.paxjulia.org; Largo de São João 1) This cinema and theatre hosts regular concerts, dance performances and film screenings. A program guide is available at the *turismo* or the theatre's box office.

🛍 Shopping
An *artesenato* cooperative has a range of goods for sale within the Igreja de Misericórdia (Praça da República; ⊘10am-1pm & 2-5.30pm Mon-Fri, 10am-1pm Sat), a unique style of store.

ℹ Information
Several banks near the *turismo* have ATMs.

Biblioteca Municipal (Rua Luís de Camões; ⊘2.30-10.30pm Mon, 9.30am-12.30pm & 2.30-11pm Tue-Fri, 2.30-8pm Sat) Free internet.

Espaço Internet (Rua Luis de Camões; ⊘2-5.30pm Mon-Fri) Free internet access. Enter through Casa da Cultura.

Hospital (☑284 310 200; Rua Dr António Covas Lima)

Police station (☑284 322 022; Largo Dom Nuno Álvares Pereira)

Post office (Rua Luís de Camões; ⊙8.30am-6.30pm Mon-Fri) Has NetPost.

Turismo (☑/fax 284 311 913; Rua Capitão João Francisco de Sousa 25; ⊙10am-1pm & 2-6pm Mon-Sat) Within the castle premises, provides a good city map and information on Beja.

❶ Getting There & Away

BUS From the **bus station** (☑284 313 620) buses run to regional towns and villages. Weekends see fewer services. The bus station is in the southern part of town, about 600m from the historic centre.

Évora (€7.50, 1¼ hours, hourly)

Mértola (€5, 1¼ hours, three daily except weekends)

Serpa (€3.15, 40 minutes, five to six daily) From Serpa, some continue to Moura (€5.10, 65 minutes, four daily).

Buses also run to destinations that are further afield:

Albufeira (€12.30, three hours, three daily)

Faro (€12.70, three hours, three daily)

Lisbon (€12, 3¼ hours, eight daily).
Around half this number operate on weekends.

TRAIN Beja is on the Lisbon–Funcheira (near Ourique) railway line. At the time of research, the line was undergoing major maintenance works; when functioning, express trains run to/from Lisbon (2½ hours).

Serpa

POP 6000

Planted among the rolling hills of vineyards and dusty fields, Serpa is a sleepy, atmospheric town of bleached-white walls and narrow cobblestone streets. At its medieval heart is a small, pretty plaza carefully guarded by the elderly folk who have long called Serpa home. Locals are renowned for their love of food, and several factory outlets produce the town's culinary jewel, *queijo Serpa,* a cheese made from curdled sheep's milk.

Those arriving by car must brave tight gateways into the old town and breathtakingly narrow streets (or park outside the walls).

◉ Sights

Castelo   CASTLE
(admission free; ⊙9am-12.30pm & 2-5.30pm) You enter the small castle through a dramatic entrance: a heavy cracked piece of wall. Inside it feels domestic in scale. You can walk around the battlements for long views over the flat plains, the aqueduct, town walls, rooftops and orange trees, and the slow life of Serpa residents.

Town Walls & Aqueduto   AQUEDUCT
Walls still stand around most of the inner town. Along the west side (follow Rua dos Arcos) run the impressive remains of an 11th-century **aqueduct**. At the southern end is a huge 17th-century wheel pump (aka *noria*), once used for pumping water along the aqueduct to the nearby **Palácio dos Condes de Ficalho** (still used by the de Ficalho family as a holiday home).

Museu Etnográfico   MUSEUM
(Ethnographic Museum; Largo do Corro; admission free; ⊙9am-12.30pm & 2-5.30pm) No traditional rural trade is left unturned in the exquisite exploration of Alentejan life found at Serpa's Museu Etnográfico. Occupying the former town market (in use from 1887 to 1986), the museum beautifully presents restored items donated by locals. Polished tools used by former wheelwrights, saddle makers, cheese makers, barrel makers and ironmongers – among others – are on display.

TOP CHOICE **Museu do Relógio**   MUSEUM
(☑284 543 194; www.museudorelogio. com; Rua do Assento 31; adult/under 10yr €2/free; ⊙2-5pm Tue-Fri, 10am-noon & 2-5pm Sat & Sun) The Watch Museum houses an amazing collection of watches and clocks, dating from a 1630 Edward East clock to the museum's own 2010 wristwatch model (also for sale). Napoleonic gilded timepieces and Swiss cuckoo clocks are among the 2000 pieces ticking away in the cool surroundings of the former Convento do Mosteirinho.

✦ Festivals & Events

Festas de Senhora de Guadalupe RELIGIOUS
Celebrations of Serpa's patron saint take place in March/April from Good Friday to the following Tuesday – there is a pilgrimage to bring the saint's image down to the parish church, and on the last day a procession takes it back to the chapel.

On the Tuesday roast lamb is the traditional meal.

Noites na Nora
CULTURAL

This festival features nightly local theatre and music shows on a terrace tucked behind the aqueduct. Check with the tourist office – dates change annually.

🛏 Sleeping

Monte da Morena
RURAL INN €€€

(☎917 629 010; www.montemorena.com; s/d €45/65, 4-person apt €130; 🏊) Only 1.5km from the camping ground, this converted *quinta* offers simple, modern rooms arranged in a stable-like design. Because it's new, it's slightly stark but has wonderful agricultural surrounds (it's a working farm). There's a swimming pool and a very friendly labrador. Two-night minimum stays in high season. Breakfast features local produce from Serpa.

Casa da Muralha
GUEST HOUSE €€

(☎284 543 150; www.casadamuralha.com; Rua das Portas de Beja 43; r €65; ❄🐾) Nestled beside the town walls, which loom overhead, this place is atmospheric, although one senses it's seen better days. Rooms vary in size and decor. Some of its whitewashed rooms have beamed ceilings, others have traditional Alentejan (brightly painted wooden) furniture. Most rooms face onto an overgrown courtyard with lemon and orange trees.

Residencial Pulo do Lobo
GUEST HOUSE €

(☎284 544 664; www.residencialpulodolobo .com; Estrada de São Brás 9A; s/d €30/45) Handy to the bus station, this sparkling place and its house-proud owners provide plain but modern rooms. Excellent value if you don't mind being slightly out of the centre.

Residencial Beatriz
GUEST HOUSE €

(☎284 544 423; www.residencialbeatriz.com; Largo do Salvador 10; s/d incl breakfast €32/45, apt from €52) Overlooking the pretty square, this small guest house provides simple, but adequate, rooms of varying sizes. If there's more than two of you, the apartments provide good-value stays.

Casa de Serpa
GUEST HOUSE €€

(☎284 549 238; www.casadeserpa.com; Largo do Salvador 28; s €40, d €56-65) This friendly guest house has handsomely furnished rooms of varying sizes (some without external windows). Rooms at the back are smaller but open onto a courtyard. Homemade breakfasts include local produce.

Casa de Hóspedes Virgínia
GUEST HOUSE €

(☎284 549 145; Largo 25 de Abril; s/d €20/30) This small guest house has basic, but spotless, rooms and en-suite bathrooms, though the walls are somewhat thin. It faces a square dotted with orange trees.

Parque de Campismo
CAMPGROUND €

(☎284 544 290; Largo de São Pedro; sites per adult/tent/car €2/1.80/1.50) The municipal camp site is on dusty ground 400m northeast of the bus station. There's a restaurant and disabled access; rates include admission to the nearby pool.

🍴 Eating

All the local restaurants serve *tapas de queijo de Serpa* (the salty and creamy local cheese) or *queijadas* (small cheesecakes). Cheap eats can be found in several decent snack bars at the roundabout near the bus station.

Molhó Bico
PORTUGUESE €€

(Rua Quente 1; mains €8.50-14; ⏱lunch & dinner Thu-Tue) This enticing place pulls a crowd; kitchen odours hit you on entry to its arched, rustic space. It has wagon-wheel lights, huge wine urns, and a friendly ambience. Eating here is a pure, traditional gastronomic experience. There are hearty half serves.

Pedra de Sal
PORTUGUESE €€

(Estrada da Circunvalação s/n; mains €10-16; ⏱lunch & dinner Tue-Sun) This smart place is a win–win food-lover's scenario. The owner-chef conjures up Alentejana specialities using quality produce, including her own home-grown greens. Modern art, a candelabra and wood trim grace the interior, and there's an attractive bamboo-covered outdoor patio.

Restaurante O Alentejano
PORTUGUESE €€

(Praça da República; mains €8-15; ⏱lunch & dinner Tue-Sun) This handsome place, above a cafe of the same name, in a former mansion, serves local cuisine. Go for the daily specials – anything from braised hare in red wine to pigs' trotters.

O Nay
GRILL HOUSE €

(Rua de Santo António 10; mains €6-8; ⏱lunch & dinner Mon-Sat) A small, cheerful *churrasqueira*, serving up basic grills. It's one of the few places open on a Monday.

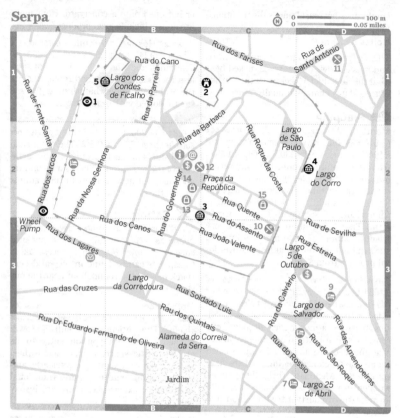

Shopping

Small artisan shops and delicatessens are dotted around town. You can buy good *queijadas* and a range of oils, honey, herbs and handicrafts at **Dom Luis** (Praça da República 15; ⊘closed Mon & Tue morning), as well as **Sabores da Terra** (Praça da República; ⊘8am-8pm) and **Casa de Artesanato** (Rua dos Cavalos 33; ⊘10am-7pm).

Information

On the fourth Tuesday of the month a country market sprawls beside Rua de Santo António on the town's northeastern outskirts.

Caixa Geral de Depósitos Bank & ATM (Largo Conde de Boavista) Around the corner from the *turismo*.

Espaço Internet (Rua Pedro Anes 14; ⊘10am-5pm Mon-Fri, 10am-1pm Sat) Free internet access with helpful staff.

Post office (Rua dos Lagares)

Turismo (☑284 544 727; www.cm-serpa.pt; Largo Dom Jorge de Melo 2; ⊘10am-7pm Jun-Aug, 9am-12.30pm & 2-5.30pm Dec-Feb) In the centre; staff provide a map of the old town with good listings, and sell local handicrafts.

Getting There & Away

Buses (☑284 544 740) run to/from Lisbon (€13.50, four hours, three to five daily) via Beja (normal/express €3.20/5.40, one to six daily). There are no direct buses to Évora. The bus station is a couple of kilometres south of town – head south on Avenida da Paz.

Moura

POP 8500

This pleasant working-class city, a flattish fortified town, has an ageing castle, graceful buildings and a well-preserved Moorish neighbourhood. Well placed near water sources and rich in ores, Moura has been a

Serpa

farming and mining centre and a fashionable spa in previous incarnations, and is currently experiencing a new lease of life; the world's largest solar-power generation plant is located nearby. Moura is also the nearest large town to the Barragem do Alqueva, 15km to the north.

The Moors' 500-year occupation came to an end in 1232 after a Christian invasion. Despite the reconquest, Moorish presence in the city remained strong – they only abandoned their quarter in 1496 (after Dom Manuel's convert-or-leave edict).

The town's name comes from a legend related to the 13th-century takeover. Moorish resident Moura Salúquiyya opened the town gates to Christians disguised as Muslims. They sacked the town, and poor Moura flung herself from a tower.

◉ Sights & Activities

There are several cafes with outdoor seating around Praça Sacadura Cabral, where you'll also find the *mercado municipal* in a huge glass building. Some good restaurants are located in the streets further south from the Praça.

FREE **Museu Municipal**   MUSEUM
(☎285 253 978; Rua da Romeira; ⏰9.30am-12.30pm & 2.30-5.30pm Tue-Fri, 10am-noon & 2-4pm Sat & Sun) In an appealing residential quarter off a lane about 200m east of the *praça* (head up Rua do Espírito Santo, behind the tourist office), this tiny museum contains local prehistoric and Roman remains, such as 1st- and 2nd-century needles, as well as Moorish funerary tablets.

FREE **Lagar de Varas do Fojo (Museu do Azeite)**   MUSEUM
(Rua João de Deus 20; ⏰9.30am-12.30pm & 2.30-5.30pm Tue-Sun) With a system of production that would have been similar to that of Roman times, the oil press re-creates the oil-pressing factory that functioned here between 1841 and 1941, with giant wooden and stone-wheel presses, vats and utensils.

Igreja de São Baptista   CHURCH
This 16th-century church has a remarkable Manueline portal. Set against the plain facade, it is a twisting, flamboyant bit of decoration, with carvings of knotted ropes, crowns and armillary spheres. Inside are some fine deep-blue and yellow 17th-century Sevillian *azulejos*. It's just outside Jardim Dr Santiago.

Jardim Dr Santiago & Spa   GARDEN
The lovely, shady Jardim Dr Santiago, at the eastern end of Praça Sacadura Cabral, is a delightful place to wander. There are good views, a bandstand, shady, flowering trees and it's a favourite spot for elderly men to sit and chat. The **thermal spa** (⏰9am-noon), at the entrance to the garden, is open and you can join the locals for a soak in a basic bath. Bicarbonated calcium waters, said to be good for rheumatism, burble from the richly marbled **Fonte das Três Bicas** (Fountain with Three Spouts) by the entrance to the *jardim*.

Mouraria   MOORISH QUARTER
The old **Moorish quarter** (Poço Árabe) lies at the western end of Praça Sacadura Cabral. It's a well-preserved tight cluster of narrow, cobbled lanes and white terraced cottages with chunky or turreted chimneys.

The **Núcleo Árabe** (Travessa da Mouraria 11; admission free; ⏰9.30am-12.30pm & 2.30-5.30pm), just off Largo da Mouraria, is a pocket collection of Moorish ceramics and other remains, such as carved stone inscriptions and a 14th-century Arabic well. Visits here must be arranged through the Museu Municipal.

Castelo   CASTLE
(admission free; ⏰closed Mon & Tue morning) The castle offers fabulous views across the

THE ALENTEJO MOURA

DAM STATISTICS

The 250-sq-km Alqueva reservoir, Europe's largest, created by an enormous dam (Barragem do Alqueva) near Moura, is undeniably beautiful. But there is something strange and otherworldly about it: it's not so much a lake as drowned land, with islands poking out of the water and roads disappearing into nowhere.

It is hoped that this huge water mass will save the arid Alentejo. One of Portugal's major agricultural regions, and its poorest, it employs a host of irrigation schemes and reservoirs to bring water to the soil, as well as hydroelectricity that supplies the national grid. The most important source of water is the Rio Guadiana, which rises in Spain and flows through the Alentejo. Various agreements with Spain were meant to ensure that its waters were fairly shared. But successive droughts strained the arrangement. Although the idea for the dam was first mooted in 1957, the Portuguese finally took matters into their own hands in 1998 and started work on the giant dam to guarantee both irrigation water and electricity for years to come. It flooded 2000 properties, including those of the village of Luz (rebuilt elsewhere but strangely antiseptic). The project cost €1.7 billion.

Critics say that the dam may not even fulfil its remit, that irrigation schemes are vastly expensive, and that it is an ecological disaster (many birds and animals had to be moved as part of the initial agreement). Ancient rock art was enveloped in the waters and menhirs were moved elsewhere. Plans are afoot for tourism projects, including resorts and associated activities.

Completed in 2002, the dam created an 83km-long reservoir, with a perimeter of 1100km. It's well worth driving to the dam wall for a look if you have your own transport (no buses head here). A Centro de Informação (☺10am-7pm Dec-Feb, 9.30am-6.30pm Jun-Aug, closed 1-2.30pm) provides technical (read: public relations) information.

Alternatively, take a boat trip from one of two marinas, one near the dam wall, the other 15km northwest at Amieira Marina (where there's also a snack bar and restaurant with lovely views). The company, Amieira Marina (☏266 611 173/4; www.amieira marina.com, www.gescruzeiros.com), offers a range of watery adventures, from kayak rentals (€17.50 per half-day) to short boat excursions (€35 including lunch). Some trips head to medieval villages, such as Monsaraz; restaurant owners will ferry you to and from the marina (after meals you are permitted to briefly peruse the sights). For those with more time and dosh, another fun option is to hire a houseboat (from around €200 per night). For other boat trips see p214.

countryside. One of the towers is the last remnant of a Moorish fortress. Rebuilt by Dom Dinis in the 13th century and again by Dom Manuel I in 1510, the castle itself was largely destroyed by the Spanish in the 18th century. There's a ruined convent inside the walls.

🛏 Sleeping

There are some great-value places around town.

Hotel Santa Comba HOTEL €
(☏285 251 255; www.residencialsantacomba. com; Praça Sacadura Cabral 34; s/d incl breakfast from €24/35; ✷) On the main square, this smart place opened in 2004 and has clean rooms overlooking the square. There's disabled access and a pleasant dining room.

Hotel Passagem do Sol HOTEL €
(☏285 250 080; www.hotelpassagemdosol.com; Largo José Maria dos Santos 40; s/d incl breakfast €26/38; ✷ @ ☎) The key holders – jugs embedded into walls – are the most novel things in this modern, but comfortable and spotless place. It's near the bus station – look for an ordered, green-shuttered house.

Hotel de Moura HOTEL €
(☏285 251 090; www.hoteldemoura.com; Praça Gago Coutinho; s/d incl breakfast from €38/48; ✷) Moura's lovely old dame of a hotel is housed in a former military hospital and overlooks a pretty square. It's a grand place, covered in tiles on the outside, and with sweeping staircases and tall windows on the inside. Rooms, however, vary considerably, from the classically furnished to the

rather sterile. It's worth paying extra for a superior room. Prices increase slightly on weekends and 'special' days.

🍴 Eating & Drinking

O Trilho PORTUGUESE €€
(Rua 5 de Outubro 5; mains €8.50-12.50; ⊕lunch & dinner Tue-Sun) Three streets east of Rua Serpa Pinto, O Trilho is a local favourite, with excellent regional mains and mouth-watering daily specials in pleasant, starched table clothed surroundings.

Patos & Infantes PORTUGUESE €€
(Rua Primero Dezembro 34; mains €8-12; ⊕lunch & dinner Wed-Sun, lunch Mon) Another establishment offering *cozinha tradicional* (traditional cuisine), but the difference here is the top quality produce and a more manageable (read: smaller) menu. Half servings are available for those who can't stomach consuming half an animal in one sitting.

Fronteiro Mar GRILL HOUSE €€
(Rua dos Ourives 13; mains €7-12; ⊕lunch & dinner Mon-Sat) This down-to-earth grill house serves up a big daily feed (locals tend to head here for lunch).

ℹ️ Information

There are banks on the *praça* and along Rua Serpa Pinto, directly north of the *turismo*.
Espaço Internet (🖱Rua 5 de Outubro 18) Free internet access.
Post office (Rua da República) East of Rua Serpa Pinto.
Turismo (📞285 251 375; www.cm-moura. pt; Patio dos Rolins 13; ⊕9am-12.30pm & 2-5.30pm Mon-Fri, 10am-1pm & 2.30-5.30pm Sat & Sun) Has a map of town.

ℹ️ Getting There & Away

Buses run to/from Beja (€5, one hour, five to six weekdays, less on weekends) via Serpa (€3.20, 40 minutes). Rede Expressos runs to Lisbon (€14.20, four hours, daily) via Évora (€9.50, 1½ hours); these leave from Praça Sacadura Cabral.

COASTAL ALENTEJO

Porto Côvo

POP 1100
Perched on low cliffs with views over the sea, Porto Côvo is the first enticing coastal town you'll reach after heading south of the Setúbal Peninsula. The old town, a former

fishing village, has a pretty square and cobbled streets lined with sun-bleached houses.

Paths along the cliffs lead down to the harbour at the town's southern end and to interesting rock formations to the north, with access down to various beaches such as **Praia do Somouqueira**. The official nudist beach is Praia do Salto.

The **turismo** (📞269 959 124; www.fregue siadeportocovo.com; ⊕9am-noon & 1-5pm Mon-Fri Dec-Feb, 10am-1pm & 3-7pm Jun-Aug) is on the edge of the old town, just one block north of the main square and next to a car park. Diving trips can be arranged through **Ecoalga** (📞964 620 394; www.ecoalga.com). In summer, a boat shuttles between Porto Côvo and the diminutive island of Ilha do Pesseguiero.

🛏️ Sleeping & Eating

Refúgio da Praia GUEST HOUSE €€€
(📞269 959 063 Praia do Queimado; r incl breakfast €90-125) Located several kilometres outside of town, this remote house (a converted restaurant) has neat, pine-filled rooms. You pay more for the setting – a slice of beach paradise – than luxury, here. It sits in countryside 50m from the water's edge.

Parque de Campismo da Ilha do Pesseguiero CAMPGROUND €
(📞269 905 178; www.ilhadopessegueirocamping .com; sites per adult/tent/car €4/4/2, bungalows €44-55) This well-equipped camp site is several kilometres northeast of Porto Côvo opposite Ilha do Pesseguiero and near an historic fort. For those without wheels, another small camp site is on the outskirts of town.

Zé Inácio GUEST HOUSE €€
(📞269 905 977; www.zeinacio.com; Rua Vasco da Gama 38; d €72.50) Above a restaurant of the same name, these attractive rooms have contemporary decor, tile floors, bamboo ceilings and white stucco walls.

Restaurante Marquês SEAFOOD €€
(Largo Marquês de Pombal; mains €12-19; ⊕lunch & dinner Wed-Mon) Porto Côvo's overwhelmingly favourite dining spot is set on the town's main square, with inviting outdoor tables, a smart tiled interior, and scrumptious plates of grilled fish and seafood salads. No reservations.

ℹ️ Getting There & Away

During summer at least five buses a day travel to/from Lisbon (€12.20, 2¾ hours). There are also regular connections to Vila Nova de Milfontes (around €5.20, 25 minutes).

Vila Nova de Milfontes

POP 3200

One of the loveliest towns along this stretch of the coast, Vila Nova de Milfontes has an attractive, whitewashed centre, sparkling beaches nearby and a laid-back population that couldn't imagine living anywhere else. Milfontes remains much more low-key than most resort towns in the Algarve, except in August when it's packed to the hilt with surfers and sun-seekers. It's located in the middle of the beautiful Parque Natural do Sudoeste Alentejano e Costa Vicentina and is still a port (Hannibal is said to have sheltered here) alongside a lovely, sand-edged limb of estuary.

Milfonte's narrow lanes and tiny plazas harbour varied eating and drinking options, with even more scenic restaurants out on the beach.

Sights

Praia do Farol, the lighthouse beach just by the town, is sheltered but gets busy. Beaches on the other side of the estuary are less crowded. Be careful of the strong river currents running through the estuary. If you have your own transport, you could head out to the fantastic **Praia do Malhão**, backed by rocky dunes and covered in fragrant scrub, around 7km to the north (travel 2.5km to Bruinheras, turn left at the roundabout just before the primary school, then travel another 3km – at the time of research it was signed to the left). The more remote parts of the beach harbour nudist and gay areas. The sea can be quite wild here, but the rugged coast is strikingly empty of development.

Activities

There are some gorgeous beaches around, both near the town and extending out along the coast. Scuba diving is possible through **Ecoalga** (☏964 620 394; www.ecoalga.com) in nearby Porto Côvo.

Recommended:

Sudaventura   EXCURSIONS, SURFING LESSONS
(☏283 997 231; www.sudaventura.com; Rua Custódio Brás Pacheco 38A; ◷10am-7pm, closed Mon Dec-Feb) Offers a range of excursions, including canoe trips, riverboat outings and bike hire. Surf lessons cost €30 per class.

Surf Milfontes   SURFING LESSONS
(☏969 483 334; www.surfmilfontes.com; Rua António Mantas 26) Surf lessons are available.

Sleeping

The tourist office has a list of official sleeping options. High-season (August) prices are listed here; at other times of the year prices are significantly lower. In August, you'll need to book in advance.

Casa do Adro   GUEST HOUSE €€
(☏283 997 102; www.casadoadro.com.pt; Rua Diário de Notícias 10; d €85; ☏) Set in a house dating from the 17th century, this special option is chock-a-block with antiques and artwork. It has six elegantly furnished bedrooms, some with private balconies (others have access to shared terraces). Foodies will love the breakfasts – and you can turn up to this scrumptious spread at any time in the morning (a nice touch).

Naturarte   RURAL INN €€€
(☏913 619 939; www.naturarte.pt; São Luis; r €145-180; ✳☀) There's definite attitude at this place, 12km from Milfontes – it's smart, sassy and has been well designed by an architect member of the family. The property is spread over two locations – Naturarte Camp offers a more classic option, whose rooms are modern, but have family antiques and heirlooms as talking points. Several kilometres away overlooking a river, Naturarte Rio is a more contemporary option.

Casa da Eira   GUEST HOUSE €€€
(☏283 990 010; www.alentejoadventures.com; Rua Casa da Pedra; r €60, apt €120-240) Housed in a refurbished building, this lovely place boasts a range of contemporary-style rooms and apartments (two to four person), each decked out in a funky colour scheme and fun decor. Stripes, squares and tasteful touches, from lamps to cushions, add to a colourful experience.

Casa Amarela   HOSTEL €€
(☏283 996 632; www.casaamarelamilfontes. com; Rua Dom Luis Castro e Almeida; dm €20, d/tr/q €60/80/92.50; @☏) This privately run, cheery yellow place is set with eclectic knick-knacks belonging to the genial English-speaking owner, Rui. You'll find bright rooms, a lounge space and shared (if slightly messy) kitchens. The annexe nearby has attractive dorm rooms, a courtyard and solar-heated showers.

Mil Reis   GUEST HOUSE €€
(☏283 998 233; http://milreis.tipod.com; Largo do Rossio; d/tw €60/70) Recently renovated, this pleasant place is decked out in contemporary blond woods and white. Be aware,

this isn't for large (that goes for up and out) people; rooms are a bit cramped. The terrace has a fabulous views.

Casa dos Arcos
GUEST HOUSE €€

(☑283 996 264; fax 283 997 156; Rua do Cais; d/ tr €70/85; ❄) Jauntily painted in blue and white, this airy and spotless (if dated) guest house has comfortable beds, tiled floors and small balconies.

Campers can take their pick of two grounds:

Campiférias
CAMPGROUND $

(☑283 996 409; www.roteiro-campista. pt; Rua da Praça; sites per adult/tent/car €3.95/3.20/4; ❄) Shady, and 800m from the beach.

Parque de Campismo Milfontes
CAMPGROUND $

(☑283 996 140; www.campingmilfontes.com; sites per adult/tent/car €4/3.80/4.40; ❄) North of Campiférias, in a pine forest close to the beach.

✖ Eating

TOP CHOICE **Tasca do Celso**
PORTUGUESE €€

(☑283 996 753; Rua dos Aviadores; mains €13.50-20; ☺lunch & dinner Tue-Sun) *The* choice. Locals and travellers from far and wide rave about the excellent cuisine produced within the kitchen of this charming, 'upmarket rustic' blue-and-white building. You're safe trying anything here. Great service, too.

Restaurante A Fateixa
SEAFOOD €€

(☑283 996 415; Largo do Cais; mains €7-14; ☺lunch & dinner Thu-Tue) A Fateixa delivers good grills and seafood dishes – try the *tamboril* (monkfish) rice for two – and it has breezy outdoor tables. It's excellent value given its perfect setting down by the river.

Portal da Vila
PORTUGUESE €€

(☑283 996 823; Largo do Rossio; mains €9-14; ☺lunch & dinner Tue-Sun) This cosy restaurant decorated in colourful tiles has been around for 26 years – it must be doing something right. It serves up sizzling grilled fish as well as *naco na pedra* (pork served on a hot stone) and other unusual plates.

Restaurante Choupana
SEAFOOD €€€

(☑283 996 643; Praia do Farol; dinner for 2 €55; ☺lunch & dinner) In a wooden building right on the beach, this rustic spot is renowned for its fresh grilled fish. You pay by the kilo here so you feel it in your hip pocket, but the quality is top-notch. You can just stop in for a drink on a pleasant little open-air terrace and watch the grill master in action.

Pica Tapa
CONTEMPORARY €€

(Travessa da Sociedade 1; mains €13-17; ☺lunch & dinner) This new eatery offers tapas and contemporary takes on traditional cuisine. Its modern setting makes a fun change from the usual farm tool–clad walls.

Conversas com Sal
CONTEMPORARY €€

(Travessa da Sociedade 1; mains €13-17; ☺11am-2am) Milfontes goes cosmopolitan at this hip abode, which screams 'chill out' and where anything goes: candelabra, surfboards, retro sofas, guitars, board games. And we haven't even got to the food, an esoteric range of *petiscos,* delicious desserts and tea infusions. Alentejan produce is used where possible.

⬤ Drinking

Café Azul
BAR

(Rossio 20) Always lively, whatever the time of year, even if the rest of the town is dead, this is a jovial bar with a pool table and lots of papier-mâché sharks, octopuses and squid hanging from the ceiling.

Discoteca SudWest
DISCO

(Estrada do Canal; ☺midnight-6am) In season this is the local disco nightspot, with a packed dance floor and diverse crowds.

ⓘ Information

Police station (☑283 998 391; Rua António Mantas)

Turismo (☑283 996 599; Rua António Mantas; ☺10am-6pm Dec-Feb, to 8pm Jun-Aug) Off the main road, opposite the police station. Buses stop 100m along the same road.

ⓘ Getting There & Away

Vila Nova has three bus connections daily on weekdays to/from Odemira (€3, 20 minutes). Rede Expressos buses runs daily from Lisbon (€14, four hours, three daily) via Setúbal (€12.70, three hours) and once daily from Portimão (€11.80, two hours), Aljezur (€9.40, 1¼ hours) and Lagos (€11.40, 1½ hours). The ticket agent for **Rede Expressos** (☑917 790 634; www.rede-expressos.pt) is located in Travessa dos Amadores.

Zambujeira do Mar

POP 850

Enchantingly wild beaches backed by rugged cliffs form the setting of this sleepy seaside village. The main street terminates at the cliff; paths lead to the attractive sands below. Quieter than Vila Nova, Zambujeira attracts a backpacker, surfy crowd, though in August the town is a party place and hosts the massive music fest, **Festa do Sudoeste**. The high-season crowds obscure Zambujeira's out-of-season charms: fresh fish in mom-and-pop restaurants, blustering cliff-top walks and a dramatic, empty coast.

A new 3km-long walking and biking path runs between Zambujeira do Mar and Porto de Pesca. At Porto de Pesca there are a couple of excellent eateries.

Sleeping & Eating

TOP CHOICE Herdade do Touril   RURAL INN €€€
(937 811 627; www.herdadedotouril.pt; r from €130; ❄ @) Four kilometres north of Zambujeira do Mar is this upmarket *quinta* building with the rooms and apartments of the fluffy-pillow variety. Some are located within the original building (built in 1826), others are converted farm cottages. The rustic and contemporary design of this tranquil place has an African safari-lodge feel – without the lions. Instead, storks nest in nearby cliffs (note, this area is not safe for children). There's a seawater pool, a buffet breakfast and free bikes. Good taste, good choice.

Parque de Campismo Zambujeira
    CAMPGROUND €
(283 961 172; www.campingzambujeira.com. sapo.pt; sites per adult/tent/car €5.50/6/5) Just 800m east of the village, this is a wooded,

well-appointed site. It's near the beach and also has bungalows for rent.

Residencial Mira Mar   GUEST HOUSE €€
(283 961 352; Rua Miramar; d €60) In Zambujeira's main street, next to a cafe of the same name. Rooms are basic, but tiled and large and light. Some have access to balconies. No English is spoken.

Anywhere in town offers a reasonable, if repetitive, feed. Your best bet is to head to Porto de Pesca where there are a couple of wonderful fishermen's tavernas serving up sublime seafood dishes.

Restaurante Sacas   SEAFOOD €€
(283 961 151; meals €10-15; ❧lunch & dinner Thu-Tue) The fish and shellfish make up for the car-park view.

A Barca Tranquitanas   SEAFOOD €€
(283 961 186; meals €10-15) A fun fishermen's cabana.

🛈 Information

There's a small **turismo** (283 961 144; ❧10am-6pm Tue-Sat) on the main street, which closes to traffic from July to mid-September.

🛈 Getting There & Away

In summer, Zambujeira has one daily connections with Vila Nova de Milfontes (€7.50, 45 minutes) and one daily connection with Lisbon (€15, 3¾ hours) through **Rede Expressos** (www.rede-expressos.pt) – buy tickets at the **bookshop** (Rua Miramar 9). Buses also run to Odemira (40 minutes) and Beja (three hours, one weekdays); for these you buy your ticket on the bus.

Estremadura & Ribatejo

Best Places to Stay

» Quinta de Rio Alcaide (p277)

» Casa das Marés (p257)

» Casa d'Óbidos (p261)

» Challet Fonte Nova (p268)

Best Places to Eat

» A Tasquinha (p266)

» Malagueta Afrodisiáca (p272)

» Mar à Vista (p254)

» O Saloio (p281)

» Vinho em Qualquer Circunstância (p271)

Why Go?

Stretching from the Rio Tejo to the Atlantic Ocean, Estremadura and Ribatejo constitute Portugal's heartland, but their central importance goes beyond geography. These fertile lands have formed the backdrop for every major chapter in Portuguese history, from the building of key fortified settlements in the 12th century to the release of Salazar's political prisoners in 1974. Two of medieval Portugal's critical battles for autonomy – against the Moors at Santarém and the Spaniards at Aljubarrota – were fought and won here, and remain commemorated in the magnificent monasteries at Alcobaça and Batalha, both Unesco World Heritage Sites. A third Unesco site, Tomar's Convento de Cristo, was long the stronghold of the venerable Knights Templar.

These days, the region draws visitors not only to these renowned monasteries, but also to its vineyards, beaches, castles and historic villages – and the new cathedral at Fátima, modern Portugal's premier religious shrine.

When to Go

Leiria

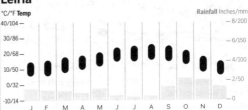

April & May Beat the summer heat with a springtime visit to the region's World Heritage Sites.

June & September For warm beaches at cooler prices, visit the coast in early summer or fall.

October World-class waves and competitions well up at Peniche, Ericeira and other prime surf spots.

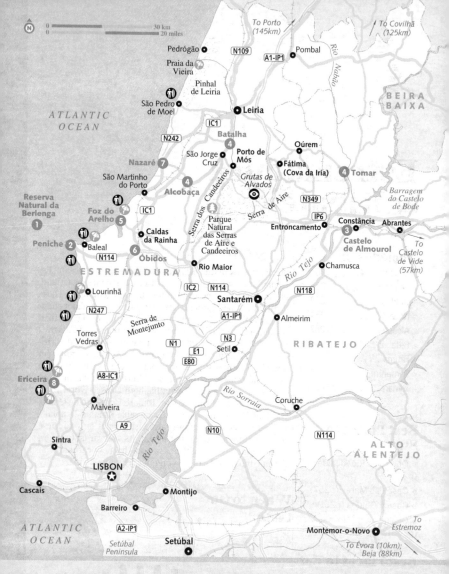

Estremadura & Ribatejo Highlights

① Cross the narrow arched bridge to the island fort on **Berlenga Grande** (p259)

② Watch the pros in action at Supertubos, the gnarliest spot in surfing **Peniche** (p256)

③ Survey the Rio Tejo from the crenellated heights of 12th-century **Castelo de Almourol** (p281)

④ Explore the region's three World Heritage Sites: the monasteries at **Batalha** (p269), **Alcobaça** (p267), and **Tomar** (p287)

⑤ Sail across the lagoon at sunset in **Foz do Arelho** (p263)

⑥ Sample *ginja* (cherry liqueur) in a chocolate cup

while strolling the flowery lanes and medieval walls of **Óbidos** (p259)

⑦ Catch Carnaval or New Year's fireworks at **Nazaré** (p264), one of Estremadura's most picturesque beach-party settings

⑧ Feast on the region's best seafood at **Ericeira** (p254)

ESTREMADURA

Running up the Atlantic coast from the mouth of the Rio Tejo almost to the Rio Mondego, Estremadura has long been a land of plenty, its rolling hills and valleys offering up some of Portugal's richest farmland. For proof, visit the elaborate kitchens that fattened up the monks at Alcobaça's extraordinary monastery. The coast is blessed with miles-long strands, which also catch some of Europe's best surf.

Estremadura earned its name the same way as Spain's Extremadura: for a time, it represented the furthest reaches of the Reconquista.

Ericeira

POP 6600

Picturesquely draped across sandstone cliffs above the blue Atlantic, sunny, whitewashed Ericeira is popular with *lisboêtas* seeking a quick weekend getaway. It's renowned as much for its spectacular ocean vistas as for its excellent seafood restaurants, where you choose your own freshly caught fish from the case and watch it grilled on the spot. Ericeira is also a mecca for surfers, who come here for the great waves and camaraderie of beaches like São Sebastião and Ribeira d'Ilhas – witness the amusing surfer-dude statue catching a wave just north of town!

The town's old centre is clustered around Praça da República, with the chaos of newer development spreading south and north.

☉ Sights & Activities

There are three beaches within walking distance of the *praça* (town square). **Praia do Sul**, also called Praia da Baleia, is easiest to get to and has a protected pool for children. **Praia do Norte** (also called Praia do Algodio) and **Praia de São Sebastião** lie to the north. Some 5km north is unspoilt **Praia de São Lourenço**, while **Praia Foz do Lizandro**, a big bite of beach backed by a small car park and a couple of restaurants, is 3km south.

The big attraction in Ericeira is **surfing**. Serious aficionados congregate 3km north of town at **Praia da Ribeira d'Ilhas**, a World Qualifying Series (WQS) site and frequent host to Portuguese national surfing championships; most amateurs will find the waves at the nearer Praia de São Sebastião challenging enough.

TOP CHOICE **Ribeira Surf Camp** SURFING LESSONS
(www.ribeirasurfcamp.com; Praia da Ribeira d'Ilhas; board rentals per day/week €20/95, 1-/5-lesson package €30/100) This highly recommended place runs surf classes and camps from its privileged location directly across from central Portugal's premier surfing beach. Weekly packages including breakfast, dinner and accommodation costs from €175 per week for campers, or €315 for bungalows.

🛏 Sleeping

Book ahead in July and August. During the low season, expect discounts of 30% to 50%.

TOP CHOICE **Blue Buddha** HOSTEL €
(☎910 658 849; www.bluebuddhahostel.com; Moinhos do Mar; dm €25, d with private/shared bathroom €68/50; @[☎]) Like having your very own beach house, this welcoming hostel in a condo development between Praia São Sebastião and the campground has a bright, spacious living room with couches, cable TV, DVD player and free internet, plus a guest kitchen and barbecue area. Multilingual proprietress Luzia is generous in sharing her knowledge of the local area, and her abundant attention to the smallest details really shows, including the comfortable mattresses and bold happy colours on the walls. Even the eight-person dorm downstairs manages to feel cheerful, thanks to the unusually wide spacing between the beds. Other services include surf lessons and surfboard and wetsuit storage. At time of research the owners were opening a second hostel right on the waterfront.

Residencial Vinnus GUEST HOUSE €€
(☎261 866 933; www.residencialvinnus.com; Rua Prudêncio Franco da Trindade 19; r without breakfast €60-70; ☎) Friendly, bright, modern and centrally located, Residencial Vinnus offers great value, with simple and comfortable whitewashed rooms, some with pretty, blue-tiled bathrooms. Triples with kitchenette are especially nice.

Hotel Vila Galé HOTEL €€€
(☎261 869 900; www.vilagale.pt; Largo dos Navegantes; d from €140, with ocean view from €168; [P][✳][@][☎][≋]) Proudly advertising itself as Europe's westernmost four-star hotel, the spiffy Vila Galé is an imposing edifice whose green mansard roof dominates Ericeira's skyline. Although its classic fin-de-siècle core has been rendered unrecognisable

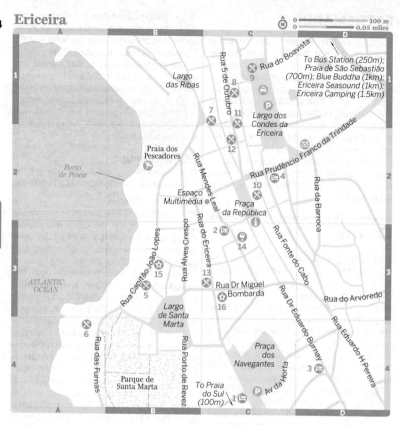

by recent remodelling, the hotel's modern amenities compensate for any lost historic charm, and they include comfortable bedrooms, a fine cliffside pool and panoramic vistas.

Residencial Fortunato
GUEST HOUSE €€
(☎261 862 829; www.pensaofortunato.com; Rua Dr Eduardo Burnay 45; d €55-70, with ocean view €65-80; ℗) A well-run, well-kept place with light, bright and all-white rooms. The best digs upstairs have small terraces with lovely sea views for €10 extra. Parking under the building costs €3 per night.

Ericeira Camping
CAMPGROUND €
(☎261 862 706; www.ericeiracamping.com; sites per adult/child/tent/car €6/3/6.50/6, cabins from €110) On the coastal highway 800m north of Praia de São Sebastião, this high-quality site has two-bedroom cabins, lots of trees, a playground, disabled access and a municipal swimming pool next door.

Pensão Gomes
GUEST HOUSE €
(☎/fax 261 863 619; Rua Mendes Leal 11; d €40-50) This old-fashioned boarding house, once featured in a popular Portuguese soap opera, has smallish rooms, creaky floors and homey touches including a friendly watchdog and patio full of potted plants.

✕ Eating

Seafood is one of Ericeira's big tourist draws, and restaurants are everywhere.

TOP CHOICE Mar à Vista
SEAFOOD €€€
(Largo das Ribas 16; mains €12-20; ⊙lunch & dinner Thu-Tue) Crustaceans of every kind are on full display at this hearty local place known for its shellfish. Order simple *doses* of oysters, clams or garlic shrimp accompanied by beer on tap, indulge in a *massada*, *feijoada*, *açorda* or *cataplana* for two, or choose your very own crab or lobster from the stainless steel

Ericeira

counter up front, where the chaotic mix of claws and legs is truly impressive.

Mar d'Areia · SEAFOOD €€
(Rua Fonte do Cabo; mains €8.50-13; ⊘lunch & dinner Tue-Sun) They keep the decor simple – blue-and-white checked tablecloths and tile designs of fish in nets – and let the excellent grilled fish do the talking at this locally popular, family-friendly seafood eatery adjacent to the Mercado Municipal.

Tik Tak · INTERNATIONAL €€
(Rua 5 Outubro 7; mains €9-13; ⊘dinner Mon-Thu, lunch & dinner Fri-Sun) On a picturesque corner in the pedestrian zone, Tik Tak draws a young, hip clientele with its well-stocked bar, open kitchen, jazzy music and atmospheric tables overhung by red ladybug lights on the cobblestones. The varied menu offers a nice break for those unmoved by Ericeira's seafood fetish; there are more fresh vegetables than you'll find at most places, plus abundant non-fishy options: serious carnivores will love the *parrilhada real* – a veritable cornucopia of grilled meat. The dessert menu is also wide-ranging, with everything from fresh fruit to apple pie.

Esplanada Furnas · SEAFOOD €€€
(Rua das Furnas; grilled fish per kg €35-48; ⊘lunch & dinner) As close to the sea as you can get without a boat, Furnas is all about

freshly caught fish and spectacular ocean views. They'll show you the catch of the day and then barbecue your choice on the spot. The per-kilogram price on the board covers the fish, plus all the accompaniments.

Restaurante Prim · INTERNATIONAL €€
(Rua 5 de Outubro 12; mains €8-13; ⊘lunch & dinner) This bright, contemporary place with outdoor seating dishes up high-quality, Brazilian-style grilled meats and potent *caipirinhas*. Side dishes such as rice and black beans make welcome alternatives to the ubiquitous Portuguese potato. Try the all-inclusive €8.50 midweek lunch special.

A Canastra · SEAFOOD €€
(Rua Capitão João Lopes 8A; grilled fish per kg €25-49; ⊘lunch & dinner) A Canastra specialises in grilled fish and *caldeiradas* (seafood stews). Eat inside or grab one of the alluring sidewalk tables overlooking the ocean just across the street.

Tik Tapas · TAPAS €
(Rua do Ericeira 15; tapas €3-7; ⊘dinner Mon-Thu, lunch & dinner Fri-Sun) Decked out with orange walls, colourful wooden tables and a glowing blue bar, this place sells meat, fish and vegie tapas, full meals, sangria and draught beer.

Pão da Vila · BAKERY €
(Praça da República 12; ⊘7am-10pm) Self-caterers can find tasty bread, pastries, croissants and mini-quiches at this bakery on the main square.

Mercado Municipal · MARKET €
(Largo dos Condes da Ericeira) Head through the giant M-shaped doorway for fresh produce and other foodstuffs at Ericeira's municipal market.

🍸 Drinking & Entertainment

At Praia Foz do Lizandro, south of town, a cluster of bars line the brand new boardwalk overlooking the beach and river mouth, perfect for a late afternoon drink.

Neptuno Pub · PUB
(Rua Mendes Leal 12; ⊘7.30pm-2am) This cosy neighbourhood pub features live fado (traditional, melancholic Portuguese singing) on Monday nights in summer.

Disco-Bar Ouriço · NIGHTCLUB
(Rua Caminho Novo 9; ⊘11pm-6am Fri & Sat, nightly Jul & Aug) One of Portugal's oldest discos caters to night owls of all ages, with a mix of pop, dance, oldies and disco standards.

Ponto Sete JAZZ BAR
(cnr Rua do Ericeira & Rua Dr Miguel Bombarda; ⊙8pm-2am) This laid-back little club specialises in jazz, blues and bossa nova.

Bar 121 BAR
(Rua Eduardo Burnay 9D; ⊙11pm-late Fri & Sat, nightly Jul & Aug) This underground DJ bar has a loyal following on summer nights. Depending on your taste, you may find it appealingly intimate or downright claustrophobic.

ⓘ Information

Espaço Multimédia (Biblioteca Municipal, Rua Mendes Leal; ⊙10am-1pm & 2-6pm Tue-Sat) Free internet in the ornate blue-and-white public library, one block west of Praça da República.

Police station (☑261 866 700; Largo Domingos Fernandes)

Post office (Rua do Paço 2; ⊙9am-12.30pm & 2.30-6pm Mon-Fri)

Turismo (tourist office; ☑261 863 122; turismo .ericeira@cm-mafra.pt; Rua Dr Eduardo Burnay 46; ⊙10am-6pm)

ⓘ Getting There & Away

BUS Mafrense (☑261 862 717; www.mafrense. pt) buses stop at the bus station 800m north of the *praça*, off the N247 highway. Buses arriving from Lisbon and Sintra will sometimes stop to let passengers off at other bus stops more convenient to the centre along the N247.

Connections to northern destinations such as Peniche and Coimbra are best made through Torres Vedras (€3.40, one hour, six on weekdays, three on Saturday and one on Sunday). Other destinations, with services roughly on the hour, are Lisbon–Campo Grande station (€5.40, 1¼ hours), Mafra (€1.95, 25 minutes) and Sintra (€2.95, 50 minutes).

CAR & MOTORCYCLE There is paid parking under Praça dos Navegantes and by the sea just north of the town centre near Praia de São Sebastião.

ⓘ Getting Around

Regular local buses to Torres Vedras go past Praia da Ribeira d'Ilhas (€1.10). For Praia Foz do Lizandro (€0.80), take any Sintra-bound bus to a stop on the N247 above the beach.

You can rent bicycles from **Ericeira Seasound Guest House** (☑965 100 883; www. ericeiraseasound.com; Moinhos do Mar 3; per day/week €15/70), inland from the main road just north of the Praia de São Sebastião traffic circle. There's a taxi stand in Largo dos Condes da Ericeira.

Peniche
POP 16,000

Popular for its nearby surf beaches and also as a jumping-off point for the beautiful Ilhas Berlengas nature reserve, the coastal city of Peniche remains a working port, giving it a slightly grittier and more 'lived-in' feel than its beach-resort neighbours. The town's walled historic centre makes for pleasant strolling, and the seaside fort where Salazar's regime detained political prisoners is a must-see for anyone with an interest in Portuguese history. Outdoors enthusiasts will love the beaches east of town, where lessons and rentals for every sport under the sun are available.

From the bus station, it's a 10-minute walk west to the historic centre. Cross the Ponte Velha (Old Bridge) into the walled town, then turn left on Rua Alexandre Herculano towards the *turismo*. The fort, harbour and Av do Mar – where you'll find most of the seafood restaurants – are just a short distance further south. Passenger boats for Ilha Berlenga depart from the harbour.

◎ Sights

FREE **Fortaleza** FORT
(⊙9am-12.30pm & 2-5.30pm Tue-Fri, from 10am Sat & Sun) Dominating the southern end of the peninsula, Peniche's imposing 16th-century fortress was in military use as late as the 1970s, when it was converted into a temporary home for refugees from the newly independent African colonies.

Twenty years earlier it served as one of dictator Salazar's infamous jails for political prisoners. By the entrance, where prisoners once received visitors – the stark booths with their glass partitions are all preserved – is the **Núcleo-Resistência**, a grim but fascinating display about those times. It includes the flimsy leaflets of the Resistance; educational materials for schools where pupils would learn phrases such as 'Viva Salazar!'; prisoners' poignant, beautifully illustrated letters to their children; and some secret letters, written in incredibly small handwriting.

Museu Municipal MUSEUM
(admission €1.50; ⊙9am-12.30pm & 2-5.30pm Tue-Fri, from 10am Sat & Sun) Housed in another part of the fort, this museum's most striking features are the desolate prison yard outside, and the chilling, sinister interrogation chambers and cells on the top

floor, some used for solitary confinement. Floors below this contain a municipal mishmash, from Roman archaeological artefacts to shipwreck finds.

Baleal
BEACH

About 5km to the northeast of Peniche is this scenic island-village, connected to the mainland village of Casais do Baleal by a causeway. The fantastic sweep of sandy beach here offers some fine surfing. Surf schools dot the sands, as do several bar-restaurants.

Escola de Rendas de Bilros
LACE MAKING

(⊙9am-12.30pm & 2-5.30pm Mon-Fri) At this school attached to Peniche's *turismo* building, you can watch the nimble (and chatty) ladies in action as the chaos of their bobbins produces some of the world's most exquisite lace.

☆ Activities

Surfing

Long renowned as a prime surfing destination, Peniche burnished its celebrity status in 2009 and 2010 when **Supertubos** beach, south of town, was selected as a stop on the ASP World Tour, the most prestigious international circuit of competitive surfing.

Meanwhile, surfers of all abilities continue to sing the praises of **Baleal**, a paradise of challenging but, above all, consistent waves that make it an ideal learners' beach. Depending on the season, surf camps at Baleal charge from €222 to €495 for a week of classes, including equipment and shared self-catering lodging. You can also take individual two-hour classes (€50) and rent boards and wetsuits (from €25/119 per day/week). There are a zillion surf operations; well-established ones include **Baleal Surfcamp** (www.baleal surfcamp.com), **Maximum Surfcamp** (www. maximumsurfcamp.com) and **Peniche Surfcamp** (www.penichesurfcamp.com).

Diving

There are good opportunities for diving around Peniche, especially at Berlenga. Expect to pay about €60 to €70 (less around Peniche) for two dives with **Acuasuboeste** (www.acuasuboeste.com; Porto de Pesca) or **Haliotis** (www.haliotis.pt; Av Monsenhor Bastos).

Kitesurfing

Kitesurfing is big in Peniche. On the far side of high dunes about 500m east of the walled town, **Peniche Kite & Surf Center** (www.penichekitecenter.com) offers lessons with equipment for €70.

☞ Tours

From the harbourfront kiosks in Largo da Ribeira, an ever-increasing number of companies offer day tours to Berlenga (see Getting There and Away under the Reserva Natural da Berlenga section), plus other activities such as fishing.

Associação de Operadores Marítimo-Turística
BOAT TOURS

(☑262 789 997; associacaopescadesportiva@ gmail.com) Runs privately organised cruises on demand throughout the year, ranging from €7.50 per person for a trip to Cabo Carvoeiro, to €50 per person to the Farilhões, the twin outer islands of the Berlenga chain. They also organise fishing trips: a full-day excursion for up to 11 people, including licences, bait and equipment costs €550; half-day excursions on a smaller boat cost €35 per person (maximum 6 passengers).

Nautipesca
FISHING

(www.nautipesca.com.pt) Organises similarly priced fishing trips from their kiosk at the harbour.

⌂ Sleeping

Prices quoted below are for high season; expect discounts of up to 30% outside July and August. Surfers can also find cheap lodging at the many surf camps in Baleal.

TOP CHOICE Casa das Marés
B&B €€

(☑262 769 255/200/371; www.casadas mares2.com, www.casadasmares1.com; Praia do Baleal; d €80; ☎) At the picturesque, wind-swept tip of Baleal stands one of the area's most unique accommodation options. Three sisters inherited this imposing house from their parents and divided it into three parts – each of which now serves as its own little B&B. The breezy, inviting rooms all have great sea views, the downstairs sitting areas are extremely cosy and the entire place is loaded with character. Worth reserving ahead.

Peniche Hostel
HOSTEL €

(☑969 008 689; www.penichehostel.com; Rua Arquitecto Paulino Montês 6; dm/d €20/45; @☎) This cosy little hostel, only steps from the tourist office and a five-minute walk from the bus station, has colourfully decorated and breezy rooms with tall windows overlooking the town wall. The friendly owners make you feel at home immediately, as do the comfortable common areas and small sundeck. Surfboards and bikes are available for hire, and there's an attached surf school.

Residencial Maciel HOTEL €
(☑262 784 685; www.residencial-maciel.com; Rua José Estevão 38; d €45-55; ☎) Recently spiffed up with new paint, blinds and soundproof windows to go with its polished wood floors and carpeted hallways, Maciel is a cut above the other downtown sleeping options. The annexe around the corner costs €10 less.

Residencial Rimavier GUEST HOUSE €
(☑262 789 459; www.rimavier.com; Rua Castilho 6; s/d €30/40) This immaculate *pensão* (guest house) – run by the helpful family in the souvenir shop downstairs – has small but spruce rooms, nautically themed linens and hallways decorated with lovely tile paintings of Peniche.

Parque de Campismo Peniche Praia
CAMPGROUND €
(☑262 783 460; www.penichepraia.pt; Estrada Marginal Norte; sites per adult/child//tent/car €3.60/1.80/3.60/3.20; ☎▨) On the high, windy, north side of the peninsula, 1.7km from town and the beach, and 2km from Cabo Carvoeiro, this site has decent facilities but lacks shade.

Eating

Restaurante A Sardinha SEAFOOD €€
(Rua Vasco da Gama 81; mains €6.50-12.50; ☉lunch & dinner) This simple place on a narrow street parallel to Largo da Ribeira does a roaring trade with locals and tourists alike. The fixed-price menu, featuring soup, bread, main course, dessert, wine and coffee, is a good deal at €9.50.

Restaurante Popular SEAFOOD €€
(Largo da Ribeira 40; mains €12-17; ☉lunch & dinner Tue-Sun) This harbourside spot serves up delicious, freshly caught fish grilled before your eyes.

Hó Amaral PORTUGUESE €€
(Rua Dr Francisco Seia 7; mains €8-14; ☉lunch & dinner Fri-Wed) Still going strong after 35 years, this snug wood-panelled eatery reliably does some of the best seafood in Peniche.

Katekero II SEAFOOD €€
(Av do Mar 68-70; mains €6.50-12; ☉lunch & dinner Wed-Mon) One of several restaurants forming a long strip near the harbour, this place serves good seafood without an excessive price tag.

Drinking & Entertainment

The area around Igreja de São Pedro is the old town's drinking hub (think four walls, cold beer and a home stereo system). For nightlife, you're really better off in Baleal, where you'll find several laid-back surfer bars right on the beach. Good choices include the rather stylish wood-and-glass **Danau Bar**, offering hot snacks, ocean views and sometimes live music on weekends, and **Bruno's Bar**, whose beach party atmosphere revolves around regular DJ gigs ranging from reggae to rock, world music to hip hop.

ℹ Information

Espaço Internet (Rua Dr João de Matos Bilhau; ☉10am-1pm & 3-10pm Mon-Sat, 10am-noon & 3-8pm Sun) Free internet access.

Hospital (☑262 780 900; Rua General Humberto Delgado) About 600m northwest of the market.

Police station (☑262 790 310; Rua Heróis Ultramar) About 400m west of the market.

Post office (Rua Arquitecto Paulino Montês 53)

Turismo (☑262 789 571; turismo@cm-peniche.pt; ☉9.30am-1pm & 2-5.30pm) Main branch in the public garden alongside Rua Alexandre Herculano, plus a second branch on the waterfront at Praia da Gamboa, halfway between Baleal and Cabo Carvoeiro.

ℹ Getting There & Away

BUS Peniche's **bus station** (☑968 903 861) is located 400m northeast of the *turismo* (cross the Ponte Velha connecting the town to the isthmus). It's served by **Rodotejo** (www.rodotejo.pt) and **Rede Expressos** (www.rede-expressos.pt). Destinations include Coimbra (€13, 2¾ hours, three daily), Leiria (€11.80, two hours, three daily), Lisbon (€8.20, 1½ hours, every one to two hours) and Óbidos (€2.75, 40 minutes).

CAR & MOTORCYCLE Driving into Peniche, the main highway (N114/IP6) reaches a roundabout shortly before town, where you can bear left towards the centre, right for Baleal and the eastern beaches, or straight for 3km along the northern cliffs to Cabo Carvoeiro and its lighthouse. Most days you can find ample free parking on the road that runs along the harbour.

ℹ Getting Around

Local buses connect Peniche with Baleal (€1.50, 10 minutes) during the week, but service is spotty on weekends outside summer.

Cycling is a great way to get to the eastern beaches. Bikes can be rented from **Duas Rodas** (☑262 781 385; Rua da Ponte Velha; per day €5; ⊙9am-1pm & 3-7pm Mon-Fri) near the bus station.

Reserva Natural da Berlenga

Sitting about 10km offshore from Peniche, Berlenga Grande is a spectacular, rocky and remote island, with twisting, shocked-rock formations and gaping caverns. It's the only island of the Berlenga archipelago you can visit – the group consists of three tiny islands surrounded by clear, calm, dark-blue waters full of shipwrecks that are great for snorkelling and diving.

In the 16th century Berlenga Grande was home to a monastery, but now the most famous inhabitants are thousands of nesting sea birds, especially guillemots. The birds take priority over human visitors: the only development that has been allowed includes housing for a small fishing community, a lighthouse, a shop and a restaurant-*pensão*. You can camp here – book at the *turismo* in Peniche. Paths are clearly marked to stop day trippers trespassing on the birds' domain.

Linked to the island by a narrow causeway is the 17th-century Forte de São João Baptista, now one of the country's most dramatic (but barren) hostels.

🛌 Sleeping & Eating

If you want to sleep on the island, you'll need to book well ahead. The two park facilities can only be reserved starting in May. Most places are already booked solid by the end of May.

There's a small grocery store on the island for self-catering.

Forte de São João Baptista Hostel
HOSTEL €
(☑912 631 426; berlengareservasforte@gmail. com; d/tr/q €28/42/56; ⊙Jun-Sep) This was once a fine historic inn, but was abandoned for many years – and you can feel it. It's a dramatic but dead-basic hostel, with limited water supply and antiquated bathrooms; you need to bring your own sleeping bag and cooking equipment, although there is a small shop and a bar. Advance payment by wire transfer is required. Bring a torch, as the generator goes off at midnight.

Berlenga Campground
CAMPGROUND €
(☑262 789 571; turismo@cm-peniche.pt; 2-/3-/4-person tent sites €10/14.50/19; ⊙May-Sep) This simple camping area is just above a pretty beach near the boat dock; book in advance at the Peniche *turismo*.

Mar e Sol
HOTEL, RESTAURANT €€
(☑919 543 105; www.restaurantemaresol.com; d/q €80/130; ⊙mid-Apr-Oct) The decent, if simple, rooms at Mar e Sol would seem overpriced anywhere else, but when you consider the location just a few steps above Berlenga's boat dock and directly adjacent to its only restaurant, the place starts looking a bit more appealing.

ℹ️ Getting There & Away

Viamar (☑262 785 646; www.viamar-berlenga. com; round-trip adult/child €18/10; ⊙20 May-15 Sep) is the longest established of several harbourside outfits, all making the 40-minute trip to the island on roughly the same schedule and for the same round-trip fare. Viamar sails three times daily during July and August, at 9.30am, 11.30am and 5.30pm, returning at 10.30am, 4.30pm and 6.30pm. During the remainder of the season there's one sailing daily, departing at 10am, returning at 4.30pm. Tickets tend to sell out quickly in summer, as only 300 visitors are allowed each day. All sailings are weather-dependent. Some companies also offer add-ons such as a guided hike on the island (per person €2 extra) or a sea cave visit (€3.50 extra).

If you're prone to seasickness, choose your day carefully – the crossing to Berlenga can be rough.

Óbidos

POP 3100 / ELEV 80M

Surrounded by a classic crenellated wall, Óbidos' gorgeous historic centre is a labyrinth of cobblestoned streets and flower-bedecked, whitewashed houses livened up with dashes of vivid yellow and blue paint. It's a delightful place to pass an afternoon, but there are plenty of reasons to stay overnight, including atmospheric medieval bars and a hilltop castle now converted into one of Portugal's most luxurious *pousadas* (up-market inns).

It's especially enjoyable to visit during one of the town's festivals – celebrating everything from opera to chocolate to Óbidos' medieval heritage – when you'll find yourself rubbing shoulders with Portuguese tourists as much as those from other countries.

Hill-town aficionados looking to savour Óbidos' 'lost in time' qualities may find the nearby superhighway (in plain view just east of town) and the copious souvenir shops lining the main street a bit jarring. For a more bucolic approach, visitors can arrive at the sleepy Óbidos train station 2km west of town and walk up the zig-zagging country lanes to the town gate, through a rural landscape more in keeping with the town's medieval flavour.

The town's main gate, Porta da Vila, leads directly into the main street, Rua Direita.

History

When Dom Dinis first showed Óbidos to his wife Dona Isabel in 1228, it must have already been a pretty sight, because she fell instantly in love with the place. The king decided to make the town a wedding gift to his queen, initiating a royal tradition that lasted until the 19th century.

Any grace it had in 1228 must be credited to the Moors, who had laid out the streets and had only recently abandoned the strategic heights. The Moors had chased out the Visigoths, who in turn had evicted the Romans, who also had a fortress here.

Until the 15th century Óbidos overlooked the sea; the bay gradually silted up, leaving the town landlocked.

⊙ Sights

Castelo, Walls & Aqueduct　　HISTORICAL SITE
You can walk around the unprotected **muro** (wall) for uplifting, if nail-biting, views over the town and surrounding countryside. The walls date from the time of the Moors (later restored), but the **castelo** (castle) itself is one of Dom Dinis' 13th-century creations. It's a stern edifice, with lots of towers, battlements and big gates. Converted into a palace in the 16th century, it's now a deluxe *pousada*.

The **aqueduct**, southeast of the main gate, dates from the 16th century and is 3km long.

Igreja de Santa Maria　　CHURCH
(Praça de Santa Maria; ⊙9.30am-12.30pm & 2.30-7pm) The town's elegant main church, near the northern end of Rua Direita, stands on the foundations of a Visigothic temple later converted into a mosque. Begun in the 12th century but restored several times since, it dates mostly from the Renaissance. It had its 15 minutes of fame in 1444 when 10-year-old Afonso V married his eight-year-old cousin Isabel here.

Inside is a wonderful painted ceiling and walls done up in beautiful blue-and-white 17th-century *azulejos* (hand-painted tiles). Paintings by the renowned 17th-century painter Josefa de Óbidos are to the right of the altar. There's a fine 16th-century Renaissance tomb on the left, probably carved by the French sculptor Nicolas Chanterène.

Museu Municipal　　MUSEUM
(Solar da Praça de Santa Maria; admission €1.50; ⊙10am-1pm & 2-6pm) Located in an 18th-century manor house just next to Igreja de Santa Maria, the town's museum houses a small collection of paintings spanning sev-

JOSEFA DE ÓBIDOS

In an age when the only acceptable vocations for a woman were nun, or wife and mother, Josefa de Óbidos managed to establish herself not just as one of 17th-century Portugal's best artists but also as one of its most respected. The daughter of minor Portuguese painter Baltazar Gomes Figueira, she was born in Seville but returned to Portugal as a child after the country regained its independence from Spain. She studied at the Augustine Convento de Santa Ana but left the convent and eventually settled in Óbidos, where she remained famously chaste and religious until her death in 1684.

A number of factors enabled Josefa to carve out her unlikely public position. First, her father was a painter, so she was able to receive an education within her home – the only 'respectable' place a woman might have received training. Second, she allied herself closely with the church without ever taking vows. In this way, she never subjected her talents to the whims of a nay-saying mother superior, yet still could appear as a humble representative of the Mother Church rather than an independent woman hawking her own works. Finally, there was the sheer appeal of her paintings. Often they ignore established iconography in favour of a certain domestic sweetness, but at the same time they combine a masterful use of colour and form.

Óbidos goes crazy for chocolate during the annual **Festival Internacional do Chocolate** (www.festivalchocolate.cm-obidos.pt). This scrumptiously decadent 12-day celebration draws over 200,000 people each March with events for every age and taste. There's an international chocolate recipe contest, a chocolate-themed fashion show, the Portuguese Chocolatier of the Year awards, a chocolate sculpture exhibit and even a kids' playhouse made entirely of chocolate (sorry, older kids, only the youngest toddlers get to taste the merchandise!).

If your trip to Óbidos doesn't coincide with the festival, no worries. A gaggle of shops open year-round along Óbidos' main street will be happy to ease your pain with a chocolate cup full of *ginja* (the local cherry liqueur).

eral centuries. The highlight is a haunting portrait by Josefa de Óbidos, *Faustino das Neves* (1670), remarkable for its dramatic use of light and shade.

✦ Festivals & Events

Festival Internacional do Chocolate FOOD
Celebrates the sweet temptation of the cocoa bean for almost two weeks in early March.

Semana Santa RELIGIOUS
In March or April, Holy Week (the week leading up to Easter Sunday) is celebrated with religious re-enactments and processions.

Mercado Medieval MEDIEVAL FAIR
In July, this two-week medieval fair – held inside the castle grounds and below the town's western wall – includes live entertainment, jousting matches, plenty of grog and pigs roasting on spits, and the chance to try your hand at scaling the town walls with the help of a harness and rope. Dress in medieval attire and the €7 admission fee is waived.

Festival de Ópera de Óbidos OPERA
Since 2005, this August festival has brought opera to the masses, staging open-air performances at Óbidos' castle and the vast lagoon northwest of town.

🛏 Sleeping

Several places around town rent out private rooms; look for signs, or pick up a comprehensive list of accommodations at the tourist office.

Casa d'Óbidos RURAL INN €€
TOP CHOICE
(☎262 950 924; www.casadobidos.com; Quinta de São José; s/d €75/90, 2-/4-/6-person apt without breakfast €90/140/175; P 🛜 🌊) In a whitewashed, 19th-century villa at the

foot of the old town, this delightful place is clearly a labour of love for its friendly owners. It features spacious, breezy rooms with good new bathrooms and period furnishings, plus tennis courts, a swimming pool and lovely grounds with sweeping views of Óbidos' bristling walls and towers. Home-raised honey and fruit are served at breakfast, and trails lead through the orchards up to town.

Casas de São Thiago B&B €€
(☎262 959 587; www.casas-sthiago.com; Largo de São Thiago; s/d €65/80; P 🛜) This ridiculously charming labyrinth of snug, 18th-century rooms and tiled, flower-filled courtyards in the shadow of the castle has its own wine cellar and billiards room. Rooms vary, but all offer standard midrange comforts, plus some nice antique touches.

Pousada do Castelo INN €€€
(☎262 955 080; www.pousadas.pt; d/ste from €210/284; 🌡 🛜) One of Portugal's best *pousadas* occupies a charming convent hidden within the town's forbidding 13th-century castle. The whitewashed rooms are mostly done up with sleek contemporary furnishings. Book well in advance for the split-level rooms in the two castle towers – especially room 203, which is popular with honeymooners.

ÓbidoSol GUEST HOUSE €
(☎262 959 188, 914 283 155; Rua Direita 40; d €40-50) This centrally located, neatly kept old town house, with cosy and comfortable rooms surrounding a snug living room, is a good option for the budget-minded. Best are the two east-facing rooms, with views across town to the adjacent hills. Less expensive rooms have their own private bathrooms down the hall. Avoid the darker units on the ground floor.

Casa das Senhoras Rainhas INN €€€

(📞262 955 360; www.senhorasrainhas.com; Rua Padre Nunes Tavares 6; s/d €166/179; ❀📶) This classy inn with a flowery courtyard directly abutting the town walls is more luxurious than most lodgings in the historic centre and has an excellent restaurant attached.

Casa do Relógio GUEST HOUSE €€

(📞262 958 554; www.casadorelogio.com; Rua da Graça 12; s/d/tr €45/70/90; 📶) Just east of the town walls, this 18th-century house (named for a nearby sundial) has eight smallish, but spotless, traditionally furnished rooms with handsome tile floors, plus a pretty shared terrace.

✗ Eating & Drinking

In touristy Óbidos, restaurants are generally long on atmosphere but short on value. Visitors with limited funds can snack at one of the town's medieval bars. The larger inns, including the *pousada,* have good, if pricey, dining rooms.

Bar Lagar da Mouraria BAR €

(Rua da Mouraria; snacks €3-8; ⊙11am-2am) Enjoy the simple menu of tapas, cheese, sausage, sandwiches or fish soup – plus a few daily specials (€8 to €10) – in this lovely traditional bar behind the post office. It's housed in a former winery, with beamed ceiling, a flagstone floor and seats around a massive old winepress.

Cozinha das Rainhas

CONTEMPORARY PORTUGUESE €€€

(Rua Padre Nunes Tavares 6; mains €14-22; ⊙lunch & dinner) Attached to the Casa das Senhoras Rainhas hotel, this elegant restaurant offers some of the finest dining in Óbidos, with main courses like *bacalhau das rainhas* (codfish in a *fines herbes* crust with extra-virgin olive oil) and desserts like *dueto de chocolate* (white and dark chocolate mousse scented with orange and lime peel).

Alcaide PORTUGUESE €€

(Rua Direita 60; mains €12-17; ⊙lunch & dinner Thu-Tue) This upstairs restaurant with windows overlooking the town features creative dishes such as *requinte de bacalhau* (saltcod with cheese, chestnuts and apples).

ⓘ Information

Espaço Internet (Rua Direita 107; ⊙10am-7pm Mon-Fri, 11.30am-6.30pm Sat & Sun) Free internet access.

Post office (Praça de Santa Maria; ⊙9am-12.30pm & 2.30-6pm Mon-Fri)

Turismo (📞262 959 231; posto.turismo@cm-obidos.pt; ⊙9.30am-7.30pm) Just outside Porta da Vila near the bus stop. Helpful multilingual staff offer town brochures and maps in four languages. Bike rentals (per day/half day €10/5) also available.

ⓘ Getting There & Away

BUS Buses stop on the main road just outside Porta da Vila. There are frequent departures for Caldas da Rainha (€1.50, 15 minutes) and Peniche (€2.75, 45 minutes). There are a dozen-plus weekday runs to Lisbon (€6.75, 65 minutes), plus five on Saturday and Sunday.

CAR & MOTORCYCLE There is a fee-charging car park just outside the gate, while the one just across the road is free.

TRAIN Óbidos' train station has at least six daily trains to Lisbon (€7.30, 2½ hours) via connections at Mira Sintra-Meleças station on the suburban Lisbon line. The station is located at the foot of the castle end of town. It's rather a hoof uphill.

Caldas da Rainha

POP 25,000 / ELEV 90M

Now that its sulphurous waters are restricted to patients at the local hospital, dowdy historic spa town Caldas da Rainha is of limited interest to the traveller, though its old centre – particularly the leafy Parque Dom Carlos I – is pleasant enough. It's also a convenient transport hub for the nearby beaches of Foz do Arelho and São Martinho do Porto.

If ceramics are your bag, the **Museu de Cerâmica** (📞262 840 280; mceramica@imc-ip.pt; Rua Ilídio Amado; admission €2, 10am-12.30pm Sun free; ⊙10am-12.30pm & 2-5pm Tue-Sun) makes an interesting stop. In a delightful, 19th-century holiday mansion, it features fantastic works by native son Rafael Bordalo Pinheiro, whose intricate creations often involve effusions of flora and fauna. Most memorable are the fabulous jars and bowls encrusted with animals, lobsters and snakes.

Good-value accommodation is in short and dwindling supply; for a list of options, check the **turismo** (📞262 839 700; turismo@cm-caldas-rainha.pt; ⊙9am-7pm Mon-Fri, 10am-1pm & 3-7pm Sat & Sun) on Praça 25 de Abril, a block from the bus station and five blocks east of the train station.

Rápida Verde buses run frequently to Lisbon (€7.90, 1¼ hours) and twice daily to

Alcobaça (€3.75, 30 minutes). Regular buses also run to/from Óbidos (€1.50, 15 minutes), Peniche (€3.15, 45 minutes), Nazaré (€3.15, 45 minutes) and Leiria (€8, 50 minutes).

Four to six regional trains run daily to/from Óbidos (€1.10, four minutes), continuing to Lisbon (€7.65, 2½ hours) via connections at Mira Sintra-Meleças station on the suburban Lisbon line.

Foz do Arelho

POP 1300

With a vast, lovely beach backed by a lagoon ideal for windsurfing, Foz do Arelho remains remarkably undeveloped. It makes a fine place to laze in the sun, and outside July and August it'll often be just you and the local fishermen.

Escola de Vela da Lagoa (www.escoladeveladalagoa.com) rents out sailboards (€14 to €22 per hour), sailboats (€16 per hour), kayaks (€8 per hour) and catamarans (€20 to €30 per hour). The school also provides private windsurfing and sailing lessons (two hours, €60 each) and group kayak lessons (€14 per person for a three-hour session), and houses a bar serving snacks and drinks with nice views of the lagoon. From the village, turn left on the road that follows the lagoon's inland edge and continue 2.5km.

Sleeping

Hotel Penedo Furado   HOTEL €€
(262 979 610; www.hotelpenedofurado.com; Rua dos Camarções 3; s/d €50/70; P) Situated in the village, this smart, efficient and modern hotel offers bright, newly remodelled rooms with tiled floors, some with verandahs and distant lagoon views.

O Facho   HOTEL €€
(262 979 110; ofachoguesthouse@hotmail.com; Rua Francisco Almeida Grandela; rear-view/ocean-view d €65/85) This funky 100-year-old waterfront hotel has seen better days, but still retains some of its historic character, including high ceilings, creaky wooden floors, and checkerboard tiles and tubs in some bathrooms. The best rooms are the front-facing ones on the 2nd floor, with terrific ocean views.

Parque de Campismo Foz do Arelho
                                    CAMPGROUND €
(262 978 683; infofozarelho@orbitur.pt; sites per adult/child/tent/car €5.40/2.70/6.10/5.30,

4-person cabins €89;) This good, shady camp-site, 2km from the beach, is run by Orbitur. It has a restaurant, a bar, laundry facilities and a market.

Eating & Drinking

Cabana do Pescador   SEAFOOD €€€
(Av do Mar; mains €13-23) The service may be a bit lackadaisical, but this renowned restaurant with its ocean-view terrace serves excellent meals featuring every imaginable form of sea life.

Café Caravela   PUB €
(Rua Francisco Almeida Grandela 89; pub food €3-7) With its Guinness sign shining like a beacon in the night, this pink-hued Irish pub opened in the heart of the village in 2010. Guinness and Kilkenny on tap pair up nicely with sandwiches, curry, chilli and homemade burgers, and there's a big-screen TV for football matches.

Cais da Praia   BAR-CAFE €€
(Av do Mar; mains €9.50-11.50; lunch & dinner) The trendiest of Foz do Arelho's waterfront joints, Cais da Praia serves everything from sandwiches to salads to full meals, but the real draws are the great lagoon views and a drinks list that just won't quit.

Getting There & Away

Buses connect Foz do Arelho with Caldas da Rainha (€1.85, 20 minutes, nine daily, fewer on weekends).

São Martinho do Porto

POP 2700

Families seeking a safe place for their kids to swim can't do much better than São Martinho do Porto. The town's moon-shaped bay is ringed by sandy beaches, and cradled between twin headlands that shield it from the Atlantic's notorious undertow. Midrise development isn't making the place any more charming, but São Martinho still has a small centre of cobbled streets and open-air seafood restaurants to remind you of quieter days.

Sleeping & Eating

Palace do Capitão   B&B €€€
(262 985 150; www.palacecapitao.com; Rua Capitão Jaime Pinto 6; d €100-140, ste €180;) This perfectly preserved, 19th-century sea captain's home directly across from the beach is the town's only place of

distinction, with much of its original Victoriana still intact. The upstairs suite (room 6) has its own sun terrace, accessed by a whimsical spiral staircase. Afternoon tea, complete with scones, is served downstairs at 5pm daily (€5 extra).

Residencial Atlântica HOTEL **€€**
(📞262 980 151; www.residencial-atlantica.com; Rua Miguel Bombarda 6; s/d €55/80; @🛜) In a modern building, Residencial Atlântica has spotless white-and-blue rooms with tiled floors to match. Downstairs, the affiliated Restaurante Carvalho serves simple but good fish and meat dishes accompanied by a wider variety of vegetables than you'll find in most Portuguese restaurants. Room rates drop dramatically outside July and August.

Colina do Sol CAMPGROUND **€**
(📞262 989 764; www.colinadosol.net; sites per adult/child/tent/car €4.50/2.30/4.50/4; 🐕) This well-equipped, friendly camp site is 2km north of town, and about the same distance from the beach, with disabled access, a children's playground, a pool and some sections shaded by pine trees.

ℹ️ Information

The **turismo** (📞262 989 110; pit-smporto@rt-leiriafatima.pt; Rua Vasco da Gama; ⊙10am-1pm & 3-7pm) is in the middle of the little town, a block back from the beach.

ℹ️ Getting There & Away

The train station is about 700m southeast of the centre. Buses stop on Rua Conde de Avelar, a block inland from the waterfront.

BUS Rede Expressos runs at least five buses daily to/from Lisbon (€10, 1½ hours).

CAR & MOTORCYCLE Street parking is plentiful, though it gets competitive on summer weekends.

TRAIN There are five daily trains northbound to Leiria (€3.15, 45 minutes) and southbound to Caldas da Rainha (€1.30, 15 minutes), with onward connections in both directions.

Nazaré
POP 15,000

With a warren of narrow, cobbled lanes running down to a wide, cliff-backed beach, Nazaré is Estremadura's most picturesque coastal resort. The sands are packed wall-to-wall with multicoloured umbrellas in July and August, but the party atmosphere isn't limited to the summer beach scene – Nazaré is one of Portugal's top draws for New Year's Eve and Carnaval celebrations as well.

The town centre is jammed with seafood restaurants, bars and local women in traditional dress hawking rooms for rent, especially near seafront Av da República. To escape the crowds and get a different perspective on the town, take the funicular up to Promontório do Sítio, where picture-postcard coastal views unfold from the cliff tops.

◉ Sights

Until the 18th century the sea covered the present-day site of Nazaré; locals lived inland at **Promontório do Sítio**, the cliff-top area 110m above the beach. Today this promontory is popular for its tremendous views and, among Portuguese devotees, its mystical associations. According to legend it was here that a long-lost statue of the Virgin, brought back from Nazareth in the 4th century, was finally rediscovered in the 18th century.

Even more famously, it's said the Virgin appeared here on a foggy day in 1182. Local nobleman Dom Fuas Roupinho was in pursuit of a deer when the animal disappeared off the edge of the Sítio precipice. Dom Fuas cried out to the Virgin for help and his horse miraculously stopped right at the cliff's edge.

Dom Fuas built the small **Hermida da Memória** chapel on the edge of the belvedere to commemorate the event. It was later visited by a number of VIP pilgrims, including Vasco da Gama. The nearby 17th-century baroque **Igreja de Nossa Senhora da Nazaré** replaced an earlier church, and is decorated with attractive Dutch *azulejos*.

From Rua do Elevador, north of the *turismo*, an **ascensor** (funicular; adult/child €0.90/0.65; ⊙7.15am-9.30pm every 15 min, 9.30pm-midnight every 30 min) climbs up the hill to Promontório do Sítio.

✨ Festivals & Events

Carnaval MARDI GRAS
One of Portugal's brashest Mardi Gras celebrations, with lots of costumed parades and general irreverence.

Arte Xávega TRADITIONAL FISHING
On Saturday afternoons in May and June, traditional fishing methods are on display along Nazaré's waterfront.

FISHING, THE OLD-FASHIONED WAY

Long gone are Nazaré's days as a traditional fishing village, but tourists can still get a taste of the old ways on Saturdays throughout May and June during the **Arte Xávega** festival. In the morning, locals set off in pointy-prowed *xávega* boats to lay out the gigantic nets typical of this stretch of coast, a process that takes many hours. Then at 4pm, townspeople gather on the beach, men in berets and women in shawls and kerchiefs, and begin to draw the nets in – sometimes with the help of teams of oxen. Watching is colourful enough, but adventurous tourists are also welcome to help haul the ropes. If you fancy frying up your own dinner, bring your wallet – fish is sold on the spot as soon as it comes out of the net!

Festa do Mar   RELIGIOUS

Held every year on the first weekend in May, this festival features fireworks at midnight, a parade with floats dedicated to local fishermen's patron saints and a procession of decorated boats around Nazaré's harbour.

Bullfights   BULLFIGHTING

Held in the *praça de touros* (bullring) about every other weekend from August to mid-September; check with the *turismo* for times and ticket availability.

Nossa Senhora da Nazaré   RELIGIOUS

This annual pilgrimage, held in Sítio on 8 September and the following weekend, is Nazaré's big religious festival, featuring sombre processions, folk dances and bullfights.

🛏 Sleeping

You'll likely be hit up by local women offering rooms for rent. It never hurts to bargain and see what the going rate is. Prices below are for July and August. Expect a 30% to 50% discount at other times.

Vila Conde Fidalgo   APARTMENTS, ROOMS €

(☑262 552 361; http://vilaturisticacondefidalgo. blogspot.com; Av da Independência Nacional 21A; d €40-50, 2-person apt €50-70, 5-person apt €80-100) Built around a series of courtyards and patios decorated with broken-china mosaics and adorned with flowers and plants, this pretty family-run complex a few blocks up from the beach was a former fishermen's colony. Friendly manager Ana offers 10 clean, colourful and comfortable rooms with mini-fridges, plus a dozen apartments of varying sizes, each with dining table and fully equipped kitchenette. Breakfast (freshly squeezed orange juice, bread and seasonal fruit) is available for €5 extra, served in your room or on the terrace outside.

Adega Oceano   HOTEL €€

(☑262 561 161; www.adegaoceano.com; Av da República 51; d €50-60; ✳🗺) This little oceanfront place offers much nicer amenities than you'd expect from the price and exterior appearance. The 15 recently remodelled rooms at the back come with flat-screen TVs and ultra-modern bathroom fixtures, while those at the front have nice views across the beach to the cliffs and waterfront. As with any place this close to the action, street noise can be a problem.

Residencial Ribamar   HOTEL €€

(☑262 551 158; www.ribamar.pa-net.pt; Rua Gomes Freire 9; d €65-75) Rooms at this seafront hotel are brighter, frillier and airier than the musty and lugubrious halls might suggest. Bathrooms are clean and nicely tiled, and the two corner rooms (11 and 21) have little balconies with great ocean views.

Hospedaria Ideal   GUEST HOUSE €

(☑262 551 379; www.hospedariaideal.com.sapo. pt; Rua Adrião Batalha 98; d with shared bathroom €40, with full board €75) The gracious French-speaking landlady has a little restaurant downstairs and six humbly old-fashioned rooms upstairs that are a little bigger than the beds. Doubles cost as little as €20 most of the year. It's booked solid in August, when full board is sometimes mandatory.

Albergaria Mar Bravo   LUXURY HOTEL €€€

(☑262 569 160; www.marbravo.com; Praça Sousa Oliveira 71; d €100-140; 🅿✳@🗺) Facing Nazaré's busiest square on one side and the sea on the other, this recently remodelled four-star hotel offers calmly luxurious, if not tremendously large, rooms with ocean views and some with balconies. There's a good attached restaurant, and free parking is available at its sister hotel a few blocks away. While the location is perfect, the service sometimes leaves something to be desired.

Nazaré

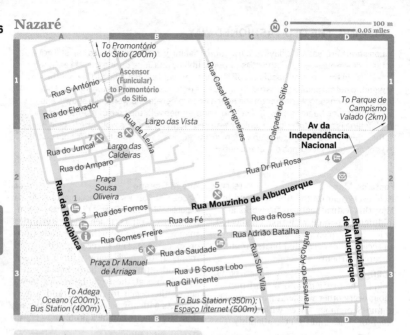

Parque de Campismo

Valado   CAMPGROUND €

(📞262 561 111; infovalado@orbitur.pt; sites per adult/child/tent/car €4.40/2.20/4.90/4; 🛜🏊) This shady, well-equipped Orbitur site has a restaurant, bar and brand new swimming pool. It's 2km east of town, off the Alcobaça road.

✕ Eating & Drinking

Seafood is the star in Nazaré.

TOP CHOICE **A Tasquinha**   SEAFOOD €€

(Rua Adrião Batalha 54; mains €6.50-11; ⏰lunch & dinner Tue-Sun) This family operation serves excellent seafood in a pair of

snug but pretty tiled dining rooms. High quality and reasonable prices make it hugely popular. Expect queues on summer nights.

A Lanterna   SEAFOOD €€

(Rua Mouzinho de Albuquerque 59; mains for 2 €18-32; ⏰lunch & dinner) This cosy, if touristy, place specialises in paella-like *cataplana* (seafood simmered with herbs, toma-toes, onions and wine), served in its low-ceilinged dining room.

Conchinha da Nazaré   SEAFOOD €€

(Rua de Leiria 17D; mains €6.50-10; ⏰lunch & dinner) This simple place on a backstreet square serves good-value seafood, includ-ing wood-grilled fish and delicious *açorda de marisco* (thick bread soup with seafood). Many nights there are more locals than tourists.

To drink with the locals, check out the bars around Travessa do Elevador.

Casa O Santo   BEER BAR €

(Travessa do Elevador 11; seafood appetisers from €5; ⏰noon-late) An immensely enjoyable *cervejaria* (beer house) serving beer, wine and tasty seafood snacks – especially recom-mended are the garlicky steamed *ameijoas* (clams). Grab a table on the pavement, or eat under the stone arches of the cosy interior rooms beside the bustling bar.

ℹ Information

Centro de Saúde (☑262 569 125; Urbanização Caixins) Medical centre on the eastern edge of town.

Espaço Internet (Biblioteca Municipal, Av do Municipio; ☺9.30am-1pm & 2-7pm Mon-Fri, 3-6pm Sat & Sun) Free internet and wi-fi in Nazaré's spiffy new public library.

Police station (☑262 550 070; Rua Sub-Vila)

Post office (Av da Independência Nacional; ☺9am-12.30pm & 2.30-6pm Mon-Fri)

Turismo (☑262 561 194; www.cm-nazare.pt; Av da República; ☺9.30am-12.30pm & 2.30-6.30pm)

ℹ Getting There & Away

BUS Rodotejo (www.rodotejo.pt) and **Rede Expressos** (www.rede-expressos.pt) serve the following destinations several times daily from Nazaré's bus station, a couple of blocks in from the ocean: Alcobaça (€1.85, 20 minutes), Caldas da Rainha (€3.15, 45 minutes), Leiria (express/local €3.90/3.40, 40/60 minutes), Lisbon (€9.50, 1¾ hours) and Peniche (€8.50, 70 minutes).

CAR & MOTORCYCLE Parking and, in summer, even driving, can be frustrating. There's a large, paid car park one block south of the municipal market, plus a large free car park a few blocks east of the market, near the junction of Av Vieira Guimarães and the EN242.

Alcobaça

POP 6200

Only 100km north of Lisbon, the little town of Alcobaça is pleasant but unassuming, yielding centre stage to the magnificent 12th-century Mosteiro de Santa Maria de Alcobaça, one of Portugal's most easily accessible Unesco World Heritage Sites. Hiding behind the imposing if uninspired baroque facade lies a bright forest of unadorned 12th-century Cistercian arches rising to ethereal heights, adjoined by a graceful ensemble of courtyards, kitchens and former monks' living quarters.

From the bus station and car park in the new town, descend 500m along Av dos Combatentes to cross the Rio Alcôa and reach the monastery. Prominent bell towers provide the only guidance needed to reach the grand square before the church; the *turismo*, restaurants and hotels are all clustered nearby.

(☑262 505 126; cloisters, kitchen & refectory adult/child/senior €6/free/3, 9am-2pm Sun & holidays free; ☺9am-7pm Apr-Sep, to 5pm Oct-Mar) This monastery was founded in 1153 by Dom Afonso Henriques, first king of Portugal, to honour a vow he'd made to St Bernard after the capture of Santarém from the Moors in 1147. The king entrusted the construction of the monastery to the monks of the Cistercian order, also giving them a huge area around Alcobaça to develop and cultivate.

Building started in 1178 and by the time the monks moved in, some 45 years later, the monastery estate had become one of the richest and most powerful in the country. In those early days the monastery is said to have housed 999 monks, who held Mass nonstop in shifts.

Switching from farming to teaching in the 13th century, the monks used the estate's abundant rents to carry out further enlargements and changes to the monastery to suit the fashions of the day. Towards the 17th century, the monks turned their talents to pottery and the sculpting of figures in stone, wood and clay.

Revived agricultural efforts in the 18th century made the Alcobaça area one of the most productive in the land. However, it was the monks' growing decadence that became famous, thanks to the writings of 18th-century travellers such as William Beckford, who, despite his own tendency to exaggerate, was shocked at the 'perpetual gormandising…the fat waddling monks and sleek friars with wanton eyes…'. The party ended in 1834 with the dissolution of the religious orders.

Church

Much of the original facade was altered in the 17th and 18th centuries (including the addition of wings), leaving only the main doorway and rose window unchanged.

However, once you step inside, the combination of Gothic ambition and Cistercian austerity hits you immediately: the nave is a breathtaking 106m long but only 23m wide, with huge pillars and truncated columns. It is modelled on the French Cistercian abbey of Clairvaux.

Tombs of Dom Pedro & Dona Inês

Occupying the south and north transepts are two intricately carved 14th-century

As moving as *Romeo and Juliet* – and far more gruesome – is the tragic story of Dom Pedro. The son of Dom Afonso IV, he fell madly in love with his wife's Galician lady-in-waiting, Dona Inês de Castro. Even after the death of his wife, Pedro's father forbade his son from marrying Inês, wary of her Spanish family's potential influence. Various suspicious nobles continued to pressure the king until finally he sanctioned her murder in 1355, unaware that the two lovers had already married in secret.

Two years later, when Pedro succeeded to the throne, he exacted his revenge by ripping out and eating the hearts of Inês' murderers. He then exhumed and crowned her body, and ordered the court to pay homage to his dead queen by kissing her decomposing hand.

tombs, the church's greatest possessions, which commemorate the tragic love story of Dom Pedro and his mistress.

Although the tombs themselves were badly damaged by rampaging French troops in search of treasure in 1811, they still show extraordinary narrative detail and are embellished with a host of figures and scenes from the life of Christ. The Wheel of Fortune at the head of Dom Pedro's tomb and the gruesome Last Judgment scene at the foot of Inês' tomb are especially amazing. The tombs are inscribed *Até ao Fim do Mundo* (until the end of the world) and, on Pedro's orders, placed foot to foot so that, when the time comes, they can rise up and see each other straight away.

Kitchen & Refectory

The grand kitchen, described by Beckford as 'the most distinguished temple of gluttony in all Europe', owes its immense size to alterations carried out in the 18th century, including a water channel built through the middle of the room so that a tributary of the Rio Alcôa could provide a constant source of fresh fish to the monastery – they swam directly into a stone basin. The water was also useful for cooking and washing.

Even now, it's not hard to imagine the scene when Beckford was led here by the abbey's grand priors ('hand in hand, all three together'). He saw:

> …pastry in vast abundance which a numerous tribe of lay brothers and their attendants were rolling out and puffing up into a hundred different shapes, singing all the while as blithely as larks in a corn field.

The adjacent refectory, huge and vaulted, is where the monks ate in silence while the Bible was read to them from the pulpit. Opposite the entrance is a 14th-century *lavabo* (bathroom) embellished with a hexagonal fountain. The monks entered through a narrow door on their way to the refectory. Those who could not pass through were forced to fast.

Claustro do Silencio & Sala dos Reis

The beautiful Cloister of Silence dates from two eras. Dom Dinis built the intricate lower storey, with its arches and traceried stone circles, in the 14th century. The upper storey, typically Manueline in style, was added in the 16th century.

Off the northwestern corner of the cloister is the 18th-century Sala dos Reis (Kings' Room), so called because statues of practically all the kings of Portugal line the walls. Below them are *azulejo* friezes depicting stories relevant to the abbey's construction, including the siege of Santarém and the life of St Bernard.

🎊 Festivals & Events

Now in its second decade, the **Cistermúsica festival** (www.cistermusica.com) runs from late May to late July, featuring classical concerts in the monastery and other local venues.

🛏 Sleeping & Eating

Cafes are clustered under the sycamores on pretty Praça Dom Afonso Henriques – just to the left (north) of the monastery's facade. The best streets for restaurant browsing are Rua Frei António Brandão and Travessa da Cadeia, both feeding off the main square, Praça 25 de Abril.

TOP CHOICE **Challet Fonte Nova** B&B €€€
(☎262 598 300; www.challetfontenova. pt; Rua da Fonte Nova 8; s/d €85/120; P ✳ @ 🛜)
Set amid pretty gardens, this elegant and charming 19th-century chalet has grand

common areas with gleaming wood floors, carpets and period furnishings. The main house is especially attractive, with sumptuously decorated rooms, tall French windows, and a downstairs self-serve bar with billiard table; there's also a whitewashed modern annexe.

Parque de Campismo CAMPGROUND €
(☑262 582 265; Av Professor Vieira Natividade; sites per adult/child/tent/car €2.10/1.45/1.45/1.55; ☺Feb-Dec) The small, simple municipal site is located 500m north of the bus station. It has some tree shade and disabled access.

Hotel Residencial Santa Maria HOTEL €
(☑262 590 160; www.hotelsantamaria.com.pt; Rua Dr Francisco Zagalo 20-22; s/d/tr €40/50/60; [P][✳][☎]) Popular with tour groups, this well-appointed, modern place sits just across from the monastery. Book ahead for the front rooms with impressive views of the monastery's facade and square.

A Casa PORTUGUESE €€
(Praça 25 de Abril 51-54; mains €6.95-9.75; ☺9am-7pm) Enjoy the local speciality, *frango na púcara* (stewed chicken) in the attractive beamed dining room just off the main square or escape the crowds on the pretty back patio. The adjacent wine shop sells vintages from all over Portugal, including a bottle of port dating to 1890 – don't drop it or you'll be out €1719.50! There's a second location just around the corner on Travessa da Cadeia.

❶ Information

Hospital (☑262 590 400; Rua Hospital) On the eastern edge of the new town, off Rua Afonso de Albuquerque.

Police station (☑262 505 650; Rua de Olivença)

Post office (Praça 25 de Abril; ☺9am-12.30pm & 1.30-6pm Mon-Fri) Almost next door to the *turismo*.

Turismo (☑262 582 377; Praça 25 de Abril; ☺10am-1pm & 3-7pm) Opposite the monastery's main entrance, providing assistance in multiple languages, plus free internet access for 15 minutes.

❶ Getting There & Away

BUS Coming from Leiria it's possible to see both Batalha and Alcobaça in a single, carefully timed day. All buses run less frequently on weekends. Destinations include Batalha (€2.75,

30 minutes, every hour or two), Lisbon (€9.80, two hours, six per weekday), Leiria (€3.45, 50 minutes, six per weekday) and Nazaré (€1.85, 20 minutes, every hour or two).

CAR & MOTORCYCLE There's a public car park near the roundabout at the end of Av dos Combatentes da Grande Guerra, as you arrive via the EN8 from Leiria.

Batalha

POP 7500 / ELEV 120M

Among the supreme achievements of Manueline architecture, Batalha's monastery nowadays looks strangely out of place, surrounded by a rather nondescript modern town, and flanked by a national highway passing 100m from its facade. But walk through the doors and you're immediately transported to another world, where solid rock has been carved into forms as delicate as snowflakes and as pliable as twisted rope.

Beyond the monastery, the town's charms are limited. For anyone disinclined to linger, Batalha makes an easy day trip from Leiria, Alcobaça or other places along the N8.

❂ Sights

**Mosteiro de Santa Maria
da Vitória** MONASTERY
(cloisters & Capelas Imperfeitas adult/child/senior €6/free/3, 9am-2pm Sun & holidays free; ☺9am-6pm Apr-Sep, to 5pm Oct-Mar) This extraordinary abbey was built to commemorate the 1385 Battle of Aljubarrota (fought 4km south of Batalha), when 6500 Portuguese, commanded by Dom Nuno Álvares Pereira and supported by a few hundred English soldiers, repulsed a 30,000-strong force of Juan I of Castile, who had come claiming the throne of João d'Avis.

João called on the Virgin Mary for help and vowed to build a superb abbey in return for victory. Three years later he made good on his promise, as work began on the Dominican abbey.

Most of the monument – the church, Claustro Real, Sala do Capítulo and Capela do Fundador – was completed by 1434 in Flamboyant Gothic, but Manueline exuberance steals the show, thanks to additions made in the 15th and 16th centuries. Work at Batalha only stopped in the mid-16th century when Dom João III turned his attention to expanding the Convento de Cristo in Tomar.

Exterior

The glorious ochre-limestone building bristles with pinnacles and parapets, flying buttresses and balustrades, and Gothic and Flamboyant carved windows, as well as octagonal chapels and massive columns, after the English perpendicular style. The western doorway positively boils over – layers of arches pack in the apostles, various angels, saints and prophets, all topped by Christ and the Evangelists.

Interior

The vast, vaulted Gothic interior is plain, long and high like Alcobaça's church, warmed by light from the deep-hued stained-glass windows. To the right as you enter is the intricate Capela do Fundador (Founder's Chapel), a beautiful, achingly tall, star-vaulted square room lit by an octagonal lantern. In the centre is the joint tomb of João I and his English wife, Philippa of Lancaster, whose marriage in 1387 cemented the alliance that still exists between Portugal and England. If you stand on tiptoes, you can see that the two monarchs' sculpted figures are still holding hands. The tombs of their four youngest sons line the south wall of the chapel, including that of Henry the Navigator (second from the right).

Claustro Real

Afonso Domingues, the master of works at Batalha during the late 1380s, first built the Claustro Real (Royal Cloisters) in a restrained Gothic style, but it's the later Manueline embellishments by the great Diogo de Boitac that really take your breath away. Every arch is a tangle of detailed stone carvings of Manueline symbols, such as armillary spheres and crosses of the Order of Christ, entwined with exotic flowers and marine motifs – ropes, pearls and shells. Three graceful cypresses in the central courtyard echo the shape of the Gothic spires atop the adjacent chapter house.

Claustro de Dom Afonso V

Anything would seem austere after the Claustro Real, but the simple Gothic Claustro de Dom Afonso V is like being plunged into cold water – sobering you up after all that frenzied decadence.

Sala do Capítulo

To the east of the Claustro Real is the early-15th-century chapter house, containing a beautiful 16th-century stained-glass window. The huge, unsupported, 19-sq-metre vault was considered so outrageously dangerous to build that only prisoners on death row were employed in its construction. The Sala do Capítulo contains the tomb of the unknown soldiers – one killed in France in WWI, the other in Mozambique – now watched over by a constant guard of honour and by the 'Christ of the Trenches', a partially shattered statue that also fell victim to war.

Capelas Imperfeitas

The roofless Capelas Imperfeitas (Unfinished Chapels) at the eastern end of the abbey are perhaps the most astonishing, and certainly the most tantalising, aspect of Batalha. Only accessible from outside the abbey, the octagonal mausoleum with its seven chapels was commissioned by Dom Duarte (João I's eldest son) in 1437. However, the later Manueline additions by the architect Mateus Fernandes overshadow everything else, including the Renaissance upper balcony.

Although Fernandes' original plan for an upper octagon supported by buttresses was never finished, the staggering ornamentation gives a hint of what might have followed, and is all the more dramatic for being open to the sky. Most striking is the 15m-high doorway, a mass of stone-carved thistles, ivy, flowers, snails and all manner of 'scollops and twistifications', as William Beckford noted. Dom Duarte can enjoy it for all eternity: his tomb, and that of his wife, lie opposite the door.

🛏 Sleeping & Eating

Casa do Outeiro   BOUTIQUE HOTEL €€

(☎244 765 806; www.casadoouteiro.com; Largo Carvalho do Outeiro 4; s/d €55/70; P ❄ @ 🛜 ⛱) This colourful contemporary place sits just uphill from the town centre. The airy rooms, some with balconies overlooking the abbey and one equipped for guests with disabilities, are individually decorated with flair. The guest book and lobby walls are plastered with praise from former customers. Book ahead in summer.

Pensão Gladius   GUEST HOUSE €

(☎244 765 760, 919 103 044; Praça Mouzinho de Albuquerque; s/d/tr without breakfast €25/30/40) In the square right next to the abbey, friendly older proprietor Dona Eglantina runs this snug but attractive place. It's got a vaguely Alpine feel, with flower-filled window boxes and spotless, modern rooms tucked under the eaves. Some upstairs rooms overlook the equestrian statue in the abbey square.

Churrasqueira Vitória   GRILL HOUSE €

(Largo da Misericórdia; mains €6.50-9; ⊘lunch & dinner) In the square adjacent to the bus stop, this simple, friendly place serves excellent grilled meat and other Portuguese standards.

Vinho em Qualquer Circunstância

TAPAS €€

(☑244 768 777; www.circunstancia.com.pt; Estrada de Fátima 15; mains €10-15; ⊘dinner Mon-Sat, lunch Sat & Sun) Sleek and stylish, this wine bar serves delicious tapas and full meals along with an amazing array of Portuguese wines.

ℹ Information

Facing the back (eastern) end of the abbey, the **turismo** (☑244 765 180; info@rt-leiriafatima. pt; ⊘10am-1pm & 3-7pm Jul-Sep, 10am-1pm & 2-6pm Oct-Jun) has helpful, multilingual staff.

ℹ Getting There & Away

BUS Rodotejo (www.rodotejo.pt) and **Rede Expressos** (www.rede-expressos.pt) leave from the stop in Largo 14 de Agosto, 200m east of the abbey. Destinations served at least four times daily include Alcobaça (€2.75, 35 minutes), Fátima (€2.15, 25 minutes), Leiria (€1.80, 20 minutes), Lisbon (€10.50, two hours) and Nazaré (€3.45, one hour) and Tomar (€5.10, 1½ hours).

CAR & MOTORCYCLE There is street parking just east of the abbey, as well as a paying public car park a little further on.

Leiria

POP 43,000

Leiria is an agreeable mixture of medieval and modern influences, a lively university town built at the foot of a promontory fortified since Moorish times. The town's dramatically sited castle is a commanding presence above the narrow streets and red-tiled roofs of the historic centre, built along the lazy curves of the Rio Liz.

Dom Afonso III convened a *cortes* (Portugal's early parliament) here in 1254; Dom Dinis established his main residence in the castle in the 14th century; and in 1411 the town's sizeable Jewish community built Portugal's first paper mill.

Modern-day Leiria has a pleasant, low-key urban buzz. Good restaurants, bars and cafes abound, and back alleys hide a bevy

of shops selling skateboards and clubwear to the town's student population. The old town is focused on Praça Rodrigues Lobo, with hotels and restaurants nearby. The castle is perched on a wooded hilltop a short walk to the north.

Leiria makes a convenient base for visiting several nearby sights, including Alcobaça, Batalha, Fátima and the beaches and pine forests of the Pinhal de Leiria – all easily accessible by bus.

⊙ Sights

This long-inhabited cliff-top site got its first **castelo** (☑244 813 982; adult/child €2/1; ⊘10am-6pm) in the time of the Moors. Captured by Afonso Henriques in 1135, it was transformed into a royal residence for Dom Dinis in the 14th century. Inside the walls is a peaceful garden, overgrown with tall trees, and the ruined but still lovely Gothic **Igreja de Nossa Senhora da Penha**, originally built in the 12th century and rebuilt by João I in the early 15th century. It has beautiful leaflike carvings over one arch. The castle's most spectacular feature, however, is a gallery with small corner seats. It provides a fantastic vantage point over the town's red-tiled roofs, though the current structure is largely the result of overeager restoration by early-20th-century Swiss architect Ernesto Korrodi.

The **sé** (cathedral), to the southeast of the castle, was started in the 16th century, and the cloister, sacristy and chapter houses date from 1583 to 1604. It's a plain, cavernous place. Opposite is the wonderfully tiled **Pharmácia Leonardo Paiva** – the beautiful *azulejos* depict Hippocrates, Galen and Socrates. Novelist Eça de Queirós used to live in Travessa Tipografia next to the cathedral, and he and his literary group met regularly in the pharmacy. These days, it's an Irish-style pub (p273).

✪ Festivals & Events

Leiria celebrates the joy of eating with the nine-day **Festival de Gastronomia** in early September. Expect folk dancing, as well as stalls of mouth-watering traditional food.

🛏 Sleeping

Hotel Leiriense   HOTEL €

(☑244 823 054; www.hotelleiriense.com; Rua Afonso de Albuquerque 6; s/d €28/40; ❀🛜) On a cobbled street in the historic centre, this place had just undergone extensive renovation at the time of research. New

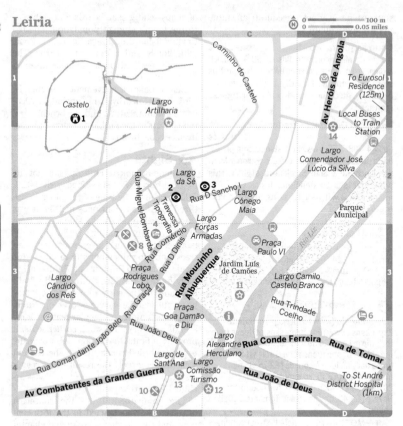

features – including double-glazing to keep out street noise, fresh coats of paint in cheerful colours and new shower curtains to match – complement the retro appeal of its marble steps, tiled hallways and parquet wood floors. Rooms are small but all are kept in fine fettle.

Pousada da Juventude HOSTEL €
(☎244 821 840; leiria@movijovem.pt; Largo Cândido dos Reis 9; dm €12, d with shared/private bathroom €28/30; ☎) In an attractive, 18th-century town house on a charming central square, this friendly hostel offers kitchen and TV privileges, a filling breakfast, and high-ceilinged (if basic) dorms. Doubles are in the adjacent newer wing.

Residencial Dom Dinis HOTEL €
(☎244 815 342; www.residencialddinis.com; Travessa de Tomar 2; s/d €24/37; ❄@☎) Across the river from the old town, this friendly, modern *residencial* has small, spotless and mostly bright rooms; several on the top floor have terraces and fine views (especially room 301) across town to the castle. French is spoken.

Eurosol Residence APARTMENT HOTEL €€
(☎244 860 460; www.eurosol.pt; Rua Commisão da Iniciativa 13; s/d from €83/95; P❄@☎≋) Downtown Leiria's only high-end option has comfortable if unexceptional business-class mini-apartments, all with kitchens and many with pleasant views across the riverside park to the castle.

✗ Eating

TOP CHOICE **Malagueta Afrodisíaca**
INTERNATIONAL €€
(Rua Gago Coutinho 17; mains €12-15; ⊙dinner; ☑) For a rare deviation from standard Portuguese fare, head to this trendy, slinkily decorated place, tucked down a narrow street in the historic centre. The eclectic 15-page menu features aphrodisiac teas, flam-

ing desserts, mixed drinks, and a dizzying collection of Brazilian, Mexican and other ethnic dishes.

Cardamomo INDIAN, PORTUGUESE €€
(Rua Barão de Viamonte 43; mains €9-13; ◷lunch & dinner Tue-Sun; 🖉) The owner's Goan roots are evident at this air-conditioned upstairs restaurant serving a fusion of Indian and Portuguese cuisine. Start with bacon-wrapped asparagus or salad greens with apples and honey, then feast on stuffed eggplant, sea bass with mango, Goan *xacuti* curry or arugula-beet risotto.

Martin & Thomas Padaria Gourmet
BAKERY €
(Praça Rodrigues Lobo 8-9; snacks & pastries from €1; ◷8am-8pm Sun & Mon, 8am-midnight Tue-Sat) This gourmet bakery with outdoor tables on Leiria's prettiest square features tasty bread and pastries, as well as light meals, all served with a dazzling castle view. A great place to pick up snacks for a day trip to Batalha or Alcobaça.

Restaurante A Toca PORTUGUESE €
(Rua Dr Correia Mateus 42; mains €6-11; ◷lunch & dinner Sun-Fri) Along pedestrianised Rua Dr Correia Mateus are several traditional restaurants, including this friendly, no-nonsense spot with a pretty tiled interior and a long menu featuring meat and fish prepared on a wood grill.

🍷 Drinking & Entertainment
Bars are scattered throughout the historic centre, and the student population keeps things hopping.

Pharmácia PUB
(Largo da Sé 9; ◷9.30pm-2am Mon-Sat) Set inside a marvellous 19th-century pharmacy,

this Irish-style bar features a mellow vibe, darts and a vast universe of drinks.

Teatro José Lúcio da Silva ARTS CENTRE
(www.teatrojlsilva.pt; Av Heróis de Angola) Newly reopened after extensive remodelling, this venerable 723-seat performance space regularly features dance, theatre, comedy, highbrow cinema and other cultural events.

Mercado Sant'Ana Centro Cultural
CULTURAL CENTRE
(Largo de Sant'Ana) This market-turned-cultural-complex is built around a pleasant courtyard, where you'll find cafes, restaurants, free wi-fi and the **Teatro Miguel Franco,** a smaller performance venue affiliated with Teatro José Lúcio da Silva.

Suite BAR, NIGHTCLUB
(Rua Machado dos Santos; www.clubesuite.com; ◷bar from 10pm, club 2-5am Thu-Sat) Party into the wee hours at this club in the heart of town.

Club Glam NIGHTCLUB
(Jardim Luís de Camões) A popular Latino dance club in the riverfront square.

ℹ **Information**
Biblioteca Municipal (Largo Cândido dos Reis 6; ◷2-8pm Mon, 10am-8pm Tue-Fri, 10.30am-6pm Sat) Free internet access at the public library.

Police station (☎244 859 859; Largo de São Pedro 4) By the castle.

Post office (Av Heróis de Angola 99; ◷8.30am-6.30pm Mon-Fri, 9am-12.30pm Sat)

St André District Hospital (☎244 817 000) About 1.5km east of town.

Turismo (☎244 848 770; www.rt-leiriafatima. pt; ◷10am-1pm & 3-7pm) Provides a free town map, plus reams of information about local attractions and events.

ESTREMADURA & RIBATEJO LEIRIA

❶ Getting There & Around

BUS **Rodotejo** (www.rodotejo.pt) and **Rede Expressos** (www.rede-sinexpressos.pt) both serve the **bus station** (Largo 5 de Outubro) in the heart of town. Buses run every hour or two to Alcobaça (€3.45, 50 minutes), Batalha (€1.80, 20 minutes), Coimbra (€8.50, 50 minutes), Fátima (€3, 25 minutes), Lisbon (€11, two hours) and Nazaré (€3.45, one hour).

CAR & MOTORCYCLE Street parking is fairly easy along Rua João de Deus.

TRAIN Leiria is on the train line that runs about three times daily from Figueira da Foz (€4.75, one hour) to the Mira Sintra-Meleças station near Lisbon (€11.35, 2½ to 3½ hours). Leiria's train station is 4km northwest of town. Local bus 4 runs here frequently from Largo José Lúcio da Silva near the long-distance bus station (€1.10, 10 to 15 minutes, schedule posted at bus stop). A taxi from downtown to the train station costs about €4.

Pinhal de Leiria

First planted by a forward-looking monarch some 700 years ago, the Pinhal de Leiria is a vast forest of towering pines whose fragrance and stippled shade make this one of the loveliest stretches of Portugal's Atlantic coast. Dom Dinis expanded it significantly as a barrier against encroaching dunes and also as a source of timber for the maritime industry – a great boon during the Age of Discoveries.

Today, the protected forest covers more than 100 sq km along the coast west of Leiria. Narrow roads and well-maintained bike paths cut through the serene stands of pine, leading to a number of excellent beaches and three resort towns: **São Pedro de Moel**, 20km west of Leiria; **Praia da Vieira**, 16km north of São Pedro along the coastal highway; and **Pedrógão**, 2km further north.

Be aware that here, as elsewhere on the Atlantic coast, seas and currents can be strong; ask around before venturing into the waters.

🛏 Sleeping & Eating

All places listed below are in São Pedro de Moel, the most appealing of the three towns for an overnight stay.

Parque de Campismo Orbitur

CAMPGROUND €

(☑244 599 168; infospedro@orbitur.pt; sites per adult/child/tent/car €5.40/2.70/6.10/5.30; 🖥🏊) In among the pine trees 500m above town, this well-equipped, pretty site includes a swimming pool, disabled facilities and a playground. You can also rent two-/four-/six-person bungalows for €89/99/109 in August or €56/66/76 the rest of the summer.

Hotel Mar e Sol

HOTEL €€

(☑244 590 000; www.hotelmaresol.com; Av da Liberdade 1; r €80-115; 🖥🏊) This recently refurbished seafront hotel is comfortable and sparkling clean, with minimalist modern decor. The best rooms, with grand views over the tussling sea, cost €35 to €45 extra. Wi-fi is free in the lobby, paid in the rooms.

O Pai dos Frangos

PORTUGUESE €€

(Praia Velha; mains €9.50-15; ⊗lunch & dinner Tue-Sun) 'The Father of Chickens' sits in splendid isolation above the sands of Praia Velha, just north of the lighthouse. Specialities include *arroz de marisco* (paella-like rice and seafood stew) and, naturally, grilled chicken.

Estrela do Mar

SEAFOOD €€€

(Av Marginal; mains €13-20; ⊗lunch & dinner) Food prices here reflect the unbeatable view; the restaurant is perched on wave-battered cliffs above São Pedro's town beach.

Bambi Café

CAFE-BAR €

(⊗11am-3am Jul-Sep, 1pm-2am Fri-Sun Oct-Jun) Guinness on tap, wi-fi, and comfy couches on an outdoor deck are the big draws at this cool glass-walled cafe behind the *turismo*.

❶ Information

Turismo (⊗10am-1pm & 3-7pm Tue-Sun Jul & Aug) São Pedro de Moel (☑244 599 633); Praia da Vieira (☑244 695 230); Pedrógão (☑244 695 411)

❶ Getting There & Away

From Leiria there are at least six daily buses to São Pedro de Moel (€2.65, 40 minutes) and Praia da Vieira (€3, 45 minutes).

Fátima

POP 10,000 / ELEV 320M

What you see in Fátima will depend on what you come looking for. Aesthetically, it's hard to get past the town's bland and monolithic architecture, and outside the main pilgrimage dates (the 12th and 13th of each month from May to October) the vast parking lots ringing the basilicas have the feel of a forlorn desert. Yet for Catholic pilgrims Fátima has a magnetic appeal like few places on earth, and a trip here will provide any visitor with new insights into Portugal's religious culture. If you're travelling anywhere within a 100km radius near the dates of the important May and October pilgrimages, you'll find the highways lined with throngs of fluorescent-clad wanderers, making the spiritual journey to Fátima from all over Portugal and the world.

Whatever your beliefs, you can't help but be impressed by the vast reserves of faith that every year lead as many as six million people to the glade where, on 13 May 1917, the Virgin Mary is said to have first appeared to three awestruck peasant children (for the full story see p491). Where sheep once grazed there are now two huge churches on opposite ends of a vast 1km-long esplanade twice the size of St Peter's: the earliest 1953 basilica topped with a golden crown and a cross; and the modernist Basilica da Santíssima Trindade, inaugurated on 12 October 2007, with room for 9000 worshippers.

The focus of the pilgrimages, known as Cova da Iria, is just east of the A1 motorway. Several major roads ring the area, including Av Dom José Alves Correia da Silva to the south, where the bus station and *turismo* are located. To reach the sanctuary, turn right from the bus station and walk 300m, then left along Rua João Paulo II for 500m.

The town itself is packed with boarding houses and restaurants for the pilgrim masses, and shop windows crowded with glow-in-the-dark Virgins and busts of the Pope.

◉ Sights

At the east end of the sanctuary is the 1953 basilica, a triumphantly sheer-white building with a *praça* and a colonnade reminiscent of St Peter's in Rome. On the left side, the Capela das Apariçoes (Chapel of the Apparitions) marks the site where the Virgin appeared. It is the focus of intense devotion, and supplicants who have promised penance (for example, in return for helping a loved one who is sick, or to signify a particularly deep conversion) regularly shuffle on their knees across the vast esplanade, following a long marble runway polished smooth by thousands of previous penitents.

Near the chapel is a blazing pyre and a candle-lighting area. Here people can throw offerings on the fire, leave gifts – which are collected at the end of the day and donated to charities – or simply light candles in prayer. As you approach, the sound of melting wax from so many hundreds of candles is like a rushing waterfall.

Inside the basilica are 15 altars dedicated to the mysteries of the rosary. Attention is focused on the tombs of Blessed Francisco (died 1919, aged 11) and Blessed Jacinta (died 1920, aged 10), both victims of the flu epidemic, who were beatified in 2000. Lúcia, the third witness of the apparition, entered a convent in Coimbra in 1928, where she died in 2005.

At the entrance of the sanctuary, to the south of the rectory, is a segment of the Berlin Wall, donated by a Portuguese resident of Germany and a tribute to God's part in the fall of communism, as some say was predicted at Fátima.

Eight Masses are held daily in the basilica, and seven daily in the Capela das Apariçoes. At least two Masses daily are held in English; check at the information booth by the chapel for details.

The new Basilica da Santíssima Trindade (Basilica of the Holy Trinity), inaugurated in October 2007, sits at the west end of the esplanade. A central passageway hung with golden angels leads to a long etched-glass window spelling out scriptural verses in dozens of languages. Twelve 30ft bronze doors run around the edges of the monumental round marble structure, each with a Biblical quote dedicated to one of Jesus' disciples. Inside, the church's cavernous and impersonal feel is redeemed by Irish artist Catherine Green's striking altarpiece depicting a wild-haired and gaunt Jesus on the cross, backed by the beautiful gold-and-terracotta mosaic work of Slovenian artist Marko Ivan Rupnik.

Fátima's several Catholic-themed museums include Museu de Arte Sacra e Etnologia (http://masefatima.blogspot.com; Rua Francisco Marto 52; adult/child €2.50/1.50; ⏰10am-7pm Tue-Sun) – displaying religious art and artefacts from around the world – and duelling wax museums on either side of the basilica: the Museu de Cera de Fátima (www.mucefa.pt; Rua Jacinta Marto; adult/child €6/3.50; ⏰9.30am-6.30pm), which gives a blow-by-blow, starry-eyed account of the story of Fátima; and the Museu Vida de

Cristo (www.vidadecristo.pt; Rua Francisco Marto; adult/child €7/4; ⊙9am-7pm), representing 33 scenes from the life of Christ.

🍴 Sleeping & Eating

There are dozens of restaurants, *pensões* (guest houses) and interchangeable pilgrim lodges in the thick of the shops east of the basilica, most geared for visiting groups of hundreds and very few with any character.

Residencial Aleluia   HOTEL €

(📞249 531 540; www.residencialaleluia.com; Av Dr José Silva 120; s/d with shared bathroom from €15/20, s/d with private bathroom from €30/36, breakfast per person €3) Bargain-hunters and penniless pilgrims will rejoice at the reasonably priced rooms at this centrally located place. As bland as everything else in Fátima but squeaky clean and directly across from the basilica, it offers a few spartan rooms with shared bathrooms on the top floor to supplement the cushier en-suite rooms downstairs. Other pluses include the friendly English-speaking owner and in-house laundry service (€10 per load).

ℹ️ Information

The **turismo** (📞249 531 139; ⊙10am-1pm & 3-7pm) is on Av Dom José Alves Correia da Silva, 600m southeast of the bus station.

ℹ️ Getting There & Away

BUS Fátima (sometimes called Cova da Iria on timetables) is a stop on most major north–south bus runs. The following destinations are served at least hourly: Coimbra (€10, one to 1¼ hours), Leiria (€3 to 5.90, 25 to 45 minutes), Lisbon (€10.50, 1½ hours) and Porto (€16, two to three hours).

TRAIN Fátima's train station is 21km east of town. Travelling by bus is a much better option.

Porto de Mós

POP 24,000 / ELEV 260M

Dominated by a 13th-century hilltop castle, Porto de Mós is an untouristy town on the little Rio Lena that makes a good base for exploring the mountains and caves of the adjacent Parque Natural das Serras de Aire e Candeeiros.

Porto de Mós became a major Roman settlement whose residents used the Lena to ferry millstones from a nearby quarry and, later, iron from a mine 10km northeast at Alqueidão da Serra. Today, the region remains an important centre for quarrying the black-and-white stones used in *calçada portuguesa*, the mosaic-style pavements seen throughout Portugal. The windswept plateaus surrounding town are dotted with ancient stone windmills alongside sleek modern ones generating electricity for Portugal's power grid.

The town spreads south from a cluster of streets just below the castle to a newer area around the *mercado municipal* on Av Dr Francisco Sá Carneiro, where buses also stop. Walk west from here towards the river and you'll hit Alameda Dom Afonso Henriques, the main road through town.

DINOSAUR FOOTPRINTS

For years a huge quarry 10km south of Fátima yielded nothing more interesting than chunks of limestone. But when the quarry closed in 1994 a local archaeologist discovered huge footprints embedded in the sloping rock face. These, the oldest and longest sauropod tracks in the world, record a 147m walk in the mud a trifling 175 million years ago.

The sauropods (those nice herbivorous dinosaurs with small heads and long necks and tails) would have been stepping through carbonated mud, later transformed into limestone. As you walk across the slope you can clearly see the large elliptical prints made by the *pes* (feet) and the smaller, half-moon prints made by the *manus* (hands).

Another major dinosaur discovery – a partial skeleton of a flesh-eating *Allosaurus fragilis* – was made in April 1999 at nearby Pombal (26km northeast of Leiria). It proved to be the same species as fossils found in the western USA, throwing into disarray the theory that the Atlantic Ocean opened only during the late Jurassic period.

You can follow in the footsteps of the dinosaurs at Fátima's **Monumento Natural das Pegadas dos Dinossáurios** (📞249 530 160; www.pegadasdedinossaurios.org; adult/child €1.50/0.50; ⊙10am-5pm Tue-Sun) in Pedreira do Galinha, 9km east of the N360 running south of Fátima; follow the brown signs marked 'Pegadas da Serra de Aire'.

Sights

FREE **Castelo**   CASTLE
(⊙10am-12.30pm & 2-6pm Tue-Sun)
The green-towered castle was originally a Moorish stronghold. Conquered definitively in 1148 by Dom Afonso Henriques, it was largely rebuilt in 1450 and again after the 1755 earthquake. These days it's too pristine to be convincingly medieval, especially the overneat green tiles of its pitched roof. Still, it's fun to climb around and has pleasant views across the valley to the Serras de Aire e Candeeiros. Stick around till closing and watch 'em lock up with a key the size of your forearm!

Estrada Romana   ROMAN RUINS
Fifteen minutes northeast of Porto de Mós by car, a section of ancient Roman road has been converted into a walking trail. Marked with red and yellow blazes, the old road bed meanders through the hills for 9km; the most impressive section is at the signposted trailhead just above the town of Alqueidão da Serra.

Sleeping & Eating

TOP CHOICE **Quinta de Rio Alcaide**   RURAL INN €€
(☏244 402 124; rioalcaide@mail.telepac. pt; 2-/4-/6-person apt from €55/85/120; P🅿🛜🏊) One kilometre southeast of Porto de Mós, this terrific inn is set in a converted 18th-century paper mill. The rooms and apartments are charming, including one in a hilltop windmill, and another that in 1973 served as a meeting place for Portuguese captains plotting the Revolution of the Carnations. The lovely grounds feature a pool, citrus trees, hiking trails and a cascading stream. Many languages spoken.

Residencial O Filipe   GUEST HOUSE €
(☏244 401 455; www.ofilipe.com; Largo do Rossio 41; s/d/ste €35/45/60; 🛜) Porto de Mós' only *pensão* offers 13 trim if slightly grandmotherly rooms. The guest house is located at the town's main intersection.

Adega do Luis   PORTUGUESE €€
(☏964 103 287; www.adegadoluis.pt; Rua Principal, Livramento; mains €7.50-12.50; ⊙lunch & dinner Wed-Mon) Three kilometres southeast of town, this delightful place with high ceilings, stone walls and a roaring fire in the brick oven serves grilled bacon, lamb chops, Iberian pork and *picanha* (rump steak), with pear tart for dessert. Outside summer call ahead, as hours fluctuate according to demand.

Esplanada Jardim   CAFE €
(lunch €4.50-6.50; ⊙10am-2am) This pleasant cafe in the leafy municipal gardens near the *turismo* serves excellent, reasonably priced lunches on weekdays.

ℹ Information

The **turismo** (☏244 491 323; ⊙10am-1pm & 3-7pm Tue-Sun) is near the town's main roundabout in the *jardim público* (public park) and offers 15 minutes' free internet access.

ℹ Getting There & Away

There are at least three buses each weekday to/from Leiria (€2.80, 45 minutes) via Batalha (€1.90, 15 minutes). There are also three to four daily buses to Alcobaça (€2.80, 35 minutes). You can buy tickets in the municipal market.

Parque Natural das Serras de Aire e Candeeiros

With its barren limestone heights crisscrossed by hiking trails, this natural park east of Porto de Mós is a popular place for outdoor pursuits.

Once the haunt of dinosaurs, the park is famous for its cathedral-like caves, but above ground it's also scenic, particularly the high Planalto de Santo António (starting 2km south of the Grutas de Santo António). Gorse- and olive grove–covered hills are divided by dry-stone walls and threaded by cattle trails, all making for tempting rambles. Numerous *percursos pedestres* (walking trails), ranging from 1km to 17km, are described in the English-language *Guide to Walking Tours in the Aire and Candeeiros Mountain Ranges,* available for €5 from the park offices.

Sights

Mira de Aire   CAVE
(☏244 440 322; adult/child €5.50/3.20; ⊙9.30am-7.30pm) Portugal's largest cave system, at Mira de Aire, 14km southeast of Porto de Mós, was discovered in 1947 and opened to the public in 1971. The 45-minute guided tour apparently hasn't changed much since then, although the caves themselves are impressive. A spiralling 110m descent leads through psychedelically lit chambers with names like the Spaghetti Room and Organ Pipe Room, to a final cavern containing a lake with a rather hokey fountain display.

On weekdays year-round, there are three buses daily from Porto de Mós to Mira de Aire (€2.30, 35 minutes). From July to mid-September there's also weekend service (two buses on Saturday, one on Sunday).

Grutas de Alvados & Grutas de Santo António
CAVES

(☎244 440 787, 249 841 876; www.grutasalva dos.com, http://grutassantoantonio.com; adult/child per cave €5.20/3, both caves €9/6; ☺10am-5.30pm Tue-Sun) These caves are about 15km southeast of Porto de Mós, and 2km and 3.5km, respectively, south of the N243 from Porto de Mós to Mira de Aire. They were discovered by workmen in 1964, and are the spiky smaller cousins of Mira de Aire, with similarly disco-flavoured lighting.

Buses between Porto de Mós and Mira de Aire can drop you at the caves turn-off on the N243, but it's a steep uphill walk from there.

🛏 Sleeping

From June through September, the park operates four rustic lodgings known as **centros de acolhimento** (☎966 599 867, 244 491 904; pnsacvisitas@gmail.com; 4-/8-person house €64/128) in its southern section. This accommodation should be booked at least a week in advance at the park's *ecoteca* in Porto de Mós.

Alvados Hostel
HOSTEL €

(☎244 441 202; alvados@movijovem.pt; dm €13, d with private/shared bathroom €38/32; 🅿🛜) This friendly, sparkling new place 8km southeast of Porto de Mós has four-bed dorms, doubles with and without private bathrooms, a guest kitchen and wheelchair-accessible facilities. During the week, buses from Leiria (€4, 55 minutes) stop at the Alvados traffic circle in front of the hostel twice daily.

Parque de Campismo
CAMPGROUND €

(☎966 599 867, 244 491 904; sites per adult/child/tent €2.50/1.25/0.75; ☺May-Sep) Remote, basic and beautifully set at Arrimal, 17km south of Porto de Mós, this place has only 50 pitches, so advance reservations are essential. It's accessible by a weekday bus to Porto de Mós (€3, 35 minutes).

ⓘ Information

Ecoteca (☎244 491 904; ☺9.30am-12.30pm & 2-6pm Tue-Sun) Main information office near the Porto de Mós *turismo*, where you can pick up information and hiking maps.

Administrative headquarters (☎243 999 480; pnsac@icnb.pt; Rua Dr Augusto César Silva Ferreira) In Rio Maior, at the south of the park.

RIBATEJO

Literally meaning 'Above the Tejo', Ribatejo is the only Portuguese province that doesn't border either Spain or the open ocean. A string of Templar castles are proof of its strategic importance, though these days its clout is economic, thanks to industry along the Tejo and the rich agricultural plains that spread out from the river's banks. This is also bull country – most of Portugal's fighters are bred in and around the capital, Santarém.

Santarém

POP 29,000 / ELEV 110M

Contemplating the staggering views from Santarém's Portas do Sol garden atop the old town walls, it's easy to understand why Roman, Visigoth, Moorish and Portuguese armies all wanted to claim this as their strategic stronghold above the Rio Tejo. Dom Afonso Henriques' storming of these heights in 1147 marked a turning point in the Reconquista and quickly became the stuff of Portuguese national legend. The city's name refers to Santa Iria, the martyred saint who washed up on these shores after being thrown into the Tejo upstream near Tomar.

A group of beautiful Gothic buildings recalls Santarém's glory days, though it was quickly eclipsed by Lisbon. These days, the Ribatejan capital's main claims to fame are bullfights and a large agricultural fair in June.

History

One of the most important cities of Lusitania under Julius Caesar, and prized by the Moors under the name Xantarim for almost 400 years, Santarém already had centuries of history under its belt before passing to Portuguese rule in 1147. So great was Dom Afonso Henriques' joy at conquering this legendarily impenetrable citadel that he built the magnificent Mosteiro de Santa Maria de Alcobaça (p267) in gratitude.

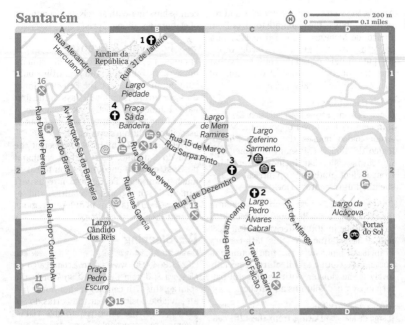

Under the Portuguese, Santarém became a favourite royal residence (hunting was the main draw), and its palace served as the meeting place of the *cortes* during the 13th, 14th and 15th centuries. A 400-year royal hiatus ended in 1833 – when Dom Miguel used it as his base during his brief (unsuccessful) war against his brother Pedro.

Pedestrianised Rua Serpa Pinto and Rua Capelo e Ivens constitute the heart of Santarém's old town, where you'll find the *turismo* and most of the restaurants, shops and cheap accommodation. Signposts to the Portas do Sol lookout lead visitors on a walk past most of the churches of interest.

◉ Sights

Unless noted otherwise, attractions below are open from 9am to 12:30pm and from 2pm to 5:30pm Wednesday through Sunday.

Portas do Sol   GARDEN
(Gates of the Sun; ⊘9am-6pm Oct-Apr, to 10pm May-Sep) Occupying the site of the Moorish citadel, the Portas do Sol garden proffers by far the town's best views over the Rio Tejo and the great spread of plains that surround it. The garden's shady walks make a fine place for a picnic or afternoon linger.

FREE **Museu Arqueológico**   MUSEUM
(Largo Zeferino Sarmento) This archaeological museum is housed in the enchanting 12th-century Igreja de São João de Alporão.

Among the stone carvings, *azulejos* and rotating exhibits is the elaborate tomb of Dom Duarte de Menezes, who died in 1464 in a battle against the Moors in North Africa. It's quite grand – especially considering that once the Moors had finished with him, all that was left for burial was a tooth!

Torre das Cabaças MUSEUM
(Largo Zeferino Sarmento; admission €1) This 15th-century bell tower opposite the Museu Arqueológico houses the Núcleo Museológico do Tempo (Museum of Time). The museum's collection includes everything from ancient sundials to an intricate, glass-sheathed, 19th-century clock.

Convento de São Francisco MONASTERY
(Rua 31 de Janeiro; €2) Restored and reopened to the public in 2009 after years of neglect and a devastating fire, this 13th-century Franciscan monastery is a fine example of Portuguese Gothic architecture. Especially lovely is the cloister, with its graceful pattern of twinned columns and arches.

Igreja de Marvila CHURCH
(Largo de Marvila) Dating from the 12th century but with 16th-century additions, this endearing little church has a fine, twisted Manueline doorway, while the interior is completely awash in brilliant, dramatically patterned *azulejos* dating from the 17th century.

Igreja da Graça CHURCH
(Largo Pedro Álvares Cabral) Just south of the Igreja de Marvila is Santarém's early-15th-century church, with its delicately carved facade of multilayered arches. Inside, a rose window spills light across the beautifully spare interior of stone columns and white walls. Note especially the tombs of Pedro Álvares Cabral (the 'discoverer' of Brazil, who lived in Santarém) and Dom Pedro de Menezes (the first governor of Ceuta, who died in 1437). The de Menezes family founded the church, which explains why Dom Pedro's funerary monument – supported by a pride of lions – is considerably more ornate than that of the more prominent explorer.

Igreja de Nossa Senhora da Conceição
CHURCH
(Praça Sá da Bandeira) This baroque, 17th-century Jesuit church, built on the site of the former royal palace, looms over the town's most impressive square, Praça Sá da Bandeira. The church now serves as the town's cathedral. Inside is a lush baroque ceiling bursting with angels, plus a number of elaborately gilded altars.

🎺 Festivals & Events
Famous nationwide for its merriment, horse races, bullfights and night-time bull-running in the streets, the **Feira Nacional da Agricultura** lasts for 10 days in the first half of June and mostly takes place 2km west of the town centre. There are lots of associated children's events.

Held over a fortnight in October at the Casa do Campino, the **Festival Nacional de Gastronomia** encourages you to eat as much traditional Portuguese fare as you can. Stalls sell regional specialities, and selected restaurants from 18 different regions present their finest cuisine.

🛏 Sleeping
Casa da Alcáçova INN €€€
(☑243 304 030; www.alcacova.com; Largo da Alcáçova 3; d from €125; P 🛜 🛝) Worth the splurge, this 17th-century manor house has an enviable position near the Portas do Sol garden, with the same remarkable vistas. Rooms are impeccable, large, bright and beautifully furnished, while the handsome, walled garden includes an inviting pool.

Residencial Muralha GUEST HOUSE €
(☑243 322 399; Rua Pedro Canavarro 12; s/d without breakfast €30/35) By the old town walls, this simple and centrally located place offers cheerful, good-value rooms with tiled floors and rather eclectic ornaments.

Pensão José Rodrigues GUEST HOUSE €
(☑962 837 909; Travessa do Frois 14; r per person without breakfast €15-20) On a quiet cobbled alley between Santarém's two pedestrianised thoroughfares, Dona Arminda rents out a few simple rooms, most with shared bathroom. Look for the *'quartos/dormidas'* sign out front.

Residencial Vitória GUEST HOUSE €
(☑243 309 130; Rua 2 Visconde de Santarém 21; s/d €25/45; ❄) This night-at-your-great-aunt's-type place is run by Dona Vitória, assisted by various elderly hangers-on. It has clean and well-kept rooms with old-fashioned amenities, including parquet wood floors and writing desks.

Hotel Alfageme GUEST HOUSE €
(☑243 377 240; www.hotelalfageme.com; Av Bernardo Santareno 38; s/d €59/69; P ❄ @) This place offers standard business-class comforts, but the location in a high-rise

district 2km north of the centre leaves a lot to be desired.

✗ Eating & Drinking

As you'd expect of a student-packed agricultural town, Santarém is well off for good-value restaurants.

TOP CHOICE O Saloio   PORTUGUESE €

(Travessa do Montalvo 11; mains €5.50-7.50; ⊙lunch & dinner Mon-Fri, lunch Sat) This cosy, tiled, family-friendly *tasca* (tavern) is a neighbourhood favourite thanks to its authentic Portuguese dishes. Drop your inhibitions and discover local specialities like *enguias de caldeirada* (eel stew).

Taberna do Quinzena   PORTUGUESE, BAR €

(www.quinzena.com; Rua Pedro de Santarém 93; mains €6-9; ⊙lunch & dinner Mon-Sat) If you don't mind drawing a few locals' stares, this atmospheric neighbourhood hang-out is well worth a visit. Walls plastered with brightly coloured bullfighting posters are a reminder that this was once a macho refuge, though women can now join the boys for a simple plate of grilled meat or fish, washed down with local Ribatejo wine straight from the barrel. A second branch near the bus station, **Taberna do Quinzena II** (Cerca da Mecheira 20) is slightly less intimidating for tourists squeamish about sticking out like a sore thumb.

Aromatejo   PORTUGUESE €€

(www.aromatejo.pt; Travessa Bairro do Falcão 21; mains €9-12; ⊙lunch & dinner Wed-Sun) Overlooking the Tejo, this garden restaurant commands a fantastic river-and-rural view from its outside terrace. The house speciality is aromatically grilled wild game, from partridge to deer to wild boar.

O Quintal do Beco

PORTUGUESE, INTERNATIONAL €

(Beco dos Fiéis de Deus 15; mains €5-6.50; ⊙lunch & dinner Mon-Sat) This cheerful, modern place with lots of natural light draws in local crowds for its €7.50 midday specials including a main meal, beer and dessert.

ⓘ Information

Esp@çonet (Sala de Leitura Bernardo Santareno, Rua Pedro Canavarro; ⊙10am-6pm Mon-Fri) Free internet access.

Hospital (✆243 300 200; Av Bernardo Santareno) On the northern edge of town.

Police station (✆243 322 022; Av do Brasil)

Post office (Rua Dr Teixeira Guedes; ⊙8.30am-6.30pm Mon-Fri, 9am-12.30pm Sat)

Turismo (✆243 304 437; posto.turismo@cm-santarem.pt; Rua Capelo e Ivens 63; ⊙9am-7pm Mon-Fri, 10am-12.30pm & 2.30-5.30pm Sat & Sun)

ⓘ Getting There & Around

The **train station** is 2.4km northeast and steeply downhill from the centrally located **bus station** (Av do Brasil). Local buses run regularly between the two stations on weekdays and Saturday mornings (€1.25, 10 minutes). **Taxis** (✆243 332 919) charge about €4 for the trip.

BUS **Rede Expressos** (www.rede-expressos.pt) and **Rodotejo** (www.rodotejo.pt) operate at least three times daily (more frequently to Lisbon) to the following destinations: Coimbra (€13, 2¼ hours), Fátima (€8.80, 45 minutes), Leiria (€11.50, 1¼ hours), Lisbon (€7.50, one hour).

CAR & MOTORCYCLE There is usually sufficient street parking; there are also a few public car parks near the bullring.

TRAIN Very frequent IC (€9.50) and local (€5.65) trains go to Lisbon (45 minutes to one hour).

Constância & Castelo de Almourol

POP 3800

Constância's compact cluster of whitewashed houses, cobbled lanes and narrow staircases spills picturesquely down a steep hillside to the confluence of the Rios Tejo and Zêzere. Its leafy riverfront promenade, main square and gardens make a lovely place for lunch or a stroll before moving on to the biggest draw in these parts, the neighbouring Castelo de Almourol.

⊙ Sights

Castelo de Almourol   CASTLE

(⊙10am-5.30pm) Like the stuff of legend, the 10-towered Castelo de Almourol seems to have broken away from the land and floated out into the middle of the Rio Tejo. Set on an island that was once the site of a Roman fort, the castle was built by Gualdim Pais, Grand Master of the Order of the Knights Templar, in 1171. It's no surprise that Almourol has long caught the imagination of excitable poets longing for the Age of Chivalry.

The *castelo* is 5km from Constância. Boats (€1.25, five minutes) leave regularly from a riverside landing directly opposite the castle. Once on the island, a short walk leads up to the ramparts, where you're free to linger as long as you like.

WINES OF RIBATEJO

For years, Ribatejo wines were considered good, honest jug stuff, while the really good vintages came from Alentejo. Indeed, alluvial soil and a temperate climate historically made these wines fruity and eminently drinkable, if unexciting, and prone to rough, tannic edges. However, the 21st century has seen vintners pursuing more experimental techniques and exploiting more labour-intensive, higher-quality terrains on the stony hillsides. In 2000 the region won DOC (Denominação de Origem Controlada; the best wine certification in Portugal) status, with six regions of particular distinction: Tomar, Santarém, Coruche, Chamusca, Cartaxo and Almeirim.

For more information about vineyards and suggested do-it-yourself itineraries, head to www.viniportugal.pt, or pick up one of Vini Portugal's free wine-route maps, available at tourist offices throughout the region.

🛏 Sleeping & Eating

Casa João Chagas HOTEL €
(☎249 739 403; www.constancia.info; Rua João Chagas, Constância; r midweek/weekend €47/49; ❄ ❒ ☞) Once the town hall, this 18th-century house offers rather plain but neat, high-ceilinged rooms just off the main square near the river. João Chagas also runs the Café da Praça nearby; try the fantastic *queijinhos do Céu* (sweets from heaven), still made by local nuns.

Remédio d'Alma PORTUGUESE €€
(Largo 5 de Outubro, Constância; mains €11-15; ☺lunch Tue, lunch & dinner Wed-Sun) For fine regional cooking, try this elegant little place, set in a pretty stucco house with a lovely garden shaded by orange trees. It's 200m upriver from Constância's main square.

ℹ Information

Constância's **turismo** (☎249 730 052; turismo@cm-constancia.pt; ☺9.30am-1pm & 2.30-5.30pm Mon-Fri, 2.30-6pm Sat & Sun) is beside the river in the centre of town.

ℹ Getting There & Away

By public transport, a combined visit to both Constância and Castelo de Almourol is possible but somewhat tricky. The bus and train routes described below can be joined into a loop with the insertion of an intermediate rail leg between Constância's Praia do Ribatejo station and Almourol station (€1.10, three minutes); however, there's a substantial walk involved at the Constância end of this short train journey.

BUS Constância is easily reached by bus from Tomar (€2.30, 40 minutes). There's no regular bus service to Castelo de Almourol.

CAR & MOTORCYCLE If driving your own vehicle, exit the A23/IP6 at Constância and follow signs to the riverside ferry landing directly opposite Castelo de Almourol.

TRAIN To visit the castle only, take a local train (changing at Entroncamento) from Tomar (€2.50, 55 minutes) or Santarém (€2.95, 45 minutes) to tiny Almourol station, then walk 1km downhill to the ferry landing. The train station nearest Constância – known as Praia do Ribatejo – is 2km outside town, so the bus is a better option if you're only visiting Constância.

Tomar

POP 16,000

Tomar is one of central Portugal's most appealing small cities. With its pedestrian-friendly historic centre, its pretty riverside park frequented by swans, herons and families of ducks, and its charming natural setting adjacent to the lush Mata Nacional dos Sete Montes (Seven Hills National Forest), it wins lots of points for aesthetics.

But to understand what makes Tomar truly extraordinary, cast your gaze skyward to the crenellated walls of the Convento de Cristo, which forms a beautiful backdrop from almost any vantage point. Eight-and-a-half centuries after its founding, this venerable headquarters of the legendary Knights Templar still rules the hill above town, casting Tomar in the role of supporting actor. Now a Unesco World Heritage Site, Tomar's crown jewel is a rambling concoction of Gothic, Manueline and Renaissance architecture that bears extravagant witness to its integral role in centuries of Portuguese history, from the founding of Portugal as a nation-state to the Age of Discoveries.

The Rio Nabão neatly divides the town, with new developments largely concentrated on the east bank and the old town to the west. The monastery looks down on it all from a wooded hilltop at the town's western edge.

Given the good train connections from Lisbon, Tomar makes a very appealing place to base yourself for a few days, or even a pleasant first destination to get over your jet lag.

◉ Sights

Convento de Cristo MONASTERY, CASTLE
(☏249 313 481; adult/child/senior €6/free/3, 9am-2pm Sun & holidays free; ☺9am-6pm Jun-Sep, to 5pm Oct-May) Wrapped in equal parts splendour and mystery, the Knights Templar held enormous power in Portugal from the 12th to 16th centuries, and largely bankrolled the Age of Discoveries. Their headquarters are set on wooded slopes above the town and enclosed within 12th-century walls. The Convento de Cristo is a stony expression of magnificence combined with the no-holds-barred theatricality that long lent the order its particular fascination.

The monastery was founded in 1160 by Gualdim Pais, Grand Master of the Templars. It has chapels, cloisters and chapter houses in widely diverging styles, added over the centuries by successive kings and Grand Masters. You can follow a short route (45 minutes) or take a more comprehensive 90-minute tour.

Charola

This 16-sided Templar church, thought to be in imitation of the Church of the Holy Sepulchre in Jerusalem, dominates the complex. The interior is otherworldly in its vast heights – an awesome combination of simple forms and rich embellishment. It's said that the circular design enabled the knights to attend Mass on horseback. In the centre stands an eerily Gothic high altar, like a temple within a temple. Restored wall paintings date from the early 16th century. A huge funnel to the left is an ancient organ pipe (the organ itself is long gone).

Dom Manuel was responsible for tacking the nave on to the west side of the Charola and for commissioning the architect Diogo de Arruda to build a chapter house with a *coro alto* (choir) above it. The main western doorway into the nave is a splendid example of Spanish plateresque style (named after the ornate work of silversmiths), and is the work of Spanish architect João de Castilho. The same team repeated its success at Belém's Mosteiro dos Jerónimos.

THE ORDER OF THE KNIGHTS TEMPLAR

Founded in about 1119 by French crusading knights to protect pilgrims visiting the Holy Land, the Templars got their name when King Baldwin of Jerusalem housed them in his palace, which had once been a Jewish temple. The Knights soon became a strictly organised, semireligious gang. Members took vows of poverty and chastity, and wore white coats emblazoned with a red cross – a symbol that eventually came to be associated with Portugal itself. By 1139 the Templars came under the pope's authority and were the leading defenders of the Christian crusader states in the Holy Land.

In Portugal, Templar knights played a key role in expelling the Moors. Despite their vows of poverty, they gladly accepted land, castles and titles in return for their military victories. Soon the order had properties not just in Portugal but all over Europe, the Mediterranean and the Holy Land. This geographically dispersed network enabled them to take on another influential role: bankers to kings and pilgrims.

By the early 14th century, the Templars had grown so strong that French King Philip IV – eager for their wealth or afraid of their power – initiated an era of persecution (supported by the French pope Clement V). He arrested all of the knights, accusing many of heresy and seizing their property. In 1314 the last French Grand Maître (Master) was burned at the stake.

In Portugal, Dom Dinis followed the trend by dissolving the order in 1314, but a few years later he cannily re-established it as the Order of Christ, though now under the royal thumb. It was largely thanks to the order's wealth that Prince Henry the Navigator (Grand Master from 1417 to 1460) was able to fund the Age of Discoveries. In the 16th century, Dom João III took the order into a humbler phase, shifting it towards monastic duties. In 1834, together with all of the other religious orders, it was finally dissolved.

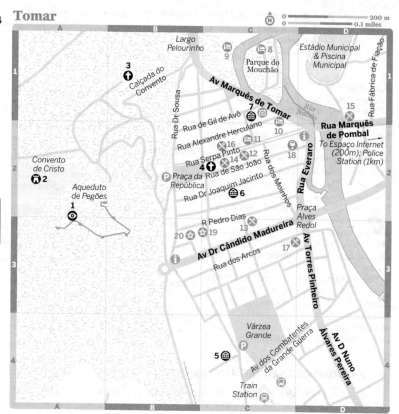

ESTREMADURA & RIBATEJO RIBATEJO

Claustro do Cemitério & Claustro da Lavagem

Two serene, *azulejo*-decorated cloisters to the east of the Charola were built during the time when Prince Henry the Navigator was Grand Master of the order in the 15th century. The Claustro do Cemitério (Burial-Ground Cloisters) contains two 16th-century tombs and some pretty citrus trees, while the two-storey Claustro da Lavagem (Ablutions Cloisters) affords nice views of the crenellated ruins of the Templars' original castle.

Chapter House

Seeming to have grown from the wall like a frenzied barnacle, the window on the western side of the chapter house is the most famous and fantastical feature of the monastery. It's the ultimate in Manueline extravagance, a celebration of the Age of Discoveries: a Medusa tangle of snaking ropes, seaweed and cork boats, on top of which

floats the Cross of the Order of Christ and the royal arms and armillary spheres of Dom Manuel. These days it's covered in ochre-coloured lichen – appropriate given the seaworthy themes. It's best seen from the roof of the adjacent Claustro de Santa Bárbara. Follow signs to the *janela* (window).

Unfortunately obscured by the Claustro Principal is an almost-equivalent window on the southern side of the chapter house.

Claustro Principal

The elegant Renaissance Claustro Principal (Great Cloisters) stands in striking contrast to the flamboyance of the monastery's Manueline architecture. Commissioned during the reign of João III, the cloisters were probably designed by the Spaniard Diogo de Torralva but completed in 1587 by an Italian, Filippo Terzi. These foreign architects were among several responsible for introducing a delayed Renaissance style into Portugal. The Claustro Principal is arguably the country's finest expression of that style: a sober ensemble of Greek columns and Tuscan pillars, gentle arches and sinuous, spiralling staircases.

The outlines of a second chapter house, commissioned by João III but never finished, can be seen from the cloisters' southeast corner.

FREE Museu Luso-Hebraico Abraham Zacuto MUSEUM
(Rua Dr Joaquim Jacinto 73; ⊙10am-7pm Tue-Sun) On a charming cobbled lane in the old town, you'll find the country's best-preserved medieval synagogue. Built between 1430 and 1460, it was used for only a few years before Dom Manuel's convert-or-leave edict of 1496 forced most Jews to do the latter. The synagogue subsequently served as a prison, chapel, hayloft and warehouse until it was classified as a national monument in 1921.

Mostly thanks to the efforts of Luís Vasco (who comes from one of two Jewish families left in Tomar and is often present), the small, plain building has been remodelled to look something like it would have in the 15th century. It's named after the Jewish mathematician and royal astrologer who helped Vasco da Gama plan his voyages. Inside, among various stones engraved with 13th- and 14th-century Hebraic inscriptions, is a rose-coloured limestone block from the Great Synagogue of Lisbon, dating from 1307. The walls are adorned with

gifts and contributions from international Jewish visitors. The upturned jars high in the wall were a device to improve acoustics.

FREE Museu dos Fósforos MUSEUM
(⊙10am-7pm Tue-Sun) This museum, reached via the lovely courtyard of the Convento de São Francisco, contains Europe's largest collection of matchboxes. Amassed by local 'phillumenist' Aquiles da Mota Lima, the 40,000-plus matchboxes from countries around the world depict everything from bullfighters to bathing beauties, dinosaurs and French cuisine.

Aqueduto de Pegões AQUEDUCT
This impressive aqueduct, striding towards the monastery from the northwest, was built between 1593 and 1613 to supply water to thirsty monks. Its 180 arches, some of which are double-decker, are thought to have been designed by Italian Filippo Terzi. It's best seen just off the Leiria road, 2.3km from town.

Igreja de São João Baptista CHURCH
(⊙10am-7pm Tue-Sun) The old town's most striking church faces Praça da República, itself an eye-catching ensemble of 17th-century buildings. The recently restored church dates mostly from the late 15th century. It has an octagonal spire and richly ornamented Manueline doorways on its northern and western sides. Inside are 16th- and 17th-century *azulejos;* Gregório Lopes, one of 16th-century Portugal's finest artists, painted the six panels hanging inside.

FESTA DOS TABULEIROS

Tomar's Festival of the Trays is a weeklong celebration with music, drinking, dancing and fireworks. But the highlight is definitely the procession of about 400 young, white-clad women (traditionally virgins) bearing headdresses of trays stacked as tall as they are with loaves of bread and ears of wheat, decorated with colourful paper flowers and, finally, topped with a crown, cross or white paper dove. Young male attendants, dressed in black and white, help the girls balance the load, which can weigh up to 15kg. The following day, bread and wine are blessed by the priest and handed out to local families. The festival is believed to have roots in pagan fertility rites, though officially it's related to the saintly practices of 14th-century Dona Isabel (Dom Dinis' queen).

The festival is held every four years during the first two weeks of July. As this book goes to press, the next one is scheduled for 2–11 July, 2011.

Igreja de Nossa Senhora da Conceição
CHURCH

Downhill from the monastery is this strikingly simple Renaissance basilica (closed for renovation at the time of research). It's attributed to Diogo de Torralva, architect of the Convento cloisters.

FREE Núcleo De Arte Contemporânea
MUSEUM

(Rua de Gil de Avô; ☺10am-7pm Tue-Sun) This recently opened museum showcases the work of modern artists from all over Portugal.

🏃 Activities

Via Aventura
KAYAKING

(www.via-aventura.com) Organises kayak trips on the Rio Nabão as well as to Constância and Castelo de Almourol (€15 per person).

🎊 Festivals & Events

Tomar's most famous event is the quadrennial Festa dos Tabuleiros. It is next scheduled for early July 2011.

The Nossa Senhora da Piedade, another important religious festival, features a candlelit procession and a parade of floats decorated with paper flowers. It's held on the first Sunday in September.

🛏 Sleeping

TOP CHOICE Residencial União
HOTEL €

(☎249 323 161; www.hotel-ami.com/hotel/uniao; Rua Serpa Pinto 94; s/d/q €25/38/45; ☎) Tomar's most atmospheric budget choice, this once-grand town house features large and sprucely maintained rooms with antique furniture and fixtures. Especially pleasant are the expansive old-fashioned parlour and bright breakfast room. New, French-speaking owners had just purchased the place at time of research.

Estalagem de Santa Iria
INN €€

(☎249 313 326; www.estalagemsantairia.com; Parque do Mouchão; s/d/ste €65/85/125; ☎) Centrally located on an island in Tomar's lovely riverside park, this slightly kitsch, '40s-style country inn has large comfortable rooms, most with balconies overlooking the leafy grounds or the river. Downstairs are a restaurant and bar, both with roaring fireplaces in the winter.

Quinta do Valle
RURAL INN €€

(☎249 381 165; www.quintadovalle.com; 2-/4-person apt €89/109; P☎) With parts dating back to the 15th century, this manor house 7km south of Tomar, together with its outbuildings, has been turned into an upmarket inn, with large grounds, chapel, swimming pool and quaint two- to four-bedroom apartments featuring fireplaces and kitchenettes.

To get here from Tomar, take the N110 south to Santa Cita, then follow the signs.

Camping Redondo
CAMPGROUND €

(☎249 376 421; www.campingredondo.com; sites per adult/child/tent/car €3.50/2/2.80/2.10, 4-person chalet €60-75; ☎☎) This lovely Dutch-run campground with four chalets plus two additional units in a stone cottage is 10km northeast at Poço Redondo. Amenities include a bar, pool and sun terrace.

For transport details and driving directions in English, consult the website.

Hotel dos Templarios
HOTEL €€€

(☎249 310 100; www.hoteldostemplarios.pt; Largo Cândido dos Reis 1; s/d/ste €108/128/199; P☎☎) If Tomar's summer heat has you gasping for air-con and a swimming pool, look no further than this comfortable if somewhat dated four-star hotel at the river's edge, just outside the historic centre. Rooms are enormous and most have terraces. There are indoor and outdoor pools, the latter adjacent to a small but stylish hotel bar.

Residencial Cavaleiros Cristo HOTEL €€
(☎249 321 203; www.cavaleirosdecristo.pt; Rua Alexandre Herculano 7; s/d €37/52; ✳☎) In a newer building down a side street near the river, this place offers comfortable, modern rooms with writing desks and mini-bars. Wireless access costs €2 per day.

Residencial Luz GUEST HOUSE €
(☎249 312 317; www.residencialluz.com; Rua Serpa Pinto 144; s/d €20/30; @) Tomar's cheapest downtown option offers grandmotherly, threadbare and doleful rooms with spongy faux-wood floors. The best have front balconies with views of Tomar's main pedestrian thoroughfare and the castle beyond.

 Eating

Calça Perra INTERNATIONAL €€
(Rua Pedro Dias 59; mains €8-13; ☺lunch & dinner Tue-Sun) At this charming backstreet eatery, you can dine in the pretty pink-walled dining room or the breezy courtyard below. The menu is diverse and innovative, and guest chefs and occasional fado nights keep things lively. Lunch specials (€9) include beer or wine, soup, main course and coffee.

Restaurante Tabuleiro PORTUGUESE €
(Rua Serpa Pinto 140; mains €6.80; ☺lunch & dinner Mon-Sat) Located just off Tomar's main square, this family-friendly local hang-out features warm, attentive service, good traditional food and ample portions.

Restaurante Tomaz PORTUGUESE €
(Rua dos Arcos 31; mains €4-8; ☺lunch & dinner Mon-Sat) Popular with locals, this simple, appealing place has unbeatable prices plus a cosy tiled dining room and outdoor seating on a wide, leafy street.

Restaurante Bela Vista PORTUGUESE €€
(Rua Marquês de Pombal 68; mains €6-11; ☺lunch & dinner Wed-Sun, lunch Mon) The views are lovely from Bela Vista's wisteria-bedecked terrace overlooking the river, although service and food (standard Portuguese fare) are somewhat less dependable.

La Bella ITALIAN €€
(Rua Serpa Pinto 149; mains €7.50-12; ☺lunch & dinner Tue-Sun) People flock to this brightly

THEATRE IN THE MONASTERY

For a completely different take on Tomar's Convento de Cristo, catch a performance of Umberto Eco's *The Name of the Rose* by hometown theatre troupe Fatias de Cá. From the first strains of Gregorian chants wafting through the monastery's entry hall, to the torch-lit finale in the Great Cloisters, this performance takes you to places (literally and figuratively) that you won't get to during a daytime tour.

Not for the faint of heart or weak of leg, the play is a multi-hour workout. Although performed in Portuguese, its plot is easy enough to follow for anyone who has read the novel, and roaming the monastery by night is a wonderful experience regardless of your linguistic abilities. As the drama unfolds, actors lead you from room to room and back again, eventually taking you to almost every corner of the monastery. The presentation is punctuated by five meal breaks, each taking place in the old refectory, where chanting black-robed monks preside at the head of long stone tables. The first course involves a little tongue-in-cheek medieval humour: diners are presented with a rock and a pile of walnuts and left to their own devices. Subsequent courses are more substantial and accompanied by free-flowing wine.

As the sun sets, a mood of meditative contemplation creeps in with the crepuscular light. Walking the hallways in this altered state, it's easier to summon up images from centuries past: the Knights Templar mounted on horseback in their torch-lit octagonal chapel, or the royal wedding that took place in the half-finished chapter house under a roof improvised from sailcloth. The play's last few scenes, staged in obscure attic-like spaces off the public tour circuit, are guaranteed to jolt you out of this reverie.

Fatias de Cá stages performances in other atmospheric sites throughout Portugal, including the Sete Montes national forest, the Roman ruins of Conimbriga and the old quarry full of fossilised dinosaur footprints near Porto de Mós. For full details, see www.fatiasdeca.com.

lit, mirror-walled pizzeria just behind Igreja de São João Baptista for excellent pasta, pizza and meat dishes.

🍷 Drinking & Entertainment

Theatro Café Concerto Bar das Artes BAR (www.theatro.uffportugal.pt; Rua do Teatro; ☺10pm-4am Wed-Sat) Right next door to the movie theatre, this eclectic bar features jazz, classical music and weekend DJ sets running the gamut from electronic to lounge to alternative sounds.

Fatias de Cá THEATRE TROUPE (☎960 303 991; www.fatiasdeca.com) This Tomar-based theatre company presents highly innovative and entertaining weekend performances of works such as *The Name of the Rose* and *The Tempest,* often in amazing locations (see the boxed text p287).

Cine Teatro Paraíso CINEMA, THEATRE (cnr Ruas Infantaria 15 & do Teatro) Showing movies five nights a week, the community-run Cine Teatro Paraíso also hosts occasional live music and drama performances.

Akiákopus Bar BAR (Rua de São João 28; ☺9.30pm-4am) This cosy little drinking hole has stone walls, beamed ceilings and an infinite range of libations.

Café Paraíso BAR-CAFE € (Rua Serpa Pinto 127; snacks from €3; ☺9pm-2am Mon, 8am-2am Tue-Sat, 8am-8pm Sun) This old-fashioned, high-ceilinged deco cafe serves as a refuge for anyone in need of a mid-afternoon snack and a shot of caffeine or whisky.

ℹ Information

District hospital (☎249 320 100; Av Maria de Lourdes Mello e Castro) A new hospital 1km east of town.

Espaço Internet (Rua Amorim Rosa; ☺10.30am-12.30pm & 2.30-7pm Mon-Sat) Free internet access.

Police station (☎249 328 040; Rua Dom Lopo Dias de Sousa)

Post office (Av Marquês de Tomar; ☺8.30am-6.30pm Mon-Fri)

Regional turismo (☎249 329 000; info@visittemplarios.com; Rua Serpa Pinto 1; ☺9am-7pm) For information the surrounding region, visit this air-conditioned office with comfy armchairs and free internet.

Turismo (☎249 322 427, 249 329 823; turismo@cm-tomar.pt; Av Dr Cândido Madureira; ☺10am-7pm) Offers a good map of the town and an accommodation list with prices.

ℹ Getting There & Away

The bus and train stations are next door to each other, about 500m south of the *turismo*. You will also find several large car parks here.

BUS Two to four daily buses serve Fátima (€4.25, one hour), Batalha (€5.10, 1½ hours), Alcobaça (€6.50, two to 2½ hours), Nazaré (€7, 2½ to three hours) and Leiria (€3.70, one hour).

TRAIN Trains run to Lisbon's Santa Apolónia and Oriente stations (€8.35, two hours) via Santarém (€4.35, 55 minutes) every hour or two between 6am and 10pm.

Food & Wine

Cheeses on display at the bustling Mercado do Balhao, Porto

Eat! Eat!

The Portuguese eat with gusto; food is positively relished.

The culinary day starts mid-morning, when peckish folk nibble on a fresh pastry or three from a *pastelaria* (pastry and cake shop) or cafe, and gulp down a *bica* (espresso) while standing at a bar. There's a cracking coffee culture in Portugal: coffee quality is high and baristas are good.

Lunch is a serious past time. As the main meal of the day – usually taken some time between midday and 3pm – lunches are big and hearty. Much Portuguese cuisine is prepared simply, dished up without pretension and served in massive portions; *meia dose* (half-portion) is an expression worth knowing.

Late afternoon sees another sugar hit. Increasingly, dinner is also on the Portuguese agenda, and can be more of the same – large portions of meat-based dishes.

Opening hours for most eateries – *restaurantes* (restaurants), *tabernas & adegas* (literally 'taverns & wine cellars' but, these days, a restaurant by another name), *churrasqueiras* (grill houses) and *marisqueiras* (seafood restaurants) – are noon to 3pm and 7pm to 10pm. *Cervejarias* (beer hall) stay open all day and well into the night. Cafes and snack bars are open all day – at any time of day you can opt for a trusty *tosta mista* (toasted ham and cheese sandwich).

So, how to savour Portugal? Loosen your belt a notch, eat (or risk offending), and take your tastebuds on a trip... Prepare to spend plenty of hours at the table.

Below
Traditional Portuguese breakfast: cofee and cake

Portuguese Staples

Bread, cheese, pork, fish and wine are the clear winners in the Portuguese staples. That's not to leave out chicken (especially grilled or with piri-piri), olives and olive oil, and sweet pastries.

Traditionally, Portuguese meals were served on slabs of bread *(pão)* instead of plates. These days, bread is integral to every meal. *Pão caseiro* is home-baked bread, usually with a crusty outer. Bread turns up in *açorda* (bread soup), *migas* (bread pieces prepared as a side dish) and *ensopados* (stews with toasted or deep-fried bread).

Cheese – usually made of ewe's or goat's milk – is a common appetiser with a bowl of olives or as a snack. Regions have their own cheese varieties.

Pork meat and pork-based products form the basis of many meals. Portuguese pork (especially *porco preto* – black pork) will have you oinking happily all the way home.

As for seafood, even if you think you don't like *bacalhau* (salted cod), there are two words for you: learn to. *Bacalhau* is bound up in myth, history and tradition, in everything from everyday dishes to important celebrations; it would be bad form to pass it up. Nowadays, the cod is imported, mainly from Scandinavian countries. But this hasn't stopped the local consumption of massive amounts of the trusty fish. There are over 365 recipes for cod – one for each day of the year.

Above
Fresh-baked crusty loaves in a Porto shop window

Bite-Sized Regions

Vegetable jam. Savoury cakes. Pork sweets. Meat with seafood. Portugal's distinct regional delights feature a mix of textures and tastes. Recalibrate your expectations and enjoy a tasty journey.

Lisbon

Lisbon has some of the country's best cuisine, from local *tascas* (taverns) to large hotels and traditional Portuguese to modern international. But traditions live on: this is home of the legendary *pastéis de nata* (see p294) and grilled sardines.

Algarve

A culinary conundrum: tragically, nowhere in the country is the bland internationalisation of local food so apparent; yet, conversely, the region boasts more Michelin-starred restaurants than anywhere else in Portugal.

This is a bivalve zone, with hordes of fresh clams, oysters, mussels, cockles and whelks. Don't go past the seafood *cataplana* (a Portuguese version of the Spanish paella) and *xerém* (corn mash made with cockles).

Alentejo

Warning to vegetarians: pork will confront you at every repast. Bread also figures heavily; you'll find it in gazpacho or *açorda* (bread soup with garlic, herbs and a poached egg). In hunting season, *perdiz* (partridge), *lebre* (hare) and *javali* (wild boar) are the go.

Estremadura & Ribatejo

Seafood dominates the culinary palate in Estremadura; *caldeiradas de peixe* (fish stews) rule the menus, closely followed by *escabeche* (marinated vinegar fish stew) and *sopas de mariscos* (shellfish soups). Carnivores should head to Ribatejo – this is meat and tripe country. *Enguias* (eels) slip down a treat, too.

Beiras

There's plenty of *bacalhau* and *ovos moles* (thickened sweet egg yolks), egg cakes and *chanfana* (goat or lamb stews), plus Atlantic seafood. Sausages are the go here, as are cheeses, especially Rabaçal cheese and *Queijo Serra da Estrela* (Serra cheese).

Minho

This region produces the (in)famous *vinho verde* (green wine – 'green' because it's made from immature grapes, either red or white), *Caldo verde* (Galician kale and potato soup), *broa de Milho* (golden corn loaf), thrifty *sopa seca* (dry soup) and the seasonal eel-like lamprey, trout and salmon dishes.

Douro & Trás-os-Montes

Region of the *tripeiros* (tripe eaters), this is also the place to pig out, with great *presunto* (ham) and pork dishes – even the rich desserts pack a porky punch. The pork-free *alheira* (a bread and meat sausage) was invented by the Jewish people during the Inquisition. Crops of figs, cherries, almonds, chestnuts and oranges abound.

Clockwise from top left
1. *Sardinhas gerlhadas* (grilled sardines) 2. A fresh and fruity *vinho verde* 3. *Caldo verde* – green soup with your green wine?

2

QUINTA
DE
CARRAPEÇOS

2006
REGIONAL MINHO

O / TRAJADURA
WHITE WINE

12.5% vol.   750 ml

3

Sweet Habits

When indulging in Portuguese cakes and pastries – served in the country's excellent *pastelarias* and cafes – three rules apply:

One, any time is a good time to partake. Two, consume with an espresso or cup of tea (look out for the traditional tea rooms). Three, do what the locals do – never stop at one...

With every bite of a Portuguese sweet you are consuming history. Portugal's sweets industry was crystallised when the Arabs introduced sugar to the country. In medieval times, enterprising nuns and monks made – and sold – *doces conventuais* (literally, convent sweets). The best known of these is the *pastel de nata*, a creamy, dreamy, egg-based custard tart.

Why the 'eggy emphasis'? The story goes that nuns stiffened their habits with egg whites and, to consume the leftover yolks, devised special recipes. In those convents attended by wealthy women (many of whom were sent by their fathers to avoid expensive marriages), cooking became a pursuit to fill the days. The animals and produce of the convents provided handy ingredients.

Don't think twice about indulging in this irresistible experience – it may be 'sinful', but it's oh so sweet.

HEAVENLY TREATS

Wonderful egg-based convent legacies:
» *pastéis de Tentugal* (heavenly pastry parcels)
» *toucinho do céu* ('heaven's lard'; almond cake with a smidgeon of pork fat)
» *papos de anjo* ('angel's chins'; sugared egg-yolk ribbons)
» *barriga de freira* ('nun's belly'; egg tart)

Below
Irresistable cinnamon-dusted *pastéis de nata*

The Grape Escape

The Portuguese have been growing grapes for at least 2000 years. The country boasts some of the oldest and most unique grape varieties on the planet, grown and processed within hundreds of formal wine estates.

These days, the world of viticulture is acknowledging Portugal's wines, from table wines to superlative fortified drops including, of course, port wine. Since joining the EU in 1986 the country's wine industry has modernised rapidly, and it isn't holding back.

The Portuguese are really pushing their viticulture industry, as well they should. Portugal's wine trade association ViniPortugal (www.viniportugal.pt) has marked an excellent range of regional wine routes (complete with maps and details), highlighting *adegas* (wineries) that welcome visitors. *Adega*-hopping is a great way to see the countryside and several have accommodation options and good restaurants attached.

Enthusiastic boozing also extends to beer; two brands – Sagres and Super Bock – fight it out for market share. Beer is strong (5% alcohol) and inexpensive. Regions, too, boast their own spirited *aguardentes* (firewaters), which kick like a mule.

Above
Flat-bottomed *barcos rabelos* boats were traditionally used to transport port wine from the vineyards

---

WINE WAYS

Treat your palate to these indigenous Portuguese grape varieties:
» **Whites** – Alvarinho, Arinto (Pedernã), Encruzado, Fernão Pires (Maria Gomes), Loureiro
» **Reds** – Aragonês (Tinta Roriz), Baga, Castelão, Touriga Franca, Touriga Nacional, Trincadeira (Tinta Amarela)

Contemporary Cuisine

Portuguese cuisine may not be on the world's gastronomic radar along with nearby France or Spain, but it should be.

Often ignored by outsiders, Portuguese cuisine has always been celebrated by the proud food-loving locals themselves. As many locals attest, who cares about fancy presentation when you've got taste and quality? Think oodles of fresh, local and seasonal produce from both land and sea.

Furthermore, many traditional Portuguese products have been accorded Protected Geographical Status (along the lines of French camembert and Italian parmigiana). These include Serpa cheese and Moscatel de Setúbal.

And the country is by no means behind the culinary times. New young Portuguese chefs are embracing the world of gastronomy. Some are adding contemporary twists to traditional recipes, others are embracing international cuisine using fresh Portuguese produce. Lisbon, Porto and the Algarve in particular boast fine international restaurants (some Michelin starred) serving top-class, innovative cuisine.

TOP CONTEMPORARY PICKS

» **Vila Joya** (p167) Delightful two-Michelin-star restaurant by the sea.

» **100 Maneiras** (p88) The place for a creative tasting menu.

» **Alma** (p90) A heavenly experience in all-white surrounds.

» **Kyodai** (p373) Brazilian-owned Sushi extravaganza, featuring a daily set menu.

» **Vinho em Qualquer Circunstância** (p271) Sleek and stylish wine bar.

» **Batel** (p322) The place to have fun with food.

Below
The glossy interior of Vinho em Qualquer Circunstância

The Beiras

Best Places to Stay

» Casa Pombal Guesthouse (p306)

» Aveiro Rossio Hostel (p321)

» Quinta dos Três Rios (p345)

» Quinta das Cegonhas (p335)

Best Places to Eat

» Batel (p322)

» O Albertino (p337)

» O Hilário (p346)

» Restaurante Área Benta (p353)

Why Go?

Three worlds rolled into one, the Beiras offer as much diversity as any region in Portugal.

Along the Atlantic, the Beira Litoral (Coastal Beira) lures surfers and sun-seekers with scores of sandy beaches. Here, the Beiras' top two tourist destinations – the sophisticated university town of Coimbra and the brash casino-party town of Figueira da Foz – arm-wrestle for visitors' attention.

Move inland to the Beira Alta (Upper Beira) and the mood shifts entirely. Stoic stone villages cling to the slopes of Portugal's highest mountains – the Serra da Estrela – casting their gaze down at the fertile wine country of the Dão valley.

East of the mountains, in the hypnotically beautiful Beira Baixa (Lower Beira), vast expanses of olive and cork oak forest spread across a hotter, lonelier landscape. Here, surveying the borderlands from the ramparts of nearly abandoned medieval fortress-towns, you feel centuries away from the coast you just left behind.

When to Go

Coimbra

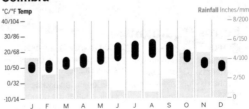

Early May Queima das Fitas fills Coimbra's streets with students in dashing black capes.

June Before summer crowds descend, Beiras beaches are warm enough for a swim.

July Clear mountain air and low-season prices coalesce in the Serra da Estrela.

BEIRA LITORAL

Coimbra

POP 101,000

The medieval capital of Portugal for over a hundred years, and site of the country's greatest university for the past five centuries, Coimbra wears its weighty importance in Portuguese history with gritty dignity. Its historic core straggles down a hillside on the east bank of the Rio Mondego, a multicoloured collage of buildings spanning nearly a millennium, from the Moor-

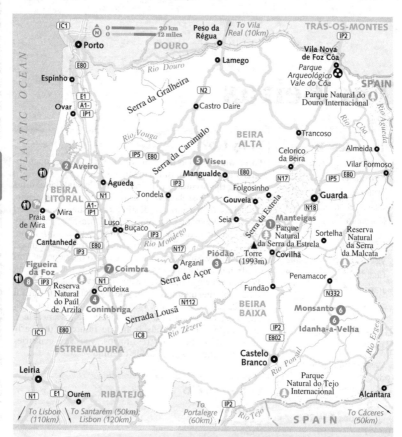

Beiras Highlights

❶ Hike alongside the glistening Rio Zêzere outside **Manteigas** (p336), past shepherds' huts and soaring peaks

❷ Admire the art nouveau facades lining the canals of **Aveiro** (p319), then hit the streets for some of the Beiras' most animated nightlife

❸ Switchback your way up terraced slopes to **Piódão** (p324), the most picturesque of the Beiras' stone villages

❹ Conjure up a vanished civilisation at the Roman ruins of **Conimbriga** (p311)

❺ Sip fine Dão wine in the flowery civic gardens of **Viseu** (p342)

❻ Savour the golden light in the cork oak forest as you climb from ancient **Idanha-**a-Velha to the craggy cliff-top castle at **Monsanto** (p327)

❼ Listen for the first notes of the *serenata*, a midnight fado performance staged annually by students in **Coimbra** (p303)

❽ Catch a wave, a casino show or a few rays at the poolside bar in **Figueira da Foz** (p314)

ish Arco de Almedina at the base of town to the 18th-century clock tower crowning the courtyard of the old university.

If you visit during the academic year, you'll be sure to feel the university's influence. Students throng the bars and cafes of the old town and Praça da República; posters advertise talks on everything from genetics to genocide; and graffiti scrawled outside *repúblicas* (communal student dwellings) addresses the political issues of the day. If you can, come during the Queima das Fitas in early May, a raucous weeklong celebration featuring live music every night. Or stroll the streets on a summer evening, when the city's old stone walls reverberate with the haunting metallic notes of the Portuguese *guitarra* (guitar) and the full, deep voices of fado singers.

Take a few steps outside the historic centre and you'll also see the city's modern side – a brand new riverfront park with terrace bars and restaurants, a spiffy pedes-

trian bridge across the Mondego, and vast shopping complexes offering everything you'd expect in a major European city.

Coimbra makes a fine base for day visits to the remarkable Roman ruins at Conimbriga, the medieval hilltop fortress of Montemor-o-Velho, or the outlandishly ornate Palace Hotel do Buçaco.

History

The Romans founded a city at Conimbriga, though it was abruptly abandoned in favour of Coimbra's more easily defended heights. The city grew and prospered under the Moors, who were evicted definitively by Christians in 1064. The city served as Portugal's capital from 1139 to 1255, when Afonso III decided he preferred Lisbon.

The Universidade de Coimbra, Portugal's first university (and among the first in Europe), was actually founded in Lisbon by Dom Dinis in 1290 but settled here in 1537. It attracted a steady stream of teachers,

Beira Litoral

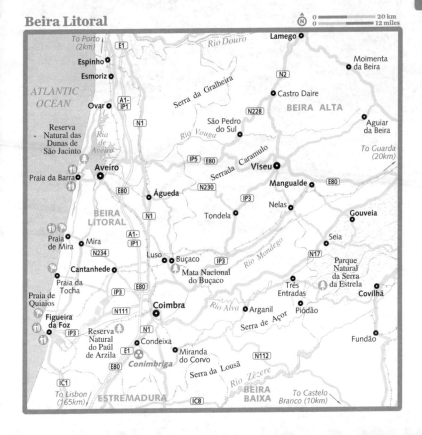

THE BEIRAS BEIRA LITORAL

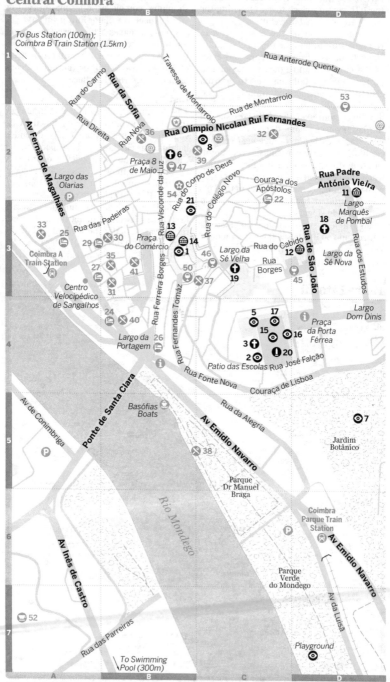

To Bus Station (100m);
Coimbra B Train Station (1.5km)

Rua do Carmo
Rua da Sofia
Rua Direita
Rua Nova
Travessa de Montarroio
Rua Anterode Quental
Rua de Montarroio
53
Av Fernão de Magalhães
Rua Olímpio Nicolau Rui Fernandes
36
8
6
39
47
32
Praça 8 de Maio
Largo das Olarias
Rua das Padeiras
54
Rua do Corpo de Deus
21
Rua Visconde da Luz
Couraça dos Apóstolos
22
Rua Padre António Vieira
11
Largo Marquês de Pombal
18
33
25
29 30
35
27 41
31
Praça do Comércio
13
14
1
46
50
37
Rua do Colégio Novo
Largo da Sé Velha
19
Rua do Cabido
Rua Borges
12
Rua de São João
Largo da Sé Nova
45
Largo dos Estudos
Coimbra A Train Station
Centro Velocipédico de Sangalhos
24 40
Largo da Portagem
26
Rua Ferreira Borges
Rua Fernandes Tomáz
5
17
15
3
2
16
20
Praça da Porta Férrea
Largo Dom Dinis
Rua José Falção
Patio das Escolas
Rua Fonte Nova
Couraça de Lisboa
Ponte de Santa Clara
Av de Coimbriga
Basófias Boats
Rua da Alegria
Av Emídio Navarro
38
7
Jardim Botânico
Parque Dr Manuel Braga
Rio Mondego
Coimbra Parque Train Station
Av Emídio Navarro
Av Inês de Castro
52
Parque Verde do Mondego
Av da Luísa
Rua das Parreiras
To Swimming Pool (300m)
Playground

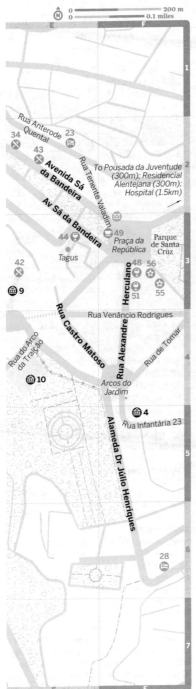

artists and intellectuals from across Europe. The 16th century was a particularly heady time thanks to Nicolas Chanterène, Jean de Rouen (João de Ruão) and other French artists who helped create a school of sculpture here that influenced styles all over Portugal.

Today Coimbra's university remains Portugal's most prestigious – and one of its most traditional. Students still attend class in black robes and capes – often adorned with patches signifying course of study, home town or other affiliation – while a rigorously maintained set of rites and practices called the *codigo de praxe* (praxe code) governs all aspects of student life, including the schedule of the annual Queima das Fitas.

Crowning Coimbra's steep hilltop is the university, around and below which lies a tangle of lanes marking the limits of the old town. The new town, locally called 'Baixa', sprawls at the foot of the hill and along the Rio Mondego.

From the main bus station on Avenida Fernão de Magalhães it's about 1.2km to the old centre. There are three train stations: Coimbra B (also called *estação velha*, or old station), 2km northwest of the centre; central Coimbra A (also called *estação nova*, or new station, and on timetables called just 'Coimbra'); and Coimbra Parque, south of the centre. Coimbra A and B are linked by a rail shuttle, free for those with an inbound or outbound long-distance ticket.

Pick up a map of the city centre in any of Coimbra's *turismos* (tourist offices).

◉ Sights

Compact Coimbra is best toured on foot. Sights of interest across the river are also accessible on foot via the Ponte de Santa Clara. Seniors pay the same price as students at all museums.

Upper Town HISTORICAL NEIGHBOURHOOD
Long a Moorish stronghold and for a century the seat of Portugal's kings, Coimbra's upper town rises abruptly from the banks of the Rio Mondego. The most picturesque way to enter Coimbra's labyrinth of lanes is via **Arco de Almedina** – the city's heavy-duty Moorish gateway – and up the staggered stairs known as Rua Quebra Costas (Backbreaker). People have been gasping up this hill (and falling down it) for centuries; local legend says that it was the 19th-century writer Almeida Garrett who persuaded the mayor to install the stairs.

THE BEIRAS COIMBRA

Central Coimbra

Sights
1 Arco de Almedina ... B3
2 Biblioteca Joanina ... C4
3 Capela de São Miguel ... C4
4 Casa Museu Bissaya Barreto ... F5
5 Clock Tower ... C4
6 Igreja de Santa Cruz & Cloisters ... B2
7 Jardim Botânico ... D5
8 Jardim da Manga ... C2
9 Museu Acadêmico ... E3
10 Museu Botânico ... E4
11 Museu da Ciência ... D2
12 Museu Nacional Machado de Castro ... D3
13 Núcleo da Cidade Muralhada/Torre de Almedina ... B3
14 Palácio de Sub Ripas ... B3
15 Patio des Escolas ... C4
16 Porta Férrea ... C4
17 Sala dos Capelos ... C4
18 Sé Nova ... D3
19 Sé Velha ... C3
20 Statue of João III ... C4
21 Torre de Anto ... B3
Velha Universidade ... (see 15)

Sleeping
22 Casa Pombal Guesthouse ... C2
23 Grande Hostel de Coimbra ... E2
24 Hotel Astória ... B4
25 Hotel Oslo ... A3
26 Pensão Residencial Larbelo ... B4
27 Pensão-Restaurante Flôr de Coimbra ... A3
28 Residencial Botânico ... F6
29 Residencial Domus ... A3

Eating
30 Adega Paço dos Condes ... B3
31 Churrasqueira Giro ... B3
32 Mercado Municipal Dom Pedro V ... C2
33 Minipreço Supermarket ... A3
34 Molho de Brócolos ... E2
35 Porta Larga ... B3
36 Restaurante Democrática ... B2
37 Restaurante do Gil ... C3
38 Restaurante Italia ... C5
39 Restaurante Jardim da Manga ... C2
40 Restaurante Zé Manel ... B4
41 Restaurante Zé Neto ... B3
42 Student Cantina ... E3
43 Zé Carioca ... E2

Drinking
44 AAC Pub ... E3
45 Bar Bigorna ... D3
46 Bar Quebra Costas ... C3
47 Café Santa Cruz ... B2
48 Café Tropical ... F3
49 Cartola Esplanada Bar ... F3
50 Fangas Mercearia & Bar ... B3
51 Feitoconceito ... F3
52 Galeria Bar Santa Clara ... A7
53 Shots Bar ... D1

Entertainment
54 À Capella ... B2
55 Noites Longas ... F3
56 Via Latina ... F3

To the left up Rua Sub Ripas is the grand Manueline doorway of the early-16th-century **Palácio de Sub Ripas**; its Renaissance windows and stone ornaments are the work of Jean de Rouen, whose workshop was nearby. Further on is the **Torre de Anto**, a tower that once formed part of the town walls.

Backtrack and climb via Largo da Sé Velha up to the Museu Nacional Machado de Castro and the 'new' campus, much of it founded by the Marquês de Pombal in the 18th century. Dominating Largo da Sé Nova in front of the museum is the severe **Sé Nova** (New Cathedral; ⌚9.30am-12.30pm & 2-6.30pm Tue-Sat), started by the Jesuits in 1598 but only completed a century later.

The **Museu Acadêmico** (Colégio de São Jerónimo; adult/student €1/0.50; ⌚10am-12.30pm & 2-5pm Mon-Fri), just uphill from Largo Dom Dinis, has some interesting displays on Coimbra student life, including vintage Queima das Fitas posters from decades past (especially noteworthy is the 27 May 1926 poster showing hordes of student revellers one day before the coup d'état that ushered in the Salazar era). The museum is also adorned with some grand *azulejos* (hand-painted tiles).

For a glimpse of student life, stroll along any of the alleys around the *sé velha* (old cathedral) or below the *sé nova*. Flags and graffiti mark the cramped houses known as *repúblicas,* each housing a dozen or so students from the same region or faculty.

Velha Universidade

In every way the university's high point, the Old University consists of a series of remarkable 16th- to 18th-century buildings, all set around the vast **Patio das Escolas**. You enter the patio by way of the elegant 17th-century **Porta Férrea**, which occupies the same site as the main gate to Coimbra's Moorish stronghold. In the square is a **statue of João III**, who turns his back on a sweeping view of the city and the river. It was he who re-established the university in Coimbra in 1537 and invited big-shot scholars to teach here.

The square's most prominent feature is the much-photographed 18th-century **clock tower**. This tower is nicknamed *a cabra* (the goat) because, when it chimed to mark the end of studies, the first-year undergrads were pounced upon by swaggering elder students and then humiliated without mercy – that is, unless they leapt their way home like mountain goats in order to avoid them.

From the courtyard gate take the stairway on the right up to the rather grand **Sala dos Capelos** (Graduates' Hall), a former examination room hung with dark portraits of Portugal's kings, and heavy patchwork, quiltlike decoration. Better yet is the adjacent catwalk, which affords visitors excellent city views.

Back outside, take a peek to the left below the clock tower, where you'll find the entrance to the fanciful **Capela de São Miguel**, an ornate baroque chapel with a brightly painted ceiling and a gilded baroque organ. Concerts still take place here on occasion – ask at the *turismo* for a schedule.

However, all else pales before **Biblioteca Joanina** (João V Library) next door. A gift from João V in the early 18th century, it seems too extravagant and distracting for study with its rosewood, ebony and jacaranda tables, elaborately frescoed ceilings and gilt chinoiserie bookshelves. Its 300,000 ancient books deal with law, philosophy and theology, though they might as well be painted onto the walls for all the study they receive now.

Admission to both the Biblioteca Joanina and the Sala dos Capelos is €7/4.90/4.90 for adults/seniors/students, or you can visit just one for €5/3.50/3.50. Entry to the Capela de São Miguel costs €3/2.10/2.10.

Visitors are only admitted in small numbers and on a timetable (from 9am to 7pm April to October; from 9.30am to 5pm Monday to Friday and 10.30am to 4pm on Saturday and Sunday from November to March), and you may find that some rooms are closed during degree ceremonies. Groups of more than four may want to book a few days ahead through the **ticket office** (239 859 884; reservas@ci.uc.pt) adjacent to the municipal *turismo,* in the square just

---

FIRED UP

In the first week of May, Coimbra marks the end of the academic year with **Queima das Fitas** (www.queimadasfitas.org) – a weeklong party that serves as the country's biggest and best excuse to get roaring drunk. Literally, the name means 'Burning of the Ribbons', because graduates ritually torch the colour-coded ribbons worn to signify particular courses of study.

In the wee hours of Friday morning, the Queima kicks off with the **Serenata Monumental**, a hauntingly beautiful midnight fado performance on the steps of the Sé Velha. The agenda continues with sports events, private black-tie balls, nightly concerts at the so-called **Queimodromo** across the Ponte de Santa Clara, and a beer-soaked Sunday-afternoon parade called the **Cortejo dos Grelados** that runs from the university down to Largo da Portagem.

In their rush to sponsor the various festivities, Portuguese breweries provide ultracheap beer, which is distributed and drunk in liberal quantities. Relations between students and police are amazingly friendly, but the strain on local hospitals is heavy, with a strong emphasis on stomach pumping.

outside the Porta Férrea. Individuals and smaller groups can generally get in with minimal waiting time.

Sé Velha
CATHEDRAL

(Largo da Sé Velha; ⊙10am-6pm) Coimbra's stunning old cathedral is considered to be one of the finest examples of Romanesque architecture in all of Portugal. Its crenellated exterior and narrow, slit-like lower windows serve as reminders of the nation's embattled early days, when the Moors were still a threat. Since its construction in the late 12th century, the building has been only slightly altered. Even the 16th-century Renaissance portal in the northern wall is so eroded you hardly notice it. The austere majesty of the interior is broken only by a 16th-century gilded altarpiece.

Museu da Ciência
MUSEUM

(www.museudaciencia.org; Largo Marquês de Pombal; adult/student €3/1.50; ⊙10am-6pm Tue-Sun) This wonderful science museum occupies a centuries-old former monastery converted by Pombal into the university's chemical engineering building. With a couple of awards under its belt since opening in 2006, it features intriguing state-of-the-art interactive science displays coexisting with 18th-century lab sinks. Don't miss the giant glowing globe in a room paved with medieval stones, or the psychedelic insect's-eye view of flowers. Displays are English/Portuguese bilingual.

Museu Nacional Machado de Castro
MUSEUM

(www.ipmuseus.pt; Largo Dr José Rodrigues; adult/student €2/1; ⊙10am-6pm) In a former bishop's palace, complete with a 16th-century loggia overlooking the *sé velha* and the old town, this art museum houses one of Portugal's most important collections of 14th- to 16th-century sculpture. Long closed for renovations, the museum's lower level has recently reopened, displaying a remarkably vast set of Roman foundations known as the Cryptoporticum, which used to sit below the forum of Roman Aeminium. The rest of the museum is officially slated to reopen in 2011, although it could be later than that.

Baixa & Around

Igreja de Santa Cruz
CHURCH

(Praça 8 de Maio; adult/student €2.50/1.50; ⊙9am-noon & 2-5pm Mon-Sat, 4-5.30pm Sun) From the trendy shops out on Praça 8 de Maio, this church plunges you back to Man-

ueline and Renaissance times. Step through the Renaissance porch and flamboyant 18th-century arch to discover some of the Coimbra School's finest work, including an ornate pulpit and the elaborate tombs (probably carved by Nicolas Chanterène) of Portugal's first kings, Afonso Henriques and Sancho I. The most striking Manueline work is in the restrained 16th-century cloister.

Behind the church is the **Jardim da Manga** (once part of the cloister) and its curious fountain: a lemon-yellow, four-buttressed affair.

Núcleo da Cidade Muralhada/Torre de Almedina
MUSEUM

(cidade.muralhada@cm-coimbra.pt; Pátio do Castilho; adult/student €1.70/1.10; ⊙10am-1pm & 2-6pm Tue-Sat) Housed in the medieval tower directly above the Arco de Almedina, this historical museum displays a plaster reproduction of Coimbra's old-town layout, complete with castle. A multilingual audiovisual presentation traces the fate of the many towers that used to line Coimbra's walls, each lit in red on the map as its story is told. There are fine city views upstairs, but the real fun is looking down through the *matacães* (dog killers), big holes cut in the watchtower's stone floor, through which hot oil was traditionally poured on unsuspecting enemies below.

Praça da República & Around

Leafy Praça da República is the unofficial student social centre. The surrounding neighbourhood, laid out in the 19th century and still dominated by prim bourgeois homes of the period, is a relaxing break from the high density of both the university and the Baixa area.

Jardim Botânico
GARDEN

(⊙9am-8pm Apr-Sep, 9am-5.30pm Oct-Mar) A serene place to catch your breath, the lovely botanical garden sits in the shadow of the 16th-century Aqueduto de São Sebastião. Founded by the Marquês de Pombal, the gardens combine formal flowerbeds, meandering paths and elegant fountains. The green-fingered can also visit the lush greenhouses (admission €0.50) and the adjacent **Museu Botânico** (Botanical Museum; adult/student & senior €2/1.50; ⊙9am-noon & 2-5pm Mon-Fri).

Casa Museu Bissaya Barreto
MUSEUM

(www.fbb.pt; Rua Infantaria 23; adult/child or senior €2.50/1.25; ⊙3-6pm Tue-Sun) Bissaya

Barreto was a local surgeon, scholar and obsessive hoarder of fine arts, and his handsome, late-19th-century mansion has been turned into an art museum. A guide (not necessarily English-speaking) accompanies guests through rooms jam-packed with Portuguese sculpture and painting, Chinese porcelain, old *azulejos* and period furniture.

Along & Across the River

In a kind of ecclesiastical counterweight to the university, a cluster of convents, together with several other sights, sits on the far side of the Rio Mondego. A new pedestrian bridge connects these west-bank attractions to one of the city's prettiest green spaces, stretching south from the historic centre along the east side of the river.

Convento de Santa Clara-a-Velha CONVENT
(Rua das Parreiras; admission €5; ☺10am-7pm Tue-Sun May-Sep, to 5pm Oct-Apr) In 2009, after two decades of steady renovation work, this Gothic convent was reopened to the public after finally being cleared of the river ooze that had drowned it since the 17th century. Founded in 1330 by the saintly Dona Isabel, Dom Dinis' wife, it served as her final resting place until flooding and mud forced her to move uphill to Convento de Santa Clara-a-Nova. The new museum adjacent to the convent displays archaeological finds from the excavation, and shows two films, one about the nuns who lived here, the other documenting the renovation work itself.

Convento de Santa Clara-a-Nova CONVENT
(admission cloister €1.50; ☺8.30am-6pm) Begun on higher ground in the 17th century to replace its flooded twin, this convent is devoted almost entirely to the saintly Isabel's memory. Aisle panels tell her life story, while her solid-silver casket is enshrined above the altar. Even her clothes hang in the sacristy. Her statue is the focus of the Festa da Rainha Santa.

Quinta das Lágrimas GARDEN
(admission €2; ☺10am-7pm Tue-Sun, closed Jan) Legend says Dona Inês de Castro met her grisly end in the gardens of this private estate (see boxed text, p268). It's now a deluxe hotel, although anyone can take a turn about the gardens and track down the Fonte dos Amores (Lovers' Fountain), which marks the spot where the king's unwitting mistress was struck down. Also note the

sequoia tree planted by English hero, the Duke of Wellington.

Parque Dr Manuel Braga & Parque Verde do Mondego PARKS
Lovely green spaces stretch south from the Ponte de Santa Clara along the eastern bank of the river. Parque Dr Manuel Braga provides a haven of serene shade under stately rows of old sycamores, while the newer Parque Verde do Mondego, opened in 2004, features riverfront bars and eateries, a pedestrian bridge across the Rio Mondego and a small playground for kids.

🏃 Activities

Several organisations offer opportunities for canoeing, rafting and other outdoor sports in the region surrounding Coimbra. Many trips begin in nearby Penacova.

O Pioneiro do Mondego KAYAKING
(☑239 478 385; www.opioneirodomondego. com) Rents out kayaks for paddling the Rio Mondego between Penacova and Torres de Mondego, an 18km trip costing €20 per person.

Transserrano ADVENTURE
(☑235 778 938; www.transserrano.com) Leads adventure and cultural discovery tours in the nearby Serra da Lousã and Serra do Açor, including hiking, climbing and tours focused on traditional cheese-making and olive-oil production.

Coimbra for Children

Aside from the engaging Portugal dos Pequenitos, Coimbra is short on children's play spaces. The best bet near the city centre is the small playground in the Parque Verde do Mondego. Across the river, via the new pedestrian bridge, there's also a brand new swimming pool (adult/child €5/3).

Portugal dos Pequenitos AMUSEMENT PARK
(www.portugaldospequenitos.pt; Rossio de Santa Clara; adult/child €8.95/5.50; ☺10am-7pm) The brainchild of local collector Bissaya Barreto, Portugal dos Pequenitos is an impossibly cute theme park where kids clamber over, into and through doll's-house versions of Portugal's most famous monuments, while parents clutch cameras at the ready. There's an extra charge to visit the marginally interesting mini-museums of marine life, clothing and furniture. You can also hop aboard one of the frequent river trips with Basófias.

QUEEN-SAINT ISABEL

One of Portugal's most popular saints, Isabel is most often depicted with a scattering of roses falling across her garments. Legend has it that one day while she was bringing food to the poor, her less-than-saintly husband (Dinis I) accused her of stealing food from the royal kitchens. When the king angrily demanded to see the contents of her apron, out fell nothing but flowers. Rainha Isabel – not surprisingly, given the tenor of the apocryphal tale – is credited with founding homes for abused wives and abandoned children. When eldest son Afonso challenged Dom Dinis for the throne, Isabel rode on horseback between the two lines of opposing forces, daring both father and son to attack her first.

☞ Tours

Basófias   BOAT TRIPS
(www.basofias.com; ☉Tue-Sun) Basófias runs boat trips (€6, 55 minutes) on the Rio Mondego. They depart from beside Parque Dr Manuel Braga hourly from 3pm to 7pm May to September, and at 3pm and 4pm only October to April.

Carristur   BUS TOURS
(www.carristur.pt, in Portuguese; adult/child €9/5; ☉Sat & Sun mid-Mar–mid-May, Tue-Sun mid-May–Oct) Carristur runs hour-long hop-on, hop-off bus tours of Coimbra with recorded multilingual commentary. The double-decker open-top buses originate near the *turismo* at Largo da Portagem. The bus ticket (available at the *turismo* and some local hotels, as well as at the offices of Coimbra's local transport company, SMTUC) entitles you to a Basófias boat tour and free or discounted admission to several other city attractions.

Tuk Tuk City Tour   TUK-TUK TOURS
(☎969 830 664; adult/under 10yr €9.50/free; ☉10.30am, 11.30am, then hourly 2.30-5.30pm Tue-Sun) New in summer 2010, this hour-long circuit takes you whizzing deftly through the old town's narrow streets aboard an eight-seater Thai *tuk-tuk,* then explores the city's outskirts before depositing you back at Largo da Portagem. Tickets – purchased from the driver at the embarkation point in Largo da Portagem – include a free Basófias boat tour.

✯✯ Festivals & Events

Queima das Fitas

Coimbra's biggest bash celebrates the end of the academic year in great style. The festivities take place every year during the first week in May.

Festa da Rainha Santa

Held around 4 July in even-numbered years, this festival commemorates Santa Isabel. A Thursday-night candlelit procession carries her statue from the Convento de Santa Clara-a-Nova across the Ponte de Santa Clara to Largo da Portagem and through the streets of Coimbra to Igreja do Carmo; a second procession the following Sunday returns her to the convent. The festival also coincides with the Festa da Cidade (Town Festival), celebrated with music, folk dancing and fireworks.

Festival das Artes

Initiated in 2009, this two-week festival in late July brings classical music to the Quinta das Lágrimas, jazz to the riverboats on the Mondego, famous guest chefs to the local restaurants and other forms of merriment to Coimbra's streets.

🛏 Sleeping

⬛ Casa Pombal Guesthouse
TOP CHOICE   GUEST HOUSE €€
(☎239 835 175; www.casapombal.com; Rua das Flores 18; d with shared/private bathroom €52/68; ☉closed 2-3 weeks in Jan; @🛜) Hidden down a narrow lane near the university, this winning, Dutch-run guest house squeezes tons of charm into a small space. The cosy wood-floored rooms are simple, fresh and brightly coloured, and a couple of attic eyries boast superb views. The friendly owners provide multilingual advice about local cultural events, plus an ample morning buffet in the gorgeous blue-tiled breakfast room. Single rooms cost €5 less. Book ahead during the busy season (Easter to October).

Quinta das Lágrimas   HOTEL €€€
(☎239 802 380; www.quintadaslagrimas.pt; Rua António Augusto Gonçalves; r from €169; 🅿✳🛜🏊) This splendid historical palace is now one of Portugal's most enchanting upper-crust hotels. Choose between richly furnished rooms in the old palace, or Scandinavian-style minimalist rooms in the modern annexe – complete with ja-

cuzzi. A few rooms look out onto the garden where Dona Inês de Castro reputedly met her tragic end (see boxed text, p268). Significant discounts are sometimes available online, even in high season.

Hotel Astória   HOTEL €€€
(☏239 853 020; www.almeidahotels.com; Av Emídio Navarro 21; s/d/ste €92/112/155; P❄🛜) The Astória's unmistakable art nouveau facade contemplates the river and Largo da Portagem. It has bags of personality and professional staff, though some of the quiet, plush rooms are a tad dog-eared. The round tower suites (room numbers ending in 9) cost €25 extra but score fabulous panoramic views from the Mondego up to the university. Wi-fi is available only in the lobby, not in the rooms.

Pensão-Restaurante Flôr de Coimbra
GUEST HOUSE €
(☏239823865; http://flordecoimbrahr.com.sapo.pt; Rua do Poço 5; s/d/tr with shared bathroom €20/35/45, with private bathroom €50/60/70; 🛜) This once-grand 19th-century home with its own restaurant (mains €10 to €12) offers loads of character in a great location. It's clean and friendly, if occasionally behind on maintenance. The low-ceilinged upstairs rooms, popular with Fátima pilgrims and partially occupied by foreign students during the academic year, have wi-fi, shared bathrooms with ancient plumbing and a community kitchen. Main-floor rooms are larger with private bathrooms.

Hotel Oslo   HOTEL €€
(☏239 829 071/2/3; www.hotel-oslo.web.pt; Av Fernão de Magalhães 25; s/d €60/70; P❄🛜) This outwardly bland, modern hotel block redeems itself with well-maintained rooms, a free garage with complimentary valet parking, satellite TV, double-paned windows and a popular 5th-floor bar with views up to the university. Recently remodelled 'superior' rooms have larger bathrooms, big-screen TVs and balconies.

Residencial Alentejana   GUEST HOUSE €€
(☏239 825 903; www.residencialalentejana.com; Rua Dr António Henriques Seco 1; s €39-55, d €45-68; ❄🛜) Worth the uphill walk, this prominent old town house offers wood-panelled, high-ceilinged older rooms, plus some less charming but still comfortable newer ones.

Residencial Domus   GUEST HOUSE €
(☏239828584; www.residencialdomus.com; Rua Adelino Veiga 62; s/d €30/38; ❄🛜) Clean, well-maintained Domus is a family-run place in a quiet pedestrian shopping zone near Coimbra A. The best rooms are the front-facing ones upstairs, which get plenty of natural light.

Pensão Residencial Larbelo   GUEST HOUSE €
(☏239 829 092; residencialarbelo@sapo.pt; Largo da Portagem 33; s/d €30/40; ❄) In a pleasant and impeccably maintained 19th-century building, Larbelo is bang in the centre and boasts high-ceilinged rooms with wooden floors and modern furnishings. Front rooms with windows opening onto the Largo da Portagem are especially nice.

Residencial Botânico   GUEST HOUSE €
(☏239 714 824; residencialbotanico@mail.telepac.net; Bairro de São José 15; s/d €38/48; ❄🛜) This irreproachably kept guest house is a bit far from the centre, but delightful in every other way. It has friendly staff and spacious, elegantly sparse rooms, including some family suites. There's wi-fi in the lobby and double-paned glass to keep out street noise.

Grande Hostel de Coimbra   HOSTEL €
(☏239 108 212; www.grandehostelcoimbra.com; Rua Antero Quental 196; dm €18, d €40; @🛜) You won't find a hostel more laid-back than this – in fact, service may be too lax for some – but it's hard to beat the location in a grand, century-old town house near the nightlife of Coimbra's university campus.

Pousada da Juventude   HOSTEL €
(☏239 829 228; coimbra@movijovem.pt; Rua Dr António Henriques Seco 14; dm €12, d with shared/private bathroom €28/30; 🛜) Coimbra's HI-affiliated hostel is in a leafy neighbourhood 500m northeast of Praça da República. No meals other than breakfast are served, but there are self-catering kitchen facilities. Do your best to avoid the gloomy basement dorms. From Coimbra A station take northbound bus 6, 7 or 29.

Hotel Tivoli   HOTEL €€€
(☏239 858 300; www.tivolihotels.com; Rua João Machado 4; s/d from €85/95; P❄@🛜🏊) If you require unimpeachable 'business-class' comforts and are willing to give on aesthetics, consider the Tivoli. Occupying an ugly modern building in a rather unappealing and trafficky stretch of the Baixa, it has huge rooms with all the expected frills, a pool and a small gym. Superior rooms upstairs have big-screen LCD TVs, broadband wi-fi and (ahem!) electric blinds.

Eating

If you're feeling gutsy, or simply penniless, you can try your luck at the university's student cantinas (AAC, Av Sá da Bandeira; meals €4.60; ☺lunch & dinner), two of which are off the courtyard of the Associação Acadêmica de Coimbra (AAC). Cheap and filling cafeteria food abounds, although cafeteria personnel have recently begun more stringently enforcing the official policy banning diners not affiliated with the university.

TOP CHOICE Restaurante Zé Manel

PORTUGUESE €€

(Beco do Forno 12; mains €7-9; ☺lunch & dinner Mon-Fri, lunch Sat) Tucked down a nondescript alleyway, this little gem, which is papered with scholarly doodles and scribbled poems, is easy to miss. Despite its location, it's highly popular, so come early or be ready to wait. Try the good *feijoada á leitão* (a stew of beans and suckling pig).

TOP CHOICE Restaurante Zé Neto PORTUGUESE €€

(Rua das Azeiteiras 8; mains €6-10; ☺lunch & dinner Mon-Sat) This marvellous family-run place specialises in homemade Portuguese standards, including *cabrito* (kid). Come in the late morning and you'll catch the elderly owner – a fixture here since 1952 – tapping out the menu on a typewriter of similar vintage

Restaurante do Gil

CONTEMPORARY PORTUGUESE €€

(☎922 040 194; Rua Joaquim d'António d'Aguiar 49; mains €10-15; ☺dinner Tue-Sun) Since buying this low-key neighbourhood tavern a couple of years back, experienced chef Gil has been lovingly converting it into a one-of-a-kind restaurant, featuring traditional Portuguese cuisine with a personal twist. There's no menu; Gil decides what to cook and what wine to serve on a daily basis as he visits local markets. There's also no sign – just look for the only restaurant on the downhill side of this backstreet below the Sé Velha.

Zé Carioca

BRAZILIAN €€€

(Av Sá da Bandeira 89; mains €15-20; ☺lunch & dinner, closed Sun in Aug) Set in a handsome old town house, this Brazilian eatery is both relaxed and elegant. The grilled meats, *moqueca de camarão* (shrimp stewed with coconut milk, tomatoes and coriander) and *caipirinhas* are all superb. The weekday lunch buffet (€16.50 per kilogram) is a good deal, as is the *feijoada* buffet on weekend afternoons (€9 for all you can eat).

Restaurante Jardim da Manga CAFETERIA €

(Rua Olímpio Nicolau Rui Fernandes; dishes €6.50-8.50; ☺lunch & dinner Sun-Fri) Student-friendly and tailored to tight budgets, this cafeteria-style restaurant serves up tasty meat and fish dishes, with pleasant outdoor seating beside the Jardim da Manga fountain.

Porta Larga

SANDWICH SHOP €

(Rua das Padeiras 35; sandwiches €4.50; ☺9am-8pm Mon-Sat) For a quick snack with a hefty dose of local flavour, António's *sandes de leitão* (roast pork sandwich) can't be beat, although it's best avoided if you're squeamish about little piggies turning on spits.

Restaurante Democrática PORTUGUESE €

(Travessa da Rua Nova 5; mains €6-10; ☺lunch & dinner Mon-Sat) A down-to-business, family-friendly place offering good-value standards, Democrática is a Coimbra classic and always filled with hungry students.

Restaurante Italia

ITALIAN €€

(Parque Dr Manuel de Braga; mains €8-15; ☺noon-midnight) Cheery Italia serves reasonably good Italian food, but what really draws the crowds is its incomparable location. The sunny glass-walled dining room is cantilevered out over the Rio Mondego, while breezy outdoor tables bask in the shade of giant sycamores in the adjacent riverside park.

Molho de Brócolos

VEGETARIAN €

(Galerias Avenida, Av Sá da Bandeira 33, 2nd fl, Loja 230; mains €6.50-8; ☺noon-2pm & 8-10pm Mon-Sat; ☑) *Feijoada* with vegan 'sausage'? Miso soup in Portugal? It's enough to make a vegetarian swoon! Hidden on the 2nd floor of a movie theatre-turned-shopping mall, this unassuming eatery serves reasonably priced organic and vegetarian food.

Adega Paço dos Condes

GRILL HOUSE €

(Rua do Paço do Conde 1; mains €5-9; ☺lunch & dinner Mon-Sat) Usually crowded with students and Coimbra locals, this straightforward family-run grill is one of the city's best budget eateries.

Mercado Municipal Dom Pedro V MARKET €

(Rua Olímpio Nicolau Rui Fernandes; ☺Mon-Sat) A colourful stop for self-caterers. this market is full of lively fruit and vegetable stalls and butcher shops displaying Portuguese cuts of meat, hooves, claws and all. Watch out for the bunny eyes!

Churrasqueira Giro

GRILL HOUSE €

(Rua das Azeiteiras 39; mains €7-12; ☺lunch & dinner Mon-Sat) This back-alley place serves wonderful traditional Portuguese fare in a pleasant tiled dining room.

Minipreço SUPERMARKET €
(Rua António Granjo 6C; ☺9am-8pm) Convenient supermarket behind Coimbra's downtown train station.

🍷 Drinking

The big nights are Thursday to Saturday – but during university term time, any night is game.

Cafes

TOP CHOICE **Café Santa Cruz** CAFE
(Praça 8 de Maio; ☺Mon-Sat) Few cafes in Portugal offer such an atmospheric backdrop. The interior, set in a dramatically beautiful high-vaulted former chapel, features stained-glass windows and graceful stone arches, while the outdoor patio area affords one of the city's best vantage points over the popular Praça 8 de Maio. Popular with tourists and locals alike, the cafe periodically hosts free evening music events and talks. You'll pay a bit extra here for the atmosphere, but it's worth it.

Galeria Bar Santa Clara BAR, CAFE
(www.galeriasantaclara.com; Rua António Augusto Gonçalves 67; ☺2pm-2am Sun-Thu, 2pm-3am Fri & Sat) Arty tearoom by day and chilled-out bar at night, this terrific place across the Mondego has good art on the walls, a series of sunny rooms and a fine riverfront terrace.

Cartola Esplanada Bar BAR, CAFE
(Praça da República; ☺8am-2am Mon-Sat; 9am-1am Sun) Equally popular for morning coffee and late-night beers, this perennially packed cafe with a great plaza-side location is the ideal place for a spot of student-watching.

Fangas Mercearia & Bar BAR, TEAROOM
(Rua Fernandes Thomas 45; ☺1pm-1am Tue-Sun) Tucked away on a backstreet off Rua Quebra Costas, this cosy tearoom also doubles as a bar, with a wide selection of teas and a welcoming vibe.

Bars

For a late-afternoon drink, the cluster of bars along the Mondego waterfront in Coimbra's Parque Verde do Mondego makes a pleasant stop. Otherwise, the action is mostly up by the university, near Praça da República and Praça da Sé Velha, where students spill onto the cobblestones outside

classic pubs like **Bar Bigorna** (Rua Borges Carneiro 11) and **O Moelas** (Rua dos Coutinhos 14). For a full list of local clubs and bars, see www.coimbranight.net.

Bar Quebra Costas BAR
(www.quebra.eu; Rua Quebra Costas 45-49; ☺Mon-Sat) In the perfect position to sip a cold beer as you watch people puff and pant up the Quebra Costas, this Coimbra classic has a sunny cobblestoned terrace, an artsy interior, friendly service and chilled-out tunes playing on the sound system.

Feitoconceito BAR
(Rua Alexandre Herculano 16A; ☺Mon-Sat) Entered through the Tabacaria Pavão downstairs, this hip little hideaway near Praça da República woos a student-heavy crowd with regular DJ sets, plus ridiculously low prices on *caipirinhas*, mojitos, gin and tonics, vodka and beer. Hang out at the bar, or decamp to one of the high-ceilinged back rooms, all decorated with eye-catching, one-of-a-kind wallpaper. The vintage barbershop and design store next door are equally fun.

AAC Pub PUB
(Av Sá da Bandeira) Join the black-cape-clad students at their student-union bar, where beers are under €1 and everyone is welcome. The new open-air esplanade out back, with wood decking and a grassy lawn, makes an agreeable refuge from the busy streets outside.

Café Tropical BAR
(Praça da República 35; ☺Mon-Sat) A bare-bones student place with pleasant outdoor seating, bohemian wall decor, cheap beers and lively crowds.

Shots Bar BAR
(Rua da Saragoça) With eight shots going for €5, this is a popular place for students to start (or finish) the night.

☆ Entertainment
Music

If Lisbon represents the heart of Portuguese fado music, Coimbra is its head. The local style is more cerebral than the Lisbon variety, with a greater emphasis on *guitarra*-led instrumental pieces.

Free fado performances take place periodically at Café Santa Cruz – consult the weekly schedule of events posted at the cafe. From late June to mid-September, you'll also find evening folk music and dancing in Praça 8 de Maio.

À Capella
FADO HOUSE

(www.acapella.com.pt; Rua do Corpo de Deus; admission €10; ☺10pm-2am) A tiny, 14th-century chapel transformed into a candlelit cocktail lounge, À Capella regularly hosts the city's most renowned fado musicians. The setting is as intimate as the music itself, with heart-rendingly good acoustics. Be forewarned that these shows cater directly to a tourist crowd, but the atmosphere and music are both superb.

Nightclubs

Late-night activity is concentrated on Rua Almeida Garrett and Av Sá da Bandeira.

Via Latina
DANCE CLUB

(Rua Almeida Garrett 1; ☺Tue-Sat) Students swear by the DJs at this simple, sweaty dance club. Fridays are particularly good, when there's occasional live music. Also worth a look is the **Noites Longas** club next door, which goes till 6am.

Information

Emergency

Police station (☎239 822 022; Rua Olímpio Nicolau Rui Fernandes)

Internet Access

Ciberespaço (Galerias Avenida, Loja 4, Av Sá da Bandeira; per hr €2; ☺10am-midnight Mon-Sat, 1pm-midnight Sun) Paid access with plenty of computers, on ground floor of shopping centre.

Espaço Internet (Praça 8 de Maio 37; ☺10am-2pm & 3-8pm Mon-Fri, 10am-2pm & 3.30-10pm Sat & Sun) Free access.

Laundry

Lavandaria Lucira (Av Sá da Bandeira 86; wash & dry per kg €2; ☺9am-7pm Mon-Fri, 9am-1pm Sat)

Medical Services

Hospital da Universidade de Coimbra (☎239 400 400; Praceta Mota Pinto) Located 1.5km northeast of the centre.

Post

Post office Main branch (Av Fernão de Magalhães 223; ☺8.30am-6.30pm Mon-Fri, 9am-12.30pm Sat); Praça da República (☺9am-6pm Mon-Fri); Rua Olímpio Nicolau Rui Fernandes (☺8.30am-6.30pm Mon-Fri, 9am-12.30pm Sat)

Tourist Information

Good town maps as well as a very detailed bimonthly cultural agenda are available from *turismos*.

Municipal turismo (☎239 834 158; http://turismodecoimbra.pt; Praça da Porta Férrea; ☺10am-5.30pm) Adjacent to the Velha Universidade ticket office, just outside the Porta Férrea.

Regional turismo (☎239 488 120; geral@turismodocentro.pt; Largo da Portagem; ☺9am-6pm Mon-Fri, 9.30am-12.30pm & 1.30-5.30pm Sat & Sun)

Travel Agencies

Tagus (coimbra@viagenstagus.pt; Rua Padre António Vieira; ☺9.30am-6pm Mon-Fri) In the AAC; head here for student and youth travel discounts.

Getting There & Away

Bus

From the main **bus station** (Av Fernão de Magalhães; **Rede Expressos** (☎239 855 270) runs at least a dozen buses daily to Lisbon (€12, 2½ hours) and to Porto (€10.70, 1½ hours), with almost as many to Braga (€11.90, 2¾ hours) and to Faro (€21.50, six to seven hours). There's also regular service (more frequent in summer) that runs to Seia (€10, 1¾ hours), Guarda (€11.80, three hours) and other points around the Parque Natural da Serra da Estrela.

Joalto Mondego (☎239 820 141; Rua João de Ruão 18) has bus service to the Roman ruins at nearby Conímbriga.

Car

Several car-rental agencies are concentrated just south of the bus terminal.

Auto Jardim (Rua Abel Dias Urbano 6)

Hertz (Edifício Tricana, Rua Padre Estevão Cabral)

Train

Long-distance trains stop only at **Coimbra B** station, north of the city. Cross the platform for quick, free connections to more-central **Coimbra A** (called just 'Coimbra' on timetables). There's no left-luggage office at either station.

Coimbra is linked by regular Alfa Pendular (AP) and *intercidade* (IC) trains to Lisbon (AP/IC €21.50/15.50, 1¾/two hours) and Porto (€15.50/11, one/1¼ hours); IC trains also stop at intermediate destinations north and south. Additional *interregional* (IR) services cost slightly less but take at least 30 minutes longer. IR trains also run at least hourly to Figueira da Foz (€2.05, one hour).

Getting Around

Bicycle

For mountain-bike rental, **Centro Velocipédico de Sangalhos** (Rua da Sota 23; ☺9am-12.45pm & 2-7pm Mon-Fri, 9am-1pm Sat) charges €7.50 per day.

Bus

Between them, buses 27, 28 and 29 run about every half-hour from the main bus station and the Coimbra B train station to Praça da República.

You can purchase multi-use tickets (three/11 trips €2/6.10), also usable on the *elevador* (see below), at the **SMTUC office** (www.smtuc.pt; Largo do Mercado; ☺7am-7pm Mon-Fri, 8am-1pm Sat) at the foot of the *elevador*, at official kiosks and also at some *tabacarias* (tobacconists-cum-newsagents). Tickets bought on board cost €1.60 per trip.

You'll also see *patufinhas* (electric minibuses) crawling around pedestrian areas in the centre of Coimbra, between Baixa and Alta Coimbra and through the medieval heart of the city. These accept the same tickets as other SMTUC buses.

Car

If you come by car, prepare for snarled traffic and scarce parking. The best free parking near the Baixa is on the west bank of the river, in a dirt lot just across Ponte de Santa Clara from Largo da Portagem. Nearer the university, free street parking is available on side streets around Praça da República. If you're willing to pay, look for the blue 'P' signs in the Baixa district, and buy your ticket from the machine. Make sure you're legal, as enforcement is strict. There are also parking garages along Avenidas Fernão de Magalhães and Emídio Navarro.

Elevador do Mercado

The **elevador** (☺7.30am-10pm Mon-Sat, 10am-10pm Sun) – a combination of elevator, walkway and funicular between the market and the university – can save you a tedious uphill climb. Use regular city bus tickets, which you punch once for each ascent or descent. You can't buy tickets at the top.

Around Coimbra

CONIMBRIGA

Hidden amid humble olive orchards in the rolling country southwest of Coimbra, Conimbriga boasts Portugal's most extensive and best-preserved Roman ruins, and ranks with the best-preserved sites on the entire Iberian Peninsula. It tells the poignant tale of a town that, after centuries of security, was first split in two by quickly erected walls and then entirely abandoned as the Roman Empire disintegrated.

HISTORY

Though Conimbriga owes its celebrity to the Romans, the site actually dates back to Celtic times (*briga* is a Celtic term for a defended area). However, when the Romans settled here in the 1st century AD, it blossomed into a major city on the route from Lisbon (Olisipo) to Braga (Bracara Augusta). Its prosperity is revealed by well-to-do mansions carpeted with elaborate mosaics and scattered with fountains.

In the 3rd century the townsfolk, threatened by invading tribes, desperately threw up a huge defensive wall right through the town centre, abandoning the residential area. But this wasn't enough to stop the Suevi seizing the town in 468. Inhabitants fled to nearby Aeminius (Coimbra) – thereby saving Conimbriga from destruction.

☉ Sights

Museum   MUSEUM
(adult/student incl ruins €4/2, 10am-1pm Sun free; ☺10am-6pm Tue-Sun) To get your head around Conimbriga's history, begin at the small but well-organised and informative historical museum. Displays present every aspect of Roman life from mosaics to medallions. There's a sunny cafe-restaurant at the back.

Ruins   ROMAN RUINS
(☺10am-6pm daily) The sprawling Roman ruins, included in museum admission, tell a vivid story. On the one hand, their domesticity is obvious, with elaborate mosaics, heated baths and trickling fountains that evoke delightful, toga-clad dalliances. But smack through the middle of this scene runs a massive defensive wall, splitting and cannibalising nearby buildings in its hasty erection to fend off raids.

It's the disproportionately large wall that will first draw your attention, followed by the patchwork of exceptional mosaic floors below it. Here you'll find the so-called Casa dos Repuxos (House of Fountains); though partly destroyed by the wall, it contains cool pond-gardens, fountains and truly extraordinary mosaics showing the four seasons and various hunting scenes.

The site's most important villa, on the other side of the wall, is said to have belonged to one Cantaber, whose wife and children were seized by the Suevi in an attack in 465. It's a palace of a place, with baths, pools and a sophisticated underground heating system.

Excavations continue in the outer areas. Eye-catching features include the remains of a 3km-long aqueduct, which led up to a hilltop bathing complex, and a forum, once surrounded by covered porticoes.

ⓘ Getting There & Away

You can catch a **Joalto Transdev** (☎239 823 769) bus from Coimbra directly to the ruins site (€2.15, 45 minutes) at 9am or 9.30am (only 9.30am on weekends). Buses depart for the return trip at 12.45pm and 5.45pm (only 5.45pm on weekends).

LUSO & MATA NACIONAL DO BUÇACO

A retreat from the world for almost 2000 years, the slopes of the Serra do Buçaco are now home to the 105-hectare Mata Nacional do Buçaco (or Bussaco). Harbouring an astounding 700 plant species, from huge Mexican cedars to tree-sized ferns, this national forest is equally fecund in terms of the poetry it has inspired. Generations of Coimbra's literary types have enshrined the forest in the national imagination with breathless hymns to its mystical marriage of natural and spiritual beauty.

The high stone walls that for centuries have encircled the forest have no doubt helped reinforce its sense of mystery. And in the midst of the forest stands a royal palace completed in 1907; despite the extravagance of its fairy-tale neo-Manueline facade, the dynasty fell just three years later.

Outside the forest walls lies the old-fashioned little spa town of Luso, whose waters are considered a balm for everything from gout to asthma. The forest and spa make an easy day trip from Coimbra. If you want to linger, Luso has a handful of *residenciais* (guest houses). Those with the wherewithal can stay at the astonishing royal palace, right in the forest.

HISTORY

The Luso and Buçaco area probably served as a Christian refuge as early as the 2nd century AD, although the earliest known hermitage was founded in the 6th century by Benedictine monks. In 1628 Carmelite monks embarked on an extensive program of forestation. They planted exotic species, laid cobbled paths and enclosed the forest within high stone walls. The forest grew so renowned that in 1643 Pope Urban VIII decreed that anyone damaging the trees would be excommunicated.

The peace was briefly shattered in 1810, when Napoleon's forces under Masséna were soundly beaten here by the Anglo-Portuguese army of the future Duke of Wellington (the battle is re-enacted here every 27 September). In 1834, when religious orders throughout Portugal were abolished, the forest became state property.

From the Luso/Buçaco train station it's a 15-minute walk into town. Turn left (uphill) and climb gradually to the N234 before descending via Rua Dr António Granjo to the *turismo* and spa in the centre of Luso.

Buses from Coimbra stop on Rua Emídio Navarro, near the *turismo*.

By road the Portas das Ameias, the nearest gate into the forest, is 900m south of the *turismo*. From May to October there's a charge of €5 per car entering the forest, though walkers and cyclists enter free.

⊙ Sights & Activities

Forest   FOREST

The aromatic forest is crisscrossed with trails, dotted with crumbling chapels and graced with ponds, fountains and exotic trees from palms to sequoias. Popular paths lead to the pretty **Vale dos Fetos** (Valley of Ferns) and the **Fonte Fria**, where swans swim beneath a grand staircase. Among several fine viewpoints is **Cruz Alta** (545m), reached by a route called the Via Sacra.

What most visitors come to see is the fairy-tale **Palace Hotel do Buçaco**. Now a luxury hotel, it was originally built in 1907 as a royal summer retreat on the site of a 17th-century Carmelite monastery. This wedding cake of a building is over the top in every way: outside, its conglomeration of turrets and spires is surrounded by rose gardens and swirling box hedges in geometrical patterns; inside you'll find neo-Manueline carving, suits of armour on the grand staircases and *azulejos* illustrating scenes from *Os Lusíados* (The Lusiads; see p511), in which Portuguese armies win glorious battles at sea amid the dismayed looks of their stupefied opponents. Gawping nonguests are officially discouraged, although you can generally sneak a peek if you're subtle enough about it. By road, the hotel is 2.1km from the Portas das Ameias.

Maloclinic Spa Luso   SPA

(www.maloclinicspa.com; Rua Álvaro Castelões; ⊙8am-7pm) Just the ticket after a long walk in the forest, the Termas de Luso – re-opened under new management in summer 2010 – welcome drop-in visitors for therapies ranging from full-body massages (€25) and steam baths (€9) to body wraps (€18) and a kind of high-velocity shower called *duche de Vichy* (€12).

Fonte de São João   NATURAL SPRING

People come from far and wide to fill their bottles for free at this crystal-clear natural spring adjacent to the spa. A glass skylight allows you to peer down and see the limpid waters rippling over pretty grey and white stones.

🛌 Sleeping

Luso's glut of accommodation, coupled with a struggling Portuguese economy, tends to drive down prices. The best place to shop for bargains is Rua Emídio Navarro, Luso's main street, lined with several *pensões* and *residenciais* beyond those listed below.

Hotelaria Alegre   BOUTIQUE HOTEL €€
(☎231 930 256; www.alegrehotels.com; Rua Emídio Navarro 2; s €40-45, d €55-65; P🅿🛜🏊) This grand, peach-coloured 19th-century town house wears its age much better than Luso's other in-town lodgings. Replete with period touches, its large doubles boast plush drapes, decorative plaster ceilings and polished period furniture. Its appeal is enhanced by an elegant entryway, formal parlour and pretty vine-draped garden with pool.

Palace Hotel do Buçaco   HOTEL €€€
(☎231 937 970; www.palacehoteldobussaco.com; Mata Nacional do Buçaco; standard/superior d midweek €150/170, weekend €175/200; P🅿) If you can afford it, treat yourself to a night at this delightfully ostentatious king's palace. Rooms abound in varying degrees of period finery, some of it a touch threadbare. Common areas are stunning and will put you in a royal mood, and the meals here are truly memorable (see boxed text, below). Significant discounts are sometimes available for bookings via the hotel's website.

Casa de Hóspedes Familiar   GUEST HOUSE €
(☎231 939 612; paulcoelho@sapo.pt; Rua Ernesto Navarro 34; d/tr €35/45) You feel (and are) a guest of the family at this handsome, late-Victorian country house just above town. Personal touches include lacy bedspreads and curtains made by the owner's mother, homemade jams at breakfast and eclectic amenities such as room 6's huge bathroom filled with house plants or room 5's extra bedroom under the eaves for kids.

Astória   GUEST HOUSE €
(☎231 939 182; pensaoastorialuso@sapo.pt; Rua Emídio Navarro 144; s/d €25/35; 🛜) Beside the *turismo,* this rambling, homely place features clean, comfortable rooms with wood floors, slightly tired-looking beds and frilly decor. The O Selas restaurant downstairs serves traditional Portuguese standards.

🍴 Eating

In touristy Luso, restaurant service is often lacklustre. Most *pensões* have reasonable restaurants of their own.

Palace Hotel do Buçaco
                 PORTUGUESE, INTERNATIONAL €€
(☎231 937 970; Mata Nacional do Buçaco; 7-/8-course meals €35/40) Hands down the region's spiffiest dining option, this royal retreat-turned-hotel serves a blow-out seven-to eight-course menu offering a creative take on regional dishes (see boxed text, below).

Restaurante Lourenços   PORTUGUESE €€
(Av Emídio Navarro; mains €9-11; ⊙lunch & dinner) This blandly bright modern place across from the Termas de Luso serves good regional specialities with amusing if unintelligible English translations (really, who could resist a plate of 'sweated skrimp'?).

Restaurante Imperial   PORTUGUESE €
(Rua Emídio Navarro 25; mains €6.90-8.90; ⊙lunch & dinner) The grilled meats and

---

DINNER AT THE PALACE

For a truly memorable dinner, it's hard to beat the elegant spread at the **Palace Hotel do Buçaco**'s dining room. Better come hungry – the meal spans seven to eight courses: appetisers, soup, pasta, fish and/or meat, a salad trolley, a selection of local cheeses, the dessert trolley and finally an evening *cafezinho* (espresso). Specialities on offer at the time of writing included cold melon soup with crunchy Serrano ham, suckling pig ravioli with candied orange zest, marinated sardines with raspberry vinaigrette and kiwi mousse, and codfish confit with sautéed scallops, corn bread, turnip sprouts and black-eyed peas. The dining room itself is a work of art, with natural light pouring over the parquet wood floors through a graceful faux-Manueline window studded with rosettes and overlapping arches.

You'll probably be too full to move afterwards, but never fear – the palace also rents out rooms, for a 'mere' €150 (and up).

other simple Portuguese fare are good value here, but steer clear of the vinegary house red.

ℹ️ Information

The **turismo** (☎231 939 133; info.luso-bucaco@turismodocentro.pt; Rua Emídio Navarro 136; ⏰9am-12.30pm & 2-5.30pm) has accommodation information, town and forest maps, and leaflets (in English) detailing flora and points of historical interest. It also offers internet access on a single terminal.

ℹ️ Getting There & Away

BUS Transdev/RBL buses (more convenient than the train) run five times each weekday and twice daily on Saturdays from Coimbra's main bus station to Luso (€3.20, 40 minutes) and the Palace Hotel do Buçaco (€3.45, 50 minutes).

TRAIN IR trains run four times daily from **Coimbra B** to Luso/Buçaco station (€1.80, 25 minutes), but the inconvenient schedule makes a same-day round trip nearly impossible. From Luso/Buçaco station it's a solid 15-minute walk to the Luso *turismo*, plus another half-hour uphill through the forest to the Palace Hotel do Buçaco.

MONTEMOR-O-VELHO

Perched high atop a rugged hill 25km west of Coimbra, the glowering walls of the **Castelo do Montemor-o-Velho** (admission free; ⏰10am-6.30pm) dominate the surrounding marshland far out to the horizon. Whether seen from a distance or from atop the castle walls themselves, it's easy to imagine this site as an early bastion in the Reconquista. Ferdinand I of Castilla y León recaptured Montemor-o-Velho from the Moors in 1064, and within less than a century his great-grandson Afonso Henrique claimed it as part of his new Kingdom of Portugal. Over the intervening centuries the castle was rebuilt and expanded several times, with most of the current structure dating from the 14th century.

Today you can walk around the castle's crenellated battlements, explore the 'killing ground' between the inner and outer perimeter, and survey the lush rice fields lying alongside the Rio Mondego far below. Inside the walls almost no buildings remain except for a small portion of the ruined **Paço das Infantas** (Princesses' Palace), which was built by Afonso Henrique's aunt Urraca, and the beautifully tiled **Igreja de Santa Maria de Alcáçova**, a small Romanesque church that was founded in 1090 and was rebuilt most recently with Manueline

touches in the 16th century. The site's strategic importance as a fortification dates back at least two millennia, and archaeologists have identified elements of Roman stonework in the castle's keep.

The village below is small, though there are restaurants and parking beneath the castle's southern and eastern walls. **Residencial Abade João** (☎239 687 010; burgomedieval@sapo.pt; Rua dos Combatentes da Grande Guerra 15; s/d €35/45) is a beautiful old town house for anyone looking to hang their hat.

Trains between Coimbra B (€1.45, 35 minutes) and Figueira da Foz (€1.65, 30 minutes) stop every hour or two at Montemor station, 4km southeast of the castle. Moisés Correia de Oliveira **buses** between Coimbra (3.20, 50 minutes) and Figueira (€2.35, 30 minutes) stop closer to the castle, five to eight times daily (fewer on Sunday).

RESERVA NATURAL DO PAÚL DE ARZILA

Birdwatchers and other nature fans may wish to make a detour to the 535-hectare Reserva Natural do Paúl de Arzila. Halfway between Coimbra and Montemor-o-Velho, this marshy natural reserve is home to some 120 species of resident and migratory birds, as well as otters. The **on-site centre** (rnpa.santosmf@icn.pt; ⏰9am-5.30pm) serves as the base for a two-hour interpretive walk.

Figueira da Foz

POP 28,000

Popular with Portuguese holidaymakers for over a century, the beach resort of Figueira da Foz (fi-*guy*-ra da *fosh;* Figueira) continues to attract big summer crowds – including increasing numbers of Spaniards lured by the easy superhighway access, as well as surfers drawn to the championship-calibre waves at Cabedelo. For most visitors, the star attractions are Figueira's outlandishly wide beach and a casino featuring big-name acts on summer evenings. The local sands are so vast that it takes a five-minute walk across creaky boardwalks simply to reach the sea. Out of season, the place feels a bit desolate, but come here in summer and things are much more upbeat, with sizzling bodies and candy-striped beach huts filling every square inch of beach.

Just inland from the beach and the 16th-century Forte de Santa Catarina is a knot of streets with the *turismo*, accommodation and restaurants, and the casino. Seafront development continues clear to Buarcos, a former fishing village 3km to the north.

◎ Sights & Activities

Beaches BEACHES

Despite its size, Figueira's main city beach gets packed in August. For more character and some terrific surf, head north to **Buarcos**. From Figueira's *turismo* it's a 2km stroll along the pleasant beachfront promenade to the south end of Buarcos. Alternatively, **AVIC** (☑233 422 828) runs buses (€1.20) from the train station every 45 minutes or so.

For more seclusion, continue on around the Cabo Mondego headland to **Praia de Quiaios**, about 10km north of Figueira da Foz. **Joalto** (☑233 422 648) buses run from the bus station to Quiaios (€2.15, 30 minutes) seven times daily (less often on weekends).

South across the mouth of the Rio Mondego is **Praia de Cabedelo**, Figueira's prime surfing venue; classes and rentals are available here from **Escola de Surf da Figueira da Foz** (www.surfingfigueira.com; Cabedelo; group/individual class €25/35, short-/longboard rental per day €25/30).

A little further on is **Praia de Gala**. AVIC buses run from the train station via the *mercado municipal* to Cabedelo and Gala (both €1.20) every hour or so on weekdays (less often on weekends).

Museu Municipal Santos Rocha MUSEUM

(Rua Calouste Gulbenkian; adult/student or senior €2/1; ⊙9.30am-5.15pm Tue-Fri, 2-6.45pm Sat) This modern museum, beside Parque das Abadias, houses a wonderfully wide-ranging collection featuring local archaeological finds, Roman coins, medieval statues, outlandish Indo-Portuguese furniture, objects documenting Portugal's early African explorations, and rotating art exhibits.

Serra da Boa Viagem SCENIC HEADLAND

For those with wheels, this headland, found 4km north of Figueira and carpeted in pines, eucalyptus and acacias, is a fine place for panoramas, picnics and cool walks. Take the coastal road to Buarcos, turn right at the lighthouse and follow the signs to Boa Viagem.

★☆ Festivals & Events

Festas da Cidade The Town Festival carries on for two weeks at the end of June, with folk music, parades and concerts.

Mundialito de Futebol de Praia The town is mobbed for about a week in late July or August most years for the World Beach-Football Championships.

🛏 Sleeping

Prices listed are for the high season (July and August). Expect discounts of up to 40% in winter. Touts may approach you at the bus or train stations with their own offers.

TOP CHOICE Foz Holidays Surf House
GUEST HOUSE €€

(☑917 903 367; www.fozholidays.com; Rua dos Cravos; dm/s/d with shared bathroom €25/30/60, d with private bathroom €70; 🛜) Affable young hosts Kate and Jacques offer this home away from home for surfers and anyone else looking to kick back and appreciate life by the water. The comfortably renovated private house can accommodate up to seven people, with two doubles, a single and a small bunk room. Guests are welcomed into the living room with comfy couches, loads of DVDs and a PlayStation, while the sunny deck out back is perfect for barbecues, and the downstairs board and wetsuit storage is designed to please the surfer crowd. Afternoon cake and tea is always on offer, and for only €10 more per day, they'll cook you a three-course evening meal (including wine)! Book ahead by phone or internet.

TOP CHOICE Paintshop Hostel HOSTEL €

(☑233 436 633; www.paintshophostel. com; Rua da Clemência 9; s/tw/d €20/45/45; @🛜) In an old, pink town house, this top-of-the-line hostel offers small, attractive rooms, plush quilts, free wi-fi, a great bar out back, and a nice shared kitchen and barbecue for self-caterers. Bike, skateboard and body-board rentals are available, as are excellent services for surfers. Steve and Debbie are generous with their time and love to show people around town.

Residencial Aviz GUEST HOUSE €€

(☑233 422 635; www.residencialaviz.pt.to; Rua Dr A L Lopes Guimarães 16; s/d €45/55; ❄🛜) Run by a charming, well-travelled older couple, this squeaky-clean guest house two blocks from the beach has lovely wood floors, high ceilings and some nice period details. Reserve ahead in summer.

Hotel Wellington HOTEL €€

(☑233 426 767; www.lupahoteis.com; Rua Dr Calado 25; s/d/ste €75/85/120; ❄🛜) Near the

beach and casino action, this comfortable hotel offers immaculate rooms with minibars and writing desks, along with off-street parking at a nearby car park (€5 per night).

Orbitur Gala CAMPGROUND €
(☎233 431 492; infogala@orbitur.pt; Praia de Gala; sites per adult/child/tent/car €4.50/2.25/5.10/4.40) The best of the local camp sites, flat and shady Orbitur Gala is next to a great beach. It's south of Foz do Mondego and 1km from the nearest bus stop. Bungalows here cost €56 to €81 for two to seven people in the high season.

Hotel Mercure HOTEL €€€
(☎233 403 900; www.mercure.com; Av 25 de Abril 22; d with city/ocean view €99/109; P❄@🛜) One of a pair of high-end chain hotels side by side on the beachfront; rows of balconies boast sweeping views of the vast beach.

Parque de Campismo Figueira da Foz
CAMPGROUND €
(☎233 402 810; www.campingfigueira.blogspot.com; Quinta da Calmada; sites per adult/child/tent/car €5/3/3.70/3.90) Northeast of the centre and 2km inland from Buarcos beach, this camping ground has a pool, tennis courts and a supermarket.

✗ Eating

Restaurante Caçarola I SEAFOOD €€
(Rua Cándido dos Reis 65; specials €6.50, mains €8.50-15; ⊗lunch & dinner) Locals belly up to the bar all day long for good-value *combinados do dia balcão* (daily lunch-counter specials) at this popular seafood restaurant. In addition to the counter seating, there are tables on the pedestrian boulevard outside.

Núcleo Sportinguista do Concelho
PORTUGUESE €
(Rua Praia da Fonte 14; all-you-can-eat €7.50; ⊗lunch & dinner) Sitting under the awning

here, surrounded by enthusiastic locals and a sea of tables draped in checked tablecloths, feels a bit like crashing a Portuguese family's private barbecue. The waitresses bring round plate after plate of grilled meat and fish and you eat as much as you like of everything. With wine at €1.50 a pitcher, it's an unbeatable deal.

Restaurante Forte de Santa Catarina
SEAFOOD €€€

(☎233 428 530; Tennis Club, Av 25 de Abril; allyou-can-eat per person €18.50; ⊗lunch & dinner Wed-Mon) At this seafront eatery, crowds pack in nightly for the *rodizio de mariscos* (all-you-can-eat seafood) and to chat with the turbaned owner, who is something of a local celebrity. Dinner reservations are recommended in summer and on weekends.

Pizzeria Claudio
PIZZERIA €

(Largo do Carvão 11e; pizzas from €6; ⊗lunch & dinner) Figueira's best pizzeria generates lines out the door in summer.

Estúdio 24
FAST FOOD €

(Rua Dr Calado 24; ⊗6pm-6am) If all you really need is a late-night burger as big as your face, and maybe a beer or two to keep you hydrated, this is the place.

Mercado municipal
MARKET €

(Passeio Infante Dom Henrique; ⊗Mon-Sat) Self-caterers will find everything they need at the market, opposite the Jardim Municipal.

🍷 Drinking & Entertainment

Zeitgeist Caffé
BAR

(www.myspace.com/zeitgeistcaffe; Rua Francisco Antonio Dinis 82; ⊗4pm-4am) Glamorous Zeitgeist features comfy couches and chairs, wi-fi and windows overlooking the popular strip of bars that line adjacent Rua Académico Zagalo. There's live music every Wednesday, plus some Fridays and Saturdays – jazz guitar, drums and sax being the instruments of choice.

Casino Figueira
CASINO

(www.casinofigueira.pt, in Portuguese; Rua Dr Calado 1; ⊗3pm-3am) Shimmering in neon and acrylic, Figueira's casino is the epicentre of the city's nightlife. Crawling with cash-laden holidaymakers in search of a quick buck, it has roulette and slot machines, occasional free cabaret shows and a sophisticated piano bar with live music after 11pm most evenings. Dress up at night – beach attire, thongs (flip-flops) or sports shoes may keep you out.

Complexo Piscina de Mar
BAR, POOL

(Av 25 de Abril; ⊗10am-8pm Jul & Aug) Kick back on a lounger or dive into the pool at this waterfront bar with great beach views, resident DJ and a big-screen TV for those must-see football matches.

Discoteca Pessidónio
DANCE CLUB

(www.discotecapessidonio.com; Condados, Tavarede; ⊗Fri & Sat) Still going strong after four decades, Pessidónio is in the suburbs east of the municipal campground. Its four distinct dance venues include the Capela Club, whose poolside Sala da Piscina is popular for tropical drinks on hot summer nights.

Bergantim Discoteca
DANCE CLUB

(www.bergantim.com; Rua Dr AL Lopes Guimarães 28; ⊗Fri & Sat) This lively disco/nightclub spinning mostly pop, rock and electronic has a party atmosphere and a perfect downtown location one block from the beach.

Centro de Artes e Espectáculos

ARTS CENTRE

(www.cae.pt) Behind the museum, CAE hosts big-name bands, theatre and art-house cinema. Check the website or pick up a schedule at the *turismo*.

ⓘ Information

Biblioteca Municipal (Rua Calouste Gulbenkian; ⊘2-7.15pm Mon, 10am-7.15pm Tue-Fri, 2-6.45pm Sat) Free internet on four computers at town library.

Main post office (Passeio Infante Dom Henrique; ⊘9am-6pm Mon-Fri)

Turismo (⌨233 422 610; www.figueiraturismo.com; Av 25 de Abril; ⊘9am-10pm Jun-Aug, 9am-12.30pm & 2-5.30pm Sep-May)

ⓘ Getting There & Away

The train and bus stations are right next to each other, 1.5km east of the beach.

BUS Figueira's bus terminal is served by two long-distance companies. Moisés Correia de Oliveira (⌨233 426 703) has at least hourly service (fewer on weekends) via Montemor-o-Velho (€2.35, 30 minutes) to Coimbra (€3.95, 1½ hours.

Rede Expressos (www.rede-expressos.pt) has buses to Lisbon (€12.50, 2¾ hours, three daily), Aveiro (€9, 70 minutes, two daily) and Leiria (€8.40, one hour, three daily).

CAR High-season parking is a headache in the centre, even in the evenings, thanks to the casino. A good bet for street parking is the area between the Jardim Municipal and the train station.

TRAIN Train connections to/from Coimbra (€2.05, one hour, hourly) are superior to buses. There are also direct trains to Leiria (€4.30, one hour, four daily), with connecting service to Mira Sintra-Meleças station on the suburban Lisbon line.

Praia de Mira

For a few days of sunny, windblown torpor, head for Praia de Mira, the best-equipped town along the mostly deserted 50km coastal strip between Figueira da Foz and Aveiro. Sandwiched between a long, clean beach and a canal-fed lagoon, this small resort has little to distract you from the main business at hand: sun, sea and seafood. You may still glimpse local fishermen hauling in their colourful *xávega* boats in summer, though they're a vanishing species. For an interesting glimpse of Mira's past, check out the 1:32 scale model of the erstwhile fishing village, c 1940, at **Centrarte –**

a beachfront warehouse just north of **Igreja da Nossa Senhora Conceição**, the town's picturesque candy-striped church.

Praia de Mira is 7km west of Mira on the N109, itself 35km north of Figueira da Foz. Praia de Mira's axis is Avenida Cidade de Coimbra (also called the N342).

🛏 Sleeping

Rates given here are for the high season (mid-July to August). At other times the rates drop by up to 40%. The town abounds in summer – *quartos* (private rooms), are typically €30 to €40 per double. Watch for signs, or ask at the *turismo*.

Residencial Maçarico   HOTEL €€
(⌨231 471 114; www.residencial-macarico.com; Av Arrais Batista Cêra; r €65-75; ⓟ) Mira's best lodging option, this attractive yellow villa sits back from the beachfront promenade, a stone's throw from the Atlantic. It's clean and friendly, and front rooms have little balconies with sea views. At the time of research, a major remodelling project was scheduled for winter 2010–11; prices may have risen by the time you read this.

Orbitur   CAMPGROUND €
(⌨231 471 234; www.orbitur.pt; sites per adult/child/tent/car €5/2.50/5.80/5; ⊘Jan-Nov; 🛜) This well-equipped, shady site is at the southern end of the lagoon. Bungalows are available from €78 in August, or €49 the rest of the summer.

Pousada da Juventude   HOSTEL €
(⌨231 471 199; mira@movijovem.pt; dm/d €10/25; ⊘mid-May–mid-Sep) Near Orbitur, this hostel is super-cheap but barebones – no guest kitchen or restaurant. Reception is open from 8am to midnight. Beware noisy school groups during the June end-of-term period.

🍴 Eating & Drinking

Restaurante Caçanito   SEAFOOD €€
(Av do Mar; mains €10-15; ⊘lunch & dinner Apr-Sep, closed midweek dinner Oct-Mar) Neighbourhood cats wait expectantly outside the door of this great little seafood restaurant, an unadorned wood and glass cube right on the beach. Caçanito wins universal acclaim from locals for its superb charcoal-grilled seafood.

Jôbaló   GRILL HOUSE €€
(Av Manuel Milheirão 115; all-you-can eat rodizio €14.50; ⊘lunch & dinner) Fans of grilled meat should make the 1.5km trek inland to this

Brazilian-style *churrasqueria* (barbecue house) with indoor-outdoor seating on the town's main entrance road. House specialities like *picanha* (rump steak, served with or without garlic) are excellent. Better yet, try the all-you-can-eat *rodizio*, where itinerant waiters ply you with every grilled meat imaginable till you beg for mercy.

Marisqueira Tezinho　　　　SEAFOOD **€€**
(Av da Barrinha 9; mains €7.50-13; ☺lunch & dinner; ☺closed Tue Sep-Jun) Bustling and friendly, with only two small rooms, this place opposite the lagoon is recommended for its ultrafresh seafood.

Polar Cervajaria　　　　BAR, SEAFOOD **€€**
(Av Arrais Batista Cêra 34; bar snacks €4, mains €10-12.50; ☺noon-4am) Half bar, half restaurant, with occasional live music and DJs on the weekend, ever-popular Polar is an inviting place with a breezy terrace just across the street from the Atlantic.

Sixties Irish Pub　　　　PUB **€**
(Travessa Arrais Manuel Patrão 14; ☺7.30pm-2am Sun-Thu, to 4am Fri & Sat) Tucked into a classic pub-crawler's alley a block back from the beachfront, this cosy spot has multiple beers on tap and a lively old-school Irish atmosphere.

ⓘ Information

The **turismo** (☏231 472 566; turismo@cm-mira.pt; Av da Barrinha; ☺10am-1pm & 2-6pm), 450m south of Avenida Cidade de Coimbra beside the lagoon, shares a wooden house with a little ethnographic exhibition.

ⓘ Getting There & Away

Aveirense (☏234 423 513) runs direct Praia de Mira buses from Aveiro's train station (€3.55, 50 minutes, at least two daily). However, most coastal transport stops inland only at Mira (7km east). Joalto (☏233 422 648) also offers service from Figueira da Foz to Mira (€3.40, one hour, about five daily).

Taxis (☏231 471 257; €7) can ferry you between Mira and Praia de Mira, or Joalto runs occasional buses between the two towns (€1.80).

Aveiro

POP 55,000

Hugging the edge of the Ria, a shallow coastal lagoon rich in bird life, Aveiro (uh-*vey*-roo) is a prosperous town with a youthful, energetic buzz, thanks to a student population numbering nearly 15,000. The town has occasionally been dubbed the

Venice of Portugal thanks to its high-prowed boats, humpbacked bridges and a small network of canals. It's certainly not Venetian in scale, but Aveiro and its surroundings make a pleasant day trip from Porto or Coimbra. The town is best explored on foot, on a free municipal bicycle, or aboard a *moliceiro* – the traditional seaweed-harvesting boat that has now been converted to tourist use.

A prosperous sea port in the early 16th century, Aveiro suffered a ferocious storm in the 1570s that blocked the mouth of the Rio Vouga, closing it to ocean-going ships and creating fever-breeding marshes. Over the next two centuries, Aveiro's population shrank by three-quarters. But in 1808 the Barra Canal forged a passage back to the sea, and within a century Aveiro was rich once more, as evidenced by the spate of art nouveau houses that still define the town's old centre.

From the *azulejo*-clad train station it's a 1km stroll southwest down the main street, Avenida Dr Lourenço Peixinho and Rua Viana do Castelo (together called Avenida by all), to Praça Humberto Delgado, straddling the Canal Central. Nearby are the *turismo* and a pedestrianised centre dominated by the flashy Forum Aveiro shopping mall.

◉ Sights & Activities

At the time of research, the **Museu Arte Nova** – a brand-new museum celebrating Aveiro's art nouveau architecture – was scheduled to open in 2011. For details, check with the *turismo*.

Museu de Aveiro　　　　MUSEUM
(www.ipmuseus.pt; Av Santa Joana; admission €4, 10am-2pm Sun free; ☺10am-5.30pm Tue-Sun) This fine, if somewhat single-minded museum, in the former Mosteiro de Jesus opposite the Catedral de São Domingos, owes its finest treasures to Princesa (later beatified as Santa) Joana, daughter of Afonso V. In 1472, 11 years after the convent was founded, Joana 'retired' here and, though forbidden to take full vows, she stayed until her death in 1490.

Her tomb, a 17th-century masterpiece of marble mosaic, takes centre stage in an equally lavish room (actually the remodelled choir stalls of this former Dominican convent). The adjacent chapel is decorated with *azulejos* depicting Princesa Joana's life. The museum's paintings include a late-15th-century portrait of her, attributed to Nuno Gonçalves.

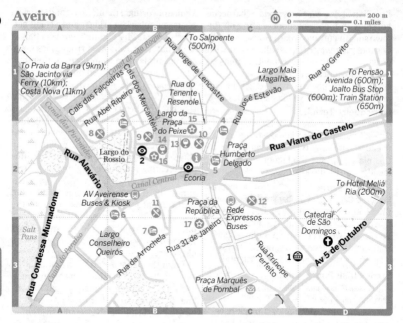

Reserva Natural das Dunas de São Jacinto
NATURE RESERVE

Stretching north from São Jacinto towards Ovar, between the sea and the N327 about 10km west of Aveiro, is this supremely peaceful little 6.7-sq-km wooded nature reserve, equipped with trails and birdwatching hides. Entry is via an **interpretive centre** (rndsj.visitas@icnb.pt; ☺Mon-Sat) on the N327. Self-guided visits along a meandering 7km loop trail through the pines and dunes are possible anytime the reserve is open (9am to 3pm in winter, later in other seasons). A trail map is posted at the entrance, with interpretive displays along the trail itself, and the helpful staff can answer questions to help you make the most of your visit. The best birdwatching is from November to February.

To get here, take a Forte da Barra bus from the **AV Aveirense kiosk** (Rua Clube dos Galitos) to the end of the line, from where a small *lancha* (passenger boat) crosses to the port of São Jacinto (combined boat and bus ticket: €3.50). Alternatively, drivers can take a car ferry across from Forte da Barra to São Jacinto (€5.25). Schedules for both boats are at www.moveaveiro.pt; bus schedules are posted at the AV Aveirense bus stop in town.

From São Jacinto port the reserve entrance is 1.3km north along the lagoonside road (follow signs for Torreira). Drivers can also circumnavigate the lagoon and arrive from the north via Ovar, but it's a much longer journey – a full 50km from Aveiro!

Beaches
BEACHES

Though not the Costa de Prata's finest beaches, the surfing venues of **Praia da Barra** and **Costa Nova**, 13km west of Aveiro, are good for a day's outing. The prettier Costa Nova has a beachside street lined with cafes, kitsch gift shops and picturesque candy-striped cottages.

AV Aveirense buses go via Gafanha da Nazaré to Costa Nova (€2, hourly) from the kiosk on Rua Clube dos Galitos; the last bus returns at around midnight.

Wilder and more remote is **Praia de São Jacinto**, on the northern side of the lagoon. The vast beach of sand dunes is a 1.5km walk from São Jacinto port, through a residential area at the back of town.

Oficina do Doce
CULINARY CENTRE

(www.oficinadodoce.com; Rua João Mendonça 23; ☺10-7pm) Part living museum and part cooking school, Oficina do Doce aims to introduce visitors to Aveiro's proudest culinary tradition – *ovos moles:* eggy, sugary

Aveiro

sweets originally developed by local nuns. You can watch as modern-day confectioners work their magic or, better yet, learn about the process first-hand by making your very own *ovo mole*.

☞ Tours

O Cicerone   WALKING TOURS
(☎234 094 074; www.o-cicerone-tour.com; Rua Trindade Coelho 6) This dynamic young company leads two-hour **walking tours** (€7) of downtown Aveiro as well as cultural tours elsewhere in the region.

Ecoria   BOAT TRIPS
(www.ecoria.pt) Near the *turismo,* this is one of several canalside operators offering 45-minute **moliceiros trips** (adult/child €5/3.50) around the Ria, with departures subject to passenger numbers. Tickets are available at the *turismo.* Longer *moliceiros* (boat) trips to São Jacinto may also be on offer in July and August; ask at the *turismo.*

⚑ Festivals & Events

Feira de Março Held from 25 March to 25 April, this festival dates back 5½ centuries. Nowadays it features everything from folk music to rock concerts.

Festas do Município Aveiro sees two weeks of merrymaking around 12 May in honour of Santa Joana.

Festa da Ria Aveiro celebrates its canals and *moliceiros* from mid-July to the end of August. Highlights include folk dancing and a *moliceiros* race.

🛏 Sleeping

Summer accommodation is even tighter than parking here; consider booking a week or so ahead in peak season.

TOP CHOICE **Aveiro Rossio Hostel**   HOSTEL €
(☎234 041 538; www.aveirorossiohostel. com; Largo do Rossio; dm €18-21, r with shared/private bathroom €52/65; ❋@➅✈⊘) Unquestionably one of Portugal's nicest hostels, this converted three-storey family home is the brainchild of brother-sister team José and Ana Rita and their designer friend Raquel. Creatively decorated with family heirlooms, recycled furniture and found objects, it also overflows with homey touches (from the waffle iron to the honour-system minibar) and splashes of colour (antique original tiles, gorgeous wooden floors, and brightly painted walls – even the bathrooms are beautiful!). There's a back patio for lounging, and breakfast often includes fresh croissants or organic fruit from the family farm. Solar energy is used wherever possible, earning the hostel recognition as Portugal's first 'green hostel'. Dorm rooms come with plush mattresses, individual reading lamps and bedside storage racks for mobile phones and glasses, and there are a couple of air-conditioned rooms under the eaves where bunk beds are replaced by regular twins. Still need more? How about bike and surfboard storage, wheelchair access, and free olive oil in the kitchen? OK, enough said.

Hotel das Salinas   HOTEL €€
(☎234 404 190; www.grupoalboi.com; Rua da Liberdade 10; s/d/studio €48/70/78; ✈) This immensely comfortable little hotel was already one of Aveiro's best, but a recent remodel has got it feeling downright homey. Angle for one of the 'studio' units, complete with kitchenettes, couches and plasma TVs for only €8 more than a regular double. Some rooms offer nice canal views.

Hotel Arcada   HOTEL €€
(☎234 421 885; www.hotelarcada.com; Rua Viana do Castelo 4; s/d from €59/69; ❋✈) The ornate facade promises more than the unimaginative rooms deliver, but you couldn't ask

for a more central location. Picturesequely perched above the canal, this vintage building is directly opposite the historic centre's main bridge, and the best front-facing rooms (costing €10 more) have full-on views of the *moliceiro* boats below. Internet costs extra.

Hotel Meliá Ria
HOTEL €€€

(234 401 000; www.solmelia.com; Cais da Fonte Nova; s/d €95/105; P ❄ @ 🛜) This spiffy four-star sits alone at the eastern end of the main canal. Its cubelike exterior is shrouded in intriguing brises-soleil, while inside it's all contemporary lines and business-friendly comforts. Check online for 'no breakfast' specials, as low as €79 in summer, or €69 the rest of the year. There's a spa too; guests pay extra to use the pool.

Pensão Avenida
GUEST HOUSE €

(234 423 366; Av Dr Lourenço Peixinho 256; s with shared bathroom €20, d with shared/private bathroom €25/35) This handsome art nouveau building is directly across from the train station, about a 15-minute walk from the centre. The owners, who also run the adjacent *pastelaria* (pastry and cake shop), have fixed up the bright, high-ceilinged rooms simply but tastefully.

Orbitur São Jacinto
CAMPGROUND €

(234 838 284; infosjacinto@orbitur.pt; sites per adult/child/tent/car €4.40/2.20/4.90/4; ☉late Dec–mid-Oct) Orbitur is a very nice, shady site with good facilities and a 20-minute footpath leading to a deserted beach just north of the Reserva Natural das Dunas de São Jacinto. You'll need your own transport, as there's no bus service along this road; it's a full 5km north of the São Jacinto ferry dock.

Hotel Aveirocenter
HOTEL €€

(234 380 390; www.hotelaveirocenter.com; Rua da Arrochela 6; s/d €48/70; @ 🛜) Down a quiet lane in the heart of town, Aveirocenter is more conservatively decorated and less cosy than its sister Hotel das Salinas, but still offers solid midrange comfort.

Barra Camping
CAMPGROUND €

(234 369 425; www.cacampings.com; Rua Diogo Cão 125, Praia da Barra; sites per adult/child €3.50/1.90, tent €3.60-4.30) A well-equipped, sandy and flat site next to the beach about 10km from Aveiro.

Hospedaria dos Arcos
GUEST HOUSE €

(234 383 130; Rua José Estêvão 47; s/d €25/35) One of several budget options along this street, Hospedaria dos Arcos has a just-like-grandma's-house atmosphere, with several floors of spotless little rooms.

Eating

TOP CHOICE Batel
INTERNATIONAL €€

(Travessa Tenente Resende 21; mains €12-15; ☉lunch & dinner Tue-Sat, lunch Sun) From curry cook-offs to sardine parties in the street, these guys know how to have fun with food. The intimate, newly opened eatery is clearly a labour of love for its multilingual, well-travelled owners, one a native of Greece, the other recently returned from France. A weekly gathering of friends helps field-test new recipes, resulting in an eclectic, international menu where ultra-fresh ingredients – locally sourced and organic whenever possible – are put to creative use in everything from tsatsiki to steak with cognac and caramelised onions. Rounding out the experience are an excellent wine list, and scrumptious desserts like *tarte Filadelfia com doce de pêra*, a smooth-as-silk cheesecake with homemade pear compote, based on a recipe from the owner's aunt. The lunchtime *prato do dia* (main, soup and drink for only €8.50) is a great deal.

Maré Cheia
SEAFOOD €€

(Rua José Rabumba 8-12; fish/shellfish per kg from €30/35; ☉lunch & dinner Thu-Tue) *Maré cheia* means 'high tide' in Portuguese, but the adjective *cheia* (full) applies equally to the counter and dining room at this fabulously popular seafood eatery. You'll often have to elbow your way through a crowd of locals just to get your name on the waiting list. It's a great place to try the local *enguias* (eels), served fried, grilled or *caldeirada* (stewed).

Salpoente
CONTEMPORARY PORTUGUESE €€

(Canal São Roque 83; mains €12.50-18; ☉lunch & dinner Mon-Sat) This old salt warehouse has been remodelled into one of Aveiro's classiest restaurants. Giant sepia-toned photos on the walls and a cavernous roof lend it a grand atmosphere, but it's the little details that really count in the cooking – from delicious appetisers like *patanhiscas de bacalhau* (codfish fritters) to the not-to-be-missed *arroz do mar* – a cornucopia of prawns, shrimp, mussels, clams and fish, bubbling away in bright orange broth.

Adega Típica O Telheiro
PORTUGUESE €€

(Largo da Praça do Peixe 20-21; mains €8.50-14; ☉lunch & dinner Tue-Sun) An Aveiro institution, this cosy place has red wine by the jug, grilled seafood and a long bar where locals convene.

À Linha SEAFOOD €€
(Rua João Afonso 13-15; mains €6.50-12; ☺closed Sun dinner & all day Tue) With casual-chic decor featuring brick walls and dark wood, this little fish restaurant makes a great lunch stop. Daily specials including soup and bread go for €7.

Pingo Doce SUPERMARKET €
(☺9am-10pm) For self-caterers there are plenty of supermarkets, including this one in the Forum Aveiro mall.

🍷 Drinking & Entertainment

A big student population and a generally party-friendly culture make for some raucous nightlife. Action radiates outward from Largo da Praça do Peixe, with several places clustered on Rua do Tenente Resende.

Toc Aqui PUB
(Largo da Praça do Peixe) This raucous, friendly pub opposite the fish market regularly hosts live music of various types. It's especially fun on winter nights, when there's usually a blazing fire and people start grabbing instruments off the back wall for impromptu jam sessions.

Decante Wine Bar WINE BAR
(www.decantebar.com; Rua do Tenente Resende 28) People congregate out on the streetside tables to sip wine during the early evening, then move inside for live music most nights, including everything from Latin rhythms, rock and blues to jazz and world music.

Mercado Negro ALTERNATIVE ARTSPACE
(Rua João Mendonça; ☺3pm-12.30am Tue-Sun) With a high-ceilinged upstairs cafe overlooking the canal, and a performance venue on the floor below, this quirky alternative artspace attracts a largely bohemian crowd.

Clandestino PUB
(www.clandestinobar.blogspot.com; Rua do Tenente Resende 35; ☺Mon-Sat) A cosy little pub attracting a youthful crowd with chilled-out music and imported DJs.

Teatro Aveirense ARTS CENTRE
(www.teatroaveirense.pt; Rua Belem do Para) Celebrating 125 years at the heart of Aveiro's cultural scene, this recently renovated historic theatre regularly hosts dance, music and theatre performances.

ℹ️ Information

Aveiro Digital (Praça da República; ☺9am-7pm Mon-Fri, 10am-6pm Sat) Free internet.

Hospital (☎234 378 300; Av Artur Ravara)

Net7 (Av 5 de Outubro 45; per hr €3; ☺9.30am-11pm Mon-Fri, 3-11pm Sat)

Police station (☎234 302 510; Praça Marquês de Pombal)

Post office (Praça Marquês de Pombal; ☺8.30am-6.30pm Mon-Fri)

Regional turismo (☎234 423 680; www.turismodocentro.pt; Rua João Mendonça 8; ☺9am-8pm Mon-Fri, 9am-6pm Sat & Sun) Extremely helpful office with multilingual staff in an art nouveau gem beside the Canal Central.

ℹ️ Getting There & Away

BUS Few long-distance buses terminate here – there isn't even a bus station.

Rede Expressos has at least three daily services to/from Lisbon (€15.50, three to four hours) and Coimbra (€5.90, 45 minutes). Get tickets and timetables at the **Loja das Revistas newsagent** (Praça Humberto Delgado; ☺7am-8pm) and catch the bus around the corner.

Joalto goes three to four times a day to Figueira da Foz (€4.65, one hour) from Rua Viana do Castelo and the train station. Aveirense serves Praia de Mira (€3.55, 50 minutes).

TRAIN Aveiro is within Porto's *suburbano* network, which means there are commuter trains to/from Porto at least every half-hour (€2.20, 50 to 60 minutes); much pricier IC/AP links (€9.50/13) are only slightly faster. There are also at least hourly links to Coimbra (€5.65, one hour) and several daily IC (€16.50, 2½ hours) and AP (€25, two hours) trains to Lisbon.

ℹ️ Getting Around

BICYCLE Loja BUGA (Bicicleta de Utilização Gratuita de Aveiro; ☺9am-7pm Mon-Fri, 10am-1pm & 2-7pm Sat & Sun) provides free bikes for residents and vistors alike. Give your details at the kiosk beside the Canal do Cojo, take a bike and ride it within the town limits, then return it to the kiosk before it shuts, all for free.

BUS Local bus routes converge on the Avenida and the train station. It's an easy 15-minute walk southwest from the station into town.

CAR Free street parking is available but competitive. For paid parking, try the underground lots below Praça Marques de Pombal and the Forum Aveiro shopping mall, or at Largo do Rossio near the *turismo*. The *turismo* offers a map showing other car parks.

Piódão

POP 225 / ELEV 690M

Remote Piódão (*pyoh*-down) offers a chance to see rural Portugal at its most pristine. This tiny traditional village clings to a terraced valley in a beautiful, surprisingly remote range of vertiginous ridges, deeply cut valleys, rushing rivers and virgin woodland called the Serra de Açor (Goshawk Mountains).

Until the 1970s you could only reach Piódão on horseback or by foot, and it still feels as though you've slipped into a time warp. The village is a serene, picturesque composition in schist stone and grey slate; note the many doorways with crosses over them, said to offer protection against curses and thunderstorms.

Houses descend in terraces to Largo Cônego Manuel Fernandes Nogueira – smaller than its name. Here you'll find the fairy-tale parish church, the Igreja Nossa Senhora Conceição.

◉ Sights & Activities

The tiny Núcleo Museológico de Piódão (admission €1; ☉10am-1pm & 2-6pm), just upstairs from the *turismo*, offers a glimpse of traditional village life in Piódão, displaying reconstructions of typical rooms in local homes, complete with tools, pottery and furniture. There are also historic photos of Piódão and its residents.

A signposted network of hiking trails connects Piódão to the nearby villages of Foz d'Égua (6.3km, two-hour loop hike) and Chãs d'Égua (4km, one hour each way). Foz d'Égua has some lovely old stone bridges, schist houses and a precarious-looking footbridge over the river gorge. Chãs d'Égua is home to over one hundred examples of rock art spanning the period from the Neolithic to the Iron Age.

✴ Festivals & Events

The area's patron saint, São Pedro do Açor, is honoured with a Mass, religious procession, ball, and a handicrafts fair during the **Santos Populares no Piódão** in late June or early July.

⌂ Sleeping & Eating

Turihab (a nationwide organisation marketing private accommodation) rents rooms with breakfast from €35 to €40 in properties such as Casa da Padaria (☎235 732 773; casa.padaria@sapo.pt) – a former bakery within the village limits – and Casa do Malhadinho (☎235 731 464), on a hillside west of town. Several cafes around the *largo* (small central square) serve pastries, sandwiches and light meals.

There are *quartos* everywhere, but quality is uneven; the most dependable options are listed below. A full list is available from Piódão's *turismo*.

Casas da Aldeia   RENTAL HOUSES €
(☎235 731 424; d €25, d with kitchenette €40, 2-room house €65) Piódão's village improvement committee has kitted out these two schist houses near the centre with TV, private bathroom, kitchenette and fireplace. You can rent just a room, or an entire house.

Estalagem do Piódão   HOTEL €€
(☎235 730 100; inatel.piodao@inatel.pt; s/d €90/95; 🅿@🕾) Looming unaesthetically on a ridge above the village, this unsightly, mammoth, government-run caricature of a local schist house has rather luxurious, modern rooms and the town's only decent restaurant.

Solar dos Pachecos   ROOMS €
(☎235 731 424; Largo Cónego Nogueira; r from €30) This cafe on the main square rents out a few rooms and serves snacks.

Campismo de Ponte de Três Entradas
                    CAMPGROUND €
(☎238 670 050; www.pontedastres entradas.com; sites per adult/child/tent/car €3.20/1.70/2.80/2.80) This delightful, shady riverside site 22km from Piódão near Avô also has bungalows from €45 for two people.

ⓘ Information

On the main square, the village **turismo** (☎235 732 787; geral@cm-arganil.pt; ☉10am-1pm & 2-6pm) provides info on Piódão itself as well as walks in the surrounding area – check upstairs in the museum if there is nobody minding the *turismo* below.

ⓘ Getting There & Away

The only transport other than car or bicycle is a bus from Arganil (41km to the west) that stops in Piódão's *largo* (€3, 1¼ hours) on Thursday and Sunday. Check current times with Piódão's *turismo*.

The area's breathtaking views, narrow roads and sheer drops are a lethal combination for drivers. Note that side roads marked '4WD' are axle-breakers for ordinary cars.

BEIRA BAIXA

Beira Baixa closely resembles neighbouring Alentejo, with hospitable locals, fierce summer heat and rolling plains that stretch out to the horizon. It's also home to sprawling agricultural estates, humble farming hamlets and several stunning fortress towns that for centuries guarded the vulnerable plains from Spanish aggression.

Castelo Branco

POP 31,000

With its sweltering heat and surrounding waves of high-rise construction, the provincial capital of Castelo Branco isn't big on charm, although as the region's transport hub it makes a good jumping-off point for outlying attractions such as Monsanto and Idanha-a-Velha. The best reasons to visit nowadays are the town's excellent museum and gardens, but it's also worth walking up to the ruined *castelo* (castle) for a better appreciation of Castelo Branco's historic importance – these once-strategic heights afforded views across the surrounding plains to the Spanish border 20km away. Unfortunately, Castelo Branco's position made it a regular target of aggression, and as a result much of its historic fabric has been destroyed. Still, there are some charming medieval streets clustered in the centre, and the town's modern development includes an attractive series of tree-lined squares and boulevards.

From the bus station, turn right down Rua do Saibreiro to central Alameda da Liberdade. From the train station the Alameda is 500m north on Avenida Nuno Álvares.

◉ Sights

Palácio Episcopal MUSEUM
(www.ipmuseus.pt; Largo Dr José Lopes Dias; adult/under 14yr/student €2/free/1; ◷10am-12.30pm & 2-5.30pm Tue-Sun) The Palácio Episcopal (Bishop's Palace), in the north of town, is a sober 18th-century affair housing the **Museu de Francisco Tavares Proença Júnior**. Downstairs, the museum's centrepiece is an excellent display of archaeological finds from the surrounding area.

If you're a fan of embroidery you'll also be wowed by the upstairs exhibition of Castelo Branco's famous *colchas:* silk-embroidered linen bedspreads and coverlets made with patterns and techniques inspired by fabrics brought back by early Portuguese explorers. The museum has a stunning collection of Indian and Chinese originals, plus a workshop where on weekdays you can watch women practising the art.

THE BEIRAS CASTELO BRANCO

Beira Baixa

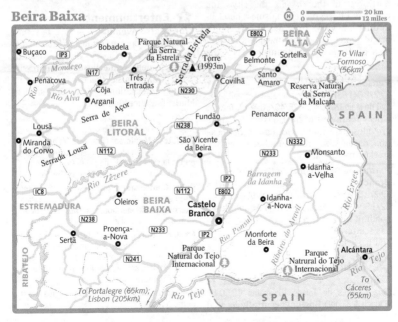

Jardim Episcopal GARDEN
(Bishop's Garden; admission €2; ⊙9am-7pm) Beside the museum is this baroque whimsy of clipped box hedges and little granite statues. Notice that the statues of Portugal's Spanish-born kings Felipe I and II are smaller than those of the Portuguese monarchs!

At the bottom of the kings' stairway, there's a hidden, clap-activated fountain, sadly out of order at the time of research. It was built by a loutish 18th-century bishop who liked to surprise maidens by soaking their petticoats. Ask the attendant if it's back in operation and he'll show you where to clap.

Castelo CASTLE
There's little left of the castle, which was built by the Knights Templar in the 13th century and extended by Dom Dinis. However, the **Miradouro de São Gens** garden, which has supplanted the walls, offers grand views over town and countryside. The old lanes that lead back down to the town centre are also picturesque.

🛏 Sleeping

Tryp Colina do Castelo HOTEL €€
(☎272 349 280; www.solmelia.com; Rua da Piscina; s/d/ste €79/90/110; P ✳ @ 🛜 ⛶) Soulless but nicely positioned on the hillside northwest of the *castelo,* the city's top choice is a huge, modern, business hotel affording fine views from most of its comfy, bright rooms. Amenities include a nice indoor pool, squash and tennis courts and a gymnasium.

Pensão Residencial Arraiana HOTEL €
(☎272 341 637; residencialarraiana@gmail.com; Av 1 de Maio 18; s/d/tr €25/40/50;✳) A few blocks southwest of the *turismo,* Arraiana provides good value, with its central location, decent-sized rooms and generously stocked minibars.

Parque de Campismo de Castelo Branco CAMPGROUND €
(☎272 322 577; sites per adult/child/tent/car €2/1.30/1.75/2; ⊙Jan–mid-Nov) About 3km north of the town centre, this dusty site has scattered trees, mostly grassy pitches and basic facilities.

🍴 Eating & Drinking

Kalifa PORTUGUESE €€
(Rua Cadetes de Toledo 10; mains €8.50-13; ⊙lunch & dinner) Bustling, centrally located Kalifa is a Castelo Branco institution. Formally clad waiters buzz around the large dining room, serving generous portions of hearty, regional fare. Especially pleasant is the lively grapevine-shaded patio on the cobblestones out back. It's just off Alameda da Liberdade near the *turismo.*

Restaurante O Jardim PORTUGUESE €€
(Rua Figueira 29A; meals €7-12.50; ⊙lunch & dinner Mon-Sat) Given the sheer volume of helpings (order pork and expect half a pig!), this cosy, friendly restaurant down a backstreet near Largo da Sé is fantastic value. Daily specials include soup, main course, drink, dessert and coffee for under €10.

Praça Velha PORTUGUESE €€€
(Praça Luís de Camões 17; dishes €12.50-17; ⊙lunch & dinner Tue-Sat, lunch Sun) This atmospheric former Knights Templar abode in the old town includes a medieval wooden ceiling, stone floors and pillars, and a long buffet table heaped with platters. Try the all-inclusive lunch specials (€12.50) or the fantastic Sunday buffet (€19).

Self-Catering

Self-caterers can find supplies, including the *queijo de ovelha* (sheep's cheese) for which this region is famous, in the mercado municipal (Av 1 de Maio) or nearby Pingo Doce supermarket (Av 1 de Maio; ⊙8.30am-9pm).

☆ Entertainment

Cine-Teatro Avenida ARTS CENTRE
(www.culturavibra.com; cnr Rua do Sabreiro & Av Humberto Delgado) Castelo Branco's leading entertainment venue hosts an impressive array of film, music, theatre and dance, including international performers such as Madrid's Ballet Flamenco.

ⓘ Information

Biblioteca Municipal (Praça do Município; ⊙10am-4.30pm Mon-Fri) Free internet in the public library, across the plaza from the *turismo* in a courtyard behind the yellow facade.

Cyber Centro Municipal (Praça do Município; internet per hr €1; ⊙9am-11pm Mon-Fri) Paid internet with longer hours, across the courtyard from the library.

Parque Natural do Tejo Internacional office (☎272 348 140; pnti@icnb.pt; 2nd fl, Centro de Interpretação Ambiental Bldg, Rua da Bela Vista s/n) In a spiffy new white building just west of the *turismo.*

Police station (Rua Espírito Santo) Just west of the *turismo.*

THE BEIRAS BEIRA BAIXA

Post office (Rua da Sé; ⊙8.30am-6.30pm Mon-Fri, 9am-12.30pm Sat)

Turismo (☑272 330 339; turismo.cmcb@mail.telepac.pt; Alameda da Liberdade; ⊙9.30am-7.30pm Mon-Fri, 9.30am-1pm & 2.30-6pm Sat & Sun) Slick new quarters on the town's main square.

ⓘ Getting There & Away

BUS Rede Expressos (☑272 340 126; www.rede-expressos.pt) serves several destinations.

Coimbra (€12.30, 2½ hours, one to four daily)

Covilhã (€4.40, one hour, at least six daily)

Guarda (€9.20, 1½ hours, at least six daily)

Lisbon (€12, 3¾ hours, one to four daily)

TRAIN Castelo Branco is on the Lisbon–Covilhã line. Three daily IC trains to Lisbon (€14, 2¾ hours) are supplemented by three slower regional services (€11.75, 3¾ hours). IC/regional trains also serve Covilhã (€8/5.40, one hour/90 minutes).

Parque Natural do Tejo Internacional

Still one of Portugal's wildest landscapes, this 230-sq-km natural park shadows the Rio Tejo and the watersheds of three of its tributaries: the Rio Ponsul, Ribeira do Aravil and Rio Erges. While not aesthetically remarkable, it shelters some of the country's rarest bird species, including black storks, Bonelli's eagles, royal eagles, Egyptian vultures, black vultures and griffon vultures. The park was established in 2000, after a major push by private environmental organisation Quercus.

The park headquarters in Castelo Branco can sometimes provide a Portuguese-language brochure with background information, although supplies are limited.

The park's best-marked hiking trail, known locally as the Rota dos Abutres (Route of the Vultures), descends from Salvaterra do Extremo (60km east of Castelo Branco) into the dramatic canyon of the Rio Erges.

Drivers can get a taste of the park's natural beauty by following the unnumbered road between Monforte da Beira and Cegonhas (southeast of Castelo Branco), which passes through a beautiful cork oak forest on either side of the Ribeira do Aravil.

🖋 **Quercus** (☑272 324 272; www.quercus.pt; Travessa da Ferradura 14, Castelo Branco) organises birdwatching, walking and other programs, and offers basic accommodation at Rosmaninhal and Monte Barata. At Castelo Branco's *turismo* you can also buy Quercus' 250-page *Guia de Percursos Tejo Internacional,* a guide (in Portuguese) to regional geology, climate, flora and fauna, villages, trails and transport.

Monsanto

POP 200 / ELEV 600M

Like an island in the sky, the stunning village of Monsanto towers high above the surrounding plains. A stroll through its steeply cobbled streets, lined with stone houses that seem to merge with the boulder-strewn landscape, is reason enough to come. But to fully appreciate Monsanto's rugged isolation, climb the shepherds' paths above town to the abandoned hilltop castle, whose crumbling walls command vertiginous views in all directions. Walkers will also appreciate the network of hiking trails threading through the vast cork-oak-dominated expanses below.

Monsanto is so small that there are really only two directions to worry about – up towards the castle or down towards the parking lot. The rest is a compact cluster of lanes perfect for aimless wandering. A handy brochure and map from the *turismo,* available in English, helps to identify routes and sights and describes historic details. The *turismo* also lends out a limited number of free hand-held GPS devices that provide multilingual audio-visual commentary as you stroll about town.

⊙ Sights

Village   VILLAGE

Since winning a national competition in 1938 as the country's most 'Portuguese' village, Monsanto has been largely shielded from modernisation. Several houses near the village entrance are surprisingly grand, some sporting Manueline doorways and stone crests. Halfway to the castle you'll come across the **gruta**, a snug cavern apparently once used as a drinking den – and still used as such, judging by the half-empty glasses of beer inside. Other caves around town double as barns for the local sheep and goats.

Castelo   CASTLE

This formidable stone fortress seems almost to have grown out of the boulder-littered hillside that supports it. It's a beautiful site, windswept and populated by lizards and wildflowers. Immense vistas (marred only by mobile-phone masts) include Spain to the east and the Barragem da Idanha dam to the southwest.

There was probably a fortress here even before the Romans arrived, but after Dom Sancho I booted out the Moors in the 12th century it was beefed up. Dom Dinis refortified it, but after centuries of attacks from across the border it finally fell into ruin.

Just below the castle stands what's left of the Romanesque Capela de São Miguel, with its cluster of sarcophagi carved into solid rock eerily lying just outside the chapel portal.

Hiking Trails

Monsanto is crisscrossed by long-distance hiking trails, including the GR-12 from Lisbon to Constancia, Bulgaria, and the GR-22, a 540km circuit of Portugal's historic villages. For a beautiful, relatively easy walk (one hour return), descend the GR-12 along the stone road to the Capela de São Pedro de Vir-a-Corça, a medieval chapel surrounded by giant boulders. You can follow this same trail all the way to Idanha-a-Velha, a beautiful but exposed 7km walk best undertaken in cooler weather.

✦ Festivals & Events

On 3 May each year Monsanto comes alive in the **Festa das Cruzes**, commemorating a medieval siege. The story goes that the starving villagers threw their last lonely calf over the walls, taunting their besiegers as if they had plenty to spare. And apparently, their attackers were hoodwinked, because they promptly abandoned the siege. These days, young girls throw baskets of flowers instead, after which there's dancing and singing beside the castle walls.

🛏 Sleeping & Eating

Accommodation in Monsanto is limited. Advance reservations are advisable in high season.

Pousada de Monsanto   HOTEL €€
(☎277 314 071; pousadamonsanto@hotmail.com; s/d/tr €60/70/95; ✲@☎) Reopened under new management in early 2010, this is the only hotel in the old town. The best reason to stay here (aside from the sheer pleasure of being in Monsanto overnight) is room 103, whose large balcony commands fabulous views of the town and surrounding countryside.

Casa do Chafariz   ROOMS €
(☎914 253 793; casadochafariz1@sapo.pt; Rua Marquês da Graciosa; s/d/tr €35/45/50) A stone's throw from the *turismo,* these four rooms in a renovated old house cluster around an unadorned cobblestoned courtyard. All have nice wood floors and massive slabs of exposed stone, plus TV and electric heat. The two upstairs units are nicest, with high ceilings and atmospheric – if non-functioning – fireplaces. Penny-pinchers can save €5 by staying in the rather claustrophobic smaller room at the foot of the stairs.

Casa da Maria   RENTAL HOUSE €
(☎965 624 607; Av Fernando Ramos Rocha 11; r per person without/with breakfast €20/25; P✲) Depending on group size, you can rent one, two or all three rooms in this well-equipped house just below town, with optional access to a kitchen and living room. It's not quite as atmospheric as places in the pedestrian zone, as it's squeezed between the main road and the embankment above, and all of the small windows face the traffic below. Town is a five-minute walk uphill.

Taverna Lusitana   CAFE, ROOMS €
(☎927 892 768; www.tavernalusitana.com; Rua do Castelo 19; mains €6; ☉lunch & dinner) A few paces up towards the castle from the town centre, this cafe (run by a friendly French-Portuguese couple) serves simple *pratos do dia* (daily specials like codfish, lasagne or duck with rice) along with sweet and savoury crêpes and beer on tap. The 270-degree view from the little terrace upstairs is *magnifique,* especially at sundown, and they also rent out two rooms with private bathroom (single/double €35/50).

Petiscos e Granitos   PORTUGUESE €€
(☎277 314 029; Rua Pracinha; mains €7.50-15; ☉lunch & dinner) Wedged between gigantic boulders, Petiscos e Granitos' back terrace provides a fantastic backdrop for sipping a *copo de vinho* (glass of wine) at sunset, with incomparable views over the plains below. Waiters sometimes move at a geological pace, but specialities like grilled lamb chops with roasted potatoes are delicious. There are also souvenir shops selling homemade honey cakes, some laced with a wicked *aguardente* (alcoholic 'firewater').

ⓘ Information

Post office (Largo do Cruzeiro; ☉9am-noon Mon-Fri) Near the town centre.

Turismo (✆277 314 642; turismomonsanto@ hotmail.com; Rua Marquês da Graciosa; ◷10am-1pm & 2-6pm) A few doors east of the post office.

ℹ️ Getting There & Away

Without a car, Monsanto can be difficult to reach. **Rodoviária da Beira Interior** (✆272 340 126; www.rbi.pt) has one direct bus daily between Castelo Branco and Monsanto (€5.15, one hour), leaving Castelo Branco at 5.15pm weekdays and 11.35am on weekends, returning from Monsanto at 7.15am daily. Ask at the *turismo* in either Monsanto or Castelo Branco for the latest schedules.

Idanha-a-Velha

While very different from hilltop Monsanto, neighbouring Idanha-a-Velha is just as extraordinary. Nestled in a remote valley of patchwork farms and olive orchards, Idanha-a-Velha was founded as the Roman city of Igaeditânia. Rome's ramparts still define the town, though it only reached its apogee under Visigothic rule. They built a cathedral and made Idanha their regional capital. It's also believed that their legendary King Wamba was born here.

Moors were next on the scene, and the cathedral was turned into a mosque during their tenure. They, in turn, were driven out by the Knights Templar in the 12th century. The mystical knights constructed the town's small but imposing keep, which sits on the remarkably preserved pedestal of a Roman temple.

It's believed that a 15th-century plague virtually wiped out the town's population, with survivors going on to found Idanha-a-Nova about 20km to the southwest. However, the townspeople's misfortune is our luck, since they left the town virtually intact. A few brave souls eventually returned, and today a small but hardy population of shepherds and farmers live amid the Roman, Visigothic and medieval ruins.

⊙ Sights

Near the southwest corner of the walled town, directly across from the *turismo*, sits the 6th-century Visigothic **cathedral**, surrounded by a jigsaw puzzle of scattered archaeological remains. The church has undergone heavy restoration, but its early roots are evident everywhere: foundation stones bearing Latin inscriptions, Moorish brick arches (now plastered over), salvaged Roman columns along the right side of the

nave and Visigothic elements such as the baptistry visible through glass near the entrance. Of the frescos within, the best preserved features São Bartolomeu with a demon at his feet.

Adjacent to the *turismo* are two equally worthy sights: the **Lagar de Varas** (◷10am-1pm & 2-5.30pm) hosts an impressive olive-oil press made in the traditional way with ruddy great tree trunks providing the crushing power. Just outside, you'll find a narrow **epigraphic museum** densely packed with over 200 stones from the area bearing Latin inscriptions. Touch-screen interpretive displays in English, Spanish and Portuguese explain the meaning, purpose and historical context of the collection, with in-depth studies of three particularly noteworthy stones.

The only evidence of the Knights Templar is the **Torre des Templários**, made of massive chunks of stone and now surrounded by clucking hens. It sits on top of what was likely the pedestal of a Roman temple. Other Roman remains include the gracefully arched **Roman bridge** on the east side of town, the old **Roman wall and gate** on the north side (accessible via a metal catwalk) and a row of stones on the south side used for two purposes: crossing the river on foot, and measuring river depth to ensure safe passage of horse-drawn carts.

After all this history it's a delight to come across the **Forno Comunitário** (communal bakery; Rua do Castelo) and discover villagers sliding trays of biscuits and enormous loaves of bread into the huge stone oven, blackened from use.

With advance notice, walking tours of town can be organised through the nearby **Idanha-a-Nova turismo** (✆277 202 900).

🛏️ Sleeping & Eating

Idanha-a-Velha has no tourist accommodation and only a couple of small cafes serving snacks and drinks. Monsanto (16km northeast) and Idanha-a-Nova (20km southwest) are your best bets for a hot meal and a place to bed down. The latter has a comfortable new **hostel** (✆277 208 051; idanha@movijovem. pt; Praça da República 32, Idanha-a-Nova; dm €12, d with shared/private bathroom €28/34).

ℹ️ Information

Idanha-a-Velha's **turismo** (✆277 914 280; Rua da Sé; ◷10am-1pm & 2-6pm) is directly opposite the cathedral.

❶ Getting There & Away

Without your own transportation, getting to Idanha-a-Velha is difficult indeed. There's occasional **school bus** service to/from Idanha-a-Nova (40 minutes), from where you can catch onward buses to Castelo Branco (€3.65, 45 minutes, two to three daily). Alternatively, you can hike the beautiful but exposed 7km trail from Monsanto. The *turismo* can also arrange a **taxi** to Idanha-a-Nova or Monsanto, but prices are steep (about €30).

Sortelha

POP 800 / ELEV 760M

Perched on a rocky promontory, Sortelha is the oldest of a string of fortresses guarding the frontier east of Guarda and Covilhã. Its fortified 12th-century castle teeters on the brink of a steep cliff, while immense walls encircle a village of great charms. Laid out in Moorish times, it remains a winning combination of stout stone cottages, sloping cobblestone streets and diminutive orchards.

These days the walled village has few permanent residents, giving it an eerie silence. A scramble along the ramparts affords views over a landscape of steep valleys and forbidding, boulder-strewn peaks that is just as beautiful and just as haunting as the town itself.

'New' Sortelha lines the Santo Amaro–Sabugal road, along which are several Turihab properties and a restaurant. The medieval hilltop fortress is a short drive, or a 10-minute walk, up one of two lanes signposted 'castelo'.

◉ Sights

The entrance to the fortified old village is a grand, stone **Gothic gate**. From here, a cobbled lane leads up to the heart of the village, with a *pelourinho* (stone pillory) in front of the remains of a small **castle** to the left and the parish **church** to the right. Higher still is the **bell tower**. Climb it for a view of the entire village (but heed the sign begging visitors not to ring the bells). For a more adventurous and scenic climb, tackle the **ramparts** around the village (beware precarious stairways and big steps!). As you walk, keep your eyes open for the weather-worn Arabic script above the doorway of the **Casa Árabe** at the very top of town.

⌂ Sleeping

Sortelha boasts several atmospheric Turihab properties, complete with kitchens,

thick stone walls and heating. The *turismo* has a full list. Calling a week or two ahead is essential in July and August.

Casa da Cerca HOUSE, ROOMS €€
(✆271 388 500; cercasitur@gmail.com; Largo de Santo António; s/d/tr €45/60/75; P❋☎) Just off the main road, below the old town, this 17th-century house is Sortelha's top choice. Rooms are comfortable and attractive if not luxurious, with wood floors and traditional furnishings. The same owners rent out apartments just across the courtyard in the Casa do Páteo (two/four people with kitchen €60/80).

Casa da Villa HOUSE, ROOMS €€
(✆271 388 113; Rua Direita; d downstairs/upstairs €45/65, whole house for 4/6/8 people €120/160/180; ☎) This delightful stone cottage has a privileged place within the village walls. You can rent the downstairs only (somewhat claustrophobically built into the rock, with shower only, no kitchen and no windows in the back bedroom), the upstairs only (much nicer, with kitchenette, small terrace overlooking the town walls and larger bathroom with tub) or the entire house. It's owned by the same people that run Casa da Cerca and Casa do Páteo.

Casas do Campanário RENTAL HOUSES €€
(✆271 388 198; luispaulo55@sapo.pt; Rua Mesquita; d €50-65, house for 4/6 people €100/150; ☎) Nicely sited at the top of the village, adjacent to the bar of the same name, Sortelha's other 'inside-the-walls' lodging option includes a house for two people and another for up to six; ask at Bar Campanário, just above the bell tower.

✗ Eating & Drinking

Restaurante Dom Sancho I PORTUGUESE €€
(Largo do Corro; mains €10-17; ◷lunch & dinner Tue-Sat, lunch Sun) Sortelha's favourite eatery sits just inside the main Gothic gates. Prices for the regional cuisine are high, but the food is renowned and the dining room rustically elegant. For lighter snacks and drinks, head to the beamed, stone-walled bar downstairs.

Bar As Boas Vindas BAR €
(◷noon-late Fri-Sun) Uphill and to the right of the *turismo*, this cosy little stone house with couches, rustic farm decor, a cute old German shepherd and a well-stocked bar makes a good place to cool off on a hot summer afternoon.

Bar Forno Esplanada

CAFE €

(Travessa do Forno; snacks from €3; ⊙9am-midnight daily Jun-Sep, weekends Oct-May)
Suitable for a simple afternoon snack, this terrace cafe directly below the castle walls commands sweeping views of the rugged landscape below.

ⓘ Information

The town's **turismo** (☑271 750 080; turismo@sabugalmais.com; Largo do Corro; ⊙10am-12.30pm & 1.30-6pm) is an incongruous modern wood-and-glass cube (air-conditioned in summer) in Largo do Corro, just inside the old town gate. It provides a wide range of brochures on Sortelha and the surrounding area.

ⓘ Getting There & Away

Regional trains on the Covilhã–Guarda line (three to four daily) stop at **Belmonte-Manteigas** station, 12km to the northwest, where you can catch a local **taxi** (☑936 259 107) to Sortelha (around €20). There's no regular bus service.

PARQUE NATURAL DA SERRA DA ESTRELA

Fascinating both for its natural and cultural history, Parque Natural da Serra da Estrela was one of Portugal's first designated natural parks, and at 1011 sq km remains the country's largest protected area. The rugged boulder-strewn meadows and icy lakes of its high country form one of Portugal's most unique and unexpected landscapes. On the slopes below, rushing rivers historically provided hydro power to spin and weave the Serra's abundant wool into cloth. Nowadays, shepherds still roam a landscape of terraced fields and traditional one-room, stone *casais* (huts) thatched with rye straw, but traditional sheep-herding is fast giving way to a service economy catering to weekending tourists.

The presence of 1993m Torre – Portugal's highest peak – at the centre of the park is both a blessing and a curse. It forms an undeniably dramatic backdrop, but as the only place in Portugal where snow dependably falls, it also tends to lure vast winter hordes with little consciousness of their impact on the high country's ecosystems. The fragility of the mountain environment is underscored by the devastation wrought by forest fires in recent years, while the fragility of the economy is evidenced by the large numbers of residents who have emigrated elsewhere, leading to a notable greying of the local population.

The Serra abounds in hiking and climbing opportunities. Although the underfunded park service struggles to keep trails marked, and the best books and maps on the region regularly go out of print due to lack of funding, these mountains remain one of Portugal's most alluring destinations for outdoors enthusiasts. Hikers – and everyone else – will also appreciate the Serra's excellent mountain cheese and hearty rye bread.

⊙ Sights & Activities

Wildlife

The park harbours many endangered or vulnerable species – especially feathered ones. These include the black stork, Montagu's harrier, chough, turtle dove and 10 species of bats. If you're lucky you may also catch a glimpse of miniature high-altitude frogs, mountain geckos or rare birds such as the peregrine falcon, eagle owl and black-shouldered kite.

The flora, too, is interesting. Popularity as medicinal remedies has put several of the park's plants in the list of endangered or vulnerable species, including mountain thrift *(Armeria transmontana)*, great yellow gentian *(Gentiana lutea)* and juniper *(Juniperus communis)*.

Walking

Crisp air and immense vistas make this a trekking paradise for those willing to make the effort. In part because of limited infrastructure, surprisingly few people get off the main roads. Even in summer, walkers will generally feel they have the park to themselves.

While still very chilly and possibly damp, late April has the hillsides bright with wildflowers. The weather is finest from May to October. Winter is harsh, with snow at the higher elevations from November or December to April or May.

Whenever you come, be prepared for extremes: scorching summer days give way to freezing nights, and chilling rainstorms blow through with little warning. Mist is a big hazard not only because it obscures walking routes and landmarks, but because it can also stealthily chill you to the point of hypothermia. You may set out on a warm, cloudless morning and by noon find yourself fogged in and shivering, so always pack for the cold – and the wet, too.

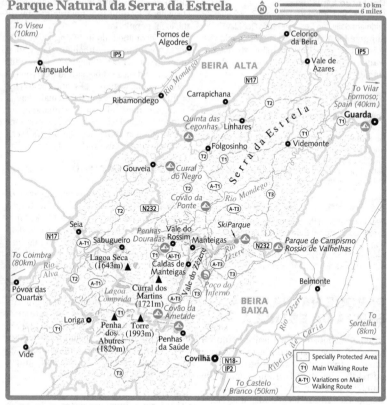

There are three main 'official' routes through the park, as well as branches and alternative trails. For downloadable Portuguese-language brochures and topo maps for the three main trails, see www.rt-serradaestrela.pt/ROTAS_SITE/index.html. The TSE1 runs the length of the park (about 90km) and is the easiest to follow, taking in every kind of terrain, including the summit of Torre. TSE2 and TSE3 (both around 80km) run respectively along the western and eastern slopes. All of the trails pass through towns and villages, each of which offers some accommodation. Many of the finest walks start around Manteigas.

Within a zone of special protection (which includes almost everything above 1200m altitude), camping and fires are strictly prohibited except at designated sites, all of which are on the main trails. Cutting trees and picking plants are also forbidden.

Skiing

The ski season typically runs from January to March, with the best conditions in February.

Biking & Other Activities

Several companies specialise in outdoor activities in the park, including **Adriventura** (www.adriventura.com), which organises groups for biking, rock climbing, hiking and more. **Turistrela** (www.turistrela.pt) also organises biking adventures and can offer information about the new Vodafone Bike Park around Torre (half-/full day €15/20). SkiParque, east of Manteigas, offers many activities, including summertime 'dry skiing', paragliding, rock climbing, mountain biking and hiking.

ℹ Information

There are park offices at Manteigas (headquarters), Seia, Gouveia and Guarda, though not all staff speak English. Some local *turismos* can also provide park information.

Finding up-to-date printed information about the park can be frustrating. A free pamphlet (last published in 2006) offers a general introduction in English to the park as well as two suggested walks, but supplies are scarce due to lack of funds.

Likewise, the best resource for serious hikers – the 1:50,000 topographic map *Carta Turística: Parque Natural da Serra da Estrela* – has been out of print for years. Until the government's **Instituto de Conservação da Natureza e da Biodiversidade** (icnb@icnb.pt) provides funding for a reprint, your best bet is to snap a digital photo of the map at one of the park offices.

An English-language booklet, *Discovering the Region of the Serra da Estrela* (€4.25), has trail profiles, walking times, historic notes and flora and fauna basics, but is of limited use due to its 1992 publication date. A recommended, more-scientific guide to local flora and fauna is *Geobotanical Guide of the Serra* (€10), published in 2002. Park offices offer other books and brochures in Portuguese on geography, geology, medicinal plants and archaeology.

The best bets for understanding the Serra's natural history are Seia's Centro de Interpretaçaõ da Serra da Estrela and the park service's small but well-done interpretive exhibit atop Torre.

Accommodation

While Seia, Gouveia, Manteigas, Covilhã and Guarda all provide useful bases with comfortable accommodation options, those wanting a true mountain experience should opt for Manteigas, because the others – situated as they are on the Serra's outer slopes – feel as if they are more a part of the surrounding plains.

Whereas camping grounds drop their rates or close in winter, many hotels, *pensões* and *residenciais* actually increase their rates, typically from late December to March.

The park also rents out a couple of basic houses in **Penhas Douradas** (2-/4-person house €40/80), high on the ridgeline between Manteigas, Gouveia and Seia. For reservations, contact the park office in Manteigas.

There are hostels at Penhas da Saúde and Guarda, and at least eight camping grounds near the centre of the park. Turismo Habitação properties, which are concentrated on the western slopes, can be booked through local *turismos*.

ⓘ Getting There & Around

Express buses run daily from Coimbra to Seia, Guarda and Covilhã, and from Aveiro, Porto and Lisbon to Guarda and Covilhã. There are daily IC trains from Lisbon and Coimbra to Guarda (plus IR services calling at Gouveia) and from Lisbon

to Covilhã (with IR services on to Guarda). See town listings for more details.

There are regular, though infrequent, bus services around the edges of the park but none directly across it.

Driving can be hairy, thanks to mist and wet or icy roads at high elevations, and stiff winds. The Gouveia–Manteigas N232 road is one of the most tortuous in all of Portugal. Be prepared for traffic jams around Torre on weekends.

Seia

POP 5700 / ELEV 532M

Despite its sweeping views over the surrounding lowlands, modern Seia feels largely like a charmless strip of contemporary buildings slapped onto a hillside. The best reasons to visit are the local museums, especially the Serra da Estrela Interpretive Centre, and the attractive rural lodgings in the surrounding hills. The town itself also has enough restaurants and hotels to make it a convenient stop if you're arriving from the west and aren't quite ready for switchbacking drives into the mountains.

◉ Sights & Activities

Centro de Interpretaçaõ da Serra da Estrela MUSEUM
(CISE; Serra da Estrela Interpretive Centre; www.cise-seia.org.pt; Rua Visconde Molelos; adult/child €2/1.50; ☺10am-6pm Tue-Sun) Opened in 2007 with partial EU funding, this regional museum provides an excellent introduction to the Serra da Estrela region. A nine-minute film in English or Portuguese (don your 3D glasses at the door!) takes you flying around the mountains' main points of interest. Multimedia displays in the museum next door include a topographic scale model of the Serra with push buttons allowing you to light up rivers and fault lines, or see which features are granite and which are schist. CISE also provides free information on local hikes.

Museu do Pão MUSEUM
(www.museudopao.pt; admission €2; ☺10am-6pm Tue-Sun) This museum has all the information you'll ever need on local bread production. The highlight is the traditional-style shop, which sells local goodies (including freshly ground flour and bread baked on the premises). It's 1km northeast of the centre on the road to Sabugueiro.

Museu do Brinquedo MUSEUM
(museu.brinquedo@cm-seia.pt; Largo de Santa Rita; admission €1.50; ☺10am-6pm Tue-Sun)

THE BEIRAS SEIA

Near the *turismo*, this museum traces the history of toys in Portugal, from the Victorian to the contemporary. There's a playroom, a collection of toys from other countries and a workshop where kids can watch toys being made or repaired.

🛏 Sleeping

Casas da Ribeira   RENTAL COTTAGES **€€**
(☎238 311 221, 919 660 354; www.casasdaribeira.com; Póvoa Velha; 2-/4-person cottages incl breakfast & firewood from €65/100) In the hills above Seia, this charming collection of vine-draped, stone cottages equipped with kitchenettes and fireplaces is highly recommended if you have your own vehicle. There's a two-night minimum stay, but prices drop significantly for additional nights. From Seia, climb the Sabugueiro road for about 5km, then follow signs into the tiny hamlet of Póvoa Velha, where you'll find the rental office. Call ahead to arrange your visit.

Casas da Lapa   INN **€€€**
(☎934 560 401; www.casasdalapa.com; Rua da Eira de Costa 10, Lapa do Dinheiro; r midweek/weekend €90/115, 2-/3-bedroom house €180/210; P✳@🛜❄) This lovely boutique inn 9km south of Seia is a study in contrasts, blending ancient stone architecture with colourful modern decor. There are eight rooms in the renovated main house, with two larger self-catering units off-site in the same village. Guests have access to a sauna, Turkish bath, massage room and weight room, although plenty of folks are happy just chilling by the infinity pool, on a sunny terrace where the rush of a nearby waterfall provides the background music. Meals are provided on request, including a full-fledged multi-course dinner with wines and other drinks for €25, or lighter fare for €12 to €15.

Casa das Tílias   INN **€€**
(☎238 390 055; www.casadastilias.com; Rua das Tílias, São Romão; r €70, 1-/2-bedroom apt €80/140; P🛜❄) This gorgeous 1850s-era mansion with polished wooden floors and high ceilings (some with lovingly restored friezework) has six rooms and a grand parlour in the main building, plus three self-catering apartments in the modern adjacent annexe.

Hotel Eurosol Seia-Camelo   HOTEL **€€**
(☎238 310 100; www.eurosol.pt; Av 1 de Maio 16; s/d €47/64; P✳@🛜❄) This well-functioning but nondescript business-class hotel has large rooms, pink-marble bathrooms with abundant hot water, a large sandy children's play area, a pool with lounge chairs and free off-street parking. Inquire about discounts for longer stays.

🍴 Eating

Restaurante Central   PORTUGUESE **€**
(Av 1 de Maio 12B; mains €6-10; ⊙lunch & dinner) Family-friendly, with warm and attentive service, this plain-faced restaurant near Hotel Eurosol Seia Camelo serves dependably good if basic Portuguese fare.

Restaurante Regional da Serra
    PORTUGUESE **€€**
(Av dos Combatentes da Grande Guerra 14; mains €7-11; ⊙lunch & dinner Fri-Wed) This trim place is well known for hearty regional specialities, including local cheeses and sausages as well as *chanfana à serrana* (highland goat).

Restaurante Borges   PORTUGUESE **€€**
(Travessa do Funchal 7; mains €9-14; ⊙lunch & dinner Fri-Tue, lunch Wed) Tucked away in a tight corner off the main street, this country-style place offers large portions of delicious traditional Portuguese fare and is popular with locals celebrating special events. The TV conspicuously blaring in other Portuguese restaurants is blessedly absent here.

ℹ Information

Espaço Internet (⊙10am-6pm Tue-Sun) Free internet adjacent to the CISE interpretive centre.

Parque Natural da Serra da Estrela office (☎238 310 440; pnse@icnb.pt; Praça da República 30; ⊙9am-12.30pm & 2-5.30pm Mon-Fri)

Post office (Av 1 de Maio; ⊙8.30am-12.30pm & 2-6pm Mon-Fri)

Turismo (☎238 317 762; turismo@cm-seia.pt; Rua Pintor Lucas Marrão; ⊙9am-12.30pm & 2-5.30pm Mon-Sat, 9am-1pm Sun)

ℹ Getting There & Away

Rede Expressos (☎238 313 102) goes to Lisbon (€17.50, 4½ hours), Coimbra (€10, 1¾ hours) and Guarda (€9.70, 70 minutes). It also runs one direct bus weekly to Covilhã (€12, 1¾ hours). Rede Expressos has a central **ticket office** (Praça da República 52).

  Marques (☎238 312 858) serves Gouveia (€2.35, 25 minutes) and Guarda (€4.55, two hours) several times each weekday.

Sabugueiro

POP 700 / ELEV 1050M

Attracting tourists from far and wide thanks to its title as Portugal's highest village, Sabugueiro is more noteworthy as a place to shop for *queijo da serra* (mountain cheese) and Serra da Estrela dogs (see boxed text, p336) than as a destination in itself. While the hills around town are still inhabited by sturdy farmer-shepherd families living in slate-roofed granite houses, casual passers-by are more likely to encounter the motley strip of charm-free *pensões* and souvenir shops straggling along the main highway between Seia and Torre.

You can buy some excellent cheese here, although it's mostly made with milk from outside the Serra da Estrela due to diminishing local supply and skyrocketing demand. Pet lovers, and children especially, will find it hard to resist stopping to look at the Serra da Estrela puppies peering wistfully from their roadside cages. Local families also sell delicious smoked ham, rye bread, juniperberry firewater and cosy fleece slippers for the chilly mountain nights.

🛈 Getting There & Away

Sabugueiro is a 15-minute drive uphill from Seia. A taxi from Seia costs around €10.

Gouveia

POP 3800 / ELEV 650M

Gouveia (goh-*vay*-ah), draped across a hillside 5km from the N17, is a charming blend of the contemporary and historic in a smaller-town setting. Pleasantly laid out, with parks and public gardens, it offers sufficient accommodation, food and transport to be a good base for exploring the northwestern side of the *parque natural*.

From the bus station, it's 450m south via Avenida 1 de Maio and Rua da República to Praça de São Pedro, the town centre.

🛏 Sleeping & Eating

TOP CHOICE **Quinta das Cegonhas**

CAMPGROUND, ROOMS €€

(☑238 745 886; www.cegonhas.com; Nabainhos; sites per adult/child/tent/car €4.20/2.20/4.10/3, d with breakfast €57.50, 3-/4-person apt without breakfast €65/86; @🛜🏊) Meaning 'House of the Storks', this restored 17th-century *quinta* (country estate) 6km northeast of Gouveia has nice views, terraced tent sites and a few private rooms and self-catering apartments.

Meals are available by arrangement (adult/child €15/7.50). The Dutch owners offer a wealth of information about local hikes, and have a couple of copies of the long-out-of-print topographic map of Serra da Estrela to lend out to guests – worth its weight in gold! They can also help arrange two-night walking excursions with stays at a nearby farm where meals include homemade produce and goat cheese. If you'd rather just kick up your feet and relax, the pool and lounge area in the old stone house – complete with guest computers and free wi-fi – offer plenty of opportunity for self-indulgent lazing about.

Casas do Toural

RENTAL HOUSES €€

(☑238 492 132; www.casasdotoural.com; Rua Direita 74; 2-person cottages €60-74, 4-person cottages €100-108, 6-person cottages €151; 🏊) This gorgeous ensemble of restored houses surrounds an immaculately kept hillside garden near the centre of town. Most rooms feature exposed stone walls, kitchens, fireplaces and living rooms. Book in advance on weekends. For longer-term guests, owner Maria José offers guided hikes into the Serra da Estrela.

Parque de Campismo Curral do Negro

CAMPGROUND €

(☑961 350 810; www.curraldonegro.com; sites per adult/child/tent/car €3/1.50/2.50/4; 🏊) Generously shaded with oaks, pines and chestnuts, this scenically located place offers camp sites plus three brand-new bungalows sleeping six to eight. It's reached via a steeply winding climb 3km southeast of town.

Residencial Monteneve

HOTEL €€

(☑238 490 370; www.moteneveresidencial. com; Av Bombeiros Voluntários 12; s/d without breakfast €55/80, with breakfast €65/90; 🅿🌡) This old granite building in the heart of town has been converted into a rigorously clean hotel with comfortable rooms and a pleasant breakfast area.

Restaurante O Júlio

PORTUGUESE €€

(☑238 498 016; Travessa do Loureiro 11A; dishes €7.50-12; ⓒlunch & dinner Wed-Mon) Tucked away in a narrow downtown street, this place is popular for its regional cuisine. House specialities include *cabrito à serrana* (mountain-style kid) and *batatinhas do céu* (heavenly potatoes).

Mercado Municipal

MARKET €

(ⓒMon-Sat morning) Self-caterers will find the market straight uphill from the *turismo,* at its best on Thursday.

A SHEPHERD'S BEST FRIEND

Any animal lover travelling through the Serra da Estrela will be hard-pressed to resist the 'take-me-home-now' feeling prompted by the region's indigenous Cão da Serra da Estrela, or **Estrela mountain dog** (EMD). It's not just the adorable fuzzy golden and black puppies; the massive adults are as handsome as they are reputed to be strong and smart, loving and loyal.

The importance of these beautiful animals to local culture is epitomised in the bronze statue outside Gouveia depicting a shepherd with his faithful dog. Widely recognised as one of the most ancient breeds on the Iberian Peninsula, the EMD is thought to have descended from dogs brought by the Romans or Visigoths. Over the centuries, shepherds chose the best dogs to guard their goats and sheep and perform in harsh mountain conditions. The dogs are massive, with males weighing over 45kg; they have a warm coat to protect against the frigid mountain winters, can survive on minimal diets, and possess the endurance and agility to trek over boulder-strewn terrain. Fiercely resisting any predator daring enough to attack its flock, the EMD can also be gentle as a lamb, especially in its nurturing attitude towards the young of both the human and goat/sheep variety. Traditionally the dogs were outfitted with spiked collars to protect their throats against an attacking wolf or bear.

While today the EMD is one of the most popular pets in Portugal, its traditional use has declined drastically. In an ironic twist, the wolf-recovery organisation **Grupo Lobo** (http://lobo.fc.ul.pt) has become one of Portugal's leading advocates for reviving the EMD's role as herd guardian. Biologists worldwide now see herd-guarding dogs as one of the best strategies for protecting flocks while promoting wolf recovery.

ⓘ Information

Biblioteca Municipal (Praça de São Pedro 5; ⊙9.30am-12.30pm & 2-6pm Mon-Fri, 9.30am-1pm Sat) Free internet.

Centro do Cidadão Espaço Net (Rua da República; ⊙9.30am-12.30pm & 2-6pm Mon-Fri, 9.30am-12.30pm Sat) Free internet across the square from the *turismo*.

Parque Natural da Serra da Estrela office (☑238 492 411; pnse@icnb.pt; Av Bombeiros Voluntários 8; ⊙9am-12.30pm & 2-5.30pm Mon-Fri) A block south of the centre.

Post office (Av 1 de Maio 3; ⊙9am-12.30pm & 2-6pm Mon-Fri) One block downhill from Praça de São Pedro.

Turismo (☑238 083 930; turismo@dlcg.pt; Jardim da Ribeira; ⊙9.30am-12.30pm & 2-6pm Mon-Sat, 10am-12.30pm & 2-5pm Sun) On a pleasant square five minutes' walk downhill from Praça de São Pedro.

ⓘ Getting There & Away

BUS **Rede Expressos** (☑238 493 675) and **Marques** (☑238 312 858) stop at Gouveia's **bus station** (Rua Cidade da Guarda), a 10-minute walk north of the centre. Marques runs to Seia (€2.35, 25 minutes, four per weekday) and Guarda (€4.15, 1½ hours, one daily). Rede Expressos goes two or three times daily to Coimbra (€12, two hours) and Lisbon (€17.50, 4¾ hours).

TRAIN The Gouveia railway station, 14km north near Ribamondego, is on the Beira Alta line between Coimbra (€7.60, 1¾ hours) and Guarda (€4.85, 50 minutes) – regional trains stop here three to four times daily. A taxi between Gouveia and the station will cost around €10.

Manteigas

POP 4100 / ELEV 720M

Cradled at the foot of the beautiful Vale do Zêzere, with high peaks and forest-draped slopes dominating the horizon in all directions, Manteigas feels more like a true mountain town than any of the other major Serra da Estrela gateways. There has been a settlement here since at least Moorish times, probably because of the nearby Caldas de Manteigas hot springs.

As headquarters for the Parque Natural da Serra da Estrela, Manteigas makes an excellent base for hikers looking to explore the region. Walk through the glacial valley above town and you'll still encounter terraced meadows, stone shepherds' huts and tinkling goat-bells, while in Manteigas itself cobblestoned streets and older homes still hold their own against the high-rise development that has taken root elsewhere on the Serra's fringes.

From Seia or Gouveia you approach Manteigas down a near-vertical switchback, the N232. South of town, the N338 snakes up the Zêzere valley into the high country between Torre and Penhas da Saúde.

Manteigas has no real centre, but buses will set you down between the Galp petrol station and the *turismo,* near the park headquarters, the town church and a cluster of hotels and restaurants.

Sights & Activities

Poço do Inferno
WATERFALL
In springtime, this waterfall in the craggy gorge of the Ribeira de Leandres – about 10km outside Manteigas by car – makes a beautiful sight. From Manteigas town centre, drive approximately 4km along the signposted main road towards Torre. Just beyond Caldas de Manteigas, look for a sign on your left for Poço do Inferno (Hell's Well) and climb up a narrow road 6km further to the falls, passing through a lush remnant of evergreen forest that was spared by the 2004 forest fire.

There's also a hiking trail from Manteigas to the falls, starting with a long descent along the cobbled road between the *turismo* and the Galp petrol station. However, at the time of writing it was extremely poorly marked.

In summer the waterfall slows to a trickle, and with trash and misuse the site's beauty is considerably dampened.

Walking Trails
WALKING
Recently, Manteigas' town government has begun improving several local trails and developing new ones as part of an ambitious program called **Green Trails**, which ultimately aims to create over 300 hours of well-signposted walking opportunities in the area. For details, inquire at Manteiga's *turismo* or the park office.

Following are the outlines of three recommended walks in the mountains surrounding Manteigas.

Vale do Zêzere
The relatively easy ramble through this magnificent, glacier-scoured valley at the foot of Torre is a highlight of any trip to Manteigas. Its only drawback: the trail is shadeless and baking in clear summer weather. The valley suffered a massive forest fire in 2004, and recovery has been very slow. Still, the Zêzere valley remains one of the park's most beautiful and noteworthy natural features.

From the park office, follow the N338 for 2.8km towards Caldas de Manteigas, leaving the road at the brown-and-white 'Roteiro Rural Palhotas' sign just beyond the spa hotel. From here, a part-cobbled, part-dirt road leads upstream through irrigated fields dotted with typical stone *casais*. About 4km along, the unpaved road crosses the Rio Zêzere just above a popular local swimming hole. A park service sign here (marked 'Reserva Biogenética') signals the beginning of a trail closed to vehicles. Drivers can park in the small dirt lot beside the road.

THE BEIRAS MANTEIGAS

HILL TOWNS OF THE NORTHERN SERRA

Two of the Serra da Estrela's prettiest towns are tucked high in the hills between Gouveia and Guarda. Neither **Linhares** nor **Folgosinho** has much in the way of tourist infrastructure – which is part of their appeal.

Linhares, designated an *aldeia histórica* (historic village) by the Portuguese government, is best known for its imposing castle, which commands remarkable bird's-eye views over the surrounding countryside. Aside from that, it's the kind of place where shepherds still drive their flocks down the middle of the road and older women come out to chat in their gardens at sunset. Poke around in the warren of stone houses, terraced hillsides and twisting lanes below the castle and you'll find signs advertising rooms for rent, including those at **Casa Pissarra** (271 776 180; r from €35, house €100); weekend visitors can eat and drink at **Taberna do Alcaide** (271 776 578; www.cvrdao.pt; Rua Direita, Linhares; mains €8-10; 9am-midnight Sat & Sun).

Folgosinho's biggest draw, aside from its miniature hilltop castle, is its pretty main square, where you'll find **O Albertino** (238 745 266; prix fixe menus €12; lunch & dinner Tue-Sat, lunch Sun), a cosy stone-walled restaurant specialising in down-to-earth mountain cuisine. Dinner is an all-you-can-eat affair, featuring gamey favourites like *feijoada de javeli* (beans stewed with wild boar). Albertino also rents rooms around town from €40.

The 4km trail follows the Rio Zêzere upstream along its eastern bank, climbing gradually through a wide-open landscape dotted with stone shepherds' huts and backed by spectacular views of the looming mountains on either side. Eventually the path, marked with cairns and red and yellow paint, narrows and steepens as you scramble up to meet the N338 (11km from Manteigas).

Once at the N338, backpackers wanting to overnight amid this dazzling scenery can continue uphill on the paved road 1.1km to the Covão da Ametade camp site. Thirsty day trippers should descend 900m along the pavement to Fonte Paulo Luís Martins, a crystalline spring whose delightfully cold water (constantly 6°C) is bottled in Manteigas and sold nationally as Glacier mineral water – but you can drink as much as you want here at the source for free! If you've left a car at the swimming hole, you can walk an additional 3.2km back downhill along the N338, although it's usually easy to hitch a ride from someone filling their bottles at the springs.

Penhas Douradas & Vale do Rossim

A more demanding walk goes to Penhas Douradas, a collection of windblown holiday houses. The track climbs northwest out of town via Rua Dr Afonso Costa to join a sealed, switchback forestry road and, briefly, a wide loop of the Seia-bound N232. Branch left off the N232 almost immediately, on another forestry road to the Meteorological Observatory. From there it's a short, gentle ascent to Penhas Douradas.

You're about 700m above Manteigas here, and you mustn't miss the stunning view from a stub of rock called Fragão de Covão; just follow the signs. You can also drive up the N232 just for the view: about 18km from Manteigas, then left at the first turning after the one marked *observatório*, and 1km to the sign for Fragão de Covão. Save your car's oil-pan and walk the rest of the way.

Walking back the same way makes for a return trip of about 5½ hours.

Vale do Rossim to Lagoa Comprida

If you've got a vehicle and want a taste of the high country without having to climb on foot from Manteigas, consider this trek through the boulder-strewn hillsides and sheep-grazing meadows between two artificial lakes: the Vale do Rossim reservoir and Lagoa Comprida. To reach the trailhead,

drive up the steep N232 to Penhas Douradas, where signs on your left will point to the Vale do Rossim.

From the trailhead, follow the T1 trail towards Torre, then veer off onto the T13. Total hiking time to Lagoa Comprida is approximately three hours each way. Elevation gain is relatively moderate, starting at 1425m on the Vale do Rossim side and climbing to 1700m before descending to 1600m at Lagoa Comprida.

SkiParque   DRY-SKI RUN

(www.skiparque.pt; N232; ☺10am-5pm) A surreal-looking dry-ski run 7.5km east of Manteigas, SkiParque has a lift, gear rental, snowboarding, a cafe and a treeless, functional camp site. The price for lifts and equipment rental is €10/22 per hour/day in low season, €14/26 in high season. Group lessons are also available.

To further compensate for the lack of snow in summer, SkiParque organises other outdoor activities such as **rock climbing**, **hiking**, **mountain biking** and **paragliding** lessons for first-timers.

🛏 Sleeping

Casa das Obras   B&B €€

(☎275 981 155; www.casadasobras.pt; Rua Teles de Vasconcelos; r summer/winter €64/80; P☎️☎️) Manteigas' nicest in-town lodging, this lovely 18th-century town house has been carefully renovated to preserve its original grandeur and stone-walled charm. The antique-filled rooms are well kept, and breakfast includes local cheese, honey and jams. Other pluses include the friendly hotel dog Beirão, the cave-like stone bar and the pool in a grassy courtyard across the street.

Albergaria Berne   HOTEL €€

(☎275 981 351; www.albergariaberne.com; Quinta de Santo António; s €35-65, d €55-65; P✱@☎️☎️) Going for a Swiss feel, this lovely hotel at the bottom of town was completely remodelled in 2009, with red pillows and curtains brightening up the spotless, wood-accented rooms. Many units have balconies and double-hinged windows opening onto views of Manteigas and the mountains above.

ⓉⓄⓅ CHOICE Covão da Ametade   CAMPGROUND €

(sites €1; ☺Jul–mid-Sep) The wilder of two idyllic, bare-bones campgrounds tucked away in the mountains surrounding Manteigas, this tents-only site sits in a grove of birch trees near the head of the Vale do Zêzere, with awe-inspiring views up to the looming Cántaro Magro. It's signposted at a hairpin bend 12km west of Manteigas along the N338. There are toilets (sometimes poorly maintained), picnic tables and cement barbecues, but don't expect electricity or hot water.

TOP CHOICE **Covão da Ponte** CAMPGROUND €
(sites per adult/child/tent/car €1.50/1/1.50/1; ☉Aug) At this lovely, shaded spot along the Mondego, you can wade, picnic or simply relax by the river's tranquil headwaters. Hikers can also explore the surrounding fields and mountains on three loop trails of varying lengths described on a park service sign at the camp-site entrance. To get here, take the N232 5.4km uphill from Manteigas, then continue an additional 5km from the signposted turn-off. The poorly marked park entrance is on the right. There's an intermittently open snack bar as well as showers.

Pousada de São Lourenço LUXURY HOTEL €€€
(☎275 980 050; www.pousadas.pt; s/d €113/125, with mountain view €138/150; P) Pitching for the Beiras' most stupendous view, but hemmed in on both sides by a hairpin curve along the busy main road, this luxurious modern hotel features plush rooms with a woodsy, alpine feel. It's 13km above and north of town, topping the wiggly switchbacks on the N232. The restaurant (open to nonguests) shares the hotel's glorious views; on a clear day, you can see all the way into Spain.

Pensão Serradalto HOTEL €
(☎275 981 151; Rua 1 de Maio 15; s/d winter €40/45, summer €30/35) In the heart of town, the Serradalto offers rooms with wood floors and simple antique furnishings, plus fine valley views from a sunny, grapevine-shaded upstairs terrace. Multinight stays earn a €5 discount.

Parque de Campismo Rossio de Valhelhas CAMPGROUND €
(☎275 487 160; jfvalhelhas@clix.pt; Valhelhas; sites per adult/child/tent/car €2.50/1.25/2/2; ☉May-Sep) About 15km from Manteigas, in a pretty cottonwood grove by the Rio Zêzere, this municipal site along the N232 is flat and shady, if somewhat dusty, with a river beach nearby.

✕ Eating

Most of Manteigas' eateries are clustered within a block of the park office.

Dom Pastor PORTUGUESE €€
(☎275 982 920; Rua Sá da Bandeira; mains €10-13; ☉lunch & dinner Wed-Mon) Set idyllically on the parklike banks of the town's millstream, Manteigas' top-rated restaurant puts fine local ingredients, from cheese to mountain-raised meats, to creative use.

Pastelaria Padaria Floresta BAKERY, CAFE €
(Rua 1 de Maio; ☉6am-midnight Mon-Sat, 8am-1pm Sun) Open bright and early, this little bakery is a hiker's best friend, with simple sandwiches on homemade bread plus delicious trail snacks for sale for around €1. Taste the *empadas de frango* (pastry dough filled with chicken), *queijadas de requeijão* (half-sweet, half-savoury cheese tarts) and the house speciality *pastéis de feijoca* (bean cakes).

Luso Pizza PIZZERIA €€
(☎275 982 930; Rua Dr Manuel Duarte Leitão; pizzas from €7-16; ☉11am-11pm) This tiny place makes great pizza, although locals tend to get preferential treatment over visitors. Pasta appears on the menu but isn't always available.

Clube de Compras SUPERMARKET €
(Rua 1 de Maio; ☉9am-1pm & 2-8pm Mon-Fri, 9am-8pm Sat, 9am-6pm Sun) Provides groceries for self-caterers, just up the street from the park office.

❶ Information

Parque Natural da Serra da Estrela office (☎275 980 060; pnse@icnb.pt; Rua 1 de Maio 2; ☉9am-12.30pm & 2-5.30pm Mon-Fri)

Turismo (☎275 981 129; Rua Dr Esteves de Carvalho 2; ☉9am-12.30pm & 2-5.30pm Tue-Sat)

❶ Getting There & Away

Two regular weekday buses connect Manteigas with Guarda. Check with Manteigas' *turismo* for up-to-the-minute details.

Manteigas is a fairly easy 20-minute drive from the IP2, or a more winding 40-minute drive from Covilhã.

Torre

In winter, Torre's road signs are so blasted by freezing winds that horizontal icicles barb their edges. Portugal's highest peak at 1993m, Torre ('Tower') produces a winter freeze that's so reliable you'll also find the small **Estância Vodafone ski resort** (www.skiserradaestrela.com/index1.php; half-/full day €15/25; ☉9am-5pm during ski season), with three creaky lifts that serve a small set of beginners' slopes. Ski-gear rental is also available, including skis, poles and boots (€25 per day) and snowboards (€15 per day).

If you come outside of the snowy season (mid-December to mid-April), Portugal's windy pinnacle is rather depressing – occupied by several ageing golf-ball radar domes, and a sweaty, smelly shopping arcade. And then there's the 7m-high, neo-classical obelisk, erected by João VI in the early 19th century so that Portugal could cheekily claim its highest point was exactly 2000m.

The summit's most redeeming feature is the **Centro de Interpretação do Parque Natural da Serra da Estrela** (admission €2), a park service visitor centre filled with maps, photos and informational displays about the natural and cultural history of the region.

Even if you decide to give Torre itself a miss, it's worth making the trip up in this direction just to survey the astoundingly dramatic surroundings. The drive from Manteigas or Covilhã is especially breathtaking, passing as it does through the Nave de Santo António – a traditional high-country sheep-grazing meadow – before climbing abruptly through a surreal moonscape of crags and gorges. The area's most remarkable rock formation, visible near the turn-off for Torre, is Cántaro Magro. Rising 500m straight up from the valley below, it's a spectacular spot, popular with rock climbers.

A taxi to Torre will cost around €30 from Covilhã, €35 from Seia or €25 from Manteigas. In August, **Autotransportes do Fundão** (☑275 336 448) runs a 2pm bus service from Covilhã's bus station to Torre (€2.65, 1½ hours), arriving around 3.30pm and returning down the mountain an hour later.

Penhas da Saúde

Penhas, the closest spot in which to hunker down near Torre (about 10km from Covilhã), isn't a town but a weather-beaten collection of chalets sited strip-like along the N339 at an elevation of about 1500m. It sits just uphill from a burned-out tuberculosis sanatorium and downhill from the Barragem do Viriato dam. Supplies are limited; if you plan to go walking, do your shopping in Covilhã.

🍴 Sleeping & Eating

There are several cafes along the N339.

Pousada da Juventude   HOSTEL €
(☑275 335 375; penhas@movijovem.pt; dm/d summer €10/28, winter €13/45; P) Penhas' first-rate mountaintop hostel has a communal kitchen and cafeteria, giant stone fireplaces and a games room featuring billiards and table tennis. The deluxe doubles in the new building (opened in late 2009) are especially nice. Book well ahead in winter.

ℹ️ Getting There & Away

Daily throughout August, and on weekends in late July and early September, local **Autotransportes do Fundão** (☑275 336 448) runs buses from Covilhã's bus station to Penhas (€1.90) at 8.50am and 2pm, returning down the mountain at 5.35pm.

A **taxi** from Covilhã to Penhas costs €15 to €20.

Covilhã

POP 35,000 / ELEV 700M

Easily accessible from Lisbon by train and superhighway, modern Covilhã is awash in suburban sprawl, its 18th-century textile factories having given way to 20th-century high-rise apartment blocks. Despite these rather dreary outskirts, Covilhã's pleasant historic core remains intact, and the presence of the Universidade da Beira Interior lends it an air of modern urban vitality. The city's geographic setting – on steeply canted terraces directly below Penhas da Saúde and Torre – provides phenomenal views eastward towards Spain.

Covilhã received a major ego boost in 2010 when the Portuguese national football team chose it as their official World Cup training site.

👁 Sights

The narrow, winding streets to the west of Praça do Município have a quiet charm, and set in the midst of them is the **Igreja de Santa Maria**, with a startling facade covered in *azulejos*.

Commanding fabulous views, the leafy **Jardim Público**, just north of Praça do Município, is a popular local gathering place and a pleasant spot for a drink at sunset.

Covilhã used to be the centre of one of Europe's biggest wool-producing regions. However, the industry has long since fallen on hard times. Stray outside the centre and you'll see the town's ghostly mills standing empty and forlorn.

of the municipal gardens. All rooms have leafy views of the park or sweeping panoramas of the surrounding mountains (room 10 has both!), and one is wheelchair-accessible. The cafe downstairs is another plus.

Hotel Solneve HOTEL €
(☑275 323 001/2; www.solneve.pt; Rua Visconde da Coriscada 126; s/d/tr/q Noc-Mar €35/53/68/83, Apr-Oct €25/43/58/73; P❄@🛜⛱) With views of Covilhã's main square, this grand pink hotel in the heart of town has spotless, high-ceilinged, old-style hotel rooms with bathtubs and good hot water. There's a decent restaurant and a swimming pool downstairs, plus off-street parking (€2.50). Pricier rooms include jet baths.

Parque de Campismo do Pião
CAMPGROUND €
(☑275 314 312; www.clubecampismo covilha.pt; sites per adult/child/tent/car €2.85/1.45/3.45/2.10, 2-/4-person bungalows from €45/60; ⛱) Some 4km up the N339 towards Penhas da Saúde, this snug, wooded municipal camp site also offers bungalows with kitchen facilities.

Hotel Covilhã Parque HOTEL €€
(☑275 329 320; www.covilhaparquehotel. com.pt; Av Frei Heitor Pinto; s/d/tr winter €44/63/90, summer €31/50/69; ❄@🛜) Ten floors of uninspired but comfortable rooms enjoy nice city views in this modern apartment block next to the *turismo*. Internet is available but expensive.

✕ Eating & Drinking

Restaurante Zé do Sporting PORTUGUESE €€
(Rua Comendador Mendes Veiga 19; mains €8-14; ◷lunch & dinner Tue-Sat, lunch Sun) Grilled

Sited in the former royal textile factory, founded in 1764 by the Marquês de Pombal, the **Museu de Lanifícios** (Museum of Wool-Making; www.museu.ubi.pt; Rua Marquês de Ávila e Bolama; admission €2; ◷9.30am-noon & 2.30-6pm Tue-Sun) traces the proud but vanishing history of wool production and cloth dyeing in the Serra da Estrela. A map shows the 100-plus wool producers that once thrived in this region, while other displays demonstrate how cochineal and indigo from the New World were used to dye Portuguese soldiers' uniforms red and blue. Even if yarn makes you yawn, you may be impressed by the gigantic old looms and dyeing vats.

🛏 Sleeping

TOP CHOICE **Residencial Covilhã Jardim** HOTEL €
(☑275 322 140; www.residencialcovilhaja rdim.com; Jardim Público 40; s/d Apr-Dec €30/45, Jan-Mar €35/55; ❄@) This bright, modern family-run place sits on the quietest corner

meats – including local favourites such as *coelho* (rabbit) and *cabrito* (kid) – share the menu with other Portuguese classics. Try the *feijoada á transmontana,* a hearty stew of beans, cabbage, pork and smoky sausage.

Pastelaria Restaurante Montiel

CAFE, PORTUGUESE €

(Praça do Município 33-37; daily specials €7-8; ☺cafe all day, restaurant lunch & dinner) The upstairs dining room here serves up decent regional cooking, with an emphasis on meat dishes.

Covilhã Jardim Café-Bar

CAFE €

(Jardim Público 40; ☺all day) With comfy couches inside and tree-shaded tables on its parkside terrace, this trendy little cafe makes an enjoyable place to watch the world go by.

Mercado municipal

MARKET €

(Rua António Augusto d'Aguiar) Self-caterers will find abundant fruit and vegetables most mornings at the market.

☆ Entertainment

Companhia Club

BAR, DANCE CLUB

(www.companhiaclub.com; Rua Indústria 33) This sleek DJ bar and club is one of a cluster of late-night venues popular with students, set in the abandoned-looking mill zone north of the municipal gardens.

ⓘ Information

Hospital (☏275 330 000; Quinta do Alvito)

Police station (☏275 320 920; Rua Conde de Ericeira)

Ponto Já (cnr Rua da Olivença & Rua António Augusto d'Aguiar; ☺10am-7pm Mon-Fri) Free internet access.

Post office (Praça do Município; ☺8.30am-6.30pm Mon-Fri, 9am-12.30pm Sat)

Regional turismo (☏275 319 560; www. turismoserradaestrela.pt; Av Frei Heitor Pinto; ☺9am-5.30pm Mon-Fri, 9am-12.30pm & 2-5.30pm Sat)

ⓘ Getting There & Away

BUS From the long-distance **bus station** (☏275 313 506), **Joalto** (☏275 336 700) and **Rede Expressos** (www.rede-expressos.pt) run jointly to Guarda (€4.40, 45 minutes, several times daily), and via Castelo Branco (€4.40, one hour) to Lisbon (€13, 3¾ hours) at least three times daily. There are also multiple daily services to Porto (€14, three to four hours).

TRAIN Three daily IC trains run to/from Lisbon (€15.50, four hours) via Castelo Branco (€8, one

hour). Regional trains serving this same route are slower and only slightly cheaper.

ⓘ Getting Around

From the train and long-distance bus stations, it's a punishing 2km climb to Praça do Município, the town centre. A taxi up the hill from either station will cost about €5, or you can catch a yellow local bus (€1.10) operated by **Covibus** (www. covibus.com). For the centre, take bus 10 or 11 and get off in Praça do Municipio or at the local bus terminal on Rua António Augusto d'Aguiar (just south of Praça do Município).

Parking is available at the public garage underneath Praça do Municipio.

BEIRA ALTA

Heading north and west from the Serra da Estrela, mountains give way quickly to rolling plains that stretch up to the Douro valley and east to Spain. Threat of invasion from its not-always-friendly neighbour marks both the region's history and its landscape. A series of fearsome fortress-towns are the biggest draw for travellers, though the cities of Viseu and Guarda also have their charms, from excellent local wines to troves of Renaissance art.

Viseu

POP 47,000

One of the Beiras' most appealing cities, Viseu easily rivals the more-visited Coimbra for sheer charm and vitality. Its well-preserved historical centre offers numerous enticements to pedestrians: cobbled streets, meandering alleys, leafy public gardens and a central square – Praça da República, aka the 'Rossio' – graced with bright flowers and fountains. Viseu sits beside the Rio Pavia, a tributary of the Mondego. Sweeping vistas over the surrounding plains unfold from the town's highest point, the square fronting the late-Gothic and Manueline cathedral, built on the site of a former mosque.

Nowadays capital of the Beira Alta province, and a bishopric since Visigothic times, Viseu has a proud and multilayered history. The former bishop's palace now houses a museum dedicated to the works of Renaissance painter Vasco Fernandes and his contemporaries. Viseu is also a great place to eat and drink: the reds from the surrounding Dão region (see boxed text,

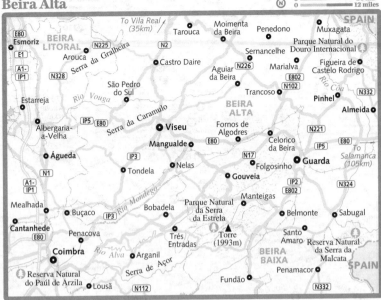

p348) are considered to be some of Portugal's finest.

The bus station is 500m northwest of the Rossio along Avenida Dr António José de Almeida.

History

According to legend, Viriato, chief of the Lusitani tribe (p476), took refuge in a cave here before the Romans hunted him down in 139 BC, though there's no cave now.

The Romans built a fortified camp just across the Rio Pavia from Viseu, and some well-preserved segments of their roads survive nearby. The town, conquered and reconquered in the struggles between Christians and Moors, was definitively taken by Ferdinand I, king of Castilla y León, in 1057.

Afonso V completed Viseu's sturdy walls in about 1472. The town soon spread beyond them, and grew fat from agriculture and trade. An annual 'free fair' declared by João III in 1510 carries on today as one of the region's biggest agricultural and handicrafts expositions.

◎ Sights

Sé   CATHEDRAL

(◎8am-noon & 2-7.30pm) Resplendent on a rock above town is the 13th-century granite cathedral, whose gloomy Renaissance facade conceals a splendid 16th-century interior, including an impressive Manueline ceiling.

Stairs in the northern transept climb to the **Museu de Arte Sacra**. The museum itself (closed for renovation at the time of research) is a lacklustre assemblage of vestments and religious paraphernalia, but its lofty setting offers a nice perspective on the church's architecture; sweeping panoramas of Viseu's historic centre are also available from the upper gallery of the adjacent **Claustro Jónico** (Ionian Cloister).

The original lower level of the cloister is one of Portugal's earliest Italian Renaissance structures. Note the Romanesque-Gothic portal on one corner, rediscovered during restoration work in 1918.

Facing the cathedral is the 1775 **Igreja da Misericórdia**, whose bright rococo exterior contrasts markedly with its neoclassical, severe and rather dull interior.

Museu Grão Vasco   MUSEUM

(mgv.se@imc-ip.pt; admission €4; ◎2-5.30pm Tue, 10am-5.30pm Wed-Sun) Adjoining the cathedral is the severe granite box of the Paço de Três Escalões (Palace of Three Steps), probably a contemporary of the cathedral and originally built as the bishop's palace. In 1916 it reopened as a splendid museum

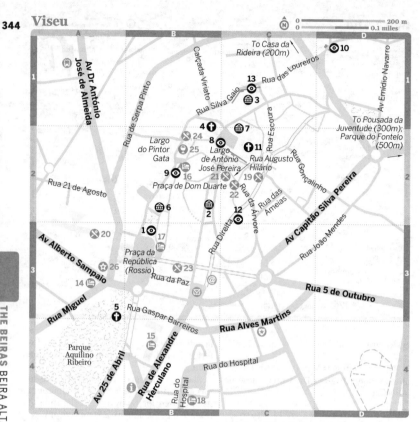

featuring Viseu's own Vasco Fernandes, known as Grão Vasco, 'the Great Vasco' (1480–1543) – one of Portugal's seminal Renaissance painters.

The recently renovated museum houses other bright lights of the so-called Viseu School. Vasco's colleague, collaborator and rival Gaspar Vaz merits special attention. Together they spurred each other on to produce some of Portugal's finest artwork. After five centuries their rich colours and luminous style are still as striking as ever.

Around the Rossio

At the southern end of Praça da República is the late-18th-century **Igreja dos Terceiros**, all heavy, gilded baroque but for the luminous *azulejos* portraying the life of St Francis.

Fine modern **azulejos** at the northern end of the Rossio depict scenes from regional life, and beyond these is the

azulejo-adorned **Museu Almeida Moreira** (apoio.municipe@cm-viseu.pt; Rua Soar de Cima; 10am-12.30pm & 2-5.30pm Wed-Sun, 2-5.30pm Tue), genteel home to the first director of the Museu Grão Vasco, with fine furnishings and art. The museum was about to close for renovations at the time of research but expected to reopen in mid-2011.

From here the grandest route into the old town is through the **Porta do Soar de Cima**, a gate set into a section of Afonso V's town walls.

Around the Sé

North of the cathedral along Rua Silva Gaio is the longest remaining stretch of the old **town walls**. To the east, across Avenida Emídio Navarro, is another old town gate, the **Porta dos Cavaleiros**.

South of the cathedral beneath the **Passeio dos Cônegos** (Curates Walk, on part of the old wall) is **Praça de Dom Duarte**, named after the Portuguese monarch (brother of Prince Henry the Navigator) born in Viseu. Several of the square's mansions show off wrought-iron balconies and genteel contours.

Southward is **Casa de Dom Duarte** (Rua Dom Duarte; ⊗ closed to public), a house with a beautiful Manueline window and traditionally regarded as the king's birthplace.

Rua Augusto Hilário runs southeast through the former **judiaria** (14th- to 16th-century Jewish quarter). **Rua Direita**, Viseu's most appealing street and once the most direct route to the hilltop, is a lively melee of shops, souvenir stands, restaurants and old town houses.

Mansions

The most handsome of Viseu's many old town houses is the 18th-century **Solar dos Condes de Prime** (Rua dos Andrades), now serving web-surfing citizens as an Espaço Internet.

Among other stately homes are the 18th-century **Solar dos Viscondes de Treixedo** (Rua Direita), now a bank, and the 16th-century **Casa do Miradouro** (Calçada da Vigia), just off Largo de António José Pereira. Neither is open to the public.

Parque do Fontelo   PARK
A haven of woodland and open space sprawls beyond the Portal do Fontelo. Here are the 16th-century **Antigo Paço Episcopal** (former Bishop's Palace), now home to

the Dão Regional Vintners' Commission (CVRD; see boxed text, p348), together with once-lovely Renaissance gardens, a stadium and a recreation complex.

✯ Festivals & Events

Viseu's biggest annual get-together is the **Feira de São Mateus** (St Matthew's Fair), a jamboree of agriculture and handicrafts from mid-August to mid-September, augmented by folk music, traditional food, amusement-park rides and fireworks. This direct descendant of the town's old 'free fair' still takes place in the riverside Campo da Feira de São Mateus, set aside for the event by João III in 1510.

🛏 Sleeping

TOP CHOICE **Quinta dos Três Rios**   INN €€€
(☑232 959 189; www.minola.co.uk; Rua Francisco de Oliveira 239, Parada de Gonta; 2-/4-person apt from €100/150; 🅿🛜) At this remarkable getaway about 10km southwest of Viseu, every room is a suite with 5m-high ceilings and 4m French doors opening onto a symphony of frogs and nightingales by night and vistas of the surrounding olive trees, vineyards and river by day. Hosts Hugh and Jane Forestier-Walker make fabulous dinners with their own homemade olive oil and wine, and with the help of their daughter Caroline, a Michelin-star pastry chef. Hugh leads impromptu tours of the surrounding area that encompass everything from wineries to traditional net

THE BEIRAS VISEU

fishing and barrel-making to grape stomp-ing during the harvest season. One suite (the Oaks) is wheelchair-equipped and pet-friendly as well – reserve ahead.

Pensão Rossio Parque　GUEST HOUSE **€**
(☑232 422 085; Praça da República 55; s €20-25, d €30-35, tw €40; ✸⊛) A no-brainer for budget-minded travellers, this small, old-fashioned hotel directly above the Rossio features a bright, bustling restaurant downstairs and nice views from the front rooms. All rooms are discounted €5 per night for stays of a week or longer. Serious penny-pinchers should ask about the one interior room without bathroom or windows (€20 single or double).

Palácio dos Melos　BOUTIQUE HOTEL **€€**
(☑232 439 290; www.hotelpalaciodosmelos.pt; Rua Chão Mestre 4; s/d €80/90, ste €125-145; P✸@⊛) This very central hotel enjoys a remarkable location, in a renovated man-sion built right into the town walls. Rooms incorporate all the modern comforts you'd expect from a five-star, but the most atmo-spheric rooms in the original older building also have grand high ceilings, carpets and chandeliers that speak of a different time. All guests have access to a small grassy yard where drinks are served, reached by a catwalk across the top of the old town gate. Look for money-saving multi-night pack-ages online, which typically include local Dão wines and meals in the hotel's gourmet restaurant.

⊘Campismo Moinhos do Dão
　CAMPGROUND, COTTAGES **€**
(☑232 610 586; www.moinhosdodao.nl; Tibald-inho, Mangualde; sites per adult/child/car €3.50/1.75/1, tent €3-4) This tranquil spot at the end of a dirt road 20km southeast of Viseu offers camping on the banks of the Rio Dão, plus rustic indoor lodgings with propane stoves and fridges (per week €245 to €375). Built amid a cluster of restored water-mills, it's a place where you truly get away from it all – swimming and boating by day, dining by candlelight at outdoor tables by night (three-course dinners in-cluding Dão wine run at €15/7.50 per adult/child). Clientele is almost exclusively Dutch, but the hosts speak excellent English; call ahead for directions.

Pousada de Viseu　LUXURY HOTEL **€€€**
(☑232 457 320; www.pousadas.pt; Rua do Hos-pital; r from €240; P✸@⊛⊛) Viseu's lat-est touch of luxury, and one of the newest additions to Portugal's government-run network of *pousadas* (upmarket inns), this monumental neoclassical 1793 hospital was completely remodelled over a period of several years and opened for business in early 2009. The original three floors, all with ridiculously high ceilings and spa-cious rooms, have been enhanced with a 4th floor dedicated to special suites with panoramic terraces. The central courtyard, complete with bar, is as vast as an aircraft hangar, while the elegant former pharmacy has been converted into a smokers' lounge. Indoor and outdoor pools, plus a spa with sauna, jacuzzi and Turkish bath complete the luxurious picture.

Hotel Avenida　HOTEL **€**
(☑232 423 432; www.hotelavenida.com.pt; Av Alberto Sampaio 1; s/d €40/50; @⊛) Proudly proclaiming its presence with a vintage neon sign visible from the Rossio, this friendly, modestly elegant hotel has a grand spiral staircase, stately common areas and slightly creaky rooms deco-rated in regal colours.

Hotel Grão Vasco　HOTEL **€€**
(☑232 423 511; www.hotelgraovasco.pt; Rua Gaspar Barreiros; s/d €66/76; P✸@⊛⊛) This handsome, modern granite hotel is set back in leafy grounds above the Ros-sio. Rooms are properly plush, though a little shy of luxurious.

Pousada da Juventude　HOSTEL **€**
(☑232 413 001; viseu@movijovem.pt; Rua Aristides Sousa Mendes; dm €10, d with shared/private bathroom €22/25; ⊛) A 10-minute walk east of the centre, Viseu's boxy and rather basic hostel has friendly, helpful staff but no cooking facilities. You'll find free internet and a decent restaurant across the street.

✗ Eating

Viseu is awash in good food for any budget.

TOP CHOICE O Hilário　PORTUGUESE **€**
(Rua Augusto Hilário 35; mains €3.50-6.80; ⊙lunch & dinner Mon-Sat) Named for the 19th-century fado star who once lived down the street, this highly recommended eatery wins points for its excellent food, cosy at-mosphere, righteous prices and attentive service.

O Cortiço　PORTUGUESE **€€**
(Rua Augusto Hilário 45; mains €9-17.50; ⊙lunch & dinner) This heartily recommended stone-walled eatery specialises in traditional reci-

pes collected from surrounding villages. Generous portions are served in heavy tureens, and the good house wine comes in medieval-style wooden pitchers. Finish your meal with a glass of the local firewater made from olives.

Casa dos Queijos PORTUGUESE €
(Travessa das Escadinhas da Sé 7; mains €6-9; ⊙lunch Mon-Sat) Despite the owner's rather gruff attitude, this stone-walled old place, hidden up narrow stairs, gets top marks for atmosphere and for its carefully prepared grills and *cozidos* (stews). The shop downstairs, stacked high with tempting wines and cheeses, is a neighbourhood hang-out where locals chat all afternoon over glasses of wine.

Restaurante Muralha da Sé PORTUGUESE €€€
(Adro da Sé 24; mains €11-20; ⊙lunch & dinner Tue-Sat, lunch Sun) Go ahead: bust your budget at this unabashedly upper-crust spot under the looming Igreja da Misericórdia. It boasts fine regional cuisine made with ingredients from the nearby Serra da Estrela, plus cathedral-square views from its terrace.

Pastelaria Horta BAKERY €
(Rua Formosa 22; ⊙7am-8pm) This popular bakery serves traditional sweets made of egg yolk and almonds, and offers pleasant outdoor seating on Viseu's main pedestrian thoroughfare.

Mercado municipal MARKET €
(Rua 21 de Agosto; ⊙Mon-Sat) Self-caterers will find fruit, vegetables and other goodies at the market.

⚐ Drinking & Entertainment

A clutch of bars near the cathedral overflows onto the streets and makes for a merry atmosphere on summer nights.

Irish Bar PUB
(Largo do Pintor Gata 8; ⊙9am-2am Mon-Sat, 1pm-2am Sun) The Irish Bar offers Guinness on tap, occasional live Irish music and terrace seating on a charming square near the old town gate.

Minus 5° Ice Lounge BAR
(www.minus5experience.com; Palácio do Gelo Shopping; ⊙2-11pm) Don your winter garb (provided) and step into the cold at this theme bar specialising in vodka drinks and ever-changing decor. Everything's made of ice, from the cups to the tables and chairs, and the temperature's kept constant at a

bone-tingling -5°C. It's in the brand-new Palácio do Gelo shopping centre south of town.

NB Club DANCE CLUB
(www.noitebiba.pt; Rua Conselheiro Afonso de Melo 31; ⊙Thu-Sat) Centrally located one block from the Rossio, popular NB spins a mix of house, pop, hip hop and rock. The owners run a number of other nightspots around town – check the website for details of other venues.

🛍 Shopping

Handicrafts here are cheaper than in more-touristy towns.

Casa da Ribeira HANDICRAFTS
(Largo Nossa Senhora da Conceição; ⊙9am-12.30pm & 2-5.30pm Tue-Sat) In this municipal space north of the river, local artisans work and sell their products, including lace, ceramics and the region's distinctively black earthenware.

ℹ Information

Espaço Internet (Solar dos Condes de Prime, Rua dos Andrades; ⊙10am-8pm Mon-Fri, 10am-1pm & 2-7pm Sat, 2-7pm Sun) Free internet in a centrally located historic mansion.

Espaço Internet Pórtico do Fontelo (Rua Aristides Sousa Mendes; ⊙8.30am-11pm Mon-Sat, 8.30am-9pm Sun) Free internet, newly opened near the youth hostel.

Police station (☑232 480 380; Rua Alves Martins)

Post office (Rua dos Combatentes da Grande Guerra; ⊙9am-7pm Mon-Fri, 9am-12.30pm Sat)

Regional turismo (☑232 420 950; www.turismodocentro.pt; Av Calouste Gulbenkian; ⊙9am-6pm Mon-Fri, 9.30am-1pm & 2.30-6pm Sat & Sun)

São Teotónio Hospital (☑232 420 500; Av Dom Duarte)

ℹ Getting There & Away

BUS Between them, **Rede Expressos** (☑232 422 822) and **Joalto** (☑232 426 093) serve the following destinations from their shared bus station at the western edge of town.

Braga (€12.30, three hours, one daily)
Bragança (€13, 3¼ hours, three daily)
Coimbra (€7.50, 75 minutes, 10 daily)
Lisbon (€14.50, 3½ hours, at least 14 daily)
Porto (€9.50, two hours, five daily)
Trancoso (€6.30, 1½ hours, two daily)

WINES OF THE DÃO REGION

The velvety red wines of the Dão region (within the Rio Mondego and tributary Rio Dão, south and east of Viseu) have been cultivated for over 2000 years, and are today among Portugal's best drops. Vineyards are mostly sheltered in valleys at altitudes of 200m to 900m just west of the Serra da Estrela, thus avoiding the rain of the coast but also the harsh summer heat that comes further inland. This, together with granitic soil, helps the wines retain their natural acidity. Dão wines are often called the burgundies of Portugal because they don't overpower but, rather, are subtle and full of finesse.

Some three-dozen Dão vineyards and producers offer multilingual cellar tours and tastings; most require advance bookings. You can pick up a list in Viseu's *turismo*. Two popular wineries near Viseu are **Casa da Ínsua** (☑232 420 000; www.casadainsua. pt; Penalva do Castelo), 30km east on the IP5 and N329-1, and **Casa de Santar** (☑232 942 937; http://casadesantar.com; Santar), 15km southeast on the N231. Both have fine grounds and lovely architecture, and the former operates a lovely five-star country hotel.

Coordinating them all is the **Comissão Vitivinícola Regional do Dão** (CVRD; ☑232 410 060; www.cvrdao.pt; Av Capitão Homem Ribeiro 10, Viseu), which eventually plans to open its headquarters – Viseu's 16th-century Antigo Paço Episcopal – as a posh Solar do Dão where the public can sample a range of Dão wines.

White Dão wines are also available, though the full-bodied reds are the best (and the strongest). Also try the sparkling white wines of the separate, small Lafões region, northwest of Viseu.

Vila Real (€9.80, 75 minutes, three daily)

CAR Parking is available just north of the Rio Pavia around the town's fairgrounds and at an underground garage adjacent to Igreja do Carmo, east of the Rossio.

Guarda

POP 26,000 / ELEV 1056M

Fria, farta, forte e feia (cold, rich, strong and ugly): such is the popular description of Portugal's highest full-fledged city. Hunkered down on a hilltop, it was founded in 1197 to guard young Portugal against both Moors and Spaniards (hence the name).

Nowadays stripped of its military functions, this granite-grey district capital is a delightful place to spend an afternoon. Highlights include the looming cathedral and enormous square, Praça Luís de Camões (also called Praça Velha); the narrow lanes and town gates of the historic Jewish quarter; a good museum and sweeping views of the plains stretching to Spain.

Old Guarda is perched on a steep hill, a rambling climb from the IP5 or the train station, both roughly 5km northeast of the old centre. From the bus station on Rua Dom Nuno Álvares Pereira, it's 800m northwest to the cathedral square and the heart of the old town.

◉ Sights

Sé　　　　　　　　　　　　　　CATHEDRAL
(Praça Luís de Camões; ◷9am-noon & 2-5pm) Powerful in its sobriety, this Gothic fortress of a cathedral squats heavily by a large square in the city centre. The earliest parts date from 1390 but it took 150 years to finish; it's dotted with Manueline doors and windows and Renaissance ornamentation, while its facade is girded by two handsomely hexagonal bell towers.

The most striking feature in the immense, granite interior of the Sé is a four-storey Renaissance altarpiece attributed to Jean de Rouen (João de Ruão), one of a team of 16th-century French artists who founded an influential school of sculpture at Coimbra. Also impressive are the twisted Manueline columns found at each transept.

Museu da Guarda　　　　　　　　MUSEUM
(http://museudaguarda.imc-ip.pt; Rua Alves Roçadas 30; admission €2, 10am-12.30pm Sun free; ◷10am-12.30pm & 2-5.30pm Tue-Sun) The museum occupies the severe, 17th-century Episcopal Seminary, adjacent to the old bishop's palace. The collection runs from Bronze Age swords to Roman coins, from Renaissance sculpture to 19th- and 20th-century Portuguese painting.

In the adjacent, 18th-century courtyard, the handsome **Paço da Cultura** (☺irregular hours) features temporary art exhibitions.

FREE **Torre de Menagem** CASTLE KEEP (☺10am-4pm) Opened to the public in late 2009, Guarda's castle keep, on a hilltop above the cathedral, is open for daily tours; the best reason to visit is for the amazing views up top, all the way to Spain and the Serra da Estrela. Check in at the small **Guarda Patrimonium museum** just down the hill, which houses a very small collection of archaeological finds from the surrounding area. The tour includes a rather overproduced (and technologically fragile) 3D movie that sends you soaring through virtual renditions of Guarda's main monuments, with a few flapping pigeons and swirling leaves thrown in for good measure.

Old Town

With its 16th- to 18th-century mansions and its overpowering cathedral, Praça Luís de Camões is the town's centrepiece. Plenty of medieval atmosphere survives in the cobblestone lanes and huddled houses north of the cathedral, centred around Rua de São Vicente.

Of the old walls and gates, the stalwart **Torre dos Ferreiros** (Blacksmiths' Tower; Rua Tenente Valadim) is still in good condition. Two other surviving gates are the **Porta d'El Rei**, the steps of which you can still climb for views over town, and the **Porta da Erva**. A walk between these two gates takes you through the heart of Guarda's historic **judiaria** (Jewish quarter; see boxed text, p349). Sharp-eyed visitors will notice crosses and other symbols scratched into a few 16th-century vaulted doorframes – look for examples along Ruas Rui de Pina and Dom Sancho I – which identified the homes of *marranos* (New Christians) during the Inquisition.

Guarda for Children

The **Parque Urbano do Rio Diz**, set in 21 hectares of green space by Guarda's train station, has an astoundingly large, modern playground that can keep kids happily engaged for hours.

★ Festivals & Events

Guarda hosts a jazz festival called **Ciclo de Jazz de Guarda**, with several performances each week from March to May.

THE JEWS OF BELMONTE

When the Moors ruled Portugal, it's estimated that 10% of the country's population was Jewish. Jews remained vital to the young Christian state, serving as government ministers and filling key roles in Henry the Navigator's school devoted to overseas exploration. Even the current Duke of Bragança, hereditary king of Portugal, proudly acknowledges his own Jewish parentage.

When Portugal embraced Spain's Inquisitorial zeal beginning in the 1490s, thousands of Jews from both Portugal and Spain fled to northeast Portugal, including the Beiras and Trás-os-Montes, where the arm of the Inquisitors had not yet reached. Eventually the Inquisitors made their presence felt even here, and Jews once again faced conversion, expulsion or death.

However, in the 1980s it was revealed that in the town of Belmonte, 30km south of Guarda, a group of families had been practising Jewish rites in secret since the Inquisition – more than 500 years. While it's believed that many such communities continued in secrecy well into the Inquisition, most slowly died out. But Belmonte's community managed to survive five centuries by meticulously ensuring marriages were arranged only among other Jewish families. The transmission of Jewish tradition was almost exclusively oral and passed not from father to son but from mother to daughter. Each Friday night families descended into basements to pray and celebrate the Sabbath. Now that the community is out in the open, they have embraced male-dominated Orthodox Judaism, though the women elders have not forgotten the secret prayers that have been doggedly transmitted these past 500 years.

The modest **Museu Judaico de Belmonte** (Rua Portela 4; admission free; ☺9.30am-12.30pm & 2-6pm Tue-Sun) tells the story of the Belmonte families and Judaism generally. Ask here about visits to the town's synagogue.

There are frequent daily bus connections between Belmonte and Guarda.

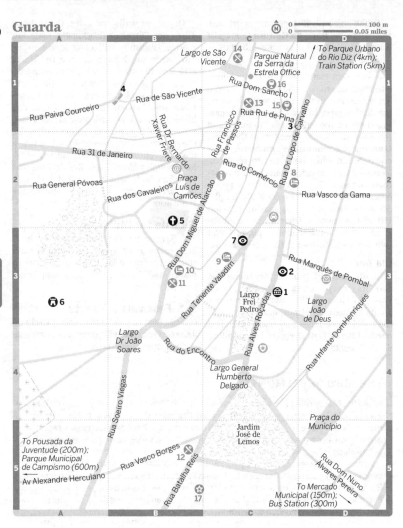

🛏 Sleeping

There's no winter high-price season here, though Guarda is almost as close to the snow as the park's other main towns.

TOP CHOICE **Residencial Santos** HOTEL **€**
(☏271 205 400; www.residencial santos.com; Rua Tenente Valadim 14; s/d/tr/q €30/45/55/65; 🛜) Santos is warmly recommended for its spotless, newly furnished rooms, good prices, generous breakfast and welcoming staff. Its ultramodern interior resembles an Escher drawing, with interconnecting walkways, stairs and glass

walls that incorporate both a handsome 19th-century granite building and the town's medieval walls. For nice views of the cathedral, book ahead for room 307 on the top floor.

Solar de Alarcão INN **€€**
(☏271 214 392; solaralarcao@gmail.com; Rua Dom Miguel de Alarcão 25-27; d €80; 🅿) Easily Guarda's most refined choice, this beautiful 17th-century granite mansion has its own courtyard and loggia, sits within spitting distance of the cathedral, and offers a handful of gorgeous rooms stuffed with antique furniture and drapes.

Guarda

Sights
Guarda Patrimonium.....................(see 6)
1 Museu da Guarda C3
2 Paço da Cultura C3
3 Porta da Erva C1
4 Porta d'El Rei...B1
5 Sé..B2
6 Torre de Menagem A3
7 Torre dos Ferreiros C3

Sleeping
8 Residência Filipe.................................C2
9 Residencial Santos C3
10 Solar de Alarcão B3

Eating
11 O Bule B3
12 O Caçador B5
13 Restaurante A Floresta C1
14 Restaurante Belo Horizonte C1

Drinking
15 Aqui Jazz C1
16 Bar Noctis C1

Entertainment
17 Teatro Municipal da Guarda B5

Pousada da Juventude   HOSTEL €
(☎271 239 014; guarda@movijovem.pt; Av Alex
andre Herculano; dm €10, d with shared/private
bathroom €22/25; [P][☎]) The modern, rather
clinical youth hostel is a short walk to the
centre. The dorms have only four beds each,
some upper rooms enjoy nice vistas and
there's 24-hour reception; on the downside,
there's no guest kitchen.

Parque Municipal de Campismo
                               CAMPGROUND €
(☎271 221 200; Rua do Estádio Municipal; sites
per adult/child/tent/car €2/1.50/2/2.50) Very
close to the town centre and next to a
leafy park, this municipal site has free
hot showers and plenty of shade.

Residência Filipe   GUEST HOUSE €
(☎271 223 658; Rua Vasco da Gama 9; s/d/tr
€20/35/45;[P]) This funny mix of old
and new offers mostly bright, attractive
rooms, brisk service and garage parking
across the street (€2.50).

🍴 Eating
Rua Francisco de Passos is the historic
centre's best street for restaurant-browsing.

Restaurante A Floresta   PORTUGUESE €€
(Rua Francisco de Passos 40; mains €7.50-12.50;
☺lunch & dinner) Just north of the cathedral,
this snug and friendly (if well-touristed)
place serves up hearty regional cuisine, including the marvellous *chouriçada*, a heap-
ing portion of grilled sausages from the
nearby Serra da Estrela. *Meia-doses* (half-
portions) of most menu items are available
for €5 to €8.50.

O Caçador   PORTUGUESE €€
(Rua Batalha Reis 121; mains €7.50-12.50; ☺lunch
& dinner Tue-Sun) Drawing in dinner guests
with a happy red neon sign and a glass-
walled front room vaguely reminiscent of
Parisian brasseries, O Caçador specialises
in seafood brought straight from the coast.

Restaurante Belo Horizonte PORTUGUESE €€
(Largo de São Vicente 1; mains €7-14; ☺lunch &
dinner Tue-Sat, lunch Sun) Granite-fronted Belo
Horizonte packs them in for lunch and dinner, with regional specialities such as *chouriçada* and *cabrito grelhado* (grilled kid).

O Bule   BAKERY, CAFE €
(Rua Dom Miguel de Alarcão; ☺8am-8pm
Mon-Fri, 9am-8pm Sat, 10am-8pm Sun) This
lovely, traditional cafe near the cathedral
specialises in local pastries, including the
delicious *queijadas de canela,* cinnamon-
tinged tarts made with sheep's milk.

Self-caterers can head to the **mercado municipal** near the bus station.

🍷 Drinking
Guarda's historic centre has a surprising
number of nightspots for its size – all small
and unlikely-looking from the outside, but
welcoming within.

Aqui Jazz   BAR
(Rua Rui de Pina 29; ☺10.30pm-3am) Aqui Jazz
attracts arty types with live jazz.

Bar Noctis   BAR
(Rua Dom Sancho I 9; ☺10.30pm-3am) Just
around the corner from Aqui Jazz is this
other popular late-night hang-out.

☆ Entertainment
Teatro Municipal da Guarda   ARTS CENTRE
(www.tmg.com.pt; Rua Batalha Reis 12) Guarda's
shiny new theatre complex, a boxy modern
building of grayish-green glass just south
of the historic centre, regularly hosts high-
quality theatre, dance and music, including
frequent international acts.

ℹ Information

CyberCentro Guarda (Rua General Povoas; per hr €1.50; ☺9am-8pm Mon-Fri) The historic centre's most conveniently located internet, directly opposite the *turismo*.

Municipal turismo (☎271 205 530; posto deturismo@mun-guarda.pt; Praça Luís de Camões; ☺10am-1pm & 2.30-6.30pm)

Parque Natural da Serra da Estrela office (☎271 225 454; pnse@icnb.pt; Rua Dom Sancho I 3; ☺9am-12.30pm & 2-5.30pm Mon-Fri) Modestly helpful, with a couple of English-language books about the park for sale.

Police station (☎271 222 022; Rua Alves Roçadas 15)

Ponto Já (Av Alexandre Herculano; ☺9am-8pm Mon-Fri) Free internet adjacent to the youth hostel.

Post office (Largo João de Deus; ☺8.30am-6pm Mon-Fri, 9am-12.30pm Sat)

ℹ Getting There & Away

BUS **Rede Expressos** (☎271 212 720) runs services at least three times daily via Covilhã (€4.40, 45 minutes) to Castelo Branco (€9.20, 1¾ hours) and Lisbon (€14.50, 5½ hours), and several times daily to Viseu (€7.80, 1¼ hours), Porto (€11.80, three hours) and Coimbra (€11.80, three hours).

Marques (☎238 312 858) goes daily via Gouveia (€4.15, 1½ hours) to Seia (€4.55, two hours). Rede Expressos also goes to Seia (€9.70, 70 minutes) once daily Sunday to Friday.

TRAIN Guarda's spiffy modern train station is served by at least two fast IC trains daily from Lisbon (€17.50, 4¼ hours) and Coimbra (€10.50, two hours). Trains to Porto (€15.50 to €21, four to five hours) all involve a change at Pampilhosa.

ℹ Getting Around

BUS Buses (€0.80) between the train station and the centre are infrequent; if one isn't waiting (look to the right as you exit the train station), you're probably better off taking a **taxi** (€4 to €5). There's a rank to the left as you exit the train station; and another just outside the historic centre on Rua Alves Roçadas.

CAR Parking, both paid and unpaid, is competitive in the centre. Try your luck around Largo Dr João Soares.

Trancoso

POP 2300 / ELEV 870M

A warren of cobbled lanes squeezed within Dom Dinis' 13th-century walls make peaceful, hilltop Trancoso a delightful retreat from the modern world. The town also served as a refuge for Spanish Jews fleeing the Inquisition – until Portugal, too, adopted Spain's persecutory zeal. As elsewhere along the border, you can generally spot Jewish houses by looking for a pair of doors: a smaller one for the private household and a larger one for a shop or warehouse.

Although it's predominantly a medieval creation, the town's castle also features a rare, intact Moorish tower, while just outside the walls are what are believed to be Visigothic tombs.

Dinis underscored the importance of this border fortress by marrying the saintly Dona Isabel of Aragon here in 1282. But the town's favourite son is Bandarra, a lowly 16th-century shoemaker and fortune-teller who put official noses out of joint by foretelling the end of the Portuguese monarchy.

Sure enough, shortly after Bandarra's death, the young Dom Sebastião died, heirless, in the disastrous Battle of Alcácer-Quibir in 1558. Soon afterwards, Portugal fell under Spanish rule.

⊙ Sights

The **Portas d'El Rei** (King's Gate), surmounted by the town's ancient coat of arms, has always been its principal entrance, and its guillotine-like door long sealed out unwelcome visitors. The **town walls** run intact for over 1km around the medieval core, which is centred on the main square, Largo Padre Francisco Ferreira (also called Largo do Pelourinho, or Largo Dom Dinis). The square, in turn, is anchored by an octagonal **pelourinho** (stone pillory) dating from 1510. Another important gate, **Portas do Prado**, serves as the western entrance to the walled town.

Like many northern towns, Trancoso acquired a sizeable Jewish community following the expulsion of Jews from Spain at the end of the 15th century. The **old judiaria** (Jewish quarter) covered roughly the southeast third of the walled town. Among dignified reminders of that time is a former rabbinical residence called the **Casa do Gato Preto** (House of the Black Cat; Largo Luís Albuquerque), decorated with the gates of Jerusalem and other Jewish images. It's now private property.

On a hill in the northeast corner of town is the now-tranquil, 10th- to 13th-century **castelo** (admission free; ☺10am-1pm & 2-6pm Tue-Sun), with its crenellated towers and the distinctively slanted walls of the squat, Moorish **Torre de Menagem**.

Across the road from the Portas do Prado, beside the courthouse, is an untended rock outcrop carved with eerie, body-shaped cavities, thought to be **Visigothic tombs** dating back to the 7th or 8th century.

About 150m northward is Trancoso's prettiest church, the 13th-century **Capela de Santa Luzia**, with heavy Romanesque door arches and unadorned dry-stone construction. Trancoso abounds with other churches heavy with baroque make-up, most prominently the **Igreja de São Pedro**, behind the *pelourinho* on Largo Padre Francisco Ferreira.

🛌 Sleeping

Ask at the *turismo* about the possibility of *quartos* for rent.

Hotel Turismo de Trancoso   HOTEL **€€**
(☎271 829 200; www.hotel-trancoso.com; Rua Professora Irene Avillez; s/d/ste €80/95/130; 🅿❄@🛜🏊) Forming an anachronistic counterpoint to the walled city two blocks away, this brand-new, chalk-white mono-lith offers stylish modern rooms, most with verandahs and rural vistas around a semi-circular courtyard. Special deals are often available midweek or online.

Residencial Dom Dinis   HOTEL **€**
(☎271 811 525; www.domdinis.net; Av da República 10; s/d/tr €28/33/42; 🅿) In a drab apartment block behind the post office, the Dom Dinis has spotless, if spiritless, newly remodelled rooms with wooden floors, plus a downstairs bar and restaurant.

Residencial Vale a Pena   GUEST HOUSE **€**
(☎271 811 219; Largo Senhora da Calçada; s/d €20/40) This simple, slightly grandmotherly place near the Portas de São João offers clean, modern rooms with tile floors and newish furnishings.

🍴 Eating & Drinking

Restaurante Área Benta   CONTEMPORARY PORTUGUESE **€€**
(Rua dos Cavaleiros 30A; mains €9.50-15; ⏲lunch & dinner, closed Sun dinner & Mon Oct-Apr) For regional cuisine presented with contemporary flair, try this swish, minimalist restaurant

---

DETOUR – AROUND THE PLANALTO

While Trancoso and Almeida are the quintessential Planalto fortress-villages, three other towns are well worth a gander, though only if you have your own wheels – bus connections would be maddening in this sparsely populated region. With a car, you could see all three in a single, long day.

Located 30km northwest of Trancoso, **Sernancelhe** has a wonderfully preserved centre fashioned out of warm, beige-coloured stone. Sights include a 13th-century church that boasts Portugal's only free-standing Romanesque sculpture; an old Jewish quarter with crosses to mark the homes of the converted; several grand 17th- and 18th-century town houses, one of which is believed to be the birthplace of the Marquês de Pombal; and hills that bloom with what are considered to be Portugal's best chestnuts.

Heading northeast another 16km, you arrive at little **Penedono**, with its small but splendid **Castelo Roqueiro** (Roqueiro Castle; free admission; ⏲9am-6pm). This irregular hexagon, with its picturesque crenellation, has fine views over the Planalto. It probably dates back to the 13th century. It's a remarkable sight.

Perhaps most impressive of all is **Marialva**, 25km southeast of Penedono. It's dominated by a forbidding, 12th-century **castelo** (admission €1.50; ⏲10am-1.30pm & 3-6.30pm May-Sep, 9am-12.30pm & 2-5.30pm Oct-Apr) that guards over the rugged valley of the Rio Côa. Below its walls lies a haunting little village populated almost exclusively by black-clad widows knitting in the timeless shade.

If you want to make an overnight trip of it, consider staying at Sernancelhe's 17th-century **Casa da Comenda de Malta** (☎254 559 189; d from €65; ❄), near the church in the old town, with well-equipped rooms, walled gardens and a pool. In Penedono, **Residencial Flora** (☎254 504 411; flora.residencial@gmail.com; s/d €20/35), a short walk downhill from the *castelo*, offers plain but modern rooms with bathroom. The downstairs restaurant serves hearty Portuguese fare (mains €8 to €10). Marialva has the cushiest digs of all, at the luxurious **Casas do Côro** (www.casasdocoro.com.pt).

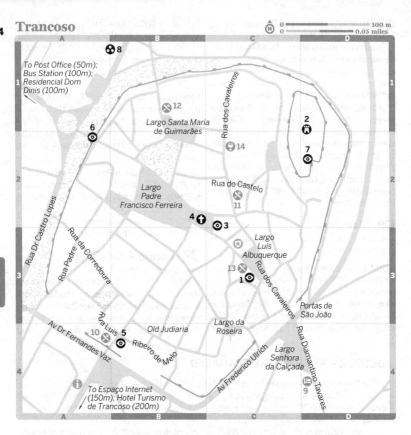

Trancoso

0 ——— 100 m
0 ——— 0.05 miles

To Post Office (50m);
Bus Station (100m);
Residencial Dom
Dinis (100m)

Largo Santa Maria
de Guimarães

Rua dos Cavaleiros

Largo
Padre
Francisco Ferreira

Rua do Castelo

Largo
Luís
Albuquerque

Rua dos Cavaleiros

Rua Dr Castro Lopes

Rua Padre da Corredoura

Rua Luís
Ribeiro de Melo

Av Dr Fernandes Vaz

Old Judiaria

Largo da
Roseira

Portas de
São João

Largo
Senhora
da Calçada

Rua Diamantino Tavares

Av Frederico Ulrich

To Espaço Internet
(150m); Hotel Turismo
de Trancoso (200m)

---

in an ancient stone town house. Specialities include *feijoada à transmontana* (a stew of red beans, pork and cabbage) and *cabrito assado com castanhas* (roast kid with chestnuts). Daily specials (from €8) are a bargain, and the wine list is excellent.

Restaurante O Museu   PORTUGUESE **€€**
(Largo Santa Maria de Guimarães; dishes €6.50-13; ⊙lunch & dinner Mon-Sat, lunch Sun) Stone-walled O Museu goes for quaint appeal, with its rustically elegant upstairs dining room and wisteria-draped front terrace. Along with Portuguese standards, it serves fondue and regional specialities such as *porco grelhado com murcela* (grilled pork with blood sausage).

Casa da Prisca   SPECIALITY GROCERY **€**
(Rua da Corredoura 1; ⊙9am-7pm) This shop specialising in regional cheeses and smoked meats just inside the Portas d'El Rei is a fun place to browse. Try the *sardinhas doces*

(sweet sardines), a local fish-shaped confection made with eggs, almonds, cinnamon and chocolate.

Restaurante São Marcos   PORTUGUESE **€€**
(Largo Luis Albuquerque; mains €7-12; ⊙lunch & dinner Mon-Sat, lunch Sun) This down-to-earth place next door to Casa do Gato Preto draws a local clientele with its tasty Portuguese fare.

Bar Água Benta   BAR
(Rua dos Cavaleiros 36A; ⊙noon-3pm & 8.30pm-3am Mon-Thu, to 4am Fri & Sat) Tucked away in the backstreets is this little cafe-bar, with a cheerful and youthful atmosphere, international beers, and occasional live music and karaoke.

ℹ Information
Espaço Internet (⊙9am-12.30pm & 1.30-6pm Mon-Fri) Free internet in Trancoso's Centro Cultural, two blocks south of the *turismo*.

Trancoso

Police station (☎271 811 212; Largo Luis Albuquerque)

Post office (Av da República; ◷9am-12.30pm & 2-6pm Mon-Fri)

Turismo (☎271 811 147; www.cm-trancoso.pt/turismo; ◷9.30am-12.30pm & 2-5.30pm)

❶ Getting There & Away

BUS From Trancoso's brand new **bus station** (Av Calouste Gulbenkian), just northwest of the walled town, **Rede Expressos** (www.rede-expressos.pt) has service to Viseu (€6.30, 70 minutes, twice daily, extra bus on Sunday), with connections via Celorico da Beira to Guarda (€7.70, 1¼ hours, daily except Sunday).

CAR There is plentiful free parking just outside the town gates.

TRAIN The closest train station is at Celorico da Beira, 15km to the south.

Almeida

POP 1500 / ELEV 760M

After Portugal regained independence from Spain in the 1640s, the country's border regions were on constant high alert. Tiny Almeida, along with Elvas and Valença do Minho, became a principal defence against Spanish incursions. Almeida's vast, star-shaped fortress – completed in 1641 on the site of its medieval predecessor, 15km from Spain – is the least famous but the most handsome of the three.

When its military functions were largely suspended in 1927, Almeida settled into weedy obscurity. Nowadays, the fortified old village – designated as a national monument and recently scrubbed up for tourism – is a place of great charm, where you'll find flowery green spaces interspersed with old stone houses. The town may have the disquieting calm of a museum, but it also has enough history and muscular grandeur to set the imagination humming.

⊙ Sights

The **fortress** is on the northern side of 'new' Almeida. Most visitors arrive via the handsome **Portas de São Francisco**, two long tunnel-gates separated by an enormous dry moat.

The long arcaded building just inside the Portas de São Francisco is the 18th-century **Quartel das Estradas** (Infantry Barracks), which still serves as military housing.

In a bastion 300m northeast of the *turismo* is the **Museu Histórico Militar de Almeida** (admission €2; ◷10.15am-12.15pm & 2.15-5.15pm Tue-Sun), built into the *casamatas* (casemates or bunkers), a labyrinth of 20 underground rooms used for storage, barracks and shelter for troops in times of siege. In the 18th century these *casamatas* also served as a prison. Piles of cannonballs fill a central courtyard of the museum, with British and Portuguese cannons strewn about nearby.

The fort's **castle** was blown to smithereens during a French siege in 1810, when Britain's and Portugal's own ammunition supplies exploded. You can still see the foundations, 300m northwest of the *turismo,* from an ugly catwalk. Below the ruins is the former Royal Riding Academy.

🛏 Sleeping & Eating

Casa de Pedra　　　　　　　　B&B €€€

(☎914 843 760; www.casadepedra.com.pt; Praça da Liberdade 9; house for up to 6 people €130-150; ❄🅟) On the same pretty square as Almeida's town hall, courthouse and post office, this comfortable apartment occupies a restored 17th-century stone house smack in the historic centre. Full of natural light and smartly done up with modern furnishings, it has a fully equipped kitchen, two rooms with double beds upstairs and a sofa bed in the living area on the main floor. Breakfast is included in the price.

Hotel Parador de Almeida INN €€€

(☑271 574 283; www.hotelparadordealmeida. com; d midweek/weekend €85/110; P❄@☎) Ugly from the outside, if entirely respectable on the inside, the Parador de Almeida sits on the site of former cavalry quarters near the north bastion. Rooms here are large and comfortable, all with giant windows and/or balconies. The modern *pousada* also offers some creative takes on regional cuisine in the dining room (mains €15 to €18.50).

Pensão-Restaurante
A Muralha HOTEL, RESTAURANT €

(☑271 574 357; www.amuralha.pt; Bairro de São Pedro; s/d €25/40; P❄) This functional, modern place sits 250m outside the Portas de São Francisco on the Vilar Formoso road. It has quiet, personality-free rooms and a large restaurant serving straightforward, belly-filling platters (mains €6.50 to €9.50).

ℹ Information

The **turismo** (☑271 570 020; turismo.almeida@ cm-almeida.pt; ☺9am-12.30pm & 2-5.30pm, from 10am Sat & Sun) is impressively located in an old guard-chamber within the Portas de São Francisco. Here you can get a map of the fortress and town.

ℹ Getting There & Around

BUS Nondrivers will almost certainly have to stay the night due to limited bus connections.

Rede Expressos (www.rede-expressos.pt) has weekday-only service to Celorico da Beira, with connections to Viseu (€10, three hours), Coimbra (€12.30, five hours) and Lisbon (€15.80, 7½ hours). On Sunday afternoons there's a faster direct service to Lisbon (€15.80, 5½ hours).

Rodoviária da Beira Interior (☑271 212 720; www.rbi.pt) has direct morning service at 8.30am from Almeida to Guarda (€4.95, one hour), returning to Almeida at 2pm and 4.30pm.

CAR Drivers are better off parking outside the gates and negotiating the inner town on foot.

Porto & the Douro

Best Places to Stay

» Guest House Douro (p369)
» Yeatman (p372)
» Hotel Infante de Sangres (p371)
» Aquapura (p389)
» Casa Cimeira (p396)

Best Places to Eat

» A Grade (p373)
» Taberna São Pedro (p374)
» Kyodai (p373)
» Adega Gavina (p384)
» Restaurante Ponte Romana (p396)

Why Go?

The face of the Rio Douro always changes. One day it's deeply grooved, folding and rippling in swells. The next it's dimpled glass with just a sheen of wind providing definition but not obscuring the reflection of the granite bluffs, fortresslike wine caves, medieval stone houses and steep, terraced mountain vineyards that seem to have been engineered by some superhuman force.

The river is dynamic precisely because of the sheer diversity of the province it has defined. Romantic Porto, Portugal's second-largest city, is at its mouth; the world's oldest demarcated vineyards are close to the source; and scores of friendly villages and towns in between have always relied on it for water, food and commerce. Its legacies are the intricately carved cathedrals, baroque churches, palatial *quintas*, beaux-arts boulevards and 18th-century wine cellars that are all here, ripe for the tasting.

Note that a few towns in this chapter are not actually in the Douro region, but lie along the Rio Douro.

When to Go

Porto

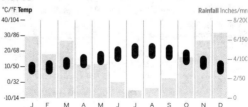

June 24	July	August–September
Festa de São João, Porto's biggest party: music, fireworks and plastic mallets	For 18 years Vila Do Conde has hosted Curtas, an edgy short-film fest	Lamego's Festa de Nossa Senhora dos Remédios runs for weeks

Highlights

1 Wine-taste your way around the picturesque vineyards of the **Alto Douro** (p395)

2 Lose yourself amid the medieval alleys and riverfront promenades of Porto's cinematic district, **Ribeira** (p359)

3 Sample a tawny at a port-wine lodge in **Vila Nova de Gaia** (p366)

4 Relax beside the Rio Tâmega and its medieval bridge in the charming town of **Amarante** (p385)

5 Come face to face with Palaeolithic artwork at **Parque Arqueológico do Vale do Côa** (p397)

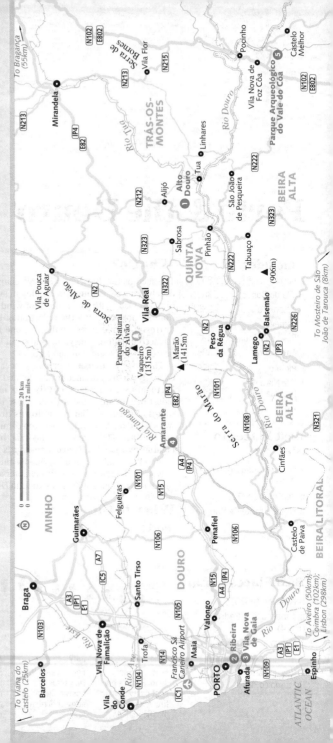

Porto

POP 263,000

From across the Rio Douro at sunset, romantic Porto, the country's second-largest city, looks like a pop-up town. A colourful tumbledown dream with medieval relics, soaring bell towers, extravagant baroque churches and stately beaux-arts buildings piled on top of one another, illuminated by streaming shafts of sun. If you squint you might be able to make out the open windows, the narrow lanes and staircases zigzagging to nowhere.

Porto's historic centre is the Ribeira district, a Unesco World Heritage Site where *tripeiros* (Porto residents) mingle before old storefronts, on village-style plazas and in the old houses of commerce where Roman ruins lurk beneath the foundations. On the downside, here and in other parts of the city centre stand many dilapidated early-20th-century town houses, left to crumble as the young and moneyed flee to the sprawling suburbs by the sea.

Yet despite signs of decay, in the last two decades Porto has undergone a remarkable renaissance – expressed in the hum of its efficient metro system and the gleam of Álvaro Siza Vieira's Museu de Arte Contemporânea and Rem Koolhaas' Casa da Música.

Culturally, Porto is more relevant than much larger global cities. The birthplace of port, it's a long-running mecca for wine aficionados. Riverside wine caves jockey for attention in nearby Vila Nova de Gaia, with scores of cellars open for tastings. With tasty new kitchens springing up regularly, its palate is slowly growing more cosmopolitan. And thanks to a number of superb venues, Porto residents dance to many of the world's top rock, jazz and electronic artists. On warm summer nights many a plaza can feel like one enormous block party.

Of course, you'll be forgiven if what you remember most are the quiet moments: the slosh of the Douro against the docks; the snap of laundry lines drying in river winds; the shuffle of a widow's feet against cobblestone; the sound of wineglasses clinking under a full moon; the sight of young lovers discreetly tangled under a landmark bridge, on the rim of a park fountain, in the crumbling notch of a graffiti-bombed wall...

History

Porto put the 'Portu' in 'Portugal'. The name dates from Roman times, when Lusitanian settlements straddled both sides of the Rio Douro. The area was briefly in Moorish hands but was reconquered by AD 1000 and reorganised as the county of Portucale, with Porto as its capital. British-born Henri of Burgundy was granted the land in 1095, and it was from here that Henri's son and Portuguese hero Afonso Henriques launched the Reconquista (Christian reconquest), ultimately winning Portugal its status as an independent kingdom.

In 1387 Dom João I married Philippa of Lancaster in Porto, and their most famous son, Henry the Navigator, was born here. While Henry's explorers groped around Africa for a sea route to India, British wine merchants – forbidden to trade with the French – set up shop, and their presence continues to this day, evidenced in port-wine labels such as Taylor's and Graham's.

Over the following centuries Porto acquired a well-earned reputation for rebelliousness. In 1628 a mob of angry women attacked the minister responsible for a tax on linen. A 'tipplers riot' against the Marquês de Pombal's regulation of the portwine trade was savagely put down in 1757. And in 1808, as Napoleon's troops occupied the city, Porto citizens arrested the French governor and set up their own short-lived junta. After the British helped drive out the French, Porto radicals were at it again, leading calls for a new liberal constitution, which they got in 1822. Demonstrations in support of liberals continued to erupt in Porto throughout the 19th century.

Meanwhile, wine profits helped fund the city's industrialisation, which began in earnest in the late 19th century, when elites in the rest of Portugal tended to see trade and manufacturing as vulgar. Today the city remains the economic capital of northern Portugal and is surpassed only by muchlarger Lisbon in terms of economic and social clout.

◎ Sights

RIBEIRA

The Ribeira district – Porto's riverfront nucleus – is a remarkable window into Porto's history. Along the riverside promenade, *barcos rabelos* (the traditional boats used to ferry port wine down the Douro) bob beneath the shadow of the photogenic Ponte de Dom Luís I. From here you have a fine perspective onto port-wine lodges across the river in Vila Nova de Gaia. Despite flocks of tourists, the neighbourhood remains easygoing and surprisingly ungentrified.

Sé
CATHEDRAL

(Cloister per adult/student €3/€2; ☺cathedral 9am-12.30pm & 2.30-7pm daily, to 6pm Nov-Mar) From Praça da Ribeira rises a web of medieval alleys and stairways that eventually reach this hulking, hilltop fortress overlooking the river and city below. Founded in the 12th century, this cathedral was largely rebuilt a century later and then extensively altered in the 18th century. However, you can still make out the church's Romanesque contours. Inside, you'll see soaring stone arches, a 14th-century Gothic cloister with thick timbers in the ceiling, and carved reliefs wrapped in gold leaf.

Igreja de São Francisco
CHURCH

(Praça Infante Dom Henrique; adult/student €3.50/2.50; ☺9am-7pm Oct-Mar, to 8pm Apr-Sep) Sitting on the Praça Infante Dom Henrique, it looks from the outside to be an austerely Gothic church, but inside hides one of Portugal's most dazzling displays of baroque finery. Originally built between 1383 and 1410, a 1425 remodel brought the rose window and reticulated domes. Subsequent work in the 17th and 18th centuries smothered the eight altars in 100kg of gold leaf.

Palácio da Bolsa
HISTORICAL BUILDING

(Stock Exchange; Rua Ferreira Borges; tours adult/student/senior €6/3/3; ☺9am-7pm May-Sep, 9am-1pm & 2-6pm Oct-Apr) This splendid neoclassical monument (built from 1842 to 1910) honours Porto's past and present money merchants. Just past the entrance hall is the glass-domed **Pátio das Nações** (Hall of Nations), where the exchange once operated. But this pales in comparison with rooms deeper inside, and to visit them you must join one of the guided tours given in Portuguese, English and French, which set off every half-hour and last for about 30 minutes. The highlight is a stupendous ballroom called the **Salão Árabe** (Arabian Hall), with stucco walls that have been teased into complex Moorish designs, then gilded with some 18kg of gold. There's also a restaurant and wine bar (the appropriately named 'O Comercial', p373).

Casa do Infante
HISTORICAL BUILDING, MUSEUM

(www.cm-porto.pt; Rua Alfândega 10; adult/student/senior €3/2/2, Sat & Sun free; ☺10am-noon & 2-5pm Tue-Sat, 2-5pm Sun) Just back from the river is the handsomely renovated medieval town house where according to legend Henry the Navigator was born in 1394. The building later served as Porto's first customs house. Today it houses three floors of exhibits on the complex activities of the customs house throughout the centuries. In 2002 the complex was excavated, revealing Roman foundations as well as some remarkable mosaics – all of which are now on display.

FREE Instituto dos Vinhos do Douro e do Porto
NOTABLE BUILDING

(www.ivdp.pt; Rua Ferreira Borges; ☺11am-7pm Mon-Fri) When area vintners apply for the certification that ultimately christens their casks with the term 'Port' they bring vials to the labs set in this attractive relic just uphill from the river. Those labs are off-limits to visitors, but you're welcome to explore the lobby exhibits, and the attached wine shop offers free tastings.

Igreja da Misericórdia
CHURCH

(Rua das Flores 15; adult/student €1.50/free; ☺9.30am-12.30pm & 2-5.30pm Tue-Fri, 9am-noon Sat & Sun) North of the square on the distinctly Parisian Rua das Flores, you'll find the rococo facade of this 16th-century church designed by the Italian baroque architect Nicolau Nasoni. The church's original nucleus is now a museum boasting a superb Renaissance painting known as *Fons Vitae* (Fountain of Life). The painting depicts Dom Manuel I and his family around a fountain of blood from the crucified Christ.

Praça da Ribeira
PLAZA

Back down by the river, narrow streets open out onto a plaza framed by austerely grand, tiled town houses overlooking a picturesque stretch of the Rio Douro. From here you have fine views of the port-wine lodges across the river as well as the monumental, double-decker Ponte de Dom Luís I.

PORTO CARD

If you plan to do a lot of sightseeing, the **Porto Card** (1-/2-/3-day card €7.50/11.50/15.50) may save you money. It holders free or discounted admission to city museums, free travel on public transport, and discounts on cruises, tours and cultural events, as well as at some restaurants and shops. The card is sold at *turismos* (tourist offices) throughout Porto.

Ponte de Dom Luís I
LANDMARK

Completed in 1886 by a student of Gustave Eiffel, the bridge's top deck is now reserved for pedestrians as well as one of the city's metro lines; the lower deck bears regular traffic, with narrow pedestrian walkways lining the road. Its construction was significant, as the area's foot traffic once travelled across a bridge made from old port boats lashed together. To make matters worse, the river was wild back then, with no upstream dams. When Napoleon invaded in 1809, scores were crushed and drowned in the rushing river as a panicked stampede proved too much for the makeshift bridge.

Palacio das Artes
MUSEUM

(www.fjuventude.pt; Largo de S Domingos 19; ⊙10am-8pm Tue-Sat, 3-7pm Mon) Rotating exhibitions of mixed media, sculpture, photography and video art are curated by the cultural ministry and are usually worth a peek.

Igreja de Santa Clara
CHURCH

(Largo 1 de Dezembro; ⊙9.30-11.30am & 3-6pm Mon-Fri) East of the Sé, this humbler (but not too humble) church was part of another Franciscan convent. Gothic in shape, with a fine Renaissance portal, its interior is dense with elaborately gilded woodwork.

ALIADOS, BATALHA & BOLHÃO

Rua Santa Catarina
STREET

Absurdly stylish and romantic with trim boutiques, striped stone sidewalks and animated crowds. At its southern end, it opens out onto the lovely, eclectic **Praça da Batalha**, framed by Nasoni's gracefully baroque **Igreja de Santo Ildefonso** (⊙9am-noon & 3-6.30pm Mon-Sat, 9am-1pm Sun) with its twin bell towers, and the lavishly romantic **Teatro Nacional São João** (p378), built in the style of Paris' Opéra-Garnier.

Avenida dos Aliados
STREET

Lined with bulging, beaux-arts facades and capped by the stately **câmara municipal** (municipal council), this *avenida* recalls grand Parisian imitators like Buenos Aires and Budapest. Its central plaza was restored a few years back and often hosts pop-up-book, comic and art festivals and exhibitions.

Torre dos Clérigos
LANDMARK

(Rua dos Clérigos; admission €2; ⊙9.30am-1pm & 2.30-7pm Apr-Oct, 10am-noon & 2-5pm Nov-Mar)

DON'T MISS

THE AZULEJO-HUNTER'S GUIDE TO PORTO

Porto has some stunning tilework, with a wide range of stories unfolding on the city's old walls. One of the largest and most exquisite displays of *azulejos* (hand-painted tiles) covers the **Igreja do Carmo** (Praça Gomes Teixeira; ⊙8am-noon & 2-5pm Mon-Fri, 8am-noon Sat). Silvestre Silvestri's magnificent 1912 panel illustrates the legend of the founding of the Carmelite order.

Along pedestrianised Rua Santa Catarina, the **Capela das Almas** (Rua Santa Catarina 428; ⊙irregular) is a close second to Igreja do Carmo. Magnificent panels here depict scenes from the lives of various saints, including the death of St Francis and the martyrdom of St Catherine. Interestingly, Eduardo Leite painted the tiles in a classic 18th-century style, though they actually date back only to 1929.

Hidden inside the Sé (p360), on the upper storey of the cloister (reached via a Nasoni-designed stairway), is Vital Rifarto's 18th-century masterpiece of *azulejos* that lavishly illustrate scenes from the *Song of Songs*.

Just off Av dos Aliados lies São Bento train station. Completed in 1903, it seems to have been imported straight from 19th-century Paris, thanks to its mansard roof and imposing stone facade. But the dramatic *azulejos* in the front hall are the real attraction. Designed by Jorge Colaço in 1930, some 20,000 tiles depict historic battle scenes (including Henry the Navigator's conquest of Ceuta), as well as a history of transport.

Bringing the art of the *azulejo* up to date, the modernist, polychromatic *Ribeira Negra* by Júlio Resende celebrates life in the Ribeira district in a huge, tiled mural. Created in 1987, it's located at the mouth of the tunnel to the lower deck of the Ponte de Dom Luís I.

For more on the Portuguese art of tilework, see p509.

Central Porto

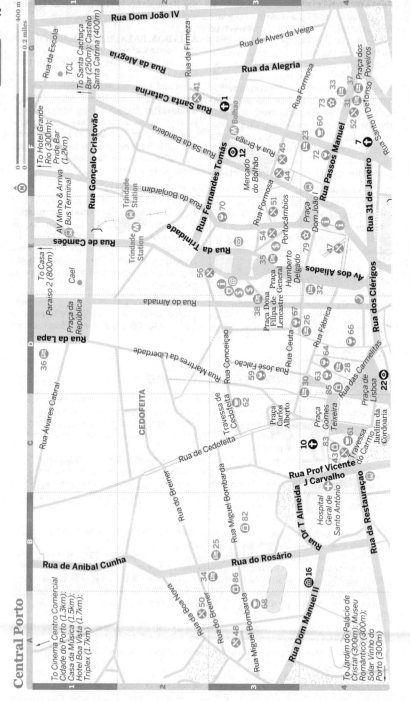

To Cinema Centro Comercial
Cidade do Porto (1.3km);
Casa da Música (1.5km);
Hotel Boa Vista (1.7km);
Triplex (1.7km)

Rua de Anibal Cunha

CEDOFEITA

Rua de Cedofeita

Rua do Breiner

Rua do Rosário

Rua Miguel Bombarda

Rua Dom Manuel II

To Jardim do Palácio de
Cristal (300m); Museu
Romântico (300m);
Solar Vinho do
Porto (300m)

Rua Álvares Cabral

Rua da Lapa

Praça da
República

To Casa
Paraiso 2 (800m)

Cael

Rua de Camões

AV Minho & Arriva
Bus Terminal

Trindade Station

Trindade
Station

To Hotel Grande
Rio (300m);
Pride Bar
(1.2km)

Rua Gonçalo Cristóvão

Rua Fernandes Tomás

Rua da Trindade

Rua do Bonjardim

Rua Sá da Bandeira

Rua A Braga

Mercado
do Bolhão

Rua Formosa

Rua Formosa

Rua da Alegria

Rua da Alegria

Rua Santa Catarina

Rua Dom João IV

Rua da Firmeza

Rua de Alves da Veiga

To Santa Cachaça
Bar (250m); Castelo
Santa Catrina (400m)

Rua da Escola

TCL

Praça dos
Poveiros

Rua Passos Manuel

Rua 31 de Janeiro

Rua dos Clérigos

Rua das Carmelitas

Rua da Restauração

Rua Prof Vicente
J Carvalho

Rua Dr T Almeida

Hospital
Geral de
Santo António

Praça
Gomes
Teixeira

Praça
Carlos
Alberto

Travessa de
Cedofeita

Rua Martires da Liberdade

Rua Conceição

Rua José Falcão

Rua Ceuta

Rua Fábrica

Praça Dona
Filipa de
Lencastre

Praça General
Humberto
Delgado

AV dos Aliados

Praça
Dom João I

Portocâmbios

Jardim da
Cordoaria

Praça
de Lisboa

Travessa
do Carmo

Rua de Almada

Rua Miguel Bombarda

Rua do Breiner

Rua da Boa Nova

Rua do Breiner

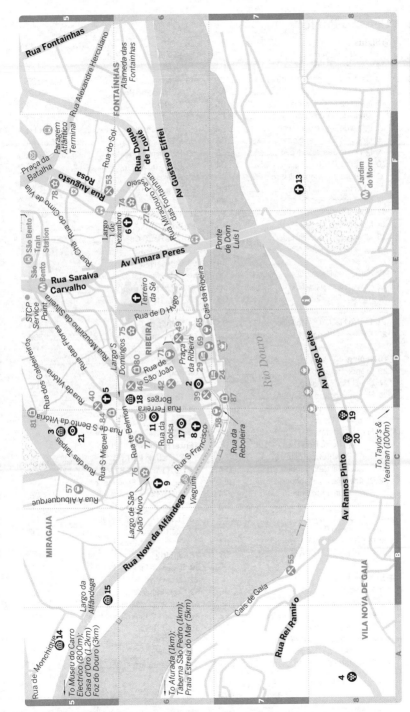

G5

Rua Fontainhas

FONTAINHAS
Alameda das
Fontainhas

Paragem
Atlântico
Terminal

Rua do Sol

Rua Alexandre Herculano

Praça da
Batalha

Rua Duque
de Loulé

78
53

Rua
Rosa

Rua
Augusto

74
27

Largo
1 de
Dezembro
6

Rua das Fontainhas

Av Gustavo Eiffel

Rua Miragaia do Passeio

13

Jardim
do Morro

Av Vimara Peres

Ponte
de Dom
Luís I

São Bento
Train
Station

São
Bento

Rua Chã Rua do Cimo de Vila

Rua Saraiva
Carvalho

STCP
Service
Point

Terreiro
da Sé

Rua Mouzinho da Silveira

Rua de D Hugo

Cais da Ribeira

Rua das Flores

Largo S
Domingos

RIBEIRA

75

80

Rua de
São João

49

71

Praça
da Ribeira

65

69

29

Rua dos Caldeireiros

Rua da Vitória

40

5

18

46

42

Rua Ferreira Borges

2

39

24

87

Rio Douro

3

84

81

Rua de S Bento da Vitória

11

Rua da
Bolsa

77

17

8

58

Av Diogo Leite

21

Rua S Miguel

Rua das Taipas

76

Rua S Francisco

Rua da
Reboleira

19

Rua A Albuquerque

57

Largo de São
João Novo

9

Vieguini

20

MIRAGAIA

Rua Nova da Alfândega

Av Ramos Pinto

To Taylor's &
Yeatman (100m)

Largo da
Alfândega

15

Cais de Gaia

55

VILA NOVA DE GAIA

Rua Rei Ramiro

Cais de Gaia

14

Rua de Monchique

To Museu do Carro
Electrico (800m);
Casa d'Oro (1.2km);
Foz do Douro (3km)

To Afurada (1km);
Taberna São Pedro (1km);
Praia Estrela do Mar (5km)

4

Central Porto

Just uphill from Aliados you can get your bearings and bird's-eye photographs from this vertigo-inducing tower, which looms over all of Porto. Italian-born baroque master Nicolau Nasoni designed the 76m-high tower in the mid-1700s. To reach the top you must scale its 225-step spiral staircase.

Mercado do Bolhão   MARKET
(Rua Formosa; ⊙8am-5pm Mon-Fri, 8am-1pm Sat) It's open most of the day but you should come in the morning, when local crowds jostle for fresh produce, cheese, olives, smoked meats, fresh flowers and more. There is a tremendous little fish grill (p373) on the market floor, and the entirety of Rua Formosa is lined with gorgeously dusty gourmet shops.

CORDOARIA

FREE **Centro Português de Fotografia**   MUSEUM
(Portuguese Photography Centre; www.cpf.pt; Campo dos Mártires da Pátria; ⊙exhibition hall 3-6pm Tue-Fri, 3-7pm Sat & Sun) On the south side of Cordoaria is a stately yet muscular building (1796) that once served as a prison and now houses this photography museum. You actually walk through the thick iron gates and into the cells to see the work, which lends the intriguing exhibits even more gravitas. Immediately south of the museum are the narrow, atmospheric lanes that were once part of Porto's *judiaria* (Jewish quarter).

Teatro Nacional São Joáo   THEATRE
(www.tnsj.pt; Rua de São Bento da Vitória) Immediately south of the photography museum, and set in an old synagogue turned church, is this gorgeous branch of Porto's Teatro Nacional. Shows are scheduled sporadically and take place in a spectacular interior courtyard framed by 50ft stone walls.

FREE **Igreja do São João Novo**   CHURCH
Set up a narrow maze of stone stairs, this medieval church with magnificent views was built in 1539 on land that was originally part of Porto's old Jewish quarter. It's a nice place to stop, take a breath and listen to sad fado tunes riding the wind.

Jardim da Cordoaria   PARK
Uphill from Aliados and past the Torre dos Clérigos lies the pleasantly leafy park known simply as 'Cordoaria'. The romantic, narrow lanes that run north from the Cordoaria and the Torre are the domain of Porto's hippest bars.

FREE **Igreja do Carmo**   CHURCH
Almost adjacent to the Cordoaria stands this striking *azulejo*-covered church, and one of Porto's best examples of rococo architecture (for more on *azulejos* see the boxed text, p361).

Museu Nacional Soares dos Reis MUSEUM
(http://mnsr.imc-ip.pt; Rua Dom Manuel II 44; adult/student/senior €5/2/2.50, 10am-2pm Sun free; ⊙10am-6pm Wed-Sun, 2-6pm Tue) Porto's most comprehensive art collection is just a short walk west of Cordoaria. It ranges from Neolithic carvings to Portugal's take on modernism and is housed in the formidable Palácio das Carrancas. Requisitioned by Napoleonic invaders, the neoclassical palace was abandoned so rapidly that the future Duke of Wellington found an unfinished banquet in the dining hall. Transformed into a museum of fine and decorative arts in 1940, its best works date from the 19th century, with sculpture by António Soares dos Reis – including his famous *O*

BOMBED OUT LOUD

It glows everywhere. Alien words contorted into visual language that all see and few understand. This three-dimensional scrawl appears on garage doors, crumbling ancient walls, empty storefront glass, neglected stucco. Maybe it's some postmodern, evolutionary art cycle, wherein the city chooses its worthy, salvageable relics and lets the bandit artists fix the rest. Usually they do it with loud blocky neon melting into a signature, other times it's all straight lines and clear cut: a stencilled pilgrim here, a cloaked bodhisattva there to make us see things some other kind of way. These 'statements' (and what else can you call them?) are left untouched for days, weeks, sometimes years. There's no getting around it, when graffiti tolerance is this high, it becomes a sort of passive celebration. And in Porto the graffiti art deserves to be celebrated. It's massive and ubiquitous and spectacular – especially at the **Lapa** metro station.

Desterrado (The Exile) – and António Teixeira Lopes, and the naturalistic paintings of Henrique Pousão and António Silva Porto.

BOAVISTA & WEST PORTO

The sprawling roundabout at Praça de Mousinho de Albuquerque roughly marks the boundary between 'old' and 'new' Porto. Here you'll find Casa da Música (see the boxed text, p378), Porto's extraordinary concert hall.

Museu de Arte Contemporânea   MUSEUM
(Fundação de Serralves, Museum of Contemporary Art; www.serralves.pt; Rua Dom João de Castro 210; museum & park €3; ☺10am-7pm Tue-Wed & Fri-Sun, to 10pm Thu Oct-Mar, 10am-7pm Tue-Thu, to 10pm Fri & Sat, to 8pm Sun Apr-Sep) Set in a leafy, upmarket neighbourhood, off the grand Av da Boavista, is Porto's other great work of contemporary architecture. Designed by the eminent Porto-based architect Álvaro Siza Vieira, the Museu de Arte Contemporânea is an arrestingly minimalist construction of vast, whitewashed spaces bathed in natural light. Most of the museum is devoted to cutting-edge exhibitions, though there's also a fine permanent collection featuring works from the late 1960s to the present day. With a single admission fee, you can also visit the nearby **Casa de Serralves**, a delightful pink art deco mansion that also hosts temporary exhibitions.

Both museums are located within the marvellous 18-hectare **Parque de Serralves**. Lily ponds, rose gardens, formal fountains and whimsical touches – such as a bright-red sculpture of oversized pruning shears – make for a bucolic outing in the city.

The estate and museum are 4km west of the city centre; take bus 207 from in front of Praça Dom João I, one block east of Av dos Aliados.

PALÁCIO DE CRISTAL TO FOZ DO DOURO

While it can get jumping on weekends, Foz do Douro is often peaceful on weekdays, especially if wisps of fog blow in off the Atlantic, bathing the cobbled upper reaches in cool mist.

Museu do Carro Eléctrico   MUSEUM
(Tram Museum; www.museudocarroelectrico.pt; Alameda Basílio Teles 51; adult/child €3.50/2; ☺9.30am-12.30pm & 2.30-6pm Tue-Fri, 3-7pm Sat & Sun) Housed in an antiquated switching-house, the museum displays dozens of beautifully restored old trams. Ticket price includes free Andante transport for four hours. See p382 for details of Porto's surviving tramlines, and p382 for information on the Andante Card.

Museu dos Transportes   MUSEUM
(www.amtc.pt; Rua Nova da Alfândega; adult/student/senior €3/1.50/1.50; ☺10am-6pm Tue-Fri, 3-7pm Sat & Sun; P) Set in the gorgeous 19th-century riverside customs house, this new museum traces the motorcar from inception to the future. It does the same for radio and telecom.

Museu do Vinho do Porto   MUSEUM
(Port Wine Museum; www.cm-porto.pt; Rua de Monchique 45-52; adult/student/senior €2/1/1, Sun free; ☺11am-7pm Tue-Sun) Down by the river in a remodelled warehouse, this modest museum explores the impact of the famous tipple on the region in a series of largely interactive exhibits. It has plenty of antique wine-making hardware too.

Jardim do Palácio de Cristal   PARK
(Rua Dom Manuel II; ☺8am-9pm Apr-Sep, 8am-7pm Oct-Mar) Sitting atop bluffs just west of Porto's old centre, this leafy park is home to a domed sports pavilion, the hi-tech Biblioteca Municipal Almeida Garrett (p379) and pleasant tree-lined footpaths with fantastic river views.

Museu Romântico   MUSEUM
(Quinta da Macieirinha; off www.cm-porto.pt; Rua Entre Quintas 220; admission €2, Sat & Sun free; ☺10am-12.30pm & 2-5.30pm Tue-Sat, 2-5.30pm Sun) Nestled on the south slopes of Jardim do Palácio de Cristal, beneath cathedral oaks and sycamores, is the small but stately home where the exiled king of Sardinia spent his final days holed up in 1843. The upstairs has been turned into a modest museum featuring the king's belongings and dainty period furnishings. Downstairs is the wonderful Solar do Vinho do Porto (see p377).

VILA NOVA DE GAIA

While technically its own municipality, Vila Nova de Gaia ('Gaia') sits just across the Rio Douro from Porto and is woven into the city's fabric both by a series of stunning bridges and by its shared history of port-wine making. Since the mid-18th century, port-wine bottlers and exporters have been obliged to maintain their 'lodges' – basically dressed-up warehouses – here. Today

PORT WINE 101

With its intense flavours, silky textures and appealing sweetness, port wine is easy to love, especially when it is taken with its proper accompaniments: cheese, nuts and dried fruit. Ports are also wonderfully varied, and even non-connoisseurs can quickly learn to tell an aged tawny from a late-bottled vintage (LBV). For a friendly primer on all things port, head to the convivial Vinologia (p375), where the learned owner gives an enlightening lesson with each glass he pours (English and French spoken). From here, you can also head across the Douro to Vila Nova de Gaia to taste the output of particular houses (p366). Finally, impress friends and loved ones by leading your own tour through the offerings at the remarkable Solar do Vinho do Porto (p377).

Until you've become an authority, we've prepared this quick cheat sheet.

PORTO SIGHTS

History

It was probably Roman soldiers who first planted grapes in the Douro valley some 2000 years ago, but tradition credits the discovery of port itself to 17th-century British merchants. With their own country at war with France, they turned to their old ally Portugal to meet their wine-drinking habits. The Douro valley was a particularly productive area, though its wines were dark and astringent. According to legend, the British threw in some brandy with grape juice, both to take off the wine's bite and to preserve it for shipment back to England – and port wine was the result. In fact, the method may already have been in use in the region, though what's certain is that the Brits took to the stuff. Their influence has been long and enduring, a fact that is still evidenced in some of port's most illustrious names, including Taylor's, Graham's and Cockburn's.

The Grapes

Port-wine grapes are born out of adversity. They manage to grow on rocky terraces with hardly any water or even soil, and their roots must reach down as far as 30m, weaving past layers of acidic schist (shale-like stone) to find nourishment. Vines endure both extreme heat in summer and freezing temperatures in winter. These conditions produce intense flavours that stand up to the infusions of brandy. The most common varietals are hardy, dark reds such as *touriga, tinto cão* and *tinto barroca*.

The Wine

Grapes are harvested in autumn and immediately crushed (often still by foot) and allowed to ferment until alcohol levels reach 7%. At this point, one part brandy is added to every five parts wine. Fermentation stops immediately, leaving the unfermented sugars that make port sweet. The quality of the grapes, together with the ways the wine is aged and stored, determines the kind of port you get. The most common include the following:

» **Ruby** – made from average-quality grapes, and aged at least two years in vats; rich, red colours and sweet, fruity flavours.

» **Tawny** – made from average-quality grapes, and aged for two to seven years in wooden casks; mahogany colours, drier than ruby, with nuttier flavours.

» **Aged tawny** – selected from higher-quality grapes, then aged for many years in wooden casks; subtler and silkier than regular tawny; drinks more like brandy or cognac than wine.

» **Vintage** – made from the finest grapes from a single year (and only select years qualify), aged in barrels for two years, then aged in bottles for at least 10 years (and up to 100 or more); dark ruby colours, fruity yet extremely subtle and complex.

» **Late-bottled vintage (LBV)** – made from very select grapes of a single year, aged for around five years in wooden casks, then bottled; similar to vintage, but ready for immediate drinking once bottled, and usually smoother and lighter bodied.

some 60 of these lodges clamber up the steep riverbank.

From Porto's Ribeira district, a short walk across Ponte de Dom Luís I lands you on Gaia's inviting riverside promenade. Lined with beautiful *barcos rabelos* – flat-bottomed boats specially designed to carry wine down the Douro's once-dangerous rapids – the promenade offers grandstand views of Porto's historic centre. Here you'll find Gaia's **turismo** (www.cm-gaia.pt; Av Diogo Leite 242; ☺10am-6pm Mon-Sat, 10am-1pm & 2-6pm Sun Jul & Aug, 10am-6pm Mon-Fri, 10am-1pm & 2-6pm Sat Sep-Jun), which dispenses a good town map and a brochure listing all the lodges open for tours.

Most people come here to taste the tipple, of course, and about 20 lodges oblige them. If you come in high season (June to September), you may feel yourself rushed in the largest lodges. Then again, you won't have to wait long for a tour in your native tongue. Note that more and more large houses are charging for their tours (€2 to €3), though these invariably include free tastings.

TOP CHOICE **Taylor's** WINERY
(www.taylor.pt; Rua do Choupelo 250; free admission; ☺10am-6pm Mon-Fri Sep-Jun, 10am-6pm Mon-Sat Jul & Aug) Up from the river and one of the first wineries in Portugal, British-run Taylor's boasts lovely grounds with fine views of Porto. Its tours are free and even include a tasting of one top-of-the-range LBV – your reward for the short huff uphill. Its on-site restaurant is tasty and at time of research it was about to open the region's first five-star resort across the road (p372).

Graham's WINERY
(www.grahamsportlodge.com; Rua Rei Ramiro 514; per person €3; ☺9:30am-6pm Mon-Fri Mar-Oct, 9:30am-1pm & 2-6pm Mon-Sat Nov-Feb) Another of the original British-founded Gaia wine caves, and a popular choice for tours and tastings.

Ramos Pinto WINERY
(www.ramospinto.pt; Av Ramos Pinto 400; tour & tasting €5-10; ☺10am-6pm Mon-Fri Jun-Sep, 9am-1pm & 2-5pm Mon-Fri Oct-May) Right on the riverfront you can visit the rather grand Ramos Pinto, including a look at its historic offices and ageing cellars. Book your tours in advance at the Gaia *turismo*.

Sogevinus TASTING ROOM
(www.sogevinus.com; Av Ramos Pinto 280; ☺10am-7pm Jun-Sep, 10am-5.30pm Mon-Fri Oct-May) Sogevinus is the port-wine holding company that owns the Kopke label, among others. Founded in 1638, Kopke is the oldest brand on the hill, but its lodge is not open to the public. Which is why you should stop here for the smooth caramelised bite of a seriously good aged tawny. The 10-year is tasty; the 20-year is spectacular.

Mosteiro da Serra de Pilar CHURCH
Watching over the entire scene is this severe 17th-century hilltop church, with its striking circular cloister. Requisitioned by the future Duke of Wellington during the Peninsular War (1807–14), it still belongs to the Portuguese military and is closed to the public. The church is open for Mass every Sunday morning from 10am to noon.

AFURADA & PRAIA ESTRELA DO MAR
Near the mouth of the Rio Douro, the picturesque, traditional fishing village of Afurada has salt in the blood and fog on the nose. Houses are decked with *azulejos*, and cafes are redolent with hearty *caldeirada* (fish stew). This old-fashioned way of life is depicted in Pedro Neves' 2007 documentary *A Olhar O Mar* (Gazing out to Sea).

There are several ways to get here. You can take a tram from the Ribeira to the stop just west of the Ponte da Arrábida then catch a small **ferry** (per person/bicycle €1/1; ☺6am-midnight) across the river to the village. Alternatively, buses 93 and 96 from Cordoaria stop just across the bridge in Vila

---

DON'T MISS

BOHEMIAN PORTO

For a glimpse of Porto's bohemian side, take a stroll two blocks north of Igreja do Carmo to Rua Miguel de Bombarda. Heading west along this street, you'll soon pass a growing number of art galleries, a few cafes, curio and record shops and some edgy local-designer boutiques. The neighbourhood is liveliest in the afternoon and early evening – particularly as the weekend nears.

Nova de Gaia. From here, it's a short walk along the boardwalk to Afurada.

Or you could rent a bicycle (they are allowed on the ferry), propel yourself there, and continue west. You'll come upon the last swath of intact estuary, which runs into the back of a wide blonde beach that arcs perfectly to receive rolling surf. It's stunning, but given its proximity to the river, head south for another 400m, past the smooth boulders and rocky beaches to soft, golden, sheltered Praia Estrela do Mar. Technically in Gaia, this is the best swimming beach in Porto. It's a 15-minute bike ride or 40-minute walk from Afurada, or you can take bus 902 from Boa Vista for Lavadores (via Ponte Arrábida), get off at the pedestrian path and walk 800m south.

Porto for Children

The best spots for kids to let off some steam are Porto's numerous parks – the fenced, expansive Parque de Serralves (p366) is particularly kid-friendly. For beach fun, head to Praia Estrela do Mar (p368). Kids might also enjoy a rattling journey in one of Porto's old trams (p366). The *turismo* offers a brochure called *Famílias Nos Museus* (Families in Museums), which lists a wide variety of activities designed just for kids throughout the city's museums.

Tours

Eco Tours   WALKING
(220 108 096; www.ecotours.com.pt; Rua do Passeio Alegre 20; 4hr tour per person €20) This outfit offers English-language walking excursions that take in the highlights of historic Porto before heading to Vila Nova de Gaia for port tasting.

Porto Tours   VARIOUS
(222 000 073; www.portotours.com; Torre Medieval, Calçada Pedro Pitões 15; 10am-7pm Mon-Fri, 10am-1pm & 2-6pm Sat & Sun Apr-Sep, 10am-5pm Mon-Fri, to 2pm Sat Oct-Mar) This excellent municipal service provides details of all the recommended tour operators, from city walking tours and Douro cruises to private taxi tours and helicopter rides over the city. As well as providing impartial advice, Porto Tours will make bookings.

River Cruises

Several outfits offer cruises in ersatz *barcos rabelos*, the colourful boats that were once used to transport port wine from the vineyards. Cruises last 45 to 55 minutes and depart at least hourly on summer days. You can board at Porto's Cais da Ribeira or Cais da Estiva, or at Vila Nova de Gaia's Cais de Gaia or Cais Amarelo. By far the largest carrier is Douro Azul (www.douroazul.com); Barca Douro (www.barcadouro.pt) is another solid choice.

Festivals & Events

There's a stream of cultural events throughout the year; check the main tourism website, www.portoturismo.pt, for more details. Some highlights:

Fantasporto   FILM
(Porto International Film Festival; www.fantasporto.com) Two weeks of fantasy, horror and just plain weird films in February/March.

Festival Internacional de Teatro de Expressão Ibérica   THEATRE
(International Theatre Festival of Iberian Expressions; www.fitei.com) Two weeks of contemporary theatre in Spanish and Portuguese; held in late May/early June.

Serralves em Festa   ARTS
(http://serralvesemfesta.com) This huge event runs for 40 hours nonstop over one weekend in early June. Parque de Serralves hosts the main events, with concerts, avant-garde theatre and kiddie activities; other open-air events happen all over town.

Festa de São João   RELIGIOUS
(St John's Festival) Porto's biggest party. For one night in June the city erupts into music, competitions and riotous parties; this is also when merrymakers pound each other on the head with squeaky plastic mallets (you've been warned).

Festival Internacional de Folclore   MUSIC
(International Folk Festival) A weeklong festival in late July/early August attracting international groups.

Noites Ritual Rock   MUSIC
(Festival of Portuguese Rock; www.noitesritual.com) A weekend-long rock extravaganza in late August.

Sleeping
RIBEIRA

TOP CHOICE   **Guest House Douro**

                              BOUTIQUE HOTEL €€€
(222 015 135; www.guesthousedouro.com; Rua Fonte Taurina 99-101; r €130-170; ※ @ 🛜) Owner-operated and set in a restored relic overlooking the Douro, these eight rooms have

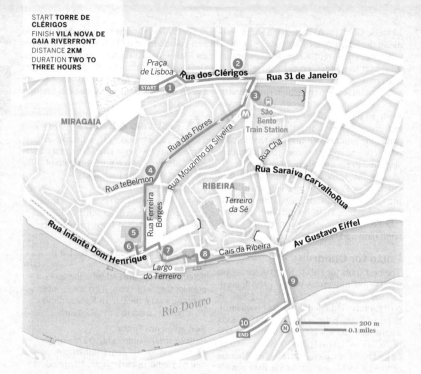

START **TORRE DE CLÉRIGOS**
FINISH **VILA NOVA DE GAIA RIVERFRONT**
DISTANCE **2KM**
DURATION **TWO TO THREE HOURS**

Walking Tour
Porto a Pé

❭ Begin at the baroque ① **Torre de Clérigos**, which offers unrivalled views over Porto. Next, head down Rua dos Clérigos, passing the foot of ② **Avenida dos Aliados** and pausing to admire the avenue's beaux-arts splendour. Just ahead, you'll see the French-inspired ③ **São Bento train station**. Check out the astounding *azulejos* in its main hall. Now cross over to Rua das Flores, a lovely street dotted with second-hand booksellers, old-fashioned stationers and some enticing cafes.

Near the end of the street is Nicolau Nasoni's baroque masterpiece, the ④ **Igreja da Misericórdia**. Cross Largo São Domingos to Rua Ferreira Borges, where you will pass the neoclassical ⑤ **Palácio da Bolsa**. You can check out its main courtyard – once Porto's stock exchange – for free or stay on for a tour of its elaborate interior. Just next door is the ⑥ **Igreja de São Francisco**, with a severe Gothic facade hiding a jaw-dropping golden interior.

Head back up Rua Infante Dom Henrique and turn right on Rua da Alfândega, where you'll find the medieval ⑦ **Casa do Infante**, the birthplace of Henry the Navigator and the site of some remarkable Roman ruins. Continue into the shadowy Ribeira district, following narrow, medieval Rua de Fonte Taurina as it opens onto the lovely ⑧ **Praça da Ribeira**. From here, take a stroll along the Rio Douro, admiring Vila Nova de Gaia's port-wine lodges across the river. Next, walk across the Eiffel-inspired ⑨ **Ponte de Dom Luís I** to Gaia's ⑩ **waterfront esplanade**. Grab an outdoor table at one of the waterfront cafes and enjoy the splendid city views across the Ribeira over a much-deserved drink.

been blessed with gorgeous wooden floors, plush queen beds, marble baths and flat-screen TVs. Riverfront rooms aren't huge but picture windows usher in the breeze, while larger backside rooms have romantic alleyway views. Breakfasts are marvellous, and the hosts will tip you off to all things Porto beautiful. With a 1am curfew, it's not for night owls.

Pestana Porto Hotel BOUTIQUE HOTEL €€€
(☎223 402 300; www.pestana.com; Praça da Ribeira 1; r €171-329; ﷯﷯) Right on the Douro and one of Porto's most sophisticated sleeps. Rooms are a fine balance between plush contemporary and traditional. Be aware that they vary widely in terms of size, light and views (the best face the river). It has a fine breakfast buffet.

ALIADOS

A new Intercontinental Hotel was under construction in a 250-year-old building in Aliados at time of research. It was scheduled to open in early 2011.

TOP CHOICE **Hotel Infante de Sagres**
BOUTIQUE HOTEL €€€
(☎223 398 500; www.hotelinfantesagres.pt; Praça Dona Filipa de Lencastre 62; s/d from €175/195; ﷯﷯) An exquisite time warp with well-coiffed doormen, crystal chandeliers and ornately decorated common areas, this place feels like a royal getaway in the heart of the city. Digs are modern and chic, though standard rooms are a little care-worn; superiors are quite up to scratch.

Porto Downtown Hostel HOSTEL €
(☎222 018 094; www.portodowntownhostel.com; Praça Guilherme Gomes Fernandes 66; r €16-19; ﷯﷯﷯) Set in a restored office building with gleaming marble floors, large dorms have new beds, shag rugs and bean-bag chairs strewn about, and get lots of light. Private rooms lack private baths, but the public kitchen is dynamite with granite counters and new fixtures.

Pensão Cristal GUEST HOUSE €
(☎222 002 100; www.pensaocristal.com; Rua Galeria de Paris 48; r €35-60; ﷯﷯﷯) The new budget favourite in town, Pensão Cristal lies on a romantic street that can get rowdy on weekends when the nearby galleries and bars get rolling. Corridors are narrow but decorated with artwork, and the rooms are clean and cosy with tile floors and simple wooden furnishings.

Residencial Rex GUEST HOUSE €
(☎222 074 590; www.residencialrex.com; Praça da República 117; r €48-59; ﷯﷯) Overlooking a peaceful plaza, Residencial Rex is set in a 150-year-old belle époque manor with a wide range of rooms. Floors 2 and 3 are best, with handsome old details, high ceilings and plenty of space. Fourth-floor rooms are small, carpeted and charmless. It's popular with a good mix of travellers.

Residencial dos Aliados GUEST HOUSE €
(☎222 004 853; www.residencialaliados.com; Rua Elísio de Melo 27; r €40-70; ﷯﷯) Set in one of Porto's marvellous beaux-arts buildings, it offers spiffy rooms with polished wooden floors, decent beds and tasteful if vaguely austere furnishings of dark-stained wood. Plaza-facing rooms are bright but can be noisy.

Residencial Vera Cruz GUEST HOUSE €€
(☎223 323 396; www.residencialveracruz.com; Rua Ramalho Ortigao 14; r €56-105; ﷯﷯) Homey rooms with high ceilings off the *avenida*. The carpeting can be a bit aged, but suites have wood-tiled floors. The top-floor breakfast room is special.

Residencial Paulista GUEST HOUSE €
(☎222 054 692; Av dos Aliados 214; r €27-75; ﷯) Cute, cream-coloured rooms, accessed by a grated old lift, with wooden trim, double beds and French doors that open onto the Av dos Aliados.

Hotel Grande Rio HOTEL €
(☎225 094 032; www.hotel-grande-rio.com; Rua do Bonjardim 977; r €30-65; ﷯﷯﷯) A cosy, well-run three-star nest with plain but modern rooms in a quiet neighbourhood near the lovely Rua Santa Catarina. It has bikes for rent and are often fully booked.

BATALHA & BOLHÃO

TOP CHOICE **Pensão Astória** GUEST HOUSE €
(☎222 008 175; Rua Arnaldo Gama 56; r €25-35) In an austere but elegant town house atop vertiginous stairs that lead down to the Rio Douro, this spotless place has no frills but great charm. Rooms vary in size and only a few have full bathroom, but all are decorated with antiques, have high ceilings, and several have great river and bridge views. Reservations recommended.

Castelo Santa Catarina BOUTIQUE HOTEL €€
(☎225 095 599; www.castelosantacatarina.com.pt; Rua Santa Catarina 1347; r €35-95; ﷯)

And now for something completely different: Castelo Santa Catarina is a whimsical, late-19th-century, pseudo-Gothic castle, a fabulously over-the-top hideaway in palm-shaded, *azulejo*-smothered gardens complete with its own chapel. Choose between more-elegant, period-furnished doubles in the castle and smaller rooms in a modern annexe. Reserve well in advance for summer weekends and holidays.

Residencial Santo André GUEST HOUSE €
(✆222 000 115; www.residencialsantoandre.com; Rua Santo Ildefonso 112; r €30-40) A charming four-floor walk-up with spiralled staircase and 10 oddly curvaceous rooms, some with bathrooms. They're all spic and span, but it's the smaller rooms that catch the most light. Set on a quiet street, it really is a splendid cheapie.

Residencial Belo Sonho GUEST HOUSE €
(✆222 003 389; Rua Passos Manuel 186; r €20-35; 🖵) Homey, if a touch dark, it has parquet floors, cable TV and wi-fi in tidy rooms with bathrooms. Management is warm and friendly.

Residencial Escondidinho GUEST HOUSE €
(✆222 004 479; www.residencialescondidinho.com.pt; Rua Passos Manuel 135; r €30-80) A cheap and groovy option ideal for young vampires of the night, it's set in the art deco Coliseu complex. Rooms are often fully booked and come with satellite TV and bathrooms.

Grande Hotel do Porto HOTEL €€€
(✆222 076 690; www.grandehotelporto.com; Rua Santa Catarina 197; r €100-250; 🅿❄🖵) Open since 1880, this proud old institution preserves a good deal of its grandeur, especially in its cavernous dining room and gilded parlour. Its rooms are less distinguished but still plush.

CORDOARIA & AROUND

Residencial Lusitana GUEST HOUSE €
(✆222 012 696; Rua do Rosario 241; r €27-37) A well-restored town house with bright, reasonably spacious rooms featuring stone-framed windows, forest-green carpeting and wooden furnishings. It's not fancy, but it is very clean and great value.

Hotel Eurostars das Artes HOTEL €€
(✆222 071 250; www.eurostarshotels.com; Rua do Rosário 160; r €74-204; 🅿❄🖵) This stylish hotel has something of a boutique feel, with handsomely outfitted rooms featuring spare contemporary furnishings, sparkling marble bathrooms and in-room wi-fi. There's also a lounge and a peaceful terrace that's ideal for an afternoon drink. Service is excellent.

BOAVISTA & WEST PORTO

TOP CHOICE **Hospedaria Boavista** GUEST HOUSE €
(✆226 098 376; Av Boavista 880; r €25) Eight spacious budget rooms await in your Porto grandma's house. The carpet may be industrial but the furniture is antique, the ceilings are high, the bathrooms gleaming, and the beds firm in this Tivoli town house. Rooms overlook *senhora*'s blooming veggie garden. A superb cheapie.

Hotel Boa Vista BOUTIQUE HOTEL €€
(✆225 320 020; www.hotelboavista.com; Esplanada do Castelo 58; r €73-122; 🅿🖵) A classic, 19th-century seaside inn outside and a thoroughly modern if somewhat characterless hotel inside, the Boa Vista sits at the mouth of the Douro and one block from the beach in the tiny Foz do Douro neighbourhood. It's worth the extra €10 for a view of the fort and the sea.

Pousada da Juventude HOSTEL €
(✆226 177 257; http://microsites.juventude.gov.pt; Rua Paulo da Gama 551; dm/r €14/33; 🅿@🖵) In a bright, modern building on bluffs above the Rio Douro, the crown jewel of Portugal's hostels offers basic but handsome doubles with sweeping views of the river, as well as clean, well-maintained dorms and 24-hour access. The hitch: it's 4km from central Porto.

VILA NOVA DE GAIA

TOP CHOICE **Yeatman** RESORT €€€
(✆220 134 200; www.the-yeatman-hotel.com; Rua do Choupelo; r €305-575; ❄🖵❄♨) Named for one of Taylor's original founders, the Yeatman is a brand-new resort, terraced and tucked into the Gaia hillside with massive Douro and Porto views. It is the first five-star hotel in town. There's a Michelin-starred chef, huge guest rooms and suites with private terrace, a decanter-shaped pool, sunken roman baths in the spa, and all the amenities you desire. Internet discounts available.

✖ Eating

Porto's restaurant scene has grown in leaps and bounds in recent years. Diners can enjoy traditional recipes from the north, contemporary Portuguese fusion fare or a medley of Italian, Indian and vegetarian dishes, and even sublime sushi. For dessert or breakfast, the cafes and patisseries around town keep locals in *pastéis de nata* (custard tarts).

Self-Catering

Those wanting to self-cater should check out Porto's fantastic municipal market, the **Mercado do Bolhão** (Rua Formosa; ⊗8am-5pm Mon-Fri, 8am-1pm Sat), which is most alive in the morning and is a bastion of fresh fruit, flowers and fish. Don't miss the nearby grocery-cum-bakery **Confeitaria do Bolhão** (Rua Formosa 305) and the best of the speciality food grocers on Rua Formosa, **Comer e Comer por más** (Rua Formosa 300). As well as stinky cheese, their shelves buckle under the weight of aged port; baskets of cherries and almonds crowd the doorway; and the rafters dangle with sausage and prosciutto. Among the central *supermercados* (supermarkets) are the well-stocked **Minipreço** (Rua Sá da Bandeira 355; ⊗9am-8pm Mon-Sat) and **Pingo Doce** (Rua Passos Manuel 213; ⊗8.30am-9pm Mon-Sat, 9am-8.30pm Sun).

RIBEIRA

TOP CHOICE **A Grade** PORTUGUESE €€
(☑223 321 130; Rua da Saoicolau 9; meals €10-20; ⊗lunch & dinner Mon-Sat) Both a humble mum-and-dad operation and a masterwork of traditional fare. Padre Ferreira works the room like your affectionate uncle. Madre Elena works her tiled kitchen with quiet grace as she bakes octopus in butter and wine, stews sardines and presents special roast veal and grilled seafood dinners in gorgeous casseroles alongside sautéed kale, boiled cabbage and crispy potatoes. The meal ends with free nips of house-aged *aguardente* (firewater), and dessert. Do not skip dessert. Reservations recommended.

Kyodai SUSHI €€€
(☑936 335 483; Rua dos Mercadores 36; per person €25; ⊗lunch & dinner Mon-Sat) We know it's hard to believe that sushi prepared by Brazilian chefs and served in a back-alley Porto hole-in-the-wall can wind up being one of the best sushi meals of your life. But collectively these charming chefs have 54 years of fish-carving and rolling experience. They hand-select their fish every day, and create an ever-changing set menu with two constants: melt-in-your-mouth sushi sweetness and warm service. Reservations mandatory.

DOP PORTUGUESE €€€
(☑222 014 313; http://ruipaula.com; Largo de S Doimngos 18; meals €25-50; ⊗lunch & dinner) The Ribeira's newest restaurant flickers with candles and is blessed with excellent service. Sit at the 'long table' and watch the chef prepare tapas tableside, or find a romantic corner and linger over duck risotto and a bottle of Douro red. Porto's upper crust digs it.

Churrasqueira do Infante PORTUGUESE €
(Rua Mouzinho da Silveira 20; dishes €5-6; ⊗lunch & dinner Mon-Sat) Popular with locals and for good reason. Its *platos do dia* (€5 to €6) are filling and fresh. If they have it, get the grilled *robalo* (sea bass). It falls of the bone.

A Parte TAPAS €€
(www.aparte-lounge.com; Rua das Flores 46; tapas €5-12; ⊗lunch & dinner) Think: gourmet tapas like veal and salmon carpaccio, and *milojas* with brie and purple onion. The room is wallpapered in local art and groovy tunes. The downstairs lounge hosts DJs and pretty people on weekends when they stay open until 2.30am.

O Comercial PORTUGUESE €€
(☑223 322 019; Palácio da Bolsa, Rua Ferreira Borges; dishes €12-20, set menu €25; ⊗lunch & dinner Mon-Fri, dinner Sat) Hidden at the back of the stock-exchange building, this one-of-a-kind restaurant boasts towering arches, old-world service and a stylish, fireside lounge. At dinner, the food has been known to disappoint, but the three-course lunch menu is great value.

ALIADOS, BATALHA & BOLHÃO

Casa Paraiso 2 PORTUGUESE €
(Rua do Paraiso, Largo de Lapa; mains €6-9; ⊗lunch & dinner) This cute, *azulejo*-pasted, family-run, stone-wall dining room is easy to miss (as is its more pedestrian predecessor across the street), but if you are hungry for Porto roast-meat classics or want to make like Bourdain and tuck into the blood-blended savouriness that is *frango con arroz*, you'll find it.

Cafeteria Pintainho SEAFOOD €
(Mercado do Bolhão, Barraca 36; mains €5-7; ⊗breakfast & lunch Mon-Sat) A cheap and cheerful fish grill in the heart of Porto's romantic market. No frills here, just the freshest of fish – salted, grilled and squeezed with lemon.

Padeirinha Doce
CAFE €

(Rua Augusto Rosa 46; pastries €1-3; ⊘breakfast & lunch daily, dinner Mon-Sat; 🖶) Croissants are stuffed with ham and cheese. Muffins are packed with walnuts. The chocolate éclairs are sinful, baguettes crusty, *pastéis de nata* flaky and sweet, the orange juice fresh squeezed and the espresso rocket fuelled. Naturally, this hole-in-the-wall is crammed with locals every morning.

O Escondidinho
PORTUGUESE €€

(www.escondidinho.com.pt; Rua Passos Manuel 144; mains €13-20; ⊘lunch & dinner) Amid *azulejos,* dark-wood furnishings and starched white place settings, O Escondidinho serves excellent traditional cuisine. Chefs here combine fresh ingredients and a wood-burning oven to create classic *bacalhau* dishes and flavourful baked octopus, while grilled seafood dishes are equally impressive.

Flor dos Congregados
PORTUGUESE €€

(Travessa dos Congregados 11; mains €9-15; ⊘dinner daily, breakfast & lunch Sat & Sun) There's a shock of green grass leading you into the alley, where you'll find a canvass flag menu and a narrow iron-and-glass entry into a dining room with a Slow Food ethos.

Restaurante Migalha
PORTUGUESE €

(Rua Conceiçao; mains €5-8; ⊘lunch & dinner Mon-Sat) Popular among lunching locals, this chef-owned mum-and-dad diner serves traditional seafood and the roast-meat dishes you've come to expect with abundant portions and charm.

Churrasqueira Papagaio
GRILL €€

(Travessa do Carmo 30A; mains €9-15; ⊘lunch & dinner) Walk in past the market-case packed with cuts of beef, scalloped pork, spicy chorizo and fresh seafood, then sit in the old stone dining room and order what looks good.

Aquarela
CAFE €

(Rua Santa Catarina 534; mains €4-6; ⊘breakfast & lunch Mon-Sat; 🖶) There are so many cafes and bakeries in Porto, it's hard to know which to explore. Our advice? Look for the locals, and they pack this joint for bacon and sausage baguettes, burgers and some of the richest, flakiest pastries in the city.

Pedro dos Frangos
GRILL €

(Rua do Bonjardim 219; mains €4-7; ⊘lunch & dinner Wed-Mon) *Frango no espeto* (spit-roasted chicken) is the name of the game at this extremely popular and inexpensive grill. Grab a spot at the stand-up counter and join the good ol' boys for a filling meal (abundant chips included). Other grills are nearby. They close at 7pm.

O Caçula
ECLECTIC €€

(www.ocacula.com; Travessa do Bonjardim 20; mains €6-15; ⊘lunch & dinner Mon-Sat; 🖉) Tucked down a narrow lane, O Caçula serves healthy-tasting lighter fare in a trim, contemporary, bi-level space. In addition to a few vegetarian dishes (veggie curry), it serves bruschetta with melted goat cheese, grilled fish, lamb steak smothered in Thai sauce, and fresh juices.

CORDOARIA & MASSARELOS

TOP CHOICE Casa d'Oro
ITALIAN €€

(Alameda Bastio Teles 797; pizzas €8-12; ⊘lunch & dinner) A concrete and glass clay-oven pizzeria leaning over the Rio Douro just upriver from the mouth. It does terrific classics like *diavola* (spicy salami and oregano) and *Vesuvio* (sausage and broccoli), but the prize is the sweet and salty *fichi e prosciutto* (prosciutto and fig). They serve pasta, salads and calzones, too.

Nakité
VEGETARIAN €

(Rua do Breiner 396; mains €6-9; ⊘breakfast, lunch & dinner; 🖉) This pleasant vegetarian restaurant has satisfying daily specials featuring tofu, seitan and tempeh paired nicely with goat cheese, shiitake mushrooms and other fresh ingredients. Nakité also has fresh juices and good desserts. Dine inside (amid piped-in New Age tunes) or on the back patio next to a gurgling fountain.

Guernica
FUSION €€

(🖉226 062 179; Rua Miguel Bombarda 598; mains €14-20; ⊘lunch & dinner Tue-Sat) Guernica brings a self-conscious dash of style to Porto, with excellent international cooking in a slim Manhattan-style bistro. Recent favourites include lasagne with mushrooms and brie, codfish with sausage, wild boar and seafood pasta.

VILA NOVA DE GAIA & AFURADA

TOP CHOICE Taberna São Pedro
SEAFOOD €€

(Rua Agostinho Al Baño 84, Afurada; meals €6-12; ⊘lunch & dinner) Fado scales the *azulejo* walls, toddlers tear through the dining room, plump and oily sardines (and other fresh fish) are roasted on sidewalk grills, and you can almost smell the tart snap of *vinho verde* in the air. There's much to love in this forever-packed, salt-of-the-earth local seafood house. It's located one block inland from the ferry pier.

Real Indiana INDIAN €€
(www.realindiana.pt; Cais de Gaia; meals €12-17; ⊙lunch & dinner; P ♨) Above Pizza Hut, in a glass box dining room at the end of the Gaia strip, is Porto's best Indian kitchen. Locals and tourists alike rave about the fluffy naan and aromatic curries. With 10 meatless dishes to choose from, this is the vegetarian's Porto salvation.

FOZ DO DOURO

Foz Velha CONTEMPORARY PORTUGUESE €€€
(☎226 154 178; www.fozvelha.com; Esplanada do Castelo 141; mains €12-20; ⊙lunch & dinner Tue-Sat, dinner Mon) Expect upscale and updated Portuguese cooking, and an exclusive local scene, at this long-running Foz favourite. The dishes (like sea bass with squid-ink puree, and veal cheek in bread dough) are seriously gourmet, the wine list extraordinary and the desserts (popcorn ice cream anyone?) extremely creative. Arguably the best splurge in town. Reservations recommended.

Shis FUSION €€
(☎226 189 593; http://shisrestaurante.com; Esplanade do Castelo; mains €9-18; ⊙lunch & dinner) Perched above the thrashing sea is this fashionable white dining room with funky Chinese lanterns, Eames chairs and lighthouse views. The sushi bar is very good, and so are the creative mains, like duck ravioli and tuna with balsamic-infused teriyaki sauce. But the vibe and the view are what make it special.

 Drinking

They may have a strong work ethic, but that doesn't stop *tripeiros* from partying – the city has a club scene that is at once sophisticated and largely devoid of elitism. Porto also boasts a rich theatre and music scene. To keep pace pick up *Agenda do Porto,* a monthly cultural events brochure, or scan the daily *Jornal de Notícias.*

RIBEIRA

Vinologia PORT-WINE BAR
(www.lamaisondesporto.com; Rua de São João 46; ⊙2-9pm Mon-Wed, 2pm-midnight Thu-Sat, 6-9pm Sun) This oaky, subterranean wine bar is an excellent place to sample the fine quaffs of Porto, with over 200 different bottles on offer, including a spectacular aged white,

bottled in 1952 (per glass €20). If you fall in love with a certain wine, you can usually buy a whole bottle (or even send a case home).

Café Bar O Cais BAR
(Rua Fonte Taurina 2A; ⊙10pm-2am Sun-Thu, to 4am Fri & Sat) A funky, classic-rock-drenched basement bar with old stone walls, vinyl booths and a loyal following that descends for a steamy stream of good vibrations. When everywhere else is dead, there is fun to be had here. They put out streetside tables on weekend nights.

La Taverna BAR
(Praça da Ribeira; ⊙noon-2am) Set on the edge of Praça da Ribeira, it does carafes and glasses of sangria, pours local wines and port and some decent rum, too – though most of the throng opts for icy draughts. It's the most popular outdoor watering hole in the Ribeira, and usually draws a crowd.

Sahara Bar LOUNGE
(Caís da Estiva 4; ⊙10pm-4am Mon-Sat) Decked out like an Arabian hideaway, this loungey place has hookahs, a young garrulous crowd, the occasional belly dancer (Friday at 11pm) and sidewalk seating for taking in the passing people parade.

ALIADOS & BOLHÃO

Nightlife rules in central Porto, with some eclectic bar-gallery spaces leading the way. It's worth exploring the narrow cobblestone streets just north of Rua das Carmelitas, which become an all-out street party (especially Rua Galeria de Paris) on warm summer nights and on weekends throughout the year. Nearby, there is also a lively (downmarket) scene at open-air cafe-restaurants on Praça de Parada Lentão, around the corner from the Jardim da Cordoaria.

TOP CHOICE Casa do Livro BAR
(Rua Galeria de Paris 85; ⊙11.30am-2am Mon-Sat) Vintage wallpaper, gilded mirrors, polka-dot ceilings and walls of books give a discreet charm to this perfectly lit bar – with good beer and wine and fine spirits. On weekends DJs spin funk, soul, jazz and retro sounds in the back room for pretty people. They host occasional live acts too.

Rota do Chá TEAROOM
(www.rotadocha.pt; Rua Miguel Bombarda 457; tea €2; ⊙noon-8pm Mon-Thu, noon-midnight Fri & Sat, 1-8pm Sun; ♨) This proudly bohemian cafe has a verdant but rustic back garden

where students and the gallery crowd sit around low tables sampling from an enormous tea menu divided by region. Tasty snacks include broccoli and cheese crêpes and vegie *empanadas* (stuffed pastries).

Cafe Piolho Douro
CAFE

(Praça Parada Leitão 41; ⊗8am-midnight Mon-Thu, to 2am Fri & Sat) Old school, still cool, and crazy popular on weekends when college kids pack the communal tables, lean against thick columns, and sip cold, cheap draughts or strong coffee. Take your poison inside or out in the glass box dining room on the plaza.

Praça
BAR

(Praça D Filipa de Lencastre 193; ⊗6pm-2am Mon-Sat) The busiest of a string of usually happening bars across from Hotel Infante do Sangres. It is a bit too bright inside, but the white walls, marble bar, reggae tunes and tropical cocktails (think mojitos, margaritas and *caipirinhas*) keep the young and hip lubricated and happy.

Plano B
CAFE, LOUNGE

(www.planobporto.com; Rua Cândido dos Reis 30; cover €3-12; ⊗4:30-10pm Tue & Wed, 4:30pm-4am Thu & Fri, 2:30pm-4am Sat, closed Aug; ☎) This creative space has an art gallery and cafe upstairs, and a cosy downstairs where DJs and some terrific international indie rock bands hold court. Much like the crowd, the programming is truly eclectic, with performance art, theatre and art openings held regularly.

Galeria de Paris
CAFE

(Rua Galeria de Paris 56; ⊗6pm-3am Mon-Sat) Two years old and still popular, it's a whimsically decorated spot, with toys, old phones and other assorted memorabilia lining the walls, which shake to a hip-hop soundtrack. In addition to cocktails and draught beer, you'll find an expensive, passable lunch buffet and decent coffee during the day.

Villa
NIGHTCLUB

(Travessa dos Congregados 64; ⊗vary) Brand new at research time, this block-long club was opened by Ibiza promoters. It can feel empty on any given night, but it is known to get wild when they pack the place for special events.

Casa de Lo
CAFE

(Tv de Cedofeita 20 A; ⊗noon-12:30am Mon-Thu, noon-2am Fri, 2pm-2am Sat) Hidden off a narrow alley is this boho coffee house beloved by area hipsters. Think thick stone walls,

old timber-beamed ceilings, funky downbeat tunes and a pretty and pouty, frequently androgynous, guitar-toting, literary, politicised crowd. DJs spin on Saturday and Sunday.

Café Guarany
CAFE

(www.cafeguarany.com; Av dos Aliados 89; ⊗9am-midnight) With a sunny, tiled interior, marble-top tables and an Afro-Brazilian mural, this classy affair has attracted the business and literary elite since the 1930s. It regularly has live music, and serves full meals.

Café Majestic
TEAROOM

(www.cafemajestic.com; Rua Santa Catarina 112; ⊗9.30am-midnight Mon-Sat) Porto's best-known tearoom is graced with opulently gilded woodwork, leather seats and gold-braided waiters who serve an elegant set breakfast, afternoon tea or any number of snacks and beverages. It's well located on fabulous Rua Santa Catarina, but largely a tourist scene.

Taberna do Bonjardim
BAR

(Rua do Bonjardim 450; ⊗8am-2am Mon-Sat) It's coffee by day and wine, port or whisky by night at this hip, two-storey spot with DJs on the decks, local art on the walls and a mostly young and hip clientele. It serves tapas, too.

Santa Cachaça Bar
BAR

(Rua Santa Catarina 191; ⊗9am-midnight) Here's a quirky, funky departure from the high-browness of port and wine swilling. Sip one of over 50 *cachaça* (Brazilian-style rum) in cramped, kitschy environs as the '80s tunes wash over you.

BOAVISTA & WEST PORTO

Indústria
NIGHTCLUB

(www.myspace.com/industriaporto; Av do Brasil 843; ⊗11.30pm-4am Thu-Sat) This basement club, owned by Antonio Pereira, aka DJ Vibe, and his girlfriend and Portugal celebrity, Merche Romero, was recently remodelled and still serves up deep house to a crowd that generally skews young. Take the bus and get off at the Molhe stop.

Vogue
NIGHTCLUB

(www.vogueporto.com; Av Fontes de Pereira de Melo 481; ⊗11.30pm-4am Wed-Sat) This was the only place to dance on Wednesday nights at research time. The crowd is often trendy, and the music bounces from electronica to house.

PALÁCIO DE CRISTAL TO FOZ DO DOURO

All of the places listed here can be reached via the night bus 1M from Aliados.

Solar do Vinho do Porto PORT-WINE BAR
(www.ivp.pt; Rua Entre Quintas 220; ☺4pm-midnight Mon-Sat) In a 19th-century house near the Palácio de Cristal, this upmarket *solar* (manor house) has a manicured garden offering picturesque views of the Douro. There are hundreds of ports available as well as refreshing aperitifs, such as *portônico* (white port and tonic water).

Twins NIGHTCLUB
(Passeio Alegre 1000; ☺11pm-6am Thu-Sat) Set in a quaint 19th-century seaside home, this club rumbles into the wee hours as great house tunes keep the party rolling for the pretty people. It's a bit out of the way, but that breeze does feel good at dawn.

Praia da Luz RESTAURANT, BAR
(Av Brasil; ☺9am-2am) Praia da Luz is a worthwhile stop when out exploring Porto's coastline. It rambles over tiered wooden decks to its own private rocky cove, and while you should probably skip the food, you should definitely enjoy a cocktail. Bring a sweater. It's about 500m north of the Castelo de São João.

Era uma Vez no Porto EXPERIMENTAL
(www.eraumaveznoporto.com; Rua das Carmelitas 162; ☺9:30pm-2am Mon-Sat) Part tearoom, part nightclub, part experimental-art gallery and part vintage-clothing shop, this place in an airy riverfront town house feels as if you've entered a private party with a cash bar.

☆ Entertainment

Cinemas

You can head by metro to the multiscreen **Cinema Centro Comercial Cidade do Porto** (www.shoppingcidadedoporto.com; Rua Gonçalo Sampaio 350, Boavista).

Fado

Porto has no fado tradition of its own, but you can enjoy the Lisbon or Coimbra version of 'Portuguese blues' into the wee hours at **Restaurante O Fado** (www.ofado.com; Largo de São João Novo 16; ☺8.30pm-2am Mon-Sat). The more low-key **Restaurante Fado Menor** (☑222 010 991; Largo dos Grilos, Ribeira; ☺noon-10pm Mon-Sat), overlooking a hidden plaza in the Ribeira, hosts fado several nights a week.

Music & Theatre

The Casa da Música (p378) has quickly become the city's premier music venue.

GAY & LESBIAN PORTO

Porto's gays and lesbians keep it discreet in the streets, but let their hair down in Porto's numerous gay-friendly night spots. Most venues are clustered around Jardim da Cordoaria. Gay Pride festivities take place in the first or second weekend in July. Consult http://portugalgay.pt for listings, events and other information. Note that while there are no exclusive women's bars or clubs, all the places listed here are at least somewhat mixed.

» **Zoom** (Beco Passos Manuel; ☺11pm-4am Fri & Sat) Located in an old warehouse, this is the gay dance hall of the moment, with some of the best electronic dance music in town and an often-mixed crowd.

» **Pride Bar** (www.pride-bar.blogspot.com; Rua do Bonjardim 1121; ☺midnight-late Fri-Sun) Another newish favourite has live music, drag shows and go-go boys. Open very late.

» **Café Lusitano** (www.cafelusitano.com; Rua José Falcão 137; ☺noon-1.30am Mon-Thu, to 3.30am Fri & Sat) In a handsomely designed throwback to 1950s Paris, this intimate space hosts a mixed gay-straight crowd. Live music on Wednesday nights.

» **Triplex** (www.triplex.com.pt; Av Boavista 911; ☺10pm-4am Thu-Sat) This popular nightspot in a pink, three-storey mansion has a regular line-up of '80s, electronica and '60s sounds (plus karaoke on Thursday). Triplex draws a mixed gay-straight crowd.

» **Boys 'R' Us** (Rua Dr Barbosa de Castro 63; ☺11pm-4am Wed & Fri-Sun) They've been pumping pop and electronica and holding raucous drag shows downstairs for years. Usually best from 1am to 3am.

Hot Five Jazz & Blues   JAZZ, BLUES
(www.hotfive.eu; Largo Actor Dias 51; ⊘10pm-3am Wed-Sun) True to its name, this new spot hosts live jazz and blues as well as the occasional acoustic, folk or all-out jam session. It's a modern but intimate space, with seating at small round tables fronting the stage and on an upper balcony.

Teatro Nacional São João   THEATRE
(www.tnsj.pt; Praça da Batalha) One of Porto's premier performing-arts organisations hosts international dance, theatre and music groups in two theatres.

Coliseu do Porto   ROCK CONCERTS
(www.coliseudoporto.pt; Rua Passos Manuel 137) This frayed yet still stylish art deco theatre hosts major names – like Air and Slash – as well as grand theatre productions. If something big is going down here, you'll see posters all over town.

Teatro Rivoli   BROADWAY PLAYS
(www.filipelaferia.pt; Praça Dom Joáo I; 🖪) In the mood for a musical? This stage serves up mainstreamed, translated classics, like *Annie*, from Broadway's yesteryear.

Teatro de Belmonte   PUPPET SHOWS
(www.marionetasdoporto.pt; Rua Belmonte 57) Specialises in puppet shows that range from fairy tales like Cinderella to non-violent political theatre.

Football

The flashy, fairly new, 52,000-seat Estádio do Dragão is home to heroes-of-the-moment **FC Porto** (www.fcporto.pt). It's northeast of the centre, just off the VCI ring road (metro stop Estádio de Dragão).

Boavista FC (www.boavistafc.pt) FC Porto's worthy cross-town rival. Its home turf is the Estádio do Bessa, which lies west of the centre just off Av da Boavista (take bus 3 from Praça da Liberdade). Check the local editions of *Jornal de Notícias* newspapers for upcoming matches.

Shopping

Porto shopping ranges from dusty food shops to chic fashion boutiques. In some areas, entire streets specialise in particular items (try Rua da Fábrica for bookshops). Rua Santa Catarina near Praça da Batalha

---

DON'T MISS

PORTO'S MUSIC MECCA

Grand and minimalist, sophisticated yet populist, dreamt up by local nobility and beloved by young bohemians, skate punks and ravers, Porto's **Casa da Música** (House of Music; www.casadamusica.com; Av da Boavista 604) finally opened its doors in 2005 – four years late but every bit worth the wait. Like a gigantic piece of raw crystal, the cloud-white concrete exterior is at once rigorously geometric and defiantly asymmetrical. But that monolithic sheathing doesn't prepare you for the surprisingly varied delights inside.

At the building's heart is a classic shoebox-style concert hall, meticulously engineered to accommodate everything from jazz duets to Beethoven's Ninth. It's also home to most of the building's right angles. The rest of the rooms – from classrooms to group rehearsal spaces to professional soundproof practice studios to a light-filled VIP lounge – wind around the central hall in a progression of trapezoids and acute angles. It's as if architect Rem Koolhaas has deliberately crushed and twisted the sombre geometry of high modernism, then added narrative touches such as *azulejos* and gilded furnishings – though always refracted through his own peculiar vision.

The hall holds concerts most nights of the year, from classical to jazz, fado to electronica (look out for one of the Casa's all-night raves popular among local beat freaks), with occasional summer concerts staged outdoors in the adjoining plaza. It also offers one-hour guided **tours** (per person €3, ⊘tours 4pm daily) in English led by students from Porto's highly regarded school of architecture.

Other ways to interact with the space: have a coffee or a light meal in the 1st-floor café **Bar dos Artistas** (⊘10am-7pm Wed-Sat, to 6pm Sun & Mon; 🛜), head to the 7th floor for fine dining at the stylish **Restaurant Casa Da Música** (🗩220 115 912; ⊘lunch & dinner Mon-Sat), or jack into the lobby's dozen-seat digitopia where you can tickle keyboards linked to Macs souped up with pro-grade mixing and beat-making software, and leave with a demo CD, all for free.

is a bustling, all-purpose shopping street, and style hounds will love Rua da Bombarda, home to nearly a dozen art galleries and a growing collection of clothing and interior boutiques.

CC Bombarda
MALL

(Rua Miguel Bombarda) Amid the galleries along Rua Miguel Bombarda, the small, unique CC Bombarda doesn't look like much from the exterior, but inside you'll find stores blaring indie rock and global funk and selling locally designed, fair-trade urban wear, stylish home knick-knacks and other hipster-pleasing delights. There's a cafe (Pimenta Rosa) serving light fare on an inner courtyard.

Shopping Cidade do Porto
MALL

(www.shoppingcidadedoporto.com; Rua Gonçalo Sampaio; P) Porto's largest mainstream mall sprawls for a few blocks in Boavista, featuring major European and international brands.

Livraria Lello
BOOKS

(Rua das Carmelitas 144; ⊙10am-7:30pm Mon-Sat) Even if you're not after books, don't miss this 1906 neo-Gothic confection that's stacked to the rafters with new, second-hand and rare books. Up the sensational butterfly staircase is a pleasant cafe. Look for the bookshop's monogram in the stained glass.

Miau Frou Frou
CLOTHING

(www.miaufroufrou.blogspot.com; Rua Miguel Bombarda 416; ⊙9:30am-12:30pm & 2-6pm Mon-Fri, to 4:30pm Sat) It happens to all of us. Our gear fades and frays as road miles pile up, lending a certain frump to our days. If you're in need of a slinky, funky fashion infusion come to this local designer's boutique for sexy dresses, chunky beaded jewellery and cute handbags.

Prometeu Artesano
HANDICRAFTS

(Muro dos Bacalhoeiros 125, Ribeira; ⊙9:30am-8pm) A collective of artisans from across Portugal, this antiquated stone-house riverside shop has a fun collection of *azulejos*, and while not everyone will be a fan of the Jesus sticks (passion of the twigs, if you will), you shouldn't miss the lovely ceramic dishes downstairs.

Livraria Chamme da Mota
BOOKS

(Rua das Flores 28, Ribeira; ⊙10am-6pm) Those who continue to appreciate the poetry of the printed word would do well to leaf through these leather-bound volumes, vintage postcards and sheet music. Here is history tied in pink string, sealed in handmade envelopes, kissed with style and elegance.

Lobo Taste
HANDICRAFTS

(lobotaste@gmail.com; Largo de S Domingos 20, Ribeira; ⊙10am-8pm) A small but groovy shop set in the Palacio das Artes. It specialises in contemporary handicrafts, like ceramic sculpture, wooden radios and a terrific selection of baskets and sun hats. Seriously, if you need a sun hat but hate the 'I'm a tourist' look, you'll find style here.

Port & Other Wines

It's great fun buying direct from the warehouses in Vila Nova de Gaia, but you can also try **Garrafeira do Carmo** (222 003 285; Rua do Carmo 17), specialising in vintage port and high-quality wines at reasonable prices. Other good sources are **Cabaz do Infante Garrafeira** (Rua do S Joáo 132), a humble looking minimart with a massive port annexe; and the photogenic **Casa Oriental** (Campo dos Mártires da Pátria 111).

ℹ Information

Emergency

Police station (222 006 821; Rua Augusto Rosa) South of Praça da Batalha.

Tourist police (222 081 833; Rua Clube dos Fenianos 11; ⊙8am-2am) Multilingual station beside the main city *turismo*.

Internet Access

Biblioteca Municipal Almeida Garrett (Jardim do Palácio de Cristal; ⊙2-6pm Mon, 10am-6pm Tue-Sat) A public library with free internet access.

On Web (Praça General Humberto Delgado 291; per hr €1.60; ⊙10am-2am Mon-Sat, 3pm-2am Sun)

Internet Resources

Porto Turismo (www.portoturismo.pt) Useful and complete guide from the city's tourist office.

Porto XXI (www.portoxxi.com) Cultural guide with restaurant listings.

Medical Services

Hospital Geral de Santo António (222 077 500; www.hgsa.pt; Rua Prof Vicente J Carvalho) Has some English-speaking staff.

Money

There is a currency exchange, open from 5am to 1am, as well as several 24-hour ATMs, in the airport arrivals hall. If you need a private exchange, consider the following:

Intercontinental (☑222 005 557; Rua de Ramalho Ortigão 8; ⊘9am-noon & 2-6.30pm Mon-Fri, 9am-noon Sat)

Western Union (www.westernunion.pt; Rua Sá da Bandeira 39; ⊘8.30am-6.45pm Mon-Fri, 9am-1pm & 2-5.45pm Sat & Sun) Currency exchange, plus internet access (€3 per hour) and phone booths for international calls.

Post

Main post office (☑223 400 200; Av dos Aliados; ⊘8am-9pm Mon-Fri, 9am-6pm Sat, 9am-12.30pm & 2-6pm Sun) Opposite the main city *turismo* office.

Post office branches Praça da Batalha (⊘8.30am-6pm Mon-Fri); Rua Ferreira Borges 67 (⊘8.30am-6pm Mon-Fri).

Telephone

Post offices, kiosks and newsagents sell Portugal Telecom phone cards, which can be used from most public phones.

Portugal Telecom office (PT; www.telecom. pt; Praça da Liberdade 62; ⊘8am-8pm Mon-Sat, 10am-8pm Sun) The handiest place for long-distance calls using card phones or payafterward *cabines* (phone boxes).

Tourist Information

ICEP turismo (Investimentos, Comércio e Turismo de Portugal; www.visitportugal.com) City (Praça Dom João I 43; ⊘9am-7.30pm, to 3.30pm Sat & Sun Sep-Jun); Airport (⊘8am-11pm) For countrywide queries, visit this national *turismo*.

Loja da Mobilidade (Mobility Store; www. cm-porto.pt; Rua Clube dos Fenianos 25; ⊘9am-5.30pm Mon-Fri) Located in the main city *turismo*, it dispenses a handy brochure, *Guia de Transportes* (English version available), sell tickets and passes, and can provide details on everything from bus timetables to car parks and metro stations.

Turismo (www.portoturismo.pt; ⊘9am-7pm Jul & Aug, 9am-5.30pm Mon-Fri, 9.30am-4.30pm Sat & Sun Sep-Jun) City (Rua Clube dos Fenianos 25); Ribeira (Rua Infante Dom Henrique 63) The main city *turismo*, opposite the *câmara municipal*, has a detailed city map, a transport map and the *Agenda do Porto* cultural calendar.

Travel Agencies

When booking a tour, see p369 for details of government-run organisation Porto Tours, which acts as an impartial intermediary between tour operators and travellers.

Tagus (☑226 094 146; www.viagenstagus.pt; Rua Campo Alegre 261; ⊘9am-6pm Mon-Fri, 10am-1pm Sat) Youth-oriented agency selling discounted tickets, rail passes and international youth and student cards.

Top Atlântico (☑222 074 020; www.topatlantico.com; Praça General Humberto Delgado 269; ⊘9.30am-7pm Mon-Fri, 10am-1pm Sat)

Getting There & Away
Air

The gleaming **Francisco Sá Carneiro airport** (www.ana.pt), ominously named after a beloved politician who was killed in a plane crash, is 19km northwest of the city centre. Portugália and TAP have multiple daily flights to/from Lisbon. There are also low-cost carriers, such as EasyJet and Ryanair, with nonstop services to London, Madrid, Paris, Frankfurt, Amsterdam and Brussels; see p527 for more details. Note that there is no left-luggage facility at the airport.

Bus

As in many Portuguese cities, bus service in Porto is regrettably dispersed, with no central bus terminal. The good news is that there is frequent service to just about everywhere in northern Portugal, as well as express service to Coimbra, Lisbon and points south.

DOMESTIC **Renex** (www.renex.pt; Campo dos Mártires da Pátria 37) is the choice for Lisbon (€18, 3½ hours), with the most direct routes and eight to 12 departures daily, including one continuing to the Algarve. Renex also has frequent services to Braga (€5, 1¼ hours). **Rede Expressos** (www.rede-expressos.pt; Rua Alexandre Herculano 370) has services to the entire country from the smoggy Paragem Atlântico terminal.

For fast Minho connections, mainly on weekdays, three lines run from around Praceta Régulo Magauanha, off Rua Dr Alfredo Magalhães. **Transdev-Norte** (www.transdev.pt) runs chiefly to Braga (€5, one hour) and Guimarães (€4.60, 50 minutes). **AV Minho** (www.avminho.pt) goes mainly via Vila do Conde (€3.50, 50 minutes) to Viana do Castelo (€6, 2¼ hours). **Rodonorte** (☑222 005 637; www.rodonorte.pt; Rua Ateneu Comercial do Porto 19) has multiple daily departures (fewer on Saturday) for Amarante (€6.40, one hour), Vila Real (€8, 1½ hours) and Bragança (€12.20, 3½ hours).

INTERNATIONAL There are **Eurolines** (www. eurolines.com; Centro Comercial Central Shopping, Campo 24 Agosto 215) services to/from cities all over Europe. Northern Portugal's own international carrier is **Internorte** (www.internorte.pt; Praça da Galiza 96). Take bus 302 or 501 from Aliados. Most travel agencies can book outbound buses with either operator.

Car & Motorcycle

All major Portuguese and international car-hire companies have offices at the airport (some have offices in town, as well) including the always helpful and reliable **Cael** (☎220 104 245; www.cael.pt; Rua Gonacalo Cristovão 360; per day from €40), **TCL** (☎222 076 840; www.tcl.pt; Rua Santa Catarina 922; per day from €40) and **Europcar** (☎808 204 050, 222 057 737; www.europcar.com; Rua Antonio Bessa Leite 1478; per day from €45).

Train

Porto is the principal rail hub for northern Portugal. Long-distance services start at Campanhã station, which is 2km east of the centre. Most *urbano*, regional and *interregional* (IR) trains depart from the stunning indoor-outdoor São Bento station, though all these lines also pass through Campanhã.

For destinations on the Braga, Guimarães and Aveiro lines, or up the Douro valley as far as Marco de Canaveses, take one of the frequent *urbano* trains. Don't spend extra money on *interregional, intercidade* (IC) or Alfa Pendular (AP) trains to these destinations (eg Porto to Braga costs €2.20 by *urbano*, but €13 by AP train). Direct IC destinations from Porto include Lisbon (2nd class €20, three hours, hourly).

There are information points at both **São Bento** (⊙8.30am-8pm) and **Campanhã** (⊙9am-7pm) stations. Alternatively, call toll-free ☎808 208 208 or consult www.cp.pt.

ℹ️ Getting Around

To/From the Airport

The metro's 'violet' line provides a handy service to the airport. A one-way ride from the centre costs €1.45 and takes about 45 minutes.

A daytime taxi costs €20 to €25 to/from the centre. Taxis authorised to run *from* the airport are labeled 'Maia' and/or 'Vila Nova de Telha'; the rank is just outside the arrivals hall. In peak-traffic time, allow an hour or more between the city centre and the airport.

Bicycles

Despite the narrow alleyways, steep hills and cobbled streets, cyclists are ubiquitous in Porto, and there are some particularly great rides along the Douro on dedicated bike paths from the Ribeira to Foz or from Vila Nova de Gaia to Afurada and beyond.

Vieguini (☎914 306 838; Rua Nova da Alfandega 7; bikes per hr/day €4/13.50; ⊙10am-7pm Tue-Sat, from 10:30am Sun) It has a great selection of high-quality mountain bikes and rents motor scooters (per day €18.50), too.

Car & Motorcycle

Avoid driving in central Porto if possible. Narrow, one-way streets, construction and heavy traffic can turn 500m into half a morning. Street parking is tight, with a two-hour maximum stay on weekdays. There is no limit on weekends and parking spaces are more readily available. Most squares have underground, fee-charging lots – follow the blue Ps. Beware that men may guide you into places and then expect tips. They can be very disagreeable if you don't comply. They also may direct you into an illegal spot – be sure to double-check signs. The Loja da Mobilidade (p380) provides a map devoted exclusively to parking.

Public Transport

BUS Porto's transport agency **STCP** (Sociedade de Transportes Colectivos do Porto; ☎information 808 200 166; www.stcp.pt) runs an extensive bus system, with central hubs at Praça da Liberdade (the south end of Av dos Aliados), Praça Almeida Garrett (in front of São Bento train station) and Cordoaria. Special all-night lines also run approximately hourly, leaving Aliados on the hour and returning on the half-hour from 1am to 5.30am. City *turismos* have maps and timetables for day and night routes.

A ticket bought on the bus (one way to anywhere in the STCP system) costs €1.50. But you get steep discounts if you buy multiple tickets in advance from the STCP service point or many newsagents and *tabacarias* (tobacconists). For two/10 trips within Porto city limits you pay €1.80/7.50; those to outlying areas cost €2.25/9.35, and longer trips (including to or from the airport) cost €2.60/11.40. Tickets are sold singly or in discounted *cadernetas* (booklets) of 10. Many key lines accept the Andante Card (see the boxed text, p382).

Also available is the *bilhete diário* (day pass), valid for unlimited trips within the city on buses and trams. For 24/72 hours, it costs €5/11.

FUNICULAR The restored **Funicular dos Guindais** (one way/with Metro transfer €0.95/1.45; ⊙8am-10pm Sun-Wed, 8am-midnight Thu-Sat Jun-Sep, 8am-8pm Sun-Wed, 8am-midnight Thu-Sat Oct-May) shuttles up and down a steep incline with tremendous river and bluff views from Av Gustavo Eiffel opposite Ponte de Dom Luís I, to Rua Augusto Rosa, near Batalha and the cathedral. The funicular is part of the Andante Card scheme.

METRO Porto's fairly new metro system provides speedy service around town. The central hub is Trindade station, a few blocks north of the Aliados corridor. Three lines – Linha A (blue, to Matosinhos), Linha B (red, to Vila do Conde and Póvoa de Varzim) and Linha C (green, to Maia) – run from Estádio do Dragão via Campanhã train station through the city centre, and then on to far-flung northern and western suburbs. Linha D (yellow) runs north–south from Hospital São João to João de Deus in Vila Nova de Gaia, crossing the upper deck of Ponte de Dom Luís I. Key stops include Aliados and São Bento station. Linha E (violet) connects via Linha B with the airport.

ANDANTE CARD

For maximum convenience, Porto's transport system offers the rechargeable Andante Card (www.linhandante.com), allowing smooth movement between tram, metro, funicular and many bus lines.

The card itself costs only €0.50 and can be recharged indefinitely. Once you've purchased the card, you must charge it with travel credit according to which zones you will be travelling in. It's not as complicated as it sounds. A Z2 trip covers the whole city centre east to Campanhã train station, south to Vila Nova de Gaia and west to Foz do Douro. And each 'trip' allows you a whole hour to move between different participating methods of transport without additional cost. Your time begins from when you first enter the vehicle or platform: just wave the card in front of a validation machine marked 'Andante'.

You can purchase credit at metro ticket machines and staffed TIP booths at central hubs such as Casa da Música and Trindade, as well as the STCP office, the funicular, the electric tram museum and a scattering of other authorised sales points.

One/11 'trips' in Z2 (including central Porto, Boavista and Foz do Douro) cost €1/9.65. Alternatively, you can choose to roam freely for 24 hours for €3.45. If you want to go further out than two zones, pick up a map and explanation of zones at any metro station.

Metro trains run from approximately 6am to 1am daily. For information on prices and tickets, see the Andante Card boxed text.

TRAM Porto's trams used to be one of its delights. Only three lines remain, but they're very scenic. The Massarelos stop, on the riverfront near the foot of the Palácio de Cristal, is the tram system's hub. From here, line 1 trundles along the river to near Praça Infante Dom Henrique (Ribeira). Line 1E (appears as a crossed-out '1') heads down the river in the opposite direction, towards Foz do Douro. And line 18 heads uphill to the Igreja do Carmo and Jardim da Cordoaria. Trams run approximately every 30 minutes from 9am to 7pm. For fare information see the Andante Card boxed text.

Taxi

There are taxi ranks throughout the centre, or you can call a **radio taxi** (☎225 076 400/029 898). Count on paying around €5 to €7 for trips within the centre during the day, with a 20% surcharge at night. There's an extra charge if you leave the city limits, which includes Vila Nova de Gaia.

Vila do Conde

POP 31,000

With its quaint historic heart, poetic folk hero, glassy river mouth, luscious beaches and salty past, you can understand why Vila do Conde is a popular weekend getaway for Porto residents. An important salt exporter during Roman times and a prime shipbuilding port during the Age of Discoveries, the town still drips history. Looming over it is the immense hilltop Mosteiro de Santa Clara, which, along with surviving segments of a long-legged medieval aqueduct, lends the town an air of monumentality. At the same time, Vila do Conde's beaches are some of the best north of Porto, and a metro link makes getting here an easy afternoon jaunt from downtown Porto.

Vila do Conde sits on the north side of the Rio Ave, where it empties into the sea. From the metro station, look for the aqueduct (about 100m away) and follow it towards the large convent (another 400m). From here it's a few steep blocks downhill to the town's historic centre. From the centre it's another kilometre via Av Dr Artur Cunha Araúja or Av Dr João Canavarro to Av do Brasil and the 3km-long beach.

◉ Sights & Activities

Beaches   SWIMMING

Vila do Conde's two best beaches, **Praia da Forno** and **Praia de Nossa Senhora da Guia**, are wide, blond and picturesque even when the winds howl, and most of the year seas are calm and suitable for young children. Buses marked 'Vila do Conde' from Póvoa de Varzim stop at the station and continue to the beach, about half-hourly all day. Surfers can sometimes ride swells near the 17th-century Castelo de São João Baptista (see p384), at the river mouth. Once a castle, it's now a small deluxe hotel with a glamorous, hard-partying reputation.

Mosteiro de Santa Clara CONVENT
Peering down over the town centre and the Rio Ave, the imposing Mosteiro de Santa Clara, founded in 1318, still has a severe-looking Gothic chapel, though the main building is an 18th-century affair. Currently the entire complex remains closed to visitors. Outside the convent are the poetic remains of a towering **aqueduct** that once brought water to the convent's 100 resident nuns from Terroso, 7km away.

Alfandega Resia Museu da Construção Naval NAVAL MUSEUM
(Museum of Shipbuilding; www.cm-viladoconde. pt; Largo da Alfândega; adult/child €1/0.50; ⊕10am-6pm Tue-Sun) Shipbuilding has been in Vila do Conde's bones since at least the 13th century. This museum, occupying the former customs house on the banks of the Rio Ave, just west of Praça da República, is mildly interesting, with exhibits on trade, and models of hand-built *nau* (a sort of pot-bellied caravel once used for cargo and naval operations). The real attraction, however, is the replica of a 16th-century *nau* moored opposite the museum. Visitors can wander across the various decks of the ship, peeking in rooms that give a faint taste of ship life in the 1500s.

FREE **Casa do Barco** NAVAL MUSEUM
(Cais das Lavandeiras; ⊕10am-1pm & 2-6pm) A glass-box museum on the south-west corner of Praça Republica. The basement level offers up models, photo displays, old fishing gear and one full-sized boat that provide a glimpse into the city's shipbuilding past. The entry level is a **Nelo** (www.nelo.eu) high-performance kayak showroom. Seems someone is still building boats around here.

Capela da Nossa Senhora de Socorro CHAPEL
(Largo da Alfândega; ⊕irregular) The tiny but striking 17th-century chapel has a crisp, mosquelike dome. The interior is covered in *azulejos* that date back to the church's founding.

Igreja Matriz CHURCH
(Parish Church; Rua 25 de Abril; ⊕9am-noon & 2-6pm Tue-Sun) At the heart of old town, the Manueline *igreja matriz* dates mostly from the early 16th century and has an ornate doorway carved by Basque artist João de Castillo.

Casa de José Régio HOUSE MUSEUM
(www.geira.pt; Rua de São Bento; admission €1; ⊕10am-noon & 2-6pm Tue-Sat) Religious art, as well as antique furnishings, ceramics and early 20th-century contemporary art – including some stunning Julio canvases, can be glimpsed at the Casa de José Régio. Named after the distinguished local-born poet, playwright and healer José Régio (1901–69), who lived and worked here, admission includes a guided tour (in Portuguese) through each floor of the town house. The stunning upstairs office and library, and rooftop garden are highlights.

FREE **Museu de Arte Sacra** ART MUSEUM
(⊕10am-noon & 2-4pm Jun-Sep, 2-4pm Oct-May) Outside is a *pelourinho* (stone pillory) topped by the sword-wielding arm of Justice. Inside is an interesting, if modest, collection of ecclesiastical art.

FREE **Centro de Memoria** GALLERY
(www.cm-viladoconde.pt; Rua da Lapa 14; ⊕9am-noon & 2-5pm Mon-Fri; ☏) This slick limestone gallery, uphill from the town centre, is home to the city's archives. The wide lawn out the front, framed by the spectacular aqueduct, hosts frequent art installations. Downstairs, you'll find rotating art exhibits. The whole space is penetrated by skylights, there's a groovy old-school horse carriage in the updated carriage house, and free public internet access.

Museu das Rendas de Bilros LACE MUSEUM
(Museum of Bobbin Lace; www.geira.pt; Rua São Bento 70; admission €1; ⊕10am-noon & 2-6pm Mon-Fri)
It's no accident that seafaring fingers, so deft at making nets, should also be good at lace making. Vila do Conde is one of the few places in Portugal with an active school of the art, founded in 1918. Housed in a typical 18th-century town house in the town centre, the school includes the Museu das Rendas de Bilros with eye-popping examples of work from Portugal and around the world.

★ Festivals & Events

Festival Ollin Kan Portugal MUSIC
(www.ollinkanportugal.com) Held in June, on the shores of the Rio Ave. Musicians from the Americas, Africa and throughout Europe rock Vila do Conde with three nights of free music.

Festa de São João RELIGIOUS
The town's biggest event takes place on the days leading up to 23 June, with fireworks,

concerts, a traditional boat parade and a religious procession through the streets.

Curtas FILM

(www.curtas.pt) For 18 years running, this seaside hamlet and sometimes Porto playground has been hosting an edgy and popular short film fest each July.

Feira Nacional de Artesanato HANDICRAFTS

(http://fna.vconde.org) A major fair of Portuguese handicrafts during the last week of July and the first week of August.

🛏 Sleeping

Forte São João Baptista BOUTIQUE HOTEL €€€

(☎252 240 600; www.forte.com.pt; Av Brasil; r €250-400; P❋◉🛜) Hidden within the forbidding, metres-thick stone walls of a 17th-century fort is this oasis of luxury. The hotel's eight rooms are cosy but plush, and popular on party nights, even if you do have to forfeit your keys until 6am.

Villa C Hotel & Spa BOUTIQUE HOTEL €€

(☎252 240 420; www.villachotel.com; Av Mouzinho de Albuquerque, Azurara; r €109-202; P❋@🛜🏊) A boutique property set on the hill above town. Rooms are minimalist and stylish with wooden floors and marble baths. Those on the seaside have spectacular views, but you can glimpse lovely village views from the street side. Stay off the 1st floor to avoid the roaring highway.

Estalagem do Brasão GUEST HOUSE €€

(☎252 642 016; Av Dr João Canavarro; r €38-100; P❋❋) Set in a restored 16th-century nobleman's house, this guest house has added onto at various times over the years, making it a patchwork of old and new. Rooms are spacious and comfortable, with sea-green carpeting and crown mouldings. Situated 200m west of the Rua 25 de Abril *turismo,* it's excellent low-season value.

Pensão Patarata GUEST HOUSE €

(☎252 631 894; Cais das Lavandeiras 18; s/d €30/35) Looking over the river, off the southwest corner of the square, this place has simple but sweet rooms with high ceilings and wooden furnishings, and all have river views.

Casa de Hospedes O Manco d'Areia GUEST HOUSE €€

(☎252 631 748; Praca de Republica 84; s/d/tr €25/35/50; ❋) Up an *azulejo*-clad staircase, this renovated old town house has clean, quiet, simply furnished rooms. We don't love the 'wooden' floors, but the larger ones come with ceiling fans. Expect 40% discounts in low season.

Santana Hotel BOUTIQUE HOTEL €€

(☎252 640 460; www.santanahotel.net; Monte Santana, Azurara; r €73-136; P❋🛜🏊) On a hillside across the river, this ageing modern hotel has comfortable rooms boasting excellent views over town. The amenities are the best part of Santana, with a small gym, jacuzzi, indoor pool, decent restaurant and spa. It's 1km from the centre; take Av José Régio across the bridge and turn left up Calçada de Sant'Ana.

Parque de Campismo da Árvore CAMPGROUND €

(☎252 633 225; www.cnm.org.pt; Rua do Cabreiro, Árvore; camp sites per adult/tent €7/5; 🏊) Tightly packed and well shaded, this campsite is 3km from town, right next to Praia da Árvore.

🍴 Eating & Drinking

Around the corner from the *turismo,* Praça José Régio, a rather ugly modern plaza in the middle of the quaint old town, has an assortment of outdoor cafes, bars and restaurants, and on weekends pop-up bars sprout to serve sugary *caparinhas* to the masses.

TOP CHOICE Adega Gavina SEAFOOD €

(Rua Cais das Lavandeiras 56; meals €5-7; ⊘lunch & dinner Mon-Sat) The top choice in town offers tremendous roast-chicken lunches for a song, and burns some damn good steaks, but first and foremost it's a seafood grill. Step one: stroll into the kitschy interior and peruse the chalkboard menu. Step two: choose your catch and watch the chef grill it perfectly on his streetside barbecue. Excellent value lunch specials (€5 to €7) come with potatoes, rice and steamed greens. Ask for the house-made vinaigrette dressing. It makes everything even better.

O Canghalho SEAFOOD €€

(Rua Cais das Lavandeiras 48; meals €10-15; ⊘lunch & dinner Mon-Sat) The funky, tricked-out vintage Land Rover parked out front may catch your eye, and as you come close you'll notice the stylish bistro interior and fresh fish on ice. Great style, great vibe, tasty seafood.

Restaurante Le Villageois FRENCH-PORTUGUESE €€

(mariaalicelisson@hotmail.com; Praça da República 94; meals €9-18; ⊘lunch & dinner Tue-Sun) The popular Villageois has been preparing terrific steaks and fresh seafood in French-

Portuguese style since 1977. The airy dining room is appointed with *azulejos*, the appealing sun-drenched patio is classy and the bar is full. It hosts live fado on Friday and Saturday nights.

Caximar
SEAFOOD €€

(www.restaurantecaximar.pai.pt; Av Brasil; mains €9-16; ⊙lunch & dinner Tue-Sun) For tasty seafood in a modern, unfussy place with tables overlooking the crashing waves, head to the beach, 1km west of Forte São João Baptista.

Cacau
CAFE, BAR

(Praca de Republica 42; ⊙9am-2am) Running deep into the hollowed-out ground floor of an old stone relic, it's a cafe by day and bar by night, with electro-funky tunes and a young crowd.

Forte São João Baptista
CLUB

(☑252 240 600; www.forte.com.pt; Av Brasil; ⊙Jul-Sep) Not just the best party in Vila do Conde, this is the best night out in the Porto orbit. Think mighty, seasonal blinged-out electronica throwdowns with international DJs, Bedouin tents, spinning disco balls and up to 2000 people spilling onto the windswept sands and dancing on the ancient fortress walls. Parties last until 6am. Make arrangements in advance to get on that door list.

ℹ Information

The friendly Vila do Conde **turismo** (www.cm-viladoconde.pt; Rua 25 de Abril 103; ⊙9am-6pm Mon-Fri, 9.30am-1pm & 2.30-6pm Sat & Sun) has maps and some nice examples of local lace, but the staff does not speak much English.

ℹ Getting There & Away

Vila do Conde is 33km from Porto, and it's a straight shot on the IC1 Hwy. It's now served by Porto's Linha B (red) metro line to Póvoa de Varzim, stopping about 400m from the town centre. A one-way trip from central Porto costs €1.95 and takes about an hour – the trip is a little faster if you catch the express service.

Buses stop on Rua 5 de Outubro, near the *turismo*. AV Minho express buses stop hourly (fewer on weekends) en route to Porto (€3, 50 minutes) and Viana do Castelo (€4, one hour).

Amarante

POP 11,300

Handsomely set on a bend in the Rio Tâmega, the sleepy village of Amarante is dominated by a striking church and monastery, which sit theatrically beside a rebuilt medieval bridge that still bears city traffic. The willow-lined riverbanks lend a pastoral charm, as do the balconied houses and switchback lanes that rise quickly from the narrow valley floor.

The town enjoys some small degree of fame for being the hometown of São Gonçalo. Portugal's St Valentine, he is the target for lonely hearts who make pilgrimages here in hope of finding true love. Surrounded by prized vineyards, Amarante is also something of a foodie mecca. As well as wine, the region produces excellent cheeses, smoked meats (*fumeiros*) and rich eggy pastries.

Self-drivers can use Amarante as an alternate base to explore the *quintas* (estates) of the Alto Douro. There is free parking just east of the *turismo* where the *mercado municipal* (municipal market) is held; avoid parking there overnight before crowded market days (Wednesday and Saturday).

History

The town may date back as far as the 4th century BC, though Gonçalo, a 13th-century hermit, is credited with everything from the founding of the town to the construction of its first bridge.

Amarante's strategically placed bridge (Ponte de São Gonçalo) almost proved to be its undoing in 1809, when the French lost their brief grip on Portugal. Marshal Soult's troops retreated to the northeast after abandoning Porto, plundering as they went. A French detachment arrived here in search of a river crossing, but plucky citizens and troops held them off, allowing residents to escape to the far bank. The French retaliated by burning down much of the town.

Amarante has also suffered frequent natural invasions by the Tâmega. Little *cheia* (high water level) plaques in Rua 31 de Janeiro and Largo Conselheiro António Cândido tell the harrowing story.

◉ Sights & Activities

Ponte de São Gonçalo
LANDMARK

Symbol of the town's heroic defence against the French (marked by a plaque at the southeastern end), the granite Ponte de São Gonçalo is Amarante's visual centrepiece. The original bridge, allegedly built at Gonçalo's urging in the 13th century, collapsed in a flood in 1763; this one was completed in 1790.

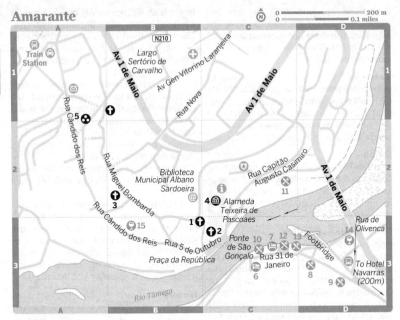

Mosteiro de São Gonçalo MONASTERY

(Monastery of São Gonçalo; ⊙8am-6pm) Founded in 1543 by João III, the Mosteiro de São Gonçalo and **Igreja de São Gonçalo** weren't completed until 1620. Above the church's photogenic, multitiered, Italian Renaissance side portal is an arcaded gallery, 30m up, with 17th-century statues of Dom João and the other kings who ruled while the monastery was under construction: Sebastião, Henrique and Felipe I. The bell tower was added in the 18th century. The best view of the royal statues is from the steep lane just west of the church entrance.

Within the lofty interior is an impressive gilded baroque altar, pulpits, an organ casing held up by fishtailed giants, and Gonçalo's tomb in a tiny chapel (left of the altar). Tradition has it that those in search of a mate will have their wish granted within a year if they touch the statue above his tomb. Sure enough, its limestone toes, fingers and face have been all but rubbed away by hopefuls.

Museu Amadeo de
Souza-Cardoso ART MUSEUM

(www.amarante.pt/museu; Alameda Teixeira de Pascoaes; adult/child €1/free; ⊙10am-12.30pm & 2-5.30pm Tue-Sun) Hidden in one of the monastery's cloisters is the Museu Amadeo de Souza-Cardoso. Its delightfully eclectic collection of modernist and contemporary art is a pleasant surprise in a town this size. The museum is named after Amarante's favourite son, artist Amadeo Souza-Cardoso (1889–1918) – one of the best-known Portuguese artists of the 20th century. He abandoned naturalism for home-grown versions of Impressionism and cubism. This museum is full of his sketches, cartoons, portraits and abstracts. Notable works by other local artists include Acácio Lino's enormous *O Grande Desvairo*, depicting the burial of Dom Pedro I, and Carneiro's evocative 1901 painting of Ponte de São Gonçalo.

Rio Tâmega WALKING

For an idyllic river stroll, take the cobbled path along the north bank. A good picnic or daydreaming spot is the rocky outcropping overlooking the rapids, 400m east of the bridge.

You can also potter about the peaceful Rio Tâmega in a paddle or row boat; **boat hire** (per 30min/1hr €5/10; ⊙9am-8pm) is available along the riverbank.

Solar dos Magalhães RUINS

This burned-out skeleton of an old manor house situated above Rua Cândido dos Reis,

Amarante

near the train station, has been left in ruins – a stark and uncaptioned memento from Napoleon's troops.

Parque Aquático Amarante   WATER PARK
(www.tamegaclube.com; A4 exit 15; adult/child €13/7; ⊙10.30am-7pm Jun-Sep) A good place for little (and big) kids to splash around, Parque Aquático Amarante is located above the river, about 2km southwest of the centre. It has a choice of three chutes, plus swimming pools and sunbathing areas.

Igreja de São Domingos   CHURCH
(⊙irregular) Rising beside São Gonçalo are several impressively steep switchbacks topped by this round, 18th-century church. The views from here are stunning.

Igreja de São Pedro   CHURCH
(Rua Miguel Bombarda; ⊙2-5pm) A baroque church, the nave is decorated with beautiful authentic 17th-century blue-and-yellow *azulejos*.

🎉 Festivals & Events

Held during the first weekend in June, Festas de Junho highlights include an all-night drumming competition, a livestock fair, a handicrafts market and fireworks, all rounded off with Sunday's procession in honour of the main man – São Gonçalo.

🛏 Sleeping

TOP CHOICE Casa da Calçada   BOUTIQUE HOTEL €€€
(☎255 410 830; www.casadacalcada.com; Largo do Paço 6; r €150-270; P ❋ 🌐 ⓢ ⚟) Oozing class and boasting every creature comfort, this 16th-century palace (rebuilt following Napoleon's destructive campaign) rises royally above the Ponte de São Gonçalo. Past the antique-filled parlours lie spacious, elegantly furnished rooms with marble bathrooms. The jacuzzi and pool overlook the hotel's vineyards. It's easily Amarante's top choice.

Residencial Estoril   GUEST HOUSE €
(☎255 431 291; mnestoril@hotmail.com; Rua 31 de Janeiro 49; r €30-45) Jutting out over the riverbank, Estoril has basic wooden-floored rooms with small bathrooms and sweet views of São Gonçalo's bridge. It is one of only three spots to offer rooms year round.

Hotel Navarras   HOTEL €€
(☎255 431 036; www.hotelnavarras.com;http://www.whotelnavarras.com/Rua Antonio Carneiro; r €87-110) Oddly located above the new town mall, this modern three-star affair is worth a look, and is always receiving. Rooms tend to be dark but have built-in wooden furnishings and sparkling new tiles in the baths.

Parque de Campismo de Penedo da Rainha   CAMPGROUND €
(☎255 437 630; ccporto@sapo.pt; Rua Pedro Avelos; sites per adult/tent/car €3.50/2.75/2.25; ⊙Feb-Nov; ⚟) A big, shady site that cascades down to the river. It has a *minimercado* (grocery shop) and bar. It's about 1km upstream (and uphill) from the town centre.

🍴 Eating

You can get picnic fixings at shops along Rua 31 de Janeiro or at the mercado municipal (Rua Capitão Augusto Casimiro).

TOP CHOICE Zé da Calçada   PORTUGUESE €€
(Rua 31 de Janeiro; mains €9-10; ⊙lunch & dinner) Excellent northern cuisine served in an elegant country-style dining room or on a veranda with idyllic views of the Moistero and the bridge. Top picks here include the fall-off-the-bone *jarretes e dordeiro* (roast lamb shank), and the savoury *açorda de camarãoes* (shrimp stew in bread bowl).

Restaurante Lusitana   PORTUGUESE €€
(Rua 31 de Janeiro; mains €8-12; ⊙lunch & dinner Wed-Mon) Roasted kid and stewed tripe are house specialities at this traditional

Portuguese restaurant with a pretty riverside terrace.

Cafe Principe
CAFE €

(Largo Conselheiro Atónio Candido 73; sandwiches €3-5; ⏲lunch & dinner) If you're hankering to try the smoked meats Amarante is famous for, you might consider this modernised new town bar and cafe, where the barman treats his sandwiches like a gentleman and keeps his Cintra beer icy.

Confeitaria da Ponte
BAKERY €

(Rua 31 de Janeiro; pastries €1-1.50; ⏲breakfast, lunch & dinner) Boasting a peaceful, shaded terrace overlooking the bridge, this traditional bakery has the best ambience for enjoying Amarante's famous pastries and eggy custards.

Adega A Quelha
PORTUGUESE €€

(Rua de Olivença; mains €5-10; ⏲lunch & dinner Tue-Sun, lunch Mon) One of several low-key *adegas* (wine taverns) proffering Amarante's fine smoked meats and cheese, A Quelha is a good place to sample the local delicacies. Grab a bite and a jug of red wine at the bar, or sit down to a simple but filling meal.

Drinking & Entertainment

Open-air cafes and bars pop up every summer on the riverside along Av General Silveira, opposite the monastery.

TOP CHOICE Travo & Canela
WINE BAR

(Rua Cândido dos Reis; ⏲1pm-2am) This inviting wine bar combines trim decor with festive red-and-yellow walls. DJs spin and live bands perform on occasion. And that inviting sunken stone terrace is Amarante's hipster hang of choice.

Spark Bar
BAR, RESTAURANT

(Av Alexandre Herculano 25; ⏲12.30pm-4am) A contemporary, multilevel bar-restaurant turns into a makeshift disco on Friday and Saturday nights.

Information

Banks with ATMs are along Rua 5 de Outubro and Rua António Carneiro.

Biblioteca Municipal Albano Sardoeira (Rua Capitão Augusto Casimiro; ⏲10am-12.30pm & 2-6.30pm Mon-Sat) In the newly refashioned former convent, Casa da Cerca, set behind the crumbling 16th-century remains of the Capula Santa Clara; provides free internet access.

Hospital (☑255 410 500; Largo Sertório de Carvalho) North of the centre.

Police station (☑255 432 015; Rua Capitão Augusto Casimiro)

Post office (Rua João Pinto Ribeiro; ⏲8.30am-6pm Mon-Fri)

Turismo (www.amarante.pt/turismo; Alameda Teixeira de Pascoaes; ⏲9am-7pm Jul-mid-Sep, 9am-12.30pm & 2-5.30pm mid-Sep-Jun) Next to the museum, in the former cloisters of São Gonçalo. It offers city maps, but very little English.

Getting There & Away

Bus

At the small but busy **Estação Quemado** (www. rodonorte.pt; Rua Antonio Carneiro), buses stop at least five times daily from Porto (€6.40, one hour) en route to Vila Real (€6.30, 40 minutes) and Bragança (€12, 2¾ hours). There are also daily buses to Braga (€7.80, 1½ hours), and Lisbon (€18, 4¼ hours).

Lamego

POP 11,100 / ELEV 550M

Most people come to Lamego – a prim, prosperous town 10km south of the Rio Douro – to see (and possibly to climb) the astonishing baroque stairway that zigzags its way up to the Igreja de Nossa Senhora dos Remédios. The old town centre itself has a mix of winding narrow lanes and tree-lined boulevards, with uplit medieval landmarks looming from almost every angle. Connoisseurs also swear by Lamego's *raposeira,* the town's famously fragrant sparkling wine, which provides a fine break between bouts of port.

Though often quiet midweek, Lamego is a university town, and there's usually some fun to be had in area bars on weekends. It's also a natural base for exploring the half-ruined monasteries and chapels in the environs, one of which dates back to the time of the Visigoths.

Self-drivers take note: parking can be tight in Lamego.

History

Lamego was an important centre even in the time of the Visigoths and has had a cathedral since at least the 6th century. The city fell to the Moors in the 8th century and remained in their hands until the 11th. In 1143 Portugal's first *cortes* (parliament) was convened here to confirm Afonso Henriques as Portugal's first king. The little town grew fat thanks to its position on trading routes between the Douro and the

Beiras and, thanks to its wine, was already famous in the 16th century.

Sights & Activities

Igreja de Nossa Senhora dos Remédios
CHURCH

(☉7.30am-8pm May-Sep, 7.30am-6pm Oct-Apr) One of the country's most important pilgrimage sites, the twin-towered 18th-century church has a trim blue-and-white stucco interior with a sky-blue rococo ceilings and a gilded altar. The church, however, is quite overshadowed by the zigzagging monumental **stairway** that leads up to it. The 600-plus steps are resplendent with *azulejos*, urns, fountains and statues, adding up to one of the great works of Portuguese rococo.

It's a dramatic sight at any time, but the action peaks in late summer when thousands of devotees arrive and ascend the steps in search of miracles during the Festa de Nossa Senhora dos Remédios. Most offerings are made at the rear altar where Mother Mary reigns supreme.

If you can't face the climb by foot, a road (turn off 1km out on the Viseu road) winds up the hill for about 3km before reaching the top.

Sé
CATHEDRAL

(Cathedral, Largo da Sé; ☉8am-1pm & 3-7pm) Older than Portugal itself, Lamego's striking *sé* has been declared a national monument. There is little left of the 12th-century original except the base of its square belfry. The rest of the structure, including the brilliantly carved, Gothic triple portal, dates mostly from the 16th and 18th centuries. Arresting biblical frescoes seem to leap off the ceiling. Both these and the high choir stalls are the work of 18th-century Italian baroque architect Nicolau Nasoni, who left his mark all over Porto. With luck you will find the door open to the peaceful 16th-century cloisters, located just around the corner.

Igreja Santa Maria de Almacave
CHURCH

(Rua de Almacave; ☉7.30am-noon & 4-7.30pm) This unassuming little church is Lamego's oldest surviving building, much of it dating back to the 12th century. It's thought that after winning independence from Spain, Portugal's first king assembled his initial *cortes*, an early version of Portugal's proto-democratic assembly of nobles and clergy, here from 1142 to 1144. It occupies the site

of a Moorish cemetery; some of its grave markers are now in the Museu de Lamego.

Museu de Lamego
MUSEUM

(www.ipmuseus.pt; Largo de Camões; admission €2; ☉10am-12.30pm & 2-5pm Tue-Sun) Occupying a grand, 18th-century Episcopal palace, the Museu de Lamego is one of Portugal's finest regional museums. The collection features five entrancing works by renowned 16th-century Portuguese painter Vasco Fernandes (Grão Vasco), richly worked Brussels tapestries from the same period, and an extraordinarily diverse collection of heavily gilded 17th-century chapels rescued in their entirety from the long-gone Convento das Chagas.

Castelo
CASTLE

(Rua do Castelinho; admission by donation; ☉irregular) Climb the narrow, winding Rua da Olaria to the modest medieval castle, encircled by a clutch of ancient stone houses. What little remains – some walls and a tower – has belonged to the Boy Scouts ever since their mammoth 1970s effort to clear the site after years of use as a glorified rubbish tip. Unfortunately, the site isn't always open (stop in the tourist office for the latest details). Still, the walk through narrow, kitten-patrolled stone lanes, and views from the castle's perch make it worth your while.

Festivals & Events

Lamego's biggest party, the **Festa de Nossa Senhora dos Remédios**, runs for several weeks from late August to mid-September. In an afternoon procession on 8 September, ox-drawn carts rattle through the streets carrying *tableaux vivants* (religious scenes represented by costumed people), and devotees slowly ascend the stairway on their knees. Less-pious events in the run-up include rock concerts, folk dancing, car racing, parades and at least one all-night party.

Sleeping

TOP CHOICE **Aquapura**
RESORT €€€

(☎254 660 600; www.aquapurahotels. com; Quinta Vale de Abraão; r €230-305; P❋☎) This stunning 50-room property nestled on an idyllic bend in the river north of Lamego, wrapped by terraced vineyards and dotted with swaying palms, is the grand dame of the Douro. Chic modernist rooms are set in an antiquated villa that's also outfitted with a top-shelf spa and stunning black-bottom infinity pool.

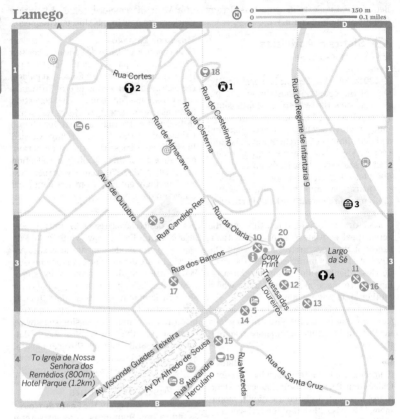

0   150 m
0   0.1 miles

Albergaria Solar dos Pachecos

GUEST HOUSE €

(☏254 600 300; Av Visconde Guedes Teixeira 27; s/d €35/45; ❄☎) Occupying an impressive, 18th-century nobleman's city home, this central place offers clean, carpeted rooms with exposed stone walls, ample light, high ceilings and wide terraces out the back.

Hotel Parque

BOUTIQUE HOTEL €€

(☏254 609 140; www.hotel-parque.com; s/d €40/70; ☐❄☎) Set in a former convent next to the Igreja de Nossa Senhora dos Remédios, the Hotel Parque offers tastefully decorated rooms with wooden floors and a few antique flourishes. The best rooms overlook Lamego. Best to have your own car; the turn-off is 1km out on the Viseu road (N2).

Residencial Solar da Sé

GUEST HOUSE €

(☏254 612 060; Av Visconde Guedes Teixeira 7; s/d €24/39; ❄) There are great deals to be

had on rooms with French windows opening onto the Sé. The carpet is a bit aged, but there's a funky modernist groove you might like. Or love.

Residencial São Paulo

GUEST HOUSE €

(☏254 613 114; Av 5 de Outubro 22; s/d €20/35; ☐) Although it's a bit out of the way, this guest house is one of the best of the budget options. The rooms are clean and bright, with parquet floors and somewhat dated bathrooms. Corner rooms have extra windows and verandas, and some rooms even have views.

Residencial Solar do Espírito Santo

GUEST HOUSE €

(☏254 655 233; Rua Alexandre Herculano 8; d incl breakfast €37; ☐❄☎) The common areas feature old-world touches like wooden floors and *azulejo*-lined walls. Rooms are cramped but clean with parquet floors. There's wi-fi in the tearoom.

Lamego

✕ Eating & Drinking

Like most regions that produce good wines, Lamego delivers food to match. Its *fumeiros* (smoked meats) are justly famous and can be found in one of several wonderful gourmet food shops on Rua de Olaria. Hit the **Mercado Municipal** (Av 5 de Outubre) early for fresh fruit and veggies if you're packing a picnic.

Sé Cristina   PORTUGUESE €€
(restaurante-sechristia@hotmail.com; Rua do Mazeda 11-12; mains €8-12; ☺lunch & dinner) Lamego's best restaurant occupies an elegant dining room, with outdoor tables above a small plaza. Recipes are traditional Portuguese, and service is excellent.

Restaurante Trás da Sé   PORTUGUESE €
(Rua Virgílio Correia 12; mains €5-6; ☺lunch & dinner) Congratulations to the chef line the walls at this *adega*-style place, where the atmosphere is friendly, the menu short and

simple, the food good and the *vinho maduro* (matured wine) list long.

O Brasilero   PORTUGUESE €
(Rua de Olaria 1-3; mains €5; ☺lunch & dinner) A corner-shop cafe with roast pork, beef, goat and rotisserie chicken plates on the cheap, especially at lunch (€5). Order downstairs and munch in the upstairs dining room.

Scala Cafe   CAFE €
(Av Visconde Guedes Teixeira; pastries €1-2; ☺breakfast, lunch & dinner) The charming wooden booths and tables are almost always crammed with locals who descend for great coffee and better pastries.

Podé Café   CAFE/BAR
(Rua Alexandre Herculano; ☺8am-2am; 🛜) Students tend to gather here for billiards, beer and thumping Euro tunes at this expansive patio cafe turned bar. The music isn't for all, but there is a scene here most nights.

Casa do Castelo   BAR
(Rua do Castelinho 25; ☺noon-2am Tue-Sun) A more hidden drinking spot lies inside the walls of the *castelo*. This atmospheric landmark bar is subdued during the week, but packs in a festive student crowd on weekends.

☆ Entertainment

Teatro Ribeiro Conceição   THEATRE
(www.teatroribeiroconceicao.com; Largo Camões; tickets €5-48) This handsomely restored theatre and cultural space hosts a wide range of programs throughout the year, from children's puppet shows to classical concerts, orchestral concerts and ballets. There's also a cafe with outdoor seating.

ℹ Information

Biblioteca Municipál (Municipal Library; Rua de Almacave 9; ☺9.30am-12.30pm & 2-5.30pm Mon-Fri) Provides free internet access in 30-minute chunks.

C@fenet (Av 5 de Outubro 153; internet per hr €1.50; ☺8am-midnight)

Hospital (📞254 609 980; Lugar da Franzia)

Police station (📞254 612 022; Rua António Osório Mota)

Post office (Av Dr Alfredo de Sousa; ☺8.30am-6pm Mon-Fri)

Turismo (www.cm-lamego.pt; Av Visconde Guedes Teixeira; ☺10am-12.30pm & 2-6pm Mon-Fri, 10am-12.30pm & 2-5pm Sat & Sun, closed Sat afternoon & Sun Oct-Jun) This fantastic tourist office is full of solid suggestions from warm, knowledgeable, English-speaking staff.

ℹ️ Getting There & Away

The most appealing route to Lamego from anywhere in the Douro valley is by train to Peso da Régua (p394) and by bus or taxi from there. A taxi from Régua costs about €12 to €15.

From Lamego's **bus station**, Joalto/EAVT is the only operator. Buses travel about hourly to Peso da Régua (€1.95, 30 minutes) and daily to Viseu (€7.70, 1¼ hours), and Lisbon (€15.50, 5¾ hours). The Lisbon bus also passes through Chaves (€10.50, 2¼ hours) and Vila Real (€5.50, one hour). **Copy Print** (Av Visconde Guedes Teixeira; ⊙8am-8pm), a newsagent beside the *turismo*, sells tickets for these services.

Around Lamego

CAPELA DE SÃO PEDRO DE BALSEMÃO

Older than Portugal itself, this mysterious little **chapel** (⊙10am-12.30pm & 2-6pm Wed-Sun, 2-6pm Tue, closed 3rd weekend of month) was probably built by Visigoths as early as the 6th century. With Corinthian columns, round arches and intriguing symbols etched into the walls, it certainly predates the introduction of even Romanesque architecture to Portugal. More-ornate 14th-century additions were commissioned by the Bishop of Porto, Afonso Pires, who's buried under a slab in the floor. Check out the ancient casket dominating the entrance chamber: supported by lions and intricately engraved, it depicts the Last Supper on one side and the Crucifixion on the other.

The chapel is tucked away in the hamlet of Balsemão, 3km southeast of Lamego above the Rio Balsemão. It's a pleasant downhill walk from Lamego through an old world village, then a riparian corridor full of flowers, grapevines and wild shrubs, though it is a rather steep return trip. From the 17th-century Capela do Desterro at the end of Rua da Santa Cruz, head southeast over the river and follow the road to the left.

MOSTEIRO DE SÃO JOÃO DE TAROUCA

The stunning, massive yet skeletal remains of Portugal's first Cistercian monastery, the **Mosteiro de São João de Tarouca** (⊙10am-12.30pm & 2-5.30pm Wed-Sun, to 6pm May-Sep), founded in 1124, stand eerily in the wooded Barosa valley below the Serra de Leomil, 15km southeast of Lamego. There's beauty in the decay, as a stream bisects the walls backed by a bowl of terraced hills. The monastery fell into ruin after religious orders were abolished in 1834.

Only the church, considerably altered in the 17th century, stands intact among the ghostly ruins of the monks' quarters. Closed for renovations at research time, its treasures include the gilded choir stalls, 18th-century *azulejos,* and the church's pride and joy – a luminous *São Pedro* painted by Gaspar Vaz, contemporary and colleague of Grão Vasco (p343).

From Lamego, Joalto/EAVT has several services each weekday (fewer on weekends) to São João de Tarouca (€2.20).

MOSTEIRO DE SALZEDAS

Another Cistercian monastery, its pink stone arches picturesquely mouldering in the sun, the **Mosteiro de Salzedas** (⊙9am-12.30pm & 2-5pm Wed-Sun Nov-Apr, 10am-12.30pm & 2-6pm Wed-Sun May-Oct) is located about 3km further up the Barosa valley from Ucanha.This was one of the grandest monasteries in the land when it was originally built in 1168 with funds from Teresa Afonso, governess to Afonso Henriques' five children. The enormous church, which was extensively remodelled in the 18th century, is today a bit scruffy with decay, particularly its roofless cloisters next door, and those feaux crystal chandeliers are an odd sight. Across from the church lies the old *judiaria,* with dark narrow lanes skirting around the gloomy centuries-old dwellings.

From Lamego, Joalto/EAVT runs three buses each weekday to Vila Salzedas (€2.60).

Peso da Régua

POP 9400

Lamego's businesslike alter ego, the sun-bleached town of Régua abuts the Rio Douro at the western edge of the demarcated port-wine region. As the region's largest riverside town, it grew into a major port-wine entrepôt in the 18th century, and remains an important transport junction – thanks in part to the hulking IP3 bridge that soars above the river valley. The town itself, set along a busy highway above the river, doesn't have a lot of charm, and most visitors stop in just long enough to get recommendations, maps and directions to nearby wineries, but it makes a convenient base to visit the port-wine country, cruise the Rio Douro and ride the Corgo railway line to Vila Real. Most tourists stick to the scenic riverfront, but the quaint old town one block uphill is an almost exclusively local scene, and well worth a wander.

There is a public car park at the eastern end of the riverfront promenade, a few blocks from the *turismo*.

⊙ Sights

TOP CHOICE **Museu do Douro** MUSEUM
(www.museudodouro.pt; Rua Marqués de Pombal; admission €5; ⊙10am-6pm Oct-Jun, to 8pm Jul-Sep) It's not all about the wine. Sometimes it's about contemporary canvases, impressionistic landscapes, old leather-bound texts, vintage port-wine posters and the remains of an old flat-bottomed port hauler. You'll find it all in a gorgeous converted riverside warehouse. The gift shop, stocked with wine, cheese and some terrific silver, is brilliant.

Solar do Vinho do Porto WINE MUSEUM
(Rua da Ferreirinha; admission with/without audio guide €4/2; ⊙10am-12.30pm & 2-6pm Tue-Sun) A good place to learn about the history of port is this small museum housed in another of Regua's 18th-century warehouses. Props like an ox cart, delicate old decanters and enormous, fragrant barrels help illuminate the centuries-old winemaking traditions in the Douro. The Solar hosts frequent wine tastings.

🏃 Activities

River Cruises BOAT TRIPS
Peso da Régua is a major stop on the Douro cruise line (see p369). Your best bet is to reserve through Porto Tours in Porto (p369). In Régua, you can inquire about trips at the Rota do Vinho do Porto (p394). You could also try hopping aboard one of the frequent daily 50-minute cruises to Pinhão offered by Tomaz do Douro (www.viadouro -cruzeiros.com; cruises €20). You'll find them at the **pier**. Locals also operate smaller boats from the pier, which can be less comfortable, yet more intimate and often a better choice for an hour's cruise.

Steam Train to Tua STEAM TRAIN
(Comboio Vapor; www.cp.pt; adult/child return €43/21.50 ⊙trains depart Regua 2:45pm Sat May-Oct) While the gorgeous Linha da Tua line remains out of service, you can still ride in this lovingly restored steam train, which travels along the Douro from Régua to Tua, making a 20-minute stop in Pinhão. You cannot catch the train in Pinhão, however. You'll be back at 6:30pm.

🛏 Sleeping

Quinta do Vallado RURAL INN €€€
(☏254 323 147; www.quintadovallado.com; Vilalinho dos Freiras; r €95-140; P ❄ ☃) About 3km from Régua, this 70-hectare winery offers five rooms in an old stone manor. The exposed stone alcove, reclaimed doors and tiled bath set the Yellow Room apart, but all have terracotta floors, and share a common living room and gorgeous pool. Overnights come with breakfast, but do not serve lunch or dinner.

Dom Quixote GUEST HOUSE €
(☏254 321 157; residencialdquixote@sapo.pt; 1st fl, Av Sacadura Cabral 1; s/d €25/30; P ❄) Located 1.5km west of the *turismo,* the modern Dom Quixote is arguably Régua's best budget option. It offers simple but comfortable – if forgettable – rooms.

Hotel Régua Douro HOTEL €€
(☏254 320 700; www.hotelreguadouro.pt; Largo da Estação; r €60-120; P ❄ ☃) This industrial-sized hotel sits by the river and is steps from the train station. It has plush, carpeted rooms in ruby (or is that tawny?) colour schemes and windows overlooking the Douro. The pool is much appreciated on hot days.

🍴 Eating

Castas Pratos PORTUGUESE, TAPAS €€
(Rua José Vasques Osorio; tapas €3-7; ⊙lunch & dinner) The coolest new dining room in town is set in a restored wood-and-stone rail-yard warehouse with original timbers exposed. You can order grilled *alheira* sausage or octopus salad from the tapas bar downstairs or perhaps you'd rather have the roasted ox tail or the spinach lasagne in the mezzanine?

Don Quixote PORTUGUESE €
(Av João Franco; mains €5-6; ⊙lunch & dinner) Run in conjunction with the guest house but in a different location next to EuropCar, this humble diner serves all the fish and roasted-meat dishes you crave, along with a nice selection of table wines.

Douro In PORTUGUESE €€
(www.wonderfulland.com/douro-in; Av Joáo Franco; mains €14-16; ⊙lunch & dinner) A step up

DRINKING IN THE DOURO

Pinhão offers some enticing exploring for wine-lovers, with picturesque 18th-century manor houses overlooking steeply terraced vineyards leading down to the Rio Douro. To explore the *quintas* on your own, you'll need a vehicle. Ask the tourist office about lodges open for tours and tastings. It's worth shelling out €2 for a map (*Rota do Vinho do Porto;* www.rvp.pt) – available at most *turismos* in the Douro – listing 50 or so vineyards accepting visitors. A few good places to start the viticultural journey are listed here:

Quinta do Panascal (www.fonseca.pt; ◷10am-6pm Mon-Fri Nov-May, daily Jun-Oct) Producer of Fonseca ports, this lovely estate offers free self-guided audio tours (in English, French or Portuguese) through some beautifully situated vineyards. The estate is located about 10 minutes' drive west of Pinhão, and is well signposted from the N222.

Quinta do Portal (www.quintadoportal.com; ◷10am-1pm & 2-6pm) Quinta do Portal is an award-winning vineyard producing ports, red and white table wines, and a little-known muscatel. The surrounding region is one of the only places in the country producing muscatel (the other is Setúbal). There's a restaurant and guest house (doubles from €125). The winery lies about 12km north of Pinhão, along EN323 in the direction of Vila Real.

Quinta do Crasto (☎254 920 020; www.quintadocrasto.pt; ◷tours by appointment) They've been making wine since 1615 on this gorgeous property set high in the Alta Douro with delicately laced vineyards overlooking the river and layers of mountains. Their dusty hounds are sweet, the wine is special and they do receive guests, but only during the week and with advance reservation.

Quinta Seara D'ordens (☎254 906 415; www.quintasearadordens.pa-net.pt; ◷tours by appointment) A 60-hectare property run by three charming brothers who make some of the most quaffable and affordable table wines in the valley. Make an appointment and Fernando will tour you through their product line, pouring glass after glass, and if you buy a bottle the tasting is free.

Quinta do Tedo (www.quintadotedo.com; ◷10am-6pm) Blessed with sublime real estate carved by two rivers – the Douro and Tabua, this American-French-Portuguese-owned estate is equipped with a restaurant and winery – which you can see on a short 20-minute tour, with eight excellent table wines and a port to sample in the tasting room. Be warned, they do get some package tourists, but service is excellent even for indie types.

in price and quality from most Régua options is the stylish Douro In. Elegant place settings and sizeable windows overlooking the river set the scene for feasting on *arroz de tamboril* (monkfish rice), roast loin with asparagus risotto, and other flavourful dishes. It has a superb wine list.

ℹ️ Information

Pick up a town map and local information at the **Rota do Vinho do Porto** (www.rvp.pt; Largo da Estação; ◷9am-12.30pm & 2-6pm Feb-Oct, Mon-Fri only Nov-Jan), conveniently located in a converted warehouse right next to the train station. It has a terrific map of its participating *quintas*. There's also a less useful **turismo** (www.cm-pesoregua.pt; Rua da Ferreirinha 505; ◷9am-12.30pm & 2-5.30pm daily Jul–mid-Sep,

Mon-Fri mid-Sep–Jun), 1km west of the station. For the *cais fluvial* (river terminal) bear left at the Residencial Império.

ℹ️ Getting There & Around

Rodonorte (www.rodonorte.pt) buses run regularly to/from Lamego (€1.80, 20 minutes) and four times daily to Vila Real (€5.50, 30 minutes).

There are around 12 trains daily from Porto (€7.75, two hours); some go up the valley to Pinhão (€1.80, 25 minutes, five daily). Around six trains depart daily for Tua (€2.80; 40 minutes). If you've taken a train this far and suddenly realise you need a car to visit the vineyards, your best bet is **Europcar** (☎254 321 146; www.europcar.com; Av João Franco), with car rentals from €80 per day.

Alto Douro

Heading upriver from Peso da Régua, terraced vineyards blanket every hillside, with whitewashed *quintas* perched high above the Douro. This dramatic landscape is the jaw-dropping by-product of over 2000 years of winemaking. While villages are small and architectural monuments few and far between, it's worth the trip simply for the ride itself (scenic by car, train or boat), with panoramic vistas lurking around nearly every bend. Its allure has clearly not gone unnoticed. In 2001 Unesco designated the entire Alto Douro wine-growing region a World Heritage Site.

Further east towards Spain, the soil is drier, and the sculpted landscape gives way to more-rugged terrain. But despite the aridity – and the blisteringly hot summers – the land around Vila Nova de Foz Côa produces fine grapes and excellent olives and nuts.

Many port and table wine *quintas* offer rural accommodation, though rooms grow scarce in late September and early October during the *vindima* (grape harvest).

Daily trains run from Porto, with a change at Régua, up to Pinhão, Tua and Pocinho. Travellers with their own wheels can take the river-hugging N222 from Régua to Pinhão, beyond which the roads climb in and out of the valley. For information on river cruises, see p393.

PINHÃO
POP 960

Encircled by terraced hillsides that produce some of the world's best port – and some damn good table wines too, little Pinhão sits on a particularly lovely bend of the Rio Douro, about 25km upriver from Peso da Régua. Wineries and their competing signs dominate the scene. Even the delightful train station has *azulejos* depicting the grape harvest. The town itself, cute though it is, holds little interest, but does makes a fine base for exploring the many surrounding vineyards.

In addition to drinking your fill, this is a good setting for country walks, and there are some fine day-trip possibilities. Except on high-season weekends, street parking is straightforward. Look around the train station or down by the river (first left after passing the train station).

◎ Sights & Activities

Driving the Alto Douro   DRIVING
(Hwy N222 & N322) One of the region's biggest thrills is simply driving the Douro's winding roads, navigating hairpin turns, climbing terraced ridges and cruising village back roads patrolled by mobs of latter-day Romeos. This road teases the adventurous driver, taking you away from the river and into the shadows of another impossibly huddled village, then back into direct sunlight that streams through trees and bathes the steep drop to the river in surreal golden light. In between, of course, you will need to stop at a *quinta* or three.

Quinta Nova   HIKING
(☎254 730 430; www.quintanova.com; up to 4 people €15; ◎8am-dusk) Set on a stunning ridge, surrounded by luscious, ancient vineyards, overlooking the deep green Douro river with mountains layered in the distance, the Quinta Nova estate is well worth an in-depth exploration. While it has easier loops, the 12km of hiking trail (three hours) is the best in the region, and fans of *The Amazing Race* will want in on their Geocaching Challenge. Guests use a GPS to locate five wine caches, replacing the corks in each. If you complete the task, you'll win a prize! To get here, head 9km west of Pinhão, along the north bank of the Douro (EN322-2). Hotel guests roam free.

Train to Pocinho   TRAIN TRIP
(round-trip €6.20; ◎trains depart 9:45, 11:45 daily) With the Linha do Tua still out if service, the most beautiful train trip in the area is this one-hour chug upriver along the most stunning section of the Tua line. Trains depart from the Pinhão train station twice per day.

Port Boat to Tua   BOAT TRIPS
(Aris Douro; ☎937 355 595; www.arisdouro.com; per person €20) One of the cheapest, easiest and sweetest thrills in the area demands that you simply lie back and cruise upriver into the heart of the Alta Douro aboard a traditional flat-bottomed port boat. Catch the boat just outside Vintage House (p396). Cruises last an hour.

Quinta Nova Wine Museum & Shop
                    WINE MUSEUM
(Aris Douro; www.quintanova.com; Largo da Estacão 14; tours & tastings €2.50; ◎tours 11am, 3pm & 5pm Apr-Oct) This collection of vintage winemaking gear offers a glimpse into early days viniculture and cooperage (bottling and labelling), but is only available by 25-minute tours offered three times per day. It's owned and operated by Quinta Nova, and you can taste the table and port wines here, too.

Sleeping & Eating

TOP CHOICE **Casa Cimeira** RURAL INN €€
(☑254 732 320; www.casacimeira
-douro.com; r €60; P ❋ ☲) Set in a 200-year-
old home at the top of the stunning hilltop town of Valença – its cobbled streets
wrapped with vineyards and olive trees
and alive with old country warmth – this is
the domain of the charming Nogueira family. Rooms are quaint and spotless, there's
a small pool and sun deck and family-style
dinners featuring their own house wine.

Casa de Casal de Loivos RURAL INN €€
(☑254 732 149; www.casadecasaldeloivos.com;
s/d €80/100; P ❋ ☲) The house has been
in this winemaking family for nearly 350
years. The halls are enlivened by museum-
level displays of folkloric dresses, and the
perch – high above the Alto Douro and 7km
from Pinhão, with vineyard-terraced hills
spread out in all directions – is spectacular.

Quinta Nova RURAL INN €€€
(☑254 732 430; www.quintanova.com; r
€125-165; ◷tours 11am & 4pm Tue-Sun) This
120-hectare vineyard offers first-rate lodging on a historic estate on the north side
of the Douro, 9km from Pinhão. Rooms are
sizeable and plush. Views are massive and
the atmosphere – in the rooms, by the pool,
throughout the grounds – is extremely romantic. The restaurant is fair at best, but
the wine is special. They also have several
walking trails.

Vintage House BOUTIQUE HOTEL €€€
(☑254 730 230; www.csvintagehouse.com; Lugar
da Ponte; r €117-188, ste €168-375; P ❋ ☎ ☲)
Occupying a string of 19th-century buildings right on the river, this luxurious sleep
is actually very modern once you get past
the distinctly English facade (a reminder of
the key role Brits played in the port trade).
This is where BB King stayed when he
rocked the Douro. All rooms have terraces
or balconies with river views.

Quinta San Antonio RURAL INN €€
(☑254 789 177; www.quintasanantonio.pt; r €85;
P ❋ ☲) Yet another stunning 40-hectare
property, this one owned by the former
winemaker for Sandeman. The drive up the
steep, rutted dirt road is exciting, the perch
high, the river and mountain views jaw
dropping, and the price fair. Dinner is to
be avoided, but the wines they pour... Don't
leave until you've sipped their 25-year-old
tawny. Get here via the road to Tabuaço.

Hotel Douro GUEST HOUSE €€
(☑254 732 404; www.hotel-douro.com; Rua Antonio Manuel Saraiva 39; r €50-55; ❋☎) This
cheery, well-kept guest house – the nicest of
its kind in Pinhão – has several river-facing
rooms, other large rooms facing a quiet rear
courtyard, and a miniterrace covered with
flowering vines.

TOP CHOICE **Restaurante Ponte Romana**
PORTUGUESE €€
(Rua Santo António 2; mains €8-12; ◷lunch &
dinner Mon-Sat) For nicely prepared traditional Portuguese food, Ponte Romana is
the place, with tasty fresh grilled sea bass,
tender and buttery grilled octopus, and
cabrito assado (roasted kid). From the train
station, turn left and follow the main road
for 600m; cross the stone bridge and you'll
see it on the right.

Veladouro PORTUGUESE €
(Rua Praia; mains €6-8; ◷lunch & dinner Mon-
Sat) Simple Portuguese food, such as wood-
grilled meats, is served inside this quaint
schist building or outside under a canopy of
vines. From the train station, turn left and
go along the main road for 150m, then left
again under a railway bridge, and right at
the river.

DOC PORTUGUESE €€€
(☑254 858 123; www.ruipaula.com; Casi da Folgo-
sa; mains €15-30; ◷lunch & dinner) DOC serves
haute cuisine to the well-to-do (check those
Ferraris and Astons in the parking lot) on
an outdoor deck over the Douro. The changing menu features creative dishes such as
monkfish with tomato jam, and lamb with
emulsified apple and sautéed mushrooms.
It's located 13km west of Pinhão, on the
south side of the river.

ⓘ Information

The summer-only **turismo** (☑254 731 932;
Largo do Estação; ◷10am-noon & 2-6pm Tue-
Sun) is open from May to September and housed
in the train station.

ⓘ Getting There & Away

Regional trains go to and from Peso da Régua
(€1.80, 25 minutes, five daily), where you can
catch one to Porto.

VILA NOVA DE FOZ CÔA
POP 2800

In the heart of the Douro's *terra quente* (hot
land), this once-remote, whitewashed town
has been on the map since the 1990s. That's
when researchers – during an environmental

SAN JOÃO DE PESQUEIRA

Driving between Pinhão and Foz Côa, you'll pass through this sprawling, almost suburban city, but if you follow the brown signs to the historic centre you'll discover an old theatre, a crumbling plaza and a historic church, all of which feed narrow stone lanes; a network from another era.

impact study for a proposed dam – stumbled across an astounding collection of Palaeolithic art. These mysterious rock engravings, which number in the thousands, blanket the nearby Rio Côa valley. Yet they were very nearly lost when the power company tried to insist on completing the dam. Archaeologists brought the petroglyphs to the world's attention, and the dam builders finally backed down when the whole valley was declared a Unesco World Heritage Site.

The *turismo* in Vila Nova de Foz Côa (p398) also offers free brochures for a **self-guided archaeological tour** of the region. Oh, and that stark James Bond–esque construct on the rim of the mountain outside Foz Côa is the **Museu do Côa**. Seemingly complete, but still shuttered at research time, it's anybody's guess when the doors will finally open. Locals aren't optimistic.

You may find the climate startlingly Mediterranean if you've just come from the mountains. Summers here are infernally hot, with temperatures regularly exceeding 45°C. But if you come in late March, you'll be treated to cooler climes, wildflowers and blooming almond trees.

Long-distance coaches stop at the bus station about 150m north of the *turismo* at Av Gago Coutinho. From here the town stretches eastward along Av Gago Coutinho, pedestrianised Rua Dr Juiz Moutinho de Andrade, Rua São Miguel and Rua Dr Júlio de Moura to the old town's centre, Praça do Município.

There is usually plenty of free parking along Av Gago Coutinho between the *turismo* and park headquarters.

◉ Sights & Activities

Parque Arqueológico do Vale do Côa
PETROGLYPHS

(www.igespar.pt; in Foz Côa: Av Gago Coutinho 19 A; per person €8.50; ☉9am-12.30pm & 2-5.30pm Tue-Sun) Most visitors to Vila Nova de Foz Côa come for one reason: to see its world-famous gallery of rock art. Although the park is currently an active research zone, the

three sites are open to the public: **Canada do Inferno** from the **park office** (☏279 768 260; ☉tours depart 9-10:30am) in Vila Nova de Foz Côa; **Ribeira de Piscos** from the **Muxagata visitor centre** (☏279 764 298; ☉9.30am-3pm Tue-Sun) on the western side of the valley; and **Penascosa** from the **Castelo Melhor visitor centre** (☏279 713 344; ☉1:30-430pm Tue-Sun) on the eastern side, which also offers night tours. While Castelo Melhor has some of the most significant etchings, Canada do Inferno – which sits by the half-constructed dam – is the ideal place to understand just how close these aeons-old drawings came to disappearing.

Because the entire valley is a working archaeological site, all visitors must enter with a guided tour. Visitors gather at the various visitor centres, where they're taken, eight at a time, in the park's own 4WDs, for a guided tour of one of the sites (1½ hours at Canada do Inferno and Penascosa; two hours at Ribeira de Piscos). Visitors with mountain bikes may go on guided bike tours (bring your own bike) in similar-sized groups. The price in either case is €8.50 per person.

Visitor numbers are strictly regulated, so from July to September book a tour well in advance or you may miss out. You must book at least a few weeks ahead for bicycle trips at any time. You can make bookings through the park office.

Old Town
WALKING

The sleepy old quarter makes for a pleasant stroll in the early evening. Highlights are the Praça do Município, with its impressive granite *pelourinho,* and the elaborately carved portal of the Manueline-style parish church. Just east off the square is the tiny Capela de Santa Quitéria, once the town's synagogue.

Museu da Casa Grande
MUSEUM

(www.acdr-freixo.pt; admission €1.50; ☉9am-noon & 2-6pm Tue-Sun) Archaeological finds from the Stone Age to the 18th century have been uncovered in the region around Freixo de

SAN SALVADOR DEL MUNDO

Here's another stunning diversion between Pinhao and Foz Côa. Follow the signs to a short series of stone turnouts with special hill, vineyard and river views. Some have stone slab tables and benches surrounded by wildflowers, serenaded by birdsong, and demand a picnic. After lunch continue to the top of the road and stroll to the chapel on the pinnacle. Spectacular.

Numão, 12km west of Vila Nova de Foz Côa. A good little display can be viewed in this baroque town house with Roman foundations. Some English and French are spoken. Guided tours are available by arrangement with the museum.

Capula San Gabriel   CHAPEL
(Hwy N332) About 14km from Foz Côa, on the way to Castelo Milhor, an antiquated chapel sits on the rim of a ridge with commanding views of both the Douro and Foz river valleys from an altitude of 1500m. The chapel is almost always closed, but you're here for the view. There are plenty of picnic tables on the ledge below the chapel.

🛏 Sleeping & Eating

Pousada da Juventude   HOSTEL €
(✆279 768 190; www.pousadasjuventude.pt; Caminho Vicinal Curruteles 5; dm €12, r €28-30; 🅿) This fairly new hostel in a modern, pink-brick building is well worth the 800m-walk north from the town centre (1.4km by road). Its basic but handsome doubles have views over a rugged valley; four-bed dorms are clean and well maintained. Amenities include bar, open kitchen, laundry, cafeteria, games room and large patio with sweeping views.

Residencial Marina   GUEST HOUSE €
(✆279 762 112, 968 407 642; Av Gago Coutinho 4; s/d €20/30) Another good budget choice, this relatively bright and well-kept guest house is in the old town centre. Call the mobile if it looks like nobody's home.

Albergaria Vale do Côa   HOTEL €
(✆279 760 010; www.albergariavaledocoa.net; Av Cidade Nova 1A; s/d €45/55; 🅿❄) This modern hotel opposite the tourist office offers comfortable, air-conditioned rooms with clean-swept wooden floors. Most rooms have verandas with views of the hilly countryside.

Cafenteria Ritz   PORTUGUESE €
(Rua de São Miguel 14; mains €5-7; ⊙breakfast, lunch & dinner Mon-Sat) Popular among the locals for locally styled roast-meat (and only roast meat) dishes. Ritz stays open until midnight.

António & Julia   GOURMET FOOD €
(Rua de São Miguel 50; ⊙breakfast & lunch Mon-Sat) Top-quality local hams, sausages, cheese and honey are available for picnics in this charming shop on the São Miguel strip.

Casa Regional Guida   GOURMET FOOD €
(Rua Moutinho de Andreade 10; ⊙breakfast & lunch Mon-Sat) Another quirky shop crammed with artisan handicrafts and, more importantly, artisan food. You can pack a fine lunch from its abundant selection of almonds, olives, sausages, prosciutto and cheese.

Restaurante A Marisqueira PORTUGUESE €€
(Rua de São Miguel 35; mains €7-25; ⊙lunch & dinner Mon-Sat) Located on a pleasant pedestrian street in the old town, this cheery place serves good Portuguese meat dishes and just enough *mariscos* (shellfish) to justify the name in a small but bright contemporary dining room.

☆ Entertainment

Although there isn't a lot going on in Foz Côa, the **Centro Cultural** (www.fozcoactiva. pt; Av Cidade Nova 2) hosts concerts, temporary art exhibitions and film screenings throughout the year. It's in the same building as the *turismo*.

ⓘ Information

Biblioteca Municipal de Vila Nova de Foz Côa (✆279 760 300; Av Cidade Nova 2; ⊙9am-noon & 2-5.30pm Mon-Fri) Free internet access in the same building as the *turismo*.

Municipal Turismo (www.cm-fozcoa.pt; Av Cidade Nova 2; ⊙9am-12.30pm & 2-5.30pm) Opposite Albergaria Foz Côa.

ⓘ Getting There & Away

One daily bus each connects Vila Nova de Foz Côa with Bragança (€7.50, 1¾ hours) and Miranda do Douro (€5.70, 2½ hours). Three buses per day travel via Trancoso (€4.40) from Viseu (€9.20, two hours).

Five daily trains run to Pocinho, at the end of the Douro valley line, from Porto (€10.65, 3½ hours) and Peso da Régua (€6) through Pinhão (€3.20). A taxi between Pocinho and Vila Nova de Foz Côa costs about €6 to €8, and there are two daily buses (€2 to €4.40, 20 minutes).

 Getting Around

There are no direct buses to Muxagata or Quinta da Ervamoira. However, a twice-daily bus passes the outskirts of Castelo Melhor (€1.90, 15 minutes); and from here it's an easy walk to the visitor centre. Alternatively, there is a taxi stand on the square in front of the parks office, and park guides often help organise carpools, too.

The Minho

Best Places to Stay

» Margarida da Praça (p421)

» Residencial Portas do Sol (p425)

» Convento dos Capuchos (p427)

» Pacos de Gloria (p434)

» Hotel de Peneda (p438)

Best Places to Eat

» Churrasqueira da Sé (p406)

» Flor de Tangerina (p415)

» Taberna do Valentim (p422)

» Restaurante Santos (p422)

» Restaurante Fortaleza (p425)

Why Go?

The Minho delivers world-class natural beauty with a knowing smile. Here are lush river valleys, sparkling beaches and granite peaks patrolled by locals – who, whether they are charging 2m waves along the Costa Verde or shepherding their flock into high mountain meadows, seem particularly in tune with their homeland. This is, after all, the birthplace of the Portuguese kingdom, and it would be hard to find better-preserved landmarks than those uplit and on display in the Minho's gorgeous old cities. Then there's the bold, sharp and fruity *vinho verde* to consider. This young wine is fashioned from the fruit of miles of vineyards that wind along rivers, over foothills and into Minho mountain villages. The crops are eventually crushed and bottled in community *adegas* (wineries), giving each destination its own flavour. Of course, if you sip enough along the way, they may all blend into one delicious memory.

When to Go

Braga

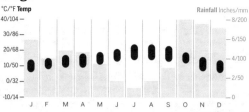

May (first week) Festa das Cruzes turns Barcelos into a fairground

June 23 & 24 Braga's Festas de São João bursts with pagan energy and fireworks

September (first week) Festas de Senhora, Peneda, features candlelit processions and a gushing waterfall

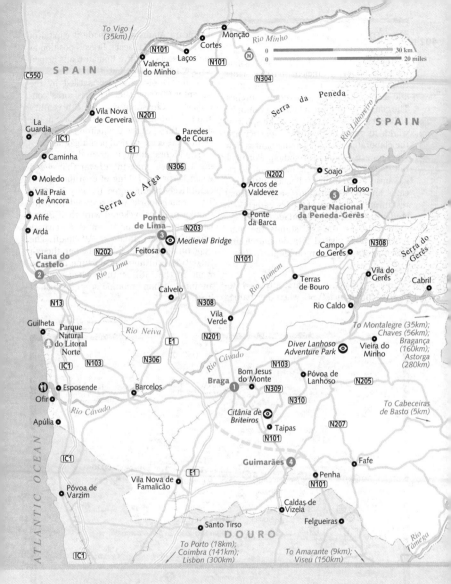

Minho Highlights

① Visit historic monuments, followed by dinner at a top restaurant in **Braga** (p402)

② Stroll the atmospheric streets of **Viana do Castelo** (p417), then catch sunset on the beach

③ Lounge at a cafe overlooking the medieval bridge and lush countryside beyond in **Ponte de Lima** (p428)

④ Delve into medieval history inside the striking old quarter of **Guimarães** (p412)

⑤ Hike the boulder-strewn peaks and gorse-clad moorlands of the **Parque Nacional da Peneda-Gerês** (p435)

Braga

POP 133,000 / ELEV 200M

Portugal's third-largest city is an elegant town laced with ancient narrow lanes closed to vehicles and strewn with plazas and a splendid array of baroque churches. The constant chiming of bells is a reminder of Braga's age-old devotion to the spiritual world. Its religious festivals – particularly the elaborately staged Semana Santa (Holy Week) – are famous throughout Portugal. But don't come expecting piety alone: Braga's upscale old centre is packed with lively cafes and trim boutiques, some excellent restaurants and low-key bars catering to students from the Universidade do Minho.

Just outside the city stands the magnificent, much-visited hillside church and sanctuary of Bom Jesus do Monte (p408).

History

Founded by Celts, Braga first attracted Roman attention in 250 BC, when they named it Bracara Augusta and made it capital of their province Gallaecia. Braga's position at the intersection of five Roman roads helped it grow fat on trade, but it fell to the Suevi around AD 410, and was sacked by the Visigoths 60 years later. The Visigoths' conversion to Christianity in the 6th century and the founding of an archbishopric in the next century put the town atop the Iberian Peninsula's ecclesiastical pecking order.

The Moors moved in around 715, sparking a long-running tug of war that ended when Fernando I, king of Castilla y León, definitively reconquered the city in 1040. The archbishopric was restored in 1070, though prelates bickered with their Spanish counterparts for the next 500 years over who was Primate of All Spain. The pope finally ruled in Braga's favour, though the city's resulting good fortune began to wane in the 18th century, when a newly anointed Lisbon archdiocese stole much of its thunder.

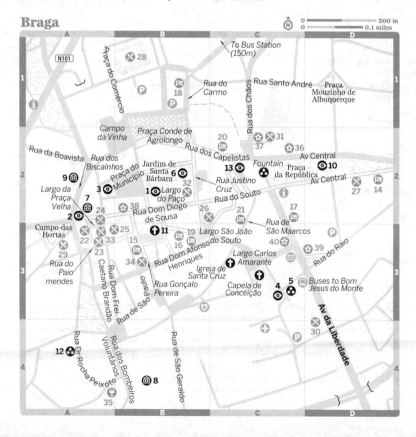

Braga

Not surprisingly, it was from conservative Braga that António de Oliveira Salazar, with his unique blend of Catholicism and fascism, gave the speech that launched his 1926 coup, introducing Portugal to half a century of dictatorship.

◉ Sights

Sé   CATHEDRAL
(www.se-braga.pt; Rua Dom Paio Mendes; ⊙8.30am-6.30pm) Braga's extraordinary cathedral, the oldest in Portugal, was begun when the archdiocese was restored in 1070 (probably on the ruins of a mosque) and completed in the following century. It's a rambling complex made up of differing styles, and architectural buffs could spend half a day happily distinguishing the Romanesque bones from Manueline musculature and baroque frippery. The original Romanesque style is the most interesting and survives in the cathedral's overall shape, the southern entrance and the marvellous west portal, which is carved with scenes from the medieval legend of Reynard the

Fox (now sheltered inside a Gothic porch). The most appealing external features are the filigree Manueline towers and roof – an early work by João de Castilho, who went on to build Lisbon's Mosteiro dos Jerónimos.

You can enter the cathedral through the west portal or via a courtyard and cloister that's lined with Gothic chapels on the north side. The church itself features a fine Manueline chapel, a tall chapel with *azulejos* (hand-painted tiles) telling the story of Braga's first bishop, and fantastic twin baroque organs held up by formidable satyrs and mermen.

Connected to the church is the **Tesouro** (Treasury; adult/child €3/2; ⊙9am-12.30pm & 2-6.30pm), housing a goldmine of ecclesiastical booty, including the lovely *Nossa Senhora do Leite* of the Virgin suckling Christ, attributed to 16th-century French sculptor Nicolas Chanterène. Other highlights are the iron cross that was used in 1500 to celebrate the very first Mass in Brazil, and a flowery pair of high-heeled (10cm) shoes made for a particularly diminutive archbishop.

Braga

To visit the choir (adult/child €2/1), visitors must purchase a separate ticket and join a guided tour (some guides speak English), which gives an up-close look at the mesmerising organs and gilded choir stalls. Visitors will then be led downstairs and into the cathedral's showpiece **Capela dos Reis** (Kings' Chapel), home to the tombs of Henri of Burgundy and Dona Teresa, parents of the first king of Portugal, Afonso Henriques. You'll also visit the *azulejo*-covered **Capela de São Geraldo** (dating from the 12th century but reworked over the years) and the 14th-century **Capela da Glória**, whose interior was painted in unrepentantly Moorish geometric motifs in the 16th century.

Museu Dom Diogo de Sousa
MUSEUM
(http://mdds.imc-ip.pt; Rua dos Bombeiros Voluntários; admission €3, 10am-2pm Sun free; ⊙10am-5.30pm Tue-Sun) The relatively new archaeological museum houses a nicely displayed collection of fragments from Braga's earliest days. The four rooms feature pieces from Palaeolithic times (arrowheads, funerary objects and ceramics) through the days of Roman rule (when Braga was known as Bracara Augusta) and on up to the period dominated by the Suevi-Visigoth kingdom (5th through 7th centuries). The most fascinating pieces are the huge *miliários* (milestones), carved with Latin inscriptions, that marked the Roman roads. There is also a section of mosaic flooring recovered from a local site, which dates from the 1st century AD.

Termas Romanas do Alto Cidade
ROMAN RUINS
(Roman Baths; Rua Dr Rocha Peixoto; adult/student €1.70/free; ⊙9am-12.30pm & 2-5.30pm Tue-Fri, 11am-5pm Sat & Sun) A short walk from the archaeological museum are these ruins of an extensive bathing complex – with an attached theatre – dating from the 2nd century AD, and probably abandoned in the 5th century. The helpful receptionist speaks English and will show you a quick seven-minute introductory video in English or Portuguese.

Fonte do Idolo
ROMAN RUINS
(Idol Spring; Rua do Raio; adult/student €1.70/free; ⊙9am-12.30pm & 2-5.30pm Wed-Fri, 11am-5pm Sat & Sun) Another Roman ruin recently opened to the public, this spring is set underneath a mod lobby. An essential community water source, it was carved into a fountain during pre-Roman times by Celicus Fronto, an immigrant from the city-state of Arcobriga. One carving is of a toga-clad pilgrim thought to be holding the horn of plenty. There's an introductory video here too.

Antigo Paço Episcopal & Around
NOTABLE BUILDINGS
(Archbishop's Palace; ⊙9am-12.30pm & 2-7.30pm Mon-Fri) Facing the cathedral is the severe Antigo Paço Episcopal. Begun in the 14th century and enlarged in the 17th and 18th centuries, it's now home to university offices and the municipal library. A heavily carved, painted and gilded ceiling looks down on the library's computer room; this and the *azulejos* lining the main stairway are well worth a peek.

Outside the spiky-topped, medieval north wing is the 17th-century square known as Jardim de Santa Bárbara, with narrow paths picking their way through a sea of flowers and topiary. On sunny days, the adjacent pedestrian-only streets fill with buskers and cafe tables.

At the western end of neighbouring Praça do Município, Braga's câmara municipal (town hall) sports one of Portugal's finest baroque facades, designed by André Soares da Silva. A more extroverted Soares work is the Casa do Raio (Casa do Mexicano; Rua do Raio), its rococo face covered in *azulejos*. They're both closed to the public, but still worth seeing from the outside.

Arco da Porta Nova
LANDMARK
West of the old centre on Rua Dom Diogo de Sousa, this diminutive but elegant 18th-century 'arch of the new gate' once served as the city's main entrance. It displays the ostentatious coat of arms of the archbishop who commissioned it, Dom José de Bragança.

Museu dos Biscaínhos
MUSEUM
(Rua dos Biscaínhos; admission €2, Sun morning free; ⊙10am-12.15pm & 2-5.30pm Tue-Sun) An 18th-century aristocrat's palace is now home to the enthusiastic municipal museum, with a nice collection of Roman relics and 17th- to 19th-century pottery and furnishings. The palace itself is the reason to come, with its polychrome, chestnut-panelled ceilings and 18th-century *azulejos* depicting hunting scenes. The ground floor is paved with deeply ribbed flagstones on which carriages would have once rattled through to the stables.

DON'T MISS

EASTER IN BRAGA

Braga hosts the most elaborate Easter celebrations in Portugal. It kicks off with **Semana Santa** (Holy Week), when Gregorian chants are piped throughout the city centre and makeshift candlelit altars light the streets at night. The action heats up during Holy Thursday's **Procissão do Senhor Ecce Homo**, when barefoot, hooded penitents – members of private Catholic brotherhoods (think Opus Dei) – march through the streets spinning their eerie rattles. The **Good Friday Mass** in the cathedral is a remarkable, elaborately staged drama with silk canopies, dirgelike hymns, dozens of priests and a weeping congregation. On Saturday evening, the **Easter Vigil Mass** begins dourly, the entire cathedral in shadow, only to explode in lights and jubilation. Finally, on Sunday, the people of Braga blanket their thresholds with flowers, inviting passing priests to enter and give their home a blessing.

Praça da República PLAZA
The cafes and restaurants on this broad plaza are a pleasant place to start or finish your day. An especially mellow atmosphere descends in the evening, when coloured lights spring up and people of all ages congregate to enjoy the night air.

The square-shaped, crenulated tower behind the cafes is the walled-up **Torre de Menagem** (Castle Keep; Largo Terreiro do Castelo), which is all that survives of a fortified medieval palace.

FREE **Museu do Imagem** MUSEUM
(Campo das Hortas 35-37; ⌚11am-7pm Wed-Fri, 2:30-6:30pm Sat & Sun) A minimalist, ancient and beautiful stone relic, outfitted tastefully with steel and wood stairs, shows off impeccably lit, international photography exhibits on three floors.

Festivals & Events

Semana Santa RELIGIOUS
Elaborate Easter celebrations.

Festa de São João CULTURAL
A pre-Christian solstice bash dressed up to look like holy days, this festival still bursts with pagan energy. Held on 23 and 24 June, it features medieval folk plays, processions, dancing, bonfires, fireworks – and thousands of little pots of basil. Basil is the symbol of São João (John the Baptist), and traditionally people write poems to loved ones and then conceal them in their pots. Locals also bust out squeaky plastic hammers and whack each other mercilessly.

Sleeping

Reservations are essential during Semana Santa.

TOP CHOICE **Casa Santa Zita** GUEST HOUSE €
(☎253 618 331; Rua São João 20; s €25-30, d €40) This impeccably kept pilgrim's lodge (look for the small tile reading 'Sta Zita') is open to all and has an air of palpable serenity. The sweet sisters offer bright, spotless rooms, nice touches such as ironed cotton sheets, and breakfast in a stone arched dining room. The only drawback is a midnight curfew. Very warmly recommended.

Albergaria da Sé GUEST HOUSE €€
(☎253 214 502; www.albergaria-da-se.com.pt; Rua Gonçalo Pereira 39; s/d €45/55; P ❄) As the name promises, this simple, friendly, three-storey guest house is around the corner from the cathedral. Its dark-wood floors, large and airy rooms, and scattering of *azulejos* make it one of the best accommodation choices in Braga. The bright breakfast room and patio are particularly pleasant.

Pousada da Juventude HOSTEL €
(☎253 616 163; www.pousadasjuventude.pt; Rua de Santa Margarida 6; dorm/r €10/25; P @ ᯤ) Braga's rather institutional but lively youth hostel (with pool table), a 700m walk from the *turismo* (tourist office), has frill-free, eight-bed dorms with high ceilings and huge windows. Reception is open from 8am to noon and 6pm to midnight.

Residencial dos Terceiros GUEST HOUSE €
(☎253 270 466; www.terceiros.com; Rua dos Capelistas 85; r €25-45; ᯤ) On a quiet pedestrian street near Praça da República, this guest house has great deals on recently repainted and updated rooms overlooking a small square. Most rooms have one full and twin bed each, and can sleep up to three people.

Residencial Avenida
GUEST HOUSE €

(☎253 609 020; www.residencialavenida.net; 2nd fl, Av da Liberdade 738; r €23-52; ❄☻) Cobbled together from a few big apartments in an art-deco building, this friendly, family-run place offers decent, simply furnished accommodation. Rooms vary greatly in size and light; some have balconies.

Residencial São Marcos
GUEST HOUSE €

(☎253 277 177; Rua de São Marcos 80; r €25-75; ❄) This welcoming place in a fine old town house has large, comfortable rooms with high ceilings and parquet floors. The marble staircase lends a touch of grandeur.

Albergaria Senhora-a-Branca
GUEST HOUSE €

(☎253 269 938; www.albergariasrabranca.pt; Largo da Senhora-a-Branca 58; r €40-60; ❄☻) Removed from the city centre, this converted town house has well-kept rooms (some on the small side), all with bathroom and double-glazed windows. It's above a pastry shop (bonus), overlooking a busy little square.

Hotel-Residencial Dona Sofia
HOTEL €€

(☎253 263 160; www.hoteldonasofia.com; Largo São João do Souto 131; r45-75; ❄☻) On a pretty, central square, Dona Sofia has doable, if a bit dated, carpeted rooms of varying sizes. Aim for one of the airy rooms with nice French windows overlooking the square.

Hotel Ibis
HOTEL €€

(☎253 204 800; www.ibishotel.com; Rua do Carmo 38; €45-65; ❄@☻) The rooms in this smart, modern midranger all have wood floors, floating desks, bath-tubs and queen beds. They aren't huge, but have all the mod cons, and those from the upper reaches have panoramic views of surrounding monuments. Walk-in prices dip as low as €45, and at that price, it's a steal.

Albergaria Bracara Augusta
BOUTIQUE HOTEL €€

(☎253 206 260; www.bracaraaugusta.com; Av Central 134; r €130-160; ❄@☻) This stylish, grand town house offers bright, modern rooms with parquet floors and French doors opening onto decorative balconies. Its restaurant has an excellent breakfast buffet, with open-air dining by a gurgling fountain in back. Service could be better.

✖ Eating

Some of Braga's best restaurants lie along a narrow alley (Largo da Praça Velha) just west of the cathedral.

Churrasqueira da Sé
GRILL HOUSE €

(Rua do Paio Mendes 25; mains €4; ☻lunch & dinner) If for some reason you've skipped breakfast and arrived in Braga after all the other restaurants have closed for their afternoon break, head to this Brazilian-style *churrasqueira* (grill restaurant). Get half a bird (or ribs) grilled to perfection and smothered in spicy barbecue sauce, with fries made to order. Then find a park bench, channel your inner caveman (or woman), and enjoy the best lunch in Braga. Of course, if you're eating at a traditional hour, grab a table in the tiled dining room and feel free to use cutlery.

Livraria Café
CAFE €

(www.centesima.com; Av Central 118; mains €4; ☻breakfast & lunch Mon-Sat) Tucked inside Centésima Página, an absolutely splendid bookshop with foreign-language titles, this charming cafe serves a rotating selection of tasty quiches along with salads and desserts, and has outdoor tables in the pleasantly rustic garden.

Cozinha da Sé
PORTUGUESE €€

(☎253 277 343; www.cozinhadase.com; Rua Dom Frei Caetano Brandão 95; mains €4-9; ☻lunch & dinner Tue-Sun) Contemporary artwork hangs from the exposed stone walls at this intimate, cheery and upscale Braga dining room. Sé serves traditional, high-quality dishes (including one vegetarian selection), with flavourful standouts such as baked *bacalhau* (dried salt-cod) and *açorda de marisco* (seafood stew in a bread bowl).

Copa 1/2
TAPAS €€

(☎253 265 475; Rua Dom Frei Cateano Brandão 118; dishes €7-15; ☻dinner daily, lunch Fri & Sat) The hip new kid at research time, this swanky, gourmet tapas bar with a cute upstairs stone dining room gets packed with local moneyed types.

Frigideiras do Cantinho
CAFE €

(Largo São João do Souto 1; mains €4-7; ☻breakfast, lunch & dinner) Set on a sweet, quiet plaza, with pleasant indoor and outdoor seating, this humble cafe is favoured by loyal locals for great coffee, inexpensive fish and meat plates, omelettes, freshly squeezed orange juice and a superb selection of pastries.

O Alexandre
PORTUGUESE €€

(☎253 220 185; Campo das Hortas; mains €12-14; ☻lunch & dinner) A handsomely appointed dining room sets the stage for the top-notch cuisine at one of Braga's best Portuguese restaurants. Grilled meats, *bacalhau com nata* (baked codfish) and an excellent *cabrito assado* (roasted kid) are particularly recommended.

Salão de Chá Lusitana TEAROOM €
(Rua Justino Cruz 119; mains €4-6; ⊘breakfast, lunch & dinner) Next to sweet-smelling Jardim de Santa Bárbara, this sunny, well-preserved art-deco tearoom is another local favourite with all, but especially ladies who lunch.

Anjo Verde VEGETARIAN €
(www.anjoverde.com; Largo da Praça Velha 21; mains €6-9; ⊘lunch & dinner Mon-Sat; 🍴) Braga's vegetarian offering serves up generous, elegantly presented plates in a lovely, airy dining room. Vegetarian lasagne, risotto and vegetable tarts are among the choices here. Mains can be bland, but that spiced chocolate tart is a superstar.

Taberna do Felix FRENCH-PORTUGUESE €
(🕿253 617 701; Largo da Praça Velha 19; dishes €7-10; ⊘dinner Mon-Sat) Situated near the Arco da Porta Nova, this attractive country-style tavern prepares unusual Franco-Portuguese dishes; try the tapas or delicious *pataiscas* (fish fritters).

Taperia Palatu PORTUGUESE €€
(🕿253 279 772; Rua Dom Afonso Henriques 35; mains €8-12; ⊘lunch & dinner Mon-Sat) A Spanish-Portuguese couple serves up delectable Spanish tapas and classic Portuguese dishes in a pleasantly minimalist dining room or an airy courtyard in front.

The boisterous mercado municipal (municipal market; Praça do Comércio; ⊘8am-3pm Mon-Fri, 6am-1pm Sat) buzzes on weekdays and Saturday mornings, and is ideal for self-caterers. You can also hit Pingo Doce supermarkets in the rapidly ageing Bragashopping centre (⊘10am-11pm) and on Av da Liberdade (⊘9am to 9pm), or one of several fruit-and-vegetable shops along Rua de São Marcos.

🍷 Drinking

Colinatrum Café CAFE
(www.colinatrum.com; Rua dos Bombeiros Voluntários; ⊘8am-2am; 🖎) On a hill overlooking the countryside, this sleek glass-and-wood cafe is a fine meeting spot for a coffee or two, sunset cocktails or late-night flirtations. From the sleek, muslin-shaded outdoor terrace, you'll have a splendid view

of Bom Jesus do Monte. At 10pm the place turns into a rather happening lounge that breezes until 2am.

☆ Entertainment

Espaço Cultural ARTS CENTRE
TOP CHOICE (www.myspace.com/ruadoschaos14; Rua dos Chãos 14; ⊘9pm-2am) Just north of the Praça da República, this youthful arts space hosts exhibitions, concerts, film screenings and other cultural fare. There's also a shop selling fair-trade items and a cafe where you can linger over a bite or a drink.

Meu Café LIVE MUSIC
(Rua Dom Diogo de Sousa 97) An otherwise ordinary stone-wall cafe becomes a singalong fado bar at 9pm on Friday and Saturday nights when a passionate axeman sings his Iberian blues.

Teatro Circo de Braga THEATRE
(www.teatrocirco.com; Av da Liberdade 697) One of the most dazzling theatres in the country reopened in late 2006 following a lengthy restoration. Inside the grand fin de siècle building you can catch concerts, theatre and dance, with offerings ranging from the staid to the truly avant-garde.

Bragashopping Cinema CINEMA
(www.cinemascinemax/bragaini; Av Central) The rundown mall has seen better days, but this cinema is the only game in town. It shows the usual first-run Hollywood fare.

Sporting Clube de Braga SPORTS
(www.scbraga.pt; Av da Liberdade; ⊘10am-1pm & 2.30-7pm Mon-Fri, 10am-1pm Sat) Buy your tickets here at the team shop in the Centro Comercial Galeries do Bingo, then cheer on Braga's football team in the 30,000-seat Estádio Municipal de Braga, which was built to host the 2004 UEFA European Football Championships (Euro 2004). It's 2km north of the centre off the N101.

ℹ️ Information

Biblioteca Lúcio Craveiro da Silva (www.blcs.pt; Rua de São Paulo 1; ⊘9am-6pm Mon-Sat) Free wi-fi and internet access on public computers.

Hospital de São Marcos (🕿253 209 000; Rua 25 Abril) A block west of Av da Liberdade.

Police station (🕿253 200 420; Rua dos Falcões)

Post office (Rua Gonçalo Sampaio; ⊘8.30am-6pm Mon-Fri, 9am-12.30pm Sat) Just off Av da Liberdade.

Turismo (www.cm-braga.pt; Praça da República; ◎9am-7pm Mon-Fri, to 12.30pm & 2-5.30pm Sat & Sun Jun-Sep, to 6.30pm Mon-Fri, to 5.30pm Sat Oct-May) Braga's helpful tourist office is in an art-deco-style building facing the fountain.

❶ Getting There & Around

Bus

Braga has a centralised bus station that serves as a major regional hub.

Empresa Hoteleira do Gerês (✆253 262 033) Serves Campo do Gerês (€4, 1½ hours) about hourly during the week and six times on Saturday and Sunday.

Rede Expressos (www.rede-expressos.pt) Has up to 12 daily buses to Lisbon (€18.50, 4½ hours).

Transdev Norte/Arriva (✆253 209 401) Has at least eight buses per day to Viana do Castelo (€4, 1½ hours), Barcelos (€2.30, one hour), Guimarães (€2.75, 50 minutes) and Porto (€4.50, one hour), plus four per day to Campo do Gerês (€3.35, 1½ hours). Service drops by half at weekends.

Car & Motorcycle

The A3-IP1 motorway makes Braga an easy day trip from Porto. The N101 from Braga to Guimarães is congested and poorly marked.

Because of one-way and pedestrian-only streets, driving in central Braga is difficult, and parking is maddening. There is a large, fee-charging lot under Praça da República. You might also try side streets east of Av da Liberdade.

AVIC (✆253 203 910; www.avic.pt; Rua Gabriel Pereira de Castro 28; ◎9am-12.30pm & 2.30-6.30pm Mon-Fri) An efficient agency for several car-rental companies, with prices starting at €35 per day.

Train

Braga is at the end of a branch line from Nine and also within Porto's *suburbano* network, which means commuter trains travel every hour or so from Porto (€2.20, about one hour); don't waste €18.50 on an Alfa Pendular (AP) train.

Useful AP links include Coimbra (€19, 2¼ hours, five to seven daily) and Lisbon (€31, four hours, two to four daily).

Around Braga

BOM JESUS DO MONTE

The goal of legions of penitent pilgrims every year, Bom Jesus do Monte is one of Portugal's most recognisable icons. A rather windswept and glamorous pilgrimage site,

lying 5km east of central Braga, this sober neoclassical church stands atop a forested hill that offers grand sunset views across the city. However, most people don't come simply for the church or even the view. They come to see the extraordinary baroque staircase, Escadaria do Bom Jesus.

The photogenic climb is made up of tiered staircases, dating from different decades of the 18th century. The lowest is lined with chapels representing the Stations of the Cross. **Escadaria dos Cinco Sentidos** (Stairway of the Five Senses) features allegorical fountains with water gurgling from ears, eyes, nose and mouth of different statues. Highest is **Escadaria das Três Virtudes** (Stairway of the Three Virtues), with chapels and fountains representing Faith, Hope and Charity.

The area around the church has become something of a resort, with sumptuous hotels, tennis courts and flower gardens. It's choked with tourists on summer weekends. They come to explore the church, cobblestone roads and trails on foot, horseback (€5 per 15 minutes) or bicycle. You can find the horse-riding salesmen on the main Bom Jesus plaza – you can't miss them. They also gather at Largo Mae de Agua.

🛏 Sleeping

Reservations are recommended in summer.

Hotel Grande BOUTIQUE HOTEL €
(✆253 281 222; www.grandehotel.com.pt; Largo Mãe da Água, Bom Jesus, Tenões; d €52; P❄☎) This sleek hotel, with its minimalist exterior and nouveau Renaissance interior, is 1km from the church (at the fork before reaching Bom Jesus, veer left). Its spacious doubles are by far the best choice in the area.

Hotel do Elevador BOUTIQUE HOTEL €€
(✆253 603 400; www.hoteisbomjesus.pt; Bom Jesus do Monte; d €99; P❄@☎) Set in an antiquated villa, rooms here have romantic old-world touches and magical views. The **restaurant** (mains €10 to €16) has a stunning perch too.

Hotel do Templo BOUTIQUE HOTEL €€
(✆253 603 610; www.hoteisbomjesus.pt; Bom Jesus do Monte; d €99; P❄☎☎) One of four Bom Jesus hotels owned by the same company, this is the only one with wi-fi and a swimming pool. It rents mountain bikes, upon which you can explore the network of wooded dirt and cobble paths, and rooms

are modern, but, and this is nitpicking, Hotel do Elevador has better views.

✗ Eating

Aside from the hotel restaurants, eating options are scarce.

Restaurante Central do Bom Jesus
PORTUGUESE €€

(Largo Mãe da Água; mains €9-14; ☺lunch & dinner Tue-Sun) With stone walls, a slender outdoor patio, charming staff and an array of perfectly prepared chicken, fish and roast-meat dishes, this is the best choice on the mountain. It's near the Hotel Grande, 1km uphill from the church.

Restaurante Casavelha
PORTUGUESE €€

(Largo Mãe da Água; mains €8-14; ☺lunch & dinner Tue-Sun) This traditional restaurant next to Hotel Grande offers good Portuguese dishes, with live music on Friday and Saturday nights.

ⓘ Getting There & Away

City bus 2 runs from Braga's Av da Liberdade to the bottom of the Bom Jesus steps (€1.45, 20 minutes) – the end of the line – every half-hour all day (hourly on Sunday). From here you can hoof it up the steps or hop aboard the newly restored **ascensor** (funicular; ☑253 281 222; Largo Mãe da Água; one-way €1.10; ☺8am-8pm), which whisks visitors up to the top every half-hour. Alternatively, a taxi from central Braga to the top of the steps costs €7 to €10.

Barcelos

POP 21,000 / ELEV 100M

The Minho is famous for its sprawling outdoor markets, but the largest, oldest and most celebrated is the Feira de Barcelos, held every Thursday in this ancient town on the banks of the Rio Cávado. Tour buses arrive by the dozen, spilling their contents into the already brimming marketplace. Even if you don't come on a Thursday, you'll find that Barcelos has a pleasant medieval core, with old stone towers perched over the river. It also harbours an ancient but still-thriving pottery tradition.

◉ Sights & Activities

Feira de Barcelos
MARKET

(Campo da República; ☺7am-6pm Thu) You'll need at least a couple of hours to see all the goods in this sprawling market. Despite attracting travellers, the market retains its rural soul. Villagers hawk everything from scrawny chickens to hand-embroidered linen, and Roma women bellow for business in the clothes section. Snack on sausages and homemade bread as you wander among the brass cowbells, hand-woven baskets and carved ox yokes.

Pottery is what most outsiders come to see, especially the yellow-dotted *louça de Barcelos* ware and the gaudy figurines à la Rosa Ramalho, a local potter known as the Grandma Moses of Portuguese pottery, whose work put Barcelos on the map in the 1950s. The trademark Barcelos cockerel motif is everywhere.

FREE Museu Arqueológico & Around
MUSEUM

(☺9am-12.30pm & 3-5pm) On a ledge above Barcelos' 14th-century bridge over the Rio Cávado are the roofless ruins of the former palace of the counts of Barcelos and dukes of Bragança. Practically obliterated by the 1755 earthquake, the palace ruins now serve as an alfresco archaeological museum.

Among the mysterious phallic stones, Roman columns and medieval caskets, you'll find a 14th-century stone cross, the **Crucifix O Senhor do Galo**, depicting the gentleman of the cockerel story and said to have been commissioned by the lucky pilgrim himself. Near the entrance is a late-Gothic *pelourinho* (stone pillory) topped by a granite lantern.

ROOSTER RESCUE

His colourful crest adorns a thousand souvenir stalls – and you will notice the great and brilliant cocks sprinkled along the Barcelos streets like bigger-than-life chess pieces – but just how and why did the proud Portuguese cockerel become a national icon? It seems that a humble pilgrim, plodding his way to Santiago de Compostela in the 16th (some say 14th) century, stopped to rest in Barcelos, only to find himself wrongfully accused of theft and then swiftly condemned to be hanged. The outraged pilgrim told the judge that the roast on the judge's dinner table would affirm the pilgrim's innocence. As it would happen, just as the judge was about to tuck in, the cooked cock commenced to crow. The pilgrim, needless to say, was set free.

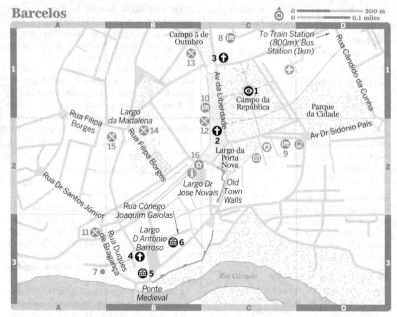

Eastward along the bluffs is a remnant of the medieval **town walls**, and west of here a slender, leafy **riverside park** blooms with plenty of bench seating and shady nooks for cooing and smooching and watching the languid green river flow.

Peek inside the **igreja matriz** (⊙10am-5.30pm Tue-Fri, 9.30-11.45am & 3.30-7.30pm Sat & Sun), the stocky Gothic parish church behind the Museu Arqueológico, to see its 18th-century *azulejos* and gilded baroque chapels.

Museu de Olaria   MUSEUM
(www.cm-barcelos.pt; Rua Cónego Joaquim Gaiolas; adult/child €1.40/free, Sun morning free; ⊙10am-12.30pm & 2-5.30pm Tue-Sun) This good pottery museum features ceramics in most of Portugal's regional styles. At research time it was under renovation and set to reopen at the end of 2010. If it's been delayed, the bulk of its wares will be on display for free in the *câmara municipal*.

Igreja do Senhor Bom Jesus da Cruz
      CHURCH
(Templo do Bom Jesus; ⊙8.30am-noon & 2-5.30pm Wed-Mon) On a corner of the Campo da República, this arresting octagonal church, built in 1704, overlooks a garden of obelisks. Its baroque interior includes some bright *azulejos* depicting scenes from Christ's last days.

Igreja do Terço   CHURCH
(Av dos Combatentes da Grande Guerra; ⊙10am-noon & 2-4pm) Smothering the walls of this deceptively plain church, which was once part of a Benedictine monastery, is an overwhelming display of *azulejos* on the life of St Benedict by the 18th-century master António de Oliveira Bernardes.

Yoga Space   YOGA
(Nas Margens do Rio Cavado; ⊙10-11am Sun May-Sep) On summer Sunday mornings, the serene riverside park becomes a free public yoga space. Instruction is in Portuguese, but, you know, body language is universal. Look for the signs around town.

✪ Festivals & Events

Festa das Cruzes   CULTURAL
(Festival of the Crosses) In the first week of May, this festival turns Barcelos into a fairground of flags, flowers, coloured lights and open-air concerts. The biggest days are generally the first three days of the month.

Festival de Folclore   CULTURAL
This celebration of folk song and dance in this tradition-loving town takes place

on the last weekend in July or the first weekend in August.

🛏 Sleeping

Accommodation is always tight on Wednesday and Thursday because of the market.

Quinta do Convento da Franqueira

RURAL INN €€

(☑253 831 606; www.quintadafranqueira.com; r €70-100; ⊙Apr-Oct; ℗ ✿) Six kilometres north of Barcelos lies this remarkable 16th-century convent turned vineyard and up-market inn. The complex includes cloisters, a bell tower and a gatehouse (now a self-catering apartment). Rooms are prim, antique affairs, and all have garden views, while the surrounding property yields a fine *vinho verde* (a young, slightly sparkling white or red wine). Minimum two-night stay.

Residencial Arantes

GUEST HOUSE €

(☑253 811 326; residencialarantes@sapo.pt; Av da Liberdade 35; s/d €30/45) A fantastic choice fronting the Campo da República, this friendly, family-run spot offers clean, tidy rooms with flowery window treatments. Most have plenty of light and some have nice views over the green plaza (and market tents on Thursday). Double rooms sleep three. Our favourite is room 2 – check out that bathroom tile.

Hotel do Terço

HOTEL €

(☑253 808 380; www.hoteldoterco.com; Edifício do Terço, Rua de São Bento 7; r €31-59; ℗ ✿) This sleek, modern option sits atop its namesake shopping centre (take the lift round the back). The stylish, squeaky-clean rooms feature dark-wood floors, tiny balconies

and furnishings straight out of an IKEA catalogue.

Hotel Bagoeira

HOTEL €€

(☑253 809 500; www.bagoeira.com; Av Dr Sidónio Pais 495; r €45-99; ✳ ✿) A business-class hotel just across from the market site, with decent contemporary digs, although some rooms can smell musty. Prices rise significantly in August.

🍴 Eating & Drinking

There are plenty of equally inviting cafes and bakeries on the Old Town walking-only streets and plazas.

TOP CHOICE **Churrasqueira Arantes**

GRILL HOUSE €€

(Av de Liberdade 33; mains €6-8; ⊙lunch & dinner) A deep, linoleum-tiled, mustard-tinted dining hall sizzling with grilled chicken, steaks and fish as well as some tasty smoked meats. Prices: reasonable; service: no-nonsense; the wine: local. What's not to love?

Casa dos Arcos

PORTUGUESE €€

(Rua Duques de Bragança 185; mains €6-9; ⊙lunch & dinner Tue-Sun) Set in a stone-walled dining room, this cosy restaurant has been around for 50 years. All the traditional favourites are here, including eight cod dishes, suckling pig and *picanha* (rump steak).

Pérola

PORTUGUESE €€

(Av Álvares Pereira 50; mains €5-10; ⊙lunch & dinner) The restaurant and bar of choice at research time, Pérola is known for its seafood dishes, and the menu has decent crêpes and omelettes too, but lately the pretty people have been sliding into the dated vinyl booths to sip one of the six draught beers. It's not fancy, but very groovy.

Restaurante Galliano PORTUGUESE €€
(www.restaurantegalliano.com; Campo 5 de Outubro 20; mains €8-14; ⊙lunch & dinner) Near the Campo da República, Galliano serves some of Barcelos' best cuisine. The menu features regional delicacies like *barrosã grelhado* (grilled steak), *costeletas* (ribs) and other grilled meats, as well as seafood and salads. Lunch specials (€7) are excellent value. There are pavement tables and an airy, elegant dining room.

Two stops for self-caterers are the mercado municipal (Largo da Madalena; ⊙7am-7pm Mon-Fri, 7am-1pm Sat) and a nearby Pingo Doce (Rua Filipa Borges 223; ⊙8.30am-9pm Mon-Sat, 9am-8.30pm Sun) supermarket.

☆ Entertainment

Biblioteca Municipal de Barcelos
DANCE PARTY
(www.subscuta.blogspot.com; Largo Dr Jose Novais; €3-5; ⊙Sat Jul-Sep) Oddly enough, on summer Saturdays the municipal library, set in a stunning mid-16th-century fort with a gorgeous stone stairway, hosts a dance party, with a roster of international live acts and DJs.

ℹ Information

Biblioteca Municipal de Barcelos (Largo Dr Jose Novais; ⊙9am-6pm; 📶) The library has free internet access in the basement.

Hospital Santa Maria Maior (✆253 809 200; Campo da República)

Police station (✆253 802 570; Av Dr Sidónio País)

Post office (✆253 811 711; Av Dr Sidónio País; ⊙8.30am-6.30pm Mon-Fri, 9am-12.30pm Sat)

Turismo (www.cm-barcelos.pt; Largo Dr Jose Novais 8; ⊙9.30am-6pm Mon-Fri, 10am-1pm & 2-5pm Sat, 10am-1pm & 2-4pm Sun Mar-Sep, 9.30am-5.30pm Mon-Fri, 10am-1pm & 2-5pm Sat Oct-Feb)

ℹ Getting There & Around

Bus

The centralised bus station is 1km east of the centre. Many buses also depart from Av Dr Sidónio País across from the Campo da República. **Transdev Norte/Arriva** (Av Dr Sidónio País 445) had the only reliable bus service to/from Barcelos at the time of research, with at least eight buses to Braga (€2.30, one hour) on

weekdays and about four on weekends. It also has services to Ponte de Lima (€3.10, one hour) and Porto (€3.80, two hours).

Car & Motorcycle

Parking is very tight on Thursdays, so avoid driving if you can. Other days, look for spots around the Campo da República.

Train

Barcelos' station is on the Porto–Valença do Minho line. There are three to five direct trains a day to/from Porto (€3.80, 55 minutes), and commuter trains every hour or two that change at Nine (€3.20, 1¼ hours). There is similar service via Nine to Braga (€2.60, 45 to 60 minutes).

Guimarães

POP 54,000 / ELEV 400M

The proud birthplace of Afonso Henriques, the first independent king of Portugal (he was born here in 1110 and later used the city to launch the main thrust of the Reconquista against the Moors), and, thus, the Portuguese kingdom, Guimarães has beautifully preserved its illustrious past. Its medieval centre is a warren of labyrinthine lanes and picturesque plazas framed by 14th-century edifices, while on an adjacent hill stands a 1000-year-old castle and, next to it, the massive palace built by the first duke of Bragança in the 15th century. Guimarães' glory was officially recognised in 2001, when Unesco declared its old centre a World Heritage Site. It has also been chosen by Portugal to be the European capital of culture in 2012.

The city, however, is more than just the sum total of its historical treasures. There are museums, cafe-filled plazas, atmospheric guest houses and delightful restaurants. Plus, Guimarães is a university town, and its students lend much vitality to the place – particularly during the celebratory Festas de Cidade e Gualterianas in August.

◉ Sights

Paço dos Duques de Bragança PALACE
(Ducal Palace; ✆253 412 273; adult/child €5/ free; ⊙10am-6pm Tue-Sun) Looming over the medieval city, the crenulated towers and cylindrical brick chimneys of the Paço dos Duques have pushed the palace into the foreground on Guimarães' hilltop. Built in 1401 by a later and equally famous Afonso (the future first duke of Bragança), it fell into ruin after his powerful family upped sticks to Vila Viçosa in the Alentejo.

Pompously restored – often too perfectly – as a presidential residence for Salazar, it still contains a clutch of original treasures. Visitors can wander freely through the rooms, which house a collection of Flemish tapestries, weapons from the 15th and 16th centuries, and a chapel with glittering stained-glass windows. The real treasures, however, are reproductions: four enormous tapestries which relate various episodes in the Portuguese attempt to conquer North Africa.

Castelo
CASTLE

(castle tower adult/student €1.50/.75; ⊙10am-6pm Tue-Sun) Built in the 11th century and still in fine form, the seven-towered castle is thought to be the birthplace of the great man himself, Afonso Henriques. It's free to walk around the windswept ramparts of the castle, but you must pay to scale the narrow steps to the bird's-nest heights of Countess Mumadona's keep.

Sandwiched between the palace and castle is the little Romanesque Igreja de São Miguel do Castelo (Church of St Michael of the Castle), where Afonso Henriques was probably baptised. Under its floor rest many of the king's companions-at-arms, their graves marked with worn crosses, spears and shields.

Igreja de São Gualter
CHURCH

(Church of St Walter; Largo da República do Brasil; ⊙7.30am-noon & 3-5pm Mon-Sat, 7.30am-noon Sun) This slender 18th-century construction with its 19th-century twin spires and blooming run-up from central Guimarães has the most striking appeal of all the city's churches.

Igreja de Nossa Senhora da Oliveira
CHURCH

(Our Lady of the Olive Tree; ⊙7.15am-noon & 3.30-7.30pm) Founded by Countess Mumadona in the 12th century and rebuilt four centuries later, the beautiful Largo da Oliveira is dominated by the convent church of Igreja de Nossa Senhora da Oliveira.

The proud **monument** outside the church is a Gothic canopy and cross, said to mark the spot where the great Wamba the Visigoth, victorious over the Suevi, drove his spear into the ground beside an olive tree, refusing to reign unless a tree sprouted from the handle. In true legendary fashion, it did just that.

Built around the church's serene Romanesque cloister, the Museu Alberto Sampaio (www.ipmuseus.pt; Rua Alfredo Guimaraes; adult/child €3/free, Sun morning free; ⊙10am-1pm, 2-6pm Tue-Sun) has an excellent collection of ecclesiastical art and religious finery. Highlights include the tunic reputedly worn by João I at the Battle of Aljubarrota (1385).

Antigos Paços do Concelho
HISTORIC BUILDING

Guimarães' 14th-century former town hall sits above an arcaded portico providing a most graceful communication between cosy Largo da Oliveira and the more rambling Praça de Santiago. It also serves as home to the Museu de Arte Primitiva Moderna (Museum of Modern Primitive Art), which historically has hosted temporary art exhibitions, but was under renovation when we visited.

Museu Arqueológico Martins Sarmento & Igreja de São Domingos
MUSEUM

(www.csarmento.uminho.pt; Rua Paio Galvão; admission €1.50; ⊙9.30am-noon & 2-6pm) This fantastic collection of mostly Celtiberian artefacts is housed in a former convent and named after the archaeologist who excavated Citânia de Briteiros (p417) in 1875. Hefty stone artefacts, including thick Roman columns and milestones, and a mossy Celtic sarcophagus, are spread around the cloister. Look for the impressive *pedras formosas* (beautiful stones) thought to have adorned Celtiberian bathhouses in the surrounding region, and the impressive case of Palaeolithic and Neolithic tools.

Penha
PARK

Some 7km southeast up a twisting, cobbled road – or a short ride on an ageing cable car – is the wooded summit of Penha (617m), overlooking Guimarães and the highest point for miles. Its cool woods make it a wonderful escape from the city and summer heat. Kids love losing themselves amid the massive boulders, many cut with steps, crowned with flowers and crosses or hiding in secret grottoes.

On the lower slopes of the hill lies the Mosteiro de Santa Marinha da Costa, 1.5km east of Penha's centre. It dates from 1154, when Dona Mafalda, wife of Afonso Henriques, commissioned it to honour a vow she made to the patron saint of pregnant women. Rebuilt in the 18th century, it's now a flagship Pousada de Portugal.

The easiest and finest route to the top of Penha is aboard the **Teleférico da Penha** (cable car; return €4.10; ⊙10am-7pm Mon-Fri, to

Guimarães

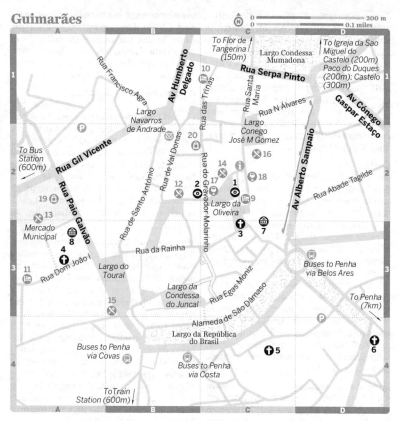

8pm Sat & Sun), which starts from Parque das Hortas, 600m east of Guimarães' old centre. You can also get there on the rare municipal bus 51 or 52 to São Roque (€2.50, three daily Monday to Saturday, hourly on Sunday), which departs from the south side of the public gardens; get off at Costa. A taxi costs €7.

Igreja de São Francisco CHURCH
(Church of St Francis of Assisi; ◐9.30am-noon & 3-5pm Tue-Sat, 9.30am-1pm Sun) This 13th-century has a striking interior, along with a lovely Renaissance cloister and 18th-century *azulejos* depicting scenes from the saint's life.

FREE **Galeria de Arte Jose Gomes Alves** ART GALLERY
(Rua do Gravador Molarinho; ◐10:30am-1pm & 3:30-7:30pm Tue-Sat) A bright, airy gallery in a medieval stone compound, it rotates intriguing exhibitions of modern work.

✺ Festivals & Events

Encontros de Primavera MUSIC
This series of classical and early music concerts is held at historic venues in late May and June.

Festas de Cidade e Gualterianas CULTURAL
(www.aoficina.pt) Marked by a free fair (held in Guimarães since 1452 to honour its patron saint), this festival also features folk dancing, rock concerts, bullfights, fireworks and parades. It takes place on the first weekend in August.

Jazz Festival MUSIC
One of the country's top festivals, this jazz extravaganza runs for about three weeks in November.

🛏 Sleeping

Pousada da Oliveira INN €€€
(☎253 514 157; www.pousadas.pt; r €77-122; Ⓟ❋) Offering the most atmospheric stay

in medieval Guimarães, this small, elegant *pousada* is set in a converted manor house overlooking the Largo da Oliveira. The superb rooms (if a bit dark) are set with wide plank floors, dark-panelled wood, classical furnishings and elegant window treatments. Guests can use the beautifully situated pool at the Pousada de Santa Marinha.

Hotel de Guimarães   HOTEL €€
(☎253 424 800; www.hotel-guimaraes.com; Rua Eduardo de Almeida; r €105-154; P🅿🛜❄) A stylish, relatively new business hotel near the train station. Think large rooms with lush linens, chic paint jobs and flat-screen TVs, along with a health club and spa. It's a bit removed from the old town for some, but still excellent value and an easy two-minute walk to the train.

Villa Hotel   HOTEL €€
(☎253 421 440; www.villa-hotel.net; Av São João IV 631; r €80-100; P🅿🛜) Another frosted-glass block hotel is the newest nest in town. Rooms are minimalist, maybe a bit bland for some, but the black-tiled bathrooms are sleek. It's wired, offers plenty of parking and guests can use the gym next door.

Pousada da Juventude   HOSTEL €
(☎253 421 380; www.pousadasjuventude.pt; Largo da Cidade 8; dm/d/apt €13/34/60) Set in the palatial 18th-century home of a prosperous factory owner, this terrific hostel has hardwood floors, bright dorms and doubles that are downright stylish. It also has kitchen and laundry facilities, and two wheelchair-

accessible rooms. Management and service are first rate.

Residencial das Trinas   GUEST HOUSE €
(☎253 517 358; www.residencialtrinas.com; Rua das Trinas 29; s/d €25/30; ❄) This renovated house in the historical zone offers likeable little rooms with double-glazed windows, satellite TV, plenty of natural light and patterned ceramic-tile floors. You won't get a better position for the price.

Residencial Mestre d'Aviz   GUEST HOUSE €
(☎253 422 770; www.residencialmestredavis. com; Rua Dom João I 36; r €25-75; ❄🛜) Fronted by curlicue ironwork, this renovated town house has bright rooms on a quiet cobbled street in the town centre. Interiors are a strange mix of modern and antique, but it's a solid-value option.

Pousada de Santa Marinha   RURAL INN €€€
(☎253 511 249; www.pousadas.pt; €111-176; P🅿❄) This former monastery overlooking the city from the slopes of Penha is a magnificent, sprawling structure. The gardens are stunning and you'll want to wander around the cloister, past dribbling fountains and masterful *azulejos*, but the rooms (former monks' cells) feel cramped and oddly arranged, and the vibe is *munto* stuffy.

✕ Eating

Flor de Tangerina   VEGETARIAN €€
⊡TOP CHOICE (www.cor.de.tangerina.blogspot. com; Largo Martins Sarmento 89; mains €6-11; ⊙lunch & dinner Tue-Sat, lunch Sun; ✈) This charming restaurant sits above a co-op and

THE MINHO

whips up a good selection of cuisine you won't find elsewhere in Guimarães. Among the standouts: a hearty vegetarian pizza with grilled pineapple and tofu, carrot and orange soup, and vegetable fusilli. Changing art exhibitions decorate the walls, while the wild, jazz-washed garden (with tangerine tree) produces much of the herbs used in the ancient stone kitchen. The chef is something of an herbal alchemist capable of brewing all manner of teas and tonics too. He even teaches workshops to local doctors.

Pastelaria Clarinha
BAKERY €
(Largo do Toural 86; pastries €0.80-1.50; ☺breakfast, lunch & dinner Tue-Sun) Guimarães' best pastry shop has filled its window with fresh-baked tarts and cakes to tempt passers-by since 1953. There are a few pavement tables, a heavenly *touchino do ceu* (almond cake) and a spectacular *torta de Guimaraes* (a flaky, glazed pastry stuffed with ground almonds soaked in honey).

Pensao Penha
PORTUGUESE €€
(Penha; mains €9-15; ☺lunch & dinner) Not just the best kitchen on the mountain, this is one of the best restaurants in all Guimarães. Meals are of the traditional roast-meat, grilled-seafood variety, but they are fresh and perfectly prepared. Views are outstanding and service is some of the best we had in northern Portugal.

Paraxut
PORTUGUESE €€
(Rua Santa Maria 21; mains €7-12; ☺lunch & dinner; ✎) If you're hungry for traditional northern dishes like *feijoada a Transmontana* (beans with pork, veal and vegetables served over rice) served in tasteful modernised environs, or better yet outdoors on an old stone plaza, come here. It's popular with locals for a reason.

Restaurante Solar do Arco
PORTUGUESE €€
(www.solardoarco.com; Rua de Santa Maria 50; mains €10-20; ☺lunch & dinner Mon-Sat, lunch Sun; ✿) With a handsomely panelled dining room under a graceful arcade, this is a top central choice. Portuguese classics made with straight-from-the-market ingredients add to the allure.

Histórico by Papaboa
PORTUGUESE €€
(www.papaboa.pt; Rua de Val Donas 4; pastries €1, mains €9-13; ☺lunch & dinner) The soundtrack is cheesy, but the setting – in a medieval fort with breezy courtyard seating and glassed-in stone dining room – is tremendous. Service is top-notch and the fare is

dressed up yet traditional. You could also simply stop by the *gelataria*.

Self-caterers should go in the morning to the bustling **mercado municipal** (Rua Palo Galvão).

🍷 Drinking & Entertainment

Tásquilhado Bar
BAR
(Rua de Santa Maria 42; ☺9pm-2am Wed-Sat, to midnight Sun) One of a swath of bar-hopping venues in the historic centre, the cosy, ever-popular Tásquilhado Bar plays alternative sounds and offers enticing drink specials during the week.

El Rock
BAR, LIVE MUSIC
(www.elrock.blogspot.com; Praça de Santiago; ☺2pm-close) Dug into a narrow stone room and spreading onto the plaza is this funky beer bar. It hosts touring DJs and occasional live bands, and is the destination for many a pretty, wild-haired hipster when night falls.

Tunel 29
BAR
(www.tunel29.com; Praça de Santiago 29; ☺6pm-close) A reggae- and electronica-infused, mosaic-tiled cave that sees its share of Guimarães party people.

🛍 Shopping

A big flea market takes over Praça de Santiago and Largo da Oliveira on the first Saturday of each month.

Meia Tigela
GIFTS
(www.meiatigela.com; Rua de Santa Maria 35; ☺10am-1pm, 2-7pm) It sells artisan wine, food and crafts from the Minho and Douro along with imported chocolate, scented candles and lotions. It's one of those feel-good *lojas* (shops) that shouldn't be missed.

A Oficina
HANDICRAFTS
(www.aoficina.pt; Rua Paio Galvão 11; ☺9am-6pm Mon-Sat) Today, as in medieval times, Guimarães is renowned for its linen. Other crafts contributing to its prosperity are embroidery, worked gold and silver, and pottery. For quality work by Guimarães artisans, visit this municipal outlet near the municipal market.

ℹ Information

There's free wi-fi in the main squares.

Espaço Internet (Praça de Santiago; ☺9am-12.30pm & 2-10pm Mon-Fri, to 7pm Sat, to noon Sun) Free internet access. It's up a flight of stairs near Largo da Oliveira.

Hospital (☑253 512 612; Rua dos Cotileros, Creixomil) Opposite the bus station.

Livraria Ideal (Rua da Rainha 34; ◷9am-1pm & 3-7pm Mon-Fri, 9am-1pm Sat) The city's best bookshop has a terrific selection of area maps.

Police station (☑253 519 598; Av Dr Alfredo Pimenta)

Post office (Largo Navarros de Andrade 27; ◷8.30am-6.30pm Mon-Fri, 9am-12.30pm Sat)

Turismo (www.guimaraesturismo.com; Praça de Santiago; ◷9.30am-6.30pm Mon-Fri, 10am-6pm Sat, to 1pm Sun) The excellent, informative staff speaks English, French and Spanish.

ℹ Getting There & Around

There is street parking in front of the Convento do Carmo at the foot of the Paço dos Duques. If you wish to explore Guimarães and the surrounds on two wheels or four, go to **Quality Tours** (www.qualitytours.pt; Largo Martins Sarmento 89; ◷9am-7:30pm), which rents bikes (€12), scooters (€30) and four-wheelers (€90) by the day.

Bus

Transdev (☑253 423 500) has buses leaving at least hourly for Braga (€2.75, 50 minutes) on Monday through Saturday, and eight buses on Sunday. It also has services to Porto (€4.60, 50 minutes) running approximately hourly on weekdays but less often on weekends, and to Lisbon (€17, five hours) daily. **Rodonorte** (☑253 514 476; www.rodonorte.pt) heads for Amarante (€6.50, one hour), Vila Real (€7.50, two hours) and Bragança (€14, four hours).

Train

Guimarães is the terminus of a branch of Porto's wide *suburbano* network. Commuter trains potter out to Guimarães from Porto (€2.20, 75 minutes) 11 to 15 times daily. Try to avoid the once-daily *intercidade* (express) train, which costs €9.50 and departs at 7.20am.

Around Guimarães

CITÂNIA DE BRITEIROS

One of the most evocative archaeological sites in Portugal, Citânia de Briteiros (www.csarmento.uminho.pt; admission incl museum adult/student €3/1.50; ◷9am-6pm May-Sep, to 5pm Oct-Apr), 15km north of Guimarães, is the largest of a liberal scattering of northern Celtic hill settlements, called *citânias* (fortified villages), dating back at least 2500 years. It's also likely that this sprawling 3.8-hectare site, inhabited from about 300 BC to AD 300, was the

Celtiberians' last stronghold against the invading Romans.

When archaeologist Dr Martins Sarmento excavated the site in 1875, he discovered the foundations and ruins of more than 150 rectangular, circular and elliptical stone huts, linked by paved paths and a water distribution system, all cocooned by multiple protective walls. Highlights include two reconstructed huts that evoke what it was like to live in the settlement, and – further down the hill – a bathhouse with a strikingly patterned stone doorway.

Some artefacts are on display in the Sede e Museu Arqueológico in Guimarães, but the Museu da Cultura Castreja (Museum on Pre-Roman Culture; www.csarmento. uminho.pt; Solar da Ponte; adult/student €3-1.50; ◷9.30am-12.30pm & 2-6pm) also has important artefacts from various sites housed in Sarmento's 18th- and 19th-century manor house. It's about 2km back down the hill towards Guimarães in the village of Briteiros Salvador.

ℹ Getting There & Away

From Guimarães, **Transdev/Arriva** (☑253 516 229) has about six weekday buses that pass within 1km of the site; get off between the towns of Briteiros Salvador and Santa Leocádia. Check at the bus station for current schedule information.

Viana do Castelo

POP 15,600

The jewel of the Costa Verde, Viana do Castelo is blessed with both an appealing medieval centre and lovely beaches just outside the city. The old quarters seem downright sophisticated, with leafy, 19th-century boulevards and narrow lanes crowded with Manueline manors and rococo palaces. It's also the place where conservative Minho comes to let its hair down, with raucous traditional festivals complemented by a few sleek local nightclubs catering to university students who give the city a shot of life. The town's setting just by the Rio Lima estuary means that Viana do Castelo is only a short hop from some excellent beaches, and also makes it a handy base for exploring the lower Lima valley.

History

The remains of Celtic hill settlements on Monte de Santa Luzia, overlooking the contemporary town centre, and the name

THE MINHO

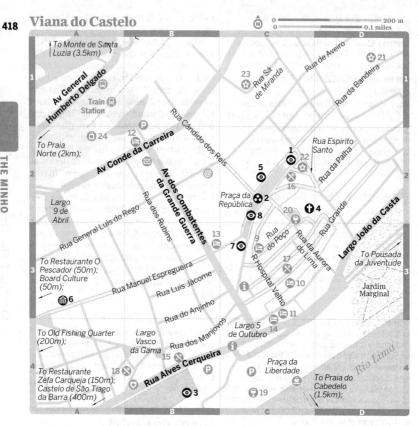

Viana – a nod to its Roman past when this once-humble settlement was called Diana – convey Viana do Castelo's deep historical roots, while its Manueline mansions and monasteries recall its 16th-century prosperity as a major cod-fishing port. In fact, by the mid-17th century it had bloomed into Portugal's biggest overall port, with merchants trading as far afield as Russia.

More riches arrived in the 18th century, with the advent of the Brazilian sugar and gold trade. But with Brazil's independence and the rising importance of Porto, Viana's golden age stuttered and faded. These days Viana earns much of its current living and reputation as the Minho's favourite resort town.

◉ Sights & Activities

Praça da República & Around   PLAZA
The fine Praça da República, the hub of seven narrow laneways, is at the heart

of the old town's well-preserved zone of mansions and monuments. An especially elegant example is the *praça*'s **Chafariz**, a Renaissance fountain that was built in 1554 by João Lopes the Elder. The fountain is topped with Manueline motifs of an armillary sphere and the cross of the Order of Christ. The fortresslike **Antigos Paços do Concelho** is the old town hall – another 16th-century creation. These days it usually hosts temporary contemporary art exhibitions.

Situated at right angles to this is the striking former Misericórdia almshouse, designed in 1589 by João Lopes the Younger. Adjoining the almshouse is the Igreja de Misericórdia (◷10am-12.30pm & 2-5pm Mon-Fri Aug, 11am-12.30pm Sun year-round), which was rebuilt in 1714 and is adorned with some of Portugal's finest *azulejos,* created by the master António de Oliveira Bernardes.

THE MINHO VIANA DO CASTELO

Praia do Cabedelo
BEACH

One of the Minho's best beaches has little development to spoil its charm. Think a 1km-long arch of blond powdery sand, which folds into grassy dunes and is backed by a grove of wind-blown pines. It's across the river from town, and one way to get there is by passenger **ferry** (one-way adult/child €1.20/0.60) from the pier south of Largo 5 de Outubro. The five-minute trip goes about hourly between 9am and 6pm daily. Alternatively, **TransCunha** (☑258 821 392) has multiple daily buses to Cabedelo (€0.75) from the bus station. Check at the station or *turismo* for current schedules.

Igreja Matriz
CHURCH

(Rua da Aurora do Lima; ⊙vary) This elegant parish church – also known as the *sé* – dates back to the 15th century, although it has since been through several reincarnations. Check out its unusually sculpted Romanesque towers and Gothic doorway, carved with figures of Christ and the Evangelists.

Capela de Nossa Senhora de Agonia
CHAPEL

(Rua do Monserrate; ⊙9am-6pm) This serene 18th-century chapel with an onion dome and gilded octagonal nave is the centre of an August festival of the same name (see the boxed text, p421).

Museu de Arte e Arqueologia
MUSEUM

(www.cm-viana-castelo.pt; Largo de São Domingos; admission €2; ⊙10am-1pm & 3-7pm Jun-Sep, to 6pm Oct-May) The 18th-century Palacete Barbosa Maciel bears witness to Viana's affluent past. It houses an impressive collection of 17th- and 18th-century ceramics (especially blue Portuguese china) and furniture. Most impressive are three 2nd-floor rooms lined with *azulejos,* depicting scenes of hunting and palace life.

Museu do Traje
MUSEUM

FREE (Costume Museum; www.cm-viana-costelo.pt; Rua Manuel Espregueira 27; ⊙10am-1pm & 3-7pm Tue-Sat) This attractive new museum houses the traditional wear used for farming, fishing and seaweed harvesting in centuries past. You'll see costumes worn during the Romaria de Nossa Senhora d'Agonia (see the boxed text, p421) and cool antique looms. The then-and-now mural-sized photos on the 2nd floor are pretty special too.

Castelo de São Tiago da Barra
CASTLE

(Campo de Castelo; ⊙9am-5pm Mon-Fri) You can still scoot around the ramparts of this squat castle, a short walk west of the centre, which began in the 15th century as a smallish fort. It was integrated into a larger fort, commissioned by Felipe II of Spain (Felipe I of Portugal) in 1592, to guard the prosperous port against pirates.

Monte de Santa Luzia   HILL

There are two good reasons to visit Viana's 228m, eucalyptus-clad hill. One is the wondrous **view** down the coast and up the Lima valley. The other is the fabulously over-the-top, 20th-century, neo-Byzantine **Templo do Sagrado Coração de Jesus** (Temple of the Sacred Heart of Jesus; ⊘8am-7pm Apr-Sep, to 5pm Oct-Mar). You can get a little closer to heaven on its graffiti-covered roof, via a lift, followed by an elbow-scraping stairway (€0.80) – take the museum entrance on the ground floor.

There's a gaudy **Pousada de Portugal** (Pousada do Monte de Santa Luzia) up here too, behind and above the basilica. Behind that is another attraction, the **Ruinas da Cidade Velha** (adult/student €1.50/.75; ⊘10am-noon & 2-6pm Apr-Sep, to 5pm Oct-Mar), ruins of a Celtiberian *citânia* from around the 4th century BC. You'll see the stones peeking out above the wind-blown savannah. Most of the site is accessible via a boardwalk.

You can get up the mountain by the restored **funicular** (one-way/return €2/3; ⊘8am-8pm Jun-Sep, 8am-6pm Oct-May), which departs from near the train station every 15 minutes. You can also drive or take a taxi (3.5km) to the top, or hike 2km of steps (only for the fit and/or penitent). The road starts by the hospital, and the steps begin about 200m up the road.

Gil Eannes   MUSEUM

(www.fundacaogileannes.pt; admission €2; ⊘9am-7pm Mon-Fri Jul-Sep, to 5.30pm Oct-Mar) Demanding attention on the waterfront near Largo 5 de Outubro is a pioneering naval hospital ship, the *Gil Eannes* (zheel *yan*-ish). Now restored, the ship once provided on-the-job care for those fishing off the coast of Newfoundland. Visitors can clamber around the steep decks and cabins, though a scattering of old clinical equipment may make your hair stand on end. The ship even houses a novel – if cramped – youth hostel.

Kite House   KITESURFING

(⊘926 897 595; http://kitehouse.wordpress.com; Praia do Cabedelo) Set in a condo opposite the harbour on the road to Praia do Cabedelo, this excellent kitesurfing outfitter is owned and operated by João Fontainhas, Portugal's 2007 kitesurfing champion. He offers six-day courses for beginners, intermediate and advanced students (with/without accommodation €750/300) and rents gear by the day (€150). Lessons usually take place off Cabedelo, but location depends on wind and wave conditions.

Viana Locals   SURFING, KITESURFING

(⊘258 325 168; www.vianalocals.com; Praia do Cabedelo) Another friendly, full-service board-sports outfitter and school set in a modern tower complex right on Praia do Cabedelo. It has surfboards, kite gear and paddle boards for rent and sale, and does overnight repairs too.

River Trips   BOAT TRIPS

(www.passeiofluvial.com; ⊘May-Sep) If there are enough passengers, boats run up and down the Rio Lima daily in summer, from the pier south of Largo 5 de Outubro (the same dock where ferries depart to Praia do Cabedelo). The most common trip takes 45 minutes (adult/child €7/4). Longer excursions (adult/child €12/6.50) take in the old shipyards and stop at Praia do Cabedelo.

★★ Festivals & Events

Viana has a knack for celebrations. The **Romaria de Nossa Senhora d'Agonia**

SURFING & KITESURFING IN MINHO

Praia do Cabedelo (p419) is an excellent kitesurfing destination, with consistent on-shore wind year-round. It's a great teaching site, but also fun for intermediate surfers thanks to the lagoonlike conditions created by the southern headland and harbour breakwater, which is a full kilometre north. Seventeen kilometres south of Cabedelo, there's good kiting and some traditional surfing at **Esposende**, but conditions are iffy. Among the fine beaches strung north along the 25km of coast between Viana do Castelo and Caminha, **Afife** has the best surf breaks, with waves topping out at 2m during peak swells. Four daily regional trains (€1.05, 12 minutes) make their way up the coast to Afife from Viana. Advanced kitesurfers will want to drive a bit further north to **Moledo** where the wind and waves are at their fiercest and finest. For tips and gear rental head to Viana do Castelo and contact the Kite House, hit Board Culture (p423), or stop by Viana Locals at Praia do Cabedelo.

(www.festas-agonia.com), held in August, is the region's biggest annual bash and **Carnaval** festivities here are considered northern Portugal's best. The town also goes a little nuts in mid-May during **Semana Académica** (or Queima das Fitas), a week of end-of-term student madness.

The *turismo* has details of other annual events, including the following:

Encontros de Viana   FILM
A week-long festival of documentaries and short films; held in the first half of May.

Festival Maio   DANCE/CULTURAL
A national folk-dance extravaganza that takes place at the end of May.

🛏 Sleeping

Melo Alvim   BOUTIQUE HOTEL **€€€**
(📞258 808 200; www.meloalvimhouse.com; Av Conde da Carreira 28; d from €140; P ❄) Melo Alvim offers 20 four-star rooms in a stately 16th-century mansion. No two rooms are alike, but it is worth the extra €15 for the deluxe rooms, which have huge ceilings and ornately carved beds. There's a top-notch Portuguese restaurant (mains €12 to €18) on the ground floor.

TOP CHOICE **Margarida da Praça**
                          BOUTIQUE HOTEL **€€**
(📞258 809 630; www.margaridadapraca.com; Largo 5 de Outubro; r €65-75; ❄🛜) Fantastically whimsical, this boutique inn offers rooms in striking pinks, sea greens and whites, accented by stylish floral wallpaper, candelabra lanterns and lush duvets. It's all very nouveau Renaissance and the kind of place Sofia Coppola might dream up. The equally stylish lobby glows with candlelight in the evening. Staff is warm and helpful.

Residencial Jardim   GUEST HOUSE **€€**
(📞258 828 915; www.residencialjardim.com. sapo.pt; Largo 5 de Outubro 68; d €65; ❄🛜) In a stately 19th-century town house, this quirky place has spacious rooms with wooden floors, stone-framed French windows overlooking the historic centre or the river, comfy beds and sizeable bathrooms with bath-tub and shower. It's one of the best-value options in town.

Flôr de Sal   BOUTIQUE HOTEL **€€€**
(📞258 800 100; www.hotelflordesal.com; Av de Cabo Verde 100, Praia Norte; r €115-140;

DON'T MISS

CELEBRATION OF SORROWS

Streets decorated with coloured sawdust. Women decked out in traditional finery of scarlet and gold. Men drinking till they keel over. Viana do Castelo's **Romaria de Nossa Senhora d'Agonia** (Festival of Our Lady of Sorrows; www.festas-agonia.com) is one of the Minho's most spectacular festivals. Expect everything from emotive religious processions to upbeat parades with deafening drums and lumbering carnival *gigantones* (giants) and *cabeçudos* (big heads). The festival takes place for three or four days around 20 August. Accommodation is very tight at this time, so book well ahead.

P ❄🛜🏊) Perched on a windswept stretch of rocky coastline, this sleek, designer offering has whitewashed rooms, all the modern touches, and huge balconies. There's a spa, a workout centre, two heated, black-bottom pools, and a pleasant restaurant on-site. It's 2km west of the centre.

Hospedaria Senhora do Carmo
                            GUEST HOUSE **€**
(📞258 825 118; batistaesilva@sapo.pt; Rua Grande 72; r with/without bathroom €30/17) Cute and cosy, clean and bright, freshly painted rooms, parquet floors and a warm welcome. It's in a four-floor walk-up hidden above a small newsstand and is one of the best-value options in town. Not all rooms have private bathrooms, but even those with shared bathrooms are a steal.

Pousada da Juventude   HOSTEL **€**
(📞258 800 260; www.pousadasjuventude.pt; Rua da Lima; dorm €13, r with/without bathroom €34/28; P @🛜) The exterior may need a paint job, but the interiors of this Carrilho Graça–designed hostel overlooking the marina are decked out nicely. Think black concrete floors and chic marble baths. Four-bed dorms have lockers and the doubles have either shared or private bathrooms. It's 1km from the centre.

Dolce Vianna   GUEST HOUSE **€€**
(📞258 824 860; pizzariadolcevianna@gmail.com; Rua do Poço 44; r from €40; ❄) Set above a popular pizzeria, the quiet rooms at Dolce Vianna are spick and span, with tiled floors

and sturdy furnishings. It's decent value for being in the town centre.

Casa Santa Filomena
RURAL INN €€

(258 981 619; soc.com.smiths@mail.telepac.pt; Estrada Avelino Ramos Meira de Votado Afifense 621, Afife; d incl breakfast from €50) Located 11km north of Viana, this stone-walled B&B offers simple but pleasant rooms that open onto a beautiful garden. Breakfast is served on the grassy lawn amid fruit trees, sunflowers and twittering birds. It's a 15- to 20-minute walk from Afife's train station, and a 30-minute walk to the beach. Reservations are essential.

Pousada do Monte de Santa Luzia
RURAL INN €€€

(Pousada de Viana do Castelo; 258 800 370; www.pousadas.pt; r €119-210; P ❄ @ ❅ ⛱) This regal 1918 hotel sits squarely atop Monte de Santa Luzia, peering down at the basilica's backside and beyond it to some of the best coastal views in Portugal. Common areas are splendid, while the rooms themselves are comfortable, if less inspired than the views.

Pensão Laranjeira
GUEST HOUSE €

(258 822 258; Rua Manuel Espregueira 24; s/d €30/40; ❄) This bright town house is a nice new choice in the old centre, with rooms that are spare but comfy. There's an attractive restaurant on the ground floor.

Pousada da Juventude Gil Eannes
HOSTEL €

(258 821 582; www.pousadasjuventude.pt; Gil Eannes; s/d €16/24; 📶) Sleep in the oily bowels of a huge, creaky hospital ship where men were stitched up and underwent emergency dentistry. The floating *pousada da juventude* scores well for novelty, but don't expect easy access, luxury or more natural light than fits through a few portholes.

Orbitur
CAMPGROUND €

(258 322 167; info@orbitur.pt; Praia do Cabedelo; ❂year-round; ⛱) Nestled on the inland side of lovely sand dunes, this shady site is within walking distance of the ferry pier, and also has two- to six-person bungalows (€24 to €75). It heaves with holidaymakers in summer, and is a two-minute walk to the sea.

✖ Eating

Viana do Castelo whips up some excellent seafood – among the region's best.

Although you can find fresh fish at restaurants throughout the old town, the best joints are in the old fishermens quarter on the west side of town.

TOP CHOICE Taberna do Valentim
SEAFOOD €€

(Rua Monsignor Daniel Machado 180; mains €12-14; ❂lunch & dinner Mon-Sat) Hidden within the old fishermens quarter you'll find this fantastic seafood restaurant. Fresh grilled fish is available by the kilo, and equally well loved are the rich seafood stews – *arroz de tamboril* (monkfish rice) and *caldeirada* (fish stew). In a good eating town, no place does it better.

Restaurante Zefa Carqueja
GRILL HOUSE €€

(Campo do Castelo; mains €7.50-25; ❂lunch & dinner) Barbecue aficionados should find this grill house for some of the best barbecue chicken and ribs in northern Portugal. You can also get barbecued seafood – including lobster. Dine in or line up at the grill and take it away.

Restaurante Santos
PORTUGUESE €

(Rua dos Poveiros 48; meals from €5; ❂lunch & dinner) This backstreet pink *casa* pours forth the smoky essence of grilled chicken and the laughter of a packed house here for €5 lunch specials. There are baskets of fresh bread and cloths on the tables and ready smiles from the ladies that lord over the kitchen and dining room.

Castelo Velho
PORTUGUESE €€

(Largo Vasco da Gama; mains €7-12; ❂lunch & dinner) An old riverside warehouse turned all-things-to-all-people restaurant and bar is stocked with good wine and fresh catch, and roasts a damn fine chicken too.

Dolce Vianna
ITALIAN €

(Rua do Poço 44; pizzas €6-9; ❂lunch & dinner) This pleasant local favourite cooks up thin-crust, cheese-heavy pizzas in a wood-burning oven. Lasagne, calzones and fettucine also provide a nice respite from Portuguese standards.

Doce Lima
BAKERY €

(Rua Frei Bartolmeu de Martires 176; pastries €0.75-2; ❂breakfast & lunch) There's no denying the popularity of this tiny pastry shop, which is positively flooded with locals in the morning. This is where Viana cops come for coffee and doughnuts.

Os 3 Potes
PORTUGUESE €€

(Rua Beco dos Fornos 7; mains €8-12; ❂lunch & dinner) Set in the former public kiln, this atmospheric restaurant serves traditional Minho delicacies such as oven-roasted lamb, lamprey eels (in season) and grilled fish. An ample wine cellar adds to the restaurant's appeal.

Restaurante O Marques
PORTUGUESE €
(Rua do Marques 12; meals from €5; ⊙lunch & dinner Tue-Sat) Another tremendous back-street find, this place is absolutely jammed with locals for the *platos do dia* (plates of the day; €5). Think baked cod with white beans or roasted turkey leg with potatoes and salad. It's a friendly, satisfying, family-run affair.

Restaurante O Galeao do Mar
SEAFOOD €
(Rua Grande 73; meals from €6.50; ⊙lunch & dinner Mon-Sat) This restaurant's streetside cooler is packed with fresh catch; its dining room is packed with locals and tourists alike, and patrolled by the owner-operator who pours wine liberally. It offers inexpensive seafood lunches (€6.50).

Restaurante O Pescador
SEAFOOD €€
(Largo de São Domingos 35; mains €9-13; ⊙lunch & dinner Tue-Sat, lunch Sun) A simple, friendly, family-run restaurant admired by locals for its good seafood and tasty lunch specials (from €6).

Drinking
There is a handful of upmarket bars, trendy beer bars and more-casual open-air spots on the waterfront.

Lunas Cervejaria
BEER BAR
(Rua do Poço; ⊙3pm-2am Mon-Thu, to 4am Fri & Sat) Situated mere footsteps from the holy stone flower that is Igreja Matriz, the (mostly) young crowd gathers here beginning in the late afternoon and sips into the wee hours.

Foz
CAFE
(Praça da Liberdade; ⊙noon-2am) This glass-box cafe with a massive menu and even better views is a gathering point for locals late in the evening. It's a good place for a sundowner, a crêpe or even an ice cream. The wine list is substantial.

☆ Entertainment
Teatro Municipal Sá de Miranda
THEATRE
(www.cm-viana-castelo.pt; Rua Sá de Miranda) Viana do Castelo's cultural epicentre, this pink-washed neoclassical theatre hosts a regular line-up of music, theatre, dance and the occasional opera.

Nazomi
NIGHTCLUB
(Rua Espirito Santo; ⊙10pm-4am Thu-Sat) Under-ground indie rock fills the historic 18th-century rococo environs of the Capula Malheiras where you can shake your ass free of all sin and self-doubt.

Off
NIGHTCLUB
(www.offdanceclub.com; Rua de Monserrate; cover men/women €7/5; ⊙midnight-6am Thu-Sat) The new choice dance spot hosts resident and occasional international DJs spinning pop and house tunes.

Look
NIGHTCLUB
(www.look-club.com; Av de Cabo Verde, Praia Norte; ⊙11pm-4am Thu-Sat) Still a good choice if you're looking to groove into the wee hours. This boxy space has a spacious dance floor ringed by an upstairs gallery for checking out the scene below. It's next door to the Flôr de Sal hotel.

Glamour
NIGHTCLUB
(Rua da Bandeira 179-185; ⊙10.30pm-4am Tue-Sat) This nightlife mainstay is Viana's longest-running nightclub featuring live acts that usually cover the rock and blues classics. Bands take the stage at midnight. Wednesdays are for karaoke.

Shopping
Board Culture
SURF SHOP
(☑258 400 508; www.abcescoladesurf.com; Largo de São Domingos 49; ⊙10am-1pm & 2.30-7pm) Physically, it's in old town. Spiritually, it's one with the waves. This well-equipped board shop can send you to the right break, link you up with an instructor and outfit you with all the gear.

Estação
MALL
(www.estacaoviana.pt; Av General Humberto Delgado 101; ⊙10am-10pm Sun-Wed, to 11pm Thu, to midnight Fri & Sat; ℗) Chic and gleaming, this attractive new mall is conveniently fused with the train and bus stations. All the international fashion chains are here, and there's a decent food court and a cinema too.

Information
Esp@ço.net (Rua General Luis do Rego 21; per hr €1; ⊙9am-7pm Mon-Fri, to 6pm Sat) Internet access.

Hospital (☑258 829 081; Estrada de Santa Luzia) North of the train station.

Police station (☑258 822 022; Rua Alves Cerqueira)

Post office (Av dos Combatentes da Grande Guerra; ⊙8.30am-6pm Mon-Fri, 9am-12.30pm Sat)

Regional turismo (www.cm-viana-costelo. pt; Rua Hospital Velho; ⊙9am-12.30pm & 2-5.30pm Mon-Fri, 9.30am-1pm & 2-5.30pm Sat, 9.30am-1pm Sun Oct-Apr, 9am-12.30pm & 2.30-6pm Mon-Fri, 9.30am-1pm & 2-6pm Sat, 9.30am-1pm Sun May-Jul & Sep, 9.30am-7pm daily Aug) Housed in a 15th-century inn.

Viana Welcome Centre (www.vivexperiencia. pt; Rotunda da Liberdade; ⊙10am-7pm) This private outfit run by a young tourism entrepreneur offers creative city tours (€15) in multiple languages, as well as regional food, wine and culture itineraries in the Douro and Minho. Canyoneering, surfing and mountain biking are also on offer, and bike rental are available for €2.50/11 per hour/day.

ℹ Getting There & Around

Bus

Long-distance *expresso* buses operate from the shiny, centralised bus station, which is just across the tracks from the train station.

AV Cura/Transcolvia (☑258 800 340) Runs up the Lima valley to Ponte de Lima (€3, 1 hour), Ponte da Barca (€3.75, 1½ hours) and Arcos de Valdevez (€4, 1½ hours) at least hourly on weekdays (less at weekends).

AV Minho (☑258 800 341) Runs a line from Porto (€6.00, 2¼ hours) at least four times daily, passing through Esposende (€3, 40 minutes); one to three daily buses run to Valença do Minho (€4, 1¼ hours) and Monção (€5, 1½ hours).

Transdev Norte (☑258 825 047) Has at least eight weekday and four weekend runs to Braga (€4, 1½ hours).

Car & Motorcycle

Parking can be a challenge – most locals opt for paid underground lots sprinkled about the centre (including lots on either end of Av dos Combatentes da Grande Guerra). There's ample free parking next to the Castelo de São Tiago da Barra. If you need wheels to hit the beaches north of Viana, **Orbita** (☑258 813 513; www.orbitaviagens.com; Rua Alves Cerqueria 216; ⊙9am-6pm) rents cars from €29 per day, but they must be reserved at least one day in advance.

Train

Daily direct services from Porto include five IR/international trains (€6.65, 1½ hours) and five regional services (€4.95, two hours). For Braga (€4.35, 1½ to two hours, 12 daily), change at Nine. There are also seven to 10 daily trains to Valença do Minho (€3.45, 45 minutes to one hour).

Valença do Minho
POP 5200

Now you're really in the Minho, where all is green, fertile and rustling in shared Spanish–Porto winds and waters. And no place has a better view of it all than this atmospheric fort village occupying strategic heights above the picturesque Rio Minho. Valença do Minho (Valença) sits just a cannonball shot from Spain, and its impressive pair of citadels long served as the Minho's first line of defence against Spanish aggression. But history insists on repeating itself, and these days the town is regularly overrun by Spanish hordes. They come armed with wallets and make away with volumes of towels and linens that are stacked high along cobbled streets.

The good news is that on even the busiest days, you can sidestep the towel touts and discover that these two interconnected forts also contain a fully functioning village where locals shop, eat, drink and gossip among pretty squares and narrow, medieval lanes. And when in the evening the weary troops retreat back to Spain with their loot, the empty watchtowers return once again to the silent contemplation of their ancient enemy – the glowering Spanish fortress of Tui just across the river.

Visitors can easily see the sights of Valença as a day trip, but there are two atmospheric sleeps within the fortress walls that allow you to see and feel peaceful Valença when it empties at sunset. That's when you can hear the footsteps of kittens in the laneways while birdsong echoes off ancient stone walls.

An uninspiring new town sprawls at the foot of the fortress. From the bus station it's 800m north via Av Miguel Dantas (the N13) and the Largo da Trapicheira roundabout (aka Largo da Esplanada) to the *turismo*. The train station is just east of Av Miguel Dantas.

◉ Sights & Activities

There are in fact two **fortresses**, bristling with bastions, watchtowers, massive gateways and defensive bulwarks, connected by a single bridge. The old churches and Manueline mansions inside testify to the success of the fortifications against several sieges, some as late as the 19th century. The earliest fortifications date from the 13th-century reign of Dom Afonso III, though largely what you see today was built in the 17th century, its design inspired by the French military architect Vauban.

Zip past the tacky gift shops and towel merchants, and follow the cobbled lanes to the far end of the larger northern fortress, which incorporates Dom Afonso's original stronghold and contains almost everything else that's of interest. From Praça da República bear right, then left, into Rua Guilherme José da Silva. On the left, opposite the post office, is the Casa da Eira, with a handsome Manueline window somewhat marred by that horrendous corrugated tin room that peeks out above the crenulated walls. The 14th-century Igreja de Santo Estevão, with its neoclassical facade, is at the end of the street. Nearby is a 1st-century Roman milestone from the old Braga–Astorga road.

From the milestone continue north to the end of Rua José Rodrigues and the now-decrepit Romanesque parish church, Igreja de Santa Maria dos Anjos (Church of St Mary of the Angels), dating from 1276. At the back is a tiny chapel with Romano-Gothic inscriptions on the outside. After years of being left crumbling and closed to the public it did appear to be in the midst of renovation at research time.

To the left of the parish church is the Capela da Misericórdia and beyond it the Pousada de São Teotónio.

But the best fun can be had rambling on and around the series of exterior walls. In fact, if you turn right by the *pousada* you'll descend the atmospheric lane through one of the original gates, with a trickling stream running below, and an impressive echo. Keep going and you'll pass through several thick, mossy layers to the outside world.

Sleeping

Residencial Portas do Sol

GUEST HOUSE €

(☑251 837 134; www.residencialportasdosol. com; Rua Conselheiro Lopes da Silva; s/d/tr €30/35/45; ❄) The best option in the fortress is set in an antiquated stone building that's been refurbished and outfitted with all things IKEA-esque, but that's not necessarily a bad thing. The ceilings are high, and the old stone window frames lend enough old-world panache. It's in the north fort, a half block from the bridge.

Pousada de São Teotónio   RURAL INN €€€

(☑251 800 260; www.pousadas.pt; Rua de Baluarte do Socorro; d from €100; P❄) Perched on the outermost post of the fortress and surrounded by green ramparts, this bright, modern *pousada* has large, luxurious rooms, most with prime views overlooking the walls and river to Spain; a few have balconies.

Hotel Lara   HOTEL €

(☑251 824 348; www.hotellara.com; Av dos Bombeiros; r from €35; P❄) The ageing bones of this business hotel in the new town cloak some great-value and spacious rooms, with Japanese wallpaper and tremendous views from the upper reaches. It's directly opposite the fort.

Val Flores   HOTEL €

(☑251 824 106; Av dos Bombeiros; s/d €25/30; ❄) On a busy road facing the fortress, Val Flores is a slightly less charming new town habitat that has clean trim rooms graced with cork-tiled floors and sizeable windows.

Eating

Restaurante Fortaleza

PORTUGUESE €€

(Rua Apolinário da Fonseca; meals €8-13; ⊗lunch & dinner) Set in the south fortress, with tables inside and on a wide patio with sublime views overlooking the edge of the fort, this place does a superbly grilled, melt-in-your-mouth *truta* (trout). Highly recommended.

Restaurante Baluarte   PORTUGUESE €€

(Rua Apolinário da Fonseca; mains €8-11; ⊗lunch & dinner Sat-Thu) Baluarte enjoys a peaceful fortress setting with outdoor tables fronting a plaza. A decent assortment of Minho specialities is on hand, including *truta* and seafood rice.

Churrasqueira Valença   GRILL HOUSE €

(Rua Augusto Dias 9; mains €4-7; ⊗lunch & dinner) Come to this cavernous north-fort dining room if you're looking for tasty grilled chicken. There's no patio dining, which means there's no view, but the local scene inside is worthy of your contemplation.

Shopping

There is no shortage of cheap and tacky gift shops and stalls in Valença's hallowed walls, but there's also plenty of interesting fabric shops and interiors boutiques, such as the shabby-chic Da Vinci (davinciinteriores@sapo.pt; Rua Albuquerque 139), and one superb antique store Loja Maria & Luis Maria (Viscinde da Guaratiba) deals in such treasures as 18th-century telescopes, 17th-century parasol frames made from bone, a

GOING GREEN IN VINHO VERDE COUNTRY

Outside Portugal, *vinho verde* (literally, 'green wine') gets a bum rap, but often for good reason – exports tend to sit on shelves far too long. The stuff is made to be drunk 'green' – that is, while it is still very young, preferably less than one year old.

While the wine is made from fully ripe rather than still-green grapes as is sometimes believed, the straw-coloured whites can indeed achieve greenish tints – a visual reminder of the green landscape from which they come. Served well chilled on a hot summer day, its fruity nose, fine bubbles and acidic bite make *vinho verde* one of the great delights of travelling in northern Portugal.

Vinho verde is grown in a strictly demarcated region of the Minho that occupies the coastal lowlands between the Rio Douro and the Spanish border. There are actually more vines here than in the Douro, but the *quintas* (estates) are subdivided to such a degree that most growers simply sell their fruit, or their wine, to community *adegas* (wineries).

Traditionally, the vines are trained high both to conserve land and to save the grapes from rot, and you can still see great walls of green in the summer months. Like German wines, *vinho verde* tends to be aromatic, light-bodied and low in alcohol. There are red *vinho verdes*, though you may find them chalky and more of an acquired taste. White is both the most common and the easiest to appreciate. Alvarinho grapes, grown around Monção, are also used to make a delightful *vinho verde*.

For more information about the wine, its history and visiting particular regions and vineyards, check out www.vinhoverde.pt.

---

wooden altar from a 17th-century church and a fantastic ship captain's log made from wood and elephant skin.

❶ Information

Espaço Internet (◷10am-12.30pm & 2-6.30pm Mon-Fri) By the bus station; free internet access.

Post office (Travessa do Eirado; ◷9am-12.30pm & 2-5.30pm Mon-Fri) The fortress has its own post office.

Turismo (www.cm-valenca.pt; Av de Espanha; ◷9.30am-12.30pm & 2-5.30pm Mon-Sat)

❶ Getting There & Around

Bus

AV Minho (☎251 652 917) has two daily weekday runs and one daily weekend run beginning in Monção (€2, 20 minutes) and going all the way to Porto (€9, 3½ hours) via Viana do Castelo (€4, 1¼ hours).

Car & Motorcycle

There is free parking in lots just west of the fortresses, though they can fill to capacity at weekends. If you're spending the night inside, you should be able to find free street parking within the fort.

Train

Five to 10 trains run daily to Valença from Porto (€9.30, 3½ hours), two of which continue on as far as Vigo in Spain.

Monção

POP 2600

Like Valença do Minho to the west, Monção (mohng-*sowng*) was once an important fortification along the border with Spain. It has a modest but attractive historic centre – which includes the remains of its 14th-century fortifications still watching over the river – that sees far fewer visitors than Valença's. The town's big claim to fame is its fine *vinho verde*, with signs touting Monção as the cradle of the refreshing Alvarinho wine (Spain's Galicia makes similar claims).

It is said that during a siege by Castilian soldiers in 1368, a local townswoman named Deu-la-Deu Martins managed to scrabble together enough flour from starving citizens to make a few loaves of bread, and in a brazen show of plenty tossed them to the enemy with the message, 'if you need any more, just let us know'. The disheartened Spaniards immediately withdrew back to Spain.

From the bus station it's 600m east to the defunct train station, then another two blocks north up Rua General Pimenta de Castro to the first of the town's two main squares, Praça da República. Praça Deu-la-Deu and the heart of the old town lie just one block further.

⊙ Sights & Activities

Old Monção   NEIGHBOURHOOD
The best part of Monção's old town is the utter lack of tourism. It's almost exclusively a local scene in chestnut-shaded Praça Deula-Deu, where a hand-on-breast statue of its namesake tops a **fountain** and looks hungrily down over the surrounding cafes. The **Senhora da Vista** bastion at the northern end offers a gentle view across the sinuous Rio Minho into Spain. The **Capela da Misericórdia** at the square's southern end has a coffered ceiling painted with cherubs.

East of the square is the snug, cobbled old quarter. Two blocks along Rua da Glória is the pretty little Romanesque igreja matriz (parish church), where Deu-la-Deu is buried (look for the stone-carved alcove to the left of the entrance).

Adega Cooperativa de Monção   WINERY
(www.adegademoncao.pt; ⊘10am-noon & 2-5pm Mon-Fri) Alvarinho is the delicious, tart and full-bodied variety of white *vinho verde* produced around Monção and neighbouring Melgaço. If you'd like a tasting, stop by this *adega* 1.8km south of Monção on the N101 to Arcos de Valdevez. Otherwise, the clutch of bars around Monção's principal squares will be happy to oblige.

Termas de Monção   SPA, THERMAL SPRINGS
(www.tesal.com, in Portuguese; Av das Caldas; admission €24; ⊘9:30am-7pm Mon-Sat, to 2:30pm Sun; P) Monção's *termas* (thermal springs) reopened in 2008 under Galician management. This modern centre has a large aquatic area with Jacuzzis, tiny waterfalls and a childrens swimming area. In addition to dips in the warm springs, a wide variety of spa treatments are available, with day packages starting at €49. Those wanting the aquatic experience without the fuss can head across the road to the newly inaugurated piscina municipal (Largo das Caldas).

✯✯ Festivals & Events

Feira do Alvarinho   CULTURAL
(www.feiraalvarinho.pt.vu) The self-described cradle of Alvarinho, Monção hosts a five-day fair in honour of its wine. Music, folk dancing and much eating and drinking rule the day. It's held in late May.

Festa do Corpo de Deus   RELIGIOUS
The town's biggest party is held on Corpus Christi (the ninth Thursday after Easter). Events include a religious procession and medieval fair, with a re-enactment of St George battling the dragon.

Festa da Nossa Senhora das Dores
                                    RELIGIOUS
A big five-day celebration in the third week of August, headed by a pious procession.

🛏 Sleeping

Convento dos Capuchos BOUTIQUE HOTEL €€€
(☑251 640 090; www.conventodoscapuchos.com; Quinta do Convento de São Antonio; r €103-145; P⊕ 🛜 ⛱) Monção's newest and most captivating property is set in a restored 18th-century hilltop monastery with a glimmering infinity pool overlooking the river below. The stone bones are accented nicely in the deluxe rooms with wooden floors and French doors opening onto a splendid riverfront terrace. Less expensive rooms are set in a newly constructed annexe. They are large with chic furnishings, but lack the former's majesty and views. In low season, 20% discounts are common.

Solar de Serrade   RURAL INN €€
(☑251 654 008; www.solardeserrade.pt; Mazedo; d from €70; P) One of two manor houses on area estates producing Alvarinho grapes and delicious wines, this rather magnificent 17th-century mansion has whimsical gardens and a few suites with elaborately furnished digs. Good for romantic getaways.

Hospedaria Beco da Matriz GUEST HOUSE €
(☑251 651 909; Beco da Matriz; d €35) Just left of the facade of the *igreja matriz,* this place offers simple but impeccable rooms, with comfortable beds and spotless tile floors. Some rooms have excellent views over the adjacent ramparts to Spain. Check in at the bar downstairs if there's no answer at the door.

Residencial Esteves   GUEST HOUSE €
(☑251 652 386; Rua São Antonio; d with/without €25/20) Around the corner from the Praça da República, this guest house is run by two sweet grannies and the whole vibe is infused with their laid-back warmth. You'll also find simple, spotless rooms with antique furnishings scattered throughout. No breakfast.

Fonte da Vila   BOUTIQUE HOTEL €€
(☑251 656 296; www.fontedavila.com; Beco da Matriz; s €40, d €55-65, ste €80) The Spanish-owned Fonte da Vila has cheerfully painted

rooms with wooden floors and an overall clean, contemporary look in a renovated and remodelled manor house. There's an upscale tapas and seafood restaurant on the ground floor.

Eating

For the pick of local specialities, try fresh shad, salmon and trout from the Rio Minho, and lamprey eels in spring.

Restaurante Cabral   PORTUGUESE €€
(Rua de Zenbro 1; mains €6-18; ⊙lunch & dinner) Cabral grills fresh fish and does a tasty *arroz do marisco* (rice and seafood stew) too. It's all served in an attractive stone-walled dining room, almost always packed at lunch, down a narrow lane from Praça Deu-la-Deu.

Sete á Sete   PORTUGUESE €€
(For a de Portas; mains €10-17; ⊙lunch & dinner Tue-Sat) About 600m south of the old centre, this place serves up top-notch *bacalhau* as well as Minho specialities made with the finest, freshest ingredients.

O Escondinho   CAFE €
(Praça Deu-la-Deu 18; pastries €1; ⊙breakfast, lunch & dinner) Monção's best pastry shop has tempting fresh-baked goods with outdoor tables overlooking the plaza.

Restaurante O Ardo   PORTUGUESE €€
(Rua dos Neiris; plates from €11; ⊙lunch & dinner) Expect more of the same traditional plates on the ground floor of this old stone relic. The tourist menu offers a choice of meat or fish served with a glass of the local *vinho verde*. Or you could just belly up to the circle bar and sip it from the tap (€0.80).

ⓘ Information

Post office (Praça da República; ⊙9am-12.30pm & 2-5.30pm Mon-Fri)

Turismo (www.cm-moncao.pt; Praça Deu-la-Deu; ⊙9.30am-12.30pm & 2-6pm Mon-Sat) Housed in the Casa do Curro, the *turismo* also sells a small but high-quality selection of pottery and lacework from artisans of northern Portugal.

ⓘ Getting There & Around

You'll find street parking around Praça da República.

AV Minho (☑251 652 917) operates one weekend and two weekday buses that stop here en route from Melgaço (€2.20, 35 minutes) to Porto (€8, four hours) via Viana do Castelo (€4, 1½ hours).

Ponte de Lima

POP 2800 / ELEV 175M

This photogenic town by the sweet and mellow Rio Lima springs to life on weekends when Portuguese tourists descend in droves, and every other Monday, when a vast market spreads along the riverbank. All the action happens within sight of Portugal's finest medieval bridge. And even if you can't make the market, Ponte de Lima's small, historic centre dotted with cafes, and vast riverside gardens and greenways are well worth visiting. Even the outskirts are romantic, as vineyards tumble down to bustling avenues, and at sunset swallows take flight, singing and diving until night finally falls.

When a Roman regiment first passed through here, soldiers were convinced that the Rio Lima was Lethe itself – the mythical 'river of oblivion'. Alas, no such luck. Decimus Junius Brutus forced his men to plunge ahead, and yet they still remembered all their sins upon reaching the far side. The impressive Ponte Romana (Roman Bridge) – part of the Roman road from Braga to Astorga in Spain and the town's namesake – supposedly marks their crossing. Though largely rebuilt in medieval times, it still contains traces of its Roman antecedent.

◉ Sights

Ponte Romana & Arcozelo   LANDMARKS
The city's pièce de résistance, this elegant 31-arched bridge across the Rio Lima is now limited to foot traffic. Most of it dates from the 14th century, though the segment on the north bank by the village of **Arcozelo** is bona fide Roman.

In Arcozelo you'll find the extremely photogenic little **Igreja Santo António**, built in 1814, and the kitsch **Parque do Arnado** (admission free; ⊙10am-7pm), an architecturally themed park that crams in styles from all around the world.

In Ponte de Lima, **Largo de Camões**, with a fountain resembling a giant bonbon dish, makes a fine spot to watch the sun set over the bridge.

FREE **Museu dos Terceiros & Around**
    MUSEUM
(www.museudoterceiros.com; Av dos Plátanos; ⊙10am-noon & 2-5.30pm Tue-Sun) Downriver, the 18th-century Igreja de São Francisco dos Terceiros is now a rambling museum full of ecclesiastical and folk treasures,

although the highlight is the church itself, with its gilded baroque interior. The Renaissance-style **Igreja de Santo António dos Frades**, once a convent church, is now a wing of the museum. Both churches just benefited from an extensive renovation and are well worth a visit.

Town Walls & Towers   LANDMARKS
Two crenulated towers (part of the fortifications made in the 14th century) face the river at the end of Rua Cardeal Saraiva. The **Torre da Cadeia Velha** (Old Prison Tower; admission free; ☉2-6pm Tue-Sun) now houses temporary art exhibitions, plus a host of pigeons on its window ledges.

Fragments of the walls survive behind and between this and the other tower, the **Torre de São Paulo**. Note the somewhat bizarre *azulejo* image on its front wall, entitled *Cabras são Senhor!* (They're goats m'lord!) – a reference to a local story in which Dom Afonso Henriques almost attacked a herd of goats, apparently mistaking them for Moors!

Behind the tower is the rather staid, mostly 15th-century **igreja matriz** (Rua Cardeal Saraiva; ☉daily), sporting a pretty Romanesque doorway.

Lagoas de Beritandos e São Pedro d'Arcos   NATURE RESERVE
(www.lagoas.cm-pontedelima.pt, in Portuguese; admission €1; ☉9am-12.30pm & 2-5.30pm Mon-Fri, 2.30-6pm Sat & Sun) This 350-hectare nature reserve is set in a wildlife-rich humid zone just north of the Rio Lima. There's a wildlife interpretation centre and five hiking trails, ranging from an easy lakeside loop (1.6km) to a longer 12.5km hike. To get there, take the A27 4km west from Ponte de Lima, taking exit 3.

Jardins Temáticos   GARDEN
(Thematic Gardens; admission €1; ☉10:30am-7pm) Green space is abundant in Ponte de Lima, but this small, intriguing garden with rose bushes and lemon-filled trellises next to a public swimming pool on the west side of the river is notable because each May it hosts a competition where 12 artists create temporary gardens built around a theme. The winning garden is chosen in October and it remains rooted for the year.

FREE **Museu de Carlos de Cavalos** MUSEUM
(☎258 731 162; Quinta da Bouca, Santa Leocádia de Geraz do Lima; ☉3-7pm Sat & Sun) A private museum owned by a local, carriage-obsessed physician, it's stocked with more than 50 antique carriages spanning the horse-drawn traditions of the UK, Holland, Italy, Spain, the US and, of course, Portugal. Admission is by reservation only (get directions when you ring).

🏃 Activities

Ecovia   WALKING, CYCLING
On both sides of the Rio Lima you'll find riverside paths. On the left bank it follows the river east for 5km to **Bertiandos**. On the right bank it runs east for 14.1km to the settlement of **Bravães**. West of Ponte de Lima, the *ecovia* (greenway) begins again off Av dos Plátanos and runs 13.3km to **Deano**. The big government dream is to eventually follow the Lima all the way to Viana do Castelo, but for a day's whirl, this will do just fine. Given the distances it's best to explore the paths by bike. Rent wheels (per hour €2) at Clube Náutico.

Village Walks   WALKING
There are several charming walks through the countryside, past ancient monuments and along cobbled lanes trellised with vines. The *turismo* has literature on routes ranging from 5km to 14km. Pack water and a picnic – cafes and restaurants are rare.

A steep 5km climb north of Arcozelo yields panoramic views up and down the Lima valley from a tiny and bizarre **chapel** (open irregular hours) dedicated to Santo Ovídio, patron saint of ears. Yes, you read that right. The interior is covered with ear-shaped votive candles offered in hope of, or as thanks for, the cure of an ear affliction. You can also drive up; the turn-off from the N202 is about 2.5km upstream of the N201 bridge.

Clube Náutico   CANOEING, KAYAKING
(www.cnplima.com; kayaks & canoes per hr €3; ☉10am-1pm & 2.30-7pm Jul-Sep, 10am-1pm & 3-7pm Sat & Sun Oct-Jun) Across the river and 400m downstream from town, this aquatic outfitter rents canoes and plastic kayaks for exploring the mellow river as it spreads over willowed sand bars, glistens blue in the sun and fades to deep green at dusk. It also rents bicycles (per hour €2).

🎉 Festivals & Events

Vaca das Cordas & Corpus Christi
                    CULTURAL
On the ninth Wednesday after Easter, another tradition probably dates back at least to Roman times and possibly has

Ponte de Lima

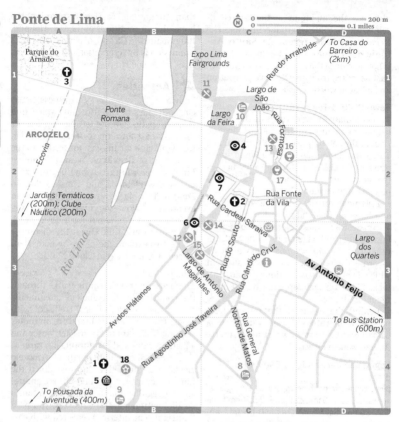

Phoenician origins. It features a kind of bull-running in which young men goad a hapless bull (restrained by a long rope) as it runs through the town. It's followed the next day by the more pious Festa do Corpo de Deus, with religious processions and flowers carpeting the streets.

Feiras do Cavalo　　　　HORSE RACING
(www.feiradocavalo.com) Held annually in the third week of June, this horse fair is one of the town's most raucous festivals, when the Expo Lima, the riverside fairgrounds, becomes a race track and stage for horseman, carriages and musicians.

Feiras Novas　　　　CULTURAL
(New Fairs) Held here since 1125, this is one of Portugal's most ancient ongoing events. Stretching over three days during the third week of September it centres on the riverfront, with a massive market and fair, and features folk dances, fireworks, brass bands and all manner of

merrymaking. Book accommodation well ahead.

🛏 Sleeping

Casa do Pinheiro　　TOP CHOICE　　GUEST HOUSE €€
(☎258 943 971; www.manorhouses.com/manors/portugal/casadopinheiro.html; Rua General Norton de Matos 50; d €65; ❈☎❋)
The unsigned Casa do Pinheiro is set in a painstakingly restored private house, whose seven elegant rooms boast high ceilings, antique beds and touches of religious art. Some rooms have balconies, while others open onto the splendid back garden with pool and fruit trees. You can use the house computer for internet access. It's a stunning place and breakfast is fabulous. Don't let the animal heads in the foyer put you off.

InLima　　　　BOUTIQUE HOTEL €€
(☎258 900 050; www.inlimahotel.com; Rua Agostinho José Taveira 6; s/d €75/85; ❈🛜☎)

Floating above the *ecovia* like some white-washed frosted glass pod from the future is the newest, flashiest hotel in town. These 30 chic rooms all have woven floors, blond-wood desks, lush linens, rain showers and wide terraces. At these prices, it's a steal.

Casa do Arrabalde   RURAL INN €€
(☑258 742 442; www.casadoarrabalde.com; Arcozelo; r €80, cottages €80-130; P 🅿 🐕 🏊) This terrific option sits conveniently just across the Ponte Romana in Arcozelo. The main quarters are still inhabited by the family who built the place in the 18th century. Rooms are grand and furnished with period antiques; cottages are more contemporary. There are huge grounds and an inviting pool.

Quinta de Pentieiros
         CAMPGROUND, BUNGALOWS €
(☑258 733 553; www.lagoas.cm-pontedelima. pt, in Portuguese; camp sites €3-10, casas €20-90; P 🏊) Inside the Lagoas nature reserve, this estate has campgrounds and more comfortable bungalows and casas (€20 to €90) with kitchen units that work well for families. There's also an inviting swimming pool, horse riding and bike rental available. Prices are lower (and crowds fewer) on weekdays.

Pousada da Juventude   HOSTEL €
(☑258 751 321; www.pousadasjuventude.pt; Rua Papa João Paulo II; dorm €12, r €28-30; P @ 🛜) Built of concrete, wood and glass, this striking, contemporary youth hostel is a pleasant 800m walk from the centre of town along the river. Facilities are limited, but rooms are clean and attractive.

Casa do Barreiro   RURAL INN €€
(☑258 948 137; www.casadobarreiro.net; Quinta de Pias, Gemeira; r €70, apt €70-120; P 🏊) Particularly elegant, this 17th-century manor house about halfway between Ponte de Lima and Ponte de Barca features original details, including stone mantles and *azulejos*. Rooms are spare but lovely, and the grounds gush with fountains, are surrounded by vineyards and include a pool and tennis courts.

Residencial São João   GUEST HOUSE €
(☑258 941 288; restaurante_sjoao@spo.pt; Largo de São João; d from €30) This welcoming, family-run guest house offers a decent collection of clean, serviceable and mostly bright rooms (no TV) with wooden floors. Some have private bathrooms. Quarters are tight but the location can't be beat. Ask at the restaurant on the ground floor.

✕ Eating

Restaurante Muralha   PORTUGUESE €€
(Largo da Picota; mains €9-16; ⏱lunch & dinner) Tucked into an alcove behind one of the town's old towers, this somewhat divey dining room also serves up tasty seafood dishes (those salmon steaks rock). They brag about their *cabrito* too. Believe it.

Restaurante A Tulha   PORTUGUESE €
(Rua Formosa; mains €6-10; ⏱lunch & dinner Tue-Sat, lunch Sun; ❄) All dark wood, stone and terracotta tiles inside, this restaurant serves excellent meat and fish dishes with plenty of vegetables. Try the *medalhão á Tulha* – a thick steak wrapped in bacon.

Casa Almeida   PORTUGUESE €
(Almeida de São João 44; mains €6-12; ⏱lunch & dinner Tue-Sat) With its glorious riverside

perch north of the bridge, locals swear this is the best place in town to eat roast octopus.

Sabores do Lima
PORTUGUESE €€

(Largo de António Magalhães 64; mains €8-13; ⊙lunch & dinner) A few steps from the river, the inviting Sabores do Lima has exposed stone walls that give a dash of style to its open dining room. The first-rate cooking features grilled meats, cod dishes and a few assorted seafood plates.

Pimenta & Reis
DELI €

(Passeio 25 de April; ⊙lunch & dinner) If you're looking for a loaf of bread, a wedge of cheese and a hunk of smoked protein to include in your self-catering kit, stop by this boutique sausage factory. You won't be disappointed.

Restaurante A Carvalheira
PORTUGUESE €€

(☑258 742 316; mains €12-18; ⊙lunch & dinner Tue-Sun; P✸) On the N202 at the northern end of Arcozelo, country-style A Carvalheira is generally agreed to serve the area's best food. Order ahead if you want the regional favourite – *arroz de sarrabulho* (stewed rice with pork and pork blood).

Drinking

Arte e Baco
WINE BAR

(Rua Formosa 19; ⊙1pm-2am Jun-Sep, 4pm-2am Tue-Sun Oct-May) The hippest bar in town is a black-floored, chalkboard-walled lounge featuring rotating art exhibitions, the finest wine from the Minho (mostly *vinho verde*) and Douro, fine cigars, better port and occasional live music.

Bar Che
BAR

(Rua Formosa; ⊙4pm-2am) Images of the bar's namesake revolutionary decorate this cosy place, which has long attracted alternative types.

☆ Entertainment

Teatro Diogo Bernardes
THEATRE

(www.cm-pontedelima.pt; Rua Agostinho José Taveira) Behind the Museu dos Terceiros, the galleried Teatro Diogo Bernardes, built in 1893, is the pride of the town, with interesting music and theatre performances throughout the year.

❶ Information

Caixa Geral de Depósitos (☑258 909 300; Rua Inácio Perestrelo 40) ATMs and currency exchange.

Espaço Internet (☑258 900 400, ext 415; Av António Feijó; ⊙1-8pm Mon-Fri, 10am-8pm Sat) Free internet access.

Hospital (☑258 909 500; Rua Conde de Bertiandos)

Police station (☑258 941 113; Rua Dr Luís da Cunha Nogueira)

Post office (Praça da República; ⊙8.30am-5.30pm Mon-Fri)

Turismo (www.cm-pontedelima.pt; Praça do Marquês; ⊙9.30am-12.30pm & 2.30-6pm Mon-Sat, 10am-12.30pm Sun Jun-Aug, 9.30am-12.30pm & 2-5.30pm Mon-Sat, 10am-12.30pm Sun Sep-May) This exceptionally friendly and well-organised tourist office shares an old tower with a small handicrafts gallery. The lower floor has glass walkways over the excavated layers of an ancient tower.

❶ Getting There & Away

There is street parking uphill from Praça da República; higher up, it's free.

Board long-distance buses on Av António Feijó (buy tickets on board) or at the bus station. All services thin out on Sunday.

AV Cura/Transcolvia (☑258 800 340) has a service to Viana do Castelo (€3.50, 50 minutes). **Rede Expressos** (☑258 942 870) has one daily run to Braga (€4, 30 minutes), Valença do Minho (€7, 25 minutes) and Lisbon (€19, 6½ hours) via Porto (€8, 2¼ hours).

Ponte da Barca
POP 2100 /ELEV 178M

Peaceful and friendly Ponte da Barca, named after the *barca* (barge) that once ferried pilgrims and others across the Rio Lima, has an idyllic, willow-shaded riverfront (perfect for cycling into the wooded valley), a handsome 16th-century bridge, a tiny old centre and the best source of information on the Parque Nacional da Peneda-Gerês.

The old town, just east of the bridge, is packed into narrow lanes on both sides of the main road, Rua Conselheiro Rocha Peixoto. Wednesday is market day.

◉ Sights & Activities

The riverfront is the focal point of the town (and a good place for a picnic), with picturesque weeping willows lining the banks of the Rio Lima, and a green lawn that beckons sunbathers. The lovely, 10-arched ponte (bridge) originally dates from the 1540s. Beside it is the old arcaded marketplace and a little garden, **Jardim dos Poetas**, dedicated to two 16th-century poet brothers, Diogo Bernardes and Agostinho da Cruz, who were born in Ponte da Barca.

It's now a strip of occasionally happening bars with ample, shady park-bench riverside seating.

The *turismo* has a booklet called *Historia, Patrimonia & Cultura* with regional information, including details of hikes in the surrounding valley, some of them punctuated with ancient sites. A simple stroll west for 4km leads to Bravães, a village famous for its lovely, small Romanesque Igreja de São Salvador. Its west portal is adorned with intricate carved animals, birds and human figures; its interior shelters simple frescoes of the Virgin and of the Crucifixion.

✨ Festivals & Events

Festa de São Bartolomeu   CULTURAL
Held from 19 to 24 August, this festival sees folk music and dancing aplenty, not to mention parades and fireworks.

🛏 Sleeping

TOP CHOICE Casa Nobre do Correio Mor   INN   €€
(📞258 452 129; www.correiomorlaceme. pt; Rua Trás do Forno 1; r €80; P🛜❄) Lovingly restored, this 17th-century manor house on the street above the town hall offers 10 gorgeous rooms, most with stone-framed windows, wide timber floors, antique furnishings and French windows with city and river views.

Pensão Restaurante Gomes   GUEST HOUSE   €
(📞258 452 288; Rua Conselheiro Rocha Peixoto 13; d without bathroom €25) Welcome to your sweet Barca granny's house. Incredibly cheap, old-world rooms have worn wooden floors, sloping ceilings and tons of charm, and there are fabulous river and bridge views from the rooftop terrace.

Residencial San Fernando   GUEST HOUSE   €
(📞258 452 580; www.residencialsfernando.com; Rua de São Antonio; d €28; P) At the very top of the new town, about 800m beyond Pensão Restaurante Gomes, this more-modern, businesslike *residencial* has smart, bright rooms with up-to-date comforts, up a marble staircase. It's a very good-value option. If you can't find anyone at the desk, pop into the furniture shop next door.

Residencial Os Poetas   GUEST HOUSE   €€
(📞258 453 578; Largo dos Poetas 49; d from €50; 🕑Jul-Sep) A short stroll east of the bridge, this summer-only place has 10 pleasant rooms and an excellent riverside location.

🍴 Eating & Drinking

Restaurante Veranda do Lima
PORTUGUESE   €€
(Campo do Cúrro; mains €9-18; 🕑lunch & dinner) The recently remodelled main dining room is one of Barca's grandest options, with fresh fish and all the traditional meat dishes served on pressed tablecloths. If you want something lighter, pop into the restaurant's popular cafe next door.

O Desejo   PORTUGUESE   €
(Rua Peixoto; mains €6-12; 🕑lunch & dinner Tue-Sun) Tucked up a narrow stone lane from Rua Peixoto, this tiny dining room is a local favourite for traditional *chouriços* (sausages), *bacalhau a casa* (house cod) and *costeletao de novilho* (breaded veal chop). There are some nice wines here too.

Belião Bar   CAFE, BAR   €
(www.myspace.com/beliaobar; Jardim dos Poetas; mains €6-8; 🕑10am-2am Sun-Thu, to 4am Fri & Sat; 🎵) On a pretty plaza overlooking the bridge, diners can enjoy vegetable lasagne, Mexican burritos, vegetable quiche, hamburgers and big salads made with market-fresh ingredients. At night the bar frequently hosts live bands and DJs.

Exlibris Bar   BAR
(Rua Doutor Alberto Cruz 27; 🕑4pm-2am Sun-Thu, to 4am Fri & Sat) Housed in an old stone relic, this fashionable oasis was the new hot spot when we came through. DJs spin on weekends.

ℹ Information

Adere-PG (Parque Nacional da Peneda-Gerês Regional Development Association; www. adere-pg.pt; Largo da Misericórdia 10; 🕑9am-12.30pm & 2.30-6pm Mon-Fri) Park information and bookings (see p436).

Espaço Internet (Rua Doutor José Lacerda Emegre 17; 🕑10am-6pm Mon-Sat) Free internet access.

Post office (Rua das Fontaínhas; 🕑9am-12.30pm & 2-5.30pm Mon-Fri)

Turismo (www.pontedabarca.com.pt; Rua Dom Manuel I; 🕑9.30am-12.30pm & 2.30-6pm Mon-Sat) The tourist office is about 750m east of the bridge down a small street, and has a town map and accommodation information. The adjacent shop sells local wine, honey and jam.

ℹ Getting There & Away

You'll find free parking in the shady square at the western end of the bridge.

AV Cura buses run to Arcos de Valdevez (€1.10, 15 minutes), Ponte de Lima (€2.50, 40 minutes) and Viana do Castelo (€3.80, 1½ hours) four to five times daily from Monday to Friday, and once or twice a day on weekends.

Salvador buses travel through Ponte da Barca twice a day Monday to Friday on their way from Arco of Valdevez to Soajo (€2.40, 45 minutes) in Parque Nacional da Peneda-Gerês. Buses stop in front of Pensão Restaurante Gomes, just west of the old bridge. Enquire at the *turismo* for the current schedule.

Arcos de Valdevez

POP 2300 / ELEV 200M

Drowsy little Arcos de Valdevez is home to a couple of interesting old churches and several stately homes in a small, almost tourist-free old centre. It also has a vibrant, willow-shaded riverfront. While it doesn't merit a special trip, it's a handy gateway to the northern end of Parque Nacional da Peneda-Gerês.

Sleeping

TOP CHOICE Pacos de Gloria   RURAL INN €€€

(www.manorhousesofportugal.com; São Paio de Jolda; r €80-110; P ⊛) A restored 18th-century manor house, built on 13th-century foundations in what was then the cradle of Portuguese nobility, can be your nest in the vineyard-draped hills outside Arcos. There are two choices here. Rooms inside the house are massive, with stone fireplaces and huge marble bathrooms, while those in the 17th-century staff annexe are older and cosier. There's a fantastic 1730s chapel with a gilded altar on the property too, and the pool is glorious. Reservations must be made via the website.

Casa da Breia   RURAL INN €€

(📞258 751 751; www.casadabreia.com; São Paio de Jolda; r €35-65; P 🛜⌗) This sweeping 17th-century *quinta* nestled in a village just 10km from Arcos is owned by a sweet family who offer up the charming, historic stone staff quarters to guests. Hosts offer terrific tips for visiting the nearby national park.

Residencial Tavares   GUEST HOUSE €

(📞965 181 226; Rua Padre MJ Cunha Brito; d €30; ⌗) In the historic centre, Tavares is excellent value for its clean, bright rooms, though the building itself is modern and unappealing. Some rooms have balconies. It's near the *câmara municipal*.

Hotel Ribeira   BOUTIQUE HOTEL €

(📞258 531 358; hoteldaribeira@gmail.com; Largo dos Milagres; s/d €40/50; P ⊛ @ 🛜) Except for its picturesque fairy-pink facade, this early-1900s town house has, unfortunately, been largely gutted of its original character, but it does have spotless, comfortable rooms with big windows, high ceilings and an excellent position by the river.

Eating

TOP CHOICE Doçaria Central   BAKERY €

(Rua General Norton de Matos 47; pastries €1; ⌚breakfast & lunch) Founded in 1830, this wonderful confectioner stocks the town's favourite sweet (*rebuçados dos arcos*; enormous, jaw-breaking, hard-boiled sweets) and pastry (*charutos da Barcos*; preserved egg wrapped in a sugary dough). To get here take the street to the right of the tourist office, past the post office.

Matadouro   STEAKHOUSE €€

(Campo do Trasladário; mains €9-18; ⌚lunch & dinner) Set in a stately house on the riverside, Matadouro serves some of the best steaks in the Minho. When we visited there were plans to introduce a less expensive barbecue menu on summer nights. It's located about 500m south of the *turismo* on the river.

Restaurante Minho Verde   PORTUGUESE €€

(Rua Mário Júlio Almeida Costa 37; mains €6-12; ⌚lunch & dinner Mon-Sat) One of Arcos' finest restaurants is in an unlikely location in an ugly block down the waterfront from the *turismo*. However, it serves excellent Minho specialities ranging from *posta de vitela* (veal steak) to *arroz de sarrabulho*.

Entertainment

Azenha Club   NIGHTCLUB

(www.azenha.com.pt; Campo do Trasladário; ⌚10pm-4am) In an old stone house perched over the river, this club is a popular destination for the young partiers of Arcos de Valdevez.

ℹ Information

Turismo (www.portonorte.pt; Campo do Trasladário; ⌚9.30am-noon & 2.30-6pm Mon-Sat) This helpful, English-speaking tourist office is across from the town fountains (legless horses).

ℹ Getting There & Away

The bus station is almost 1km north of the town centre, but regional buses will stop on request in front of the *turismo*.

AV Cura buses run to Ponte da Barca (€1.10, 15 minutes), Ponte de Lima (€2.65, 40 minutes) and Viana do Castelo (€4, 1½ hours) four to five times daily Monday to Friday, and once or twice on weekends.

Salvador buses roll at least twice on weekdays to Soajo (€2.40, 40 minutes) in Parque Nacional da Peneda-Gerês. There is no weekend service into the park.

PARQUE NACIONAL DA PENEDA-GERÊS

Spread across four impressive granite massifs in Portugal's northernmost reach, this 703-sq-km park encompasses boulder-strewn peaks, precipitous valleys, and lush forests of oak and fragrant pine. It also shelters more than 100 granite villages that, in many ways, have changed little since Portugal's founding in the 12th century. Established in 1971, Parque Nacio-

nal da Peneda-Gerês – Portugal's first and most important national park – has helped to preserve not just a unique set of ecosystems but also an endangered way of life for its human inhabitants.

Many of the park's oldest villages are found in the Serra da Peneda and remain in a time warp, with oxen trundled down cobbled streets by black-clad widows, and horses shod in smoky blacksmith shops. You can get the good kind of lost amid the hard-handed, open-hearted shepherds of old Portugal who still maintain the practice of moving livestock, and even entire villages, to high pastures for up to five months each year. Yet, despite joint governmental and private initiatives, this rustic scene is in danger of fading away, as young people head for the cities and village populations continue to shrink. The steeper, more pristine Serra do Gerês sees the most tourism, in the form of hiking and water sports such as kayaking and rafting.

Parque Nacional da Peneda-Gerês

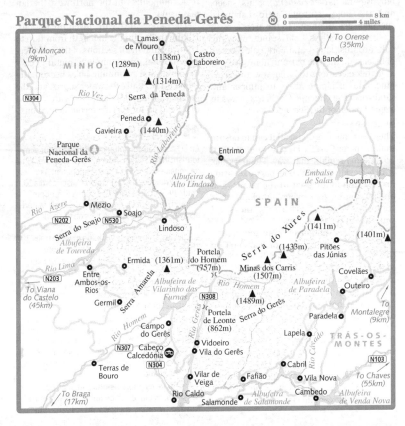

ℹ HONEY

Local honey (*mel*) is on sale everywhere. The best – unpasteurised, unadulterated and with a faint piny taste – is from small dealers; look for signs on private homes.

Environment

WILDLIFE

In the more remote areas a few wolves still roam, as do wild boar, badgers and otters. With luck, you may catch a quick glimpse of roe deer and a few wild ponies. Closer to the ground are grass snakes and the rare venomous black viper. Birders should look out for red kites, buzzards, goshawks, golden eagles and several species of owl.

The park's domestic animals are also of interest – and don't tend to run away so fast. In particular, primitive local breeds of long-horned cattle (the mahogany-coloured *barrosã* and darker *cachena*), goats, sheep, and the huge, sturdy Castro Laboreiro sheepdog are all unique to the area.

Sheltered valleys hold stands of white oak, arbutus, laurel and cork oak. Forests of black oak, English oak and holly give way at higher elevations to birch, yew and Scots pine, and in alpine areas to juniper and sandwort. The endemic Gerês iris grows in a small patch of the Serra do Gerês.

PROTECTED AREAS

The government is doing all it can to ensure that Peneda-Gerês' largely undisturbed ecosystems remain that way. The park has a high-elevation inner zone, partly set aside for research and closed to the public, and an outer buffer zone, where development is controlled. Most villages, roads, tracks and trails are in the latter area.

The most assiduously protected area is the Mata de Albergaria, north of Vila do Gerês. Ironically, it's crossed by the N308 highway, which, because it serves an EU-appointed border crossing, cannot simply be closed. Motorised traffic is tolerated on a 6km stretch of road above Gerês but forbidden to linger. At checkpoints at either end, drivers must pay €1.50 to enter the road from June to September. Daily patrols ensure that motorists don't park on the road. Two side roads are also no-go areas for non-residents: southwest down the Rio Homem valley and east from Portela do Homem into the high Serra do Gerês.

Campers must use designated sites or risk the wrath of park rangers. There are also restrictions on the type of boats allowed in the park's *albufeiras* (reservoirs), and no boats at all are allowed on the Vilarinho das Furnas and Paradela. Even swimming is prohibited in Vilarinho das Furnas.

◉ Sights & Activities

The ancient, remote granite villages, still inhabited by farmers and shepherds (and now small doses of tourists), are the park's real treasure. So are their distinctive *espigueiros* (stone granaries; see p437).

There is a scattering of Stone Age dolmens and antas (megaliths) on the high plateaux of the Serra da Peneda and Serra do Gerês, near Castro Laboreiro, Mezio, Paradela, Pitões das Júnias and Tourém. Not all are easily accessible, but there is a good road from the park gateway in Mezio to Gaio. Once home to the Mezio people, it's considered to be one of the most important rock compounds in the northwest Iberian peninsula.

The park is alive with adventure options. Hiking trails ranging in length from 1km to 17km abound in all sections of the park. Signage is solid, mountain-bike rental is easy to source, and swimming holes beckon. Rio Caldo is the centre for water sports, and the thermal springs of Vila do Gerês are worth a dip. Read on for specific recommendations.

ℹ Information

An EU-assisted consultancy formed to spur eco-tourism in the region, **Adere-PG** (Parque Nacional da Peneda-Gerês Regional Development Association; www.adere-pg.pt; Largo da Misericórdia 10, Ponte da Barca; ⏰9am-12.30pm & 2.30-6pm Mon-Fri) is the best resource on the park. Materials available include pamphlets on the park's natural, architectural and human landscapes, and about village-to-village walks on marked trails. There's also a booklet on accommodation.

Adere-PG is also the booking agent for many camp grounds, shelters and rural houses located in the park. You can peruse pictures, read about, and book accommodation online (in Portuguese) at www.adere-pg.pt.

Adere-PG also offers an informative gateway station at Mezio (⏰10am-7pm Jun-Sep, to 5pm Oct-May), 13km from Arcos and now the main park gateway from Arcos de Valdevez and Ponte da Barca. It has solid maps, but can't book rural accommodation.

Another even more helpful and information-packed park office can be found at Lamas de Mouro (www.cm-melgaco.pt; ⏰10am-7pm

Jun-Sep, to 5pm Oct-May) gateway, on the way to Castro Laboreiro.

ℹ️ Getting There & Around

Bus

Empresa Hoteleira do Gerês (✆253 262 033) buses go from Braga to Vila do Gerês (€3.50, 1½ hours) hourly during the week and six times on Saturday and Sunday.

Salvador buses pass through Ponte da Barca twice on weekdays on their way from Arco de Valdevez to Soajo (€2.10, 45 minutes) and Lindoso (€2.20, one hour) in Parque Nacional da Peneda-Gerês.

Car & Motorcycle

Paved roads are well maintained throughout the park, but back roads can be axle-breakers. There's no practical way to travel by car or motorcycle between the Peneda and Gerês sections of the park, except from outside it – most conveniently via Spain, or back through Braga.

Serra da Peneda

The least visited, northernmost end of the park is ripe for exploration. It is here where lower-lying forested hills fade into massive glacially formed peaks. Some are topped with powerful 21st-century windmills, others sit idly watching over vast boulder fields. Old stone houses huddle in the shadows, wild horses and cattle gather and wander free, old stone fences sprout haphazardly and wind through wildflower prairies.

👁 Sights & Activities

Hiking is the principal activity in this end of the park, but there's a certain amount of old-world history to explore on these trails too. The easiest walk can be found opposite the Lamas de Mouro gate. This **interpretative trail** winds past watermills, stone churches and community ovens, and along a stream for 4km.

Driving from here, bear right at the intersection and you'll head into the somewhat sprawling village of **Castro Laboreiro**, named for its endemic sheepdogs but more notable for the picturesque ruins of its 16th-century **castle**, built in 1505 on the foundations of a 12th-century Moorish castle. You can access it from a short and faint 800m trail. Views are stunning. Castro Laboreiro also has three other trails to explore. The shortest is a moderate 3km **interpretative trail**, but the more strenuous and spectacular are the **Trilho Castrejo**, a 17km ramble

over some of the oldest trails in these mountains, and the equally beautiful but less demanding 7km **Trilho Curro da Velha**. Maps and brochures with trail descriptions are available in Lamas de Mouro, but you can also download the brochures for free from the website www.cm-melgaco.pt. Castro Laboreiro has one strikingly modern hotel, which rents bicycles (€3/17 per hour/day) to all comers if you'd rather see the sights, such as the area's unimproved **thermal springs**, on two wheels.

Further south, almost halfway between Lamas De Mouro and Soajo, is one of the park's most stunning mountain villages, and the *serra's* namesake. Set on both sides of a deep ravine, and backed by a domed mountain and gushing waterfall, **Peneda** will take your breath away. The village's only hotel, a former pilgrims lodge, is set next to the historic **Igreja Senhora de Peneda**. This historic church is the centre of the **Festas de Senhora**, which takes place during the first week of September when villagers converge on the plaza for candlelit processions and long nights of music, dance and prayer. It's possible to climb the face of Peneda's gorgeous domed peak, but you'll need to bring your own climbing gear. Otherwise, a short but steep **1km trail** begins from behind the church and winds past, up and over the dome to a man-made but still scenic **lake** high in the hills where wild horses graze the savannah.

ESPIGUEIROS

They look hauntingly like mausoleums, but *espigueiros* are in fact the stuff of life. New World corn was a great innovation in these low-yielding lands when it was introduced in the 18th century. But there was a catch – it ripened late, when autumn rains threatened harvests with rot. *Espigueiros* – granite caskets on stilts with slotted sides – were created to dry and store the valuable kernels. Usually built in clusters, covered with moss and topped with little crosses, they look like the village graveyard. Neither the washing lines lashed to them nor the squat, long-horned cattle grazing at their feet can entirely dispel their eerie charm.

If you stay on the trail past the lake you can make an 8km loop that leads back to the main highway just uphill from Peneda.

Sleeping & Eating

Hotel de Peneda BOUTIQUE HOTEL €€
(☎251 460 040; www.hotelpeneda.com; Lugar da Peneda; r €40-75; P❀) Once a nest for Igreja Senhora de Peneda's pilgrims, these days Hotel de Peneda is one hell of a mountain lodge, with a waterfall backdrop, a gushing creek beneath and ultracosy rooms with blond-wood floors, French windows and views of quaint Peneda village across the ravine. If you'd rather save a few bucks, stay in the even more atmospheric but less improved stone quarters in the Anja de Guarda wing (singles/doubles €40/45); these rooms get very cold in the winter. The hotel also has a decent restaurant. If you only have one night to spend in the park, come here.

Hotel Castrum Villae BOUTIQUE HOTEL €€
(☎251 460 010; www.castrumvillae.com; Castro Laboreiro; s/d €53/63; P❀) A fairly modern, comfy hotel just off the highway and a short hoof to the *castro* (castle, p437). The tiled rooms are bright and have accent wallpaper but are just a cut above basic. However, the hotel also has a restaurant and rents bikes.

Parque do Campismo Lamas de Mouro
CAMPGROUND €
(☎251 465 010; www.cm-melgaco.pt; Lamas de Mouro; per adult/tent/car €3.20/3.10/3.10; ☉Jul-Sep) There are some tremendous, shady, creekside campsites here near boulder fields and flowering meadows. There are also a few restaurants not too far away in the village northwest of the park gate.

Getting There & Away

This is self-driving country. The park office at Mezio provides general park information and can supply a map, but you'll get more specific hiking advice at the brilliant Lamas de Mouro gate.

Soajo

POP 500 / ELEV 300M

Sturdy Soajo (soo-*ahzh*-oo), high above the upper Rio Lima, is best known for its photogenic *espigueiros*. It has splendid views over the surrounding countryside, with scenic walks providing a fine opportunity to take in the beauty of this protected region. Although it lacks the majesty of the Serra da Peneda high country, it's accessible by public transport and thanks to village enterprise and the Turismo de Aldeia, you can stay in one of Soajo's restored stone houses and glimpse a vanishing way of life.

Soajo is 21km northeast of Ponte da Barca on the N203 and N530, or the same distance from Arcos de Valdevez via the scenic N202 and N304. Buses stop by Restaurante Videira at the intersection of these two roads. A few hundred metres down the N530 towards Lindoso are Soajo's trademark *espigueiros*.

Soajo's small main square, Largo do Eiró – with a *pelourinho* topped by what can only be described as an ancient smiley face – is down a lane in the opposite direction from the bus stop.

Activities

Soajo is filled with the sound of rushing water, a resource that has been painstakingly managed over the centuries. A steep walk on the eastern slopes shows just how important these streams once were.

On the N304, 250m north of the bus stop, is the signed trailhead for the **Trilho do Ramil**. Initially paved with immense stones and grooved by centuries of oxcart traffic, it ascends though a landscape shaped by agriculture, taking in granite cottages, *espigueiros*, and superb views. Further up are three derelict **watermills** for grinding corn, stone channels that once funnelled the stream from one mill to the next, and the reservoir that fed them. Once you reach the old guardhouse at 500m, the trail parallels Laceiras Creek and runs through oak and pine groves to **Branda Ramil**. (A *branda* was a settlement of summer houses for villagers, who drove their livestock to high pastures and lived with them all summer.)

Another walk, along the **Caminho do Pho** and **Caminho do Fé** takes you downhill from Soajo village to the **Ponte da Ladeira**, a simple medieval bridge. Hike another 500m upstream and you'll find perfect swimming holes at **Poyo de Luzio**, an ideal antidote for Soajo's soaring summer mercury. Ask for a map at the Adere-Soajo office.

Sleeping & Eating

 Restaurante Espigueiro de Soajo
PORTUGUESE €
(☎258 576 136; espigueirodosoajo@hotmail.com; Av 25 de Abril; mains €7-10; ☉lunch & dinner Tue-

Sun) Just out of town, this modern place serves terrific Minho fare, with outdoor seating on a vine-covered terrace. Management is English speaking (local by way of Boston), very friendly, and pours some sensational port. It's about 200m north of the centre on the N304. The restaurant also rents out several simple, attractive rooms (€35 per night), and a special mountain house (€100) accessible by a 2km trail.

Village houses   HOUSES €€
(cottages €50-180) About a dozen houses (sleeping two to eight) are available for tourist accommodation under the Turismo de Aldeia scheme. Each has a fireplace or stove (with firewood in winter) and a kitchen stocked with breakfast food, including fresh bread on the doorstep each morning. Stays of more than one night are preferred on weekends. Book through Adere-PG in Ponte da Barca (p436).

Casa do Adro   RURAL INN €
(⊉258 576 327; www.casadoadroturismorural. com; d €50; P @) This manor house (rather than a cottage), located off Largo do Eiró by the parish church, dates to the 18th century. Rooms are huge, furnished with antiques, and blessed with sweet vineyard and village vistas. There is a minimum three-night stay in July and August.

Saber ao Borralho   PORTUGUESE €€
(www.saberaoborralho.com; plates for 2 €18-20; ⊙lunch & dinner Wed-Mon) A further 200m beyond Restaurante Espigueiro, the handsomely set Saber ao Borralho features excellent local dishes like the Minho *barrosã* steak as well as three codfish dishes and a tempting dessert counter. Village house rentals are available here (€50 per night).

Restaurante Videira   PORTUGUESE €€
(mains €7-10; ⊙lunch daily Jul-Sep, Fri-Sun Oct-Jun) Locals rave about Videira's authentic regional smoked meats and sausage. Its shady, arched patio is outfitted with sturdy, polished wooden tables. It's situated by the bus stop.

ℹ Information

The **Adere-Soajo** (www.adere-pg.pt; Largo da Cardeira; ⊙9am-noon & 2-7pm Mon-Fri, 9am-1pm Sat) is the village's de facto *turismo;* follow the signs west from the bus stop for 150m. Here you can book a room, get tips on good walks and pick up a basic map of the region. There's an ATM below the parish council office, off the far side of the square.

ℹ Getting There & Away

On weekdays there are two Salvador buses from Arcos de Valdevez (€2.40, 45 minutes) via Ponte da Barca (€2.20, 35 minutes). A taxi from Arcos or Ponte da Barca costs €15 to €20.

Vila do Gerês

POP 800 / ELEV 350M

Big nature rises in steep wooded pinnacles, gushes with cold streams, and pools into crystalline swimming holes in the Gerês end of the park. Its beating heart is the bustling tourist resort town of Vila do Gerês, commonly referred to simply as Gerês and the park's busiest settlement. Sandwiched tightly into the Rio Gerês valley, this spa town has a rather charming fin de siècle core surrounded by a ring of less appealing, modern *pensões* (guest houses). Most accommodation remains shuttered from November to April, as does the spa itself. By the same token, it's packed in July and August.

The town is built on an elongated, one-way loop, with the *balneário* (spa centre) in the pink buildings on the lower road. The original hot spring, some baths and the *turismo* are in the staid colonnade at the northern end (where the road takes a sharp U-turn). Buses stop at a traffic circle just south of the loop.

🏃 Activities

There are several hiking trails within a short drive. Following are a few of our favourites.

Cascada do Arado   HIKING
This scenic and somewhat challenging 12km trail penetrates a gorgeous highland boulder field and thick fern gullies to a waterfall. It begins in Pedra Bella, 200m north of the park office.

Roman road trails   HIKING
There are several trails that link to an old Roman road that once stretched 320km between Braga and Astorga (in Spain), and now has World Heritage status. Most are marked only as Trilho de Geira. The trail at Portela de Homem is an out-and-back 6km round-trip in the steep, wooded Mata de Albergaria range. Milestones – inscribed with the name of the emperor during whose rule they were erected – remain at miles XXIX, XXX and XXXI. Another Trilho de Geira, in the Terras de Bouro region, leaves from São Sebastiao, roughly 6km from Campo de Gerês.

Trilho da Preguiça   HIKING

This park-maintained loop trail starts on the N308 about 3km above Gerês. For 5km it rolls through the valley's oak forests. A leaflet about the walk is available from the park office (€0.60). You can also carry on – or hitch – to the **Portela de Leonte**, 6km north of Gerês.

Agua do Gerês   SPA, THERMAL SPRINGS

(www.aguasdogeres.pt; admission €18; ☺8am-noon & 2.30-6pm Mon-Sat, 9am-1pm Sun May-Oct) After a long hike, finish the day by soaking away aches and pains in the town's thermal springs. In addition to the sauna, steam bath and pool (available with basic admission), you can indulge with a full range of treatments, including massage and facials.

🛏 Sleeping

Gerês has plenty of *pensões,* though in summer you may find some are block-booked for spa patients and other visitors. Outside July and August, prices plummet.

Quinta Souto-Linho   RURAL INN €€

(☏253 392 000; www.oocities.com/souto_linho; d €50-60; P❄☀) This delightful Victorian manor house has been simply but tastefully remodelled into the town's one genuinely nonbland option. The four rooms are cosy and spotless with hardwood floors; some have views. There's also a large swimming pool with fine vistas.

Pensão Central Jardim   GUEST HOUSE €

(☏253 391 132; Av Manuel F Costa 141; s/d €40/50; P) Set in a stone building with ample glass to take in the nearby swaying oaks and cascading stream. Rooms are quite spacious if oddly configured with sloping ceilings. The warm service and central location make it a winner.

Pensão Adelaide   GUEST HOUSE €

(☏253 390 020; www.pensaoadelaide.com.pt; Rua de Arnaçó 45; s/d €30/45; ❄☀) This big, modern, lemon-yellow guest house wins for value. The rooms are cosy – almost cramped – but have parquet floors and new beds and some have massive valley views. It is uphill from the southern end of the town loop.

Hotel Apartamentos Gerês Ribeiro   HOTEL €€

(☏253 900 060; www.ehgeres.com; Av Manuel F Costa 115; s/d €45/55; P❄☀☀) Bringing a touch of loft-ish modernism to stony old Gerês, these studio apartments have sleek furnishings, high ceilings, a full kitchen and ergonomic bathrooms. Not to mention a pool and tennis court.

Pensão Baltazar   GUEST HOUSE €

(☏253 391 131; www.pensaobaltazar.com; Rua Emy José Lagrifa Medes 6; s/d €30/40) In a fine old granite building, this ultrafriendly, family-run place just up from the *turismo* has basic rooms, many of which look out onto a pleasant wooded park. The downstairs restaurant is excellent.

Pensão Pedra Bella   GUEST HOUSE €

(☏253 392 114; Rua Manuel F Costa; d €20) At the southernmost *pensão* in the lower circuit, the rooms are clean and bright with high ceilings, plasma TVs, funky bathroom tiles and wide balconies with sweet mountain vistas. And at this price the Pedra Bella is terrific value.

Aparthotel Gerês   HOTEL €

(☏253 397 000; www.aparthotelgeres.pt; Rua do Pedrogao 5; r €45-60; P❄☀☀) This is a new spot on the town's upper ridge, 1.3km from the *turismo,* that rents one-bedroom apartments by the night and week. They come with ceramic-tile floors in the sitting room, granite countertops in the kitchen and a terrace with mountain views off the bedrooms.

Hotel Universal   HOTEL €€

(☏253 390 220; www.ehgeres.com; Av Manuel F Costa 115; s/d €45/59; P❄☀☀) Yes, it's kitschy, but it's still got class. The mosaic stone atrium is wired with wi-fi; rooms are large and sport headboard radios of a bygone era.

Hotel Águas do Gerês   HOTEL €€

(☏253 390 190; www.aguasdogeres.pt; Av Manuel F Costa 136; s/d €55/70; P❄) In a grand fin de siècle building, this slightly upmarket place has decent spacious, carpeted rooms with high ceilings and modern decor that don't live up to the exterior. The hotel also runs the *termas* and offers special packages.

Parque de Campismo de Vidoeiro   CAMPGROUND €

(☏253 391 289; www.adere-pg.pt; per adult/tent/car €3.20/3.10/3.10; ☺mid-May–mid-Oct) This cool and shady hillside, park-run facility is next to the river, about 1km north of Vila do Gerês. Book ahead through Adere-PG in Ponte da Barca (p436).

X Eating & Drinking

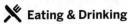
TOP CHOICE **Lurdes Capela** PORTUGUESE €€
(📞253 391 208; Av Manuel F Costa; mains
€6-18; ⊘lunch & dinner) Family owned and
operated, and almost always packed. Expect top-end service and even better food.
We're talking massive fresh-fish platters
with buttered potatoes and vegetables,
fluffy, savoury omelettes and all the beef
and cod dishes too.

Churrasqueira Parque GRILL HOUSE €
(Lugar de Brufe; mains €6-11; ⊘lunch & dinner)
Grilled meats are the speciality at this
family-run place about 1km uphill from
the *turismo*. It does a pretty mean *frango*
(chicken). Dine on the patio or have it
wrapped for the trail.

Adega Regional BAR, CAFE €
(Av Manuel F Costa 115; tapas €5-9; ⊘lunch & dinner Tue-Sun) Set behind Hotel Apartmentos
Gerês Ribeiro, and just above a roaring
stream, this historic stone *adega* serves
tapas and wine. Saturday-night karaoke
kicks off at 7pm.

ℹ Information

Espaço Internet (⊘9:30am-1pm & 2-5.30pm
Mon-Fri) Free internet access up the stairs
across from Hotel Universal.

Park office (www.adere-pg.pt; Centro de
Educação Ambiental do Vidoeiro; ⊘9am-noon
& 2-5.30pm Mon-Fri) About 1km north of the
village on the track leading to the campground.

Post office (⊘9am-12.30pm & 2-5.30pm Mon-
Fri) By the roundabout at the southern end of
the village.

Turismo (www.portoenorte.pt; ⊘9.30am-
12.30pm & 2.30-6pm Mon-Wed, Fri & Sat)
Located in the colonnade.

ℹ Getting There & Away

Empresa Hoteleira do Gerês (📞253 390 220;
www.ehgeres.com) runs between six and 10
buses daily from Braga to Gerês (€3.90, 1½
hours), passing through Rio Caldo (€1.80, 1¼
hours). Buy tickets at Hotel Universal.

Rio Caldo

POP 1000 / ELEV 160M
Just below Vila do Gerês, this tiny town
sits on the back of the stunning Albufeira
de Caniçada, making it the park's centre for
water sports.

English-run **AML** (Água Montanha e Lazer;
📞965 000 917; www.aguamontanha.com; Lugar

de Paredes) rents single/double kayaks for
€4.50/7.50 for the first hour (€22/35 for
the day), plus pedal boats, rowing boats
and small motorboats. It will also take you
wakeboarding (€40 per 20 minutes) or organise kayaking trips along the Albufeira
de Salamonde, and rents three **cottages** (d
€75-140), all with balconies, kitchen units
and lake views. The shop is 100m from the
N304 roundabout, but staff is often down
by the water on the other side of the bridge
to Vila do Gerês.

There are now dozens of guest houses
set on the ridge encircling the Albufeira
de Caniçada, but none have a more spectacular setting than the lovely **Pousada do
Gerês-Caniçada/São Bento** (📞253 649
150; www.pousadas.pt; Caniçada; d from €140;
P❅⊠), a splendid retreat at eagle's-nest
heights. The plush rooms have beamed
ceilings, and some have balconies with
magnificent views. There's a pool, gardens,
a tennis court and an excellent restaurant.
To get there, head south 3km from Rio
Caldo, along the N304, following signs to
Caniçada.

Campo do Gerês

POP 200 / ELEV 690M
Campo do Gerês (called São João do Campo
on some maps, and just Campo by most) is
a humble huddle of stone houses high in the
mountains in the middle of a wide, grassy
basin. It has more hikers than shepherds
once the weather turns warm, thanks to
easy access to some spectacular trails.

Coming from Vila do Gerês, you first arrive at a little traffic circle. The tiny village
centre is another 1.5km straight on, while
the youth hostel is 1km up the road to the
left.

⊙ Sights

The neighbouring village of **Vilarinho
das Furnas** was for centuries a remarkably democratic and fiercely independent
village, with a well-organised system of
shared property and decision-making. But
the entire town was submerged by the
building of a dam in 1972. In anticipation
of the end of their old way of life, villagers
collected stories and objects for a moving
memorial that is on display at the **Museu
Etnográfico** (www.visitgeres.com; adult/stu-
dent €2/1; ⊘9:30am-12.30pm & 2-5pm Tue-Sun).
The recently expanded museum also offers

exhibits on local flora and fauna. All exhibit explanations are in Portuguese. It's located at the park gate.

In late summer and autumn when the reservoir level falls, the empty village walls rise like spectres from the water. You can visit the spooky remains about 2.5km beyond the dam, which is a comfortable three-hour return hike.

🏃 Activities

There are several well-marked hiking trails around Campo do Gerês, lasting from three to six hours. You can pick up maps and trail information (€0.10) at the information desk of the Museu Etnográfico.

Trilho da Cidade da Calcedónia   HIKING

A narrow, sealed road snakes over the ridge from Vila do Gerês to Campo do Gerês, offering short but spectacular, high-elevation walks from just about anywhere along its upper reaches. One of these is the Cidade da Calcedónia trail, a moderate, signposted, 7km (four-hour) loop that climbs a 912m viewpoint called the **Cabeço Calcedónia**, with views to knock your socks off.

Trilho dos Currais   HIKING

'The Corrals Trail' is a moderate 10km loop that takes about four hours to complete. Along the way you'll wind beneath oak and pine and glimpse boulder fields, sublime valley views and – if you leave early enough and get lucky – resident deer, wolf or wild boar. The trailhead is located and signposted in Vidoeiro.

Equi Campo   HIKING, BIKING

(📞253 357 022; www.equicampo.com; ⊙9am-4pm) One of two Campo-based outfitters located on the right just before you arrive in town. Guides lead horse-riding trips (one/two hours €17/30), hikes (half-day €7 per person) and combination hiking-climbing-rappelling excursions (€20 per person). You can also rent mountain bikes here if you'd like to head off on your own (€5/17.50 per hour/day).

🛏️ Sleeping & Eating

The road to Cerdeira is lined with signs advertising houses for rent (€40 to €60 for up to four people).

Parque Campismo de Cerdeira
CAMPGROUND €

(📞253 351 005; www.parquecerdeira.com; camp sites €3-4.50, bungalows €50-65; P☀) This private facility has oak-shaded sites, a laun-

dry, a pool, a *minimercado* (grocery shop), tennis courts, a particularly good restaurant (open to the public) and bikes to hire. Best of all are the lovely new ecofriendly bungalows, with French doors opening onto unrivalled mountain views. Book ahead in August. Look for the turn-off just before you reach the village.

Pousada da Juventude de Vilarinho das Furnas   HOSTEL €

(📞253 351 339; www.pousadasjuventude.pt; dm €13, bungalows for 4 €49-54; P@) Campo's woodland hostel began life as a temporary dam-workers' camp and now offers a spotless selection of spartan dormitories, simply furnished doubles (with bathrooms) and roomier bungalows with kitchen units.

Albergaria Stop   GUEST HOUSE €

(📞253 350 040; www.albergariastop.com; Rua de São João 915; s/d €40/50; P☀) More mountain motel than lodge, this guest house has spotless rooms with balconies, wooden floors and mountain views. The modest restaurant and bar is what passes for Campo nightlife. It's located just before the village.

O Abocanhado   PORTUGUESE €€

(📞253 352 944; www.abocanhado.com; Brufe; mains €15-18; ⊙lunch & dinner) This beautifully situated restaurant is a temple to the finest ingredients that the surrounding countryside has to offer, including *javali* (wild boar), *veado* (venison) and *coelho* (rabbit), as well as beef and goat raised in the adjacent fields. Finish with *requeijão* – a soft goat's cheese so fresh it's actually sweet. The only drawback: off-season, the restaurant keeps irregular hours, so call ahead before making the trip. It's located 6km east of Campo do Gerês (across the dam) on a panoramic spot above the Rio Homem.

ℹ️ Getting There & Away

From Braga, Transdev has five daily buses (€4, 1½ hours; fewer at weekends) stopping at the museum crossroad and the village centre.

Eastern Peneda-Gerês

Cabril, on the eastern limb of the national park, and Montalegre, just outside the park, are actually in Trás-os-Montes, but you're unlikely to visit either unless you're coming in or out of the park.

CABRIL
POP 700 / ELEV 400M

Although it hardly looks the part, peaceful Cabril – set with its outlying hamlets in a wide, fertile bowl backed by soaring peaks – is the administrative centre of Portugal's biggest *freguesia* (parish), stretching up to the Spanish border. Your best reference point is **Largo do Cruzeiro**, with its old *pelourinho*. To one side is the squat but stately **Igreja de São Lourenço**, said to have been moved five centuries ago, brick by brick, by villagers of nearby São Lourenço. Some 400m southwest is a bridge over an arm of the Albufeira de Salamonde where you'll find **Restaurante Ponte Nova** (mains €7-12; ⊙breakfast, lunch & dinner). It does good river trout (in season) and, if you order ahead, *cabrito* or *javali assada*. There's an outdoor deck right over the water. While Cabril is a lovely place to stop for lunch, there's no reason to stay the night.

There are no buses to Cabril, but you could take any Braga–Montalegre or Braga–Chaves bus service and get off at the Ruivães bus stop, then hike the last 4km. Drivers can cross into the park from the N103 via the Salamonde dam; alternatively, a longer but far more scenic route is via the Venda Nova dam, 14km east of Salamonde at Cambedo.

Further west in nearby **Fafião**, you'll find the adventure outfitter, **Javsport** (www.javsport.pt). It operates popular canyoning expeditions down the Rio Arado and Rio Conho.

MONTALEGRE
POP 2100 / ELEV 1000M

Technically in Trás-os-Montes, Montalegre is the park's eastern gateway, and if ever there was a hamlet with a castle on the hill this is it. The small but particularly striking **castle**, part of Dom Dinis' 14th-century ring of frontier outposts, looms over the town and the surrounding fertile plains fed by so many rivers. The future Duke of Wellington made use of it in his drive to rid Portugal of Napoleon's troops in 1809. Today visitors can only wander around its perimeter, taking in the lovely views. Just below the castle lies the old town centre.

From the bus station it's 500m uphill on Rua General Humberto Delgado to a five-way roundabout, beside which you'll find the town hall and *turismo*. Keep heading uphill to reach the crown.

☉ Sights

FREE **Barroso Eco Museu**   MUSEUM
(www.ecomuseu.org; Praça do Município; ⊙10am-12:30pm & 2-6pm) Next to the castle, this new museum hosts exhibits that showcase regional history, rural traditions and folklore. There are also exhibits highlighting local flora and fauna, and a gallery rotating contemporary canvases from local artists.

🛏 Sleeping & Eating

Montalegre Hotel   HOTEL €€
(📞276 510 220; www.montalegrehotel.com; Rua do Avelar 100; s/d from €42/58; P ❋ ☎ ☎) Situated just southwest of the roundabout at the top of town, this somewhat out-of-place business hotel has spacious and sunny rooms with wooden floors and fine views. It also features an indoor swimming pool, sauna and gym. Oh, and did we mention that it used to be a political prison during Salazar's reign?

Casa Zé Maria   RURAL INN €
(📞276 512 457; www.casazemaria.centrobar rosao.com; Rua Dr Victor Branco 21; d from €45; P) This converted 19th-century granite manor features old-fashioned charm in its wooden-floored rooms with lacy bedspreads and dark-wood furnishings. It's located one block east and one block south of the *turismo*.

Tasca do Açougue   TAPAS €
(Terreiro do Açougue; tapas €7-10; ⊙lunch & dinner Tue-Sun) In a charming stone cottage just below the castle, Tasca do Açougue serves tasty Iberian tapas dishes, including grilled octopus and smoked meats, as well as heartier plates. It's a lively place for a drink in the evening.

Pastelaria São Paulo   BAKERY €
(Rua Direita 27; pastries €0.75-2; ⊙breakfast, lunch & dinner) If you're just in town long enough for a cup of something strong and a nibble of something sweet, then search out this luscious bakery where the interior decor verges on hip and the ovens work overtime.

O Castelo Piano Bar   PORTUGUESE €
(📞276 511 237; Terreiro do Açougue; mains€7-10; ⊙dinner Tue-Sun) On the castle's doorstep, O Castelo serves good smoked meats, trout from the Rio Cávado, roast pork and the like. Diners can enjoy the peaceful setting at outdoor tables, and there's live music on most weekend nights.

ⓘ Information

Biblioteca Municipal (Rua General Humberto Delgado; ⊙1-7pm Mon, 9am-12.30pm & 2-5.30pm Tue-Fri) Free internet access.

Park information office (www.adere-pg.pt; Praça do Municipal; ⊙9am-12.30pm & 2-5.30pm Mon-Fri) Next door to the Barroso Eco Museu.

Post office (⊙9am-12.30pm & 2-5.30pm Mon-Fri) Located 400m northeast of the roundabout, down Av Dom Nuno Álvares Pereira.

Turismo (www.cm-montalegre.pt; ⊙10am-12.30pm & 2-6pm) In the Eco Museu complex.

ⓘ Getting There & Away

Transdev (☑253 209 400; www.transdev.pt) buses stop at Montalegre between Braga (€7, 2½ hours) and Chaves (€4.60, 1¼ hours) three times daily Monday to Friday; they run less frequently on weekends. Change at Chaves for Bragança or Vila Real.

Trás-os-Montes

Best Places to Stay

» A Lagosta Perdida (p463)
» Casa Agrícola da Levada (p447)
» Quinta Entre Rios (p465)
» Quinta da Mata (p465)
» Barreiro de Cima (p451)

Best Places to Eat

» Flor de Sal (p465)
» A Lareira (p470)
» Solar Bragançano (p460)
» Terra de Montanha (p448)

Why Go?

Sandwiched between the Rio Douro and the Spanish border in Portugal's extreme northeast corner, ruggedly beautiful Trás-os-Montes is named for its centuries-long isolation 'behind the mountains'. Despite pockets of wine-based prosperity and EU-supported 21st-century development, it remains one of Portugal's poorest and most remote regions. Young people continue to emigrate in droves, leaving behind ancient stone villages with a tantalisingly lost-in-time quality.

A handful of attractive cities with Roman and medieval roots offer worthy urban diversions, but rural life is still the region's heart and soul, from the southwest's steep vineyard-clad hillsides, to the olive groves, almond orchards and rugged canyonlands of the sun-baked east, to the chestnut-shaded, heathery highlands of the north.

In the hinterlands, millennial traditions persist, including ancient Latin-derived dialects, pagan winter solstice revels and robust *transmontano* hospitality, expressed in the phrase *'entre quem é'* ('come in, whoever you may be').

When to Go

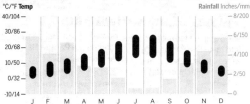

Bragança

March White petals float over the orchard-covered hills of Mirandela during almond-blossom season.

September Terraced hillsides hang heavy with grapes; hiking abounds in the natural parks.

December & January Bonfires and masked dancers fill village streets during solstice festivals.

Vila Real

POP 24,000 / ELEV 445M

Clinging to steep hillsides above the confluence of the Rios Corgo and Cabril, the university town of Vila Real is short on charm, although its historic centre, dotted with picturesque old churches, is pleasant enough. Its key attractions lie just beyond the city limits: the dramatically rugged highlands of the Parque Natural do Alvão; and the resplendent Palácio de Mateus, one of Europe's most elegant country houses, surrounded by lovely vineyard country east of town.

◉ Sights

Palácio de Mateus   WINERY
(www.casademateus.com, in Portuguese; admission gardens/palace & gardens €4.50/7.50; ⊙9am-7pm) Famously depicted on bottles of Mateus rosé, the 18th-century Palácio de Mateus is one of Portugal's great baroque masterpieces – probably the work of Italian-born architect Nicolau Nasoni.

Its granite wings ('advancing lobster-like towards you', wrote English critic Sir Sacheverell Sitwell) shelter a lichen-encrusted forecourt dominated by an ornate stairway and guarded by rooftop statues. Surrounding the palace is a fantasy of a garden, with tiny boxwood hedges, prim statues and a fragrant cypress tunnel that's blissfully cool on even the hottest days. (Don't miss the fanciful 5m-tall curved ladders used to prune the tunnel's exterior branches!)

Guided tours of the mansion (in English, French, Spanish and German) take you through the main quarters, which combine rusticity with restrained grandeur.

Trás-os-Montes Highlights

❶ Stroll the formal gardens and taste fine Portuguese wines at the stately 18th-century **Palácio de Mateus** (p446)

❷ Survey the steep granite walls of the Rio Douro gorge from bird's-eye viewpoints in the **Parque Natural do Douro Internacional** (p468)

❸ Hike across a medieval bridge or climb heather-draped hills to 21st-century windmills in **Parque Natural de Montesinho** (p461)

❹ Delight in the devilish grins of winter carnival masks at the Museu Ibérico da Máscara e do Traje in **Bragança** (p456)

❺ Swim and slide into natural pools above the dramatic Fisgas de Ermelo waterfall in **Parque Natural do Alvão** (p449)

❻ Take in the medieval tower and the 17th-century fortifications from the pedestrianised Roman bridge in **Chaves** (p452)

❼ Watch the sheep return home at sundown in **Rio de Onor** (p462), a town built squarely on the Portugal–Spain border

The library contains one of the first illustrated editions of Luís Vaz de Camões' *Os Lusíadas* (p511), Portugal's most important epic poem, and one room houses an unintentionally droll collection of religious bric-a-brac, including three dozen macabre relics bought from the Vatican in the 18th century: a bit of holy fingernail, a saintly set of eyeballs, and the inevitable piece of the true cross – each with the Vatican's proof of authenticity.

Near the guided tour starting point, a wine shop offers tastings of three locally produced wines for €1 (waived with the purchase of a bottle). Especially interesting is the Alvarelhão, which is essentially the same fine rosé originally bottled by Mateus in the 1940s (see p450).

The palace is 3.5km east of the town centre. Take local Corgobus bus 1 (€1, 20 minutes) towards the university (UTAD). It leaves from Largo de Camões, just north of the *turismo,* roughly half-hourly between 7.30am and 8pm, with fewer buses on weekends. Ask for 'Mateus' and the driver will set you down about 250m from the palace (if you don't ask, he may not stop).

Churches CHURCHES
Once part of a Dominican monastery, the Gothic **sé** (cathedral; Travessa de São Domingos) has been given a lengthy facelift that has restored the 15th-century grandeur of its rather spare interior.

Northeast of the cathedral is the magnificent baroque facade of the 17th-century **Capela Nova** (cnr Ruas Central & Direita). Inside are fine, 18th-century *azulejos* (hand-painted tiles) and large-headed cherubs with teddy-boy coifs.

More baroque, and more *azulejos*, are on view at the **Igreja de São Pedro** (Largo de São Pedro), one block north of Capela Nova.

Museu Etnográfico de Vila Real MUSEUM
(Largo de São Pedro 3; admission €1.50; ⊙9.30am-12.30pm & 2-6pm) This small but colourful museum documents the traditional culture of the surrounding highlands, with exhibits on linen-making, ceramics, farming techniques, games, musical instruments and local festivals.

Miradouro de Trás-do-Cemitério
VIEWPOINT
For a fine view across the gorge of the Rio Corgo and Rio Cabril, walk south to this panoramic viewpoint, just beyond a small cemetery and chapel.

🛏 **Sleeping**

Appealing budget and midrange options in downtown Vila Real are in short supply. The best accommodations, including some charming semirural guest houses, are on the city's outer fringes.

TOP CHOICE **Casa Agrícola da Levada** RURAL INN €€
(☏259 322 190; www.casadalevada.com; Rua da Capela, Timpeira; s/d/4-person apt €60/80/130; P@🛜🏊) Just north of the centre, at the end of a long, shady drive lies this little gem of an inn. A collection of tastefully renovated old houses surrounds grounds that include rose gardens, a large grassy lawn and swimming pool. The friendly, multilingual owners have deep roots in the region and are generous in sharing their knowledge of the area's natural beauty, viticulture, cuisine and cultural attractions.

Quinta de São Martinho RURAL INN €€
(☏259 323 986; www.quintasaomartinho.com; Lugar de São Martinho, Mateus; s/d €60/75, 2-/4-person apt €95/140; P🏊) Only 400m from the Palácio de Mateus, this rambling granite farmhouse-turned-inn is surrounded by pretty gardens. Rooms aren't fancy but have wood-beamed ceilings and are traditionally furnished. Three-course dinners are served for €17.50 with advance notice, and wi-fi is available down the street at the owners' wine store.

Residencial Real HOTEL €
(☏259 325 879; www.residencialreal.com; Rua Central 5; s/d/tr €30/40/50) Most appealing of the limited budget options downtown, this family-run place is nicely positioned in the middle of a pedestrian zone, above a popular *pastelaria* (pastry shop). Some of the bright, neatly kept rooms have high ceilings and French windows.

Hotel Miracorgo BUSINESS HOTEL €€
(☏259 325 001; www.hotelmiracorgo.com; Av 1 de Maio 78; s/d/ste €49/71/98; P❄@🛜🏊) Boasting fine views of the Rio Corgo canyon, this central, modern, midrise business hotel has well-appointed if unexciting rooms, all with large verandahs.

Pousada da Juventude HOSTEL €
(☏259 373 193; vilareal@movijovem.pt; Rua Dr Manuel Cardona; dm €10, d with shared/private bathroom €21/25) Perched atop Vila Real's youth centre, in a dreary high-rise residential neighbourhood about 20 minutes' walk from the town centre, this hostel is rather

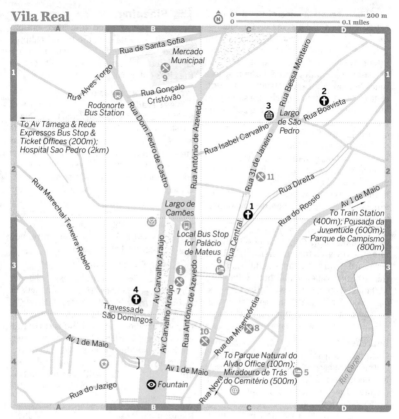

Vila Real

Vila Real

basic, but the clean rooms all come with balconies and the staff is friendly and helpful. No meals are available, but you can use the kitchen, and there are a few cafes nearby.

Parque de Campismo de Vila Real

CAMPGROUND **€**

(☎259 324 724; Rua Dr Manuel Cardona; sites per adult/child/tent/car €3.75/1.88/2.30/2.65; ⊙Mar-Nov) This simple, shady hillside camp site above the Rio Corgo, 1.2km northeast of the centre, has a small restaurant and pool nearby.

🍴 Eating

Numerous eateries are clustered in the historic centre, along the narrow streets just east of Av Carvalho Araújo.

Terra de Montanha PORTUGUESE **€€**

(Rua 31 de Janeiro 16; mains €9.50-12; ⊙lunch & dinner Mon-Sat, lunch Sun) From the black crockery to the halved wine casks that serve as booths, everything here is rigorously *transmontana*. The hearty local cuisine includes specialities such as *posta barrosã* (grilled veal steak) and *cabrito assado no forno* (oven-roasted goat, served only on weekends). Weekday lunch specials are a great deal at €6.50, including bread, main dish, fruit and coffee.

Restaurante Transmontano PORTUGUESE €€
(Rua Teixeira de Sousa 37; mains €8.50-13; ⊙lunch & dinner Mon-Sat) Popular with locals, this plain-faced, family-run place in the central pedestrian zone serves delicious, belly-filling regional dishes. At lunchtime, *pratos do dia* (daily specials) go for €4.75 to €6.50.

Casa Lapão TEAROOM €
(Rua de Misericórdia 54; pastries from €1; ⊙8.30am-7pm Mon-Sat, to 1pm Sun) This spruce tearoom specialises in traditional local sweets, including *cristas de galo* (almond and egg paste in a buttery pastry dough), *pitos de Santa Luzia* (made with pumpkin and cinnamon) and *pastéis de Santa Clara* (made with eggs, almond and cinnamon).

Café Pastelaria Nova Pompeia BAKERY €
(Av Carvalho Araújo 82; mains €5.25-8.80; ⊙8am-11pm) A few doors down from the tourist office, this large, bright cafe and bakery serves omelettes and light meals at reasonable prices. Free wi-fi is icing on the cake.

Mercado Municipal MARKET €
(Rua de Santa Sofia; ⊙Mon-Sat) Self-caterers can stock up on rural produce at the market.

☆ Entertainment

Teatro de Vila Real ARTS CENTRE
(www.teatrodevilareal.com, in Portuguese; Alameda de Grasse) This slick, modern building, in a parklike area across the Corgo from the city centre, stages high-quality dance and theatre performances, as well as classical, jazz and world music. It also screens biweekly films and serves as a venue for the **Douro Jazz Festival** (www.dourojazz.com) during wine harvest season. At the back, the theatre's bright cafe overlooking the Corgo is popular with Vila Real's beau monde.

ℹ Information

Espaço Internet (Av 1 de Maio; ⊙10am-1pm & 2-6pm Mon-Fri) Free internet near Hotel Miracorgo.

Hospital de São Pedro (☑259 300 500; Av da Noruega, Lordelo)

Parque Natural do Alvão office (☑259 302 830; pnal@icnb.pt; Largo dos Freitas; ⊙9am-12.30pm & 2-5.30pm Mon-Fri)

Police station (☑259 330 240; Largo Conde de Amarante)

Post office (Av Carvalho Araújo; ⊙8.30am-6pm Mon-Fri, 9am-12.30pm Sat)

Regional Turismo (☑259 322 819; turismo dodouro@gmail.com; Av Carvalho Araújo 94; ⊙9.30am-12.30pm & 2-6pm) Located in a Manueline house in the town centre.

ℹ Getting There & Around

BUS Several companies serve Vila Real. **Rodonorte** (☑259 340 710; www.rodonorte.pt, in Portuguese) buses leave from a station on Rua Dom Pedro de Castro, 300m northwest of the turismo. **AV Tâmega** (☑259 322 928; www.avtamega.pt, in Portuguese) and **Rede Expressos** (☑962 060 655; www.rede-expressos.pt, in Portuguese) both operate from a lot slightly west of the Rodonorte station, at the corner of Rua Dr António Valente Fonseca and Av Cidade de Ourense. Destinations include Bragança (€9.10 to €9.40, two hours), Chaves (€6.90 to €7.20, 70 minutes), Lamego (€5.50 to €5.70, 45 minutes), Lisbon (€17.50 to €18, five to 5½ hours), Miranda do Douro (€10.60, three to 3½ hours) and Porto (€7.50, 1½ hours).

CAR & MOTORCYCLE There's pay parking downtown along Av Carvalho Araújo and in the parking garage below the *câmara municipal* (town hall).

TRAIN Vila Real's train station is 1km from the centre, across the Rio Corgo. The rail link to Peso da Régua – a scenic 26km narrow-gauge route along the Rio Corgo – was closed for repairs at the time of research, with five daily buses replacing the train until further notice. For updates on the railway's status, inquire at Vila Real's turismo.

Parque Natural do Alvão

With its rock-strewn highlands, schist villages, waterfalls and verdant pockets where cows graze in stone-walled pastures, the pristine Parque Natural do Alvão comes as a delightful revelation to travellers climbing from the hotter, drier country below. A drive of less than half an hour brings you from Vila Real to this extraordinary park straddling the central ridgeline of the Serra de Alvão, whose highest peaks reach more than 1300m. The small (72 sq km) protected area remains one of northern Portugal's best-kept secrets and shelters a remarkable variety of flora and fauna, thanks to its position in a transition zone between the humid coast and the dry interior.

The Rio Ôlo, a tributary of the Rio Tâmega, rises in the park's broad granite

MATEUS REVISITED

If 'Mateus' conjures up images of sickly sweet pink 'starter wine' and ubiquitous 1970s wine-bottles-as-candleholders, think again and try a sip of Alvarelhão. This distinctive Portuguese grape is the original base for Mateus rosé, which in the 1950s was retooled for mass marketing in North America, where palates were considerably less sophisticated. Now the growers and vintners of Lavradores de Feitoria, whose numbers include the current Count of Vila Real and heir to the famous Palácio de Mateus itself, are producing an Alvarelhão rosé that more fully honours the legacy of this uniquely Iberian varietal.

Some growers describe Alvarelhão as a grape that is impractical and near-impossible to grow. It matures late, well into October, and is easy prey to mildews and other pathogens – so much so that growers traditionally grew it closest to their homes and estates so they could be more easily alerted to possible outbreaks of disease. As one Lavradores producer puts it, 'Here in Portugal, we love tradition. But we are not efficient. We are not practical. We grow something because our fathers and our grandfathers and their grandfathers did. It's said that because of this we still have hundreds of varietals which have died out in other places. So we are still growing this Alvarelhão because we love it.'

Because of its temperamental nature, Alvarelhão – like many of Portugal's best wines – is bottled in small quantities, mostly for use in Portugal. Until these delicious and deserving wines get wider international distribution, do yourself a favour while touring the Palácio de Mateus (p446) and sip it while you can!

basin. A 300m drop above Ermelo gives rise to the spectacular Fisgas de Ermelo falls, the park's major tourist attraction.

Exploring the park on your own is not simple, as maps, accommodation and public transport are limited. Whether you plan to walk or drive in the park, it's worth visiting one of the park offices beforehand.

◉ Sights

Fisgas de Ermelo   WATERFALLS
Just north of the town of Ermelo, on the N304 between Vila Real and Mondim de Basto, is a turn-off to the dramatic Fisgas de Ermelo waterfalls. From this junction, the road climbs 4km to an overlook with picture-perfect views of the falls and the rugged terrain surrounding them.

To see the falls from above, return to the main road and climb to a T-junction with a right-hand turn marked Varzigueto. Follow the Varzigueto road a short distance until you see signs on the right-hand side for Piocas de Cima. There are actually two footpaths, the first marked '1.5km', the second marked '600m'. Either path leads down into the river gorge, where you'll find not only hair-raising views of the river plunging off a cliff face, but also (further up) a natural waterslide and a series of pools perfect for cooling off on a hot day.

Ermelo   VILLAGE
The 800-year-old town of Ermelo is famous for its schist cottages capped with fairy-tale slate roofs that seem to have been constructed from broken blackboards. Once the main village of the region, it boasts traditional *espigueiros* (stone granaries; see p437), an ancient chapel, a sturdy granite *pelourinho* (pillory), a workshop that still practises the ancient local art of linen-making, and **Ponte de Várzea** – a Roman bridge rebuilt in medieval times.

The Ermelo turn-off is about 16km south of Mondim de Basto on the N304. The heart of town is about 1km uphill.

Lamas de Ôlo   VILLAGE
Set in a wide, verdant valley some 1000m above sea level, somnolent Lamas de Ôlo is the park's highest village, best known for its photogenic thatched roofs, as well as a nearby mill that was long driven by water from a crude aqueduct.

🕴 Activities

There are a number of fine hikes in the park. A 7km, three-hour jaunt around the southern village of **Arnal** is described in the Portuguese-language leaflet *Guia do Percurso Pedestre,* available at park offices. The signposted hike delivers views east beyond Vila Real to the Serra do Marão.

While you're in Arnal, track down the slate-roofed centre for traditional handicraft techniques.

Another popular route is the 13km, five-hour loop through the high country starting just north of the Cimeira dam along the **Vila Real-Lamas de Ôlo road**. The trail, marked with red and yellow blazes, traverses the rock-strewn *planalto* (high plateau) for 8km to the village of Barreiro. From here, you can return 5km by road to your starting point, passing through Lamas de Ôlo en route.

With your own vehicle it's much easier to explore the network of small hillside villages within the park's borders. A particularly attractive drive connects Lamas de Ôlo to Ermelo via the traditional agricultural communities of Pioledo, Varzigueto and Fervença.

Sleeping & Eating

Camping is prohibited in the natural park, and other food and lodging options are scarce. In Lamas de Ôlo, a few steps from the town bus stop, Café Albina (259 341 959; s/d €20/25) rents out simple rooms and serves limited food. In Ermelo, Dona Benedita (255 381 221; r €30) also rents out rooms with shared bathroom. It's also worth inquiring at the Mondim de Basto *turismo* for possible bookings of private houses within the park. Otherwise, your best bet is to use Vila Real or Mondim de Basto as your base.

In Bobal, halfway between Lamas de Ôlo and Mondim de Basto, A Tasca da Alice (255 381 381; Oct-Aug) is recommended for its all-day snacks and can also arrange full meals for groups of six or more with advance notice.

Information

There are park offices in Vila Real (p449) and Mondim de Basto (p452).

Getting There & Away

Public transport within the park is extremely limited.

FROM VILA REAL **Rodonorte** (259 340 710) operates weekday-only buses at noon and 6.30pm to Lamas de Ôlo (€2.15, 30 minutes), returning to Vila Real at 12.30pm.

FROM MONDIM DE BASTO **Auto Mondinense** (255 381 296) runs to Ermelo (€2.35, one hour) three times each weekday, and to Lamas de Ôlo (€3.20, 50 minutes) twice on Tuesdays and Fridays.

POP 3400 / ELEV 200M

Sitting in the Tâmega valley at the intersection of the Douro, Minho and Trás-os-Montes regions, low-lying Mondim de Basto has no compelling sights beyond a few flowery squares, but it makes an attractive base from which to explore the heights of the Parque Natural do Alvão. The vineyards surrounding town cultivate grapes used in the fine local *vinho verde* (young wine).

Activities

Hiking

Hikers wanting to feel a little burn in their thighs should consider the long haul up to the 18th-century **Capela da Senhora da Graça** on the summit of pine-clad Monte Farinha (996m). It takes about two hours to reach the top. The path starts east of town on the N312 (the *turismo* has a rough map). By car, turn off the N312 3.5km from Mondim towards Cerva; from there it's a twisting 9.5km to the top.

Swimming

At Senhora da Ponte, 2km south of town on the N304, there's a rocky swimming spot by a disused watermill on the Rio Cabril. Follow signs to the Parque de Campismo de Mondim de Basto and then take the track to the right.

Wine-Tasting

Eight kilometres north of town in Atei, the 17th-century Casa Santa Eulalia (www.casasantaeulalia.com), set amid 32 hectares of vineyards, offers tastings of their refreshing local *vinho verde* with advance notice.

Sleeping

Barreiro de Cima   RURAL INN €€
(255 386 491; www.barreirodecima.com; Atei; s/d/4-person house €70/80/130; P) Chirping birds and fragrant boxwood hedges greet you at this agreeable hideaway, tucked down a side road in the wine country 6km north of Mondim de Basto. The 17th-century granite manor house is full of period charm, although the rooms are a little on the small side. More appealing are the secluded and grassy grounds across the street from the inn – punctuated with *espigueiros* and a cool blue pool that offers lovely views over the surrounding hills and nearby vineyards.

Quinta do Fundo
RURAL INN €€

(☑255 381 291; www.quintadofundo.com; Vilar de Viando; d/ste €50/75; P ✹ ☒) This pleasant spot, set amid a sea of vineyards 2km south on the N304, has decent rooms (if you can overlook the shiny, vinyl-like flowered bedspreads), fine mountain vistas, a tennis court and a swimming pool. The *quinta* (estate) also produces its own *vinho verde*. Ask about discounts for multinight stays.

Casa das Mourôas
GUEST HOUSE €€

(☑255 381 394, 938 711 272; www.casadasmouroas.com; Rua José Carvalho Camões; r €55; P) Occupying an old stone house on the same flower-filled square as the *turismo,* this little place has three humble but neat rooms arranged around a delightful, vine-covered terrace. English is spoken. Reservations are recommended on weekends and in summer.

Casa do Campo
RURAL INN €€

(☑255 361 231; www.casadocampo.pt; Molares, Celorico de Basto; s/d/ste €75/90/110; P ✹ ☒) If you have wheels and funds, consider this antique-packed, whitewashed 17th-century manor house with its own crenellated stone tower, chapel and extravagant topiary gardens. Rooms are modest but pleasant, with wood floors and plain country furnishings. Suites include a small living room with TV and *frigobar*. It's 7km west of Mondim.

Parque de Campismo de Mondim de Basto
CAMPGROUND €

(☑255 381 650; mondim.basto@fcmportugal.com; sites per adult/tent/car €4.30/2.85/2.85; ☺Feb-Nov) This shady, well-run facility is about 1km south of town, near a medieval bridge over the Rio Cabril. The river offers a cool plunge on hot summer days and there's a snack bar (but no restaurant).

Residencial Carvalho
GUEST HOUSE €

(☑255 381 057; Av Dr Augusto Brito; s/d/q €20/30/45; P ✹) For low-cost indoor accommodation, your best bet is this graceless, modern *residencial* (guest house) west of the *turismo*, next to the GALP petrol station.

✗ Eating

Adega Sete Condes
PORTUGUESE €€

(Rua Velha; mains €7.50-12; ☺lunch & dinner Tue-Sun, lunch Mon) Tucked into a tiny corner near the *turismo,* this rustic, granite-walled spot has a small menu of well-prepared traditional dishes, including *bacalhau* (dried salt-cod) and a very tasty *feijoada* (pork and bean stew).

Adega São Tiago
PORTUGUESE €€

(Zona Velha; mains €7.50-11; ☺lunch & dinner Mon-Sat) Very similar to Adega Sete Condes, this restaurant is just up the street. The all-inclusive lunch special is a good deal at €6.

ℹ Information

Parque Natural do Alvão office (☑255 381 209; pnal@icnb.pt; Lugar do Barrio; ☺9am-12.30pm & 2-5.30pm Mon-Fri) About 700m west of the *turismo*.

Turismo (☑255 389 370; turismo@cm-mondimdebasto.pt; Largo Conde de Vila Real; ☺9am-1pm & 2-5pm Mon-Fri, 10am-1pm & 2-6pm Sat & Sun) Has loads of local information and rents bikes (per hour/day €1/5).

ℹ Getting There & Around

BUS Buses stop behind the *mercado municipal,* 150m east of the *turismo* and what remains of the old town. **Auto Mondinense** (☑255 381 296) has seven weekday and two to three weekend buses to Porto (€6.05, 2¾ hours) via Guimarães (€4, 1½ hours). For Vila Real, take a Mondinense bus to Campeã (€3.40, 50 minutes, three daily) and change there for the short-hop Rodonorte bus to Vila Real.

CAR & MOTORCYCLE There is street parking just west of the centre along Av Augusto Brito.

Chaves

POP 18,000 / ELEV 340M

A spa town with a long and fascinating history, Chaves (*shahv*-sh) is a pretty and engaging place, straddling the mountain-fringed banks of the Rio Tâmega only a few kilometres south of the Spanish border. Its well-preserved historic centre is anchored at the edges by a 16-arched Roman bridge dating back to Trajan's reign, a beautiful medieval tower (the Torre da Menagem) and the rock-solid Forte de São Francisco.

All of these remnants testify to Chaves' earlier strategic importance in controlling the small but fertile plain that surrounds it. Romans built a key garrison here, and it was subsequently contested by the Visigoths, Moors, French and Spanish. The city saw particularly fierce fighting during the Napoleonic invasion, when it was at the forefront of resistance against French domination.

Nowadays Chaves is a placid backwater – where the Portuguese come not to defend the national honour but to pamper themselves in the natural hot springs that bubble up in the city's heart.

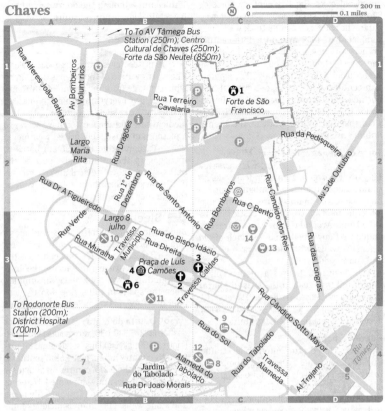

Chaves

⊙ Sights

1 Forte de São Francisco C1
2 Igreja da Misericórdia........................... B3
3 Igreja Matriz C3
4 Museu da Região Flaviense B3
   Museu Militar .... (see 6)
5 Ponte Romana D4
6 Torre de Menagem B3

Activities, Courses & Tours

7 Termas de Chaves A4

🛏 Sleeping

Forte de São Francisco Hotel ....(see 1)

8 Residencial Jardim das
   Caldas C4
9 Residencial Restaurante
   Kátia C4

🍴 Eating

10 Hospedaria Florinda............................. B3
11 João Padeiro Forno
    Regional B3
12 Restaurante Carvalho C4

🍷 Drinking

13 Adega Faustino C3
14 Biblioteca C3

The backbone of Chaves' old town is Rua de Santo António, which runs southeast from the *turismo* to the Roman bridge. The spa is near the river, just south of the centre.

⊙ Sights

Forte de São Francisco & Forte de São Neutel
FORTS
Reached by a drawbridge and bordered by a park with floral designs, hedges and

grand old oaks, the 17th-century Forte de São Francisco is the centrepiece of Chaves' old town. The fort, with its thick walls, was completed in 1658 around a 16th-century Franciscan convent. These days it's a top-end hotel, though nobody minds if you snoop around inside the walls. The smaller, 17th-century Forte de São Neutel, 1.2km northeast of the centre, is open only for occasional summertime concerts. Both forts were inspired by the work of the French military architect Vauban.

Torre de Menagem & Museu Militar
HISTORICAL SITE, MUSEUM

The lovely Torre de Menagem (castle keep) stands alone on a grassy embankment behind the town's main square, the only major remnant of a 14th-century castle built by Dom Dinis. Around the tower are attractive manicured flowerbeds and a stretch of old defensive walls, with views over the town and countryside.

The *torre* now houses a motley collection of military gear in the **Museu Militar** (admission incl Museu da Região Flaviense €1; ⊙9am-12.30pm & 2-5.30pm; ⊙closed holidays), accessed via a series of creaky stairs.

Ponte Romana
HISTORICAL SITE

Recently closed to automobile traffic, Chaves' handsome, 140m-long, Roman-era bridge makes a lovely place for a stroll. The span was completed in AD 104 by order of Emperor Trajan (hence its other name, Ponte Trajano). It likely served as a key link on the important road between Braga and Astorga (Spain), as two engraved Roman milestones on the centre of the bridge indicate.

Museu da Região Flaviense
MUSEUM

(☎276 340 500; Praça de Luís Camões; admission incl Museu Militar €1; ⊙9am-12.30pm & 2-5.30pm; ⊙closed holidays) Small but interesting, this regional archaeological-ethnographic museum has lots of Roman artefacts, plus a collection of pre-Roman jewellery, bronze tools, grinding stones and menhirs, some dating back over 2500 years. There are also temporary art displays upstairs.

Churches
CHURCHES

The 17th-century **Igreja da Misericórdia** (Praça de Luís Camões) has an eye-catching facade with distinctive, twisting columns, plus some huge 18th-century *azulejos* inside.

Also on the square is the **igreja matriz** (parish church), which is Romanesque in form. It was thoroughly remodelled in the 16th century, though the doorway and belfry retain some original features.

🏃 Activities

Termas de Chaves
SPA

(www.termasdechaves.com; Largo das Caldas) The warm waters of the Termas de Chaves, which emerge from the ground at 73°C, are said to relieve everything from rheumatism to obesity. After shelling out the initial €65 medical consultation fee, you have access to a plethora of reasonably priced treatments (€5 to €23), ranging from steam baths to massage. In the rotunda just outside the baths, spa employees distribute free glasses of the warm, bicarbonate-heavy waters, though they taste pretty awful.

🛏 Sleeping

Budget accommodation is clustered along Rua do Sol in the historic centre. For a bit more character and charm, consider the slew of attractive rural inns in the hills surrounding town. Book ahead in summer, when the spa is in full swing. Most places offer big discounts from September to May.

Quinta da Mata
RURAL INN €€

TOP CHOICE (☎276 340 030; www.quintadamata.net; Nantes; d €80; ⓟ🐾🏊) This isolated and family-friendly country haven, just 4.5km southeast of Chaves off the N213, centres on a lovingly restored and elegantly appointed 17th-century manor house with terracotta tile floors and stone walls. The grounds include tennis courts, a sauna and beautiful, flower-filled gardens on the lush hills overlooking the city. The excellent breakfast includes local ham and other regional specialities.

Quinta de Santa Isabel
RURAL INN €€

(☎276 351 818; www.quintadesantaisabel.com.pt; Santo Estevão; self-catering 2-/4-person apt €60/90; ⓟ🛜) This cluster of lovely stone houses – some dating back to the 16th century and converted from haylofts or stables – sits at the foot of a vineyard-covered hillside in the tiny town of Santo Estevão, 7km northeast of Chaves. The five apartments – each with a fireplace or woodstove, plus kitchenette or kitchen – are filled with historic charm, including ancient wood floors, stone walls and antique furniture. The common rooms, including billiards and foosball tables, are built around the massive old wine press downstairs. Pets are welcome, there are hiking trails out the back and proprietor Luísa Sarmento speaks flawless English.

Forte de São Francisco Hotel

LUXURY HOTEL €€€

(☑276 333 700; www.forte-s-francisco-hoteis.pt; s/d/ste €120/135/165; P✳@🌊) For stylish digs in downtown Chaves, look no further than this remarkable historic inn. Housed in a 16th-century convent within the walls of the city's 17th-century fort, this extraordinary blend of four-star hotel and national monument has flawless rooms, tennis courts and a sauna, not to mention a rare-bird aviary, a centuries-old private chapel with piped-in Gregorian chants and an upscale restaurant and bar.

Casa de Samaiões

HOTEL €€

(☑276 340 450; www.hotel-casasamaioes.com, in Portuguese; Samaiões; s/d/ste €83/93/134; P🌊🌊) Set amidst spacious grounds at the foot of lovely mountains, this manor house turned luxury hotel in the village of Samaiões (5km south of Chaves) is replete with historic decor, including a full suit of armour in the front parlour, and a 19th-century chapel. The rooms, while comfortable, are blandly modern by contrast.

Quinta do Rebentão

CAMPGROUND €

(☑276 322 733; www.cccchaves.com, in Portuguese; Vila Nova de Veiga; sites per adult/child/tent/car €3.20/2/2.60/3, 2-/4-person bungalows €40/52; ☺Jan-Nov; 🌊) Six kilometres southwest of Chaves, just off the N2, is this grassy, partly shaded, suburban camping facility with free hot showers, pool access and basic supplies. Bike rentals are also available.

Residencial Jardim das Caldas

HOTEL €

(☑276 331 189; www.jardimdascaldas.com; Alameda do Tabolado 5; s/d €35/40; 🌊) In a modern building facing Chaves' riverside park, this guest house has tidy rooms with patterned wood floors and dependable in-room wi-fi. If there's nobody at reception, ask at the restaurant on the ground floor.

Residencial Restaurante Kátia

GUEST HOUSE €

(☑276 324 446; Rua do Sol 28; s/d €30/35) One of several guest houses on this street, this family-run place offers small, prim, spotless rooms – some with verandahs – plus a decent restaurant downstairs.

🍴 Eating

For self-caterers, there's a **supermarket** upstairs from the AV Tâmega bus station.

Restaurante Carvalho

PORTUGUESE €€

(Alameda do Tabolado; mains €8-14; ☺lunch & dinner Tue-Sat, lunch Sun) Carvalho's top-notch regional dishes have earned recognition as some of Portugal's best. It's hidden away amid the cluster of parkside cafes opposite the Jardim do Tabolado.

Hospedaria Florinda

PORTUGUESE €€

(Rua dos Açougues; meals €10; ☺lunch & dinner) On a narrow street near the Torre de Menagem, Florinda's unpretentious downstairs

---

GHOST TOWNS: THE TRANSMONTANA EXODUS

Portugal is one of the few European countries to experience mass emigration well into the 20th century. In the 1970s alone, it's estimated that 775,000 people left the country – nearly 10% of the total population.

With difficult agricultural conditions and little industry, it's little surprise that Trás-os-Montes (along with the neighbouring Minho) contributed more than its share to the exodus. The region's population shrank by nearly 33% between 1960 and 2001. To get an idea of the kinds of conditions they were fleeing, consider this: 60% of the region's workforce was engaged in agriculture into the 1990s – a figure higher than in many developing nations.

At the turn of the 20th century, the lion's share of emigrants headed to Brazil, which was undergoing a coffee boom. Later, many left for Portugal's African possessions, which received increased investment and interest during Salazar's regime. Then as Europe's postwar economy heated up in the 1960s and '70s, *transmontanas* began to stick closer to home, finding work as labourers in Germany, Belgium and especially France.

The effect of this exodus is still visible, especially in rural areas. Many villages have been abandoned wholesale, left to a few widows and a clutch of chickens. Around others you'll find a ring of modern construction, almost always paid for not by the fruit of the land but by money earned abroad. And don't be surprised to meet a villager, scythe in hand and oxen in tow, who speaks to you in perfect Parisian argot.

dining room serves top-notch regional meals, including meats cooked over the open fire and traditional homemade desserts. The lady of the house (who also runs the guest house upstairs) is a paragon of *transmontana* hospitality.

João Padeiro Forno Regional   BAKERY €
(Rua do Postigo; ☺9am-8pm) Snack on tasty regional treats at this corner bakery, including the trademark *folar de Chaves* (big pillowy loaves filled with bacon, linguiça and local *salpicão* sausage) and the ridiculously affordable *pasteis de Chaves* (flaky turnovers filled with ground meat, €0.60 each).

🍷 Drinking & Entertainment

There's a cluster of lively bars across from the park and the spa at the bottom of town, and another on Travessa Cándido dos Reis near the fort.

Adega Faustino   WINE BAR €
(Travessa Cândido dos Reis; snacks €3-7.50; ☺noon-11pm Mon-Sat) Resembling a fire station from the outside, this cavernous ex-winery oozes atmosphere inside, with cobblestoned floors and gigantic wine casks lined up behind the bar. The menu features a long list of carefully prepared regional snacks, from *salpicão* (small rounds of smoked ham) to pig's ear in vinaigrette sauce, plus an excellent selection of quaffable local wines.

Biblioteca   BAR
(Travessa Cândido dos Reis) This bar-cum-disco with a name meaning 'library' attracts a raucous and decidedly nonliterary younger crowd.

Centro Cultural de Chaves   ARTS CENTRE
(☎276 333 713; Largo da Estação) Chaves' brand-new cultural centre stages regular concerts, plays and other events, most of them free of charge. For details on current shows, see the monthly *Agenda Cultural*, available at the tourist office.

ℹ️ Information

Biblioteca Municipal (Largo General Silveira; ☺9am-7pm Mon-Fri) Free internet at the town library.

District hospital (☎276 300 900; Av Francisco Sá Carneiro) Northwest of the centre.

Police station (☎276 323 125; Av Bombeiros Voluntários)

Post office (Largo General Silveira; ☺8.30am-6pm Mon-Fri, 9am-12.30pm Sat)

Regional turismo (☎276 348 180; turismo@ portoenorte.pt; Terreiro de Cavalaria; ☺9am-12.30pm & 2-5.30pm Mon-Sat) Helpful multilingual tourist office.

ℹ️ Getting There & Around

BUS AV Tâmega (☎276 332 384; www.avtamega.pt) and **Rodonorte** (☎276 328 123; www.rodonorte.pt; Av de Santo Amaro) have terminals just north and west of the centre respectively. Only Tâmega serves all of the following destinations: Bragança (€10, three hours, one daily at 4pm), Coimbra (€13.50, 3¾ hours, three daily), Lisbon (€19.10, six to seven hours, three daily), Porto (€11.90, 2¼ hours, several daily) and Vila Real (€7.30, 1¼ hours, several daily).

CAR & MOTORCYCLE There's plenty of free public parking below the Torre da Menagem and around Jardim do Tabolado.

Bragança

POP 20,000 / ELEV 650M

The historical capital of Trás-os-Montes, Bragança is at once a modern city of broad sterile avenues and suburban high-rises, and an overgrown medieval village from whose crenellated heights one can still survey the surrounding countryside and see small farms, fields, and oak-chestnut forest. While many streets – especially some in the older *centro* – give the appearance of a town down on its luck, new construction and civic projects express Bragança's enduring pride and dynamism. Recent additions to the city's cultural life include a new municipal theatre; museums dedicated to contemporary art and regional folk traditions; and eye-catching public sculptures such as the bronze postman outside the *correio* (post office) and the massive fighting bulls in the Rotunda do Lavrador Transmontano.

For the visitor, the main attraction remains the ancient walled Cidadela (citadel), high atop the hill at Bragança's eastern edge. Walk through the arched gates into this extraordinarily well-preserved medieval quarter, with its tangle of narrow streets, multistorey keep and towering pig pillory, and it's easy to imagine life in the Middle Ages unfolding around you. The view from the topmost tower – for those brave enough to climb a steep, ancient wooden ladder – is truly astounding.

History

Known as Bragantia to the Celts and Juliobriga to the Romans, Bragança is an ancient

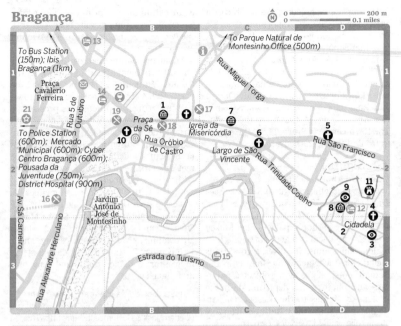

Bragança

◉ Sights
1 Centro de Arte Contemporânea Graça Morais	B1
2 Cidadela	D3
3 Domus Municipalis	D3
4 Igreja de Santa Maria	D2
5 Igreja de São Bento	D2
6 Igreja de São Vicente	C2
7 Museu do Abade de Baçal	C2
8 Museu Ibérico da Máscara e do Traje	D2
Museu Militar	(see 11)
9 Pelourinho	D2
10 Sé	B2
11 Torre de Menagem	D2

🛌 Sleeping
12 Arco da Velha	D2

13 Hotel Tulipa	A1
14 Pensão Rucha	A1
15 Pousada de São Bartolomeu	C3
Residencial Poças	(see 18)

🍴 Eating
16 O Pote	A2
17 Restaurante Lá Em Casa	B1
18 Restaurante Poças	B2
19 Solar Bragançano	B1

🍷 Drinking
20 Moderno	B1

✴ Entertainment
21 Teatro Municipal	A1

city. Its location, mere kilometres from the Spanish border, made it an important post in the centuries-long battles between Spain and Portugal. The walled citadel was built in 1130 by Portugal's first king, Afonso Henriques I. His son and successor, Sancho I, improved the fortifications by building Bragança's castle, with its watchtowers, dungeons and keep, in 1187, after reclaiming the city from the king of León.

In 1442 Afonso V created the Duchy of Bragança for his uncle, an illegitimate son of the first Avis king João I, thus launching one of Portugal's wealthiest and most powerful noble families. The Braganças assumed the Portuguese throne in 1640, ending Spain's 60-year domination of Portugal. The family went on to reign in Portugal until the dissolution of the monarchy in 1910.

During the Napoleonic Wars, Bragança again served as an important strategic point against foreign invaders: it was from here that Sepúlveda launched his call to resistance against French forces.

The city's main axis road – alternately called Av João da Cruz, Rua Almirante Reis, Rua Combatentes da Grande Guerra and Rua Trindade Coelho – winds southeast from the bus station up to the citadel. The town centre is Praça da Sé, the square in front of the old cathedral.

◉ Sights

Museu do Abade de Baçal   MUSEUM

(www.ipmuseus.pt, in Portuguese; Rua Abílio Beça 27; admission €2, 10am-2pm Sun free; ☺10am-5pm Tue-Fri, to 6pm Sat & Sun) Set in a restored 18th-century bishop's palace, the Museu do Abade de Baçal is one of Portugal's best regional museums. Its diverse collections include local artefacts from the Celtic and Roman eras, along with objects, paintings and photographs depicting daily life in Trás-os-Montes to the present. Of particular interest are the handful of Iron Age stone pigs called *berrões* (see the boxed text, p464). The museum also features works by Portuguese naturalist painter Aurelia de Sousa and her contemporaries, as well as Christian pieces from India, which depict Jesus in a style highly influenced by Hindu and Buddhist art.

Cidadela   MEDIEVAL CITADEL

Keep climbing uphill from Largo de São Vicente and you'll soon set foot inside the astonishingly well-preserved 12th-century citadel. People still live in its narrow, atmospheric lanes, unspoilt by the few, low-key handicrafts shops and cafes that have crept in.

Within the ruggedly ramparted walls is the original castle – built by Sancho I in 1187 and beefed up in the 15th century by João I, then heavily restored in the 1930s. The stout **Torre de Menagem** was garrisoned up until the early 20th century. It now houses a **Museu Militar** (Military Museum; admission €1.50, Fri morning free; ☺9-11.30am & 2-4.30pm Tue-Sun), whose four floors are filled with swords, guns and suits of armour spanning several centuries, from medieval times to WWI and the Salazar dictatorship's colonial exploits. The price of admission is well worth the chance to climb to the top of the crenellated tower, with great views all around. In front of the *torre*

is an extraordinary, primitive **pelourinho** (stone pillory) atop a granite boar similar to the *berrões* (see the boxed text, p464) found around the province.

Squatting at the rear of the citadel is an odd pentagonal building known as the **Domus Municipalis** (Town House; admission free; ☺9am-4.45pm Fri-Wed), the oldest town hall in Portugal – although its precise age is a matter of scholarly disagreement – and one of the few examples of civil Romanesque architecture on the Iberian Peninsula. Bragança's medieval town council once met upstairs in an arcaded room studded with weathered faces of man and beast and scratched with symbols of the stonemasons.

Beside the Domus Municipalis is the early-16th-century **Igreja de Santa Maria**. Of particular interest are its brick Mudéjar columns, vividly painted ceiling, and a 17th-century Santa Maria Madalena at the high altar, with her traditional long hair and ragged garb.

Museu Ibérico da Máscara e do Traje

MUSEUM

(Iberian Mask & Costume Museum; http://museu damascara.cm-braganca.pt, in Portuguese; Rua Dom Fernão o Bravo 24/26; admission €1; ☺10am-12.30pm & 2-6pm Tue-Sun) This visually appealing little museum displays a colourful and fascinating collection of masks and costumes from the ancient pagan-based solstice and Carnaval festivities celebrated in Trás-os-Montes and neighbouring Zamora (Spain). Costumes are displayed across three floors, with the upper exhibits dedicated to the work of local artisans.

Centro de Arte Contemporânea
Graça Morais   ART MUSEUM

(http://centroartegracamorais.cm-braganca. pt; Rua Abílio Beça 105; admission €2; ☺10am-12.30pm & 2-6.30pm Tue-Sun) The Centro de Arte Contemporânea Graça Morais, which opened in 2008, is another cross-border collaboration between Portugal and Spain. Its permanent collection features local painter Graça Morais' haunting portraits of Trás-os-Montes residents, alongside more abstract work. The modern annexe showcases rotating special exhibitions.

Igreja de São Bento   CHURCH

(Rua São Francisco) Bragança's most attractive church has a Renaissance stone portal, a wonderful *trompe l'œil* ceiling over the nave and an Arabic-style inlaid ceiling above the chancel.

Igreja de São Vicente CHURCH

(Largo de São Vicente) Romanesque in origin but rebuilt in the 17th century, this church may have played host to a chapter in Portugal's favourite – and grisliest – love story. Tradition has it that the future Dom Pedro secretly married Inês de Castro here around 1354 (see the boxed text, p268, for the whole tragic tale).

Sé CATHEDRAL

(Praça da Sé) Bragança's modest old cathedral started out in 1545 as the Igreja de São João Baptista, but moved up the ranks to become a cathedral in 1770 when the bishopric moved here from Miranda do Douro. It was then downgraded again when Bragança's contemporary cathedral, the Igreja de Nossa Senhora Rainha, opened just west of the centre.

★☆ Festivals & Events

Bragança's biggest annual market, Feira das Cantarinhas, runs for three days in early May. It's a huge street fair of traditional handicrafts (a *cantarinha* is a small terracotta pitcher) held in and around the Cidadela.

⌂ Sleeping

Bragança's central hotels are largely dreary low-budget affairs whose glory days seem to have been sometime in the early 1970s. There are also two campgrounds in the nearby Parque Natural de Montesinho – see p463 and p464.

Arco da Velha APARTMENT €

(☏966 787 784; www.turismobraganca.com; Rua Dom Fernão o Bravo; 2-bedroom apt €90; ᴘ) The only place to stay within Bragança's atmospheric medieval citadel, this comfy split-level apartment sleeps up to four, allows pets and has its own parking spot just outside. The original stone-walled building has been thoroughly remodelled, with modern furniture and a wood-pellet stove for chilly winter evenings. Minimum stay is two nights.

Hotel Tulipa HOTEL €

(☏273 331 675; www.tulipaturismo.com; Rua Dr Francisco Felgueiras 8-10; s/d/tr €35/45/55; ᴘ✳🛜) Nicely remodelled in 2010, the Tulipa offers clean and comfortable – if uninspiring – modern rooms, most with big flat-screen TVs, and some adapted for visitors with disabilities. An additional plus is the central location between the bus station and downtown.

Pousada de São Bartolomeu
LUXURY HOTEL €€€ **459**

(☏273 331 493; recepcao.sbartolomeu@pousadas.pt; Estrada do Turismo; d €220; ᴘ✳@🛜♨) This whitewashed modern affair may not, in itself, be the most arresting *pousada* (upmarket inn) in Portugal, but its views over the Cidadela and countryside are way up there. It sits proudly alone, on a hilltop 1.5km southeast of the centre, and boasts lots of creature comforts, including a great restaurant and bright contemporary rooms with balconies overlooking the pool and the castle.

Ibis Bragança HOTEL €€

(☏273 302 520; www.ibishotel.com; Rotunda do Lavrador Transmontano; r without breakfast €59;✳🛜) Just off the IP4 north of town, the Ibis is nicer than most hotels in the centre, despite its bland chain-hotel predictability. The recently constructed rooms are small but bright and cheery. Wi-fi is available in the lobby (free) or in the rooms (€5 per hour), and breakfast costs €5 extra. Rates drop dramatically outside the summer season.

Pousada da Juventude HOSTEL €

(☏273 304 600; braganca@movijovem.pt; Av 22 de Maio; dm €12, d with private/shared bathroom €34/28; ᴘ🛜) This modern – if sometimes inattentively run – hostel offers self-service laundry, free wi-fi, comfy common areas, and an on-site bar and restaurant. The two-bedroom apartment (€64) with its own kitchen and washer-dryer is a great option for families. It's located in the nondescript suburbs west of the centre, about a 30-minute walk from the Cidadela.

Residencial Poças GUEST HOUSE €

(☏273 331 428; Rua Combatentes da Grande Guerra 200; s/d/tr/q without breakfast €15/25/35/45) The high-ceilinged rooms here are cheap and spacious, even if the mismatched and battered furniture looks like it was salvaged off a truck. Check out the hundreds of swallows' nests under the eaves as you enter; the building is reputed to be the second-biggest urban nesting site in Europe.

Pensão Rucha GUEST HOUSE €

(☏273 331 672; Rua Almirante Reis 42; s/d with shared bathroom €15/25) The kind proprietor at this simple *pensão* (guest house) offers spotless but lacklustre rooms with shared bathroom at a good price. No breakfast.

The people of Portugal are, in my book, the least ego-driven in Europe. That is not to say they're saints immune to concerns of status or always perfectly patient or generous. However, they value amiability above all things, and since 'attitude' is an impediment to this, it's not considered a show of power but as very poor form. Travels in Portugal's former colonies have only confirmed this impression. Brazil vs Argentina, Guinea-Bissau vs Senegal, Macau vs Hong Kong – every time, the former Portuguese colony comes out on top, at least in terms of easy sociability.

In the hills of the Parque Natural de Montesinho, I encountered the logical extension of my theory. As I stepped out of my car in a town whose main road had only recently been paved, an old man greeted me and asked what I was doing in his town. 'What business is it of his?' I thought. 'Why is he trying to make me feel unwelcome?' Within half an hour I was, happily, proven so very wrong as he poured me glasses of port, then homemade cherry hooch (it was April and the hills all around us were in high bloom with next year's batch). His wife arrived, scythe in hand, and encouraged me to take pictures of her goats. 'They're so beautiful', she said. At one point, she pointed at her wrist, where there was no watch. 'We don't have to worry about that here.'

As we stood there together, it dawned on me that this man had asked what I was doing not to mark his territory (as would have been the case in my country) but merely so he could help me find whatever it was that I'd been seeking. I'd had no idea that what I wanted above all was simply to spend this moment with him and his wife and then his neighbours who, as the shadows lengthened, were returning from their fields and soon joining us with their hoes and staffs, pleased to have a stranger among them.

Robert Landon is a travel writer and Lonely Planet author; he co-wrote the 6th edition of the Portugal guide.

Eating

Solar Bragançano PORTUGUESE €€
(Praça da Sé 34; mains €8.50-14; ☺lunch & dinner Tue-Sun) Upstairs in a manor house opposite the cathedral square, this elegant eatery boasts oak-panelled rooms, chandeliers, wide plank floors, a leafy and sun-dappled outdoor terrace and a seasonal menu weighted towards local game, with specialities including wild boar, partridge with grapes and pheasant with chestnuts.

O Pote PORTUGUESE €€
(Rua Alexandre Herculano 186; mains €7.50-14; ☺lunch & dinner Mon-Sat) This friendly eatery is divided into a formal upstairs dining room and a more relaxed downstairs cafe, both serving excellent regional specialities. The olive oil, some of the wine and much of the produce is sourced from the owners' farm outside town. The all-inclusive weekday lunch menu for €7.50 is almost too good to be true. For dessert, try the *peras bêbadas* ('drunk' pears soaked in wine).

Restaurante Poças PORTUGUESE €
(Rua Combatentes da Grande Guerra 200; mains €6.50-10; ☺lunch & dinner) Despite the touristy multilingual menus, Restaurante Poças serves very good *transmontano* food at nontouristy prices, from charcoal-grilled lamb and goat to stewed partridge with chestnuts.

Restaurante Lá Em Casa PORTUGUESE €€
(Rua Marquês de Pombal; mains €9-15; ☺lunch & dinner) This place serves platters heaped with excellent, wood-grilled local meats in a stone-walled, pine-panelled dining room with fireplace. The veal and lamb are especially savoury.

Mercado Municipal MARKET €
(☺8am-7pm Mon-Sat) It's a longish walk to this new, rather antiseptic market behind the *câmara municipal*.

Drinking

There are atmospheric bars in the Cidadela where you can down shots of *ginja* (cherry liqueur) with Bragança's version of good ole boys.

Moderno NIGHTCLUB
(Rua Almirante Reis; ☺midnight-4am) This is the city's principal disco, with DJs spinning an eclectic mix of tunes.

⭐ Entertainment

Teatro Municipal ARTS CENTRE
(http://teatromunicipal.cm-braganca.pt, in Portuguese; Praça Cavaleiro Ferreira) The boxy new Teatro Municipal has given the city's cultural life a great boost, by hosting high-quality music, theatre and dance shows, plus afternoon performances for children. There's a multi-screen cinema next door.

ℹ️ Information

Biblioteca Municipal (Praça Camões; ⊙9am-12.30pm & 2-7pm Mon-Fri) Free internet (one hour maximum) at the public library.

Cyber Centro Bragança (1st fl, Mercado Municipal; per hr €1; ⊙10am-11pm Mon-Fri, 10am-7pm Sat, 2-7pm Sun) Evening and weekend internet access.

District Hospital (☑273 310 800; Av Abade de Baçal) West of the centre.

Parque Natural de Montesinho office (☑273 300 400; pnm@icnb.pt; Rua Cónego Albano Falcão 5; ⊙9am-12.30pm & 2-5.30pm Mon-Fri) Northeast of the *turismo*.

Police station (☑273 303 400; Rua Dr Manuel Bento) Just north of the *câmara municipal*.

Post & telephone office (Largo dos Correios; ⊙8.30am-5.30pm Mon-Fri, 9am-12.30pm Sat)

Turismo (☑273 381 273; turismo@cm-braganca.pt; Av Cidade de Zamora; ⊙9am-12.30pm & 2-5pm Mon-Fri, 10am-12.30pm Sat) An extremely helpful office, run by the knowledgeable and multilingual Anabela.

ℹ️ Getting There & Away

BUS Bragança's spiffy modern bus station, housed in the former train depot at the top of Av João da Cruz, is served by **Rede Expressos** (☑966 482 215; www.rede-expressos.pt, in Portuguese), **Rodonorte** (☑273 326 552; www.rodonorte.pt, in Portuguese) and **Eurolines** (☑273 326 211; www.eurolines.com). Station offices tend to be open only at departure times. Services to the following destinations are daily, except as noted: Braga (€13.50, four hours, Rodonorte), Guimarães (€13.50, 3½ hours, Rodonorte), Lisbon (€18.50, seven hours, Rede Expressos), Mirandela (€6.10, one hour, Rodonorte), Nice (€112, 23 hours, Eurolines, thrice weekly), Paris (€86, 19 hours, Eurolines, daily except Sunday), Porto (€12, three hours, Rodonorte and Rede Expressos), Vila Nova de Foz Côa (€7.50, 1¾ hours, Rede Expressos), Vila Real (€9.10, two hours, Rodonorte), Viseu (€13, 3¼ hours, Rede Expressos) and Trancoso (€9.80, 2¼ hours, Rede Expressos).

CAR Parking is generally not difficult. There are lots of paid spots in the square just south of the *sé*, with free overnight parking for motor homes in the lot just east of the Cidadela.

Parque Natural de Montesinho

The peaceful highlands along Portugal's northeastern border with Spain constitute one of Trás-os-Montes' most appealing natural and cultural landscapes – it's a patchwork of rolling grasslands, giant chestnut trees, oak forests and deep canyons, sprinkled with ancient stone villages where an ageing population still ekes out a hard-scrabble existence.

The 750-sq-km Parque Natural de Montesinho was established to protect the area's 88 lean villages as much as their natural setting. This harsh, remote *terra fria* inspired early Portuguese rulers to establish a system of collective land tenure and then leave the villagers to their own devices, allowing for a remarkably democratic, communal culture, which persists today.

Unfortunately, remote villages continue to be deserted by their young, and many have not a single resident under the age of 60. However, these settlements – mostly just small clusters of granite houses roofed in slate and sheltering in deep valleys – retain an irresistible charm, especially in late April, when cherry and chestnut trees are in flower. In some towns, the government has helped preserve traditional slate-roofed stone houses as well as churches, forges, mills and the characteristic, charming *pombals* (dovecotes).

Villages that retain lashings of character include Pinheiro Novo, Sernande, Moimenta and Dine in the west, and Montesinho, Varge, Rio de Onor and Guadramil in the east.

The natural base from which to explore the park is Bragança. Smaller villages within the park also offer accommodation, but public transport is patchy.

⊙ Sights

The most famous inhabitant of the eastern Serra de Montesinho is the rust-coloured Iberian wolf. Indeed, this natural park and the adjoining Spanish park together form the last major refuge for this seriously endangered animal. Other threatened species include the royal eagle and the black stork.

In vast forests of Iberian oak and chestnut, and among riverside alders, willows, poplars and hazel, there are also roe deer, otters and wild boar; in the grasslands are

partridges, kites and kestrels. Above 900m the otherwise barren ground is carpeted in heather and broom in spring.

Rio de Onor
VILLAGE

This lovely little town of 70 souls situated in the eastern half of the park is entirely unfazed by the Spanish–Portuguese border splicing it down the middle. It's interesting not just for its rustic stone buildings, whose ground floors still house straw-filled stables for goats, sheep and donkeys, but also for its staunch maintenance of the communal lifestyle once typical of the region. Spend an afternoon here and you'll see elderly locals trundling wheelbarrows from the well-tended community gardens surrounding town, pitchforking hay onto horse-drawn carts, stopping in at the local cafe whose communally shared proceeds are used to fund town festivals, or trading jobs with each other – one cousin staying to mind the store while the other goes to bring in the sheep. The twinned village also has one other claim to fame – a hybrid Portuguese–Spanish dialect known as Rionorês.

The border runs east–west through the middle of the village, while the Rio de Onor trickles along perpendicular to it. The road from Bragança continues north through town into Spain, branching right just before the border to cross an old stone bridge to the prettiest part of the village, where you'll find the community cafe.

From Bragança, STUB bus 5 (€1.20, 45 minutes) heads to Rio de Onor three times daily.

Montesinho
VILLAGE

Hidden at the end of the road in a narrow valley wedged between forbidding granite heights, this tiny village is one of the park's best-preserved, thanks to a program to restore old dwellings and stop construction of new ones. The village is also the jumping-off point for the 8km **Porto Furado hiking trail** through the rugged hills to a nearby dam. STUB bus 7 (€1.20, one hour) runs from Bragança to Montesinho at least once daily.

Dine & Moimenta
VILLAGES

Dine and Moimenta, two of the prettiest villages in the western half of the park, are connected by a high-altitude road with panoramic views of the windmill-speckled hills along the Spanish border. In well-preserved Dine, you can visit a tiny **archaeological museum**, which documents the 1984 find by a Danish diplomat of Iron Age remains in a nearby cave. The museum is usually locked, but just ask around and someone will rustle up the French-speaking caretaker, Judite, who may also lead you around to the cave itself – pointing out traditional lime kilns and wild-growing medicinal herbs along the way.

Moimenta has a lovely core of granite houses roofed in terracotta, plus a small baroque church – a rare dose of luxury in this austere corner of Portugal. The pretty 7km **Calçada loop trail** descends from town into the nearby river gorge, following sections of an old stone roadway across a remarkably well-preserved **medieval bridge** with a single impressive arch.

🏃 Activities

There are plenty of opportunities for biking and hiking. Park offices offer free brochures detailing 11 marked hiking trails around the park (although some of these seem to be chronically out of print!).

If you come here in the summer, you can always cool off in the park's plentiful (if chilly) rivers and streams. Look for signs pointing to *praias fluviais* (river beaches) throughout the park; one of the nicest such swimming spots is near the centre of the park, just northwest of the town of Fresulfe.

🛏 Sleeping & Eating

Park headquarters rents out several houses throughout the park. Known as *casas-retiro* and *casas-abrigo,* these generally sleep six or more people. Check with the park offices for price details, or Google 'casas retiro abrigo Montesinho' and click on the 'Onde Ficar – ICNB' link for photos.

For a more complete list of local sleeping options, check out the *Alojamento* (lodging) section of the free *Nordeste Transmontano* booklet available from Bragança's tourist office.

Eastern Park

There are a number of self-catering stone cottages in the village of Montesinho. Note that rooms book up in July and August.

TOP CHOICE **A Lagosta Perdida** B&B €€€
(☑273 919 031; www.lagostaperdida.com; Montesinho; s/d incl breakfast & dinner €94/125; P @ 🏊) The region's most luxurious accommodation is this refurbished stone-walled house, run by a friendly Anglo-Dutch couple. It retains numerous period features, including high, beamed ceilings and an old stone water trough downstairs. The comfortable rooms come equipped with cable internet connections, tea-making facilities, flat-screen TVs and beautifully tiled modern bathrooms with tubs. Other amenities include mountain bikes, a nice piano, a library full of books about local trails, flora and fauna, a swimming pool heated by solar power and incinerated olive pits, and six hiking trails right out back. Two meals a day from the vegetarian-friendly kitchen are included in the price. Kids will love the ping-pong table, not to mention the sheepdogs, cats, bunny, Scottish Highland ponies, horse and donkey.

Casa de Onor ROOMS €
(☑273 927 163, 937 592 762; www.casadeonor.com, in Portuguese; Rio de Onor; s/d €40/50) In a pretty stone house overlooking the river in the centre of Rio de Onor, Senhora Rita Rego rents five rooms sleeping one to six people, each with private bathroom. Breakfast is included, and additional meals are available upon request for €15 per person.

Inatel Parque de Campismo de Bragança CAMPGROUND €
(☑273 001 090; pc.braganca@inatel.pt; N103-7, km 6; sites per adult/child/tent/car €5/4/3.50/5; ☉Jun–mid-Sep) The nicest of the local campgrounds, tucked into a cottonwood grove on the banks of the Rio Sabor, has featureless but shady and quiet sites, plus hot showers and a restaurant. From Bragança take STUB bus 7 (€1.20, 20 minutes, four daily).

Café Montesinho CAFE €
(☑273 919 219; Montesinho) A cosy spot at the hub of the village, stone-walled Café Montesinho serves snacks and drinks, and also rents an upstairs two-bedroom apartment (€50) that sleeps up to four people, complete with kitchen and a pleasant verandah.

Casa das Pedras RENTAL COTTAGES €€
(☑919 860 500; www.casadaspedras.com, in Portuguese; Montesinho; d with/without kitchen from €55/40) Senhor Antero Pires rents out four rustic stone and wood cottages ranging from a basic studio to multi-room units with kitchenettes.

Casa Alta ROOMS €
(☑273 927 128; Rio de Onor; r without breakfast €35) Senhor António Preto rents out three simple rooms in this old stone house on the west side of the river in downtown Rio de Onor.

Western Park

Casa dos Marrões RURAL INN €€
(☑273 999 550; www.casadosmarroes.com, in Portuguese; Vilarinho; d €50-60, self-catering house €125; P 🏊) In Vilarinho, 17km northwest of Bragança, this 18th-century home built of oak, chestnut and schist has lovely beamed ceilings and exposed-stone walls. Across the street is a self-catering house sleeping up to six. A spring-fed outdoor pool, plus nearby hiking trails and riverside beaches, enhance its appeal.

Moinho do Caniço RENTAL HOUSE €€
(☑273 323 577; www.bragancanet.pt/moinho; N103, km 251, Castrelos; 4/5/6 people €80/90/100; P) This tastefully refurbished

PIG MYSTERIES

Hundreds of crudely carved granite pigs, or boars, known as *berrões* (singular: *berrão*) are still scattered around the more remote parts of Trás-os-Montes and over into Spain. While they're widely acknowledged to be Celtic in origin, nobody knows for sure what purpose they served. Theories abound: they may have been symbols of fertility or prosperity, grave guardians, offerings to Iron Age gods, manifestations of the gods themselves or simply property markers.

You can see these mysterious pigs in museums in Bragança, Chaves and Miranda do Douro, or in situ in Bragança's citadel, where a weather-beaten porker supports a medieval pillory. The best-preserved example sits heavily atop a pedestal in the central square of tiny **Murça**, 30km northeast of Vila Real.

watermill – complete with centuries-old kitchen and open fireplace – is 12km west of Bragança on the N103. The rustically furnished stone-floored cottage sleeps up to six people, with trout fishing in the Rio Baceiro just outside the door. STUB bus 2 (€1.20, 55 minutes) stops nearby.

Parque de Campismo Cepo Verde
CAMPGROUND €
(☑273 999 371; www.cepoverde.montesinho.com, in Portuguese; Gondesende; sites per adult/child/tent/car €3.25/1.60/3/2; ☺Apr–mid-Sep; ☒) This medium-sized rural facility is 12km west of Bragança near the tiny village of Gondesende on the park's southern border. Sixty camp sites, some shaded and some in full sun, are set on a hillside above a central cafe and swimming pool. STUB bus 4 passes within 1km of the site (€1.20, 40 minutes).

Estúdio da Moimenta STUDIO APARTMENT €
(☑273 300 400; pnm@icnb.pt; Moimenta; d €35) The smallest and least expensive of the park-administered lodgings, this two-person studio, complete with kitchenette, is right in the heart of Moimenta village.

Casa da Bica ROOMS €
(☑273 999 454; www.bragancanet.pt/casadabica; s/d/q €30/35/60) In Gondesende, 12km northwest of Bragança, this schist cottage offers five rather spartan rooms upstairs, plus a downstairs sitting area with fireplace, where breakfast is served.

ⓘ Information

PARK OFFICES at **Bragança** (☑273 300 400; pnm@icnb.pt; Rua Cónego Albano Falcão 5; ☺9am-12.30pm & 2-5.30pm Mon-Fri) and **Vinhais** (☑273 771 416; cipnm@cm-vinhais.pt; Casa da Vila, Centro Histórico; ☺9am-12.30pm & 2-5.30pm) distribute a free park map. Brochures on flora, archaeology, handicrafts and

park walks are in Portuguese, although English-speaking staff at Bragança are happy to answer questions.

ⓘ Getting Around

Exploring the park is difficult without a car, a bike or sturdy feet. The free park map clearly indicates which roads are paved – unpaved roads can be dicey both during and after rains.

Only parts of the park are served by bus. For up-to-date schedules, check with Bragança's municipal bus company, STUB (www.stub.com.pt, in Portuguese). Trips to towns within the park cost €1.20 and generally take an hour or less.

Mirandela

POP 11,000 / ELEV 270M

Built along the Rio Tua in the centre of Trás-os-Montes' agricultural heartland, Mirandela makes a pleasant way-station for travellers looking to break the journey between Vila Real and Bragança, or those coming up from the Alto Douro via Tua. While primarily a down-to-business market town, Mirandela offers a couple of delightful places to stroll: a picturesque, flower-bedecked medieval bridge, and a downtown pedestrian zone where shop windows are hung with the region's renowned sausages and smoked hams.

Rua Dom Afonso III runs in front of the newly combined train and bus stations. To reach the centre of town, turn right along the river towards the medieval bridge and an adjacent modern one. Here you can either carry on along pedestrianised Rua da República to the *turismo* and market (about 800m from the train station), or turn right and uphill on Rua Dom Manuel I to the *câmara municipal* and the old town.

⊙ Sights

The star attraction in Mirandela is the 15th-century Ponte Românica (Romanesque bridge) across the Rio Tua. Featuring 20 uniquely proportioned arches and lined with flower boxes, it's a leading candidate for Portugal's most elegant and photogenic footbridge.

Old Mirandela is centred on the *câmara municipal,* in the splendiferous Palácio dos Távoras (Praça do Município), built in the 17th century for António Luiz de Távora, patron of one of northeast Portugal's powerful aristocratic families. The adjacent Praça de Outubro has a church and several palaces from the same period.

Olive oil production is big in this region, and at the time of research plans were underway for a new **olive oil museum**, but the opening date remained uncertain.

⊨ Sleeping

TOP CHOICE **Quinta Entre Rios**　　　　　RURAL INN **€€**
(☑278 263 160; www.quintaentrerios. do.sapo.pt, in Portuguese; Chelas; s/d €60/75; [P][🛜][❄][≋]) Set amid olive groves and orchards 3km outside Mirandela, this 18th-century country home is the perfect rural retreat. Handsome schist and timber construction give it plenty of rustic charm, but creature comforts also abound, including satellite TV, wi-fi, tennis courts and a nice swimming pool. The surrounding farm produces its own wine, olive oil, sausages, honey and fruit preserves, and owner Olimpia invites guests to pick cherries in June, harvest olives in January or even assist with olive oil production. Horseback riding is available for a small extra charge.

Hotel Miratua　　　　　　　　HOTEL **€€**
(☑278 200 140; www.miratuahotel.com; Rua da República 42; s/d/ste €30/55/70; [❄]) Pleasantly situated in the heart of Mirandela's pedestrian zone, this '70s-era hotel has seen some wear but is kept in good trim. Some of the smallish but comfortable midrange rooms have verandahs.

Hotel Dom Dinis　　　　　　　HOTEL **€€**
(☑278 260 100; www.hoteldomdinis.com, in Portuguese; Rua Nossa Senhora do Amparo; s/d/tr €72/88/124; [P][✳][@][🛜][≋]) Despite its run-down and charmless exterior, this oversized business hotel at the far end of the medieval bridge has comfortable rooms, many with balconies offering fine views of the bridge and river.

(☑278 263 177; www.parquedecampismodemiran dela.com in Portuguese; Maravilha; camp sites per adult/child/tent/car €3.50/2.50/3/3, 2-/4-person bungalows €50/65; [≋]) This flat, shady campground at the confluence of three rivers is 3km north of the centre on the N15. It has a restaurant and *minimercado.*

✗ Eating

Along the waterfront near the two bridges, several photogenic delicatessens sell the region's excellent olive oil, as well as the local speciality *alheira de Mirandela,* a smoky, garlicky sausage of poultry or game. The *mercado municipal* hums along every morning except Sunday, trailing off into the afternoon.

TOP CHOICE **Flor de Sal**
CONTEMPORARY PORTUGUESE **€€€**
(www.flordesalrestaurante.com, in Portuguese; Parque Dr José Gama; mains €16.50-19.50; ☺lunch & dinner Tue-Sun) With a breezy riverside terrace, fancy white tablecloths, elegant red-and-black-clad waiters and jazzy ambient music, this upmarket restaurant is pleasantly situated in a park across the new bridge. It's won high praise for creative, beautifully presented regional dishes such as stewed partridge with wild asparagus and truffle oil, or grilled octopus in an olive-bread crust with carrot purée and caramelised fava beans. On weekdays at lunchtime, there's a great *menu executivo,* including appetiser, main dish and dessert for €15.

O Pinheiro　　　　　　　　PORTUGUESE **€**
(Calçada de São Cosme; mains €5-9.50; ☺lunch & dinner) Up a little alley just off pedestrianised Rua da República, this popular local eatery serves an extensive range of Portuguese fare. The daily handwritten specials go for €6.

ⓘ Information

District hospital (☑278 260 500; Av Nossa Senhora do Amparo) Just west of the old bridge.

Espaço Internet (ground fl, mercado municipal; ☺9am-12.30pm & 3-6.30pm Mon-Fri) Free internet; bring a photocopy of your ID.

Police station (☑278 265 814; Praça 5 de Outubro) Four blocks north of the post office.

Post office (Rua Dom Manuel I; ☺8.30am-12.30pm & 1.30-6pm Mon-Fri) Just below the *câmara municipal.*

Turismo (☑278 203 143; postodeturismo@cm-mirandela.pt; Rua Dom Afonso III; ⏱9am-6pm Mon-Fri, 10.30am-4.30pm Sat & Sun) Right next to the train station; provides town maps and other local information.

ℹ Getting There & Away

BUS Rede Expressos (☑965 008 362) and **Rodonorte** (☑278 262 541) buses go to Bragança (€6.30, one hour) and Porto (€10, 2½ hours). Rodonorte also serves Vila Real (€6.10, one hour) and Miranda do Douro (€8.50, 2¾ hours).

TRAIN At the time of research, service remained suspended on the scenic narrow-gauge Linha da Tua from Mirandela to Tua in the Douro valley. Pending repair work, the train was only covering the 20-minute stretch between Mirandela and Cachão, with low-cost taxi service offered the rest of the way south. Check at the *turismo* or www.cp.pt for current schedules and status.

Miranda do Douro

POP 2000 / ELEV 560M

A fortified frontier town hunkering on the precipice of the gorgeous Rio Douro canyon, Miranda do Douro was long a bulwark of Portugal's 'wild east'. With its crumbling castle still lending an air of medieval charm, modern-day Miranda has now taken on a decidedly different role – receiving weekending Spanish tourists, as opposed to repelling Castilian attacks.

The town's beautifully hulking, 16th-century church may seem all out of proportion to the rest of the town, but it once served as cathedral for the entire region. Visitors shouldn't miss Miranda's ethnographic museum, which sheds light on the region's border culture, including ancient rites such as the 'stick dancing' of the *pauliteiros* (p469).

Street signs around town are written in Mirandês, an ancient language that developed during Miranda's long centuries of isolation from the rest of Portugal (p468). Romance-language buffs will enjoy names like 'Rue de la Santa Cruç', which read like a fantastical blend of French, Spanish and Portuguese.

History

Miranda was a vital stronghold during Portugal's first centuries of independence, and the Castilians had to be chucked out at least twice: in the early days by Dom João I, and again in 1710, during the War of the Spanish Succession. In 1545, perhaps as a snub

to the increasingly powerful House of Bragança, a diocese was created here – hence the oversized cathedral.

During a siege by French and Spanish troops in 1762, the castle's powder magazine exploded, pulverising most of the castle and killing some 400 people. Twenty years later, shattered Miranda lost its diocese to Bragança. No one paid much attention to Miranda again until the nearby dam was built on the Douro in the 1950s.

Largo do Menino Jesus da Cartolina, a roundabout perched at the edge of the river gorge, roughly divides the old and new town. The *turismo* sits on the north edge of the roundabout. The bus station lies just downhill, on the road descending towards the bridge to Spain.

Uphill (southwest) from the roundabout, past the old walls and castle ruins, are the old town and what was once the citadel. The main axis is Rua da Alfândega (also called Rua Mouzinho da Albuquerque), which runs into central Praça de Dom João III and, a little further on, Largo da Sé and the cathedral.

The new town's commercial hub is Rua do Mercado, running northeast from the roundabout and parallel to the Rio Douro gorge.

◉ Sights & Activities

It's possible to see everything in a couple of hours, but the vagaries of public transport make it almost essential for nondrivers to stay longer.

Museu da Terra de Miranda   MUSEUM
(☑273 431 164; Praça de Dom João III; admission €2, Sun morning free; ⏱9.30am-12.30pm & 2-5.30pm Wed-Sun, 2.30-5.30pm Tue) This modest but attractive museum sheds light on a unique culture that has preserved millennial traditions into the 21st century. The handsome 17th-century building (formerly Miranda's city hall) houses a fascinating collection of local artefacts: ceramics, textiles, clothing, furniture, musical instruments and tribal-looking masks, along with recreations of a traditional kitchen, a blacksmith's forge and a room dedicated to traditional wool and linen weaving, complete with massive looms.

Old Town   HISTORIC AREA
The backstreets in the old town hide some dignified 15th-century facades on Rua da Costanilha (which runs west off Praça de Dom João III) and a Gothic gate at the end of it.

Inside the right transept of the handsomely severe 16th-century sé (cathedral), look for the doll-like Menino Jesus da Cartolinha, a Christ child in a becoming top hat whose wardrobe rivals Imelda Marcos', thanks to deft local devotees. It's open the same hours as the Museu da Terra de Miranda.

Barragem de Miranda & River Cruises
BOAT TRIPS

A road crawls across this 80m-high dam about 1km east of town, and on to Zamora, 55km away in Spain. Even dammed, the gorge is dramatic.

You can take a one-hour boat trip through the gorge with **Europarques** (273 432 396; www.europarques.com; adult/child under 10yr €16/8; trips 4pm daily, plus 11am Sat & Sun). Boats leave from beside the dam on the Portuguese side. Occasional two-hour trips (€20) are also offered; check with Europarques for details.

Sleeping

Hotel Turismo
HOTEL €

(273 438 030; www.hotelturismomiranda.pt; Rua 1 de Maio 5; s/d €30/50; ❄️🛜) Offering terrific comfort for a modest price, this newer place opposite the *turismo* features large, spotless rooms – most including a separate sitting room – with cable TV, minibars and marble bathrooms. Front rooms have large windows with views across to the castle ruins.

Estalagem Santa Catarina
LUXURY HOTEL €€

(273 431 005; www.estalagemsantacatarina.pt; Largo da Pousada; s/d/ste midweek €82.50/92/122, weekend €92.50/102/133; P❄️@🛜) Every guest gets a private verandah with spectacular views of the gorge at this luxurious, modern hotel perched on the canyon's edge. Rooms are a handsome mix of traditional and contemporary, with hardwood floors, flat-screen TVs and large marble bathrooms. The attached restaurant is the most upmarket in town.

Residencial a Morgadinha
GUEST HOUSE €

(273 438 050; Rua do Mercado 57/59; s/d €25/40; ❄️) This simple place – one of several budget options along the same street – features spacious rooms with parquet wood floors and bathtubs. There are nice river views from the upstairs breakfast area and from many of the rooms; avoid those facing the street, which are noisier and more claustrophobic.

Parque de Campismo Santa Luzia
CAMPGROUND €

(273 431 273; Rua do Parque de Campismo; sites per adult/child/tent/car €1.50/0.75/2/2; Jun-Sep) This modest municipal camp site is at the end of a residential street, 2.5km west of town across the Rio Fresno.

Eating

Restaurante São Pedro
PORTUGUESE €€

(Rua Mouzinho de Albuquerque; mains €7-12; lunch & dinner Tue-Sun, lunch Mon) This spacious restaurant, just in from the main old-town gate, serves up a fine *posta á São Pedro* (grilled veal steak dressed with garlic and olive oil). The €15 tourist menu comes with soup, main, dessert, wine and coffee.

Restaurante-Pizzeria O Moinho
PORTUGUESE, PIZZA €

(Rua do Mercado 47D; pizzas €4-7.50, mains €6.50-10.50; lunch & dinner) Despite lacklustre service, this new-town spot serves up glorious Douro views along with a wide-ranging menu featuring pizza, pasta, salads and Portuguese standards. (Sadly, they've abandoned their English-language menu, which used to include cryptic and entertaining menu translations like 'sausage to the hell' and 'codfish of the bras'.)

Capa d'Honras
PORTUGUESE €€

(Travessa do Castelo 1; mains €10-15; lunch & dinner) Named after the sinister-looking cape that is traditional to the region, this more upmarket place just inside the old town gates serves local specialities like *posta* (veal steak) as well as very good *bacalhau*.

Drinking

Atalaia Bar
BAR

(Largo do Castelo; 8pm-4am) Miranda's neon-lit, old-school disco serves up pop and dance standards.

Information

Centro de Saúde (273 430 040; Rua Dom Dinis) Health centre with 24-hour emergency service.

Espaço Internet (Rua Mouzinho de Albuquerque; 10am-1pm, 2-7pm & 8-10pm Mon-Fri, 2-8pm Sat) Free internet in the Casa da Cultura Mirandesa.

Parque Natural do Douro Internacional office (273 431 457; pndi@icnb.pt; Palácio da Justiça, Rua do Convento; 9am-12.30pm & 2-5.30pm Mon-Fri) Around the block from the cathedral and across from a baroque church that has been converted into a public library.

SPEAKING MIRANDÊS

France has Provençal, Britain has Welsh and Gaelic, and Italy has dozens of distinct regional dialects. Portugal, by contrast, is one of Europe's most monolingual countries, thanks both to its long-stable borders (unchanged since the 13th century) and to the fact that it was conquered and consolidated within a very short period of time (less than 200 years).

The region around Miranda do Douro is a significant exception. Because of its proximity to Spain and long isolation from the rest of Portugal, residents of the towns and villages around Miranda still speak what linguists have now recognised as an entirely distinct language. Closely related to Astur-Leonese – the regional language of the adjacent Spanish province – Mirandês is in fact closer to Iberian Latin, the language spoken during the Roman period, than it is to either Portuguese or Spanish.

While Mirandês has largely died out in the city of Miranda do Douro itself, it's still the first language of some 10,000 people in the surrounding villages. The Portuguese government officially recognised it as a second language in 1998, and increasingly the region's road signs are bilingual.

In 1882 Portuguese linguist José Leite de Vasconcelos described Mirandês as 'the language of the farms, of work, of home and love'. The same is true today.

Resurgent local pride in the language is evident in the window display of Miranda do Douro's **Papelaria Andrade**, whose collection of Mirandês-language titles includes translations of *Asterix* comic books.

Police (☏273 430 010; Largo de São José)

Post office (Largo da Sé; ☉9am-12.30pm & 2-5.30pm Mon-Fri)

Turismo (☏273 430 025; turismo@cm-mdouro.pt; Largo do Menino Jesus da Cartolina; ☉9am-7pm Tue-Fri, 10am-6pm Sat-Mon)

❶ Getting There & Around

BUS **Rodonorte** (☏273 432 667; www.rodonorte.pt) offers service daily except Saturday to Mogadouro (€6, 45 minutes), with onward connections to Vila Nova de Foz Côa (€7.40, 2½ hours), Mirandela (€8.50, two to three hours), Vila Real (€10.60, three to four hours) and Porto (€12.40, 4½ to six hours).

CAR The quickest road from Bragança is the N218 and N218-2, a winding 80km trip. The slower but lovelier 80km route (N216/N221) from Macedo de Cavaleiros via Mogadouro crosses a *planalto* (high plateau) dotted with olive, almond and chestnut groves and includes a dramatic switchbacking descent into the Rio Sabor valley. Miranda has plenty of free parking around Largo do Menino Jesus da Cartolina.

Parque Natural do Douro Internacional

Tucked into Portugal's far northeast corner, this 852-sq-km, Chile-shaped park runs for 120km along the Rio Douro and the monumental canyon it has carved along the border with Spain. The canyon's towering, granite cliffs are the habitat for several threatened bird species, including black storks, Egyptian vultures, griffon vultures, peregrine falcons, golden eagles and Bonelli's eagles.

The human habitat is equally fragile. In the plains that run up to the canyon lip, there are some 35 villages, many inhabited by descendants of banished medieval convicts, as well as Jews who fled the Inquisition. The region's isolation has enabled its people to preserve even more ancient roots, such as the Celtic *dança dos paulitos*. Many villagers still speak Mirandês, a language distinct from both Spanish and Portuguese that linguists believe descends directly from Iberian Latin; you'll see town names written in Portuguese and Mirandês throughout the park's northern reaches.

As you move south along the river, the terrain gains a distinctly Mediterranean air, with rolling orchards of olives and chestnuts and, in the southernmost reaches, land demarcated for port-wine grapes.

Park maps, as elsewhere in Portugal, are in short supply; at the time of research, a free park overview map was available, as were a couple of detailed trail maps (€0.50 each); all other print resources had run out, with only reference copies or photocopies available. English-speaking staff at the Mogadouro headquarters can answer general questions, but printed materials are in Portuguese only.

Miranda do Douro and Mogadouro are the best places from which to explore the park.

◉ Sights & Activities

There are four marked trails in the park. The most convenient for nondrivers – and one of the most beautiful – is the 19km Miranda do Douro to São João das Arribas loop, starting and ending at Miranda's cathedral. The trail – open to hikers, cyclists and horses – passes through mixed oak woodlands and small villages, and includes striking vistas of the river at São João. Another stunning option near the south end of the park is the Vale da Ribeira do Mosteiro loop, which passes through vineyards and rugged canyon country along a small tributary of the Douro.

For fabulous, near-aerial views of the gorge and its birdlife, you can also visit six panoramic overlooks throughout the park. North to south, with the nearest village in parentheses, these are Penha das Torres (Paradela), São João das Arribas (Aldeia Nova), Fraga do Puio (Picote), Carrascalinho (Fornos), Penedo Durão (Poiares) and Santo André (Almofala).

Without your own transport, the easiest way to see the Douro gorge is on Europarques' hour-long **cruise** from Miranda do Douro (see p467).

Douro Activo (☎933 299 854; www.douroactivo.com) rents bikes (per hour/day €2.50/10) and operates a wide range of adventure trips around Miranda, including hiking, canoeing, mountain biking and horse and donkey tours.

In Torre de Moncorvo, near the park's southern end, Sabor Douro e Aventura (☎279 258 270; www.sabordouro.com; Rua Abade Tavares) offers guided hikes and kayak trips.

🛏 Sleeping & Eating

With its impressive views of the river gorge, Miranda do Douro is the most attractive base for exploring the park. Mogadouro also offers tourist services, but at nearly 15km from the Douro, it's a far less scenic option.

TRÁS-OS-MONTES PARQUE NATURAL DO DOURO INTERNACIONAL

THE HILLS ARE ALIVE: STRANGE WAYS IN TRÁS-OS-MONTES

For centuries, the remoteness of Trás-os-Montes has insulated it from central authority, helping its people preserve nonconformist ways that sometimes still raise eyebrows in other parts of Portugal.

A number of licentious – and blatantly pagan – traditions still survive in the countryside. Witness the antics of the **Caretos of Podence** (near Macedo de Cavaleiros) – where gangs of young men in caretos (leering masks) and vividly striped costumes invade the town centre, bent on cheerfully humiliating everyone in sight. Prime targets are young women, at whom they thrust their hips and wave the cowbells hanging from their belts. Similar figures are to be seen in Varge, in the Parque Natural de Montesinho.

Colourful festivals derived from ancient Celtic solstice rituals take place in many villages in the two weeks between Christmas Eve and Dia dos Reis (Epiphany). During the so-called **Festa dos Rapazes** (Festival of the Lads), unmarried men over 16 light all-night bonfires and rampage around in robes of rags and masks of brass or wood. Un-Christian indeed!

Then there are the pauliteiros (stick dancers) of the Miranda do Douro region, who look and dance very much like England's Morris dancers. Local men deck themselves out in kilts and smocks, black waistcoats, bright flapping shawls, and black hats covered in flowers and ribbons, and do a rhythmic dance to the complex clacking of paulitos (short wooden sticks) – a practice that likely survives from Celtic times. The best time to see pauliteiros in Miranda is during the **Festas de Santa Bárbara** (also called Festas da Cidade, or City Festival), which is held on the third weekend in August.

Finally, there are the region's so-called crypto-Jews. During the Inquisition, Jews from Spain and Portugal found that they could evade ecclesiastical authorities here. Many families continued to observe Jewish practices in secrecy well into the 20th century (see boxed text, p349).

Solar dos Marcos   RURAL INN €€

(☑279 570 010; www.solar-dos-marcos.com; Rua Santa Cruz, Bemposta; s/d/ste €59/75/110; P❀❀☎) About 12km northeast of Mogadouro in the ramshackle village of Bemposta, this place is the most upmarket option in the region. The reception is in an 18th-century manor house, while the comfortable rooms are in a modern annexe at the back.

TOP
CHOICE **A Lareira**   PORTUGUESE €€

(Av Nossa Senhora do Caminho 58, Mogadouro; mains €7.50-12; ⊙lunch & dinner) This recommended restaurant offers outstanding local beef and veal grilled on an open fireplace by the French-trained proprietor. The small, well-equipped rooms upstairs (single/double €20/30) are also excellent value.

ⓘ Information

PARK HEADQUARTERS are in **Mogadouro** (☑279 340 030; pndi@icnb.pt; Rua Santa Marinha 4; ⊙9am-12.30pm & 2-5.30pm Mon-Fri), with smaller park offices in **Miranda do Douro** (☑273 431 457; Palácio da Justiça, Rua do Convento) and **Figueira de Castelo Rodrigo** (☑271 313 382; Rua Artur Costa 1).

ⓘ Getting There & Around

Rodonorte (www.rodonorte.pt) offers regular bus services to Miranda do Douro and Mogadouro. However, public transport to smaller villages within the park is extremely limited, and mostly designed to serve schoolchildren; check with the park offices for current schedule information.

Understand Portugal

population per sq km

PORTUGAL   USA   UK

👤 ≈ 30 people

Portugal Today

» Population:
10.7 million

» Unemployment: 9.6%

» Highest point:
Torre (1993m)

» Largest
Portuguese
community
outside Lisbon:
Paris

» Number of
Portuguese
speakers
worldwide: 260
million

In a tiny windswept hamlet in northern Portugal, goats still trundle through the dusty streets while elderly widows in black keep watch over the village square against the backdrop of a medieval castle. The hillsides nearby bear the terraced vineyards that were probably planted by the Phoenicians, centuries before the Romans arrived. The latest buzz here revolves around the upcoming Festa de São João, where villagers will decorate statues of Catholic saints with flowers and process alongside the bishop through the streets, followed by much feasting and celebrating at the country fairgrounds.

Meanwhile, a few hundred kilometres away, a group of young friends has gathered at an art opening in the city. Mingling and cocktails are the order of the evening, then a dance party in the bar below the gallery. But after a flurry of text messages, the group heads to the seaside suburbs for a late-night meal in a chrome-and-glass lounge perched above the crashing waves. Later, around 1am, when things begin to pick up, they'll head for the new club that just opened, where a DJ from LA is spinning.

The once-great seafaring empire of Portugal is today a country straddling two very different worlds. In simplest terms, it's the struggle between old and new, long-standing tradition versus widespread modernisation – a conflict that plays out daily in many different ways and in many different settings. And no matter one's age, ideology or socioeconomic status, every person in Portugal has a stake in the outcome.

Traditional villages across the country are at the forefront of this clash, as younger generations – seeking educational and job opportunities, or simply a more modern way of life – abandon the small settlements where they grew up and strike out for the city. Yet even the cities face demographic shifts. The young and upwardly mobile largely favour

Top Books

» **The Inquisitor's Manual** (António Lobo Antunes; 1996) Story about life under Salazar.

» **Baltasar & Blimunda** (Jose Saramago; 1982) Darkly comic 18th-century love story.

» **The Book of Disquietude** (Fernando Pessoa; 1982)

Top Films

» **A Lisbon Story** (1994) Wim Wenders' love letter to Lisbon.

» **Letters from Fontainhas** (1994–2006) Pedro Costa's art-house trilogy set in Lisbon.

» **Capitães de Abril** (Captains of April; 2000) Overview of the 1974 Carnation Revolution.

Top Albums

» **Fado em Mim** (2002) Mesmerising fado album by the legendary Mariza.

» **Art of Amália** (1998) Compilation by one of fado's greats.

» **Re-Definições** (2004) Catchy album by hip-hop artists Da Weasel.

occupation of workforce
(% of population)

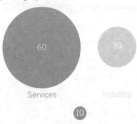

Services — 60
Industry — 30
Agriculture — 10

if Portugal were 100 people

85 would be Roman Catholic
9 would be other
4 would be no religion
2 would be other Christian

the suburbs, leaving worn and ageing city centres to the elderly – and tourists. Other places are undergoing a cultural renaissance, with shops, galleries, restaurants and bars bringing new vitality (and the complicated baggage of gentrification) to some neighbourhoods.

Portugal's economy has confronted similar challenges. Facing ultimatums from the EU to rein in its debt, Portugal had to decide between modernising its economy and keeping the social-welfare state intact. In the end it chose modernising, which meant pension reform, higher taxes and other stringent measures that made a few enemies for Prime Minister José Socrates. Although Portugal succeeded in reaching some of its EU-mandated goals ahead of schedule, it was hit hard by the global financial crisis that erupted in 2007; its surging deficit raised alarm bells in 2010, and Portugal was hailed (alongside Greece, Italy and Spain) as being a nation in grave risk of default. Stagnant economic growth and high unemployment have only made matters worse.

On other fronts, Portugal is marching head-on into the future. Over the last half decade, Portugal has invested heavily in renewable energy. It has some of the largest solar and wind power plants on the planet and has even opened an experimental wave power plant, which will harness the ocean's power to create energy. More controversial are Portugal's new and proposed hydroelectric dams, which provide abundant energy but drown much land in their creation (nine dams are slated for construction by the end of 2020) – leading once again to that struggle between old and new.

GDP

Portugal has a GDP of €178 billion, which is the lowest per-capita GDP (€16,600) in Western Europe, but typically ranks high in quality-of-life surveys.

Faux Pas

» Thinking the *couvert* (bread, cheese, olives) is free. Whatever you eat – whether ordered or not – you pay for.

» Not saying 'hello' when entering a store, restaurant, market stall etc. Say '*bom dia*' (good day), '*boa tarde*' (good afternoon) and '*boa noite*' (good evening).

» Assuming that Portugal is just a version of Spain. The history, food, language, music and celebrations are quite different. Say '*obrigado*' (or '*obrigada*' if you're female) – not *gracias*!

Greetings

» When greeting people and bidding *adeus*, women receive two kisses – one on each cheek (start to your left, her right). Gentlemen generally settle for a handshake with one another. In business, a handshake is also common for and among women.

History

The small nation on the edge of Europe has seen a long line of conquerors and foreign princes over the last 3000 years. Early traces of modern humans are 30,000-year-old stone carvings; more impressive are megaliths and other mysterious monuments left by unknown peoples after 5000 BC. Later, Celtic peoples found their way onto the Iberian stage, settling in fortified villages and mingling with Phoenician traders around 700 BC.

Next came the Romans, who built roads and bridges, cultivated vineyards, and salted and dried fish – practices not unknown today. After six centuries, the empire crumbled and Christian Visigoths and other tribes conquered the land by 500 AD. The Moors came next, sailing in from North Africa around 700 AD. They planted citrus trees and other crops, founded schools and established a peaceful regime lasting four centuries.

By the 12th century the Christian reconquest was underway, as battle-hungry European crusaders advanced and conquered the Moors. Portugal's first Christian king took the throne in 1139. Subsequent kings parried threats from Spain, founded the first university, sealed an important alliance with England and established Portugal's boundaries – still standing today. In the 15th century, Portugal turned its eyes seaward. Vasco da Gama's epic voyage to India in 1497 launched the age of discovery. More discoveries and great riches followed as Portuguese arrived in present-day Brazil, the Philippines, China, Japan and other lands. Overexpansion proved Portugal's downfall, and Spain seized the Portuguese throne in 1580. Spanish rule lasted until the mid-1600s when Portuguese conspirators helped regain independence.

In the 18th century, the Marquês de Pombal, embodying Enlightenment ideals, abolished slavery, modernised the state, and sped recovery following the devastating 1755 earthquake. By 1800 Portugal was at war with France. As Napoleon invaded, the royals fled to Brazil. Succession

The word Portugal comes from Portus Cale, a name the Romans gave to a town near present-day Porto. The word morphed into Portucale under Visigoth rule and expanded significantly in meaning.

TIMELINE 18,000 BC	5000 BC	700 BC
Ancestors of modern Iberians leave behind a gallery of Palaeolithic art, which features rock carvings in the Alto Douro and cave paintings in the Alentejo.	Little-understood Neolithic peoples build protected hilltop settlements in the lower Tejo valley. They leave behind stone monuments, including megaliths scattered around Évora in present-day Alentejo.	Celtic peoples, migrating across the Pyrenees with their families and flocks, sweep through the Iberian Peninsula. They settle in fortified villages, known as castros, and intermarry with local tribes.

troubles marked the early 1800s, with peace and prosperity returning in the 1860s. In 1900, industrialisation brought large-scale changes to Portugal, and the masses clamoured for a more equal society. The king became a target and he was assassinated in 1908. Portugal became a republic in 1910.

Political turmoil followed, and the autocratic Salazar came to power in 1926. Backed by the repressive secret police, his repressive regime lasted until the 1970s. The 1974 military coup finally ended the authoritarian state. The 1970s and '80s were unstable times in Portugal with ineffective government and a faltering economy. The 1990s brought more stability, as the EU became a reality.

The first decade of the 21st century saw Portugal enter a period of economic decline, which worsened during the Global Financial Crisis. In 2009, the economy shrank by 2.8% with unemployment rising to nearly 10%. In spite of challenges, it has invested heavily in renewable energy, becoming a leader in wind-, solar- and hydropower.

Portugal: A Traveller's History (2004), by Harold Livermore, explores some of the richer episodes from the past – taking in cave paintings, vineyards and music, among other topics.

Early Peoples

One of Europe's earliest settlements, the Iberian Peninsula was first inhabited many millennia ago, when hominids wandered across the landscape some time before 200,000 BC. During the Palaeolithic period, early Portuguese ancestors left traces of their time on earth in the fascinating stone carvings in the open air near Vila Nova de Foz Côa in the Alto Douro (p397). These date back some 30,000 years and were only discovered by accident, during a proposed dam building project

THE MYSTERY OF THE NEANDERTHALS

Scientists have never come to agreement about the fate of the Neanderthals – stout and robust beings who used stone tools and fire, buried their dead and had brains larger than those of modern humans. The most common theory was that homo sapiens drove Neanderthals into extinction (perhaps in some sort of genocidal warfare). A less-accepted theory is that Neanderthals and humans bred together and even produced a hybrid species. This idea gained credence when Portuguese archaeologists found a strange skeleton – the first complete Palaeolithic skeleton ever unearthed in Iberia – just north of Lisbon in 1999. In what was clearly a ritual burial, the team led by João Zilhão, director of the Portuguese Institute of Archaeology, discovered the 25,000-year-old remains of a young boy with traits of both early humans (pronounced chin and teeth) and of Neanderthals (broad limbs). Some believe this kind of relationship (love-making rather than war-making) happened over the span of thousands of years, and that some elements of Neanderthals entered the modern human gene pool.

197 BC	60 BC	AD 100	400
After defeating Carthage in the Second Punic Wars, the Romans invade Iberia, expanding their empire west. They face fierce resistance from local tribes, including the Lusitani, but eventually conquer them.	The Romans eliminate all traces of Lusitanian independence and establish an important capital and trade hub at Olissipo (Lisbon), a name derived from the mythical founding father Ulysses.	Romans collect taxes to build roads, bridges and other public works. They cultivate vineyards, teach the natives to preserve fish by salting and drying, and grant local communities much autonomy.	Rome crumbles as German tribes run riot in southern Europe. The Suevi, peasant farmers from the Elbe, settle in present-day Porto. Christian Visigoths follow suit, conquering the land in 469.

in 1992. Other signs of early human artistry lie hidden in the Alentejo, in the Gruta do Escoural, where cave drawings of animals and humans date back to around 15,000 BC.

Homo sapiens weren't the only bipeds on the scene. Neanderthals co-existed alongside modern humans in a few rare places like Portugal for as long as 10,000 years. In fact, some of the last traces of their existence were found in Iberia prior to their disappearance.

Neanderthals were only the first of a long line of inhabitants to appear (and later disappear) from the Iberian stage. In the 1st millennium BC Celtic people started trickling into the Iberian Peninsula, settling northern and western Portugal around 700 BC. Dozens of *citânias* (fortified villages) popped up, such as the formidable Citânia de Briteiros (p417). Further south, Phoenician traders, followed by Greeks and Carthaginians, founded coastal stations and mined metals inland.

When the Romans swept into southern Portugal in 210 BC, they expected an easy victory. But they hadn't reckoned on the Lusitani, a Celtic warrior tribe that settled between the Rio Tejo and Rio Douro and resisted ferociously for half a century. Unable to subjugate the Lusitani, the Romans offered peace instead and began negotiations with Viriato, the Lusitanian leader. Unfortunately for Viriato and his underlings, the peace offer was a ruse, and Roman agents, posing as intermediaries, poisoned him. Resistance collapsed following Viriato's death in 139 BC.

For a vivid glimpse into Roman Portugal, you won't see a better site than Conimbriga (p311), near Coimbra, or the monumental remains of the so-called Temple of Diana (p205), in Évora.

By the 5th century, when the Roman Empire had all but collapsed, Portugal's inhabitants had been under Roman rule for 600 years. So what did the Romans ever do for them? Most usefully, they built roads and bridges. But they also brought wheat, barley, olives and vines; large farming estates called *latifúndios* (still found in the Alentejo); a legal

Prehistoric Sights

» **Vila Nova de Foz Côa**, Minho

» **Citânia de Briteiros**, Minho

» **Cromeleque dos Almendres**, Alentejo

» **Gruta do Escoural**, Alentejo

» **Anta Grande do Zambujeiro**, Alentejo

» **Cromeleque do Xerez**, Alentejo

UNFORGETTABLE RIVER

When Roman soldiers reached the Rio Lima in 137 BC, they were convinced they had reached the River Lethe, the mythical river of forgetfulness that flowed through Hades and from which no man could return. Unable to persuade his troops to cross the waters leading to certain oblivion, the Roman general Decimus Junius Brutus Callaicus forged the river alone. Once on the other side he called out to his men, shouting each of their names. Stunned that the general could remember them, they followed after him and continued their campaign. Incidentally, Brutus, who led legions to conquer Iberia after Viriato's death, was later named proconsul of Lusitania.

711	800	1147
Visigoth King Witiza is assassinated. When oldest son Agila is blocked from the throne he sends for help from North African Berbers. The Muslim force arrives, establishes peace and puts down roots.	The Umayyad dynasty rules the Iberian Peninsula. The region flourishes under the tolerant caliphate. The Arabs introduce irrigation, bring new crops (including oranges and rice) and establish schools.	The Reconquista is underway as Christians attain decisive victories over the Moors. Afonso Henriques leads the attack, laying siege to Lisbon and becoming Portugal's first (self-declared) king.

» Lisbon from São Jorge

system; and, above all, a Latin-derived language. In fact, no other invader proved so useful.

Moors & Christians

The gap left by the Romans was filled by barbarian invaders from beyond the Pyrenees: Vandals, Alans, Visigoths and Suevi, with Arian Christian Visigoths gaining the upper hand in 469.

Internal Visigothic disputes paved the way for Portugal's next great wave of invaders, the Moors – North African Muslims invited in 711 to help a Visigothic faction. They quickly occupied large chunks of Portugal's southern coast.

Southerners enjoyed peace and productivity under the Moors, who established a capital at Shelb (Silves). The new rulers were tolerant of Jews and Christians. Christian small-holding farmers, called Mozarabs, could keep their land and were encouraged to try new methods and crops, especially citrus and rice. Arabic words filtered into the Portuguese language, such as *alface* (lettuce), *arroz* (rice) and dozens of place names (including Fatima, Silves and Algarve – the latter stemming from the Arabic *el-gharb*, meaning 'the west'), and locals became addicted to Moorish sweets.

Meanwhile in the north, Christian forces were gaining strength and reached as far as Porto in 868. But it was in the 11th century that the Reconquista (the Christian reconquest) heated up. In 1064 Coimbra was taken and, in 1085, Alfonso VI thrashed the Moors in their Spanish heartland of Toledo; he is said to have secured Seville by winning a game of chess with its emir. But in the following year, Alfonso's men were driven out by ruthless Moroccan Almoravids who answered the emir's distress call.

Alfonso cried for help and European crusaders came running – rallying against the 'infidels'. With the help of Henri of Burgundy, among others, Alfonso made decisive moves towards victory. The struggle continued in successive generations, and by 1139 Afonso Henriques (grandson of Alfonso VI) won such a dramatic victory against the Moors at Ourique (Alentejo) that he named himself Dom – King of Portugal – a title confirmed in 1179 by the pope (after extra tribute was paid, naturally). He also retook Santarém and Lisbon from the Moors.

By the time he died in 1185, the Portuguese frontier was secure to the Rio Tejo, though it would take another century before the south was torn from the Moors.

The Burgundian Era

During the Reconquista, people faced more than just war and turmoil: in the wake of Christian victories came new rulers and settlers.

Roman Sights

» **Conimbriga**, Beiras

» **Milreu**, Algarve

» **Templo Romano**, Évora, Alentejo

» **Termas Romanas**, Évora, Alentejo

» **Museu do Teatro Romano**, Lisbon

» **Núcleo Arqueológico**, Lisbon

» **Cidade de Ammaia**, Alentejo

» **Cromeleque do Xerez**, Alentejo

1242	1297	1348	1385
The last remaining Moors are driven out in the battle of Tavira. Portugal later establishes its border with Castile (Spain), aided by Dom Dinis: 50 fortresses line the eastern frontier.	The boundaries of the Portuguese kingdom – much the same then as they are today – were formalised with neighbouring Castile. The kingdom of Portugal had arrived.	The Black Plague arrives in Portugal (most likely carried on ships that dock in Porto and Lisbon). As in other parts of Europe, the disease devastates, killing one in three.	Intermarriage between Castilian and Portuguese royal families leads to complications. Juan I of Castile, claiming the throne, invades. The Portuguese, with English help, rout the invaders at Aljubarrota.

The Treaty of
Windsor (1386),
which established
a pact of mutual
assistance
between Portugal
and England, is
widely considered
to be the oldest-
surviving alliance
in the world.

The Church and its wealthy clergy were the greediest landowners, followed by aristocratic fat cats. Though theoretically free, most common people remained subjects of the landowning class, with few rights. The first hint of democratic rule came with the establishment of the *cortes* (parliament). This assembly of nobles and clergy first met in 1211 at Coimbra, the then capital. Six years later, the capital moved to Lisbon.

Afonso III (r 1248–79) deserves credit for standing up to the Church, but it was his son, the 'Poet King' Dinis (r 1279–1325), who really shook Portugal into shape. A far-sighted, cultured man, he took control of the judicial system, started progressive afforestation programmes and encouraged internal trade. He suppressed the dangerously powerful military order of the Knights Templar, refounding them as the Order of Christ (p283). He cultivated music, the arts and education, and founded a university in Lisbon in 1290, which was later transferred to Coimbra (p303).

Dom Dinis' foresight was spot-on when it came to defence: he built or rebuilt some 50 fortresses along the eastern frontier with Castile, and signed a pact of friendship with England in 1308, the basis for a future long-lasting alliance.

It was none too soon. Within 60 years of Dinis' death, Portugal was at war with Castile. Fernando I helped provoke the clash by playing a game of alliances with both Castile and the English. He dangled promises of marriage to his daughter Beatriz in front of both nations, eventually marrying her off to Juan I of Castile, and thus throwing Portugal's future into Castilian hands.

On Fernando's death in 1383, his wife, Leonor Teles, ruled as regent. But she too was entangled with the Spanish, having long had a Galician lover. The merchant classes preferred unsullied Portuguese candidate João, son (albeit illegitimate) of Fernando's father. João assassinated Leonor's lover, Leonor fled to Castile and the Castilians duly invaded.

The showdown came in 1385 when João faced a mighty force of Castilians at Aljubarrota. Even with Nuno Álvares Pereira (the Holy Constable) as his military right-hand man and English archers at the ready, the odds were stacked against him. João vowed to build a monastery if he won – and he did. Nuno Álvares, the brilliant commander-in-chief of the Portuguese troops, deserves much of the credit for the victory. He lured Spanish cavalry into a trap and, with an uphill advantage, his troops decimated the invaders. Within a few hours the Spanish were retreating in disarray and the battle was won.

The victory clinched independence and João made good his vow with Batalha's stunning Mosteiro de Santa Maria da Vitória (aka the Mosteiro da Batalha or Battle Abbey; see p269). It also sealed Portugal's

1411	1415	1418	1419
Newly crowned Dom João builds an elaborate monastery to commemorate his victory at Aljubarrota. João marries John of Gaunt's daughter, ushering in an English alliance lasting centuries.	Dom João's third son, Prince Henry the Navigator, joins his father in the conquest of Ceuta in North Africa. Thus begins the colonial expansion of Portugal.	Shipbuilding advances lead to the development of the caravel, a fast, agile ship that changed the face of sailing. Portuguese mariners put it to brilliant use on long voyages of exploration.	Portuguese sailors discover Madeira. More discoveries follow suit, including the Azores in 1427 and Cape Verde Islands in 1460. Explorers also chart the west coast of Africa.

alliance with England, and João wed John of Gaunt's daughter. Peace was finally concluded in 1411.

The Age of Discoveries

João's success had whetted his appetite and, spurred on by his sons, he soon turned his military energies abroad. Morocco was the obvious target, and in 1415 Ceuta fell easily to his forces. It was a turning point in Portuguese history, a first step into its golden age.

It was João's third son, Henry, who focused the spirit of the age – a combination of crusading zeal, love of martial glory and lust for gold – into extraordinary explorations across the seas. These explorations were to transform the small kingdom into a great imperial power.

The biggest breakthrough came in 1497 during the reign of Manuel I, when Vasco da Gama reached southern India. With gold and slaves from Africa and spices from the East, Portugal was soon rolling in riches. Manuel I was so thrilled by the discoveries (and resultant cash injection) that he ordered a frenzied building spree in celebration. Top of his list was the extravagant Mosteiro dos Jerónimos in Belém (p74), later to become his pantheon. Another brief boost to the Portuguese economy at this time came courtesy of an influx of around 150,000 Jews expelled from Spain in 1492.

Spain, however, had also jumped on the exploration bandwagon and was soon disputing Portuguese claims. Christopher Columbus' 1492 'discovery' of America for Spain led to a fresh outburst of jealous conflict. It was resolved by the pope in the bizarre 1494 Treaty of Tordesillas, by which the world was divided between the two great powers along a line 370 leagues west of the Cape Verde islands. Portugal won the lands to the east of the line, including Brazil, officially claimed in 1500.

The rivalry spurred the first circumnavigation of the world. In 1519 the Portuguese navigator Fernão de Magalhães (Ferdinand Magellan), his allegiance transferred to Spain after a tiff with Manuel I, set off in an effort to prove that the Spice Islands (today's Moluccas) lay in Spanish 'territory'. He reached the Philippines in 1521 but was killed in a skirmish there. One of his five ships, under the Basque navigator Juan Sebastián Elcano, reached the Spice Islands and then sailed home via the Cape of Good Hope, proving the earth was round.

As its explorers reached Timor, China and eventually Japan, Portugal cemented its power with garrison ports and trading posts. The monarchy, taking its 'royal fifth' of profits, became stinking rich – indeed the wealthiest monarchy in Europe, and the lavish Manueline architectural style symbolised the exuberance of the age.

It couldn't last, of course. By the 1570s the huge cost of expeditions and maintaining an empire was taking its toll. Young, idealistic

COLUMBUS

King João II financed voyages by Vasco da Gama and others, but he is also known for rejecting Christopher Columbus. The Italian navigator approached Portugal first (in 1485) before turning to Spain.

1443	1494	1497	1497
Explorers bring the first African slaves to Portugal; it marks the beginning of a long, dark era of slavery in Europe and later the new world.	The race for colonial expansion is on: Spain and Portugal carve up the world, with the Treaty of Tordesillas drawing the line 370 leagues west of Cape Verde.	After pressure from the church, Dom Manuel I expels commercially active Jews. Those staying must convert or face persecution. By 1536 the Inquisition is underway, and thousands will be executed.	Following Dias' historic journey around the Cape of Good Hope a few years earlier, Vasco da Gama sails to India and becomes a legend. Trade with the East later brings incredible wealth.

Exploration by the Portuguese

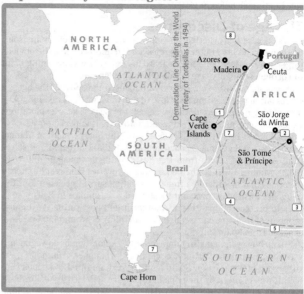

Sebastião took the throne, and the final straw came in 1578 when, determined to take Christianity to Morocco, he rallied a force of 18,000 and set sail from Lagos, to be disastrously defeated at the Battle of Alcácer-Quibir (also known as the Battle of Three Kings). Sebastião and 8000 others were killed, including much of the Portuguese nobility. His aged successor, Cardinal Henrique, drained the royal coffers ransoming those captured.

On Henrique's death in 1580, Sebastião's uncle, Felipe II of Spain (Felipe I of Portugal), fought for and won the throne. This marked the end of centuries of independence, Portugal's golden age and its glorious moment on the world stage.

Spain's Rule & Portugal's Revival

Spanish rule began promisingly, with Felipe vowing to preserve Portugal's autonomy and attend the long-ignored parliament. But commoners resented Spanish rule and held on to the dream that Sebastião was

---

1519

Fernão de Magalhães embarks on his journey to circumnavigate the globe. He is killed in the Philippines, but one of his ships returns, completing the epic voyage.

» Magalhães (Magellan)

1572

Luís Vaz de Camões writes *Os Lusiados*, an epic poem that celebrates da Gama's historic voyage. Camões dies poor and largely unrecognised, though he is later hailed as Portugal's greatest literary figure.

1578

King Sebastião raises an army and invades Morocco. The expedition ends at the Battle of Alcácer-Quibir. Sebastião and many nobles are killed; the king leaves no heir, destabilising the country.

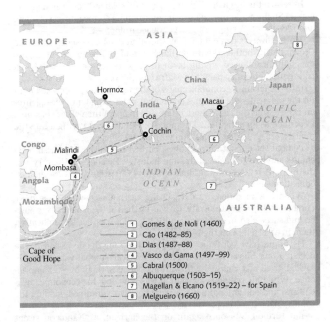

1	Gomes & de Noli (1460)
2	Cão (1482–85)
3	Dias (1487–88)
4	Vasco da Gama (1497–99)
5	Cabral (1500)
6	Albuquerque (1503–15)
7	Magellan & Elcano (1519–22) – for Spain
8	Melgueiro (1660)

still alive (as he was killed abroad in battle in Morocco, some citizens were in denial); pretenders continued to pop up until 1600. Though Felipe was honourable, his successors proved to be considerably less so, using Portugal to raise money and soldiers for Spain's wars overseas, and appointing Spaniards to govern Portugal.

An uprising in neighbouring Catalonia gave fuel to Portugal's independence drive (particularly when the Spanish King Felipe III ordered Portuguese troops to quell the uprising), and finally in 1640 a group of conspirators launched a coup. Nationalists drove the female governor of Portugal and her Spanish garrison from Lisbon. It was then that the duke of Bragança reluctantly stepped forward and was crowned João IV.

With a hostile Spain breathing down its neck, Portugal searched for allies. Two swift treaties with England led to Charles II's marriage to João's daughter, Catherine of Bragança, and the ceding of Tangier and Bombay to England.

CR Boxer's classic text, *The Portuguese Seaborne Empire* (1969), is still one of the best studies of the explorations by Portuguese mariners and the complex empire that unfolded as a result.

1580	**1622**	**1640**	**1690**
Sebastião's weak successor, the former cardinal Henrique, dies. King Felipe II of Spain invades Portugal and becomes king. Spain will rule for 80 years, draining Portugal's coffers and ending its golden age.	Portugal's empire is slipping out of Spain's grasp. The English seize Hormoz. Later in the 1650s the Dutch take Malacca, Ceylon (Sri Lanka) and part of Brazil.	When Catalonia rebels against the oppressive monarchy, Felipe III sends Portuguese troops to quell the uprising. Portuguese noblemen stage a coup and overthrow Spain. Dom João IV is crowned.	With the economy in tatters and empire fading, the Portuguese pray for a miracle. The prayer is answered when gold is discovered in Brazil; incredible riches soon flow into the royal coffers.

In return the English promised arms and soldiers: however, a preoccupied Spain made only half-hearted attempts to recapture Portugal, and recognised Portuguese independence in 1668.

Moves towards democracy now stalled under João's successors. The Crown hardly bothered with parliament, and another era of profligate expenditure followed, giving birth to projects such as the wildly extravagant monastery-palace in Mafra (see p125).

Into the ensuing economic chaos of the 18th century stepped a man for the moment – the Marquês de Pombal, chief minister to the epicurean Dom José I (the latter more interested in opera than affairs of state). Described as an enlightened despot, Pombal dragged Portugal into the modern era, crushing opposition with brutal efficiency.

Pombal set up state monopolies, curbed the power of British merchants and boosted agriculture and industry. He abolished slavery and distinctions between traditional and New Christians, and overhauled education.

When Lisbon suffered a devastating earthquake in 1755 (see p48), Pombal swiftly rebuilt the city. He was by then at the height of his power, and succeeded in dispensing with his main enemies by implicating them in an attempt on the king's life.

He might have continued had it not been for the accession of the devout Dona Maria I in 1777. The anticlerical Pombal was promptly sacked, tried and charged with various offences, though never imprisoned. While his religious legislation was repealed, his economic, agricultural and educational policies were largely maintained, helping the country back towards prosperity.

But turmoil was once again on the horizon, as Napoleon swept through Europe.

The Dawn of a Republic

In 1793 Portugal found itself at war again when it joined England in sending naval forces against revolutionary France. Before long, Napoleon threw Portugal an ultimatum: close your ports to British shipping or be invaded.

There was no way Portugal could turn its back on Britain, upon which it depended for half of its trade and the protection of its sea routes. In 1807 Portugal's royal family fled to Brazil (where it stayed for 14 years), and Napoleon's forces marched into Lisbon, sweeping Portugal into the Peninsular War (France's invasion of Spain and Portugal, which lasted until 1814).

To the rescue came Sir Arthur Wellesley (later Duke of Wellington), Viscount Beresford and their seasoned British troops, who eventually drove the French back across the Spanish border in 1811.

The Portuguese were the first Westerners to reach Japan in 1543. They founded Nagasaki, introduced the mosquito net and brought new words to the Japanese language, including *pan* (bread) and, possibly, *arrigato* (thank you).

Some historians believe Portuguese explorers reached Australia in the 1500s, 250 years before its 'official' discoverer, Captain James Cook. For the inside scoop, read Kenneth McIntyre's *The Secret Discovery of Australia* (1982).

1703	1717	1755	1770
France and England are at war. Facing (disastrous!) wine shortages, the English sign a new treaty with Portugal, and become a major player in the Portuguese economy, with port production growing exponentially.	Brazilian gold production nears its peak, with over 600,000oz imported annually. Dom João V becomes Europe's richest monarch, lavishing wealth on ostentatious projects like Mafra Palace.	Lisbon suffers Europe's biggest natural disaster in recorded history. On All Saint's Day, three massive earthquakes destroy the city, followed by a tsunami and ravaging fires that kill tens of thousands.	The king's powerful prime minister, the Marquês de Pombal, rebuilds the city following a modern grid. He abolishes slavery, builds schools and develops the economy, crushing those in his way.

Free but weakened, Portugal was administered by Beresford while the royals dallied in Brazil. In 1810 Portugal lost a profitable intermediary role by giving Britain the right to trade directly with Brazil. The next humiliation was João's 1815 proclamation of Brazil as a kingdom united with Portugal – he did this to bring more wealth and prestige to Brazil (which he was growing to love) and in turn to him and the rest of the royal family residing there. With soaring debts and dismal trade, Portugal was at one of the lowest points in its history, reduced to a de facto colony of Brazil and a protectorate of Britain.

Meanwhile, resentment simmered in the army. Rebel officers quietly convened parliament and drew up a new liberal constitution. Based on Enlightenment ideals, it abolished many rights of the nobility and clergy, and instituted a single-chamber parliament.

Faced with this fait accompli, João returned and accepted its terms – though his wife and son Miguel were bitterly opposed to it. João's elder son, Pedro, had other ideas: left behind to govern Brazil, he snubbed the constitutionalists by declaring Brazil independent in 1822 and himself its emperor. When João died in 1826, the stage was set for civil war.

Offered the crown, Pedro dashed out a new, less liberal charter and then abdicated in favour of his seven-year-old daughter Maria, provided she marry uncle Miguel and provided uncle Miguel accept the new constitution. Miguel took the oath but promptly abolished Pedro's charter and proclaimed himself king. A livid Pedro rallied the equally furious liberals and forced Miguel to surrender at Évoramonte in 1834.

After Pedro's death, his daughter Maria, now queen of Portugal at just 15, kept his flame alive with fanatical support of his 1826 charter. The radical supporters of the liberal 1822 constitution grew vociferous over the next two decades, bringing the country to the brink of civil war. The Duke of Saldanha, however, saved the day, negotiating a peace that toned down Pedro's charter, while still radically modernising Portugal's infrastructure.

The latter half of the 19th century was a remarkable period for Portugal, and it became known as one of the most advanced societies in southern Europe. Casual visitors to Lisbon, such as Hans Christian Andersen, were surprised to find tree-lined boulevards with gas street lamps, efficient trams and well-dressed residents. Social advances were less anecdotal. The educational reformer João Arroio dramatically increased the number of schools, doubling the number of boys' schools and quadrupling the number of girls' schools. Women gained the right to own property; slavery was abolished throughout the Portuguese empire, as was the death penalty; and even the prison system received an overhaul – prisoners were taught useful trades while in jail so they could integrate into society upon their release.

It was the Portuguese who started England's obsession with tea: their explorers introduced it to Europe in the mid-17th century and tea enthusiast Catherine of Bragança did the rest.

1803	1807	1815	1822
England and France are again at war. Portugal sides with England and refuses Napoleon's call to close its ports to the British. French troops are on the march across Iberia.	Napoleon invades Portugal. The Portuguese royal family and several thousand in their retinue pack up their belongings and set sail for Brazil. British warships guard their passage.	Having fallen hard for Brazil, Dom João VI declares Rio the capital of the United Kingdom of Portugal and Brazil and the Algarves, relegating Lisbon to second-class status.	In Brazil, Prince Regent Pedro leads a coup d'état and declares Brazilian independence with himself the new 'emperor'. Dom João VI, his father, returns to Portugal, to reclaim his crown.

Professional organisations, such as the Literary Guild, emerged and became a major impetus to the advancement of ideas in public discourse, inspiring debate in politics, religious life and the art world.

As elsewhere in Europe, this was also a time of great industrial growth, with a dramatic increase in textile production, much of it to be exported. Other major works included the building of bridges and a nationwide network of roads, as well as a flourish of major architectural works such as the Pena Palace (p109) above Sintra.

However, by 1900 the tides of discontent among workers began to grow. With increased mechanisation, workers began losing jobs (some factory owners began hiring children to operate the machines), and their demand for fair working conditions went unanswered. Those who went on strike were simply fired and replaced. At the same time, Portugal experienced a dramatic demographic shift: rural areas were increasingly depopulated in favour of cities, and emigration (especially to Brazil) snowballed.

Much was changing, and more and more people began to look towards socialism as a cure for the country's inequalities. Nationalist republicanism swept through the lower-middle classes, spurring an attempted coup in 1908. It failed, but the following month King Carlos and Crown Prince Luis Filipe were brutally assassinated in Lisbon.

The Inquisitor's Manual (2003), by Arnaldo Antunes, is a brilliantly written depiction of dark days under Salazar as seen through the eyes of Faulknerian characters such as 'the minister', Senhor Francisco.

Carlos' younger son, Manuel II, tried feebly to appease republicans, but it was too little, too late. On 5 October 1910, after an uprising by military officers, a republic was declared. Manuel, dubbed 'the Unfortunate', sailed into exile in Britain where he died in 1932.

The Rise & Fall of Salazar

After a landslide victory in the 1911 elections, hopes were high among republicans for dramatic changes ahead, but the tides were against them. The economy was in tatters, strained by an economically disastrous decision to join the Allies in WWI. In postwar years the chaos deepened: republican factions squabbled, unions led strikes and were repressed, and the military grew more powerful.

The new republic soon had a reputation as Europe's most unstable regime. Between 1910 and 1926 there were an astonishing 45 changes of government, often resulting from military intervention. Another coup in 1926 brought forth new names and faces, most significantly António de Oliveira Salazar, a finance minister who would rise up through the ranks to become prime minister – a post he would hold for the next 36 years.

Salazar hastily enforced his 'New State' – a corporatist republic that was nationalistic, Catholic, authoritarian and essentially repressive. All political parties were banned except for the loyalist National Union,

1832	1865	1890
Dom Pedro I returns to Portugal where he must contest his throne with his brother Miguel. Two years of civil war end with Miguel's banishment. Dom Pedro's daughter becomes queen.	Portugal enjoys peace and prosperity. Railways connect villages with Lisbon and Porto, now cities enriched by maritime trade. Advancements are made in industry, agriculture, health and education.	Portugal takes a renewed interest in its African colonies. England wants all control of sub-Saharan Africa, and threatens Portugal with war. Cowed, Portugal withdraws, causing a crisis at home.

» Dom Pedro's tomb

which ran the show, and the National Assembly. Strikes were banned and propaganda, censorship and brute force kept society in order. The sinister new secret police, Polícia Internacional e de Defesa do Estado (PIDE), inspired terror and suppressed opposition by imprisonment and torture. Various attempted coups during Salazar's rule came to nothing. For a chilling taste of life as a political prisoner under Salazar, you could visit the 16th-century Fortaleza at Peniche (p256) – used as a jail by the dictator.

The only good news was a dramatic economic turnaround. Through the 1950s and 1960s Portugal experienced an annual industrial growth rate of 7% to 9%.

Internationally, the wily Salazar played two hands, unofficially supporting Franco's nationalists in the Spanish Civil War, and allowing British use of Azores airfields during WWII despite official neutrality (and illegal sales of tungsten to Germany). It was later discovered that Salazar had also authorised the transfer of Nazi-looted gold to Portugal – 44 tonnes according to Allied records.

But it was something else that finally brought the Salazarist era to a close – decolonisation. Refusing to relinquish the colonies, he was faced with ever more costly and unpopular military expeditions. In 1961 Goa was occupied by India, and nationalists rose up in Angola. Guerrilla movements also appeared in Portuguese Guinea and Mozambique.

Salazar, however, didn't have to face the consequences. In 1968 he had a stroke, and died two years later.

His successor, Marcelo Caetano, failed to ease unrest. Military officers sympathetic to African freedom fighters – the officers had seen the horrible living conditions in which the colony lived beneath the Portuguese authorities – grew reluctant to fight colonial wars. Several hundred officers formed the Movimento das Forças Armadas (MFA), which on 25 April 1974 carried out a nearly bloodless coup, later nicknamed the Revolution of the Carnations (after victorious soldiers stuck carnations in their rifle barrels). Carnations are still a national symbol of freedom.

From Revolution to Democracy

Despite the coup's popularity, the following year saw unprecedented chaos. It began where the revolution had begun – in the African colonies. Independence was granted immediately to Guinea-Bissau, followed by the speedy decolonisation of the Cape Verde islands, São Tomé e Príncipe, Mozambique and Angola.

The transition wasn't smooth: civil war racked Angola, and East Timor, freshly liberated in 1975, was promptly invaded by Indonesia.

Former Portuguese Colonies & Year of Independence

» Brazil, 1822
» Goa, 1961
» Guinea-Bissau, 1974
» Angola, 1975
» Cape Verde, 1975
» Mozambique, 1975
» São Tomé e Príncipe, 1975
» East Timor, 1975
» Macau, 1999

HISTORY FROM REVOLUTION TO DEMOCRACY

1900	1908	1910	1916
The republican movement gains force. The humiliating Africa issue is one among many grievances against the crown. Others include rising unemployment and growing social inequalities.	The Braganças fail to silence antimonarchist sentiment by shutting down newspapers, exiling dissidents and brutally suppressing demonstrations. King Carlos and his eldest son, Luís Filipe, are assassinated.	King Carlos' younger son, 18-year-old Manuel, takes the throne but is soon ousted. Portugal is declared a republic. Chaos rules, and the country will see 45 different governments in 16 years.	Despite initial neutrality, Portugal gets drawn into the WWI, and sends 55,000 troops; nearly 10,000 perish. The war effort is devastating for the economy, creating a long postwar recession.

BEWARE THE ECONOMICS PROFESSOR

When General António Carmona was named Portugal's new president in 1926, he inherited a country in serious debt. Fearing economic catastrophe, Carmona called in an expert, a man by the name of Oliveira Salazar. At the time, Salazar was a 37-year-old bachelor, sharing spartan quarters with a priest (who would later become cardinal of Lisbon). Salazar himself was no stranger to religious life. He spent eight years studying to become a priest, and some residents from his small native village even called him 'father' on his visits. Only a last-minute decision led him to veer into law instead.

Upon graduating, he went into the then fledgling field of economics, becoming one of the country's first economics lecturers, and soon garnered wide respect for his articles on public finance. When General Carmona approached him with the job of finance minister, Salazar accepted on one condition: that the spending of all government ministries fall under his discretion. The general agreed.

Salazar achieved enormous success at firing up the national economy. He severely curtailed government spending, raising taxes and balancing the budget during his first year. Unemployment decreased significantly. Salazar quickly became one of Carmona's star ministers. He also took on adjoining posts as other ministers resigned. In this way he consolidated power until Carmona eventually named him prime minister.

Within Portugal, too, times were turbulent, with almost a million refugees from African colonies flooding into Portugal.

The country was an economic mess, with widespread strikes and a tangle of political ideas and parties. The communists and a radical wing of the MFA launched a revolutionary movement, nationalising firms and services. Peasant farmers seized land to establish communal farms that failed because of in-fighting and poor management. While revolutionaries held sway in the south, the conservative north was led by Mário Soares and his Partido Socialista (PS; Socialist Party).

It took a more moderate government, formed in 1975, to unite the country after a coup by radical leftists was crushed. At last, the revolution had ended.

The law allowing all Portuguese women to vote was only established in 1975.

The Rocky Road to Stability

Portugal was soon committed to a blend of socialism and democracy, with a powerful president, an elected assembly and a Council of the Revolution to control the armed forces.

Soares' minority government soon faltered, prompting a series of attempts at government by coalitions and nonparty candidates, including Portugal's first female prime minister, Maria de Lourdes Pintassilgo. In the 1980 parliamentary elections a new political force took the reins –

1932	1935	1943	1961
António de Oliveira Salazar seizes power. The Portuguese economy grows but at enormous human cost. Salazar uses censorship, imprisonment and torture to silence his opponents.	The largely unpublished 47-year-old poet Fernando Pessoa dies, leaving a trunk containing a staggering collection of writing. Critics later describe him as one of the greatest poets of the 20th century.	Portugal, neutral during WWII, becomes a crossroads for intelligence activities of Allied and Axis operatives. Salazar works both sides, selling tungsten to the Nazis while allowing Britain use of airfields.	The last vestiges of Portugal's empire begin to crumble as India seizes Goa. Independence movements are underway in the former African colonies of Angola, Mozambique and Guinea-Bissau.

This is when Salazar set the tone for civilian life that would last for many decades to come. He drafted a new constitution around his New State ideals, which were partly modelled on the family as a political idea. Families had no organised internal strife so there was no need for unions or for political parties; a family had a head of the household, who would determine where to spend the money. Naturally, Salazar saw himself as the father figure who would be steering the family ship; he also saw the church as the 'mother' of the family, which would continue to fulfil society's thirst for spiritual values.

Under his authoritarian rule, he did bring stability and prosperity to the country, though at enormous cost: censorship, imprisonment and, in some cases, torture of political opponents. Among his most damning attributes was his attitude towards the working class. He believed in giving them a diet of 'fado, Fátima and football' to keep them happily compliant, but had no intention of bettering their lot; at the end of his rule, Portugal had the highest rate of illiteracy and tuberculosis in Western Europe, and women were still not allowed to vote. Given the socially backward condition of the nation when Salazar relinquished power, the advancements of the last 30 years seem all the more startling.

the conservative Aliança Democrática (AD; Democratic Alliance), led by Francisco Sá Carneiro.

After Carneiro's almost immediate (and suspicious) death in a plane crash, Francisco Pinto Balsemão stepped into his shoes. He implemented plans to join the European Community (EC).

It was partly to keep the EC and the International Monetary Fund (IMF) happy that a new coalition government under Soares and Balsemão implemented a strict programme of economic modernisation. Not surprisingly, the belt-tightening wasn't popular. The loudest critics were Soares' right-wing partners in the Partido Social Democrata (PSD; Social Democrat Party), led by the dynamic Aníbal Cavaco Silva. Communist trade unions also organised strikes, and the appearance of urban terrorism by the radical left-wing Forças Populares de 25 Abril (FP-25) deepened unrest.

In 1986, after nine years of negotiations, Portugal joined the EC. Flush with new funds, it raced ahead of its neighbours with unprecedented economic growth. The new cash flow also gave Prime Minister Cavaco Silva the power to push ahead with radical economic reforms. These included labour law reforms that left many disenchanted workers; the 1980s were crippled by strikes – including one involving

Officially neutral in WWII, Portugal was a major intersection of both Allied and Nazi spying operations. British secret service agents based there included Graham Greene, Ian Fleming and double agent Kim Philby.

1974	1986	1998	1998
Army officers overthrow Salazar's successor in the Revolution of the Carnations. Portugal veers to the left, and communists and moderates struggle for power in the unstable country.	In a narrow second-round victory, Mário Soares is elected president of Portugal, becoming its first civilian head of state in 60 years. The same year, Portugal joins the EC along with Spain.	Lisbon hosts Expo 98, showcasing new developments, including Santiago Calatrava's cutting-edge train station, Europe's largest oceanarium and its longest bridge (Ponte de Vasco da Gama).	José Saramago receives the Nobel Prize in Literature for his darkly humorous tales about ordinary characters facing fantastical obstacles. A lifelong communist, his work was condemned by the church.

WOMAN

1.5 million workers – though all to no avail. The controversial legislation was eventually passed.

The economic growth, however, wouldn't last. In 1992 EC trade barriers fell and Portugal suddenly faced new competition. Fortunes dwindled as recession set in, and disillusionment grew as Europe's single market revealed the backwardness of Portugal's agricultural sector.

Strikes, crippling corruption charges and student demonstrations over rising fees only undermined the PSD further, leading to Cavaco Silva's resignation in 1995. The general elections in 1995 brought new faces to power, with the socialist António Guterres running the show. Despite hopes for a different and less conservative administration, it was business as usual, with Guterres maintaining the budgetary rigour that qualified Portugal for the European Economic & Monetary Union (EMU) in 1998. Indeed, for a while Portugal was a star EMU performer with steady economic growth that helped Guterres win a second term. But it couldn't last. Corruption scandals, rising inflation and a faltering economy soon spelt disaster. Portugal slipped into economic stagnation by the dawn of the 21st century. The next ten years have been one of hardship for the Portuguese economy, which saw little or negative GDP growth, and rising unemployment from 2001 to 2010. As elsewhere in Europe, Portugal took a huge hit during the global financial crisis, with the economy shrinking almost 3% in 2009. Ultimatums from the EU governing body to rein in its debt (to avoid a Greece-style meltdown) have brought unpopular austerity measures – pension reform, raising taxes, public sector hiring freezes – leaving some Portuguese disgruntled.

Portugal has had more success in the realm of renewable energy (harvesting solar, wind and hydroelectric power). In 2005, only 17% of electricity in Portugal's grid came from green energy. By 2010, the figure had risen to 45% – a gain unprecedented elsewhere in Europe. In 2012, Portugal expects to become the first country with a nationwide grid of charging stations for electric cars.

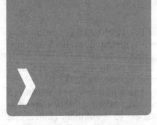

Religion

Christianity has been a pivotal force in shaping Portugal's history, and religion still plays an important role in the lives of its people. Churches and cathedrals are sprinkled about every town and city across the country, and Portugal's biggest celebrations revolve around religious events, with a packed calendar of colourful parades and concerts held on important feast days. Portugal is also home to a number of pilgrimage sites, the most important of which, Fátima, attracts over 300,000 pilgrims each year.

Church & State

Portugal has a long and deep connection to the church. Even during the long rule of the Moors, Christianity flourished in the north – which provided a strategic base for Christian crusaders to retake the kingdom. Cleric and king walked hand in hand, from the earliest papal alliances of the 11th century and up through the 17th century, when the church played a role both at home and in Portugal's expanding empire.

Things ran smoothly until the 18th century, when the Marquês de Pombal, a man of the Enlightenment, wanted to curtail the power of the church – specifically the Jesuits, whom he expelled in 1759. He also sought to modernise the Portuguese state (overseeing one of the world's first urban 'grid' systems) and brought education under the state's control. State–church relations see-sawed over the next 150 years, with power struggles including the outright ban of religious orders in 1821, and the seizing by the state of many church properties.

The separation of church and state was formally recognised during the First Republic (1910–26). But in practice the church remained

> **Biggest Religious Events**
> » Semana Santa (Braga)
> » Festa de São João (Porto & Braga)
> » Festa de Santo António (Lisbon)
> » Fátima Romaris (Fátima)
> » Romaria de Nossa Senhora d'Agonia (Viana do Castelo)
> » Festa de Nossa Senhora dos Remédios (Lamego)

LIFE UNDER MUSLIM RULE

The Moors ruled southern Portugal for over 400 years, and some scholars describe that time as a golden age. The Arabs introduced irrigation, previously unknown in Europe. Two Egyptian agronomists came to Iberia in the 10th century and wrote manuals on land management, animal husbandry, plant and crop cultivation and irrigation designs. They introduced bananas, rice, coconuts, maize and sugar cane. They also encouraged small-scale cooperatives – in olive-oil and wine production and food markets – which are still embraced in many parts of Portugal.

The Moors opened schools and set about campaigns to achieve mass literacy (in Arabic of course), as well as the teaching of mathematics, geography and history. Medicine reached new levels of sophistication. There was also a degree of religious tolerance that evaporated when the Christian crusaders came to power. Much to the chagrin of Christian slave owners, slavery was not permitted in the Islamic kingdom – making it a refuge for runaway slaves. Muslims, Christians and Jews all peacefully co-existed – at times even collaborated together, creating one of the most scientifically and artistically advanced societies the world had ever known up until that time.

intimately linked to many aspects of life. Health and education were largely under the domain of the church, with Catholic schools and hospitals the norm. Social outlets for those in rural areas were mostly church-related. And the completion of any public works project always included a blessing by the local bishop.

In 1932 António de Oliveira Salazar swept into power, establishing a Mussolini-like *Estado Novo* (New State) that lasted until the Carnation Revolution of 1974. Salazar had strong ties to the Catholic church – he spent eight years studying for the priesthood before switching to law. His college roommate was a priest who later became the Cardinal Patriarch of Lisbon. Salazar was a ferocious anticommunist, and used Roman Catholic references to appeal to people's sense of authority, order and discipline. He described the family, parish and larger institution of Christianity as the foundations of the state. Church officials who spoke out against him were silenced or forced into exile.

Following the 1974 revolution, the church found itself out of favour with many Portuguese; its support of the Salazar regime spelled its undoing in the topsy-turvy days following the government's collapse. The new constitution, ratified in 1976, again emphasised the formal separation of church and state, although this time the law had teeth, and Portugal quickly transitioned into a more secular society. Today, only about half of all weddings happen inside a church. Divorce is legal, as is abortion (up to 10 weeks; a law that went into effect following a 2007 referendum). In 2010 same-sex marriage was legalised, making Portugal the sixth European nation to permit it.

One of the more unusual rituals celebrated around Easter is the *enterro do bacalhau* (burying of the codfish), which marks the end of Lent (a time when much fish is eaten).

The Inquisition

'After the earthquake, which had destroyed three-fourths of the city of Lisbon, the sages of that country could think of no means more effectual to preserving the kingdom from utter ruin than to entertain the people with an auto-da-fé, it having been decided by the University of Coimbra that burning a few people alive by a slow fire, and with great ceremony, is an infallible secret for preventing earthquakes.'

Candide *(Voltaire, 1759)*

One of the darkest episodes in Portugal's history, the Inquisition was a campaign of church-sanctioned terror and execution that began in 1536. It was initially aimed at Jews who were either expelled from Portugal or forced to renounce their faith. Those who didn't embrace Catholicism risked facing the auto-da-fé (act of faith), a church ceremony consisting of a Mass, a procession of the guilty, the reading of their sentences and later their burning at the stake.

'Trials' took place in public squares in Lisbon, Porto, Évora and Coimbra in front of crowds sometimes numbering in the thousands. At the centre atop a large canopied platform sat the Grand Inquisitor, surrounded by his staff of aristocrats, priests, bailiffs, torturers and scribes, who meticulously recorded the proceedings.

The victims usually spent years in prison, often undergoing crippling torture, before seeing the light of day. They stood accused of a wide variety of crimes – such as skipping meals on Jewish fast days (signs of 'unreformed' Jews), leaving pork uneaten on the plate, failing to attend mass or observe the Sabbath, as well as straight-up blasphemy, witchcraft and homosexuality. No matter how flimsy the 'evidence' – often delivered to the tribunal by a grudge-bearing neighbour – very few were found innocent and released. After a decade or so in prison,

PAGAN

Portugal still has a few good old-fashioned pagan celebrations. The most famous is the *Festa dos Rapazes* (Festival of the Lads), which features young men in rags and wooden masks rampaging around Miranda do Douro.

When Manuel I banned the practice of Judaism, most Jews fled or converted. Some however, simply hid their faith from public view and wore the facade of being a New Christian (the name given to Jewish converts). Religious ceremonies were held behind closed doors, with the Sabbath lamp placed at the bottom of a clay jar so that it could not be seen from outside. Within their Catholic prayer books they composed Jewish prayers, and even overlaid Jewish prayers over Catholic rituals (like the making of the sign of the cross). Clever food preparations also helped hide their faith, such as the eating of pork-free *alheiras,* which were seasoned garlicky sausages made of a mixture or chicken, rabbit, partridge or veal mixed with bread dough for consistency.

One Crypto Jewish community in Belmonte managed to maintain its faith in hiding for over 400 years, and was only revealed in 1917. Through centuries of endogamy (intermarriages), many of the 200 Jews in this community suffer from hereditary diseases. No longer underground (Belmonte now has its own synagogue and Jewish cemetery), they still remain quite secretive about the practices they maintained in hiding.

the condemned were finally brought to their auto-da-fé. Before meeting their judgment, they were dressed in a *san benito* (yellow penitential gown painted with flames) and *coroza* (a high conical cap) and brought before the tribunal.

After the sentence was pronounced, judgment was carried out in a different venue. By dawn the next morning, for instance, executioners would lead the condemned to a killing field outside town. Those who repented were strangled first before being burned at the stake. The unrepentant were simply burned alive.

During the years of the Inquisition, the church executed over 2000 victims and tortured or exiled tens of thousands more. The Portuguese even exported the auto-da-fé to the colonies – burning Hindus at the stake in Goa, for instance.

As Voltaire sardonically suggested, superstition played no small part in the auto-da-fé. Some believers thought that the earthquake of 1755 was the wrath of God upon them – and that they were being punished not for their bloody auto-da-fés, but because the Holy Office hadn't done quite enough to punish the heretics.

The Apparitions at Fátima

For many Portuguese Catholics, Fátima represents one of the most momentous religious events of the 20th century, and it transformed a tiny village into a major pilgrimage site for Catholics across the globe. On 13 May 1917, the 10-year-old Lúcia Santos and her two younger cousins, Jacinta and Francisco Marto, were out tending their parents' flocks in the fields outside the village of Fátima. Suddenly a bolt of lighting struck the earth, and a woman 'brighter than the sun' appeared before them. According to Santos, she came to them with a message exhorting people to pray and do penance to save sinners. She asked the children to pray the rosary every day, which she said was key to bringing peace to one's own life and to the world. At the time, peace was certainly on the minds of many Portuguese, who were already deeply enmeshed in WWI. She then told the children to come again on the 13th of each month, at the same time and place, and that in October she would reveal herself to them.

Word of the alleged apparition spread, although most who heard the tale of the shepherd children reacted with scepticism. Only a handful of observers came to the field for the June 13 appearance but on the month

The last auto-da-fé was held in 1765, which ironically enough was levied against 10 Jesuit priests who dared oppose the autocratic and anticlerical Marquês de Pombal.

RELIGION THE APPARITIONS AT FÁTIMA

following several thousand showed up. That's when the apparition apparently entrusted the children with three secrets. In the weeks that followed, a media storm was loosed, with the government accusing the church of fabricating an elaborate hoax to revive its flagging popularity. The church for its part didn't know how to react. The children were even arrested and interrogated at one point, but the three refused to change their story.

On 13 October 1917, some 70,000 gathered for what was to be the final appearance of the apparition. Many witnesses there experienced the so-called Miracle of the Sun, where the sun seemed to grow in size and dance in the sky, becoming a whirling disc of fire, shooting out multicoloured rays. Some spoke of being miraculously healed; others were frightened by the experience; still others claimed they saw nothing at all. The three children claimed they saw Mary, Jesus and Joseph in the sky. Newspapers across the country reported on the event, and soon a growing hysteria surrounded the event.

Only Lúcia made it into adulthood. Jacinta and Francisco, beatified by the church in 2000, were two of the more than 20 million killed during the 1918 influenza epidemic. Lúcia later became a Carmelite nun and died at the age of 97 on 13 February 2007.

The Three Secrets

Much mystery surrounds the three secrets told to the children at Fátima on 13 July 1917. Lúcia revealed the first two in 1941 at the request of the Bishop of Leira, who was publishing a book on Jacinta. The first secret depicted a vision of demons and human souls suffering in the fires of hell. The second secret predicted that an even more disastrous war would follow WWI should the world – and in particular Russia – not convert. Given months before the Bolshevik takeover in St Petersburg, this secret was considered particularly inflammatory, as it went on to say that if her call for repentance goes unheeded Russia will spread its terrors through the world, causing wars and persecution of the church. Lúcia was reluctant to reveal the third secret, claiming that she was told by the Virgin Mary never to reveal it. Stricken with illness and convinced she was going to die – and under pressure from the Bishop of Leira – Lúcia finally agreed to write the secret down in 1944.

The bishop who received the secret then passed it on to the Vatican, who kept it hidden away for decades. Lúcia requested that the last secret be revealed in 1960 or upon her death, whichever came first. She picked 1960 as she figured that by then the secret would be more clearly understood. The Vatican, however, had other plans and announced in 1960 that the secret would probably remain sealed forever. Fátima followers meanwhile offered wild speculations on what the third secret might reveal – from nuclear holocaust to WWIII, catastrophic global

Fátima Books & Films

» *The Fourth Secret of Fátima* (2006), written by Antonio Socci

» *The 13th Day* (2009), directed by Ian and Dominic Higgins

» *Miracle of Our Lady of Fátima* (1952), directed by John Brahm

FAITH ON THE DECLINE

The percentage of Portuguese who consider themselves Catholics (85%) ranks among the highest in Western Europe. The number of the faithful, however, has been on a steady decline since the 1970s (when over 95% of the nation was Catholic). Today nearly half a million residents describe themselves as agnostic, and less than 20% of the population are practising Catholics.

Regional differences reveal a more complicated portrait: around half of northern Portugal's population still attend Sunday Mass, as do more than a quarter in Lisbon – with noticeably fewer churchgoers on the southern coast.

financial crisis, famine, the apocalypse. The church kept them in suspense until 2000, when it was finally revealed.

The last secret was the most mystical and controversial of the three. Lúcia described seeing an angel holding a flaming sword who pointed at the earth and cried out 'penance'. Then she saw a ruined city full of corpses and beyond that a steep mountain, up which climbed a bishop dressed in white – whom she took to be the pope. At the top he knelt before a cross made of rough-hewn tree trunks, and was killed by soldiers who gunned him down.

Some claim that this predicted the assassination attempt on Pope John Paul II in 1981. The attempt happened on May 13 – the anniversary of the apparitions – and the pope himself claimed the Virgin of Fátima saved him from death. (According to some reconstructions of the shooting, the assassin's bullet followed a bizarre elliptical path rather than a straight line, thereby avoiding the pope's vital organs). Conspiracy theorists, meanwhile, claim that the church was hiding the 'real' third secret, which related to the apocalypse and a great apostasy within the church – a breakdown that begins at the top. Recent scandals, including the Catholic sex-abuse cases in various parts of the world, have only fuelled the speculation among some 'Fátimists' that the third secret has yet to be revealed.

Portugal's favourite holy man, Santo Antonio, is the go-to for lonely hearts. Unmarried women and men light candles to him to find love, and on his feast day in June, Lisbon hosts free mass marriages for those too poor to spring for a private celebration.

Art & Architecture

Home to one of Europe's oldest cities, Portugal has a long and storied art history dating back at least 20,000 years – when early artists clambered out of caves and first pounded stone against stone in an attempt to record the world around them. Following the earliest peoples, waves of foreign conquerors all left their mark on the Iberian nation – megaliths made by mysterious Neolithic tribes, walled villages of Celtic peoples, elaborate mosaics and carefully designed theatres and temples of the Romans, Visigothic churches, Moorish cityscapes and the imposing fortresses by early Christian crusaders.

Things really started to get interesting around 1500, when the spice trade showered enormous wealth on the kingdom, giving birth to an age of grand cathedrals and lavish palaces. In the 500 years that followed, Portugal became a canvas for the great architects and artisans of Europe – both home-grown and foreign, with memorable works in a dizzying array of styles – Manueline, mannerist, baroque, art nouveau, modernist and postmodernist. Meanwhile, painters, sculptors, poets and novelists have all made contributions to Portugal's artistic heritage – all rather astounding given the country's small size.

Prehistoric Relics

» Vila Nova de Foz Côa, the Douro

» Citânia de Briteiros, the Minho

» Cromeleque dos Almendres, the Alentejo

The Palaeolithic Palette

A most mysterious group of 95 huge monoliths forms a strange circle in an isolated clearing among Alentejan olive groves near Évora. It's one of Europe's most impressive prehistoric sites: the Cromeleque dos Almendres.

All over Portugal, but especially in the Alentejo, you can visit such ancient funerary and religious structures, built during the Neolithic and Mesolithic eras about 6000 years ago. Most impressive are the dolmens: rectangular, polygonal or round funerary chambers, reached by a corridor of stone slabs and covered with earth to create an artificial mound. King of these is the Anta Grande do Zambujeiro, also near Évora, and Europe's largest dolmen, with six 6m-high stones forming a huge chamber. Single monoliths, or menhirs, often carved with phallic or religious symbols, also dot the countryside like an army of stone sentinels. Their relationship to promoting fertility seems obvious.

Roman Ruins

» Conimbriga, the Beiras

» Temple of Diana, Évora

» Teatro Romano, Lisbon

» Milreu, the Algarve

With the arrival of the Celts (800–200 BC) came the first established hilltop settlements, called *castros*. The best-preserved example is the Citânia de Briteiros in the Minho, where you can literally step into Portugal's past. Stone dwellings were built on a circular or elliptical plan, and the complex was surrounded with a dry-stone defensive wall. In the *citânias* (fortified villages) further south, dwellings tended to be rectangular.

The Romans

The Romans left Portugal their typical architectural and engineering feats – roads, bridges, towns complete with forums (marketplaces), villas, public baths and aqueducts. These have now largely disappeared from the surface, though the majority of Portugal's cities are built on Roman foundations. Today you can descend into dank foundations under new buildings in Lisbon and Évora, and see Roman fragments around Braga. At Conimbriga, the country's largest Roman site, an entire Roman town is under excavation. Revealed so far are some spectacular mosaics, along with structural or decorative columns, carved entablatures and classical ornamentation, giving a sense of the Roman high life.

Portugal's most famous and complete Roman ruin is the Templo Romano, the so-called Temple of Diana in Évora, with its flouncy-topped Corinthian columns, nowadays echoed by the complementary towers of Évora cathedral. This is the finest temple of its kind on the Iberian Peninsula, its preservation the result of having been walled up in the Middle Ages and later used as a slaughterhouse.

Architectural Movements

Great Gothic

Cistercians introduced the Gothic trend, and this reached its pinnacle in Alcobaça, in one of Portugal's most ethereally beautiful buildings. The austere abbey church and cloister of the Mosteiro de Santa Maria de Alcobaça, begun in 1178, has a lightness and simplicity strongly influenced by Clairvaux Abbey in France. Its hauntingly simple Cloisters of Silence were a model for later cathedral cloisters at Coimbra, Lisbon, Évora and many other places. This was the birth of Portuguese Gothic, which flowered and transmuted over the coming years as the country gained more

Gothic Architecture

» Mosteiro de Santa Maria de Alcobaça, Estremadura

» Convento do Carmo, Lisbon

» Mosteiro de Santa Maria da Vitória, Estremadura

ART & ARCHITECTURE THE ROMANS

A SERENDIPITOUS DISCOVERY

In 1989 researchers were studying the rugged valley of the Rio Côa, 15km from the Spanish frontier, to understand the environmental impact of a planned hydroelectric dam that was to flood the valley. In the course of their work, they made an extraordinary discovery: a number of petroglyphs (rock engravings) dating back tens of thousands of years.

Yet it wasn't until 1992, after dam construction was underway, that the importance of the find began to take root. Archaeologists came across whole clusters of petroglyphs, mostly dating from the Upper Palaeolithic period (10,000 to 40,000 years ago). Local people joined the search and the inventory of engravings soon grew into the thousands. Despite the extraordinary collection, Portugal's main power company insisted on completing the dam, but eventually backed down in the face of an international campaign. In 1998 the future of the collection was safeguarded when Unesco designated the valley a World Heritage Site.

Today Rio Côa holds one of the largest-known collections of open-air Palaeolithic art in the world. Archaeologists are still puzzling over the meaning of the engravings – and why this site was chosen. Most of the petroglyphs depict animals: stylised horses, aurochs (extinct ancestors of domesticated cattle) and long-horned ibex (extinct species of wild goat). Some animals are depicted with multiple heads – as if to indicate the animal in motion – while others are drawn so finely that they require artificial light to be seen. Later petroglyphs begin to depict human figures as well. The most intriguing engravings consist of overlapping layers, with successive artists adding their touches thousands of years after the first strokes were applied. A kind of Palaeolithic palimpsest in which generations of hunters worked and reworked the engravings of their forebears.

and more experience of the outside world. For centuries Portugal had been culturally dominated and restricted by Spain and the Moors.

By the 14th century, when the Mosteiro de Santa Maria da Vitória (commonly known as Mosteiro da Batalha or Battle Abbey) was constructed, simplicity was a distant, vague memory. Portuguese, Irish and French architects worked on this breathtaking monument for more than two centuries. The combination of their skills and the changing architectural fashions of the times, from Flamboyant (late) Gothic to Renaissance and then Manueline, turned the abbey into a seething mass of carving, organic decorations, lofty spaces and slanting stained-glass light. It's a showcase of High Gothic art. It exults in the decorative (especially in its Gothic Royal Cloisters and Chapter House), while the flying buttresses tip their hat to English Perpendicular Gothic.

Secular architecture also enjoyed a Gothic boom, thanks to the need for fortifications against the Moors and to the castle-building fervour of the 13th-century ruler, Dom Dinis. Some of Portugal's most spectacular, huddled, thick-walled castles – for example, Estremoz, Óbidos and Bragança – date from this time, many featuring massive double-perimeter walls and an inner square tower.

Portugal has few Renaissance buildings, but some examples of the style are the Great Cloisters in Tomar's Convento de Cristo, designed by Spanish Diogo de Torralva in the late 16th century; the nearby Igreja de Nossa Senhora da Conceição; and the Convento de Bom Jesus at Valverde, outside Évora.

Manueline

Manueline is a uniquely Portuguese style, a specific, crazed flavour of late Gothic architecture. Ferociously decorative, it coincided roughly with the reign of Dom Manuel I (r 1495–1521) and is interesting not just because of its extraordinarily imaginative designs, burbling with life, but also because this dizzyingly creative architecture skipped hand in hand with the era's booming confidence.

During Dom Manuel's reign, Vasco da Gama and fellow explorers claimed new overseas lands and new wealth for Portugal. The Age of Discovery was expressed in sculptural creations of eccentric inventiveness, drawing heavily on nautical themes: twisted ropes, coral and anchors in stone, topped by the ubiquitous armillary sphere (a navigational device that became Dom Manuel's personal symbol) and the cross of the Order of Christ (symbol of the religious military order that largely financed and inspired Portugal's explorations).

Manueline first emerged in Setúbal's Igreja de Jesus, designed in the 1490s by French expatriate Diogo de Boitaca, who gave it columns like trees growing into the ceiling, and ribbed vaulting like twisted ropes. The style quickly caught on, and soon decorative carving was creeping, twisting and crawling over everything (aptly described by 19th-century English novelist William Beckford as 'scollops and twistifications').

Outstanding Manueline masterpieces are Belém's Mosteiro dos Jerónimos, masterminded largely by Diogo de Boitaca and João de Castilho; and Batalha's Mosteiro de Santa Maria da Vitória's otherworldly Capelas Imperfeitas (Unfinished Chapels).

Other famous creations include Belém's Torre de Belém, a Manueline-Moorish cake crossed with a chess piece by Diogo de Boitaca and his brother Francisco, and Diogo de Arruda's fantastical organic, seemingly barnacle-encrusted window in the Chapter House of Tomar's Convento de Cristo, as well as its fanciful 16-sided Charola – the Templar church, resembling an eerie *Star Wars* set. Many other churches sport a Manueline flourish against a plain facade.

The style was enormously resonant in Portugal, and reappeared in the early 20th century in exercises in mystical romanticism, such as Sintra's Quinta da Regaleira and Palácio Nacional da Pena, and Luso's over-the-top and extraordinary neo-Manueline Palace Hotel do Buçaco.

(Continued on page 505)

Elevador de Santa Justa, Lisbon (p52)

Lisbon's only vertical street lift is a neo-Gothic creation by Raul Mésnier, apprentice of Gustave Eiffel.

1. Bom Jesus do Monte, Braga (p408)
This neoclassical church plays second fiddle to the
stupendous baroque Bom staircase leading up to it.

2. Igreja de São Francisco, Porto (p360)
The dazzling baroque interior of this Gothic church uses
100kg of gold leaf.

3. Gare do Oriente, Lisbon (p72)

This space-age, geometric train station is the handiwork of architect Santiago Calatrava.

4. Mosteiro dos Jerónimos, Lisbon (p74)

The fantastical Manueline monastery was built in tribute to the explorers of the Age of Discoveries.

5. Velha Universidade, Coimbra (p303)

The 'Old University' of Coimbra is a cluster of remarkable buildings constructed around a hilltop between the 16th and 18th centuries.

1. Praça do Comércio, Lisbon (p49)

Verissimo da Costa's triumphal Arco da Victória is the crowing glory of Lisbon's riverfront plaza.

2. Convento de Cristo, Tomar (p283)

The Great Cloisters are a fine example of the Renaissance style.

3. Rossio, Lisbon (p52)

The neo-Manueline horseshoe-shaped arches feature at Rossio train station.

4. Castelo, Guimarães (p413)

The 11th-century hilltop castle is the supposed birthplace of the great Afonso Henriques.

1. Mosteiro de Santa Maria, Alcobaça (p267)
The monastery's baroque facade belies the Gothic ambition and Cistercian austerity of its interiors.

2. Palacio Nacional, Mafra (p125)
German Friedrich Ludwig's baroque masterpiece covers a staggering 4 sq km.

3. Torre de Belém, Lisbon (p69)
The Manueline fortress, designed in 1515 to defend Lisbon's harbour, is World Heritage listed.

4. Palácio de Queluz, Queluz (p124)

Portugal's answer to Versailles, designed for Prince Dom Pedro in the 1750s.

5. Casa da Mùsica, Porto (p378)

Rem Koolhaas' minimalist white-concrete concert hall rests in Porto like a gigantic piece of raw crystal.

ADINA TOVY AMSEL

3

4

Templo Romano, Évora (p205)
These Corinthian columns, capped with Estremoz marble, form one of the best-preserved Roman ruins in Portugal.

(Continued from page 496)

Baroque

With independence from Spain re-established and the influence of the Inquisition on the wane, Portugal burst out in baroque fever – an architectural style that was exuberant, theatrical and fired straight at the senses. Nothing could rival the Manueline flourish, but the baroque style – named after the Portuguese word for a rough pearl, *barroco* – cornered the market in flamboyance. At its height in the 18th century (almost a century later than in Italy), it was characterised by curvaceous forms, huge monuments, spatially complex schemes and lots and lots and lots of gold.

Financed by the 17th-century gold and diamond discoveries in Brazil, and encouraged by the extravagant Dom João V, local and foreign (particularly Italian) artists created mind-bogglingly opulent masterpieces. Prodigious *talha dourada* (gilded woodwork) adorn church interiors all over the place, but it reached its most extreme in Aveiro's Convento de Jesus, Lisbon's Igreja de São Roque and Porto's Igreja de São Francisco.

The baroque of central and southern Portugal was more restrained. Examples include the chancel of Évora's cathedral and the massive Palácio Nacional de Mafra. Designed by the German architect João Frederico Ludovice to rival the palace-monastery of San Lorenzo de El Escorial (near Madrid), the Mafra version is relatively sober, apart from its size – which is such that at one point it had a workforce of 45,000, looked after by a police force of 7000.

Meanwhile, the Tuscan painter and architect Nicolau Nasoni (who settled in Porto around 1725) introduced a more ornamental baroque style to the north. Nasoni is responsible for Porto's Torre dos Clérigos and Igreja da Misericórdia, and the whimsical Palácio de Mateus near Vila Real (internationally famous as the image on Mateus rosé wine bottles).

In the mid-18th century a school of architecture evolved in Braga. Local artists such as André Soares built churches and palaces in a very decorative style, heavily influenced by Augsburg engravings from southern Germany. Soares' Casa do Raio, in Braga, and much of the monumental staircase of the nearby Bom Jesus do Monte, are typical examples of this period's ornamentation.

Only when the gold ran out did the baroque fad fade. At the end of the 18th century, architects flirted briefly with rococo (best exemplified by Mateus Vicente's Palácio de Queluz, begun in 1747, or the palace at Estói) before embracing neoclassicism.

Manueline Architecture

» Mosteiro dos Jerónimos, Belém

» Torre de Belém, Belém

» Chapter House, Tomar

» Igreja de Jesus, Setúbal

Baroque Architecture

» Palácio Nacional de Mafra

» Igreja de São Roque, Lisbon

» Igreja de São Francisco, Porto

» Palácio de Mateus, Vila Real

ART & ARCHITECTURE ARCHITECTURAL MOVEMENTS

PORTUGAL'S FAVOURITE ARCHITECT

One of Portugal's great contemporary architects, Álvaro Siza Vieira (born 1933) remains fairly unknown outside his home country. This is surprising given his loyal following in the architecture world, his long and distinguished career over the past five decades and his award-winning designs (which garnered him the coveted Pritzker Prize in 1992). Part of the reason perhaps is the deceptive simplicity of his minimalist creations.

On the surface, his work may seem less than dazzling. Stucco, stone, tile and glass are Siza Vieira's building materials of choice, and his designs might seem to the casual observer like low-rising boxlike structures. Yet, once inside, it's a different story: the whole trumps the parts, and everything – inside and out – morphs into a smoothly integrated work. Place means everything in Siza Vieira's work, with geography and climate carefully considered before any plans are laid, regardless of the size or scale of the project.

The Modern Era

The Salazar years favoured decidedly severe, Soviet-style, state commissions (eg Coimbra University's dull faculty buildings, which replaced elegant 18th-century neoclassical ones). Ugly buildings and apartment blocks rose on city outskirts. Notable exceptions dating from the 1960s are Lisbon's Palácio da Justiça in the Campolide district, and the gloriously sleek Museu Calouste Gulbenkian. The beautiful wood-panelled Galeto cafe-restaurant is a time capsule from this era.

The tendency towards urban mediocrity continued after the 1974 revolution, although architects such as Fernando Távora and Eduardo Souto de Moura have produced impressive schemes. Lisbon's postmodern Amoreiras shopping complex, by Tomás Taveira, is another striking contribution.

Portugal's greatest contemporary architect is Álvaro Siza Vieira. A believer in clarity and simplicity, his expressionist approach is reflected in projects such as the Pavilhão de Portugal for Expo 98, Porto's splendid Museu de Arte Contemporânea and the Igreja de Santa Maria at Marco de Canavezes, south of Amarante. He has also restored central Lisbon's historic Chiado shopping district with notable sensitivity, following a major fire in 1988.

Spanish architect Santiago Calatrava designed the lean organic monster Gare do Oriente for the Expo 98, architecture that is complemented by the work of many renowned contemporary artists. The interior is more state-of-the-art spaceship than station. In the same area lies Lisbon's architectural trailblazer the Parque das Nações, with a bevy of unique designs, including a riverfront park and Europe's largest aquarium. The longest bridge in Europe, the Ponte de Vasco da Gama built in 1998, stalks out across the river from nearby.

Since the turn of the millennium, Portugal has seen a handful of architecturally ambitious projects come to fruition. One of the grander projects is Rem Koolhaas' Casa da Música in Porto (2005). From a distance, the extremely forward-looking design appears like a solid white block of carefully cut crystal. Both geometric and defiantly asymmetrical, the building mixes elements of tradition (like *azulejos* hidden in one room) with high modernism (enormous curtains of corrugated glass flanking the concert stage).

Literary Giants

In 2010, Portugal lost one of its greatest writers when José Saramago died at the age of 87. Known for his discursive, cynical and darkly humorous novels, Saramago gained worldwide attention after winning the Nobel Prize in 1998. His best works mine the depths of the human experience and are often set in a uniquely Portuguese landscape. Sometimes his quasi-magical tales revolve around historic events – like the Christian Siege of Lisbon or the building of the Mafra Palace – while at other times he takes on grander topics (writing, for instance, of Jesus' life as a fallible human being) or even creates modern-day fables (in *Blindness*, everyone on earth suddenly goes blind). As a self-described libertarian communist, Saramago's political views sometimes landed him in trouble. After his name was removed from a list of nominees for a European literary prize, he went into self-imposed exile, spending the last years of his life in the Canary Islands.

Under the shadow of Saramago, António Lobo Antunes is Portugal's other literary great – and many of his admirers say the Nobel committee gave the prize to the wrong Portuguese writer. Antunes produces magical, fast-paced prose, often with dark undertones and vast historical sweeps; some critics compare his work to that of

Modern Architecture

» Casa da Música, Porto

» Boa Nova Casa-Chá, Porto

» Gare do Oriente, Lisbon

» Torre Vasco da Gama, Lisbon

Alvaro Siza (2001) by Brigitte Fleck is a handy monograph on the great contemporary architect, whose nationwide projects include the clean cubism of Porto's Museu de Arte Contemporânea.

The Sin of Father Amaro is a powerful 19th-century novel by Eça de Queirós. The book is set in Portugal, though it was relocated for a popular Mexican film, *El Crimen del Padre Amaro* (2002).

'There's no such man known as Fernando Pessoa', swore Alberto Caeiro, who, truth be told, didn't really exist himself. He was one of more than a dozen heteronyms (identities) adopted by Fernando Pessoa (1888–1935), Portugal's greatest 20th-century poet.

Heralded by literary critics as one of the icons of modernism, Pessoa was also among the stranger characters to wander the streets of Lisbon. He worked as a translator by day (having learned English while living in South Africa as a young boy), and wrote poetry by night – but not just Pessoa's poetry. He took on numerous personas, writing in entirely different styles, representing different philosophies, backgrounds and levels of mastery. Of Pessoa's four primary heteronyms, Alberto Caeiro was regarded as the great master by other heteronyms Alvaro de Campos and Ricardo Reis (Fernando Pessoa was the fourth heteronym, but his existence, as alluded to earlier, was denied by the other three). Any one style would have earned Pessoa renown as a major poet of his time, but considered together, the variety places him among the greats of modern literature.

Pessoa for many is inextricably linked to Lisbon. He spent his nights in cafes, writing, drinking and talking until late into the evening, and many of his works are set precisely in Lisbon's old neighbourhoods. Among Pessoa's phobias: lightning and having his photograph taken. You can see a few of the existing photos of him at the Café Martinho da Arcada, one of his regular haunts.

Despite his quirks and brilliance, Pessoa published very little in his lifetime, with his great work *Livro do Desassossego* (Book of Disquietude) only appearing in 1982, 50 years after it was written. In fact, the great bulk of Pessoa's work was discovered after his death: thousands of manuscript pages hidden away inside a wooden trunk. Scholars are still poring over his elusive works.

William Faulkner. Antunes' writing reflects his harrowing experience as a field doctor in Angola during Portugal's bloody colonial wars, and he often turns a critical gaze on Portuguese history – setting his novels around colonial wars, the dark days of dictatorship and the 1974 revolution. Slowly gaining an international following, Antunes is still active today, and many of his earlier novels are finally being translated into English.

Fine Arts

As Gothic art gave way to more humanistic Renaissance works, Portugal's 15th-century painters developed their own style. Led by the master Nuno Gonçalves, the *escola nacional* (national school) took religious subjects and grounded them against contemporary backgrounds. In Gonçalves' most famous painting, the panels of Santo Antonio, he includes a full milieu of Portuguese society – noblemen, Jews, fishermen, sailors, knights, priests, monks and beggars.

Some of Portugal's finest early paintings emerged from the 16th-century Manueline school. These artists, influenced by Flemish painters, developed a painting style known for its incredible delicacy, realism and luminous colours. The most celebrated painter of his time was Vasco Fernandes, known as Grão Vasco (1480-1543). His richly hued paintings (still striking five centuries later) hang in a museum dedicated to his work – as well as that of his Manueline school colleague Gaspar Vaz. Meanwhile sculptors including Diogo de Boitaca went wild with Portuguese seafaring fantasies and exuberant decoration on some of Portugal's icons.

The 17th century saw a number of talented Portuguese artists emerge. One of the best was the talented female painter Josefa de Óbidos, who

Baltasar and Blimunda (1982) is José Saramago's Nobel Prize–winning novel about the Mafra, a convent-palace dreamed up by size-junkies and compulsive builders.

enjoyed success as a female artist – an extreme rarity in those days. Josefa's paintings were unique in their personal, sympathetic interpretations of religious subjects and for their sense of innocence. Although she studied at an Augustine convent as a young girl, she left without taking the vows and settled in Óbidos (where she got her nickname). Still she maintained close ties to the church, which provided many of her commissions, and remained famously chaste until her death in 1684. Josefa left one of the finest legacies of work of any Portuguese painter. She excelled in richly coloured still lifes and detailed religious works, ignoring established iconography.

In the 19th century, naturalism was the dominant trend, with a handful of innovators pushing Portuguese art in new directions. Columbano Bordalo Pinheiro, who hailed from a family of artists, was a seminal figure among the Portuguese artists of his time. He played a prominent role in the Leã d'Ouro, a group of distinguished artists, writers and intellectuals who gathered in the capital and were deeply involved in the aesthetic trends of the day. A prolific artist, Pinheiro painted some of the luminaries of his day, including the novelist Eça de Queirós and Teófilo Braga (a celebrated writer who later became president of the early republic). One of his best-known works is a haunting portrait of the poet Antero de Quental, who later committed suicide.

Building on the works of the naturalists, Amadeo de Souza-Cardoso lived a short but productive life, experimenting with new techniques emerging in Europe. Raised in a sleepy village outside of Amarante, he studied architecture at the Academia de Belas Artes in Lisbon, but soon dropped out and moved to Paris. There, he found his calling as a painter, and mingled with the leading artists and writers of the time, including Amedeo Modigliani, Gertrude Stein, Max Jacob and many others. He experimented with Impressionism and later cubism and futurism, and created a captivating body of work, though is little known outside of Portugal.

José Sobral de Almada Negreiros delved even deeper into futurism, inspired by the Italian futurist Filippo Tommaso Marinetti. His work encompassed richly hued portraits with abstract geometrical details (such as his famous portrait of Fernando Pessoa from 1954), and he was also a sculptor, writer and critic. He managed to walk a fine line during the Salazar regime, creating large-scale murals by public commission as well as socially engaged works critical of Portuguese society.

Top Museums for Portuguese Art

» Museu Nacional do Azulejo, Lisbon

» Casa das Histórias, Cascais

» Museu Nacional de Arte Antiga, Lisbon

» Museu Amadeo de Souza-Cardoso, Amarante

» Museu Grão Vasco, Viseu

THE EVOCATIVE WORLD OF PAULA REGO

The conservative Salazar years of the mid-20th century didn't create the ideal environment to nurture contemporary creativity, and many artists left the country. These include Portugal's best-known modern artist, Paula Rego, who was born in Lisbon in 1935 but has been a resident of the UK since 1951. Rego's signature style developed around fairy-tale paintings given a nightmarish twist. Her works deal in ambiguity and psychological and sexual tension, such as *The Family* (1988), where a seated businessman is either being tortured or smothered with affection by his wife and daughter. Domination, fear, sexuality and grief are all recurring themes in Rego's paintings, and the mysterious and sinister atmosphere, heavy use of chiaroscuro (stark contrasting of light and shade) and strange distortion of scale are reminiscent of surrealists Max Ernst and Giorgio de Chirico.

Rego, now in her 70s, is considered one of the great early champions for painting from a female perspective and she continues to add to a substantial volume of work. Her acclaim also continues to grow, particularly with the opening of a new museum in Cascais that showcases her work.

The Art of the Tile

Portugal's favourite decorative art is easy to spot. Polished painted tiles called *azulejos* (after the Arabic *al zulaycha,* meaning polished stone) cover everything from churches to train stations. The Moors introduced the art, having picked it up from the Persians, but the Portuguese wholeheartedly adopted it.

Portugal's earliest 16th-century tiles are Moorish, from Seville. These were decorated with interlocking geometric or floral patterns (figurative representations aren't an option for Muslim artists for religious reasons). After the Portuguese captured Ceuta in Morocco in 1415, they began exploring the art themselves. The 16th-century Italian invention of majolica, in which colours are painted directly onto wet clay over a layer of white enamel, gave works a frescolike brightness and kicked off the Portuguese *azulejo* love affair.

The earliest home-grown examples, polychrome and geometric, date from the 1580s, and may be seen in churches such as Lisbon's Igreja de São Roque, providing an ideal counterbalance to fussy, gold-heavy baroque.

The late 17th century saw a fashion for huge panels, depicting everything from saints to seascapes. As demand grew, mass production became necessary and the Netherlands' blue-and-white Delft tiles started appearing.

Portuguese tile-makers rose to the challenge of this influx, and the splendid work of virtuoso Portuguese masters António de Oliveira Bernardes and his son Policarpo in the 18th century springs from this competitive creativity. You can see their work in Évora, in the impressive Igreja de São João.

By the end of the 1700s, industrial-scale manufacture began to affect quality, coupled with the massive demand for tiles after the 1755 Lisbon earthquake. (Tiling answered the need for decoration, and was cheap and practical – a solution for a population that had felt the ground move beneath its feet.)

From the late 19th century, the art nouveau and art deco movements took *azulejos* by storm, providing fantastic facades and interiors for shops, restaurants and residential buildings. Today, *azulejos* still coat contemporary life, and you can explore the latest in *azulejos* in the Lisbon metro. Maria Keil designed 19 of the stations, from the 1950s onwards – look out for stunning block-type prints at Intendente (considered her masterpiece) and Anjos. Oriente also showcases extraordinary contemporary work by artists from five continents.

The Lisbon metro is not just about transport – it's an art gallery, showcasing the best of Portuguese contemporary art and architecture, with especially wonderful *azulejos*. Check out Metro Lisboa's website at www.metrolisboa.pt.

Portuguese Decorative Tiles (1998) by Rioletta Sabo is an all-out wallow in the dazzling colours and diversity of Portugal's favourite wall-covering.

ART & ARCHITECTURE FINE ARTS

Saudade: the Portuguese Blues

The Portuguese psyche is a complicated thing, particularly when one tries to comprehend those not easily translatable concepts like *saudade*. In its purest form, *saudade* is the nostalgic, often deeply melancholic longing for something. The object of one's longing can be a person, a place or just about anything that's no longer obtainable – youth, a dead loved one, a childhood home. It's an evocative, deep-rooted sadness for which there is often no remedy.

Scholars are unable to pinpoint exactly when the term first arose. Some trace it back to the grand voyages during the Age of Discoveries, when sailors, captains and explorers spent many months out at sea, and gave voice to the longing for the lives they left behind. Yet even before the epic sea voyages across the ocean, Portugal was a nation of seafarers, and *saudade* probably arose from those on terra firma – the women who longed for the men who spent endless days out at sea, some of whom never returned.

Naturally, emigration is also deeply linked to *saudade*. Long one of Europe's poorest peoples, the Portuguese were often driven by hardship to seek better lives abroad. Until recently, this usually meant the men leaving behind their families to travel to Northern Europe or America to find work. Families sometimes waited years before being reunited, with emigrants facing years of experiencing the painful longing for their homeland – for the familiar faces, the foods and village life. Many did eventually return, but of course things had changed and so *saudade* reappeared, this time in the form of longing for the way things were in the past.

No matter its roots, *saudade* remains deeply intertwined with Portuguese identity. The elusive emotion has played a starring role in some of Portugal's great works of art – in film, literature and most importantly music.

A Nation of Emigrants

The great discoveries of Portuguese seafarers had profound effects on the country's demographics. With the birth and expansion of empire, Portuguese settled in trading posts in Africa and Asia, but the colony of Brazil drew the biggest numbers of early Portuguese emigrants. They cleared the land (harvesting the Brazil wood that gave the colony its name), set up farms, and set about the slow, steady task of nation-building – with help of course from the millions of enslaved blacks stolen from Africa. Numbers vary widely, but an estimated half a million Portuguese settled in Brazil during the colonial period, prior to independence in 1822, and over 400,000 flooded in during the second half of the 19th century.

DOM JOÃO VI

The most famous Portuguese emigrant to Brazil was the king himself. When Napoleon invaded in 1807, the royal family and thousands of their retinue fled to Brazil, where they installed themselves in Rio de Janeiro. Many royal retainers never returned home; Dom João VI returned only in 1822.

By the 1900s, Portuguese began emigrating in large numbers to other parts of the world. The US and Canada received over half a million immigrants, with huge numbers heading to France, Germany, Venezuela and Argentina. The 1960s saw another upsurge of emigrants, as young men fled the country in order to avoid the draft that would send them to fight bloody colonial wars in Africa. The 1974 revolution also preceded a big exodus as those associated with the Salazar regime went abroad rather than face reprisals.

What all these emigrants had in common was the deep sadness of leaving their homeland to struggle in foreign lands. Those left behind were also in a world of heartache – wives left alone to raise children, villages deserted of young men, families torn apart. The numbers are staggering: over three million emigrants between 1890 and 1990; no other European country aside from Ireland lost as many people to emigration.

Saudade in Literature

One of the first great Portuguese works of literature that explores the theme of *saudade* is *Os Lusiadas* (The Lusiads, aka The Portuguese). Luiz Vaz de Camões mixes mythology with historical events in his great verse epic about the Age of Discoveries of the 15th and 16th centuries. The heroic adventurer Vasco da Gama and other explorers strive for glory but many never return, facing hardship (sea monsters, treacherous kings) along the way. First-hand experience informed Camões' work. He served in the overseas militia, lost an eye in Ceuta in a battle with the Moors, served prison time in Portugal and survived a shipwreck in the Mekong (swimming ashore with his unfinished manuscript held aloft, according to legend).

The great 19th-century Portuguese writer Almeida Garrett wrote an even more compelling take on the Age of Discoveries. In his book *Camões*, a biography of the poet, he describes the longings Camões felt toward Portugal while in exile. He also captured the greater sense of *saudade* that so many felt as Portugal's empire crumbled in the century following the great explorations.

More recent writers also explore the notion of *saudade*, though take radically different approaches from their predecessors. Contemporary writer António Lobo Antunes deconstructs *saudade* in cynical tales that expose the nostalgic longing for something as being a form of neurotic self-delusion. In *The Return of the Caravels* (1988), he turns the discovery

Goa, India, still has vestiges of its past as a Portuguese colony. In Margão, the largest city in Goa, one finds a street named 'Rua das Saudades'. On this street, one finds a Christian cemetery, a Muslim cemetery and a Hindu cremation ground – Saudade being the most apt name for a street where people come to long for those who've died.

Saudade of the Jews

Until the end of the 15th century, Jews enjoyed a prominent place in Portuguese society. The treasurer of King Afonso V (1432–81) was Jewish, as were others who occupied diplomatic posts and worked as trade merchants, physicians and cartographers. Jews from other countries were even welcomed in Portugal, such as those expelled from Spain in 1492. Eventually, pressure from the church and from neighbouring Spain forced the king's hand, and in 1497 Manuel I decreed that all Jews convert to Christianity or leave the country. A catalogue of horrors followed, including the massacre of thousands of Jews in 1506 by mobs run riot and two centuries of bloody inquisition that kicked off in 1536.

Aside from a secretive Crypto-Jewish group in Belmonte that managed to successfully preserve their faith, the Judaic community slowly withered and perished. Those who converted felt the heart-rending *saudade* of deep loss: essentially the loss of one's identity. Once flourishing Jewish neighbourhoods died as neighbours went into exile or perhaps suffered arrest, torture and even execution. The personal losses paralleled the end of a flourishing and tolerant period in Portugal's history, and effectively ended Jewish presence in Portugal.

myth on its head when, four centuries after da Gama's voyage, the great explorers, through some strange time warp, become entangled with the *retornados* (who returned to Portugal in the 1970s, after the loss of the country's African empire) as the Renaissance era achievements collapse in the poor, grubby, lower-class neighbourhoods of Lisbon.

Saudade in Film

Portugal's oldest and most prolific film-maker, Manoel de Oliveira, is known for his carefully crafted, if slow-moving, films that delve deep into the world of *saudade* – of growing old, unrequited loves and longing for things that no longer exist. In *Voyage to the Beginning of the World* (1998), several companions make a nostalgic tour through the rugged landscapes and traditional villages of the north – one in search of a past that he knows only in his dreams (having heard only of his ancestral land from his Portuguese-born father), and another haunted by a world that no longer exists (the places of his childhood uprooted). Past and present, nostalgia and reality collide in this quiet, meditative film. It stars a frail, 72-year-old Marcello Mastroianni as Oliveira's alter ego, in the actor's final film before he died.

One of the finest love letters to the capital is the sweet, meandering *Lisbon Story* (1994) directed by German filmmaker Wim Wenders. The story follows a sound engineer who goes in search of a missing director, discovering the city through the footage his friend left behind. Carefully crafted scenes conjure up the mystery and forlorn beauty of Lisbon (and other parts of Portugal, including a wistful sequence on the dramatic cliffs of Cabo Espichel). *Saudade* here explores many different realms, inspired in large part by the ethereal soundtrack by Madredeus – band members also play supporting roles in the film.

Fado

'I don't sing fado. It sings me.'

Amália Rodrigues

Portugal's most famous style of music, fado (Portuguese for 'fate') couldn't really exist without *saudade*. These melancholic songs are dripping with emotion – and revel in stories of the painful twists and turns of fate, of unreachable distant lovers, fathomless yearning for the homeland, and wondrous days that have come and gone. The emotional quality of the singing plays just as an important role as technical skills, helping fado to reach across linguistic boundaries. Listening to fado is perhaps the easiest way of understanding *saudade*, in all its evocative variety.

Although fado is something of a national treasure – in 2009 Portugal even put in an application to have it named a Unesco 'intangible heritage' – it's really the music of Lisbon. (In the university town of Coimbra, fado exists in a different, slightly more cerebral form: it's exclusively men, often students or alumni, who sing of love, bohemian life and the city itself.) No one quite knows its origins, though African and Brazilian rhythms, Moorish chants and the songs of Provençal troubadors may have influenced the sound. What is clear is that by the 19th century, fado could be heard all over the traditional working-class neighbourhoods of Mouraria and the Alfama, usually in brothels and seedy taverns. It was the anthem of the poor, and maintained an unsavoury reputation until the late 19th century when the upper classes took an interest in the music and brought it into the mainstream.

Fado remained an obscure, mostly local experience until the 20th century, when it received national and later international attention. One

---

The national music of Cape Verde, a former Portuguese colony, is *morna*, a distant cousin of fado, with plaintive songs often revolving around themes of homesickness and deep longing. Renowned 'barefoot diva' Cesária Évora is the country's prime *morna* ambassador; her song 'Sodade' (Creole for 'saudade') is one of many poignant hits.

MORNA

In Brazil, 30 January is set aside as the *Dia de Saudade* (Saudade Day). It's a fine day to engage in a bit of nostalgic longing for past lovers, distant homelands and better days.

Brazilian Saudade & Bossa Nova

Brazilian identity is also deeply connected to *saudade*, which is not surprising given the influence Portugal has had on the country – nearly every inhabitant in Brazil can trace Portuguese roots somewhere in the family tree. In Brazil, *saudade* means much the same thing, and it has played a role in shaping the country's music – in particular, bossa nova. The 1958 hit 'Chega de Saudade' (often poorly translated as 'No More Blues') by legendary song-writing team Tom Jobim and Vinícius de Moraes is considered one of the first bossa nova songs ever recorded. In it, the singer pines for his lover who has left him, and commands his sadness to go out and bring her back. Melancholic chords and a slow, wistful singing style are hallmarks here, as they are of nearly all bossa nova tunes. And even if you can't understand Portuguese, you'll still feel the sadness and deep sense of loss.

singer who played a major role in its popularisation was Amália Rodrigues, the 'queen of fado', who became a household name in the 1940s. Born to a poor family in 1920, Amália took the music from the tavern to the concert hall and then into households via radio, and onto film screens (starring in the 1947 film *Capas Negras*). She had some of Portugal's best poets and writers of the day writing songs for her. Yet, along the way, she had her share of ups and downs – depression, illness, failed love affairs – and her heart-rending fado was more than an abstraction.

Amália enjoyed wide acclaim, although her reputation was sullied following the 1974 revolution – when she was criticised for tacitly supporting the Salazar regime (although there is little evidence of that). Fado's popularity slid off the map in the post-revolution days when the Portuguese were eager to make a clean break from the past. (Salazar spoke of throwing the masses the three F's – fado, football and Fátima – to keep them happily occupied.) The 1990s however saw a resurgence of fado's popularity, with the opening of new fado houses and the emergence of new fado voices. Amália's reputation was also rehabilitated. Upon her death at age 79 in 1999, Portugal declared three days of national mourning and suspended the general election campaign in her honour. Today she is buried in the National Pantheon.

While fado may bring to mind dark bars of the Salazar years, this is not a musical form stuck in time. Contemporary performers and exponents of a new fado style include the dynamic *fadista* Mísia, who broke new ground by experimenting with full band instrumentation. The Mozambique-born singer Mariza has earned accolades for her extraordinary voice and fresh eclectic approach. She continues to break new ground in albums like *Terra* (2008) that bring in world music – African rhythms, flamenco, Latin sounds and jazz. Another one to watch is Carminho, a young singer with a powerful and mournful voice. Fado runs deep in her veins – her mother was the owner of one of Lisbon's most traditional fado houses (now closed), where as a young girl she heard the best *fadistas* of the time. Her first album *Fado* (2009) is superb. The men aren't outdone: one of the great male voices in traditional fado these days is Camané.

Fados are traditionally sung by one performer accompanied by a 12-string Portuguese *guitarra* (a pear-shaped guitar). When two *fadistas* perform, they sometimes engage in *desgarrada,* a bit of improvisational one-upmanship where the singers challenge and play off one another. At fado houses, there are usually a number of singers, each one traditionally singing three songs. For the lowdown on the live fado scene in Lisbon, see p97.

For more on Amália, check out the fine documentary *The Art of Amália* (2000), directed by Bruno de Almeida. The more recent biopic *Amália* (2008) by Carlo Coelho da Silva provides an in-depth portrait of Rodrigues that few ever saw.

The film *Fados* (2007) is Spanish director Carlos Saura's love letter to the great Portuguese music. The film features the singing of fado legends like Camané and Mariza as well as genre-defying singers not often associated with the art – Brazilian singers Caetano Veloso and Chico Buarque, among others.

Spectator Sports

In Portugal sport means football. The season lasts from September to May, with every sizeable village and town fielding a team to compete at the local or regional level.

Portugal's national team, the Selecção Nacional, appears regularly in international tournaments, and has carved a name for itself as a contender. As of 2010, the team enjoyed a FIFA ranking of third internationally – its best ranking ever – which surprised many in Portugal and beyond.

The only other event that draws big crowds is bullfighting, which differs considerably from the Spanish version. Here the most important aspect of the fight happens on horseback, and the bull is not killed in the ring.

The website www.portugoal.net has excellent info on Portugal's football clubs, player stats and team standings as well as in-depth articles on Portuguese players abroad.

STATS

Football

Football is not a game: it's a national obsession. Life – and often the national economy – come to a near standstill during any big match, with bar and restaurant TVs showing nothing else. During big events, like the World Cup and the European Football Championship, many towns put up big-screens TVs on the main plazas so hundreds can gather to watch the games.

Boozy post-match celebrations are a tradition in themselves, with fans taking to the streets, honking car horns, setting off fireworks and gridlocking entire town centres until the wee hours.

Football madness well and truly took hold in 2004 when Portugal hosted the European Football Championship, the biggest sporting event ever staged there. Sports authorities were counting on the tournament to provide a big shot in the arm for Portuguese football, and they got it. Local clubs, with mounting debts and ageing stadiums, had long watched the country's star players earn a fortune abroad, but sure enough, the authorities set about building and sprucing up Portuguese stadiums and building vital new transport links to the venues. Unfortunately, many of these new and upgraded stadiums sit more than half empty during games, and local teams are finding them too costly to maintain.

VOLTA A PORTUGAL

First held in 1927, the Volta a Portugal is one of Europe's oldest cycling events. The 10-stage tour happens over two weeks in August. Once a major draw for top international cyclists, the tour has waned in popularity in recent years, largely owing to its timing – sandwiched between the bigger-purse events of the Tour de France and the Vuelta a España. The course changes periodically, but its most recent incarnation kicked off in Viseu and ran some 1600km over 11 days of racing, with the final day featuring a blazing finale from Sintra into Lisbon.

With government coffers empty in the wake of the global financial crisis, city officials are pressed to find ways to cut ballooning deficits. One item under consideration in several townships is the demolition of little-used stadiums that were built by Portugal to host the 2004 Euro championship. Portugal spent €600 million to build or upgrade several arenas, many of which fill to only about 25% capacity during league games.

The cities of Aveiro and Leira cite monthly maintenance costs of €1.2 million, a substantial investment to cash-strapped communities. The team Beira Mar can't afford the upkeep of the 31,000-seat, €62 million Estádio Municipal de Aveiro. Likewise, the team União de Leira isn't earning enough revenue to maintain its 30,000-seat, €90 million stadium. Supporters of the demolition plan say the stadiums are a symbol of the country's wasteful spending and shouldn't have been built in the first place.

Needless to say, tearing down stadiums isn't a well-liked idea by residents in the afflicted towns, and local officials are seeking creative ways to keep them intact – from hosting concerts and corporate events, to renting out space to schools and businesses.

In the end, though, economic realities may trump local nostalgia, and the wrecking ball may be hard to avoid.

The most recent bout of football hysteria happened in 2010, as Portugal competed in the FIFA World Cup. Although they almost failed to qualify, they were ranked 10th going into the tournament, and there were high hopes that the team could pull off a dark-horse victory. Unfortunately, the team gave a rather lacklustre performance, with a scoreless draw in games against Côte d'Ivoire and Brazil. They did however pummel 105th-ranked North Korea 7–0, a shock for the communist nation, particularly as it was allegedly the first match aired live in the nation's history.

After the round of 16, Portugal played against old archrival Spain, who knocked them out of the tournament (and went on to become World Cup champions) in a 1–0 loss. Star player Cristiano Ronaldo disappointed fans with a weak showing at the World Cup, and head coach Carlos Queiroz also came in for a drubbing, particularly following the loss to Spain. (Ronaldo publicly blamed Queiroz for the loss; an incensed Queiroz said he was welcome to leave if he felt he was bigger than the team.)

On a national level, the story of Portuguese football is mainly about Lisbon and Porto. Although 16 teams compete for top honours each year in the Liga Portuguesa, the big three – Lisbon's Sporting (Sporting Clube de Portugal), Benfica (Sport Lisboa e Benfica) and Porto's FC Porto (Futebol Clube do Porto) – have among them won every national championship but two since the 1920s (Porto's upstart Boavista Futebol Clube briefly broke the spell in 2001). Regional titles haven't been lacking either for the country's top teams, with FC Porto picking up the 2004 European Champions League title.

Despite long-standing rivalries, Portugal and Spain really are good neighbours at heart. In 2009, Spain and Portugal joined forces and submitted a bid to co-host the 2018 FIFA World Cup. Portugal has never hosted, although Spain played host nation to the big event in 1982.

Bullfighting

Love it or loathe it, bullfighting is a national institution. First recorded in Portugal a staggering 2000 years ago by a Roman historian, it was honed in the 12th century, when the *tourada* (bullfight) became a way to maintain military fitness and prepare nobles for battle on horseback. But the gory death of a nobleman in 1799 resulted in a less bloodthirsty version, in which the bull's horns are covered in leather or capped with metal balls and the animal is not killed publicly.

A *tourada* starts with an enraged bull charging into the ring towards a *cavaleiro*, a dashing horseman dressed in 18th-century finery and plumed tricorn hat. The *cavaleiro* sizes up the animal as his team of *peões de brega* (footmen) distract and provoke the bull with capes.

WORLD CUP

RAGS TO RICHES

In 2009, Portugal's team captain and star player Cristiano Ronaldo (b 1985) became the world's most expensive football player after Real Madrid paid the staggering sum of €96 million for the Portuguese winger. In addition, Ronaldo's six-year contract amounts to €13 million per year. The multimillionaire and widely touted playboy has certainly come a long way from his roots growing up in a poor community on the Portuguese island of Madeira.

The youngest of four children born to a working-class family, Ronaldo was named after US President Ronald Reagan, and lived in a tiny tin-roof shack in the parish of Santo Antonio overlooking Funchal and the Atlantic Ocean. He was only 11 when he left home to pursue his dream of playing professionally for Sporting Lisbon. After maturing, he quickly rose to prominence. Ronaldo became Manchester United's first Portuguese player ever, when at age 18, he signed for some €17 million in 2003. He set out to prove his worth, racking up player-of-the-year awards and helping Man U win the Premier League in 2007, 2008 and 2009.

Paralleling his football success, life has changed dramatically for his family back home. His mother, who once struggled to support herself and her family as a cleaner, now lives in the affluent district of Livramento in Funchal. Ronaldo has also opened a boutique with his sister, called CR7 (Ronaldo's initials and his number for Man U).

Meanwhile, Ronaldo's family keeps growing. Less than a week after Portugal's exit from the 2010 World Cup, Ronaldo announced that he had fathered a baby boy and would have sole guardianship of the child, as agreed with the baby's mother, who wanted her identity to remain confidential. Rumours have since swirled regarding the mother's identity and the specifics of the arrangement.

Then, with superb horsemanship, he gallops within inches of the bull's horns and plants several *bandarilha* (spears) in the creature's neck.

The next phase, the *pega,* features eight brave (read: foolhardy) young *forcados* dressed in breeches, white stockings and short jackets, who face the weakened bull bare-handed (Portuguese-American *forcados* in the US call themselves the 'suicide squad'). The leader swaggers towards the bull, provoking it to charge. Bearing the brunt of the attack, he throws himself onto the animal's head and grabs the horns while his mates rush in to grab the beast, often being tossed in all directions. Their success wraps up the contest and the cows are sent in to the arena to lure the bull out. Though Portuguese bullfighting rules prohibit a public kill, the animals are killed after the show by a professional butcher – you just don't witness the final blow. On very rare occasions, bulls who show particular bravado are sent out to pasture for breeding.

Despite its long history in the nation, bullfighting is waning in popularity. In 2009 Viana do Castelo became the first city in Portugal to ban bullfighting, and the mayor announced the arena would be torn down to build a cultural centre. Other municipalities followed suit and a handful of towns, including Sintra, Cascais and Braga have banned the practice. In the central part of the country, bullfighting remains popular despite pressure from international animal-welfare organisations and Portugal's own antibullfighting lobby, the Liga Portuguesa dos Direitos dos Animais (LPDA; Portuguese League for Animal Rights).

The season runs from March or April to October. The most traditional contests take place in bull-breeding Ribatejo province, especially in Santarém during the June fair, and in the otherwise-unexceptional Vila Franca de Xira during the town's July and October festivals. Frequent *touradas* in the Algarve and Lisbon are more tourist-oriented. There are also unusual festivals like the Vaca das Cordas, where a bull on a rope runs wild through the streets of Ponte de Lima.

Since traditional bullfighting is outlawed in the US, Portuguese emigrants in central California invented a bloodless bullfight using Velcro-tipped spears. Read more on this bizarre sport at www.ranchcardoso.biz.

Survival Guide

Directory A–Z

Accommodation

There's an excellent range of good-value, inviting accommodation in Portugal. Budget places provide some of Western Europe's cheapest rooms, while you'll find atmospheric accommodation in farms, palaces, castles, mansions and rustic town houses – usually giving good mileage for your euro.

Turismos (tourist offices) hold lists of accommodation and *quartos* (private rooms), but they overlook anywhere not registered with them – which can sometimes be excellent options. The government grades accommodation with a star system that's bewildering and best ignored. Good websites for browsing include www.manorhouses.com and www.innsofportugal.com.

Prices

In popular tourist destinations, prices rise and fall with the seasons. Mid-June to mid-September are firmly high season (book ahead); May to mid-June and mid-September to October are midseason; and other times are low season, when you

can get some really good deals. Outside the resorts, prices don't vary much between seasons.

In the big Algarve resorts, you'll pay the highest premium for rooms from mid-July to the end of August, with slightly lower prices from June to mid-July and all of September, and substantially less (as much as 50%) if you travel between November and April. For example, a room that is listed as €120 in July may cost €160 in August, €100 in June and September, €85 in May and October, and €70 during the rest of the year. Note that a handful of places close in winter.

We list July prices throughout this book. Unless otherwise indicated, rooms have en-suite bathroom.

In general, we categorise hotels or guest houses costing less than €50 for a double room as budget accommodation, and include camping grounds and hostels in this category. In some budget places, you might have to share a bathroom.

In the middle range, a double room runs from €50 to €100. For this you'll almost always get an en-suite bathroom, TV (sometimes

satellite), often air-conditioning and telephone.

In the top end of the lodging category you'll pay anywhere from €100 to €300, with the odd stratospheric place where you can chill by the pool with visiting royals or football stars.

We list rack rates for places in this book, but often you won't be charged the full whack, particularly if you do some searching online. Most *pousadas* are cheaper during the week; they have lots of discount deals and prices.

Your bargaining power depends on what season it is and how much choice you have. If it's low season or echoingly empty, people will usually drop prices without you even needing to ask. If you plan to stay more than a few days, it's always worth inquiring whether lower rates are available for longer stays. If you're looking for somewhere cheaper than the room you have been shown, just say so; frequently the management will show you the cheaper rooms they previously forgot to mention.

Camping & Caravan Parks

Camping is popular in Portugal, with many excellent camping grounds, often in good locations and near beaches. Prices for camp sites usually range from about €3.20 to €5 per adult, around €3 to 4.50 per tent and €3 to €5 per car.

The swishest camping grounds are run by **Orbitur** (www.orbitur.pt) but there are lots of other good companies, such as **Inatel** (www.inatel.pt). Most towns have municipal camp sites, which vary in quality.

For detailed listings of camp sites nationwide, pick up the **Roteiro Campista** (www.roteiro-campista.pt; €7), updated annually and sold at *turismos* and bookshops. It contains details of most Portuguese camping grounds, with maps and directions.

The Camping Card International (CCI) can be presented instead of your passport at camping grounds affiliated with the Federation Internationale de Camping et de Caravanning (FICC). It guarantees third-party insurance for any damage you may cause and can be good for discounts. Sometimes certain camp sites run by local camping clubs may be used by foreigners *only* if they have a CCI, so it's handy if you plan to camp a lot. The CCI is available to members of most national automobile clubs, except those in the USA. It is also issued by FICC affiliates such as the UK's **Camping & Caravanning Club** (www.campingandcaravanningclub.co.uk) and the **Federação de Campismo e Montanhismo de Portugal** (☎218 126 890; www.fcmportugal.com; Av Coronel Eduardo Galhardo 24D, Lisbon).

Guest Houses

Guest houses are small-scale budget or midrange accommodation, with the personal feel that can be lacking in larger hotels. The best ones are often better than the cheapest hotels. High-season *pensão* (guest house) rates are roughly €50 to €80 for a double.

Residenciais (guest houses) may be more expensive, and usually include breakfast. The title *residencial* means that the venue hasn't received the official approval that a *pensão* has, but this doesn't mean that it's a bad place to stay. *Hospedarias* and *casas de hóspedes* (boarding houses) are usually cheaper, with shared bathrooms.

Hostels

Portugal has a growing number of hostels, particularly in Lisbon, where the hostel scene has exploded in recent years. Although the accommodation is basic, hostels offer excellent value and are often in lovely settings or historic buildings. Many of the hostels outside of Lisbon are part of the *pousadas da juventude* (youth hostels) network affiliated with Hostelling International (HI).

High-season dorm beds cost around €20. Most hostels also offer simple doubles with shared bathrooms and some have small apartments. Bed linen and breakfast are usually included in the price. Standard features are kitchens, lounges with wi-fi access, and computers for guest use; some have swimming pools, such as those in Alcoutim and Portimão.

In summer you'll need to reserve, especially for doubles. Contact **Movijovem** (☎707 203 030; www.pousadasjuventude.pt; Rua Lúcio de Azevedo 27, Lisbon).

If you don't have a HI card, you can get a guest card, which requires six stamps (€2 per time) – one from each hostel you stay at – after which you have paid for your membership.

Most hostels open 8am to midnight, though some are open 24 hours (nearly all in Lisbon stay open 24 hours). Staff will usually let you stash your bags and return at check-in time (usually 8am to noon and 6pm to midnight).

Pousadas

In 1942 the government started the **pousadas network** (www.pousadas.pt), turning castles, monasteries and palaces into luxurious hotels, roughly divided into rural and historic options. July prices range from €130 to €250; prices in August are €10 to €20 more. You can pick up a comprehensive list at any of the sites. You may be able to take advantage of frequent special offers, such as reduced prices for those aged over 55.

Private Rooms

In coastal resorts, mostly in summer, you can often rent a *quarto* in a private house. These usually have a shared bathroom, are cheap and clean, and might remind you of a stay with an elderly aunt. If you're not approached by an owner or don't spot a sign *(se aluga quarto)*, try the local *turismo* for a list. Prices are generally from €35 to €45 per double.

Rental Accommodation

Plenty of villas and cottages are available for rent. The site www.chooseportugal.com lists hundreds of private houses and apartments for rent, with the majority found in the Algarve. You'll find characterful houses in the north on www.casasnocampo.net.

Turihab Properties

These charming properties are part of a government scheme, either Turismo de Habitação, Turismo Rural or Agroturismo, through which you can stay in a farmhouse, manor house, country estate or rustic cottage as the owner's guest.

Divided into historic, heritage and rustic categories, these properties provide some of the best bargains in Portugal. Though they are more expensive than some other options, you will usually be staying in splendid surroundings. A high-season double room ranges from

---

BOOK YOUR STAY ONLINE

For more reviews by Lonely Planet authors, check out hotels.lonelyplanet.com/. You'll find independent reviews, as well as recommendations on the best places to stay. Best of all, you can book online.

€70 to €120. Many properties have swimming pools and usually include breakfast (often with fresh local produce).

Turismos keep detailed information of Turihab properties in the area. You can also look them up online at www.turihab.pt or www.solaresdeportugal.pt.

Business Hours

Reviews won't list operating hours unless they deviate from the following normal opening times:

Sights 10am–12.30pm & 2–5pm Tue–Sun

Restaurants noon–3pm & 7–10pm

Cafés 9am–7pm

Shops 9.30am–noon & 2–7pm Mon–Fri, 10am–1pm Sat

Bars 7pm–2am

Nightclubs 11pm–4am Thu–Sat

Malls 10am–10pm

Banks 8.30am–3pm Mon–Fri

Post offices 8.30am–4pm Mon–Fri

Children

The great thing about Portugal for children is its manageable size and the range of sights and activities on offer. There's so much to explore and to catch the imagination, even for those with very short attention spans. The Portuguese are generally quite laid-back about breast-feeding as long as some attempt at discretion is made. Formula (including organic brands) and disposable nappies (diapers) are widely available at most pharmacies and grocery stores.

The Algarve has to be the best kid-pleasing destination in Portugal, with endless beaches, zoos, water parks, horse riding and boat trips. Kids will also be happy in

PRACTICALITIES

» Portugal uses the metric system for weights and measures. (See the inside front cover for a metric conversions chart.) Decimals are indicated by commas, thousands by points.

» The electrical current is 220V, 50Hz. Plugs are rounded with two prongs (sometimes with a third middle prong), as used elsewhere in Continental Europe.

» Portugal uses the PAL video system, incompatible with both the French SECAM system and the North American NTSC system.

» Main newspapers include *Diário de Noticias*, *Público*, *Jornal de Noticias* and the tabloid bestseller *Correio da Manhã*.

» English-language media includes the long-running daily the *Portugal News* (www.theportugalnews.com) and the weekly *Algarve Resident* (www.portugalresident.com).

» TV channels in Portugal include Rádio Televisão Portuguesa (RTP-1 and RTP-2), Sociedade Independente (SIC) and TV Independente (TV1), with RTP-2 providing the best selection of foreign films and world news coverage. Other stations fill the airwaves with a mix of Portuguese and Brazilian soaps, game shows and dubbed or subtitled foreign movies.

» Portugal's national radio stations are comprised of the state-owned Rádiodifusão Portuguesa (RDP), which runs the stations Antena 1, 2 and 3 and plays Portuguese broadcasts and evening music (Lisbon frequencies are 95.7, 94.4 and 100.3). For English-language radio there is the BBC World Service (Lisbon 90.2) and Voice of America (VOA), or a few Algarve-based stations, such as Kiss (95.8 and 101.2).

Lisbon and its outlying provinces. There are trams, puppet shows, a huge aquarium, a toy museum, horse-drawn carriages, castles, parks and playgrounds.

As for fairy-tale places, Portugal has these in spades. Some children enjoy visiting churches if they can light a candle. They'll enjoy the make-believe of the castles and palaces sprinkled about the country.

In towns, hop-on, hop-off tours can be good for saving small legs, and miniature resort trains often cause more excitement than you

would have thought possible.

Kids will like Portugal almost as much as they like sweets, and they are welcome just about everywhere. They can even get literary: Nobel Prize–winner José Saramago, the great Portuguese novelist, has written a charming children's fable, *The Tale of the Unknown Island*, available in English. For an entertaining guide packed with information and tips, turn to Lonely Planet's *Travel with Children*.

Turismos can often recommend local childcare, and

branches of the youth-network **Instituto Português da Juventude** (IPJ; ☑707 203 030; Av da Liberdade 194, Lisbon) sometimes advertise babysitting.

Customs Regulations

You can bring as much currency as you like into Portugal, though €10,000 or more must be declared. Customs regulations say anyone who needs a visa must bring in at least €50 plus €10 per day, but this isn't enforced.

The duty-free allowance for travellers more than 17 years old from non-EU countries:

» 200 cigarettes or the equivalent in tobacco

» 1L of alcohol that's more than 22% alcohol, or 2L of wine or beer.

Allowance for nationals of EU countries:

» 800 cigarettes or the equivalent

» 10L of spirits, 20L of fortified wine, 60L of sparkling wine or a mind-boggling 90L of still wine or 110L of beer.

Discount Cards

Portugal's network of *pousadas da juventude* (p519) is part of the HI network. An HI card from your hostelling association at home entitles you to the standard cheap rates.

A student card will get you reduced admission to almost all sights. Likewise, those aged over 65 with proof of age will save cash.

If you plan to do a lot of sightseeing in Portugal's main cities, the Lisboa Card (p53) and Porto Card (p360) are sensible investments. Sold at tourist offices, these cards allows discounts or free admission to many attractions and free travel on public transport.

Electricity

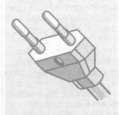

230V/50Hz

230V/50Hz

Embassies & Consulates

Your embassy or consulate is the best first stop in any emergency. Most can provide lists of reliable local doctors, lawyers and interpreters. Foreign embassies

and consulates in Portugal include the following:

Australia (☑213 101 500; www.portugal.embassy.gov.au; 2nd fl, Av da Liberdade 200, Lisbon)

Canada Lisbon (☑213 164 600; www.canadainternational.gc.ca; 3rd fl, Av da Liberdade 198, Lisbon); Faro (☑289 803 757; Rua Frei Lourenço de Santa Maria 1, Faro)

France Lisbon (☑213 939 292; www.ambafrance-pt.org; Calçada Marques de Abrantes 123, Lisbon); Porto (☑226 078 220; Av da Boavista 1681, 4100-132 Porto)

Germany (☑218 810 210; www.lissabon.diplo.de; Campo dos Mártires da Pátria 38, 1169-043 Lisbon)

Ireland (☑213 929 440; www.embassyofireland.pt; Rua da Imprensa a Estrela 1, Lisbon)

Netherlands (☑213 914 900; www.emb-paisesbaixos.pt; Av Infante Santo 43, 1399-011 Lisbon)

New Zealand There's no New Zealand consular in Portugal. The nearest New Zealand embassy is in Madrid (☑34 915 230 226; www.nzembassy.com).

Spain Lisbon (☑213 220 500; www.maec.es; Rua do Salitre 1, Lisbon); Porto (☑225 363 915; Rua de Dom João IV 341, Porto) Also in Valença do Minho and Vila Real de Santo António.

UK (☑213 924 000; http://ukinportugal.fco.gov.uk; Rua de São Bernardo 33, Lisbon) Also in Portimão.

USA (☑217 273 300; http://portugal.usembassy.gov; Av das Forças Armadas, 1600-081 Lisbon)

Gay & Lesbian Travellers

In 2010, Portugal legalised gay marriage, becoming the sixth European country to do so. Most Portuguese profess a laissez-faire attitude about same-sex couples, although how out you can be depends on where you are in Portugal. In Lisbon, Porto and the Algarve, acceptance has increased, whereas in most other areas, same-sex couples would be met with incomprehension. In this conservative Catholic country, homosexuality is still outside the norm. And while homophobic violence is extremely rare, discrimination has been reported in schools and workplaces.

Lisbon has the country's best gay and lesbian network and nightlife (see p98). Lisbon, Porto and Leiria hold Gay Pride marches, but outside these events the gay community keeps a discreet profile.

Health

Prevention is the key to staying healthy while abroad. A little planning before departure, particularly for pre-existing illnesses, will save trouble later. See your dentist before a long trip, carry a spare pair of contact lenses and glasses, and take your optical prescription with you. Bring medications in their original, clearly labelled, containers. A signed and dated letter from your physician describing your medical conditions and medications, including generic names, is also a good idea. If carrying syringes or needles, be sure to have a physician's letter documenting their medical necessity.

Availability of Health Care

Good health care is readily available and for minor illnesses pharmacists can give valuable advice and sell over-the-counter medication. Most pharmacists speak some English. They can also advise when more specialised help is required and point you in the right direction. The standard of dental care is usually good, but it is sensible to have a dental check-up before a long trip.

Health Insurance

If you're an EU citizen, be sure to get the European Health Insurance Card (EHIC), which is available online at www.ehic.org.uk. It will not cover you for non-emergencies or emergency repatriation. Citizens from other countries should find out if there is a reciprocal arrangement for free medical care between their country and Portugal. If you do need health insurance, consider a policy that covers you for the worst possible scenario, such as an accident requiring an emergency flight home. Find out in advance if your insurance plan will make payments directly to providers or reimburse you later for overseas health expenditures. The former option is generally preferable, as it doesn't require you to pay out of pocket in a foreign country.

Heat Exhaustion & Heat Stroke

Heat exhaustion occurs following excessive fluid loss with inadequate replacement of fluids and salt. Symptoms include headache, dizziness and tiredness. Dehydration is already happening by the time you feel thirsty – aim to drink sufficient water to produce pale, diluted urine. To treat heat exhaustion, replace lost fluids by drinking water and/or fruit juice or an oral rehydration solution, such as Dioralyte, and cool the body with cold water and fans. Treat salt loss with salty fluids such as soup (*canja de galinha*, or chicken soup, works wonders) or Bovril, or add a little more table salt to foods than usual.

Heat stroke is much more serious, resulting in irrational and hyperactive behaviour and eventually loss of consciousness and death. Rapid cooling by spraying the body with water and fanning is ideal. Emergency fluid and

electrolyte replacement by intravenous drip is recommended.

Jellyfish, Sea Urchins & Weever Fish

Stings from jellyfish are painful but not dangerous. Douse the wound in vinegar to deactivate any stingers that haven't 'fired'. Applying calamine lotion, antihistamines or analgesics may reduce the reaction and relieve the pain.

Watch for sea urchins around rocky beaches. If you get their needles embedded in your skin, immerse the limb in hot water to relieve the pain. To avoid infection visit a doctor and have the needles removed.

Thankfully, it is very rare to find the dangerous weever fish that inhabit shallow tidal zones along the Atlantic coast. They bury themselves in the sand with only their spines protruding and inject a powerful toxin if trodden upon. Soaking your foot in very hot water breaks down the poison, but you should seek medical advice in any event, since in rare cases this can cause permanent local paralysis.

Rabies

Rabies, though rare in Portugal, is a risk, and transmissible via the bite of an infected animal. It can also be transmitted if the animal's saliva comes in contact with an open wound. If you've been bitten by a wild animal, a treatment of shots must begin at once.

Tap Water

Tap water is generally safe to drink in Portugal.

Traveller's Diarrhoea

If you develop diarrhoea, be sure to drink plenty of fluids, preferably an oral rehydration solution (eg Dioralyte). A few loose stools don't require treatment, but if you start having more than four or five stools a day, you

TRAVEL HEALTH WEBSITES

It's a good idea to consult your government's travel health website before departure, if one is available:
Australia (www.smartraveller.gov.au)
Canada (www.hc-sc.gc.ca)
UK (www.doh.gov.uk)
USA (www.cdc.gov/travel)

» Municipal Espaços Internet
(www.espacosinternet.pt)
» Cybercafes, common in cities and towns, charge from around €2 per hour
» Some post offices have terminals for NetPost, an internet facility payable with a special card.

should start taking an antibiotic such as Norfloxacin, Ciprofloxacin or Azithromycin. Antidiarrhoeal agents such as loperamide are just 'stoppers' and don't get to the root of the problem. If diarrhoea is bloody, persists for more than 72 hours or is accompanied by fever, shaking, chills or severe abdominal pain you should seek medical attention.

Vaccinations

The WHO recommends that all travellers should be covered for diphtheria, tetanus, measles, mumps, rubella and polio, regardless of their destination. Since most vaccines don't produce immunity until at least two weeks after they're given, visit a physician at least six weeks before departure.

Insurance

Don't leave home without a travel-insurance policy to cover theft, loss and medical problems. You should get insurance for the worst-case scenario; for example, an accident or illness requiring hospitalisation and a flight home.

Check the small print, as some policies specifically exclude 'dangerous activities' such as scuba diving, motorcycling or even trekking. If these activities are in your sights, either find another policy or ask about an amendment (usually available for an extra premium) that includes them.

Make sure you keep all documentation for any

claims later on. Some policies ask you to call back (reverse charges) to a centre in your home country, where an immediate assessment of your problem is made.

Citizens of the EU are eligible for free emergency medical treatment if they have a European Health Insurance Card (EHIC), which replaces the no-longer-valid E111 certificate. In the UK, you can apply for this card online (www.ehic.org.uk) or pick up an application at a post office.

Worldwide travel insurance is available at www.lonelyplanet.com/bookings. You can buy, extend and claim online anytime – even if you're already on the road.

See also p528 for information about motor-vehicle insurance.

Internet Access

Throughout this guide, the @icon indicates places that have a physical computer where guests can access the internet. The 🛜icon indicates where wireless access (wi-fi) is available. Free internet access is not prevalent in Portugal. If you have your own laptop, a small number of hotels offer wireless access. There are also a few locations in Lisbon and Porto where you can find wi-fi.

Other options:
» Local branches of the Instituto Português da Juventude (IPJ), some of which are attached to IPJ hostels
» *Bibliotecas municipais* (municipal libraries)

Language Courses

You can take a crash course in Portuguese at the **Centro de Informação e Documentação Anti-Colonial** (CIDAC; ☎213 172 860; www.cidac. pt; Rua Pinheiro Chagas 77) in Lisbon. The capital is a good base for studying (p72).

Legal Matters

Fines for illegal parking are common. If you're parked illegally you'll be towed and will have to pay around €100 to get your car back. Be aware of local road rules, as fines for other transgressions will also be enforced.

Narcotic drugs were decriminalised in 2001 in an attempt to clear up the public-health problems among drug users, and to address the issue as a social rather than a criminal one. You may be brought before a commission and subject to fines or treatment if you are caught with up to 10 doses of a drug. Drug dealing is still a serious offence and suspects may be held for up to 18 months before coming to trial. Bail is at the court's discretion.

Legal Ages

Consent 16
Driving 18
Drinking 16
Voting 18

Travellers should note that it is possible for them to be prosecuted under the law of their home country regarding age of consent, even when abroad.

Maps

National and natural park offices usually have simple park maps, though these are of little use for trekking or cycling. Other local sources for topographic maps are noted in the text. The following offer a good range of maps:

Omni Resources (www. omnimap.com) US company that sells excellent maps, including 1:25,000 topographic maps.

Stanfords (www.stanfords. co.uk) Good selection of Portugal maps and travel products in the UK.

Money

Portugal uses the euro, along with most other European nations.

Banks and *bureaux de change* are free to set their own rates and commissions, so a low commission might mean a skewed exchange rate.

ATMs & Credit Cards

The most convenient way to get your money is from an ATM. Most banks have a Multibanco ATM, with menus in English, that accept Visa, Access, MasterCard, Cirrus and so on. You just need your card and PIN. Your home bank will usually charge around 1% to 2% per transaction. But it's wise to have a back-up source of money; sometimes ATMs temporarily stop accepting a certain type of card, usually a hiatus lasting a day or so. You'll be asked for a six-digit PIN, but it still works fine if yours is only four digits.

Credit cards are accepted at smarter hotels and restaurants and in larger towns, but won't be any use to pay for things in the budget arena or in rural outposts.

Tipping

Portuguese aren't big tippers. If service was satisfac-

tory, they usually tip 5% to 10%. Bills at pricier restaurants may already include *serviço* (service charge). After a snack at a bar or cafe, some shrapnel is enough. Taxi drivers are not generally tipped, but 10% for good service would be appreciated.

Travellers Cheques

These are a safe way to carry money, as they will be replaced if lost or stolen, but are less convenient than the card-in-machine method. Amex, Thomas Cook and Visa are most widely recognised. It's best to get cheques in euros, and keep a record of the ones you've cashed in case you do mislay them. However, although travellers cheques are easily exchanged, with better rates than for cash, they are poor value because commission is so high.

Post

Post offices are called **CTT** (www.ctt.pt). *Correio normal* (ordinary mail) goes in the red letterboxes, *correio azul* (airmail) goes in the blue boxes. Automated red postal stands dispense stamps, saving you the hassle of waiting in line at the post office. Postcards and letters up to 20g cost €0.80/0.68/0.32 outside Europe/within Europe/locally. International *correio azul* costs €1.85 for a 20g letter. Post to Europe takes up to five working days, and the rest of the world up to seven. Economy mail (or surface airlift) is about a third cheaper, but takes a week or so longer.

You can send mail to poste restante in main post offices of cities and large towns.

Public Holidays

Banks, offices, department stores and some shops close on the public holidays listed

here. On New Year's Day, Easter Sunday, Labour Day and Christmas Day, even *turismos* close. For details of festivals and events see p23.

New Year's Day 1 January

Carnaval Tuesday February/March – the day before Ash Wednesday

Good Friday March/April

Liberty Day 25 April – celebrating the 1974 revolution

Labour Day 1 May

Corpus Christi May/June – ninth Thursday after Easter

Portugal Day 10 June – also known as Camões and Communities Day

Feast of the Assumption 15 August

Republic Day 5 October – commemorating the 1910 declaration of the Portuguese Republic

All Saints' Day 1 November

Independence Day 1 December – commemorating the 1640 restoration of independence from Spain

Feast of the Immaculate Conception 8 December

Christmas Day 25 December

Safe Travel

Once behind the wheel of a car, the otherwise mild-mannered Portuguese change personality. Macho driving, such as tailgating at high speeds and overtaking on blind corners, is all too common. Portugal has one of the highest road accident rates in Europe. Police have responded by aggressively patrolling certain dangerous routes, such as on the cheerfully named 'highway of death' from Salamanca in Spain.

Smoking

In 2008 Portugal passed a law that bans smoking in public indoor areas. Some restaurants and bars are entirely smoke-free, while others have separate smoking sections (sometimes with less than adequate ventilation). Meanwhile, many hotels still offer smoking rooms.

Telephone

To call Portugal from abroad, dial the international access code (☑00), then Portugal's country code (☑351), then the number. All domestic numbers have nine digits, and there are no area codes. Most public phones accept phone cards only – available at most news-stands – though a few coin-operated phones are still around. You can also make calls from booths in Portugal Telecom offices and some post offices – pay when your call is finished.

Long-distance and international calls are cheaper from 9pm to 9am weekdays, all weekend and on holidays.

Directory Inquiries & Reverse-Charge Calls

Portugal's directory inquiries number is ☑118; operators will search by address as well as by name. The international directory inquiries number is ☑177.

To make a *pagar no destino* (reverse-charge call) with the help of a multilingual operator, dial ☑120.

International Calls & Cards

From Portugal Telecom, you can get a PT Hello Card in denominations of €5 or €10, which offer good long-distance rates. You call an access number then key in the code on the back of the card. There are lots of competing cards offering much the same service. Note that peak and off-peak periods vary from company to company.

Local, Regional & National Calls

The cheapest way to call within Portugal is with a Portugal Telecom *cartão telefónico* (phone card). These are available for €3, €5 and €10 from post and telephone offices and many newsagents. A youth or student card should get you a 10% discount.

Local calls cost around €0.09 per minute to land lines and €0.30 per minute to mobile phones. Numbers starting with ☑800 (*linha verde;* green line) are toll free. Those starting with ☑808 (*linha azul;* blue line) are charged at local rates from anywhere in the country.

Mobile Phones

Portugal uses the GSM 900/1800 frequency, the same as found in Australia, the UK and the rest of the EU. Mobile-phone usage is widespread in Portugal, with extensive coverage provided in all but the most rural areas. The main domestic operators are Vodafone, Optimus and TMN. All of them sell prepaid SIM cards that you can insert inside a GSM mobile phone and use as long as the phone is not locked by the company providing you service. If you need a phone, you can often buy one at the airport and shops throughout the country with a package of minutes for under €50. This is generally cheaper than renting a phone. Note that mobile-phone numbers usually begin with a 9.

It's illegal in Portugal to drive while talking on a mobile phone.

Time

Portugal, like Britain, is on GMT/UTC in winter and GMT/UTC plus one hour in summer. This puts it an hour earlier than Spain year-round (which is a strange thought when you are crossing the border). Clocks are set forward by an hour on the last Sunday in March and back on the last Sunday in October.

Tourist Information

Turismo de Portugal, the country's national tourist board, operates a handy website: www.visitportugal.com.

Locally managed *postos de turismo* (tourist offices, usually signposted *'turismo'*) are everywhere, offering brochures and varying degrees of help with sights and accommodation. For tourist office locations, see the Information sections in the relevant chapter.

Travellers With Disabilities

The term *deficientes* (Portuguese for disabled) gives some indication of the limited awareness of disabled needs. Although public offices and agencies are required to provide access and facilities for people with disabilities, private businesses are not.

Lisbon airport is wheelchair accessible, while Porto and Faro airports have accessible toilets. The useful website www.allgohere.com has information on facilities offered by all airlines.

Parking spaces are allotted in many places but are frequently occupied. The EU parking card entitles visitors to the same street-parking concessions given to disabled residents. If you're in the UK, contact the **Department for Transport** (☎020-7944 8300; www.dft.gov.uk/transportforyou/access).

Newer and larger hotels tend to have some adapted rooms, though the facilities may not be up to scratch; ask at the local *turismo*. Most camping grounds have accessible toilets and some hostels have facilities for people with disabilities.

Lisbon, with its cobbled streets and hills, may be difficult for some travellers with disabilities, but not impossible. The Baixa's flat grid and Belém are fine, and all the sights at Parque das Nações are accessible.

For more details, contact the following:

Accessible Portugal (☎217 203 130; www.accessibleportugal.com; Rua João Freitas Branco 21D, Lisbon) This Lisbon-based tour agency offers a wide range of itineraries and can arrange accommodation, transfers, overnight trips and outdoor activities such as tandem skydiving and hot-air balloon trips.

Cooperativa Nacional de Apoio Deficientes (☎218 595 332; www.cnad.org.pt; Praça Dr Fernando Amado, Lote 566-E, Lisbon) This is a private organisation that can help with travel needs.

Dial-a-ride Disabled Bus Service Lisbon (☎217 585 676); Porto (☎226 006 353)

Secretaria do Nacional de Reabilitação (☎217 929 500; www.inr.pt; Av Conde de Valbom 63, Lisbon) The national

governmental organisation representing the disabled supplies information, provides links to useful operations and publishes guides (in Portuguese) that advise on barrier-free accommodation, transport, shops, restaurants and sights.

Taxi Services for Disabled Persons Braga (☎253 684 081); Coimbra (☎239 484 522)

Wheeling Around the Algarve (☎289 393 636; www.player.pt; Rua Casa do Povo, 1, Almancil) Another private set-up, with great advice on accommodation, transport, care hire, sport and leisure facilities, and equipment.

Visas

Nationals of EU countries don't need a visa for any length of stay in Portugal. Those from Canada, New Zealand, the USA and (by temporary agreement) Australia can stay for up to 90 days in any half-year without a visa. Others, including nationals of South Africa, need a visa unless they're the spouse or child of an EU citizen.

The general requirements for entry into Portugal also apply to citizens of other signatories of the 1990 Schengen Convention (Austria, Belgium, Denmark, Finland, France, Germany, Greece, Iceland, Italy, Luxembourg, the Netherlands, Norway, Spain and Sweden). A visa issued by one Schengen country is generally valid for travel in all the others, but unless you're a citizen of the UK, Ireland or a Schengen country, you should check visa regulations with the consulate of each Schengen country you plan to visit. You must apply for any Schengen visa while you are still in your country of residence.

To extend a visa or 90-day period of stay after arriving in Portugal, contact the **Foreigners' Registration Service** (Serviço de Estrangeiros e Fronteiras; ☎213 585 545; Rua São Sebastião da Pedreira 15, Lisbon); major tourist towns also have branches. As entry regulations are already liberal, you'll need convincing proof of employment or financial independence, or a pretty good story if you want to stay longer.

Women Travellers

Women travelling alone in Portugal report few serious problems. As when travelling anywhere, women should take care – be cautious about where you walk after dark and don't hitch.

If you're travelling with a male partner, people will expect him to do all the talking and ordering, and pay the bill. In some conservative pockets of the north, unmarried couples will save hassle by saying they're married.

If you're a victim of rape or violence while you're in Portugal, you can contact the **Associação Portuguesa de Apoio à Vítima** (APAV; Portuguese Association for Victim Support; ☎213 587 900; www.apav.pt; Rua José Estêvão 135), which offers assistance for rape victims. Visit the website for office locations nationwide.

Work

The most likely kind of work you will be able to find is teaching English, if you have Teaching English as a Foreign Language (TEFL) certification. If you're in the UK, contact the British Council, or get in touch with language schools in the area where you want to teach as possible avenues of work.

Bar work is a possibility in the Algarve, particularly in Lagos; ask around. You can also try looking in the local English press for job ads (see boxed text, p520).

Transport

GETTING THERE & AWAY

Entering the Country

From within Europe, you'll have no problems entering Portugal by land, sea or air. If arriving from further afield, check p526 to see if you need a visa before arrival.

Flights, tours and rail tickets can be booked online at lonelyplanet.com/bookings.

Air

Airports & Airlines

Most international flights arrive in Lisbon, though Porto and Faro also have international flights. For more information, including live flight arrival and departure schedules, see www.ana-aeroportos.pt.

Lisbon airport (LIS; ☎218 413 500)

Porto airport (OPO; ☎229 432 400)

Faro airport (FAO; ☎289 800 800)

Airlines flying to/from Portugal:

Aer Lingus (www.aerlingus.com)

Air Berlin (www.airberlin.com)

Air France (www.airfrance.fr)

Alitalia (www.alitalia.com)

British Airways (www.britishairways.com)

British Midland/bmibaby (www.bmibaby.com)

Continental Airlines (www.continental.com)

Delta (www.delta.com)

EasyJet (www.easyjet.com)

Finnair (www.finnair.com)

Grupo SATA (www.sata.pt)

Iberia (www.iberia.com)

KLM (www.klm.nl)

Lufthansa (www.lufthansa.com)

Monarch Airlines (www.flymonarch.com)

Regional Air Lines (www.regional.com)

Ryanair (www.ryanair.com)

Swiss International Air Lines (www.swiss.com)

TAP Air Portugal (www.tap.pt) Portugal's international flag carrier as well as its main domestic airline.

Transavia Airlines (www.transavia.com)

Tunisair (www.tunisair.com.tn)

Land

Bus

The major long-distance carriers that serve European destinations are **Busabout** (www.busabout.com) and **Eurolines** (www.eurolines.com) Lisbon (☎218 957 398; Loja 203, Gare do Oriente); Porto (☎225 189 299; Rua Formosa 76); Bragança (☎273 327 122; bus station, Av João da Cruz). Unfortunately, Portugal is not currently included in either company's multicity travel passes.

CLIMATE CHANGE & TRAVEL

Every form of transport that relies on carbon-based fuel generates CO_2, the main cause of human-induced climate change. Modern travel is dependent on aeroplanes, which might use less fuel per kilometre per person than most cars but travel much greater distances. The altitude at which aircraft emit gases (including CO_2) and particles also contributes to their climate change impact. Many websites offer 'carbon calculators' that allow people to estimate the carbon emissions generated by their journey and, for those who wish to do so, to offset the impact of the greenhouse gases emitted with contributions to portfolios of climate-friendly initiatives throughout the world. Lonely Planet offsets the carbon footprint of all staff and author travel.

CONTINENTAL EUROPE BUSES TO PORTUGAL

FROM	TO	FREQUENCY	DURATION (HR)	COST (€)
Amsterdam	Porto	3 times weekly	32	110-140
Amsterdam	Faro	3 times weekly	36	138-164
Barcelona	Lisbon	3 times weekly	18	69
Brussels	Porto	3 times weekly	28	132-139
Brussels	Faro	3 times weekly	31	164-171
Hamburg	Porto	3 times weekly	36	156
Hamburg	Lisbon	3 times weekly	39	159
Hamburg	Faro	3 times weekly	41	175
Madrid	Porto	daily	8½	50
Madrid	Lisbon	daily	8	40-50
Seville	Lisbon	daily	7	35-48
Seville	Faro	daily	4½	20
Paris	Faro	3 times weekly	27	91-120
Paris	Lisbon	daily	26	91-100
Paris	Porto	daily	22	91-100

For some European routes, Eurolines is affiliated with the big Portuguese operators **Internorte** (www .internorte.pt) and **Eva Transportes** (www.eva-bus.com).

CONTINENTAL EUROPE

Eurolines has services to Portugal from destinations all across Europe, typically running about twice a week. From Paris, hefty surcharges apply to one-way or return tickets for most departures from July to mid-August and also on Saturday year round.

UK–Portugal and France–Portugal Eurolines services cross to Portugal via northwest Spain. Spanish lines with services to Portugal include the following:

Alsa (www.alsa.es)

Avanza (www.avanzabus.com)

Damas (www.damas-sa.es).

UK

Eurolines runs several services to Portugal from Victoria coach station in London, with a stopover and change of bus in France and sometimes Spain. These include two buses a week to Viana

do Castelo (34 hours), five to Porto (33 hours), five via Coimbra to Lisbon (35 hours) and two via Faro to Lagos (38 hours). These services cost around £169 return.

Car & Motorcycle

Of more than 30 roads that cross the Portugal–Spain border, the best and biggest do so near Valença do Minho (E01/A3), Chaves (N532), Bragança (E82/IP4), Vilar Formoso (E80/IP5), Caia (E90/A6/IP7), Serpa (N260) and Vila Real de Santo António (E1/IP1). There are no longer any border controls. Petrol is significantly cheaper in Spain (around €1.20 per litre).

See p531 for more on driving in Portugal.

LICENCES & INSURANCE

Nationals of EU countries, the USA and Brazil need only their home driving licence to operate a car or motorcycle in Portugal. Others should get an International Driving Permit (IDP) through an automobile licensing department or automobile club in their home country.

If you're driving your own car or motorcycle into Portugal, you need the following:

» vehicle registration (proof of ownership)

» insurance documents

» motor vehicle insurance with at least third-party cover.

Your home insurance policy may or may not be extendable to Portugal, and the coverage of some comprehensive policies automatically drops to third party outside your home country unless the insurer is notified.

If you hire a car, the rental firm will provide you with registration and insurance papers, plus a rental contract.

UK

The quickest driving route from the UK to Portugal is by car ferry to northern Spain. Take **P&O Portsmouth** (www.poferries.com) from Portsmouth to Bilbao (35 hours, twice weekly mid-March to mid-December), or **Brittany Ferries** (www .brittany-ferries.com) from

Plymouth to Santander (18 hours, twice weekly from March to November). From Bilbao or Santander it's roughly 1000km to Lisbon, 800km to Porto and 1300km to Faro. Fares are wildly seasonal and start at around £900 return.

An alternative is to catch a ferry across the Channel (or the Eurotunnel vehicle train beneath it) to France and motor down the coast. The fastest sea crossings travel between Dover and Calais, and are operated by P&O Portsmouth. For travel through the Channel Tunnel, visit **Eurotunnel** (www.euro tunnel.com).

Train

Trains are a popular way to get around Europe – comfortable, frequent and generally on time. But unless you have a rail pass the cost can be higher than flying.

There are two standard long-distance rail journeys into Portugal. Both take the *TGV Atlantique* from Paris to Irún (in Spain), where you must change trains. From there the *Sud-Expresso* crosses into Portugal at Vilar Formoso (Fuentes de Oñoro in Spain), continuing to Coimbra and Lisbon; change at Pampilhosa for Porto. The other journey runs from Irún to Madrid, with a change to the *Talgo Lusitânia*, crossing into Portugal at Marvão-Beirã and on to Lisbon. For trips to the south of Portugal, change at Lisbon.

Two other important Spain–Portugal crossings are at Valença do Minho and

at Caia (Caya in Spain), near Elvas.

You will have few problems buying long-distance tickets as little as a day or two ahead, even in the summer. For those intending to do a lot of European rail travel, the exhaustive *Thomas Cook European Timetable* is updated monthly and is available from **Thomas Cook Publishing** (www .thomascooktimetables.com).

TRAIN PASSES

Many of the passes listed here are available through **Rail Europe** (www.raileurope. co.uk); most travel agencies also sell them, though you will save a little by buying directly from the issuing authority. Note that even with a pass you must still pay for seat and couchette reservations and express-train supplements.

InterRail Pass (www.inter railnet.com) allows a certain number of travel days within a set time frame. The network includes 30 countries. A pass for five days of travel over 10 days costs €249 for 2nd class, €374 for 1st class. A month of unlimited travel runs €599/899. The InterRail Pass is available to anyone residing in Europe for six months before starting their travels. You cannot use it in your home country.

Eurail (www.eurail.com) sells passes to non-European residents. The Global pass is valid for unlimited travel in 21 European countries, including Portugal, and ranges from 15 days (1st/2nd class €511/332) to three months (€1432/933). The Select

pass allows you to travel between three, four or five of your chosen Eurail countries (which must be directly connected by Eurail transport). You can choose from five to 10 travelling days (or up to 15 days for five countries), which can be taken at any point within a two-month period.

Iberic Rail Pass (www .europeanrailguide.com), available only to non-European residents, is also valid for a specified period of 1st-class travel in Spain and Portugal during a two-month period, from three days (US$284) to 10 days (US$547).

CONTINENTAL EUROPE

The train journey from Paris (Gare d'Austerlitz) to Lisbon takes 21 hours and stops in a number of Spanish cities along the way. You can buy tickets direct from **SNCF** (www.voyages-sncf.com).

UK

The fastest and most convenient route to Portugal is with **Eurostar** (www.eurostar .com) from London Waterloo to Paris via the Channel Tunnel, and then onward by TGV.

River

Car ferries cross the Rio Guadiana border from Ayamonte in Spain to Vila Real de Santo António in the Algarve every 20 minutes from 8.30am to 7pm Monday to Saturday, and from 9.15am to 5.40pm on Sunday; buy tickets from the waterfront office (€1.50/5/0.90 per person/car/bike).

CONTINENTAL EUROPE TRAINS TO PORTUGAL

FROM	TO	FREQUENCY	DURATION (HR)	COST (€)
Badajoz	Lisbon	daily	5	25
Madrid	Lisbon	daily	10½	120
Paris	Lisbon	daily	21	170

Sea

There are no scheduled sea-going ferries to Portugal, but many to Spain. For details on those from the UK to Spain, see p528.

The closest North African ferry connections are from Morocco to Spain; contact **Trasmediterranea** (www.trasmediterranea.es) and **Euro Ferrys** (www.euroferrys.com) for details. Car ferries also run from Tangier to Gibraltar.

GETTING AROUND

A helpful website for schedules and prices to assist with your trip planning is www.transpor.pt.

Air

Flights within mainland Portugal are expensive and, for the short distances involved, not really worth considering. Nonetheless, **TAP Air Portugal** (www.tap.pt) has multiple daily Lisbon–Porto and Lisbon–Faro flights (taking less than one hour) year round. For Porto to Faro, change in Lisbon.

Bicycle

Mountain biking is hugely popular in Portugal, even though there are few dedicated bicycle paths. Possible itineraries are numerous in the mountainous national/natural parks of the north (especially Parque Nacional da Peneda-Gerês), along the coast or across the Alentejo plains. Coastal trips are easiest from north to south, with the prevailing winds. More demanding is the Serra da Estrela (which serves as the Tour de Portugal's 'mountain run'). You could also try the Serra do Marão between Amarante and Vila Real.

Local bike clubs organise regular Passeio BTT trips; check their flyers at rental agencies, bike shops and *turismos* (tourist offices). Guided trips are often available in popular tourist destinations. For jaunts arranged from abroad, see p39.

Cobbled roads in some old-town centres may jar your teeth loose if your tyres aren't fat enough; they should be at least 38mm in diameter.

Documents

If you're cycling around Portugal on your own bike, proof of ownership and a written description and photograph of it will help police in case it's stolen.

Hire

There are numerous places to rent bikes, especially in the Algarve and other touristy areas. Prices range from €8 to €20 per day.

Information

For listings of events and bike shops, buy the bimonthly Portuguese-language *Bike Magazine* (www.bikemagazine.pt), available from larger newsagents.

For its members, the UK-based **Cyclists' Touring Club** (CTC; www.ctc.org.uk) publishes useful and free information on cycling in Portugal, plus notes for half a dozen routes around the country. It also offers tips, maps, topography guides and other publications by mail order.

Transporting Your Bicycle

Boxed-up or bagged-up bicycles can be taken free on all *regional* and *interregional* trains as accompanied baggage. They can also go unboxed on a few suburban services on weekends or for a small charge outside the rush hour. Most domestic bus lines won't accept bikes on board.

Boat

Other than river cruises along the Rio Douro from Porto (p393) and the Rio Tejo from Lisbon (p73), Portugal's only remaining waterborne transport is cross-river ferries. Commuter ferries include those across the Rio Tejo to/from Lisbon (p105), and across the mouth of the Rio Sado (p133).

Bus

A host of small private bus operators, most amalgamated into regional companies, run a dense network of services across the country. Among the largest companies are **Rede Expressos** (www.rede-expressos.pt), **Rodonorte** (www.rodonorte.pt) and the Algarve line **Eva Transportes** (www.eva-bus.com).

Bus services are of four general types:

Alta Qualidade A fast deluxe category offered by some companies.

Expressos Comfortable, fast buses between major cities.

Carreiras Marked 'CR'; slow, stopping at every crossroad.

Rápidas Quick regional buses.

Even in summer you'll have little problem booking an *expresso* ticket for the same or next day. A Lisbon–Faro express bus takes four hours and costs just under €20; Lisbon–Porto takes about four hours for around €18. By contrast, local services can thin out to almost nothing on weekends, especially in summer when school is out.

Don't rely on *turismos* for accurate timetable information. Most bus-station ticket desks will give you a little computer printout of fares and all services.

Car & Motorcycle

Portugal's modest network of *estradas* (highways) is gradually spreading across the country. Main roads are sealed and generally in good condition. The downside is your fellow drivers. The country's per-capita death rate from road accidents has long been one of Europe's highest, and drinking, driving and dying are hot political potatoes.

The good news is that recent years have seen a steady decline in the road toll, thanks to a zero-tolerance police crackdown on accident-prone routes and alcohol limits. The legal blood-alcohol level is 0.5g/L, and there are fines of up to €2500 for drink-driving.

It's also illegal in Portugal to drive while talking on a mobile phone.

Driving can be tricky in Portugal's small walled towns, where roads may taper down to donkey-cart size before you know it, and fiendish one-way systems can force you out of your way.

A common occurrence in larger towns is down-and-outers, who lurk around squares and car parks, waving you into the parking space you've just found for yourself, and asking for payment for this service. It's wise to do as Portuguese do, and hand over some coins (€0.50) to keep your car out of 'trouble' (scratches, broken windows, etc).

For information on what to bring in the way of documents, see p528.

Accidents

If you are involved in a minor 'fender bender' with no injuries, the easiest way for drivers to sort things out with their insurance companies is to fill out a *Constat Aimable* (the English version is called a European Accident Statement). There's no risk in signing this: it's just a way to exchange the relevant information and there's usually one included in rental-car documents. Make sure it includes any details that may help you prove that the accident was not your fault. To alert the police, dial ☏112.

Assistance

Automóvel Club de Portugal (☏213 180 100; www.acp.pt), Portugal's national auto club, provides medical, legal and breakdown assistance for its members. Road information and maps are available to anyone at ACP offices, including the head office in Lisbon and branches in Aveiro, Braga, Bragança, Coimbra, Évora, Faro, Porto and elsewhere.

ROAD DISTANCES (KM)

	Aveiro	Beja	Braga	Bragança	Castelo Branco	Coimbra	Évora	Faro	Guarda	Leiria	Lisbon	Portalegre	Porto	Santarém	Setúbal	Viana do Castelo	Vila Real	Viseu
Aveiro	---																	
Beja	383	---																
Braga	129	504	---															
Bragança	287	566	185	---														
Castelo Branco	239	271	366	299	---													
Coimbra	60	329	178	314	191	---												
Évora	305	78	426	488	191	251	---											
Faro	522	166	643	732	437	468	244	---										
Guarda	163	369	260	197	102	161	291	535	---									
Leiria	126	273	244	402	179	72	195	412	233	---								
Lisbon	256	183	372	530	264	202	138	296	402	146	---							
Portalegre	276	178	403	390	93	222	100	344	193	172	219	---						
Porto	71	446	58	216	308	123	368	585	202	189	317	339	---					
Santarém	188	195	309	464	181	134	117	346	295	78	80	147	251	---				
Setúbal	299	143	420	575	316	246	105	256	406	189	47	186	362	123	---			
Viana do Castelo	144	519	56	241	382	191	441	658	275	262	387	412	73	324	435	---		
Vila Real	169	528	94	120	261	199	450	683	159	282	412	352	98	349	460	150	---	
Viseu	86	415	185	228	177	86	366	554	75	158	288	268	127	220	331	241	113	---

If your national auto club belongs to the Fédération Internationale de l'Automobile or the Alliance Internationale de Tourisme, you can also use ACP's emergency services and get discounts on maps and other products. Among clubs that qualify are the AA and RAC in the UK, and the Australian, New Zealand, Canadian and American automobile associations.

The 24-hour ACP emergency help number is ☑707 509 510.

Fuel

Fuel is expensive – about €1.40 (and rising) for a litre of *sem chumbo* (unleaded petrol) at the time of writing. There are plenty of self-service stations, and credit cards are accepted at most. If you're near the border, you can save money by filling up in Spain, where it's around 20% cheaper.

Highways & Toll Roads

Top of the range are *auto-estradas* (motorways), all of them *portagens* (toll roads); the longest of these are Lisbon–Porto and Lisbon–Algarve. Toll roads charge cars and motorcycles a little over €0.06 per kilometre (around €20 from Lisbon to Porto and €19 from Lisbon to Faro).

Nomenclature can be baffling. Motorway prefixes indicate the following:

PARKING

Parking is often metered within city centres, but is free on Saturday evening and Sunday. Central Lisbon has car parks, and these cost around €10 per day. For more details on driving and parking in Lisbon see p106.

A prefixes Indicate Portugal's toll roads.

E prefixes Europe-wide designations.

N prefixes Indicate main two-lane *estradas nacionais* (national roads); prefix letter used on some road maps only.

IC (itinerário complementar) Indicates subsidiary highways.

IP (itinerário principal) Indicates main highways.

Numbers for the main two-lane *estradas nacionais* (national roads) have no prefix letter on some road maps, whereas on other maps they're prefixed by N.

Hire

To rent a car in Portugal you must be at least 25 years old and have held your driving licence for more than a year (some companies allow younger drivers at higher rates). The widest choice of car-hire companies is at Lisbon, Porto and Faro airports. Competition has driven Algarve rates lower than elsewhere.

Some of the best advance-booking rates are offered by internet-based brokers such as Holiday Autos (www.holidayautos .com). Other bargains come as part of 'fly/drive' packages. The worst deals tend to be those done with international firms on arrival, though their prepaid promotional rates are competitive. Book at least a few days ahead in high season. For on-the-spot rental, domestic firms such as Auto Jardim (www.auto-jardim.com) have some of the best rates.

Renting the smallest and cheapest available car for a week in high season costs as little as €135 (with tax, insurance and unlimited mileage) if booked from abroad, and a similar amount through a Portuguese firm. It can cost up to €400 if you book through Portuguese branch-es of international firms such as Hertz, Europcar and Avis.

For an additional fee you can get personal insurance through the rental company, unless you're covered by your home policy. A minimum of third-party coverage is compulsory in the EU.

Rental cars are especially at risk of break-ins or petty theft in larger towns, so don't leave anything of value visible in the car. The ultra-cautious unscrew the radio antenna and leave it inside the car at night; they might also put the wheel covers (hubcaps) in the boot (trunk) for the duration of the trip.

Motorcycles and scooters can be rented in larger cities, and all over coastal Algarve. Expect to pay from €30/60 per day for a scooter/ motorcycle.

Road Rules

Despite the sometimes chaotic relations between drivers, there are rules. To begin with, driving is on the right, overtaking is on the left and most signs use international symbols. An important rule to remember is that traffic from the right usually has priority. Portugal has lots of ambiguously marked intersections, so this is more important than you might think.

Except when marked otherwise, speed limits for cars (without a trailer) and motorcycles (without a side-car) are 50km/h in towns and villages, 90km/h outside built-up areas and 120km/h on motorways. By law, car safety belts must be worn in the front and back seats, and children under 12 years may not ride in the front. Motorcyclists and their passengers must wear helmets, and motorcycles must have their headlights on day and night.

The police can impose steep on-the-spot fines for speeding and parking offences, so save yourself a big hassle and remember to toe the line.

Hitching

Hitching is never entirely safe anywhere, and we don't recommend it. In any case it isn't an easy option in Portugal. Almost nobody stops on major highways, and on smaller roads drivers tend to be going short distances so you may only advance from one field to the next.

Local Transport

Bus

Except in Lisbon or Porto, there's little reason to take municipal buses, as most attractions are within walking distance. Most areas have regional bus services, for better or worse (see p530).

Metro

Both Lisbon and Porto have ambitious underground systems that are still growing; see p107 and p381.

Taxi

Taxis offer fair value over short distances, and are plentiful in large towns and cities. Ordinary taxis are usually marked with an 'A' (which stands for *aluguer*, for hire) on the door, number plate or elsewhere. They use meters and are available on the street and at taxi ranks, or by telephone for a surcharge of €0.75.

The fare on weekdays during daylight hours is about €2.50 *bandeirada* (flag fall) plus around €0.80 per kilometre, and a bit more for periods spent idling in traffic. A fare of €6 will usually get you across bigger towns. It's best to insist on the meter, although it's possible to negotiate a flat fare. If you have a sizeable load of luggage you'll pay a further €1.50.

Rates are about 20% higher at night (9pm to 6am), and on weekends and holidays. Once a taxi leaves the city limits you also pay a surcharge or higher rate.

In larger cities, including Lisbon and Porto, meterless taxis marked with a T (for *turismo*) can be hired from private companies for excursions. Rates for these are higher but standardised; drivers are honest and polite, and speak foreign languages.

Tram

Tram lovers shouldn't miss the charming relics rattling through the narrow streets of Lisbon (p106) and Porto (p381).

Tours

Bus

The following companies offer bus tours:

AVIC (www.avic.pt) Runs tours in Porto, the Douro and the Minho.

Cityrama (www.cityrama.pt) Based in Lisbon, but offers countrywide excursions.

Diana Tours (www.diana tours.pt) Specialises in Lisbon and Sintra.

Megatur (www.megatur.pt) Offers a variety of Algarve tours.

Train

Caminhos de Ferro Portugueses (www.cp.pt), the state railway company, organises Saturday day trips up the Douro valley on an old steam engine during the summer months. See p393 for more details.

Specialist Tours

Locally run adventure tours are noted in individual town listings; activity-based tours are listed in Portugal Outdoors (p32). Try the following for special-interest tours:

Destination Portugal (www.destination-portugal. co.uk) Will tell you all you need to know and can help with flights, car hire and accommodation, separately or together.

Martin Randall Travel (www.martinrandall.com) UK cultural specialist that

arranges first-rate escorted tours, including a historical and architectural tour of Central Portugal.

Naturetrek (www.nature trek.co.uk) Specialist in birdwatching and botanical tours; runs an eight-day excursion around southern Portugal.

Train

Portugal has an extensive railroad network, making for a scenic way of travelling between destinations. **Caminhos de Ferro Portugueses** (CP; www.cp.pt) is the state railway company.

Three of the most appealing old railway lines on narrow-gauge tracks climb out of the Douro valley:

Linha da Corgo From Peso da Régua to Vila Real (p449).

Linha da Tâmega From Livração to Amarante.

Linha da Tua From Tua to Mirandela (p466).

Discounts

Children aged under five travel free; those aged five to 12 go for half-price. A youth card issued by Euro26 member countries gets you a 20% discount on *regional* and *interregional* services on any day. For distances above 100km, you can also get a 20% discount on *intercidade* (express) services and a 10% discount on Alfa Pendular (AP) trains – though the latter applies only from Tuesday to Thursday. Travellers aged 65 and over can get 50% off any service by showing some ID.

Information & Reservations

You can get hold of timetable and fare information at all stations and from CP. You can book *intercidade* and Alfa Pendular tickets up to 30 days ahead, though you'll have little trouble booking for the next or even the

Train Routes

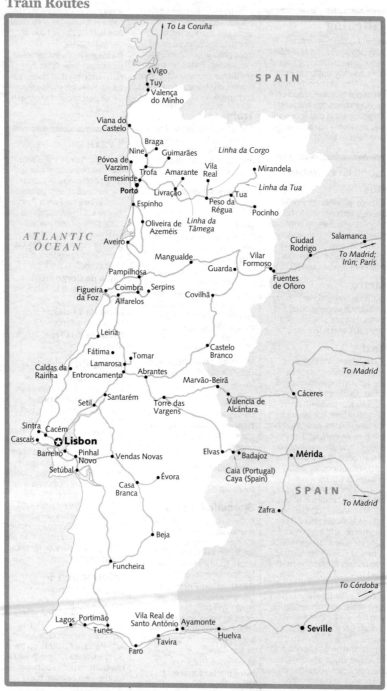

same day. Other services can only be booked 24 hours in advance. A seat reservation is mandatory on most *intercidade* and Alfa trains; the booking fee is included in the price.

Types & Classes of Service

There are four main types of long-distance service. Note that international services are marked IN on timetables.

Regional (R) Slow, stop everywhere.

Interregional (IR) Reasonably fast.

Intercidade (IC) *Rápido* or express trains.

Alfa Pendular Deluxe This service is marginally faster than express and much pricier.

Lisbon and Porto have their own *urbano* (suburban) train networks. Lisbon's network extends to Sintra, Cascais and Setúbal, and up the lower Tejo valley. Porto's network takes the definition of 'suburban' to new lengths, running all the way to Braga, Guimarães and Aveiro. *Urbano* services also travel between Coimbra and Figueira da Foz. The distinction matters where long-distance services parallel the more convenient, plentiful and considerably cheaper *urbanos*.

Only the Faro–Porto *Comboio Azul* and international trains like *Sud-Expresso* and *Talgo Lusitânia* have restaurant cars, though all IC and Alfa trains have aisle service and most have bars.

Train Passes

The One Country Portugal Pass from **InterRail** (www .interrailnet.com) gives you unlimited travel on any three, four, six or eight days over a month period. The price for three/four/six/ eight days on 2nd class is €71/89/119/139. A 1st-class pass costs about 35% more. It's available to all travellers who hail from outside of Portugal. It can be purchased from many travel agents in Portugal or in advance from the website.

Language

WANT MORE?
For in-depth language information and handy phrases, check out Lonely Planet's *Portuguese Phrasebook*. You'll find it at **shop.lonelyplanet. com**, or you can buy Lonely Planet's iPhone phrasebooks at the Apple App Store.

Portuguese is the official language of Portugal, Brazil, and the African nations of Angola, Mozambique, Cape Verde, Guinea-Bissau and São Tomé e Príncipe. In Asia it's spoken in Macau and East Timor, and in enclaves around Malaka, Goa, Damão and Diu.

Most sounds in Portuguese are also found in English. The exceptions are the nasal vowels (represented in our pronunciation guides by ng after the vowel), which are pronounced as if you're trying to make the sound through your nose; and the strongly rolled r (represented by rr in our pronunciation guides). Also note that the symbol zh sounds like the 's' in 'pleasure'.

In Portuguese stress generally falls on the second-last syllable of a word. In our pronunciation guides stressed syllables are indicated with italics.

Keeping these few points in mind and reading the coloured pronunciation guides as if they were English, you won't have problems being understood.

Portuguese has masculine and feminine forms of nouns and adjectives. Both forms are given in this chapter where necessary, and indicated with 'm' and 'f' respectively.

BASICS

Hello.	Olá.	o·laa
Goodbye.	Adeus.	a·de·oosh
How are you?	Como está?	ko·moo shtaa
Fine, and you?	Bem, e você?	beng e vo·se
Excuse me.	Faz favor.	faash fa·vor
Sorry.	Desculpe.	desh·kool·pe

Yes./No.	Sim./Não.	seeng/nowng
Please.	Por favor.	poor fa·vor
Thank you.	Obrigado.	o·bree·gaa·doo (m)
	Obrigada.	o·bree·gaa·da (f)
You're welcome.	De nada.	de naa·da

What's your name?
Qual é o seu nome?   kwaal e oo se·oo no·me

My name is ...
O meu nome é ...   oo me·oo no·me e ...

Do you speak English?
Fala (inglês)?   faa·la (eeng·glesh)

I (don't) understand.
(Não) entendo.   (nowng) eng·teng·doo

ACCOMMODATION

Do you have a single/double room?
Tem um quarto de solteiro/casal?   teng oong kwaar·too de sol·tay·roo/ka·zal

How much is it per night/person?
Quanto custa por noite/pessoa?   kwang·too koosh·ta poor noy·te/pe·so·a

Is breakfast included?
Inclui o pequeno almoço?   eeng·kloo·ee oo pe·ke·noo aal·mo·soo

campsite	parque de campismo	paar·ke de kang·peezh·moo
guesthouse	casa de hóspedes	kaa·za de osh·pe·desh
hotel	hotel	o·tel
youth hostel	pousada de juventude	poh·zaa·da de zhoo·veng·too·de

air-con	ar condicionado	aar kong·dee·syoo·naa·doo
bathroom	casa de banho	kaa·za de ba·nyoo
bed	cama	ka·ma
cot	cama de grades	ka·ma de graa·desh
window	janela	zha·ne·la

DIRECTIONS

Where's (the station)?
Onde é (a estação)?   ong·de e (a shta·sowng)

What's the address?
Qual é o endereço?   kwaal e oo eng·de·re·soo

Could you please write it down?
Podia escrever   poo·dee·a shkre·ver
isso, por favor?   ee·soo poor fa·vor

Can you show me (on the map)?
Pode-me mostrar   po·de·me moosh·traar
(no mapa)?   (noo maa·pa)

at the corner	na esquina	na shkee·na
at the traffic lights	nos semáforos	noosh se·maa·foo·roosh
behind ...	atrás de ...	a·traash de ...
in front of ...	em frente de ...	eng freng·te de ...
far	longe	long·zhe
left	esquerda	shker·da
near	perto	per·too
next to ...	ao lado de ...	ow laa·doo de ...
opposite	do lado oposto ...	doo laa·doo oo·posh·too ...
right	direita	dee·ray·ta
straight ahead	em frente	eng freng·te

EATING & DRINKING

What would you recommend?
O que é que   oo ke e ke
recomenda?   rre·koo·meng·da

What's in that dish?
Quais são os   kwaish sowng oosh
ingredientes   eeng·gre·dee·eng·tesh
daquele prato?   da·ke·le praa·too

I don't eat ...
Eu não como ...   e·oo nowng ko·moo ...

Cheers!
Saúde!   sa·oo·de

That was delicious.
Isto estava   eesh·too shtaa·va
delicioso.   de·lee·see·o·zoo

Bring the bill/check, please.
Pode-me trazer   po·de·me tra·zer
a conta.   a kong·ta

KEY PATTERNS

To get by in Portuguese, mix and match these simple patterns with words of your choice:

When's (the next bus)?
Quando é que sai   kwang·doo e ke sai
(o próximo   (oo pro·see·moo
autocarro)?   ow·to·kaa·rroo)

Where do I (buy a ticket)?
Onde é que eu   ong·de e ke e·oo
(compro o bilhete)?   (kong·proo oo bee·lye·te)

I'm looking for (a hotel).
Estou à procura de   shtoh aa proo·koo·ra de
(um hotel).   (oong o·tel)

Do you have (a map)?
Tem (um mapa)?   teng (oong maa·pa)

Please bring (the bill).
Pode-me trazer   po·de·me tra·zer
(a conta).   (a kong·ta)

I'd like (the menu).
Queria (um menu).   ke·ree·a (oong me·noo)

I'd like (to hire a car).
Queria (alugar   ke·ree·a (a·loo·gaar
um carro).   oong kaa·rroo)

I have (a reservation).
Eu tenho   e·oo ta·nyoo
(uma reserva).   (oo·ma rre·zer·va)

Could you please (help)?
Pode (ajudar),   po·de (a·zhoo·daar)
por favor?   poor fa·vor

Do I need (a visa)?
Preciso de   pre·see·zoo de
(um visto)?   (oong veesh·too)

I'd like to reserve a table for ...	Eu queria reservar uma mesa para ...	e·oo ke·ree·a rre·zer·vaar oo·ma me·za pa·ra ...
(eight) o'clock	as (oito da noite)	ash (oy·too da noy·te)
(two) people	(duas) pessoas	(doo·ash) pe·so·ash

Key Words

appetisers	aperitivos	a·per·ee·tee·voosh
bar	bar	baar
bottle	garrafa	ga·rraa·fa
bowl	tigela	tee·zhe·la
breakfast	pequeno almoço	pe·ke·noo aal·mo·soo
children's menu	menu das crianças	me·noo dash kree·ang·sash
cold	frio	free·oo
delicatessen	charcutaria	shar·koo·ta·ree·a

Signs

Aberto	Open
Encerrado	Closed
Entrada	Entrance
Fechado	Closed
Informação	Information
Lavabos/WC	Toilets
Proibido	Prohibited
Saída	Exit

dinner	jantar	zhang·taar
food	comida	koo·mee·da
fork	garfo	gar·foo
glass	copo	ko·poo
hot (warm)	quente	keng·te
knife	faca	faa·ka
lunch	almoço	aal·mo·soo
main course	prato principal	praa·too preeng·see·paal
market	mercado	mer·kaa·doo
menu (in English)	menu (em inglês)	me·noo (eng eeng·glesh)
plate	prato	praa·too
restaurant	restaurante	rresh·tow·rang·te
spicy	picante	pee·kang·te
spoon	colher	koo·lyer
vegetarian food	comida vegetariana	koo·mee·da ve·zhe·ta·ree·aa·na
wine list	lista dos vinhos	leesh·ta doosh vee·nyoosh
with/without	com/sem ...	kong/seng ...

Meat & Fish

beef	carne de vaca	kaar·ne de vaa·ka
chicken	frango	frang·goo
duck	pato	paa·too
fish	peixe	pay·she
lamb	cordeiro	kor·day·roo
pork	porco	por·koo
turkey	peru	pe·roo
veal	novilho	noo·vee·lyoo

Fruit & Vegetables

apple	maçã	ma·sang
apricot	alperce	aal·per·se
artichoke	alcachofra	aal·ka·sho·fra
asparagus	espargos	shpar·goosh
beetroot	beterraba	be·te·rraa·ba

cabbage	couve	koh·ve
capsicum	pimento	pee·meng·too
carrot	cenoura	se·noh·ra
celery	aipo	ai·poo
cherry	cereja	se·re·zha
corn	milho	mee·lyoo
cucumber	pepino	pe·pee·noo
fruit	fruta	froo·ta
grapes	uvas	oo·vash
lemon	limão	lee·mowng
lettuce	alface	aal·faa·se
mushrooms	cogumelos	koo·goo·me·loosh
nut	oleaginosa	o·lee·a·zhee·no·za
onion	cebola	se·bo·la
orange	laranja	la·rang·zha
peach	pêssego	pe·se·goo
peas	ervilhas	er·vee·lyash
pineapple	ananás	a·na·naash
plum	ameixa	a·may·sha
potato	batata	ba·taa·ta
prune	ameixa seca	a·may·sha se·ka
pumpkin	abóbora	a·bo·boo·ra
spinach	espinafres	shpee·naa·fresh
strawberry	morango	moo·rang·goo
tomato	tomate	too·maa·te
turnip	nabo	naa·boo
vegetable	hortaliça	or·ta·lee·sa
watermelon	melancia	me·lang·see·a

Other

bread	pão	powng
butter	manteiga	mang·tay·ga
cheese	queijo	kay·zhoo
egg	ovo	o·voo
honey	mel	mel
lentils	lentilha	leng·tee·lya
oil	óleo	o·lyoo
pasta/noodles	massas	maa·sash
pepper	pimenta	pee·meng·ta
rice	arroz	a·rrosh
salt	sal	saal
sugar	açúcar	a·soo·kar
vinegar	vinagre	vee·naa·gre

Drinks

beer	cerveja	ser·ve·zha
coffee	café	ka·fe
juice	sumo	soo·moo

milk	leite	lay·te
tea	chá	shaa
(mineral) water	água (mineral)	aa·gwa (mee·ne·raal)
(red) wine	vinho (tinto)	vee·nyoo (teeng·too)
(white) wine	vinho (branco)	vee·nyoo (brang·koo)

EMERGENCIES

| Help! | Socorro! | soo·ko·rroo |
| Go away! | Vá-se embora! | vaa·se eng·bo·ra |

Call ...!	Chame ...!	shaa·me ...
a doctor	um médico	oong me·dee·koo
the police	a polícia	a poo·lee·sya

I'm lost.
Estou perdido. shtoh per·dee·doo (m)
Estou perdida. shtoh per·dee·da (f)

There's been an accident.
Houve um acidente. oh·ve oong a·see·deng·te

I'm ill.
Estou doente. shtoh doo·eng·te

It hurts here.
Dói-me aqui. doy·me a·kee

I'm allergic to ...
Eu sou alérgico/ e·oo soh a·ler·zhee·koo/
alérgica a ... a·ler·zhee·ka a ... (m/f)

SHOPPING & SERVICES

I'd like to buy ...
Queria comprar ... ke·ree·a kong·praar ...

I'm just looking.
Estou só a ver. shtoh so a ver

May I look at it?
Posso ver? po·soo ver

I don't like it.
Não gosto. nowng gosh·too

How much is it?
Quanto custa? kwang·too koosh·ta

It's too expensive.
Está muito caro. shtaa mweeng·too kaa·roo

Question Words		
How?	Como?	ko·moo
What?	Quê?	ke
When?	Quando?	kwang·doo
Where?	Onde?	ong·de
Who?	Quem?	keng
Why?	Porquê?	poor·ke

Can you lower the price?
Pode baixar o preço? po·de bai·shaar oo pre·soo

There's a mistake in the bill.
Há um erro na conta. aa oong e·rroo na kong·ta

ATM	caixa automático	kai·sha ow·too·maa·tee·koo
credit card	cartão de crédito	kar·towng de kre·dee·too
internet cafe	café da internet	ka·fe da eeng·ter·ne·te
post office	correio	koo·rray·oo
tourist office	escritório de turismo	shkree·to·ryoo de too·reezh·moo

TIME & DATES

What time is it?
Que horas são? kee o·rash sowng

It's (10) o'clock.
São (dez) horas. sowng (desh) o·rash

Half past (10).
(Dez) e meia. (desh) e may·a

morning	manhã	ma·nyang
afternoon	tarde	taar·de
evening	noite	noy·te
yesterday	ontem	ong·teng
today	hoje	o·zhe
tomorrow	amanhã	aa·ma·nyang

Monday	segunda-feira	se·goong·da·fay·ra
Tuesday	terça-feira	ter·sa·fay·ra
Wednesday	quarta-feira	kwaar·ta·fay·ra
Thursday	quinta-feira	keeng·ta·fay·ra
Friday	sexta-feira	saysh·ta·fay·ra
Saturday	sábado	saa·ba·doo
Sunday	domingo	doo·meeng·goo

January	Janeiro	zha·nay·roo
February	Fevereiro	fe·vray·roo
March	Março	maar·soo
April	Abril	a·breel
May	Maio	maa·yoo
June	Junho	zhoo·nyoo
July	Julho	zhoo·lyoo
August	Agosto	a·gosh·too
September	Setembro	se·teng·broo
October	Outubro	oh·too·broo
November	Novembro	no·veng·broo
December	Dezembro	de·zeng·broo

Numbers

1	*um*	oong
2	*dois*	doysh
3	*três*	tresh
4	*quatro*	kwaa·troo
5	*cinco*	seeng·koo
6	*seis*	saysh
7	*sete*	se·te
8	*oito*	oy·too
9	*nove*	no·ve
10	*dez*	desh
20	*vinte*	veeng·te
30	*trinta*	treeng·ta
40	*quarenta*	kwa·reng·ta
50	*cinquenta*	seeng·kweng·ta
60	*sessenta*	se·seng·ta
70	*setenta*	se·teng·ta
80	*oitenta*	oy·teng·ta
90	*noventa*	no·veng·ta
100	*cem*	seng
1000	*mil*	meel

TRANSPORT

Public Transport

boat	*barco*	baar·koo
bus	*autocarro*	ow·to·kaa·roo
plane	*avião*	a·vee·owng
train	*comboio*	kong·boy·oo
tram	*eléctrico*	ee·le·tree·koo

I want to go to (Braga).
Queria ir a (Braga).   ke·ree·a eer a (braa·ga)

Does it stop at (Amarante)?
Pára em (Amarante)?   paa·ra eng (a·ma·rang·te)

What time does it leave/arrive?
A que horas sai/chega?   a ke o·rash sai/she·ga

Please tell me when we get to (Évora).
Por favor avise-me   poor fa·vor a·vee·ze·me
quando chegarmos   kwang·doo she·gaar·moosh
a (Évora).   a (e·voo·ra)

Please stop here.
Por favor pare aqui.   poor fa·vor paa·re a·kee

aisle seat	*lugar na coxia*	loo·gaar na koo·shee·a
cancelled	*cancelado*	kang·se·laa·doo
delayed	*atrasado*	a·tra·zaa·doo
platform	*plataforma*	pla·ta·for·ma

ticket office	*bilheteira*	bee·lye·tay·ra
timetable	*horário*	o·raa·ryoo
train station	*estação de caminhos de ferro*	shta·sowng de ka·mee·nyoosh de fe·rroo
window seat	*lugar à janela*	loo·gaar aa zha·ne·la

a ... ticket	*um bilhete de ...*	oong bee·lye·te de ...
1st-class	*primeira classe*	pree·may·ra klaa·se
2nd-class	*segunda classe*	se·goong·da klaa·se
one-way	*ida*	ee·da
return	*ida e volta*	ee·da ee vol·ta

Driving & Cycling

I'd like to hire a ...	*Queria alugar ...*	ke·ree·a a·loo·gaar ...
4WD	*um carro com tracção às quatro rodas*	oong kaa·rroo kong traa·sowng aash kwaa·troo rro·dash
bicycle	*uma bicicleta*	oo·ma bee·see·kle·ta
car	*um carro*	oong kaa·rroo
motorcycle	*uma mota*	oo·ma mo·ta

bicycle pump	*bomba de bicicleta*	bong·ba de bee·see·kle·ta
child seat	*cadeira de criança*	ka·day·ra de kree·ang·sa
helmet	*capacete*	ka·pa·se·te
mechanic	*mecânico*	me·kaa·nee·koo
petrol/gas	*gasolina*	ga·zoo·lee·na
service station	*posto de gasolina*	posh·too de ga·zoo·lee·na

Is this the road to ...?
Esta é a estrada   esh·ta e a shtraa·da
para ...?   pa·ra ...

(How long) Can I park here?
(Quanto tempo) Posso   (kwang·too teng·poo) po·soo
estacionar aqui?   shta·see·oo·naar a·kee

The car/motorbike has broken down (at ...).
O carro/A mota   oo kaa·rroo/a mo·ta
avariou-se (em ...).   a·va·ree·oh·se (eng ...)

I have a flat tyre.
Tenho um furo no   ta·nyoo oong foo·roo noo
pneu.   pe·ne·oo

I've run out of petrol.
Estou sem gasolina.   shtoh seng ga·zoo·lee·na

adegas – wineries

Age of Discoveries – the period during the 15th and 16th centuries when Portuguese sailors explored the coast of Africa and finally charted a sea route to India

albergaria – upmarket inn

albufeira – reservoir, lagoon

aldeia – village

alta – upper

anta – see *dolmen*

arco – arch

armillary sphere – celestial sphere used by early astronomers and navigators to chart the stars; a decorative motif in Manueline architecture and atop *pelourinhos*

arrayal, arraiais (pl) – street party

artesanato – handicrafts shop

avenida – avenue

azulejo – hand-painted tile, typically blue and white, used to decorate buildings

bairro – town district

baixa – lower

balneário – health resort, spa

barcos rabelos – colourful boats once used to transport port wine from vineyards

barragem – dam

beco – cul de sac

biblioteca – library

bilhete diário/turístico – day pass/tourist ticket

câmara municipal – city or town hall

caldas – hot springs

Carnaval – Carnival; festival that takes place just before Lent

casa de hóspedes – boarding house, usually with shared showers and toilets

casais – huts

castelo – castle

castro – fortified hill town

cavaleiro – horseman

CCI – Camping Card International

Celtiberians – descendants of Celts who arrived in the Iberian Peninsula around 600 BC

centro de saúde – state-administered medical centre

cidade – town or city

citânia – Celtic fortified village

claustro – cloisters

concelho – municipality, council

cortes – Portugal's early parliament

couvert – cover charge added to restaurant bills to pay for sundries

CP – Caminhos de Ferro Portugueses (the Portuguese state railway company)

cromeleque – circle of prehistoric standing stones

cruz – cross

direita – right; abbreviated as D, dir or Dta

dolmen – Neolithic stone tomb (*anta* in Portuguese)

Dom, Dona – honorific titles (like Sir, Madam) given to royalty, nobility and landowners; now used more generally as a very polite form of address

elevador – lift (elevator), funicular

espigueiros – stone granaries

esplanada – terrace, sea-front promenade

estação – station (usually train station)

estalagem – inn; more expensive than an *albergaria*

expressos – comfortable, fast buses between major cities

estradas – highways

fadista – singer of *fado*

fado – traditional, melancholic Portuguese style of singing

feira – fair

festa – festival

FICC – Fédération Internationale de Camping et de Caravanning (International Camping & Caravanning Federation)

fortaleza – fortress

GNR – Guarda Nacional Republicana (the national guard) – the acting police force in rural towns without *PSP* police

guitarra – guitar

gruta – cave

hospedaria – see *casa de hóspedes*

IC (intercidade) – express intercity train

ICEP – Investimentos, Comércio e Turismo de Portugal, the government's umbrella organisation for tourism

igreja – church

igreja matriz – parish church

ilha – island

IR (interregional) – fairly fast train that doesn't make too many stops

jardim – garden

judiaria – quarter in a town where Jews were once segregated

largo – small square

latifúndios – Roman system of large farming estates

litoral – coastal

livraria – bookshop

lisboêtas – Lisbon dwellers

loggia – covered area or porch on the side of a building

lugar – neighbourhood, place

Manueline – elaborate late Gothic/Renaissance style of art and architecture that emerged during the reign of Dom Manuel I in the 16th century

mantas alentejanas – handwoven woollen blankets

marranos – 'New Christians', ie Jews who converted during the Inquisition

menhir – standing stone monument typical of the late Neolithic Age

mercado municipal – municipal market

mesa – table

MFA – Movimento das Forças Armadas, the military group that led the Revolution of the Carnations in 1974

minimercado – grocery shop or small supermarket

miradouro – viewpoint

Misericórdia – derived from Santa Casa da Misericórdia (Holy House of Mercy), a charitable institution founded in the 15th century to care for the poor and the sick; it usually designates an old building that was founded by this organisation

moliceiro – high-prowed, shallow-draft boats traditionally used for harvesting seaweed in the estuaries of Beira Litoral

mosteiro – monastery

mouraria – the quarter where Moors were segregated during and after the Christian *Reconquista*

museu – museum

paço – palace

parque de campismo – camping ground

parque nacional – national park

parque natural – natural park

pelourinho – stone pillory, often ornately carved; erected in the 13th to 18th centuries as symbols of justice and sometimes as places where criminals were punished

pensão, pensões (pl) – guest house, the Portuguese equivalent of a B&B, though breakfast is not always served

planalto – high plain

pombal – dovecote, a structure for housing pigeons

ponte – bridge

portagem – toll road

pousada – government-run upmarket inn, often a converted castle, convent or palace

pousada da juventude – youth hostel; usually with kitchen, common rooms and sometimes rooms with private bathroom

praça – square

praça de touros – bullring

praia – beach

PSP – Polícia de Segurança Pública, the local police force

quinta – country estate or villa; in the Douro wine-growing region it often refers to a wine lodge's property

R (regional) – slow train

Reconquista – Christian reconquest of Portugal (718–1249)

reservas naturais – nature reserves

residencial, residenciais (pl) – guest house; slightly more expensive than a *pensão* and usually serving breakfast

ribeiro – stream

rio – river

romaria – religious pilgrimage

rua – street

saudade – melancholic longing for better times

sé – cathedral

sem chumbo – unleaded (petrol)

senhor – man

senhora – woman

serra – mountain, mountain range

solar – manor house

tasca – tavern

termas – spas, hot springs

terra quente – hot country

torre de menagem – castle tower, keep

tourada – bullfight

Turihab – short for Turismo Habitação, a scheme for marketing private accommodation (particularly in northern Portugal) in cottages, historic buildings and manor houses

turismo – tourist office

vila – town

behind the scenes

SEND US YOUR FEEDBACK

We love to hear from travellers – your comments keep us on our toes and help make our books better. Our well-travelled team reads every word on what you loved or loathed about this book. Although we cannot reply individually to postal submissions, we always guarantee that your feedback goes straight to the appropriate authors, in time for the next edition. Each person who sends us information is thanked in the next edition – and the most useful submissions are rewarded with a free book.

Visit **lonelyplanet.com/contact** to submit your updates and suggestions or to ask for help. Our award-winning website also features inspirational travel stories, news and discussions.

Note: We may edit, reproduce and incorporate your comments in Lonely Planet products such as guidebooks, websites and digital products, so let us know if you don't want your comments reproduced or your name acknowledged. For a copy of our privacy policy visit lonelyplanet.com/privacy.

OUR READERS

Many thanks to the travellers who used the last edition and wrote to us with helpful hints, useful advice and interesting anecdotes:

Trine Ahlgreen, Giorgio Allegretto, Marika Arban, Stasiek Arendarski, Andrew Atchley, Mirjam Bakker, Steve Barnett, Guilherme Barreto, Cynthia Barriault, Joe Bazinet, Johan Benesch, Monica Bessone, David Blood, Anne-Cathrine Bojsen, Fred Boley, Michelle Bottazzi, Renato Braz, Peter Brinkman, Carolina Brito, Lawson Bronson, Alexander Buchanan, Shane Buckham, Johnny Bugler, Len Buurman, Rui Caeiro, Phileem Calder-Potts, David Cartwright, Ana Carvalho, Miguel Carvalho, Sherryl Casella, Mary Cave, Vicki Christini, Natalia Chudinovskikh, Kai Chuen Law, Bjørn Clasen, Isabella Coelho, Rodolfo Coelho, Sandra Contente, Danyl Cook, Fiona Cortland, Nathalie Costa, Graham Courtenay, Eurico Covas, Bruce Crow, Bart Crum, Luis Da Silva, Lisa Davis, Carla De Beer, Hans De Clercq, Maurice De Heus, Vitor De Souza, Esther De Waal, Monique Dehaese, Joost Descheemaeker, Nicole Dicke, Heather Dickson, Nick Dillen, Helen Dodd, Remi Durand, Zdena Dvorakova, Steve Emmott, Jay Espejo, Bastian Etzold, Sandra Faustino, Yelin Fernandez, Ana Ferreira, Sérgio Ferreira, Martin Ferro, Fabio Fiorini, Michael Fischer, Faya Frederiek, Ketil Froyn, Aaron Gafner, Joao Galhardo, John Gallagher, Teresa Maria Barreiros Garcia, Leigh Gates, Jay Geller, Maggie Gore, Steve Gorton, Ingmar Griffioen, Pedro Guimarães, Heiko Günther, Molly Hamilton, Kaspar Hanni, Craig Hill, Gary Hill, Marion Höllriegl, Anna Holmberg, Louise Hora, Deborah Hughes, Navid Imani, Jennifer Isaak-Harrington, Carl Jacquemyn, Sheryl James, Femke Janssen, Anders Jeppsson, Maria João Arriscado Nunes, Camilla Johannessen, Ursa Jozelj, Kate Karpf, Edward Keefe, Anke Kessler, Helena Kopova, Bart Korsten, Wojciech Kosiorek, Ilona Kotala, Raffaello Lapucci, Kiersten Larsen, Halcyon Leonard, Jorge Leote, Julia F Li, Alesa Lightbourne, Colin Little, Marcus Lloyd, Joao Paulo Lourenco, Anabel Loyd, Robert Lynch, Thomas Maher, Charles Manton, Zoe Marcham, Carma Maria, John Markwell, Catarina Matos, Albert Mcmurdie, Claudia Melo, Sarah Menne, Maaike Merens, Matthew Metcalfe, Eileen Midgley, Richard Mieli, Jens Møller, Graeme Mooney, Alice Moura, Jens Müller, Emma Neill, Keith Newitt, Vivienne Nielssen, Catherine Noack, Karin Nygaard, Katherine Ohlsen, Ricardo Oliveira, Ellen O'Neill, Carsten Ottesen, Palheirãobar Palheirãobar, Anna Pamula, RF Parsons, Artur Pegãs, Adelino Pereira, Marcos Pereira Da Silva, Marco Peruzzi, Lorraine Peters, Hans Pettersson, Thibault

Philibert, Cynthia Phipps, Vanessa Pinto, Pat Pires, Joao Prudencio, Beth Pullman, Albert Rapp, Paulo Ribeiro, Mike Robinson, Sandra Robinson, Carmen Rodriguez, Francesco Russo, Annelotte Rutgers, Tiago Sá, Aaron Sagers, Sahba Sanai, Paulo Sanchez, Susana Santos, Paolo Scheffer, Jurriaan Schoorl, Frank Schroen, Carlos Seixas, Alexandra Serôdio, Jacinta Shaw, Roy Shergold, Terry Shubkin, Telmo Silva, Hugo Silvestre, Katrin Sippel, Fiona Slater, Vic Sofras, Margarida Spry, Peter Steckelmacher, Maurits Stuyt, Darius Sunawala, Nanda Talsma, Monique Teggelove, Filipe Teles, Olinda Teresa, Regis Titeca, Jim Toth, Lise Trap, Steven Tung, Sergei Tupailo, Beverley Tyler, Kristina Ulgemo, Alexander Unwin, Iker Urbina, Liselot Van Delden, Glenn Van Der Knijff, Rob Van Der Linden, Selinde Van Der Spek, Julie Anne Van Eijk, Martijn Van Geelen, Ernst Van Nieuwburg, Joris Van Voorst Tot Voorst, Wim Vandenbussche, André Vaughan, Esther Veen, Paula Verlinden, Vincenzo Vigilante, Teresa Vilas Boas, Richard Walker, Charles Wardell, Chris Web, Stefanie Weber, Simone Wilczek, Vivienne Wild, Bev Wilson, Klaus Witzmann, Anneli Wrethling, Felix Würkert, Edson Yazejy, Miroslava Zilkova

AUTHOR THANKS

Regis St Louis
Big thanks to editor Lucy Monie for inviting me on board, Herman So for cartographic magic and co-authors Kate, Gregor and Adam, who proved a stellar team to work with. I'd like to thank João for insight into all things Lisboa, Marco and friends for the memorable trip out to Cabo da Roca, Paolo for the insightful Castelo walking tour and memorable meals, Bruno for the cruise around town in the radical UMM, and the friendly folks at Pensão Imperial. As always *beijos* to Cassandra and daughters Magdalena and Genevieve for their support.

Kate Armstrong
Thanks to the generous Portuguese people and travellers. A massive thanks to Laura Stansfeld, Guida Gonçalves, Rui Virgínia and Frank Schroen, Isabel Almeida, Victor Cariço, Ana Palma, Luis Coelho, and all those – unfortunately too numerous to name – in the *turismos*. Special *obrigada* to Antonio Pedro and Mina, *minha família Portuguesa*.

Gregor Clark
I would like to thank Else and Anja in Coimbra, Anabela in Bragança, Inês in Vila Real, Cristina in Santarém, Silvia in Aveiro, Hugh in Viseu, and Kate, Jacques, Debbie and Steve in Figueira. Thanks also to my coordinating author Regis St Louis, as well as commissioning editors Lucy Monie and Joe Bindloss for their steadfast support throughout this project. Finally, big hugs to my loving family and sometimes travel companions Gaen, Meigan and Chloe, for helping me stay sane and reminding me to eat more *gelado*.

THIS BOOK
The 8th edition of *Portugal* was coordinated by Regis St Louis. Regis (Plan Your Trip, Lisbon & Around, Understand Portugal, Survival Guide) headed up a team of expert authors including Gregor Clark (Portugal Outdoors, Estremadura & Ribatejo, The Beiras, Trás-os-Montes) Kate Armstrong (The Algarve, The Alentejo, Food & Wine) and Adam Skolnick (Porto & The Douro, The Minho). *Portugal 7* was written by Regis, Gregor and Kate with the additional help of Kerry Walker, while the following authors made significant contributions to previous editions: Robert Landon, Dr Caroline Evans, Abigail Hole, Charlotte Amelines (nee Beech), Richard Sterling, John King and Julia Wilkinson. This guidebook was commissioned in Lonely Planet's London office and produced by the following:

Commissioning Editors Lucy Monie, Joe Bindloss, Dora Whitaker
Coordinating Editors Erin Richards & Louisa Syme
Coordinating Cartographer Xavier Di Toro
Coordinating Layout Designer Carlos Solarte
Managing Editors Imogen Bannister, Brigitte Ellemor
Managing Cartographers Shahara Ahmed, Herman So
Managing Layout Designers Indra Kilfoyle, Celia Wood
Assisting Editors Carolyn Bain, Jackey Coyle, Jessica Crouch, Victoria Harrison, Helen Koehne, Gabrielle Stefanos
Assisting Cartographer Joelene Kowalski

Cover Research Sabrina Dalbesio
Internal Image Research Aude Vauconsant
Language Content Annelies Mertens, Branislava Vladisavljevic

Thanks to Mark Adams, David Connolly, Melanie Dankel, Frank Deim, Stefanie Di Trocchio, Diana Duggan, Janine Eberle, Joshua Geoghegan, Mark Germanchis, Chris Girdler, Michelle Glynn, Lauren Hunt, Laura Jane, David Kemp, Yvonne Kirk, Lisa Knights, Nic Lehman, John Mazzocchi, Wayne Murphy, Katie O'Connell, Susan Paterson, Trent Paton, Adrian Persoglia, Piers Pickard, Andy Rojas, Lachlan Ross, Michael Ruff, Wibowo Rusli Julie Sheridan, Mandy Sierp, Laura Stansfeld, John Taufa, Sam Trafford, Gina Tsarouhas, Jeanette Wall, Juan Winata, Emily Wolman, Nick Wood

Adam Skolnick

Thanks first and foremost to my family in Porto: that means you Carmen, João, Padre Fereira and Madre Elena. Thanks also to Adrian Bridge at Taylor's, Ambassador Bob and Alex Illing, Artur Pintoleite in Foz, the Welcome Centre and the Kite House in Viana, Isabel at Casa Arrabalde in Ponte de Lima, Casa da Breia and Cecilia with the *turismo* in Arcos, to the rest of the LP team, and to the sweet and gorgeous Georgiana Johnson.

ACKNOWLEDGMENTS

Climate map data adapted from Peel MC, Finlayson BL & McMahon TA (2007) 'Updated World Map of the Köppen-Geiger Climate Classification', Hydrology and Earth System Sciences, 11, 163344.

Cover photograph: Albufeira beach, Algarve, Portugal/Neale Clark, Photolibrary

Many of the images in this guide are available for licensing from Lonely Planet Images: www.lonelyplanetimages.com.

NOTES

NOTES

index

Map Pages **p000**
Photo Pages **p000**

INDEX C

how to use this book

These symbols will help you find the listings you want:

- ◉ Sights
- 🛉 Activities
- 🢢 Courses
- 👉 Tours
- ⚓ Festivals & Events
- 🛏 Sleeping
- 🍴 Eating
- 🍷 Drinking
- ☆ Entertainment
- 🛍 Shopping
- ℹ Information/ Transport

Look out for these icons:

- TOP CHOICE — Our author's recommendation
- FREE — No payment required
- 🌿 — A green or sustainable option

Our authors have nominated these places as demonstrating a strong commitment to sustainability – for example by supporting local communities and producers, operating in an environmentally friendly way, or supporting conservation projects.

These symbols give you the vital information for each listing:

- ☎ Telephone Numbers
- ⊙ Opening Hours
- Ⓟ Parking
- ⊖ Nonsmoking
- ✳ Air-Conditioning
- @ Internet Access
- 🛜 Wi-Fi Access
- ☷ Swimming Pool
- 🌶 Vegetarian Selection
- 📖 English-Language Menu
- 👪 Family-Friendly
- 🐾 Pet-Friendly
- 🚌 Bus
- ⛴ Ferry
- Ⓜ Metro
- Ⓢ Subway
- ⊖ London Tube
- 🚋 Tram
- 🚆 Train

Reviews are organised by author preference.

Map Legend

Sights
- 🏖 Beach
- 🛕 Buddhist
- 🏰 Castle
- ✝ Christian
- 🕉 Hindu
- ☪ Islamic
- ✡ Jewish
- 🗼 Monument
- 🏛 Museum/Gallery
- 🏚 Ruin
- 🍇 Winery/Vineyard
- 🐾 Zoo
- ◎ Other Sight

Activities, Courses & Tours
- 🤿 Diving/Snorkelling
- 🛶 Canoeing/Kayaking
- ⛷ Skiing
- 🏄 Surfing
- 🏊 Swimming/Pool
- 🚶 Walking
- 🏄 Windsurfing
- • Other Activity/ Course/Tour

Sleeping
- 🛏 Sleeping
- ⛺ Camping

Eating
- 🍴 Eating

Drinking
- 🍷 Drinking
- ☕ Cafe

Entertainment
- ☆ Entertainment

Shopping
- 🛍 Shopping

Information
- ✉ Post Office
- ℹ Tourist Information

Transport
- ✈ Airport
- ⊗ Border Crossing
- 🚍 Bus
- 🚠 Cable Car/ Funicular
- 🚲 Cycling
- ⛴ Ferry
- Ⓜ Metro
- 🚝 Monorail
- Ⓟ Parking
- Ⓢ S-Bahn
- 🚕 Taxi
- 🚆 Train/Railway
- 🚋 Tram
- Ⓣ Tube Station
- Ⓤ U-Bahn
- • Other Transport

Routes
- Tollway
- Freeway
- Primary
- Secondary
- Tertiary
- Lane
- Unsealed Road
- Plaza/Mall
- Steps
- Tunnel
- Pedestrian Overpass
- Walking Tour
- Walking Tour Detour
- Path

Boundaries
- International
- State/Province
- Disputed
- Regional/Suburb
- Marine Park
- Cliff
- Wall

Population
- ◉ Capital (National)
- ◉ Capital (State/Province)
- ● City/Large Town
- ○ Town/Village

Geographic
- 🏠 Hut/Shelter
- 🚨 Lighthouse
- ◎ Lookout
- ▲ Mountain/Volcano
- ◯ Oasis
- 🏞 Park
-)(Pass
- 🍽 Picnic Area
- 🏞 Waterfall

Hydrography
- River/Creek
- Intermittent River
- Swamp/Mangrove
- Reef
- Canal
- Water
- Dry/Salt/ Intermittent Lake
- Glacier

Areas
- Beach/Desert
- + + + Cemetery (Christian)
- × × × Cemetery (Other)
- Park/Forest
- Sportsground
- Sight (Building)
- Top Sight (Building)

OUR STORY

A beat-up old car, a few dollars in the pocket and a sense of adventure. In 1972 that's all Tony and Maureen Wheeler needed for the trip of a lifetime – across Europe and Asia overland to Australia. It took several months, and at the end – broke but inspired – they sat at their kitchen table writing and stapling together their first travel guide, *Across Asia on the Cheap*. Within a week they'd sold 1500 copies. Lonely Planet was born.

Today, Lonely Planet has offices in Melbourne, London and Oakland, with more than 600 staff and writers. We share Tony's belief that 'a great guidebook should do three things: inform, educate and amuse'.

OUR WRITERS

Regis St Louis

Coordinating Author, Lisbon & Around Regis' admiration for Portugal began years ago on a magical trip through Lisbon's Alfama district. Since then he's returned frequently for fado fixes, decadent seafood meals and coastal explorations. On his most recent journey, he feted Lisbon's favourite saint at the Festa de Santo António, explored gorgeous beaches in Parque Natural da Arrábida and ate way too many *pastéis de nata* (including six in one day – oops). Regis has written two previous editions of *Portugal* along with 30 other guidebooks for Lonely Planet, and his articles have appeared in the *LA Times* and *Chicago Tribune* among other publications. He lives in Brooklyn, New York.

Read more about Regis at:
lonelyplanet.com/members/regisstlouis

Kate Armstrong

The Algarve, The Alentejo A regular visitor to Portugal, Kate first backpacked around the country over 20 years ago and fell for the Alentejan countryside, Algarvian seafood and Portuguese hospitality. Lured by the language of fado, she later returned to study Portuguese. For this edition Kate surfed the west coast, hiked sections of the Via Algarviana, and consumed kilos of convent cakes. Kate also contributes to Lonely Planet's *Africa*, *Greece* and *South America* titles. She is published regularly in Australian newspapers and magazines – see www.katearmstrong.com.au.

Read more about Kate at:
lonelyplanet/members/kate_armstrong

Gregor Clark

Estremadura & Ribatejo, The Beiras, Trás-os-Montes Since first visiting Portugal in 1986, Gregor Clark has loved the country's end-of-the-world feeling, its kind-hearted people, its *azulejos* (hand-painted tiles) and its incomparably tasty fish-and-wine-based cuisine. A lifelong polyglot with a degree in Romance Languages, Gregor has contributed to Lonely Planet's *Italy* and *Brazil* guides. Gregor's favourite experience while researching this book was getting an impromptu lesson in the nearly extinct Mirandês language from old folks on a park bench at sunset in Trás-os-Montes.

Read more about Gregor at:
lonelyplanet.com/members/gregorclark

Adam Skolnick

Porto & the Douro, The Minho Adam Skolnick writes about travel, culture, health and the environment for Lonely Planet, *Men's Health*, *Outside* and *Travel & Leisure*. He has travelled and worked in 40 countries on six continents and authored or coauthored 10 previous Lonely Planet guidebooks. While on assignment in Portugal he made Porto his second home, living as just another Ribeira local while making satellite trips throughout the north. You can read more of his work at www.adamskolnick.com. His web series, *Aspiring*, is online at www.youtube.com/user/TheHoldingpattern.

Published by Lonely Planet Publications Pty Ltd
ABN 36 005 607 983
8th edition – March 2011
ISBN 978 1 74179 600 1
© Lonely Planet 2011   Photographs © as indicated 2011
10 9 8 7 6 5 4 3
P   d in China